# FINANCIAL ACCOUNTING:
## Basic Concepts

The Robert N. Anthony / Willard J. Graham Series in Accounting

# FINANCIAL ACCOUNTING:
## Basic Concepts

**Earl A. Spiller, Jr.**
Ph.D., CPA
Professor of Accounting
Indiana University

**Martin L. Gosman**
Ph.D., CPA
Associate Professor of Accounting
Boston University

Fourth Edition

1984

**RICHARD D. IRWIN, INC.**
Homewood, Illinois 60430

ISBN 0-256-02803-6
Library of Congress Catalog Card No. 83–82142

*Printed in the United States of America*

1 2 3 4 5 6 7 8 9 0 K 1 0 9 8 7 6 5 4

# PREFACE

In this fourth edition of *Financial Accounting: Basic Concepts*, we have endeavored to retain the strengths of prior editions and improve the weaknesses. We have tried to resist making changes just to be different.

The overall purpose of the text and its main features remain the same. The book is intended for a one-semester introductory financial accounting course to be offered to MBA students or to highly motivated undergraduates. The text assumes no prior knowledge of accounting so it can also be used in Executive MBA programs and has been used successfully in management development programs.

This edition maintains the same conceptual-analytical approach that was the hallmark of previous editions. The book stresses more than just an "appreciation" of accounting. Both the "why" and the "how" are emphasized in the chapter discussions and problem material. The attention given to theoretical considerations and analytical operations is significant. They will require a mature, intelligent, and motivated readership.

The primary aim is to develop the reader's ability to understand, interpret, and analyze the financial statements of business organizations. Several secondary objectives support the achievement of this overall goal.

1. Familiarity with accounting terminology, so as to communicate using accounting as a language.
2. Knowledge of the measurement rules and disclosure regulations governing the recording and reporting of business activity.
3. Understanding of the impact of alternative accounting principles on the financial statements, so as to know what the statements mean and do not mean.
4. Ability to use the conceptual structure of financial accounting, both extant and prospective, as a benchmark for evaluation.
5. Acquisition of a working knowledge of the accounting process, so as to reason using accounting as a logical framework.

## CHANGES IN THE FOURTH EDITION

We have tried to accomplish these objectives with a clear and direct writing style, challenging problem material, interesting and up-to-date discussions, and an improved explication of our ideas. Perhaps the greatest innovation has been the inclusion of the 1981 Annual Report of Armco,

Inc., as an *integrated* teaching device. The entire financial section of the report is reproduced in an appendix to Chapter 5. Each chapter thereafter ends with a discussion that relates the material discussed in that chapter to the reporting practices of Armco in 1981. These Armco sections in Chapters 5–19 feature a detailed, in-depth analysis (two to seven pages) of Armco's financial statements and notes. They help to relate the textbook concepts and procedures to real-world situations and greatly increase the reader's confidence in his or her ability to understand actual corporate financial reports.

Other important changes in the fourth edition include the following:

1. Rewriting of all chapters to improve clarity and to incorporate the latest accounting thought and authoritative pronouncements.
2. Updating of Chapters 1–2 in particular to tie the definitions and discussion to the conceptual framework statements issued by the Financial Accounting Standards Board.
3. Inclusion of credit card sales and long-term service contracts in the discussion of revenue recognition in Chapter 6.
4. Elimination of the appendix to Chapter 7, which covered detailed cost accounting procedures. This material was rarely used by adopters. The space has been devoted to an expansion of the discussion and examples in Chapter 7 concerning marketable equity securities and capitalization of interest.
5. Incorporation of the highlights of the disclosures of *FASB Statement No. 33* within Chapters 8 and 9 dealing with inventories and plant assets.
6. Introduction of the accelerated cost recovery system (ACRS) mandated for tax purposes in Chapter 9 and a thorough discussion of it in Chapter 13.
7. Coverage of bonds as an investment in Chapter 10 to tie in with the chapter's discussion of bond liabilities.
8. Reorganization of Chapter 11 on leases to facilitate a comparison of the recording by lessees and lessors for each of the major types of leases.
9. Inclusion in Chapter 12 on pensions of a discussion of reporting problems of defined-benefit pension plans. This chapter also received extensive rewriting to incorporate recent pronouncements and discussions of proposed pronouncements.
10. Revision of the discussion of the various disclosure issues in Chapter 16 to reflect new principles and procedures. Particular subjects receiving extensive updating include extraordinary items and prior period adjustments, earnings per share, and foreign currency adjustments. The discussion of the auditor's role in accounting is also expanded.
11. Creation of a new appendix to Chapter 17 to cover some of the more

difficult material related to the funds statement. This change increases the usefulness of the chapter to some adopters who do not assign all chapters or who do not want an in-depth discussion of the more theoretical areas.

12. Inclusion in Chapter 18 of a description of research on the predictive ability of financial ratios and the use of ratios by credit evaluators.

13. Extensive rewriting of Chapter 19 on income measurement and changing prices to explain the disclosure requirements of *FASB Statement No. 33* and their relationship to a complete set of constant dollar or current cost statements.

In this fourth edition we also have included a glossary at the end of the text. The glossary contains the names and definitions of almost 300 technical terms and phrases used in financial accounting. The items are arranged in alphabetical order for easy reference by the user. Not only are clear, concise definitions provided for each item, but also the reader is directed to the first text chapter in which the item is discussed in greater depth.

A well-written accounting text without an adequate number of suitable problems accomplishes only half its intended purpose. We have tried to keep that idea paramount in our revision of the problem material. The number of problems is about the same as in the prior edition. Almost 50 percent of the problems in this edition are totally new, and many more have been significantly changed. The number of problems which follow fairly directly from text discussions and illustrations has been increased so the user can better see if he or she has mastered the basic material.

The great majority of problem material in this text stresses the application of conceptual knowledge and the development of analytical skills. They will require thought but should prove to be interesting, relevant, and challenging.

A significant number of them (over 25 percent of the problems in Chapters 5–19) comes from the annual reports of actual companies. Many chapters contain a number of problems of this nature. Also we have included some problems taken from the CPA and CMA examinations. These often have been tailored to the specific discussions in the text.

The basic organization of the book remains as in prior editions. Section One contains the first five chapters. These establish the fundamental concepts and procedures, including the accounting cycle. The emphasis, however, remains on understanding procedures as an aid in analysis and communication. Sections Two and Three discuss selected areas involved in the measurement of assets and equities. The material in these sections builds on the conceptual framework presented in Chapter 1. Current accounting principles and procedures are critically examined. Section Four contains five chapters which concern problems of analysis, disclosure, and interpretation in the financial statements.

**ACKNOWL-EDGMENTS**

A successful revision results only when users of prior editions are willing to share their experiences and ideas with the authors. We have been fortunate to receive numerous suggestions for improvements, both large and small, in this edition. Some of this information was solicited in a survey of users; other suggestions came from adopters who were kind enough to write about their specific satisfactions and complaints. The list is too long to mention each one individually. Hopefully, they will recognize some changes made in response to their advice.

James M. Fremgen of the Naval Postgraduate School deserves a special mention of appreciation. He made the suggestion that we include an annual report in the book and use it as a formal part of the textual discussion. We believe this feature adds significantly to the relevance, clarity, and challenge of the book. We would also thank Marsha Murphy of Armco, Inc., for her assistance. She supplied supplementary information, clarified our misunderstandings, and corroborated many of our analyses.

Professors Michael L. Fetters (Babson College), James J. Linn (Tulane University), and Phillip T. May (Wichita State University) read the entire manuscript. They were of great help in suggesting material in need of clarification and/or revision and in evaluating our implementation of changes in this edition.

As she had in the two preceding editions, Jane Warren reviewed the entire manuscript for grammar, punctuation, consistency in style, and overall readability. It never ceased to amaze us how much better our material read after it had emerged from under the scrutiny of her pencil.

We also were aided by some very able graduate assistants. Marilyn Hill at Boston University and Chuu-Yun (Nancy) Yin at Indiana University verified references and numbers, critiqued text and problem material, assisted in the preparation of the index, and provided other valuable help.

We are grateful to the American Institute of Certified Public Accountants and the Institute of Management Accounting for allowing us to adapt problem material from their uniform examinations.

Last, but certainly not least (although it may have seemed that way to them for the last two years), we express great appreciation to our families. Their understanding, encouragement, and support have made our efforts worthwhile.

All of the foregoing people share in the completion of this book and in any improvements that it contains. The remaining deficiencies are ours alone. Comments and suggestions from users are most welcome.

**Earl A. Spiller, Jr.**
**Martin L. Gosman**

# CONTENTS

# FUNDAMENTAL CONCEPTS AND PROCEDURES

# CHAPTER 1

# THE FRAMEWORK AND ENVIRONMENT OF ACCOUNTING

One important key to rational conduct in human affairs is the availability of information. Information helps people to decide what to believe and what to do. The soundness of our judgments—personal, political, social, and economic—reflects directly the quality, quantity, and timeliness of the information we have.

Accounting systems communicate economic information. This chapter defines accounting and its role as an information supplier. It also examines the objectives and environmental context of a major subset of accounting—financial accounting. The chapter concludes with a description of the conceptual framework on which subsequent chapters rest.

**INTRODUC-TION TO ACCOUNTING**    Accounting consists of the concepts and processes by which financial and economic data, primarily quantitative in nature, are gathered and summarized in reports that are useful in decision making. In the quest to communicate about the economic events of various entities, the accountant undertakes a variety of tasks:

1. *Identification*—The accountant must select from the myriad of economic activities those transactions and events that are relevant to accounting. Even the most ambitious information system cannot encompass all financial data. Criteria must be established for choosing the data to be gathered.
2. *Measurement*—Financial information normally is communicated in monetary terms. To report the relevant economic transactions and events, the accountant must develop measurement rules for assigning

dollar values. As we shall see, a number of different valuation bases can be employed; the choice depends on what information the accountant is trying to communicate and to whom.

3. *Recording*—The accountant analyzes the character of a transaction and provides a systematic method for keeping track of it. A simplified bookkeeping procedure for recording in financial accounting is described in Chapter 3.

4. *Classification*—The accountant must fit the financial data into a logical, useful framework. Huge masses of figures have little significance unless they are ordered and their relationships highlighted. The asset-equity framework, the subject of the next chapter, provides the basic foundation for the classification of financial accounting data.

5. *Reporting*—The collected and classified financial information must be periodically summarized in financial statements and reports. These are the instruments for communication in accounting.

6. *Interpretation*—Presentation of information in reports is not sufficient. In addition, an explanation of the accounting process—its meanings, uses, and limitations—to the users of these statements is a most necessary final task. Understanding the process enables one to interpret the results of accounting, and this is the crucial goal of its study.

In this book we will emphasize the identification, measurement, reporting, and interpretation functions. The system for recording and classifying accounting data is called *bookkeeping*. Although it may require some analytical skills, bookkeeping is concerned primarily with procedures—the "how to." The field of accounting, while encompassing bookkeeping, goes beyond these techniques into the conceptual issues and rationale involved in applying the procedures—the "why" and "what for."

## Users of Accounting Information

Accounting is often called the language of business. A language implies the existence of both a message and an audience. Ideally the message, or financial information, is attuned to the needs and characteristics of those to whom it is directed. However, the audiences of accounting information include diverse groups:

1. Owners—present and prospective investors and their representatives (e.g., professional security analysts and investment advisors).
2. Managers.
3. Creditors and lenders.
4. Employee and labor organizations.
5. Customers.
6. Tax authorities.
7. Regulatory agencies—the Securities and Exchange Commission (SEC), stock exchanges, various governmental commissions, and courts.

8. Information agencies—the financial press and reporting agencies, trade associations, and accumulators of economic statistics.

In a broad sense all these audiences share a common desire for information about the economic resources of an organization. The allocation of financial capital and the distribution of real resources among competing uses are basic economic decisions. Consequently, accounting for the economic resources controlled by an organization and reporting on their use to all interested parties are vital tasks. They are essential for both profit-making business ventures and nonprofit organizations, such as universities and hospitals.

In another sense, however, the audiences listed above have different needs for and abilities to obtain information. Their desire for knowledge about the nature and use of an organization's resources reflects quite different objectives. For example, current and prospective owners must decide whether to increase, retain, or reduce their investment in the business. They are interested in the current state of their investment as well as information from which to forecast the future success of the business. Bankers and lenders, on the other hand, must judge whether to grant a loan and, if so, on what terms. They may be primarily interested in current financial solvency and information from which to predict the ability of a firm to pay its debts as they become due. Managers must select among alternative courses of future action relating to products, processes, and operating techniques. They need very detailed information to plan and control an organization's human and material resources effectively. Taxation authorities have a specific interest in determining how much tax the business is legally obligated to pay. Employees and their unions make decisions about whether the firm is able to pay higher wages and hire more people. The list of varying decisions and different informational needs could easily be extended for the other users on the list.

**The Many Facets of Accounting**

One result of the foregoing differences in the accounting audience has been a partitioning of the accounting process into a number of overlapping yet distinct activities differentiated by the type of information being communicated and the audience to whom it is reported. Figure 1-1 depicts this partitioning. The center consists of all types of financial information about the acquisition, financing, and use of resources. The spokes represent the major branches of accounting, the reports they prepare, and the audiences they serve.

**Financial Accounting.** Our focal point will be the type of accounting activity known as financial accounting. Its primary concern is the provision of information to investors and other groups not directly involved in operating the business or empowered to dictate the presentation and content of the reports prepared for them. Its output consists of general-purpose financial statements directed at a variety of external users.

FIGURE 1-1   The Many Facets of Accounting

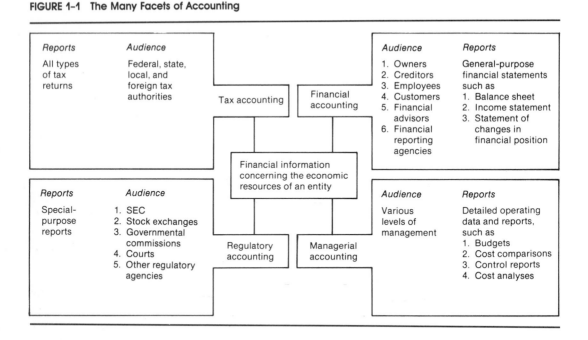

Of these, stockholders and creditors are dominant; other external parties are assumed to share the informational needs of the direct investors.

Although specifically oriented to these external audiences, the reports of financial accounting are of interest to practically all audiences. In addition, the fundamental concepts of financial accounting provide a basis for the recording process. For these two reasons, financial accounting provides a natural starting point for our discussion.

**Managerial Accounting.**   Unlike external audiences making decisions about the business firm as a whole, management makes decisions about the resources within the entity. Management directs the activities of the firm through its acquisition and use of economic resources. To be sure, managers must grasp the basic concepts of financial accounting. The financial statements are the principal means that management uses to communicate the results of its endeavors to external parties. Like all of us, managers are interested in what their scorecards, the financial statements, reveal.

At the same time, managers need additional detailed information of a different kind in making decisions about current and future operations. Financial accounting reports primarily on "what is" and "what was." Internal management needs to know "what will be" for planning purposes and "what should have been" for control purposes. Managerial accounting consists of the additional procedures and techniques for supplying detailed operating data and projections.

**Regulatory Accounting.** Regulatory agencies constantly call on accountants to prepare a variety of special-purpose reports. They need these reports to judge whether an enterprise is meeting its legal obligations and conforming to various social and economic regulations issued by federal, state, and local governments.

The regulatory authorities usually are in a position to dictate exactly what information they desire and how it is to be arranged. The informational needs of these groups determine the varied specialized procedures which collectively are referred to as regulatory accounting. To some extent the reports filed with the Securities and Exchange Commission and with the stock exchanges parallel financial accounting statements. Reports prepared for other regulatory agencies have less in common.

**Tax Accounting.** This aspect of the accounting process covers the preparation of records and reports necessary for the filing of tax returns. Often different from the concepts underlying financial accounting, tax regulations are a complex set of ever-changing laws and rules. Keeping up to date on tax regulations and their implications for business planning and decision making ranks high on the list of tasks occupying accountants' energies. Because of their different audience, their complexity, and their changeability, detailed income tax reports do not play an important role in this book. Nevertheless, we will be alert to some possible distortions caused by the intrusion of tax concepts in the measurement of business income.

**NATURE OF FINANCIAL ACCOUNTING AND ITS AUDIENCE**

In general the audience for financial accounting reports consists of external users, in particular stockholders and creditors. Of course, even this latter group includes many different types of investors with varying investment objectives and degrees of interest and expertise. Consequently, financial accounting and reporting must build upon certain assumptions about their general characteristics and purposes. These assumptions exert a directing influence on what information is recorded and how.

**Audience Characteristics**

The paramount characteristic assumed by conventional financial reporting is the aforementioned idea that the investor audience cannot dictate the presentation and content of financial reports. While managers know or can directly obtain detailed information necessary for internal operating decisions, stockholders must rely on reports prepared for them by management. They are usually not involved in the actual operations of the firm and therefore lack the authority to demand specific financial information or to check directly on its reliability.

In addition, three other characteristics of the investor audience are usually presumed:

1. *Technical competence*—Users of general-purpose financial statements are presumed to be familiar with business and economic activities and to understand accounting language and information. "Financial information . . . cannot be of much direct help to those who are unable or unwilling to use it. . . . Financial reporting should not exclude relevant information merely because it is difficult for some to understand."[1]

2. *Comparative analyses*—In their analyses, investors and creditors wish to compare one business entity with another and the results of one entity over successive periods of time.

3. *Interpretive preference*—This characteristic concerns the degree to which users are willing to have preparers of information inject their judgments or interpretations of future events into the financial statements. For the most part, financial accounting operates on the assumption that its audience desires to retain the bulk of the interpretive task and certainly wishes a clear distinction to be made between information that is primarily factual and that which is primarily interpretive. Financial accounting should therefore furnish information which emphasizes transactions and events that have already happened and which minimizes the influence of management's expectations on the financial reports.

**Objectives of Financial Reporting**

The overall purpose of financial accounting is to provide information that is useful and understandable to its external audiences. The most recent authoritative statement about the objectives of general-purpose financial reporting lists the following three specific aims:[2]

1. To provide information that is useful to present and prospective investors and creditors and other users in making rational investment and credit decisions.

2. To furnish information to aid users in assessing the amounts, timing, and uncertainty of prospective cash receipts associated with investments in the enterprise.

3. To report information about the economic resources of an enterprise, the claims to those resources, and the effects of transactions and events that change those resources and claims to them.

The first two objectives are general. The first one recognizes that financial information is used primarily in the determination of the attractiveness of a firm as an investment outlet. Investors and creditors must evaluate the earnings potential and financial strength of various competing firms in order to allocate financial capital rationally. Owners must decide

---

[1] Financial Accounting Standards Board, *Statement of Financial Accounting Concepts No. 1*, "Objectives of Financial Reporting by Business Enterprises" (Stamford, Conn., November 1978), par. 36.

[2] The discussion in this section relies on *FASB Concepts No. 1*, par. 32–53.

whether to buy, sell, or retain their ownership interests; lenders must decide whether to make loans, in what amounts, and on what terms.

The second objective asserts that critical to these decisions is information concerning prospective cash receipts from dividends or interest and from the proceeds associated with the sale, redemption, or maturity of securities and loans. Rational investment and credit judgments depend directly on predictions of future cash flows to the investor and creditor. These, in turn, are tied to the future cash flows of the enterprise. Financial accounting should supply inputs, primarily in the form of information on past performance and existing financial position, to allow users to assess the amounts, timing, and uncertainty of net cash flows to the enterprise.

The third objective becomes more specific. Indeed, it is divided into four sub-objectives which detail specific kinds of information to be reported:

*a.* Information about an enterprise's economic resources, obligations, and the difference between them (which accountants call owners' equity).
*b.* Information about an enterprise's financial performance during a period as measured by earnings.
*c.* Information about how an enterprise obtains and uses funds, about its borrowings and repayments, and about other factors that may affect its liquidity and solvency.
*d.* Information about how the management of the enterprise has discharged its *stewardship* responsibility.

Financial accounting has three primary reports that respond to the specific needs in *(a)*, *(b)*, and *(c)*. These will be discussed later in the chapter and will continue to be the center of attention throughout the rest of this book.

Objective *(d)* is a long-standing one in financial accounting. Control over resources often rests with individuals or groups who act on behalf of those who furnish or are the beneficiaries of the resources. Those who control resources are accountable to others for their stewardship over those resources. In our specific context owners commit funds and other properties to the business enterprise. In turn, management is responsible for protecting this financial commitment and using the resources for the purposes intended. Moreover, managers have an obligation to provide information concerning their stewardship over invested funds. This reporting objective is satisfied directly by historical information which owners can use to appraise the effectiveness of management in administering the resources of the enterprise.

**FINANCIAL ACCOUNTING PRINCIPLES**

One important step in the achievement of these three objectives is the establishment of a set of basic concepts to guide the preparation and interpretation of financial accounting reports. With the rise of the large corporation in which absentee owners entrust operating control to professional managers, investors and creditors require financial information that adheres to some general standards that are consistently applied and understood. Otherwise the content, format, and basis of the financial information could vary drastically from one situation to another, from one time period to another, and from one management source to another.

Therefore, financial accounting rests on a framework of concepts and conventions that act as general guides in the identifying, measuring, classifying, and reporting processes. The elements in this framework collectively are called *generally accepted accounting principles (GAAP)*. They are not immutable laws of nature. Rather, they are man-made guides that determine what information is to be recorded, how measurements are to be made, and how the data are to be presented in the financial statements. Being widely accepted, they help to ensure that financial information is understood by users and that different firms use substantially uniform principles in reporting similar events. This uniformity is absolutely essential for the comparative analyses so frequently carried out by investors.

## Development of Accounting Principles

Financial accounting principles (GAAP) have risen from the interaction between two distinct and often independent sources—the theoretical and the practical. Over a period of more than 500 years, accounting has developed as a practical art of collecting and reporting certain data relating to business operations; more recently it has also evolved as a body of theoretical knowledge founded on assumptions and containing logically derived and internally consistent conclusions. In both accounting theory and accounting practice, general principles are developed for dealing with the real world of business transactions and events. However, the approaches are quite different.

**Development of Practice.** The development of accounting practice can be characterized as a four-stage process:

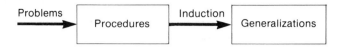

As problems arise in connection with individual business events, practicing accountants design particular procedures to solve these specific problems. The history of accounting practice consists of a problem-procedure evolution—the development of new procedures or modification of old ones as different problems occur.

The search for basic concepts in accounting practice involves generalizing from a detailed analysis of these individual procedures. Through induction—the derivation of a broad pattern or conclusion from a number of specific instances—generalizations can be developed concerning accounting practice. In other words, "Accounting is what accountants do." The generalizations derived from a study of existing accounting procedures and practices are considered sound because they are accepted and used. By and large, accounting has developed as a practical art with its history dominated by the inductive approach of the practitioner. For this reason it is difficult to compile a definitive list of GAAP, much of which is simply implicit in accounting practice.

**Development of Accounting Theory.**   Theoretical formulations of accounting principles have arisen from a very different process:

The first step in the development of a theory is to abstract from the existing real world of business events. Rising above the myriad of specific events, the theorist attempts to set forth some basic assumptions about business activities. From these assumptions, conclusions can be developed concerning accounting activities through the use of deductive logic. These conclusions present the theoretical answer to the query, "What should accountants do?"

This process is identified as model building, quite similar to that employed in mathematics and economics. The models are not as abstract in accounting as in these other disciplines, however.

Actually, a number of accounting models have been advanced by various individuals. The initial assumptions and objectives are diverse. Some are normative; others are primarily descriptive. Our concern centers on what can be called "conventional theory," the system of reasoning that appears to underlie present-day financial reporting. This attention does not necessarily imply that the existing theoretical framework is the best one; we explore some alternatives in Chapter 19.

**Interaction between Theory and Practice.**   Ideally, the *conclusions* developed from accounting *theory* should agree with the *generalizations* developed from a study of accounting *practice*. Unfortunately, the ideal world does not exist. Generally accepted accounting principles are often established by political compromise among conflicting parties rather than being based on strict logic.

Accounting theory provides three major aids in the development of accounting principles: (1) a framework for organizing existing ideas and practices so they can be better understood, (2) criteria for evaluating the internal consistency of accounting practice, and (3) guidelines for resolving new accounting problems and practices that develop in the future. When accounting practices are not firmly rooted in a logical foundation, generalizations in one problem area appear inconsistent with recommended treatments in other areas. Seemingly similar items may be treated differently by different reporting companies but with equal acceptability. The result is likely to be a lack of comparability among the statements of different companies.

If accounting theory is at variance with observable practice, then the basic postulates are not descriptive of the real world, the logic used in deriving conclusions from the assumptions is not sound, or other influences in the environment operate to counteract the reason and logic of the theoretical model. The assumptions underlying accounting theory must be based on common sense and relate to the existing business world. Their validity must be continually checked empirically. Indeed, some of the assumptions themselves may result from observations of practice. In addition, any errors in logic must be weeded out. Differences in fact which might justify alternative procedures must not be assumed away. A critical examination of differences between theory and practice may be helpful.

Theory and practice complement one another and provide a check-and-balance element in the development of accounting principles. At any particular time the set of concepts which we know as generally accepted accounting principles represents the consensus arising from this interaction.

**AUTHORITA-TIVE BODIES INFLUENCING ACCOUNTING THOUGHT**

In the evolutionary process from which emerge the generally accepted accounting principles, the pronouncements and publications of major accounting organizations and other groups and individuals play key roles. Currently, the two most influential bodies are the Securities and Exchange Commission (SEC), a governmental organization, and the Financial Accounting Standards Board (FASB), a private sector group. In a formal sense, generally accepted accounting principles are what these organizations say they are.

**Securities and Exchange Commission.** Under the securities laws of 1933 and 1934, Congress established this agency in an attempt to regulate the nation's securities markets and to assure that investors had adequate information on which to base their decisions. Congress empowered the SEC to establish the accounting principles to be followed by companies which issue new securities directly to the general public or whose securities are traded on the organized exchanges. Over 10,000 firms, including practically all of the large, dominant corporations in the United States, fall under SEC jurisdiction and must comply with its regulations.

One reporting requirement is that these firms must file *Form 10-K* after the close of each fiscal year. The 10-K must include a complete set of financial statements audited and prepared in accordance with *Regulation S-X*. First issued in 1940, Regulation S-X remains the SEC's principal accounting regulation. It standardizes the definitions, format, and content of the financial statements required by the SEC. Additionally, over 300

*Accounting Series Releases* have been issued since 1937. These ASRs report the Commission's official policy on accounting questions. Through them the Commission has articulated standards for the full and fair reporting of financial information both in SEC reports and firms' annual reports to stockholders.[3]

In *Accounting Series Release No. 4,* issued in 1938 and reaffirmed in 1973 in *ASR No. 150,* the SEC formally stated that accounting principles underlying the financial statements must have "substantial authoritative support." Although possessing statutory power to regulate accounting procedures, the SEC traditionally has looked to the accounting profession to supply this authoritative support. Historically, the principles promulgated by the SEC either have reflected existing ones set forth by the accounting profession or have been worked out in close conjunction with authoritative groups in the private sector. Nevertheless, the impact of the SEC is great because of the authority vested in it, and its pronouncements are not taken lightly.

**Financial Accounting Standards Board.** Since 1973 the FASB has been the authoritative force in the private sector in the setting of standards for financial accounting reports. The FASB is composed of seven full-time professionals appointed by an independent group, the Financial Accounting Foundation, for renewable five-year terms. Four of the seven must be certified public accountants, and the FASB is responsible only to the Foundation. The Foundation trustees are chosen by various accounting organizations and user groups.

The Financial Accounting Standards Board issues three types of accounting pronouncements:

1.  *Statements of Financial Accounting Standards (SFAS)*—These authoritative statements spell out the current generally accepted accounting principles. Over 70 of them have been issued to date.
2.  *Statements of Financial Accounting Concepts*—This series of publications attempts to lay the groundwork for a conceptual framework for financial accounting and reporting. They do not establish standards for particular procedures and practices. Rather, the four statements issued to date describe concepts and ideas that will guide the development of future accounting standards.
3.  *Interpretations of Statements of Financial Accounting Standards*—As their name implies, these publications explain, clarify, and sometimes amend previously issued statements of standards. The standards sometimes are general guidelines, and the interpretations provide needed elaboration. Over 40 of them have been issued to date.

Prior to the establishment of the FASB, generally accepted accounting

---

[3] The staff of the SEC also periodically issues *Staff Accounting Bulletins,* which discuss accounting reporting issues in a detailed yet less official medium than its *Accounting Series Releases.*

principles were promulgated through the American Institute of Certified Public Accountants (AICPA). This organization represents over 150,000 professionally trained accountants responsible for issuing opinions on the financial statements prepared by management. Each member has met certain minimum requirements as to education and experience and has passed a national examination to earn the designation, *certified public accountant* (CPA).

Between 1939 and 1960 the AICPA issued over 50 *Accounting Research Bulletins* (ARBs) and *Accounting Terminology Bulletins* (ATBs) through its Committee on Accounting Procedure. Then in 1960 the Institute created an *Accounting Principles Board* (APB) to issue authoritative opinions and to publish research studies. The APB had 18 part-time members elected by the Council governing the AICPA. Prior to its dissolution in 1973, the APB issued 4 statements and 31 opinions, the latter becoming part of GAAP.

Despite its 13 years of contribution to the establishment of accounting principles, the APB suffered almost continuous criticism from within the accounting profession, from management, and from user groups as well. The criticisms were aimed at the unwieldy size and part-time nature of the APB and its concomitant lack of productivity. In addition, the APB was criticized for being dominated by CPAs and hence not sufficiently responsive to the needs of users and management. The structural changes involved in the establishment of the FASB were designed to make it more productive, more independent, more autonomous, and more respresentative than was the APB.

An essential ingredient of the FASB's method of operation is to encourage as much input as possible from all parties interested in a particular accounting problem. Before publishing a standard, the FASB normally appoints a task force to define the problem carefully and to identify the issues. Task forces include persons from the FASB organization as well as outsiders who are knowledgeable about the topic. Then the FASB distributes discussion memoranda. It solicits written comments from interested parties and conducts public hearings. After consideration of all views, the FASB publishes an exposure draft of its proposed statement. The draft is widely circulated among public accountants, educators, business executives, investors, analysts, and others. The FASB reviews the feedback, makes any revisions it feels are warranted, and issues a statement after an affirmative vote of four of its seven members.

Both the Council of the American Institute of Certified Public Accountants and the Securities and Exchange Commission have taken formal action to increase the importance of the FASB standards. The AICPA in its *Rules of Conduct* has resolved that members generally may not express an opinion that financial statements are presented in conformity with generally accepted accounting principles if such statements contain any departure from an accounting principle promulgated by the FASB. In a similar vein, the SEC in *Accounting Series Release No. 150* explicity stated that standards and interpretations of the FASB constitute substantial authoritative support and that accounting principles contrary to FASB standards will not have such support.

**Overview.**   In the future, generally accepted accounting principles officially will consist of *Statements of Financial Accounting Standards* issued by the FASB. However, some pronouncements from earlier authorities remain in effect in their original or modified form. Current accounting practice must look therefore to a mixture of SFASs, APBs, ARBs and ATBs for its authoritative guidelines. References to many of these different authoritative pronouncements appear throughout the remaining chapters.

Figure 1–2 identifies various groups that influence the formulation of accounting principles and reporting standards. The SEC and the FASB form the central source of authoritative pronouncements. As a rule the former has focused on disclosure matters, and the latter has been concerned with measurement issues. However, many other groups and individuals contribute formally and informally to the deliberations. In addition, many of these groups publish research results and statements of their own which over time may have a subtle and continual impact on the development of accounting principles.

**FIGURE 1–2   Groups Involved in the Establishment of Accounting Principles**

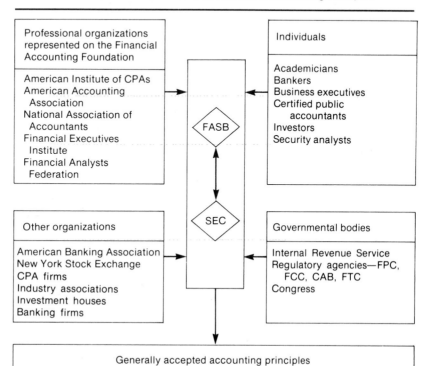

A detailed description of all these sources of influence is beyond our scope. Nevertheless, a few comments about some of the major professional organizations may help explain the environment of financial accounting.

1. *American Institute of Certified Public Accountants*—This body was discussed earlier. Since authority to set standards has been transferred to the FASB, the AICPA provides extensive input through its Accounting Standards Executive Committee. It also has the major responsibility for developing *auditing* standards and overseeing the professional conduct of practicing CPAs. It publishes a monthly periodical called *The Journal of Accountancy* as well as numerous other studies and materials on accounting problems and practices.

2. *American Accounting Association*—This group represents the views primarily of accounting educators. Its quarterly publication, *The Accounting Review,* is one of the major outlets for writers of conceptual literature. In addition the AAA periodically issues statements on the standards or concepts which *should* underlie financial statements and sponsors individual research projects by outstanding scholars. Both the periodic statements of standards and the research monographs tend to be normative declarations about the directions in which financial reporting should be moving and not necessarily a reflection of current accounting thought.

3. *National Association of Accountants*—This association represents primarily internal managerial accountants. However, in recent years it has broadened the scope of its research and educational programs to include the problems of external reporting. Its monthly publication, called *Management Accounting,* is supplemented occasionally by research studies or monographs which it sponsors. Its Committee on Management Accounting Practices expresses the official views of NAA on relevant accounting matters to other professional groups, including the FASB and SEC.

4. *The Financial Executives Institute*—Perhaps the most influential association on the management side, FEI is composed of the financial executives of large corporations. It has a direct interest in the external reporting principles imposed on businesses by the SEC and FASB. It contributes directly to discussions of accounting principles through statements from its Panel on Accounting Principles. *The Financial Executive,* its monthly publication, provides indirect input in the form of accounting literature. Also, its research arm, the *Financial Executives Research Foundation,* has sponsored several relevant and highly influential studies.

5. *Financial Analysts Federation*—The FAF represents a major group of users of accounting information. Composed of professional financial analysts, this organization has begun to exert influence on the development of accounting principles and reporting standards. Frequently in the past, analysts have been critical of corporate financial disclosure.

The FAF provides a collective voice for these criticisms. It publishes the bimonthly *Financial Analysts Journal*.

## A FRAMEWORK FOR FINANCIAL ACCOUNTING PRINCIPLES

The primary concern of this section is the conceptual framework for the conventional financial accounting model. Figure 1-3 depicts the overall framework and the interrelationships of its major elements. Many influences, both theoretical and practical, impact on the development of generally accepted accounting principles. Not all accountants or accounting organizations would agree entirely with this particular arrangement or identification of elements. Many of the ideas come from the series of *Statements of Financial Accounting Concepts* published by the Financial Accounting Standards Board. The rest reflect concepts appearing fre-

**FIGURE 1-3  A Framework for Financial Accounting Principles**

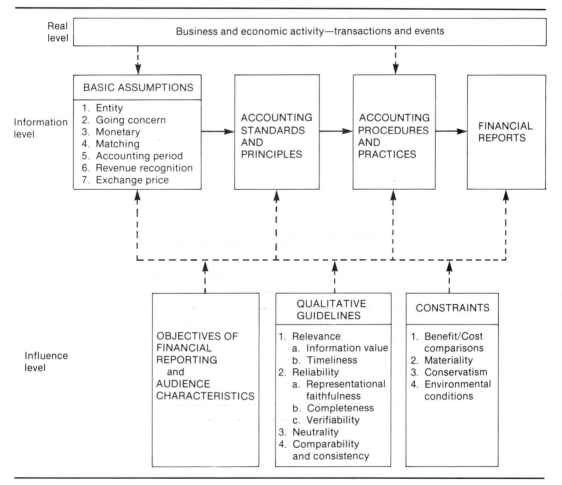

quently in accounting literature and accounting practice. Together they form an interrelated structure upon which we can build in subsequent chapters.

Before discussing the particular elements, let us take an overview of the entire framework in Figure 1–3. The real-world domain of financial reporting consists of actual business transactions and other economic events. The financial accounting process, the middle level, attempts to provide information about this stream of economic activities. First, some basic assumptions about the business environment and about the accounting process itself are established. From these assumptions follow some general principles and standards. These in turn lead to procedures and practices which accountants use to describe real-world events as they construct financial reports.

But this process of *selecting assumptions, deriving principles, applying procedures,* and *preparing reports* is not carried out in a vacuum. Overriding the whole process of financial accounting are a number of other factors and conditions. Their influence is shown by the broken lines in Figure 1–3. First, the overall objectives of financial reporting and the assumed audience characteristics discussed earlier in this chapter play a significant role in the adoption of the particular assumptions and the setting of general standards. Second, a group of normative characteristics—relevance, reliability, neutrality, and comparability—provide qualitative guidelines for all parts of the information process. Last, certain environmental factors and conventions modify the basic theory derived from the underlying assumptions and constrain its application.

## Qualitative Guidelines

Conventional accounting is characterized by certain normative ideas of what "good" accounting ought to be. These doctrines specify qualities or characteristics that make reported information useful, desirable, proper, and so on. *Relevance* and *reliability* are the paramount, although sometimes conflicting, guidelines that help accountants to judge when events should be recorded in the accounting system and what dollar values should be used to measure them. Comparability, on the other hand, relates more to the actual reporting process. Neutrality attempts to assure that the choices made by accountants are guided by evenhandedness and economic fact and not by ulterior motives. Together these four exert a pervasive influence on financial accounting theory and practice.

**Relevance.** The idea of relevance is elusive because it is a subjective measure of information content. Relevant information is that which is responsive to the audience's information needs. It is capable of making a difference to the user of the information.

To be relevant, information must possess two subqualities. First, it must have value to the user—either predictive value or feedback value. Information with predictive value improves the user's ability to make forecasts about the outcome of events of interest. Information with feedback value reduces uncertainty by confirming or altering prior expectations. The second subquality of relevance is timeliness. Timely information is reported before it ceases to affect decisions. "Timeliness alone cannot make information relevant, but a lack of timeliness can rob information of relevance it might otherwise have had."[4]

One major problem with the guideline of relevance is that accountants have only begun to understand what it means. Apart from generalized notions about the perceived needs of investors and creditors, we know little about what specific information and measurements are relevant to users' actual or hypothesized decision models. For example, in a warehouse a steel wholesaler has 10 tons of steel which cost $60 per ton three months ago. Because of a slowdown in the economy, similar steel can be acquired from the mills at $53 per ton. Deliveries from the warehouse to retail customers have been made recently at a selling price of $68 per ton. However, recent sales activity has been sluggish, and management is considering instituting retail price cuts or extensive sales promotional activity. What dollar value per ton—$60, $53, $68, or some other figure—should the accountant assign to this steel in reporting to investors and creditors? Which of these figures is relevant to the audience?

**Reliability.**     This guideline plays the most important role in conventional accounting. Financial accounting information should be "reasonably free from error and bias and faithfully represent what it purports to represent."[5] Financial accounting statements should be based on actual, verifiable events and should be reported in an unbiased manner. In this way they will serve an audience that we assume desires to make its own interpretations and will offer protection to an audience that we assume lacks authority to dictate the content of financial reports.

Three conditions contribute to the existence of reliability:

1.     *Representational faithfulness* implies a correspondence between accounting measures and the underlying economic events they are representing. Bias occurs in financial reporting when measurement methods fail to capture the essence of the economic variables they are measuring. In pursuing representational faithfulness to minimize any potential measurement error, accountants should stress economic substance over legal form.

A financial statement is analogous in many ways to a map. To have representational faithfulness, the map should portray accurately what it represents. A geopolitical map cannot represent topography well, but it can and should show countries clearly. Likewise, a topographical map may not show political boundaries, but the reader should be able to depend on it to delineate validly the mountains and river valleys.

2.     *Completeness* means that financial statements should present information that is complete and understandable to users of the reports. A

---

[4] FASB, *Statement of Financial Accounting Concepts No. 2*, "Qualitative Characteristics of Accounting Information" (Stamford, Conn., May 1980), par. 56.

[5] Ibid., p. xvi.

highway map that shows all roads but omits a number of thruway interchanges lacks reliability. One without scales or legends suffers similarly.

In financial accounting the term *full and fair disclosure,* which arose from the securities laws of 1933 and 1934 creating the SEC, is often used to describe this characteristic. Full disclosure requires that all material accounting data that might be significant to a reasonably intelligent user be disclosed. There should be no unnecessary summarization. Moreover, the quantitative information should be supplemented by narrative explanations necessary for accurate interpretation by the reader. Included would be identification of accounting policies followed, departures from generally accepted accounting principles, changes in accounting procedures from one period to the next, and other supplementary data exploring the assumptions or estimations behind the statements. The information given must not only be complete; it must be clearly presented as well. Reasonable condensation is desirable; supporting schedules should be amply used. Moreover, statement titles and footnote terminology should be understandable to the reader of the statement.

3. *Verifiability* means that accounting information and measurement methods can be independently confirmed by other competent measurers. Another potential source of reporting bias in financial accounting is unintentional error on the part of the accountant. When accounting is done so that two or more independent parties can reach the same conclusion about a measurement, possible measurer-bias is significantly reduced. The desire for verifiability (objectivity) is one reason why accountants, when preparing financial statements, place great importance on transactions arising out of arm's-length negotiations between independent parties, rather than relying on management's plans, expectations, or dreams of the future.

These three conditions—representational faithfulness, completeness, and verifiability—make up what accountants call reliability, It is, of course, a relative concept, utilized in specific situations in varying degrees. Nonetheless, its general influence is strong.

Although reliability and relevance have been established as the primary qualitative characteristics, accounting theorists have not established how they interact or how trade-offs between them are to be made. Relevance in accounting practice more often than not takes a back seat to reliability. As we shall see, conventional financial accounting resolves the valuation problem in our steel example in the last section in favor of the $60 purchase cost on the grounds of reliability and an *assumption* that historical cost is relevant to the investor's needs. But because $53 and $68 more nearly reflect current values, a case can be made that they are relevant, albeit less reliable, than the cost of $60.

Both relevance and reliability are desirable, and more of either adds to the usefulness of accounting information. However, the dilemma caused by the interaction and conflicts between them will not be resolved until we learn more about user decision models.

**Neutrality.** This qualitative characteristic pervades all aspects of the accounting process. "Neutrality means that either in formulating or implementing standards, the primary concern should be the relevance and reliability of the information that results, not the effect that the new rule may have on a particular interest."[6] Accounting policies should be chosen without any specific purpose other than to measure economic variables accurately. When judgments are needed to make the statements useful, those judgments should be free from any purposeful bias favoring any particular group. Financial statements should present information fairly and impartially.

Neutrality does not mean that financial statements have no purpose or that various parties may not be affected differently by their disclosures. Rather, it means that in the measuring-reporting process no attempt should be made to influence behavior in a particular direction. A road map designed to encourage people to travel on a tollroad, say by omitting alternative routes, would not be neutral. Similarly, the choice of an accounting method solely because it would discourage (or encourage) companies from merging would not be appropriate under this standard. Neutrality attempts to minimize intentional bias in financial reporting.

**Comparability.** The desire to conduct comparative analyses among firms and between accounting periods is one of the major characteristics assumed for the audience of financial accounting. Comparability calls for like events to be reported in the same manner and unlike events to be reported differently. Some of the obvious reporting conventions that promote comparability are uniform measurement practices; relatively standardized formats for financial statements; uniform definitions, terminology, and classifications; and regular reporting periods. Comparability also requires that changes in accounting principles be restricted to situations in which the new principle is *clearly preferable* to the old. When a change has been made, its nature, effect, and justification should be explained.

Comparability obviously deals with the quality of the relationship between two pieces of information and not with the individual pieces. Controversy arises over its achievement in the interfirm context. Some uniformity in accounting practices among firms is necessary. Only then will reported differences in the financial statements reflect variances in the economic circumstances of the firms. Comparative analyses may be frustrated if differences arise from differences in accounting methods applied to like events. On the other hand, an overly rigid or mechanistic quest for uniformity of techniques almost certainly would result in a masking of underlying economic differences, causing unlike items to be measured and reported as though they possessed the same characteristics.

Closely allied to comparability is *consistency*. Indeed, it is an essential ingredient of comparability over time within a single firm. Measurement methods and reporting procedures in accounting should be consistently

---

[6] Ibid., par. 98.

applied from one report to another. It is imperative that the choices and judgments the accountant makes regarding alternative methods and practices be the same from period to period for the same enterprise. Otherwise, users will not be able to analyze trends or to discern changing relationships over time. Consistency does not bar a change to more accurate or correct procedures. However, if no change has been reported, the reader should be able to feel confident that the same concepts and procedures underlie each period's statements. The quality of consistency does bar indiscriminate switching from practice to practice.

## Basic Assumptions

Seven fundamental concepts can be identified as basic to the deductive formulation of financial accounting. Three of them—the entity concept, the going-concern concept, and the monetary concept—are *environmental* in nature. They postulate some fairly obvious conditions for business activity. The other four assumptions concern *operational* processes—assertions as to the best way of carrying out the major tasks of financial accounting. The strong influence of the qualitative guidelines on the selection of these assumptions is readily apparent.

**Entity Concept.** This assumption states that *accounting reports and records pertain to a specifically defined business entity, separate and distinct from the people or groups concerned with it*. The accounting entity can be any identifiable organizational unit with control over resources and with economic activities of interest to someone. It is not necessarily synonymous with any specific legal or taxable organization. For example, accounting records are maintained for a one-owner business (single proprietorship), which is not recognized as a separate entity for the levying of taxes or for most legal purposes. In this situation the entity concept would direct that the accounting records reflect only the activities of the business and not be mixed with the personal affairs of the owners, for example, the personal consumption expenditures of the proprietor.

The large modern corporation is recognized by legal and tax authorities as a separate organization. In this case the accounting entity and the legal entity are the same. Because of its importance, the private, profit-directed corporation is the accounting entity referred to in the remainder of this book. We focus on events in which the corporation is an actual participant. The entity concept forces us to distinguish between gains (losses) of the corporation and gains (losses) of the individual stockholder. In Chapter 15 we modify the single-corporation definition of the entity and look at a *consolidated entity,* a group of interrelated corporations under a single control. That discussion also explores some of the difficulties in the selection of an appropriate entity.

**Going-Concern Concept.** This assumption describes the accounting entity more fully. Under the going-concern, or *continuity,* concept, *in the absence of evidence to the contrary, the entity is assumed to remain in operation sufficiently long to carry out its objectives and plans*. Thus the accountant does not focus on liquidation values at any particular date. Rather, as we shall see, the central activity is the *matching process* in which the costs of economic resources are allocated over their useful lives. This type of allocation implies that the concern will be in existence at least as long as the useful lives of its various resources.

Of course, we are describing only an assumption, not reality for all businesses. If there is evidence that an entity's existence will terminate in the foreseeable future, then a different assumption should be selected and different accounting procedures developed. For instance, special accounting procedures are used for concerns in liquidation or bankruptcy. Financial accounting, however, is interested in those firms that are expected to remain in operation.

**Monetary Concept.** This assumption contains two basic ideas about the unit of measurement used in accounting. The first states that *because money is the common denominator for the expression of economic activity, it should be used to measure and analyze accounting events and transactions.* No other means of expression is so universal, simple, and adaptable. However, this part of the postulate excludes from financial accounting the recording of events which are not monetarily quantifiable. Such events or conditions (e.g., a heart attack suffered by the company president, employee morale, and the competence or charisma of the sales manager) may be of great importance; nevertheless, they are not communicated through the accounting system.

The second part of this assumption states that *fluctuations in the value of the dollar can be ignored without significant impairment of the usefulness or validity of the financial statements.* The value in *purchasing power* of the monetary unit declines whenever the quantity of goods and services that people will exchange decreases significantly over time. We call this inflation. The monetary concept assumes that any distortions caused by inflationary price-level changes (changes in the value or size of the monetary unit) will not undermine the reliability of the financial statements. Although soundly criticized and attacked as invalid in the last 40 years, this assumption remains an integral though contentious cornerstone of conventional accounting theory.

**Matching Concept.** The general nature of business affairs can be described as an acquisition-consumption-recovery cycle. Stripped of embellishments, the conduct of any business enterprise involves acquiring economic resources, called *assets* (raw materials, labor, equipment, etc.), in anticipation of using them to produce a product or a service, which is then sold. A resource inflow, usually in the form of cash or claims to cash, results from the sale. Measuring accounting income involves matching against the total amount of resource inflow *(revenues)* received from the period's operations the cost of resources *(expenses)* that were consumed in the production of the inflow.

The central operational assumption of financial accounting is that *net income is best measured by a matching of costs against the revenues to which the costs have given rise.* In this way, we are associating the total resources used up in operations with the total resources received from operations. Costs are divided into two groups—those applicable to the production of revenues in the current period (expenses) and those applicable to the production of revenues in future periods (assets). Costs, in theory, should be allocated between the present and the future wholly on the basis of when they contribute to the process of revenue generation.

In practice, uncertainties and difficulties in assigning costs cause departures from this theory. Nevertheless, the general concept is that a cost becomes an expense when the resource (asset) is consumed in the production of revenues. In a broad sense, revenues provide a monetary measure of the *accomplishment* of a firm in satisfying the wants and desires of consumers. Likewise, expenses can be viewed as a monetary expression of *effort,* in the sense of resources used, in satisfyng consumer desires. By coupling the two flows of revenue and expense, we relate effort and accomplishment to obtain a meaningful measure of performance (net income).

This matching concept is, of course, only one possible assumption. There are other approaches to income measurement. For example, the business could be valued at the end of selected periods of time, and net income could be defined as the increase or decrease in value. Alternatively, we could employ some subjective approach to determine the present value of expected future net receipts, as in theoretical economics.

The matching assumption is selected, however, because it incorporates greater reliability and historical perspective than do other alternatives. Although not completely free from judgmental factors, the basic information used in the matching concept—revenues and expenses—is rooted in actual market transactions and events. To the extent that the matching concept ignores changes in value or future expectations, its usefulness may be limited. Nevertheless, financial accounting currently accepts this fundamental assumption.

**Concept of the Accounting Period.**   To fulfill its communication function, financial accounting must operate in a time framework. The complexity of the modern business environment requires interim measures of economic progress; users of financial reports rely on timely data and cannot wait until the entity's life has ended to ascertain net income. The *periodicity concept assumes that economic activity can be meaningfully divided into arbitrary time periods.*

Considering the continuous nature of enterprise activity, the time periods selected are to some extent artificial. Periodic reports serve only as indices of the stream of economic activity of the entity. Measurements of operating results (costs matched against revenues) for any short period of time are tentative. They involve estimates and approximations, but accountants make them in order to supply needed information for current decision making. Many of the procedures, expedients, and conventions that accountants use to make estimates derive from this concept of the accounting period.

In the employment of this concept, a balance must be achieved between reliability and timeliness. The accounting period must be long enough to provide reasonably accurate results yet short enough to supply currently usable information. For reporting to investors, quarterly and yearly accounting periods are commonly used. Usually the time periods, which are identified in the accounting reports, are of equal length in order that comparisons may be facilitated. The period concept reflects directly the characteristics and needs of those who use accounting reports. It is linked closely to the qualitative guidelines of timeliness and comparability.

**Revenue-Recognition Concept.** If we are to match costs (expenses) against the revenues to which they give rise, we need to know when to recognize the revenues themselves. Two tests are established in this concept. *Revenue should be recognized only when it has been earned and can be measured with a reasonable degree of reliability.* Revenues are effectively earned when substantially all of the activities necessary for and associated with the production of revenues have been completed. More is needed than just a knowledge that the revenues have been earned, however; they must be measurable. Because reliability in measurement is sometimes lacking, revenues are not always recognized as they are economically earned. Instead, the accountant waits for some verifiable evidence, such as a legal sale plus the acquisition of some well-defined asset. With few exceptions, the accountant finds this evidence when transactions with outside customers are completed. In most cases, the point of sale has become the most generally accepted time for revenue recognition. Usually, both criteria are met there. We explore some ramifications of the revenue recognition concept in greater depth in Chapter 6.

**Exchange-Price Concept.** This operational assumption establishes the valuation measures to be applied as data enter the accounting process. *The resources (assets) held by a firm and the claims against those resources (liabilities) are to be recorded at the prices (values) agreed upon or inherent in the exchanges in which they originated.* Assume that a business acquired a new piece of equipment, paying $60,000 for it. To the firm, the equipment possesses greater value than $60,000 over its life; otherwise, it would not have been acquired. Once purchased and installed, it might be worth very little if the firm tried to sell it to someone else. On the other hand, its value might increase as happened with used aircraft in the 1970s. The exchange-price concept dictates that the equipment be recorded at $60,000; no other figure is assumed to be a valid measure for financial accounting. One can see the strong influence exerted by the qualitative guideline of verifiability in the selection of this particular measurement standard.

Similar exchange-price valuations are applied to other types of accounting data. In addition, the measurement concept is extended to include transfers and exchanges not involving money prices, as in barter transactions or those between the firm and its owners. In such cases the initial valuation measure is called *fair market value* and is defined as the value which would have prevailed in a bona fide exchange.

**Constraints**

The factors to be discussed in this section are practical influences on the theoretical framework of financial accounting. Accounting practice may be constrained in its attempts to follow the basic theory derived from the underlying assumptions. Four such constraints present in the real world are benefit/cost comparisons, the time-honored traditions of materiality and conservatism, and the social and legal environment of accounting. Together they help to explain differences between accounting theory and accounting practice in the handling of items.

**Benefit/Cost Comparisons.** Accounting information costs money to gather, process, and report. It should be collected and disclosed only if the benefits to be derived from its use are greater than the cost of generating it. All information must attain some minimum level of relevance and reliability to be useful. However, often marginal increases in relevance or reliability can be attained only at great cost. For example, at times the cost of measuring the current values of economic resources instead of their exchange prices may exceed the gains from improved decision making.

To be sure, the benefits and costs of disclosing information are very difficult to quantify. Usually no explict calculation is made. Rather, the constraint is considered subjectively by individual business enterprises and by the Financial Accounting Standards Board. Business entities weigh it in deciding how detailed an accounting system to maintain and how much information to report voluntarily to outside parties. The FASB should be cognizant of the benefit/cost constraint each time it mandates a change in reporting requirements. However, the benefit/cost comparison is different in internal reporting from external reporting. In the latter, the groups benefited are different from the groups that incur the costs of reporting.

**Materiality.** This criterion both influences the manner of recording items and sets a guideline for reporting. Materiality refers to the relative importance or magnitude of a piece of accounting information. Any amount or transaction that has a significant (material) effect on the financial statements should be recorded correctly and reported. However, items trivial in amount need not be recorded in strict accordance with accounting theory. In addition, minor items (immaterial ones) do not need to be reported in detail.

Materiality serves as a threshold for the recognition of information. In the FASB's definition an item is material if "in the light of surrounding circumstances, the magnitude of the item is such that it is probable that the judgment of a reasonable person relying on the report would have been changed or influenced by the inclusion or correction of the item."[7] Even with this definition, decisions about what is material or immaterial vary from situation to situation and often require the accountant's careful judgment based on extensive experience.

**Conservatism.**    This constraint grows out of the uncertain environment and the tentative measurements of accounting. Historically it has been viewed, and sometimes applied, as a rule requiring understatement of income and assets. In modern financial accounting it calls for due caution and a careful assessment of risks and uncertainties. The old adage, "Don't count your chickens before they hatch," is in keeping with the spirit of conservatism in financial reporting. When a decision requires judgment, accountants tend to select those procedures that result in smaller measures of resources or income. Accountants feel that the possible consequences of overstating these items (bankruptcy, loan defaults, subsequent stock-market declines, lawsuits, etc.) are more severe than those associated with an understatement.

**Environmental Conditions.**    The legal environment of business includes certain precedents and procedures. In addition, practically all firms are regulated to some degree by governmental bodies. These legal and governmental influences affect the accounting procedures used in business. In the extreme situation, accounting procedures may be dictated by governmental bodies, as in the case of railroads and public utilities.

Income tax regulations are another of the environmental factors that currently play an exceedingly important role in accounting practice. Tax rulings are designed to achieve a multiplicity of political and economic purposes. Financial accounting procedures, on the other hand, attempt to achieve the proper matching of costs and revenues to measure business income. Where the two sets of concepts are not the same, the business entity faces a dilemma. Either separate records must be maintained for tax accounting and for financial accounting, with the attendant inconvenience and expense, or procedures designed to implement particular goals of taxation end up being used in the measurement of periodic business income. In the latter situation the purposes of financial accounting may be undermined.

**Financial Accounting Information**

As depicted in Figure 1-3, the outputs of the accounting process are financial reports or statements. These are the means through which selected information about the entity's economic activity can be communicated to external audiences. Recall from our earlier discussion that one major objective of financial reporting is to communicate information about the economic resources of the enterprise, the claims to those resources, and the effect of transactions and events that change those re-

---

[7] Ibid., par. 132.

sources and claims to them. A detailed subdivision of this objective indicated that investors and creditors need information in three specific, basic areas—present financial condition, changes in financial condition over time, and income measurement.

It is not surprising, therefore, that the reporting function in financial accounting centers principally on three financial statements, one directed to each of these information areas. Figure 1–4 shows diagramatically how these three statements are related in time.

**FIGURE 1-4  Financial Accounting Statements**

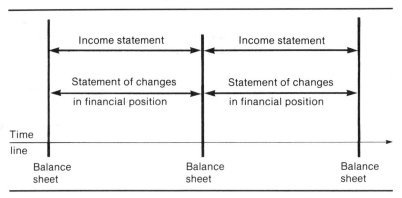

The *balance sheet,* or statement of financial position, presents the financial condition of the entity as of a moment in time. It is akin to the photographer's snapshot. It portrays in monetary terms the economic resources controlled by the business and the claims on and interests in those resources as of a specific date.

In the time intervals between the issuance of statements of financial position, two major types of transactions of interest to stockholders and creditors occur. Many involve the acquisition and financing of productive resources. We can call these *financing-investing* or *capital activities.* The other activities of major concern relate to the production and sale of goods and services. We call these *operating activities.* Knowledge of both types of activities is important in the assessment of future cash flows associated with investments in the business enterprise.

The *income statement* summarizes the major changes in the resources of the business as a result of the operating, or earning, activities. It attempts to report on the performance achieved by the enterprise during a particular period. The FASB, in *Statement of Financial Accounting Concepts No. 1,* explicitly affirmed that the interest of investors and creditors "in an enterprise's future cash flows and its ability to generate favorable cash flows leads primarily to an interest in information about its earnings rather than information directly about its cash flows."[8] It goes on to say that "infor-

---

[8] *FASB Concepts No. 1,* par. 43.

mation about enterprise earnings and its components (as measured on the income statement) generally provides a better indication of enterprise performance than information about current cash receipts and payments."9

The *statement of changes in financial position* (SCFP or funds statement) is designed to disclose the major financing and investing transactions undertaken by the firm. Like the income statement, it covers a period of time. The statement shows the firm's sources of capital during the period and the major areas to which these financial resources were committed. In so doing, the statement discloses causes of changes in financial position during the period. Although it does not depict short-run performance as effectively as the income statement, the SCFP "may be useful in understanding the operations of the enterprise, evaluating its financing activities, assessing its liquidity or solvency, or interpreting earnings information provided."10 For pedagogical reasons, we shall defer discussion of the statement of changes in financial position until Chapter 17.

**Auditing.**   Financial accounting reports are prepared by management and presented to groups who are not connected intimately with the daily operations of the firm. Management is at the same time being judged through the reports it presents. Inherent in this situation is a potential conflict of interest that only an independent attestation can resolve. The function of verifying and appraising the accuracy, integrity, and authenticity of the financial statements is called auditing.

Auditing is a major present-day accounting activity. Certified public accountants are licensed by each state and charged with the responsibility of passing expert judgment on financial statements. Many firms are required by law to submit audited financial statements to the SEC. In addition, most published financial statements for stockholders and creditors are accompanied by an auditor's report or opinion. It adds significantly to the credibility and, hence, usefulness of the financial information by affirming that the statements are a fair representation and have been prepared on a consistent basis in accordance with GAAP. (A typical auditor's report is illustrated in Chapter 16.) The standards and procedures auditors use in making these judgments form the subject matter of separate accounting courses and books.

**SUMMARY**

The purpose of this chapter is to open the door to financial accounting. From our brief exploration of its environmental and theoretical setting, we reach some general observations:

1.   Accounting is a communication system designed for the accumulation

---

9 Ibid., par. 44.
10 Ibid., par. 49.

and reporting of financial information. Financial accounting is only one aspect, albeit an important one, of this many-faceted system.

2. Financial accounting has the task of providing relevant and reliable information primarily to an external audience composed of owners and creditors.

3. The audience of financial accounting reports uses them in making rational investment and credit decisions, in assessing the nature of the prospective cash receipts associated with the enterprise, in evaluating the earnings potential and financial strength of the firm, and in judging the effectiveness of management's administration of the resources of the firm.

4. Financial accounting reports comprise three statements—a balance sheet, which provides information concerning the existing resource base of the enterprise and how the resources were financed; an income statement, which presents information about the historical results of the profit-directed activities of the enterprise; and a statement of changes in financial position, which relates information about changes in resources and obligations from financing-investing transactions.

5. Financial statements are prepared according to generally accepted accounting principles and standards which have evolved from an interaction of theory and practice. They promote uniformity in the application of procedures, reliability in measurements, comparability in reporting, and increased usefulness of the information.

6. Generally accepted accounting principles and standards are currently established by the Financial Accounting Standards Board. However, their determination is heavily influenced by other groups, particularly the Securities and Exchange Commission.

7. Financial accounting principles and procedures rest on a network of seven underlying assumptions. This network is interlaced with four qualitative guidelines—relevance, reliability, neutrality, and comparability—and with many practical conventions and environmental constraints. These also heavily influence the totality we call accounting.

In subsequent chapters our primary emphasis is on the conceptual framework of financial accounting. Procedures are studied only if they enhance understanding or are likely to be useful analytical tools. By focusing on a sound understanding of basic concepts, we may avoid much of the ambiguity and mystery that so often accompany the study of accounting. Nevertheless, we must recognize our limitations. Accountants know so little about the impact of information on people's decision processes. Consequently, our framework consists only of a thin web of interrelated assumptions about what investors want and how they behave. To make matters worse, we often lack the measurement techniques to fully utilize the theoretical framework we do possess.

Financial reporting is both an art and a science. To the extent that it attempts to develop a theoretical body of knowledge that can be applied logically, it can be called a science. This aspect is stressed in the following pages. However, because these concepts are not fixed by laws of nature or human behavior, judgment must be used in their application to specific circumstances. In this sense accounting remains an art. We invite the reader to enter with us into this extremely important yet elusive world of financial reporting with all of its postulates, conventions, procedures, doctrines, and rules.

## QUESTIONS AND PROBLEMS

**1–1.** Financial accounting has been described alternatively as (1) an information system, (2) a measurement science, (3) an economic model, and (4) a communication medium. Which of these descriptions explains the nature of accounting as you see it?

**1–2.** The following quotation is attributed to one of the leaders in the development of accounting practice in the first half of this century: "The allocation of income to periods of time would be indefensible if it were not indispensable."

*Required:*

a. Explain the use of the terms *indefensible* and *indispensable* in relation to two basic accounting concepts.
b. What are the advantages and disadvantages of long and short reporting periods?

**1–3.** Each of the following situations describes an action that affects the financial accounting reports. Indicate the assumption(s) of financial accounting that would justify the action taken. Describe how the assumption(s) may detract from the realism of the accounting.

1. A panel truck to be used for repair calls is purchased for $15,000 at the beginning of the year. At the end of the year, the accounting records report it at $12,000, although its current market value as a used truck is only $10,000.
2. Gourmet Restaurant, Inc., sells books of 10 coupons for $100 as a promotional scheme. Each coupon entitles the holder to enjoy two dinners for the price of one. The $7,500 received from the sales of those coupon books is reported as a liability rather than as revenue.
3. A retail store bought a three-year insurance policy for $1,500. During the first year, only $500 was charged to operations even though the entire $1,500 was paid in cash that year.
4. Sue Flay purchased 300 shares of stock in Eggs and Cakes, Inc., for $30 a share upon the advice of her investor advisor. She sold half of them for $48 during the year. Nevertheless, the firm's annual report shows 10,000 shares outstanding all year with an average book value of $27.32.
5. In 1947 a company acquired for $280,000 a plot of land on which to construct its home office building. In 1985 it still reports the land at $280,000 although the land is located in a prime commercial area of Dallas.

6. A business office purchased 20 wastebaskets for $4.95 each. It charged the entire $99 to operations even though the wastebaskets are expected to last at least four years.

7. Over the last decade the inflation rate has varied greatly. However, no adjustments were entered in the accounting records or reports to reflect these changes in the economic environment.

8. Wes Harper owns a construction firm, a real estate holding company, and a management consulting firm. He participates actively in each business but has a separate bank account and separate accounting records for each one.

**1-4.** In addition to financial accounting, Chapter 1 briefly describes managerial accounting and tax accounting.

*Required:*

a. Outline the distinctions among these three areas.
b. Does a firm need to have three separate accounting systems, one for each area?
c. Why are there seemingly no generally accepted accounting principles in managerial and tax accounting?

**1-5.** The Financial Accounting Standards Board and the Securities and Exchange Commission are the two organizations that currently have the greatest impact on the development of GAAP.

*Required:*

a. Describe each of these organizations and the role it plays in the process of formulating accounting principles.
b. Which organization should set accounting principles? Explain why.

**1-6.** The following comment was made by a local proprietor operating a small family business: "I don't have to get all tangled up in revenue postulates, matching concepts, or subjective guesses. In my business, we record revenue when we get cash and expenses when we pay cash. My accounting records are simpler to keep, easier to understand, and accurate besides." Analyze and comment on this viewpoint.

**1-7.** Each of the following situations describes an action that affects the financial accounting reports. Indicate the assumptions, qualitative guidelines, etc., of financial accounting that are *violated* by the action taken.

1. A firm specializes in the construction of roller coasters for amusement parks. Each roller coaster takes about three years to build, and the firm works on only two or three at a time. The president decides, therefore, to prepare a set of financial statements only upon completion of each roller coaster project.

2. Slow-Drain Corporation prepares tentative financial statements for the calendar year of 1985. However, before the audit is completed and the statements are issued formally to the public in February 1986, the owners decide to liquidate the company. The statements are issued as originally prepared, however.

3. A business owns 500 acres of land, purchased at a cost of $300 an acre, which it is holding for investment purposes. The owner of a very similar tract of land across the road just recently sold that property for $400 an acre. Based on this evidence the business increases the recorded value of its land from $150,000 to $200,000.

4. A retail establishment rents a store building on an annual lease. It spends $20,000 remodeling the inside of the store, installing fixtures, etc. These costs will enable the establishment to operate for at least five years before the work would have to be redone. However, the entire $20,000 is charged to operations the first year because legally under the rental agreement, all permanent fixtures and remodeling done by a tenant revert to the landlord upon termination of the lease.

5. A firm borrowed $100,000 at a 10 percent rate of interest. The president wanted to record only $4,000 of interest cost. He argued that because the general price level increased 6 percent, the $100,000 debt now represented "cheaper" dollars. The $6,000 gain from being able to pay off in cheaper dollars offset an equal amount of the $10,000 interest cost leaving only a net cost of $4,000.

6. The president and sole owner of Monumental Express Company purchases five new units to be added to the company's fleet of delivery trucks. While buying them, she decides to acquire a new pick-up truck to be used on her farm and for personal transportation. All six trucks are purchased with a company check.

7. Greens and Beans is a national franchiser of restaurants featuring rare and unusual salads. For $50,000 it sells franchises to local investors entitling them to use the name and recipes of the national organization. In addition, the national company agrees to train the franchisee's employees, install accounting systems, and provide continuing management consulting services for a period of five years. The entire $50,000 received from the sale of each franchise is recorded as income in the year of sale.

8. After investigating outside estimates for the construction of a new conveyor belt, Greenlee Coal Company decides to build the conveyer belt itself. The cost is $550,000. However, the firm records the equipment at $700,000, the lowest of the outside bids received.

**1–8.** The accounting department of a privately owned corporation might be called upon to prepare accounting reports for (1) a bank loan officer, (2) an agent for the Internal Revenue Service, (3) an investor in stock of the firm, and (4) an analyst of a large insurance company that makes long-term loans to the corporation.

*Required:*

a. Describe how the reports presented to each of these individuals might differ and how each of them might use the accounting reports.

b. What role does the certified public accountant (independent auditor) play in the provision of information to each of these persons?

**1–9.** Relevance and reliability are presented as major qualitative standards for accounting information.

*Required:*

a. Discuss the ingredients of each of these concepts.

b. Describe the relationship between each of these qualitative guidelines and the operational assumptions of matching, accounting period, revenue recognition, and exchange price.

c. A company has a piece of machinery which cost $80,000. It would cost $90,000 to replace, and it is estimated that the net value (sales less all other additional costs) of the goods produced on it is $110,000. If the company were liquidated, it could be sold as a used piece of equipment for $70,000. Discuss the relative relevance and reliability of each of these measures of the equipment.

1-10. Generally accepted accounting principles result from the interaction of reporting objectives, audience characteristics, qualitative guidelines, underlying assumptions, and practical constraints.

*Required:*

a. In your own words, define and explain the term *generally accepted accounting principles.*
b. What advantages and benefits are derived from having a broad set of reporting objectives and qualitative guidelines such as those issued by the Financial Accounting Standards Board?
c. Give an example of how each of the constraints might modify the application of a basic assumption?

# CHAPTER 2

# ASSETS AND EQUITIES

Business entities engage in two basic types of activities. They acquire various financial and productive resources. Then they operate by using these resources to produce an inflow of additional property in hopes of augmenting the original stock of resources. A comparison of the cost of the resources used (expenses) and the total resources received from the sale of a product or a service (revenues) provides a measure of net income under our matching assumption.

Therefore, fundamental to the study of financial accounting is an understanding of these resources—what they are, where they come from, how they are valued, and how subsequent changes in their form and valuation are recorded. In the technical terminology of accounting, the resources of a business are called its *assets*. The acquisition of assets gives rise to corresponding financial interests on the part of various groups. A financial interest may be a legal claim, such as a bank loan, or a residual interest such as that of the owner of a share of stock. Accountants use the term *equities* to describe the general financial interests (sources of assets) in the business entity. Then the terms *liabilities* and *owners' equity* are used as subdivisions to indicate the financial interests of outside parties (creditors) and of the owners, respectively.

The financial condition of the business entity consists of its assets and related equities. As we noted in the first chapter, one major reporting task of financial accounting is periodically to inform investors and creditors of the financial position of the firm. For this purpose, a financial statement called a *position statement* or *balance sheet* is prepared as of particular moments in time.

## BASIC EQUATION OF THE POSITION STATEMENT

The information which appears on a position statement (balance sheet) can be arranged in the following basic equations:

$$\text{Assets} = \text{Equities}[1]$$
$$\text{Assets} = \text{Liabilities} + \text{Owners' Equity}$$

In this manner, the balance sheet portrays the dual analysis of business capital. It denotes the resources that the particular business entity will use in the conduct of its activities and also the financial claims or interests created by the commitment of capital to that business enterprise. Assets and equities have to be equal; every asset comes from somewhere. For every resource a business entity obtains, there is a financial interest, legal or beneficial, represented as well. Of course, subsequent changes in assets and equities make it almost impossible to identify particular sources with particular assets. At the outset, however, each asset had a source; therefore, in the aggregate resources equal sources.

The position statement provides a starting point for our discussion of financial accounting. In this chapter our attention centers on a description and classification of the items—assets and equities—on that financial report. In addition, we tie the concepts of revenue and expense, which are incorporated in the matching assumption, to changes in the accounting equation.

## ASSETS

As the term is used in financial accounting, assets are "probable future economic benefits obtained or controlled by a particular entity as a result of past transactions or events."[2] Assets can be looked upon as the form taken by the financial capital which is invested in the entity. Note the following four considerations:

1. Assets encompass all types of economic resources. Included is property such as cash, land, and machinery. Also, however, they may embody the right to receive certain services. For example, a company purchases a three-year insurance policy. This entitles the firm to transfer the risk of loss to the insurance company. The economic resource is in the form of a service to be received over a three-year period; hence, prepaid insurance qualifies as an asset.

2. We are concerned only with items that hold future economic benefit, that are expected to contribute to the firm's future cash flows. The capacity to be exchanged for cash and other resources or to provide future

---

[1] Occasionally one will see a balance sheet which employs the term *liabilities* in a generic sense to describe all financial interests. Nevertheless, it is more precise and modern to restrict "liabilities" to creditors' equity. The single term *equities* should be used as the general description of asset sources.

[2] FASB, *Statement of Financial Accounting Concepts No. 3,* "Elements of Financial Statements of Business Enterprises" (Stamford, Conn., December 1980), par. 19.

services gives resources value or utility. When the value (service potential) has been used up or has expired, the items no longer appear as assets. Indeed, our matching concept is formulated with the idea of relating the consumption of assets to the benefits received during each accounting period.

3. Assets are acquired as a result of a specific event, called a transaction, in which the business entity participates. The transaction may result in legal ownership, as in the case of a purchase of merchandise, or only in a right to use property, as in the case of a payment of rent in advance. In both cases, the transaction culminates a process of negotiation with some independent party and confers control over the economic benefit upon the business entity. Contrast this with labor services which the firm will receive from its employees in future years. Even though these services probably will be used productively in the future, no asset has been acquired as of the present time. Similarly, items such as public streets which are not assignable to the specific accounting entity are not accounting assets, because there has been no past transaction.

4. Assets must be measurable in monetary terms with a reasonable degree of precision. Some valuable resources do not entail a measurable dollar outlay. For this reason, advantages such as being located in a city with a large pool of skilled labor or with good fire and police protection would not qualify as part of a firm's accounting assets. Expenditures on employee training over a number of years may lead to the existence of a valuable service potential. In most cases, though, the dollar value of this benefit would be extremely difficult to quantify, so it would not appear among the assets on the balance sheet.

## Monetary and Nonmonetary Assets

The future economic benefit of an asset to an enterprise may consist of either exchange value (purchasing power) or use value. Those which provide the first type of potential value are called *monetary assets*. Included in this division are cash, short-term security investments being held as a temporary backlog for cash, and accounts and notes receivable. These assets furnish general service potential to an enterprise because they can be exchanged for cash or other productive resources. Temporary investments (called marketable securities) can be converted into cash practically at a moment's notice. For most purposes, the business entity views them as the equivalent of cash. Receivables represent legal claims to cash. The benefit they represent is a right to receive a certain amount of purchasing power.

Probably the largest portion of a firm's assets consists of *nonmonetary* items which the entity has acquired to help produce revenues in future periods. These assets have value to the business because each possesses some specific service potential to be used over a period of time to generate additional assets. It is hoped that the cost of these assets will be recovered as their stored-up services are consumed in the production of revenues. Some may supply services in the short term (e.g., inventories, prepaid rent, prepaid insurance), while others, such as land, buildings, and equipment, may provide benefit for many years. These resources perform the same basic economic function, regardless of the duration; their capacity to be combined with other resources to produce and sell exchangeable goods and services gives them use value.

## Classification of Assets

When assets are presented on a balance sheet, a reasonable classification of the individual items enhances communication. Over the years, certain arrangements have evolved and have received sanction through use in financial and accounting circles and through formal pronouncements by authoritative bodies. Normally, these classifications distinguish between current and all other assets.

**Current Assets.** Current assets include cash and other resources that will be converted into cash or used in the normal operations of the business within a relatively short period of time. *Cash, marketable securities, short-term receivables,* various kinds of *inventories,* and *prepayments* make up the capital that is continually being "turned over" during the *operating cycle* of a firm. When presented on the position statement, these current assets are usually listed in the foregoing order of decreasing liquidity (speed with which the item can be converted to cash or liquidated).

The operating cycle is usually described as the time needed by the business to acquire (purchase or make) the product or service, sell it, and collect the receivables. An operating cycle of a business may be depicted as follows:

$$\text{Cash} \rightarrow \text{Inventory} \rightarrow \text{Receivables} \rightarrow \text{Cash}$$

Of course, for each type of business the operating cycle may be of a different length, anywhere from a few weeks to several years. Therefore the American Institute of Certified Public Accountants has recommended the use of a one-year period *or* the operating cycle, whichever is longer, as the cutoff time for current assets. This definition prevails in current financial reporting; as a result, current assets may include inventories and prepayments applicable to time periods as long as three years. Nevertheless, in general the definition of "a relatively short period of time" used in the identification of current assets is one year or less.

**Other Asset Categories.** Accounting practice is not so uniform in classifying noncurrent assets. However, one reasonable and fairly common subdivision includes the following three groupings:

1. *Investments*—long-term security investments (stocks and bonds of other companies), moneys restricted for special purposes, land held for future use or speculation, and long-term loans to other parties.
2. *Property, plant, and equipment*—land, buildings, machinery, equipment, and furniture and fixtures.

3. *Intangibles*—nonphysical rights and privileges such as patents, long-term prepayments, copyrights, licenses, and franchise costs.

We will generally adhere to this particular classification scheme. However, remember that arrangements and terminology may vary. The term *fixed assets* frequently is used synonymously for "property, plant, and equipment," and intangible assets often are lumped together in a nondescript category labeled "other assets" or "deferred charges." Statement form is primarily a matter of convention. All that can be asked is that the classification of assets be reasonable, consistent, and understandable to the reader of the statement.

**Recording of Assets**

Monetary assets generally are recorded at their current cash equivalent. This measurement derives directly from their use as providers of current purchasing power.

Except in rare instances, *nonmonetary assets are recorded at their acquisition cost*. This practice is in keeping with the basic exchange-price assumption in the financial accounting model discussed in Chapter 1. Moreover, adherence to this *cost principle* facilitates income measurement—the matching of dollar acquisition costs against revenues. Acquisition costs provide relevant information as monetary measures of effort. Presumably, management decides that the estimated value in future use or sale of a particular asset to the business is *at least* equal to its cost. Then users of the statements can base their own judgments about management's performance on this matching of costs with related revenues as reported on the income statement. In brief, recording assets at cost is assumed to meet the audience's needs for reliable information about management's accountability for financial resources.

*Cost is the sacrifice made, the benefits foregone, or the resources consumed in the acquisition of an asset.* Acquisition cost is commonly measured by the cash paid or promised or, if acquisition is not a direct cash purchase, by the cash equivalent exchanged. For instance, if a firm purchases merchandise, paying $4,000 in cash immediately and promising to pay (incurring a liability of) $7,000 within 30 days, the proper amount of asset cost is $11,000. If a partner invests equipment having a current market value of $18,000 in the business enterprise, the asset should be entered at that amount in the accounting records. In each of these cases the cash-equivalent figure is a measure of the values exchanged or the price inherent in the transaction between the entity and another party.

Acquisition cost and fair market value of an asset are assumed to be identical at the date of acquisition. Although the market value of the asset may subsequently change, normally no attempt is made in the accounting records to show such fluctuations. Any further transactions relating to the eventual consumption or disposition of the asset are based on the actual cost invested by the firm.

Over the years numerous suggestions have appeared in accounting literature that financial accounting should depart from the cost principle and formally embrace changing money values in the accounting records.[3] Advocates claim that these valuations are relevant to the decision processes of investors. In many instances such current values can be measured with sufficient reliability.

To date, these suggestions have met with only limited acceptance. In most cases the thrust for alternative valuation schemes is toward supplementing rather than replacing historical cost as the basic accounting measurement. Chapter 7 briefly touches on some of these alternative valuations in a detailed discussion of cost measurement. Briefly in Chapters 8 and 9 and extensively in Chapter 19 we consider what the requirements are for supplementary disclosure of changing prices under generally accepted accounting principles. In addition we explore how alternative concepts of income *could* be implemented formally in financial accounting.

## EQUITIES

The equities of a firm represent the sources of assets. They measure the financial investment in or claim on the business by particular groups or individuals. Equities are subdivided into two categories—liabilities and owners' equity. Liabilities indicate the financial interest of creditors (those from whom the firm has borrowed) and usually reflect some type of legal obligation. Owners' equity, on the other hand, reflects the financial investment of the owners of the business. Let us take a closer look at each of these types of equities and at some of the common items they include.

## Liabilities

Liabilities are the debts and other amounts owed by the business entity. Most liabilities represent definite amounts owed to specific groups or individuals. Such is the case with accounts payable, bank loans, mortgages payable, and so on. These liabilities arise out of a transaction between the business enterprise and a creditor and are legally enforceable.

The accounting concept of liability is broader, however, than just legal commitments. It includes all obligations to disburse cash, convey other assets, or perform services, providing that these obligations have arisen from transactions in past or current periods and are subject to reasonably accurate monetary measurement. Included are constructive obligations requiring a future sacrifice of resources. An example is a liability for vacation pay in the current year in a firm whose long-standing practice has been to pay for vacations although no legal contract requires it to do so. Excluded, however, are obligations arising from promises that both par-

---

[3] Some accountants advocate the restatement of original cost to recognize only changes in the value of money caused by general inflation. Others would recognize changes in the replacement cost of assets, and still others would value assets at their current sales price (exit value).

ties will fulfill in the future. A company may sign a contract with its president agreeing to pay $100,000 each year for the next five years. However, no liability is recorded for the services to be received in the future, for a transaction has not yet occurred.

**Accrued Liabilities.** Certain liabilities grow progressively in amount until a payment date is reached, at which time the debt is liquidated. For example, employees normally are paid after they have performed services. The liability Wages Payable increases each day that employees work. Then, on payday, the liability is satisfied. This type of liability is called an *accrued liability* and is illustrated by Figure 2-1.

**FIGURE 2-1   Time Pattern of Accrued Wages Payable**

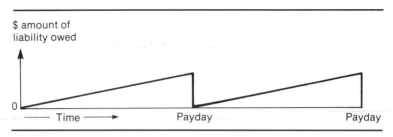

Interest payable is another good example. Interest is the charge for the use of borrowed money. The interest owed increases as time passes, until periodic cash payments are made for the total interest related to the elapsed time. Often it may not be convenient to record the daily increase in the liability. However, if a balance sheet is to be prepared before the date of payment, we must be sure to recognize all of these accrued liabilities to the extent that they have accumulated. In Chapter 4 we explore the accounting procedures whereby the accrued claims are brought up to date and formally recognized on position statement dates.

**Advances.**   Most liabilities represent claims to be settled by a cash payment. Occasionally, however, a claim against the business arises that is to be satisfied by the delivery of some product or the performance of some service in the future. For example, magazine subscriptions normally are paid in advance. The publisher is under an obligation to provide the magazine during the entirety of the subscription period. The claim, though not for cash, is real and should be shown on the position statement. The source of the asset Cash is the liability Subscriptions Received in Advance. The liability is gradually decreased as the magazine is delivered. Such liabilities fall under the general label of *advances,* although each one usually carries a separate account title—Rent Received in Advance, Advances by Customers, Partial Payments on Uncompleted Contracts, and so on.

**Estimated Liabilities.**   Sometimes an obligation or claim exists when the amount owed and/or the identity of the claimant is not known precisely. If the amount can be reasonably measured, it should be shown as an estimated liability. For example, a company that issues trading stamps redeemable later for various types of merchandise has a definite obligation to convey goods in the future. The number of stamps that eventually will be redeemed and the cost of the premiums to be delivered may have to be estimated. Nevertheless, a claim which arose from sales in the current or past periods exists now.

Similar examples of estimated liabilities include refundable deposits, liabilities under product warranty programs, and estimated income taxes payable. In the later case, the *payee* is known, but the exact amount may be established only at a later date, perhaps after extended discussion with tax authorities. The accountant shows that a liability for taxes exists by making a reasonable estimate of the amount due.

The estimated liability must be distinguished from *potential* and *contingent* liabilities, which are *not* recognized on the position statement. Potential liabilities relate solely to future events—for example, future purchases of merchandise on credit or future wage payments under a labor contract. No debt actually exists now. Contingent liabilities may relate partially to past actions, but the *existence* of a claim depends on the outcome of some future event outside the direct control of the entity. Pending lawsuits, disputes over past taxes, and guarantees of another's debts are common examples of events giving rise to contingent liabilities. Unless and until the future event materializes, no actual claim, estimated or otherwise, exists. Contingent liabilities frequently are mentioned as *supplementary information* in notes to the position statement. The factor that distinguishes the estimated liability from the contingent liability is that the future asset outlay, which can be reasonably estimated, has to be made *because of an event which has already occurred*.

**Classification and Measurement of Liabilities.** Arrangement of liabilities on the balance sheet closely parallels that of the assets. Liabilities are normally divided into two categories—current and noncurrent (long-term). The former includes amounts payable to employees (wages payable), to suppliers (accounts payable), to owners (dividends payable), to lenders (notes payable and interest payable), and to government (taxes payable). Current liabilities represent obligations that will be paid within one year or within the operating cycle of the firm when that is longer. The presumption is that current liabilities will be satisfied through the use of current assets or the creation of other current liabilities. Their dollar measurement is generally the amount due.

Long-term liabilities represent those debts that fall due after one year from the date of the position statement.[4] Bonds payable and mortgage liabilities are recorded at the *present value* of the amounts due in the future.

---

[4] Ordinarily the portion of any long-term bond issue that is payable within one year is classified as a current liability. The FASB allows an exception if the firm has a definite, noncancelable agreement from a lender to refinance the bonds as they become due.

Present value is the amount which theoretically would liquidate the claim today. Procedures for its calculation will be discussed in Chapter 10.

**Owners' Equity**

The other major source of assets is the equity of the owners. "Equity [owners' equity] is the residual interest in the assets of an entity that remains after deducting its liabilities. In a business enterprise, the equity is the ownership interest."[5] If a business owns a $500,000 warehouse with a $300,000 mortgage, the warehouse is the asset, the mortgage is a liability, and the $200,000 remainder is the owners' equity in the building. Sometimes the accounting equation is reformulated to emphasize that equity is the residual interest in assets.

$$\text{Assets} = \text{Liabilities} + \text{Owners' Equity}$$
$$\text{Assets} - \text{Liabilities} = \text{Owners' Equity}$$
$$\text{Net Assets} = \text{Owners' Equity}$$

In this text, we use the term *owners' equity* as a general description. When appropriate, we can restrict our reference to particular types of business organizations through the use of the terms *proprietor's equity, partners' equity,* or *stockholders' equity.* Indeed, the major differences in the accounting records of single proprietorships, partnerships, and corporations lie in the owners' equity section. Because corporations are the dominant form of business organization in this country, we set our discussion in this and subsequent chapters in a corporate context. Most of it, however, is equally applicable to other forms of business organization.

Two prominent sources of owners' equity exist. The first is the voluntary commitment of capital to the business enterprise by its owners in an explicit transaction between these parties. In a corporation, shares of stock are issued to the owners as tangible evidence of their direct investment of capital. Consequently, the caption "capital stock" is used to reflect this particular equity. Any subsequent sales or exchanges of those shares among individual shareholders are irrelevant in measuring owners' equity, because they do not involve the corporate entity as one of the parties to the transaction.

Owners' equity can also increase as a result of activities undertaken by the entity. For instance, a firm that operates profitably experiences a net increase in assets. Asset increases, usually in the form of cash and accounts receivable, from the sale of goods and services exceed the asset decreases from the consumption of various productive resources. If this net asset increment is not distributed to the owners, then their total financial interest in the business rises. Retained Earnings is the account used to reflect the additional owners' equity arising from the retention of earned assets in the business. In this sense, retained earnings are an indirect interest, as opposed to the direct, capital stock investment. Alternative

[5] *FASB Concepts No. 3,* par. 43.

terms for retained earnings are *earnings reinvested in the business* or *earned surplus,* although the latter has lost popularity because of the erroneous impression the term *surplus* may give.

Similar sources of owners' equity exist in individual proprietorships and in partnerships. The titles used may vary in noncorporate businesses, but the concepts are the same. The owner's equity section of the position statement for Jones Drug Store might be composed of two elements: Jones, capital, and Jones, retained income. These correspond roughly to capital stock and retained earnings in a corporation. However, in partnerships and proprietorships, they often are combined into a single capital account representing the total owner's equity of a particular individual. In Chapter 14 we discuss some of the legal and conceptual reasons for maintaining the distinction in corporate businesses.

## RELATION OF INCOME MEASUREMENT TO ASSETS AND EQUITIES

The preceding discussion emphasizes the fact that assets are secured from two activity sources—capital-raising and operations. Income measurement deals only with the latter. One basic assumption of financial accounting states that net income is best measured by the matching of expenses against revenues. Revenues represent the total inflow of resources received by the entity as compensation for goods and services rendered to customers during the period. Expenses measure the acquisition cost of the assets consumed or transferred out in the provision of goods and services. Net income becomes the net increase in assets.

When we consider inflows and outflows of assets in the form of revenues and expenses in light of the basic accounting equation, an additional aspect of income transactions becomes apparent. Revenues and expenses must cause changes in owners' equity as well. For example, assume that a firm sells some merchandise it has in inventory for $800 cash. The merchandise originally cost $550. The asset inflow or revenue from this event obviously is $800; the asset outflow or expense is $550. The firm's total assets increase by the net amount of $250.

However, it is not possible to increase just one side of the accounting equation. Because these asset increases and decreases are unaccompanied by changes in any other assets or liabilities, there has to be a corresponding change in owners' equity. This can be seen in the diagram below:

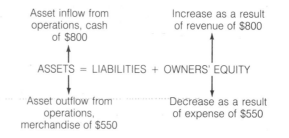

The net increase in assets of $250 is counterbalanced by a net increase in owners' equity of $250, which would appear as retained earnings if a position statement were prepared immediately after this event.

Many individual revenues and expenses cannot be related uniquely to one another as in this example. Rather, the expenses *for the period* are matched against the revenues *for the period*. Nevertheless, every revenue causes owners' equity to increase, and every expense causes owners' equity to decrease. For this reason, the owners' financial interest in the business which arises out of income-generating operations is the residual element in the accounting equation. Changes in assets (or liabilities) which are not offset by equal changes in other assets or liabilities effect a change in owners' equity. Consequently, throughout much of this text we focus on the measurement of assets and liabilities, knowing full well that, as long as the accounting equation remains intact, proper measurement of total owners' equity will result.

## POSITION STATEMENT OR BALANCE SHEET

We have now discussed in some detail the kinds of items that appear on the position statement. The basic equality of assets and equities is the reason the position statement often is called a balance sheet. Its purpose, however, is to present financial information, not just to balance. (Again, we use the terms *position statement* and *balance sheet* interchangeably.)

## Illustration of Balance Sheet and Income Statement

Tables 2–1 and 2–2 present financial statements of Marsh Supermarkets, Inc., taken from the company's actual 1982 annual report to shareholders.[6] When the *account form* is used, the position statement shows the assets on the left side and the equities on the right. Often it is more convenient and easier to show detailed classifications if the equities appear below the assets. This arrangement, called the *report form,* is used for the Marsh Supermarkets balance sheet in Table 2–1.

The heading of the balance sheet contains the name of the company, the name of the statement, and the date. Remember that the position statement is like a snapshot; it displays the assets as of a particular date. In this case the annual accounting period does not coincide with the calendar year. Marsh Supermarkets, Inc., uses a *natural* business year, which corresponds more closely to the natural ebb and flow of its operations. Nevertheless, the balance sheets still are prepared as of the last day of each accounting period.

A few comments about these financial statements are in order. The balance sheet (Table 2–1) is usually issued in comparative form, covering

---

[6] Accompanying the financial statements in the annual report are a large number of notes which provide explanations or detailed schedules for certain items. The notes have not been reproduced.

**TABLE 2-1**

MARSH SUPERMARKETS, INC., AND SUBSIDIARIES
Consolidated Balance Sheet
($000)

| | April 3 1982 | March 28 1981 |
|---|---|---|
| *Assets* | | |
| Current assets: | | |
| Cash and temporary investments | $ 6,346.2 | $ 4,699.7 |
| Notes and accounts receivable | 2,217.9 | 3,060.2 |
| Inventories | 31,835.0 | 32,067.6 |
| Prepaid expenses | 1,647.1 | 717.7 |
| Total current assets | 42,046.2 | 40,545.2 |
| Other assets: | | |
| Land held for expansion | 1,927.6 | 1,790.5 |
| Investments | 848.6 | 610.8 |
| Cash value of life insurance | 196.7 | 168.9 |
| Long-term receivables | 1,343.6 | 579.3 |
| Sundry accounts | 858.3 | 600.1 |
| Total other assets | 5,174.8 | 3,749.6 |
| Property and equipment: | | |
| Land | 4,085.3 | 3,170.7 |
| Buildings | 15,926.4 | 13,263.5 |
| Fixtures and equipment | 34,790.2 | 29,600.6 |
| Leasehold improvements | 7,628.5 | 7,100.5 |
| Construction in progress | 5,943.2 | 2,515.5 |
| | 68,373.6 | 55,650.8 |
| Allowances for depreciation and amortization | (20,174.9) | (17,398.4) |
| Total property and equipment | 48,198.7 | 38,252.4 |
| Capitalized lease property | 22,659.7 | 20,105.8 |
| Total assets | $118,079.4 | $102,653.0 |
| *Liabilities and Shareholders' Equity* | | |
| Current liabilities: | | |
| Accounts payable | $ 20,124.2 | $ 19,162.9 |
| Salaries, wages, and payroll withholding | 5,539.7 | 4,893.0 |
| State and local taxes | 2,800.3 | 2,383.5 |
| Other accounts payable and accrued expenses | 1,718.8 | 2,929.9 |
| Dividends declared | 357.8 | 292.7 |
| Current maturities of long-term debt | 1,363.9 | 294.7 |
| Current portion of lease obligations | 1,359.4 | 1,093.8 |
| Total current liabilities | 33,264.1 | 31,050.5 |
| Other liabilities: | | |
| Long-term debt of Marsh Supermarkets | 9,310.5 | 9,600.0 |
| Long-term debt of real estate subsidiaries | 10,469.1 | 7,720.0 |
| Capital lease obligations | 24,087.1 | 21,161.9 |
| Deferred federal income taxes | 3,505.3 | 2,133.7 |
| Other deferred items | 1,354.3 | 714.3 |
| Total other liabilities | 48,726.3 | 41,329.9 |
| Total liabilities | 81,990.4 | 72,380.4 |
| Shareholders' equity: | | |
| Common stock | 9,115.0 | 9,115.0 |
| Retained earnings | 28,467.4 | 22,651.0 |
| | 37,582.4 | 31,766.0 |
| Cost of common stock in treasury | (1,493.4) | (1,493.4) |
| Total shareholders' equity | 36,089.0 | 30,272.6 |
| Total liabilities and shareholders' equity | $118,079.4 | $102,653.0 |

**TABLE 2-2**

MARSH SUPERMARKETS, INC., AND SUBSIDIARIES
Consolidated Statement of Income
For the Years Ended March 28, 1981, and April 3, 1982
($000)

|  | 1982 | 1981 |
|---|---|---|
| Income: |  |  |
| Net sales | $535,364.6 | $491,610.3 |
| Other income | 2,736.0 | 1,497.6 |
| Gain on disposal of certain drugstores | 1,686.7 | — |
|  | 539,787.3 | 493,107.9 |
| Costs and expenses: |  |  |
| Cost of merchandise sold, including warehousing and transportation | 421,634.0 | 388,010.6 |
| Selling, general, and administrative expenses | 103,575.5 | 94,415.0 |
| Interest expense | 3,956.3 | 3,639.7 |
|  | 529,165.8 | 486,065.3 |
| Income before federal income taxes | 10,621.5 | 7,042.6 |
| Federal income taxes | 3,439.0 | 2,542.0 |
| Net income | $ 7,182.5 | $ 4,500.6 |
| Net income per share | $2.21 | $1.39 |
| Dividends per share | .42 | .36 |

two years, so that the reader can see trends developing or major changes that have taken place in the capital structure (equity sources) and in the deployment of capital in various assets. The subsidiaries referred to in the title of the balance sheet are all the other corporations owned or controlled by Marsh Supermarkets, Inc. Together they comprise the accounting entity.

Observe the equality of assets and equities on the balance sheet. The classification of assets and liabilities conforms quite closely to the traditional arrangements described earlier. Do not be concerned now with the meaning and use of some of the special terms appearing on the balance sheet, such as Cash Value of Life Insurance, Allowances for Depreciation and Amortization, Capital Lease Obligations, and Cost of Common Stock in Treasury. Most of them are explained in subsequent chapters.

Marsh Supermarkets' income statement, Table 2–2, summarizes the operating activity during each of two business years. Notice that it consists of two major categories—revenues (income) and expenses. Like many companies, the company highlights its income tax deduction in a separate expense category. At the bottom of the statement the after-tax earnings are also expressed on a per share basis.

The net income of $7,182,500 in 1982 is the amount by which net assets and retained earnings increased as a result of income-seeking activities. During the year, however, Marsh Supermarkets distributed $1,366,100 of assets to the owners (shareholders) in the form of dividends. The change in retained earnings on the comparative balance sheet, therefore, reflects only the net change of $5,816,400.

**Uses of the Balance Sheet**

The position statement provides information about the present resource base and the pattern of resource financing. Useful knowledge about management's stewardship of invested capital in the past and about the solvency and liquidity of an enterprise can be derived from a study of its balance sheet. A review of the equities reveals the nature of the financial commitments the entity has made and the relative interests of the owners and creditors. Such information may have a bearing on the firm's *financial strength* (ability to meet its long-term obligations) and its financial flexibility.

By examining the current assets and current liabilities, analysts can judge the entity's *liquidity* (ability to meet its short-term financial obligations). The difference between current assets and current liabilities is called *working capital*. It is often the focus of analysis, for it is viewed as a measure of financial safety. Working capital is the liquid defense against uncertain drains of financial resources in the future. The working capital for Marsh Supermarkets, Inc., on April 3, 1982, is $8,782,100 ($42,046,200 − $33,264,100). More is said concerning the analysis of working capital in Chapter 17.

By comparing earnings from the income statement with the investment shown on the balance sheet, we can measure the past profitability of the business entity. This relationship of income to investment is called *rate of return on investment*. As one of the central measures of the earning power of the firm, it provides a benchmark for evaluating performance during a period. For Marsh Supermarkets, Inc., it would be 6.5 percent for 1982—the net income of $7,182,500 divided by the average total assets of $110,366,200. A comprehensive discussion of return on investment and other financial measures is reserved for Chapter 18.

**Limitations of the Position Statement**

Before moving into Chapter 3 which deals with how assets and equities are recorded, let us consider some major limitations of the position statement. An informed reader of financial statements must be aware of what a statement does *not* show as well as what it does.

First, the balance sheet does not indicate the current *value* of the firm's assets or of the firm itself. The amount listed for any individual asset does not necessarily correspond to the market value of that asset. For many assets the position statement simply shows the unexpired cost of the investment the business entity has made in them. Likewise, owners' equity does not reflect market values either. This fact is illustrated in the case of Marsh Supermarkets, Inc. The total shareholders' equity shown on the balance sheet at April 3, 1982, is $36,089,000. There are 3,699,227 shares of stock outstanding; hence, the *book value per share* is about $9.76. The market value of a share of common stock on the New York Stock Exchange on that date was $12.75. Book value represents the amounts invested in the firm, not the amounts the owners will get out of it.

Second, some elements of value to a business may never appear on the position statement because they cannot be expressed in dollars. A brand name that through the years has attracted customer loyalty, an industry reputation for quality products, a decline in demand, or increasing environmental regulations which could lead to the eventual closing of a productive facility are examples. The positive or negative value of these elements would rarely show explicitly on the financial statements. Yet, if one were assessing the *value* of the entity as an economic unit, these factors certainly would have to be considered.

Financial accounting attempts to record only those resources representing a measurable *monetary* commitment of capital arising out of a definite event or transaction. Even this attempt is frustrated when the dollar itself, which is used as the measuring unit, fluctuates in value. In a pure measurement sense, many of the dollar amounts shown on the balance sheet cannot logically be added together if the resources they represent have been acquired at different times when the purchasing power (real value) of the dollar has been changing.

A final limitation of the position statement is that it represents just one moment in time. A single position statement may be influenced by seasonal factors or unusual circumstances occurring just before it is prepared. Although the statement may be accurate, it may not be representative of the typical assets and equities of the firm. In addition, very often we are more interested in *changes* that have occurred in balance sheet items. Even when position statements are presented in comparative form (showing the beginning and end of the year or the end of each of a series of years), they do not provide much detail about *why* changes occurred, particularly in the area of operations. Accordingly the income statement and statement of changes in financial position are useful complements to the balance sheet.

**SUMMARY**

In this chapter we establish the analytical framework for financial accounting. This framework consists of the assets and equities of the enterprise. Different assets represent the varying forms of future economic benefits acquired by the firm. Equities denote the sources of those assets and claims against them and therefore the financial interest of various parties in the entity.

Periodically the assets and equities (liabilities and owners' equity) are formally presented on a financial statement called a position statement, balance sheet, or statement of financial condition. The arrangement illustrated in this chapter stresses the fundamental relationship:

$$\text{Assets} = \text{Liabilities} + \text{Owners' Equity}$$

Format and classification of items on the position statement are influenced by accounting convention and expediency. However, reasonable subdivisions of asset, liability, and owners' equity items arranged in a clear manner can enhance the usefulness and understandability of the report.

Revenues and expenses represent the changes in assets *and* owners' equity arising from the operating activities of the firm. The income statement summarizes these changes and, in so doing, helps to explain the net increase or decrease in the retained earnings that appears on a comparative balance sheet.

The equality of assets and equities not only forms the basic structure for the position statement but also provides the foundation for the recording processes employed in accounting. Each new topic to be discussed in future chapters can be accommodated in the asset-equity classification system. The recording process of *double-entry bookkeeping* is built on that framework and is one subject in the next chapter.

## QUESTIONS AND PROBLEMS

**2-1.** Supply the dollar amounts indicated by the numbers (1) through (15) in the following tabulations. Each case is an independent situation.

|  | Case No. 1 | Case No. 2 | Case No. 3 | Case No. 4 | Case No. 5 |
|---|---|---|---|---|---|
| Assets, beginning | $28,000 | $ (4) | $ (7) | $42,300 | $42,000 |
| Assets, end | 28,000 | 25,000 | 38,800 | 51,700 | (13) |
| Liabilities, beginning | 15,800 | 6,000 | 9,100 | (10) | 19,500 |
| Liabilities, end | (1) | (5) | 7,400 | 18,700 | 12,000 |
| Owners' equity, beginning | (2) | 4,000 | 16,500 | 29,700 | (14) |
| Owners' equity, end | 10,000 | (6) | (8) | (11) | 22,500 |
| Additional direct investment | (3) | 2,700 | (9) | 3,300 | 2,000 |
| Revenues | 30,000 | 29,300 | 58,300 | 21,400 | (15) |
| Expenses | 31,500 | 26,000 | 56,100 | (12) | 39,800 |

After you are finished, explain as succinctly as possible how net income is related to changes in assets, owners' equity (net assets), and cash.

**2-2.** The following alphabetical listing of assets and equities is obtained from the accounting department of Dimlight Corporation as of December 31, 1985:

| | | | |
|---|---|---|---|
| Accounts payable | $16,000 | Inventories | $ 8,000 |
| Accounts receivable | 6,000 | Land | 20,000 |
| Accrued interest on mortgage bonds | 1,500 | Mortgage bonds payable | 40,000 |
| | | Patents | 6,700 |
| Buildings | 80,000 | Prepaid insurance | 1,100 |
| Capital stock | 55,000 | Temporary investments | 600 |
| Cash | 6,300 | Retained earnings | ? |
| Equipment | 16,400 | Wages payable | 2,000 |
| Estimated income taxes owed | 10,300 | | |

*Required:*

*a.* From the above information, prepare a balance sheet in acceptable form and determine the proper amount to be shown as retained earnings.

*b.* The president of Dimlight Corporation is heard to comment, "Our biggest liability is our antiquated facilities, and our most important asset is our reputation for quality products." Discuss this comment in relation to the statement you prepared in part *(a).*

**2-3.** For each of the following events, indicate the effect on the elements in the accounting equation. Use $+$, $-$, and 0 to signify increase, decrease, or no effect, respectively. Use the following format:

| Event | Current Assets | + | Noncurrent Assets | = | Current Liabilities | + | Long-term Liabilities | + | Owners' Equity |
|-------|---------|---|---------|---|---------|---|---------|---|---------|
| 1. | +60,000 | | +100,000 | | | | | | +160,000 |

1. In the formation of a corporation, the owners contribute a building worth $100,000 and cash of $60,000.
2. Equipment costing $10,000 is purchased. A down payment of $4,000 cash is made, with the balance due in 90 days.
3. Advertising supplies are purchased for $1,200 on account. Half of them are used immediately; the other half will be used in future periods.
4. Merchandise costing $80,000 is purchased on account.
5. Merchandise costing $46,000 is sold on account for $70,000.
6. Sales commissions of $3,200 are incurred and are still owed.
7. Marketable securities are purchased for $10,000 cash.
8. A customer makes a deposit of $3,000 cash to apply toward the purchase of merchandise next period.
9. Remodeling costs of $20,000 are incurred on the building. The bill must be paid within 90 days.
10. The Department of Interior constructs a dam across a nearby stream, creating a large lake and water recreation area. The development creates a whole new unforeseen market for the company's products. Anticipated sales should be at least $75,000 a year from this market alone.
11. One stockholder who originally invested $5,000 wishes to withdraw from the business. The corporation writes a check for $5,000 and retires (cancels) the stock certificate.
12. Marketable securities originally costing $5,000 are sold for $7,000 cash.
13. Creditors' accounts in the amount of $40,000 are paid by check.
14. The president of the corporation sold one third of her shares to the new executive vice president for $10,000 cash. The president originally had invested a total of $24,000 as part of entry 1.

**2-4.** What is an asset and a liability? The following four situations have been taken from company records or industry descriptions. For each situation discuss whether the company should record the item on its balance sheet.

**CBS Inc.** The company makes millions of dollars of advance royalty payments to artists in its recorded music operations. The advance royalties are deducted from future royalties due the artists on successful recordings. However, the artist usually has no obligation to return the advance royalties if the recordings turn out not to be successful in the consumer market. Should the advance royalties be recognized as an asset or as an expense?

**Cable TV Industry.** When cable TV companies buy small cable TV systems in business mergers, they are willing to pay $900 to $1,000 for each subscriber that the smaller company has (*The Wall Street Journal*, May 20, 1983, p. 57). Should a small cable TV system with 2,000 subscribers record an asset of $1,800,000?

**Esmark, Inc.** Estech (a division of Esmark) has two take-or-pay contracts with a major chemical company. Under these contracts, Estech is required to purchase 135,000 tons of phosphate chemical products each year *or* make alternative payments. The alternative payments could amount to $8 or $9 million a year, for the nine-year contract. During the first three years of the contract, Estech purchased the minimum amounts of phosphate chemical products; no alternative payments were made. Should Estech record the amount of the alternative payments under these take-or-pay contracts as a liability or perhaps as an offsetting asset and liability at the beginning of year four?

**Concord Fabrics, Inc.** The company has employment contracts with five officers. The contracts provide for basic annual salaries aggregating $642,000 a year. The contracts expire at various times over the next four years. Should the company show a liability for the basic salary payments required under the contracts for the next four years?

**2–5.** The following descriptions and amounts represent a complete list of assets and equities of Listless Enterprises, Inc., as of July 31, 1985:

| | |
|---|---:|
| City of Indianapolis securities maturing in 1999, held as a long-term investment | $ 35,000 |
| Vacation pay owing to employees based on time already worked | 2,000 |
| Increase in stockholders' equity from reinvestment of earned assets | 45,200 |
| Claims of suppliers for amounts due them for merchandise | 230,400 |
| Checking account in bank | 8,800 |
| Cost of tools, dies, and structures used in operations | 311,200 |
| Initial payments made to sales personnel to be deducted from subsequent commissions earned | 5,000 |
| Unused packing materials (boxes, cartons, bags, etc.) | 3,400 |
| Accrued interest on amounts borrowed | 7,800 |
| Claims on customers for products sold | 124,600 |
| Amount spent to acquire patent rights | 21,600 |
| Debt securities issued to investors, payable in installments beginning in 1990 | 125,000 |
| Interest earned on city of Indianapolis securities but not yet received in cash | 3,000 |
| Deposits received from customers to cover future servicing of products sold | 14,600 |
| Amounts paid six months in advance for rental of warehouse | 24,000 |
| Estimated amount still owed to the Internal Revenue Service for income taxes | 37,600 |
| Building location site | 60,000 |
| Finished products awaiting sale | 96,000 |
| Special bank account set aside for construction of building addition | 90,000 |
| Amounts initially contributed by stockholders | ? |

*Required:*

a. Using the above data, prepare a position statement in a form suitable for formal reporting. Employ appropriate account titles.

b. The position statement above reflects numerous estimates and probably fails to reflect the true value of the firm. Explain which items on your statement are subject to the largest degree of estimation and why the statement may not reflect true value.

**2–6.** The bookkeeper for Byorsell Trading Company prepared the following statement at the end of 1985.

BYORSELL TRADING COMPANY
Statement of Financial Worth
For the Year 1985

Current assets:

| | | |
|---|---:|---:|
| Inventory of merchandise | $ 47,900 | |
| Inventory of delivery vans | 32,000 | |
| Inventory of store fixtures | 18,000 | |
| Cash | 13,300 | $111,200 |

Long-term assets:

| | | |
|---|---:|---:|
| Investment in marketable securities | 10,700 | |
| Notes receivable | 20,000 | 30,700 |

Fixed assets:

| | | |
|---|---:|---:|
| Land and building | 120,000 | |
| Less mortgage payable | (80,000) | 40,000 |

Deferred charges:

| | | |
|---|---:|---:|
| Goodwill | | 4,000 |
| | | 185,900 |

Debts:

| | | |
|---|---:|---:|
| Serial notes payable | 50,000 | |
| Accounts Payable | 18,000 | |
| Unpaid wages | 1,200 | 69,200 |
| Net worth of the stockholders | | $116,700 |

*Additional information:*

1. The inventory of merchandise includes the $3,200 cost of two barrels of spoiled merchandise that must be thrown away. Because they had not yet been discarded, the bookkeeper included them in the inventory.
2. The inventory of delivery vans represents the cost of the fleet of three new delivery trucks purchased at the end of 1985.
3. The inventory of store fixtures represents the cost of new display cabinets and shelves purchased on December 23, 1985.
4. The investment in marketable securities represents the current market value of some short-term government securities being held as a temporary backlog of cash. The securities originally cost $9,300.
5. The note receivable is from a former employee of the firm. The person was declared bankrupt last year; the court judgment indicated that the person's debts would be settled at a rate of 40 cents for every dollar.
6. The land and buildings were partially financed by borrowing from an insurance company using a 20-year mortgage note payable. The yearly interest of $9,000 on the mortgage has not been paid for 1985. At the time of purchase, it was estimated that the land was worth $20,000.
7. The goodwill represents a $4,000 payment made at the beginning of 1985 to a former owner. In exchange for the $4,000 payment, the former owner agreed not to start a competing business for four years (1985, 1986, 1987, and 1988).
8. The serial notes payable represent borrowings from a local bank. The $50,000 is to be paid in five annual installments of $10,000. The first installment is due on February 20, 1986.
9. In January 1985, 8,000 shares of stock were issued to the current owners of the company for $10 a share. The money was used to buy the assets of the former owners and to start current operations.

*Required:*

a. Prepare a corrected, properly classified balance sheet.

b. The bookkeeper does not understand the statement you prepared. He notes that the value of the stockholders' interests on your balance sheet is significantly less than the market value of the 8,000 shares of stock at the *end* of 1985. Explain why this apparent discrepancy exists.

2–7. You recently inherited a substantial sum of money. In your town there is a nine-hole, par-three golf course for sale. The course is lighted for night play. For $200,000 you can buy the grounds, clubhouse, and lighting equipment. The clubhouse contains a small snack shop, a pro shop where golf equipment would be displayed and sold, and an office. Attached to the clubhouse is a storage shed where golf carts and maintenance equipment are stored.

Assume you decide to invest in this business venture. Identify the assets and equities that you would expect to be reported on the balance sheets in future years.

2–8. Indicate which of the following items would be classified as assets or liabilities on an accounting position statement. Give reasons for your answers.

1. Interest earned on a bank account but not yet received in cash.
2. The signing of a contract to sell merchandise to a particular customer.
3. The cost of an old machine in good physical condition but no longer used because of technological obsolescence. It would cost as much to remove it as it could be sold for.
4. The increase in the market value of land held for future plant expansion.
5. Expenditures associated with the development and installation of new service locations.
6. Costs of relocating machinery as part of a plant modernization program.
7. Gift certificates sold to customers but not yet redeemed.
8. The right to use a suite in an office building during the coming year. The rent has already been paid.
9. The amount payable by a company for accounting services that were received but for which payment does not have to be made until the middle of next month.
10. The legal fees that the company expects to pay its law firm to defend the company in an upcoming breach of contract suit.
11. The cost of tuition and books incurred by the vice president to obtain an M.B.A. degree in an executive program. The company paid all costs.
12. The expressway which is located directly in front of the firm's manufacturing plant, thus facilitating shipment of its products by truck.

2–9. You have been employed by John Bath to help organize the financial affairs of the Waters Company which he inherited from his Uncle Soapy, who kept very few formal records.

You uncover the following facts. The bank statement shows a balance of $2,700 as of August 31, 1985. No checks have been written since July, when Uncle Soapy died. Consequently, you are reasonably sure that all checks from earlier months have cleared the bank. The cash register contains $180 in currency plus two checks from customers. One check for $1,200 is dated June 28 and represents payment of an account by a major and excellent customer, Acme Toys. The other check for $375 is dated January 13, 1979, and is from a customer who died penniless in 1982.

Uncle Soapy kept a list of people who owed him money on a large piece of cardboard. When cash was received, he would cross off the customer's name; new debts would be added at the bottom of the card. As of August 31, the total amount on the card is $11,535 (the $1,200 and $375 amounts had not been crossed off because the checks had not been cashed yet). The entire $11,535 represents customers' accounts except for a $150 advance to an employee and a $1,500 note representing a loan to a manufacturer-supplier. Also attached to the cardboard are two signed sales contracts totaling $6,000 from customers who ordered merchandise to be delivered in September.

A stack of supplier invoices is kept on a spindle. An analysis of these reveals that $9,450 is owed to suppliers for merchandise and supplies and $4,500 is owed for store equipment. The equipment had been purchased only recently and remains in the storeroom awaiting unpacking. Also on the spindle is a memo that $7,500 of merchandise has been ordered from a supplier. The order had been accompanied by a check for $1,000 as a deposit. The merchandise has not yet been received.

A careful survey of the store indicates merchandise of $70,500 and store supplies of $2,100 on hand. Store equipment *currently in use* is estimated to be $14,100. Also, advertising displays in the store are found to have been leased for one year beginning on January 1, 1985. The rental fee of $3,600 was paid in January by Uncle Soapy. The store building itself is also rented at a yearly cost of $24,000, payable semiannually. One of the last checks written was for $12,000 on June 28 to cover the second six-month period.

A cigar box full of miscellaneous documents discloses that the Waters Company owes the bank $8,000 on a short-term note. This fact is verified by the bank, which indicates that $500 in interest has accrued on the note through August 31. The box also contains an employment contract between Waters Company and a longtime employee. The contract, dated July 1, 1984, and signed by the employee and Uncle Soapy, promises the employee a salary of $15,000 a year for three years. The employee had been paid through June but had received no salary in July and August although she almost single-handedly kept the business going during those two months. Also in the box are architects' plans for remodeling the store; Bath estimates that it would cost $6,700 to do the remodeling but that operating costs would be reduced $4,000 a year as a result. At the bottom of the box are the legal titles to a delivery truck, valued at $4,600 and used in the business, and to Uncle Soapy's car, valued at $3,300. John Bath plans to use the latter as his personal automobile.

*Required:*

a. Prepare a position statement for the Waters Company as of August 31, 1985.
b. For any of the items excluded from the statement, explain why.

**2–10.** For each of the following events, indicate the effect on the elements in the accounting equation. Use +, −, and 0 to signify increase, decrease, or no effect, respectively. Use the following format:

| Event | Current Assets | + | Noncurrent Assets | = Current Liabilities | + Long-term Liabilities | + | Owners' Equity |
|-------|----------------|---|-------------------|------------------------|--------------------------|---|----------------|
| 1. | +120,000 | | | | | | +120,000 |

1. The corporation receives $120,000 cash from investors in exchange for shares of stock of the corporation.
2. Merchandise is bought on credit for $38,000.
3. The firm acquired two plots of land for $30,000 each, paying $12,000 in cash and giving a $48,000, 20-year mortgage note for the balance.
4. Merchandise which cost the company $12,000 is sold on credit for $16,000.
5. The corporation signed a contract with a golf celebrity promising to pay her a 6 percent royalty on the sale of any products bearing her endorsement.
6. A cash payment of $18,000 is made for the merchandise purchased in item 2.
7. U.S. government securities to be held as a temporary investment are purchased for $6,000 cash.
8. Merchandise which cost $2,000 is stolen; half of the loss will be recovered from the insurance company.
9. Salaries and wages totaling $24,000 were paid in cash.
10. One of the plots of land purchased in item 3 is sold for $36,000. The company receives $12,000 in cash, and the purchaser agrees to assume responsibility for paying $24,000 of the mortgage note.
11. The purchaser of the land in item 10 turns around and resells it to someone else for $40,000. The plot of land held by the company is identical in all respects.
12. The firm receives $2,400 in cash which represents its compensation for service calls made.
13. Customers pay $10,000 cash in partial settlement of their accounts.
14. Interest of $200 has built up (accrued) during the period on the U.S. government securities.

**2–11.** Assume that Canary Clothing Company uses the following headings to classify items on its balance sheet:

| | | | |
|---|---|---|---|
| A | Current assets | E | Current liabilities |
| B | Investments | F | Long-term liabilities |
| C | Property, plant, and equipment | G | Contributed capital |
| D | Intangibles | H | Retained earnings |

*Required:*

Indicate by letter how each of the 20 items shown below should be classified. If the item should not be reported in one of the classifications indicated, use the letter X. For each of the latter items explain why you excluded it.

1. An issue of bonds payable which matures in 10 years.
2. Unexpired insurance.
3. Factory building.
4. Investment in 100,000 shares of stock of U.S. Steel Corporation.
5. Estimated liability for product warranties.
6. Shares of stock issued by Canary Clothing Company.
7. Bank account on which payroll checks are written.
8. Clothing racks, display cases, and shelving.
9. Unsettled lawsuit for damages filed by an employee who was fired.
10. Cash in the store registers.
11. Commissions owed to sales personnel.
12. Semiannual interest due on bonds referred to in item 1.
13. Equipment retired from regular use and being held for resale.

14. Cost of purchasing the exclusive use of certain trademarks.
15. An extremely high credit rating assigned by the local credit agency.
16. Six-month money market certificates of deposit.
17. Company automobiles used by the merchandise buyers and sales staff.
18. A note receivable due in three months.
19. Unfilled customer orders.
20. A note receivable due in three years.

**2–12.** Hardy Lee Able, upon graduation from college, decided to establish a coffeehouse near his alma mater. He took a small inheritance of $30,000 and opened a bank account for the business, which he called Cafe Grosso. On June 1, he made the following cash payments: six months' rent on a building $12,000; kitchen supplies, $4,000; and an inventory of various blends of exotic coffees, $1,500. Also on that date he purchased $16,000 worth of furniture (tables, chairs, rugs, bamboo mats for the customers to sit on, etc.). He paid $5,600 in cash and gave a $10,400 note to the supplier for the balance.

During June, Hardy operated the coffeehouse but kept no formal accounting records. All sales and wages were received and paid in cash, as were many purchases. During the month, he invested an additional $7,000 of his own funds.

At the end of June, the bank balance stood at $8,400. All but $2,700 of the note payable had been paid off during the month. His inventories of coffees and kitchen supplies amounted to $700 and $1,600, respectively. He owed $400 for coffee purchases during the month which were not paid in cash, $200 to the college newspaper for advertisements run during July, and $800 to an electric sign company for a neon sign purchased and installed on June 30. As a promotional scheme, books of coupons that could be redeemed for various types of coffee were sold. Hardy estimated that $100 of these coupon books were still outstanding. He felt that $300 was a proper estimate of the monthly charge for the use of the furniture.

*Required:*

a. Prepare a position statement on June 1, taking into account the above data.
b. Prepare a second position statement as of June 30.
c. How successful was the venture during the month? How do you know?

**2–13.** Indicate where the following items would appear on the balance sheet, if at all. Explain why.

1. Cost incurred in grading a piece of land to make it suitable for use.
2. A lawsuit filed against the corporation by the state environmental protection agency.
3. A piece of equipment financed by an equipment trust note payable. Under this financing method legal title to the equipment does not pass to the purchaser until the note is paid in full.
4. A loan that is payable at the rate of $2,000 each year. The repayment may be in cash or equivalent service, at the option of the borrower. (Analyze from the viewpoint of the borrower).
5. Amounts to be paid to key employees under the company's bonus plan. Bonuses are based on the operating results of the preceding period.
6. Trading stamps issued to customers to be redeemed in the future for merchandise premiums.

7. Costs of interviewing and training a new group of management trainees recruited from college campuses.
8. Cash surrender value of a life insurance policy on the president's life. The policy is owned by the corporation, which is the beneficiary.
9. Investment in the securities (stocks and bonds) of another firm.
10. Contract with a construction firm for remodeling work to be done on the third floor of the company's office building.

# CHAPTER 3

# COLLECTING FINANCIAL INFORMATION

The analytical framework for financial accounting, as described in the last chapter, is the basic equation

$$Assets = Liabilities + Owners' Equity$$

This equality, when presented in statement form, shows the position of the entity as of a particular moment in time. Of course, business activity is not static. Assets and equities are continually changing as various events affect the entity. The position statement prepared yesterday becomes out of date with the first financial activity (transaction) of today. It would be highly impractical to prepare a new position statement each time an asset or equity changes. Consequently, we need to develop some other procedures for recording the changes in these items systematically.

Two general types of information about business transactions and events are called for. First, we want a separate record of each event, in order to have a chronological history of the transactions that affect the business enterprise. Secondly, we want a record of the changes that take place in individual assets and equities as the result of the various events. To provide this dual information, two basic recording media are used in accounting—*journals* and *ledgers*. Journals report the transactions as they occur. Ledgers are used to accumulate the effects of various transactions on individual asset, liability, and owners' equity items. In a journal the transaction itself is the focal point of the recording function; in a ledger the individual assets and equities become the center of attention.

Journals and ledgers constitute the bookkeeping instruments in accounting. Our primary interest in them, however, is not as recording devices. Therefore, we will not focus on elaborate forms. Rather we shall examine only their purposes and basic operations. This knowledge will enable the student to analyze accounting information in an orderly manner and to communicate the results of that analysis concisely.

**LEDGER ACCOUNTS**

Let us first look at the ledger. The ledger is a collection of summarizing devices called accounts. A separate ledger account is established for each asset, each liability, and each element of owners' equity. The individual accounts serve as the mechanical media for the recording of increases, decreases, and balances for each item in the accounting equation. The accounts comprise the heart of the recording system, for ultimately all accounting changes are entered in them. In a manual accounting system the general ledger usually consists of a binder or book (hence, the term *books* or *books of account*), with a separate page for each ledger account.

Within the general ledger the individual accounts are identified by both title and number. Numbered accounts can be classified into various subgroupings and arranged in logical sequence. Moreover, a numbering system facilitates the recording process, particularly with machine accounting or computerized methods.

Ledger accounts usually are divided into two sides. The *left half* of the account is called the *debit* side; the *right half* is called the *credit* side. To debit (or to charge) an account means to make an entry on the left side of that ledger account; crediting the account means the opposite—making a right-hand entry. A formal ledger account in a simple accounting system might look like Figure 3-1. Notice that the details of the debit and credit sides of the account are the same, each containing a place for the date, room for any explanatory material, and a money column. The small column labeled PR (posting reference) indicates the source of the information entered in the account. Its use is explained more fully later in the chapter.

**FIGURE 3-1 Formal Ledger Account**

| | | | | Account Title | | | Account No. |
|---|---|---|---|---|---|---|---|
| Date | Explanation | PR | Amount | Date | Explanation | PR | Amount |
| | | | | | | | |

For analytical and communicative purposes, we do not have to be concerned with the precise format of a ledger account. The essential element of a ledger account is the two sides, one for entering increases and the other for decreases. Consequently, in subsequent discussions, we use a simple form called a T-account. It is illustrated below.

|  | Title |  |
|---|---|---|
| Debit (Dr.) |  | Credit (Cr.) |

Although the T-account shows how a ledger account functions, it is not a representation of an actual account.

**Rules for Entering Transactions**

We now are ready to establish a procedure for recording in ledger accounts the changes in assets, liabilities, and owners' equity. The following rules regulate the entering of transactions in the ledger accounts:

*Asset* accounts:

1. *Increases* are shown as *left-hand* or *debit* entries.
2. *Decreases* are shown as *right-hand* or *credit* entries.

*Equity* accounts (liabilities and owners' equity):

1. *Increases* are shown as *right-hand* or *credit* entries.
2. *Decreases* are shown as *left-hand* or *debit* entries.

Although these rules could be changed without impairment to the theoretical framework of accounting, they provide a very simple, effective recording system with built-in checks and balances. The short time required for you to memorize these rules will more than pay for itself in added ability to understand, analyze, and communicate accounting data. Expressed in a slightly different way, the rules are:[1]

| *Debit* | *Credit* |
|---|---|
| 1. Records increases in assets. | 1. Records decreases in assets. |
| 2. Records decreases in liabilities. | 2. Records increases in liabilities. |
| 3. Records decreases in owners' equity. | 3. Records increases in owners' equity. |

**Illustration of Ledger Entries**

By following the effect of various transactions on a few individual accounts, we can see how the system operates. Two different types of assets and a liability account serve as our examples.

**Inventory Account.** Assume that the following four transactions affect this asset during the period:

1. Inventory costing $2,000 is purchased on account (payment to be made at a later date).

---

[1] It is clear from the above rules that the terms *debit* and *credit*, when used in accounting, refer only to left and right, respectively. They do not consistently indicate either increase or decrease because how they affect an account varies with the type of account. No favorable or unfavorable connotations should be ascribed to the terms, either. The terms can be used as verbs as in "debit cash," as adjectives as in "make a credit entry to accounts payable," or occasionally as nouns as in "record a credit to cash."

2. Inventory with a cost of $100 is found to be unsatisfactory and is returned to the supplier.
3. Additional inventory worth $800 is purchased for cash.
4. Inventory costing $1,200 is sold to customers.

These transactions would be entered in the ledger account as follows.[2]

**Inventory**

| | | | |
|---|---|---|---|
| (1) | 2,000 | (2) | 100 |
| (3) | 800 | (4) | 1,200 |

The first and third transactions cause the asset to increase and therefore are recorded on the left or debit side. The second and fourth transactions are credited to the account, because, according to the rules, decreases in assets are recorded on the right-hand side of the ledger. Of course, other accounts besides Inventory are also affected by these four transactions. For example, the first one involves an increase in a liability account, Accounts Payable (credit entry). The Cash account is credited also, as a result of transaction 3, since that asset decreases when the inventory goes up. The purpose of an individual asset or equity ledger account, however, is to record only the changes to that account caused by a number of transactions.

At the end of the period, the remaining inventory should appear as an asset on the position statement. We determine the amount by calculating the *balance* in the account. A comparison of the debit and credit entries reveals that the Inventory account has a debit balance of $1,500 ($2,800 − $1,300). This is to be expected. If any asset remains on hand at the end of the period, the increases (debits) must have exceeded the decreases (credits). For similar reasons, liability and owners' equity accounts normally have credit balances.

Usually once a year the ledger accounts are formally balanced and ruled. The balance is entered on the opposite side of the account, and the two sides are totaled. Then, after the account is ruled, the balance is brought down on the correct side as the opening balance for the following period. This procedure is illustrated below for the Inventory account. A check mark (√) indicates that no new transaction is being recorded.

**Inventory**

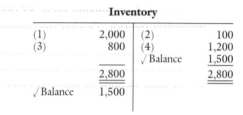

| | | | |
|---|---|---|---|
| (1) | 2,000 | (2) | 100 |
| (3) | 800 | (4) | 1,200 |
| | | √ Balance | 1,500 |
| | 2,800 | | 2,800 |
| √ Balance | 1,500 | | |

---

[2] The identifying numbers in parentheses are used for illustrative purposes only and would not actually appear in practice. With T-accounts, the use of key numbers and letters enables us to identify individual transactions. In a sense, they take the place of dates and other information recorded in a formal ledger account.

Balancing and ruling an account are mechanical processes, of course, often done by machine. They serve a useful purpose in an actual bookkeeping system by separating the entries of different accounting periods in the ledger accounts. The only *analytical* purpose served by these procedures is formally to emphasize an algebraic truism—the beginning balance plus the additions to an account equal the deductions from the account plus the ending balance (0 + \$2,800 = \$1,300 + \$1,500). We sometimes have occasion to use this equality to reconstruct various accounts to obtain information that otherwise would not be directly available.

**Equipment Account.**   Increases (debits) and decreases (credits) to an asset account may represent physical changes, as in the inventory example, or may reflect less apparent changes in economic usefulness. The asset account Equipment is an example. The types of items normally debited and credited to that account are indicated in the ledger account below.

**Equipment**

| | |
|---|---|
| Invoice price | Depreciation |
| Freight charges | |
| Installation costs | |

The total cost of an asset consists of the sum of all costs incurred in the acquisition of the service potential of the asset. Although the freight charges and installation costs may cause little physical change in the asset, they do increase the use value of the equipment. Consequently, they are properly charged to the left side of the Equipment account. As the equipment is used, a portion of that service potential expires. According to the matching concept, the total cost of the equipment should be allocated to the various accounting periods in which it is consumed. In each period a portion of the cost should be removed from the asset account to reflect this use. Such a periodic allocation of cost is called *depreciation*. The depreciation charge is credited to the asset account in each accounting period, for, even though the asset may not change a great deal physically, economically part of its service potential has been utilized.[3]

**Accounts Payable Account.**   One more example, an equity account, should suffice to illustrate basic ledger entries. At the beginning of the period the company owes \$8,000 to its suppliers from purchases in preceding periods. During the current period the following events occur:

1.   Supplies costing \$4,700 are purchased on account.
2.   Checks are written in payment of invoices totaling \$6,400.
3.   A note payable of \$800 is given to one supplier to substitute for an existing account payable.

The entries necessary to record the effect of these events on the liability

---

[3] In Chapter 4 we modify this procedure of crediting the asset account directly for the depreciation charge. The modification, however, is made for practical reasons and does not change the concept of depreciation as the using up of a noncurrent asset.

account Accounts Payable are shown in the following ledger account. The first entry is a credit because the liability account is increasing. The other two cause decreases in the liability and therefore are entered on the left-hand (debit) side. The account has a credit balance of $5,500 at the end of the period.

**Accounts Payable**

| | | | | |
|---|---|---|---|---|
| (2) | 6,400 | √ Balance | 8,000 |
| (3) | 800 | (1) | 4,700 |
| √ Balance | 5,500 | | |
| | 12,700 | | 12,700 |
| | | √ Balance | 5,500 |

## ACCOUNTING TRANS-ACTIONS

We now have both a conceptual and a procedural framework in which to record business events. The conceptual framework states that Assets = Equities; the procedural framework encompasses the system of ledger accounts and the rules for making entries in them.

*Accounting transactions* are those financial activities and events involving the business entity that cause a measurable change in asset or equity accounts. For example, offers to buy and sell (purchase orders and sales orders) normally do not constitute accounting transactions. A customer may indicate plans to buy a large quantity of merchandise. However, only the payment of cash in advance, the delivery of the merchandise, or the creation of a legal claim for payment (accounts receivable) would trigger an entry in the accounting records. Events that do not call for an accounting entry are not necessarily unimportant. A backlog of sales orders may be a significant factor for a particular business. It is one, however, that does not fit immediately into the information-reporting system of financial accounting.

Accounting transactions are of two types—external and internal. The former consist of exchanges between the business entity and some external party. The purchasing of merchandise, the borrowing of money from a bank, the incurring of a liability for labor services received, and so on, are examples of external transactions. Usually they are readily apparent. Internal transactions are changes in assets and equities that do not involve an outside party. Depreciation (the using up of the service potential of plant assets) and the gradual expiration of prepaid insurance are examples. In this chapter most of the accounting transactions are of the external variety. In Chapter 4 we record numerous internal transactions. Both types, however, must meet a fundamental criterion: *A measurable change in assets and/or equities must occur.*

## Nine Basic Types of Transactions

Every business transaction entered in the accounting records must retain the basic equality of assets and equities. Inasmuch as all economic resources have corresponding sources or claims, no transaction can arise which will invalidate the equality of the two sides of the accounting equation. Among the three different types of accounts—assets, liabilities, and owners' equity—nine possible basic transactions can occur without violating the position statement equation. Some of these nine occur only infrequently. However, in order to convey a complete picture and to further the understanding of ledger account analysis, let us illustrate each of these possibilities with an actual entry. Notice that the increases and decreases in the examples have been recorded in conformity with the rules given on page 61.

    **1. Asset Increase, Owners' Equity Increase.** A corporation receives cash of $60,000 from a group of investors and issues shares of stock as evidence of the ownership interest.

| Cash | | Capital Stock | |
|---|---|---|---|
| (1)   60,000 | | (1)   60,000 | |

    **2. Asset Increase, Liability Increase.** The corporation buys a new piece of machinery costing $17,000 but does not pay for it immediately.

| Machinery | | Accounts Payable | |
|---|---|---|---|
| (2)   17,000 | | (2)   17,000 | |

    **3. Asset Increase, Asset Decrease.** In this type of entry one asset is replaced by another asset. No change occurs on the equity side. The purchase of $9,600 of merchandise for cash is an example.

| Merchandise | | Cash | |
|---|---|---|---|
| (3)   9,600 | | 60,000 | (3)   9,600 |

    **4. Asset Decrease, Owners' Equity Decrease.** Assume that $1,300 of the merchandise purchased in item (3) is destroyed by fire. The asset obviously has disappeared. Because the claims of creditors are unaffected by the inventory loss, the financial interest of the owners in the firm must correspondingly decrease. Although the account reflecting the original capital contributions could be reduced, more commonly this particular type of owners' equity decrease is reflected in Retained Earnings.

| Merchandise | | Retained Earnings | |
|---|---|---|---|
| 9,600 | (4)   1,300 | (4)   1,300 | |

    **5. Asset Decrease, Liability Decrease.** The company pays outstanding accounts of $2,400.

| Cash | | | Accounts Payable | |
|---|---|---|---|---|
| 60,000 | | 9,600 | (5) 2,400 | 17,000 |
| | (5) | 2,400 | | |

**6. Liability Increase, Liability Decrease.** This relatively rare type of transaction arises when one liability, say a note payable, is substituted for another liability, perhaps an account payable. If a $6,000 note were given to cancel an open account of the same amount, the entry would be:

| Notes Payable | | Accounts Payable | |
|---|---|---|---|
| | (6) 6,000 | 2,400 | 17,000 |
| | | (6) 6,000 | |

**7. Liability Increase, Owners' Equity Decrease.** In corporations, withdrawal of assets from the business by the owners is accomplished by the payment of dividends to stockholders. Dividends are usually declared some time prior to their actual distribution in cash. At the time of *declaration* a legal liability is created. A portion of owners' equity is transformed into creditors' equity. Assume that $3,000 of dividends is declared but made payable at some later date.[4]

| Dividends Payable | | Retained Earnings | |
|---|---|---|---|
| | (7) 3,000 | 1,300 | |
| | | (7) 3,000 | |

Then, when the cash payment is actually made, the entry is of the type illustrated in item (5)—asset decrease, liability decrease.

**8. Owners' Equity Increase, Liability Decrease.** Again, this transaction is rare, arising only when some element of creditors' equity is replaced by an ownership interest. Occasionally, notes or bonds payable (liability) are issued which can be exchanged for (converted into) stock at the investors' option. *If* and *when* any of the notes or bonds are converted, the liability ceases, and shares of capital stock are issued. The entry to record such a conversion of the notes issued in item (6) is:

| Capital Stock | | Notes Payable | |
|---|---|---|---|
| | 60,000 | (8) 6,000 | 6,000 |
| | (8) 6,000 | | |

**9. Owners' Equity Increase, Owners' Equity Decrease.** This rare transaction involves a reclassification of some portion of owners'

---

[4] In most states it is illegal to decrease Retained Earnings to reflect a dividend declaration unless the account already has a credit balance. This requirement stems from the assumption that the assets to be withdrawn have arisen from profitable operations. If the firm has operated profitably, Retained Earnings will have a credit balance, as we will see shortly. For purposes of illustration, we will ignore this important legal constraint here.

equity from one account to another. The main instance of it is the "stock dividend," the distribution of additional shares of stock to the stockholders without any additional capital contribution on their part. More is said about this phenomenon in Chapter 14. For the time being, let us simply illustrate the entry. Assume that the amount is $12,000.

| Capital Stock | | Retained Earnings | |
|---|---|---|---|
| | 60,000 | | 1,300 |
| | 6,000 | | 3,000 |
| (9) | 12,000 | (9) | 12,000 |

Table 3–1 gives a complete picture of these nine combinations of increases and decreases. Notice in each case that the two sides of the equation balance. A transaction involves either changes in the same direction affecting opposite sides of the equation or changes in opposite directions affecting the same side of the equation. As a result the total for all nine transactions also maintains the position statement equality.

**TABLE 3–1   Summary of Basic Transactions**

| Transaction | Assets | = | Liabilities | + | Owners' Equity |
|---|---|---|---|---|---|
| 1. | +60,000 | | | | +60,000 |
| 2. | +17,000 | | +17,000 | | |
| 3. | +9,600; −9,600 | | | | |
| 4. | −1,300 | | | | −1,300 |
| 5. | −2,400 | | −2,400 | | |
| 6. | | | +6,000; −6,000 | | |
| 7. | | | +3,000 | | −3,000 |
| 8. | | | −6,000 | | +6,000 |
| 9. | | | | | +12,000; −12,000 |
| Totals | 73,300 | = | 11,600 | + | 61,700 |

**Equality of Debits and Credits**

These nine types of entries are the only possible basic transactions that can occur without upsetting the equality of assets and equities. Of course, complex transactions may occur involving a number of asset, liability, and owners' equity accounts. Nevertheless, even the most complicated accounting events can be broken down into a combination of two or more of these basic types.

A quick review of these transactions reveals one trait in common: *each recording involves equal debits and credits.* The rules for increasing and decreasing accounts ensure that the left-hand entries always equal the right-hand entries. For all of the basic types of transactions, *every debit has a corresponding credit.* Because all transactions consist of one or a combination of the basic types, the total dollar value of the debits must agree with the total dollar value of the credits for any given transaction, regardless of the number of individual accounts involved. Because each transaction involves equal debits and credits, it follows that the total of all accounts with debit balances at the end of the period will equal the total of all accounts with credit balances. In our example, debit-balance accounts (Cash, $48,000; Machinery, $17,000, Merchandise, $8,300, and Retained Earnings, $16,300) and credit-balance accounts (Accounts Payable, $8,600; Dividends Payable, $3,000; and Capital Stock, $78,000) both total $89,600.

This particular method of recording is known as *double-entry bookkeeping*, because every transaction has at least two aspects—a debit and a credit. Contrast this system with a single-entry one, which most of us practice when we keep the stubs on our checkbooks. On the stub we maintain a running record of the increases and decreases in the asset Cash in Bank. However, for each change in the Cash account, there exists a corresponding change in some other asset, liability, or owners' equity which normally goes unrecorded. The double-entry system provides a powerful tool for ensuring that a complete analysis of each transaction is made and for checking the numerical accuracy of the analysis. Most bookkeeping systems used by businesses of some size and complexity are based on the double-entry principle.

## TRANS-ACTIONS INVOLVING REVENUE AND EXPENSE

In the framework of double-entry bookkeeping, we can record any accounting transaction, including those associated with profit-seeking operations. The main objective of a business enterprise is to increase the total stock of resources by receiving more in assets through the sale of products or services than is used up in their provision to the customer. Let us see how this kind of activity can be analyzed with the tools developed to this point.

The conceptual approach to income measurement in accounting, developed in earlier chapters, is one of relating particular asset inflows (revenues) and asset outflows (expenses). From the standpoint of income measurement, our concern is with those asset changes during the period broadly connected with operating activities. However, asset accounts are used to record *all* changes in assets during the period. *Although revenues represent a source of assets, not all inflows of cash or other assets necessarily represent revenues. Similarly, although expenses represent a use of assets, not all outflows of cash or other assets necessarily represent expenses.* Effective measurement of net income only through asset accounts would require an analysis of each one for a determination of which of the asset inflows and outflows are relevant.

## Direct Reflection in Retained Earnings

In Chapter 2 we observe that asset increases and decreases from revenue and expense transactions cause corresponding increases and decreases in owners' equity. Therefore, whenever assets come into the firm from the sale of products or services, an equal increase in owners' equity could be recorded by a credit to Retained Earnings. The converse is true with expenses. As an asset is consumed in the generation of revenues, the asset could be credited and Retained Earnings could be debited to reflect the equal decrease in owners' equity.

**Illustration.**   Assume that during the month of May the following transactions take place:

1.  Quality Products Company is organized. Stockholders invest $12,000 in cash and receive shares of stock.
2.  The company leases a building, paying $2,000 in cash for a month's rent.
3.  Merchandise costing $16,000 is purchased on account.
4.  Two salespersons are hired at a cost of $2,500 each for the month, paid in cash.
5.  The firm sells half of the merchandise, receiving $6,000 in cash and $10,000 of accounts receivable.

The first four transactions are relatively easy to analyze and require little explanation. Each one involves an increase in some asset, with either an accompanying increase in owners' equity (item 1), an increase in a liability (item 3), or a decrease in another asset (items 2 and 4).

Transaction 5 relates to the profit-making endeavors of the firm during the month. As a result of these activities, cash and accounts receivable flow into the business. At the same time, other resources—merchandise, pre-paid rent, and salespersons' services—are given up. One way of recording these events is to debit and credit Retained Earnings directly, to reflect the changes in owners' equity corresponding to the individual asset outflows and inflows relating to operations. For example, the cash sale of product could be recorded as a debit to Cash and a credit to Retained Earnings. Likewise, the credit sale could be recorded separately by a debit to Accounts Receivable and a credit to Retained Earnings. These transactions are of the "asset increase, owners' equity increase" type. Likewise, whenever assets are consumed, Retained Earnings could be debited and the respective asset credited (asset decrease, owners' equity decrease).

Table 3–2 shows the results of recording these transactions in ledger accounts. The ending credit balance of $1,000 in Retained Earnings reflects the matching of revenue and expense transactions for the month. The excess of assets gained in operations ($16,000) over assets used up in operations ($15,000) causes owners' equity to increase.

If the firm operates unprofitably, the opposite situation occurs. Asset decreases exceed asset increases. Accordingly, the corresponding decreases in owners' equity, which are recorded on the left side of Retained Earnings, would exceed the increases recorded on the credit or right-hand side. On the position statement the debit balance in Retained Earnings would be subtracted from Capital Stock and is termed a *deficit*.

**TABLE 3-2  Use of Retained Earnings Account to Reflect Operating Transactions**

| Asset Accounts | | | | Equity Accounts | |
|---|---|---|---|---|---|
| **Cash** | | **Merchandise** | | **Accounts Payable** | |
| (1)  12,000 (5a)  6,000 | (2)  2,000 (4)  5,000 | (3)  16,000 | (5d)  8,000 | | (3)  16,000 |
| **Accounts Receivable** | | **Prepaid Rent** | | **Capital Stock** | |
| (5b) 10,000 | | (2)  2,000 | (5e)  2,000 | | (1)  12,000 |
| **Salespersons' Services** | | | | **Retained Earnings** | |
| (4)  5,000 | (5c)  5,000 | | | (5c)  5,000 (5d)  8,000 (5e)  2,000 | (5a)  6,000 (5b) 10,000 |

**Uses of Revenue and Expense Accounts**

Our previous discussion makes clear that the income-measurement concept is implemented in the accounting system through a matching of increases and decreases in owners' entity. These changes in owners' equity mirror particular increases and decreases in assets, namely those related to operating activities. Entering these owners' equity changes directly in Retained Earnings is conceptually sound. However, the actual procedures used in financial accounting make use of temporary accounts called revenue and expense accounts. They are introduced in the accounting system as subcategories of Retained Earnings to aid in keeping track of each kind of operations-related asset flow.

As assets from the sale of products and services flow in, the asset accounts are debited, with the corresponding credits going to separate *revenue* accounts. When asset outflows relating to the generation of revenues are recorded, the assets are credited and special *expense* accounts are debited. *Revenue accounts measure the relevant asset inflows, thereby reflecting the accomplishment of the firm. Expense accounts reflect the applicable asset consumptions, measuring the effort of the entity.* Therefore, revenue and expense accounts represent the tools for implementing the matching concept. Although the theory is based on asset changes, the execution occurs through owners' equity changes.

**Reasons for Revenue and Expense Accounts.**  The use of revenue and expense accounts in lieu of direct entries to Retained Earnings provides more detailed and better classified information about the conduct of the periodic operating affairs of the firm. Between position statement dates, owners, creditors, managers, and others need knowledge about the nature of the changes, not just the end results. Direct recording in Retained Earnings conceals the different reasons that assets are increased or decreased as a result of operations. How much of the asset increase has resulted from the sale of products, from interest earned on investments, from rentals, and so forth? How does the cost of merchandise sold compare with the selling price? What is the relationship between the selling expenses and the dollar amount of sales in the current period? What other assets have been consumed during the period and in what amounts? These and similar questions cannot be answered easily when all operating activities are commingled in Retained Earnings. The detailed information necessary for the evaluation of performance is not readily available. When separate ledger accounts are maintained for each type of revenue and expense, asset flows can be usefully classified and summarized.

Revenue and expense accounts also enable us to record asset changes separately without having to match revenues and expenses on each individual sale. Even when some costs applicable to each sale could be determined, it may be very inconvenient to record the asset outflow at the time of sale. Consider the situation of a large supermarket. Crediting the Merchandise account as each customer passes the check-out clerk would be too difficult and time-consuming. Instead, we measure the expense side only at the end of the accounting period.[5]

Revenue and expense accounts provide a procedure within the double-entry framework for recording each asset inflow and outflow relating to operations independently at the time it occurs or whenever it is convenient. Then net income is measured by the excess resulting from the matching of revenue transactions and expense transactions for any given period.

**Illustration.**   In Table 3-2 we used only position statement accounts to register the transactions for Quality Products Company during the month of May. In Table 3-3 we use revenue and expense accounts to record the *same* transactions. The fifth transaction, summarizing the operating activities of the period, has been broken down into its separate components. Notice that as assets are received from operations (items 5*a* and 5*b*), a revenue account is credited; as each asset is used up during the period (items 5*c,* 5*d,* and 5*e*), a separate expense account is debited. In this manner we can accumulate in these special retained earnings accounts additional information about the nature of the period's activities.

**Relationship to Owners' Equity.**   We can see clearly from Table 3-3 that these new accounts are merely temporary retained earnings accounts reflecting provisional changes in owners' equity arising from periodic operations. Revenue accounts record increases in owners' equity because assets—usually cash or some type of receivable—are received from the sale of a product or service. Expense accounts, on the other hand,

---

[5] We determine the cost of merchandise sold for the period by counting the merchandise left at the end of the period *(taking a physical inventory)* and subtracting its cost from the total cost of merchandise available for sale. More is said about this procedure in Chapter 8.

**TABLE 3-3  Use of Revenue and Expense Accounts**

| Cash | | Salespersons' Services | | Sales Revenue | |
|---|---|---|---|---|---|
| (1)  12,000 | (2)    2,000 | (4)    5,000 | (5c)  5,000 | | (5a)  6,000 |
| (5a)  6,000 | (4)    5,000 | | | | (5b) 10,000 |

| Accounts Receivable | | Accounts Payable | | Cost of Goods Sold | |
|---|---|---|---|---|---|
| (5b) 10,000 | | | (3)   16,000 | (5d)  8,000 | |

| Merchandise | | Capital Stock | | Salary Expense | |
|---|---|---|---|---|---|
| (3)   16,000 | (5d)  8,000 | | (1)   12,000 | (5c)  5,000 | |

| Prepaid Rent | | Retained Earnings | | Rent Expense | |
|---|---|---|---|---|---|
| (2)    2,000 | (5e)  2,000 | | | (5e)  2,000 | |

record the decreases in owners' equity because assets are consumed, used up, or given up in earning revenue.

Being owners' equity accounts, revenues and expenses follow the rules for increasing and decreasing equities. *Revenue accounts are normally credited,* inasmuch as they are positive items of owners' equity; and *expense accounts,* reflecting negative changes in owners' equity, *are normally debited.*

With the introduction of revenue and expense accounts, the accounting equation is expanded:

$$\text{Assets} = \text{Liabilities} + \text{Owners' Equity} \begin{cases} \text{Capital  Stock} \\ \text{Plus} \\ \text{Retained Earnings} \end{cases} \begin{cases} \text{Revenues} \\ \text{Less} \\ \text{Expenses} \end{cases}$$

Revenue accounts temporarily substitute for the credit side of Retained Earnings; and expense accounts, for the debit side.

**Retained Earnings**

| Decrease (Dr.) | | Increase (Cr.) | |
|---|---|---|---|
| **Expense** | | **Revenue** | |
| Increase (Dr.) 8,000 5,000 2,000 | Decrease (Cr.) | Decrease (Dr.) | Increase (Cr.) 16,000 |

The revenue and expense accounts by nature are *single-period accounts.*

Their function is to collect information applicable to the operations of one period. At the end of the period their balances are summarized, and the net result is formally transferred to Retained Earnings in order to bring the latter account up to date.[6] For this reason, they are often called *nominal* owners' equity accounts, as contrasted with Capital Stock and Retained Earnings. Referring to the distinction made in Chapter 1 between status reports (position statements) and change reports (income statements), we can say that, with respect to owners' equity, Capital Stock and Retained Earnings are the status accounts, and the revenues and expenses are the change accounts.

**The Income Statement**

We have been discussing procedures for analyzing and recording those periodic activities of the business directed toward the generation of net income. Chapter 1 indicates that the income statement is the financial report used to show the results of the matching process for the period—the amounts and kinds of revenues and costs (expenses) reasonably assignable to the revenues and the difference between them, which we call net income or net loss. A simplified format for the income statement is given in Table 3-4. The figures are based on Table 3-3.

**TABLE 3-4**

QUALITY PRODUCTS COMPANY
Income Statement
For Month of May

| | | |
|---|---|---|
| Revenue: | | |
| Sales of products . . . . . . . . . . . . . . | | $16,000 |
| Expenses: | | |
| Cost of goods sold . . . . . . . . . . . . . . | $8,000 | |
| Salary expense . . . . . . . . . . . . . . . | 5,000 | |
| Rent expense . . . . . . . . . . . . . . . | 2,000 | 15,000 |
| Net income . . . . . . . . . . . . . . . . . . | | $ 1,000 |

The reader may wish to look again at Table 2-2 and review the actual income statement of Marsh Supermarkets, Inc.

The heading of the income statement contains the name of the business entity and the *period* covered by the statement. The latter point is particularly important. A $1,000 net income for the month of May is quite different from a $1,000 net income for the year. Every figure on the income statement, under the concept of the accounting period, relates to a particular, ascertainable time span. The length of the period may vary with the needs of the business and the desires of the audience.

---

[6] The procedure to accomplish this is called closing the books and is described in the next chapter.

Because the income statement provides the major source of information about periodic operating activities, it often tends to become the focal point. The amounts on the balance sheet become residuals, resulting from income determination decisions. Nevertheless, the two statements are very closely related. For the owners' equity section of the position statement, the association is direct. The income statement is a summary of changes in retained earnings due to the current period's operations. Because revenues and expenses relate to asset inflows and outflows, respectively, the income statement also partially explains changes in the size of assets during the period.

## Costs and Expenses

One special problem in interpretation arises from confusion among the terms *costs, assets, expenses,* and *expenditures,* which unfortunately are sometimes used interchangeably. *Cost* is the broadest term. It measures the amount of resources used or sacrificed to obtain some objective. An *expenditure* involves a monetary sacrifice to acquire a productive resource. In this context, cost is the amount of cash or cash equivalent expended to acquire economic benefits. Hence, assets acquired through expenditure decisions are sometimes called costs.

*Expense* refers to the consumption of assets in the generation of revenues. In this context, cost is the amount of asset given up in the obtaining of revenues. Expenses can be viewed as *expired costs;* assets can be viewed as *unexpired costs*. The cost of an economic resource that benefits the future is an asset; the cost of a resource used up in generating the period's revenue is an expense.

The first step in tracing the life of an asset is to record the acquisition of the asset (incurrence of cost). After acquisition, several things can happen to an asset—nothing, conversion into another asset, use to liquidate a liability, or consumption in an attempt to generate revenue. Only in the last instance is there an expense. From the standpoint of periodic income measurement we are concerned with two stages in the life of most assets—acquisition and consumption (expiration). When an asset is acquired, a debit entry is made to the asset account, and a corresponding credit is made, usually to cash or some liability account. When the asset is *consumed in the production of revenue,* a credit entry is made to the asset and a debit entry to an expense account.

In the case of some assets, the period in which they are consumed in the production of revenues is the same as the period of cost incurrence. For example, the salary cost of a delivery person for the month of August is applicable to the revenues during that month. We cannot store these services for later use. They will be consumed, thus becoming an August expense. Similarly, the monthly rental payment on a building applies only to the particular month for which it is made. In these cases the cost incurred during the period is the same as the cost consumed during the period.

For these assets that become expenses almost instantaneously, we can simplify the bookkeeping, with no practical objections, by recording the expense at the time the asset is acquired. If we know that an asset will in all probability become an expense during the period in which it is acquired, we often debit its cost directly to an expense account. This shortcut can be employed in the case of salespersons' services in the example in Table 3–3. When the cash is paid out, a single entry is made:

| Cash | | Salary Expense | |
|---|---|---|---|
| | 5,000 | 5,000 | |

An expense is recognized at the time of use, because use is related to the current period's revenues. A theoretical portrayal of what happens is reflected in the *two* entries in Table 3–3. An asset or productive resource is acquired; then it is consumed in the generation of revenue. The single entry, however, eliminates the formal recording of the asset acquisition. Similar examples include other types of periodic services which very probably will become expenses entirely in the period of incurrence—rent, insurance, and maybe even supplies.

Obviously, this shortcut generally would not apply to assets which are used in more than one accounting period (those that appear on the position statement). Buildings, equipment, and merchandise are normally handled in at least two steps—acquisition and expiration. Also, this bookkeeping shortcut should not be allowed to confuse the fundamental relationship between asset and expense. Neither the payment of cash nor the incurrence of a liability necessarily gives rise to the expense, although the shortcut recording procedure may leave that impression. "Business enterprises acquire assets, not expenses, to carry out their production operations; and most expenses are at least momentarily assets."[7]

**JOURNALS**

Let us now turn to the other recording medium used in accounting, the journal. In the preceding section transactions are entered directly in the ledger accounts. In a more realistic situation, with hundreds of different ledger accounts, this procedure becomes unwieldy. In making entries directly in the individual ledger accounts, we lose the identity of the individual transaction. A particular ledger account contains only one part of a transaction. Consequently, relating individual debits and credits in various ledger accounts to one another in order to reconstruct the separate events of the period becomes almost an impossibility.

Therefore, to maintain a record of each transaction intact, we first record it in a journal. Each such recording is called a journal entry. The use of a journal in addition to the ledger provides three benefits: (1) a

---

[7] FASB, *Statement of Financial Accounting Concepts No. 3,* "Elements of Financial Statements of Business Enterprises" (Stamford, Conn., December 1980) par. 64, footnote 31.

chronological history of the period's activities, (2) a complete record of each transaction that can be used to trace errors, and (3) room for explanatory information about the entry.

**General Journal**

Because transactions are first recorded in journals, the latter are often called *books of original entry*. Then, by a process called *posting*, the debits and credits indicated in the journal entries are entered in the respective ledger account. The simplest journal is the two-column general journal shown in Table 3–5. We shall use the example in the preceding section to illustrate the journalizing and posting process.

**TABLE 3–5  Recording of Transactions in General Journal**

| GENERAL JOURNAL | | | | | Page 3 |
|---|---|---|---|---|---|
| Date | Accounts | PR | Debit | Credit |
| 1984 May 1 | Cash ................................. <br>     Capital Stock ........................ <br>     Issuance of shares to original investors. | 4 | 12,000 | 12,000 |
| 1 | Prepaid Rent ........................... <br>     Cash ............................. <br>     One month's lease on store building on Elm Street. | 4 | 2,000 | 2,000 |
| 2 | Merchandise .......................... <br>     Accounts Payable .................. <br>     Invoice No. 8079 received from Acme Wholesale Suppliers. | | 16,000 | 16,000 |
| 2 | Salary Expense ........................ <br>     Cash ............................. <br>     Two salespersons hired at a monthly salary of $2,500 each. | 4 | 5,000 | 5,000 |
| 10 | Cash ................................. <br>     Sales Revenue ..................... <br>     Cash sales. | 4 | 6,000 | 6,000 |
| 18 | Accounts Receivable .................. <br>     Sales Revenue ..................... <br>     Sales made on open account. | | 10,000 | 10,000 |
| 31 | Cost of Goods Sold .................... <br>     Merchandise ...................... <br>     Cost of the merchandise sold during May. | | 8,000 | 8,000 |
| 31 | Rent Expense ......................... <br>     Prepaid Rent ...................... <br>     To record expiration of lease. | | 2,000 | 2,000 |

When journal entries are made, the accounts to be debited are normally listed first, with the credits following and indented. When more than one account is being debited or credited, the entry is called a *compound journal entry.* The dollar amounts are entered in the respective money columns. Under each entry is an explanation giving detailed information about it. Usually the explanations are much more specific than those illustrated in Table 3–5.

**Posting**

Posting involves taking the component parts of the journal entries and transcribing them to the individual ledger accounts. To post the debit to Cash, for example, in the first entry, the bookkeeper selects the ledger page or card for the Cash account and enters $12,000 on the debit side. Also, in the PR (posting reference) column of the ledger account, the journal page number (and the particular journal if more than one journal is used) is entered to indicate the source of the ledger entry. Then, in the PR column (also sometimes labeled LF for ledger folio) of the journal, the account number of the Cash account is entered. The posting reference in the journal provides a convenient cross-reference to the ledger and indicates which debits and credits are yet to be posted. To illustrate this procedure, a formal ledger account for Cash (see Table 3–6) is shown, and the *portions* of the entries recorded in the journal affecting Cash have been posted. (Normally posting would be done entry by entry.) Similar procedures would be followed for the other accounts.

**TABLE 3-6   Illustration of Posting to Ledger Account**

|  |  |  | | Cash |  |  | | Account No. 4 |
|---|---|---|---|---|---|---|---|---|
| Date | Explanation | PR | Amount | Date | Explanation | PR | Amount |
| May 1 |  | J-3 | 12,000 | May 1 |  | J-3 | 2,000 |
| May 10 |  | J-3 | 6,000 | May 2 |  | J-3 | 5,000 |
|  |  |  | 18,000 |  |  |  | 7,000 |
|  |  |  |  | May 31 | Balance | √ | 11,000 |
|  |  |  | 18,000 |  |  |  | 18,000 |
| June 1 | Balance | √ | 11,000 |  |  |  |  |

**SUMMARY**

Journals and ledger accounts are the two technical devices used in the recording process. The journal contains a chronological analysis of specific business transactions recorded intact and accompanied by explanatory information. Through the posting process, the debit and credit elements of the journal entries are transcribed to the ledger, where they are organized according to account classification.

The ledger accounts, one for each individual asset, liability, and owners' equity element, comprise the underlying fabric of the entire accounting system. The use of special-purpose owners' equity accounts, called revenues and expenses, to measure relevant asset changes supplies us with additional valuable information. Summarized on the income statement, these accounts not only show what the net income is but give a reasonably detailed picture of how the income has been earned.

In actual business practice the exact form of the journals and ledgers varies tremendously. Only in a relatively simple, manual accounting system might they appear as illustrated in this chapter. Ledgers may consist of trays of punched cards (each card representing a specific account), computer printout sheets in a binder, or a group of memory cells within a large computer. Similarly, a journal may consist of a bound volume of printed forms of varying types, a stack of punched cards (each card representing a journal entry), or a reel of magnetic tape. Nevertheless, the important aspect is not the format of these devices but the particular function that each performs. They furnish an orderly record, cross-indexed by events (journal) and accounts (ledger).

In subsequent chapters we use both journal and ledger entries. Both require the ability to break a business event into its component parts. The sequence in analyzing and recording a transaction is:

1. Determine how assets, liabilities, or owners' equities are affected by the transaction, remembering that the equality of assets and equities cannot be overturned.
2. Determine what particular accounts are to be increased or decreased, keeping in mind that the effects on owners' equity from operating transactions are recorded in revenue and expense accounts.
3. Translate these increases and decreases into left-hand (debit) and right-hand (credit) entries.
4. Record the debits and credits in journal or ledger form, as the case may be.
5. Verify that debits equal credits in order to check on the completeness of the analysis and on numerical accuracy.

In later chapters many additional ledger accounts are introduced. However, these, of necessity, must represent embellishments of the existing asset-equity system. There are only three basic types of accounts—assets, liabilities, and owners' equity. Revenue and expense accounts are subdivisions of the latter. Each new account will be either a subdivision also or a modification of one of these. Consequently the procedural rules for recording increases and decreases can be applied to every account, once the nature of the account is determined. The following bookkeeping rules apply to the various types of accounts introduced in this chapter:

| Type of Account | Increase | Decrease |
|---|---|---|
| Assets ................. | Debit | Credit |
| Liabilities .............. | Credit | Debit |
| Owners' equity .......... | Credit | Debit |
| Revenues ............. | Credit | Debit |
| Expenses .............. | Debit | Credit |

A good knowledge of these debit and credit rules, along with the concept of the asset-equity framework, will facilitate greater understanding as we expand our discussion. New terms, accounts, procedures, and concepts should be related to the underlying foundation established in Chapters 2 and 3.

## QUESTIONS AND PROBLEMS

**3-1.** Your college roommate has been perusing your accounting textbook and after reading about the rules for debits and credits says, "Debits and credits seem very confusing to me. For example, explain these inconsistencies I've found."

1. "Both asset and expense accounts have debit balances. One arises from the acquisition of assets; the other arises from the use of assets. How can accountants use debits to reflect both increases and decreases in assets?"
2. "Revenue accounts normally have credit balances. Back in Chapters 1 and 2, the book says that revenues are asset inflows from the sale of goods and services. But, asset inflows are supposed to be recorded as debits."
3. "I just received my bank statement. Each time I make a deposit, the bank credits my account. The checks I wrote and the service charges I incurred for printed checks and for falling below my minimum balance are shown as debits. It seems to me that the exact opposite should apply to my asset account."

**3-2.** The General Electron Company is organized on March 15, 1985. Following is a summary of its dealings prior to the commencement of operating activities on April 1:

1. Shares of stock are issued to various individuals who invest $100,000 in cash.
2. Land and a building are purchased for $60,000 of which $15,000 is deemed applicable to the land. Of the total purchase price, $20,000 is paid in cash, and a 10-year mortgage is given for the remainder.
3. A landscape architect grades the land and installs permanent drainage at a cost of $6,000, to be paid in 30 days.
4. A secondhand delivery truck is purchased for cash in the amount of $8,000.
5. The truck is completely overhauled and repainted at a cost of $1,300, which is paid in cash.
6. The firm interviewed Izzy Everslow for the position of sales manager at a monthly salary of $2,000.

7. Office equipment is purchased on account for $1,600.
8. Inventory is purchased for $32,000; cash of $7,000 is paid, and a six-month, 10 percent note for the difference is given to the supplier.
9. One of the original stockholders has a change of heart. He would prefer to loan the money to the corporation rather than be an ultimate risk taker. The other stockholders agree to the request. Accordingly, his stock certificate for $10,000 is surrendered and canceled, and the loan agreement is substituted.
10. A corrected invoice is received in connection with the purchase in item 8. The cost of the inventory was actually only $31,000; the supplier sends a $1,000 refund check.
11. Insurance premiums of $1,800 are paid by check.
12. A check for $500 is received from a customer to apply against purchases she expects to make in April.

*Required:*

a. Prepare general journal entries to record the above events.
b. Establish a ledger (T-) account for Cash and post the relevant portions of the journal entries to it. At what amount would cash appear on the March 31 balance sheet?

**3–3.** The following account balances existed on January 1, 1985:

| | | | |
|---|---|---|---|
| Cash | $ 45,800 | Accounts payable | $ 24,000 |
| Accounts receivable | 18,600 | Notes payable | 1,600 |
| Merchandise inventory | 15,600 | Wages payable | 500 |
| Supplies inventory | 1,100 | Interest payable | 200 |
| Prepaid insurance | 2,500 | Capital stock | 84,000 |
| Equipment | 48,600 | Retained earnings | 49,900 |
| Buildings | 28,000 | | |
| | $160,200 | | $160,200 |

During the first quarter of 1985 the following changes took place:

1. Purchases on account amounted to $72,000 for merchandise and $1,000 for supplies.
2. Sales of merchandise on account were as follows: sales price, $96,000; cost of merchandise sold, $45,500.
3. Cash receipts:
   a. Issuance of more capital stock, $9,000.
   b. Collected from customers, $57,400.
   c. Sale of excess equipment, $5,400 (this was $1,800 less than its book amount of $7,200).
   d. Refund of insurance premium of $300. Insurance policy was canceled since it represented duplicate coverage.
4. Cash disbursements:
   a. To merchandise and supplies vendors, $47,100.
   b. To bank for note and interest accrued in 1984, $1,800.
   c. To employees for services rendered last year *and* in 1985, $6,500.
   d. For supplies, $800.
   e. For heat, light, and other utilities, $2,500.
   f. To local newspaper for advertisements during the first quarter of 1985, $600.

5. Other changes:
   a. Supplies used, $1,400.
   b. Insurance expired, $500.
   c. Equipment depreciation, $1,900.
   d. Building depreciation, $600.
   e. Employee services used in 1985 but not paid for, $1,100.

*Required:*

a. Set up ledger (T-) accounts for each of the accounts listed and enter the opening balances.
b. Record the changes occurring during the three months. Record all income transactions directly in retained earnings (do *not* use revenue and expense accounts).
c. Prepare a position statement as of March 31, 1985.
d. Did the firm operate profitably during this period? How do you know? How much income or loss did it make?
e. "Revenue and expense accounts are not necessary, but they are useful." Explain the meaning of this statement in the context of your answers to this problem.

**3–4.** Shown below is the position statement of Neverready Delivery Service, Inc., as of April 30, 1985:

NEVERREADY DELIVERY SERVICE
Statement of Financial Position
April 30, 1985

| *Assets* | | *Equities* | |
|---|---:|---|---:|
| Cash | $ 600 | Accounts payable | $ 900 |
| Supplies | 1,200 | Capital stock | 15,000 |
| Prepaid rent | 3,000 | Retained earnings | 8,900 |
| Equipment | 20,000 | | |
| | $24,800 | | $24,800 |

1. On May 1 the stockholders invested another $15,000 in the business in exchange for shares of stock.
2. The officers of the firm contacted the local bank on May 2 and arranged a line of credit whereby the business could borrow up to $20,000 as needed.
3. The business ordered $600 of supplies on May 3.
4. Accounts payable of $500 were paid in cash.
5. On May 15 the garage and office building, which heretofore had been rented, were purchased for $12,700. The rent that had been prepaid as of April 30 was to apply against the purchase price, with the remainder paid in cash.
6. Two new employees were hired. Their salaries, beginning on June 1, were to be $1,200 a month each. However, to be sure of their availability, each was advanced $400 on May 20.
7. The supplies ordered on May 3 were delivered on May 21 along with an invoice for $600.
8. A careless accident by an employee destroyed equipment with a book value of $3,000.
9. On May 30, a $15,000 loan was taken out at the bank under the previously arranged line of credit.

10. One third of the supplies delivered on May 21 were found to be defective and were returned to the supplier.

*Required:*

a. Prepare journal entries for the above events.
b. Set up ledger (T-) accounts, enter the opening balances, and post the journal entries.
c. Prepare a position statement as of May 31, 1985.

**3–5.** During the month of October the following transactions took place concerning Auntie Pasto's Pizza Parlor:

*October 1–5:*

1. The business is formed as a partnership by two brothers. One brother, I. M. Dense, contributed a restaurant location valued at $60,000. The land was appraised at $24,000, and the building at $36,000, although I. M. had originally purchased the location five years ago for only $50,000. The other brother, U. R. Dense, invested $45,000 in cash and securities having a current market value of $15,000 (original cost to U. R. was $9,000).
2. Ingredients costing $40,500 were purchased, $16,500 for cash and $24,000 on open account.
3. Mixers, ovens, and other equipment worth $30,000 were acquired on open account.
4. Circulars advertising the grand opening were printed and distributed at a cost of $600. A check for $1,200 was given to a rock band to secure its services to play each evening during opening week.
5. The brothers offered to buy for $6,700 an adjacent piece of land for a parking lot. No reply was received.

*October 6–30:*

6. Cash received in connection with pizzas served to customers was $41,500.
7. Salaries and wage costs amounting to $11,700 were incurred; $10,200 of this was paid in cash.
8. Other miscellaneous services (utilities, etc.) acquired and used during the month were $1,300, paid in cash.
9. A counteroffer from the owner of the adjacent land (see item 5) was received to sell the land for $9,000 cash. The brothers Dense accepted the offer, and title to the land passed to the business.
10. Accounts payable in the amount of $9,500 were paid in cash.
11. A refund of $100 was received from the printer for faultily printed advertising circulars (see transaction 4).

*October 31:*

12. A note payable for $30,000 was offered in payment of the open account created by the equipment purchases in transaction 3. The supplier accepts the note.
13. Pizza ingredients remaining on hand amounted to $18,600.
14. Entries were made to record the cost of asset services consumed (depreciation) during October of $300 on the restaurant building and $600 on the mixers, ovens, and other equipment.
15. Interest revenue accrued on the securities invested by U. R. amounted to $100.

*Required:*

a. Prepare journal entries for the above events.
b. Post the journal entries to ledger accounts.
c. Prepare an income statement for the month of October and a position statement as of October 31.
d. What assumption did you make with respect to the advertising expenditures in transaction 4?

**3–6.** Every exchange transaction involves two parties. Both parties record the impact of the transaction on their assets, liabilities, and owners' equity. For each of the transactions below, prepare the journal entry that would be made by *each* party to the transaction.

1. Acme Corporation issues shares of its stock to Hy Ball for $2,000.
2. Camelot Company receives a $500 cash payment from Deadbeat, Inc., in partial payment of an account.
3. Eclectic Corporation purchases theater tickets from Fanta Ticket Agency for $200 cash. Eclectric uses the tickets to entertain customers from out of town. Fanta is entitled to a 10 percent commission; the balance of the ticket price must be remitted to the theater at the end of the month.
4. Gates Computer Repair Company leases space from Heavenly Realty Company for $2,000 a month. Gates writes a check for $12,000 to cover the first six months' rent.
5. Inner Spirits Distributing Company supplies liquid refreshments for a sales conference run by Jaded Enterprises. The cost of the beverages is $350. In addition, a $50 deposit is required on the containers; the deposit is refundable upon return of the bottles, kegs, etc.
6. King Corporation borrows $50,000 on a long-term mortgage note from Last National Bank of Medusa.
7. Mammoth Motors, an automobile dealer, sells five trucks to Natural Delivery Systems, Inc., for $15,000 each. The trucks cost Mammoth Motors $9,000 apiece.

**3–7.** In Problem 2–7 you were asked to identify the asset and equity accounts that one would expect to appear on the balance sheet of a golf course. Review the information given in that problem.

*Required:*

a. Identify some of the major revenue and expense accounts that would appear on the periodic income statements of the golf course.
b. The following transactions have been summarized in terms of their debit-credit impact on general categories of accounts. Using the accounts you have identified in part *(a)* and in Problem 2–7, describe the nature of a possible underlying event that would cause the indicated changes. Do not use the same description for more than one transaction.

1. Debit a current asset and credit a current liability for $6,000.
2. Debit a current asset and credit a temporary owners' equity account for $800.
3. Debit a temporary owners' equity account and credit a noncurrent asset for $400.
4. Debit a noncurrent asset and credit a current liability for $8,000.
5. Debit a current asset for $2,500, credit another current asset for $2,000, and

make entries in two temporary owners' equity accounts—one a credit for $2,500 and another a debit for $2,000.

6. Debit a temporary owners' equity account and credit a current liability for $1,400.

7. Debit a current liability and credit a current asset for $700.

**3–8.** Using your knowledge of how various transactions affect particular ledger accounts, determine the item of missing information in each of the seven situations below:

1. Accounts receivable are $32,400 and $42,800 at the beginning and end of the period respectively. If $106,000 cash is collected from customers during the period, what were the total credit sales?

2. Accrued wages payable of $14,200 appeared on the balance sheet at the beginning of March. Wage expense for March was $37,800, and total cash payments to employees during March amounted to $33,600. How much is owed to employees at the end of the month?

3. The income statement shows a net income of $18,800. Retained earnings at the beginning and at the end of the year are $17,800 and $30,600, respectively. How much was declared in dividends during the year?

4. The position statement on November 30 shows a balance in the inventory of repair parts of $6,400, an increase of $4,300 since the beginning of the month. The income statement for November indicates that $9,000 of repair parts were used in making service calls. What quantity of repair parts was purchased in November?

5. A liability account, Rent Received in Advance, had a balance of $18,800 on July 1. By July 31, the balance was $8,000 higher. If rent revenue for July were $12,000, how much cash was received from rental customers during the month?

6. The position statements on January 1 and January 31 show $438,000 and $482,000 for plant and equipment. Capital expenditures on new plant and equipment in January totaled $75,000. There were no retirements of old plants. How much depreciation expense for plant and equipment should appear on the January income statement?

7. Prepaid insurance on October 31, is $7,400. Insurance premiums paid in October amounted to $5,200. The income statement for the month shows insurance expense of $1,900. At what amount did the asset Prepaid Insurance appear on the *October 1* balance sheet?

**3–9.** The T-accounts below show the transactions of Cardinal company during the month of May:

| Cash | | | | | Accounts Payable | | | | | Sales | | |
|---|---|---|---|---|---|---|---|---|---|---|---|---|
| (1) | 60,000 | (2) | 600 | | (8) | 29,000 | (3) | 30,700 | | | (4) | 40,900 |
| (6) | 2,500 | (5) | 12,300 | | (11) | 500 | | | | | (6) | 2,500 |
| (9) | 7,800 | (7) | 1,800 | | | | | | | | | |
| (13) | 33,600 | (8) | 29,000 | | | | | | | | | |

| Inventory | | | | | Salaries and Wages | | | | | Capital Stock | | |
|---|---|---|---|---|---|---|---|---|---|---|---|---|
| (3) | 30,700 | (11) | 500 | | (5) | 12,300 | | | | | (1) | 60,000 |
| | | (14) | 26,500 | | (15) | 700 | | | | | (10) | 4,000 |

| Depreciation | | | Cost of Goods Sold | | | Furniture and Fixtures | |
|---|---|---|---|---|---|---|---|
| (12) | 200 | | (14) | 26,500 | | (2) 6,600 | (12) 200 |

| Notes Payable | | | Rent Expense | | | Accounts Receivable | |
|---|---|---|---|---|---|---|---|
| (10) 4,000 | (2) 6,000 | | (16) | 300 | | (4) 40,900 | (13) 33,600 |

| Advances from Customers | | | Wages Payable | | | Unexpired Rent | |
|---|---|---|---|---|---|---|---|
| | (9) 7,800 | | | (15) 700 | | (7) 1,800 | (16) 300 |

*Required:*

a.  For each of the above entries (1) to (16) explain the nature of the underlying event. Be as specific as possible.

b.  Prepare an income statement and a position statement.

**3–10.**  At the close of business on December 31, 1984, the accounts of the Prince Toy Company had the following balances:

| | Debit | Credit |
|---|---|---|
| Cash | $ 12,000 | |
| Accounts receivable | 28,000 | |
| Inventory | 66,000 | |
| Office supplies | 1,100 | |
| Unexpired insurance | 800 | |
| Store equipment | 8,000 | |
| Delivery equipment | 12,000 | |
| Accounts payable | | $ 10,000 |
| Wages payable | | 4,000 |
| Rent payable | | 6,000 |
| Capital stock | | 100,000 |
| Retained earnings | | 7,900 |
| | $127,900 | $127,900 |

The following transactions, in summary form, occurred in the calendar year 1985:

1.  Purchased inventory on account, $300,000.
2.  Insurance premiums paid, $800.
3.  Delivery equipment purchased on account, $1,000.
4.  Purchased supplies, $2,400, half for cash and half on account.
5.  Wages paid in cash during year, $46,000; and wages payable on December 31, 1985, $12,000.
6.  Advertising expenses paid for in cash, $3,600.
7.  Payments on account, $280,000.
8.  Rent paid during the year, $10,000; and rent payable on December 31, 1985, $8,000.
9.  Sales of toys on account, $440,000.
10.  Cost of inventory sold during the year, $360,000.
11.  Cash collected from customers, $346,700.
12.  Toys returned by customers and accepted by Prince Toy, $6,700 selling price and $4,000 cost. The customers had not paid their accounts arising from

these purchases. Prince Toy Company donates the toys to a nearby day-care center.

13. Unused supplies, $1,400.
14. Insurance expired during the year, $1,200.
15. Equipment services used up: store, $800; and delivery, $2,400.

*Required:*

a. Set up ledger (T-) accounts for the above accounts and enter the opening balances for 1985.
b. Make ledger entries to record the transactions for 1985, using revenue and expense accounts.
c. Prepare in good form an income statement for 1985 and a position statement as of December 31, 1985.

**3–11.** In May 1984, Andy James opened an automobile parts distributorship. In summary form below are the transactions for the first six months of operations:

1. Invested $50,000 in cash.
2. Paid $18,000 rent in advance to cover 12 months.
3. Purchased storage bins and shelves costing $50,000 on account. These are expected to last 10 years.
4. Purchased parts for the stockroom in the amount of $30,000 on account.
5. Received an order for $11,400 of parts to be delivered in three months.
6. Purchased for cash a supply of 600 oil filters for $3 each. These are given away to the first 600 customers as a promotional scheme.
7. Sold parts for cash, $9,800, and on account, $14,200. The parts cost $17,600.
8. Paid in cash $4,800 for wages, $1,400 for advertising, and $800 for utility bills.
9. Delivered the parts mentioned in transaction 5. Their cost was $7,500.
10. Collected $3,600 from charge customers.
11. Invested $10,000 of idle cash in a six-month money market certificate of deposit at the bank.
12. Paid $12,300 of accounts payable and gave a $6,000 note payable in settlement of another account.
13. Recognized additional unpaid liabilities at the end of the period of $900 for wages and $100 for utilities.
14. Recognized rent applicable to the current accounting period.
15. Depreciation on the storage bins and shelves is recorded for the current accounting period in the amount of $2,500.
16. Recorded the accrual of $300 of interest on the money market certificate.

*Required:*

a. Prepare journal entries to record these transactions, employing revenue and expense accounts wherever necessary.
b. Prepare an income statement for the six months ended October 31, 1984.

**3–12.** One of your mathematically inclined colleagues has summarized financial accounting in the following sets of formulas (Δ stands for "change in"):

1.
$$A = L + OE$$
$$A - L = OE$$
$$(A - L) + \Delta(A - L) = OE + \Delta OE$$
$$\Delta(A - L) = \Delta OE$$

2.
$$R = +\Delta OE$$
$$E = -\Delta OE$$
$$R - E = \Delta OE$$
$$R - E = NI$$
$$NI = \Delta OE$$

where $A$, $L$, and $OE$ stand for assets, liabilities, and owners' equity; and where $R$, $E$, and $NI$ stand for revenues, expenses, and net income.

By substituting item 2 in item 1, your colleague reasons that $NI = \Delta(A - L)$. Therefore, he concludes that the only accounts necessary in a bookkeeping system are assets and liabilities. Keeping track of the changes in these will produce the net income figure.

*Required:*

a. Is he correct? Why or why not?
b. Are there other reasons for the use of revenue and expense accounts which your colleague has failed to understand?

**3–13.** Leif E. Maple and his wife, Sugar, decided to open a candy store on August 1, 1984. The following were the transactions for August:

1. On August 2, they deposited their savings of $9,000 in a bank account for the new firm.
2. On August 3, Leif purchased new equipment for $6,600, paying $600 down and promising to pay the rest in 60 days.
3. Utilities were hooked up. The firm had to pay a $360 deposit which could be subtracted from its monthly utility bills in equal amounts over the next year.
4. Leif had alterations and improvements made to the inside of the store building which cost $4,500 paid in cash.
5. Candy was ordered and delivered to the store by a wholesaler. The cost was $2,600, payable in 30 days.
6. Candy sales for cash amounted to $900 during the first 15 days of August.
7. Candy, which cost $100, was returned to the wholesaler because of spoilage. The anticipated selling price of that candy was $150.
8. Employee salaries of $600 were paid for the month.
9. Additional purchases of candy during the month were $1,140, unpaid as of the end of the month.
10. Supplies costing $360 were purchased for cash. Of these, approximately two thirds were used during the month.
11. Sales in the last half of the month were $2,100. This included $1,200 of credit sales, of which $1,040 had been collected by the end of the month.
12. It was estimated that the cost of candy on hand on August 31 was $1,300.
13. The *unexpired* cost of equipment on August 31 was $6,440. Leif estimated that $80 of the cost of improvements should be allocated to operations in August.
14. The utility bill for $270 was received. This amount less the allocated deposit is payable on September 10.
15. Rent for the month of August was $900 and was due on September 1.

*Required:*

a. Enter the above transactions in ledger accounts.

b. Prepare an income statement for August and a position statement as of August 31.

c. From these statements, do you foresee any financial difficulties for the Maples?

**3–14.** The following alphabetical listing of account balances has been taken from the ledger accounts of Payless Markets, Inc., at the end of 1984:

|  | Debit | Credit |
|---|---|---|
| Accounts payable | | $ 19,500 |
| Accounts receivable | $ 13,700 | |
| Accrued wages and salaries | | 600 |
| Advances from customers | | 1,500 |
| Advances to suppliers | 1,300 | |
| Buildings and equipment | 60,000 | |
| Capital stock | | 30,000 |
| Cash | 6,000 | |
| Commissions and royalties | 10,200 | |
| Cost of product delivered | 144,000 | |
| Depreciation | 6,300 | |
| Earnings reinvested in business | | 38,000 |
| Employee compensation | 46,800 | |
| Insurance expired | 1,500 | |
| Investment income | | 1,200 |
| Investments | 7,000 | |
| Land | 15,000 | |
| Liability for commissions and royalties | | 1,400 |
| Merchandise | 25,600 | |
| Mortgage loan payable (due in 10 equal annual installments) | | 35,000 |
| Prepaid insurance | 600 | |
| Sales of product | | 210,800 |
| | $338,000 | $338,000 |

*Required:*

a. Prepare an income statement for the year 1984 and a balance sheet as of December 31, 1984. Use appropriate form and terminology.

b. Why do the two "advances" accounts have different balances? Should they be offset and only a net credit of $200 shown?

c. Why is the amount shown on the balance sheet for commissions and royalties different from the amount shown on the income statement?

d. Buildings and equipment were $63,200 on January 1, 1984. Why does the depreciation charge of $6,300 not agree with the decline in the asset of $3,200?

e. The balance sheet on January 1, 1984, showed assets of $105,800; total liabilities of $46,200; and total stockholders' equity of $59,600. Explain carefully why the income figure for 1984 does not equal the change in assets or the change in stockholders' equity.

**3–15.** On January 1, 1985, the account balances of Luslerun Corporation were as follows:

|  | Debit | Credit |
|---|---|---|
| Cash | $ 6,300 | |
| Accounts receivable | 67,600 | |
| Merchandise | 96,150 | |
| Supplies | 2,550 | |
| Prepaid insurance | 3,000 | |
| Land | 47,250 | |
| Buildings | 94,500 | |
| Equipment | 31,600 | |
| Accounts payable | | $ 78,750 |
| Salaries payable | | 3,150 |
| Capital stock | | 200,000 |
| Retained earnings | | 67,050 |
|  | $348,950 | $348,950 |

During the year the transactions summarized below took place:

Purchases on account:
| | |
|---|---|
| Merchandise | $567,000 |
| Supplies | 4,200 |

Cash receipts:
| | |
|---|---|
| Services rendered to customers | 73,500 |
| Collections of customers' accounts | 630,000 |

Cash disbursements:
| | |
|---|---|
| Supplies | 2,750 |
| Delivery charges on outgoing merchandise | 4,650 |
| Insurance premium | 1,700 |
| Payments on account | 598,500 |
| Salespersons' salaries | 39,700 |
| Utility services | 4,450 |
| Equipment to be delivered and installed in 1986 | 25,000 |

| | |
|---|---|
| Sales of product on account | 721,000 |

Other information:
| | |
|---|---|
| Depreciation for year on building | 3,150 |
| Depreciation for year on equipment | 2,550 |
| Insurance expired during year | 2,800 |
| Inventory of supplies on December 31 | 1,900 |
| Merchandise on hand on December 31 | 136,500 |
| Unpaid salespersons' salaries | 2,100 |

*Required:*

a. Prepare general journal entries to record the transactions for the year.
b. Open ledger (T-) accounts, enter the beginning balances, and post the journal entries from part *(a)*.
c. Prepare an income statement for the year and a position statement as of the end of the year.

# CHAPTER 4

# ELEMENTS
# OF THE
# ACCOUNTING
# CYCLE

Financial accounting is called upon to gather and communicate financial data. Chapter 3 discusses two important elements of the recording process—journals and ledgers. These media are used to accumulate and classify the results of transactions affecting the business entity. Each serves a unique recording purpose and is cross-referenced to the other in the posting process. The financial statements, adequately explained, are vehicles for the major goal of communication. They signify the culmination of the accounting efforts.

In a sense, then, the journals and ledgers stand at the beginning of the accounting process, and the financial statements stand at the end. The purpose of this chapter is to expand our knowledge of other accounting functions performed in between and then to place the bookkeeping and accounting procedures in their proper relationship. Specifically, the first half of the chapter discusses one additional aspect of the recording process—adjusting entries. These not only are essential to an understanding of the accounting system but also increase our ability to use accounting as an analytical tool. The second half of the chapter concludes the discussion of accounting techniques by arranging the various steps in a systematic sequence called the accounting cycle. An appendix then considers special journals, work sheets, electronic data processing, and internal control.

**ADJUSTING
ENTRIES**

Accounting transactions are classified as external and internal in Chapter 3. The former consist of explicit dealings with parties outside of the business entity. In most cases the external transaction is signaled by some discrete event—the receipt of an invoice, the writing of a check, the signing of a note payable at the bank, and so forth. Normally, an entry is made at the time these transactions occur. Barring some error in the recording, the accounts are usually accurate and up to date with respect to these events.

Internal transactions, on the other hand, tend to be of a more continuous nature. They reflect changes in assets and equities that are taking place gradually. A portion of the prepaid rent expires each day. Inventories of supplies are being consumed throughout the entire period. Labor costs are incurred each day, and a liability gradually is building. If the entity lends money, interest revenue is being earned throughout the entire period in which the money is lent. An asset, interest receivable, gradually accrues with the passage of time.

It would be tremendously time-consuming and expensive to record these internal changes in the journal and ledger accounts each day. Often it is easier to enter them as cumulative totals periodically as part of an explicit, external transaction. For instance, recognition of the labor costs is deferred until payday, when an entry is made for the entire period's cost. Similarly, the interest revenue may be accumulating each day, but its recording may be deferred until the total amount is received in cash. Simply stated, it may not be convenient or necessary to keep all asset, liability, revenue, and expense accounts up to date at all times.

## Adjusting Entries Defined

However, this prevalent clerical shortcut may conflict with the purpose of accounting to furnish audiences with accurate and timely financial statements. Before financial statements are prepared, all external and internal transactions of the period should be collected in the accounts. Otherwise, the account balances and resultant financial statements will be incomplete, inaccurate, and hence, misleading to their audience. Unless all asset and equity events have been recorded, the balance sheet will not portray financial condition as of the end of the accounting period. Likewise, the income statement cannot present a realistic picture of the period's operations unless all revenues and expenses of the period are taken into consideration.

Accuracy and timeliness in the accounts are achieved prior to the preparation of financial statements through the use of adjusting entries. *Adjusting entries are those made at the end of the accounting period to record transactions that have taken place but have not yet been recorded and to revise entries that were made incorrectly*. The recording of adjusting entries is a logical adjunct of *accrual accounting*. Revenues and expenses and their related effects upon financial position are identified and reported in the period when they occur and not when cash receipts and disbursements are made. The latter points may be used sometimes for recording convenience, but they do not govern which accounting events shall be presented on the financial statements.

Although a variety of situations may call for adjustments, let us study some of the fairly common types first. Most adjusting entries for continuous transactions involve either the apportionment between accounting periods of some element already recorded on the books or the accruing of some unrecorded element that has been changing during the period. Apportionment or accrual can apply to both revenues and expenses; thus there are in total four general types:

1. Apportioning the cost of assets already acquired to reflect the expense applicable to the current period.
2. Accruing the cost of expired assets (expenses) which have not yet been recorded.
3. Apportioning the amount received in advance for products or services to reflect the revenue applicable to the delivery of the product or the performance of the service in the current period.
4. Accruing the amount of unrecorded asset increases (revenues) resulting from operations during the current period.

As noted above, apportionments and accruals adjust for those situations in which the bookkeeper has found it convenient to operate temporarily under the cash basis of accounting. Because the cash effects of transactions are incorporated in the accounts when the cash receipts or disbursements occurred, the forthcoming apportionments and accruals never feature a debit or credit to the Cash account. Also, for each of the illustrations, observe that each apportionment and accrual journal entry involves at least one income statement account and at least one balance sheet item. Consequently, any failure to adjust the books properly will result in distortions to *both* major financial statements.

**Cost Apportionments**

Numerous examples exist of this first type of adjustment. Many of the nonmonetary assets in Chapter 2 fall into this category. They represent expenditures which will benefit more than one accounting period. As a portion of the asset's services is used up in each period, part of the cost has to be allocated as an expense of that period.

Suppose that on December 31 a ledger account for Prepaid Insurance has a debit balance of $4,300, representing the beginning balance plus the premiums paid on new insurance policies acquired during the year. Although all of the insurance policies have been expiring gradually throughout the year, no entries have yet been made. A careful analysis of the insurance policies on December 31 reveals that the unexpired cost of those still in force amounts to $1,400. The following adjusting entry is needed:

| | | |
|---|---|---|
| Insurance Expense | 2,900 | |
| Prepaid Insurance ($4,300 − $1,400) | | 2,900 |

Assume that a firm orders substantial quantities of office supplies. The purchases total $6,000 and are debited to an asset account. During the period, most of the supplies are consumed; however, at the end of the period $400 of supplies are left. An expense account should reflect the cost of supplies used ($5,600), and only the remaining $400 should appear as an asset on the position statement. The adjustment (in ledger form) to apportion the cost of the supplies used would be:

| Office Supplies Expense | | Office Supplies Inventory | |
|---|---|---|---|
| (1)          5,600 | | 6,000 \| (1)          5,600 | |

Similar adjustments would be required for such assets as prepaid rent, merchandise inventory, and depreciable long-lived resources.

**Assets Initially Recorded as Expenses.**  Sometimes the acquisition cost of certain assets is debited directly to expense accounts when a high probability exists that the asset will be consumed in its entirety during the period. If part of the asset does remain unused at the end of the period, then expenses are overstated and assets are understated. An adjusting entry similar to the one above is needed, except that in this case the cost apportionment is from the expense account back to the asset rather than the other way around.

For instance, assume that the firm in the preceding example debited the $6,000 purchase of supplies directly to Office Supplies Expense on the assumption that practically all of the supplies would be consumed during the period. In this case the adjusting entry would apportion to the asset account the unused part of the cost.

| Office Supplies Expense | | Office Supplies Inventory | |
|---|---|---|---|
| 6,000 \| (1)          400 | | (1)          400 | |

Although expense accounts normally are not credited, in this case the entry is proper, for we are reducing an overstated expense.

In accounting practice both procedures are used. Similar alternatives are sometimes applied to rent and to other prepayments. *However the initial entry is made, the end results have to be the same. All that must be determined is how much of the cost eventually should end up in the expense and asset accounts by the end of the period.* In the above example, under *both* options, the Office Supplies Expense account shows a $5,600 balance after adjustment, and the Office Supplies Inventory account shows a $400 balance after adjustment.

**Depreciation Expense.**  This expense represents an estimate of the cost of the services of a long-lived asset used during the period in the generation of revenues. Although the firm continuously utilizes its buildings, equipment, furniture and fixtures, and so on, a daily recording of depreciation is unnecessary and probably quite inaccurate. Rather, the firm makes an adjusting entry at the end of the period. For example, a company acquires store equipment at a cost of $35,000. The equipment is expected to last five years. At the end of each year an entry would be necessary to reflect the consumption of a year's service potential of the equipment:

| | | |
|---|---|---|
| Depreciation Expense | 7,000 | |
| Store Equipment ($35,000 ÷ 5 years) | | 7,000 |

In accounting practice, however, the credit entry is almost universally made to a separate account called *Accumulated Depreciation* or Allowance for Depreciation:

| | | |
|---|---|---|
| Depreciation Expense | 7,000 | |
| Accumulated Depreciation—Store Equipment | | 7,000 |

The Accumulated Depreciation account is called a *contra asset* account.[1] It becomes an integral part of the asset and appears as a deduction from the asset on the position statement. For example, at the end of the year this equipment would be reported as follows:

| | | |
|---|---|---|
| Store equipment | $35,000 | |
| Less: Accumulated depreciation | 7,000 | $28,000 |

Conceptually, making direct credits to the asset account would be a perfectly sound procedure. Although the asset may not have changed physically, economically a portion of its services has expired. By using the indirect procedure of a contra account, however, we are able to report more information—the original cost of the assets still in use, the estimate of the portion used, and the unexpired cost applicable to future periods. Because depreciation is at best an estimate, its placement in a contra account allows the reader roughly to judge the adequacy of the provision for depreciation and to form a general idea of the age of the asset. One could not do so if the asset were reported simply at $28,000. An extensive discussion of depreciation accounting is reserved for Chapter 9.

**Expense Accrual**

This type of adjustment is necessary whenever an asset (usually some type of service) is used during the period but is not recorded at the time of use. Rather, the entries are deferred for clerical convenience until the service is actually paid for in cash. Wages and salaries are a good case in point.

---

[1] This is our first contact with some special accounts called *valuation* accounts. Their purpose is to modify the amounts entered in some other account to which they apply. Valuation accounts are of two general types—contra accounts to record downward modifications to the main ledger account and adjunct accounts to record upward modifications. Contra and adjunct accounts can be used in conjunction with any kind of account where a need is felt to segregate particular kinds of increases or decreases. The complete record of the particular item is thus divided between at least two places. Part of it is in the main ledger account, while the rest has been isolated in a contra account (in the case of offsets) or adjunct account (in the case of additions).

Assume that salespersons' salaries are $4,000 per month, payable on the 10th of the following month. On December 31 the December salaries have not been recorded, even though the cost has been incurred. In addition, an unrecorded liability for these salaries exists on December 31. The adjusting entry to bring the accounts up to date is:

| | | |
|---|---|---|
| Salespersons' Salary Expense | 4,000 | |
| Salaries Payable* | | 4,000 |

> \* Sometimes this account is called Accrued Salaries Payable, but the term *accrued* is unnecessary. When it does appear, it usually signifies an account arising from an adjusting entry.

For another illustration, assume that the company leases a piece of copying equipment for the office. The total rental is based on the number of copies made, at a rate of three cents per copy. Payments are remitted approximately every other month, calculated from a metered count of copies prepared. Since the last payment in November, the meter shows 7,500 copies completed up to December 31. The adjusting entry is:

| | | |
|---|---|---|
| Office Expense | 225 | |
| Equipment Rentals Payable | | 225 |

## Revenue Apportionment

Mention is made in Chapter 2 of liabilities which represent customer claims to receive goods and services in future periods. These customer advances arise when cash is obtained prior to the rendering of the service or delivery of the product by the firm. For instance, a company leases a portion of its warehouse for 12 months beginning on September 1 at a monthly rental of $200. The customer pays the entire $2,400 on September 1. The $2,400 represents revenue to be apportioned one third to the current accounting period and two thirds to the following one. On September 1 the following entry is made to record the advance as a liability:

| | | |
|---|---|---|
| Cash | 2,400 | |
| Rent Received in Advance | | 2,400 |

Then, on December 31 the *adjusting* entry would be:

| | | |
|---|---|---|
| Rent Received in Advance | 800 | |
| Rent Revenue | | 800 |

Some companies use an alternative recording procedure which initially credits the entire cash receipt to a revenue account. For example, a firm sells specialty products such as napkins, coasters, and playing cards to be used for advertising and other special purposes. Each item is printed with the client's name, advertising slogan, and so on. Orders take about two weeks to process and must be accompanied by cash payment. During the year $97,800 cash is received on such orders and credited to revenue:

| | | |
|---|---|---|
| Cash | 97,800 | |
| Sales of Specialty Items | | 97,800 |

An analysis of unprocessed orders at the end of the year reveals that items selling for $6,700 have not been printed or delivered to customers. Consequently, that part of the revenue has not been earned this period. An adjusting entry should be made to recognize the unearned (deferred) revenue as a liability:

| | | |
|---|---|---|
| Sales of Specialty Items | 6,700 | |
| Customer Advances | | 6,700 |

*Whether the apportionment is from a liability account to a revenue account, as in the first example, or from a revenue account to a liability account, the purpose and end result are the same. The underlying analysis involves a determination of the amount applicable to products and services rendered this period and that applicable to future periods.*

**Revenue Accrual**

This fourth common type of adjustment is similar to the second. For clerical convenience, the recording of revenue may sometimes be deferred until the cash is collected. However, if the revenue is earned in one accounting period and the cash collection will occur in the next, an adjustment is necessary to reflect the revenue and related asset claim. For instance, interest is earned with the passage of time, but it is not recorded every day. If a finance company lends $10,000 at 12 percent interest to a manufacturer for six months beginning on December 1, one month's interest revenue of $100 ($10,000 $\times$ 0.12 $\times$ $\frac{1}{12}$) is applicable to the accounting period that ends on December 31. The finance company's claim has grown from $10,000 to $10,100. The adjusting entry shown below would be made to correct the concomitant understatement of assets and revenues:

| | | |
|---|---|---|
| Interest Receivable | 100 | |
| Interest Revenue | | 100 |

Any revenue-producing activity which is performed during the period but for which payment will be coming later may be subject to the same type of adjustment. For instance, a typewriter repair firm might receive a 10 percent commission from a manufacturer on all new typewriters sold to customers. If, during December, new typewriters having a $23,000 retail price are sold, the firm should make the following adjusting entry, even though the cash may not be received until some time in January:

| | | |
|---|---|---|
| Commissions Receivable | 2,300 | |
| Commission Revenue | | 2,300 |

**Adjusting Entries to Record Corrections**

The foregoing adjustments represent some of the more conventional ones which the accountant makes at the end of each accounting period, almost as a matter of routine. A more complex type of entry may be called for to revise transactions that have been made incorrectly. Each correcting entry requires a careful analysis of the situation. The basic approach is to determine what the proper account balances should be and to compare them with the present balances. The <u>correcting entry, then, is whatever</u> is <u>required to get from the present balances to the desired ones</u>.

Take, for instance, the following situation. On November 1, the bookkeeper erroneously records the advance payment for four-months' rent as follows:

| | | |
|---|---|---|
| Machinery ........................................ | 900 | |
|     Cash ................................. | | 900 |

This error is discovered December 31, before any depreciation was incorrectly taken on the "machinery." Half of the cost of the four-month rental should appear as an asset and half as an expense. In other words, the *correct* account balances at December 31 *should be:*

| **Prepaid Rent** | **Rent Expense** | **Cash** |
|---|---|---|
| 450 | 450 | 900 |

A comparison of where we are with where we want to be gives rise to the following correcting entry:

| | | |
|---|---|---|
| Prepaid Rent ........................................ | 450 | |
| Rent Expense ........................................ | 450 | |
|     Machinery ........................................ | | 900 |

This basic introduction to some of the more common types of adjusting entries does not exhaust the subject. Throughout the remaining chapters, we encounter other adjusting entries as well as new examples of the basic ones discussed here. Practically any entry could be subject to later adjustment under a given set of circumstances. Fundamentally, adjusting entries encompass all those entries necessary at the end of the accounting period to render the asset, liability, revenue, and expense accounts as accurate as possible.

## THE ACCOUNTING CYCLE

We have been exposed at this point to a number of accounting processes and functions—statement preparation, recording in ledgers, journalizing, and adjusting. These procedures in an accounting system are interrelated and are performed in an established order called the accounting cycle. Presented in the sequence in which they normally are performed, the *elements of the accounting cycle* are:

1. Recording transactions in a journal.
2. Posting journal entries to ledger accounts.
3. Preparing a trial balance.
4. Journalizing and posting adjusting entries.
5. Preparing an adjusted trial balance.

6. Preparing the financial statements.
7. Journalizing and posting closing entries.

The first two of these make up most of the *bookkeeping* activity *during* the period. The other five steps are performed at the *end* of the accounting period. Together, they summarize the accounting process from the initial recording function to the final reporting function. The remainder of this chapter is devoted to an elaboration of some of these elements and a discussion of their relationship to one another and to the basic functions of accounting.

## Recording Transactions in a Journal

This task, of course, begins the basic recording function in accounting. It involves separating a transaction into its component parts (asset and equity changes) and recording that analysis in the systematic debit and credit framework discussed in Chapter 3. The journal entry provides the original record of the events of the period, usually in chronological order. Following the entity concept, we record only those transactions involving the business enterprise as a separate entity.

**Source Documents.** Before a transaction can be entered formally in any type of journal, there must be an indication that the transaction has occurred. Each journal entry rests on an underlying document. Some business form must flow to the accounting department to trigger the analysis and recording process necessary for journalizing. Source documents include purchase invoices, bills of sale, check copies, cash register tapes, labor time summaries, legal documents, receiving reports, and so on. What forms are used, who initiates them, and how they are routed must be considered in the design of the particular accounting and data processing system used by a company. Often the source documents are referenced in the explanation accompanying the formal journal entry. They are filed systematically to serve as the support for the making of the entry, for they not only provide details about the transaction but also fix responsibility for the information and event. One task that an *auditor* performs is to determine, on a test-check basis, whether the entries recorded are supported by proper underlying documents.

## Posting Journal Entries to Ledger Accounts

Posting is the process of transferring to the ledger accounts the individual changes recorded in the books of original entry. The process of posting in a manual accounting system is explained and illustrated in Chapter 3. Whether done manually, by a bookkeeping machine, or automatically, as in many electronic data processing systems, posting to the ledger accounts is the beginning of the classifying function. It involves fitting the recorded data into a logical, useful framework of assets and equities.

**Chart of Accounts.** The ledger accounts used by companies vary in accordance with the nature of their activities and the type of information desired on the financial statements. The accounts required by a particular company to provide the needed information are identified in a list called the *chart of accounts*. Often the chart of accounts is expanded to include not only the accounts making up the system but also the policies to be followed for entries in each account. The resulting accounting manual provides the basic guideline for posting to the ledger accounts.

To facilitate classification of the accounts by type, a numerical coding system is frequently employed. For example, the first digit might indicate the general classification—for example, 1 for current asset, 2 for noncurrent asset, 3 for current liability. Subsequent digits in the account numbers might signify various subclassifications, functions, locations, and so on. A carefully worked-out coding system provides ready identification and an orderly arrangement by statement grouping for the ledger accounts. Moreover, the account numbering system allows easy adoption of mechanical means of posting and of machine accounting systems.

**Subsidiary Ledgers.**  Our discussion of ledger accounts and posting has been limited to the main asset and equity accounts in the general ledger. When a large amount of detailed information about a particular general ledger account must be kept, often a separate set of accounts, called subsidiary ledger accounts, is used for the purpose. For example, when a group of individual persons is involved, as is the case with accounts receivable and accounts payable, a separate record can be maintained of each person's account in a subsidiary ledger. Similarly, when a general ledger account such as an equipment account contains many different items, subsidiary ledgers can be employed to handle the detailed information applicable to each particular machine. The general ledger account shows in summary form what the subsidiary records show in detail. The general ledger account is called a *control* account.

Specialized forms and data processing equipment can be developed to facilitate the handling of the detailed information in the subsidiary ledger. For instance, each subsidiary ledger form for Accounts Receivable could be maintained in duplicate, one copy being sent to the customer each month as his or her bill. As another example, the subsidiary ledger for an Office Equipment control account might consist of a stack of punched cards. On each card would be punched the cost of a particular machine, its location, and the depreciation rate or its useful life. A run through a computer program would automatically accomplish the computation and summing of the total depreciation expense for that period.

In some instances a file of the original business forms themselves serves as the subsidiary ledger. A file of unpaid invoices arranged by number or name of supplier might be the subsidiary ledger for Accounts Payable. Other commonly used subsidiary ledgers include a file of insurance policies for Prepaid Insurance, a file of actual notes for Notes Receivable or Notes Payable, stock cards for Inventory, and a stockholders' register for Capital Stock. Although the format for the subsidiary ledgers may vary, most general ledger accounts, in other than the smallest firms, are control accounts.

Subsidiary ledgers provide numerous advantages. Operationally they allow for a distribution and specialization of the clerical tasks of bookkeeping. The general ledger is more compact and can be maintained by one person (or machine). A number of subsidiary ledgers containing the bulk of the detailed information can be employed, with different individuals responsible for each one. Total balances can be obtained from the control accounts without the need to sum all the individual accounts every time. Perhaps the major contribution of subsidiary ledgers is their aid in error location. By recording the detail in the subsidiary ledger and the same information in summary form in the general ledger control account, accountants can maintain a check on the accuracy of the records. Because the posting to the subsidiary ledger often is done directly from the source documents, any errors made in the journals or in posting from the journals to the general ledger accounts are not repeated in the detailed records. Periodic comparisons between the subsidiary ledger and general ledger control account reveal the existence of such errors. This comparison is called *proving the subsidiary ledgers*.

**Subsidiary Ledger Example.**　To illustrate the general idea and use of a subsidiary ledger, let us take the following brief and highly simplified example of accounts receivable. Assume that a subsidiary ledger is maintained for three individual customers, A, B, and C.[2]

1. During a particular day credit sales total $10,000. A summary entry would be made in the journal, debiting Accounts Receivable and crediting Sales. This would be posted later to the general ledger accounts. Duplicate copies of the sales slips would be sent to the accounts receivable clerk for sorting and posting to the individual accounts. Assume that the sales slips indicate sales to A of $6,000, to B of $3,000, and to C of $1,000.
2. On another day the total credit sales amount to $6,000. The entry would be handled the same way. The entire $6,000 would be recorded in the general ledger, with the sales slips sorted according to customer and entered in the respective subsidiary ledger accounts. Assume $4,000 of sales to B and $2,000 to C.
3. On a later date, checks for $4,000, $2,000, and $1,000 are received from A, B, and C, respectively. A list of the customers' names and amounts paid (or perhaps portions of the bill which the customers return) is sent to the accounts receivable department for entry in the subsidiary ledger. Another copy is totaled and serves as the underlying document for an entry debiting Cash and crediting Accounts Receivable for $7,000.

The ledger accounts shown in Table 4–1 reflect these transactions. Notice that there are no offsetting debits or credits to the amounts entered

---

[2] If a firm had only three customers, a subsidiary ledger would be unnecessary. Three separate accounts receivable in the general ledger could be maintained just as easily. Multiply the three accounts by a hundred thousand, and you get a practical picture of the recording problems of a typical large department store.

**TABLE 4-1  Subsidiary Ledger Example**

| | GENERAL LEDGER | | |
|---|---|---|---|
| **Cash** | **Accounts Receivable Control** | | **Sales** |
| (3)   7,000 | (1)   10,000   (3)   7,000 <br> (2)   6,000 | | (1)   10,000 <br> (2)   6,000 |

| | ACCOUNTS RECEIVABLE SUBSIDIARY LEDGER | |
|---|---|---|
| **A** | **B** | **C** |
| (1)   6,000   (3)   4,000 | (1)   3,000   (3)   2,000 <br> (2)   4,000 | (1)   1,000   (3)   1,000 <br> (2)   2,000 |

in the subsidiary ledger accounts. The subsidiary ledger simply reflects in detail what is already recorded in summary form in the general ledger accounts. The equality of debits and credits is required only for general ledger entries.

At the end of the accounting period, we would *prove the subsidiary ledger* for accounts receivable. A schedule (see Table 4-2) would be prepared showing each customer's account balance according to the subsidiary records. We would then compare the total with the balance in the control account to check on the accuracy of the records.

**TABLE 4-2  Schedule of Accounts Receivable**
**(per subsidiary ledger)**

| | |
|---|---:|
| A | $2,000 |
| B | 5,000 |
| C | 2,000 |
| Total (per control account) | $9,000 |

**Preparing a**
**Trial Balance**

The *trial balance* is the first step of the accounting cycle to be taken at the *end* of the period. It consists of a list of ledger accounts and their balances, appropriately classified as debit or credit. It provides a summary of accounts for use in the making of adjustments and the preparation of statements. The trial balance also serves as a test check on the *numerical* accuracy of the journalizing and posting process.

The actual preparation of the trial balance is a routine task. Often, preprinted forms already containing the names of accounts are used, and the calculating and transcribing of balances may be performed by accounting machines or computerized equipment. A highly condensed trial balance of the Hypothetical Company appears in Table 4-3.

**TABLE 4–3**

HYPOTHETICAL COMPANY
Trial Balance
As of December 31, 1985

|  | Debit | Credit |
|---|---|---|
| Cash | $13,000 | |
| Accounts receivable | 20,000 | |
| Inventory | 16,000 | |
| Accounts payable | | $15,200 |
| Capital stock | | 20,000 |
| Retained earnings | | 3,900 |
| Sales revenue | | 28,300 |
| Commission revenue | | 1,700 |
| Cost of goods sold | 9,250 | |
| Salary expense | 5,700 | |
| Rent expense | 2,000 | |
| Supplies expense | 280 | |
| Delivery expense | 2,870 | |
| | $69,100 | $69,100 |

The trial balance should "balance" (have equal debits and credits). Also, the control accounts in the trial balance should agree with the schedules of their subsidiary ledgers. Usually, proving the subsidiary ledgers is an ancillary activity associated with the preparation of the trial balance. If the trial balance does not balance, some recording error must have been made. On the other hand, the converse is not necessarily true. A trial balance simply portrays the *existing* balances of the accounts and indicates that the entries that *were* made had equal debits and credits. The existing balances still may be inaccurate or incomplete. The task of correcting wrong account balances or bringing them up to date falls to the adjusting entries, the next step in the accounting cycle.

## Journalizing and Posting Adjusting Entries

Determining what adjustments are necessary to the accounts listed in the trial balance is one of the primary duties of the accountant, as contrasted with the bookkeeper. Entries to adjust the accounts at the end of the period normally require the analytical abilities of someone familiar with the operation of the system, the types of accounts used, and the interrelationships among them. Once determined, the adjusting entries are handled like any other entry. They are first journalized and then posted to the appropriate ledger accounts.

The need for adjusting entries arises from the *periodicity* and *matching* concepts. However, there are no underlying documents that automatically signal that an adjusting entry must be made. Accountants have to generate the necessary information for the adjusting entries from a study of the trial balance, a review of the accounting system, and an analysis of information sources outside the accounting records themselves. They look, for example, for depreciable noncurrent assets, prepayments, revenues received in advance, and so on, in the trial balance, for these items normally require adjustment. They may analyze files of notes receivable and notes payable to determine interest adjustments. They study insurance policies to determine what portion of prepaid insurance has expired and what is still in force. The accountant may supervise or review physical counts of inventories so as to be able to make the adjusting entries for cost of goods sold or supplies expense.

## Preparing an Adjusted Trial Balance

The adjusting entry step in the accounting cycle may be followed by the preparation of another trial balance, called the *adjusted trial balance*. It presents a complete listing of all ledger accounts with current balances. The primary use of the adjusted trial balance is in statement preparation. From this listing the accountant can arrange the ledger names and balances in the proper formats for the income and position statements. Also, the adjusted trial balance may serve as a test check on whether the debit-credit equality has been maintained through the adjustment process.

## Preparing the Financial Statements

The next step in the accounting cycle is reporting the accumulated accounting information to the various audiences through the financial statements. This stage represents the fulfillment of the reporting function and the commencement of the interpretive function. Formats of these two statements have been illustrated previously. The asset, liability, and permanent owners' equity accounts (capital stock and retained earnings) appear on the position statement. The nominal owners' equity (revenue and expense) accounts are exhibited on the income statement.

## Journalizing and Posting Closing Entries

Recall from Chapter 3 that the function of revenue and expense accounts is to accumulate information about operating activities during a *single* time period. Once the income statement has been prepared, revenue and expense accounts are cleared to zero so that they are ready to function next period, and in the process retained earnings is updated for the income earned this period. The necessary entries are called closing entries.

Closing the books is a technical process of transferring and summarizing balances. Whenever an entry has been made which causes a zero balance in an account, that account is said to have been closed. The closing process necessitates making such entries in all nominal accounts and balancing and ruling the real asset, liability, and owners' equity accounts. Accountants close each temporary account by making an entry equal in amount to the balance of the account but on the opposite side. Because revenues and expenses are temporary retained earnings accounts, one might expect that the corresponding part of the journal entry to close these accounts would be to Retained Earnings. Ultimately this is the case. Often, however, accountants use a temporary summary account, called the Income Summary account (or Expense and Revenue, Profit and Loss, or

Operating Summary), to accumulate during the closing process information dispersed throughout the ledger in individual accounts.

The closing process for the accounts listed in the trial balance in Table 4–3 is illustrated in ledger form in Table 4–4 (we are assuming that the trial balance is an adjusted trial balance). Entries (1) through (7) transfer balances to Income Summary, thereby closing the revenue and expense accounts. The credit balance of $9,900 in the Income Summary account reflects the net result of the matching of revenues and expenses—the net change in owners' equity from operating activities during the month. Entry (8) transfers this net increase to Retained Earnings, the owners' equity account established for that purpose.

**TABLE 4-4  Illustration of the Closing Process**

| Sales Revenue | | | Supplies Expense | | |
|---|---|---|---|---|---|
| (1) | 28,300 | 28,300 | 280 | (6) | 280 |

| Commission Revenue | | | Delivery Expense | | |
|---|---|---|---|---|---|
| (2) | 1,700 | 1,700 | 2,870 | (7) | 2,870 |

| Cost of Goods Sold | | | Income Summary | | |
|---|---|---|---|---|---|
| | 9,250 | (3) | 9,250 | (3) | 9,250 | (1) | 28,300 |

Cost of Goods Sold

| | 9,250 | (3) | 9,250 |
|---|---|---|---|

Income Summary

| (3) | 9,250 | (1) | 28,300 |
|---|---|---|---|
| (4) | 5,700 | (2) | 1,700 |
| (5) | 2,000 | | |
| (6) | 280 | | |
| (7) | 2,870 | | |
| (8) | 9,900 | | |
| | 30,000 | | 30,000 |

Salary Expense

| | 5,700 | (4) | 5,700 |
|---|---|---|---|

Rent Expense

| | 2,000 | (5) | 2,000 |
|---|---|---|---|

Retained Earnings

| | | | 3,900 |
|---|---|---|---|
| | | (8) | 9,900 |

After closing, the revenue and expense accounts show no balances. Neither does the Income Summary account at the end of the period. However, we have summarized in this account information concerning the period's activities. If techniques exist for summarizing information elsewhere, the nominal accounts can be closed directly without the aid of any summary account.[3] From a mechanical standpoint, a single entry could close the books by debiting all revenue accounts, crediting all expense accounts, and debiting (net loss) or crediting (net income) the difference to Retained Earnings.

Of much greater importance than scrutinizing the mechanical process, though, is learning what accounts are closed and understanding why closing entries are made. All temporary owners' equity accounts are closed. The rationale for closing entries can be traced directly to the *concept of the accounting period*. This concept requires that regular summaries of the period's activities be made. The activities of each single period must be segregated in the ledger accounts. The closing process is merely the last logical step in a process dictated by the periodicity concept.

**SUMMARY**

This chapter concludes a preliminary discussion of the procedural aspects of accounting. In it we expand our knowledge of the basic accounting process. Included is an explanation of the adjusting process and its relationship to the accounting period. Then a discussion of the accounting cycle describes the relationship among the different procedural techniques. The normal progression of accounting functions is:

1. *Journalizing*—analyzing data from source documents and recording them chronologically.
2. *Posting*—transferring debits and credits to individual accounts.
3. *Preparing the trial balance*—summarizing the general ledger accounts to test equality of debits and credits and proving any subsidiary ledgers.
4. *Adjusting*—analyzing, recording, and posting entries necessary to correct or update all accounts.
5. *Preparing the adjusted trial balance*—assembling the general ledger account balances to facilitate the preparation of financial statements.
6. *Preparing the financial statements*—organizing summarized reports of income-seeking activity and financial position.
7. *Closing*—zeroing out all nominal accounts, transferring their summarized balances to Retained Earnings, and balancing and ruling the real accounts to prepare for the new accounting period.

A basic knowledge of how the parts of an accounting system are interrelated in order to generate financial information will contribute to a better understanding of the end result—the financial reports—and enable the student to *use* accounting as an analytical tool as well.

---

[3] The Appendix to this chapter describes the work sheet which the accountant employs to summarize and organize information. With a work sheet, summary accounts may be unnecessary.

# APPENDIX: Processing Accounting Data

In future chapters we shall study financial accounting primarily from a conceptual and analytical viewpoint. Our interest will be in understanding and using the end product—the financial statements. Consequently, we use very elementary methods—the simple journal entry and the T-account—in the journalizing and posting processes. Attempts to employ more complex data processing techniques would add little to our basic understanding of the concepts and functions of financial accounting. Nonetheless, these simplified techniques are not an accurate representation of the actual recording process. No business of any consequence could maintain an effective accounting system employing only a two-column journal and a group of T-accounts.

The accounting process can also be studied as a data processing and/or control system. Accounting, like any other system, consists of a group of interrelated parts functioning together to accomplish some objective. The specific objective of the accounting system is to gather, process, and report financial information. This objective points to three major components in the system:

$$\text{Input} \rightarrow \text{Processing} \rightarrow \text{Output}$$

The various source documents which flag the fact that some changes in assets/or equities have occurred serve as input. The accounting system processes these data by means of the journal and ledger entries to provide output in the form of updated accounts and financial reports. The input, processing, and output components of an effective accounting system must be designed and coordinated in such a way that accurate information is available promptly and at a reasonable cost. Moreover, the system should aid in preventing the misappropriation or misuse of the firm's assets and the falsification of its records and reports.

This appendix presents an overview of the operation and control of an accounting data processing system. Specifically we investigate some methods to streamline data accumulation, classification, and summarization. We begin with two devices—special journals and work sheets—that are used in practically all manual bookkeeping systems. We then discuss electronic data processing and its impact on the organization and procedures of the accounting system. We conclude the Appendix with a brief examination of some general principles of internal control and the contributions a well-designed accounting system can make to the implementation of those principles.

## Special Journals

The only journal form introduced so far has been the general journal, containing single debit and credit columns. In this journal an account title must be written out with each entry, and each entry has to be posted to the ledger accounts individually. The clerical effort involved in journalizing and posting under this arrangement makes it unsuitable for handling a large volume of transactions.

**Modifications of the Journal.**  To speed up the journalizing and posting processes and to allow for a division of accounting labor, most companies make two modifications to the simple journal system. First, a number of separate books of original entry, called special journals or registers, are introduced, corresponding to major types of transactions: (1) cash disbursements, (2) cash receipts, (3) sales, and (4) purchases on account. A general journal is retained for entries not fitting into the special journals.

The second modification is the introduction of special debit and credit columns in the special journals for accounts frequently used. These extra columns are specifically identified (e.g., Cash—Debit, Accounts Receivable—Credit). Accountants can record repeated debits and credits to these accounts by simply entering the dollar amount in the special column; the need to write out the name of the account with each entry is eliminated. Posting is facilitated also because they can total the special columns and post the total rather than the individual entries.

How many special columns should be employed and what accounts should have special columns in each of the journals can be answered on pragmatic grounds. The number of actively used accounts determines the number of special columns. Each journal, however, contains a "key column" which identifies the essential type of transaction recorded in that journal. For example, the key column in the cash receipts book would be a Cash-Debit column. All entries recorded in the cash receipts journal of necessity involve a debit to Cash. Similarly, the key columns in the cash disbursements, sales, and purchase journals are Cash—Credit, Sales—Credit, and Accounts Payable—Credit, respectively.

**Cash Disbursements Journal.** Figure 4A-1 shows a multicolumn cash disbursements book. Here we assume that Accounts Payable, Wages Payable, and Utility Expenses are accounts frequently debited when Cash is credited. Of course, other special columns could be included for particular business situations. Notice,

**FIGURE 4A-1   Cash Disbursements Journal**

| Date | Payee | Check Number | Cash Cr. | Accounts Payable Dr. | Wages Payable Dr. | Utility Expense Dr. | Sundry Accounts | | | |
|---|---|---|---|---|---|---|---|---|---|---|
| | | | | | | | Account | PR | Dr. | Cr. |
| 1985 | | | | | | | | | | |
| July  1 | A. Bass | 181 | 7,000 | 7,000 | | | | | | |
| 1 | Motors, Inc. | 182 | 6,000 | | | | Automobile | 10 | ·8,000 | |
| | | | | | | | Notes Payable | 30 | | 2,000 |
| 5 | Wages | 183 | 3,000 | | 3,000 | | | | | |
| 10 | B. Carp | 184 | 2,900 | 2,900 | | | | | | |
| 10 | C. Dane | 185 | 150 | 150 | | | | | | |
| 10 | City Power Co. | 186 | 500 | | | 500 | | | | |
| 10 | Wages | 187 | 3,000 | | 3,000 | | | | | |
| 13 | | 188 | 25 | | | | Sales Returns | 51 | 25 | |
| 15 | Wages | 189 | 3,000 | | 3,000 | | | | | |
| 20 | ZT&T, Inc. | 190 | 490 | | | 490 | | | | |
| 20 | Wages | 191 | 3,000 | | 3,000 | | | | | |
| 22 | C. Dane | 192 | 1,900 | 1,900 | | | | | | |
| 31 | Motors, Inc. | 215 | 30 | | | | Interest | 91 | 30 | |
| 31 | Mass Gas Co. | 216 | 780 | | | 780 | | | | |
| | | | 50,480 | 24,325 | 18,000 | 2,100 | | | 8,055 | 2,000 |
| | | | (1) | (27) | (28) | (5) | | | (√) | (√) |

however, that in addition to the special columns, a set of Sundry (or miscellaneous) columns also appears. These aid in the recording of relatively complex or rare transactions involving cash disbursements.

As each check is written, its number and the name of the payee are entered as well as the amount. For those transactions involving special columns, journalizing consists simply of entering the amounts in the appropriate columns. In essence, the journal entry is recorded horizontally on one line. Bookkeeping machines frequently are employed to enter the amounts in the appropriate columns of the journal form automatically.

This simplified procedure is used for most of the entries—all but three during the month of July. For those three transactions—on July 1, July 13, and July 31—the Sundry columns are used. The account titles have to be entered individually, but these situations occur only infrequently.

At the end of the month the journal columns are totaled and crossfooted (debit and credit column totals are compared) for numerical accuracy. Then all special columns are posted by column total. Since the individual entries are recorded in the journal, summarized information can be entered in the ledger accounts. For instance, the total credit of $50,480 for the month is made as a single entry to the Cash account. The account number of Cash (1) is placed below the column total to indicate that the posting has been done. Similar treatment is given to the other column totals for Accounts Payable, Wages Payable, and Utility Expense. Only four items, those entered in the Sundry columns, require individual posting. These are handled in the conventional manner described in Chapter 3. The PR (Posting Reference) column is used to record the number of the account to which each sundry account was posted. Of course, entries would also be made in the subsidiary ledger for accounts payable. These could be made directly from the underlying documents or from the cash disbursements journal.

**Other Special Journals.** Figure 4A-2 shows the column headings that might appear in each of the three other commonly used special journals. The mechanical process is the same as that for the cash disbursements book. The special columns indicated in the examples are only some of the more typical ones. In practice the journals are tailored to the specific needs of each business. Moreover,

**FIGURE 4A-2 Column Headings for Other Special Journals**

CASH RECEIPTS JOURNAL                                                    Page 1

| Date | Explanation | Cash Dr. | Sales Discount Dr. | Accounts Receivable Cr. | Sales Cr. | Sundry Accounts | | | |
|------|-------------|----------|--------------------|--------------------------|-----------|-----------------|---|---|---|
| | | | | | | Account | PR | Dr. | Cr. |

SALES JOURNAL                                                           Page 1

| Date | Explanation | Invoice No. | Accounts Receivable Dr. | Sales Cr. | Sales Tax Payable Cr. | Sundry Accounts | | | |
|------|-------------|-------------|--------------------------|-----------|------------------------|-----------------|---|---|---|
| | | | | | | Account | PR | Dr. | Cr. |

PURCHASES JOURNAL                                                      Page 1

| Date | Supplier Name | Accounts Payable Cr. | Merchandise Dr. | Supplies Dr. | Sundry Accounts | | | |
|------|---------------|----------------------|-----------------|--------------|-----------------|---|---|---|
| | | | | | Account | PR | Dr. | Cr. |

although these four special journals constitute the normal books of original entry, firms may employ others for sales returns, payroll transactions, or specialized types of events peculiar to their businesses. Special journals are utilitarian and may be employed whenever the need exists.

**Advantages of Journal Modifications.** The benefits of separate, multi-column journals are obvious. The increased speed and ease of data processing are enormous. These advantages lie in two areas: (1) savings in clerical time and (2) division of recording responsibilities.

Time is saved in three ways. First, several bookkeepers are able to make journal entries concurrently in the separate special journals. Secondly, account titles do not have to be written for most of the transactions. And finally, the major saving comes during posting, through the use of column totals rather than separate debits and credits.

Since the recording function is divided among individuals, efficiency is improved. The accounting system can take advantage of any specialization of labor which results from bookkeepers concentrating their attention on one particular type of transaction. Specialization has led to the development of unique forms and bookkeeping machines designed to handle particular kinds of transactions, such as sales or cash receipts. Errors are thus minimized, and those that do occur are more readily detected. Moreover, with the data segregated in separate journals, management can analyze the detailed information easily.

## Work Sheets

A work sheet is a columnar device employed as a convenient and orderly way of organizing information to be used in the preparation of adjustments and financial statements. The work sheet serves as the accountant's scratch paper (although much neater, better organized, and more formal).

**Illustration.** Work sheets are of many forms and types, depending on the complexity of the accounting system and the personal preferences of the individual accountant. The example in Figure 4A-3 is one common format, consisting of five sets of debit and credit columns. The trial balance is listed in the first set of columns instead of being reported on a separate sheet. In some cases work sheet forms containing the names of all accounts are preprinted. Alternatively, a computer can be programmed to print out those accounts having balances. If additional accounts are needed, they can be added at the bottom of the work sheet, as in Figure 4A-3.

The adjusting entries are then entered in the second set of columns. Often, adjustments may require a great deal of analysis. Rather than journalize the adjustments directly, the accountant uses the work sheet. Omissions are more likely to be detected, and errors can be corrected before they are entered in the formal accounting records. Usually somewhere on the work sheet itself or attached to it is an explanation of the adjustments, related to the entries by a key letter or number. The adjustments for our deliberately simplified example are:

a. Ending inventory of $40,900 established by physical count.
b. Expired insurance applicable to delivery equipment.
c. Depreciation on building at an annual rate of 5 percent of original cost, allocated equally between selling and administration.
d. Depreciation of $900 on delivery equipment.
e. Revenue of $2,600 on merchandise delivered for which payment had been received earlier.

**FIGURE 4A–3   Illustration of a Work Sheet**

CENTRAL SALES COMPANY
Work Sheet
December 31, 1984

| Accounts | Trial Balance Dr. | Trial Balance Cr. | Adjustments Dr. | Adjustments Cr. | Adjusted Trial Balance Dr. | Adjusted Trial Balance Cr. | Income Statement Dr. | Income Statement Cr. | Balance Sheet Dr. | Balance Sheet Cr. |
|---|---|---|---|---|---|---|---|---|---|---|
| Cash | 8,700 | | | | 8,700 | | | | 8,700 | |
| Accounts receivable | 27,700 | | | | 27,700 | | | | 27,700 | |
| Inventory | 116,700 | | | (a) 75,800 | 40,900 | | | | 40,900 | |
| Prepaid insurance | 4,200 | | | (b) 3,000 | 1,200 | | | | 1,200 | |
| Building | 50,000 | | | | 50,000 | | | | 50,000 | |
| Accumulated depreciation—building | | 20,000 | | (c) 2,500 | | 22,500 | | | | 22,500 |
| Delivery equipment | 9,000 | | | | 9,000 | | | | 9,000 | |
| Accumulated depreciation—equipment | | 3,600 | | (d) 900 | | 4,500 | | | | 4,500 |
| Accounts payable | | 8,200 | | | | 8,200 | | | | 8,200 |
| Notes payable | | 20,000 | | | | 20,000 | | | | 20,000 |
| Customers' advances | | 2,600 | (e) 2,600 | | | | | | | |
| Common stock | | 40,000 | | | | 40,000 | | | | 40,000 |
| Retained earnings | | 9,300 | | | | 9,300 | | | | 9,300 |
| Sales | | 138,600 | | (e) 2,600 | | 141,200 | | 141,200 | | |
| Administrative expenses | 8,500 | | (c) 1,250 | | 9,750 | | 9,750 | | | |
| Delivery expense | 3,000 | | (b) 3,000 | | 6,900 | | 6,900 | | | |
| | | | (d) 900 | | | | | | | |
| Selling expense | 14,500 | | (c) 1,250 | | 15,750 | | 15,750 | | | |
| | 242,300 | 242,300 | | | | | | | | |
| Cost of goods sold | | | (a) 75,800 | | 75,800 | | 75,800 | | | |
| | | | 84,800 | 84,800 | 245,700 | 245,700 | 108,200 | 141,200 | 137,500 | 104,500 |
| Net income | | | | | | | 33,000 | | | 33,000 |
| | | | | | | | 141,200 | 141,200 | 137,500 | 137,500 |

We make entries in the third set of columns, labeled Adjusted Trial Balance, by adding horizontally the amounts in the Trial Balance and Adjustments columns for each account. When the adjustments are few and relatively simple, many accountants eliminate these columns and use only an eight-column work sheet.

Columns to accumulate information for the financial statements comprise the remainder of the work sheet. The amount listed in the adjusted trial balance for each account is placed in the appropriate debit or credit column under the name of the statement on which the particular account appears. The last two sets of columns initially will not balance, because the net income for the period has not been recorded thereon. This amount, when entered as a debit in the Income Statement columns and as a credit in the Balance Sheet columns, will balance both sets and thus provides a check on the numerical accuracy of the work sheet manipulations.

**Use of the Work Sheet.**   From the information on the work sheet, the accounting cycle can be completed routinely. A bookkeeper, using the work sheet as a source document, can journalize and post the adjusting entries. Because the accounts listed in the Income Statement columns contain all the temporary accounts to be closed, a debit to Sales and a credit to each of the expenses and to Retained Earnings ($33,000) will mechanically close the books with a single entry.

No real need exists for an Income Summary account; the information is already accumulated on the work sheet. Finally, to prepare financial statements the accountant need only rearrange in proper form the accounts in the work sheet columns.

The work sheet facilitates the accounting process by permitting the accountant to summarize and review information before recording the adjusting and closing entries and formally preparing the statements. In addition, interim statements can be obtained for managerial or other purposes without formal journalizing and posting of adjusting and closing entries.

**Electronic Data Processing**

Previously we defined an accounting system as an assemblage of interrelated parts designed to gather data inputs and process them into meaningful information outputs. In this section we describe the role that electronic computers play in this cycle. Although electronic data processing (EDP) does not change the basic functions or concepts of accounting, its introduction does require quite radical changes in the format of many accounting records and in the nature and sequence of procedures.

Electronic computers and related equipment allow information to be collected and disseminated more rapidly and often more economically than is possible in manual accounting systems. Most computer systems can process data captured through terminals, magnetic ink, optical character recognition, and point-of-sale devices. Although the data can be stored electronically in the computer's *memory*, accounting information is more likely to be stored on secondary storage devices such as tape, disk, or other mass storage. A complex set of instructions, the *program*, facilitates the processing of the data and can be stored and then executed in the indicated order without operator involvement. Therefore, a single piece of basic data can be processed and reprocessed into different sets of information without being reentered. In these ways EDP systems can deal effectively with complex informational needs and problems.

**Elements of a Computer Processing System.** The diagram in Figure 4A–4 shows the elements of a computer system. The solid lines indicate actual data flows, and the broken lines signify flows of instructions.

**FIGURE 4A-4   Computer Processing System**

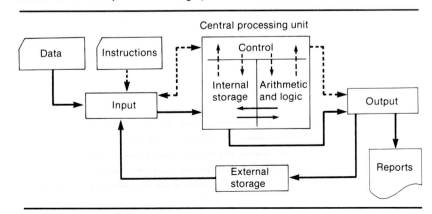

The input function in the EDP system translates instructions and data into electronic codes which the computer can understand. The input of accounting data consists of letters and numbers which are originally encoded on checks, sales slips, purchase orders, or other documents. Such input is then entered into the computer through the use of equipment such as CRT (cathode ray tube) terminals, optical character readers, magnetic ink readers, or other types of equipment.

Point-of-sale devices are being used with increasing frequency. Accounting data is recorded immediately because the data are captured in a computer-processible form as amounts are entered in electric cash registers or are typed on invoices. In some cases the underlying documents become direct inputs through the use of magnetic ink character recognition (MICR) or optical character recognition (OCR). In the first instance information is inscribed on the document in magnetic ink which can be read by special input equipment. Banks make extensive use of MICR in processing checks. In the second instance the information is recorded on the basic document in graphic characters that can be detected directly by special reading devices. Oil companies use optical scanning techniques to process charge slips from retail customers.

The *central processing unit (CPU)* consists of three components—arithmetic-logic, internal storage, and control. The arithmetic-logic unit, which need not concern us here, actually carries out the numerical manipulations, makes comparisons, and performs other processing operations.

*Internal storage* (memory) is a distinguishing feature of computerized systems. Through the use of integrated circuits, data are retained in individual memory locations or addresses. Each memory location contains magnetic bits which, in various combinations, indicate different numerical or alphabetical characters or various symbols. Internal storage capacity is used during the actual processing of data as a temporary depository for partially processed data. Permanent information may be stored on disks accessible to the system; long-term storage of accounting data frequently utilizes magnetic tape maintained outside of the processing system. This information can be reintroduced as input data. The processing capability of an electronic computer system is a direct function of its storage facilities, including capacity and access time (the time required for getting information in and out of storage).

The *control unit* enables the computer to guide itself through the actual data processing operations. It receives detailed instructions, in the form of a program, concerning the exact sequence of steps to follow in processing a given set of data. The control unit then interprets these instructions and tells the other components when and how to execute them. The control unit transmits data to and from memory and the arithmetic unit and activates the output units when necessary. With internal direction from the program, data processing on a computer most often is automatic and uninterrupted from input to output. On occasion, however, the operator through the *control console* may enter a special piece of information or check for errors along the way.

The *output* component of the EDP system translates the results of processing from machine code into various output media. It may result in the writing of an accounting file on magnetic disk or magnetic tape to allow reuse in subsequent processing. Printers produce reports, invoices, payroll checks, or other documents with exceptional speed. Another type of output equipment is the CRT, on which the output may be displayed visually. The type and form of output are major considerations in the design of the system and the writing of programs.

**Data Processing Example.**   Each electronic data processing system has different characteristics, equipment, and capabilities, of course. The selection of the proper equipment, the arrangement of the processing units, the type of input and output, and the actual internal workings of the machines are subjects of interest to those planning to enter the data processing and systems area of accounting.

Our purpose is only to gain an appreciation of the numerous uses of electronic systems. Payrolls, inventories, cash receipts, cash disbursements, sales, billings, and many other large masses of data can be processed rapidly and efficiently by computers. One brief example of how an EDP system might operate in the billing function of an electric or gas utility is shown in Figure 4A–5.

Meter readers record current readings on special forms. These could be pre-printed forms already containing the customer's name, address, meter number, and rate classification. Periodically the meter cards are entered into the accounting system through an input terminal. Input of the meter information might be accomplished through manual entry on a CRT or in many cases by input equipment capable of optically scanning the meter card.

Two other storage files are part of the input. Probably stored in a disc file is the master subsidiary ledger for each customer. The disc file contains in addition to routine information (name, address, etc.), the current dollar balance, the last meter reading, and cumulative quantities used to date. Another permanent file contains

**FIGURE 4A–5   Billing Function of a Utility Company**

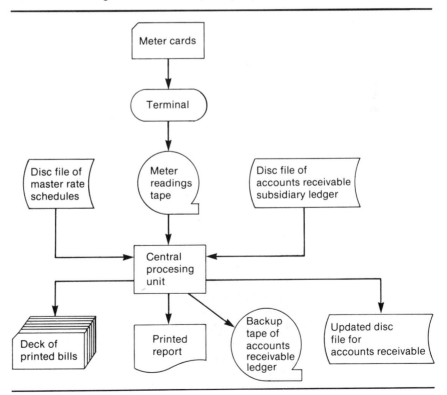

the various rates to be charged for electricity or gas, depending on customer class and quantity used. The three inputs are processed together according to the computer program.

Four major items of output result. One is a set of printed bills in punched-card form ready for direct mailing to customers. These are probably in sections, one of which is to be returned with the customer's payment, to facilitate processing of cash collections. The disc file containing the subsidiary accounts receivable ledger is updated. If the firm's general ledger is stored internally, it also can be updated by direct entries to Accounts Receivable and Sales as part of the processing routine. Usually a backup tape of the subsidiary ledger for accounts receivable will be prepared as well as a printed report of the processing run. These latter two aid in internal control of the data processing. More is said about internal control in the next section.

This particular illustration involves *batch processing* for the single function of billing only. Periodically the meter cards are run and the bills are prepared for a particular group (batch) of customers. With many computer systems, more than one processing function can be handled in a single program. These *integrated data processing* systems coordinate a number of related subsystems, making multiple use of the same input data. One source document updates all records associated with the particular item. For example, an integrated program can be formulated to include not only the sales—accounts receivable—billing function but also the maintenance of the perpetual inventory records, the computation of cost of goods sold, a test of inventory for needed replenishment, and the printing of purchase orders for replenishment and shipping orders to the customer. The customer's sales order is the initiating input to this integrated system.

Some integrated systems employ *on-line, real-time processing,* which entails processing of data practically simultaneously with their generation and immediate feedback of information from the system at any time. An on-line, real-time system has many input units and storage files in direct communication with the central processing unit. Input units may be console terminals, like those used in airline reservation systems, from which users can feed in or ask the computer for information, or electronic cash registers, hooked directly into the processing unit, with each amount being processed as it is entered, without sorting or batching. Alternatively, electronic data may be entered via wire or telephone from other computers, as when branch offices process data and communicate the output to the company's central processing unit as well.

The common data base is stored in *direct access* files, which allow the computer to retrieve desired information rapidly without having to review all items sequentially. Such systems of course require large storage facilities and specialized equipment. Careful attention must be paid to the design of the data base and to the analysis of input-output sources. All of these provisions add significantly to the cost. Nevertheless, real-time processing may offer great advantages if an updated master file must be readily available at all times.

**Microcomputers.**   An increasing number of students and accountants are spending more time with microcomputers rather than with large computer systems. In many cases, the microcomputers have sufficient storage capacity and effective software to be used as small data processors. A complete set of general ledger accounts and/or subsidiary ledger accounts can be maintained and updated through these small but powerful computers. In addition most microcomputers have "spreadsheet" software, which have become very popular in a relatively short period of time. The work sheets illustrated earlier in this chapter can be prepared easily on the computer using these software programs.

**Internal Control**

Internal control includes the *procedures and techniques used to safeguard assets, to promote operational efficiency and compliance with prescribed policy, and to achieve accurate reporting of information.* In this sense, internal control is a management function, much broader than just accounting. The role of the accounting system in internal control is to prevent fraud by making it extremely difficult to misappropriate assets without discovery, to provide assurance that errors and irregularities are detected, and otherwise to check the integrity of the accounting records. To accomplish these tasks, the accounting system must be operated according to a number of commonsense principles listed and illustrated below. A firm should strive to implement as many of these internal control procedures as are economically practicable for its scale of operations

**Systematic Organization and Procedures.** The organizational structure of the firm must be planned with clear lines of authority and responsibility. All employees should understand the extent of their own duties and accountability as well as those of the persons with whom they interact. Within the established lines of authority, a set of procedures for authorization and approval of business transactions should be understood and followed.

> *Example 1:* Authority is assigned to specific individuals for extending credit to customers, for acquiring and disposing of plant assets, for signing checks, and so on.
>
> *Example 2:* In EDP systems an up-to-date documentation for each computer routine contains systems and program flowcharts, operator instructions, input-output formats, the detailed program instructions, and an approval and change sheet. On the latter is indicated the initial approval of the program for operating use. Moreover, any modifications in the program must be entered there, and they must be properly authorized and approved by responsible officials. An operator's manual and run schedule set forth the procedures for the actual machine operation.
>
> *Example 3:* The authorization of cash disbursements and the issuance of checks often follow a formalized, uniform procedure called the *voucher system*. A voucher is a set of documents which supports the authorization for a disbursement of funds. It may be a supplier's invoice (and supporting data), a check request, a weekly payroll summary, or a travel expense report. All payments for significant amounts must be by check, and no check may be issued except in payment of an *approved* voucher showing the reason for the disbursement. Moreover, the voucher must be signed by the person authorized to make that kind of disbursement and initialed by the various individuals who have accumulated the underlying documents, compared them, and reviewed them. The purpose of the voucher system is to control cash expenditures, detect errors, and block unauthorized disbursements.[4]

---

[4] Many firms formally modify the recording mechanism to incorporate the voucher system. Standard, prenumbered voucher forms are used, the voucher numbers often corresponding to identical check numbers. Under a formal voucher system all purchases and other transactions involving an eventual cash outlay are recorded in a special journal called the *voucher register*.

**Segregation of Duties.** In the design of systematic procedures, no single individual should be responsible for all aspects of an area or transaction. The major functions of *authorization, custodianship,* and *accounting* should be separated. Persons having access to physical possession of assets should not also maintain the accounting records of those assets. Those who possess operating control over assets, that is, can authorize their use or disposition, should have neither custodial nor record-keeping responsibilities. When these functions are combined, the opportunities for misappropriation of assets and manipulation of the accounting records to cover theft increase materially. However, a high degree of segregation of duties may be difficult for a small firm to achieve.

*Example 1:* The production manager who uses raw materials, the storeroom manager who keeps them, and the inventory clerk who records additions or withdrawals are all different individuals.

*Example 2:* In the control of accounts receivable, separate persons should have the responsibility for approving credit, authorizing shipment of the goods, preparing bills, mailing statements to the customer, collecting the cash remittances, maintaining the detailed subsidiary records, and making entries in the general ledger control account.

*Example 3:* The people who receive, count, and automatically deposit all cash should not make journal or ledger entries. Similarly, the same person should not be responsible for both cash receipts and cash disbursements.

*Example 4:* The major duties in a computerized data processing system should be segregated. The *systems design and programming group* should have the responsibility for designing and modifying the system and for making and testing changes in the programs. However, it should have no access to the machines during normal operations or to the library of programs actually used to process data. The *operations group* should acquire the data to be processed and actually operate the equipment, but it should not write computer programs or maintain custody of the programs. The *control group* should perform only review and custodial functions. It should maintain and protect the files, discs, and program library and supervise the flow of data in and out of the department.

**Verification and Comparison.** Checks and balances should be designed into the standard operating procedures of the accounting system so that in the normal course of performing their duties employees verify or review the work of others.

*Example 1:* The subsidiary ledger clerk maintaining the individual accounts receivable or accounts payable provides a check on the accuracy of the entries made by the general ledger bookkeeper in the respective control accounts, and vice versa.

*Example 2:* The manager of the receiving department fills out a report on the types and quantities of goods passing through that department. Similarly, the warehouse manager maintains a record of incoming goods, often on perpetual inventory cards. A comparison of these indicates whether the merchandise received by the firm actually ends up in the company's warehouse.

*Example 3:* In a voucher system, before checks are issued to pay suppliers' invoices, someone in the accounting office compares the invoice with the purchase order and receiving report to ensure that the company is being billed for what was actually ordered and received.

*Example 4:* A formal *bank reconciliation* is prepared for each bank account by the controller's staff or the internal audit staff. It involves a systematic comparison of the bank's records of deposits and charges against the Cash in Bank account with the accounting records for cash receipts and disbursements.

**Prompt and Systematic Recording.** The origination of accounting transactions and the flow of documents and reports should follow a well-defined, orderly, preestablished pattern. Written policies governing accounting procedures should be available. The chart of accounts and the accounting manual relating to it are good examples. One of the important factors in error detection is the ability to follow a transaction through the accounting system by means of a series of underlying documents, reports, entries, and so on. This series is referred to as the *audit trail*. If record-keeping and records control are careless and slow, the chances of undetected fraud or error increase.

*Example 1:* Recording is made more prompt and systematic through the use of various mechanical devices, such as cash registers, check-writing machines, and other electronic equipment.

*Example 2:* Computerized systems possess certain characteristics that strengthen internal control in this area. The speed of the computer allows checking in more detail and facilitates more timely reporting. A computerized cash disbursements routine can compare invoices, receiving reports, and purchase orders in detail for hundreds of bills in a few minutes. In addition, the computer achieves a much higher uniformity in its execution of procedures and accuracy in its processing than is possible in manual systems. Like transactions are handled identically, and numerical computations are carried out precisely. This is not to say that computers never make mistakes, but they are far faster and more accurate than human data processors.[5]

*Example 3:* Checks, sales slips, invoices, receipts, and various other documents often are prenumbered forms. By requiring that all prenumbered documents are accounted for, management exerts very tight control over their use. In computerized systems, prenumbered output forms are also used when appropriate. Invoices in the billing routine and checks in the payroll routine are serially numbered for output control. Pages of reports are numbered and a review made to see that all pages are intact.

## QUESTIONS AND PROBLEMS

**4-1.** The following information pertains to the Regent Company and was recently made available to you:

1. Prepaid rent on January 1, 1984, was $600. On July 1, an additional $1,200 was paid to cover the rent through June 30, 1985; the amount was debited to an appropriate asset account.

---

[5] In certain instances, computer processing may conceal errors which could be more easily detected in manual systems. For example, two identical checks sent to a supplier on the same date may not disturb the computer but could make an individual suspicious.

2. Accrued wages owed to employees as of December 31, 1984, amounted to $5,000.
3. The Supplies Inventory account had a balance of $300 on January 1, 1984. In May, the firm purchased (for cash) $800 of supplies which was reflected as an asset. On December 31, 1984, only $400 of the supplies was unused.
4. Utility bills were received at the end of December. These included charges for electric service, $300, and for telephone service, $120. The bills have not yet been recorded.
5. Cash of $900, received from customers for goods to be delivered to them in 1985, has been credited to the Sales Revenue account.
6. On January 1, 1984, the company lent $4,000 to the supplier, receiving a two-year, 10 percent note. The interest for the year 1984 has not yet been received or recorded.

*Required:*

a. For each of the above items, prepare the original (nonadjusting) journal entry, *if any,* which would have been made by Regent Company during 1984 but prior to December 31.
b. For each of the above items, prepare the adjusting journal entry, *if any,* which should be made by Regent Company on December 31, 1984.

4–2. The following trial balance is prepared from the accounts of Heritage Restaurant, Inc., on December 31, 1985, the end of the first year of operations.

|  | Debit | Credit |
|---|---|---|
| Cash | $ 9,800 | |
| Inventory of food | 25,000 | |
| Operating supplies | 3,100 | |
| Equipment | 16,000 | |
| Wage expense | 13,000 | |
| Rent expense | 9,000 | |
| Utilities expense | 3,570 | |
| Insurance expense | 1,530 | |
| Customer receipts | | $48,300 |
| Accounts payable | | 12,700 |
| Capital stock | | 20,000 |
| Totals | $81,000 | $81,000 |

*Additional information:*

1. Inventories of food and operating supplies are $2,200 and $600, respectively, on December 31, 1985.
2. Unrecorded wage expense for the latter part of December is $700.
3. Utility bills received for December services are $350. These have not been paid or recorded as yet.
4. Rental expense is $500 per month, payable six months in advance on June 30 and December 31.
5. Customer receipts include $250 received from the sale of dinner tickets in December. These tickets can be exchanged for meals anytime during 1986.
6. There are two insurance policies on hand on December 31: a one-year policy purchased on September 1 for $810 and a two-year policy purchased on July 1 for $720.
7. Depreciation on the equipment for the year amounts to $1,600.

*Required:*

a. Set up ledger (T-) accounts for each account in the trial balance.
b. Make all necessary adjusting entries directly in the ledger accounts. Set up additional accounts where needed.
c. Prepare an income statement for the year and a balance sheet as of December 31, 1985.

**4-3.** The Harrison Civic Theatre group puts on dramas and concerts. One attraction is featured each month over the nine-month season, which begins in September. The following data relate to the first month of operations in the 1984–1985 season:

1. Rented the Orpheum Theatre. Rent of $1,800 per month must be paid for three months in advance. A check for the first three-months' rent is written.
2. Sent out direct-mail announcements and placed newspaper advertisements telling of the entire season's programs and soliciting season ticket orders. The cost of $12,000 was paid in cash.
3. Contracted with Lincoln Concessionaires to operate the refreshment stand. The Civic Theatre group is to receive 12 percent of all gross sales of refreshments. The amount is to be remitted on the 10th of the month for sales during the preceding month.
4. Received cash of $31,400 for season tickets to all nine scheduled attractions.
5. Purchased a specially designed insurance policy for $8,100 cash. The policy provides fire, theft, and public liability coverage during the nine months the group is active.
6. Sold individual tickets for $6,200 for September's program performances.
7. Incurred monthly salary and wage costs of $9,700, payable the fifth of the following month.
8. Printed program notes for the September performances at a cost of $2,400, paid in cash.
9. Received a report from Lincoln that September's refreshment sales were $5,000.

*Required:*

a. Assume that the group prepares monthly financial statements. Prepare journal entries to record the above transactions *as well as* any adjusting entries necessary on September 30, 1984.
b. "The matching concept dictates that the *entire* $12,000 in item 2 be expensed during September. After all, that's when *all* the ads appeared and *all* the brochures were mailed." Comment on this statement.
c. "Any person who has not recorded items 2, 4, and 5 in a consistent manner cannot possibly have come up with a completely accurate solution." Explain what might be meant by this statement. Do you agree with it?

**4-4.** The Langdon Company purchased office supplies on October 10, 1984, for $600 cash. On December 31, 1984, the end of the firm's accounting period, $250 of the supplies remained on hand.

*Required:*

a. Show two different ways in which the October 10 journal entry could be made *and* then show the adjusting entry necessary at December 31 for each.

b. Which of the two approaches you followed in (a), seems the most natural? Is either approach more accurate than the other? Explain.

**4–5.** The McNeil Clothing Company began business on April 1, 1985. The following data summarize the transactions for the first month of operations:

1. Stockholders invest $85,000 in cash and $20,000 in marketable securities.
2. Furniture and fixtures are acquired at a cost of $27,000, paid in cash.
3. Merchandise is acquired on account at a cost of $55,000.
4. Store supplies are purchased for $2,900 cash.
5. $12,000 of rent is paid.
6. Sales are $64,000 on account and $8,500 for cash.
7. Cash payments to suppliers of merchandise total $37,500.
8. Collections of accounts receivable amount to $29,000.
9. Advertising expenditures are $1,800.
10. Insurance premiums paid are $2,400.

*Additional information:*

11. Interest of $175 has been earned on the securities.
12. Insurance expense for the month is $200.
13. Advertising supplies costing $400, purchased as part of transaction 9, remain unused on April 30.
14. Sales commission equal to 15 percent of April sales are to be paid in early May.
15. The rent payment was for a 12-month period.
16. Store supplies on hand on April 30 are $400.
17. $12,000 of merchandise inventory remains on April 30.
18. Furniture and fixtures are estimated to have a 10-year life.

*Required:*

a. Prepare journal entries to record the April transactions (1–10).
b. Post your journal entries to ledger accounts.
c. Journalize and post adjusting entries for items 11–18.
d. Prepare an income statement for April and a balance sheet as of April 30, 1985.
e. Journalize and post closing entries.
f. Could you do (e) before (d)? Could you do (d) before (c)? Briefly explain.

**4–6.** A clerk for the Henry Corporation prepared the following *closing* entries on December 31, 1984:

| C1 | Sales Revenue | 80,000 | |
| | Accumulated Depreciation | 18,000 | |
| | Income Summary | | 98,000 |
| | To close accounts with credit balances. | | |

| C2 | Income Summary | 70,000 | |
| | Cost of Goods Sold | | 44,000 |
| | Depreciation Expense | | 10,000 |
| | Dividends Expense | | 9,000 |
| | Cash | | 7,000 |
| | To close accounts with debit balances. | | |

C3 Income Summary ................................... 28,000
      Owner's Capital Account .......................          28,000

*Required:*

a. Comment in detail on all errors made by the clerk.

b. Prepare the proper closing journal entries which should have been made by the clerk.

**4–7.** The trial balance of the Lake Corporation as of December 31, 1984, was as follows:

| | Debit | Credit |
|---|---|---|
| Cash ........................................ | $ 8,000 | |
| Accounts receivable ......................... | 42,000 | |
| Merchandise inventory ....................... | 68,000 | |
| Supplies inventory .......................... | 8,000 | |
| Unexpired insurance ......................... | 2,500 | |
| Notes receivable (due 1990) ................. | 60,000 | |
| Buildings ................................... | 90,000 | |
| Accumulated depreciation—buildings .......... | | $ 9,000 |
| Sales revenue ............................... | | 113,000 |
| Service fee revenue .......................... | | 12,000 |
| Interest revenue ............................ | | 4,800 |
| Salaries expense ............................ | 25,000 | |
| Insurance expense ........................... | 6,000 | |
| Expenses applicable to service fees ............ | 7,500 | |
| Capital stock ................................ | | 130,000 |
| Retained earnings ........................... | | 48,200 |
| | $317,000 | $317,000 |

The accountant of the Lake Corporation also made available the following information:

1. A physical count of merchandise disclosed that there was $32,000 of merchandise on hand at the end of the year.

2. An additional $4,500 of salaries was earned by the employees, although it had not yet been paid to them.

3. Royalty payments on merchandise sold were estimated to be $5,000. Lake must pay these by February 1, 1985.

4. The inventory of unused supplies was $3,500 at year-end.

5. The buildings had been acquired on January 1, 1982.

6. There was only one insurance policy still in force on December 31, 1984. This one-year policy cost $6,000 and runs until March 31, 1985.

7. Service fees paid in advance were credited to Service Fee Revenue; $1,200 of these were unearned at year-end.

8. The annual interest rate was 12 percent on the notes receivable. Interest was normally collected three times a year—on January 1, May 1, and September 1.

*Required:*

a. Set up ledger (T-) accounts for all accounts in the trial balance and record the existing balances.

b.  Record all adjustments directly in the ledger accounts. Use additional T-accounts if necessary.

c.  Prepare a 1984 income statement and a balance sheet at year-end.

**4–8.**  The Dayton Services Corporation was organized on January 1, 1985. The chief accountant of Dayton provides you with the following:

1.  *Unadjusted* trial balance:

| | | |
|---|---:|---:|
| Cash | $17,400 | |
| Fees receivable | 2,500 | |
| Office supplies | 300 | |
| Prepaid insurance | 700 | |
| Furniture/equipment | 5,100 | |
| Accounts payable | | $ 1,200 |
| Capital stock | | 10,000 |
| Fees earned | | 28,500 |
| Rent expense | 4,600 | |
| Office salaries expense | 9,100 | |
| Totals | $39,700 | $39,700 |

2.  1985 income statement:

| | | |
|---|---:|---:|
| Fees earned | | $31,200 |
| Less: Operating expenses: | | |
| Depreciation | $ 510 | |
| Rent | 4,300 | |
| Insurance | 450 | |
| Office supplies | 200 | |
| Office salaries | 9,850 | |
| Total | | 15,310 |
| Net income | | $15,890 |

*Required:*

a.  Prepare all the *adjusting* journal entries which Dayton Services Corporation must have made on December 31, 1985.

b.  How else could this firm initially have recorded and subsequently adjusted its rent accounts?

**4–9.**  Two students recently had the opportunity to examine the books and financial statements of a firm which had just concluded its first year of operations. Among the relationships they observed were the following:

1.  Depreciation Expense on the income statement and Accumulated Depreciation on the balance sheet were equal in amount.

2.  Sales Commission Expense on the income statement and Sales Commissions Payable on the balance sheet were equal in amount.

3.  The balance for Cash on the unadjusted trial balance was equal to the balance for Cash on the adjusted trial balance.

4.  The net income figure on the income statement was equal in amount to the Retained Earnings balance on the balance sheet.

5.  The balance for Prepaid Rent on the unadjusted trial balance was equal to the amount shown for Prepaid Rent on the adjusted trial balance.

*Required:*

a. Indicate which of the above relationships, if any, existed only because the firm was in the first period of its operations.

b. Indicate which of the above relationships, if any, would probably exist in each and every period of the firm's operations.

c. Indicate which of the above relationships, if any, might or might not exist in any period of operations, including a firm's first period.

**4–10.** The Sherman Corporation began operations on November 1, 1985. The following transactions took place in November:

Nov. 1 Issued capital stock for cash, $40,000.

1 Paid two months' rent, $2,200.

1 Purchased equipment with a useful life of 10 years for cash, $8,400.

2 Purchased merchandise from Northport, Inc., for $1,000 on account.

3 Sold merchandise on account, $950 ($625 to A. Monona and $325 to L. State).

4 Cash sales, $1,400.

6 Purchased supplies on account, $1,450 ($800 from Broom Corporation and $650 from Northport, Inc.).

8 Paid freight bill on goods shipped to customers, $90.

9 Purchased merchandise from Northport, Inc., $3,100 on account.

12 Received a check in full payment of the account of L. State.

15 Paid $1,000 to Northport, Inc.

16 Sold goods to Bassett Company on account, $3,600.

16 Paid salaries of $1,500 in cash for the first half of November.

16 Bought a delivery truck with a useful life of five years from Smart Motors, Inc., for $9,000 cash.

21 A. Monona paid for the goods purchased on November 3.

28 Paid Northport, Inc., for the supplies purchased from them on November 6.

*Additional information:*

1. On November 30, there were $250 of supplies and $1,500 of merchandise on hand.

2. Salaries for the period November 16–30 were to be paid on December 4.

*Required:*

a. Journalize the above transactions in a general journal. (Include a date and posting reference column in the journal form.)

b. Post from the journal to the ledger accounts, both general and subsidiary. (Assign account numbers to your general ledger accounts and use these in the posting process.)

c. Take a trial balance and prepare schedules of subsidiary account balances for accounts receivable and accounts payable to see that they agree with the control accounts.

d. Journalize and post all adjusting entries.

e. Prepare an adjusted trial balance.

f. Prepare an income statement and a balance sheet.

g. Journalize and post closing entries.

**4A-1.** On June 30, 1985, the end of the fiscal year, the unadjusted trial balance of Grant Bowling Alley, Inc., shows the following accounts and balances:

|  | Debit | Credit |
|---|---|---|
| Cash | $ 16,500 | |
| Supplies and accessories | 40,500 | |
| Prepaid insurance | 18,000 | |
| Prepaid rent | 24,000 | |
| Alleys | 125,000 | |
| Accumulated depreciation—alleys | | $ 25,000 |
| Furniture and fixtures | 8,000 | |
| Accumulated depreciation—furniture and fixtures | | 2,000 |
| Accounts payable | | 29,000 |
| Capital stock | | 110,000 |
| Retained earnings | | 32,000 |
| Bowling game revenues | | 91,000 |
| Sales of accessories | | 17,000 |
| Pinsetter lease expense | 15,000 | |
| Wage expense | 40,000 | |
| Utilities expense | 19,000 | |
| | $306,000 | $306,000 |

*Additional information:*

1.  An inventory of supplies and accessories amounts to $16,000 at June 30.
2.  Accrued wages on June 30 amount to $1,400.
3.  Prepaid insurance represents a three-year policy taken out on July 1, 1984.
4.  Rent expense is $18,000 for this fiscal period.
5.  Depreciation on the alleys is $12,500 per year and on the furniture and fixtures, $1,000.
6.  The company leases the pinsetting machines at a cost of $0.10 per game. Amounts have been remitted through May 1985. Meters on the machine indicate that 185,000 games have been bowled during the *fiscal year.*

*Required:*

a.  Prepare a work sheet, following the format illustrated in the Appendix.
b.  Prepare an income statement for the year ended June 30, 1985, and a balance sheet as of June 30, 1985.
c.  Did the work sheet aid you in the preparation of the financial statements? Explain.

**4A-2.** The unadjusted trial balance of Forbes Stereo Center as of December 31, 1984, appears below:

|  | Debit | Credit |
|---|---|---|
| Cash | $ 9,000 | |
| Accounts receivable | 18,200 | |
| Notes receivable (due June 30, 1985) | 14,000 | |
| Inventories | 78,800 | |
| Equipment | 28,000 | |
| Accumulated depreciation—equipment | | $ 5,600 |
| Accounts payable | | 28,500 |
| Capital stock | | 55,000 |
| Retained earnings | | 17,900 |
| Sales | | 71,700 |
| Revenue from consultations | | 5,900 |
| Repair revenue | | 6,900 |
| Selling expense | 15,000 | |
| Delivery expense | 3,000 | |
| Administrative expense | 16,600 | |
| Rent expense | 8,900 | |
|  | $191,500 | $191,500 |

In the course of reviewing the records, the accountant discovers the following facts:

1. Sales include a down payment of $2,100 on a customized sound system to be delivered in 1985.
2. Bonuses equal to 15 percent of all sales over $40,000 (excluding advances) are owed to sales personnel.
3. Accrued interest of $1,400 on the notes receivable has not yet been recorded.
4. The cost of the ending inventory is $31,200.
5. Depreciation on equipment totals $5,600 for the year, chargeable 20 percent to selling, 50 percent to delivery, and 30 percent to administration.
6. Administrative expense includes the $540 cost of a one-year insurance policy purchased on September 1, 1984.

*Required:*

a. Set up a work sheet and use it to record the adjusting entries and to organize the information for the preparation of the income statement and the balance sheet. Add accounts at the bottom of the work sheet if necessary.
b. Prepare the financial statements from the work sheet columns.
c. Prepare a single compound journal entry to close the books at the end of the period. (You may assume that the adjusting entries have already been journalized and posted.)

**4A-3.** A firm uses the following journals as its books of original entry: a cash receipts book, a cash disbursements book, a sales journal, an invoice payable register, and a general journal. Direct posting from source documents to subsidiary ledger accounts is practiced. The following transactions are selected from those occurring during the month:

1. Payment of monthly rent.
2. Depreciation expense is recorded in an adjusting entry at the end of the month.
3. A freight bill covering costs of goods shipped to customers is received.
4. Sales on account for a day.
5. Cash received from customers.
6. Purchase of office equipment on account.
7. A supplier's invoice is paid.
8. Shares of stock issued to the president of the company for cash.
9. Purchase of merchandise on account.
10. Cash sales.
11. Employees' bimonthly wages are paid.
12. Damaged merchandise is returned by the company to the supplier. The merchandise had not been paid for.
13. The company borrows from the bank, giving a six-month note payable.
14. Supplies are purchased on account.
15. A 90-day note is received from a customer in settlement of an open account.

*Required:*

For each of the above transactions, indicate:

a. What journal it would be recorded in.
b. The account(s) that would be debited and credited.
c. Whether the account(s) would be posted individually or as part of a column total.
d. The underlying source document that the accountant would probably use to support the making of the entry.

**4A-4.** Betty Post recently began thinking about internal controls as a result of two pieces of mail which she received. The first mailing advertised a new automatic teller machine which her bank was establishing several blocks from her home. Although the services advertised included both withdrawals and deposits, Betty thought she would be very reluctant to make a deposit there since proper internal controls might not have been established. The second mailing was a program guide for the public radio station which she supported. The station, WXYZ, was operated by the nearby XYZ University. The following statement appeared in the program guide:

> If you have recently joined WXYZ, make certain that your processed check contains the following endorsement: For Deposit Only to Account of WXYZ. If it does not contain such an endorsement, please contact the Internal Auditing Department of XYZ University.

*Required:*

a. What internal controls could aid in ensuring the proper recording and dispensing of cash from an automatic teller machine?

   *b.* Does controlling for the proper recording of *deposits* of cash present any additional problems and challenges?
   *c.* Evaluate the statement which appeared in the radio program guide. Does the communication of such a message to radio supporters improve the effectiveness of a system of internal controls? What past events might have led to the issuance of such a statement?

**4A–5.** Among the topics discussed in the Appendix are special journals, computers, and internal control. In the following questions, you are asked to assess the degree to which each device/concept is facilitated or impeded by the others.

*Required:*

   *a.* Can computers make the implementation and use of a system of special journals less burdensome?
   *b.* Does the use of special journals contribute to the creation of an effective internal control system within a company? Could their use be detrimental?
   *c.* Does the use of computers contribute to the creation of an effective internal control system within a company? Could their use be detrimental?

**4A–6.** Trapan Retailing, Inc., has decided to diversify operations by selling through vending machines.[6] Trapan's plans call for the purchase of 312 vending machines, which will be situated at 78 different locations within one city, and the rental of a warehouse to store merchandise. Trapan intends to sell only canned beverages at a standard price.

   Management has hired an inventory control clerk to oversee the warehousing functions, and two truck drivers, who will periodically fill the machines with merchandise and deposit cash collected at a designated bank. Drivers will be required to report to the warehouse daily.

*Required:*

   What internal controls should the auditor expect to find in order to ensure the integrity of the cash receipts and warehousing functions?

**4A–7.** The Art Appreciation Society operates a museum for the benefit and enjoyment of the community.[7] During hours when the museum is open to the public, two clerks who are positioned at the entrance collect a $5 admission fee from each nonmember patron. Members of the Art Appreciation Society are permitted to enter free of charge upon presentation of their membership cards.

   At the end of each day one of the clerks delivers the proceeds to the treasurer. The treasurer counts the cash in the presence of the clerk and places it in a safe. Each Friday afternoon the treasurer and one of the clerks deliver all cash held in the safe to the bank and receive an authenticated deposit slip which provides the basis for the weekly entry in the cash receipts journal.

   The board of directors of the Art Appreciation Society has identified a need to improve their system of internal control over cash admission fees. The board has determined that the cost of installing turnstiles or sales booths or otherwise altering the physical layout of the museum will greatly exceed any benefits which

---

   [6] Material from the Uniform CPA Examinations, copyright © 1982 by the American Institute of Certified Public Accountants, Inc., is reproduced with permission.
   [7] Material from the Uniform CPA Examinations, copyright © 1980 by the American Institute of Certified Public Accountants, Inc., is reproduced with permission.

may be derived. However, the board has agreed that the sale of admission tickets must be an integral part of its improvement efforts.

Smith has been asked by the board of directors of the Art Appreciation Society to review the internal control over cash admission fees and provide suggestions for improvement.

*Required:*

Indicate weaknesses in the existing system of internal control over cash admission fees, which Smith should identify, and recommend one improvement for each of the weaknesses identified.

Organize the answer as indicated in the following illustrative example:

| Weakness | Recommendation |
|---|---|
| 1. There is no basis for establishing the documentation of the number of paying patrons. | 1. Prenumbered admission tickets should be issued upon payment of the admission fee. |

# CHAPTER 5

# ACCOUNTING CONCEPTS OF INCOME

The preceding chapters develop the conceptual framework and some of the bookkeeping tools necessary for the measurement of accounting income. Our basic assumption states that net income is best determined by the matching of expired costs (expenses) against their related revenues. In this chapter we discuss some expansions and elaborations of this accounting concept of income as well as some of the problems associated with it. First, though, let us tie together some of the threads of thought relating to income measurement developed in earlier chapters.

**REVIEW OF THE MATCHING CONCEPT**

The accounting concept of income rests on the relationship between assets received and assets consumed in the periodic operating activities of the business. The asset inflows, usually cash or accounts receivable, from the sale of goods or services provide a monetary measure of the accomplishment of the firm in satisfying consumer needs. Similarly, the various assets consumed in this process afford a monetary expression of the effort expended. Matching the inflow and outflow of assets for particular time intervals gives us periodic readings about the performance of the business entity. This cause-and-effect relationship which exists under the matching concept is lacking if we look only at inflows and outflows of cash during a period.

Beginning with an initial equality of assets and equities, we observe that changes in assets associated with operating activities cause similar changes in owners' equity. We introduce revenue accounts to record the increases in owners' equity as assets flow into the business from operations. Revenue transactions record sources of assets. We set up various expense accounts to record the decreases in owners' equity as assets are consumed in the production of revenues. Expense transactions record the outflows or uses of assets.

The heart of the accounting concept of income rests in a matching of net asset inflows and outflows during designated time periods. In its conceptual statement on elements of financial statements, the FASB formally defines revenues and expenses in terms of asset flows:[1]

> Revenues are inflows or other enhancements of assets of an entity . . . during a period from delivering or producing goods, rendering services, or other activities that constitute the entity's ongoing major or central operations. Expenses are outflows or other using up of assets . . . during a period from delivering or producing goods, rendering services, or carrying out other activities that constitute the entity's ongoing major or central operations.

However, in double-entry bookkeeping the actual implementation of the matching concept involves associating the related owners' equity changes (revenue and expense accounts) that reflect the relevant asset changes.

The matching concept presumes that the accountant is able to do two things—to relate earned revenues to periods of time and to relate costs to revenues. Virtually all of the problems of conventional accounting theory emanate from the fact that at best we can do these tasks only imperfectly, particularly on the cost side. Chapter 6 addresses the practical problems of revenue recognition. This chapter begins the discussion of the practical difficulties associated with the determination of exactly which revenues a particular cost should be matched against. Out of this discussion comes the concept of period expense.

The second portion of this chapter focuses on the restrictive nature of the matching concept as a measure of an entity's performance. The revenue-expense model does not clearly encompass all changes in owners' equity (net assets) during a period. Out of this discussion comes an expansion of the income concept to include other nonowner transactions and events beyond just revenues and expenses.

## PERIOD EXPENSES

In implementing the matching concept accountants have developed a hierarchy for the association of costs with revenues. Costs that become classified as expenses fall into one of the three categories:

1. Expenses directly traceable to units sold or specific revenue transactions.
2. Expenses systematically and rationally allocable to time periods in which revenue is recognized.
3. Expenses for which no measurable future benefit can be discerned.

---

[1] FASB, *Statement of Financial Accounting Concepts No. 3,* "Elements of Financial Statements of Business Enterprises" (Stamford, Conn., December 1980) page xii.

When costs can be closely associated with the sale of a product, they are relatively easy to match against the revenue they help to produce. For instance, the costs of merchandise purchased for resale are attached to specific units of product. These costs may include both the direct purchase price and indirect items, such as freight charges and handling costs. By being related to units of product, these *product costs* become part of the expense "cost of goods sold" whenever the product is sold. In this way, they are fairly accurately matched against the proper revenue inflow. Another example is sales commissions. Here again, the relationship between *cost and effect* is direct; sales commission expense arises at the time a sale is made and is matched against the revenue produced from the sale.

Expenses that cannot be traced directly to units of product are called *period costs*. There are two types. Some lend themselves to a systematic and rational assignment to particular time periods. Depreciation expense, insurance expense, rent expense, and interest expense are examples. These costs benefit operations in one or more specific accounting periods. They are associated with the revenues of those identifiable periods rather than being matched against particular units of revenue. If more than one accounting period is involved, the accountant estimates a period of future benefit and a pattern of relationship between costs incurred and benefits received. Then the costs of those assets are allocated (amortized) to expense in accordance with those estimates.

The third category of expense includes costs which cannot be closely identified with specific units of product, identifiable revenue transactions, or even determinable future periods. Examples of this second type of period cost include administrative salaries, training costs, advertising, and operating costs of the firm's computer system.

## Measurement Problems with Period Costs

Period costs obviously represent the use of resources; the problem is in determining when their benefit is received. Intuitively, we would expect that many of these costs actually benefit more than one accounting period. Under ideal matching we would determine what portion of the cost is applicable to future periods, which future periods receive benefit, and to what extent each period benefits. Unfortunately, with present means of measurement this goal simply cannot be reached for certain types of costs.

As a consequence, those period costs that cannot be systematically allocated to time periods *are treated as expenses of the period in which they are incurred*. For example, the cost of conducting an institutional advertising campaign is debited to Advertising Expense in each period the cost is incurred. One could argue that a portion of the advertising cost theoretically should be deferred to the extent that the campaign stimulates revenues in future periods. The amount and length of any future benefit would be practically impossible to measure, however. Other examples of period costs which pertain to several accounting periods but which nevertheless are expensed upon incurrence are costs of market surveys, public relations, the corporate planning department, and legal and accounting services.

Although the treatment of certain costs as period expenses may be admittedly somewhat inaccurate, the practice is justified on two grounds. First, often no feasible alternative is open. The consumption of the resource bears no discernible relation to the products, services, or revenues, nor is there any rational basis for any systematic allocation to future accounting periods. To carry forward an asset value without a clearly demonstrable and reasonably measurable future period of benefit would violate the qualitative guideline of *verifiability* and the constraint of *conservatism*.

The second justification for period expenses applies in the case of recurring types of costs. Any deviations in net income from an ideal matching caused by immediate expensing are likely to be *immaterial* because of a compensating lag effect. For example, a portion of the president's salary for this period ideally should be allocated to future periods to the extent that he or she engages in forward planning. However, any such portion is counterbalanced approximately by portions of the salary cost which were incurred in past periods but are applicable to the current period. If the same type and amount of expenditure is incurred every period, probably no material asset value builds up.

## Research and Development Costs

Whether an expenditure should be recorded as an asset cost or as a period expense has been especially controversial in the treatment of research and development costs. These costs include salaries of scientists, engineers, technicians, and research administrators as well as supplies, tools, perishable equipment, and other indirect costs. Ideally these costs should be matched against the revenues to which they give rise. On the other hand, no costs should be deferred as assets unless there is a bona fide expectation that they will be recovered out of the future revenues they produce.

The link between R&D expenditures and future revenue inflows is often weakened by great uncertainty and long periods of elapsed time. In some instances substantial expenditures on research appear to yield no revenues. In other instances a small investment results in a significant breakthrough that generates large future inflows of revenue. As a result, accounting difficulties arise in the determination of whether an asset has been created by the expenditure and, if so, how many future periods will benefit.

Prior to the release of *Statement No. 2* by the Financial Accounting Standards Board, three alternative treatments existed for dealing with these difficulties. Research and development costs could be (1) collected as assets by individual project and accounted for on a case-by-case basis, (2) deferred as an intangible asset to be spread out as expense over an arbitrary time period, and (3) written off as an expense in the period incurred.

The first two procedures recognize that R&D costs are usually incurred to benefit more than one accounting period. Under the first approach the costs applicable to each individual research project would be accumulated in separate asset accounts until the project was completed. Then for successful projects the costs would be written off over the estimated period of future benefit, perhaps determined by the life of a patent or contract resulting from the project. If no lasting benefit resulted from the project, the accumulated costs would be expensed. Under the second approach all R&D costs would be charged to an intangible asset to be amortized over an arbitrary time period, such as 5 or 10 years. The assumption was that although the exact period of usefulness is not known, less distortion in net income is involved if the costs are amortized over a reasonable time interval than if they are all written off when incurred.

In 1974 the Financial Accounting Standards Board rejected the asset-oriented approaches to R&D costs and chose instead the third and most commonly used approach. It concluded that "all research and development costs . . . shall be charged to expense when incurred."[2] This treatment as period expenses is based on three major considerations: (1) Future benefits are highly uncertain, (2) a causal relationship between expenditures and benefits is often lacking, and (3) R&D expenditures do not qualify as accounting assets because future economic benefits cannot be identified and objectively measured. The exception to this general treatment is made for research and development costs specifically reimbursable under a contractual arrangement. Thus, the costs of developing a new commercial aircraft under a specific contract could allowably and logically be deferred.

Generally accepted accounting principles now require that all R&D costs be treated as period expenses. Such a treatment might be justified for the cost of *pure research* activities or for *general research* carried on continuously to improve existing products and processes. Presumably, much of the benefit is realized very shortly, and no valid basis exists for measuring the portion which may benefit future sales. Moreover, if approximately the same amount is spent each period, writing off each year's costs as an expense is probably just as accurate as attempting to allocate costs to different periods. In these cases, the approach adopted by the FASB enhances the qualitative guideline of comparability. It also reflects the constraint of conservatism.

Many accountants object, however, to the broad extension of this approach to R&D expenditures that are irregular in size and timing and that actually do give rise to future benefits.[3] They argue that immediate

---

[2] FASB, *Statement of Financial Accounting Standards No. 2,* "Accounting for Research and Development Costs" (Stamford, Conn., October 1974), par. 12.

[3] Although almost all firms elect to deduct R&D costs for tax purposes in the year incurred, income tax regulations allow as an option the amortization of such costs over a period of 60 months. It is also interesting to note that the International Accounting Standards Committee, in its *Standard No. 9,* issued July 1978, allows deferral of the identifiable costs of development projects that are clearly defined and technically and commercially feasible.

expensing may result in significant understatement of balance sheet assets, a violation of representational faithfulness. Moreover, because R&D expenditures are largely discretionary, this approach may allow management to manipulate periodic net income. The FASB attempted to mitigate this latter concern by requiring that the total R&D costs charged to expense be disclosed each period.

The difficulty in treatment of R&D costs stems clearly from two factors: (1) differences in the nature and purpose of the costs and in the particular situations faced by firms and (2) extremely difficult measurement problems. Pure research costs, if identifiable, probably should be handled differently from project-oriented development costs. Similarly, immediate expensing may be justified for new product costs in a large firm with relatively constant, recurring expenditures but not in a smaller firm where they may fluctuate substantially from year to year. However, even if this detailed classification of costs is made, accountants are still faced with measuring reliably *whether* any future benefit will be received, *how much cost* is applicable to the future, and *in what pattern* future benefit will be received.

## OTHER EQUITY CHANGES RELATED TO PERIOD OPERATIONS

Period costs represent only one problem encountered when the matching concept is applied to real-world transactions. The matching concept assumes a normal pattern and causal relationship between revenue and expense occurrence. However, certain other events, aside from capital stock transactions, may affect owners' equity during the reporting period. Many of these events relate broadly to the use of assets and the conduct of business operations but do not fit neatly into the scope of the activities we have introduced so far.

Consequently, additional temporary owners' equity accounts are needed in which these other changes may be recorded. Our concept of net income may also have to be modified and expanded to encompass some of these events. In this section we discuss certain of these special accounts—gains, losses, taxes, interest, and dividends.

### Gains

The Financial Accounting Standards Board has defined gains as "increases in equity (net assets) from peripheral or incidental transactions of an entity and from all other transactions and other events and circumstances affecting the entity during a period except those that result from revenues or investments by owners."[4] Gains represent events favorable from the stockholders' perspective and not connected with the main earning activities of the firm.

---

[4] FASB *Concepts No. 3*, par. 67.

For example, assume that a parcel of land which originally cost $8,000 is sold for $12,000 in cash. This transaction would be recorded by the following entry:

```
Cash ............................................. 12,000
      Land ........................................         8,000
      Gain on Sale of Land ...........................         4,000
```

The Gain on Sale of Land account reflects an addition to retained earnings because net assets have increased other than through owners' investments or revenues. Gain accounts are closed to Income Summary and appear on the income statement.

The example above illustrates a gain resulting from the disposition of noninventory assets. The advantageous settlement of liabilities, the winning of a lawsuit, and the receipt of donations and gifts are also events which may give rise to gains.

**Losses**

Losses are the opposite of gains. They are decreases in owners' equity other than expenses or distributions to owners. Like gains, losses usually are associated with the nonrecurring or unusual activities of the enterprise or with environmental circumstances largely beyond the control of the firm.

Most losses occur when assets disappear or are impaired and no contribution to the ordinary operations of the business is received. Examples of losses include the undepreciated cost of equipment that has to be scrapped, the uninsured cost of merchandise destroyed by fire, uninsured cash embezzled by an employee, and damages levied by a court.

To record these kinds of transactions, we use loss accounts which are debited to reflect the decrease in net assets. Assume, for instance, that a fire damages $26,000 of merchandise, and a court directs that $7,000 be paid to a customer who was injured in a fall on the firm's premises. If the business carries no insurance against these events, the losses would be recorded as follows:

```
Loss from Fire ...................................... 26,000
      Merchandise Inventory ...........................         26,000

Personal Injury Losses .................................  7,000
      Liability for Damages ............................          7,000
```

**Taxes**

Taxes are a claim on business assets by various governmental authorities. We will concern ourselves here with the more common types, such as property taxes and the corporate income tax. The latter is perhaps the most important and serves as our example.

As the tax liability accrues, there is a concomitant decrease in owners' equity. This decrease is recorded in a special temporary account. If a corporation earned income of $80,000 before taxes, the entry to record its federal income taxes would be:

```
Income Taxes  .......................................  32,000
        Income Taxes Payable  ..........................         32,000
    Calculation of federal income tax at 40 percent.
```

Taxes in some ways are similar to an expense. In a broad sense they can be viewed as a payment for government services consumed during the period or as a necessary period expense for the privilege of conducting business as a corporation. On the other hand, the amount of assets eventually distributed to governmental bodies often bears at best only an indirect and varying relationship to the amount of service received. Some accountants therefore argue that taxes are not like other expenses in the sense of assets used up in the production of revenues. They would treat taxes as a nonreciprocal transfer of wealth to the taxing authority. Probably there are elements of both concepts in tax charges.

One conclusion is sure, however. There can be no net increase in owners' equity from the activities of the period until the tax claims are provided for. Accordingly most businesses treat taxes as an expense. Also, the FASB, in its *Statement of Financial Accounting Concepts No. 3,* specifically included taxes as an expense element. We will do likewise.

## Interest

In addition to operations, a major concern to management is the financing of the firm's activities. When assets are paid or promised to various creditors for the use of borrowed money, this fact should be included on the report of the activities for the period. If assets are acquired through the incurrence of interest-bearing liabilities, than an additional legal claim on the firm's assets, for interest, accrues as time passes. This increase in an interest liability causes a corresponding decrease in owners' equity. When cash is actually distributed to the creditors, the liability is liquidated.

For instance, assume that on July 1 a firm borrows $5,000 from a bank and gives a 12 percent, one-year note payable in exchange. When the accounting period ends on December 31, the following adjusting entry is necessary to record the six months' interest that has accrued.

```
Interest Expense  .......................................  300
    Interest Payable  ...................................         300
```

Interest Expense is the temporary retained earnings account used to accumulate the total compensation for the use of funds supplied by creditors during that period. Interest Payable represents the unpaid portion of that claim as of any particular date.

**Interest Conventions and Short-Term Notes.**  Notes payable (and notes receivable) usually result from short-term transactions with a single creditor (debtor). They can arise directly from a purchase transaction when the credit period is longer than the typical 30-to-60-day charge account. Sometimes they arise indirectly from substitution for an account payable (receivable) if the usual credit period is extended. Notes payable may also result from a direct loan from a bank or other creditor as in the previous example. In any case the note represents a signed promise by the borrower to pay a certain sum on a particular date to the lender. If a note is explicitly interest bearing, the written document indicates that fact.

Because of the short time period (usually one year or less), the charge for use of the money is calculated under the simple interest formula,

$$I = P \times R \times T$$
$$\text{Interest} = \text{Principal} \times \text{Rate} \times \text{Time}$$

and the interest normally is paid at the time the principal is paid.

Businesses employ a number of conventions related to the simple interest formula. First, unless stated otherwise, the interest rate is assumed to be an annual rate. Secondly, if the time period is expressed in days, then the time period begins with the day after the date of the note and runs up to and includes the maturity date. For example, a 30-day note dated December 15 is due on January 14; a one-month note dated December 15 is due on January 15. Because of differing numbers of days in various months, most notes for less than a year are expressed in terms of days rather than months. A third convention that often influences interest calculations states that for interest purposes the year consists of 360 days. Thus, if we borrow money for 60 days, the time period is 60/360, or one sixth of a year.

To illustrate the accounting for a short-term note and its interest, assume that a firm buys machinery on March 15 for $10,000 and gives a 15 percent, 90-day note in exchange. This note promises payment on June 13 (the maturity date) of $10,000 plus interest at the rate of 15 percent, namely $375 ($10,000 × 0.15 × 90/360). The initial value of this note is its face value of $10,000. The present value will grow to $10,375 by the end of 90 days.[5] In making entries for this note payable, we must be sure to accrue the interest for the time passed in an adjusting entry whenever an accounting period ends. Because the legal document explicitly recognizes interest as a separate item, accountants accrue the contractual interest in a separate liability account.

If the firm's accounting period ends on May 31, the following entries would be made in connection with the above note:

---

[5] The conceptual valuation base for interest-bearing monetary claims is called present value. Present value concepts and procedures are explained in the Appendix to Chapter 10 and are applied to other types of short-term notes and to long-term bond liabilities in Chapter 10.

| | | | |
|---|---|---|---|
| Mar. 15 | Machinery ........................... | 10,000.00 | |
| | Notes Payable ..................... | | 10,000.00 |
| | To record purchase of machinery in exchange for a 15 percent, 90-day note. | | |
| May 31 | Interest Expense ...................... | 320.83 | |
| | Interest Payable ................... | | 320.83 |
| | To accrue interest at 15 percent for 77 days (16 days in March, 30 days in April, and 31 days in May). | | |
| June 13 | Interest Expense ...................... | 54.17 | |
| | Interest Payable ................... | | 54.17 |
| | To accrue interest at 15 percent for 13 days. | | |
| | Interest Payable ...................... | 375.00 | |
| | Notes Payable ....................... | 10,000.00 | |
| | Cash ............................ | | 10,375.00 |
| | To record the payment of liabilities for interest and principal. | | |

## Dividends

One additional temporary account, Dividends Declared, deserves mention. Dividends involve a pro-rata distribution of assets by a corporation to its stockholders. If a $50,000 dividend is declared and paid immediately, the entry is:

| | | |
|---|---|---|
| Dividends Declared .............................. | 50,000 | |
| Cash ............................................ | | 50,000 |

More commonly, the dividend is declared, but payment occurs later. At the date of declaration the corporation creates a legal obligation to distribute assets to its stockholders. This act reduces the net assets and remaining equity of the owners. The entry is:

| | | |
|---|---|---|
| Dividends Declared .............................. | 50,000 | |
| Dividends Payable .............................. | | 50,000 |

The Dividends Declared account records the decline in owners' equity when assets are withdrawn by the owners of the business entity or are promised to them. For information reasons a separate temporary account is often used instead of a direct debit to Retained Earnings.

Unlike interest, dividends do not accrue merely with the passage of time. When declared, however, the dividend represents a decrease in retained earnings and a corresponding increase in a current liability. The actual distribution of assets subsequent to the dividend declaration simply liquidates the current liability.

## Summary of Period Activities

The special-purpose accounts studied so far include the following:

| Increases in Owners' Equity | Decreases in Owners' Equity |
|---|---|
| Revenues | Operating Expenses |
| Gains | Losses |
| | Taxes |
| | Interest |
| | Dividends |

They have one trait in common; they reflect periodic increases and decreases in retained earnings. The reason for the change is different for each type of account. Each one—revenues, operating expenses, gains, losses, interest, and taxes—represents a particular aspect of periodic performance; together they affect the net change in retained earnings *via the final net income figure*. Dividends are treated as a *distribution* of a portion of the income to the owners; they are not an expense affecting the *determination* of net income.

These new temporary owners' equity accounts fit conveniently into our basic balance sheet framework. What began in Chapter 2 as a simple accounting equation now can be expanded to include the different components of the income statement. The following schema shows the relation between the flows of the income statement and the stocks of the balance sheet.

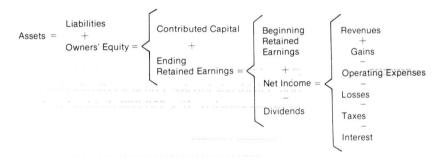

**Net Income to the Owners.**   Owners, as the ultimate risk-takers in the business, are assumed to be the major audience of financial accounting. Consistent with the overall objective of financial accounting to serve its audience, the perspective of the stockholders dominates the income calculation. The foregoing diagram and analysis reflect this viewpoint. Net income is the net asset amount available to the owners. Thus, revenues, operating expenses, gains, losses, interest, and taxes are all *determinants of net income from the owners' view*. Only dividends are treated as a *deduction from* net income.

Net income is almost always interpreted in accounting practice in this way. It is the net increase in the stockholder interest in the business caused by all periodic business activities except dividends. However, as we shall see in the next section, some definitional and disclosure issues associated with the concept of accounting income still remain unresolved.

**AN EXPANDED CONCEPT OF ACCOUNTING INCOME**

Up to this chapter our concept of accounting income has encompassed only revenues and expenses. Having introduced additional owners' equity changes, we must now address two additional questions:

1.  How broadly or narrowly should periodic business activities be defined?

2. How should these various changes in retained earnings be displayed on the financial statements?

The first question asks whether information about all activities that produce changes in retained earnings during the period should be reported on the income statement, or whether the income statement should be restricted only to the main or regular, profit-directed activities. The Financial Accounting Standards Board has coined the term *comprehensive income* to describe "the change in equity (net assets) of an entity during a period from transactions and other events and circumstances . . . except those resulting from investments by owners and distributions to owners."[6] However, the Board has left to other authoritative pronouncements, some issued and some yet to be issued, the specifications of which elements of comprehensive income should comprise *net income* in accounting reports.

The second question recognizes that, even within the array of owners' equity changes selected for inclusion in the calculation of reported net income, several relevant subtotals could be singled out for emphasis. An "operating income" figure derived from "normal" revenues and expenses could be separately disclosed. Many firms claim that an income subtotal before and after income taxes is relevant. Moreover, reporting procedures must be developed to communicate information about changes in retained earnings that are not included in net income.

There are no simple answers to these two questions. Conceivably, we may have a whole series of different income figures and formats, depending on the view or the purposes of the user. Without attempting to resolve these questions (if indeed there is a resolution), we will consider some of the basic ideas and procedures involved in the definition of income and the reporting of owners' equity changes. The first section, Reporting of Unusual Items, provides some background for the first question. The second section, Income Statement Formats, addresses the question of alternative disclosures in the financial statement. Chapter 16 discusses in much greater detail the specific problems in defining net income and reporting unusual items.

## Reporting of Unusual Items

One extremely perplexing problem related to income statement preparation is the reporting of unusual increases and decreases in retained earnings during a period. In a realistic situation, any or all of the following types of events not related to normal operations might occur during the current year.

1. The firm sells some worn-out equipment for more than its book value.
2. One entire plant is demolished by a tornado.

---

[6] *FASB Concepts No. 3*, par. 56.

3. A tax refund is received in the current period, resulting from the settlement of income tax litigation relating to income from three years ago.

4. Plant assets purchased two years ago have been erroneously charged as maintenance expense. The error is discovered and corrected in the current period.

5. The building housing the administrative headquarters is being depreciated over a 50-year useful life. In the current year, its life is revised downward to only 30 years.

6. The firm has been recognizing its extensive expenditures for the development of its computer system as an asset to be depreciated over a three-year period. In the current period, company accountants decide to treat such costs as a period expense. The existing assets are written off.

Where and how should these items be reported? Each of these events causes a change in owners' equity during the current period; they are all part of comprehensive income. However, should they all enter in the determination of current *net income*? If not, how should they be reported? Which ones would you include in net income?

Historically, there have been two schools of thought on the items to be included on the income statement. One, known as the *all-inclusive* income statement concept, argues that the income statement of the current period should reflect all transactions and events, normal or unusual, affecting owners' equity during the period—except, of course, transactions in capital stock and dividends. In this way a series of income statements gives a complete history of the retained earnings account.

The contrasting view asserts that only changes in retained earnings arising from normal, recurring operating activities should be reported on the income statement. Then the net income number would reflect only the *current operating performance* during the period. This view is founded on the belief that the primary uses of the income statement are to facilitate comparisons with other companies and periods, to enable investors to forecast future earnings and cash flows, and to measure the efficiency with which management utilized the resources of the business entity during the current period. The inclusion of unusual, nonrecurring, or nonoperating items would distort the net income figure for these purposes.

This division of thought again illustrates the basic dilemma of financial accounting in trying to serve a number of different objectives and audiences. The first belief views net income as a measure of the total change in stockholder wealth during the period. The second one emphasizes net income as an earnings predictor or a performance measurement. Which is net income to be? Both appear relevant to the overall objectives set forth in Chapter 1. Not only is knowledge lacking about the purposes financial statements serve, but also no one really knows exactly by whom they will be used and whether the user is qualified to evaluate the contents of the report. Consequently, these issues are extremely difficult to resolve theoretically.

Since 1966 the Accounting Principles Board and the Financial Accounting Standards Board have issued five major opinions and standards in an attempt to eliminate the diversity in practice in the reporting of unusual events affecting retained earnings. In general, these pronouncements are consistent with the all-inclusive view. They classify the special changes in retained earnings into various categories, for example, unusual charges and credits (tax refund), extraordinary items (tornado loss), accounting errors (treatment of plant acquisitions as a maintenance expense), and changes in accounting estimates (change in useful life). Detailed procedures are prescribed for reporting each category on the financial statements. A discussion of the resulting regulations and their current applications is better left to Chapter 16. By then we will have developed some concrete examples and analyzed many of the specific situations and events out of which the unusual items arise.

**Income Statement Formats**

In addition to the question of whether certain unusual items should be included in the calculation of net income, accountants must wrestle with a second issue. What format is best for displaying information on the income statement? Two general approaches have surfaced in accounting practice. They are called the single-step and multiple-step formats. Tables 5–1 and 5–2 illustrate these formats, using the same hypothetical income statement data of National Converters, Inc. Both statements use the most common heading, "Statement of Income." However, other titles fre-

**TABLE 5–1  Single-Step Income Statement**

NATIONAL CONVERTERS, INC.
Statement of Income
For the Year Ended December 31, 1984
($000)

| | |
|---|---:|
| Revenues and gains: | |
| Sales revenue | $1,260.2 |
| Dividend revenue | 90.4 |
| Rent revenue | 16.3 |
| Gain on sale of land | 84.9 |
| | 1,451.8 |
| Expenses and losses: | |
| Cost of goods sold | 686.5 |
| Selling expenses | 210.2 |
| Administrative expenses | 176.0 |
| Depreciation expense | 61.8 |
| Loss on sale of investments | 49.1 |
| Interest expense | 16.1 |
| Income taxes | 137.0 |
| | 1,336.7 |
| Net income | $  115.1 |

quently encountered are "Statement of Earnings" and "Statement of Operations."

**Single-Step Income Statement.** The format shown in Table 5–1 is the more common of the two. All revenues and gains are grouped together, as are the revenue deductions. Although other subtotals besides the single net income figure may be helpful for some purposes, advocates of the single-step form reason that the simplified presentation focuses attention on the most important figure while allowing intelligent readers of the statement to use the figures in whatever ways are appropriate for *their* purposes.

**Multiple-Step Income Statement.** This approach follows the view that the purpose of the income statement is to communicate information for a number of different purposes. Therefore, data are arranged to highlight significant relationships and subtotals on the statement. Notice the various "income" subtotals in Table 5–2. The operating income figure, for example, reflects the performance from the firm's main business activities.

Many analysts see the multiple-step income statement as a way of dealing with the requirements of an all-inclusive income statement. Operating income from main activities can be segregated from the impact of peripheral activities. The effect on income from abnormal or unusual events can be distinguished, and the special nature of income taxes can be highlighted. Investors and creditors will thus be better able to assess the

**TABLE 5–2  Multiple-Step Income Statement**

NATIONAL CONVERTERS, INC.
Statement of Income
For the Year Ended December 31, 1984
($000)

| | | |
|---|---:|---:|
| Sales | | $1,260.2 |
| Cost of goods sold | | 686.5 |
| Gross margin | | 573.7 |
| Operating expenses: | | |
| Selling | $210.2 | |
| Administrative | 176.0 | |
| Depreciation | 61.8 | 448.0 |
| Operating income | | 125.7 |
| Other revenue and (expenses): | | |
| Dividend revenue | 90.4 | |
| Rent revenue | 16.3 | |
| Interest expense | (16.1) | 90.6 |
| Income from recurring activities | | 216.3 |
| Gains and (losses): | | |
| Gain on sale of land | 84.9 | |
| Loss on sale of investments | (49.1) | 35.8 |
| Income before income taxes | | 252.1 |
| Income taxes | | 137.0 |
| Net income | | $  115.1 |

amounts, timing, and uncertainty of the future cash flows of the enterprise.

Some accountants object to the multiple-step approach on two grounds. First, the sequential subtraction of various expenses may erroneously imply a preferential recovery of costs. Of course, all costs rank the same in being matched against revenues. None has priority over the others, and there can be no final income unless all costs are recovered. Secondly, cluttering up the statement with numerous income subtotals may detract from, rather than add to, clarity of presentation. The latter assertion seems contrary to the technical competence assumed in Chapter 1 for the financial accounting audience.

As we shall see in Chapter 16, many authoritative pronouncements require that certain unusual events be segregated on the income statement. To this extent, some form of the multiple-step approach may be mandated. In fact, a slight drift toward multiple-step approaches seems to be building in accounting practice. Most published financial statements follow formats somewhere between the two extremes. Indeed even most single-step statements report income taxes as a separate deduction.

**Statement of Retained Earnings.** To reconcile completely the period's change in retained earnings with the balances on the comparative position statements, most firms introduce a separate statement of retained earnings. The statement starts with the balance of retained earnings at the beginning of the year, adds the amount of net income shown on the income statement, and deducts dividends. In addition, other rare direct debits and credits to retained earnings from prior period errors, restrictions of retained earnings, or adjustments associated with capital stock transactions are reported there. An example of such a statement is shown for National Converters, Inc., in Table 5–3.

**TABLE 5–3   Example of Statement of Retained Earnings**

NATIONAL CONVERTERS, INC.
Statement of Retained Earnings
For the Year Ended December 31, 1984
($000)

| | |
|---|---:|
| Retained earnings, December 31, 1983 | $1,796.3 |
| Correction of accounting error from prior period | 47.2 |
| Balance as adjusted | 1,843.5 |
| Net income | 115.1 |
| | 1,958.6 |
| Dividends | 93.8 |
| Retained earnings, December 31, 1984 | $1,864.8 |

In Chapter 16 we will define accounting errors precisely and discuss other aspects of their disclosure on the statement of retained earnings. Given the strong inclination toward an all-inclusive income statement found in regulatory pronouncements, items other than net income and dividends are rarely found on most statements of retained earnings.

**AN INTRO-
DUCTION TO
THE ARMCO
ANNUAL
REPORT**

National Converters, Inc., used in this chapter as an example, is a hypothetical company, and its statements are simplified and condensed. In the Appendix to this chapter the entire Financial Section of the Annual Report of Armco, Inc., has been reproduced. This material comprised pages 24–45 of the company's 1981 annual report.

Armco is a major worldwide company operating in a number of diversified lines of business. Many are associated with steel and would be classified as heavy industry. Armco is also active in aerospace materials and operates a number of financial services companies. Its corporate headquarters are in Middletown, Ohio.

The Armco accounting statements and other financial information will be used as a continuing example throughout the rest of this book. Beginning in this chapter and appearing in subsequent ones will be sections devoted to discussions of the Armco statements and the underlying accounting procedures. A portion of each chapter will contain a descriptive elaboration of this real-world example, relating the subject matter of that chapter to Armco's published statements. Our goal is to show that what is being discussed in the chapters has direct applicability to your understanding of actual financial reports.[7]

**An Overview of
the Financial
Section**

Armco's annual report is distributed each year to stockholders and other interested parties. In addition to the financial section, the annual report contains (1) letters to the stockholders from the chairman of the board and from the chief executive and chief operating officers, (2) some highlights concerning financial and operating data, and (3) a description with pictures of each of the company's six major lines of business. None of this information has been reproduced.

The financial section itself consists of five major parts—the accountants' opinion, the financial statements, notes to the financial statements, management's discussion and analysis, and supplementary disclosures showing the impact of inflation and presenting other pertinent information. Although we will refer often to these sections in greater detail in subsequent chapters, let us review each of them briefly here.

1. The accountants' opinion or auditor's report contains the professional judgment of the company's independent certified public accountant (CPA) concerning the financial statements. As the statement above the accountants' opinion indicates, management bears the primary responsibility for the accuracy and fairness of the information presented. The auditor, however, provides advice and guidance to management in matters

---

[7] The authors greatly appreciate the cooperation of the people at Armco and their willingness to let us use their annual report for this purpose. Armco was selected because, while its financial reporting is reasonably complex, the statements are presented in a straightforward manner, and the disclosures are quite complete. The accounting procedures and reporting practices used by Armco are chosen solely for illustration. They are not intended to represent either desirable or undesirable reporting practices.

of financial reporting and serves as an independent check on management's representations.

2. Armco shows the three primary financial statements that we introduced in Chapter 1. These are the statement of income, statement of changes in financial position, and the statement of financial position (balance sheet). In addition, there is a statement showing the changes in all the various shareholders' equity accounts. Notice that all of these statements are presented in comparative form. The term *consolidated* used in the statement titles means that Armco owns a number of other corporations whose results have been combined in the financial reports.

3. The notes to the financial statements contain a wealth of interpretive and elaborative information. They identify many of the accounting principles employed. They may also disclose the financial impact of any material changes in procedures from year to year. Significant contractual or other arrangements affecting the relationship between the business enterprise and other parties are listed and explained. The reader's attention may also be called to any material events occurring after the date of the statements. The notes often will be crucial to our understanding of some of the complex reporting issues discussed in later chapters.

4. The Securities and Exchange Commission requires that management provide in the annual report a narrative explanation of period-to-period changes in the major components of the income statement and statement of changes in financial position. Such explanations provide a meaningful backdrop against which the reader can interpret the numerical results.

5. Inflation accounting is one major type of supplementary disclosure in the annual report. It is discussed briefly in Chapters 8 and 9 and extensively in Chapter 19. The different ways of trying to report the impact of changing prices on the financial statements are explained there. Moreover, the current reporting requirements applying to Armco and other firms are reviewed and illustrated. Information relating to Armco's lines of business and other financial data are other supplementary disclosures contained in this section of the annual report. Many of these disclosures are mandated by the SEC. Some of these are examined in Chapter 16.

## An Overview of the Financial Statements

The three primary financial statements can be reviewed in light of our discussion in this chapter and previous ones. Our review here will be a general one, inasmuch as later we will be exploring many items in detail.

**Income Statement.** Armco uses a hybrid format for its income statement. All revenues are presented together except the item called Equity in Net Income of AFSG (AFSG is Armco Financial Services Group). Similarly, all expenses except income taxes are shown as a group. Notice that included in this group in 1980 were some unusual items—gains from sale of investments and from litigation settlements—as negative entries. Two income subtotals are highlighted before the overall net income figure is calculated. One reports income before taxes; and the other, income before recognition of the earnings from Armco's investment in insurance and finance leasing companies.

Under GAAP Armco must present its per share net income at the bottom of the income statement. The accounting policies that influence its calculation of net income are indicated as part of Note 1, as are the specific procedures used for the EPS calculation.

**Statement of Financial Position.**   Armco's balance sheet employs the account form, with assets on one page and equities (liabilities and shareholders' equity) on the facing page. Its assets are classified into seven sections. The current assets are typical except that prepaid expenses have been excluded. These are included with the long-term prepayments under Prepaid Expenses and Deferred Charges. The other noncurrent assets consist of investments; a long-term receivable (Due from AFSG); property, plant, and equipment; capitalized lease rights; and goodwill.

Only the latter two are new to us. Capitalized lease rights are a special class of property, plant, and equipment financed through the signing of long-term lease contracts. Detailed information on the leases is provided by Armco in Note 4; we will discuss capitalized leases in Chapter 11. Included in Note 1 is a brief explanation of the nature of the account called Excess of Cost over Equity in Net Assets of Purchased Businesses. This amount represents the amount paid by Armco for economic benefits over and above the specifically identifiable assets associated with acquired companies.

The liabilities on the Armco balance sheet are divided into current and long-term. The former classification contains a typical and detailed listing. The noncurrent liabilities have been presented in five different categories: (1) long-term debt, (2) long-term capitalized lease obligations—a special type of long-term debt, (3) deferred income taxes, (4) an amount owed to its financial and insurance companies, and (5) other. The first four illustrate concepts and procedures discussed in subsequent chapters. Notice that the portion of long-term debt that is payable during 1982 is shown as a current liability rather than as a long-term one.

The shareholders' equity section is quite complicated. There are two kinds of capital stock—preferred and common (see Chapter 14). Armco uses the title "Income retained in the business" instead of the more familiar "Retained earnings." The two subtractions at the bottom are specialized adjustments that we will discuss latter.

**Statement of Changes in Financial Position.**   In Chapter 1 we briefly introduced this statement but postponed any detailed discussion of it until Chapter 17. The statement attempts to show major sources and uses of funds. Armco's statement is atypical in two respects. First, it defines funds as cash and marketable securities rather than as working capital, the common definition. Armco then explains its major financing and investing activities in terms of inflows and outflows of cash and marketable securities. The second unusual aspect is the statement format itself. Most companies show all sources of funds together but separate from all the uses of funds. Armco intersperses sections of sources and uses; note that sequential sections often have positive totals followed by negative totals and vice versa. Moreover, with some sections (e.g., financing) both events that provide cash and events that use cash are shown.

## A REFLECTION ON ACCOUNTING INCOME

Much of the discussion in this chapter emphasizes the tentative nature of income measurement. In light of the problems associated with implementation of the matching concept and the uncertainty as to what exactly constitutes "net income," any amount so labeled must be carefully examined by readers of the financial statements. These amounts are no more accurate than the concepts on which they are founded and the solutions to the problems encountered when the concepts are put to use. These concepts are also no more concrete than the objectives to which they contribute and the characteristics of the audiences which they are designed to serve. Inasmuch as this chapter completes the first section on fundamental concepts and procedures, a brief review of the relationship between the conceptual framework and the financial statements is in order.

### Problems with the Conceptual Framework

Implicit in much of our discussion of accounting theory is that the output of the accounting system must be useful. Statements of objectives, assumptions about audience characteristics, qualitative guidelines, and generally accepted accounting principles all exist to enhance decision usefulness. The state-of-the-art thinking about a conceptual framework was discussed in Chapter 1. However, this is only a beginning. A number of fundamental issues and questions still need to be addressed or refined.

**1. Identification of Users.**   Who are the primary users of financial statements? Are they sufficiently homogeneous in their personal goals, tolerance for risk, time horizon, and expertise that a single set of general-purpose financial statements can serve their needs? Should financial accounting instead present several sets, differing in various ways? Inconsistencies remain in accounting that can be traced to a failure to distinguish between sophisticated and unsophisticated investors. The notion of general-purpose statements designed to serve common needs continually conflicts with the notion of differential disclosures designed to recognize heterogeneous needs.

**2. Specification of Information Needs.**   What are the information needs of our user groups? How should they be determined? Which of these needs can financial statements most effectively fulfill? Are existing financial statements the appropriate media for communicating this information? How is financial accounting information currently being used? How *might* it be used? How *should* it be used?

**3. Purpose of the Income Figure.** Can a single net income concept or a single income statement serve all the purposes that users currently seem to require? They use the income figure for many purposes, among them (*a*) to evaluate the overall performance of management in administering the firm's resources, (*b*) to predict future levels of profits, dividends, and cash flows, (*c*) to determine the ability of the firm to pay its debts, and (*d*) to measure the increase in the wealth of an enterprise. Which, if any, of these should be paramount in guiding the development of accounting theory and practice? How shall increases in wealth be defined? The lack of clear-cut answers to all of these questions will haunt many of our attempts to refine our techniques of income measurement.

**4. Resolution of Conflicts.** How can the accounting profession develop principles which are responsive to user needs and yet are capable of being implemented? If objectives or principles conflict, how can the differences be accommodated? Can the qualitative guidelines be made operational? We shall find numerous examples where the difficulty of making trade-offs among qualitative characteristics and among measurement principles contributes to the complexity found in accounting practice. What are the roles to be played by relevance and reliability vis-à-vis one another?

**5. Investor Reaction to Accounting Data.** How do accountants determine whether the financial statements contain useful information? Are investors misled by errors, differences, or changes in accounting methods? A large and growing body of empirical research suggests that, although changes in accounting earnings are related to changes in stock prices, investors in the aggregate see through changes and differences in accounting methods that have no economic substance or impact on future cash flows. The market for stock prices seems to be efficient; it processes new information from many sources quickly and in an unbiased manner. Do these results suggest that disclosure issues are more important than measurement issues? More fundamentally, should financial reporting swing its emphasis from individual users to aggregate users? This "capital markets" research has important but unclear implications for the development of financial accounting principles.

## Influence of Basic Assumptions

The accounting profession will be grappling with all of these questions as it forges future developments in the conceptual framework. Our concern in this section is to review the interrelationship between the extant conceptual framework and the financial statements.

In Chapter 1 we saw that seven fundamental assumptions form the basic fabric into which are woven the many principles and procedures of financial accounting. These assumptions are declaratory assertions, not discovered truths. As such, they exert an influence on financial statements only so long as and to the extent that they are accepted by the accounting profession and ultimately by the users of financial statements.

**Environmental Assumptions.** Three basic assumptions—entity concept, going-concern concept, and monetary concept—describe the environmental elements of financial accounting. The first two help set the stage for financial statements. Their initial impact is obvious. The *separate-entity concept* defines the organizational unit covered by the statements and hence determines which items are included in assets, liabilities, and so on, and which transactions get recorded. The *going-concern concept* supplies the rationale behind the matching concept. Specifically, it focuses attention away from periodic liquidation values for assets and allows for the allocation of costs, such as depreciation, over the useful lives of the noncurrent assets.

The *monetary concept* obviously supports the use of dollar amounts in the communication process. It also asserts that dollars of different vintages can be added together. Only by assuming that fluctuations in the value of the dollar can be ignored or are insignificant are we able to sum the cash in the bank, the cost of the merchandise bought in December of last year, and the amount spent on constructing a building 10 years ago into a single amount called total assets. Although the monetary postulate aids the meaningful presentation of information, it may impair interpretation in times of monetary instability. If there is an increase in the general price level, causing the size of the measuring unit to decline, the various asset items really cannot be added together. The yardstick with which the accountant measures dollar amounts changes over time. The ignoring of price-level changes in conventional accounting statements has become increasingly limiting. As a consequence, current reporting standards require that supplementary information about the impact of changing price levels be included in most annual reports. This subject is covered in greater depth in Chapter 19.

**Operational Assumptions.** The remaining four assumptions relate closely to the process of income measurement. The *matching concept* provides the major foundation for the income statement. It asserts that resources consumed during the period which have a direct association (as does merchandise) or an indirect association (as do office salaries) with the revenue of the period should be related to those revenues in the calculation of periodic net income. As a corollary, any unexpired resources appear as residuals (assets) on the position statement.

The particular matching concept underlying conventional financial accounting (matching of acquisition cost and revenue) derives from the *cost principle* for asset valuation discussed in Chapter 2. This principle in turn results from the *exchange-price concept*, which states that resources entering the accounting process should be assigned monetary values based on the prices implicit in the original exchange transactions. Expense recognition principles result from the interface of the matching and exchange-price concepts. The former determines when expenses are recognized, and the latter provides how much.

The matching concept is only one of several approaches to income measurement. Conventional accounting rejects as too uncertain and subjective concepts of "economic income" based on *expectations* about future cash flows, even though such future events are doubtless relevant to current decision making. Rather, the matching concept presumes that the basic subject matter of financial accounting is actual transactions, usually with outside parties. Therefore, it emphasizes primarily a *historical* perspective. Because of their objective tone, accounting reports may also have predictive value, but these income projections are left to the judgment of the individual user.

The resultant recording of assets at historical acquisition cost imparts a conservative bias to the interpretation of items on the balance sheet. Assets are not revalued before being matched against the revenue they produce. Other matching concepts could be used in the calculation of income. These might employ various types of current values for measuring the assets being matched against revenues. In Chapter 19 we explore some of these other concepts of income measurement.

In the area of *revenue recognition*, financial accounting usually insists on a market transaction in which the firm supplies some good or service to a consuming unit outside the entity before recognition is given to value changes in the assets. However, increases and decreases in the value of assets do not suddenly come into economic being as the firm acquires various input factors and uses them to produce a salable output. By insisting that revenue be earned and reliably measured before being recognized, financial accounting may exaggerate the importance of the sales transaction and may tend to delay the recognition of accretion in values beyond the time of their occurrence. Also, different revenue recognition expedients may cause the timing of income to vary, since revenue recognition is the initiating event in the matching process.

*The periodicity concept* also exerts a direct impact on the financial statements. By establishing a time framework within which matching occurs, it ensures that the income statement is always prepared for a specified time period. In a sense the classifications of current and noncurrent on the position statement also spring from the concept of the accounting period. The concept of the accounting period routinely causes numerous measurement problems that limit the precision of accounting net income. Although our basic data—revenues and expenses—result from market transactions, fitting them into an arbitrary time framework requires subjective judgments. The adjusting entries for accruals and prepayments and the period cost concept are two examples of such judgments. In future chapters some additional estimating procedures and assumptions are introduced, primarily for the purpose of matching costs and revenues within a specified time period. On the one hand the periodicity concept requires the accrual basis of accounting. On the other hand it increases the tentativeness of the income calculation. At best, the income figure serves only as an *index* of a continuing stream of economic and financial activity.

**A Final Note**     All of the basic assumptions of financial accounting serve simultaneously to enhance and to limit the usefulness of the statements. They are not immutable decrees; neither are they random assertions. They lead to some reasonable and useful, albeit tentative, conclusions about the nature and management of a firm's resources. They certainly do not produce precise figures or even "correct" figures according to other standards. To view the financial statements apart from the assumptions on which they rest or to use accounting measurements without being aware of their limitations is foolhardy.

One other point concerning the conventional accounting concept of income should be kept in mind. Although perhaps overall it is more certain and less subjective than alternative income systems, it is still a concept, not a precise measurement. A potential hazard to the unwary reader of an income statement is that different methods can be used for matching particular costs against revenues. Faced with inconclusive evidence as to the exact relationships between costs and revenues and with uncertainty as to how the end result is used, accountants have adopted a number of reasonable yet arbitrary procedures to implement the matching concept. The handling of period costs is one example encountered so far; many others are discussed in later chapters. If there is no single "right way" for handling particular items, there can hardly be any single resultant figure that represents *the correct* net income.

The purpose of this chapter and of this first section is to provide an insight into the items that appear on conventional financial accounting statements, particularly the income statement. With an understanding of the meaning and implications of these terms and concepts and given sufficient information through explanation or disclosure, the reader should be able to ascertain the elements comprising a particular net income figure, evaluate its usefulness, and maybe modify it for a specific purpose.

In the next section we talk in greater detail about specific problems in the measurement of accounting income. There the reader has occasion to employ many of the accounts and concepts discussed in this chapter and section.

## APPENDIX: Financial Section of 1981 Armco Annual Report

# Financial Section

**Contents**

## Responsibility for Financial Reporting

Armco Shareholders:
The information presented in this Annual Report was prepared by your Company's management. We prepared the financial statements in accordance with generally accepted accounting principles in the United States. These principles require choices among alternatives and numerous estimates of financial matters. We believe the accounting principles chosen are appropriate in the circumstances and the estimates and judgments involved in Armco's financial reporting are reasonable and conservative. We have included other financial and operating data that we think will be useful to investors.

Armco's management is responsible for the integrity and objectivity of the financial information presented in this Annual Report. We maintain a system of internal accounting control and a program of internal audits. They are designed to provide reasonable assurance that the financial reports are fairly presented and that Armco employees comply with our stated policies and procedures, including policies on the ethical conduct of business. We continually review and update our policies and system of internal accounting control as our businesses and business conditions change.

Management recommended and the Audit Review Committee of the Board of Directors approved the hiring of Deloitte Haskins & Sells as independent auditors for the Company. Deloitte Haskins & Sells expresses an informed professional opinion on Armco's financial statements. You can find it below.

The Audit Review Committee, composed solely of independent outside directors, performs an oversight role relating to Armco's public financial reporting. The Audit Review Committee meets periodically with management, Deloitte Haskins & Sells, and Armco's internal auditors, both privately and collectively, to discuss internal accounting control and financial reporting matters. Deloitte Haskins & Sells and Armco's internal auditors have free access to the Audit Review Committee to discuss any matters.

We believe Armco's internal control system, combined with the activities of the internal and independent auditors and the Audit Review Committee, provide you reasonable assurance of the integrity of our financial reporting.

*R. J. Lambrix*
R.J. Lambrix
Corporate Vice President—
Corporate Finance & Treasurer

---

*Accountants' Opinion*

**DELOITTE**
**HASKINS + SELLS**
CERTIFIED PUBLIC ACCOUNTANTS

425 WALNUT STREET
CINCINNATI 45202

Armco, Its Shareholders and Directors:

We have examined the statements of consolidated financial position of Armco and consolidated subsidiaries as of December 31, 1981 and 1980, and the related consolidated statements of income, shareholders' equity, and changes in financial position for each of the three calendar years in the period ended December 31, 1981. Our examinations were made in accordance with generally accepted auditing standards and, accordingly, included such tests of the accounting records and such other auditing procedures as we considered necessary in the circumstances.

In our opinion, such financial statements present fairly the financial position of Armco and consolidated subsidiaries at December 31, 1981 and 1980, and the results of their operations and changes in their financial position for each of the three calendar years in the period ended December 31, 1981, in conformity with generally accepted accounting principles consistently applied during the period except for the change, with which we concur, in 1981 in the method of accounting for foreign currency translation as described in Note 1 of Notes to Financial Statements.

*Deloitte Haskins & Sells*

February 11, 1982

*25*

## Statement of Consolidated Income
For the years ended December 31, 1981, 1980, and 1979
(Dollars in millions, except per share amounts)

|  | 1981 | 1980 | 1979 |
|---|---|---|---|
| **Revenues** | | | |
| Net sales | $6,906.0 | $5,678.0 | $5,035.1 |
| Interest, royalties and other income | 51.5 | 33.1 | 29.4 |
| Total | 6,957.5 | 5,711.1 | 5,064.5 |
| **Cost and Expenses** | | | |
| Cost of products sold | 5,937.4 | 4,936.7 | 4,301.9 |
| Selling and administrative expenses | 495.3 | 430.2 | 361.6 |
| Interest expense | 70.2 | 59.8 | 56.0 |
| Gain on sale of investments (Note 1) | — | (42.9) | — |
| Litigation settlement (Note 9) | — | (34.0) | — |
| Sundry other—net | 2.3 | 17.6 | 17.4 |
| Total | 6,505.2 | 5,367.4 | 4,736.9 |
| **Income Before Income Taxes** (Note 5) | 452.3 | 343.7 | 327.6 |
| **Provision for Income Taxes** (Note 5) | | | |
| Current—Federal | 68.2 | 36.1 | 16.1 |
| Foreign and state | 55.1 | 50.9 | 35.7 |
| Deferred | 64.8 | 28.6 | 70.6 |
| Total | 188.1 | 115.6 | 122.4 |
| **Income of Armco and Consolidated Subsidiaries** | 264.2 | 228.1 | 205.2 |
| **Equity in Net Income of AFSG** (Note 2) | 30.3 | 37.2 | 43.5 |
| **Net Income** | $ 294.5 | $ 265.3 | $ 248.7 |
| **Per Share** | | | |
| Common Stock | | | |
| Income | | | |
| Primary | $ 4.97 | $ 4.73 | $ 4.51 |
| Fully diluted | 4.82 | 4.52 | 4.29 |
| Dividends | 1.72 | 1.57 | 1.43 |
| Preferred Stock Dividends | 2.10 | 2.10 | 2.10 |

*See Notes to Financial Statements on pages 31 through 35.*

Armco and Consolidated Subsidiaries

## Statement of Changes in Consolidated Financial Position
For the years ended December 31, 1981, 1980, and 1979 (Dollars in millions)

| | 1981 | 1980 | 1979 |
|---|---|---|---|
| **Funds Provided From (Funds Used In):** | | | |
| Operations | | | |
| Net Income | $ 294.5 | $ 265.3 | $ 248.7 |
| Depreciation | 166.5 | 142.0 | 133.3 |
| Lease right amortization | 7.8 | 7.8 | 7.8 |
| Deferred income taxes (Note 5) | 64.4 | 27.2 | 65.2 |
| Equity in net income of AFSG | (30.3) | (37.2) | (43.5) |
| Dividends paid to Armco by AFSG | — | 40.0 | 0.3 |
| Other—net | 16.6 | 15.7 | 6.8 |
| Total | 519.5 | 460.8 | 418.6 |
| **Working Capital (excluding cash, marketable securities and notes payable)** | | | |
| Inventories—net of LIFO | (205.6) | (37.9) | (133.1) |
| Notes and accounts receivable | (137.5) | (206.2) | (40.9) |
| Accounts payable and other accruals | 12.7 | 142.1 | 19.9 |
| Ladish Co. working capital acquired | (151.5) | — | — |
| Total | (481.9) | (102.0) | (154.1) |
| **Capital Expenditures and Investments** | | | |
| Capital expenditures | (393.6) | (271.3) | (162.3) |
| Deferred blast furnace reline costs | (2.0) | (21.8) | (13.5) |
| Ladish Co. property, plant and equipment acquired | (68.1) | — | — |
| Notes receivable from sale of business | (52.4) | — | — |
| New investments | (38.4) | (33.2) | (21.3) |
| Other changes in investments—net | 12.9 | 92.3 | 5.9 |
| Change in amount due AFSG | (63.8) | (1.4) | (33.0) |
| Ladish Co. investments acquired | (10.7) | — | — |
| Translation adjustment on property, plant and equipment | 18.2 | — | — |
| Book value of property, plant and equipment retired | 25.5 | 5.6 | 3.3 |
| Total | (572.4) | (229.8) | (220.9) |
| **Financing** | | | |
| Dividends paid | (103.9) | (89.4) | (79.8) |
| Common stock issued for businesses purchased | 297.1 | 18.0 | 9.2 |
| Purchase of common stock for treasury | (29.2) | — | (21.6) |
| Other changes in shareholders' equity | (28.1) | 8.4 | 5.5 |
| Notes payable | 282.9 | 38.5 | (3.1) |
| Proceeds from issuing long-term debt | 163.0 | 11.4 | 13.1 |
| Payments on long-term debt | (25.2) | (27.6) | (46.0) |
| Payments on long-term lease obligations | (9.5) | (9.4) | (6.2) |
| Total | 547.1 | (50.1) | (128.9) |
| **Other** | | | |
| Increase in prepaid expenses and deferred charges | (11.4) | (7.7) | (9.3) |
| Miscellaneous | 7.3 | 8.9 | 11.4 |
| Total | (4.1) | 1.2 | 2.1 |
| **Increase (Decrease) in Cash and Marketable Securities** | 8.2* | 80.1 | (83.2) |
| **Cash and Marketable Securities** | | | |
| Beginning of year | 139.4 | 59.3 | 142.5 |
| End of year | $ 147.6 | $ 139.4 | $ 59.3 |

*Includes Ladish Co. cash and marketable securities acquired of $57.3.
See Notes to Financial Statements on pages 31 through 35.

27

## Statement of Consolidated Financial Position
December 31, 1981 and 1980 (Dollars in millions)

| ASSETS | 1981 | 1980 |
|---|---|---|
| **Current Assets** | | |
| Cash and short-term marketable securities | $ 147.6 | $ 139.4 |
| Accounts and notes receivable | | |
| Trade (less allowance for doubtful accounts of | | |
| $31.7 for 1981 and $27.4 for 1980) | 872.8 | 727.8 |
| Other | 143.2 | 93.2 |
| Inventories (Note 1) | 1,143.1 | 725.4 |
| Total Current Assets | 2,306.7 | 1,685.8 |
| **Investments** (Note 1) | | |
| At cost plus equity | | |
| AFSG (Note 2) | 283.3 | 265.3 |
| Associated companies | 137.1 | 98.6 |
| At cost | 79.1 | 26.2 |
| **Due from AFSG** (Note 2) | 21.7 | — |
| **Property, Plant and Equipment—At Cost** | | |
| Land, land improvements and leaseholds | 222.5 | 176.7 |
| Buildings | 346.2 | 336.7 |
| Machinery and equipment | 2,678.1 | 2,465.4 |
| Other | 171.5 | 163.3 |
| Construction in progress | 173.5 | 113.1 |
| Total | 3,591.8 | 3,255.2 |
| Less accumulated depreciation (Note 1) | 1,779.1 | 1,694.0 |
| Property, Plant and Equipment—Net | 1,812.7 | 1,561.2 |
| **Capitalized Lease Rights (less accumulated amortization of $96.4 for 1981 and $88.6 for 1980)** (Note 4) | 59.4 | 67.2 |
| **Excess of Cost over Equity in Net Assets of Purchased Businesses (Goodwill)** (Note 1) | 14.3 | 12.8 |
| **Prepaid Expenses and Deferred Charges** | 102.9 | 90.3 |
| Total | $4,817.2 | $3,807.4 |

*See Notes to Financial Statements on pages 31 through 35.*

28

Armco and Consolidated Subsidiaries ARMCO

| LIABILITIES AND SHAREHOLDERS' EQUITY | 1981 | 1980 |
|---|---|---|
| **Current Liabilities** | | |
| Notes payable (Note 3) | $ 350.8 | $ 67.9 |
| Accounts payable | | |
| Trade | 247.3 | 266.1 |
| Other | 164.1 | 79.2 |
| Accrued taxes | 121.7 | 98.1 |
| Accrued salaries, wages and commissions | 229.7 | 225.1 |
| Other accruals | 128.1 | 91.6 |
| Current portion of long-term debt and lease obligations | 22.6 | 18.7 |
| Total Current Liabilities | 1,264.3 | 846.7 |
| **Long-Term Debt** (Note 3) | 572.8 | 440.4 |
| **Long-Term Capitalized Lease Obligations** (reduced by amount representing interest of $31.4 for 1981 and $37.0 for 1980) (Note 4) | 107.4 | 115.4 |
| **Deferred Income Taxes** (Note 5) | 322.4 | 251.4 |
| **Due to AFSG** (Note 2) | — | 42.1 |
| **Other Liabilities** | 83.1 | 64.8 |
| **Shareholders' Equity** (Notes 6 and 7) | | |
| Preferred Stock | | |
| Class A—authorized 8,399,068 shares of no par value, issuable in series. Series issued: $2.10 cumulative convertible (involuntary liquidation preference equals $15 per share) | 7.6 | 10.7 |
| Class B—authorized 5,000,000 shares of $1 par value, issuable in series. None issued. | — | — |
| Common Stock—authorized 150,000,000 shares of $5 par value each | 316.5 | 276.6 |
| Additional paid-in capital | 331.2 | 63.4 |
| Income retained in the business | 1,862.0 | 1,695.8 |
| Net foreign currency translation adjustments | (40.5) | — |
| Net unrealized gains (losses) on marketable equity securities of AFSG | (9.6) | 0.1 |
| Total Shareholders' Equity | 2,467.2 | 2,046.6 |
| Total | $4,817.2 | $3,807.4 |

*See Notes to Financial Statements on pages 31 through 35.*

Armco and Consolidated Subsidiaries ARMCO

## Statement of Consolidated Shareholders' Equity
For the years ended December 31, 1981, 1980, and 1979 (Dollars in millions)

| | Preferred Stock | | Common Stock | | Additional Paid-In Capital | Income Retained in the Business | Net Foreign Currency Translation Adjustments (Note 1) | Net Unrealized Gains (Losses) (Note 2) |
|---|---|---|---|---|---|---|---|---|
| | Shares | Amount | Shares | Amount | | | | |
| Balance, December 31, 1978 (after deducting 749,142 common shares in treasury) (Note 1) | 3,399,163 | $14.4 | 53,205,261 | $266.0 | $ 34.9 | $1,366.9 | | $ (4.4) |
| Common stock purchased for treasury | | | (948,260) | (4.8) | (1.0) | (15.8) | | |
| Exercise of stock options | | | 216,465 | 1.1 | 2.8 | | | |
| Exchange of preferred shares | (26,706) | (0.1) | 33,914 | 0.2 | (0.1) | | | |
| Common stock issued in connection with businesses purchased | | | 442,489 | 2.2 | 7.0 | | | |
| Other | | | 83,664 | 0.4 | 1.2 | | | |
| Net income | | | | | | 248.7 | | |
| Cash dividends | | | | | | | | |
| Common | | | | | | (72.7) | | |
| Preferred | | | | | | (7.1) | | |
| Adjustment for net unrealized gains on marketable equity securities of AFSG | | | | | | | | 3.5 |
| Balance, December 31, 1979 (after deducting 1,210,524 common shares in treasury) | 3,372,457 | 14.3 | 53,033,533 | 265.1 | 44.8 | 1,520.0 | | (0.9) |
| Exercise of stock options | | | 436,619 | 2.2 | 6.2 | | | |
| Exchange of preferred shares | (847,483) | (3.6) | 1,076,296 | 5.4 | (1.8) | | | |
| Common stock issued in connection with business purchased | | | 685,682 | 3.4 | 14.6 | | | |
| Other | | | 79,996 | 0.5 | (0.4) | (0.1) | | |
| Net income | | | | | | 265.3 | | |
| Cash dividends | | | | | | | | |
| Common | | | | | | (83.3) | | |
| Preferred | | | | | | (6.1) | | |
| Adjustment for net unrealized gains on marketable equity securities of AFSG | | | | | | | | 1.0 |
| Balance, December 31, 1980 (after deducting 174 common shares in treasury) | 2,524,974 | 10.7 | 55,312,126 | 276.6 | 63.4 | 1,695.8 | | 0.1 |
| Adjustment to reflect beginning balance of net foreign currency translation adjustment (Note 1) | | | | | | | $ (10.5) | |
| Common stock purchased for treasury | | | (827,282) | (4.1) | (1.0) | (24.1) | | |
| Exercise of stock options | | | 290,700 | 1.5 | 7.7 | | | |
| Exchange of preferred shares | (728,787) | (3.1) | 925,512 | 4.6 | (1.5) | | | |
| Common stock issued in connection with businesses purchased | | | 7,489,427 | 37.4 | 259.7 | | | |
| Other | | | 112,764 | 0.5 | 2.9 | (0.3) | | |
| Net income | | | | | | 294.5 | | |
| Cash dividends | | | | | | | | |
| Common | | | | | | (99.5) | | |
| Preferred | | | | | | (4.4) | | |
| Adjustment for net unrealized losses on marketable equity securities of AFSG | | | | | | | | (9.7) |
| Net foreign currency translation adjustment | | | | | | | (30.0) | |
| Balance, December 31, 1981 (after deducting 171,314 common shares in treasury) | 1,796,187 | $ 7.6 | 63,303,247 | $316.5 | $331.2 | $1,862.0 | $ (40.5) | $ (9.6) |

*See Notes to Financial Statements on pages 31 through 35.*

30

## Notes to Our Financial Statements

### Note 1: Summary of Armco's Accounting Policies
**Our Consolidation Policy**
Our annual report's consolidated financial statements include the accounts of Armco and all significant subsidiaries (companies owned 51% or more by Armco) except the Armco Financial Services Group (AFSG). You can find more about AFSG in Note 2.

**Businesses Acquired**
We acquired NN Corporation and subsidiaries effective December 1, 1980, in exchange for 9,424,048 shares of Armco common stock. We accounted for the acquisition of NN as a pooling-of-interests. Armco's prior years' financial statements have been restated.

We acquired Ladish Co. effective October 16, 1981, in exchange for 7,161,594 shares of Armco common stock. We also agreed to issue on October 9, 1982, up to 1,825,504 additional shares of Armco common stock under certain conditions. The acquisition was valued at $286,500,000 and accounted for as a purchase. The value of the acquisition will not change upon issuance of any additional Armco common stock and no goodwill resulted from the acquisition. Ladish's results have been included in Armco's Statement of Consolidated Income since the date of acquisition. The pro forma results of operations for Armco had Ladish been acquired on January 1, 1980 are:

| | (dollars in millions, except per share amounts) | |
| --- | --- | --- |
| | 1981 | 1980 |
| Revenues | $7,369.9 | $6,175.6 |
| Net Income | $ 316.1 | $ 279.8 |
| Income Per Share | | |
| Primary | $ 4.76 | $ 4.29 |
| Fully Diluted | $ 4.64 | $ 4.13 |

**How We Put a Value on Our Investments**
Armco accounts for investments in two ways:
We own AFSG and are engaged in several corporate joint ventures and partnerships. We also own between 20% and 50% of numerous associated companies. We state these investments at our cost, plus our equity in their undistributed earnings since we invested in them. For practical purposes, this amount equals our share in their net equity: Our share of pre-tax earnings of associated companies has been credited to cost of products sold with the related taxes included in income taxes.

Our other investments are stated at our cost or what we could realize on their sale, whichever is lower.

In 1980, we sold an investment in Rowan Companies, Inc. preferred shares increasing our 1980 net income by $31,500,000 and primary income per share by $.57.

**How We Value Our Inventories**
Armco's inventories are valued at the lower of cost or market. Cost of inventories at most of our domestic operations is measured based on the LIFO—Last In, First Out—method. Other inventories are measured principally at average cost.

| | (dollars in millions) | |
| --- | --- | --- |
| | 1981 | 1980 |
| Inventories on LIFO: | | |
| Finished and semi-finished | $ 965.2 | $ 638.8 |
| Raw materials and supplies | 414.8 | 379.8 |
| Total | 1,380.0 | 1,018.6 |
| Less—LIFO reserve | 713.7 | 618.4 |
| Total | 666.3 | 400.2 |
| Inventories on Average: | | |
| Finished and semi-finished | 211.6 | 168.6 |
| Raw materials and supplies | 265.2 | 156.6 |
| Total | 476.8 | 325.2 |
| Total | $1,143.1 | $ 725.4 |

**How We Account for "Goodwill"**
When Armco purchases another business, we call the difference between the current value of that business' net tangible assets and the price we pay "Goodwill". We amortize this difference over 40 years or less.

**How We Record Depreciation**
Armco records depreciation and amortization for steelmaking plant and equipment using a method which adjusts, within limits, straight-line depreciation for the level of production of the particular year. Other depreciation and amortization is calculated on the straight-line method. Leasehold improvements are amortized over the shorter of the life of the related asset or the life of the lease.

**Oil and Gas Operations**
Armco's oil and gas operations (Strata Energy, Inc.) use the "successful efforts" method of accounting set forth in the Statement of Financial Accounting Standards No. 19, *Financial Accounting and Reporting by Oil and Gas Producing Companies.*

**Blast Furnace Relines**
The cost of relining blast furnaces in Armco's steel plants is amortized based on the level of production over the estimated life of the lining.

**How We Record Our Income Taxes**
Armco files a consolidated federal income tax return. This return includes all domestic companies in which Armco owns 80% or more including those in AFSG (see Note 2). We use the flow through method to account for investment and energy tax credits.

We've made no provision for foreign withholding taxes or U.S. income taxes which we might have to pay if the undistributed earnings of our foreign subsidiaries were paid as dividends to Armco. This is because substantially all of these undistributed earnings ($205,600,000 for 1981 and $167,300,000 for 1980) have been permanently reinvested in working capital and fixed assets. If they ever were distributed, foreign tax credits would be available as a reduction of U.S. income taxes.

## How We Fund Our Employee Pension Plans

Armco and domestic subsidiaries, including AFSG, have several pension plans covering substantially all employees. We define our annual pension costs as current service cost, plus amortization of prior service costs over periods of no more than 40 years. These costs are funded, and amounted to $132,300,000 in 1981, $112,100,000 in 1980, and $102,800,000 in 1979.

A summary of accumulated plan benefits for Armco's domestic plans, calculated principally using an 8½% assumed rate of return, and plan net assets at January 1, 1981 (the date of our latest actuarial determination) and 1980 follows:

| | (dollars in millions) January 1, | |
| --- | --- | --- |
| | 1981 | 1980 |
| Actuarial present value of accumulated plan benefits: | | |
| Vested ........................ | $1,135.8 | $ 926.7 |
| Nonvested .................... | 210.8 | 184.9 |
| Total ........................ | $1,346.6 | $1,111.6 |
| Net assets available for benefits ..... | $1,067.7 | $ 832.6 |

Amounts relating to Armco's foreign pension plans are not significant.

## How We Compute Income Per Share

When we compute Armco's primary income per share, we first deduct the amount of dividends on our preferred stock from our net income. Then we divide that figure by the weighted average number of common and common equivalent shares outstanding during the year. Common equivalent shares include contingent shares issuable in the Ladish Co. acquisition and dilutive stock options just as if the options were exercised and the proceeds used to acquire Armco common shares. Dilutive stock options give the optionee the right to buy shares at a price which is less than current market price.

Here is how we compute fully diluted income per share: We start with our net income, but this time we do not subtract preferred stock dividends. Second, we find the weighted average number of common shares and their equivalent. Third, we add in the effect if the outstanding preferred shares were converted into common. Finally, we divide the total we came to in Steps 2 and 3 into our net income, to compute our fully diluted income per share.

## Accounting Changes

### Translation of Foreign Subsidiaries' Financial Statements

In the fourth quarter of 1981, Armco adopted the requirements of Statement of Financial Accounting Standards No. 52, *Foreign Currency Translation*, retroactive to January 1, 1981. Prior years' financial statements have not been restated. The accounting change increased 1981 net income by $10,900,000 and primary and fully diluted income per share by $.19 and $.18, respectively.

Here is financial information relating to Armco's consolidated foreign subsidiaries:

| | (dollars in millions) | | |
| --- | --- | --- | --- |
| | 1981 | 1980 | 1979 |
| Sales ......................... | $897.0 | $938.4 | $751.7 |
| Net income ..................... | $ 51.6 | $ 53.1 | $ 47.0 |
| Total assets .................... | $585.6 | $554.1 | $454.5 |
| Total liabilities .................. | 318.3 | 293.8 | 212.9 |
| Net—representing Armco's equity ... | $267.3 | $260.3 | $241.6 |

Most of our foreign subsidiaries are on a fiscal year ending October 31. The amounts you see here are based on financial statements principally dated October 31, 1981, 1980, and 1979.

Foreign currency losses recognized in determining net income amounted to $3,100,000 in 1981, $8,700,000 in 1980, and $2,900,000 in 1979.

### Extended Vacation Plan Benefits

In the first quarter of 1981, Armco adopted the requirements of Statement of Financial Accounting Standards No. 43, *Accounting for Compensated Absences*, for extended vacation plan benefits. Income retained in the business as of December 31, 1978, has been reduced by $6,600,000 which is net of related deferred taxes of $5,700,000. Statements of consolidated income for 1980 and prior years have been restated by minor amounts.

### Note 2: Armco Financial Services Group

The following summarized financial statements include the accounts of Armco's wholly-owned insurance and finance leasing subsidiaries, plus our proportionate share of certain finance leasing joint ventures. Although the summarized statements cover calendar years, amounts for certain foreign finance leasing operations are based on their fiscal years, which end October 31.

#### Summarized Statement of Financial Position

| | (dollars in millions) December 31 | |
|---|---|---|
| | 1981 | 1980 |
| **ASSETS** | | |
| Cash and short-term marketable securities .......................... | $ 226.6 | $ 149.4 |
| Investments: | | |
| Bonds, at amortized cost ............. | 878.7 | 847.2 |
| Sinking fund preferred stock, at cost .... | — | 19.0 |
| Stocks, at market ................... | 111.2 | 68.2 |
| Real estate, at cost, net of accumulated depreciation ..................... | 4.1 | 7.2 |
| Lease and mortgage contracts receivable ...................... | 512.6 | 439.0 |
| Estimated residual value of equipment .. | 35.6 | 52.6 |
| Less: Unearned income ........... | (51.6) | (51.2) |
| Allowance for losses ......... | (25.6) | (17.8) |
| Notes receivable from aircraft sale .... | 57.8 | — |
| Less: Deferred income on sale and leaseback of aircraft .............. | (36.0) | — |
| Other ........................... | 3.0 | — |
| Total investments—net ................ | 1,489.8 | 1,364.2 |
| Premiums and agents' balances receivable. | 124.0 | 92.9 |
| Reinsurance recoverable ............... | 85.4 | 83.8 |
| Funds held by ceding reinsurers ......... | 35.3 | 39.6 |
| Deferred policy acquisition costs ........ | 72.2 | 67.6 |
| Due from Armco ...................... | — | 42.1 |
| Land, building and equipment used in operations, net of accumulated depreciation ...................... | 25.6 | 30.1 |
| Goodwill ........................... | 22.5 | 15.7 |
| Other assets ........................ | 67.0 | 89.7 |
| Total .......................... | $2,148.4 | $1,975.1 |
| **LIABILITIES & ARMCO'S EQUITY** | | |
| Unpaid losses and loss expenses ......... | $ 699.2 | $ 651.2 |
| Unearned premiums ................... | 199.5 | 190.7 |
| Life and health reserves ............... | 92.3 | 93.7 |
| Ceded reinsurance balances payable .... | 66.3 | 71.0 |
| Accounts payable and other liabilities ..... | 81.6 | 68.3 |
| Notes payable ...................... | 664.6 | 574.9 |
| Due to Armco ....................... | 21.7 | — |
| Deferred income taxes ................ | 37.4 | 57.4 |
| Deferred investment tax credits ......... | 2.5 | 2.6 |
| Total Liabilities ................ | 1,865.1 | 1,709.8 |
| Armco's equity ...................... | 283.3 | 265.3 |
| Total ......................... | $2,148.4 | $1,975.1 |

#### Summarized Statement of Income and Armco's Equity

| | (dollars in millions) Years Ended December 31 | | |
|---|---|---|---|
| | 1981 | 1980 | 1979 |
| **REVENUES** | | | |
| Premiums earned ............. | $579.3 | $574.2 | $577.6 |
| Interest, dividends and rents, net of related expenses ...... | 90.3 | 74.1 | 59.6 |
| Realized investment gains, net of related income taxes ..... | 4.1 | 0.1 | 3.6 |
| Earned income on leases and mortgages ................ | 63.0 | 47.7 | 34.4 |
| Gain on sale of leased aircraft .. | 27.5 | 9.9 | — |
| Investment tax credit amortization .............. | 0.7 | 0.9 | 1.0 |
| Interest on due from Armco ..... | 5.0 | 7.1 | 8.1 |
| Revenues of other operations ... | 41.5 | 59.2 | 54.8 |
| Other income ................ | 22.0 | 4.9 | 4.9 |
| Total ............... | 833.4 | 778.1 | 744.0 |
| **EXPENSES** | | | |
| Loss and loss adjustment expenses .................. | 426.9 | 412.6 | 403.3 |
| Underwriting expenses ......... | 207.6 | 198.1 | 186.8 |
| Interest expense ............. | 118.7 | 59.8 | 40.2 |
| Selling and administrative expenses .................. | 11.6 | 11.1 | 9.3 |
| Expenses of other operations ... | 39.9 | 60.3 | 58.9 |
| Provision for losses ........... | 23.8 | 16.2 | 2.0 |
| Provision (credit) for income taxes: | | | |
| Current ................... | (10.0) | (15.3) | 0.6 |
| Deferred .................. | (15.4) | (1.9) | (0.6) |
| Total ............... | 803.1 | 740.9 | 700.5 |
| Net income ................... | 30.3 | 37.2 | 43.5 |
| **ARMCO'S EQUITY** | | | |
| Beginning of year ............ | 265.3 | 258.1 | 204.8 |
| Capital investment by Armco ... | 3.4 | 20.0 | 13.6 |
| Capital transactions by NN prior to acquisition .......... | — | 1.5 | 2.5 |
| Dividends paid to Armco ....... | — | (40.0) | (0.3) |
| Common dividends paid by NN prior to acquisition .......... | — | (12.5) | (9.5) |
| Adjustment for net unrealized gains (losses) on marketable equity securities ........... | (9.7) | 1.0 | 3.5 |
| Net foreign currency translation adjustments ............... | (6.0) | — | — |
| End of year ................. | $283.3 | $265.3 | $258.1 |

## Note 3: Notes Payable and Long-Term Debt

Notes payable are composed of:

| | (dollars in millions) | |
| --- | --- | --- |
| | 1981 | 1980 |
| Commercial paper ............... | $282.9 | $ — |
| Foreign subsidiaries notes and overdrafts payable .............. | 67.9 | 67.9 |
| Total ...................... | $350.8 | $67.9 |

The weighted average interest rates for commercial paper issued during 1981 and outstanding at December 31, 1981, were 15.2% and 12.6%.

Under the terms of our revolving credit agreement with a group of banks, we may borrow up to $200,000,000 at prime commercial rates or, at Armco's option, the London interbank offering rate plus 3/8%. We did not borrow any amounts under this agreement in 1981. If we borrow, loans up to this maximum amount are convertible into term loans at any time prior to December 1, 1984. They are then repayable in four equal annual installments. For this revolving credit agreement, we pay an annual commitment fee equal to 3/8% of the average available credit.

In addition, we have arrangements with banks providing up to $230,000,000 in lines of credit, principally at prime commercial rates. We have an understanding to maintain an average of 5% compensating balances with these participating banks or pay a 3/8% fee. Our compensating balances on December 31, 1981, were approximately $5,000,000. Under these compensating balance arrangements, there are no legal restrictions on our use of our cash.

Here is information on our long-term debt, less current maturities:

| | (dollars in millions) | |
| --- | --- | --- |
| | 1981 | 1980 |
| Sinking fund debentures | | |
| 8.50% Due 2001 .................. | $100.0 | $100.0 |
| 9.20% Due 2000 .................. | 95.0 | 100.0 |
| 8.70% Due 1995 .................. | 70.0 | 74.5 |
| 5.90% Due 1992 .................. | 36.0 | 39.0 |
| 4.50% Due 1986 .................. | 10.0 | 12.5 |
| 4.35% Due 1984 .................. | 7.5 | 11.3 |
| Notes payable | | |
| 7.875% Due 1983-1996 ............. | 26.2 | 28.0 |
| 14.65% Due 1986 .................. | 100.0 | — |
| Pollution control and other revenue bonds—4.0% to 9.25% .............. | 136.9 | 66.2 |
| Other ............................ | 9.3 | 8.9 |
| Unamortized discount ................ | (18.1) | — |
| Total .......................... | $572.8 | $440.4 |

During the five years ending December 31, 1986, maturities of existing long-term debt will be as follows: 1982, $18,800,000; 1983, $26,100,000; 1984, $50,500,000; 1985, $22,700,000; 1986, $119,900,000.

Armco capitalized interest on projects during construction of $3,900,000 and $2,000,000 in 1981 and 1980.

## Note 4: Long-Term Leases

### Capitalized

Armco leases certain facilities constructed with the proceeds of Industrial Revenue Bonds (IRB's). These lease agreements provide for annual payments large enough to pay the principal and the interest of the IRB's (approximately $14,000,000 in 1982 through 1991 and approximately $7,000,000 in 1992 and 1993). The combined effective rate of interest on these IRB's is approximately 4.8%. Armco has options to purchase these facilities at any time during the term of the leases at the scheduled redemption prices of the IRB's. At the end of the lease periods, we can buy the facilities for nominal amounts.

### Operating

Amounts applicable to operating leases are not significant.

## Note 5: Income Taxes

Income before income taxes is composed of the following:

| | (dollars in millions) | | |
| --- | --- | --- | --- |
| | 1981 | 1980 | 1979 |
| Domestic ...................... | $361.0 | $259.4 | $252.5 |
| Foreign ....................... | 91.3 | 84.3 | 75.1 |
| Total ...................... | $452.3 | $343.7 | $327.6 |

The differences between our provision for income taxes at the statutory rate, and what we show in our statement of consolidated income, are summarized as follows:

| | (dollars in millions) | | | | | |
| --- | --- | --- | --- | --- | --- | --- |
| | 1981 | | 1980 | | 1979 | |
| | Amount | % | Amount | % | Amount | % |
| Tax at statutory rate .......... | $208.1 | 46.0 | $158.1 | 46.0 | $150.7 | 46.0 |
| Investment and energy tax credits ........ | (20.0) | (4.4) | (17.3) | (5.1) | (12.7) | (3.9) |
| Percentage depletion allowance ..... | (2.5) | (0.6) | (5.9) | (1.7) | (11.8) | (3.6) |
| State income taxes ......... | 6.3 | 1.4 | 3.7 | 1.1 | 1.5 | 0.5 |
| Foreign income tax rates different than 46% ..... | (2.3) | (0.5) | (7.5) | (2.2) | (6.4) | (2.0) |
| Capital gain difference ..... | — | — | (8.3) | (2.4) | — | — |
| Other ........... | (1.5) | (0.3) | (7.2) | (2.1) | 1.1 | 0.4 |
| Total ......... | $188.1 | 41.6 | $115.6 | 33.6 | $122.4 | 37.4 |

The provision for deferred federal income taxes results from reporting the following items in different years for financial accounting purposes and income tax purposes:

| | (dollars in millions) | | |
| --- | --- | --- | --- |
| | 1981 | 1980 | 1979 |
| Excess of tax over book depreciation .. | $35.0 | $34.9 | $38.4 |
| Pension funding .................... | — | 3.2 | 5.3 |
| Investment tax credits ................ | 35.8 | (5.0) | 14.2 |
| Blast furnace relines ................ | 0.9 | 10.0 | 6.2 |
| Gain on sale of investment .......... | — | (8.8) | — |
| Other ............................ | (7.3) | (7.1) | 1.1 |
| Total from operations ........ | 64.4 | 27.2 | 65.2 |
| Associated companies .............. | 0.4 | 1.4 | 5.4 |
| Total .................... | $64.8 | $28.6 | $70.6 |

Federal income tax returns of Armco for the years 1972 through 1974 have been examined by the Internal Revenue Service. The Service has proposed certain adjustments which we are contesting. Our tax returns for 1975 through 1979 are currently under examination. We believe Armco has made adequate provision for final settlement of any adjustments arising from these examinations.

### Note 6: Shareholders' Equity

In April 1981, the shareholders approved an amendment to the articles of incorporation authorizing an increase in the maximum number of shares of stock Armco may have outstanding to 150,000,000 shares of common, 8,399,068 shares of Class A preferred, and 5,000,000 shares of Class B preferred.

#### Preferred Stock

Armco's Class A preferred stock outstanding pays cumulative dividends at the annual rate of $2.10 per share. Preferred shareholders get one vote per share. Each share is convertible into 1.27 shares of Armco's common stock. The preferred stock may be redeemed at Armco's option for $40 per share, plus accrued but unpaid dividends. There is no Class B preferred stock outstanding.

#### Common Stock

On December 31, 1981, shares of Armco common stock were reserved for the following purposes:

| | |
|---|---|
| Conversion of preferred stock | 2,281,157 |
| Exercise of stock options | 1,198,321 |
| Ladish Co. acquisition (Note 1) | 1,825,504 |

#### Income Retained in the Business

Under the terms of the revolving credit agreement mentioned in Note 3, we agreed not to pay dividends or reacquire our capital stock in excess of specified amounts. As of December 31, 1981, $437,000,000 of income retained in the business was available for declaring cash dividends and for purchasing or redeeming our capital stock. Legal restrictions on payments of dividends to Armco by our subsidiaries are not significant. Income retained in the business as of December 31, 1981, includes $217,500,000 of undistributed earnings of unconsolidated subsidiaries and associated companies.

### Note 7: Common Stock Options

Armco shareholders adopted Common Stock Option Plans in 1969 and 1977. These plans provide generally for granting options to purchase common stock for not less than 100% of the market price on the date the option is granted. The 1977 plan provides for granting related stock appreciation rights. For options containing stock appreciation rights, the excess of the market price of the stock over the option price is accrued. Although they may terminate earlier under certain conditions, these options expire either five or ten years after they are granted. Options relating to 453,110 shares of stock were available under the 1977 plan for granting at December 31, 1981.

Here is summarized information relating to our common stock options:

| | Number of Shares | Option Price Per Share |
|---|---|---|
| Options outstanding December 31 | | |
| 1981 | 1,198,321 | $8.50-37.00 |
| 1980 | 1,399,597 | 8.05-33.44 |
| 1979 | 1,986,321 | 4.72-23.31 |
| Options exercisable December 31 | | |
| 1981 | 993,821 | 8.50-37.00 |
| 1980 | 1,234,697 | 8.08-23.31 |
| 1979 | 1,785,646 | 4.72-21.17 |
| Options exercised (including stock appreciation rights) | | |
| 1981 | 404,447 | 8.05-30.44 |
| 1980 | 711,667 | 4.72-23.31 |
| 1979 | 338,667 | 4.72-19.54 |

### Note 8: Commitments and Contingencies

Armco has guaranteed directly or indirectly through working capital maintenance agreements, certain debt of AFSG. At December 31, 1981, AFSG had total debt outstanding of $664,600,000. Of this, Armco has supported $384,800,000.

Armco has guaranteed certain liabilities up to $49,600,000 for reinsurance written by subsidiaries of AFSG with certain reinsurance companies.

Armco's principal source of iron ore is Reserve Mining Company (Reserve), a 50% owned company. Reserve has debt outstanding at December 31, 1981, of $408,500,000. Armco and Reserve's other 50% shareholder have supported these borrowings of Reserve by severally undertaking to meet Reserve's obligations to its lenders should Reserve be unable to perform. Armco purchased iron ore from Reserve totaling $168,800,000, $117,500,000 and $103,900,000 during 1981, 1980, and 1979.

A subsidiary of Armco has entered into a "take or pay" agreement to take its share (40%) of the production of iron ore by Eveleth Expansion Company. At December 31, 1981, Eveleth had outstanding First Mortgage Bonds of $192,100,000 due in 1995. Armco is committed to advance up to 40% of the funds needed for continued operation of Eveleth, including amounts for depreciation and amortization at least equal to the amounts required to pay principal and interest on such bonds. Armco purchased iron ore from Eveleth totaling $73,500,000, $65,700,000, and $57,100,000 during 1981, 1980, and 1979.

Armco's 50% portion of Reserve's and 40% portion of Eveleth's debt payments required during the five years ended December 31, 1986, are: 1982, $7,300,000; 1983, $10,500,000; 1984, $10,500,000; 1985, $20,300,000; and 1986, $20,300,000.

Armco owns 17.5% of Falconbridge Dominicana, C. Por A. (Falcondo), a nickel producer. Falcondo has debt outstanding, other than amounts payable to shareholders, of $98,700,000. Armco has guaranteed $39,500,000 of this amount. In addition, Armco has agreed to provide 40% of the net operating funds required by Falcondo. At December 31, 1981, Armco has advanced $15,700,000 under these agreements.

Armco has entered into numerous long-term supply agreements with vendors for its various manufacturing facilities. We believe that the amounts involved in these supply agreements are not material in relation to Armco's financial position.

Armco has committed to purchase property, plant and equipment (including unexpended amounts relating to projects substantially underway) amounting to approximately $419,300,000 at December 31, 1981.

### Note 9: Litigation

In January 1980, Armco and Allied Corporation reached a final agreement to settle litigation claims involving a supply contract. Under the settlement, Allied paid Armco damages of $20,000,000 in cash and transferred to Armco an operating coal mine. This settlement was valued at $34,000,000. This added $17,700,000 to our 1980 net income and $.32 to primary income per share.

There are various claims pending involving Armco and its subsidiaries with respect to product liability, environmental matters, antitrust, reinsurance arrangements, and other matters arising out of the conduct of the business. The total liability on the claims at December 31, 1981, cannot be determined, but, in our opinion, the ultimate liability resulting will not materially affect the consolidated financial position or results of operations of Armco and its subsidiaries.

### Note 10: Required Supplemental Data

Armco's industry segment information is presented on pages 42 and 43.

*35*

## Management's Discussion and Analysis

The following discussion and analysis of Armco's results of operations, changes in financial position, and liquidity should be read in conjunction with the financial statements on pages 26 through 35 and the inflation data and segment information on pages 39 through 43.

### Sales/Operating Profit

### Oilfield Equipment and Production

Sales of this segment increased 47% in 1981 compared to a gain of 45% in 1980. These increases resulted from a sharp increase in worldwide drilling activity during the same periods.

Drilling equipment operations had sales growth of 49% in 1981 versus 52% in 1980. Sales of the production equipment and distribution unit grew 45% versus 50% in 1980. Seamless tubular sales climbed 44% versus 24% in 1980. Operating profit growth of each of these units generally matched or exceeded the respective sales growth during the periods. In 1981, tubular operations had particularly strong operating profit growth due largely to significant increases in market prices for these products.

Strata Energy, Armco's oil and gas exploration and development unit, had operating losses in each of the last three years. Armco has anticipated these operating losses in that drilling expenses exceed production revenues while reserves and land positions are being developed. Strata's total exploration and development costs were $58 and $55 million for the years 1981 and 1980.

### Aerospace and Strategic Materials

Sales of this segment increased 85% in 1981 compared to a gain of 108% in 1980. The 1981 results include the fourth quarter results of Ladish Co. (Ladish) acquired in October and accounted for as a purchase. Excluding Ladish, sales grew 26%.

HITCO, a producer of composite materials for aerospace and industrial applications, had sales and operating profit growth in both 1981 and 1980.

Oregon Metallurgical Corporation (Oremet), an Albany, Oregon titanium producer 79% owned by Armco, had a sales decrease of 2% in 1981 compared to sales growth of 104% in 1980. Net income reported by Oremet grew 10% in 1981 and 274% in 1980. 1980 surge and 1981 growth were largely a result of a substantial increase in demand for and prices of titanium products during the period. This demand came principally from commercial and defense aviation markets. Titanium demand eased significantly in the latter part of 1981 because of a reduced demand for commercial aircraft.

As mentioned previously, the results of Ladish, a Cudahy, Wisconsin based producer of forgings and forged products, are included only for the fourth quarter 1981. Pro forma results of Armco for the years 1981 and 1980, including the results of Ladish, are indicated in Note 1, page 31. Sales of Ladish were $550 and $486 million and net income, after conforming accounting policies and purchase accounting adjustments, was $31 and $14 million for the years 1981 and 1980.

### Specialty Steels

Sales for this segment increased 7% in 1981 following a 4% decline in 1980. Total tons shipped increased by 13% in 1981 after a 23% decline in 1980. Average selling price per ton fell 5% in 1981 versus an increase of 24% in 1980. Operating profit increased 27% in 1981 versus a 23% decline in 1980.

Electrical steel shipments increased in 1981 following a decrease in 1980. Operating profit increased as a result of greater efficiency with a higher percent of production being continuously cast.

Stainless steel tonnage increased in 1981 after a decline in 1980. Depressed market conditions and continued foreign competition resulted in price pressures which impacted all stainless product lines in both years. Stainless steel operations were profitable in 1981 and 1980.

### Fabricated Products and Services

Sales of this segment decreased 5% in 1981 following a gain of 12% in 1980.

Sales and operating profits of U. S. construction products and metal buildings declined in both 1981 and 1980. These declines principally resulted from reduced demand and increased competition for products used in non-residential building, highway and public construction. Revenues of engineering service activities grew in 1981 and 1980, principally due to acquisitions in each of those years. Operating profits of engineering service activities had modest growth in 1981 and 1980.

International operations had lower sales in 1981 following strong growth in 1980. The 1981 decline largely related to European units which were affected by a recession throughout Europe. Operating profits of international units declined in 1981. Adoption of Statement of Financial Accounting Standards No. 52 (see Note 1, page 31 and Note 5, page 34) increased operating profits of international operations in 1981. Prior years were not restated.

### Carbon Steel

Customer sales for this segment increased 14% during 1981 following a 3% decline in 1980. Carbon steel shipments increased 9% in 1981 versus an 8% drop in 1980. Operating profits decreased 34% after a decline of 90% in 1980.

Flat-rolled mills experienced a sharp decline in demand in the second half of 1981 with deteriorating selling prices due to continued depressed conditions in the automotive and housing industries and a surge of imported steel. The impact of the coal strike during the year also contributed to operating losses in flat-rolled products in 1981.

During the third quarter of 1981, we sold our Sand Springs, Oklahoma steel works and related fabricating plants, and ceased operations of our Marion, Ohio plant. The principal products of these divested operations were reinforcing steel bars and light structural shapes. Results of these operations are included in this segment through June 30, 1981.

36

Sales from bar, wire, and rod operations increased in 1981 following a decline in 1980. Higher operating profits were reported as more tons were shipped than in either of the previous two years. Plate, bar, and structural products produced in Houston had improved sales and operating profits in both 1981 and 1980, chiefly due to an increased demand for alloy bar and plates by energy markets. 1982 results of Houston operations will be adversely affected by expiration of a long-term fixed price gas contract for natural gas. Mexican operations had higher sales and earnings in 1981 despite a strike late in the year.

Armco's mining units had an operating loss of $37 million in 1981 versus $30 million in 1980. Iron ore operations were unprofitable in 1981 and 1980, primarily due to discounted ore sales. Coal operations which were impacted by a strike, were unprofitable in 1981 versus profitable operations in 1980. Falcondo, a Dominican Republic nickel mine in which Armco has a 17.5% interest, had significant losses in 1981 versus profits in 1980. Operations at this nickel mine were suspended in February 1982. (See Note 8, page 35.)

## Corporate Expenses

Corporate general expenses increased 3% in 1981 and 55% in 1980. The 1981 increase was largely due to inflationary pressures on overheads. The 1980 increase was due, in addition to inflationary effects, to higher absorption at the corporate level of certain expenses over that reflected by operating units, higher expenses for stock appreciation rights and expenses associated with the acquisition of NN Corporation.

Interest expense increased 17% in 1981 and 7% in 1980. The 1981 increase principally resulted from higher average levels of and rates on corporate commercial paper borrowings (see Note 3, page 34). Interest expense in 1982 is expected to be significantly higher due to an increased average level of debt and higher average rates of interest.

## Other Credits/Charges

In 1981, sundry other-net included a $14 million pre-tax credit ($6 million after-tax), which represents the fourth quarter 1980 profits of Oremet. These results were recognized as a result of a change in Oremet's fiscal year. Also included is a $3 million pre-tax charge related to the closing/sale of Marion, Ohio and Sand Springs, Oklahoma steel plants.

## Income Taxes

Armco's composite income tax rate increased to 41.6% in 1981 from 33.6% in 1980. Analysis of the differences between the actual provision for income tax and the statutory rate is shown in Note 5, page 34.

## Equity in Net Income of AFSG

Armco reports the results of its financial services businesses on an equity basis. (See Note 2, page 33 for summarized financial statements.) Equity in net income of the Financial Services Group in total was down 19% in 1981 following a 15% decline in 1980.

Domestic insurance operations recorded higher underwriting losses in 1981 related to the unfavorable underwriting pressures experienced in the property and casualty industry. The combined ratio for the domestic insurance companies was 108% compared to 105% in 1980, with a 4% increase in premiums written. Net income increased as a result of higher investment income on a larger invested asset base. European insurance businesses were impacted by deteriorating underwriting results in 1981 compared to 1980.

Domestic financing businesses had a 23% increase in loans and leases outstanding over 1980. Total revenue, which included $27 million ($16 milion in net income) from the sale/leaseback of leased aircraft, was significantly higher in 1981. Net income from aircraft sales was $5 million in 1980.

The domestic financial services holding company has debt used partially to support equity in the financial services operating companies. Interest expense for the holding company was $38 and $10 million for the years 1981 and 1980.

## Cash Flow from Operations

Cash flow from operations increased 13% in 1981 and 10% in 1980.

The 1981 increase reflects increased net income, higher depreciation principally due to higher units of production charges in steel operations, and a larger increase in deferred taxes (see Note 5, page 34), offset by the impact on 1980 of a dividend from AFSG.

The 1980 increase consists chiefly of higher net income, a dividend from AFSG, offset by a lower increase in deferred taxes.

## Change in Working Capital

Working capital items, excluding cash, marketable securities, and notes payable, increased by $482 million during 1981 and $102 million in 1980.

During 1981, inventories increased $206 million. Inventory as a percent of cost of sales increased to 19% in 1981 from 15% in 1980. Significant increases in 1981 occurred in the flat-rolled steel operations (both raw materials and finished inventory), drilling equipment operations, and the oilfield production equipment and distribution unit (finished inventory). The estimated iron ore inventory in excess of normal needs was approximately $121 and $71 million at December 31, 1981 and 1980. Trade notes and accounts receivable as a percent of sales were 13% in 1981 and 1980. The acquisition of Ladish increased working capital $152 million.

## Capital Expenditures and Investments

Total capital expenditures and investments increased $342 million in 1981 and $9 million in 1980.

The 1981 increase was due primarily to:

- $122 million increase in capital expenditures, most prominent of which was a $98 million purchase of coke oven facilities in Ashland, Kentucky from the Allied Corporation, and $25 million spent on a continuous caster at our Butler, Pennsylvania steel plant (total estimated cost $54 million).
- $64 million change in balance with AFSG.
- $79 million addition to property and investments from the acquisition of Ladish.
- $52 million in notes obtained as partial consideration in the sale of Sand Springs, Oklahoma and Marion, Ohio facilities.

The 1980 increase was due to increased capital expenditures for normal replacement expenditures and expansions of various non-steel facilities, offset by net reductions of investment including $48 million from liquidation of an investment in Rowan Companies, Inc. preferred stock.

## Financing

Financing activities generated $547 million in 1981 compared to using $50 million in 1980. The 1981 increase was due to:

- $297 million issuance of common stock for businesses purchased (principally $286 million for Ladish).
- $283 million issuance of short-term commercial paper.
- $163 million issuance of new long-term debt less $35 million in payments on long-term obligations (see Note 3, page 34).

Offsetting the above items were uses of funds:

- $104 million for dividends on common and preferred stock.
- $29 million for common stock repurchases.
- $28 million in net other changes to equity, principally the effect of the adoption of Statement of Financial Accounting Standards No. 52.

The 1980 changes are essentially explained in the Statement of Changes in Consolidated Financial Position.

## Financial Condition and Liquidity

Armco judges its financial condition to be sound. Armco's ratio of long-term debt to total capitalization was 21.6% as of December 31, 1981, compared to 21.4% at December 31, 1980. During 1981, Armco added $420 million to shareholders' equity including $286 million related to the acquisition of Ladish for common stock.

Armco judges its liquidity position to be adequate to meet contingencies. Cash and marketable securities were $148 million at December 31, 1981. Armco has arranged $430 million of bank credit facilities. At December 31, 1981, a portion of these bank facilities were being used to back up short-term commercial paper borrowings of $283 million.

On December 31, 1981, Armco announced its intention to purchase from time-to-time up to 3 million shares of its common stock through the open market. As of February 23, 1982, Armco had acquired 866,800 shares as part of this program.

Armco expects to have $100-200 million of additional external financing requirements during 1982. These requirements will likely be financed through issuance of new intermediate or long-term debt, depending on prevailing market conditions.

Armco has assets and contingent obligations not recorded or fully reflected on its balance sheet. This treatment is fully in accordance with generally accepted accounting principles. Off-balance sheet assets include appreciation in the value of raw material and petroleum reserves recorded at historical costs and the higher current value of inventories as compared to amounts stated due to LIFO accounting. Our contingent liabilities include debt guarantees (see Note 8, page 35), primarily related to our raw material ventures and financing businesses, and unfunded vested pension benefits.

Armco estimates that as of December 31, 1981, the value of off-balance sheet assets exceed contingent obligations by a substantial margin.

## Capital Programs

Armco currently estimates its 1982 capital investments will be $626 million, compared to $750 million in 1981 including the $286 million acquisition of Ladish. Amounts include reinvested earnings of unconsolidated subsidiaries. The 1982 estimate includes $199 million of normal replacement type expenditures. A major portion (39%) of 1982 investments will be made in the Oilfield Equipment and Production segment. The percent of 1982 capital investments going to other segments is 27% for Carbon Steel, 11% for Fabricated Products and Services, 9% for Aerospace and Strategic Materials, 7% for Specialty Steels, and 7% for Corporate and reinvested earnings.

In March 1982, Armco announced a temporary hold on its plans to invest $671 million in a project to expand seamless tubular capacity. This action was prompted by uncertainty regarding the timing of economic recovery, continuation of high interest rates and volatile financial markets, and the proposed tax policies of the federal government.

Armco's current strategic plan calls for total net assets to grow to $5.8 billion in 1985 (expressed in constant 1981 dollars), up from $3.6 billion in 1981.

## Assessing the Impact of Inflation

Armco has always prepared its financial statements on the "historical cost accounting basis". This is the generally accepted method of accounting based on historical cost accounting measurements in actual dollars. This approach is inadequate because it doesn't show enough of the effects of inflation.

According to this view, reported profits will be sharply lower if they reflect the cost of assets at today's prices. Because current costs are not considered, reported profits may be illusory. Such illusory profits are taxed as if they were real, thus depriving companies of capital to replace assets at current prices. Failure to consider inflation may result in a tax on capital as well as one on income.

### Comparison of 1981 Results

To help readers of financial statements better understand the impact of inflation on business, the Statement of Financial Accounting Standards No. 33 requires companies to present the effects of general inflation (constant dollar) and the effects of changes in specific prices (current cost).

Below, you can see our Statement of Consolidated Income Adjusted for Changing Prices. It sets forth Armco's 1981 income statement in three ways:

1. *Historical Cost*—our normal reporting.

2. *Adjusted for General Inflation*—here we've applied the Consumer Price Index to our inventories and property, plant and equipment increasing cost of products sold and depreciation. All other items in the income statement are presumed to be stated in average 1981 dollars.

The minor adjustment of $5.9 million to Cost of

Products Sold would be considerably larger if it were not for our predominant use of the LIFO method of inventory accounting. LIFO charges current inventory cost against current sales.

The major adjustment is to depreciation. This reflects how capital intensive we are and the relatively long life of Armco's assets.

3. *Adjusted for Changes in Specific Prices*—in this calculation, inventories and property, plant and equipment are revalued to reflect the current cost of acquiring the same asset instead of using the Consumer Price Index to reflect changed values. The calculations do not reflect efficiencies or cost savings that might be gained by replacing existing facilities with new, modern facilities utilizing latest technological developments.

The statement shows, in columns (2) and (3), earnings of $137.9 million and $134.5 million, compared to the $294.5 million we report on our historical cost basis. Statement No. 33 does not permit changing the provision for income taxes, because current income tax regulations do not permit the recognition of the inflation reflected in columns (2) and (3). As a result, Armco's effective tax rate is increased from the 41.6% on an historical cost basis to 63.6% when adjusted for general inflation and to 64.4% when adjusted for changes in specific prices. To put it another way, if tax regulations permitted the utilization of the effect of either general inflation or specific price increases, our tax provisions would be $72.0 million or $73.6 million less, respectively, and net income would have increased by a similar amount.

Also reflected in this statement is $59.1 million of purchasing power gain on net monetary liabilities held

### Statement of Consolidated Income Adjusted for Changing Prices
For the Year Ended December 31, 1981
(dollars in millions)

| | (1) As Stated in the Financial Statements | (2) Adjusted for General Inflation | (3) Adjusted for Changes in Specific Prices (Current Costs) |
|---|---|---|---|
| Net sales | $6,906.0 | $6,906.0 | $6,906.0 |
| Cost of products sold | 5,763.1 | 5,769.0 | 5,769.0 |
| Depreciation and amortization | 174.3 | 325.0 | 328.4 |
| Selling and administrative expenses | 495.3 | 495.3 | 495.3 |
| Other income | (51.5) | (51.5) | (51.5) |
| Interest expense | 70.2 | 70.2 | 70.2 |
| Sundry other—net | 2.3 | 2.3 | 2.3 |
| Total | 6,453.7 | 6,610.3 | 6,613.7 |
| Income before income taxes | 452.3 | 295.7 | 292.3 |
| Provision for income taxes | 188.1 | 188.1 | 188.1 |
| Equity in net income of AFSG | 30.3 | 30.3 | 30.3 |
| Net income | $ 294.5 | $ 137.9 | $ 134.5 |
| Purchasing power gain on net monetary liabilities held during the year | | $ 59.1 | $ 59.1 |
| Increase in current cost of inventory and equipment held during the year* (based on specific price changes) | | | $ 756.2 |
| Effect of increase in general price level | | | 378.1 |
| Increase in current cost of inventory and equipment held during the year (based on specific price changes) net of changes in the general price level | | | $ 378.1 |

*At December 31, 1981, current cost of inventory was $1,942.4 and current cost of property, plant and equipment, net of accumulated depreciation, was $3,046.1.

during the year. This is defined as the increase or decrease in purchasing power resulting from holding assets or liabilities that represent claims or obligations to receive or pay fixed or determinable amounts of cash. Since Armco is in a net monetary liability position, we have a gain because we will be paying these net monetary liabilities with cheaper dollars.

The remaining figures on this schedule indicate that applying specific prices to our items of inventory and property, plant and equipment is $378.1 million more than compared to the Consumer Price Index calculation. This shows that 1981 inflation had a greater effect on Armco than it did on the Consumer Price Index. This is because 1981 general inflation has been less than our estimates of the 1981 increase in the current cost to replace our inventory and property, plant and equipment—net.

### 5-Year Comparison

Now we'll comment on our second statement, the supple-

mentary 5-year comparison of selected Financial Data Adjusted for the Effects of Changing Prices.

Despite inflation, net sales expressed in terms of average 1981 dollars show that Armco had real growth in sales during the 5-year period, although dipping slightly in 1980. Information on items (b) through (f) in this statement is required only for the years 1979 through 1981.

This summary dramatizes the effect of inflation on Armco's results as 1981 inflation adjusted income improved compared to 1980 but was below 1979. The same pattern is evident in our per share earnings. Comparing dividends per share and earnings per share when both are adjusted for general inflation shows we have paid out substantial percentages of our income in dividends. We believe this dramatically illustrates the need for an informed tax policy and the necessity to bring inflation under control. Even with the increase in our historical dividends and stock price over the past five years, our shareholders are losing ground in the fight with inflation.

### Financial Data Adjusted for the Effects of Changing Prices
(dollars in millions, except per share amounts)

|  | 1981 | 1980 | 1979 | 1978 | 1977 |
|---|---|---|---|---|---|
| **(a) Net Sales** | | | | | |
| At historical cost | $6,906.0 | $5,678.0 | $5,035.1 | $4,357.3 | $3,549.2 |
| Adjusted for general inflation* | 6,906.0 | 6,264.4 | 6,308.9 | 6,074.4 | 5,326.7 |
| **(b) Net Income** | | | | | |
| At historical cost | 294.5 | 265.3 | 248.7 | | |
| Adjusted for general inflation* | 137.9 | 102.3 | 181.9 | | |
| Adjusted to current cost* | 134.5 | 95.3 | 155.7 | | |
| **(c) Net Income per Common Share** | | | | | |
| At historical cost | 4.97 | 4.73 | 4.51 | | |
| Adjusted for general inflation* | 2.29 | 1.74 | 3.22 | | |
| Adjusted to current cost* | 2.23 | 1.62 | 2.73 | | |
| **(d) Shareholders' Equity at December 31** | | | | | |
| At historical cost | 2,467.2 | 2,046.6 | 1,843.3 | | |
| Adjusted for general inflation* | 4,272.6 | 4,020.7 | 3,940.3 | | |
| Adjusted to current cost* | 4,413.0 | 4,210.6 | 4,391.2 | | |
| **(e) Purchasing Power Gain on Net Monetary** | | | | | |
| Liabilities Held During Year* | 59.1 | 84.7 | 105.5 | | |
| **(f) Excess (Deficiency) of Increase in Specific Prices over** | | | | | |
| Increase in General Price Level | 378.1 | (249.2) | 53.1 | | |
| **(g) Cash Dividends per Common Share** | | | | | |
| At historical cost | 1.72 | 1.57 | 1.43 | 1.28 | 1.20 |
| Adjusted for general inflation* | 1.72 | 1.73 | 1.79 | 1.78 | 1.80 |
| **(h) Market Price per Common Share at Year End** | | | | | |
| At historical cost | 28.00 | 38.00 | 25.00 | 19.88 | 18.92 |
| Adjusted for general inflation* | 28.00 | 41.92 | 31.32 | 27.71 | 28.40 |
| **(i) Average Consumer Price Index** | 272.4 | 246.9 | 217.4 | 195.4 | 181.5 |

*Stated in average 1981 dollars.

The following sets forth certain information for the significant mineral reserves of Armco:

| | 1981 | 1980 | 1979 |
|---|---|---|---|
| **Proven and Probable Reserves at December 31,** | | | |
| Armco and Consolidated Subsidiaries | | | |
| Coal (tons) | 924,000,000 | 929,000,000 | 862,000,000 |
| Limestone (tons) | 48,500,000 | 52,900,000 | 59,000,000 |
| Oil (barrels) | 1,500,000 | 1,900,000 | 1,700,000 |
| Gas (MCF) | 31,000,000 | 29,900,000 | 26,300,000 |
| Associated Companies | | | |
| Iron Ore (tons) | 347,000,000 | 351,700,000 | 353,100,000 |
| Limestone (tons) | 177,000,000 | 178,000,000 | 180,000,000 |
| **Production during the year** | | | |
| Armco and Consolidated Subsidiaries | | | |
| Coal (tons) | 3,800,000 | 5,000,000 | 3,300,000 |
| Limestone (tons) | 400,000 | 550,000 | 830,000 |
| Oil (barrels) | 520,000 | 540,000 | 130,000 |
| Gas (MCF) | 3,500,000 | 3,000,000 | 2,400,000 |
| Associated Companies | | | |
| Iron Ore (tons) | 6,900,000 | 5,300,000 | 6,800,000 |
| Limestone (tons) | 890,000 | 850,000 | 670,000 |
| **Purchases/(sales) of Reserves during the year** | | | |
| Armco and Consolidated Subsidiaries | | | |
| Coal (tons) | 29,000,000 | 72,100,000 | — |
| Limestone (tons) | — | (6,600,000) | — |
| **Average Market Price during the year** | | | |
| Armco and Consolidated Subsidiaries | | | |
| Coal (price per ton) | $41.18 | $40.13 | $41.41 |
| Limestone (price per ton) | 3.40 | 3.10 | 2.85 |
| Oil (price per barrel) | 36.31 | 37.45 | 22.73 |
| Gas (price per MCF) | 3.77 | 3.03 | 1.93 |
| Associated Companies | | | |
| Iron Ore (price per ton) | 39.04 | 38.39 | 32.73 |
| Limestone (price per ton) | 2.61 | 2.61 | 2.56 |

Summary

The information contained in this section is based upon prescribed experimental techniques in an attempt to measure the economic impact of inflation. The value of this data may be enhanced when it can be reviewed in terms of trends and relationships over several periods.

Comparison of this data between companies and industries may help develop an understanding of the more significant impacts of inflation. We hope these comparisons will lead to a more enlightened tax policy, with respect both to industry's capital formation problems and the investment return to individual investors.

## Information Relating to Armco's Industry Segments and Other Financial Data*
(Dollars in millions, except per share amounts)

|  | 1981† | 1980 | 1979 | 1978 | 1977 |
|---|---|---|---|---|---|
| **Customer Sales[1]** | | | | | |
| Oilfield equipment and production | $2,379.1 | $1,614.7 | $1,111.9 | $ 924.1 | $ 651.4 |
| Aerospace and strategic materials | 385.8 | 208.1 | 100.2 | 85.2 | 73.3 |
| Specialty steels | 570.2 | 533.5 | 553.4 | 441.1 | 385.5 |
| Fabricated products and services | 1,097.4 | 1,150.2 | 1,031.0 | 877.1 | 761.8 |
| Carbon steel | 2,473.5 | 2,171.5 | 2,238.6 | 2,029.8 | 1,677.2 |
| **Intersegment Sales[2]** | | | | | |
| Oilfield equipment and production | 6.7 | .9 | 1.2 | .6 | .8 |
| Aerospace and strategic materials | 1.5 | .5 | .9 | .3 | .6 |
| Specialty steels | 24.0 | 16.9 | 35.2 | 27.0 | 16.9 |
| Fabricated products and services | 27.6 | 12.7 | 9.4 | 6.7 | 7.1 |
| Carbon steel | 310.8 | 267.6 | 237.1 | 218.5 | 188.2 |
| **Interest, Royalties, and Other Income[1]** | | | | | |
| Oilfield equipment and production | 12.5 | 10.1 | 9.0 | 5.0 | 4.8 |
| Aerospace and strategic materials | 11.1 | 2.1 | .4 | .3 | .1 |
| Specialty steels | 4.7 | 4.2 | 2.1 | .6 | .6 |
| Fabricated products and services | 12.1 | 8.7 | 10.5 | 8.2 | 6.8 |
| Carbon steel | 11.1 | 8.0 | 7.4 | 4.1 | 4.3 |
| **Eliminations[4]** | (370.6) | (298.6) | (283.8) | (253.1) | (213.6) |
| Total revenues | $6,957.5 | $5,711.1 | $5,064.5 | $4,375.5 | $3,565.8 |
| | | | | | |
| **Operating Profit[1][3][5]** | | | | | |
| Oilfield equipment and production | $ 424.1 | $ 223.2 | $ 159.8 | $ 149.9 | $ 84.1 |
| Aerospace and strategic materials | 91.3 | 57.1 | 12.5 | 8.9 | 8.8 |
| Specialty steels | 76.8 | 60.7 | 79.2 | 71.0 | 40.5 |
| Fabricated products and services | 52.4 | 73.0 | 78.5 | 73.1 | 66.9 |
| Carbon steel | 8.6 | 13.0 | 131.9 | 134.8 | 10.1 |
| LIFO adjustment[6] | (30.4) | (1.8) | (4.4) | (1.1) | (.2) |
| Adjustments and eliminations[4] | (13.9) | .9 | (3.8) | (5.0) | (1.2) |
| **Equity in Net Income of AFSG** | 30.3 | 37.2 | 43.5 | 36.4 | 28.9 |
| Total | 639.2 | 463.3 | 497.2 | 468.0 | 237.9 |
| Corporate general expense | 84.1 | 81.9 | 52.7 | 47.6 | 34.5 |
| Gain on sale of investments | — | (42.9) | — | (24.6) | — |
| Litigation settlement | — | (34.0) | — | — | — |
| Interest expense | 70.2 | 59.8 | 56.0 | 57.4 | 63.5 |
| Sundry other — net | 2.3 | 17.6 | 17.4 | 18.8 | 3.1 |
| Federal, state and foreign income taxes | 208.1 | 132.9 | 135.1 | 157.4 | 48.4 |
| Investment tax credits | (20.0) | (17.3) | (12.7) | (13.5) | (45.2) |
| Net income | 294.5 | 265.3 | 248.7 | 224.9 | 133.6 |
| Less preferred dividends | 4.4 | 6.1 | 7.1 | 7.1 | 7.1 |
| Net income applicable to common stock | $ 290.1 | $ 259.2 | $ 241.6 | $ 217.8 | $ 126.5 |
| | | | | | |
| Net income per share of common stock | | | | | |
| Primary | $ 4.97 | $ 4.73 | $ 4.51 | $ 4.07 | $ 2.43 |
| Fully diluted | $ 4.82 | $ 4.52 | $ 4.29 | $ 3.89 | $ 2.37 |
| Cash dividends per share of common stock | $ 1.72 | $ 1.57 | $ 1.43 | $ 1.28 | $ 1.20 |
| Weighted average number of shares used in computation of income per share of common stock | | | | | |
| Primary (millions) | 58.3 | 54.8 | 53.5 | 53.5 | 52.0 |
| Fully diluted (millions) | 61.1 | 58.7 | 58.0 | 57.8 | 56.4 |
| **Other Data** | | | | | |
| Net income as a percent of sales | 4.3% | 4.7% | 4.9% | 5.2% | 3.8% |
| Return on average net assets | 11.1% | 10.7% | 10.5% | 10.3% | 7.0% |
| Return on average shareholders' equity | 13.7% | 13.6% | 14.1% | 14.1% | 9.0% |
| Dividend payout percent | 34.6% | 33.2% | 31.7% | 31.4% | 49.4% |
| Book value per share | $ 38.55 | $ 36.32 | $ 33.80 | $ 30.58 | $ 28.27 |
| Cash flow from operations | $ 519.5 | $ 460.8 | $ 418.6 | $ 408.8 | $ 166.2 |
| Cash flow as a percent of long term obligations | 76.4% | 82.9% | 72.4% | 66.4% | 25.8% |
| Long-term debt and lease obligations | $ 680.2 | $ 555.8 | $ 578.5 | $ 615.8 | $ 643.0 |
| Long-term debt ratio | 21.6% | 21.4% | 23.9% | 26.8% | 29.7% |
| Interest coverage ratio | 7.9 | 7.4 | 7.6 | 7.4 | 3.1 |
| Domestic raw steel production (thousand tons) | 8,187.9 | 7,290.1 | 8,001.5 | 8,513.0 | 7,933.0 |
| Domestic steel shipments (thousand tons) | 5,767.4 | 5,390.6 | 6,004.1 | 6,017.0 | 5,483.0 |
| Flat-rolled products as a percent of carbon steel sales | 46% | 42% | 47% | 53% | 58% |
| Total employees | 67,660 | 59,975 | 57,678 | 54,808 | 51,779 |

*Amounts have been reclassified for a change in segment classification of certain products and services.
† In 1981, Armco changed the method of translating foreign subsidiaries financial statements.
See Note 1 of Notes to Financial Statements.

42

| | 1981 | 1980 | 1979 | 1978 | 1977 |
|---|---|---|---|---|---|
| **Capital Expenditures** | | | | | |
| Oilfield equipment and production .......... | $ 95.9 | $ 92.5 | $ 48.3 | $ 22.8 | $ 12.6 |
| Aerospace and strategic materials ......... | 29.2 | 22.8 | 4.8 | 2.6 | 2.8 |
| Specialty steels ......................... | 41.4 | 32.4 | 7.1 | 4.8 | 16.4 |
| Fabricated products and services .......... | 30.7 | 36.7 | 25.8 | 23.0 | 27.2 |
| Carbon steel ............................ | 179.3 | 72.6 | 64.1 | 52.8 | 78.4 |
| Corporate general ....................... | 17.1 | 14.3 | 12.2 | 4.4 | 9.0 |
| Total ................................ | $ 393.6 | $ 271.3 | $ 162.3 | $ 110.4 | $ 146.4 |
| **Depreciation, Amortization and Depletion** | | | | | |
| Oilfield equipment and production ......... | $ 24.0 | $ 20.0 | $ 11.7 | $ 10.0 | $ 5.9 |
| Aerospace and strategic materials ......... | 7.5 | 3.2 | 1.9 | 1.6 | 1.6 |
| Specialty steels ......................... | 14.7 | 13.0 | 15.6 | 15.0 | 13.2 |
| Fabricated products and services ........... | 16.0 | 15.6 | 13.3 | 13.0 | 9.8 |
| Carbon steel ........................... | 104.7 | 95.0 | 94.5 | 96.4 | 85.7 |
| Corporate general ....................... | 7.4 | 3.0 | 4.1 | 2.8 | 2.6 |
| Total ................................ | $ 174.3 | $ 149.8 | $ 141.1 | $ 138.8 | $ 118.8 |
| **Identifiable Assets**[1] | | | | | |
| Oilfield equipment and production .......... | $1,026.5 | $ 669.2 | $ 528.5 | $ 405.6 | $ 298.8 |
| Aerospace and strategic materials ......... | 575.3 | 140.7 | 56.8 | 46.2 | 32.3 |
| Specialty steels ......................... | 303.5 | 287.0 | 269.2 | 283.4 | 260.3 |
| Fabricated products and services .......... | 535.8 | 542.7 | 513.0 | 453.3 | 419.1 |
| Carbon steel ............................ | 1,918.8 | 1,734.8 | 1,663.6 | 1,638.1 | 1,688.1 |
| Investment in AFSG ..................... | 283.3 | 265.3 | 258.1 | 204.8 | 168.9 |
| Corporate general ....................... | 203.2 | 189.7 | 130.7 | 193.1 | 90.7 |
| Adjustments and eliminations[4] ........... | (29.2) | (22.0) | (25.1) | (23.8) | (19.3) |
| Total ................................ | $4,817.2 | $3,807.4 | $3,394.8 | $3,200.7 | $2,938.9 |

(1) The amounts include the following relating to Armco's consolidated foreign subsidiaries:

| | | | | | |
|---|---|---|---|---|---|
| Customer sales (7) ..................... | $ 897.0 | $ 938.4 | $751.7 | $ 609.9 | $ 550.8 |
| Interest, royalties, and other income ...... | 10.4 | 7.9 | 4.6 | 3.9 | 3.0 |
| Operating profit (5) ..................... | 116.7 | 112.2 | 97.8 | 74.6 | 60.3 |
| Identifiable assets ...................... | 585.6 | 554.1 | 454.5 | 404.7 | 372.1 |

(2) Prices are generally market less 5%.

(3) Represents total revenues less cost of products sold and other operating expenses directly related to the segments.

(4) Represents elimination of intersegment transactions or balances.

(5) Our change in the method of translating foreign subsidiaries financial statements in 1981 increased operating profit in total $17.5 and by segment: Oilfield equipment and production—$4.3; Fabricated products and services—$11.0; and Carbon steel—$2.2.

(6) We use a single steel pool for LIFO which involves four segments. Each division in the segment calculates its own LIFO provision. The total of the segments is less than is needed for the single pool. This adjustment is recorded at Corporate.

(7) Sales between foreign and domestic companies are not material.

| | 1981 | 1980 | 1979 | 1978 | 1977 |
|---|---|---|---|---|---|
| Employment Costs | | | | | |
| Wages and salaries[1] .................... | $1,353.7 | $1,182.8 | $1,065.5 | $ 900.9 | $ 787.8 |
| Cost of employee benefits | | | | | |
| Pensions .......................... | 132.3 | 112.1 | 102.8 | 94.8 | 86.5 |
| Group insurance .................... | 125.5 | 102.5 | 87.9 | 75.1 | 72.6 |
| Regular hourly and salaried vacations ..... | 115.6 | 101.8 | 87.5 | 74.5 | 67.4 |
| Social security ...................... | 107.3 | 89.7 | 77.7 | 59.5 | 51.4 |
| Hourly and salaried holiday pay .......... | 61.7 | 53.4 | 47.1 | 37.3 | 32.1 |
| Vacation benefits provided by savings and vacation plans ...................... | 13.7 | 20.3 | 15.3 | 10.9 | 8.1 |
| Thrift and profit sharing plans ........... | 18.1 | 13.6 | 13.3 | 9.8 | 8.3 |
| Worker's compensation ................ | 17.0 | 13.4 | 11.6 | 8.1 | 8.4 |
| Federal and state unemployment compensation .................... | 13.1 | 10.1 | 11.1 | 10.3 | 8.1 |
| Supplemental unemployment benefits ..... | 6.1 | 4.3 | 1.6 | 3.0 | 5.6 |
| Other ............................. | 3.8 | 1.7 | 2.0 | 1.3 | 2.1 |
| Total employee benefits ............. | 614.2 | 522.9 | 457.9 | 384.6 | 350.6 |
| Total employment costs ................. | $1,967.9 | $1,705.7 | $1,523.4 | $1,285.5 | $1,138.4 |

(1) Excludes payroll charged to construction.

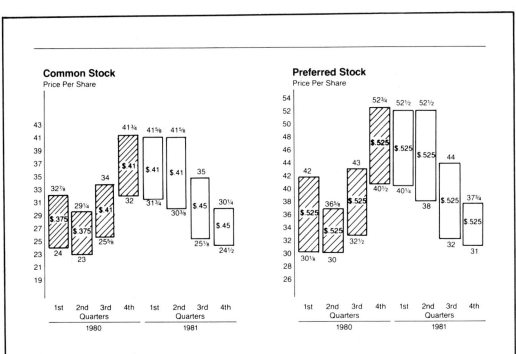

**Price Range and Dividends of Armco Stock**
(on The New York Stock Exchange, Armco's principal market—ticker symbol AS)
Dividend per share within each bar

During 1981 Mellon Bank, N.A., as trustee for the Armco Thrift Plan for Salaried Employees, the Armco Thrift Plan for Hourly Employees, and The Armco Tax Credit Employee Stock Ownership Plan for Salaried Employees, purchased 1,668,300; 190,543; and 134,660 shares, respectively, of the corporation's common stock on The New York Stock Exchange. A total of 12,605,020 shares of the corporation's common stock were traded on the exchange during 1981.

On December 31, 1981, Mellon Bank, N.A., and its nominee owned of record, but not beneficially, 9,457,269 shares of common stock and 400 shares of preferred stock of Armco. Of the total number of shares of common stock set forth above, 9,257,547 shares are owned of record, by the Mellon Bank, N.A., as trustee of the above plans, for the benefit of participants in the plans.

The number of shareholders of record of Armco's common stock on December 31, 1981, was 67,472.

## Quarterly Financial Data
(Dollars in millions, except per share amounts)

| 1981 | First Quarter | Second Quarter | Third Quarter | Fourth Quarter |
|---|---|---|---|---|
| Net sales | $1,635.2 | $1,733.6 | $1,743.4 | $1,793.8 |
| Cost of products sold[1] | | | | |
|   As originally reported | 1,402.5 | 1,469.0 | 1,520.0 | 1,563.3 |
|   As restated | 1,400.3 | 1,464.9 | 1,513.6 | 1,558.6 |
| Net income[1] | | | | |
|   As originally reported | 69.0[2] | 85.5 | 63.8 | 65.3 |
|   As restated | 69.7[2] | 87.6 | 67.1 | 70.1 |
| Income per share[1] | | | | |
|   Primary | | | | |
|     As originally reported | 1.20 | 1.49 | 1.13 | .96 |
|     As restated | 1.21 | 1.53 | 1.19 | 1.04 |
|   Fully diluted | | | | |
|     As originally reported | 1.16 | 1.44 | 1.10 | .94 |
|     As restated | 1.17 | 1.48 | 1.15 | 1.02 |
| **1980** | | | | |
| Net sales | $1,351.8 | $1,374.7 | $1,401.8 | $1,549.7 |
| Cost of products sold | 1,171.3 | 1,183.3 | 1,224.3 | 1,357.8 |
| Net income | 68.1[3] | 59.8 | 74.0[4] | 63.4[5] |
| Income per share | | | | |
|   Primary | 1.23 | 1.07 | 1.30 | 1.13 |
|   Fully diluted | 1.17 | 1.03 | 1.26 | 1.06 |

(1) In the fourth quarter, Armco adopted Statement of Financial Accounting Standards No. 52 retroactive to January 1. See Note 1 of Notes to Financial Statements.
(2) Includes $5.5 million as a result of conforming the accounting year of Oregon Metallurgical Corporation.
(3) Includes gain on settlement of litigation. See Note 9 of Notes to Financial Statements.
(4) Includes gain on sale of investments. See Note 1 of Notes to Financial Statements.
(5) Includes approximately $20,000,000 as a result of the effective income tax for the year being less than was estimated for the year.

45

## QUESTIONS AND PROBLEMS

**5-1.** Conventional financial statements cannot be interpreted apart from the concepts on which they rest. Listed below are the seven basic assumptions introduced in Chapter 1 and reviewed in Chapter 5. Indicate the concept(s) that are directly responsible for each of the following 15 items or procedures associated with the financial statements. Briefly explain the relationship.

*Basic Assumptions*

| | |
|---|---|
| Entity concept. | Accounting period. |
| Going-concern concept. | Revenue recognition. |
| Monetary concept. | Exchange price. |
| Matching concept. | |

1.  The balance sheet shows deferred training costs as a noncurrent asset.
2.  Among the current liabilities on the balance sheet is an account labeled Customers' Paid Orders, which was credited when customers made deposits on orders to be delivered in the future.
3.  On July 1, 3,000 shares of the firm's stock changes hands at various prices on the New York Stock Exchange; yet, the balance sheet on July 1 does not change.
4.  The balance sheet shows $810,000 for two testing laboratory buildings. The first was built in 1960 at a cost of $280,000; the second, identical in practically all respects to the first one, was built in 1982 at a cost of $530,000.
5.  The income statement heading contains the phrase "for the year ended July 31, 1985."
6.  Patents are shown as an intangible asset in the amount of $8 million, although they could be sold readily for twice that amount.
7.  Sales of goods "on approval," where the customer retains only certain units of product, are not recorded as revenue until the approval period ends.
8.  The goodwill shown on the balance sheet arose from the acquisition of another company. The goodwill generated internally does not appear as an asset.
9.  Even though net income is extremely low, the company still records depreciation expense.
10. The balance sheet contains a number of current assets and current liabilities with account titles beginning with the word *accrued*.
11. The three founding partners of a law firm occupy the three top positions in the organization. Collectively, they are responsible for generating a very large portion of the firm's business. Each has had a heart attack recently and is operating on a reduced schedule. On the income statement no mention is made of this loss, and no liability appears on the balance sheet.
12. Some specialized equipment appears on the balance sheet for $375,000. The plant manager admits, however, that if the firm tried to sell it, only its scrap value of $25,000 would be received.
13. Ty Coon, the president of a corporation, owns 60 percent of its capital stock and 20 percent of its outstanding bonds payable. During the year, the company makes substantial cash payments to him. Some are recorded as

salary expense, some are recorded as interest expense, and some are recorded as dividends, even though all the money goes to the same person.

14. The sales manager believes that the merchandise on hand will be sold during the following period for $180,000. It is listed on the balance sheet at $130,500.

15. The salary of the vice president for corporate planning is shown on the income statement as an expense although he spends almost all of his time working on various aspects of the five-year strategic plan for the company.

**5–2.** On its balance sheet as of December 31, 1981, Coleco Industries, Inc., a well-known maker of video games and recreational products, listed as a current asset $2,728,000 of Prepaid Advertising. The corresponding amounts as of the end of 1980 and 1979 were $2,310,000 and $3,912,000. Income before extraordinary items was $7,711,000 in 1981 and $13,065,000 in 1980.

The company explained the nature and origin of the prepaid advertising in a note to the financial statements:

> During the period 1979 to 1981, the Company entered into agreements which provided for products and cash . . . to be exchanged for media advertising. Sales for the years ended December 31, 1981, 1980, and 1979, included $2,372,000, $565,000 and $3,519,000, respectively, of shipments under these arrangements. The prepaid advertising expense resulting from these transactions was based on the fair value of the media advertising. The Company employs a process of matching advertising expense with sales revenue generated from advertised products. As a result, advertising expense is recognized as sales revenue is generated by the products advertised within the fiscal year.

*Required:*

a. Without figures give the journal entries that would summarize the recording done by Coleco Industries in connection with the prepaid advertising.

b. What would income before extraordinary items have been for 1981 and 1980 if the firm had followed the practice of treating the advertising costs as expenses of the period in which the media advertising was received? Make the simplifying assumption that the only new media advertising arising in 1980 and 1981 came in exchange for the products recorded in sales revenue. Also assume a tax rate of 46 percent.

c. An article in *The Wall Street Journal* of August 11, 1983, made the following comment: "More than [$20] million of the company's current assets included prepaid advertising . . . that, the [analysts] argue, should have been subtracted from the company's earnings. . . ." Do you agree with the analysts? Evaluate Coleco's policy.

**5–3.** The accounts listed below have been taken from the adjusted trial balance of Titus Canbe Company at the end of 1984.

| | |
|---|---:|
| Administrative expense ............................... | $ 132,800 |
| Cost of goods lost from shoplifting ..................... | 27,000 |
| Cost of goods sold to customers ....................... | 912,000 |
| Correction of errors from prior years—understatement | |
| of depreciation (1) .................................. | 26,900 |
| Dividends declared .................................... | 60,000 |
| Dividends received .................................... | 48,000 |
| Gain on sale of marketable securities ................... | 29,200 |
| Income taxes ......................................... | 51,300 |
| Interest charges ...................................... | 19,500 |
| Loss on sale of equipment ............................ | 50,200 |
| Real estate taxes ..................................... | 16,500 |
| Rent revenue ........................................ | 18,800 |
| Research and development costs ....................... | 52,000 |
| Retained earnings, January 1, 1984 .................... | 390,100 |
| Sales ................................................ | 1,470,000 |
| Selling expenses ..................................... | 191,600 |

Note 1: Generally accepted accounting principles require that this item be reported in the statement of retained earnings as an adjustment of the opening balance.

*Required:*

a. Prepare an income statement for 1984 using the multiple-step form and a separate statement of retained earnings.

b. Prepare an income statement for 1984 using the single-step form and a separate statement of retained earnings.

c. Discuss the advantages and disadvantages of the multiple-step and single-step formats. Which do you prefer?

d. In what ways are Cost of Goods Sold, Dividends Declared, Interest Charges, and Loss on Sale of Equipment similar? How do they differ?

**5–4.** Flibinite Corporation prepares a classified income statement using a multiple-step format as follows:

Operating revenues (A)

Operating expenses
  Cost of goods sold (B)
  Selling expenses (C)
  Administrative expenses (D)

Operating income
  Other revenue (E)
  Other expenses (F)

Income before gains and losses and unusual items
  Gains (G)
  Losses (H)
  Unusual charges and credits (I)

Net income

*Required:*

a. Using the above statement format, indicate where you would show each of the following items on the income statement. Use one of the key letters (A–I) applicable to each of the major sections. If the item would not appear on the income statement, identify it by using the letter X.

1. Annual depreciation on selling equipment.
2. Excess of the cash received from the sale of land over its cost.
3. Administrative salaries.
4. Cash dividends paid on capital stock.
5. Dividends received on long-term investments.
6. Costs associated with a strike.
7. Increase in the market value of temporary investments above their cost.
8. Vacation pay attributable to office staff.
9. Rental fees received from sublet of a portion of the company's warehouse.
10. Damages awarded to the firm under an antitrust settlement.
11. Expenditures on advertising.
12. Excess of the book value of equipment over the salvage value received when the equipment was scrapped.
13. Cost of office supplies used.
14. Proceeds from selling shares of the company's own stock.
15. Insurance settlement received from the insurance company for a fire that destroyed an entire warehouse. Because the insured values were based on replacement cost, the proceeds substantially exceeded the book value of the assets destroyed.
16. Costs of delivering the company's products to customers.
17. Proceeds received from a life insurance policy upon the death of an important officer in the company.
18. Sales commissions.
19. Cost of some inventory that had to be destroyed according to a new government regulation that had found the material hazardous to human health.
20. Interest paid on long-term notes payable.

*b.* What is your opinion of the income statement format used by Flibinite? What modifications would you make in it?

**5–5.** Marcia and Michael operate a children's store called Wee World. They are partners and share income equally. They do not maintain double-entry records. Prepare financial statements in good form at the end of 1985 from the following data, which you have assembled from checkbooks, deposit slips, and other sources.

1. The balance sheet as of December 31, 1984, showed the following balances:

| Assets | | Equities | |
|---|---:|---|---:|
| Cash | $ 56,300 | Accounts payable | $ 27,000 |
| Marketable securities | 14,600 | Advances from customers | 1,800 |
| Accounts receivable | 39,300 | Accrued salaries | 1,700 |
| Notes receivable | 3,000 | Partnership equities: | |
| Interest receivable | 100 | Marcia | 58,000 |
| Merchandise inventory | 54,000 | Michael | 89,500 |
| Prepayments | 2,500 | | |
| Fixtures | 14,800 | | |
| Accumulated depreciation | (6,600) | | |
| | $178,000 | | $178,000 |

2. Cash receipts for the year are summarized as follows:

| | |
|---|---:|
| Advances from customers ............................... | $ 1,400 |
| Cash sales and collections from customers ................ | 264,200 |
| Capital investment by Marcia ........................... | 12,000 |
| Collections on notes receivable: | |
| Interest ............................................ | 300 |
| Principal ........................................... | 2,000 |
| Proceeds from 12 percent, 90-day bank loan dated | |
| December 1, 1985 .................................. | 10,000 |
| Sale of all marketable securities ........................ | 16,000 |
| | $305,900 |

3. Checks written during the year are summarized as follows:

| | |
|---|---:|
| Prepayments ......................................... | $ 5,500 |
| Purchase of merchandise .............................. | 181,100 |
| Purchase of fixtures .................................. | 21,000 |
| Salaries paid to employees ............................ | 51,900 |
| Utilities ............................................. | 3,700 |
| Withdrawals by partners: | |
| Marcia ............................................ | 25,000 |
| Michael ........................................... | 25,000 |
| | $313,200 |

4. Depreciation is recognized on the fixtures at a rate of 20 percent per year; however, only a half-year's depreciation is charged on fixtures acquired during the year.

5. Selected account balances as of December 31, 1985, have been determined as follows:

| | | | |
|---|---:|---|---:|
| Accounts receivable ....... | $37,900 | Accounts payable ........ | $21,300 |
| Interest receivable ......... | 50 | Advances from | |
| Merchandise inventory ..... | 62,100 | customers ............. | 1,100 |
| Prepayments ............... | 1,400 | Accrued salaries ......... | 3,600 |

**5–6.** The Boomorbust Bomb Shelter Distributing Company was incorporated on July 1, 1984. Prepare general journal entries to record the following transactions, which summarize the activities of the company for the fiscal year ended June 30, 1985.

1. Capital stock was issued for $300,000 cash.
2. The following assets were acquired in exchange for cash and a $100,000 10-year mortgage: land, $45,000; buildings, $90,000; and equipment, $148,500. The mortgage liability was dated July 1, 1984, and bore a 12 percent rate of interest.
3. Insurance expense for the year paid in cash, $4,500.
4. Merchandise acquired on account, $742,500.
5. Promotional and entertainment costs were $89,000, paid in cash.
6. All sales of the product were made to a single foreign government, Middle Iamurpalia. A check for $75,000 was received early in the year to apply as a deposit against future deliveries.
7. Boomorbust sold some vacant land (acquired in transaction 2 for $25,000) for $37,300 cash.

8. General office and administrative work was done during the year at a cost of $54,000, paid in cash.
9. Property taxes paid in cash, $36,000.
10. Deliveries of products during the year totaled $1,312,000.
11. The cost of merchandise sold was $697,500.
12. Selling commissions were $39,300 of which $10,200 was unpaid at the end of the year.
13. Some equipment exploded while being tested. The cost of the equipment was $18,000. The loss was partially covered by insurance, and the company collected cash equal to 80 percent of the loss from the insurance company.
14. Additional equipment costing $22,000 was purchased on March 17, 1985. A cash payment of $7,000 was made, and a 10 percent, one-year note payable for $15,000 was given to the supplier.
15. Collections of cash from Middle Iamurpalia amounted to $1,222,500.
16. Depreciation amounted to $7,400 on equipment and $3,800 on the building.
17. Interest on the mortgage in transaction 2 and on the note in transaction 14 was accrued on June 30, 1985.
18. Payments to suppliers were $709,800.
19. On June 30, 1985, the board of directors declared a dividend of $100,000 payable on July 15, 1985.
20. Income taxes applicable to the fiscal year were accrued at a rate of 30 percent.

5–7. The following three notes were taken from the actual financial reports of the indicated companies.

> **International Paper Company, December 31, 1981, Report:** "Start-up costs on major projects are capitalized and charged to earnings over a five-year period. These costs are an integral part of the process of bringing a facility into commercial production, and therefore benefit future periods. At December 31, 1981, unamortized start-up costs were $49 million."
>
> **Marsh Supermarkets, Inc., April 3, 1982, Report:** "Non-capital expenditures associated with opening new stores are charged to expense as incurred."
>
> **Midland Glass Company, Inc., September 26, 1982, Report:** "Deferred pre-operating costs, net of amortization, amounted to $113,549 and $264,950 at September 26, 1982, and September 27, 1981, respectively. These costs were incurred in fiscal 1978 in connection with the expansion of a manufacturing facility and are being amortized over five years."

*Required:*

a. What circumstances make it appropriate to defer costs as assets rather than to treat them as period expenses? What is the rationale for treating costs as period expenses?
b. For each of these situations, discuss the alternative reporting procedures available to the company. Explain whether you agree or disagree with each company's policy.
c. Do you see any differences in the circumstances described by International Paper from those described by Midland Glass? Why do you think both companies chose five years as the period of benefit?
d. What factors might account for the apparent inconsistency between Marsh's

treatment of store-opening costs and the handling of start-up and preoperating costs by the other two companies?

**5–8.** The following financial statements have been prepared for Eastinghouse, Inc.—a single-step income statement for the year 1984, a balance sheet as of December 31, 1984, and a statement of cash receipts and disbursements for the year 1984.

### Income Statement
#### For 1984

| | | |
|---|---:|---:|
| Sales | | $350,000 |
| Rent revenue | | 40,000 |
| Gain on sale of marketable securities | | 13,000 |
| | | 403,000 |
| Less: Expenses, losses, and taxes: | | |
| Cost of goods sold | $228,000 | |
| Depreciation expense | 5,300 | |
| Insurance expense | 4,000 | |
| Salaries and wages | 85,200 | |
| Interest expense | 2,400 | |
| Loss on sale of land | 6,000 | |
| Taxes | 24,000 | 354,900 |
| Net income | | 48,100 |

Note: $9,000 of dividends were declared in 1984.

### Balance Sheet
#### As of December 31, 1984

| Assets | | Equities | |
|---|---:|---|---:|
| Cash | $ 27,500 | Accounts payable | $ 43,800 |
| Marketable securities | 35,000 | Interest payable | 600 |
| Accounts receivable | 63,800 | Taxes payable | 7,000 |
| Inventory | 52,500 | Rent received in advance | 15,000 |
| Prepaid insurance | 5,200 | Long-term notes payable | 40,000 |
| Land | 15,000 | Capital stock | 60,000 |
| Buildings and equipment | 55,000 | Retained earnings | 59,600 |
| Accumulated depreciation | (28,000) | | |
| | $226,000 | | $226,000 |

### Statement of Cash Receipts and Disbursements
#### For 1984

| | |
|---|---:|
| Cash receipts: | |
| Cash sales | $ 28,200 |
| Collections from charge customers | 262,500 |
| Collections from tenants | 54,000 |
| Sale of marketable securities | 28,000 |
| Sale of land | 8,000 |
| | 380,700 |
| Cash disbursements: | |
| Payments to suppliers of merchandise | 224,000 |
| Payments to insurance companies | 3,900 |
| Payments to employees | 85,700 |
| Payment of interest | 2,100 |
| Payment of taxes | 23,200 |
| Payment of dividends | 10,000 |
| Purchase of equipment | 14,000 |
| | 362,900 |
| Excess of receipts over disbursements | $ 17,800 |

*Required:*

Prepare a balance sheet as of *January 1, 1984*. You may find it helpful to use T-accounts as analytical devices and to reconstruct transactions during the period. Assume that purchases of inventory during the period were $222,300, all on account and that only inventory purchases were recorded in Accounts Payable.

**5–9.** You are in charge of the audit of the financial statements of United Soap and Tar Corporation for 1985. The audit work on each account balance has been completed, and you are satisfied that the accounts have been kept in conformity with generally accepted accounting principles. The only major part of the audit remaining, then, is to review the form of the financial statements that management proposes to use.

Presented below are the statements of profits and earned surplus that management proposes for 1985:

### Statement of Profits
### As of December 31, 1985

| | |
|---|---:|
| Sales | $649,000 |
| Selling costs | 83,800 |
| Net sales | 565,200 |
| Rent income | 16,800 |
| | 582,000 |
| Cost of goods sold | 445,000 |
| Gross profit | 137,000 |
| Profit on sale of equipment | 18,400 |
| | 155,400 |
| Operating costs: | |
| Administrative | 94,000 |
| Interest (net of interest income of $8,000) | 15,000 |
| | 109,000 |
| Net operating income | 46,400 |
| Other deductions: | |
| Depreciation | 19,400 |
| Dividend expense | 10,000 |
| | 29,400 |
| Net income | $ 17,000 |

### Statement of Earned Surplus
### As of December 31, 1985

| | |
|---|---:|
| Earned surplus, January 1 | $ 31,800 |
| Additions: Net income | 17,000 |
| | 48,800 |
| Deductions: | |
| Loss on sale of investments | 12,600 |
| Portion of net income distributed to government through taxes | 5,000 |
| | 17,600 |
| Earned surplus, December 31 | $ 31,200 |

*Required:*

a. Identify and discuss the defects in the presentation of these statements with respect to terminology, classification, and conceptual soundness. Your discussion should explain why you consider them to be defects.

  *b.*  Redraft the statements in good form.

  *c.*  The president of the company complains to you:

> Frankly, I don't understand why the accounting profession spends so much time arguing about statement format and how to report items. So long as disclosure is adequate, it doesn't matter how the item is reported. If the reader does not agree with the company's way of reporting, well, he simply can modify statements to fit his needs.

Comment on this position.

**5–10.**  U.S. Steel presented the following income statement for 1982 in its annual report for that year.

U.S. Steel
Consolidated Statement of Income
1982
($ millions)

| | |
|---|---:|
| Sales | $18,907 |
| Operating costs: | |
|   Cost of sales (excludes items shown below) | 14,194 |
|   Selling, general, and administrative expenses | 750 |
|   Pensions, insurance, and other employee benefits | 897 |
|   Depreciation, depletion, and amortization | 1,031 |
|   State, local, and miscellaneous taxes | 1,328 |
|   Exploration expenses | 304 |
|     Total operating costs | 18,504 |
| **Operating income** | 403 |
| Income from affiliates | 59 |
| Other income | 356 |
| **Total income from all operations** | 818 |
| Interest and other financial income | 291 |
| Interest and other financial costs | (911) |
| **Total income before unusual items, taxes on income, and minority interest** | 198 |
| Unusual items: | |
|   Estimated provision for costs attributable to shutdown of facilities | (123) |
|   Adjustment to provision for occupational disease claims | 31 |
|   Revaluation of investments and other assets | (30) |
|     Total unusual items | (122) |
| **Total income before taxes on income and minority interest** | 76 |
| Less: | |
|   Provision for estimated U.S. and foreign income taxes | 408 |
|   Minority interest—Marathon Oil Company | 29 |
| **Net income (loss)** | $ (361) |

Many of the items on the income statement are referenced to notes which provide detailed breakdowns and explanations. The notes have not been reproduced.

*Required:*

  *a.*  Critically evaluate the particular multistep format used by U.S. Steel. Why do you think the company showed five different income subtotals? Do you find them useful?

  *b.*  Redraft the income statement for U.S. Steel using a format that you believe is preferable. Justify your choice. Do not be concerned with items that you do not fully understand at this time such as minority interest. You may want to read parts (d), (f), (g), and (h) before completing this part.

c. Sales include $532 million of consumer excise taxes on petroleum products and merchandise. These taxes are generally levied on the manufacturer but are passed on to the consumer. U.S. Steel deducts the $532 million under the caption "State, local and miscellaneous taxes." Comment on the appropriateness of this recording of excise taxes.

d. Interest and other financial income includes $89 million of gains associated with the extinguishment of long-term debt. Should these gains be shown separately? Should the entire $291 million be included in either Operating Income or Total Income from All Operations?

e. Can you think of some reasons why U.S. Steel excludes interest and other financial costs from Operating Income or Total Income from All Operations? Do you agree?

f. U.S. Steel explains the account, Estimated Provision for Costs Attributable to Shutdown of Facilities as follows: "The Corporation approved additional permanent facility shutdowns in . . . 1982 (steel, chemicals, and specialty steel), with resultant costs of . . . $123 million. . . . The detail is as follows:"

| | |
|---|---:|
| Employee related costs | $ 71 |
| Writedown of facilities to estimated recoverable value | 48 |
| Estimated operating results during shutdown period | 4 |
| | $123 |

Do you think the classification of this item as an unusual item rather than as a normal part of the activities of a highly cyclical business is appropriate?

g. U.S. Steel offers the following explanation of the credit called Adjustment to Provision for Occupational Disease Claims:

An estimated accrual of $88 million was provided in 1979 for potential awards to those then retired for pneumoconiosis (black lung) as a result of the dramatic increase in claims following 1978 amendments to the Federal Coal Mine Health and Safety Act of 1969. Commencing in 1979, a provision for future claims is being accrued over the remaining service life of present employees. In 1982, the provision was reduced by $64 million as a result of a triennial valuation of the estimated liability for occupational disease claims. This adjustment resulted in a reduction of $33 million to Cost of sales for present employees, while $31 million was recorded as an Unusual item for pre-1979 retirees.

In general journal form (without numbers), give the entries U.S. Steel made in 1979, 1980, and 1981 in connection with this account. Do you believe that the correction of an estimate should be shown in two different places on the income statement? Do you agree that this item qualifies as an unusual item? Where would you report it?

h. The notes contain the following explanation for the deduction, Revaluation of Investments and Other Assets: "Impairment of Long-term receivables resulted in a charge of $23 million to pretax income as an Unusual item in 1982." Would you classify this item as unusual?

5–11. Northrup Corporation is an aerospace concern located in California. Early in 1983 it announced that its operating results for 1982 showed a net income of only $5.4

million compared with a 1981 income of $47.9 million. Part of the explanation for the decline concerned development expenditures as quoted from *The Wall Street Journal,* February 16, 1983.

> The Company said expenditures on the F-20 Tigershark tactical fighter plane totaled . . . $258.4 million (in 1982), compared with $153.6 million in 1981. Northrup, which still is waiting for its first F-20 order, is writing off all expenditures associated with the aircraft program as they are incurred.

DeHavilland Aircraft of Canada Ltd. is one of two major aircraft producers in Canada. In the seven months ended December 31, 1982, it reported net losses of $265.2 million (Canadian). These losses included $196.5 million of previously deferred development costs. The following comments are taken from the *The Wall Street Journal,* June 16, 1983.

> DeHavilland said its write-offs were taken because the commercial success of the two new aircraft designs is in doubt [because of] a significant reduction in demand for aircraft, which the company believes may continue for some time.
>
> Regarding previously deferred development and production costs for the company's "Dash 7" and "Dash 8" aircraft models, the company said that "there is no longer reasonable assurance that the deferred charges will be recovered." Such deferred costs were to have been applied against revenue from the sale of aircraft during the estimated life of a production run.
>
> (Earlier) . . . in testimony before a parliamentary committee, the officials indicated that DeHavilland's accounting practices were more in line with expectations. The latest write-off, therefore, came as a surprise.

*Required:*

a. What problems do these two situations suggest in making the decision whether or not to defer research and development costs? Does the DeHavilland Aircraft experience support the conservative approach mandated by the FASB in *Statement No. 2?*

b. What would Northrup's net income have been in 1981 and 1982 if it had deferred the development costs of the F-20? Assume a tax rate of 46 percent.

c. Do you believe it is appropriate for two companies in the same industry to use different accounting methods with respect to research and development costs? Are the differences justified by different economic circumstances?

d. What is meant by the testimony of DeHavilland officials that the company's "accounting practices were more in line with expectations?"

# FURTHER ASPECTS OF FINANCIAL MEASUREMENT— ASSETS

# CHAPTER 6

# ACCOUNTING FOR REVENUES AND RECEIVABLES

Revenue recognition controls the determination of periodic income. Revenues first have to be assigned to periods. Then the costs incurred to produce the assigned revenue can be measured, with appropriate accrual or deferral where necessary, and matched against it. Apart from income measurement, the revenue figure also is frequently used as a significant measure of the current volume of business activity and of the relative size and growth of business entities.

Up to this point we have recorded revenue from products whenever a sale is made. A temporary retained earnings account, Sales Revenue, is credited. If the sale does not result in the immediate receipt of cash, the debit is made to a current asset called Accounts Receivable. This account consists of all the open charge accounts used by the individual customers of a firm.

Similar entries are made for such revenues as interest and rent, which have no "point of sale" as such. These revenues are recognized at various times, usually upon receipt of cash or by year-end accrual. In any case, the debit records the inflow of assets to the business; the credit in the revenue account represents the source of assets.

In a realistic business setting, complexities arise. Revenue can be recognized at times other than the point of sale. Amounts billed to customers may include other items, such as sales taxes, in addition to the charge for products or services. Cash eventually collected from accounts receivable may be less than the amount billed because of returned merchandise, failure on the part of the customer to pay, or discounts offered for prompt payment. All of these possibilities suggest that our existing concepts, procedures, and accounts have to be clarified and expanded.

This chapter looks at the problems and procedures associated with the determination of when and how much revenue should be recognized. Separate sections of the chapter present (1) a closer look at the concept of revenue, (2) a more detailed explanation of the meaning and implications of the revenue postulate, (3) a study of some of its special applications, and (4) a description of procedures used when revenue is modified by events subsequent to the time of sale.

## THE CONCEPT OF REVENUE

In earlier chapters, revenue is defined as the inflow of assets from the provision of goods and services by the business entity.[1] The business engages in various activities in order that it may deliver products or render services. Revenue is the reward to the enterprise for performing these activities. Whether the revenue derives from a major activity (such as the sale of a product) or from a lesser, nonoperating service (such as the lending of money), one factor is common to all revenue flows. The firm is being compensated for efforts expended during the period in satisfying consumer wants. This factor distinguishes revenues from other inflows of assets—capital contributions, gifts, gains, and tax refunds.

### Revenue and Cash Receipts

Revenue being the reward to a business for efforts expended during the period, we need to know how to value the reward (asset inflow). The following observations may be helpful. The total reward over the life of the business normally cannot exceed the amount of cash collected from customers. Merchandise that is never delivered to customers and receivables that are never collected provide no compensation to the firm. The receivable arising from a revenue transaction has no intrinsic value per se. Its value, as we have seen in Chapter 2, derives from its convertibility into cash.

These observations suggest that revenue should be defined in terms of ultimate cash receipts. "Revenues represent actual or expected cash inflows (or the equivalent) that have occurred or will eventuate as a result of the enterprise's ongoing major or central operations during the period."[2] Until it is turned into cash, revenue is just an estimate. It may be represented by an inflow of assets other than cash, but the *value* of that inflow is determined by the cash equivalent received by the firm. Our concept of

---

[1] Some authors use the term *income* synonymously with revenue for such items as interest, rent, and so on. We will employ the term *revenue* for gross inflows of assets and reserve the term *income* for net flows (after various subtractions) such as operating income, income before taxes, and net income.

[2] FASB, *Statement of Financial Accounting Concepts No. 3,* "Elements of Financial Statements of Business Enterprises" (Stamford, Conn., December 1980) par. 64.

revenue for a period then will be *the cash received, cash to be received, or cash needs satisfied as a result of the firm's performance during the period.*[3]

A word of caution is necessary. The definition of revenue in terms of cash receipts does not imply that cash collections during a period equal the revenues of that period. Revenue is the compensation for performance during the period. Cash collection may be prior to the expenditure of effort, concurrent with it, or subsequent to it. The timing of revenue is determined by when the efforts necessary to provide goods and services are expended, not when the cash is actually collected.[4] However, the existence and amount of the eventual cash receipt determine how much total revenue can be recognized.

**Adjustments for Nonrevenue Receipts**

This more precise concept of revenue is helpful in later sections, where we explore the revenue recognition assumption and some associated measurement problems. Even now, however, it should be clear that only those amounts received from customers *in exchange for goods or services* can be considered revenues. Amounts billed or collected for sales taxes, customer deposits on containers, or some transportation costs are not rewards for the firm's efforts, even though a cash receipt results.

For example, a firm delivers merchandise having a sales price of $5,000. A state sales tax of 5 percent must be collected from the customer as well. The proper entry is:

| | | |
|---|---|---|
| Accounts Receivable | 5,250 | |
| Sales Revenue | | 5,000 |
| Liability for Sales Tax | | 250 |

When the $250 is remitted to the state tax authorities, the liability will be debited. The sales tax represents neither a revenue nor an expense to the business entity, which serves only as a collection agent for the government.

Transportation costs can be more complex. If delivery of the product is a necessary and vital part of the package of services being sold, the cost of performing this service is a business expense, and the total compensation received is revenue. On the other hand some sellers contact and pay the carrier merely to provide a convenience to the customer. Assume that a seller ships merchandise with a retail price of $2,000 and pays a $300

---

[3] "Cash needs satisfied" refers to those rare situations when the reward for efforts expended takes the form of a cancellation of a liability or a receipt of a tangible asset that can be used directly in the business. In such cases the revenue is measured by the amount of cash that otherwise would have been paid out, that is, the cash needs fulfilled.

[4] If a significant time period exists before cash is collected, the eventual cash receipts probably include compensation for waiting (interest) as well as for the current period's efforts. The interest element, as the reward for waiting, should be allocated to the waiting period. In this situation the revenue for the current period is actually the present value of cash to be received. Present value concepts and procedures are explained further in Chapter 10 and in the Appendix to Chapter 10.

freight bill. The goods are shipped FOB (free on board) shipping point so that the freight charges are the obligation of the buyer. Under these circumstances the following entries are appropriate:

```
Accounts Receivable  ................................    2,300
    Sales  .........................................            2,000
    Freight Paid for Customers  .......................          300

Freight Paid for Customers  ..........................      300
    Cash ..........................................             300
```

The $300 eventual cash receipt from the customer is not revenue. The seller simply serves as an agent for the customer in paying the carrier.

## CRITERIA FOR REVENUE RECOGNITION

We have laid down two criteria for recognizing revenue. One concerns the economics of earning revenue and the other the practical problem of measuring it. Our assumption states that *revenue should be recognized only when it has been earned and can be measured with a reasonable degree of reliability*. The first criterion is implicit in the definition of revenue. Because revenue is the reward for productive efforts expended, it cannot exist and therefore should not be recognized until all or a substantial portion of the earning efforts have been performed. However, during an accounting period many efforts are exerted for which the rewards may be received in subsequent periods. Only if these rewards are susceptible to reasonably precise measurement can the revenue be recognized and recorded in the period earned.

This dual approach attempts to strike a balance between the qualitative guidelines of relevance and reliability. The earning criterion tries to relate the revenue to the period in which the economic functions are performed. This provides timely and, hence, relevant monetary measures of the results of the period's efforts. The criterion of measurability confirms that a large degree of verifiability in the figures is also desirable if accounting information, particularly that communicated to external audiences, is to meet the guideline of reliability.

### Earning Criterion

Each cash receipt from a particular sale or revenue event represents the joint reward for a combination of earning efforts—organizing, purchasing, producing, selling, delivering, collecting, and others. These activities collectively are called the earning process. Because the earning process is carried out over time, the revenue may relate to activities in several accounting periods. Only that portion of the ultimate cash receipt which is compensation for efforts exerted during an accounting period should be reported as revenue for that period. One of the accounting tasks necessary in the recognition of periodic revenue is the allocation of the total estimated cash receipt to the periods in which the efforts are exerted, if not all are performed in the same accounting period.

What criterion should the accountant use for these allocations? Theoretically, the ultimate cash receipts (revenue) should be allocated on the basis of the relative importance of each function to the total efforts required for the creation and marketing of goods and services. The matching concept implies that costs are incurred to generate revenue. Therefore, accountants traditionally consider cost to be a measure of effort. As a general rule, then, if a large portion of cost has not yet been incurred, signifying that some function associated with the production of particular revenues is still unperformed, a portion of the revenue has not yet been earned. Of course, sometimes cost may not be a good measure of relative importance, in which case we must revert to some noncost measure. Nevertheless, the basic principle stands: Revenues can be recognized only to the extent that the earning process has been completed. The earning process is substantially complete when all necessary costs have been incurred or can be reliably estimated.

## Measurability Criterion

A measurement of the revenue earned in periods prior to the actual cash receipt requires a prediction of how much cash will be received. The second part of the dual standard for revenue states that it can be recognized only if this estimate is reliable. The two aspects of reliability from Chapter 1 that are relevant here are verifiability and representational faithfulness.

As a characteristic of revenue recognition, verifiability refers to the minimization of measurer bias. Artificial delay or advancement of the time of revenue recognition introduces a bias. Likewise, personal biases of management, whether optimistic or pessimistic, could affect the revenue estimate. Verifiability requires that the estimate be free from distortion and subject to independent confirmation. Consequently, accountants traditionally have accorded great weight to market transactions and arm's-length negotiations with outside parties.

Representational faithfulness concerns the probability that the revenue measure will equal the ultimate cash receipt. Of course absolute certainty in the revenue measure would have to wait upon the final receipt of cash from the customer. What the accountant must have is a sufficient degree of assurance that the amount of revenue being predicted is reasonably precise. Precision is evidenced when the sales value is ascertainable; the portion that eventually will be collected from the customer can be estimated; and when more than one accounting period is involved, the amount of revenue attributable to (earned during) each period can be determined. Again, accountants have often found such assurance in market transactions and the receipt from customers of cash, receivables, or some other asset capable of being measured (valued) reasonably accurately.

## Realization

The foregoing discussion focuses on criteria for revenue *recognition*. In accounting literature and practice, *realization* is the term most commonly associated with revenue. Some accountants state, for example, that revenues should not be recognized until they are realized. This declaration signifies little, however, for realization can be interpreted in many different ways.

Historically realization seems to have been first used with reference to the conversion of assets into cash. The concept arose in response to income tax and dividend laws, which stressed ability to pay and possession of assets in distributable form. However, its use soon broadened to include other ideas as well—liquidity (convertibility of assets into monetary assets), measurability (predictability of ultimate cash to be received), and severability (ability of the asset to be separated from the business via an exchange with an external party). The net result, unfortunately, has been that although most accountants use the term and subscribe to a realization criterion, the concept lacks a precise or common meaning. For some it means earning, for others it implies measurability, and for still others it signifies a sale. A few writers use the term to cover all of the criteria for revenue recognition, and a few still use it in its narrower sense of cash conversion. Care must be taken to interpret it correctly in context.

## APPLICATION OF THE REVENUE POSTULATE

Our earning criterion asserts that the ultimate cash receipt is a joint product of manifold activities and that revenue is earned in relation to the importance and completion of these activities. Conceptually revenue recognition should be continuous. As each stage in the earning process is completed, some increase in the value of the products and services being produced and sold by the business entity would be recorded. Gradually the goods or services would move from cost to full retail price.

As a practical matter continuous revenue recognition is impossible. Reliable determination of how much revenue is attributable to any single earning activity is extremely difficult. Therefore, accountants normally visualize revenue as arising at a particular point in the earning cycle after certain events have occurred. In a sense this expedient meshes with the measurability criterion. The longer measurement is postponed, the more certain it will be. The risk of recognizing unearned revenue or of recording revenue inaccurately is minimized. However, the postponement of recognition also increases the likelihood of earned revenue being left unrecognized.

Two conclusions seem to follow. First, the selection of a single time for revenue recognition is a useful expedient only if it does not magnify unduly either of these measurement errors. If it does, then either an alternative method which recognizes revenue in stages should be adopted, or subsequent adjustments should be made to the initial recording. Secondly, the optimum point of measurement would seem to be that which minimizes the total effects of the offsetting errors—recognition of unearned or inaccurate revenue and failure to recognize earned revenue.

According to the criteria discussed in the preceding section, if revenue is to be recognized at one point, then the *earliest* point of revenue recognition is when (1) the major revenue-producing activity has been performed *and* (2) the ultimate cash receipt can be estimated within a small margin of error. In most cases this is the point of sale, when goods are delivered or services performed. However, there are some differences from point-of-sale timing that should be discussed. These variations also derive from the revenue postulate.

**Point-of-Sale Recognition**

Recognition at the point of sale is common because for many businesses selling is the principal activity in the earning process. Once the sale is made, the probability of unearned revenue being recognized is substantially reduced. Practically all the costs associated with producing the revenue have been incurred; any additional necessary costs are either negligible or predictable, so adjustments can be made for unearned portions of the revenue. Until the actual sale (delivery of goods or performance of services) is completed, the ultimate cash receipt is largely unearned.

The accuracy of revenue measurement is also significantly enhanced at the point of sale. At any earlier time usually the expected exchange price of goods and services and/or the ability to sell them is highly uncertain. At the point of sale, on the other hand, the customer has either paid cash or pledged via an account receivable that he or she will pay cash within a short time. Adjustments for uncollectibles, returns, and discounts can usually be estimated with a sufficient degree of assurance to satisfy the measurement criteria. These adjustments and the procedures for recording them are covered in the last section in this chapter.

**Customer Advances.** The importance of the first criterion of earning in point-of-sale recognition can be seen in the case of the customer advance. The normal order in recognizing sales revenues is to delay until it can be measured with a reasonable degree of reliability. Even though the earning of revenue has taken place throughout the ordering, production, and selling phases, recognition is usually delayed until the point of sale.

However, if customers pay in cash first, say $3,000, the opposite situation arises. We have a certain measure of the revenue in the $3,000 cash receipt but have not yet earned it. Therefore, we should not yet recognize the revenue. Rather, an entry should be made:

| | | |
|---|---|---|
| Cash | 3,000 | |
| Customer Advances | | 3,000 |

Then, when the product is manufactured and delivered, the revenue will have been earned and can be recognized:

| | | |
|---|---|---|
| Customer Advances | 3,000 | |
| Sales | | 3,000 |

Until product delivery or service performance occurs, the customer has a claim against the assets of the firm. The Customer Advances account represents a liability, one that probably will be satisfied by the delivery of goods or the performance of a service. However, if the goods are not supplied or the service is not performed, the customer usually can claim a cash refund.

Similar situations exist with the sale of custom-made equipment, bus tokens, magazine subscriptions, and so on. In these cases the advances from customers may be given special account names. Nevertheless, the cash collected represents not revenue but simply an advance payment for services or goods to be received in the future. A liability account—Customers' Paid Orders, Tokens Outstanding, Unexpired Subscriptions, and so on—should be credited.[5]

**Adjustments for Cash Receipts Not Earned.** In the above case of the advance, none of the cash receipt is recognized until the major earning functions are completed. Sometimes more accurate results are obtained when some revenue is recognized at the point of sale. Any unearned portion can be determined and deducted from the total cash receipts initially or through adjustment at the end of the period. This treatment is particularly appropriate when significant additional efforts on the part of the firm are necessary after the point of sale. These efforts might include costs of installations, storage, collection, or servicing. In essence, the seller, for a single joint price, is providing a good now and a service in the future.

For example, a dealer who sells household appliances offers to provide "free" repair and maintenance service on the appliances for two years after the date of sale. Other customers can purchase such service agreements separately for $100 a year. If the total price of an appliance sold on January 1 is $900, the initial entry should be:

| | | |
|---|---|---|
| Cash (or Accounts Receivable) | 900 | |
| Sales | | 700 |
| Liability under Service Contracts | | 200 |

The service function has not been performed; therefore, the portion of the ultimate cash receipt attributable to that function has not been earned. In this case the unearned amount is $200 (two years at $100), as measured by the price of separate maintenance contracts. At the end of each year, an entry would be made:

| | | |
|---|---|---|
| Liability under Service Contracts | 100 | |
| Service Contract Revenue | | 100 |

If the actual costs of servicing are $60, this amount would be recorded as expense.

When no separate price exists for the unperformed function, in this case servicing, measurement is not so clear-cut. The portion of total

---

[5] Whether or not deposits have been received on unfilled sales orders, the magnitude and trend of such sales-order backlog is useful information. Ideally, it should be mentioned somewhere in the annual report.

revenue to be deferred to future periods may be unknown. In these cases, accountants could recognize as a liability an amount equal to the *cost* expected to be incurred under the service contract. It represents the minimum amount of the contract price to be deferred. If $60 per year is a reasonable cost estimate, the entry becomes:

| | | |
|---|---|---|
| Cash (or Accounts Receivable) | 900 | |
| Sales | | 780 |
| Liability under Service Contracts | | 120 |

This procedure may overstate sales revenue of the current period by any profit element attributable to the servicing function, but it is more accurate than treating the entire $900 as revenue. Of course, from a practical standpoint, unless the future service costs are fairly large, the revenue measurement would not be materially affected if they were not estimated.

Under the above procedure the amounts of Service Contract Revenue and Service Contract Expense are expected to be the same. Therefore, many companies do not set up separate revenue and expense accounts for the service contract. The actual costs of warranty are simply debited to the Liability under Service Contracts account. Another practical expedient used for material after-sale costs would treat the entire $900 as revenue but set up an estimated expense through the following entry:

| | | |
|---|---|---|
| Estimated Service Expense | 120 | |
| Liability under Service Contracts | | 120 |

Although following this procedure achieves the same net income effect as showing sales as $780, the treatment of the $120 as a deduction from sales (i.e., as unearned revenue) would be more in keeping with the earning criterion of the revenue concept. The estimated expense approach might be appropriate if the service contract is considered to be an incidental function. Such might be the case if the service is not sold separately and the selling price is the same whether the service is provided or not.

**Credit Card Sales.** One of the hallmarks of our modern society is the extensive use of credit cards as a means of acquiring goods and services. Major retail chains (Sears Roebuck, J. C. Penney) and oil companies (Shell, Texaco) issue their own credit cards. Banks throughout the nation sponsor MasterCard and VISA credit cards. Then, too, there are private companies, such as American Express and Carte Blanche, which have their own cards. We are indeed a society of plastic money.

How does the retailer record credit card sales? The answer depends on the type of card. In the case of the firm's own credit card, the sale is recorded as a regular sale on open account. The credit card is the means normally used to activate entries to Accounts Receivable in such businesses. The local Sears branch will record as follows a sale of $280 to a customer having a Sears charge card:

| | | |
|---|---|---|
| Accounts Receivable | 280 | |
| Sales | | 280 |

Any risk of nonpayment still rests with Sears.

In the case of bank cards and national credit card companies, the customer establishes credit with the issuer of the card (lender). As long as established procedures (validation of the card number, date, etc.) are followed, the retailer is able to transfer the risk of nonpayment and the expenses of collection to the lender. Moreover, the retailer does not have money tied up in receivable balances. For these services the issuer of the card charges a fee, which usually ranges from 2 to 5 percent of credit card sales.

The specific entries depend on whether bank cards or national credit cards are involved. In many places, MasterCard sales invoices are treated the same as cash. They are deposited in the bank just as if they were checks. Then, usually monthly, the bank reduces the retailer's bank balance by the amount of the credit card service fee. Assume that the sale for $280 referred to above was processed on MasterCard. Moreover, assume that similar sales for the month totaled $18,900 and that the fee is 3 percent. The entry to record the MasterCard sale would be:

```
Cash . . . . . . . . . . . . . . . . . . . . . . . . . . . . . . . . . . . . . . . . . . . .    280
    Sales  . . . . . . . . . . . . . . . . . . . . . . . . . . . . . . . . . . . . . . . . .           280
```

All other Master Card Sales would be recorded the same way with the total value being $18,900. The entry for the credit card service fees would be:

```
Credit Card Service Expense . . . . . . . . . . . . . . . . . . . . . . . .    567
    Cash . . . . . . . . . . . . . . . . . . . . . . . . . . . . . . . . . . . . . . . . . .           567
```

For customers' purchases made with credit cards like American Express and Diners Club, the retailer must wait for remittance from the card issuer. A receivable is set up from the credit card company, and the retailer's invoices are sent periodically to the company. The company remits the amount minus the credit card fee. If the purchases in the preceding paragraph were made with American Express cards, the following entries would be appropriate:

```
Accounts Receivable—American Express  . . . . . . . . . . . . . .    280
    Sales  . . . . . . . . . . . . . . . . . . . . . . . . . . . . . . . . . . . . . . . . .           280

Cash . . . . . . . . . . . . . . . . . . . . . . . . . . . . . . . . . . . . . . . . . .  18,333
Credit Card Service Expense . . . . . . . . . . . . . . . . . . . . . . . .    567
    Accounts Receivable—American Express  . . . . . . . . . .         18,900
```

**Completed Production**

Recognition of sales revenue before products are sold normally cannot be justified, because the revenue is not substantially earned and is not susceptible to reliable measurement. However, in some cases these conditions can be met when production is completed but before actual delivery and, perhaps, sale. For example, completed production may be an appropriate point for revenue recognition for companies which produce special orders under a binding contract. No additional selling effort is required, and the amount of revenue can be determined as soon as the major function of production is completed.

The amount of revenue recognized is the market price for the completed units less any direct marketing costs yet to be incurred. This amount is called *net realizable value*. To recognize revenue upon completion of production, the accountant debits a new inventory account and credits a revenue account for the net realizable value. The old inventory account at cost becomes an expense.

In the restricted circumstances outlined above, our dual criteria are met. When it is *unnecessary* to locate a buyer and convince him or her to purchase at a negotiated price, revenue is substantially earned when production is completed. Likewise, the selling price is a certainty. Any costs of additional functions, such as delivery, storage, servicing, and collection either are immaterial or can be estimated and the revenue figure appropriately adjusted to net realizable values.

The completed production basis also has applications in lines of business where a ready market exists to absorb all completed production at a quoted price. Examples include the extraction of precious metals or the harvesting of grains and certain other agricultural products. A farmer may value wheat, corn, or other staple crops at net selling prices because the local grain exchange provides a ready market in which the farmer can dispose of the entire output at a nearly fixed price with little additional effort. Income is recognized in the period of production, not in the period of sale or delivery. The cash reward from the production efforts can be predicted accurately at the point of completed production. Reliability of the estimate is found not in a specific transaction with a particular buyer but in the fixed price currently existing in an independent market, which will be relatively unaffected in quantity or price by the production offered by a particular seller.[6] Location of a buyer, estimation of a sales price, incurrence of material marketing costs, and other functions normally part of the earning process are of no consequence in this situation.

## Percentage of Completion

The percentage-of-completion expedient also relates revenue recognition to production rather than to sale or delivery. However, it provides for the recording of revenue as work progresses rather than when production is completed. Percentage of completion generally is employed for individual projects involving substantial amounts of revenue and considerable periods of time from inception of the project to its completion. Such projects

---

[6] If the harvested product can be sold in the current market with practically no additional effort, a seller choosing not to do so really is speculating on possible future price changes. Any gain or loss attributable to speculation properly belongs to the period between the point of completed production and the point of final sale. However, the revenue which the seller earns by *raising the product* is reliably measured by the current market price at the time production is complete.

include the manufacture of airplanes and ships and the construction of roads and bridges.

When the work span covers numerous accounting periods, reporting all of the revenue in any single period, when the project is either initially sold or finally completed, may be misleading as a measure of business activity and performance. Further, waiting until delivery occurs may not always be necessary for reliable measurement. Unlike conventional sales orders, which may be modified or canceled, a long-term construction contract usually represents a firm commitment. The amount of revenue is either established in the contract or related directly to the cost incurred, as in a cost-plus contract. Interim cash collections of portions of the sales price frequently are made as the project is worked on.

Under this recognition expedient, the *amount of revenue earned each period is based on the percentage of work done during that period*. Often the percentage of completion (work done) is measured by the ratio of the costs of the current period to the total estimated contract cost. Other measures of degree of completion include labor-hours expended, physical measures such as miles of highway laid, contract milestones reached such as number of floors erected, and engineering or architectural estimates.

**Illustration.** A construction company entered into a long-term contract for a total price of $4.5 million. Estimated costs of the contract amounted to $4,000,000. During the first year, $1,600,000 of construction costs were incurred; in the second year, $2,000,000 of such costs were incurred. The remaining work was completed in the third year at a cost of $400,000. Table 6–1 summarizes the revenue and gross margin results when percentage of completion is used.

**TABLE 6–1  Illustration of Revenue Recognition under Percentage of Completion**

|  | Year 1 | Year 2 | Year 3 | Total |
|---|---|---|---|---|
| Percentage of completion (work done) | 40% $\left(\frac{1.6}{4}\right)$ | 50% $\left(\frac{2}{4}\right)$ | 10% $\left(\frac{.4}{4}\right)$ | 100% |
| Revenue to be recognized ($4,500,000 × %) | $1,800,000 | $2,250,000 | $450,000 | $4,500,000 |
| Construction costs incurred | 1,600,000 | 2,000,000 | 400,000 | 4,000,000 |
| Gross margin | $ 200,000 | $ 250,000 | $ 50,000 | $ 500,000 |

If no revenue and income were recognized until delivery in the third year, the first two years would show no income, while the third year would show all $500,000. Percentage of completion spreads the revenue recognition over the period of construction activity in a reasonable manner. In this example, actual costs agreed exactly with the estimate. In reality, adjustments and corrections of prior revenue accruals have to be made with most contracts, but these adjustments are minor compared to the distortion of the earning process that would result if recognition were delayed until the end of the contract.[7] The percentage-of-completion method is clearly preferable when (1) reasonably dependable estimates can be made, (2) the contract specifies the rights of both buyer and seller, and (3) both parties can be expected to live up to the terms of the contract.[8] If estimates of work done or costs to complete the project are highly uncertain or if the other criteria are not met, then revenue estimates would be too unreliable. Postponement of revenue recognition until the contract is completed would be required. For example, a U.S. firm building luxury condominiums in Iran at the time of the Iranian revolution of 1979–80 shifted its accounting from percentage of completion to completed contract.

## Installment Method

Many retail businesses engage in sales transactions requiring only a nominal down payment, with the balance to be paid in monthly installments. Sometimes with these installment sales, recognition of revenue is postponed until *after* the point of sale. *Revenue is recognized only in proportion to the cash received each period.* The emphasis rests on the collection of receivables instead of their acquisition.

Two possible theoretical justifications are sometimes cited in these situations. First, the collection costs may be quite large and the waiting period long. Collecting and financing become a major part of the earning process. Therefore, revenue is substantially *unearned* at the point of sale and should not be recognized. The second justification is that the risk of uncollectibility may be very uncertain. There may be insufficient reliability in measurement for revenue recognition at the point of sale because of the high risk and unpredictable estimates associated with the ultimate cash receipt. For example, in real estate transactions the installment method is often advocated, because collectibility of the sales price cannot be estimated reasonably.

For most sale situations, however, these possible reasons for postponement of revenue recognition usually are *not* appropriate. First, a separate interest charge accompanies many installment sales. This charge, not the sales price, represents the compensation for the financing and collecting functions, which are not yet performed. Second, although there may be a great degree of uncollectibility with the installment sale, the relevant matter is the *ability to predict* the ultimate cash receipt, not the amount of uncollectibles. As long as reasonable estimates of uncollectible accounts

---

[7] The Appendix to Chapter 6 discusses in greater detail the recording problems and illustrates the accounts and actual journal entries that could be employed in accounting for construction contracts. In actual practice accountants calculate the revenue recognized each period by determining the *total* revenue earned to date less the revenue recognized in prior periods. They calculate the total revenue earned to date by multiplying the contract price by the percentage of total estimated cost incurred to date.

[8] American Institute of Certified Public Accountants, *Statement of Position 81-1,* "Accounting for Performance of Construction-Type and Certain Production-Type Contracts" (New York, July 1981).

can be made, deferral is not proper, even though the estimates may be large.

**Illustration.** An automobile dealership occasionally sells large trucks on installment contracts. On July 1, 1984, the firm sells three large trucks, each having a cost of $8,000, to a customer for a total of $30,000. The customer makes a $3,000 down payment. The balance of $27,000 will be paid at the rate of $3,000 at the end of each of the next nine quarters. The following entries are made in 1984.[9]

July 1, 1984

| | | |
|---|---|---|
| Cash | 3,000 | |
| Installment Receivables | 27,000 | |
|     Installment Sales | | 30,000 |
| | | |
| Installment Cost of Sales | 24,000 | |
|     Truck Inventory | | 24,000 |

September 30, 1984

| | | |
|---|---|---|
| Cash | 3,000 | |
|     Installment Receivables | | 3,000 |

December 31, 1984

| | | |
|---|---|---|
| Cash | 3,000 | |
|     Installment Receivables | | 3,000 |
| | | |
| Installment Sales | 30,000 | |
|     Installment Cost of Sales | | 24,000 |
|     Deferred Gross Margin—Installment Sales | | 6,000 |
| | | |
| Deferred Gross Margin—Installment Sales | 1,800 | |
|     Recognized Gross Margin | | 1,800 |

Because 30 percent of the total expected cash collections ($9,000/$30,000) is received in 1984, 30 percent of the gross margin is recognized in 1984. Another way of arriving at the same result is to apply the gross margin percentage of 20% ($6,000/$30,000) to the cash collections (20% × $9,000 = $1,800).[10] In 1985 the following entries are made:

March 31, June 30, September 30, and December 31

| | | |
|---|---|---|
| Cash | 3,000 | |
|     Installment Receivables | | 3,000 |

December 31

| | | |
|---|---|---|
| Deferred Gross Margin—Installment Sales | 2,400 | |
|     Recognized Gross Margin (20% × $12,000) | | 2,400 |

---

[9] This example excludes any interest charges on the unpaid balances. In most cases each payment has an interest element added to it. As indicated earlier, this interest revenue is the compensation for delayed payment and large collection efforts.

[10] If many sales are involved, the gross margin percentage is an average on all installment sales for 1984. This average is applied to all cash collections of 1984 installment receivables, regardless of when the cash is received. In future years cash receipts would have to be identified by year so that the gross margin percentage appropriate for each particular year could be applied.

The Recognized Gross Margin account appears on the income statement as a type of net revenue. Deferred Gross Margin—Installment Sales should appear on the balance sheet as a contra asset to Installment Receivables. Sometimes, however, it appears on the equity side among the liabilities—a curious classification, because the customer has no claim against the firm's assets. Offsetting of the Deferred Gross Margin reduces the balance of receivables to an amount equal to the unrecovered cost of the items sold. This is precisely the only asset value that can exist and still be consistent with nonrecognition of gross margin at the time of sale. No increased asset value is appropriate, because no income associated with the uncollected cash has been recognized under this method.

The installment method is permitted and widely used for *income tax purposes*. Nevertheless, except in very restricted circumstances, it should not be used for *financial reporting*. It postpones revenue recognition needlessly. The restricted circumstances are (1) when financing and collecting are the major functions and no separable estimate of interest and collection costs can be made and (2) when there is no reasonable basis for estimating the degree of collectibility. This conclusion concurs with that of the Accounting Principles Board, which has found the installment method of recognizing revenue to be unacceptable except in the second circumstance.[11]

## Challenges to Point-of-Sale Recognition

Of the previously discussed methods, point-of-sale recognition dominates the recording in most situations. So accustomed have accountants become to recognizing revenue at the point of sale that often the underlying criteria are overlooked. Overemphasis on the point of sale resulted in questionable revenue recognition practices in some companies and industries during the 1960s and 1970s. Among the industries were land development companies, franchising firms, and suppliers of long-term services.

These industry practices included (1) recognizing revenue even when a bona fide sale had not occurred, (2) recognizing revenue that was still unearned by failing to provide for functions not yet performed, and (3) overstating the revenue by failing to measure accurately the ultimate cash receipt. The net result was a "front-loading" of revenue—the recognition of too much revenue too early in the earning cycle.

A detailed description of these recording practices is beyond the scope of our discussion here. They did make necessary a reexamination of the criteria for revenue recognition. The AICPA and the FASB have both issued recommendations to guide the recording of revenue in these industries. A few of these are mentioned in the discussion of long-term service contracts later in this chapter.

---

[11] AICPA, *APB Opinion No. 10*, "Omnibus Opinion—1966" (New York, December 1966), par. 12.

## MEASUREMENT ADJUSTMENTS UNDER THE SALES METHOD

Even a strict following of the recognition postulate does not automatically solve all problems of accounting for that revenue. The original debit to Accounts Receivable and credit to Sales Revenue are at best provisional figures subject to later modification in the amount of cash to be received. This section deals with the accounting procedures necessary to handle three specific modifications—uncollectible accounts, returns, and discounts. Decreases in revenues and receivables from these modifications are often given special attention in the accounting records through segregation in contra accounts.

### Uncollectible Accounts

No matter how many precautions a firm takes to ensure against selling on credit to customers who may not pay, some accounts receivable are never collected. To the extent that this happens, both the sales revenue for the period and the trade accounts receivable at the end of the period are incorrect. Uncollectible accounts do not represent a valid claim to cash. Likewise, the sale which was originally recorded at the selling price turns out actually to have been made for nothing.

Unfortunately, a firm can specifically identify uncollectible accounts only after time has elapsed and repeated efforts at collection have failed—in short, usually in an accounting period later than the one in which the sale was originally reported on the income statement. However, to wait is contrary to both the revenue concept and the periodicity concept. It is the revenues of the period in which the sale was made that are overstated, not the revenues of the period in which the account was discovered. Uncollectible sales should be treated as adjustments of revenue in the period the sales were made. Moreover, to ignore doubtful accounts until they can be identified specifically would lead to an incorrect position statement because of the initial overstatement of accounts receivable.

Fortunately, there is an answer to this dilemma. Although businesses cannot predict at the time of sale what specific customers will not pay, many of them can estimate with a reasonable degree of accuracy the aggregate amount of uncollectible accounts arising from a period's sales. Usually a direct and reliably measurable relationship exists between the amount of uncollectibles (bad debts) and the amount of credit sales or the amount of unpaid customer balances. The estimate is based on past experience with these relationships. A firm can use its own past experience or, in the case of a new firm, the experience of similar companies in its particular line of business. By estimating doubtful accounts, the firm can adjust sales and accounts receivable in the current period.

**Recognition of Doubtful Accounts.** Assume that a company has credit sales of $250,000 during 1984, and collections during the year amount to $225,000. This leaves an outstanding balance of $25,000 in accounts receivable. Assume also that past experience indicates that one half of 1 percent of credit sales turn out to be uncollectible. The estimate of doubtful accounts would be $1,250 (0.5 percent × $250,000). An entry at the end of the period adjusts both sales and accounts receivable.

*Contra revenue account* →

| | | |
|---|---|---|
| Dec. 31 Sales Uncollectibles | 1,250 | |
| → Allowance for Doubtful Accounts | | 1,250 |

*Contra asset account* →

The $1,250 decrease in sales revenue could have been debited to the Sales account. However, for the purpose of more complete reporting of financial information, it is segregated in a special *contra revenue* account. Similarly, in the case of accounts receivable we are reducing our assets by $1,250. Nevertheless, rather than reduce the asset directly, we choose to record the credit in a separate *contra asset* account. The reason in this case is a practical one. Accounts Receivable is a general ledger account controlling numerous individual charge accounts in a subsidiary ledger. If we credit Accounts Receivable directly, it would no longer be in agreement with the total of the subsidiary ledger, unless we also reduce some specific individual accounts. However, at this point we are usually unable to identify the individuals who will not pay. All that can be said now is that of the $25,000 owed to us we expect not to collect $1,250. This is exactly the meaning of the balance in the contra asset account.

Sales and Sales Uncollectibles, being temporary accounts, are closed at the end of the period and appear on the income statement. Allowance for Doubtful Accounts (Allowance for Uncollectibles) appears on the balance sheet as a subtraction from Accounts Receivable. An alternative reporting treatment would be to show the net amount of receivables on the statement and the amount of the contra account in parentheses.

**Identification of Specific Uncollectible Accounts.** The end-of-period adjusting entry made on December 31, 1984, reduces both sales and accounts receivable by $1,250. During the following year it is reasonable to expect that specific individual charge accounts will be discovered to be uncollectible. Assume that $750 of specific accounts are so identified during 1985. The entry to write them off will be:

| | | |
|---|---|---|
| Allowance for Doubtful Accounts | 750 | |
| Accounts Receivable | | 750 |

We initially use a contra asset account because of our inability to pinpoint particular subsidiary accounts as uncollectible. We therefore reduce trade receivables by crediting the contra account rather than the control account. However, in later periods when the subsidiary accounts can be pinpointed, the need for the contra account disappears. The effect of the above entry is simply to remove the credit from the contra account and enter it in the main account. Corresponding credits are entered in the subsidiary ledger accounts also.

Accounts receivable and net income are reduced only by the original estimating entry. The write-off entry *causes no net changes in assets or in owners' equity*. To see the neutral effect of this entry, compare below the accounts receivable and contra before and after the write-off.

| | Before | After |
|---|---|---|
| Accounts receivable ..................... | $25,000 | $24,250 |
| Less: Allowance for doubtful accounts .... | 1,250 | 500 |
| Realizable value of accounts receivable .... | $23,750 | $23,750 |

The account balances after the entry simply say that of the $24,250 still owed only $23,750 is expected to be realized in cash. The firm is still unable specifically to identify the remaining $500 of individual accounts that are estimated to be uncollectible.

In our illustration we assumed that no individual accounts were written off until the years following the year of sale. This is the normal sequence. In some instances, however, specific accounts can be identified as bad debts in the period of sale. An account arising in January may be written off in July. In fact, if enough of these early write-offs are made, the contra asset, Allowance for Doubtful accounts, could temporarily have a debit balance, until the adjusting entry for that year's uncollectibles is recorded at year-end. Nevertheless, the entry to write off a specific account is still the same, regardless of when the entry is recorded. It has no impact on the financial statements. As long as an accurate estimating entry has been recorded, the income statement and balance sheet will be reliable.

**Recovery of Accounts Deemed Uncollectible.** What happens when a receivable that has previously been written off as a specific uncollectible account is collected? One very common treatment attributes the recovery to a premature write-off. The account really never should have been deemed uncollectible. Suppose that the $750 of receivables written off during 1985 includes one account of $80 which ends up being collected in December. The write-off entry should be reversed and the cash treated as an ordinary collection of a receivable:

| | | |
|---|---|---|
| Accounts Receivable ................................ | 80 | |
| Allowance for Doubtful Accounts .................... | | 80 |
| | | |
| Cash ................................................. | 80 | |
| Accounts Receivable ............................ | | 80 |

Entries would also be made in the subsidiary ledger so that a complete record of the eventual collection of the account appears.

This procedure is particularly appropriate when arbitrary policies are followed in the naming of an account as uncollectible. For example, a firm as a matter of policy might write off all accounts with balances over one year old. This policy may result in some accounts being erroneously identified as uncollectible.

Note that the recovery of an individual account does not imply that the estimate being used is inaccurate. Rather, the *write-off was a mistake;* this recovered account was not one of those inherent in the estimate.

**Adjustment Based on Credit Sales.** In our example we assume that bad debts are a direct function of credit sales. Consequently, the estimate of doubtful accounts was one half of 1 percent of credit sales. Let us pursue our example one more year. In 1985 the firm has sales on open account of $375,000 and cash collections of $345,000. The adjustment for doubtful accounts at the end of 1985 is one half of 1 percent of the credit sales for the period of $375,000 or $1,875, if we assume that our experience is unchanged.

| | | | | |
|---|---|---|---|---|
| Dec. 31 | Sales Uncollectibles | ........................ | 1,875 | |
| | Allowance for Doubtful Accounts | ........... | | 1,875 |

The year-end treatment of the accounts is the same as before. Sales and Sales Uncollectibles are closed. The T-accounts below show the effect on Accounts Receivable and on Allowance for Doubtful Accounts from the entries in 1984 and 1985.

**Accounts Receivable**

| | | | |
|---|---|---|---|
| 1984 sales | 250,000 | 1984 collections | 225,000 |
| 1985 sales | 375,000 | 1985 collections | 345,000 |
| 1985 recovery | | 1985 write off | 750 |
| of write-off | 80 | 1985 cash recovery | 80 |

**Allowance for Doubtful Accounts**

| | | | |
|---|---|---|---|
| 1985 write-off | 750 | 1984 provision | 1,250 |
| | | 1985 recovery | |
| | | of write-off | 80 |
| | | 1985 provision | 1,875 |

Both of these accounts appear on the balance sheet prepared at the end of 1985.

| | | | |
|---|---|---|---|
| Accounts receivable | ............................. | $54,250 | |
| Less: Allowance for doubtful accounts | ............ | 2,455 | $51,795 |

Of the $54,250 owed by customers, the firm expects not to collect $2,455. The specific individual subsidiary accounts that are uncollectible will be identified in 1986 and subsequent years.

Under this method of adjustment the estimate is based directly on the income statement figure of credit sales. The asset adjustment is the by-product of the revenue adjustment. An estimate based on sales is appropriate for companies having a large number of customers with relatively small receivable balances. In these cases one would expect that amounts lost through nonpayment would vary with credit sales in a reasonably stable manner from period to period. One potential defect of this approach is that the Allowance for Doubtful Accounts could grow too large or too small in relation to the end-of-period receivables if the estimate is faulty. The resultant under- or overstatement of receivables could go undetected.

**Adjustment Based on Accounts Receivable.** To estimate the amount of uncollectibles, accountants frequently use an alternative procedure which adjusts the Allowance for Doubtful Accounts to equal a preestablished percentage of the accounts receivable at the end of each period. The focus is on an accurate measurement of accounts receivable, and the adjustment of sales is the by-product. Taking the preceding example, assume that past experience indicates that of the outstanding receivables existing at the *end* of any given year 5 percent is never realized in cash. Instead of applying a percentage to total credit sales, we determine our adjustment for doubtful accounts by valuing the ending accounts receivable. Of the $25,000 of receivables outstanding at the end of 1984, 5 percent, or $1,250, is expected never to be collected. Therefore, $1,250 is the balance we desire to have in the Allowance for Doubtful Accounts to show the net realizable value of the trade receivables. Inasmuch as the contra asset account has no balance prior to the estimating entry for 1984, $1,250 is also the amount of the adjustment for doubtful accounts.

The estimate for 1985 is a little more complex. At the end of 1985, the balance in Accounts Receivable is $54,250. The estimate of 5 percent would suggest that $2,713 of this is uncollectible. Because a credit balance of $580 ($1,250 − $750 + $80) already is in the allowance account, we would make a $2,133 ($2,713 − $580) credit to Allowance for Doubtful Accounts and debit to Sales Uncollectibles for 1985.

In the interests of greater accuracy, the individual accounts receivable often are aged. *Aging* is the process of classifying account balances according to the length of time they have been outstanding. Then, instead of an *average* uncollectible percentage like the 5 percent used above, a different percentage is applied to each age group. Table 6–2 shows a hypothetical aging of the $54,250 account balances outstanding at the end of 1985. The increasing uncollectibility percentages reflect the general relationship between the length of time a balance is outstanding and the likelihood that

**TABLE 6–2  Aging Schedule for Accounts Receivable as of December 31, 1985**

| Customer Name | Total Balance | Age of Balance in Days | | | |
|---|---|---|---|---|---|
| | | *0–60* | *61–120* | *121–360* | *Over 360* |
| Anderson, K. | $ 2,700 | $ 2,100 | $   300 | $  300 | — |
| Baker, L. | 8,150 | 1,600 | 2,400 | 4,150 | — |
| Black, J. | 4,200 | 4,200 | — | — | — |
| Daube, K. | 6,400 | 4,400 | 1,500 | 500 | — |
| Light, S. | 5,250 | 4,000 | 800 | 450 | — |
| Mason, P. | 8,300 | 6,200 | 2,100 | — | — |
| Nord, Z. | 3,950 | — | 2,000 | 1,400 | $  550 |
| Rebele, J. | 5,400 | 5,400 | — | — | — |
| Smith, S. | 6,000 | 1,000 | 2,000 | 2,500 | 500 |
| Wilson, G. | 3,900 | 1,600 | 2,300 | — | — |
| Total | $54,250 | $30,500 | $13,400 | $9,300 | $1,050 |
| Uncollectible (percent) | | 1% | 5% | 10% | 50% |
| Desired balance in allowance | $ 2,430 | $   305 | $   670 | $  930 | $  525 |
| Existing credit balance | 580 | | | | |
| 1985 estimate | $ 1,850 | | | | |

the account will be collected. Aging facilitates more accurate estimates of doubtful accounts than overall percentages, because it is more sensitive to the actual condition of the accounts receivable. The aging schedule also can present information to be used by management in evaluating credit-granting policies and collection efforts.

The accounts receivable approach is widely used. Analysis of the individual accounts is particularly appropriate when some very large or unusual accounts are included in the total or when economic changes (such as recession) occur. Estimates based on accounts receivable eliminate the possibility of a disproportionate relationship developing between the asset and the contra account. At the end of each accounting period, the contra account is adjusted by *whatever amount* is necessary to make it conform to the uncollectibility situation at that time.

The defect of this method is emphasized by the italicized words. The income statement adjustment is not calculated directly but arises as a by-product of the adjustment to receivables. Consequently, any errors made in receivables—prior periods' misestimates or irregularities in the identification of specific uncollectible accounts—are automatically compensated for in the current period's estimate. For example, if the write-off of individual bad accounts follows an irregular pattern, then procedures based on outstanding accounts receivable may give an erratic estimate from year to year.

**Summary.** An adjustment based on sales asks the question, "How much of this year's sales will not be collected?" An adjustment based on accounts receivable asks the question, "How much of the year-end balance of accounts receivable will not be collected?" However, regardless of the method used for estimation, the interpretation of the accounts is the same. Sales Uncollectibles reflects the revenue adjustment applicable to the current period's sales. The Allowance for Doubtful Accounts measures the estimated amount of uncollectibles associated with the outstanding receivables, regardless of the year of origin. The contra asset account is increased by each period's adjustment for doubtful accounts. Concurrently, as individual uncollectible accounts are identified, entries are made debiting the Allowance for Doubtful Accounts. The balance in the contra account, therefore, should bear a fairly close relationship to the balance in the asset account, provided that the original estimate remains accurate. As in our example, the estimate based on credit sales and the estimate based on outstanding accounts receivable should result in very similar adjustments. Normally, only one method is used regularly, the other being used periodically as a check.

Underlying both estimating procedures is the assumption that the original entries recording sales on account are tentative. Revenue is equal to the amount of cash ultimately to be collected, not the original sales price. Because uncollectible accounts have a net realizable value of zero, these sales provide no revenue. Hence, we deduct the estimate of uncollectibles from gross sales to obtain the adjusted net revenue figure.

Many accountants and most business executives view uncollectible accounts as *expenses* instead. In practice, the debit is made to an Uncollectible Accounts Expense account in accordance with the argument that a certain amount of uncollectibles is inevitable when business is conducted on credit. Management's decision to extend credit is premised on the view that the income from the expanded sales caused by the offering of credit will far outweigh the uncollectible amounts. Nevertheless, the treatment of bad debts as an expense views the original debits to Accounts Receivable as absolute measures of value. However, it seems to us that the value of the claim to cash logically should not be divorced from the amount of cash expected to be received. Uncollectibles are not like other expenses (resources used up in the production of revenues); they represent revenue never received rather than costs incurred.

Whether the debit entry resulting from the estimate of doubtful accounts is treated as a contra revenue or as an expense, the same net income results. Moreover, the decrease in income is segregated in a special account for informational purposes in either case. Classification of this deduction on the income statement is not a major accounting issue.

What may be an issue is whether the use of any estimate introduces too much subjectivity into the recording process. Many small businesses do not estimate. They follow a procedure called *direct write-off*, under which an expense is recorded only when specific accounts are identified. Not only does direct write-off result in less accurate periodic financial statements than when timely estimates are used, but the procedure actually may be less objective as well. There is no automatic way of determining exactly when an account is uncollectible. It is a question of management's judgment. Under direct write-off, how management exercises this judgment affects income. The estimate procedure, on the other hand, allows for the specific write-off of an account without any effect on income. It thereby removes a potential distortion in income measurement arising from the purposeful speeding up or postponement of the identification of specific uncollectible accounts.

## Sales Returns and Allowances

In addition to customers who never pay their accounts, the accountant must also deal with some customers who return the merchandise they have purchased. If the returned goods are accepted by the seller, the sale is in effect canceled, and the accounts receivable claim disappears. The possibility of sales returns raises three questions that we will address in this section: How do accountants record sales returns? What about sales made at the end of the current accounting period that will be returned in the next accounting period? What implications does the return privilege have for the timing of revenue recognition?

**Recording Sales Returns.** Assume that a customer returns merchandise sold originally for $650. The return nullifies the original debit to Accounts Receivable and credit to Sales. Sometimes when the cause of customer dissatisfaction is minor imperfections in the merchandise, the seller and purchaser will agree on a price reduction or allowance in lieu of a return. The entry to record either a $650 sales return or a $650 reduction in sales price is:

| | | |
|---|---|---|
| Sales Returns and Allowances | 650 | |
| Accounts Receivable | | 650 |

The contra revenue account, as opposed to a direct debit to sales, segregates these particular decreases in revenue and highlights them for management's attention and analysis. Changes in the level of sales returns and allowances vis-à-vis sales from period to period may reflect trends in customer tastes and/or changes in the quality of merchandise or service.

Because we know the exact customers who are returning the merchandise, we normally do not need a contra asset account. When the Accounts Receivable control account is credited as in the entry above, a credit is also made in the particular customer's charge account in the subsidiary ledger.

**Estimated Sales Returns.** What about sales made at the end of the current accounting period that will be returned in the next accounting period? If we debit a contra revenue account when the return actually takes place, we shall be matching cancellations of this period's sales against the next period's sales. Moreover, the value assigned to accounts receivable on the year-end balance sheet will be overstated. Potential sales returns reduce the ultimate cash receipts to be realized through collection of the accounts.

In some industries the amount of estimated returns may be significant. Catalog sales and sales of musical records and tapes are prominent examples. In these cases accuracy in revenue recognition and income determination is enhanced by an estimation of the amount of sales at the end of the current period which normally will be canceled by returns taking place in the next period. Then an adjusting entry is made similar to the adjustment for doubtful accounts, the credit being made to a contra asset, Accounts Receivable—Allowance for Returns.

The adjustment for estimated returns differs, however, from the adjustment for uncollectibles. The former also entails a judgment concerning the *cost* of merchandise that is estimated to be returned. For example, assume that anticipated returns, based on past experience, equal about 15 percent of outstanding accounts receivable at year-end. Moreover, the cost of the returned merchandise averages 66.7 percent of the selling prices. If accounts receivable at the end of an accounting period amount to $150,000, the proper adjusting entries would be:

| | | |
|---|---|---|
| Sales Returns and Allowances | 22,500 | |
| Allowance for Sales Returns | | 22,500 |
| | | |
| Inventory—Estimated Returns | 15,000 | |
| Cost of Goods Sold | | 15,000 |

These entries reduces sales by $22,500 and net income by $7,500, the original gross margin on the sales. Assets are also reduced a net $7,500;

accounts receivable decreases by the $22,500 credited to the contra asset account, and an estimated inventory asset increases $15,000.

The foregoing adjustment is not an acceptable procedure for income tax purposes. Furthermore, for some firms the amount of estimated returns is small and relatively constant from year to year. For practical reasons, then, these firms usually do not adjust for estimated returns. If estimated returns are material, however, the adjustment is strongly recommended.

**Deferral of Revenue Recognition.** In some circumstances the existence of a right of return may call into question the appropriateness of even recognizing revenue at the point of sale. A retail firm may have a right to return to the wholesaler or manufacturer merchandise that cannot be resold to the ultimate customers. Bookstores and record stores often have this right. In these cases, the risks of ownership of the merchandise have not really passed to the retailer. The manufacturer or wholesaler has not substantially earned the revenue until the return privilege expires, nor is there likely to be a reliable measure of the ultimate cash receipt until then.

The Financial Accounting Standards Board addressed this problem in 1981. If a significant right to return a product exists, no revenue can be recognized at the point of sale unless all of the following conditions are met.[12]

1. The price is fixed or determinable at the date of sale.
2. The buyer's obligation to pay the seller is not contingent on the buyer's resale of the product.
3. Theft or destruction of the product would not change the buyer's obligation to pay the seller.
4. The buyer has economic substance apart from the seller.
5. The seller has no obligation for resale.
6. The amount of returns can be estimated.

Conditions 2, 3, and 5 concern whether there has been a legitimate transfer of risk and hence an earning of revenue. Condition 4 assures that the sale is bona fide. Conditions 1 and 6 concern issues of measurability. If all conditions are satisfied, it is acceptable to recognize revenue at the point of sale and to establish an allowance for estimated returns, as described in the preceding section. If one or more of the conditions is not satisfied, revenue recognition should be postponed until the return privilege expires.

**Sales Discounts**

One additional recording problem may arise in purchase-sale transactions; a cash discount may be offered for prompt payment of accounts. Particu-

---

[12] FASB, *Statement of Financial Accounting Standards No. 48,* "Revenue Recognition When Right of Return Exists" (Stamford, Conn., June 1981), par. 6.

larly in the wholesale trade, the seller often allows a discount from the billed amount if payment is made within a certain time. Cash discounts are offered to encourage early payment, which reduces billing and collection costs and, more importantly, lessens the risk of uncollectibles. Many business managers view cash discounts as less costly substitutes for revenue losses arising from bad debts.

The invoice price is referred to as the *gross price*. The price after the discount for prompt payment is termed the *net price*. Which amount of revenue is to be recorded at the time of the initial sale? Sales are recorded more commonly at gross prices than at net prices, but both methods are used in practice. Both methods usually also require later adjustments. If sales are entered at gross prices, then modifications are necessary whenever customers take the discount. If sales are initially recorded at net prices, then adjustments are necessary for all discounts lost by customers.

**Example.** A simple example illustrates both methods. Suppose two sales of $5,000 each (gross price) are made on October 1. One account is paid on October 9; the other is paid on November 21. Further, let us assume that the firm sells on terms which allow a 3 percent discount if the customer pays his or her account within 15 days of the invoice date. Otherwise, the full gross price is due within 60 days. These terms are abbreviated 3/15, n/60.

The journal entries in Table 6–3 show how these transactions are handled under both the gross and the net methods. Obviously an individual firm would employ one or the other, not both. Under the gross method, payment within the discount period necessitates an adjustment to revenue by means of a debit to the contra account, Sales Discounts. When payment is made after the discount period in the gross amount, no

**TABLE 6–3  Comparison of Sales Recorded at Gross and at Net Prices**

|  |  |  |  |
|---|---|---|---|
| *Gross Price Recording* | | | |
| Oct. 1 | Accounts Receivable | 10,000 | |
| | Sales | | 10,000 |
| Oct. 9 | Cash | 4,850 | |
| | Sales Discounts | 150 | |
| | Accounts Receivable | | 5,000 |
| Nov. 21 | Cash | 5,000 | |
| | Accounts Receivable | | 5,000 |
| *Net Price Recording* | | | |
| Oct. 1 | Accounts Receivable | 9,700 | |
| | Sales ($10,000 less 3%) | | 9,700 |
| Oct. 9 | Cash | 4,850 | |
| | Accounts Receivable | | 4,850 |
| Nov. 21 | Cash | 5,000 | |
| | Accounts Receivable | | 4,850 |
| | Sales Discount Revenue | | 150 |

adjustment is normally made, as gross is the basis for the original entry. In essence, the opposite occurs under the net method. No adjustment of revenue is necesssary on October 9; the sale has been recorded under the correct assumption that the customer would take the discount. Gross payments after the discount period has expired, however, require recognition of an additional $150 of revenue from those customers who elected the deferred payment privilege.[13]

Despite the greater usage of the gross method in business practice, logic seems to favor the net method. The cash discount is actually a penalty charged for late payment that customers who pay on time do not have to remit. The revenue expected from the sale of the merchandise is the "cash" price or net price. Under the net method, Sales is credited only with the pure price of the product. A separate revenue account is credited whenever additional cash is collected for late payment. Under the gross method these revenues are combined in the Sales account.[14] Both methods, of course, record the same total revenue.

## LONG-TERM SERVICE CONTRACTS

Our discussions so far in this chapter have concerned the sale of products for the most part. Some interesting revenue recognition problems exist also in the sale of services, particularly services to be provided under a long-term contract. Correspondence schools offer courses for a fixed fee; research and development laboratories provide research services under long-term contracts; health clubs supply a variety of services to members in exchange for initiation or membership fees paid in advance; maintenance firms contract to clean offices or service equipment; and computer service bureaus agree to process data.

In these and many other situations, there is a point of sale at which a contract is signed. The services, however, are usually provided later. The earning criterion suggests strongly that the point of sale is not the proper point for revenue recognition. The question we shall address is: What are the proper points or point for revenue recognition?

With long-term service contracts, abuses sometimes have occurred in revenue recognition. These abuses tended to recognize revenue as soon as possible—so called "front loading" of revenue. Such practices fell into three major categories;

1.   All revenue was recorded at the time the contract was signed. None was deferred to future periods, when services were actually per-

---

[13] Truth-in-lending laws require many merchants to disclose the effective interest rate that is hidden in the gross (delayed payment) price.

[14] Many analysts feel that this inclusion in gross sales of the revenue from discounts not taken hides significant information about a firm's credit customers. They would prefer that every discount, whether taken or not, be separately accounted for under the gross method.

formed. Indeed, in some cases not even the estimated costs of providing the services were accrued.

2.  Many such service contracts specified long periods in which the customer could cancel and receive a full or partial refund. However, no adjustment was made for this contingency.
3.  Cash collections were not always reasonably assured, and uncollectible accounts were not capable of being reliably estimated. Again, no reflection was given to this fact in the revenue measure.

A single authoritative solution to these problems has not been formulated. However, a number of worthwhile suggestions have been made by the American Institute of Certified Public Accountants through its Accounting Standards Committee.[15] With respect to the first point in the above paragraph, the timing and pattern of revenue recognition, the AICPA proposes a variety of solutions suited to differing circumstances of specific contracts. These alternatives involve practical applications of the earning criterion.

If the service transaction is a single act or consists of a series of incidental services followed by a major act, revenue should be recognized upon completion of the single or major act. For example, an employment agency which receives a fee for locating and placing an employee would recognize revenue at the time the employee is placed. An equipment services company for a fixed fee may agree to do an annual overhaul of equipment as well as provide emergency repair service if needed. If the annual overhaul is the major act, revenue recognition would not occur until the annual overhaul takes place.

In most other long-term service contracts, revenue should be recognized in accordance with some variant of the *proportional performance method*. Proportional performance measurement is the service counterpart to percentage of completion. Revenue is recognized in relation to some measure of performance or earning. The measure of performance may vary, but the underlying concept is the same.

If performance consists of a number of identical or similar acts, the total revenue under the contract would be apportioned in relation to the number of acts performed. Service bureaus that process computerized payrolls for customers or mortgage bankers who process mortgage payments would use this method. If performance consists of a number of defined but *not identical* acts (e.g., a correspondence school's provision of lessons, progress evaluations, examinations, and grading) then the ratio of direct costs incurred to total estimated direct costs of the contract could be used. This procedure is exactly the same as the one illustrated earlier in connection with percentage of completion. Finally, if performance con-

---

15 Much of the discussion to follow is based on recommendations made by the AICPA Standards Division and is contained in FASB, *Invitation to Comment*, "Accounting for Certain Service Industries" (Stamford, Conn., 1978).

sists of an unspecified number of acts within a fixed time period, revenue should be recognized on a straight-line method over the specified time. Hence, a health spa which sells two-year memberships for $1,500 would recognize revenue of $62.50 per month on each membership.

Often for long-term service contracts the costs associated with negotiating and starting the service agreements are significant. These costs, which would include commissions, legal fees, costs of credit investigation, etc., are called "initial direct costs." In accordance with the matching concept, these costs usually would be deferred and expensed in proportion to revenue recognition.

With respect to the second and third problem areas mentioned earlier, the recommendations agree with our intuition. If the buyer has the right to obtain a partial refund or if such refunds are industry practice, an allowance for expected refunds should be recorded as a reduction in revenue. Similar adjustments for estimated uncollectibles would also be required. If there is a *significant* degree of uncertainty as to collectibility of the revenue, the installment method of recognition would have to be used.

## DISCUSSION OF THE ARMCO ANNUAL REPORT

Few special revenue problems are disclosed in the Armco financial statements introduced in Chapter 5. The three-year income statement shows the dramatic increase in total revenues that occurred, from $5,064.5 million in 1979 to $6,957.5 million in 1981. Remember that this period was one of rapid price inflation; changes in sales reflect both price and volume changes. Notice that sales revenue accounts for the overwhelming majority of total revenues. Interest, royalty, and other revenue are reported as a single total. In accordance with the required segment disclosures to be discussed in Chapter 16, Armco shows in the notes the sales revenue attributable to each of its five distinct business lines.

The notes to the financial statements provide no special information about Armco's revenue recognition policies. Accordingly we may assume that sales revenues are recognized generally at the time of delivery and other revenues when they are earned and become measurable. No specific information is provided about any sales order backlogs at year-end.

On the position statement Armco shows trade receivables of $872.8 million and $727.8 million at the end of 1981 and 1980, respectively. These amounts represent the cash expected to be realized. An Allowance for Doubtful Accounts, shown in parentheses, already has been subtracted. For example, on December 31, 1981, the legal claim on customers is $904.5 million. Of this amount, $31.7 million, approximately 3.5 percent, is expected not to be collected. Armco's collection expectations as of December 31, 1980, were similar, with approximately 3.6 percent of gross receivables represented in the Allowance for Doubtful Accounts ($27.4 million out of $755.2 million).

**SUMMARY**

This chapter focuses attention on three issues: (1) what constitutes revenue, (2) when revenue should be recognized, and (3) how much revenue should be recognized.

We answer the first question by defining revenue as the cash received, cash to be received, or cash needs satisfied during a period as a result of the firm's efforts associated with supplying goods and services to customers. This definition has four elements: (1) revenue is a period concept, (2) it measures productive activity during the period, (3) the measurement is in terms of the reward resulting from the activity, and (4) the reward is expressed in terms of ultimate cash receipts or equivalent.

The definition of revenue provides a guideline for what is to be recognized and the maximum amount that may be recognized. The second question, concerning the timing of revenue recognition, is satisfied by the revenue recognition concept, which assumes that two conditions have to be met before revenue is recorded in financial accounting. Revenue must have been earned, and it must be measurable with a reasonable degree of reliability. We illustrate how this concept attempts to balance desirable but conflicting guidelines—timeliness, verifiability, and representational faithfulness. We also explore the application of this postulate to revenue recognition at times other than the point of sale as well as to special situations existing at the point of sale.

The final question of how much revenue to recognize is answered in part by the definition of revenue and the revenue recognition assumption. However, instances are identified which require adjustment of the originally recorded revenue measurement. These adjustments fall into three categories. First, part of the cash receipt may represent something other than a reward for activities associated with the supplying of goods and services to customers and hence may not be revenue, e.g., sales and excise taxes, container deposits, and freight reimbursements. Secondly, the cash received or to be received may not yet have been earned because additional efforts are required on the part of the firm after the initial entry, e.g., production, storage, financing, and servicing. Finally, events subsequent to the initial entry may alter the amount of cash eventually to be received, e.g, uncollectibles, returns, and discounts.

The theory behind each of these types of adjustments is discussed, and illustrative entries are presented. In the case of uncollectibles, returns, and discounts, contra revenue accounts are used to segregate the particular decreases in revenues for informational purposes. In some cases contra asset accounts also are used to reduce overstated trade accounts receivable. Most firms, in presenting their income statements to external audiences, condense the sales and contra revenue accounts. As a consequence, the vast majority of income statements begin with the caption "net sales," the returns and discounts already having been subtracted.

# APPENDIX: Accounting for Long-Term Construction Contracts

Long-term construction contracts such as those for buildings, ships, highways, and other major projects, present some special problems of revenue recognition. One approach suggested in Chapter 6 is called *percentage of completion*. It calls for periodic revenue recognition (and matching of expenses) as the work progresses. Income is accrued over the life of the contract in proportion to the amount earned each period. A second approach, called *completed contract,* conforms more closely to the traditional sales basis by recognizing revenue only when the constructed asset is "delivered" to the customer. During construction, the costs incurred each period are accumulated in an inventory account, to be matched against revenue only in the period when the contract is completed.

Long-term construction contracts contain other features that require careful treatment in the accounts. Under the terms of most contracts, the contractor may bill the customer periodically for partial payment. These *progress billings* may or may not conform to the amount of work completed. Of the amounts billed, it is common for the customer to withhold a specified percentage until final completion as a guarantee of performance. In addition, some contracts virtually guarantee some income; others may result in either income or loss.

## Types of Contracts

Three general types of contracts are employed on long-term construction projects. The most common type calls for a fixed total amount of revenue. The other two types provide for revenue equal to the costs incurred plus a fee. One, called cost-plus-fixed-fee, specifies the fee as a fixed *dollar* amount. The other, known as cost-plus-a-percentage, calculates the fee as a *percentage* of cost. Both cost-plus contracts guarantee a positive gross margin (revenues minus construction costs) and are found most often in government contract work. The total amount of gross margin on the cost-plus-fixed-fee contract does not require an estimate; however, its allocation to different accounting periods does. With cost-plus-a-percentage contracts, the amount of gross margin applicable to any particular accounting period is known with certainty, since it is a constant percentage of the cost incurred that period.

On a fixed-price contract, on the other hand, the ultimate gross margin may be positive or negative, depending on the amount of costs. Before the job is finished, accountants can calculate the gross margin only by *estimating* the total costs for the job and deducting them from the fixed contract price. To spread this gross margin over a number of accounting periods, as in percentage of completion, requires an additional judgment as to the proportion earned each period. Because fixed-price contracts pose more difficult problems than do cost-plus contracts and comprise the majority of long-term contracts, we will use them in the following illustrations.

To contrast the recording procedures under completed contract and percentage of completion and to serve as a common point of departure for a discussion of problems, a single numerical example is helpful. Assume that a builder contracts to construct a two-story apartment dwelling. The total contract price is $3.0 million. The estimated total cost of construction over the two and a half years' expected completion time is $2 million. The contract calls for three equal periodic billings— when the basement and foundation are completed, when the first story is com-

**TABLE 6A-1  Data for Illustration of Contract Accounting ($000)**

|  | Year 1 | Year 2 | Year 3 |
|---|---|---|---|
| Construction costs incurred | $ 800 | $ 600 | $ 650 |
| Estimated costs to complete | 1,200 | 700 | — |
| Progress billings | 1,000 | 1,000 | 1,000 |
| Collections on progress billings | — | 950 | 1,900 |
| Collection of retainer | — | — | 150 |
| Administrative expense (period charge) | 50 | 50 | 50 |

pleted, and when the entire project is completed. Each billing is collectible within 90 days, except for a 5 percent retainer to be paid upon final acceptance by the purchaser. Table 6A-1 summarizes data pertaining to the construction period.

**Completed Contract**

Summary entries to be made during each of the three years under the completed contract method appear in Table 6A-2. Only those entries unique to long-term construction contracts are illustrated.

**TABLE 6A-2  Entries under Completed Contract ($000)**

| Entry to Record | Year 1 | | Year 2 | | Year 3 | |
|---|---|---|---|---|---|---|
| 1.  Construction costs: | | | | | | |
| Contract in Progress | 800 | | 600 | | 650 | |
| Cash, Materials, etc. | | 800 | | 600 | | 650 |
| 2.  Administrative expenses: | | | | | | |
| Administrative Expenses | 50 | | 50 | | 50 | |
| Cash, Payables, etc. | | 50 | | 50 | | 50 |
| 3.  Progress billings: | | | | | | |
| Accounts Receivable | 1,000 | | 1,000 | | 1,000 | |
| Progress Billings | | 1,000 | | 1,000 | | 1,000 |
| 4.  Collections of billings: | | | | | | |
| Cash | | | 950 | | 1,900 | |
| Accounts Receivable | | | | 950 | | 1,900 |
| 5.  Collection of retainer: | | | | | | |
| Cash | | | | | 150 | |
| Accounts Receivable | | | | | | 150 |
| 6.  Revenue and expense:* | | | | | | |
| Progress Billings | | | | | 3,000 | |
| Construction Revenue | | | | | | 3,000 |
| Cost of Construction Contract | | | | | 2,050 | |
| Contract in Progress | | | | | | 2,050 |

* Sometimes in practice, the revenue and expense are not recognized separately. Only the difference between them, or gross margin, appears in the accounts. A single journal entry is made upon completion of the job ($000):

| | | |
|---|---|---|
| Progress Billings | 3,000 | |
| Contract in Progress | | 2,050 |
| Gross Margin on Construction Contracts | | 950 |

However, the *Audit and Accounting Guide for Construction Contractors* published by the AICPA recommends the more meaningful practice of a separate recording for revenues and expenses.

During Years 1 and 2 the income statement will show only $50,000 administrative expense and, consequently, a $50,000 net loss (if there are no other contracts or revenue). In Year 3, net income will be $900,000 ($950,000 gross margin from the contract minus $50,000 administrative expense). On the position statement, Accounts Receivable and Contract in Progress would be disclosed in the current asset section, the latter as a specially identified item of inventory.

The most troublesome account to classify is Progress Billings. It appears to be a type of construction advance; hence, the logical treatment is to show it as a current liability. Inasmuch as revenue is being recognized only at the completion of the contract, amounts collected from customers represent claims against assets that will be satisfied by subsequent delivery of the product.

In practice most companies treat the credit arising from progress billings as an offset to Contract in Progress. The net differences between construction costs and progress billings are shown as a current asset (amount of uncompleted contracts in excess of related billings) or as a current liability (billings on uncompleted contracts in excess of related costs). The reasoning behind this offsetting of assets and liabilities is obscure.

A basic limitation of the completed contract method for many contracts is that the method does not reflect current productive activity. Therefore, its use should be restricted to situations in which other conditions that warrant recognition of revenue and asset changes in the accounts are not present.

When dependable estimates are lacking or no signed contract exists, completed contract would be appropriate. It would be inappropriate for most cost-plus contracts. A firm may also use completed contract when it is working on a large number of short-term contracts. Then compensating lag from an almost continuous progression of completed contracts prevents the distortion on any one contract from distorting the revenue estimate for the period. Finally, because it postpones recognition of income, completed contract is of course widely used for income tax purposes.

## Percentage of Completion

There exist several slightly differing methods of recording under percentage of completion. The more common method uses the same framework of accounts as completed contract but includes a periodic revaluation of the inventory of construction in progress to reflect the earned gross margin element. This method will be illustrated. The unique feature of all methods used for percentage of completion is that the total contract price of $3.0 million is allocated over the three-year period

**TABLE 6A-3  Determination of Revenue Earned by Year under Percentage of Completion ($000)**

|  | Year 1 | Year 2 | Year 3 |
|---|---|---|---|
| Actual cost incurred to date | $  800 | $1,400 | $2,050 |
| Estimated cost to complete | 1,200 | 700 | — |
| Total cost of contract | $2,000 | $2,100 | $2,050 |
| Percentage earned to date | $\frac{\$800}{\$2,000} = 40\%$ | $\frac{\$1,400}{\$2,100} = 66.7\%$ | 100% |
| Total revenue earned to date | $1,200 (40%) | $2,000 (66.7%) | $3,000 (100%) |
| Revenue recognized in prior periods | — | 1,200 | 2,000 |
| Revenue to be recognized this period | $1,200 | $  800 | $1,000 |

**TABLE 6A-4   Entries under Percentage of Completion ($000)**

|  | Year 1 | Year 2 | Year 3 |
|---|---|---|---|
| 6.   Revenue and expense: |  |  |  |
| Contract in Progress | 1,200 | 800 | 1,000 |
| Construction Revenue |  | 1,200 | 800 | 1,000 |
| Cost of Construction Contract | 800 | 600 | 650 |
| Contract in Progress* |  | 800 | 600 | 650 |
| Progress Billings |  |  | 3,000 |
| Contract in Progress |  |  | 3,000 |

\* In Years 1 and 2 a contra asset account might be credited instead, so that Contract in Progress could act as a control account for managerial purposes.

in accordance with the calculations shown in Table 6A–3. The $950,000 gross margin on the contract is likewise spread over the three-year period.

With percentage of completion, entries 1–5 in Table 6A–2 would remain the same. Entry 6 to recognize revenue and expense each year would appear as shown in Table 6A–4.

The Construction Revenue and the Cost of Construction accounts are used to record full sales and expense information. They provide information concerning the volume of construction activity during the period, as measured by contract prices and by the amount of construction costs incurred in the earning of that revenue. Both will be closed to Income Summary each year and will appear on the income statement. Table 6A–5 contrasts the financial statements under percentage of completion with those resulting from completed contract.

The entries in Table 6A–4 cause the inventory account, Contract in Progress, to be valued at sales price earned to date rather than at the cost amount reflected by

**TABLE 6A-5   Comparative Financial Statement Information: Percentage of Completion and Completed Contract Methods ($000)**

|  | Percentage of Completion | | | Completed Contract | | |
|---|---|---|---|---|---|---|
|  | Year 1 | Year 2 | Year 3 | Year 1 | Year 2 | Year 3 |
| Income statement: |  |  |  |  |  |  |
| Construction revenue | $1,200 | $ 800 | $1,000 | — | — | $3,000 |
| Cost of contract | 800 | 600 | 650 | — | — | 2,050 |
| Gross margin | 400 | 200 | 350 | — | — | 950 |
| Administrative expense | 50 | 50 | 50 | 50 | 50 | 50 |
| Net income (loss) | $ 350 | $ 150 | $ 300 | $(50) | $(50) | $ 900 |
| Balance sheet (December 31): |  |  |  |  |  |  |
| Current assets: |  |  |  |  |  |  |
| Accounts receivable | $1,000 | $1,050 | — | $1,000 | $1,050 | — |
| Amount of uncompleted contracts in excess of related billings | $ 200 | — | — | — | — | — |
| Current liabilities: |  |  |  |  |  |  |
| Billings on uncompleted contracts in excess of related costs | — | — | — | $ 200 | $ 600 | — |

entry 1 in Table 6A–2. For example, in Year 1 the entries increase the asset from its $800,000 cost amount (Entry 1) to $1,200,000, thereby reflecting the $400,000 income element recognized in Year 1.[16] For the purpose of disclosure on the balance sheet, the Progress Billings account would be netted against the Contract in Progress account as under completed contract. With percentage of completion, the procedure has more logic behind it, however. Progress Billings is a contra asset to the inventory. The process of billing has transferred the *sales value* reflected in the inventory account to a receivable account.[17]

**Measurement Problems**

A comparison of the results under percentage of completion with those under completed contract clearly reveals the superiority of the former as to the *earning* criterion. The only factor that might prevent its use in *all* long-term construction contracts is *measurability*. Measurement problems can occur in any of four areas: (1) determination of total revenue, (2) prediction of collectibility, (3) measurement of percentage of completion, and (4) estimation of costs.

As we mentioned in Chapter 6, sufficiently reliable measurement of total revenue normally can be found in the contractual relationship between buyer and seller. The existence of an outside purchaser provides verifiability. The total price is known in advance in a fixed-fee contact or is determinable by the terms of the contract in cost-plus arrangements. Therefore, a contract and a committed customer are essential requisites for use of percentage of completion. Ordinarily, major projects are not undertaken unless a customer has agreed to purchase the completed project. Nevertheless, occasionally speculative building is undertaken without definite contracts, specified prices, or customers. Percentage of completion would not be appropriate under those circumstances.

Reliable measurement also requires that we can predict with reasonable accuracy that ultimate cash receipts equal to the total amount of revenue will be collected. Normally, the likelihood of not being able to collect from the purchaser is small. A construction project requires sizable long-term risks on the part of the contractor. These are not undertaken without a thorough review of the credit standing, reputation, financial position, and so on, of the customer. Large financially established firms and governmental bodies tend to be the ones which qualify. The risk is further reduced by progress billings. Nevertheless, instances could arise—if there were a threat of renegotiation or cancellation of a government contract—in which this aspect of measurement would not be reliable.

A third aspect of reliable measurement concerns how accurately the earned portion of total revenue may be measured. This measurement, of course, is absolutely certain on contracts covering cost plus a percentage of cost. For fixed-price and cost-plus-fixed-fee contracts, though, some estimate of the portion earned is necessary so that the revenue or fixed fee can be allocated.

---

[16] The two entries in Table 6A–4 could be combined into a single entry which would clearly reveal the upward revaluation of assets. For example, the first year would be:

| | | |
|---|---|---|
| Cost of Construction Contract | 800 | |
| Contract in Progress | 400 | |
|     Construction Revenue | | 1,200 |

[17] Under one alternative procedure used by some firms in implementing the percentage of completion method, an account called Accounts Receivable Unbilled is used. Its balance would equal the net difference between the credit balance in Progress Billings and the debit balance in Contract in Progress (at sales value).

In the examples in Chapter 6 and in this appendix we measure the portion earned according to the percentage of total cost incurred. In doing so, we assume that every dollar of cost earns an equal amount of revenue. Such an assumption may not be appropriate if one of two conditions is present. First, if the construction consists of identical or very similar segments and varying costs are incurred on different segments, it may be more reasonable to assume that each segment produces equal revenue. For example, a contract may call for the construction of three similar lakeshore cottages at a total price of $150,000. If the foundation on the second cottage has to be repoured because of shifting sand, the portion of revenue attributable to the period in which the second cottage is worked on probably should not be increased because of that fact.

The second reservation about the use of cost arises if substantial material costs or subcontracting costs are involved. Material stockpiled at a construction site does not adequately measure work done. Likewise, if revenue is to represent the reward for the contractor's efforts, large and irregular costs of subcontractors' work may distort the measurement of the prime contractor's contribution. To take a somewhat extreme case, assume that a contractor is to construct an apartment building. The laying of expensive wall-to-wall carpeting throughout is subcontracted to a rug company at a cost of $100,000. Other building costs total $900,000. The carpets are laid during the last two weeks, after all other work is complete. If cost is used as a measure of earning, only 90 percent of the revenue (and profit) is assumed to be earned by construction of the apartment building, perhaps over a two-year period. Then, in the last two weeks the contractor is assumed to earn the other 10 percent simply by contacting the subcontractor and having the subcontractor lay the carpets.

Because of these potential limitations on cost as a measure of the portion earned, other measures of earning are sometimes used. These include engineering or architectural estimates of the percentage of work completed, physical measures of completion (e.g., miles of highway), contract milestones reached, and payroll cost or labor-hours expended. Progress billings usually are not a satisfactory measure of work done, because they tend to be dictated by financial rather than production considerations. Therefore, they lead or lag behind actual performance under the contract. Nevertheless, under some government contracts the job can be broken down into a number of homogeneous physical units which are billed as the completed units are delivered. In such cases the amounts billed may be an appropriate measure of partial performance.

If cost incurred as a percentage of total cost is used as an estimate of the percentage of completion, a fourth measurement problem arises. The accuracy of the estimate depends directly on the predictability of the total cost of the project. This prediction may be uncertain or inaccurate, as in the illustration shown in Table 6A–3. The original estimate of total cost was $2 million. It was revised after the first year to $2,100,000 and finally turned out to be $2,050,000.

The particular procedure used in the illustration to determine each period's allocation of revenue contains an automatic error-correction mechanism. By estimating *total revenue earned to date* and then subtracting the portion previously recognized, we include in any particular year the portion earned that year plus any corrections of prior periods, all based on the most recent cost estimates. However, even the most recent cost estimates may turn out to be inaccurate. Table 6A–6 compares the amounts actually recognized in Table 6A–3, the amounts earned each period as determined by the most recent cost estimates without error correc-

TABLE 6A-6  Comparison of Revenue Amounts Based on Alternative Estimates

| | Revenue Earned Based on— | | |
|---|---|---|---|
| | Actual Recognition Procedure | Best Estimate Available | Perfect Foresight |
| Year 1 . . . . . . . . . . . . . . | $1,200,000 | $1,200,000 $\left(\frac{800}{2,000}\right)$ | $1,170,732 $\left(\frac{800}{2,050}\right)$ |
| Year 2 . . . . . . . . . . . . . | 800,000 | 857,143 $\left(\frac{600}{2,100}\right)$ | 878,049 $\left(\frac{600}{2,050}\right)$ |
| Year 3 . . . . . . . . . . . . . | 1,000,000 | 951,219 $\left(\frac{650}{2,050}\right)$ | 951,219 $\left(\frac{650}{2,050}\right)$ |
| | $3,000,000 | | $3,000,000 |

tion, and the amount that would have been recognized if perfect foresight had been available. Comparison of the first two columns gives the magnitude of the error correction. Comparisons of either the first or second column with the third indicates the range of inaccuracy in the revenue estimate. The percentage deviation in gross margin would be even greater, of course.

This degree of inaccuracy is caused by cost estimates that are less than 5 percent in error. Undoubtedly, the reliability of cost estimates varies considerably by industry and project. In those cases where cost estimates are subject to large errors, percentage of completion may not provide sufficiently reliable measurements, particularly for fixed-price contracts. Keep in mind, however, that the alternative may be completed contract, wherein no revenue is recognized until completion. The accountant must decide which error is more important—failure to recognize the reward for efforts expended (as under completed contract) or inaccurate and perhaps misleading measurement of periodic revenue (as under percentage of completion when cost estimates are not dependable).

## Estimated Losses on Long-Term Contracts

What should be done if the estimate of cost to complete a fixed-price project indicates that the total costs will exceed the total revenue? Weather conditions, labor disputes, shortages of crucial construction materials, and price changes are just some of the factors which could cause a contract that initially appeared worthwhile to be completed at a loss.

One approach might be to deal with the problem as a normal event. Whatever revenue-recognition procedure is being followed would be applied consistently, regardless of whether profit or a loss resulted. If revenue were being recognized under completed contract, the total revenue would be recognized in the year of completion along with the total costs (expenses). No loss would be recognized until the last year, just as no profit would be recognized until completion. If percentage of completion were being employed, the loss would be spread over the period of construction in the same manner as a positive gross margin is recognized. Revenue would be measured in the normal manner. However, the costs to be matched each period would exceed the periodic revenue; the result would be a negative gross margin on that contract each period. In both cases the fact that an additional loss is anticipated could be communicated to the reader of the income statement via a footnote.

Although the procedure described in the preceding paragraph applies revenue recognition criteria consistently, it is not generally accepted. When the current estimate of total contract costs indicates a loss, a debit to a loss account and a credit to Contract in Progress should be recorded for the *full* amount of the anticipated loss.

Assume that at the end of Year 2 in our example it is clear that total costs will amount to $3,100,000 rather than the $2 million originally estimated. The revised total estimated costs will exceed by $100,000 the total revenues of $3 million. The entire anticipated loss of $100,000 is recognized in Year 2 under *completed contract* by the following entry:

| | | |
|---|---|---|
| Anticipated Loss on Contract | 100,000 | |
| Contract in Progress | | 100,000 |

Under *percentage of completion,* the write-down (loss) would be $500,000—the anticipated total loss of $100,000 plus the positive gross margin of $400,000 already recognized in Year 1.

The rationale for this write-down is twofold. First, on grounds of conservatism, many accountants believe that all *known* losses—past, present, and future—should be recognized immediately but that profits should not be recognized until earned. Second, some accountants feel that assets should never be valued at more than their net realizable value, the net amount for which they can be sold. If a portion of the cost of the asset cannot be recovered through sale, then that portion represents a cost that has no future value. Charging the entire anticipated loss against the Contract in Progress account ensures that its value will never exceed net realizable value, provided that the new cost estimates are accurate. More is said about this concept in Chapter 8, in the section dealing with lower-of-cost-or-market valuation of inventories.

# QUESTIONS AND PROBLEMS

**6–1.** Happy Jack's Funfair Amusement Park is open from April 1 through September 30 of each year. The company sells books of admission tickets to customers at $20 per book. The book contains 10 tickets good for admission any time from April through September. The regular admission price is $3. The following statements are prepared for April, May, and June:

| | April | May | June |
|---|---|---|---|
| Sales | $6,825 | $13,650 | $18,375 |
| Expenses | 3,970 | 6,090 | 6,890 |
| Net income | $2,855 | $ 7,560 | $11,485 |

Sales include the cash received from the sale of coupon books during each month. The number of books sold were 80 in April, 250 in May, and 350 in June. An analysis of admissions reveals that 440, 1,620, and 3,410 admission-book tickets have been presented in the three months, respectively. No entries have been made for these individual tickets.

*Required:*

a. Prepare corrected income statements for each of the three months. Also, determine the liability for tickets outstanding at the end of each month.

*b.* What would you do with any balance remaining in the liability account on September 30 when the park closes down?

**6–2.** The Chaos Corporation has recently been turned down for a loan because of the "poor quality" of its accounts receivable. Hy Price, the president, has called you in as a consultant. The following report, dealing with the firm's credit sales, accounts receivable, and so forth, since the firm's founding in 1983, has been prepared for you:

| | 1983 | 1984 | 1985 |
|---|---|---|---|
| Sales on account | $165,000 | $247,500 | $157,500 |
| Cash collections: | | | |
| From 1983 sales | 135,000 | 24,700 | 2,300 |
| From 1984 sales | — | 210,000 | 31,500 |
| From 1985 sales | — | — | 135,000 |
| Estimate of bad debts | 3,300 | 4,950 | 3,150 |
| Specific accounts written off: | | | |
| From 1983 sales | 300 | 2,400 | 300 |
| From 1984 sales | — | 700 | 2,700 |
| From 1985 sales | — | — | 300 |

*Required:*

*a.* Set up ledger accounts for Sales, Accounts Receivable, Cash, Sales Uncollectibles, and Allowance for Doubtful Accounts. Record the entries over the three-year period.

*b.* How would the accounts receivable be shown on a position statement at the end of each year?

*c.* How has the company been determining its estimate of bad debts? Comment on the adequacy of this rate.

*d.* An aging schedule of accounts receivable at the end of 1985 shows the following:

| Age | Amount |
|---|---|
| Current | $10,500 |
| 0–60 days past due | 4,500 |
| 60 days—six months past due | 3,900 |
| 6 months—one year past due | 3,300 |
| Over 1 year past due | 2,600 |
| | $24,800 |

You determine from experience with similar firms in the industry that the following uncollectibility percentages are reasonable for each category: 1 percent for current accounts; 5 percent for 0 to 60 days; 10 percent for 60 days to 6 months; 25 percent for 6 months to 1 year; and 50 percent for over 1 year.

Based on an aging analysis, what balance should be in the contra asset account? Does this confirm or disagree with your conclusion in part *(c)?*

**6–3.** Rippling Road Construction Company entered into a contract for a 20-mile circumferential highway around town. The firm was to be responsible for grading and pouring cement and for constructing 10 bridges. The contract price was $1,000,000, and the estimated cost was $800,000 ($30,000 per mile and $20,000 per bridge). Payments under the contract are received according to the following schedule: $40,000 per mile at the time each mile is finished and $10,000 per mile when the entire highway is completed and approved. Final approval takes place in 1985. Data related to the contract are summarized below:

|                              |   1982   |   1983   |   1984   |
|------------------------------|----------|----------|----------|
| Costs incurred               | $240,000 | $400,000 | $160,000 |
| Number of miles finished     | 3        | 12       | 5        |
| Number of bridges constructed| 2        | 4        | 4        |

*Required:*

a. Determine the amount of revenue and gross margin to be recognized in each year under the percentage of completion method using cost incurred as a percentage of total cost as the measure of work done.

b. Determine the amount of cash payment received by the company each year under the contract.

c. The president of Rippling Road Construction Company suggests that revenues be recognized as cash is received, as in part *(b)*. "Nothing is surer than cash," he says. Explain why percentage of completion provides a better measure of revenue recognition.

d. The controller suggests a third alternative—recognition of revenue as each mile and bridge is completed. She suggests that this method does not delay recognition until cash is received but at the same time avoids the problem of making estimates that are inherent under percentage of completion. What would revenue be each year under her plan? Explain carefully how you arrived at your answer. What are the advantages and disadvantages of this plan relative to that in part *(a)?*

**6–4.** Dow Jones & Company, Inc., shows the following two accounts on its balance sheet (in thousands):

|                                                                                                                                              | December 31 1982 | December 31 1981 |
|----------------------------------------------------------------------------------------------------------------------------------------------|--------|--------|
| Current assets:                                                                                                                              |        |        |
| Accounts receivable-trade, net of allowance for doubtful accounts and book returns of $6,722,000 in 1982 and $5,515,000 in 1981             | 70,546 | 67,284 |
| Current liabilities:                                                                                                                        |        |        |
| Unexpired subscriptions                                                                                                                     | 97,298 | 85,242 |

The following note accompanies the financial statements.

> *Subscription revenue* is recorded as earned, pro rata on a monthly basis, over the life of the subscriptions. Costs in connection with the procurement of subscriptions are charged to expense as incurred. *Book returns* are provided for by charges to current operations in amounts determined on the basis of experience. Actual returns are charged to the allowance so provided.

*Required:*

a. The income statement for 1983 reported $193,930,000 in circulation revenues. How much cash was received in 1983 from subscriptions and cash payments for newspapers? (Assume no receivables from newspapers.)

b. Does the practice of charging all costs in connection with the procurement of subscriptions to expense as incurred agree with the matching concept? Explain why Dow Jones may follow this practice.

c. An alternative that Dow Jones might use would be to recognize 40 percent of the cash received as revenue on the grounds that selling the subscription is a major part of the earning function and defer the other 60 percent over the subscription period. Evaluate this alternative and compare it with the practice employed by Dow Jones.

d. What type of account is Allowance for Book Returns? Without amounts give the journal entries that are made in connection with this account.

e. Why does Dow Jones & Company use an account called Allowance for Book Returns? What other alternative practices are available? Do you prefer any of these?

**6–5.** The Lost Horizon Novelty Shop accepts two types of credit cards in addition to cash from customers purchasing its merchandise. On VISA charges (a bank credit card), Lost Horizon deposits the charge slip in the bank at the face value less a 2 percent transaction fee. On Diners Club charges the shop sends the invoices to the regional office of Diners Club, which remits 95 percent of all approved charges within four working days.

During September the following transactions took place:

Sept. 6 Total sales, $890. Cash sales were $80; VISA invoices amounted to $500, and Diners Club invoices amounted to $310.

9 Received payment from Diners Club for all charges except one for $60 which Lost Horizon erroneously had allowed to be charged on a canceled credit card.

15 Being unable to locate the customer with the canceled credit card, Lost Horizon wrote off the account to the Allowance for Doubtful Accounts.

*Required:*

a. Prepare journal entries to record the above transactions.

b. Where should the 2 percent transaction fee and the 5 percent discount appear on the income statement?

c. Assume you are a retailer who has been making credit sales for a number of years using your own credit card. MasterCard approaches you and suggests that you should accept MasterCard instead of your own credit card. What financial information would you use in deciding whether or not to change?

**6–6.** Short Circuit Appliance Company sells television sets, video recorders, and stereo systems on the installment sales basis. Selected data for 1985 and 1986 are summarized below.

|  | 1985 | 1986 |
|---|---|---|
| Installment sales | $200,000 | $270,000 |
| Cost of installment sales | 130,000 | 189,000 |
| Selling and general expenses | 31,000 | 42,000 |
| Cash collections from customers: | | |
| On 1985 sales | 105,000 | 85,000 |
| On 1986 sales | | 140,000 |

*Required:*

a. Prepare income statements for 1985 and 1986, assuming that the company recognizes revenue at the time of sale.

b. Prepare income statements for 1985 and 1986 assuming that the company recognizes revenue using the installment method.

c. Calculate the balance in the Deferred Gross Margin account(s) on December 31, 1986. Where should this be reported on the balance sheet? Why?

**6–7.** Fixit Fast Maintenance Service enters into long-term contracts with manufacturers in the high technology areas. For a fee of $8,000, payable in advance, Fixit Fast agrees to service a certain type of equipment for a two-year period. The maintenance contract covers routine maintenance and overhaul only; any fees for repairs arising from extraordinary events or damage are billed separately. Under the contract Fixit Fast is required to adjust the equipment each month for five months and then to overhaul it in the sixth month. Thus, under each contract Fixit will provide 20 adjustments and four overhauls. An adjustment costs about $150 in service labor time; an overhaul costs about $450 in service labor time and $300 in parts.

During 1985 and 1986, respectively, five and seven maintenance contracts were signed, and the advance payments were received. Fixit Fast performed all its contractual obligations under the contracts in both years. It made 40 service calls for adjustments in 1985 and 100 in 1986; it did 5 overhauls in 1985 and 17 in 1986.

The following costs were incurred in each of the two years:

|  | 1985 | 1986 |
|---|---|---|
| Commissions, legal fees, and other initial direct costs of the contracts | $2,000 | $ 2,800 |
| Service labor costs | 8,300 | 22,700 |
| Material costs | 1,400 | 5,200 |
| Other operating expenses | 2,200 | 4,600 |
| Administrative expenses | 4,000 | 4,000 |

Fixit Fast Maintenance Service decides to recognize revenue under a proportional performance method in which $200 revenue is to be recognized for each adjustment performed and $1,000 is to be recognized for each overhaul performed. Initial direct costs of the contracts are to be deferred and amortized as expense in relation to the recognition of revenue.

*Required:*

a. How was the proportional performance criteria applied to reach the $200 and $1,000 revenue figures?

b. Using the company's accounting practices as described, prepare income statements for both 1985 and 1986.

c. What amounts would appear on the December 31, 1986, balance sheet as Deferred Contract Acquisition Costs and Unearned Maintenance Revenue? How would these accounts be classified?

d. Evaluate the company's revenue recognition and other accounting practices. What alternative practices might it have used? Are these better or worse than what it chose?

**6–8.** From inception of operations to December 31, 1981, Harris Corporation provided for uncollectible accounts receivable under the allowance method.[18] Harris's usual credit terms are net 30 days.

The balance in the allowance for doubtful accounts was $130,000 at January 1, 1982. During 1982 credit sales totaled $9,000,000, interim provisions for doubtful accounts were made at 2 percent of credit sales, $90,000 of bad debts were written off, and recoveries of accounts previously written off amounted to

---

[18] Material from the Uniform CPA Examinations, Copyright © 1983 by the American Institute of Certified Public Accountants, Inc., is adapted with permission.

$15,000. Harris installed a computer facility in November 1982, and an aging of accounts receivable was prepared for the first time as of December 31, 1982. A summary of the aging is as follows:

| Classification by Month of Sale | Balance in Each Category | Estimated Percent Uncollectible |
|---|---|---|
| November–December 1982 ...... | $1,140,000 | 2% |
| July–October ................. | 600,000 | 10 |
| January–June ................. | 400,000 | 25 |
| Prior to January 1, 1982 ......... | 130,000 | 75 |
| | $2,270,000 | |

Based on the review of collectibility of the account balances in the "prior to January 1, 1982" aging category, additional receivables totaling $60,000 were written off as of December 31, 1982. Effective with the year ended December 31, 1982, Harris adopted a new accounting method for estimating the allowance for doubtful accounts at the amount indicated by the year-end aging analysis of accounts receivable.

*Required:*

a. Journalize the entries made in the allowance for doubtful accounts during 1982. Include the entry for the year-end adjustment to the allowance for doubtful accounts balance as of December 31, 1982. Show supporting computations. You may assume that the 75 percent uncollectibility percentage applies to any remaining accounts prior to January 1, 1982.

b. Klaus Trophobia, the chief accountant, objects to all estimates for doubtful accounts saying: "Accounting should record objective facts based on realized transactions, not guesses; recording a loss for accounts that we expect to go bad in the future is not sound accounting." Evaluate and reply to this argument.

c. In light of the large adjustment on December 31, 1982, Chic Kenhouse, the credit manager, suggests that immediate steps be taken to reduce uncollectibles close to zero. He suggests that credit be granted only to excellent risks, that all sales orders be accompanied by a 20 percent cash payment, and that collection efforts be intensified by turning all accounts over 45 days old over to a collection agency. Evaluate his recommendation.

**6–9.** The Harper Farm Equipment Company sells tractors and other farm apparatus primarily to individual farmers, sometimes in rather unusual deals. Three of those arrangements are described below:

1. In March the firm exchanged a new tractor for a five-year lease on some adjacent ground to the east of its present location. The tractor cost Harper $7,200 and was listed to sell at $9,000. Harper needed the ground for storage and display of equipment. The firm could have leased similar land on its west side for $1,500 a year, but Harper would have had to spend $800 for grading.

2. On May 15 the company swapped a power tiller with a cost of $600 and a list price of $750 for 30 shares of stock in a regional cattle stockyard. At the time of the exchange the shares had a market value of $23 per share. During the period from May 15 to December 31, Harper received dividends of $2.00 per share. The value of the stock was quoted at $24.50 per share on December 31.

3. Harper Farm Equipment in early September exchanged a corn picker for a

claim on 4,000 bushels of corn. The machine cost Harper $5,800 and was priced to sell at $7,000. At harvest time in late September, the corn could be sold to the local grain exchange for $1.68 per bushel. Expecting that grain prices might go up, the management of Harper stored the grain until December and then sold it for $1.85 a bushel.

*Required:*

a. In each of these instances, how much revenue should Harper Farm Equipment record? Explain.
b. How does your answer in *(a)* relate to the revenue recognition concept?

**6–10.** The financial statements for the first 11 months of the year for National Merchants Company show the following balances among the accounts.

|  | Debit | Credit |
| --- | --- | --- |
| Sales ...................................... |  | $480,000 |
| Sales returns ............................ | $ 8,900 |  |
| Sales discounts ......................... | 3,000 |  |
| Provision for doubtful accounts ................ | 9,600 |  |
| Accounts receivable ...................... | 128,800 |  |
| Allowance for doubtful accounts .............. |  | 20,600 |
| Bad debts recovered ...................... |  | 1,000 |

The company sells on terms of 1 percent cash discount allowed for all accounts paid within 15 days from the invoice date. The company's past experience indicates that 2 percent of sales on account normally are not collected, and a monthly adjusting entry is made to reflect this. All recoveries on uncollectible accounts are credited directly to a special revenue account.

During December, the following transactions occur:

1. Sales of $108,000, of which $16,000 are cash sales.
2. Gross amounts of accounts collected, $156,000, of which $134,400 represents gross accounts collected within the discount period.
3. Gross amounts of returns, $2,200.
4. Accounts charged off as uncollectible, $11,700.
5. Recoveries made of accounts previously written off, $100.
6. The adjusting entry for doubtful accounts is made.

*Required:*

a. Journalize the December transactions.
b. A detailed study of the outstanding accounts receivable at year-end indicates that 15 percent of them will eventually prove uncollectible. Assuming this information is correct, what does this suggest about the accuracy of the firm's estimate for doubtful accounts? Can you suggest a possible reason for the disparity by looking at the accounts?
c. What alternative treatment could have been employed concerning the recovery of uncollectible accounts? What would be its effect on total assets? On Net Income?
d. Assume that December sales were spread evenly over the month and that most customers do not pay until the 15th day. What adjustment could be made on December 31 with respect to sales discounts? Would you make it? Explain.

**6–11.** Downtime Computer Sales Corporation sells time-sharing computer terminals with a two-year warranty at $2,000 each. Under the warranty contract, the corporation agrees to provide at no cost to the customer all necessary repairs, both labor and replacement parts, arising from other than misuse of the equipment. From its past experience, the company estimates that labor costs under the warranty agreement will be $400 per unit and replacement parts will be $80 per unit. During 1985 Downtime sold 150 terminals evenly throughout the year. Repair costs for warranty work in 1985 amounted to $12,400 for labor and $2,500 for replacement parts.

*Required:*

a. Prepare the journal entries necessary to record the transactions for 1985. Set up an estimated liability for warranty work.

b. Indicate where the accounts employed in *(a)* would appear on the financial statements for 1985 and explain why they are so classified.

c. By how much would net income have been changed if the company treated warranty costs simply as a period expense? Which method better measures net income?

d. How might one argue that the method in *(a)* overstates revenues and hence net income?

**6–12.** Sagging Suspension Bridge Corporation erects large spans over superhighways. Most projects require 15 to 22 months to complete. During the period 1984–86, the firm worked on four major projects. Relevant data applicable to each one is presented below (in thousands of dollars):

| Project Number | Contract Price | Total Estimated Cost | Cost Incurred 1984 | 1985 | 1986 | Year Completed |
|---|---|---|---|---|---|---|
| A510 .......... | $750 | $700 | $700 | — | — | 1984 |
| A511 .......... | 900 | 720 | 120 | $420 | $180 | 1986 |
| A513 .......... | 680 | 600 | — | 300 | 300 | 1986 |
| A514 .......... | 720 | 650 | — | 195 | 325 | 1987 |

*Required:*

a. Determine the amount of gross margin to be recognized in each year if percentage of completion is used to recognize revenue.

b. What would you do if the total of the actual costs incurred under the contract differed from the estimated cost?

c. The bookkeeper of Sagging Suspension drew up the following schedule of gross margin under "conventional" accounting (in thousands):

| | 1984 | 1985 | 1986 |
|---|---|---|---|
| Sales ......................... | $750 | $    0 | $1,580 |
| Construction costs ................. | 820 | 915 | 805 |
| Gross margin ...................... | $ (70) | $(915) | $  775 |

Do you agree that this is the result from conventional accounting? Explain. Revise the figures to show the margins under a proper interpretation of the conventional completed contract (sales) basis of accounting.

d. Explain why your revised figures in *(c)* are still an unsatisfactory measure of the firm's activity.

**6–13.** In 1983 Permafrost Land Development Company purchased a plot of land for $900,000 to be developed and subdivided. During 1983 the firm spent $300,000 to put in roads and sewers and to subdivide the acreage into 150 lots. Each lot is priced to sell at $26,000, and marketing of the lots begins in 1984.

Purchasers of lots make a $2,000 cash down payment and pay $500 per month for 48 months. In addition, interest of 1 percent per month is charged on all unpaid balances. Legal title passes when all payments have been made; customers who cancel or cease making payments forfeit all rights and claims. Cancellations and uncollectibles are expected to run 10 percent of sales. This should cover the difference between the amount of uncollected contract and the cost of the recovered land.

During 1984, 100 lots are sold. A sales commission of 6 percent of the selling price is paid in cash. Cash receipts in 1984 were:

| | |
|---|---|
| 100 down payments | $200,000 |
| Collection of monthly payments | 300,000 |
| Collection of interest | 120,000 |

Two of the sales were canceled in 1984 after the customers had paid a total of $8,000, including down payments. Additional costs for completion of roads, parks, and water systems were $300,000 in 1984 and are estimated to be $100,000 annually in 1985, 1986, and 1987.

*Required:*

a. Permafrost is considering two methods of revenue recognition—(1) recognize revenue at the point of sale and (2) recognize revenue as cash is collected. What are the problems associated with each of these two methods. Are there other alternatives the company should consider?

b. If revenue is recognized at the point of sale, how would you treat sales cancellations and future development costs? Explain carefully.

c. What amount of revenue *and* expense would be shown under the sales basis in 1984? What items would appear on the balance sheet?

**6–14.** The December 31, 1984, balance sheet of Highly Distinct Industries shows among the assets the following:

| | | |
|---|---|---|
| Accounts receivable | | $306,000 |
| Less: Allowance for uncollectibles | $14,000 | |
| Allowance for returns | 12,200 | 26,200 |
| | | $279,800 |

The transactions which took place in 1985 are summarized as follows:

| | |
|---|---|
| Sales on account | $1,264,000 |
| Sales returns | 67,900 |
| Cash collected from customers | 1,086,200 |
| Accounts written off as uncollectible | 14,400 |

*Required:*

a. Prepare journal entries to record the preceding transactions.

b. Prepare the adjusting entry for 1985 uncollectibles assuming that the company were to determine them under each of the following methods:

1. 1.5% of credit sales.
2. 5% of gross accounts receivable.
3. An aging of accounts receivable indicates that $23,000 will not be collected.

Which of these methods do you prefer? Why?

c. Highly Distinct's policy is to maintain its allowance for sales returns equal to 4 percent of gross accounts receivable. Make the journal entry to record the estimate for sales returns on December 31, 1985. (Your exact journal entry may be influenced by the particular entry you made in part *(a)* for sales returns.

d.  Assume that in addition to the $14,400 of accounts written off during the year, two large customers owing a total of $67,400 went bankrupt when their businesses were completely wiped out as a result of a volcanic eruption of Mount St. Helens. These had been old, established, and very reliable customers. How would you record the write-off of these two accounts? Explain.

**6–15.**  Somewhat unusual revenue recognition practices sometimes arise in particular industries. Such is the case with companies that operate or rent oceangoing vessels to be used for cargo. Excerpts from the annual reports of two companies engaging in such operations are given below.

> **R. J. Reynolds Industries, 1982 Annual Report:**  "Transportation revenues and related vessel voyage expenses are generally recognized at the commencement of a voyage."
>
> **LTV Corporation, 1981 Annual Report:**  "Revenue from ocean shipping operations is recognized upon unloading inbound cargoes (terminated voyage basis). For voyages in process at the end of an accounting period, revenues and expenses . . . are deferred. Revenue from charter hire of vessels is recognized ratably over the terms of the contract."

*Required:*

Which of the three methods mentioned—commencement of the voyage, termination of the voyage, or ratably over the voyage—is preferable? Explain why. Are there circumstances under which each of them might be preferred or at least seem consistent with the revenue recognition postulate?

**6–16.**  Yearn to Learn Corporation offers correspondence courses in basic commercial subjects—bookkeeping, business math, computer programming, effective writing, etc. Students sign up for a course by filling out a registration form and paying the course fee of $1,200. In addition, there is a $25 application fee the first time a student takes a course. The application fee compensates the corporation for its basic record-keeping costs and is not required for subsequent courses.

For the $1,200 course fee, a student receives a textbook, a study guide, and a packet of 10 lessons. Yearn to Learn estimates that its development, production, mailing, and handling costs associated with the course materials averages $200. The student completes a lesson and mails it in. The lesson is corrected and returned to the student. The students can work at their own pace. Upon satisfactory completion of the last lesson, the student receives a certificate of completion and a brochure describing other "advanced" courses to consider.

Yearn to Learn pays local college students $30 a lesson to correct the lessons and be available three hours one evening a week to respond to students' questions via telephone calls. Students have 90 days to cancel a course. Upon cancellation within that time period, the student receives a refund of $1,000. This amount is refunded even if the student has completed two or three lessons. After 90 days there are no refunds of any kind; also the application fees are never refunded. The number of cancellations is highly unpredictable. In some years it may run up to 30 percent.

*Required:*

a. Discuss carefully how Yearn to Learn Corporation should recognize revenue. Include in your discussion how you would handle the application fee, the course fee, and the problem of cancellations.

b. Illustrate through a series of journal entries how you would record a course sold to a first-time student on July 18, 1985. During the remainder of 1985, the student completed six lessons.

c. Assume each course has a time-limit for completion of two years. After that time period a student who failed to complete a course would have to start at the beginning if he or she wished to receive a certificate of completion. However, for the second time around the course fee would be only $800. How would you modify your answer to handle this situation?

**6–17.** The Maple Corporation sells farm machinery on the installment plan.[19] On July 1, 1984, Maple entered into an installment sales contract with Agriculture, Inc., for an eight-year period. Equal annual payments under the installment sale are $100,000 and are due on July 1. The first payment was made on July 1, 1984.

*Additional information:*

1. The amount that would be realized on an outright sale of similar farm machinery is $556,000.
2. The cost of the farm machinery sold to Agriculture is $417,000.
3. The finance charges relating to the total installment period are $244,000 based on a stated interest rate of 12 percent, which is appropriate.
4. Circumstances are such that the collection of the installments due under the contract is reasonably assured.

*Required:*

a. Prepare journal entries for the 1984 transactions, assuming Maple Corporation uses the installment method of recognizing revenue.

b. How would the accounts you employed in (a) be classified on the financial statements for 1984.

c. What amount of income as a result of the above transaction would Maple record in 1984 under the conventional sales method of revenue recognition? Is this a better reflection of the firm's activities?

d. How would you handle a 20 percent sales commission that was paid on July 1, 1984, to the salesperson obtaining the order? Answer assuming first the installment method and then the sales method.

**6–18.** Anacomp, Inc., is a rapidly growing firm. It is headquartered in Indiana and has offices all over the country. Its services include software development, computer facility management and minicomputers, micrographics, and data processing.

Its revenue recognition practices are detailed in the following note from its 1981 annual report.

Revenues are generally recognized as follows:

(1) Data preparation, data processing, facility management and Com-

---

[19] Material from the Uniform CPA Examinations, Copyright © 1980 by the American Institute of Certified Public Accountants, Inc., is adapted with permission.

puter Output Microfilm (COM) services and sales are recognized as the services are performed or products are shipped. . . .

(2) Revenues from licensing of existing software systems which do not require substantial modification are recognized in accordance with the terms of the applicable contracts if performance until conversion is specified, or when the customer's records are converted to Anacomp's system if licensee has a cancellation option.

(3) Revenues from long-term contracts for development, modification, and/or implementation of software systems are recognized under methods which approximate the percentage-of-completion method, except for revenues from development contracts with certain limited partnerships which are reported on the completed contract method. . . .

Revenue recognized under items (2) and (3) may precede the date at which the customer may be billed pursuant to the contract terms. Substantially all unbilled revenue is collected in the year subsequent to the year revenue is recognized.

*Required:*

a. Evaluate Anacomp's revenue recognition practices as they relate to the earning criteria.
b. Why does one company operating basically in one line of business use so many different methods? Would it not be easier for stockholders to understand if only one method were used for all contracts?
c. Explain why the cancellation option in (2) should cause a change in revenue recognition procedures.
d. Several officers and directors of Anacomp are affiliated with and/or investors in the limited partnerships mentioned in (3). Why should this fact cause a change in revenue recognition practices for these contracts?
e. Does the frequent lack of customer billing in items (2) and (3) result in these methods failing to meet the measurability criterion? What account would the company debit when recording the revenue on these contracts?

**6A–1.** The Deytyme Construction Company began operations January 1, 1985.[20] During the year, Deytyme entered into a contract with Redbeard Razor Corporation to construct a manufacturing facility. At that time, Deytyme estimated that it would take five years to complete the facility at a total cost of $4,800,000. The total contract price for construction of the facility is $6,000,000. During the year, Deytyme incurred $1,250,000 in construction costs related to the construction project. The estimated cost to complete the contract is $3,750,000. Redbeard was billed and paid 30 percent of the contract price.

*Required:*

a. Prepare schedules to calculate the amount of gross margin to be recognized for the year ended December 31, 1985, and the amount to be shown as "cost of

---

[20] Material from the Uniform CPA Examination, Copyright © 1978 by the American Institute of Certified Public Accountants, Inc., is adapted with permission.

uncompleted contract in excess of related billings" or "billings on uncompleted contract in excess of related costs" at December 31, 1985. Assume the company uses the completed-contract method.

b. Repeat part (a) assuming Deytyme uses the percentage-of-completion method.

**6A-2.** Fantastic Flying Machine, Inc., enters into a contract with the government to produce three models of a new aircraft that can fly backward as well as forward. Because of the extreme uncertainty surrounding the venture, the company insisted on a cost-plus-fixed-fee contract. The contract is to run no longer than four years, with delivery of the models to be made as soon as they are completed. Under the terms of the contract, the government is to pay all allowable costs plus a $1.2 million fee to cover general administrative costs and profit. The company's original proposal estimated the costs at $6 million. An initial payment of $1 million is received upon signing of the contract on January 1 of the first year. Within 60 days after the close of each year, the government will pay 80 percent of the costs incurred in the preceding year. In addition, the government will pay $400,000 upon receipt of each aircraft model. The balance due under the contract will be paid at the close of the contract.

Relevant data with respect to the contract is given below (in thousands of dollars):

| | Year | | | |
|---|---|---|---|---|
| | 1 | 2 | 3 | 4 |
| Costs incurred | $1,500 | $3,000 | $1,500 | $1,500 |
| Estimated cost to complete | 4,500 | 1,800 | 1,000 | — |
| General administrative costs | 180 | 205 | 208 | 220 |

The first model was delivered at the end of Year 2; the second at the beginning of Year 4; and the third at the end of Year 4.

*Required:*

a. Prepare a schedule to determine the amount of *cash* received each year under the contract.

b. Prepare an abbreviated income statement for each year, under the assumption that the company uses percentage of completion to estimate the portion of the fee earned.

c. Indicate the accounts that would appear on each year-end position statement along with their amounts and classification.

d. Calculate the amount of revenue to be recognized each year under percentage of completion if the contract contains an incentive provision whereby the fee is increased or reduced $20,000 for every $100,000 of cost under or over $6.5 million.

**6A-3.** The current assets of Northrup Corporation as of December 31, 1982, included Accounts Receivable of $137.6 million and Inventories of $238.6 million.

Schedules accompanying the financial statements provide the following detailed information about these accounts.

*Accounts Receivable*

Long-term contracts:
Current accounts billed ................................... $ 42.1
Current accounts unbilled ............................... 70.3
Due upon negotiation of prices for customer changes,
unbilled ............................................. 7.8
Due upon contract completion ........................... 9.7
Total due, long-term contracts ..................... 129.9
Trade and other accounts receivable ....................... 26.7
156.6
Less: Allowance for doubtful accounts .................... 19.0
$137.6

*Inventories*

Costs related to long-term contracts:
Production costs ....................................... $813.4
Administrative and general costs ....................... 103.9
917.3
Less: Progress payments ............................. 690.6
226.7
Product inventories ...................................... 11.9
$238.6

The following quotations are abstracted from the narrative notes:

"Sales under cost-reimbursement, service, research and development and construction-type contracts are recorded as costs are incurred and include estimated earned fees or profits calculated on the basis of the relationship between costs incurred and total estimated costs (cost-to-cost type of percentage-of-completion method of accounting). Sales under other types of contracts are recorded as deliveries are made and are computed on the basis of the estimated final average unit cost plus profit (units-of-delivery type of percentage-of-completion method of accounting). Certain fixed-price contracts contain provisions for price redetermination or for cost or performance incentives. Such redetermined amounts or incentives are included in sales when realization is assured and the amounts can reasonably be determined. Estimated amounts for contract change orders and claims are included in sales only when realization is probable. In the period in which it is determined that a loss will result from the performance of a contract, the entire amount of the estimated ultimate loss is charged against income. Other changes in estimates of sales, costs, and profits are recognized using the cumulative catch-up method of accounting. This method recognizes in the current period the cumulative effect of the changes on current and prior periods. The effect of the changes on future periods of contract performance is recognized as if the revised estimates had been the original estimates.

"Included in accounts receivable are amounts billed and currently due from customers under all types of contracts, amounts currently due but unbilled, certain estimated contract changes and claims in negotiation, and amounts retained pending contract completion.

"Most inventoried costs represent work in process under fixed-price-type contracts. They are stated on the basis of accumulated contract costs less the portion of such costs allocated to delivered items. Accumulated contract costs include direct production costs, factory and engineering overhead, production tooling costs, and administrative and general expenses (except for general corporate expenses allocated to commercial contracts, which are charged against income as incurred). In accordance with industry practice, inventoried costs include amounts related to contracts having production cycles longer than one year."

*Required:*

a. Explain in your own words the two different types of percentage-of-completion measurements used by Northrup. Under what circumstances would each be appropriate?

b. What does the account, Due Upon Contract Completion, represent? This amount includes about $4 million that will not be collected until *1984* or later. Explain why this is so. Should these amounts still be reported as current assets?

c. Northrup Corporation uses percentage-of-completion methods, yet its inventories of long-term contracts are stated at cost and seem to include no gross profit element. Why? (Hint: You may be able to explain by reconstructing the typical journal entries that Northrup would make on a contract).

d. How is it possible to have progress payments with a credit balance and unbilled receivables with a debit balance? (Again, the explanation may be found in the reconstruction of typical journal entries).

e. Is it appropriate to charge administrative and general expenses as contract costs rather than as period expenses?

f. Describe in your own words the meaning of the "cumulative catch-up method of accounting."

# CHAPTER 7

# COST MEASUREMENT

In Chapter 1, the concept of measuring net income by matching resources used against resources received from revenue-producing operations provides the fundamental direction to financial accounting. The value of the resources used and received, according to the *exchange-price concept,* is to be measured by the prices agreed upon or inherent in the exchanges in which the resources originated. From this assumption we derived in Chapter 2 the principle that assets generally should be recorded at acquisition cost.

The acquisition cost of an asset includes all reasonable and necessary costs of acquiring the services of the asset—*the cost of the resource per se, the costs of getting it to the place of business, and other costs of rendering it available for the intended use.* Necessary expenditures encompass all outlays that increase the use value of the asset for revenue production. In economic terms, all costs that create form, place, or time utility are necessary costs. Reasonable costs include all outlays that a knowledgeable person would be willing to incur in an arm's-length transaction.

This chapter applies this general concept of cost determination to four particular types of assets—labor services, purchased inventory, manufactured inventory, and noncurrent assets. Then, after examining the manner in which the currently accepted cost concepts are handled in the accounting records, we take a brief look at current modifications when the cost principle is applied to certain marketable securities and then introduce some alternative approaches to cost determination that have become required supplementary disclosures.

**COST OF LABOR SERVICES**

Labor services, just like the various tangible properties a business uses, are a productive resource. This resource rarely appears on a position statement, because it normally is transformed immediately into some other resource or used in revenue production during the period. In fact, if we know that the labor services will be consumed in the production of revenue during the accounting period, we debit an expense account directly when the services are acquired. Nevertheless, the amount of the entry is determined by the *cost of the asset, labor services.*

There are two important factors to remember in the determination of the total labor cost:

1. The wage and salary cost usually exceeds the amounts paid to employees.
2. *Total* labor costs include more than just the wage and salary cost.

The first point arises because employers act as collecting agents for other groups by withholding certain amounts from their employees' paychecks. For instance, employers are required by law to retain a portion of the earnings for employees' income taxes and social security taxes. Workers may sanction other payroll deductions for contributory insurance and supplemental retirement programs, bond-purchase and other savings plans, union dues, and so on. The *wage and salary cost* for a period is the amount actually *earned* by the employees that period, whether or not actually paid in cash to *them*. The amounts withheld must be recognized as liabilities, to be remitted periodically on behalf of the employees to the various governmental and other agencies concerned. From the company's point of view, the total wages and salaries earned are eventually paid out.

The second point results from the recognition that the cost of various fringe benefits is part of the total cost of maintaining a labor force. For example, employers must contribute an additional amount for social security. They also must pay for unemployment compensation insurance and may spend additional sums for various employee pension and welfare programs in response to union contracts or company personnel policies. Often these fringe benefit costs are recorded for information purposes in separate cost accounts. Conceptually, however, they are costs incurred in the acquisition of labor services.

**Numerical Example**

Keeping in mind these two major points, let us assume that a company, in preparing the payroll for the week, encounters the following situation:

1. Total salaries earned amount to $20,000—$14,000 by salespersons and $6,000 by office employees.
2. The company is required to withhold 15 percent of employee earnings for income taxes and 7 percent for social security taxes.[1]

---

[1] The withholding rates used for these items are only approximations for illustrative purposes. The exact rates vary with the particular circumstances of each employee and with changes in legislation.

3. Certain employees have authorized the company to deduct from their salaries their contributions to the United Fund. These amount to $250. Also, each employee contributes 1 percent of his or her salary to the group life insurance program.

4. The company is required to match the employees' contributions for social security. It must also contribute 3.4 percent of gross salaries earned for the unemployment compensation insurance program, .7 percent to the federal government, and 2.7 percent to the state government.

5. The company contributes an additional 2 percent of gross salaries earned to the employee group life insurance program and 10 percent for a retirement program.

The following entry would be made to recognize the salary cost of labor services and the liability to employees and other agencies for the salaries earned:

| | | |
|---|---|---|
| Sales Salaries Expense | 14,000 | |
| Office Salaries Expense | 6,000 | |
| Income Tax Withholdings Payable | | 3,000 |
| Social Security Taxes Payable[2] | | 1,400 |
| United Fund Withholdings Payable | | 250 |
| Employee Insurance Premiums Payable | | 200 |
| Wages Payable | | 15,150 |

Obviously, the manner of recording the debits would vary with the type of work performed by the employee and the degree of detail desired in expense classification. A single debit to Wage Expense might suffice for a small business.

Remembering our second point that total labor cost includes the cost of various fringe benefit programs, we must also record the accruing of these costs and their related liabilities. The entries to accomplish this follow:

| | | |
|---|---|---|
| Payroll Tax Expense—Sales | 980 | |
| Payroll Tax Expense—Office | 420 | |
| Social Security Taxes Payable | | 1,400 |
| | | |
| Payroll Tax Expense—Sales | 476 | |
| Payroll Tax Expense—Office | 204 | |
| Federal Unemployment Taxes Payable | | 140 |
| State Unemployment Taxes Payable | | 540 |
| | | |
| Employee Insurance Expense—Sales | 280 | |
| Employee Insurance Expense—Office | 120 | |
| Employee Insurance Premiums Payable | | 400 |
| | | |
| Pension Expense | 2,000 | |
| Liability for Employee Pensions | | 2,000 |

All of the above debits represent costs over and above the salary cost

---

[2] This liability is often called FICA Taxes Payable (Federal Insurance Contributions Act).

incurred for the purpose of maintaining a labor force. We have recorded them in separate expense accounts in order to supply additional information about the total labor cost. In theory, we could have combined them with the related salaries in single labor service expense accounts.

The credits in the foregoing entries show the additional amounts owed to various groups for employer payroll taxes and employer-paid fringe benefits. In most cases they are current liabilities, with the possible exception of the liability for employee pensions. When they are combined with the liabilities for employee compensation and employee withholdings, we can see the total future outlays of cash that will be made to and for employees.

## COST OF PURCHASED INVENTORY

The costs necessary for acquiring inventory and placing it for sale include the net invoice price, sales and excise taxes paid, freight charges into the business, and any handling costs incurred in unloading and storage. Each of these expenditures is properly includible in the asset amount. Each adds to the usefulness of the asset in supplying its intended service. They are called *inventoriable costs*. Together with the beginning inventory, they make up a total pool of merchandise cost, eventually to be divided between the goods sold (expense) and the goods on hand at the end of the period (asset).

These costs must be distinguished from those which on occasion may be incurred *unnecessarily* in the acquisition of an asset. Examples might include rehandling costs, lost discounts, and demurrage charges for the detention of ships or railroad cars beyond the time allowed for unloading. These expenditures do not increase the utility of the merchandise and should be treated as period expenses or losses, not as part of the cost of the asset.

## Recording the Elements of Inventory Cost

Assume that a firm begins the accounting period with a merchandise inventory of $5,300. During the period the following *summary* transactions occur:

1.  Merchandise is purchased for $30,000 at net invoice prices.
2.  Freight charges of $1,800 are incurred on the incoming merchandise.
3.  The firm incurs $600 of wage costs in unloading, unpacking, inspecting, and stocking the incoming merchandise.
4.  In the receiving department, merchandise costing $3,500 is discovered to be of the wrong size and is returned.

According to our cost concept, the first three items properly could be debited to the Merchandise Inventory account. They are costs necessary to obtain the purchased merchandise delivered and ready for sale. The returned merchandise signifies a reduction in the asset and could be credited directly to it. The same treatment would be applicable to price allowances for defects or damages; they reduce the cost of the asset purchased.

On the other hand, if all of these elements of inventory cost are lumped together in one account, some desirable managerial information may be hidden. For instance, the firm may wish to record the purchases separately in order to facilitate analysis. Comparisons between total purchases and total freight charges may be desirable in the evaluation of the purchasing department's activities. For purposes of cost control, a knowledge of freight charges and handling costs on incoming merchandise would be helpful. Similarly, extensive purchase returns and allowances may indicate defects in the ordering procedures or inefficiencies on the part of the suppliers.

Many businesses, therefore, record each element of inventory cost in a separate account, as illustrated below. This procedure provides ledger accounts with the additional information needed for cost control and analysis. The Purchases, Freight-In, and Handling Costs accounts are *adjunct* accounts to the asset Merchandise—segregated increases in the asset. Purchase Returns and Allowances is a *contra* asset account.

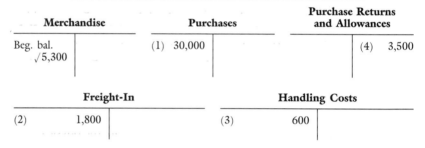

Together with the beginning inventory, all these accounts make up the total cost of goods available for sale of $34,200 ($5,300 + $30,000 − $3,500 + $1,800 + $600). At the end of the accounting period the contra and adjunct accounts, having served their purpose, are closed out. Assume, for example, that the ending inventory is counted and a cost of $7,600 (including applicable freight and handling cost) is determined for it. The adjusting entry to record cost of goods sold of $26,600 ($34,200 − $7,600) and the ending inventory would be:

| | | |
|---|---|---|
| Merchandise | 7,600 | |
| Cost of Goods Sold | 26,600 | |
| Purchase Returns and Allowances | 3,500 | |
|     Merchandise | | 5,300 |
|     Purchases | | 30,000 |
|     Freight-In | | 1,800 |
|     Handling Costs | | 600 |

In theory the cost of goods sold and the cost of the ending inventory should include all charges incurred in bringing the merchandise into its existing location and condition. Strictly interpreted, accounting theory would require the allocation of the costs of ordering, receiving, inspecting, and warehousing. In practice many of these costs are difficult to identify and trace. Therefore they are treated as period expenses. The *cost* of allocating them *exceeds* the *benefit* of increased accuracy from including them in inventoriable costs.

Even the costs which are treated as inventoriable costs in accordance with sound theory may be allocated somewhat arbitrarily. For instance, freight charges and handling costs may be divided between items sold and items on hand in proportion to the respective dollar amounts, number of units, weight, or some other variable. Indeed, some firms do not allocate any of the freight and handling cost to the ending inventory. All of it becomes part of cost of goods sold because the increased accuracy is considered not worth the work involved. When cost of goods sold is very large compared to the inventory and the latter is fairly constant, this departure from theoretical soundness probably causes no *material* difference in income.

|                          |                                                                             |
| :----------------------- | :-------------------------------------------------------------------------- |

**Purchase Discounts**

Just as a seller sometimes chooses between recording sales at gross prices or net prices, a company purchasing from suppliers who allow a discount for prompt payment has the same choice. If purchases are recorded at gross prices initially, subsequent adjustment is necessary for discounts taken. If net prices are used to begin with, adjustments are needed whenever discounts are lost. For purchases the net method seems to have all-around superiority over the gross method in terms of theoretical soundness, practicality, and managerial usefulness.

Theoretically, the net price is the actual price of the inventory. The purchasing company can acquire the physical asset for this amount, the so-called "cash price." Any amount above this is related to how the acquisition of the asset is financed. If the gross price is eventually paid, the extra amount represents the penalty for late payment—a type of financial or administrative charge—not the cost of an increase in the asset's usefulness. Recording gross prices would initially overstate the asset, necessitating downward adjustment later for the amount of the discount.

From a practical viewpoint, management determines whether purchase discounts are taken or not. (In contrast, control over the taking of sales discounts rests with the customer.) Failure to take "cash discounts" is expensive[3] and adversely reflects upon the company's creditworthiness. Under the net price procedures, we have to account only for the discounts that are lost. Since these normally are few, the bookkeeping procedure is simplified. No adjustments or special entries are needed when the bills are paid. A purchase of $6,000 gross, subject to a discount of 3 percent within

---

[3] When it loses the discount, the firm buying on terms calling for a 2 percent discount within 10 days or the full amount payable in 30 days has to pay 2 percent of the gross price for the privilege of waiting an additional 20 days to pay its bill. This is approximately equal to an annual interest charge of 36.7 percent $\left( I = P \times R \times T; 2 = 98 \times R \times \dfrac{20}{360} \right)$.

15 days and paid within the discount period, simply would be recorded as follows:

| | | |
|---|---|---|
| Purchases | 5,820 | |
|     Accounts Payable | | 5,820 |
|   To record purchase. | | |

| | | |
|---|---|---|
| Accounts Payable | 5,820 | |
|     Cash | | 5,820 |
|   To record payment within discount period. | | |

Still a third advantage of the net method exists whenever the discount is not taken. Assume that the account in the preceding example is not paid within the 15-day period. The entry under the net method would be:

| | | |
|---|---|---|
| Accounts Payable | 5,820 | |
| Purchase Discounts Lost | 180 | |
|     Cash | | 6,000 |

It is highly desirable for management to know when resources have been wasted because of negligent delay on the part of the cashier's office in paying bills or because of insufficient cash being available for prompt payment of liabilities. Under the net price procedure, any amount in excess of the net invoice price is automatically isolated in a separate account, Purchase Discounts Lost, as a natural part of the bookkeeping entry.

**Recording at Gross.** One of the disadvantages with the net method is the difficulty encountered in maintaining subsidiary inventories at net prices. The invoice above for $6,000 may consist of 20 different items. In the detailed inventory records, each one would have to be recorded at 97 percent of its invoice price. If the gross price is used instead, the supplier's invoice agrees with the inventory records. The entries for the above example would be:

| | | |
|---|---|---|
| Purchases | 6,000 | |
|     Accounts Payable | | 6,000 |
|   To record purchase. | | |

| | | |
|---|---|---|
| Accounts Payable | 6,000 | |
|     Cash | | 5,820 |
|     Purchase Discounts | | 180 |
|   To record payment *within* the discount period. | | |

| | | |
|---|---|---|
| Accounts Payable | 6,000 | |
|     Cash | | 6,000 |

| | | |
|---|---|---|
| Purchase Discounts Lost | 180 | |
|     Purchase Discounts | | 180 |
|   To record payment *after* the discount period. | | |

To reduce the asset to its actual net cost, a credit to a *contra asset*, Purchase Discounts, is made when the amount is paid. This special entry is necessary for all discounts available, whether or not they are taken. As a contra account to Purchases, Purchase Discounts would be closed when the summary entry is made segregating the cost of goods sold and the cost of the ending inventory.

In the case of lost discounts, a tendency exists in practice to make only the entry paying off the gross liability. The result is that the inefficient use of resources is never highlighted for management's attention, for the loss remains buried in an overstated asset. The net method automatically prevents this potential error. Also, when the gross method is used in practice, the contra asset account Purchase Discounts occasionally finds its way onto the income statement as a revenue, because it has a credit balance. The fallacy of this practice is clear. Revenue measures the inflow of assets from the sale of the product; it does not arise from purchases and prompt payments. A company taking all available discounts will increase its net income, but the result comes about not from an increase in the inflow of assets but from a decrease in the use of assets.

## COST OF MANUFAC-TURED INVENTORY

Our illustrations so far involve merchandising concerns, in which most of the assets used up—merchandise, labor services, equipment, and so on—are consumed in an attempt to generate the current period's revenue. Consequently, we have focused our attention on two major stages in the life of an asset—acquisition (cost incurrence) and consumption (cost expiration). In a manufacturing firm an additional aspect is introduced—*transformation or conversion*. Some assets are utilized during the period not to produce revenue immediately but to produce another asset, the manufactured product. The costs of these assets are not recorded in expense accounts at the time of utilization. Instead, they become the cost of the new asset (product) being manufactured. In the accounting system a clear separation of these three stages—acquisition, transformation, and consumption in the generation of revenues—is necessary.

Our purpose in this section is to set up the conceptual framework and introduce some new accounts and procedures appropriate for a manufacturing company. Specifically, we try to see how the cost measurement concept is implemented when the product is *made* rather than purchased.

## Nature of Manufacturing

Manufacturing activity involves the physical conversion of raw material through the application of labor and other resources into a finished product ready for sale. Cost accounting systems for manufacturing companies parallel this process. They record the flow of costs out of the accounts representing the assets used in the conversion process and into new accounts corresponding to the new asset forms which result from the manufacturing activity. The cost of a manufactured product is developed through a careful tracing of the cost of assets utilized in production to the products being manufactured.

The *costs of assets used in manufacturing affect net income (become expenses) only in the period when the products containing these costs are sold.* Consequently, the accounting system in manufacturing must be relatively detailed to allow for the accumulation of the various costs of making the product and the "storing" of these costs in inventory until the product is sold. We are concerned only with those assets associated with the production process. Costs incurred in selling or in general administration are matched against the current period's revenues, as in a merchandising firm. A clear distinction must be made, however, among the incurrence, conversion, and expiration of costs related to the *manufacture* of the product.

These *product costs* that become the inventoriable costs in a manufacturing firm are generally classified into three main categories—raw materials, direct labor, and manufacturing overhead.

*Raw material* cost includes the cost of all material directly entering into the actual production of the physical units and becoming part of the specific product being manufactured. Iron ore for a steel company, lumber for a furniture firm, and steel for an automobile manufacturer are raw materials. *Direct labor* includes the cost of labor service directly identified with specific products—the cost of laborers who actually manufacture or assemble the product or operate the machines that do so.

*Manufacturing overhead,* on the other hand, is a diverse category used to cover all manufacturing costs *except* raw materials and direct labor. It includes the indirect production costs not readily identified with any specific units but necessary to the manufacturing process. Among these facilitating costs are the following:

1. Indirect labor—factory supervisors, foremen, maintenance employees, and production engineers.
2. Indirect materials—thread, nails, glue, wax, and other materials not readily traceable to particular units of product.
3. Factory supplies—oil, coal, and maintenance supplies.
4. Utility services for the manufacturing portion of the business—heat, light, power, and water.
5. Depreciation on factory buildings and equipment.
6. Repair and maintenance of factory equipment.

**Flow of Costs in Manufacturing**

A typical cost accounting system for a manufacturing firm is depicted by the sequence of ledger accounts shown in Table 7–2. The numbers are developed from the data in Table 7–1 and can be traced from the journal entries in the next section. Separate production cost accounts are used to record utilization of the raw materials, direct labor, and manufacturing overhead and to accumulate the cost of the products being manufactured.

Raw materials, direct labor, and manufacturing overhead all represent assets that will be used in production and costs that will eventually become part of the cost of the manufactured product. The latter two are temporary assets in that they normally are utilized during the period. Manufacturing

**TABLE 7–1  Data for Manufacturing Illustration**

|  | June 1 | Transactions during June | June 30 |
|---|---|---|---|
| 1. Inventories: |  |  |  |
| Raw materials | $21,600 |  | $31,950 |
| Work in process | 23,500 |  | 17,800 |
| Finished goods | 48,600 |  | 52,200 |
| 2. Raw material purchases |  | $205,200 |  |
| 3. Wage and salary costs: |  |  |  |
| Direct factory labor |  | 139,500 |  |
| Indirect factory labor |  | 28,150 |  |
| Sales salaries |  | 19,500 |  |
| Executive salaries |  | 75,000 |  |
| 4. Other factory costs: |  |  |  |
| Depreciation on factory building |  | 4,900 |  |
| Depreciation on factory equipment |  | 6,100 |  |
| Factory supplies used |  | 15,050 |  |
| Heat, light and power (80% applicable to production operations) |  | 12,000 |  |

Overhead serves as a summary account. Individual elements may be recorded first in separate cost accounts, for example, Indirect Labor, Indirect Materials, Factory Supplies Used, Depreciation of Factory Equipment, Factory Utility Costs, and so on. Eventually, these separate cost elements are transferred to one or more Manufacturing Overhead accounts. An alternative approach often employed is to treat Manufacturing Overhead as a control account and to record the individual, detailed cost elements in subsidiary ledger accounts.

Raw Materials commonly shows a balance at the end of the period. This ending inventory represents the cost of materials acquired but not used during the period. Work in Process and Finished Goods are also inventory accounts; their ending balances represent the manufacturing costs attached to the partially completed goods and to the finished but unsold units of product, respectively. Finished Goods corresponds to the Merchandise Inventory account in a merchandising firm.

Cost of Goods Sold is the only *expense* account in the flow of manufacturing costs. Together with the selling and administrative expenses (only salaries in our example), it will be matched against sales revenue on the income statement. Part of the amount in Cost of Goods Sold may represent costs which have been incurred in production in some prior accounting period. These costs have been stored as part of work in process and finished goods until the product is sold. Then, as part of the total cost of the product, they are matched against the revenue produced this period by the product's sale. Likewise, the raw materials, direct labor, and factory overhead costs acquired and utilized during the *present* accounting period may not all flow through to Cost of Goods Sold in this period. Part may remain in the inventories (Raw Materials, Work in Process, or Finished Goods) at the end of the period and will affect Cost of Goods Sold in future periods.

**TABLE 7-2  Product Cost Flow in Manufacturing**

*Acquisition*        *Conversion*                          *Expiration*

| Raw Materials | | Work in Process | | Finished Goods | | Cost of Goods Sold |
|---|---|---|---|---|---|---|
| (1) 21,600 | (2) 194,850 | 23,500 | (3) 403,850 | 48,600 | (4) 400,250 | (4) 400,250 |
| 205,200 | | (2) 194,850 | | (3) 403,850 | | |
| | | (2) 139,500 | | | | *To Income Summary* |
| | | (2) 63,800 | | | | |

**Direct Labor**

| (1) 139,500 | (2) 139,500 |
|---|---|

**Manufacturing Overhead**

| (1) 63,800 | (2) 63,800 |
|---|---|

Explanation of the flow:

1. Entries recording the incurrence of costs for raw material, direct labor, and manufacturing overhead reflect asset acquisition. Corresponding credits are to various other asset or liability accounts.
2. These entries record the conversion of the basic cost elements into a manufactured product. The cost of the product's manufacture is accumulated by a transfer to Work in Process of the direct and indirect production costs utilized during the period.
3. As units are completed in the manufacturing process, the costs assigned to them are transferred to Finished Goods Inventory.
4. As units in finished goods are sold, a transfer of their manufacturing cost to Cost of Goods Sold reflects the expiration of cost in the generation of revenue.

**Journal Entries**

The following journal entries are necessary during the month or at month-end to record the incurrence, transformation, and expiration of the costs.

1. Raw Materials ................................. 205,200
       Accounts Payable ......................... 205,200
       To record the acquisition of additional
       raw materials.

2. Direct Labor .................................... 139,500
     Manufacturing Overhead ........................ 28,150
     Selling Expense ............................... 19,500
     Administrative Expense ........................ 75,000
       Wages and Salaries Payable ................ 262,150
       To record the incurrence of labor costs for
       the month and to classify them by type.

3. Manufacturing Overhead ........................ 26,050
       Accumulated Depreciation—
         Factory Building .......................... 4,900
       Accumulated Depreciation—
         Factory Equipment ........................ 6,100
       Factory Supplies Inventory ................... 15,050
       To record other indirect factory costs
       in Manufacturing Overhead.

4. Manufacturing Overhead ........................ 9,600
     Administrative Expense ........................ 2,400
       Accounts Payable ......................... 12,000
       To allocate heat, light, and power costs
       for the month between manufacturing cost and
       general expense.

5. Work in Process .............................. 194,850
       Raw Materials ............................ 194,850
       To record the cost of raw materials
       put into production during the month
       ($21,600 + $205,200 − $31,950).

6. Work in Process ............................. 203,300
       Direct Labor ............................. 139,500
       Manufacturing Overhead .................... 63,800
       To transfer the direct labor and total manufacturing
       overhead costs to Work in Process to record the
       utilization of these assets in the manufacturing
       process.

7. Finished Goods .............................. 403,850
       Work in Process .......................... 403,850
       To transfer the total manufacturing cost attached to
       the units of product completed during the month
       ($23,500 + $194,850 + $203,300 − $17,800).

8. Cost of Goods Sold ........................... 400,250
       Finished Goods ........................... 400,250
       To record the total manufacturing cost of the units
       of product sold during the month
       ($48,600 + $403,850 − $52,200).

**Statement of Cost of Goods Manufactured and Sold**

Normally, the income statement merely shows the single expense Cost of Goods Sold. A separate manufacturing cost report can be prepared to summarize the manufacturing activity and to present more detailed information concerning the determination of cost of goods manufactured and sold. Such a statement for the preceding illustration appears in Table 7–3.

The $398,150 total manufacturing costs represents the production costs incurred in June. Management focuses on this figure for monthly cost control. It is combined with the beginning inventories of Work in Process and Finished Goods to make up the total pool of manufacturing costs. This pool is divided among Costs of Goods Sold and the ending inventories of Work in Process and Finished Goods. The subtotal, Cost of Goods Completed, of $403,850 represents the cost of new salable products produced during the period. It is analogous to the amount in the Purchases account discussed earlier, except that in this case the cost is a production cost rather than a purchase cost. The final subtotal, Cost of Goods Sold, appears on the income statement, along with expenses associated with selling and administrative activities.

**TABLE 7–3  Statement of Cost of Goods Manufactured and Sold**
**For the Month of June, 19--**

| | | | |
|---|---:|---:|---:|
| Raw material inventory, June 1 | | $ 21,600 | |
| Plus: Raw material purchases | | 205,200 | |
| | | 226,800 | |
| Less: Raw material inventory, June 30 | | 31,950 | |
| Cost or raw materials used | | | $194,850 |
| Direct labor cost | | | 139,500 |
| Manufacturing overhead costs: | | | |
| Indirect labor | | 28,150 | |
| Factory supplies | | 15,050 | |
| Depreciation, building | | 4,900 | |
| Depreciation, equipment | | 6,100 | |
| Heat, light, and power | | 9,600 | 63,800 |
| **Total manufacturing costs** | | | 398,150 |
| Plus: Work in process, June 1 | | | 23,500 |
| | | | 421,650 |
| Less: Work in process, June 30 | | | 17,800 |
| **Cost of goods completed** | | | 403,850 |
| Plus: Finished goods, June 1 | | | 48,600 |
| | | | 452,450 |
| Less: Finished goods, June 30 | | | 52,200 |
| **Cost of goods sold** | | | $400,250 |

**COST OF NONCURRENT ASSETS**

The same cost principle that we have applied to labor services and inventory also applies to noncurrent assets. This section explores some of the problems one encounters in determining the cost of acquiring and rendering certain *noncurrent* assets available for use.

**Land**

The total initial acquisition cost of land consists of its purchase price (the amount of cash given up and any liabilities assumed) plus any other expenditures made for the purpose of acquiring ownership and use of the land. Such expenditures might include legal fees for title search, costs for registration of deeds, brokerage fees, and liens for back taxes. Any costs incurred for permanent improvements to the land also are included in the Land account as charges necessary for rendering the property available for its intended purpose. Examples include the cost of additional surveying, clearing, grading, and landscaping and one-time special assessments for sewers and drainage systems. They increase the utility of the land and hence benefit all periods in which the land is used.

A situation which may tax the analytical skills of the accountant is the purchase of land with an existing structure on it. If the original intention is to acquire the land and the building as separate assets, the purchase price should be allocated between the two assets acquired. If the original intention is simply to acquire a flat piece of land, the subsequent cost of razing the old building is added to the cost of the land. It is a necessary expenditure to render the *land* available for *its* intended use. Rational management certainly considers this additional cost in reaching its decision to acquire a particular piece of property. Presumably, it would be willing to pay a higher purchase price for the land if removal of the unwanted structure were not necessary. However, sometimes management's original intention—to acquire two assets, land and building, or to acquire a single asset, land—is not clear. Suppose the firm uses the old building one or two years and then tears it down to make a parking lot. Is the razing cost part of the cost of the asset "land" or part of the loss on destruction of the asset "building"?

One reason care must be taken in establishing the cost of land is that this asset is usually not considered to be subject to depreciation. Although the nondepreciable nature of land follows from its infinite service life, the same treatment does not apply to limited-life land improvements such as fences, pavements, sprinkler systems, and lighting systems. The costs of these items should be debited to a separate asset account, Land Improvements, and written off as expenses over their respective useful lives.

An asset with a finite life also can originate when we pay a fee for a limited interest in someone else's land. For instance, we might pay $20,000 for the privilege of using a road across a neighboring piece of property for a period of 20 years. This right is called an *easement* and really represents a long-term prepayment. Each year we use up a portion of our right, although our neighbor's land may remain unchanged. The easement has a limited life, and its cost therefore should be amortized.

**Purchased Assets[4]**

The cost of equipment, machinery, furniture, and fixtures includes the net invoice price, transportation costs, and any unloading or installation costs.

---

[4] Noncurrent assets acquired other than through purchases—for example, donations, stockholder investments, exchanges for other noncash assets, and trade-ins—are generally recorded at fair market value. Under the *exchange-price concept*, this is the value that would have prevailed in a bona fide exchange for cash. Further explanation about noncurrent asset exchanges and trade-ins appears in Chapter 9.

A machine delivered to the factory is more effective than one which rests on the supplier's loading dock. Likewise, a machine installed, tested, and ready for production is more useful than one sitting idle in the plant, waiting to be connected. Consequently, freight, installation, and testing charges represent additional *necessary* costs for putting the asset into economically useful condition and are properly debited to the asset account. A similar treatment would be accorded any costs of remodeling, renovating, or reconditioning a piece of used equipment which had been recently acquired. These costs are necessary if the business is to receive the intended benefit from use of the asset.

**Lump-Sum Acquisition.** Sometimes a business will purchase at one time practically all of the assets of another business. When more than one asset is acquired by means of a single payment, the result is called a *basket,* or *lump-sum,* purchase. The accounting problem becomes one of reasonably allocating the total purchase cost among the individual assets acquired. No single solution to this problem will suffice for all cases. The accountant must look at various sources of evidence—replacement costs, appraisal values, insurable values, valuations for tax assessments—to find a way of approximating the "net cash cost" of each asset.

Assume that a company acquires the assets of a firm going out of business. Because it is willing to buy the entire group of assets—inventory, land, warehouse, and warehouse equipment—the company is able to purchase them for a total of $330,000. The inventory consists of commonly purchased items that could be acquired on the wholesale market for $42,000. The buyer has the other assets appraised by a competent appraisal firm, whose report shows the estimated values to be: land, $105,000; warehouse, $140,000; and warehouse equipment, $70,000. The following entry might be made to record the acquisition:

| | | |
|---|---|---|
| Inventory | 42,000 | |
| Land | 96,000 | |
| Warehouse | 128,000 | |
| Warehouse Equipment | 64,000 | |
| Cash | | 330,000 |

In this case the $42,000 wholesale cost measures the current cash cost of the inventories very reliably. For the other assets, the accountant approximates the costs by allocating the remaining $288,000 cash paid among them in proportion to their appraised values (e.g., 105/315 allocated to land).[5]

---

[5] Other accountants may prefer to allocate the $330,000 to all assets, including inventory, using the total fair market value of $357,000 as a base. In this case $38,824 (42/357 of the $330,000) would be debited to inventories, $97,059 (105/357 of the $330,000) would be allocated to land, etc. In our view, when the measurement of the fair market value of one or more assets is clearly more reliable, those measurements should carry more weight in the allocation process.

**Constructed Assets**

Often a firm constructs some noncurrent asset for its own use. How do we determine the cost when there is no outright purchase? We apply concepts similar to those discussed earlier in connection with manufacturing. Just as the cost of a product being made consists of the cost of the assets used in its production, the acquisition cost of a constructed noncurrent asset includes the cost of resources, both short term and long term, which are utilized in its making.

If, for example, a firm decides to construct rather than buy a building for its home office, a special asset account, Construction in Progress—Building is established to accumulate the various costs incurred in erecting the building. Assume the following costs that would be debited to the account: $640,000 for the cost of materials used, $1,069,000 for the cost of labor services devoted to construction, $51,000 for depreciation on long-term assets used in construction, and $463,000 for subcontracting and other expenditures incurred for the purpose of creating the new asset. Upon completion of the construction project, an entry is made to transfer all relevant costs to the noncurrent asset:

| | | |
|---|---|---|
| Office Building ................................... | 2,223,000 | |
|     Construction in Progress—Building .......... | | 2,223,000 |

Ideally, we should like to be able to identify each specific cost or asset element used in erecting the building. Practical problems of measurement often arise, however, when workers normally employed in production are temporarily assigned to construction work and some of the resources normally included in manufacturing overhead are diverted to the making of some noncurrent asset. It may be difficult to determine what portion of these costs (indirect labor, power, supplies, etc.) should be debited to Construction in Progress rather than to Work in Process. At a minimum, any *increase* in overhead caused by the construction project should be assigned as part of its cost. Some accountants would stop at this point, arguing that management's decision to incur cost includes *only* the incremental costs. To charge regularly recurring manufacturing overhead to construction would reduce the costs charged to inventory and ultimately to cost of goods sold. Income would be higher in the period of construction.

In many cases the practice of charging only incremental costs seems to ignore the benefits received from the use of resources which otherwise would have been employed in other capacities or remained idle. Consequently, other accountants take the view that all manufacturing overhead costs reasonably traceable to the construction project should be added to its cost. To allocate full overhead costs when the cost of manufactured inventory is determined but to charge only incremental overhead costs when calculating the cost of self-constructed assets seems inconsistent.[6]

---

[6] *Standard 404* issued by the Cost Accounting Standards Board requires the allocation of full costs to self-constructed assets for purposes of cost determination under government contracts.

**Financial Charges**     Management's choice of how to finance the acquisition of an asset, whether by borrowed capital or stockholder capital or some combination, does not affect the service potential of that asset. Consequently, financing charges normally should be excluded from the asset's cost. The "cash" price is the initial cost of the asset. Often, however, the financing charge is implicit in the means by which the asset is bought. For instance, a firm can acquire a machine by paying $235,000 cash or making 12 monthly payments of $22,000 ($264,000 total). If the latter alternative is accepted, the accountant has to go behind the scenes to pull out the $29,000 differential. This represents the financing charge for delayed payment, not part of the asset's cost.

For many years the exclusion of financing charges from the cost of an asset was general practice. The theory was that interest expense relates to how a business acquires its financial capital and not to how much money must be expended to acquire a particular asset. Interest was treated as a general period expense, the cost of having sufficient financial capital to run the business, and not as part of the cost of a particular asset.

Two common exceptions in accounting practice existed in public utilities and retail land-sales companies. In the former, a normal interest charge on all funds tied up in the construction of an asset was included as part of the asset's cost. The argument was that these funds were committed to an asset which was not yet available for use and that some mix of capital was a necessary cost of acquiring the asset. In the latter, an interest cost was capitalized (often along with property taxes) as part of the cost of *holding* the land. These costs were matched against the eventual sales price of the land.

This practice of charging some interest expense to an asset account is called *capitalization of interest*. Under this concept interest is viewed as the cost of the money invested in a particular asset. Because the money is not available for current operations but does benefit future operations when the asset is actually used, a deferral of the interest cost of that money to future periods is argued to be appropriate.

In the early and mid-1970s the practice of capitalizing interest began to spread among industrial firms. The Securities and Exchange Commission was concerned that companies were inflating their reported incomes through this change in accounting procedure. To check the spread of this practice, the SEC in 1974 prohibited any additional firms from adopting this practice until the Financial Accounting Standards Board could study the issue.

**FASB Standard.**     In October of 1979 the FASB issued a standard recommending limited capitalization of interest costs.[7] Under this standard an asset qualifies for interest capitalization only if a significant period of time will necessarily expire between the initial expenditure for the asset

---

[7] FASB, *Statement of Financial Accounting Standards No. 34,* "Capitalization of Interest Cost" (Stamford, Conn., October 1979).

and its readiness for use. Plant assets acquired over time or constructed for internal use and assets manufactured for eventual sale under long-term construction contracts would qualify. The capitalization period begins when expenditures for the specific asset have been incurred and continues so long as activities to prepare the asset for use are in progress and interest costs are being incurred. Capitalization ends when the asset is substantially complete and ready for use.

The amount of interest to be capitalized is "that portion of the interest cost incurred during the assets' acquisition periods that theoretically could have been avoided . . . if expenditures for the assets had not been made."[8] The specific amount to be capitalized each accounting period is the product of the average monthly accumulated expenditures on the asset and the capitalization rate. This rate is the interest rate actually incurred on specific borrowings related to the asset. If the average monthly accumulated expenditures exceed the amount of specific borrowings, the excess is multiplied by a weighted-average interest rate applicable to other borrowings.

**Example.** Assume that during the current year a company spent $1,580,000 for the partial construction of its own new office building. The building will be completed in two more years. A $500,000 construction loan has been secured from a local bank at an interest rate of 15 percent. In addition, the firm has a number of interest-bearing liabilities outstanding with a weighted-average interest rate of 12 percent. The firm's total interest charges for the year are $612,500.

If the expenditures during the current year were to be made evenly throughout the year, the *average* accumulated expenditures would be $790,000 ($1,580,000/2). The interest to be capitalized on this building would be computed as follows:

$500,000 × 15% ........................... $ 75,000
290,000 × 12% ........................... 34,800
                                          $109,800

The summary entry to record interest for the year would be:

Interest Expense ................................... 502,700
Construction in Progress—Building .................. 109,800
     Cash and/or Interest Payable .................... 612,500

The amount of interest capitalized must be disclosed in the financial statements.

Limited capitalization of interest is now required under generally accepted accounting principles. However, in the eyes of some accountants the practice is still objectionable. Different assets end up with different

---

[8] *FASB Statement No. 34*, par. 12.

costs solely because they are financed differently. A building built with proceeds from the issuance of capital stock will have a lower cost than an identical building constructed with the proceeds from the issuance of bonds. In truth, it is extremely difficult to relate a particular source of cash to a particular project. Even when funds are borrowed ostensibly for a specific purpose, the result is simply to free cash from other sources and make it available for other projects. If interest is to be treated as an asset cost, then the amount capitalized should represent the implicit cost of all financial capital tied up in the asset and not just the cost of borrowed money.

## Natural Resources

Natural resources such as oil fields and mines are unique in that the additional costs over and above the initial acquisition price play a major role in cost determination. The original purchase price may be only a fraction of the total costs which the firm has to incur in order to develop the resources. Subsequent expenditures for such purposes as the sinking of shafts, construction of tunnels, and removal of topsoil (in the case of strip mining) benefit future periods. These expenditures are treated as part of the cost of the asset, for they enable the firm to use the acquired natural resources. Sometimes they are set up in asset accounts separate from the natural resource, particularly when the life of the development is different from the life of the natural resource. The services of a particular mine shaft may expire economically before the mine itself does. In this case, amortization would be easier if the two were recorded separately. Nonetheless, the major point is that these development costs are assets under the cost concept we have been developing.

A major difficulty in determining the cost of natural resources involves the handling of exploration and drilling expenditures when future benefit is uncertain. Many of the same considerations discussed in connection with research and development costs in Chapter 5 are relevant here. Should the cost of drilling oil wells, for example, be set up as an asset or be treated as a period expense? Varying circumstances may call for different answers, depending on the focal point of the expenditure.[9] If the drilling is on scattered wildcat wells, many of which will be dry holes, then it is reasonable to treat drilling costs as an operating expense except in the case of a well which is completed as a producer. On the other hand, if the drilling costs are incurred in the development of an existing oil *area,* then all costs of drilling, whether or not they always result in a producing well, can rightfully be deemed *necessary* costs of preparing the asset *"oil field"* for its intended use. However, costs of developing unproductive fields are

---

[9] This focal point of expenditure commonly is called the property unit or the unit of account. See Chapter 9 for a further discussion of ways of specifying assets in terms of property units.

expensed. Sound judgment, consistently applied, becomes extremely important in these cases for accurate income measurement in later periods.

**Successful Efforts versus Full Costing.** Most major integrated refiners follow some variation of a policy called "successful-efforts costing." Each individual well or identifiable mineral field is treated as a separate unit of account. The cost of dry holes or unproductive fields is charged to expense. Only those exploration and drilling costs traceable to successful wells or fields are set up as assets. A large number of other oil firms, however, practice "full costing." This procedure views all natural resource property as a single asset unit. Consequently, *all* expenditures, whether associated with unproductive or productive ventures, are treated as necessary asset costs. These costs enter into the determination of net income only over a substantial number of future years.

The Financial Accounting Standards Board grappled with this controversy during the 1970s. In December 1977, *Statement No. 19* was issued.[10] This standard disallowed the full-costing approach and mandated a form of successful-efforts accounting. In addition to the full-costing method's reliance on an extremely broad single-asset concept, the FASB objected to "costs that are known not to have resulted in identifiable future benefits [being] nonetheless capitalized as part of the cost of assets to which they have no direct relationship."[11] Under full costing, a firm might not reflect on its income statement for many years the fact that it had been relatively unsuccessful in exploration and drilling. The FASB felt that the financial statements should reflect the risk and uncertainty associated with oil- and gas-producing activities and that successful-efforts accounting better accomplished that objective.

In August 1978, before *Statement No. 19* became effective, the Securities and Exchange Commission issued *Accounting Series Release No. 253,* which allowed either successful efforts *or* full costing for SEC reporting purposes and required a new accounting method called reserve-recognition accounting to be used in supplementary disclosures. Pressured by the SEC, the Federal Trade Commission, and others to avoid conflicting requirements, the FASB suspended the effective date of *Statement No. 19.*[12] After a three-year experiment, the SEC abandoned reserve-recognition accounting as a potential method and requested the FASB to restudy the whole issue of disclosure standards for oil and gas producers.

The result of this restudy was *Statement of Financial Accounting Standards No. 69* issued in Fall 1982. A form of successful-efforts accounting and a form of full-costing accounting continue to be acceptable alterna-

---

[10] FASB, *Statement of Financial Accounting Standards No. 19,* "Financial Accounting and Reporting by Oil and Gas Producing Companies" (Stamford, Conn., December 1977).

[11] Ibid., par. 144.

[12] FASB, *Statement of Financial Accounting Standards No. 25,* "Suspension of Certain Accounting Requirements for Oil and Gas Producing Companies" (Stamford, Conn., February 1979).

tives. The method must be disclosed, however. In addition, the following information has to be disclosed in the supplementary information to the financial statements:

1.  Proved oil and gas reserve quantities.
2.  Capitalized costs relating to oil- and gas-producing activities.
3.  Costs incurred for property acquisition, exploration, and development activities.
4.  Results of operations for oil- and gas-producing activities.
5.  A standardized measure of discounted future net cash flows relating to proved oil and gas reserve quantities.[13]

The Board anticipates that these disclosures will assist users in assessing the degree of risk associated with different companies.

The fifth disclosure features some of the information and methodology formerly involved in reserve-recognition accounting. By standardizing the measure, the Board hoped to reduce some of the extreme subjectivity attendant to reserve-recognition accounting. The present value of future cash flows would possess some of the characteristics of a fair market value measure of oil and gas reserves; at least, it would be responsive to some of the same variables as would affect fair market value. Nevertheless, three of the FASB members dissented from the issuance of *Statement No. 69* because they believed this fifth disclosure was completely lacking in *reliability.*

**Intangible Assets**

Careful cost determination is just as important for intangible assets as for tangible assets, and the general principles are the same. When intangible assets are purchased, the amount paid is the initial measure of the asset's cost. To this amount are added any other costs that enhance the utility of the intangible. In the case of a patent, these would include the cost of a successful legal defense of the patent right.

Often intangible assets are acquired as part of a lump-sum purchase. For *specifically identifiable* intangible assets, such as patents, formulas, licenses, and copyrights, accountants determine cost by estimating the fair value of the individual assets acquired, as in any lump-sum purchase. Any excess of the total purchase price over the sum of the separate market values of the tangible assets and the specifically identifiable intangible assets is allocated to a general intangible, Goodwill. It represents the cost of the *unidentified* intangible assets.

Many intangible assets are developed internally. Determining the cost of these assets is extremely difficult, in fact often impossible. Some of the problems are discussed in Chapter 5 in the section on period costs. When these internal costs can be specifically identified with a particular intangi-

---

[13] FASB, *Statement of Financial Accounting Standards No. 69,* "Disclosures about Oil and Gas Producing Activities" (Stamford, Conn., November 1982), par. 7.

ble, the cost of the asset includes all development costs traceable to it. However, the costs of internally developed intangibles which either "are not specifically identifiable, have indeterminate lives, or are inherent in a continuing business and related to an enterprise as a whole . . . should be deducted from income when incurred."[14] These would include expenditures for the development of a favorable standing in the community, a highly trained work force, a high-technology environment, and product recognition from effective advertising.

**VALUATION OF MARKETABLE EQUITY SECURITIES**

The above discussion focuses on the determination of acquisition cost as the essential first step in the recording of assets. Cost is the almost universal valuation measure used in financial accounting. Gains and losses are not recognized until the assets are sold or used in generating revenues.

An important exception to the cost basis is required for certain marketable securities. The Financial Accounting Standards Board has ruled that in many circumstances marketable *equity* securities are to be reported in the balance sheet at the lower of acquisition cost or current market value.[15] The excess of the aggregate cost over the aggregate market value is accounted for in a contra asset account. Furthermore, changes in the valuation account related to those securities classified as *current assets* are to be reflected in the determination of net income as unrealized gains and losses. Unrealized losses result when the aggregate market value declines below aggregate acquisition cost. Gains might occur if market values subsequently were to rise. However, in no case would the securities be reported at more than their aggregate acquisition cost.

**Illustration**

The collection of marketable equity securities is called a portfolio. Let us examine how *FASB Statement No. 12* applies to the portfolio of the hypothetical Oard Corporation. Table 7–4 shows the cost and 1984 market value of Oard's current securities. Assume that the company prepares quarterly financial statements for distribution to stockholders. Securities A, B, and C were purchased during the first quarter; Security B was sold during the second quarter for $203,000; Security D was purchased during the third quarter for $40,000.

On March 31 an adjusting entry would be required to reflect the $9,000 excess cost over market value as an unrealized loss.

Net Unrealized Loss from Decline in Value of
    Marketable Equity Securities . . . . . . . . . . . . . . . . . . . . . . . . . 9,000
        Allowance to Reduce Marketable Equity
            Securities to Market Value . . . . . . . . . . . . . . . . . . . . . . . 9,000

---

[14] AICPA, *Opinion of the Accounting Principles Board No. 17*, "Intangible Assets" (New York, August 1970), par. 24.

[15] FASB, *Statement of Financial Accounting Standards No. 12*, "Accounting for Certain Marketable Securities" (Stamford, Conn., December 1975).

**TABLE 7–4  Changes in Portfolio of Current Marketable Equity Securities of Oard Corporation in 1984**

| Security | Cost | Market Value | Unrealized Loss or (Gain) |
|---|---|---|---|
| **March 31:** | | | |
| A | $105,000 | $108,000 | $ (3,000) |
| B | 216,000 | 206,000 | 10,000 |
| C | 68,000 | 66,000 | 2,000 |
| | $389,000 | $380,000 | $ 9,000 |
| **June 30:** | | | |
| A | $105,000 | $106,000 | $ (1,000) |
| C | 68,000 | 64,000 | 4,000 |
| | $173,000 | $170,000 | $ 3,000 |
| **September 30:** | | | |
| A | $105,000 | $109,000 | $ (4,000) |
| C | 68,000 | 65,000 | 3,000 |
| D | 40,000 | 40,000 | — |
| | $213,000 | $214,000 | $ (1,000) |
| **December 31:** | | | |
| A | $105,000 | $106,000 | $ (1,000) |
| C | 68,000 | 63,000 | 5,000 |
| D | 40,000 | 38,000 | 2,000 |
| | $213,000 | $207,000 | $ 6,000 |

The resultant credit goes to a contra asset account that is subtracted from the $389,000 on the balance sheet. The carrying value of the securities becomes $380,000, the lower of cost or market. Note that the unrealized loss of $9,000 is applicable to the entire portfolio; its determination involves the offsetting of unrealized gains and unrealized losses. The $9,000 reduces reported income in quarter one.

During the second quarter two entries are applicable to the current marketable securities. The first records the sale of Security B at a loss. This entry is made in the normal fashion.

| | | |
|---|---|---|
| Cash | 203,000 | |
| Loss on Sale of Security B | 13,000 | |
| Marketable Equity Securities | | 216,000 |

The recognized loss of $13,000 is the full difference between the original cost and the realized selling price and appears on the income statement. One could argue that some portion of this loss had already been recognized on the income statement for the first quarter.

The other entry on June 30 adjusts the valuation (contra asset) account so that it properly reflects the excess cost over current market value of the remaining securities, A and C.

```
Allowance to Reduce Marketable Equity
    Securities to Market Value .......................   6,000
    Net Unrealized Recovery of Losses
        on Marketable Equity Securities ...............          6,000
```

The contra asset is debited (reduced) by $6,000 so that, when its balance of $3,000 is subtracted from the original cost, the resultant carrying value is $170,000, the lower current market figure. The credit to Net Unrealized Recovery of Losses appears on the second-quarter income statement. Technically it is not a gain; it is a change in the amount of an unrealized loss. Its effect on reported income is positive, however, as with a gain. More importantly, the "recovery" actually is a combination of decreases in unrealized gains of $2,000 (A) and increases in unrealized losses of $2,000 (C) offset by the removal of the unrealized loss of $10,000 on Security B recorded in the first quarter. The *$10,000 unrealized loss* now has been recognized as part of the *realized loss of $13,000* in the second quarter.

By September 30 the market prices of the securities collectively have risen $4,000, to $1,000 more than their original cost. However, only a recovery of $3,000 is recorded, because the carrying value cannot exceed cost. The entry is:

```
Allowance to Reduce Marketable Equity
    Securities to Market Value ..........................   3,000
    Net Unrealized Recovery of Losses
        on Marketable Equity Securities ..................          3,000
```

The remaining balance in the contra asset account is eliminated, and the lower original cost figure of $213,000 appears on the balance sheet.

During the third quarter Security D was purchased for $40,000. By December 31, it had declined in value, as had the other two securities. Because the total current market value again was below cost, an entry similar to that in quarter one is necessary.

```
Net Unrealized Loss from Decline in Value
    of Marketable Equity Securities ......................   6,000
    Allowance to Reduce Marketable
        Equity Securities to Market Value ................          6,000
```

An unrealized loss is recognized on the income statement, and the valuation balance of $6,000 is subtracted on the balance sheet.

If the marketable equity securities are *noncurrent* assets, the basic entries are the same. The asset appears on the balance sheet valued at the lower of cost or market. However, the account Net Unrealized Losses on Noncurrent Marketable Equity Securities does not reduce reported income. Instead, it appears as a direct reduction in stockholders' equity on the balance sheet. The contra equity account and contra asset account will have the same balance. Presumably market declines on the noncurrent portfolio were considered not to be sufficiently imminent to be recognized in the determination of income.

**Summary and Evaluation of FASB No. 12**

Briefly stated, the following procedures are involved in recording marketable equity securities:

1. Marketable equity securities are classified into two portfolios—current and noncurrent. Each portfolio is valued at the lower of aggregate cost or aggregate market.
2. The excess of aggregate cost over aggregate market is accounted for in a contra asset valuation account.
3. Periodic changes in the balance of the valuation account for current securities are included in the determination of net income as unrealized losses and gains. These are in addition to any realized losses or gains recognized at the time of sale of securities.
4. Periodic changes in the balance of the valuation account for noncurrent securities are reflected as direct adjustments to stockholders' equity in the form of changes in a contra equity account. They bypass the income statement until the securities are sold or reclassified as current assets.

As we mentioned earlier, unrealized gains and losses on individual marketable equity securities are offset to a large extent under *Statement No. 12*. The net adjustment applies to the portfolio as a whole. However, *Statement No. 12* also requires that the total separate unrealized gains and the total separate unrealized losses be disclosed in footnotes.

*Statement No. 12* obviously is a stopgap measure awaiting a full reconsideration of the conceptual soundness and usefulness of the cost principle (exchange-price assumption). It deals solely with marketable *equity* securities. However, the same underlying reasoning would appear applicable to marketable *debt* securities. Moreover, the statement contains a number of logically objectionable provisions. For example, how a security is classified in the balance sheet determines whether changes in its value are reflected in income. One might expect that the type of value change and the reliability of its measurement would be the dominant factors, not management's intention. Also, some accountants object to the fact that increases in the market value of some current securities affect income while other increases do not. If the increases offset decreases and thereby cause a smaller net decrease, they affect income. If the increases come in a period subsequent to a decrease and thereby cause a recovery, they affect income. However, if securities increase in value so that aggregate market is above aggregate cost, they do not affect income. This inconsistency does not seem rooted in the qualitative guidelines of relevance or reliability.

On the other hand, *Statement No. 12* does mandate the use of a reliably determined alternative valuation to acquisition cost for certain assets. It also does include in reported income in highly restricted circumstances certain gains and losses which are not transaction based. Perhaps this ruling will be a forerunner of other experiments or introductions of alternative valuation measures. Some of these alternatives are explained in the next section.

**ALTERNATIVE CONCEPTS OF COST**

The concept of cost which we have been discussing embraces all actual dollar outlays necessary for acquiring the resource. Under the exchange-price concept and the monetary postulate, this figure measures the effort of the firm. When significant price changes occur, however, the propriety of continued use of historic acquisition cost as the basis for the representation of assets is called into serious question. Some accountants would prefer the use of current replacement cost as the carrying value of assets. Others would retain historic outlays but restate them to reflect inflationary changes in the general level of prices.

These alternative approaches also match costs against revenues, as does conventional accounting, to provide an income figure after consideration of the recovery of capital committed to the various assets consumed. They differ, however, in their *measurement* of the recovery of capital.

A very simple example will highlight the differences in these cost concepts. Merchandise is purchased at a cost of $2,000 when an index of the general price level stands at 100, is held until the end of the year, and then is sold for $3,000. At that time the general price index stands at 120 and the *current* acquisition cost (replacement cost) of the merchandise is $2,600. What is income? Conventionally, we subtract the *original* acquisition cost of the asset consumed ($2,000) from the selling price of $3,000 and report an income of $1,000.

**Constant Dollar Approach**

Those who advocate the constant dollar alternative view the monetary postulate as fallacious under conditions of general inflation (or deflation). The dollar is the accountant's measuring unit. When the general price level changes, the purchasing power of the monetary unit and hence its "size" change also.

In our example, the $2,000 original acquisition cost and the $3,000 revenue are not comparable in their general purchasing power. Each dollar in the $2,000 represents a greater command over goods and services than does each dollar of revenue. This situation can be corrected by restatement of the cost in terms of the present general price level. The income calculation then would be as follows:

| | |
|---|---|
| Revenues ................. | $3,000 |
| Expenses ................. | 2,400  $\left(\$2,000 \times \frac{120}{100}\right)$ |
| Income ................... | $ 600 |

Because prices *in general* have increased 20 percent, the $2,000 expended at the beginning of the year is equivalent to $2,400 of purchasing power at the end of the year. That latter amount must be recovered out of revenues measured at the end of the year for the firm to be as well off in terms of its pool of available purchasing power. Restatement of past costs in terms of present price levels, it is argued, provides a more meaningful measure of the preservation of capital. Conversely, use of unadjusted figures is analogous to subtracting apples from oranges—or Australian dollars from American dollars.

## Current Cost Approach

The current cost approach departs from original dollar acquisition cost in favor of a more immediate measure of the asset's worth. Supply and demand conditions affecting a productive resource may cause its specific value relative to other goods and services to increase or decrease. The monetary representation of assets should reflect these changes in exchange value. Likewise, no income should result until the firm recovers the current value of asset services being consumed in the generation of revenues. Under this concept the income statement might look like this:

| | |
|---|---:|
| Revenues | $3,000 |
| Expenses | 2,600 |
| Income | $ 400 |

Because it would cost $2,600 currently to replace the asset used up, this figure provides a better measure of the real sacrifice (effort) involved in its use. The $2,600 represents the opportunity cost of the asset. Unless this amount is recovered through revenue generation, the *real* capital of the business has been eroded. Current cost accounting highlights capital erosion.

A modification of this approach attempts to incorporate both original acquisition cost and current replacement cost. According to this suggestion, income consists of two parts—an operating income of $400, as previously calculated, and a price gain of $600 from holding the inventory during a time of dollar value increase, as calculated below:

| | |
|---|---:|
| Current replacement cost | $2,600 |
| Original acquisition cost | 2,000 |
| Price gain from holding inventory | $ 600 |

The constant dollar approach can also be applied to current cost measures. If recognition is given to changes in the value of the dollar in general as well as to changes in replacement cost, the $600 holding gain could be expressed in *real* terms as follows:

| | |
|---|---:|
| Current replacement cost | $2,600 |
| Original acquisition cost expressed in dollars of present purchasing power | |
| $2,000 \times \dfrac{120}{100}$ | 2,400 |
| Real increase in value from holding inventory | $ 200 |

These brief excursions into the area of alternative cost concepts do not do justice to the many theoretical ramifications, practical complexities, recording problems, or possible uses of these alternatives. The purpose of the discussion is simply to acquaint the reader with some of the options that might be used in financial accounting. This background is helpful in Chapter 8 for an understanding of the LIFO inventory procedure, which rests to some extent on these alternative cost concepts.

None of them, however, can currently be included on the financial statements proper. The reasons seem to be a lack of agreement on which concept should replace the existing postulates, the absence of legal or tax recognition of these ideas, and the existence of practical difficulties in measurement. The case is strong, nevertheless, that these alternative approaches do supply additional valuable information in the appraisal of managerial performance. For this reason, under current reporting requirements these concepts must be incorporated by many large firms as supplementary information accompanying the conventional financial statements. Chapter 19 discusses how this is accomplished and analyzes these concepts more completely.

## DISCUSSION OF THE ARMCO ANNUAL REPORT

The cost principle is very basic to the recording of assets. It is so ingrained in accounting practice that most financial statements do not emphasize it in the discussion of accounting concepts and principles. Indeed, attention usually is given only to those situations in which assets have been recorded at other than acquisition cost. For this reason, there are not many explicit references to the cost principle in the Armco financial statements for 1981. All nonmonetary assets are recorded at their acquisition cost unless otherwise stated.

However, the Armco statements do illustrate a number of the particular concepts, procedures, and practices discussed in this chapter.

### Inventories

Armco has over a billion dollars of inventories listed on its 1981 balance sheet (see Appendix to Chapter 5). In Note 1 the company tells the reader that the inventories are recorded at the lower of acquisition cost or market and that two different ways of establishing cost (LIFO and average cost) have been employed. The precise meanings of these technical inventory terms will be discussed in the next chapter. For now, simply note that the inventories are recorded at cost. Moreover, because Armco is a manufacturing company, it has more than one kind of inventory. Its Work in Process inventory is called semifinished inventory and is combined with the Finished Goods inventory. This is a common reporting practice. Similarly, Armco has combined its Raw Materials inventory with its inventories of supplies.

**Property, Plant, and Equipment**

The comparative balance sheet shows an increase in net plant assets from $1,561.2 million on December 31, 1980, to $1,812.7 million by the end of 1981. These amounts are after the deduction of accumulated depreciation. The original acquisition costs of the plant assets in service on these two dates were $3,255.2 million and $3,591.8 million, respectively.

Notes 1 and 3 to the financial statements disclose information related to two specific accounting policies discussed in this chapter. First, Armco's oil and gas operations use the successful-efforts method of accounting. Only costs incurred in the drilling of successful wells are set up as assets. Second, the cost of the asset called Construction in Progress includes $3.9 million of capitalized interest during 1981 and $2.0 million during 1980 in accordance with *FASB Statement No. 34*. If these financial costs had not been treated as part of the cost of constructed assets, interest expense on the two income statements would have been higher and income before taxes correspondingly lower.

**Goodwill**

One of the assets listed on the comparative balance sheet is called Excess of Cost over Equity in Net Assets of Purchased Businesses. In parentheses, Armco indicates that this title is just another name for purchased goodwill.

In Note 1 the company describes its accounting for goodwill. Goodwill represents the cost of unidentified intangible assets. It is recorded at acquisition cost, as measured by the difference between the total cost incurred for acquisition of the business and the current values (costs) assignable to the tangible and identifiable intangible assets.

**Marketable Equity Securities**

Any short-term marketable equity securities that might exist are combined with cash for reporting purposes. Either they do not exist, or their aggregate market value is above their cost, for we find no contra asset account anywhere and no mention made of an unrealized loss on the income statement.

Armco's recording of *noncurrent* marketable equity securities is somewhat unusual. The comparative balance sheet in the Shareholders' Equity section shows a contra equity account called Net Unrealized Gains (Losses) on Marketable Equity Securities of AFSG. (AFSG is Armco Financial Services Group.) Our discussion of marketable equity securities in this chapter indicates the presence of this account whenever *noncurrent* marketable equity securities decline in market value. Rather than being recorded on the income statement, the unrealized loss is subtracted from stockholders' equity directly on the balance sheet.

The far-right column of the Statement of Consolidated Shareholders' Equity (see page 159 in Appendix 5) shows the history of this account since December 31, 1978. It had a *debit* balance on that date of $4.4 million indicating that the portfolio of the noncurrent marketable securities had a market value $4.4 million lower than its cost. In the three subsequent years, summary entries were made as follows:

*December 31, 1979*

| | | |
|---|---|---|
| Investment in AFSG ............................ | 3,500,000 | |
| Net Unrealized Gains (Losses) on Marketable Equity Securities of AFSG ................. | | 3,500,000 |
| To record partial recovery of the market values during 1979. | | |

*December 31, 1980*

| | | |
|---|---|---|
| Investment in AFSG ............................ | 1,000,000 | |
| Net Unrealized Gains (Losses) on Marketable Equity Securities of AFSG ................. | | 1,000,000 |
| To record recovery of remaining $900,000 decline in market value and to reflect an additional $100,000 increase of market value over cost. | | |

*December 31, 1981*

| | | |
|---|---|---|
| Net Unrealized Gains (Losses) on Marketable Equity Securities of AFSG ................... | 9,700,000 | |
| Investment in AFSG ...................... | | 9,700,000 |
| To record decline in market value of security portfolio during 1981. | | |

Three aspects of these entries differ from the text discussion. The first two relate to the mechanics of the entries: (1) The asset account being revalued each year is Investment in AFSG and not directly a portfolio of noncurrent marketable equity securities and (2) increases or decreases are debited or credited directly to the asset account; no contra asset is employed. The third point is conceptual—on December 31, 1980, the equity account has a credit balance of $100,000 indicating that the investment has been recorded at an aggregate market value in excess of aggregate cost. Such a recording is generally contrary to the cost concept.

Let us take a look at each of these divergences. The noncurrent marketable equity securities that are fluctuating in values are those owned by the Armco Financial Services Group. The individual assets and liabilities of this group of companies are not shown separately on the Armco balance sheet. Rather, all the net assets together are shown as a single asset called Investment in AFSG.[16]

A review of Note 2 of the Armco financial report will show the detailed information. The net assets of AFSG are $283.3 million on December 31, 1981; this is also Armco's equity, or financial interest. Armco shows this financial interest, or investment, as an asset on its own books. Among the individual assets of AFSG are "Stocks, at market" of $111.2 million; these are the noncurrent marketable equity securities. On

---

[16] The accounting for investments in wholly owned subsidiary companies is discussed in detail in Chapter 15.

Armco's statements these securities are combined with the other assets and liabilities in the Investment account. Because the Investment account reflects fluctuations in the market value of the marketable equity securities, the provisions of *FASB Statement No. 12* are applied to it.

In the financial records of AFSG, the marketable securities are valued at market prices. The underlying asset value is modified directly rather than by means of a contra asset account. Accordingly, Armco revalues the Investment account on its books directly instead of employing a contra asset account. A contra equity account must be employed, however, to show the concomitant adjustment of stockholders' equity.

The most unusual aspect of Armco's recording is the use of market values, whether above or below cost. In the insurance industry certain investments are recorded at market value instead of at cost or at the lower of cost or market. This industry practice is widespread, and most insurance companies conform to it, even though the practice may seem to depart from the cost principle of accounting theory. This practice has come to be part of GAAP as practiced by insurance companies. As we saw in Chapter 1, accounting principles are influenced by the way accounting is practiced. Armco valued its Investment in AFSG $100,000 above cost on December 31, 1980, because the marketable equity securities held by its insurance subsidiary were valued at $100,000 above cost. The corresponding $100,000 increase in stockholders' equity is reflected in the *credit* balance of $100,000 in the Net Unrealized Gains (Losses) on Marketable Equity Securities of AFSG account. This account, which is normally a contra equity, served at the end of 1980 as an equity adjunct account.

## Alternative Concepts of Cost

Toward the end of this chapter we discussed two alternative concepts of cost—constant dollar costs and current costs. Mention was made that GAAP requires companies to incorporate these alternative cost concepts into their supplementary disclosures. Armco has done so in its annual report in the section called "Assessing the Impact of Inflation." Constant dollar cost is called "Adjusted for General Inflation," and current cost is called "Adjusted for Changes in Specific Prices."

These concepts are discussed in greater detail in Chapter 19. Accordingly, we will defer our discussion of this aspect of the Armco statements until the end of that chapter.

## SUMMARY

In this chapter we attempt to establish more detailed accounting procedures for determining the cost of specific productive resources. The general theme is that cost includes not only acquisition cost but also any necessary costs which contribute to the preparation of the asset for its intended use. In the case of most noncurrent assets, these costs are

combined directly with the net purchase price in a single account. With
labor services and inventory, the separate cost elements are accumulated in
individual ledger accounts for management's attention and analysis.

For a merchandising firm, the recording process can be summarized as
follows:

Cost of Good Sold  = Beginning Inventory + Net Purchases
                                  − Ending Inventory

where

Net Purchases            = Purchases − Returns and Allowances
                                   − Discounts + Freight-In
                                   + Handling Costs

In a manufacturing firm a quite elaborate recording system has to be
set up to collect the product costs and assign them to units sold, units
completed but not sold, and units partially completed. The recording
process in summary form is:

Cost of Goods Sold  = Beginning Inventory of Finished Goods
                                   + Cost of Goods Completed
                                   − Ending Inventory of Finished Goods

where

Cost of Goods           = Beginning Inventory of Work in Process
Completed                    + Material Used + Direct Labor
                                    + Manufacturing Overhead
                                    − Ending Inventory of Work in Process

In certain circumstances modifications are made to the general principle of recording assets at their acquisition cost. Marketable equity securities are recorded at the lower of acquisition cost or current market
value. Usually the adjustment to reduce the acquisition cost to a lower
market value or to increase the valuation to a higher market value (but not
above cost) is handled by entries to a contra asset account. The changes in
stockholders' equity corresponding to the changes in asset valuation are
recorded as unrealized losses (gains) in the income statement if the marketable equity securities are classified as current assets. If they are classified
as noncurrent assets, the changes in stockholders' equity flow directly to a
contra equity account in the owners' equity section of the balance sheet.

Original dollar acquisition cost is not the only measure in which
resources can be stated in the financial records. Constant dollar acquisition
cost and current replacement cost are two alternative measures that have
attained a degree of acceptance and understanding. In fact, many corporations are required under GAAP to show some financial information based
on these two alternatives as supplementary information to the conventional statements.

## QUESTIONS AND PROBLEMS

**7-1.** Patterson Company acquired a machine with a list price of $40,000 and debited the Machinery account for that amount. The account was paid within the 30-day discount period, and the company took the 5 percent cash discount. A credit for $2,000 was made to Purchase Discounts.

Transportation costs of $800 were paid by Patterson Company and charged to Freight Expense. This amount included $100 for delayed delivery date charges. The company had agreed to take the machine earlier, but because there was no place to put it, Patterson had to pay a penalty for having the manufacturer hold the machine.

Installation was done by a consulting engineer outside the company assisted by a few of Patterson's own employees. The fee of the consulting engineer of $1,000 was debited to the Machinery account; the wages of the employees, amounting to $400, were charged to Wage Expense.

Supplies of $300 were used in the installation and raw materials of $200 were destroyed in testing. The former cost was debited to the Supplies Expense; the latter cost, to Loss on Testing.

*Required:*

*a.* Prepare a schedule showing the total cost at which the machine should be recorded.

*b.* Prepare any adjusting entries necessary to correct the accounts.

*c.* Assume Patterson Company did not pay within the 30-day discount period. How would this affect the cost of the asset and the entries made?

*d.* Six months later, the Patterson Company decides to move the machinery to a different wing of the plant. The cost (primarily wages) is $1,500. How would you handle this relocation cost?

**7-2.** Hassell and Associates manufactures and sells sports equipment. Prepare a statement of cost of goods manufactured and sold for 1984 from the following costs and expenses incurred during the year. Use the format shown in Table 7–3.

| | |
|---|---:|
| Purchases of raw materials | $663,000 |
| Direct labor | 240,000 |
| Indirect labor | 82,500 |
| Depreciation on factory building | 49,500 |
| Property taxes on factory building | 6,000 |
| Depreciation on factory equipment | 39,000 |
| Light, heat, and power (60% applicable to manufacturing, 10% to selling, 30% to office) | 25,000 |
| Salespersons' salaries | 78,000 |
| Maintenance costs on factory equipment | 1,900 |
| Office salaries | 55,600 |
| Advertising supplies purchased and used | 7,200 |
| Factory supplies purchased | 28,200 |
| Factory manager's salary | 37,000 |

Relevant inventory accounts show the following balances:

| | Jan. 1 | Dec. 31 |
|---|---:|---:|
| Raw materials | $ 43,500 | $ 61,500 |
| Goods in process | 108,000 | 115,500 |
| Finished goods | 60,000 | 40,500 |
| Factory supplies | 5,800 | 7,700 |

**7–3.** The Modern Company buys merchandise from the New Company on terms of 3/10, n/30. Purchases during September 1985 are as follows (amounts are gross price figures):

| Purchase Date | Amount | Payment Date |
|---|---|---|
| September 7 ....... | $4,400 | September 15 |
| September 11 ....... | 3,900 | September 20 |
| September 17 ....... | 2,800 | $1,200 returned September 24; remainder paid October 10 |
| September 28 ....... | 6,600 | October 12 |

*Required:*

a. Using the net price method, record the entries that would be made on the books of the Modern Company for the months of September and October. The company prepares *monthly* financial statements.

b. Repeat part *(a)* using gross prices.

c. Record the entries for the same dates on the books of the New Company, using the net price procedure.

d. Repeat part *(c)* using gross prices.

**7–4.** On December 31, 1984, the following account balances appeared among the liabilities of Soaper Company:

| | |
|---|---|
| Wages payable .............................. | $27,360 |
| Social security taxes payable ................... | 1,040 |
| Income tax withholdings payable .............. | 4,400 |

The following selected transactions occurred during January 1985:

1. The total amount of gross wages for the month was $30,000. The company withheld 14 percent for employee income tax, 7 percent for social security taxes, and $600 under an employee stock purchase program. The $30,000 gross payroll was represented by $24,000 of direct labor wages, $3,000 of indirect labor wages, and $3,000 of administrative wages.

2. Fringe benefit costs were: employer's contribution to social security, 7 percent of gross payroll; employer's tax for unemployment compensation, 3 percent of gross payroll; employer's contribution to hospital insurance program, $1,200; and pension fund cost, $4,800. All fringe benefit costs are to be recorded as separate cost items (debit the social security and unemployment taxes to Payroll Taxes).

3. Checks drawn during the month:

| | |
|---|---|
| Employee wage checks ...................... | $49,940 |
| For income taxes withheld .................... | 8,300 |
| For social security contributions ............... | 3,200 |

*Required:*

a. Prepare journal entries for the month of January.

b. What liabilities and amounts would appear on the balance sheet as of January 31, 1985?

c. What would you do with the separate cost accounts that you established in connection with the recording of fringe benefits? On what financial statements, if any, would they appear?

**7-5.** The Poorland Company begins operations on October 1, 1984. The following selected transactions relate to purchases and sales of inventory during October:

1. Merchandise purchases on account amount to $200,000 at gross prices.
2. Merchandise costing $8,000 is returned.
3. The accounts payable from merchandise purchases are paid; $2,200 of discounts are taken, and $1,000 of discounts are lost.
4. Bills of $10,000 are received for freight charges on incoming merchandise.
5. A bill for $300 is received for demurrage charges for failure to unload and return a railroad car within the allotted time.
6. The receiving department costs are $7,000 for the month consisting of $6,000 of labor cost and $1,000 of supplies.
7. Bills in the amount of $6,500 are received for freight charges on merchandise delivered to customers during October.
8. Ninety percent of the net merchandise purchased during October is sold on account at a price of $206,000.

*Required:*

Record the selected transactions relating to purchases and sales of inventory during October in general ledger (T-) accounts. The company uses separate accounts for the individual cost elements. Include the necessary entries to determine cost of goods and the October 31 merchandise inventory.

**7-6.** The following quotations are taken from the formal descriptions of accounting policies of three oil companies contained in their 1981 annual reports.

> **Standard Oil Company of Ohio.** "The successful efforts method of accounting is followed for costs incurred in oil and gas exploration and development operations.
>
> Exploration costs other than drilling, including geological, geophysical and carrying costs, are charged against income as incurred. Exploratory drilling costs are initially capitalized. If and when they are determined to be nonproductive, such costs are charged against income.
>
> Depletion and depreciation of producing oil and gas properties . . . and depletion of mine development costs . . . are computed for each oil and/or gas reservoir or mine using the unit-of-production method based on estimated proved developed reserves."
>
> **Standard Oil of California.** "All expenditures for development wells, related plant and equipment, and mineral interests in properties are capitalized. Costs of an exploratory well are tentatively capitalized pending determination of whether the well found proved reserves. Those wells which are assigned proved reserves remain capitalized. All other exploratory wells and exploration expenditures are expensed.
>
> Depreciation, depletion and amortization expenses . . . for all capitalized oil and gas expenditures are determined on a unit-of-production method by individual fields based on proved developed reserves."
>
> **Gulf Oil Corporation.** "Provision for depreciation, depletion and amortization are calculated on a lease basis in the United States, a field basis in Canada and generally on a country basis in other foreign areas."

*Required:*

a. Standard Oil of Ohio states that it uses the successful efforts method? What does that mean? What is the alternative procedure? Can you tell what method the other companies use?

b. The first two companies initially treat the cost of exploratory wells as an asset and then write it off as expense if unproductive. Would a better procedure be to treat the cost initially as an expense to be charged later to an asset if the wells prove productive? Explain. Which procedure is more conservative?

c. Compare the policies of the three companies with respect to the asset units employed for purposes of the depreciation, depletion, and amortization of capitalized oil and gas expenditures. Why does Gulf use leases as a costing unit in the United States but fields and countries as costing units elsewhere?

**7–7.** In 1984 the Hillandale Corporation acquired a parcel of farmland on the outskirts of town for the purpose of building a new plant. Hillandale used its own resources for most of the construction work in 1985 and 1986. The following information relates to these activities:

1. The property acquired included 150 acres of land, an old farmhouse to be razed, and a timber stand to be cut and leveled.
2. Hillandale paid $460,000 cash to the owner, paid $12,000 of unpaid back property taxes, and issued 2,000 shares of its stock to the owner of the farm. The current market value of the stock was $14 a share.
3. An appraisal report on the property listed the land at $480,000, the farmhouse at $18,000, and the timber tract at $50,000.
4. Cash was received in the amounts of $5,000 representing the value of material recovered from the farmhouse and $40,000 from a lumber mill representing the net proceeds to Hillandale from cutting the timber tract and removing all stumps.
5. Labor costs incurred in razing the farmhouse were $20,000.
6. Formal construction of the new building began on January 1, 1985, and was completed on June 30, 1986. The following costs were incurred (spread evenly over the 18-month construction period):

| | |
|---|---:|
| Architect's fee | $ 210,000 |
| Labor costs | 1,200,000 |
| Materials | 600,000 |
| Subcontracting costs | 120,000 |
| Factory manager's salary (one half of the time spent supervising construction and the rest at the company's other plant) | 90,000 |

7. To help finance construction the company borrowed $500,000 on January 1, 1985, and another $500,000 on January 1, 1986. Both of these borrowings were at 12 percent. In addition, the company had $3 million of bonds outstanding with an interest rate of 10 percent and $6 million of bonds with an interest rate of 9 percent.

*Required:*

a. What is the total cost to be assigned to the Land account?

b. What is the total cost, excluding interest during construction, of the new building? Explain how you treated any costs not charged to either the land or the building.

c. Calculate the total interest that would be capitalized during construction. What effect does interest capitalization have on the financial statements in 1985, 1986, and subsequent years?

**7–8.** The *current* portfolio of marketable equity securities of Keith company contained the stocks of four different corporations. Information about their costs and market prices (on December 31 of each year) is shown below:

|  | 1984 | | 1985 | | 1986 | |
|---|---|---|---|---|---|---|
| Security | Cost | Market | Cost | Market | Cost | Market |
| AB | $13,500 | $15,000 | $13,500 | $14,500 | $13,500 | $16,000 |
| CD | 18,000 | 16,700 | 12,000* | 11,500 | 12,000 | 11,800 |
| EF | 9,200 | 7,500 | 9,200 | 7,000 | 4,600† | 4,300 |
| GH | 21,000 | 20,000 | 21,000 | 20,800 | 21,000 | 22,000 |
|  | $61,700 | $59,200 | $55,700 | $53,800 | $51,100 | $54,100 |

\* One third of the holdings in CD were sold in 1985 for $5,300.

† One half of the holdings in EF were sold in 1986 for $4,800.

*Required:*

a. Prepare any adjusting entries required on December 31, 1984, 1985, and 1986. Also record the sale of securities in 1985 and 1986.

b. What impact would the entries in part (*a*) have on the income reported in 1984, 1985, and 1986? Would this impact be different if the portfolio had been of *noncurrent* marketable equity securities?

c. Calculate the *unrealized* gains and losses that would be reported in the notes to the financial statements in each of the three years.

**7–9.** The Rebecca Corporation is a manufacturer which produces special machines made to customer specifications.[17] The following information is available at the beginning of the month of October 1984.

| Direct materials inventory, October 1 | $16,200 |
|---|---|
| Work-in-process, October 1 | 3,600 |

A review of the work-in-process inventory on October 1 revealed its composition as follows:

| Direct materials | $1,320 |
|---|---|
| Direct labor | 1,500 |
| Factory overhead | 780 |
|  | $3,600 |

Activity during the month of October was as follows:

1. Direct materials costing $20,000 were purchased.
2. Direct labor for work done totaled 3,300 hours at $5 per hour.
3. Factory overhead for October was $8,580.

On October 31, inventories consisted of the following components:

---

[17] Material from the Uniform CPA Examinations, Copyright © 1980 by the American Institute of Certified Public Accountants, Inc., is adapted with permission.

| Direct materials inventory | $17,000 |
|---|---|

Work-in-process inventory:

| Direct materials | $ 4,320 |
|---|---|
| Direct labor | 2,500 |
| Factory overhead | 1,300 |
| | $ 8,120 |

*Required:*

a. Prepare in good form a detailed statement of the cost of goods manufactured for the month of October.

b. If all the goods manufactured (finished) in October were also sold in October, how much of October's direct labor *cost* was matched against revenues as an expense?

**7–10.** On January 1, 1984, Brock Corporation purchased a tract of land (site number 101) with a building for $600,000.[18] Additionally, Brock paid a real estate broker's commission of $36,000, legal fees of $6,000, and title guarantee insurance of $18,000. The closing statement indicated that the land value was $500,000 and the building value was $100,000. Shortly after acquisition, the building was razed at a cost of $75,000.

Brock entered into a $3,000,000 fixed-price contract with Barnett Builders, Inc., on March 1, 1984, for the construction of an office building on land site number 101. The building was completed and occupied on September 30, 1985. Additional construction costs were incurred as follows:

| Plans, specifications, and blueprints | $12,000 |
|---|---|
| Architects' fees for design and supervision | 95,000 |

To finance the construction costs, Brock borrowed $3,000,000 on March 1, 1984. The loan is payable in 10 annual installments of $300,000 plus interest at the rate of 14 percent. Brock's average amounts of accumulated building construction expenditures were as follows:

| For the period March 1 to December 31, 1984 | $ 900,000 |
|---|---|
| For the period January 1 to September 30, 1985 | 2,300,000 |

*Required:*

a. Prepare a schedule which discloses the individual costs making up the balances in the land account of land site number 101 as of September 30, 1985.

b. Prepare a schedule which discloses the individual costs that should be capitalized in the office building account as of September 30, 1985. Show supporting computations in good form.

**7–11.** You are engaged to audit the accounting records of Brand X Manufacturing Company. The following figures appear at the end of the period:

| Work in process inventory | $138,900 |
|---|---|
| Finished goods inventory | 92,500 |
| Net income | 64,200 |

In the course of the investigation, you discover the following facts:

---

[18] Material from the Uniform CPA Examinations, Copyright © 1982 by the American Institute of Certified Public Accountants, Inc., is adapted with permission.

1. A purchase of raw materials in the amount of $6,000 has never been recorded, even though they have been used in production.
2. Depreciation of factory equipment has been overstated by $7,500.
3. The bookkeeper has failed to accrue $9,000 of indirect labor costs applicable to the period when making adjusting entries.
4. Direct labor costs of $15,000 have been incorrectly charged to administrative expense.
5. Rent costs of $12,000 have been charged to Manufacturing Overhead; 25 percent of this should have been allocated to selling and 25 percent to administration.

Of the production costs incurred in the period, one third are still in process. Of the finished goods manufactured during the year, 80 percent have been sold.

*Required:*

a. Prepare a schedule showing the effect of these errors on the ending inventories and net income for the period and showing the correct amounts for these items.
b. Prepare a journal entry (or entries) necessary to adjust all of the accounts, assuming the books have not been closed.

**7–12.** On November 1 the inventory of Royal, Inc., at net cost, including applicable freight and handling costs, amounted to $66,000. The company records all purchases at gross prices and initially records all elements of inventory cost in separate accounts for purposes of analysis and control. During the month of November the following transactions, in summary form, took place:

1. Inventory amounting to $254,000 gross invoice price was purchased on terms allowing a 2 percent discount if paid within 10 days.
2. The company discovered that $60,000 gross amount of inventory did not meet specifications. It returned $38,000 and was granted a purchase adjustment allowance of $6,000 by the vendor on the remaining amount.
3. The company ordered and received $30,000 gross amount of additional inventory (also subject to the 2 percent discount for prompt payment). This merchandise replaced part of that which was returned in transaction 2.
4. Transportation costs applicable to November purchases amounted to $4,000; transportation costs applicable to November sales were $9,000.
5. Wage payments made to the warehouse employees during the month were $10,000. It is estimated that 60 percent of the warehouse time is spent unloading and handling incoming purchases; the other 40 percent is spent loading and shipping merchandise sold.
6. The accounts payable were paid. All purchase discounts were taken except for a $700 discount which was lost.
7. Merchandise inventory on November 30 amounted to $51,400 at net invoice prices plus applicable transportation and handling costs.

*Required:*

a. Journalize the above transactions.
b. The chief accountant recommends that the $30,000 in item 3 be debited to Purchase Returns, because it in essence cancels part of the original return. Evaluate this suggestion.

**7–13.** Select Products Corporation engaged in several activities during 1985 with respect to noncurrent assets. Several of them are described below. Briefly explain how you would have accounted for each of the following costs both initially and in future periods if relevant.

1. Paid an advertising agency $50,000, two fifths for recurring media advertising and the remainder for a consumer behavior study that was to provide a basis for marketing strategies during the next three or so years.
2. Hired a contractor to build a new warehouse. The contract price was $400,000. Of this amount $300,000 was spent evenly over 1985 and the remaining $100,000 was paid during the first six months of 1986. Select Products borrowed $200,000 from a local bank at a 10 percent interest rate; the money was used explicitly for the warehouse. The other funds for the warehouse came from internal sources. Select Products has a $300,000 issue of bonds payable outstanding. These carry an interest rate of 8 percent.
3. Accidentally discovered that an unused portion of the company's land contained a substantial copper deposit. Immediately spent $25,000 for the services of a consulting engineer to ascertain the feasibility of mining the ore commercially. Upon receipt of the engineer's affirmative report, spent $800,000 to strip overburden and to develop the mine, plus another $70,000 for mining equipment.
4. Bought land and a building for a total cash price of $606,000. The seller agreed to accept $206,000 cash down payment and $20,000 a month for the next two years. The land had an assessed valuation for property tax purposes of $80,000; an investigation reveals that land is assessed at approximately one third of its current market value. The building has never been assessed, since it was only recently completed at a cost of $300,000 to the prior owner. The purchase agreement requires that Select Products pay half of the property taxes; the original owner had prepaid these taxes for the year in the amount of $12,000.
5. Paid $125,000 to a design firm for the creation of a new abstract logo to be used as a corporate identification and advertising symbol. Launched a broad 20-month media campaign costing $675,000 to promote the symbol. Paid $75,000 to a local firm that claimed to have developed and used the logo first. Rather than risk a court fight, Select Products bought the "rights."

**7–14.** On July 31, the following account balances existed for the Cosier Bowling Ball Manufacturing Company.

|  | Debit | Credit |
|---|---|---|
| Cash | $ 55,300 | |
| Raw materials | 29,400 | |
| Work in process | 29,700 | |
| Finished goods | 37,800 | |
| Building | 93,000 | |
| Accumulated depreciation on building | | $ 19,000 |
| Factory equipment | 60,000 | |
| Accumulated depreciation on equipment | | 12,000 |
| Accounts payable | | 38,900 |
| Capital stock | | 210,000 |
| Retained earnings | | 25,300 |
| | $305,200 | $305,200 |

During the month of August the following transactions took place:

1. Raw materials purchased on account, $120,600.
2. Raw materials used in production, $102,000.
3. Supplies (of all types) purchased on account, $42,000.
4. Supplies used, $25,100. Of this amount, $19,200 was used in production operations; $3,400, by the selling department; and $2,500, in the general office.
5. Wage and salary costs incurred: direct labor, $117,000; indirect labor, $45,000; sales department personnel, $55,500; and administration, $52,500. Amounts withheld by the company: 14 percent for federal income taxes and 7 percent for social security taxes.
6. Accrued the company's share of social security taxes and assigned it to the respective cost areas.
7. Depreciation on the building, $9,000.
8. Depreciation on factory equipment, $3,000.
9. Power cost for the month $10,000 (credit Accounts Payable).
10. Sales on account were $472,800.

*Additional information:*

1. The factory occupied three of the five floors in the building. The selling department occupied the first floor; and the general office, the remaining floor.
2. Power cost was allocated on the basis of metered amounts: 80 percent to manufacturing, 5 percent to selling, and 15 percent to general administration.
3. Inventory of work in process and finished goods on August 31 amounted to $34,900 and $38,200, respectively.

*Required:*

a. Set up ledger (T-) accounts and enter the opening balances. Record the entries during August, including any necessary entries based on the additional information provided. Use single accounts for Selling Expense, Administrative Expense, and Manufacturing Overhead.
b. Prepare a statement of cost of goods manufactured and sold and an income statement for August.

7–15. Byrd and Riley, Inc., engage in the transactions related to marketable equity securities that are summarized in the table below:

| | | | | | Market Value, Dec. 31 | |
| Security | Date Acquired | Cost | Date Sold | Selling Price | 1984 | 1985 |
|---|---|---|---|---|---|---|
| Current: | | | | | | |
| M | 2/18/84 | $26,000 | | | $20,000 | $24,000 |
| N | 2/18/84 | 24,000 | 8/15/84 | $33,000 | | |
| O | 5/23/85 | 45,000 | | | | 50,000 |
| P | 5/23/85 | 33,000 | | | | 36,000 |
| Noncurrent: | | | | | | |
| Y | 2/23/84 | 73,000 | 8/22/85 | 60,000 | 67,000 | |
| Z | 2/23/84 | 59,000 | | | 55,000 | 67,000 |

*Required:*

a. How would these securities be presented on the balance sheets as of December 31, 1984, and December 31, 1985, in conformity with *FASB Statement No. 12?* Indicate the accounts, amounts, and sections of balance sheets in which they would appear.

b. Calculate the impact of the transactions and events on income before taxes in both 1984 and 1985.

**7–16.** The following data are made available to you concerning the merchandise inventory of Grandma Crow's Discount Store:

|  | Cost |
| --- | --- |
| Inventory, January 1 | $ 57,000* |
| Purchases | 562,600 |
| Cost of goods sold | 543,000† |
| Inventory, December 31 | 76,600‡ |

* Wholesale cost on January 1, $66,000.
† Wholesale cost at date of sale, $651,000.
‡ Wholesale cost at December 31, $90,000.

Total sales for the year were $770,000, and selling and administrative expenses were $100,000.

*Required:*

a. Prepare an income statement employing conventional measures of cost.

b. Prepare a revised income statement employing a replacement cost concept and recognizing holding gains. What additional information does this statement provide?

c. The president of the company remarks that she prefers the approach in *(b)* because "it recognizes the impact of inflation." Comment on her view.

# CHAPTER 8

# ACCOUNTING FOR INVENTORIES

The discussion of inventory costs in the preceding chapter deals with the measurement of acquisition and production costs. In this chapter our concern is with the recording of the cost of inventory used or sold. In order to trace the pool of inventory cost to its eventual destinations, we need an understanding of some alternative procedures for determining costs of goods sold and ending inventory. These procedures involve decisions as to when inventory usage should be recorded and how inventory cost should be assigned. Conditions under which inventory costs should be charged to expense prior to the time of sale and procedures used to estimate inventory cost in retail establishments are also studied.

**INVENTORY FLOW**

This section deals with some elaborations and analytical techniques associated with the flow of inventory costs. Assume that a given company has a beginning inventory of $50. During the year its purchases, *including all assignable freight and handling costs*, total $253, and the ending inventory is assigned a cost of $130. The analytical procedure to reflect the accumulation and subsequent division of the pool of inventory cost can be summarized in the following convenient formula:

| | |
|---|---:|
| Beginning inventory | $ 50 |
| Plus: Net purchases | 253 |
| Equals: Cost of goods available for sale | 303 |
| Less: Ending inventory | 130 |
| Equals: Cost of goods sold | $173 |

By determining the cost of the ending inventory, we also determine the cost of what is sold, or vice versa. Actually, the emphasis is most often placed on cost of goods sold (income measurement), and the ending inventory is given secondary consideration. The procedures we discuss later in this chapter for assigning costs to the ending inventory are viewed in terms of their effects on both the income statement and the position statement.

## Impact of Inventory Errors on Income Measurement

The inventory formula serves as an effective tool for analyzing the impact of inventory errors on net income. As the formula clearly shows, if the ending inventory is inadvertently understated, cost of goods sold will be overstated and net income understated by the same amount. Moreover, if the error is not detected, the opposite effect will occur during the following period. The understated ending inventory becomes the beginning inventory. If the beginning inventory is understated, cost of goods available for sale is understated. Proper determination of the ending inventory in the second period will therefore result in cost of goods sold being understated and net income being overstated.

We can use the inventory formula to trace the effects of many types of errors affecting inventory and cost of goods sold. Assume that a firm reports net income before taxes of $68,600 in 1984 and $73,400 in 1985. Its preliminary results for 1986 indicate a net income before taxes of $74,800. However, an audit of the records made at the end of 1986 reveals the following errors:

1. *Overstated ending inventory*—When the physical inventory was counted on December 31, 1984, one lot costing $3,600 was included twice.
2. *Erroneously recorded purchases*—Merchandise costing $5,100 was received late in 1984 and was properly included in the December 31, 1984, ending inventory. However, the supplier did not send an invoice until January 1985, at which time it was first recorded as a purchase.
3. *Understated ending inventory*—The inventory total for December 31, 1985, was understated when merchandise costing $4,200 was inadvertently omitted from the physical count.

Table 8-1 depicts how each of the above errors affected the various components of the cost-of-goods-sold calculation. Observe that each inventory error affects only two accounting periods and has opposite effects in each of them. Because such errors fairly quickly "wash themselves out," it might seem tempting to view them as unimportant. However, as Table 8-2 reveals, inventory errors can cause substantial distortions in the net income of a single year and enormous deviations from the actual trend of earnings exhibited over several years. Although the corrected pretax net

TABLE 8-1  Impact of Inventory Errors on Calculation of Cost of Goods Sold and Net Income

| | ERROR 1 | | ERROR 2 | | ERROR 3 | |
|---|---|---|---|---|---|---|
| | 1984 | 1985 | 1984 | 1985 | 1985 | 1986 |
| Beginning inventory | 0 | +3,600 | 0 | 0 | 0 | −4,200 |
| Purchases | 0 | 0 | −5,100 | +5,100 | 0 | 0 |
| Goods available for sale | 0 | +3,600 | −5,100 | +5,100 | 0 | −4,200 |
| Ending inventory | +3,600 | 0 | 0 | 0 | −4,200 | 0 |
| Cost of goods sold | −3,600 | +3,600 | −5,100 | +5,100 | +4,200 | −4,200 |
| Net income | +3,600 | −3,600 | +5,100 | −5,100 | −4,200 | +4,200 |

+ signifies item is overstated as a result of the error.
− signifies item is understated as a result of the error.
0 signifies item is unaffected as a result of the error.

income still totals $216,800 for the 1984–1986 period, the great year-to-year stability previously indicated has vanished.

Although our example concerns errors in inventory, we can employ the same analytical framework to examine or predict the effect on net income of alternative costing methods or other changes in inventory determination.

TABLE 8-2  Correction of Income for Effect of Inventory Errors

| Explanation | 1984 Net Income | 1985 Net Income | 1986 Net Income | Total for 1984–1986 |
|---|---|---|---|---|
| Pretax income originally reported | $68,600 | $73,400 | $74,800 | $216,800 |
| Correction of: | | | | |
| Error 1 | (3,600) | 3,600 | | |
| Error 2 | (5,100) | 5,100 | | |
| Error 3 | | 4,200 | (4,200) | |
| Corrected pretax income | $59,900 | $86,300 | $70,600 | $216,800 |

( ) signifies deduction.

## Periodic versus Perpetual Inventory

The inventory formula illustrates the procedure followed in a *periodic* or *physical inventory* system. Cost of goods sold is recorded only at the end of the period. A physical inventory count is taken, and the cost of the units on hand is determined. This amount is then subtracted from the sum of the beginning inventory and net purchases ($BI + P - EI = CGS$).

Although widely used, particularly among merchandising concerns, the periodic procedure suffers from two disadvantages. It automatically includes in cost of goods sold the cost of merchandise which has been wasted, misappropriated, or otherwise lost. Little information to aid in the control of inventory usage is available under this accounting procedure. Secondly, the time-consuming job of taking a complete physical inventory before statements can be prepared effectively limits the frequency of accurate financial reporting.

Many companies, including most manufacturing firms, record the use of merchandise or raw material on a *perpetual* basis. Cost of Goods Sold (or Work in Process) is debited each time the inventory is decreased through sale or use, and a running, up-to-date record is kept of the number of units on hand and their cost. The perpetual inventory formula is $BI + P - CGS = EI$.

The perpetual inventory system provides more timely and accurate information about inventory balances and withdrawals. Control is enhanced by a periodic comparison of the perpetual inventory records with a physical inventory count. However, in this case the physical inventory can be taken at any convenient time, often on a rotating basis for different items in the inventory. Preparation of financial statements does not *require* a physical count of inventory.

Because of the detailed record-keeping, perpetual inventory procedures were once restricted to only a few inventory items with high unit cost, infrequently purchased and sold. However, computerization of the detailed bookkeeping function has led to wide usage of this technique.

## INVENTORY COSTING METHODS

Whether a firm employs perpetual or periodic inventory procedures, whenever it purchases units at varying prices, the accountants must decide which costs to assign to the units sold and which to the units in the ending inventory. In considering this question, we discuss a number of alternative methods by which costs may be divided. Because the periodic inventory formula better focuses attention on the relationship between cost of goods sold and ending inventory, we use it as our general framework for discussion. However, attention is drawn to points at which perpetual inventory procedures yield different results.

## Specific Identification

The inventory costing method that might first come to mind is that of relating a specific purchase cost to each item in the inventory. A tag can be attached to each unit as it is received, indicating its specific cost, or a separate invoice can be linked to each item by a serial number or a unique description. Later, when the item is sold, its specific cost can be identified and assigned to the expense account. For those items remaining unsold at the end of the period, a firm can easily determine the total cost by adding the tags or relevant invoices.

For practical reasons, specific identification is suitable primarily for high-unit-value merchandise of which purchases and sales are relatively few. For instance, an automobile dealer would have a separate invoice for each automobile in inventory. Because each car can be separately identified and its individual cost determined, assigning inventory costs to expense and ending inventory becomes a mechanical process of identifying units and cost invoices. Appliances, jewelry, and furniture are other examples of inventories often costed by specific identification.

As a method of matching resources consumed against revenues generated, specific identification appears very rational, because it adheres to the actual physical flow of inventory. Nevertheless, two criticisms are raised against this method. First, specific identification may result in biased results for completely interchangeable units. If *identical* units have different costs, management, through deliberate choice of which units to deliver, can influence the size of the cost of goods sold and, in turn, manipulate the amount of income reported.

The second criticism is a practical one. Some goods cannot be kept separate physically or be identified specifically. Gasoline in underground tanks and items stored in bins are examples. Moreover, it is usually too costly to maintain separate records for each unit when the inventory consists of numerous small items of varying types. Even when it is feasible to maintain perpetual records of units received and used, identification of the *exact* unit sold and *its* specific cost may still be difficult.

Consequently, in most cases some assumption has to be made as to which costs should be assigned to the goods left on hand at the end of the accounting period and which to the goods sold. Some of the more common of these assumptions about inventory cost flows characterize the remaining methods of inventory costing to be discussed. They are:

| Units in Ending Inventory Are Assumed to Be: | Resultant Inventory Costing Procedure |
|---|---|
| 1. Representative of all units purchased | Weighted-average cost |
| 2. Last units purchased | FIFO (first-in, first-out) |
| 3. First units purchased | LIFO (last-in, first-out) |

The data presented in Table 8–3 are used to illustrate and contrast these three inventory costing procedures.

**TABLE 8–3   Data for Illustration and Comparison of Inventory Costing Methods**

|  | Number of Units | Unit Cost | Total Cost |
|---|---|---|---|
| Beginning inventory, 1/1/84 | 50 | $10 | $ 500 |
| Add: 1984 Purchases: |  |  |  |
| March 1 | 60 | 11 | 660 |
| July 1 | 80 | 12 | 960 |
| December 1 | 70 | 13 | 910 |
| Total purchases | 210 |  | 2,530 |
| Cost of goods available for sale | 260 |  | $3,030 |
| Deduct: Ending inventory, 12/31/84 | 60 |  |  |
| Cost of goods sold | 200 |  |  |

As the accompanying diagram of the inventory formula shows, our problem is to determine how much of the $3,030 should be assigned to the 60 units in the ending inventory and how much to the 200 units sold.

**Weighted-Average Cost**

One popular assumption is that the units on hand and the units sold represent a mixture of all the units available for sale. This assumption might be particularly valid for liquids or items stored in bins. A *periodic* ending inventory under this assumption would be costed at a weighted-average unit cost. In our example, the following numbers would result:

```
Cost of goods available for sale .................................... $3,030
   Less: Ending inventory—60 units at a
      weighted-average unit cost of $11.65 .........................     699
      ($3,030 goods available/260 units = $11.65)
Cost of goods sold  ............................................... $2,331
```

Often the average cost method is used even when the units are not mixed physically. It is argued that average costing of interchangeable units minimizes possible distortions from short-term price fluctuations. If specific identification or some other alternative is used, cost of goods sold may fluctuate misleadingly from period to period. Average costing has the tendency to "normalize" the unit costs for the period. For short time periods, such a procedure may have justification.

Because the ending inventory under periodic average costing is assumed to be representative of all units purchased by the firm, costs incurred early in the period may influence its cost as much as or more than costs incurred near the end of the period. A *moving average cost*, as would be required if the average cost method were applied on a *perpetual* basis, would be better. After each purchase a new average cost would be computed for costing out units sold until the next purchase occurs. However, this procedure requires a lot of arithmetic calculations, particularly when purchases are made with great frequency. Both weighted-average (periodic) and moving-average (perpetual) cost methods are used, although they do not necessarily give identical results.

**First-in, First-out**  In the selection of criteria by which to judge an *assumed* flow of costs, one factor that often receives mention is the physical flow of goods. In this view the best inventory assumption is the one that most closely approximates the physical movement of the inventory. In most cases this view leads to the first-in, first-out (FIFO) inventory costing method. The oldest inventory (first-in) is *assumed* to be sold (first-out), and the ending inventory consists of the most recently purchased items. In our example the units sold are assumed to consist of the 50 units in the beginning inventory, the 60 units purchased on March 1, the 80 units purchased on July 1, and 10 of the units from the December 1 purchase. The ending inventory, then, is costed at the prices of the newest merchandise. The results are:

| | |
|---|---:|
| Cost of goods available for sale | $3,030 |
| Less: Ending inventory 60 units at $13 | 780 |
| Cost of goods sold | $2,250 |

In addition to its reasonableness as an approximation of the physical flow of merchandise in many businesses, FIFO has the advantage of providing the same results whether applied on a perpetual or a periodic basis. As long as the oldest merchandise is considered to be sold first, cost of sales is the same whether recorded at the end of the period or after each individual sale. Moreover, the inventory balance shown on the position statement under FIFO comes closer than the other inventory methods to the replacement cost of the asset.

The major objection to FIFO is that price gains (or losses) from the *holding* of inventory are included as part of *operating income*. Assume that the firm in our example sold merchandise in December at a price of $19.50, 150 percent of the most recent purchase cost ($13). The cost matched against it under FIFO was probably only $12 (the purchase cost on July 1). Many accountants would contend that instead of having a unit gross margin of $7.50 ($19.50 − $12.00), the firm has a unit gross margin of only $6.50 ($19.50 − $13.00) *plus a holding gain* of $1 ($13 − $12).

By assigning the oldest costs to the merchandise sold, FIFO may match low-cost inventory against high selling prices during periods of rising prices and high-cost inventory against low selling prices in periods of falling prices. Under FIFO, gains (losses) from holding inventories which increase (decrease) in cost are reflected in net income through a *cost of goods sold* that is lower (higher) than the *current* cost of the resources used. This "inventory profit (loss)" should be segregated for reporting purposes on the income statement because it is of a different nature from operating income and may result from external factors beyond management's influence.

**Last-in, First-out**

Last-in, first-out (LIFO) assumes that the cost of the most recently purchased merchandise should be matched against revenue as cost of goods sold. Correspondingly, the goods remaining on hand are assigned the costs of the oldest merchandise. Using the figures in Table 8–3 and applying LIFO on a periodic basis, we find the following results:

| | | |
|---|---:|---:|
| Cost of goods available for sale | | $3,030 |
| Less: Ending inventory: | | |
| 50 units @ $10 | $500 | |
| 10 units @ $11 | 110 | 610 |
| Cost of goods sold | | $2,420 |

The LIFO method gives us an ending inventory composed of layers. The basic layer is the oldest inventory acquired, and each succeeding acquisition is then considered in order of purchase. Schematically, the ending inventory in our example would appear as follows:

| | |
|---|---|
| 10 units at $11 | ........ Layer added this period from first purchase |
| 50 units at $10 | ........ Basic LIFO layer from beginning inventory |

If the ending inventory were 90 units at the close of the *next* accounting period, we would add an additional layer of 30 units at the cost of the first 30 units purchased in that period.[1] Conversely, since the units sold are assumed to come off the top layer, any decrease in inventory would first reduce the 10 units costed at $11. As long as the ending inventory remains at 60 units, its balance sheet amount each period will be $610. Under LIFO, inventory is viewed as a quasifixed asset, and current sales are assumed for accounting purposes to come out of current purchases.

LIFO obviously assumes a "flow of costs" which usually does not match the actual physical movement of the goods. However, many accountants and business executives claim that they can obtain more meaningful income figures by matching costs other than those approximating the acqusition cost of the actual units sold. They argue that the real cost of making a sale is the cost of *replacing* the inventory sold. While still using acqusition costs, LIFO approximates a valuation of cost of goods sold at replacement cost by matching the cost of the most recently acquired units. So, in practice, LIFO approaches a *replacement cost method* in cases where physical inventories at the end of the period are equal to or greater than

---

[1] Under current *income tax regulations* the incremental layer added during a period need not be costed at the earliest purchase prices of that period. For tax purposes the LIFO concept extends only to the layers, not to the costing within a particular layer.

the beginning inventory. In these cases, the most recently incurred costs (the cost of replacing goods) are charged to expense.

This aspect of LIFO often is characterized by the phrase "matching current costs against current revenues." By matching approximate replacement costs against revenues, LIFO provides useful information for future decisions and projections of net income. Particularly when prices are rising, LIFO charges the higher purchase costs against the higher selling prices and thereby approximates the current cost-price margin. This figure, it is claimed, is more characteristic of current operating conditions than is the historic cost-price margin. If, in fact, there were no inventory and a firm were able to purchase just the amount it sold each day, the current gross margin would *be* the gross income of the firm.

## Comparison of Inventory Costing Methods

We have seen that the three inventory-flow assumptions studied—weighted-average cost, FIFO, and LIFO—produce significantly different amounts for ending inventory and cost of goods sold based on the data in Table 8–3. Specifically, the following variations exist:

|  | Weighted Average | FIFO | LIFO |
|---|---|---|---|
| Cost of goods available for sale | $3,030 | $3,030 | $3,030 |
| Less: Ending inventory | 699 | 780 | 610 |
| Cost of goods sold | $2,331 | $2,250 | $2,420 |

The rankings evidenced in the example—FIFO ending inventory > Weighted-average ending inventory > LIFO ending inventory and LIFO cost of goods sold > Weighted-average cost of goods sold > FIFO cost of goods sold—will *typically* prevail during a period when unit costs are increasing. Accordingly, the pattern exhibited is very likely to mirror that which is being experienced by most U.S. firms. Of the three methods, LIFO produces the highest cost of goods sold during a period of rising prices. Therefore, LIFO produces the lowest gross margin (gross profit) and net income. Similarly, FIFO, during periods of price upswings, results in the highest gross margin and net income. Of course, the above pattern would usually be reversed during a period of falling prices.

Even when prices are rising, however, the rankings can reverse when the firm has been unable or unwilling to at least maintain the *physical volume* of the inventory. For example, when the oldest cost layers are represented to be the closing inventory (LIFO), a substantial depletion of inventory quantities will result in these *lower* cost layers being matched with current revenues. The resulting gross margin and net income will be high, just the reverse of what might be expected under LIFO. Depletion of inventory can be the result of voluntary management action (e.g., in response to falling sales) or such outside factors as strikes or material shortages.[2]

An expanded, multiyear example would demonstrate that the different inventory methods not only have varying effects on the amount of gross margin reported (because of the varying effects on cost of goods sold) but also produce different levels of the gross margin percentage (gross margin divided by sales revenue). A firm which sets its unit sales price at a constant percentage of the cost of its latest purchase will have a stable gross margin percentage only if it uses LIFO. The FIFO procedure will often result in significant variations in the gross margin percentage, even if the firm's pricing policy would seem to preclude such a finding; the culprit is FIFO's inclusion of holding gains and losses in the cost of goods sold.

**Selection of Inventory Costing Methods**

Because the great majority of firms are either unable or unwilling to use the specific identification procedure, they are faced with deciding among weighted-average cost, FIFO, and LIFO. A firm need not use the same inventory costing method for its entire inventory. Nevertheless, even those firms using more than one method must decide which ones to use and on what inventories to use them.

Ideally, a company should choose those inventory costing procedures which will lead to the preparation of the most relevant and reliable set of financial statements. Unfortunately, such a determination cannot be made easily. The following issues first need to be addressed and resolved by the accounting profession and the financial community:

1. The meaning and purpose of the matching concept.
2. The relative importance of the balance sheet vis-à-vis the income statement.
3. The extent to which tax regulations should influence financial reporting.
4. The feasibility of selecting accounting procedures as a means of addressing the problem of changing prices.

**Matching.** Although there is wide agreement that good matching occurs only when the costs incurred in earning revenues are deducted from those revenues, some disagreement exists concerning which costs, in the case of inventories, should be deducted. Some accountants believe that good matching can occur only if the inventory costing procedure that is adopted mirrors the actual flow of goods. Because in most businesses this flow is first-in, first-out, they argue that the supporters of matching should advocate the use of FIFO in most circumstances.

---

[2] Since inventory depletions are more common over shorter periods of time, LIFO is used on a *periodic* basis only. The likelihood of some early LIFO layers being depleted *temporarily* during the year is high, and such depletions would have to be recognized under a perpetual LIFO system.

As noted earlier, LIFO supporters suggest an entirely different line of reasoning. They point out that many firms continuously replenish their inventory during the accounting period, as sales are made. Therefore, a cost figure that is as close as possible to the cost of replacement should be matched against the sales revenue. The cost of the *last* purchase is likely to be closer to the cost of replacement than is the cost of the first purchase, so LIFO proponents consider their method preferable from a matching perspective.

Critics of LIFO raise two points in reply. First, even if the matching of current costs with current revenues accurately measures *operating income*, inventory price gains and losses are real economic changes and should not be ignored. They maintain that proper reporting on the stewardship of the owners' investment requires that effective purchasing—buying at a low price merchandise that later increases in value—be reflected as a separate component in a periodic measurement of income.

Second, through its inclusion of the increased cost of inventory replacement in cost of goods sold, LIFO implies that the income cycle is not complete until the investment is replaced. The general nature of business operations, however, is not from one investment to another investment but rather from uninvested funds back to uninvested funds available for reinvestment *or some other purpose*. Each new investment is an independent management decision based on *future* expectations. The amount and type of reinvestment are not automatically determined by the amount and type of past investment consumed. Thus LIFO, by implying reinvestment, confuses *income determination* with *income administration*. Income exists when the old investment is recovered. Whether that income is paid out in dividends or reinvested is a separate management decision dealing with the use of the income, not its measurement.

**Balance Sheet versus Income Statement.**   Accountants strive to prepare a relevant and reliable *set* of financial statements. Unfortunately, very few accounting methods provide realism simultaneously to both the balance sheet and the income statement. Even if LIFO results in better matching and a reliable gross margin and net income for the income statement, such realism hardly carries through to a LIFO-based balance sheet.

Because the LIFO ending inventory amount represents the cost of the oldest purchases ever made by the firm, the totals presented for current assets, working capital, and various other financial statistics become suspect. For example, a loan officer confronted with the position statement of a jewelry manufacturer who has used LIFO to cost the inventory of gold at $35 per ounce cannot really use the published amount to determine the firm's solvency or the collateral value of its assets. A FIFO-based balance sheet would add more realism by showing the gold inventory at the recent purchase prices of many hundreds of dollars per ounce. However, LIFO proponents would allege that the corresponding FIFO income statement would present the loan officer with significantly overstated gross margin and net income amounts, because of the matching of old costs with current revenues.

**Influence of Tax Regulations.**   Every firm which prepares financial statements for investors and creditors must also prepare a tax return for the Internal Revenue Service (IRS). A firm's taxable income is determined in accordance with the income tax regulations and almost never equals the book income reported in its published income statement. Such differences do not mean that the company has either misled its external readers or defrauded the government. Instead, a firm's two sets of books are viewed as the normal result of our tax regulations' much greater concern for fund-raising and the promotion of certain social and economic behavior than for the proper matching of accrual-basis revenues and expenses.

In the case of inventories, however, the IRS requires that companies using LIFO for tax purposes also use LIFO for published financial statements. LIFO has much appeal for tax purposes, because it usually results in higher cost of goods sold, lower gross margin, lower income, and lower taxes during inflationary times. Unfortunately, all such firms are then constrained to LIFO as the inventory costing method "chosen" for their financial statements.[3] To the extent that FIFO may have more accurately reflected the inventories, the tax code lessens the quality of financial reporting.[4]

**Changing Prices.**   Traditionally, the existence of alternative accounting methods has been welcomed by many who criticize the conventional historical cost accounting model. Among the alternatives allowed for the recording of cost of goods sold, depreciation expense (see Chapter 9), and several other items, there was always one procedure capable of producing relatively large amounts for expense. The recording of higher expense and, hence, lower net income results in performance reports that may be similar to those which would have occurred if price adjustments had been made.

LIFO incorporates features of more than one income concept. It retains the use of historical costs employed in conventional accounting theory but at the same time attempts to address the problem of changing prices. Nevertheless, LIFO costs reported on the income statement only approximate current (replacement) costs. Even when only a short time has elapsed between the purchase and sale of the product, it is unlikely that the cost of the firm's latest purchases (what is expensed under LIFO) will equal the cost of its next purchase (replacement cost). Moreover, as will be illustrated in Chapter 19, a complete replacement-cost system, unlike LIFO, recognizes inventory holding gains and losses as a separate element

---

[3] It is interesting to note that LIFO enjoys little popularity in Canada and the United Kingdom, where it is not acceptable for tax purposes, even though the rate of price increase in those countries rivals or exceeds that in the United States.

[4] During 1982 the IRS considered eliminating the LIFO conformity rule but decided to retain the requirement.

of income.[5] Accordingly, supporters of a current cost model are not enamored with LIFO, although they may favor it over FIFO.

Proponents of a constant dollar accounting model (see Chapters 7 and 19) also find LIFO lacking in certain respects. They believe that changes in the *general* level of prices need to be reflected. LIFO, however, has to do with changes in *price structure*—the relative value of goods and services—an entirely different problem, as our short example near the end of Chapter 7 illustrates. If general and specific prices move in different directions or at different rates, then LIFO fails to approximate the cost of goods sold which would be reported under a constant dollar model.

In summary, the selection of an inventory costing method can be fraught with frustration and contradiction. A firm must explicitly or implicitly address such issues as (1) the nature of the matching concept, (2) the trade-offs in realism between the balance sheet and the income statement, (3) the constraints on the selection process caused by a firm's desire legally to minimize its income taxes, and (4) the appropriateness of LIFO as a means of addressing the problem of changing prices.

Table 8–4 discloses the inventory methods used by a sample of 600 large U.S. companies for various years since 1973. A dramatic increase in the number of LIFO users occured in 1974. The double-digit inflation of

TABLE 8-4   Inventory Methods Used by a Sample of 600 Large U.S. Firms, 1973–1981

| | Number of Companies* | | | | |
|---|---|---|---|---|---|
| | 1981 | 1979 | 1976 | 1974 | 1973 |
| Methods: | | | | | |
| LIFO | 408 | 374 | 331 | 303 | 150 |
| FIFO | 371 | 390 | 389 | 375 | 394 |
| Average cost | 241 | 241 | 232 | 236 | 235 |
| Other† | 52 | 56 | 107 | 140 | 148 |
| Total disclosures | 1,072 | 1,061 | 1,059 | 1,054 | 927 |
| Use of LIFO: | | | | | |
| All inventories | 26 | 20 | 9 | 14 | 8 |
| 50 percent or more of inventories | 210 | 194 | 167 | 135 | 49 |
| Less than 50 percent of inventories | 89 | 94 | 84 | 67 | 68 |
| Extent not determinable | 83 | 66 | 71 | 87 | 25 |
| Companies using LIFO | 408 | 374 | 331 | 303 | 150 |

\* Adds up to more than 600 because many sample companies used more than one method.
† Includes unique procedures applicable to specialized industries and situations.
Source:   AICPA, *Accounting Trends & Techniques*, (New York, 1982, 1980, 1977, 1975, and 1974).

---

[5] A complete current cost system would also recognize holding gains or losses on units in the ending inventory. These are often referred to as "unrealized" holding gains or losses, "unrealized" because the units have not yet been sold. FIFO includes "realized" holding gains in the gross margin figure; LIFO attempts to exclude from income all holding gains, realized and unrealized.

1974 convinced many firms that they could no longer ignore the tax benefits provided from the use of LIFO; having made the switch for tax purposes, government regulations required the use of LIFO for financial reporting also. Since 1974, the number of sample firms using LIFO and the extent of their use of LIFO both have exhibited steady increases.

The LIFO–FIFO controversy highlights deficiencies in the existing accounting framework. Prices do change because of general inflationary pressures and specific movements in the supply/demand equilibrium for a particular product. These changes often have great economic significance. The historical cost (exchange price) concept conceals the impact of certain specific price changes, and the monetary concept ignores general price changes. Since 1976 certain firms have been required to provide readers of their financial statements with supplementary information about inventory price changes. The next section highlights these important requirements.

**REQUIRED DISCLOSURES FOR INVENTORY PRICE CHANGES**

The double-digit inflation experienced during 1974 resulted in more than just a dramatic increase in the number of firms using LIFO. The rapid rise in prices fueled long-standing efforts to require companies to disclose the replacement cost of their ending inventory and the amount of their *inventory profits*. These profits represent the realized inventory holding gains and are calculated by subtracting cost of goods sold at historical cost (using FIFO, LIFO, or weighted average) from cost of goods sold at replacement cost.

Although the difference between cost of goods sold at replacement cost and at historical cost is significantly less when LIFO has been used rather than FIFO or weighted average, not all inventory profits are eliminated through a shift to LIFO. After many such switches occurred in 1974, the government still attributed almost $38 billion of the $143.5 billion of annual corporate profits, or 26 percent, to inventory profits.[6] Companies were urged by the SEC in 1974 to disclose *voluntarily* the amount of inventory profits included in their reported net income. The SEC argued that the disclosures were necessary to prevent financial statement readers from "being inadequately informed as to the source and replicability of earnings."[7]

The first *requirements* for the disclosure of inventory price changes were established in 1976. The SEC required most large companies to disclose, among other things, the replacement cost of both the goods sold and the ending inventory. The Commission asserted that this rule "will

---

[6] U.S. Commerce Department figures. Inventory profits were approximately $25 billion (out of $151 billion of corporate profits) for 1981 and $9 billion in 1982.

[7] Securities and Exchange Commission, *Accounting Series Release No. 151*, "Disclosure of Inventory Profits Reflected in Income in Periods of Rising Prices" (Washington, D.C.; January 3, 1974).

provide investors with significant data now unavailable about the effect of current economic conditions on the business."[8] Such disclosures were required only in the annual Form 10-K filed by firms with the SEC, although disclosure in published annual reports to stockholders was not precluded.

In 1979, the Financial Accounting Standards Board expanded upon the SEC requirements in its *Statement No. 33*.[9] Applicable for some 1,200 large companies, the FASB requirements differed from the SEC's rules by calling for (1) allocation of the price changes for inventories into the portions caused by general inflation and by asset-specific factors and (2) publication of the supplementary disclosures in the annual reports prepared for stockholders. Shortly after the FASB's action, the SEC announced that it was prepared to repeal its replacement-cost rule, given that *Statement No. 33* incorporated and built upon the Commission's requirements.[10]

The FASB ruling is quite complex and has numerous provisions that address concerns other than the proper disclosure of amounts for inventories and cost of goods sold; it is comprehensively examined in Chapter 19. The required inventory disclosures do, however, concern us in this chapter. The data specifically required by *Statement No. 33* and a suggested format for their presentation are considered in depth in the forthcoming Armco section.

*Statement No. 33* is considered by many to be a constructive and long-overdue effort to increase the realism of the accounting numbers available for external decision making. The standardized disclosures facilitate a more meaningful comparison of the financial statements of companies which are using different inventory methods. Firms covered by the FASB ruling must disclose the replacement (current) cost of their year-end inventories and of their cost of goods sold. Therefore, the statement user (1) no longer needs to compare apples and oranges, (2) is made aware of the excess of current revenue over current cost of goods sold for both firms, and (3) is informed how unrealistically low the LIFO firm's inventory figure has become on its balance sheet.

## LOWER OF COST OR MARKET

The inventory methods discussed in previous sections attempt to determine the *cost* of goods on hand and the *cost* of goods sold. Although they differ in the assumptions made as to which goods are sold, they all use acquisition cost figures. Under generally accepted accounting principles,

---

[8] SEC, *ASR No. 190,* "Disclosure of Certain Replacement Cost Data" (Washington, D.C.; March 23, 1976).

[9] FASB, *Statement of Financial Accounting Standards No. 33,* "Financial Reporting and Changing Prices" (Stamford, Conn., September 1979).

[10] SEC, *ASR No. 271,* "Deletion of Requirement to Disclose Replacement Cost Information" (Washington, D.C., October 23, 1979).

inventory is actually valued according to a procedure known as *lower of cost or market* (LCM). It assigns to the ending inventory either a historical cost amount *or* a current market valuation, whichever is lower. It is applied regardless of which cost method is employed.

This procedure achieved prominence very early in accounting practice, when the balance sheet was of prime importance and conservatism was a prized virtue. If market valuation declined below acquisition cost, a loss was assumed to have occurred. The writing down of the inventory to the lower market figure "recognized" this loss and gave a more conservative value to the inventory in case the business had to be liquidated. In more recent years, as attention has shifted to the income statement and the matching concept, the interpretation of LCM appears to be that only costs possessing future use value should be carried forward to be matched against future revenues. Costs that cannot be recovered satisfactorily are seen to have lost their usefulness:

> A departure from the cost basis of pricing the inventory is required when the utility of the goods is no longer as great as its cost. Where there is evidence that the utility of goods, in their disposal in the ordinary course of business, will be less than cost, whether due to physical deterioration, obsolescence, changes in price levels, or other causes, the difference should be recognized as a loss of the current period. This is generally accomplished by stating such goods at a lower level commonly designated as market.[11]

**How LCM Operates**

Assume that a physical inventory of 100 units exists at the end of the period. The original acquisition cost assigned to each unit is $160. Market at the end of the period is determined to be $130 per unit. Assume further that cost of goods available for sale amounts to $40,000. The effects of using lower of cost or market to value the ending inventory can be seen below:

|  |  | *Cost* |  | *LCM* |
|---|---|---|---|---|
| Cost of goods available |  |  |  |  |
| for sale .................... |  | $40,000 |  | $40,000 |
| Less: Ending inventory ........ (100 at $160) | | 16,000 | (100 at $130) | 13,000 |
| Cost of goods sold ............. |  | $24,000 |  | $27,000 |

The firm makes the following journal entry to record the decline of $3,000 [100 × ($160 − $130)]:

| | | |
|---|---|---|
| Loss from Write-Down of Inventory to Market Value ....... | 3,000 | |
| Allowance to Reduce Inventory to Market Value ...... | | 3,000 |

The allowance is deducted from the inventory account. The loss account is usually closed to cost of goods sold, in this case increasing the latter

---

[11] AICPA, *Accounting Research and Terminology Bulletins, Final Edition* (New York, 1961), p. 30.

account by $3,000. Of course, the inventory decline is unrelated to the goods sold; it pertains to the inventory still on hand. Logic would suggest that, if the market decline is to be recognized, it should be segregated as a separate deduction. Rarely, however, is this method of presentation used in accounting practice.

With respect to income measurement, lower of cost or market has the effect of shifting income from one accounting period to another. A write-down to market causes charges that otherwise would appear as expenses in future periods to be recorded in the current period. However, the reduced ending inventory value, which causes cost of goods sold to be higher and income to be lower this period, becomes the beginning inventory of the following period. It has an opposite effect on income then.[12] With respect to the balance sheet, LCM prevents the inventory from being stated at a figure above its future utility.

The lower-of-cost-or-market procedures applicable to inventory are almost identical to the rules set forth in the last chapter for *current marketable equity securities*. One exception is that inventories once written down to a lower market figure are not written back up if market prices recover. Also in the case of marketable equity securities, normally only one market price exists. However, as we shall see in the next section, different market prices can exist for inventory, depending on whether we are talking about the selling market or the purchase market. Consequently, the application of LCM to inventory is more complex and subjective than in the case of marketable equity securities.

## Meaning of Market

The conceptual soundness of LCM depends to a large extent on the meaning of "utility" and on the measurement of "market." Two interpretations—one emphasizing exit values and one stressing entry values—have been advanced through the years.

**Net Realizable Value.** One reasonable meaning implied by the previous quotation is that utility should be measured by what the company will receive upon disposal of the inventory. This exit-value amount, called *net realizable value*, equals expected selling price reduced by any anticipated costs of completing and selling the inventory item. LCM, then, implies that inventory should not be stated at a figure greater than its *recoverable* cost. The inventory write-down or "loss of the current period" should include any portion of the acquisition cost which cannot be recovered out of anticipated revenue. This interpretation of market has commonly been employed for the recording of losses on damaged or obsolete merchandise in periods prior to their sale.

---

[12] For *tax* purposes *LIFO* cannot be used to determine the cost element in LCM. Under LIFO any inventory value previously written down to market would remain, as long as a minimum inventory quantity was maintained, rather than flow through cost of goods sold in the following period. Consequently, lower of *LIFO* cost or market would result in a relatively permanent inventory value at the lowest purchase price that ever existed at the end of a period.

For example, suppose that a company develops and manufactures 500 pollution control units for automobiles. Because of the firm's inexperience, the manufacturing cost is $400 per unit. Management estimates that the selling price will have to be set at $350 to be competitive with that of other devices on the market. A 20 percent dealer commission is normal for this type of good. *Net realizable value* in this case is $280 ($350 − $70 commission). Of the $400 total cost per unit, $120 ($400 − $280) will not be recovered. Consequently, that portion has no future service potential and should not be carried forward as an asset.

**Replacement Cost.** The more common definition of "market" is *replacement cost*, an entry-value amount. According to this interpretation, utility is the equivalent expenditure, as measured by the price currently being paid for the item in the wholesale market, necessary for acquiring the same use value. Replacement cost is employed as evidence of realizability when there is a close association between purchase prices and selling prices. If replacement cost has fallen below acquisition cost, the contention is that net realizable value also has declined or will decline shortly. The reader may consult the Appendix to this chapter for a more detailed analysis of alternative meanings of "market," the application of LCM under AICPA guidelines, and the theoretical implications of its many facets.

**Criticisms of LCM**

The objections to cost or market, whichever is lower, include both theoretical and practical points. Some of the theoretical criticisms arise from variations in the concept of income implied by the alternative definitions of market. These are considered in depth in the Appendix to this chapter. Two, however, are of general import.

First, the charge of inconsistency plagues lower of cost or market. The inventory may be at cost one year and at market the following year, since market prices are deemed relevant only when they are *below* cost. It seems inconsistent to many to recognize losses before sale when replacement cost or net realizable value falls below cost, and yet at the same time to maintain that gains arising from market's being above cost should be deferred until sale takes place.

Second, in some circumstances LCM will cause inventory to be written down even though the acquisition cost is still expected to be recovered out of future revenues. These circumstances occur when cost is less than net realizable value but greater than replacement cost. Many theorists argue that as long as the merchandise can be sold at some profit (net realizable value is above cost), no loss has occurred. Only a reduction in potential profit margin, not a loss, has taken place. The inventory write-down records a *hypothetical loss* for the current period, permitting a greater profit to be recorded during the following period and unnecessarily shifting income from one accounting period to another.

Three other criticisms denote practical limitations. First, LCM buries holding losses related to the *ending* inventory in cost of goods sold. Use of

LCM thus may distort income statement relationships and may make year-to-year comparisons difficult. Second, a risk exists in the use of market figures at one particular moment to measure market because they may not be representative of the future. This risk is heightened if the moment of time is the end of an accounting period, when activity (purchasing and selling) may be at a low ebb. Finally, LCM will yield *varying* results depending on whether it is applied to the inventory as a whole or to each individual item.

**RETAIL INVENTORY METHOD**

The preparation of monthly or quarterly financial statements requires either frequent physical inventory counts of the ending inventory or maintenance of perpetual inventory records. Both are arduous tasks for firms selling large quantities of many different products. Nevertheless, the need for interim financial information exists for these firms as well as for others.

Many merchandising concerns employ a method known as the retail inventory method to *estimate the dollar amount of ending inventory* when a physical count cannot conveniently be made. Retail establishments also use this procedure to find the *cost* of a physical inventory without having to go through the time-consuming job of sorting out the costs of a number of small, individual items. If the physical inventory has been taken at the current retail prices listed on the items, then the cost of that ending inventory can be estimated by means of the retail procedure. This method is also useful when insurers need to ascertain the approximate loss incurred as a result of fire or other casualty.

We can use the following monthly figures to illustrate:

|  | Cost | Retail |
|---|---|---|
| Beginning inventory | $ 20,000 | $ 26,400 |
| Net purchases | 88,000 | 117,600 |
| Goods available for sale | $108,000 | $144,000 |

The retail method employs the relationship that exists between cost and retail prices. The method requires, therefore, that a firm keep track not only of the cost of its purchases but of the selling prices assigned to them as well. Then a relationship between the *cost* of goods available for sale and the *retail price* of goods available for sale can be established and applied to the retail value of the ending inventory for an estimate of its cost. This relationship, expressed as a *cost ratio*, is 75 percent ($108,000/$144,000) in our example.

If sales for the month are $84,000, the retail price of the ending inventory is $60,000 ($144,000 retail price of goods available for sale less $84,000 retail price of goods sold). Multiplication of the $60,000 by the

75 percent cost ratio produces a $45,000 estimated cost of the ending inventory. The cost ratio can be applied either to an *estimate* of the ending inventory at retail prices, as in this case, or to an *actual physical count* of the ending inventory taken at retail prices.

Use of the cost ratio in the above manner approximates fairly accurately the *average cost* of the ending inventory if we can assume that the cost-retail relationship existing for goods available holds true for the goods sold and for the goods in the ending inventory. If different products have quite varying cost ratios and the product mix of the goods sold is not the same as the mix comprising the ending inventory, further refinements such as a partitioning of the inventory into homogeneous sections will be necessary for accurate results.[13]

**DISCUSSION OF THE ARMCO ANNUAL REPORT**

Armco's financial statements reveal a 1981 cost of products (goods) sold of $5.9 billion and an ending inventory of $1.1 billion at December 31, 1981. Additional disclosures appear in Note 1 and in the section called "Assessing the Impact of Inflation." The company's inventories are valued at the lower of cost or market, with cost for most U.S. goods determined through the use of LIFO. Because the tax benefits of LIFO are generally not available outside the United States, Armco chose the average cost method for the inventories held by its foreign subsidiaries.

The *LIFO reserve* cited in Note 1 generally measures the extra amount which a firm's ending inventory would have been valued at if either FIFO or some approximation of replacement cost had been used. Accordingly, the domestic inventories costed with LIFO at $666.3 million on December 31, 1981, would have been reported at $1.4 billion if Armco had used FIFO. The latter figure should be compared with the $1.9 billion current cost of all inventories (reported at bottom of page 168) to ascertain the percentage of the firm's inventory which is costed under LIFO; it is close to 75 percent for Armco.

The increase in the LIFO reserve during 1981 of $95.3 million ($713.7 − 618.4) represents the amount carried to cost of goods sold under LIFO which would not have gone to that account if FIFO had been used. Therefore, Armco's cost of goods sold would have been $95.3 million less and its pretax net income would have been $95.3 more if the domestic inventories had been costed using FIFO rather than LIFO. Using the 41.6 percent effective income tax rate experienced by Armco in 1981 (see Note 5), we can determine that the company's reported net income of $294.5 million would have been increased by $55.7 million

---

[13] The retail method becomes slightly more complicated when we take into consideration that changes often occur in the initial selling prices before the goods are sold. These changes are called additional markups and markdowns. Because they modify the retail price, they can also affect the cost ratio. Coverage of the technical aspects of markups and markdowns is left to later courses.

[$95.3 × (1.000 − .416)], or almost 19 percent, if FIFO had been employed. You should remember, however, that Armco's $55.7 million decline in reported net income was accompanied by a $39.6 million ($95.3 × .416) cash savings in income taxes.

Athough firms are not required to disclose amounts for the LIFO reserve, most companies now provide such information. In most cases, the data are contained in a footnote. Without a doubt, information on LIFO reserves is useful to financial statement readers. Certainly such data facilitates a more realistic comparison of the net incomes of a FIFO firm vis-à-vis a LIFO firm.

Armco's *Statement No. 33* disclosures appear on pages 168–170. The data related to inventories and cost of goods sold are as follows (all amounts are in millions of dollars):

| | As Stated in the Financial Statements | Adjusted for General Inflation | Adjusted for Changes in Specific Prices (Current Costs) |
|---|---|---|---|
| 1981 cost of products sold . . . . . . . . . . . . . | $5,763.1 | $5,769.0 | $5,769.0 |
| Increase in current cost of inventory and equipment held during the year (based on specific price changes)* . . . . . . . . . . . . . . . . . . . . . . . . . . . . . . . . . . . . | | | $ 756.2 |
| Effect of increase in general price level . . . . . . . . . . . . . . . . . . | | | 378.1 |
| Increase in current cost of inventory and equipment held during the year (based on specific price changes) net of changes in the general price level . . . . . . . . . . . . . . . . . . . . | | | $ 378.1 |

\* At December 31, 1981, current cost of inventory was $1,942.4.

Armco explains the relatively small upward adjustment for the Cost of Product Sold account ($5.9 million, or 0.1%) by noting that it "would be considerably larger if it were not for our predominant use of the LIFO method of inventory accounting." Of course, the cost of goods sold calculated under LIFO often closely approximates replacement costs. The reporting of $5,769 million in *both* the general inflation and specific prices columns is initially puzzling because it would be most unusual for the specific price changes to exactly equal the general inflation rate. However, in this case, according to authorities contacted at Armco, the specific-price-adjusted cost of goods sold was actually within one percent of the $5,769 million general-price-adjusted number. Because the former number was an estimate and was not materially different from the latter figure, the $5,769 was shown for both columns.

Additional required disclosures reveal the increase in the current cost of inventory and net property, plant, and equipment on both a gross basis and net of changes in the general price level. The 1981 figures show that Armco experienced price increases in those assets at exactly twice the general rate of inflation. It is only a coincidence that precisely one half of the $756.2 million price increase was attributable to general inflation. On occasion, the specific price change net of the general price level increase is actually a decrease. For example, in 1980 Armco reported a $225.9 million *decrease* in current cost of inventory and equipment net of a $475.8 million *increase* in the general price level.

The current cost of inventory at December 31, 1981 was $1,942.4 million. When this figure is contrasted with the $1,143.1 million reported on Armco's balance sheet, the extent to which the use of LIFO and average cost has led to unrealistically low totals for inventories and current and total assets becomes evident. In the section on "Financial Condition and Liquidity," the company stresses that it has assets which are not fully reflected on its balance sheet. Among the factors cited is "the higher current value of inventories as compared to amounts stated due to LIFO accounting."

Even when firms voluntarily provide data on LIFO reserves, the required *Statement No. 33* disclosures furnish useful additional information. A knowledge of the general and specific price changes encountered by a firm such as Armco as a result of its holding of inventory aids the financial statement reader in understanding the economic environment in which the company operates. The next chapter considers the depreciation and plant asset data for Armco emanating from *Statement No. 33*. The statement is reviewed in its entirety in Chapter 19.

**SUMMARY**

In this chapter we are primarily interested in how the pool of inventory cost is divided between the goods sold and the ending inventory. The inventory formula provides us with a helpful analytical tool for examining this and other inventory problems. In practice, a number of alternative procedures, conventions, or expedients exist for dividing the cost pool. The effects of these choices on the income statement and position statement vary with the circumstances.

With the existence of so many alternatives it behooves the firm to report clearly what its inventory policies are. Likewise, an intelligent user of financial information must understand the meaning of inventory terminology in order to assess the general impact of alternative procedures on the statements. This chapter lays a groundwork for a rational interpretation of financial statements in the inventory area.

The onset of double-digit inflation in 1974 led to an immediate, dramatic increase in the number of companies using LIFO for tax purposes. Because government regulations require conformity between book and tax inventory methods whenever LIFO is used, a greatly increased number of firms now report unrealistically low balance sheet amounts for their inventories. Fortunately, voluntary disclosures of LIFO reserves and the information required by FASB *Statement No. 33* have helped. They both increase the probability that financial statement users can intelligently interpret the inventory data and make meaningful interfirm comparisons.

# APPENDIX: Mechanics of Lower of Cost or Market

The notion of realizability or recoverability appears to underlie lower of cost or market (LCM). Nevertheless, the primary definition of market is replacement cost. The rationale for LCM under this definition appears to be as follows. If replacement cost has fallen below cost, then the net selling price of the merchandise on hand will probably decline also. Hence, the asset has lost part of its revenue-producing ability. This decline in value should be recognized as a loss upon incurrence.

## Limitations on Replacement Cost

This rationale contains some key assumptions. To the extent that these assumptions are not valid, the definition of market as replacement cost may lead to unreasonable results. Consequently, the AICPA, in formulating the cost-or-market principle, modifies replacement cost as the determinant of market by attaching upper and lower limits:

> As used in the phrase *lower of cost or market* the term *market* means current replacement cost (by purchase or reproduction, as the case may be) except that:
> (1) Market should not exceed the net realizable value (i.e., estimated selling price in the ordinary course of business less reasonably predictable costs of completion and disposal); and
> (2) Market should not be less than net realizable value reduced by an allowance for an approximately normal profit margin.[14]

These modifications provide a floor and a ceiling to the measurement of "market." The ceiling is net realizable value; the floor is net realizable value less a normal profit. Market means replacement cost only as long as it lies between the floor and the ceiling.

**Upper Limit.** When goods are obsolete or damaged, the cost of replacing them may actually be above both original cost and net realizable value. Consequently, no reduction would result under the normal definition of market as replacement cost. However, if net realizable value is below original cost, a portion of the cost cannot be recovered and a loss in this period should be recorded.

In this case replacement cost does not measure the real loss in utility due to obsolescence. A loss equal to the difference between original cost and net realizable value ultimately will occur. Many accountants claim that, because the obsolescence or damage occurred in the current period, this loss should be recognized now by a decrease in the inventory to net realizable value, even though replacement cost has risen. A write-down to net realizable value measures the *minimum* loss suffered by the firm. Consequently, if replacement cost is above net realizable value, the latter is substituted for replacement cost as the meaning of market.

**Lower Limit.** The floor placed on market attempts to resolve the problem that arises if the decline in selling prices is negligible or less than proportionate to the decline in replacement cost. In this case, a reduction in inventory to replacement cost would recognize a loss in the current period, only to show an *abnormal* income in the following period when the units are sold.

---

[14] AICPA, *Accounting Research and Terminology Bulletins, Final Edition*, p. 31.

To avoid this absurdity, the AICPA has specified that if replacement cost is below net realizable value less a normal profit margin, the latter is used as the definition of market. Only a loss equal to the difference between cost and this lower limit is to be included in the cost of goods sold of the current period. Then, if the merchandise is sold in the following period as anticipated, a normal margin will be realized. Stated differently, so long as an item can be sold at a normal profit, no additional loss has occurred, even if replacement cost has declined more. A write-down to net realizable value less a normal profit presumably measures the *maximum* loss suffered by the firm.

## Analysis of Lower of Cost or Market

Thus, the lower-of-cost-or-market rule as applied in accounting practice actually offers four different concepts of utility for inventory items: (1) acquisition cost (AC), (2) current replacement cost (RC), (3) net realizable value (NRV), and (4) net realizable value less normal profit (NRV − NP). The last three represent alternative views of market, depending on particular circumstances. Conceivably, all three concepts of market could be used by a single company at the same time for different types of inventory or at different times for the same inventory. Of course, the market figure, however determined, is applicable only if it is below cost.

The information in Table 8A–1 relates to five items in an ending inventory. Assume that we are to determine the proper dollar amount *per unit* for each item in accordance with the LCM procedure, as interpreted by the AICPA. Table 8A–2 presents the results of the LCM procedure and serves as a focal point for the analysis of each alternative.

**TABLE 8A–1  Data for Lower-of-Cost-or-Market Illustration**

| Item | Acquisition Cost | Replacement Cost | Estimated Sale Price | Estimated Cost to Sell | Normal Profit |
|------|------------------|------------------|----------------------|------------------------|---------------|
| A ..... | $ 6.00 | $ 6.50 | $ 7.50 | $0.70 | $1.20 |
| B ..... | 15.30 | 15.40 | 15.50 | 1.20 | 2.00 |
| C ..... | 10.50 | 8.20 | 11.80 | 1.10 | 1.60 |
| D ..... | 5.20 | 5.00 | 6.30 | 0.50 | 1.00 |
| E ..... | 8.60 | 8.00 | 9.40 | 1.10 | 0.50 |

**TABLE 8A–2  Computation of Lower of Cost or Market**

| | Item | | | | |
|---|---|---|---|---|---|
| | A | B | C | D | E |
| Calculation of market: | | | | | |
| Ceiling—net realizable value (estimated selling price less estimated cost to sell) ........... | $6.80 | $14.30 | $10.70 | $5.80 | $8.30 |
| Replacement cost ................. | 6.50 | 15.40 | 8.20 | 5.00 | 8.00 |
| Floor—net realizable value less normal profit ............... | 5.60 | 12.30 | 9.10 | 4.80 | 7.80 |
| Market—replacement cost as constrained by floor and ceiling ...... | 6.50 | 14.30 | 9.10 | 5.00 | 8.00 |
| Acquisition cost ..................... | 6.00 | 15.30 | 10.50 | 5.20 | 8.60 |
| Lower of cost or market ............. | 6.00 | 14.30 | 9.10 | 5.00 | 8.00 |

**Item A: Cost.** The ending inventory is valued at the acquisition cost of $6 per unit. The applicable market figure is the usual one, replacement cost, because it is between the floor and ceiling. Because it is still above cost, however, no adjustment is made. The inventory is deemed not to have suffered any decline in utility, even though the profit recognized in the next period will be only $0.80 ($6.80 NRV − $6 AC), less than the normal profit of $1.20.

**Item B: Net Realizable Value.** In this case the exit value of the item on hand is less than its entry value. Goods subject to major style or model changes and those prone to breakage or deterioration may follow this pattern. The ceiling governs the determination of market. The firm is assumed to have suffered a loss of utility at *least* equal to $1 per unit ($15.30 − $14.30). Under LCM in this instance the loss is recorded in this period—by write-down of the ending inventory to $14.30—instead of next period, when the goods are actually sold. No income or loss occurs in the next period, when the goods are actually disposed of at a net selling price of $14.30.

Of the market alternatives under LCM, this one claims the greatest use and support. Some accountants, in fact, would like to see inventories valued at net realizable values whether they are *above* or *below* cost. Even under the conventional cost valuation, most accountants agree that losses from damage, obsolescence, and similar causes are significant, measurable, economic events of the period in which they occur. Consequently, the notion that an *unrecoverable cost* is not an asset seems widely accepted. As we shall see in the next example, though, LCM often goes further than merely reducing inventory to net realizable value.

**Item C: Net Realizable Value less Normal Profit.** Here, replacement cost has declined proportionately more than selling prices. Replacement cost is below cost, but it is also below net realizable value less a normal profit. If the inventory value were reduced to replacement cost, a loss of $2.30 ($10.50 AC − $8.20 RC) would be recorded this period, and a profit of $2.50 ($10.70 NRV less the decreased inventory value of $8.20) would be recorded next period. This profit of $2.50 per unit would be much greater than the normal profit of $1.60. Therefore, the lower limit of net realizable value less normal profit becomes the applicable market figure. Through a reduction of the ending inventory to $9.10 and a concomitant charge to income this period of $1.40 ($10.50 AC less $9.10), a normal profit of $1.60 ($10.70 NRV − $9.10) is recorded in a later period.

Two major objections are raised against this result. First is the charge of profit manipulation mentioned in Chapter 8. The normal profit in the subsequent period results from an uncalled-for write-down of assets this period. Because net realizable value ($10.70) is above cost ($10.50), any "loss" recorded this period is entirely hypothetical in a conventional accounting sense. The second objection is a practical one. What, in fact, is a normal profit? The foregoing example assumes a *constant-dollar amount* regardless of changes in selling prices or costs. Should it be a *percentage* return on sales? Moreover, is normal profit a hoped-for figure, an average figure for this particular product, or an average return for the business as a whole? Grave doubts exist whether any practical quantification *could be or should be* given to a concept of "normal" in a dynamic business environment.

**Items D and E: Replacement Cost.** In both of these cases replacement cost is the applicable market figure because it is between the upper and lower limits. It is also the relevant figure for inventory valuation under LCM, because it is below the original acquisition cost. A write-down to replacement cost records a holding loss equal to the difference between cost and current cost. The precise nature of that loss depends on the circumstances. In the case of item D, the net realizable value of $5.80 remains above the acquisition cost of $5.20. Item D still will be disposed of at a profit, albeit not a normal one. Has the utility of the inventory fallen merely because an anticipated profit margin has shrunk? Even if we accept the viewpoint that unless the firm can sell at a normal profit it has suffered a loss, LCM in this instance does not achieve the objective of disposition at normal profit, either. After being reduced to a replacement-cost value of $5, the inventory will be sold at a net selling price of $5.80 for a profit of only $0.80 per unit rather than a normal profit of $1.

In the case of item E, the firm would incur an actual loss upon disposition of $0.30 per unit ($8.30 NRV less $8.60 AC). However, application of LCM results in a reduction of inventory to the replacement cost of $8. A loss of $0.60 per unit ($8.60 AC less $8 RC) is recognized in the current period, and a profit of $0.30 per unit ($8.30 NRV less the decreased inventory value of $8) will be recorded in the following period. In this case, LCM does not write the inventory down sufficiently far to allow for the normal profit of $0.50, nor does it accurately reflect the *actual* loss of $0.30 in item E.

## Summary of LCM

Lower of cost or market departs from a strict matching of original acquisition cost against revenues by recording losses on units which have not been sold. In so doing, it employs concepts of cost and income different from those which normally underlie financial accounting. These concepts, of course, are not unique to LCM, nor does their use necessarily imply a poor procedure. Actually, the real difficulty with LCM is that it adheres to no consistent concept of income. No fewer than three alternative concepts of inventory value in addition to cost— replacement cost, net realizable value, and net realizable value less normal profit— find their way into this procedure, none of them consistently.

The method basically uses replacement costs, which would imply a current cost approach to income. However, replacement cost is not used if it is above cost or below net realizable value less normal profit. The method also implies that part of an asset has expired if its original cost cannot be recovered. This argument, which also has validity, would result in a write-down to recoverable value (net realizable value). However, LCM sometimes goes further and reduces the inventory below net realizable value. The avowed purpose for a write-down below net realizable value is to allow for disposition at a normal profit later. This third procedure introduces a concept of loss that falls outside of either conventional accounting or economics. Moreover, LCM may not uniformly achieve that objective either, for, whenever replacement cost is above net realizable value less normal profit, the former is used.

Despite its inconsistencies and imprecision, lower of cost or market continues to be the most commonly used basis of valuation for inventories. In many cases LCM may give the same results as the conventional cost method, because cost is normally lower than the applicable market figure. Unfortunately, the external reader does not know the extent of the write-downs, *if any*. By burying any inventory loss that does exist in cost of goods sold, most firms prevent the reader from knowing what impact LCM has had on the financial statements.

## QUESTIONS AND PROBLEMS

**8-1.** On December 31, 1984, the Park Company discovered the following errors in the costing of its merchandise inventory:

| | | |
|---|---|---|
| December 31, 1981 | ....... | $8,000 overstatement |
| December 31, 1982 | ....... | 9,500 understatement |
| December 31, 1983 | ....... | 2,100 understatement |
| December 31, 1984 | ....... | 700 understatement |

The reported pretax income for 1982, 1983, and 1984 was $11,600, $12,400, and $13,200, respectively. Each error was independent of the others, and none had been detected or corrected as of December 31, 1984.

*Required:*

a. Using Table 8–2 as a guide, prepare a schedule showing the determination of corrected pretax income for 1982, 1983, and 1984.

b. "Making corrections for inventory errors serves no purpose. Such errors automatically counterbalance in the year following the year of error. The total income over a three- or four-year period will not differ much as a result of the corrections." Did the total income for 1982–1984 change significantly as a result of your scheduling of corrections in *(a)*? If not, what purpose does the schedule serve and what information does it reveal?

**8-2.** The Nakoma Company began business on March 1, 1985. Purchases and sales for one of its products for the first month are shown in the following tabulation. All sales were made at a price of $50 per unit.

| | Purchases | | |
|---|---|---|---|
| Date | Tag Number | Cost per Unit | Units Sold (tag numbers) |
| March 1 | 17 | $23 | |
| 3 | 22, 26 | 25 | |
| 8 | 30, 31 | 29 | |
| 12 | | | 17 |
| 17 | 37 | 31 | 26 |
| 21 | 42, 43 | 30 | |
| 24 | | | 22, 42 |
| 31 | 52 | 34 | 43 |

In order to evaluate the effect of alternative inventory costing methods, management asked a bookkeeper to prepare a summary schedule of gross margins under various alternatives. The bookkeeper prepared the following:

| | (1) | (2) | (3) | (4) |
|---|---|---|---|---|
| Sales | $250 | $250 | $250 | $250 |
| Cost of goods sold | 154 | 133 | 131 | 142 |
| Gross margin | $ 96 | $117 | $119 | $108 |

*Required:*

a. Assume that the bookkeeper neglected to label the results. You have learned that the methods considered were FIFO, LIFO, weighted-average cost, and specific identification. *Without* making computations, can you match any of the bookkeeper's results with the inventory methods considered?

b. Calculate the cost of goods sold under each of the methods and match all of the bookkeeper's results with the inventory procedures analyzed.

c. "Specific identification is the only way to go. Why introduce arbitrary inventory flow assumptions when the actual facts are evident." Do you agree with this statement? Explain.

d. If Nakoma Company asked you to recommend just *one* inventory costing procedure, which would you suggest to them and why?

**8–3.** The books of the Whitney Corporation are closed monthly. The purchases and sales for the firm's first two months of operations are given below:

| | | Purchases | | |
|---|---|---|---|---|
| | | | Cost | |
| Date | | Units | per Unit | Units Sold |
| Jan. 1 | ................ | 12,000 | $ 7 | |
| 7 | ................ | | | 4,000 |
| 12 | ................ | 18,000 | 8 | |
| 15 | ................ | | | 11,000 |
| 21 | ................ | | | 9,000 |
| 23 | ................ | 7,000 | 9 | |
| 31 | ................ | | | 5,000 |
| Feb. 6 | ................ | 6,000 | 10 | |
| 11 | ................ | | | 3,000 |
| 16 | ................ | 10,000 | 12 | |
| 19 | ................ | | | 15,000 |
| 28 | ................ | 2,000 | 13 | |

*Required:*

a. Calculate the inventory as of January 31, and the January cost of goods sold using (1) FIFO, (2) LIFO, and (3) weighted-average cost. Use periodic inventory methods.

b. Assuming that the same method is used during both months, compute cost of goods sold for the month of *February* using (1) FIFO and (2) LIFO. Use periodic inventory methods.

c. In light of the price trends during each month, do your results in (a) and (b) seem consistent with each other? Explain.

d. Assume that the number of units sold on February 19 was 21,000 instead of 15,000. Does this change affect your answer to (b)? Your answer to (c)? Explain.

**8–4.** The following information is taken from the accounts and other records of Odana Department Store, Inc.:

| | Cost | Retail |
|---|---|---|
| Beginning inventory ..................... | $ 20,000 | $ 32,000 |
| Purchases ........................... | 175,000 | 275,000 |
| Freight-in ........................... | 8,000 | |
| Purchase returns ..................... | 3,000 | 5,000 |
| Sales ............................... | | 260,000 |
| Sales returns ........................ | | 14,000 |

*Required:*

a. Use the retail inventory method to compute an ending inventory figure which approximates average cost.

*b.* Discuss carefully the assumptions inherent in any use of the retail inventory method and their validity.

*c.* How would you approximate a FIFO inventory cost?

**8–5.** *The New York Times* on February 25, 1981, carried a major article which addressed "The Question of LIFO vs. FIFO." Among the facts and opinions contained in the article were the following:

1. A U.S. Commerce Department estimate that only about one third of all manufacturing inventories are accounted for on LIFO.
2. The viewpoint of Reginald Jones, Chairman of General Electric Company, that the continuing penchant for FIFO is "the most damning piece of evidence that can be marshaled by the critics of American management."
3. The viewpoint of management author Peter Drucker that not employing LIFO is "slothful and irresponsible."
4. An estimate that Minnesota Mining & Manufacturing Co. (3M) paid $118 million extra in taxes during 1974–1978 because it remained on FIFO rather than switch to LIFO. The firm labeled the estimate "much too high."
5. A statement from Minnesota Mining's treasurer explaining his firm's affection for FIFO. He said, "We feel our management knows how to run the business on a FIFO basis, is comfortable with it, and changing could be disruptive."

*Required:*

*a.* Under what circumstances, if any, could the decision to remain with FIFO reflect well on the quality of management?

*b.* Explain the basis for the criticism leveled by Reginald Jones and Peter Drucker. Is the criticism deserved by firms that remain on FIFO?

*c.* Assume that you are a banker who has lent capital to 3M. Would the rationale for using FIFO seem to you to justify the extra taxes? Would your viewpoint change if you were a stockholder of 3M? Explain.

**8–6.** Hershey Foods Corporation, a major producer of chocolate and confectionery products, also operates a chain of restaurants and is a producer of pasta products. Safeway Stores operates more than 2,000 food supermarkets in the United States and in many foreign countries. Excerpts from their 1982 annual reports follow:

> **Hershey Foods Corporation.** "Substantially all of the Chocolate and Confectionery segment inventories are valued under the last-in, first-out (LIFO) method. . . . The remaining inventories are principally stated at the lower of first-in, first out (FIFO) cost or market."
>
> **Safeway Stores.** "Approximately 60% of consolidated merchandise inventories are valued on a last-in, first-out (LIFO) basis. Inventories not valued on a LIFO basis are valued at the lower of cost on a first-in, first-out (FIFO) basis or replacement market. Inventories on a FIFO basis include meat and produce in the U.S. and all Canadian and overseas inventories."

*Required:*

*a.* "Safeway had to make an exception for its meat and produce inventories. Valuing those items on a last-in, first-out basis would have led to an incredible amount of spoilage." Do you agree with this statement?

*b.* Why do you believe Safeway excluded meat and produce inventories?

*c.* What line of reasoning might have led Hershey Foods to conclude that its restaurant and pasta products inventories should be valued under FIFO rather than under the LIFO procedure used for chocolate and confectionery inventories?

d. "At least Hershey and Safeway value some of their inventories using FIFO. That inventory costing procedure aids in producing financial statements that are more representationally faithful for these food-related companies." Evaluate this statement.

**8–7.** The 1981 annual reports of Mead Corporation and Koppers Company included footnotes in which those firms explained the attractiveness of the LIFO inventory procedure which they had adopted. Relevant portions of those footnotes follow:

> **Mead Corporation.** "The LIFO method of valuing inventories results in a better matching of costs and revenues in periods of inflation than the FIFO method."
>
> **Koppers Company.** "LIFO accounting recognizes the current costs of labor and materials in the cost of sales (on the income statement) and thereby prevents the overstatement of earnings. . . . (The) Company uses LIFO accounting for substantially all domestic inventories, thus eliminating illusory inventory profits."

*Required:*

a. Do you agree with Mead Corporation that LIFO "results in a better matching of costs and revenues in periods of inflation"?

b. In light of your answer in *(a)*, is Koppers Company justified in stating that LIFO "prevents the overstatement of earnings"?

c. Would LIFO do an equally good or poor job of matching and income measurement during a period of *deflation?*

d. What are inventory profits? Are they illusory profits? Is Koppers correct in asserting that its use of LIFO eliminates such profits?

**8–8.** Among the firms using LIFO for inventory costing in the early 1980s were U.S. Steel and International Harvester. Excerpts from the 1982 annual report of U.S. Steel and IH's 1981 report follow:

> **U.S. Steel.** "Cost of sales has been reduced and total income from all operations increased by $621 million in 1982, $106 million in 1981, and $179 million in 1980 from the liquidations of LIFO inventories."
>
> **International Harvester.** "During 1981 and 1980, inventory quantities were reduced. As a result, 1981 and 1980 cost of sales include charges for goods carried at prior years' LIFO values which are less than current replacement costs; the effect was to reduce the 1981 and 1980 losses from continuing operations by $83.6 million ($2.60 per share) and by $7.5 million ($.24 per share), respectively."

*Required:*

a. Explain in your own words how the liquidation of LIFO inventories improves the income performance of a company.

b. Does the liquidation of LIFO inventories increase income even during periods of rising prices?

c. Were the firms' tax situations favorably or unfavorably affected by the inventory liquidations?

d. Are the above disclosures of the effect on income/loss necessary before the financial statement reader can truly interpret operating performance?

e. "The LIFO method has served U.S. Steel and International Harvester well in the early 1980s. An accounting procedure which automatically raises income or lowers losses during periods of declining sales offers an easy and convenient way of smoothing earnings." Explain what the author of this statement probably meant and indicate whether you agree with such a viewpoint.

8–9. Nina Company began operations on January 1, 1985. During its first month of operations, the firm purchased 3,000 units of merchandise at $18 each on January 2 and 1,500 units at $20 each on January 23. Operating results for the month were as follows:

| | |
|---|---:|
| Sales revenue ($30 per unit) | $60,000 |
| Less: Cost of goods sold | 39,000 |
| Gross margin | 21,000 |
| Less: Operating expenses | 18,000 |
| Net income | $ 3,000 |

The president of Nina was disturbed by the operating results because "our profits should have been at least twice the amount reported."

*Required:*

a. Which inventory method has the firm followed? Show calculations.

b. Could the company's choice of an inventory method have been motivated by income tax considerations?

c. Could Nina Company's profits for January actually have been "at least twice the amount reported"? Explain.

d. "It's incredible that firms such as Nina choose *not* to follow the weighted-average cost method. That procedure is ideal as it produces a fairly realistic income statement *and* balance sheet." Evaluate this statement.

8–10. Mayflower Company is considering the adoption of the LIFO inventory method as a way of cutting taxes. Below are the purchases and sales by quarter for 1984 and 1985.

| | Purchases | | |
|---|---|---|---|
| Period | Units | Cost per Unit | Units Sold |
| Beginning inventory, 1/1/84 | 4,000 | $5.00 | |
| 1984 quarter: | | | |
| 1 | 3,000 | 5.50 | 4,000 |
| 2 | 2,000 | 5.80 | 3,000 |
| 3 | 1,000 | 5.90 | 2,000 |
| 4 | 2,000 | 6.00 | 2,000 |
| 1985 quarter: | | | |
| 1 | 3,000 | 6.20 | 1,000 |
| 2 | 2,000 | 6.50 | 2,000 |
| 3 | 4,000 | 6.60 | 2,000 |
| 4 | 2,000 | 6.80 | 3,000 |

*Required:*

a. Determine cost of goods sold and ending inventory for the years 1984 and 1985 assuming the company uses (1) FIFO and (2) LIFO, applied on an annual basis.

    *b.*  If the corporate income tax rate is 46 percent, how much tax "savings" would Mayflower Company receive from the use of LIFO?

    *c.*  Compute cost of goods sold for 1984 and 1985 at current cost (defined as the current purchase price during the quarter the items were sold). How much price gain or loss (holding gain or loss) is included in income each year under FIFO? under LIFO?

    *d.*  Verify in detail the price (holding) gain for FIFO in 1984 that you calculated in *(c)*. Did LIFO completely eliminate the price gains in 1984 and 1985?

**8–11.**  Assume that the following letter from a company's president appeared in an annual report to stockholders:

> The inventory policy of your company has been very sound. By using the LIFO inventory costing procedure for income tax purposes, this firm is assured that it will save taxes each and every year. As you are aware, under LIFO the last goods purchased are assumed to remain in the ending inventory. We have voluntarily made the decision to use the LIFO method also on the financial statements included in this annual report. We are certain that LIFO helps us prepare for you both an excellent income statement and an excellent balance sheet.

List in numerical order and describe *all* the misconceptions which are evidenced by the above quotation.

**8–12.**  Tonka Corporation and Hasbro Industries are two well-known toy manufacturers. The following figures have been taken from their 1981 annual reports to stockholders (all amounts in thousands of dollars).

| | Hasbro Industries | Tonka Corporation |
|---|---|---|
| Sales | $104,226 | $105,162 |
| Cost of goods sold | 53,553 | 66,068 |
| Net income | 4,408 | 6,735 |
| Inventory: | | |
|   January 2, 1982 | | 13,872† |
|   December 27, 1981 | 6,901* | |
|   January 3, 1981 | | 12,736† |
|   December 28, 1980 | 6,349* | |

    \* Stated at the lower of FIFO cost or market.

    † Primarily stated at the lower of LIFO cost or market. Inventories are lower by $3,827,000 at January 2, 1982, and $3,109,000 at January 3, 1981, than such inventories determined by the FIFO method.

*Required:*

    *a.*  What would cost of goods sold and net income have been in 1981 for Tonka if it had valued its inventories at FIFO cost? Assume a 46 percent income tax rate.

    *b.*  Analysts often look at relationships between various financial statement amounts and compare them across companies, especially when the firms are in the same industry and of approximately equal size. Calculate each of the following relationships or ratios for Hasbro, for Tonka under LIFO, and for Tonka under FIFO.

       1.  Cost of goods sold as a percentage of sales.

       2.  Net income as a percentage of sales.

       3.  Inventory turnover (cost of goods sold divided by average inventory).

Does the use of different inventory methods materially distort a comparison of these relationships for Hasbro and Tonka? Explain.

c. Why do two firms in the same industry use different inventory methods? Is the use of different methods justified by underlying differences in economic circumstances? Should all firms within the same industry be required to follow the same accounting procedures?

**8A-1.** You are the chief accountant for Washington Corporation. Your assistant has gathered information about items in the ending inventory. You are to determine the proper dollar amount for each item and the total ending inventory in accordance with the lower-of-cost-or-market procedure, as interpreted by the American Institute of Certified Public Accountants.

| Item | Units | Original Cost | Replacement Cost | Estimated Selling Price | Estimated Cost to Sell | Normal Profit |
|------|-------|---------------|------------------|-------------------------|------------------------|---------------|
| A | 40 | $10.20 | $ 9.90 | $12.60 | $2.00 | $2.10 |
| B | 480 | 0.95 | 1.10 | 1.35 | 0.15 | 0.25 |
| C | 190 | 7.00 | 6.00 | 8.00 | 0.65 | 1.15 |
| D | 1,100 | 4.50 | 4.40 | 4.60 | 0.40 | 0.35 |
| E | 300 | 7.60 | 7.50 | 9.50 | 0.80 | 1.60 |
| F | 450 | 5.90 | 5.50 | 7.00 | 0.50 | 0.70 |
| G | 200 | 23.80 | 23.50 | 28.00 | 2.35 | 1.80 |

**8A-2.** Johnson Corporation uses the average cost method to assign dollar amounts to cost of goods sold and to ending inventory. Its income statement for 1985 appears below:

| | | |
|---|---:|---:|
| Sales (300,000 units at $1) | | $300,000 |
| Cost of goods sold: | | |
| Beginning inventory | $ 28,500 | |
| Purchases | 143,750 | |
| Goods available for sale (325,000 units at $0.53) | 172,250 | |
| Ending inventory (25,000 units at $0.53) | 13,250 | |
| Cost of goods sold (300,000 at $0.53) | | 159,000 |
| Gross margin | | 141,000 |
| Selling expenses (300,000 at $0.20) | | 60,000 |
| Net income (27% of sales revenue) | | $ 81,000 |

*Required:*

For each situation described below, analyze the effect of lower of cost or market. Include in your analysis a calculation of the dollar impact on net income in 1985 *and* in 1986 if (1) market is defined as replacement cost or (2) if market is defined as net realizable value. Discuss the reasonableness of using each of these two definitions in the particular situation. Indicate how the AICPA rule would apply to each situation and why.

a. On December 31, 1985, the replacement cost of a unit of inventory is $0.44 and the selling price is only $0.85. Selling expenses will increase from $0.20 to $0.25 per unit.

b. On December 31, 1985, the replacement cost of a unit of inventory is $0.52 and the selling price is only $0.71. Selling expense remains at $0.20 per unit.

# CHAPTER 9

# ACCOUNTING FOR NONCURRENT ASSETS

Accountants typically classify noncurrent assets into four major groupings—long-term investments, plant assets (property, plant, and equipment), natural resources, and intangibles. Chapter 7 sets forth the basic determinants of the cost of these various long-lived assets. This chapter shows how these costs are treated during the accounting periods following their incurrence.

We will focus on the last three groups. Plant assets, natural resources, and long-term intangibles all have a limited period of usefulness. In this chapter we study (1) methods of allocating their acquisition costs among accounting periods to reflect the use of the assets, (2) entries made upon disposition of plant assets, and (3) the treatment of expenditures made after acquisition for the purposes of repairing, partially replacing, or improving plant assets.

**DEPRECIATION, DEPLETION, AND AMORTIZATION**

Depreciation, depletion, and amortization in many respects can be discussed together, for they relate to the same accounting process. Each term refers to the estimated cost of the services of a long-lived asset consumed during the period. Every productive resource acquired represents a bundle of service potential to be realized over time. We learned in Chapter 1 that the matching concept is one of the basic assumptions underlying income measurement in financial accounting. With regard to long-lived productive resources, the matching concept dictates that a portion of their costs be allocated to each accounting period in which the asset services are consumed.

"Depreciation" is the name given to the process of rationally and systematically allocating the cost of plant assets over their useful service lives. "Depletion" and "amortization" are the names given to the cost-allocation processes for natural resources (wasting assets) and intangibles, respectively.[1] Limited-life noncurrent assets contribute to the generation of revenues in each and every accounting period in which they are used. Accordingly, part of their costs should be matched against (deducted from) revenues for all of those accounting periods as part of the measure of firm effort.

It is important to emphasize that depreciation refers only to a process of cost allocation. It is *not* a process of asset valuation. People often do refer to the decline in the market value of an asset as depreciation, e.g., a new car "depreciated" by $500 after it was driven a week. However, that is not the context in which accountants use the term. They adhere to the cost concept and do not normally reflect the market value of a firm's resources on the books. In financial statements, depreciation refers to cost allocation.

Depreciation also is not a process that generates funds for replacement of a particular asset. By matching depreciation expense against revenues, we attempt to recover the original monetary investments in noncurrent assets made in the past. If revenues are sufficient to cover all expenses, dollar capital will be recovered. Nonetheless, revenues, not depreciation, are the source of the asset inflow. Furthermore, the depreciation process is not contingent on whether past investment is recovered or whether any of the recovered capital is used for replacement.

## Depreciation Base

The depreciation base (depletion base, amortization base) is the asset cost to be allocated to the various periods in which the asset provides service. In most cases, it is defined as follows:

Depreciation Base = Acquisition Cost − Net Residual Value
Cost of Using Asset = Original Investment − Portion of Cost Recovered at
to Be Recovered End of Asset's Useful Life

Net residual value is the estimated disposal value at the end of the asset's useful life, less estimated costs of removal. For natural resources, such as oil wells or mines, the net residual value consists of the estimated value of the remaining land. For some assets a substantial amount is recovered when the asset is retired, either because the asset can supply use value to a new owner as in the case of trucks, aircraft, or office equipment or because salvage value is large as in the case of copper, aluminum, steel, or other bulk metals recovered. In other cases the assumption is frequently made that scrap value will be offset by the removal costs, so that estimated

---

[1] "Amortization" is also used as a general term in accounting to describe the periodic allocation of any cost.

net residual value is zero; the acquisition cost then becomes the deprecia-tion base.[2]

**Major Problems in Determining Depreciation**

In establishing a procedure for allocating the cost of noncurrent assets, accountants encounter two problems. They must first estimate the useful service life of the asset and then devise a systematic and rational way to spread the depreciation base over this service life.

The useful life of the asset is its period of service to the particular business entity, not necessarily its total conceivable life. Our entity concept restricts the determination of useful life to that economically justified period of service relevant to the business entity. Even so, two types of factors affecting an asset's useful life have to be considered:

1.  Physical limitations on life:
    *a.* Intensity of use (wear and tear).
    *b.* Action of elements (decay and deterioration).
    *c.* Adequacy of maintenance.
    *d.* Simple passage of time, as with legal rights protected by law for a limited period.
2.  Economic limitations on life:
    *a.* Technological development or shifts in demand for the product rendering the asset obsolete.
    *b.* Business growth or expansion for which the asset is inadequate.

The useful life of a particular asset is governed by the shortest life derived from a consideration of these factors. Each asset may be affected differently. For a natural resource, useful life is probably most often determined by intensity of use. However, situations calling for alternative treatment can readily be imagined. For example, the useful life of a mine may be determined by obsolescence (it becomes uneconomical to continue operations) rather than by physical exhaustion. In contrast, the life of a building is primarily determined by action of the elements, although in some cases obsolescence or inadequacy may be relevant. The legal life of a patent is 17 years, although economically its service potential may be exhausted much earlier because of technological change.

The point is that a determination of useful life requires a careful consideration of a number of factors. Firms review their own records of property retirements and consult the experience of others in the industry. Even then, establishing an accurate useful life is still a difficult task.

The second problem then arises. How should the cost of using the asset be allocated to the accounting periods contained in its useful life? Should each accounting period receive the same dollar charge, or should

---

[2] Under certain regulations, salvage value up to 10 percent of the cost of an asset may be ignored in computations of the depreciation base for income tax purposes. Moreover, under the accelerated cost recovery system (ACRS) enacted in the Economic Tax Recovery Act of 1981, residual value is completely ignored.

depreciation, depletion, or amortization cost be greater in some periods than in others? *The overriding consideration in selecting a depreciation method for financial accounting purposes is that it should result in a pattern of cost allocation that reasonably reflects the expiration pattern of the related services.* Because the pattern of service consumption in the various periods may be impossible to determine precisely, accountants approximate the expected pattern through the adoption of simplified formulas or depreciation methods.

## Depreciation Methods

Depreciation methods provide a rational way of systematically spreading the depreciation base over the life of an asset. There are four methods commonly encountered. These methods account for almost all of the depreciation policies used in accounting practice and can be classified by the type of periodic charge that results from their adoption:

1. Uniform charge per period—straight-line method.
2. Decreasing charge per period:
   a. Sum-of-the-years'-digits method.
   b. Declining-balance method.
3. Varying charge per period—activity method.

The term *depreciation methods* is used here in a general sense, inasmuch as the methods described are appropriate for various noncurrent assets. They are most often mentioned in connection with plant assets, but our discussion applies to wasting assets and intangibles as well. Let us use the following situation to illustrate and compare the various depreciation methods. Assume that a machine has a total acquisition cost of $13,000 and an expected residual value of $1,000 at the end of a useful life of five years.

**Straight-Line Method.** This method is the easiest to understand and compute. The depreciation base is spread evenly over the number of accounting periods in the asset's useful life. Each accounting period receives the same dollar charge for asset services consumed. The annual depreciation charge would be determined by the formula:

$$\frac{\text{Cost} - \text{Residual Value}}{\text{Useful Life}} = \frac{\$13,000 - \$1,000}{5} = \$2,400$$

Table 9–1 summarizes the changes in the accounts.

The undepreciated cost at the end of each year is commonly called *book value* and is determined by subtraction of the Accumulated Depreciation (Allowance for Depreciation) account from the original cost recorded in the Machinery account. It represents the cost of that portion of the asset's services which has not been used and charged to operations. At the end of the fifth year the asset's book value appears at $1,000, its expected residual value.

The straight-line method is widely used because of its simplicity in

**TABLE 9–1  Depreciation under Straight-Line Method**

| Year | Annual Depreciation Cost* | Year-End Balance in Accumulated Depreciation Account | Year-End Undepreciated Cost or Book Value |
|---|---|---|---|
| 0 ...... | — | — | $13,000 |
| 1 ...... | $2,400 | $ 2,400 | 10,600 |
| 2 ...... | 2,400 | 4,800 | 8,200 |
| 3 ...... | 2,400 | 7,200 | 5,800 |
| 4 ...... | 2,400 | 9,600 | 3,400 |
| 5 ...... | 2,400 | 12,000 | 1,000 |

* The depreciation *rate* can be expressed as 20 percent of the depreciation base or as 18.46 percent of cost.

concept and calculation. As a method of approximating the cost of using an asset's services, however, it implies a number of limiting assumptions. It presupposes that the services of the asset are consumed uniformly over its useful life. In addition, there should be no impairment in the efficiency or quality of the service received from the asset as it becomes older. These assumptions may not hold for many types of machinery and equipment. Conceptually, the straight-line method is most accurate when passage of time is the most important element governing the expiration of the asset's service. It could be used when the asset supplies a service capacity for a limited period of time and the availability of the service is more important than the actual extent of its use.

**Decreasing-Charge Methods.**  Two generally accepted methods result in a decreasing depreciation charge over the life of an asset. One method—sum-of-the-years' digits (SYD)—achieves a decreasing charge by applying a decreasing rate to a constant depreciation base. The other method—declining balance—applies a constant depreciation rate to a decreasing depreciation base. These two mathematical procedures have little justification in and of themselves, except that they are accepted, systematic ways of obtaining a decreasing charge.

The general rationale for a decreasing depreciation charge is that many assets contribute more service in the earlier years of their life than in the later years. Three situations might theoretically fall under this rationale.

1. An asset may become less actively used, so that the quantity of service received from it each period declines. Example—as a machine gets older, it is used less and less for mainline production and more and more for peak needs only.

2. An asset may become increasingly inefficient, so that the quality of services each period is less. Example—a precision drill press as it becomes older has difficulty maintaining its tolerances, thereby creating more rejects and causing more rework.

3.  An increasing risk of obsolescence may reduce the probability that services in the later years of an asset's life will even reach fruition. Example—as an office building ages, the initial level of rentals becomes increasingly difficult to maintain, either because renters leave for newer buildings or because management must offer rental discounts to maintain full occupancy.

The effect of any one or a combination of these factors is that the contribution to operations and ultimately to the production of revenues lessens as many assets grow older. Inasmuch as depreciation attempts to measure the consumption of asset services, in these cases we ought to charge more depreciation in the earlier years of life.

Still another reason given for the use of *accelerated depreciation methods* is to compensate for increasing repair and maintenance costs over the life of a plant asset. The *total cost* of an asset's service is viewed as consisting of the depreciation base *plus* the other costs of the asset. If the amount of service received each period is the same, the total cost should be relatively constant. However, the depreciation portion should decline as the repair and maintenance portion rises.

**Sum-of-the-Years' Digits.**  This method starts by summing the digits in the expected useful life ($N$) of the asset.[3] If the expected service life is five years, the sum is 15 ($5 + 4 + 3 + 2 + 1$). The depreciation base of the asset is viewed as representing a number of service units adding up to this sum (SYD). These service units are assumed to expire in an order determined by the fractions $N/SYD$, $(N - 1)/SYD$, $(N - 2)/SYD$, ... $1/SYD$. Used in our example, this method gives the results summarized in Table 9–2. The depreciation base and the total depreciation charge over the asset's life both still equal $12,000 (cost less residual value), as with the straight-line method. However, through a decreasing depreciation rate each year, more cost has been systematically allocated to the earlier years of life.

TABLE 9–2  Depreciation under Sum-of-the-Years' Digits

| Year | Depreciation Rate | Annual Depreciation Cost | Year-End Balance in Accumulated Depreciation | Book Value |
|---|---|---|---|---|
| 0 | — | — | — | $13,000 |
| 1 | 5/15 | $4,000 | $ 4,000 | 9,000 |
| 2 | 4/15 | 3,200 | 7,200 | 5,800 |
| 3 | 3/15 | 2,400 | 9,600 | 3,400 |
| 4 | 2/15 | 1,600 | 11,200 | 1,800 |
| 5 | 1/15 | 800 | 12,000 | 1,000 |

---

[3] A general shortcut in computing this sum for any asset is expressed by the formula:

$$SYD = N(N + 1)/2$$

**Declining Balance.** With this method we apply a uniform depreciation rate each year to a decreasing base. The depreciation base employed is *book value* (cost less accumulated depreciation). Notice that this base does not consider residual value. Even though an asset cannot be depreciated below a reasonable residual value, declining-balance methods would seem inappropriate for assets having large expected residual values. The two most common depreciation rates used with this method are 200 percent and 150 percent of the straight-line rate. These rates initially corresponded to those allowed in the income tax laws for various classes of property, and their extension into financial accounting was inevitable. For our example, the straight-line rate is 20 percent (five-year life). Double-declining balance (DDB) would call for a rate of 40 percent for this asset; 150 percent declining balance would use a rate of 30 percent. These rates give the results shown in Table 9–3 (amounts are rounded to the nearest dollar). Neither declining-balance method will reduce the net asset precisely to expected residual value.[4] For tax purposes, a firm may switch from the declining-balance method to the straight-line procedure at any time. In financial reporting as well, companies often do this to ensure that the asset is depreciated to residual value.

**TABLE 9–3 Depreciation under Declining-Balance Methods**

| | Double-Declining Balance | | | 150 Percent Declining Balance | | |
|---|---|---|---|---|---|---|
| Year | Depreciation Base or Book Value | Depreciation Rate | Annual Depreciation Cost | Depreciation Base or Book Value | Depreciation Rate | Annual Depreciation Cost |
| 1 ..... | $13,000 | 40% | $ 5,200 | $13,000 | 30% | $ 3,900 |
| 2 ..... | 7,800 | 40 | 3,120 | 9,100 | 30 | 2,730 |
| 3 ..... | 4,680 | 40 | 1,872 | 6,370 | 30 | 1,911 |
| 4 ..... | 2,808 | 40 | 1,123 | 4,459 | 30 | 1,338 |
| 5 ..... | 1,685 | 40 | 674 | 3,121 | 30 | 936 |
| | | | $11,989 | | | $10,815 |

**Activity Method.** This expedient takes a somewhat different approach. Instead of viewing depreciation initially as an allocation of cost to *time* periods, the activity method relates the cost first directly to some unit of asset service and then to periods of time. The asset's useful life is expressed in terms of *service units*, and the depreciation rate is expressed in dollars per service unit. Then the depreciation charge *per period* fluctuates

---

[4] A formula is available which will give a declining-balance depreciation rate which takes salvage into consideration and reduces the asset to salvage at the end of its life. The formula for the rate, $R$, is:

$$R = 1 - \sqrt[N]{S/C}$$

where $N$ is useful life, $C$ is acquisition cost, and $S$ is net salvage. This method is rarely used in practice; the rate used in most cases is 200 percent or 150 percent of the straight-line rate.

with the activity of the asset. Service units can be expressed in any number of ways—hours, units of production, units of output, and so on. Hence, this method also is labeled the working-hours method, the production method, the output method, and so forth, all of which share the same general objective of allocating cost in relation to asset activity.

Take the machine which costs $13,000. Assume that during its useful life it is expected to run 30,000 hours. The depreciation rate would be:

$$\frac{\text{Cost} - \text{Residual Value}}{\text{Expected Activity}} = \frac{\$13,000 - \$1,000}{30,000 \text{ Hours}} = \$0.40 \text{ per Hour}$$

Here the useful life is viewed as 30,000 service hours rather than five years. If the pattern of activity shown in Table 9–4 transpires, the relevant depreciation charge for each of the five years will be as indicated in that table. As with declining-balance methods, an adjustment to the final year's depreciation charge is often made to reduce the book value to residual value when the estimate of total service units turns out to have been slightly inaccurate.

**TABLE 9–4  Depreciation under Activity Method**

| Year | Hours Worked | Depreciation Rate | Annual Depreciation Cost | Book Value |
|------|--------------|-------------------|--------------------------|------------|
| 0 ...... | — | — | — | $13,000 |
| 1 ...... | 8,000 | $0.40/hour | $ 3,200 | 9,800 |
| 2 ...... | 5,600 | 0.40/hour | 2,240 | 7,560 |
| 3 ...... | 6,700 | 0.40/hour | 2,680 | 4,880 |
| 4 ...... | 5,200 | 0.40/hour | 2,080 | 2,800 |
| 5 ...... | 4,500 | 0.40/hour | 1,800 | 1,000 |
|  | 30,000 |  | $12,000 |  |

Although not used as widely as the other methods, the activity method seems particularly appropriate when physical use is the most important determinant of the expiration of asset services. For example, airplane engines are commonly depreciated on a flying-hour basis, and the lives of blast furnace linings are sometimes measured in terms of tons of metal produced. The cost of automobiles, trucks, or taxicabs can be allocated in relation to miles traveled during each period. Certain types of machinery—tools, dies, jigs, and patterns—for which intensity of use is a major factor also lend themselves quite readily to this expedient. The method probably has wider applicability than is currently recognized.

The major problems associated with it tend to be practical ones—difficulty in estimating life in service units and the extra effort involved in keeping track of the actual activity in each period. In addition, the activity method does not take into consideration declines in efficiency, although theoretically they could be compensated for through a declining rate per service unit. In addition, if exclusive reliance is placed on service units when useful life is established, the economic factors of inadequacy and obsolescence may be ignored. However, if these other economic factors are used to establish an asset's life, then the activity method seems to give a very reasonable allocation of the depreciation base to the various accounting periods *within that life*.

## Depletion

The activity method is most widely used in the recording of depletion costs of natural resources. The cost allocation of a wasting asset bears a definite relationship to its physical exhaustion. To see how depletion works, assume that the total cost of acquiring and developing (exploration, drilling, etc.) a natural gas well is $6.8 million. Geologists estimate that the well contains 200 million cubic feet of natural gas that can be economically withdrawn. The residual value of the land is expected to be $800,000. The depletion rate would be $0.03 per cubic foot:

$$\frac{\text{Cost} - \text{Residual Value}}{\text{Estimated Production}} = \frac{\$6,800,000 - \$800,000}{200,000,000 \text{ Cubic Feet}} = \$0.03 \text{ per Cubic Foot}$$

Each year the depletion cost would vary with the amount of gas pumped. If during the first year, for instance, three million cubic feet were pumped out, the entry to record depletion would be:

| | | |
|---|---|---|
| Depletion Cost . . . . . . . . . . . . . . . . . . . . . . . . . . . . . . . . . . . . . . . . . . . | 90,000 | |
| Accumulated Depletion—Gas Well (3,000,000 × $0.03) | | 90,000 |

Depletion cost is an inventoriable cost. It represents the "material" portion of the gas pumped. Depletion costs plus labor and other direct costs become the total cost of the inventory of unsold gas. To the extent that the pumped gas is sold during the period, depletion cost is reflected on the income statement as an expense.

Two questions can be raised concerning the above practice of calculating depreciation. First, the implication that each unit of output should have the same depletion cost may not be realistic if differing qualities of output may be recovered (e.g., high and low grades of ore) or if some units are easier and less costly to mine (e.g., ore in veins close to the surface). The second difficulty is the practical one of estimating the recoverable units contained in a natural resource. The original estimates are subject to great geological uncertainties, and the quantity of economically feasible production is a function of both future market conditions and technological changes. As a result, revisions in future estimated production ("recoverable reserves") and thus in the depletion rate are made periodically as additional knowledge becomes available.

## Amortization of Intangibles

Patents, copyrights, trademarks, franchises, and goodwill are typical of the many types of intangible assets that appear on the balance sheet. Many of the intangibles (goodwill being the major exception) represent specifically identifiable rights and privileges. The cost of intangible assets, whether acquired singly or in groups or developed internally, should be spread as expense over their estimated period of benefit.[5]

Estimating the period of benefit or useful life for these intangible assets often is a very difficult task. Some intangibles appear to have an unlimited term of existence and life (e.g., trade names, subscription lists, perpetual franchises, and organization costs). Others provide service benefits only during a useful life limited by legislation, regulation, or contract. Examples include patents, copyrights, licenses, and payments for a limited franchise. Even when the intangible appears to have a perpetual life or a specifically limited finite life, economic competition and obsolescence may introduce considerable fluctuations and uncertainty into the estimate. The result is that the lives of many intangibles are simply *indeterminate*.

Given this perplexing situation, the Accounting Principles Board established some arbitrary regulations. Reasoning that the service potential of all intangibles eventually disappears, the APB ruled that the cost of *all* intangibles must be amortized over some estimate of useful life. The estimate might vary with the type of intangible, but in no case can the period be longer than 40 years.[6]

*APB Opinion No. 17* requires straight-line amortization unless a company can demonstrate that some other method is more appropriate. The future service potential for many intangibles is highly uncertain. This fact might imply a decreasing charge for amortization. Furthermore, the amount of revenue directly attributable to an asset (e.g., royalties derived from a patent) may not be constant from period to period. Unfortunately, the accounting profession has not defined in more precise terms what is meant by the future service potential of an asset. Does a patent contribute equal service each period because it provides the same legal protection, or does it contribute decreasing service each period because the sales of the patentable item decline over time? Until more definite guidelines are established, straight-line amortization probably will prevail, particularly since this is the only *tax* method allowed for intangibles.

**Goodwill.**  One particularly thorny intangible is "purchased goodwill." Frequently in merger or acquisition transactions the price paid by the acquiring firm for the identifiable net assets of the acquired firm exceeds their fair market value. This excess is usually debited to an intangible asset called "excess cost applicable to acquired companies" or simply "goodwill." The account that receives this charge for "purchased goodwill" has been aptly described as a "master valuation" account. It is the difference between the total value of a business entity, taken as a whole, and the sum of the fair market values of its tangible and identifiable

---

[5] As we noted in Chapter 7, *internal* expenditures to develop or maintain intangibles *lacking specific identification* must be treated as period expenses according to *APB Opinion No. 17*. Consequently, the rest of our discussion relates to specifically identifiable intangible assets and externally purchased goodwill.

[6] AICPA, *APB Opinion No. 17*, "Intangible Assets" (New York, August 1970), pars. 28 and 29.

intangible assets. It is the combined value placed on the sources of future earning power which cannot be separately traced. It may include the value of trade names, a general reputation, an established clientele, strategic locations, a favorable regulatory climate, or simply a particular group of employees with special skills, knowledge, or managerial ability. In any case, the acquiring firm invests in it in order to possess the income-producing power of the acquired firm.

Under *APB Opinion No. 17,* purchased goodwill must be amortized over a period not longer than 40 years, although historically this view did not always prevail. Goodwill more commonly was treated as a permanent asset, not subject to periodic amortization.[7] This practice was justified on the grounds that the intangible factors comprising goodwill either were not consumed or were replaced by subsequent expenditures charged as period expenses. Unless and until future earnings declined, the goodwill presumably still existed as an asset. In contrast, more recent arguments have stressed the notion of purchased goodwill as a payment for certain economic factors which provide a transferable momentum to the new business. The payment for goodwill is the cost of the excess earnings accruing to the new owner as a result of this momentum built up in a going concern. As these future earnings arise, for the *new* owner they are a *recovery of investment,* not income. Amortization of the purchased goodwill reflects the fact that the momentum which produced these earnings will not persist indefinitely.

## Choice of Depreciation Methods

Under generally accepted accounting principles, a firm is permitted to choose any one of the alternative methods. They are considered equally acceptable. Consequently, the same firm may choose different methods for different assets. More disturbing and difficult to justify is the use of different methods for the same asset by different firms.

In a recent survey of 600 large companies, the methods listed in Table 9–5 were being used with the indicated frequency for at least a portion of their assets.

**TABLE 9–5  Relative Use of Depreciation Methods**

| Method | Number of Companies Indicating Usage* |
|---|---|
| Straight line | 565 |
| Declining balance | 57 |
| Sum-of-the-years' digits | 25 |
| Accelerated method (unspecified) | 68 |
| Activity | 52 |

*Adds up to more than 600 because many sample companies used more than one method.
Source: AICPA, *Accounting Trends & Techniques,* (New York, 1982).

---

[7] Such treatment is consistent with the position of current income tax regulations, which do not allow amortization of goodwill as a deductible expense.

Tables 9–1 through 9–4 reveal that wide variations can occur in the amount of depreciation cost reported by a firm in any given year, depending on the method selected. Although a firm is free to choose any one of the four generally accepted methods, each one would seem to be particularly appropriate in certain circumstances. The idea behind the depreciation calculation is the matching concept. Therefore, the general principle is to select the depreciation method with a cost allocation pattern most closely corresponding to the pattern of service consumption provided by the asset. Implementation of this theoretical concept, however, requires that accountants do two things. First, they must decide what is meant by service potential; second, they must be able to predict the expected consumption pattern of that service potential.

Until the accounting profession can generate some definite guidelines for these conceptual issues, practicing accountants must look to a variety of factors in the determination of an appropriate depreciation policy. Among these are:

1.  Pattern and extent of asset usage.
2.  Nature and amount of the asset's contribution to periodic revenue recognition.
3.  Pattern of physical deterioration of the asset over time.
4.  Expected influence of obsolescence.
5.  Anticipated policy concerning repairs and maintenance and their expected timing and size of expenditure.
6.  Degree of uncertainty concerning the asset's expected economic life.

**Depreciation and Income Taxes.** Tax considerations were not included in the above list, because—as was not the case with inventory methods—companies may use different depreciation methods for financial reporting and tax reporting. Until 1981 most firms used one of the accelerated methods for income tax purposes, for greater depreciation expense meant lower taxable income and lower income taxes in the early years of an asset's life. Even though more taxes would have to be paid in the later years, when depreciation deductions for tax purposes would be less, the company had the use of the money in the interim. Normally one would prefer to pay taxes later rather than earlier because of the time value of money. Accelerated depreciation for tax purposes was a common means of accomplishing this objective. Fortunately, firms were free to select the proper depreciation method for the financial statements without being constrained by their attempts to minimize income taxes.

For tangible assets purchased in 1981 and later, a new method of tax depreciation is used—the accelerated cost recovery system (ACRS). All assets are assigned to classes with arbitrarily established lives (recovery periods) of 3, 5, 10, or 15 years. For example, all trucks are depreciated over a 3-year period, while buildings are depreciated over 15 years. These lives, of course, may bear little similarity to the lives that are and should be used for financial reporting.

Within each asset class, an accelerated depreciation charge is computed as a percentage of cost. Residual value is completely ignored. The percentage varies with asset category and with the year the asset was placed in service. However, the rates, which are mandatory for all taxpayers, tend to follow a 150 percent declining-balance method.

The ACRS hopefully will provide strong incentives to business leaders to invest in depreciable assets. At the same time, depreciation for tax purposes becomes greatly removed from the concept of depreciation for financial statement purposes.

## DISPOSITION OF NONCURRENT ASSETS

The second major problem to be discussed in this chapter arises when the business entity disposes of a noncurrent asset. Whether disposition occurs at or before the end of an asset's original useful life and whether it is carried out with or without the acquisition of a replacement, the basic elements of the retirement entry are handled in the same way. First, depreciation is recorded up to the date of retirement, so that all charges for the use of the asset are entered.[8] Then the old asset is retired by the closing of both the main account and the accumulated depreciation account. Because the asset, in essence, is reflected in two accounts, balances in both the asset and contra asset must be removed.

## Entries to Record Asset Retirement

The basic retirement process requires us to isolate the undepreciated cost of the asset plus other factors related to the determination of the total gain or loss on retirement. For example, any costs of removing or dismantling the asset increase the potential loss on retirement. Conversely, the amount of any scrap, reusable material, salvage value, or insurance proceeds (in the case of a casualty loss) represents a gain. The aggregate of all these factors is the net gain or loss.

Let us take the example in Table 9–2. Assume that at the end of the fourth year the machinery is retired. According to the depreciation schedule in Table 9–2, under sum-of-the-years' digits, $11,200 has been allocated to the four years in which the machine has been used. The entry to record the book value of $1,800 as part of the loss would be:

```
Loss on Retirement of Machinery . . . . . . . . . . . . . . . . . . . . . . .   1,800
Accumulated Depreciation—Machinery . . . . . . . . . . . . . . . . 11,200
    Machinery . . . . . . . . . . . . . . . . . . . . . . . . . . . . . . . . . . . . . . .         13,000
```

---

[8] Some firms use simplifying expedients for charging depreciation on units used only for part of a year. For example, a full year's depreciation will be recorded in the year of acquisition, but no depreciation will be taken in the year of retirement, regardless of the specific dates involved; or the opposite policy may be followed. Still another common procedure is the half-year convention, whereby all acquisitions and retirements are treated as if they occurred at midyear. For companies with large amounts of noncurrent assets and with frequent acquisitions and retirements, these expedients probably introduce no distortion. The ACRS tax tables automatically assume a half-year convention.

In addition, assume that the firm incurs $400 of wage costs for removal and sells the dismantled machinery for $700 cash. The following entries would be made:

| | | |
|---|---:|---:|
| Loss on Retirement of Machinery | 400 | |
|     Wages Payable | | 400 |
| | | |
| Cash | 700 | |
|     Loss on Retirement of Machinery | | 700 |

The loss account now has a balance of $1,500, which represents the net decrease in owners' equity associated with the disposition of the asset. If all information about the retirement is known at the same time, a single journal entry could be made.

Any loss or gain on the sale of machinery is reported on the income statement of the period in which it is recognized. The gain or loss may be caused by an event happening in that period. However, the amount of any gain or loss reported is partially a function of the particular depreciation method originally selected by the business. For example, satisfy yourself that the firm in the example above would have reported a $3,100 loss on the sale if the straight-line method had been used rather than sum-of-the-years' digits. Accordingly, one must be careful when interpreting any gains or losses reported on the disposal of plant assets. In particular, the amount of the gain or loss reported may provide little insight into the question of whether the firm should have sold the plant asset when it did.

If the asset retirement is accompanied by a replacement purchase, we must be careful not to interpret the loss as part of the cost of the new asset. Two distinct transactions are occurring. The fact that the old asset has been retired to make way for the new one does not increase the service potential of the replacement asset. The loss, whether it be large or small, still is a measure of an asset that has disappeared without the firm's receiving full benefit from it. It should not be deferred as an expense of future periods by being buried in the acquisition cost of the new asset.

## Exchanges and Trade-Ins

An area where the separation of asset retirement from asset acquisition is particularly difficult is the exchange or trade-in. Here, two explicit events are telescoped into one. There exist a simultaneous sale of an old asset and the purchase of a new one between the business entity and the same outside party. Under these circumstances, it is sometimes difficult to determine the real economic values exchanged in the individual transactions.

Assume that on January 1, 1984, a delivery truck is purchased for $8,000. The truck is to be depreciated by the straight-line method over a useful life of four years, and it is expected to have no residual value. On June 30, 1985, the company decides to trade in the truck toward the purchase of a new one with a *list price* of $13,200. The dealer will allow $5,400 for the old truck; the company has to pay the $7,800 difference in cash.

Before any entries for the exchange are made, we first would record a half-year's depreciation for the six months' use in 1985:

```
Depreciation Expense  ...............................  1,000
      Accumulated Depreciation—Delivery Truck  .........          1,000
```

Together with the $2,000 depreciation recorded for the year 1984, this entry brings the balance in the Accumulated Depreciation account to $3,000 and the carrying value of the truck to $5,000 ($8,000 − $3,000).

In theory the economic substance of the transactions—both the disposition of the old truck and the acquisition of the new one—should be based on current exchange values. The old truck is being sold at its present fair market value; likewise, the new truck is being bought for its cash purchase price. In exchange transactions, however, the trade-in allowance may be an unreliable indicator of the current value of the old truck. Similarly, the sticker price of the new truck may be an unreliable indicator of the acquisition cost of the new truck. Adjustments to the initial list price are common in business. When a simultaneous purchase and sale are tied together, as they are in an exchange, an overallowance on the trade-in can be employed to disguise a price reduction on the new asset.

Assume that the old truck has a current market value of $3,800. This estimate may be determined from activities in a secondhand market or from a study of independent opportunities for selling the old asset. The entry below would correctly reflect the disposal of the old asset and the acquisition of the new one.

```
Delivery Truck  .....................................  11,600
Accumulated Depreciation  ...........................   3,000
Loss on Retirement  .................................   1,200
      Delivery Truck  ...................................          8,000
      Cash ..........................................             7,800
```

If the old truck had been sold in a separate transaction, $3,800 would have been received and a loss of $1,200 (book value of $5,000 less $3,800) recorded. The simultaneous acquisition of another truck should not be allowed to becloud the basic transaction. Furthermore, the real cost of the new truck consists of the current values exchanged for it. In this case the company gives up $7,800 in cash plus an old truck worth $3,800.

The above entry and analysis derive from the exchange-price concept, one of the fundamental concepts of financial accounting. When assets are acquired in exchange for nonmonetary considerations, the transaction should be based on the fair market values implicit in the exchange. This general principle is affirmed in APB *Opinion No. 29.*[9] Generally in an exchange situation the *fair market value* of the old asset given up plus the cash paid measure the resources sacrificed for the acquisition of the new asset.

**Exchange of Similar Assets.** An exception to the general rule, however, is required under *APB Opinion No. 29* whenever the exchange

---

[9] AICPA, *APB Opinion No. 29*, "Accounting for Nonmonetary Transactions" (New York, May 1973), par. 18.

involves "similar" assets and would result in a gain being recorded.[10] Suppose that in our example the current market value of the old truck was $5,200. Adherence to the exchange-price concept would have resulted in a gain on disposition of $200 ($5,200 less $5,000 book value) and a cost of the new truck of $13,000 ($7,800 + $5,200). Because the exchange involved similar assets, however, the following entry would be required:

| | | |
|---|---|---|
| Delivery Truck | 12,800 | |
| Accumulated Depreciation | 3,000 | |
|     Delivery Truck | | 8,000 |
|     Cash | | 7,800 |

No gain on the disposition of the old truck is recognized, and the cost of the new truck is the cash paid plus the *book value* of the trade-in.

If the truck had been exchanged for a *dissimilar* asset, say a piece of land, fair market values would be used, and gains or losses would be recognized. If one truck were exchanged for another similar truck and a *loss* resulted, as in our first example, fair market values would be employed. However, when the trade-in of a *similar* asset would result in a gain on disposition of the old asset, then the use of book values is required.[11]

This exception is rationalized on the grounds that an exchange of similar productive assets does not represent the culmination of an earning process, while an exchange of dissimilar assets does. Without this exception, two tool and die shops could swap drill presses and each record a gain for the difference between the carrying value and current market value. The APB reasoned that income should not increase simply from the substitution of one productive asset for a similar one. Earnings flow from the sale of goods and services which is made possible by the possession and of productive assets.

**OTHER ASSET MODIFI-CATIONS**

In Chapter 7 we introduced and illustrated the concept that all expenditures incurred to acquire a plant asset and put it into use are charged to the asset account. These expenditures are said to have been *capitalized*. The use of many plant assets requires that additional amounts be spent periodically after acquisition. Whether these postacquisition costs are capitalized depends on a number of theoretical and practical considerations.

Some of these expenditures simply keep the asset in good working condition but in no better condition than when it was purchased. These

---

[10] A similar asset is one that is the same general type, that performs the same function, or that is employed in the same line of business.

[11] This recording of an exchange using book values is known as the "income tax method." Its use is required for tax purposes for *all* exchanges of similar assets, whether a gain *or* a loss results. This approach fails to distinguish between the two separate transactions making up the exchange. Gains and losses on disposition become buried in the cost of the new asset. Clearly this approach should be acceptable for financial reporting only when neither the real cost of the new asset nor the current value of the old is determinable.

recurring maintenance and repair costs merely maintain the service initially expected from the asset. These costs are called *operating expenditures* (revenue expenditures). Costs of lubricating, cleaning, adjusting, and replacing worn-out or damaged small parts are operating expenditures. They are deemed to benefit only the current accounting period.

In contrast, other expenditures increase the quantity or quality of service through an addition to the asset, a partial replacement, or major overhaul, with new components being substituted for old ones. These expenditures are called *capital expenditures*. They benefit future periods, and accordingly the costs should be treated as assets. Nevertheless, they frequently do not represent the acquisition of any new physical item or the complete replacement of one asset by another, as we have seen in previous examples.

Different terms describe the modifications resulting from capital expenditures:

1. *Additions*—modifications that normally increase the physical size or capacity of the asset, such as an extension on a building or a labeling attachment connected to a bottle-filling machine.
2. *Improvements and betterments*—major modifications that increase the output of service, extend the useful life of the asset, or improve its economy of operation, such as substitution of concrete for wooden floors or the acquisition of a new gear system to increase the speed or efficiency of a machine.
3. *Renewals and replacements*—substitutions, often of a more or less recurring nature, of essential units and parts for similar existing units and parts, such as the relining of the inside of a chemical tank every three years or the intermittent overhaul of pumps and filter systems.

In accounting practice, these terms are often employed interchangeably. They appear to differ primarily in the magnitude of the amounts involved and the economic or physical importance of the modification.

The theoretical objectives of recording subsequent expenditures related to plant assets are fairly clear. Operating expenditures (i.e., costs incurred to maintain the original estimated service) should be charged against operations in the period incurred. Costs which modify the service by lengthening useful life, by increasing capacity or efficiency, by reducing the cost of operating, or by replacing long-term service potential which has expired are capital expenditures. They should be treated as an addition to the stock of assets. In theory any expenditure which benefits future accounting periods should be capitalized.

In practice there are limitations. Each nut or bolt, or minor part, cannot be set up as a separate asset. A company must adopt a policy specifying what costs are to be treated as capital expenditures and what ones as operating expenditures. One way of making the distinction is in terms of dollar amount. Any expenditure over a preestablished amount, say $1,000, will be capitalized. Expenditures less than that are treated as period operating costs. Alternatively, if the modification of an existing asset costs more than a certain percentage of the original cost, it will be treated as an asset replacement; otherwise, it is handled as a repair cost.

Instead of establishing dollar-amount classifications, many firms define capital expenditures in terms of physical units, called *units of property*. A depreciation unit is selected, and any subsequent modification short of the depreciation unit is handled as a periodic charge to operations. For example, trucking companies frequently classify truck chassis, tires, and engines as separate asset units. Telephone poles are an asset group for utility companies, as are the crossbars. The glass insulators attached to the crossbars are not. The replacement of a crossbar is a capital expenditure (asset replacement); costs of replacing the insulators are handled as repairs. Sometimes industry and trade groups will issue accounting guidelines specifying the commonly used units of property for that industry or trade.

As noted above, materiality plays a key role in this determination. Wastepaper baskets and pencil sharpeners, although they will probably last for more than one accounting period, are usually charged to expense. For practical purposes they are not defined as property units. Typewriters, on the other hand, frequently are a property unit, and expenditures for them are capitalized.

The establishment of policy regarding capital expenditures has a significant influence on income measurement. Sound policies must be formulated and consistently followed for the achievement of an equitable allocation of the total cost of services of noncurrent assets. Expenditures subsequent to acquisition are an integral part of this total cost. Care must be taken to see that these costs are not unreasonably charged against the revenues of a single period to distort income or treated as expenses one year but capitalized the next to manipulate income. Unless the expenditure is small or its future benefit is insignificant or unmeasurable, the presumption should be toward capitalizing the amount rather than expensing it. Unfortunately, the prospect of an immediate tax deduction and the modifying influence of conservatism often push accounting policies in the opposite direction. Also, if the same amount and type of capital expenditures are made each year, the results of a capitalize-and-depreciate policy may not be materially different from an immediate-expense policy.

**Noncurrent Asset Records**

A firm's capitalization policy governs whether an asset is recognized as a result of a subsequent expenditure. Another closely related consideration is the degree of detail used in the recording of noncurrent assets. This factor determines whether the identified capitalizable costs are recorded in separate or combined asset accounts and also influences capitalization policy. As a general goal, accounting records for plant assets should be kept in detail whenever asset components have different life expectancies or are the object of separate management decisions.

Achievement of such a goal carries with it two major advantages. First, detailed asset records facilitate more accurate estimates of depreciation. Assume that a firm acquires a piece of machinery and a group of attachments. The economic life of the machine is 10 years, while the attachments have to be replaced at the end of 5 years. Recording the expenditure in two separate asset accounts would allow the cost of the machine itself to be allocated over 10 years and the cost of the attachments over 5. On the other hand, combining the machinery and attachments as one asset results in underdepreciation of the attachments.

The second advantage, directly germane to our discussion of asset modifications, is that the use of detailed asset records helps accountants to distinguish between maintenance and asset replacement. What costs are classified as maintenance and repairs depends to a large extent on how accountants classify assets. If the attachments are part of the total cost of machinery, then their replacement could be treated as repairs—costs necessary for maintenance of the asset service. The benefit from this expenditure though will certainly be received over more than one accounting period. If the degree of detail involved in asset records provides for the attachments to be set up as a separate asset, their replacement every three years is not a maintenance charge at all. It represents a retirement of one asset and the acquisition of a replacement.

## Recording of Asset Modifications

Many additions and practically all improvements and betterments call for some change in the old asset. The enlargement of windows in the factory necessitates the complete removal of the old casements. The installation of a new air-conditioning system may require the removal of the old ducts. Even most periodic replacements—rebricking the inside of a blast furnace, for example—involve the removal of part of the old asset.

*Ideally,* if the old asset is partially removed, that part should be retired and replaced with the new one. The cost of the old part should be removed from the asset account, the accumulated depreciation on the portion displaced should be removed from the contra asset account, a gain or loss on retirement should be recognized if it has occurred, and the new cost should be debited to the asset account. Future periods are thus not burdened by depreciation charges on costs no longer in existence but are charged only with those expenditures that benefit operations in the future.

Assume that a building having a useful life of 20 years is constructed at a total cost of $140,000. Straight-line depreciation is used. After 10 years the wood-shingle roof is replaced with a slate roof costing $18,000. A study of the original construction records reveals that $12,000 is an accurate estimate of the original cost of the wood-shingle roof. It would be erroneous simply to charge the $18,000 to the Building account without recognizing the underdepreciation on the old roof. The entries to record the partial replacement are:

```
Accumulated Depreciation—Building .................... 6,000
Loss on Retirement ................................... 6,000
     Building ........................................          12,000
     To remove the shingle roof and its
     related depreciation.

Building ............................................. 18,000
     Cash (or Accounts Payable) ......................          18,000
     To record replacement with new slate roof.
```

When these entries are posted, the Building account and its related contra will appear as follows:

| Building | | Accumulated Depreciation | |
|---|---|---|---|
| √140,000 | 12,000 | 6,000 | √70,000 |
| 18,000 | | | |

The book value of the asset has increased to $82,000 ($146,000 − $64,000). This represents the cost which should be depreciated over the next 10 years (we are assuming that the new roof does not increase the useful life of the building). Depreciation rates and amounts, of course, would be revised to reflect the major modification in the asset.

Perhaps a more accurate procedure initially would have been to record the various structural elements—roof, foundation, heating system, and so on—of the building as separate assets and to depreciate the roof over 10 years rather than 20. If this had been done, the treatment of the new roof as an asset replacement would be obvious. The fact that it was not done, however, does not relieve the accountant of the responsibility to reflect accurately the exhaustion of the service potential of the old roof.

Whenever the carrying value (cost less accumulated depreciation) of the replaced asset (or portion thereof) is known or can be accurately approximated, the substitution method illustrated above is the only appropriate method. Theoretically all renewals and replacements, whether major or minor, should be handled this way. However, from a practical standpoint it may be difficult and probably is unnecessary to record each substitution of a minor part for an asset as a replacement. Consequently in accounting practice minor modifications are often treated as operating expenditures (charged to repairs or maintenance) or are capitalized indirectly by being charged to the contra account (see discussion below).

**Charging Accumulated Depreciation.** A hybrid treatment of replacements, renewals, and "extraordinary repairs" is to debit their cost to the Accumulated Depreciation account. Ostensibly, this approach reflects the rebuilding or recapture of service potential previously expired. It does recognize that the particular costs benefit future periods and should not be treated as costs of the current period only. Although this expedient departs from theoretical soundness, it is satisfactory when no significant gains and losses are involved. It is particularly useful when the accountant is unable to determine the original cost and accumulated depreciation related to the portion of the asset retired.

If the cost of the new roof in our example had been handled this way, the entry would have been:

```
Accumulated Depreciation—Building ................... 18,000
        Cash (or Accounts Payable) .......................          18,000
```

*Book value* of the asset increases by $18,000 to $88,000, although the asset account itself remains unchanged. Valid asset expenditures are brought in through the back door. The new depreciation charge will be $8,800 ([$140,000 − $52,000]/10 years remaining life).

The conceptual objection to this procedure is that it does not identify in the asset account the cost of the old asset (or portion thereof) removed from service and the cost of the new one added. It leaves net assets overstated by $6,000, the amount of the loss not recognized on retirement. Any gain or loss on the old component remains buried in the asset account, to be charged to a future period. In addition, this method ignores any difference between the cost of the replacement and that of the original part. Consequently, the asset account does not reflect the original cost of the plant *actually in service,* nor does the accumulated depreciation account provide an indication of the portion of that original cost which has been charged to operations.

## DISCUSSION OF THE ARMCO ANNUAL REPORT

The financial statements of Armco are contained in the Appendix to Chapter 5. In the balance sheet and the notes accompanying it, one can find four depreciable asset categories. By far the largest is Property, Plant, and Equipment, which has a carrying value of over $1.8 billion on December 31, 1981. The other three are much smaller—Capitalized Lease Rights, Excess of Cost over Equity in Net Assets of Purchased Businesses, and Deferred Blast Furnace Reline Costs (included in Prepaid Expenses and Deferred Charges). Capitalized Lease Rights are discussed in Chapter 11; for our purposes we can view them as a special type of plant asset. Excess of Cost over Equity in Net Assets of Purchased Businesses is the name Armco gives to its purchased goodwill. The problems associated with the amortization of goodwill were discussed in a previous section of this chapter.

Armco follows the policy suggested in this chapter of treating the blast furnace linings as a separate asset from the furnaces themselves. The former have short lives which are heavily influenced by productive activity. Indeed, the linings are depreciated by an activity method, activity being defined in terms of volume of production. On the other hand, the furnaces last much longer and are depreciated by a straight-line method. The use of separate asset classifications not only allows this differentiation in depreciation policy; it also facilitates the treatment of a lining replacement as a new asset substituting for an old one.

Contained in Note 1 is a description of the depreciation and amortization policies followed by Armco. Unfortunately, they are not very specific. Goodwill is amortized over 40 years *or less*. No indication is given of the useful lives of the various major plant-asset groupings. More detail would help readers judge the degree of conservatism inherent in these policies. In addition, as is often the case, the total amount of depreciation expense included in various expense accounts on the income statement is not clearly disclosed. However, the amount is shown in the statement of changes in financial position and in detailed schedules on pages 168 and 172.

One interesting note concerns Armco's depreciation procedures for steelmaking plant and equipment. The firm basically uses straight-line depreciation. However, the useful lives and the exhaustion of service potential for steelmaking equipment are also heavily influenced by intensity of use. Consequently, Armco modifies the straight-line depreciation charges to reflect changes from normal levels of production. In years when the facilities are run close to capacity, an additional depreciation amount is added to the straight-line charge. Conversely, when production levels drop materially in a particular year, the straight-line depreciation charge is reduced. These changes are made within limits and according to policy guidelines. Therefore, the method still meets the requirements for a rational and systematic allocation of cost.

Information about additions to the stock of plant resources also can be found on the statement of changes in financial position. Armco spent $393.6 million on new equipment in 1981. A detailed breakdown of this amount by major divisions is given on page 172. In addition, plant assets

**TABLE 9–6  Calculation of Book Value of Retired Plant ($000,000)**

| | | |
|---|---:|---|
| Original cost of plant retired | $ 106.9 | (a) |
| Accumulated depreciation applicable to retired plant | 81.4 | (b) |
| Book value | $ 25.5 | |

| | | | |
|---|---|---:|---:|
| (a) | Cost of plant assets, December 31, 1980 | | $3,255.2 |
| | Additions during 1981: | | |
| |    Capital expenditures | $393.6 | |
| |    Ladish Co. property | 68.1 | |
| |    Translation adjustment on property | (18.2) | 443.5 |
| | Cost of plant assets, December 31, 1981 | | (3,591.8) |
| | | | $ 106.9 |
| | | | |
| (b) | Accumulated depreciation, December 31, 1980 | | $1,694.0 |
| | Depreciation expense for 1981 | | 166.5 |
| | Accumulated depreciation, December 31, 1981 | | (1,779.1) |
| | Accumulated depreciation applicable to | | |
| |    retirements | | $ 81.4 |

increased $68.1 million as a result of the acquisition during 1981 of Ladish Co.

The only information available concerning asset retirements is that the book value of property, plant, and equipment retired in 1981 was $25.5 million. A knowledgeable analyst could reconstruct this figure from the financial information shown on the balance sheet and other statements and schedules in the manner shown in Table 9–6.

We may assume that any gains or losses on the property, plant, and equipment retired were reflected on the income statement in the category "Sundry other—net." It might have been useful to know what the total gain or loss on retirement was. Presumably, the amounts were immaterial. For the purposes of the statement of changes of financial position, the total proceeds received upon retirement would certainly have been more informative than just the book value.

Armco's disclosures of the impact of changing prices on depreciation and plant assets appear on pages 168–169. This information is mandated under *FASB Statement No. 33*. The items listed below are extracted from that information; they show the significant impact that changing prices can have on long-lived assets.

Depreciation and amortization for 1981:
| | | |
|---|---|---|
| As stated in the financial statements | $ | 174.3 million |
| Adjusted for general inflation | | 325.0 million |
| Adjusted for changes in specific prices | | 328.4 million |

Property, plant, and equipment (net) as of December 31, 1981:
| | | |
|---|---|---|
| As stated in the financial statements | | $1,812.7 million |
| Adjusted for changes in specific prices | | 3,046.1 million |

Armco is a capital-intensive firm; plant assets comprise a significant part of its asset structure. Because of their relatively long lives, even modest changes in prices of plant assets over time can cause material differences. Notice that the plant assets, net of accumulated depreciation, in service on December 31, 1981, had a current cost which is 168 percent of their original acquisition cost. This same general difference can be seen in the expense charge for depreciation. At historical cost, the amount is $174.3 million; at current cost, it is $328.4 million—188 percent of the historical cost figure.

The depreciation expense is approximately the same whether adjusted for general price inflation or specific price changes. This comparison suggests that the prices of Armco's plant assets over time increased generally in line with the consumer price index. However, as Armco points out at the top of page 169, in 1981 the current costs of assets *and inventory* increased faster than the consumer price index—in fact, twice as fast as evidenced by the data at the bottom of the statement of consolidated income adjusted for changing prices (also see Chapter 8's discussion of Armco disclosures). How much of the price change applied to inventory and how much applied to plant, we cannot ascertain.

**SUMMARY**

This chapter concentrates on three major topics concerning noncurrent assets—periodic use, disposition, and expenditures for modifications. Each topic includes an exploration of major concepts, a presentation and analysis of alternative procedures, and a discussion of practical influences relevant to them. The interaction between the theoretical concepts and practical necessities of record-keeping requires that accounting entities adopt policies to deal with each of the major problems:

1. Capitalization versus expensing at acquisition.
2. Estimates of useful life and residual value.
3. Choice of depreciation methods.
4. Distinction between repairs and replacements.
5. Treatment of trade-ins.

The accounting procedures and methods following from these policies have no effect on *total* noncurrent asset charges. Their important impact is on the *timing* of these charges and the form they take—depreciation, repairs, or losses (gains) on retirement.

The relative lack of precision in these policy areas does not mean, however, that any old way will suffice. Sound policy must be formulated, consistently followed, and adequately disclosed if the ultimate communication purpose of the financial statements is to be fulfilled. In recognition of the significant effects on financial position and income measurement from variations in these policies, the Accounting Principles Board stated that the following information should be disclosed in the financial statements or in the notes accompanying them:

1. Depreciation expense for the period.
2. Balances of major classes of depreciable assets at the balance sheet date.
3. Accumulated depreciation, either by major classes of depreciable assets or in total at the balance sheet date.
4. A general description of the method or methods used in computing depreciation with respect to major classes of depreciable assets.[12]

## APPENDIX: Group Depreciation Procedures

The depreciation methods described in Chapter 9 rest on the presumption that the cost of each asset is assigned *individually* to the accounting periods in which it is used. An estimate is made of each asset's expected useful life, and its specific depreciable cost is allocated in some reasonable manner over that period. If the asset is retired before the end of its useful life, a gain or loss is recorded, equal to

---

[12] AICPA, *APB Opinion No. 12*, "Omnibus Opinion—1967" (New York, December 1967), par. 5.

the difference between the remaining book value (as shown in a separate subsidiary ledger account) and the amount received upon retirement. For many large, individual assets such a *unit* depreciation procedure is reasonable.

However, a firm's depreciable assets include numerous smaller items, often acquired in groups. Examples are the telephone poles of a utility company, the typewriters in a large office, tires acquired by a trucking company, and small tools used in a manufacturing concern. These expenditures benefit more than one accounting period and should be capitalized and depreciated. However, treating each telephone pole, tire, typewriter, or tool as a separate asset would be an almost insurmountable clerical chore. In addition, *unit depreciation* based on the average life of units in the group may distort periodic charges against revenues. With a large number of units one would expect a mortality dispersion within the group around the average life. Unit depreciation fails to reflect this typical and often predictable dispersion. Unit depreciation indicates gains and losses on units retired before the average life, even though some were expected to be retired. Likewise, it records no more depreciation on units lasting longer than the average life, although, again, some might be expected to do so.

## Description of Group Depreciation

To overcome these two difficulties, many large firms employ group depreciation procedures. Although the method itself had been used for many years, income tax regulations passed in 1962 provided an increased impetus to the grouping of assets by fairly broad guideline classes. Calculating depreciation on some of these multiple-asset accounts involved a natural extension of group depreciation procedures. The chief characteristics of this method are as follows:

1. The individual costs of all units in a group are combined and treated as a single asset with one Accumulated Depreciation account.
2. A depreciation rate is based on the expected *average* life of the units in the group. The depreciation rate is applied to the asset balance in the group account for a determination of the periodic depreciation charge.
3. No gain or loss is recognized upon retirement of an individual unit from the group. This is the key procedural difference from unit depreciation.

*Example:* A typing service company purchases 50 electric typewriters, each costing $600. They are to be depreciated as a group over an average useful life of four years, each having an expected residual value of $120. Table 9A–1 shows the actual experience with the asset group.

**TABLE 9A–1  Retirement Experience for Group of 50 Typewriters**

| Year | Retirements at End of Year | Residual Value per Typewriter |
|---|---|---|
| 1 | 4 | $240 |
| 2 | 8 | 200 |
| 3 | 8 | 120 |
| 4 | 11 | 120 |
| 5 | 9 | 120 |
| 6 | 5 | 50 |
| 7 | 3 | 0 |
| 8 | 2 | 0 |
| | 50 | |

The following journal entries illustrate the basic features of the group method.

1. To record acquisition of the asset:

Typewriters .......................................... 30,000
    Cash ..........................................                30,000

2. To record depreciation for first year:

Depreciation Expense—Typewriters .................... 6,000
    Accumulated Depreciation—
    Typewriters .......................................        6,000

| | |
|---|---:|
| Cost ........................................... | $30,000 |
| Residual value ............................... | 6,000 |
| Depreciation base ............................ | $24,000 |
| Annual depreciation ($24,000 ÷ 4) .............. | 6,000 |
| Depreciation rate ($6,000 ÷ $30,000) ............ | 20% of cost |

3. To record retirement of four units at the end of first year:

Cash ............................................. 960
Accumulated Depreciation—
    Typewriters ....................................... 1,440
    Typewriters .......................................       2,400

4. To record depreciation for second year:

Depreciation Expense—Typewriters .................... 5,520
    Accumulated Depreciation—
    Typewriters [20% × ($30,000 − $2,400)] ..........       5,520

5. To record retirement of eight units at end of second year:

Cash ............................................. 1,600
Accumulated Depreciation—
    Typewriters ....................................... 3,200
    Typewriters .......................................       4,800

Similar entries are made in each of the remaining six years. Depreciation expense calculated at 20 percent of the remaining gross asset balance each year is recorded as long as some asset units are still in service. No gain or loss is recognized on units retired; Accumulated Depreciation—Typewriters is debited for the difference between original cost and actual residual value. Under the group method these early retirements were expected; consequently, more of the early years' depreciation expense applied to these units than to the units that were expected to last longer than average. Indeed, the group method assumes that sufficient depreciation has been charged for each unit retired to reduce it to actual residual value. Gains and losses caused solely by expected variations in asset lives are not true gains and losses; they should not be recognized.

Based on the information given in the problem, the changes in the ledger accounts for the group asset, Typewriters, and its related contra asset account are given in Table 9A–2. At the end of eight years the asset account shows no balance. If all estimates had been entirely accurate, the accumulated depreciation account would show no balance either. The $170 balance remains because the average

**TABLE 9A-2  Summary of Changes in Asset and Contra Asset Accounts**

| Year | Typewriters Debit | Typewriters Credit* | Typewriters Year-End Balance | Accumulated Depreciation—Typewriters Debit* | Accumulated Depreciation—Typewriters Credit† | Accumulated Depreciation—Typewriters Year-End Balance | Year-End Asset Book Value |
|---|---|---|---|---|---|---|---|
| 0 ...| $30,000 | | $30,000 | | | | $30,000 |
| 1 ...| | $2,400 | 27,600 | $1,440 | $6,000 | $4,560 | 23,040 |
| 2 ...| | 4,800 | 22,800 | 3,200 | 5,520 | 6,880 | 15,920 |
| 3 ...| | 4,800 | 18,000 | 3,840 | 4,560 | 7,600 | 10,400 |
| 4 ...| | 6,600 | 11,400 | 5,280 | 3,600 | 5,920 | 5,480 |
| 5 ...| | 5,400 | 6,000 | 4,320 | 2,280 | 3,880 | 2,120 |
| 6 ...| | 3,000 | 3,000 | 2,750 | 1,200 | 2,330 | 670 |
| 7 ...| | 1,800 | 1,200 | 1,800 | 600 | 1,130 | 70 |
| 8 ...| | 1,200 | — | 1,200 | 240 | 170 | (170) |

* These changes occur in connection with the retirement of typewriters at the end of each year. The difference between the two amounts is the debit to Cash for the residual value received.
† The credit to Accumulated Depreciation is the annual depreciation expense equal to 20 percent of the asset balance.

salvage value was slightly greater than $120 per typewriter. When the last unit in the group is retired, the balance could be closed out to a gain account.[13]

**Evaluation of Group Depreciation**

The advantage of the group method in saving clerical effort is obvious. Detailed asset and contra asset accounts for each unit are not necessary, and entries upon the retirement of individual units are simplified.

**More Accurate Periodic Depreciation.**  Perhaps not so obvious is the fact that, with a homogeneous group of items, the group depreciation method provides a more accurate assignment of cost to periods in which the items are actually used. Table 9A-3 compares the total charges against revenues under the unit depreciation method and under the group depreciation method. Under the unit method, depreciation expense is calculated only for four years, the average useful life. The retirement loss is the undepreciated cost of each typewriter less residual value at retirement. For example, at the end of Year 1, four typewriters are retired. The retirement entry for the units, *under the unit depreciation method,* would be:

| | | |
|---|---|---|
| Cash . . . . . . . . . . . . . . . . . . . . . . . . . . . . . . . . . . . . . . . . . . . . . . . . . . . | 960 | |
| Retirement Loss . . . . . . . . . . . . . . . . . . . . . . . . . . . . . . . . . . . . . . . . . | 960 | |
| Accumulated Depreciation—Typewriters . . . . . . . . . . . . . . . . | 480 | |
| Typewriters . . . . . . . . . . . . . . . . . . . . . . . . . . . . . . . . . . . . . . . | | 2,400 |

The total charge over the eight years is the same under both methods. The group method, however, distributes this total cost in closer relation to the actual usage of the assets. With a dispersion of lives around the average useful life, a uniform write-off over the life of each individual item is almost impossible, except on a postmortem basis. The significant retirement losses indicate the unattain-

---

[13] This statement is true only if the group account is a *closed-end* one. In an *open-end* group account, additions of similar assets are debited to the asset account, and the procedures described above go on indefinitely.

TABLE 9A-3  Comparison of Annual Charges under Group and Unit Depreciation Methods

| Year | No. of Units in Use | Group Depr. Expense | Unit Depreciation Method | | |
| | | | Depr. Expense | Retirement Loss | Total Charge |
|---|---|---|---|---|---|
| 1 ....... | 50 | $ 6,000 | $6,000 | $ 960 | $ 6,960 |
| 2 ....... | 46 | 5,520 | 5,520 | 1,280 | 6,800 |
| 3 ....... | 38 | 4,560 | 4,560 | 960 | 5,520 |
| 4 ....... | 30 | 3,600 | 3,600 | — | 3,600 |
| 5 ....... | 19 | 2,280 | — | — | — |
| 6 ....... | 10 | 1,200 | — | 350 | 350 |
| 7 ....... | 5 | 600 | — | 360 | 360 |
| 8 ....... | 2 | 70* | — | 240 | 240 |
| | | $23,830 | | | $23,830 |

* Includes $170 gain on retirement of group.

ability of this goal. In contrast, the group method attempts to achieve a *uniform charge per service year.* The group method expresses the life of the asset group as 200 years of service. Under a straight-line assumption, each *year of service* carries an equal charge.

$$\text{Depreciation per Service Year} = \frac{\$30,000 - \$6,000}{200 \text{ Years}} = \$120 \text{ per Year}$$

The total charge each year varies with the number of units in service that year.

**Limitations of the Group Method.**  Many of the conceptual underpinnings of the group method come from those used in insurance and actuarial calculations. The average age of an individual item is actuarially calculated just like the average life expectancy of human populations. The expected mortality distribution also is similar to that employed in life insurance computations. It is obvious, therefore, that the asset group must be sufficiently large and the units similar enough in nature so that the concepts of average life and mortality distribution have statistical validity.

The other major difficulty of the group depreciation method is that errors in average useful lives may go undetected for many years. With unit depreciation a gain or loss on retirement of an individual unit may trigger a reexamination of depreciation rates and lives of similar assets. Under the group method no such gain or loss on retirement is recorded until the last unit in the group is retired. The depreciation expense may be too large or too small for a substantial time period before the error in the depreciation estimate becomes apparent.

**Composite Depreciation**

When applied to a collection of *heterogenous* assets differing in kind and useful life, the same procedure illustrated above is called composite depreciation. The depreciation rate is based on a weighted-average life of the assets comprising the composite group. This calculation is illustrated for an Office Equipment account in Table 9A-4.

Depreciation expense each year would be 10 percent of the *gross asset balance*, and no gain or loss is recognized when a component of the account is retired. If

**TABLE 9A–4  Calculation of Composite Depreciation Rates**

| Asset | Cost | Residual Value | Depreciation Base | Estimated Life | Straight-Line Depre-ciation |
|---|---|---|---|---|---|
| Calculators ........... | $17,500 | $ 5,500 | $12,000 | 4 | $3,000 |
| Office desks .......... | 10,400 | 2,400 | 8,000 | 8 | 1,000 |
| Files ................ | 16,500 | 1,500 | 15,000 | 10 | 1,500 |
| Book shelves ......... | 20,600 | 3,600 | 17,000 | 17 | 1,000 |
| | $65,000 | $13,000 | $52,000 | | $6,500 |

Weighted-average life: 8 years ($52,000 ÷ $6,500).
Composite depreciation rate: 10% ($6,500 ÷ $65,000) on original cost or 12½%
($6,500 ÷ $52,000) on depreciation base.

$4,500 were received for the calculators upon their retirement at the end of five years, annual depreciation expense would be $6,500 for five years and the retirement entry would be:

| | | |
|---|---|---|
| Cash ........................................................ | 4,500 | |
| Accumulated Depreciation ........................... | 13,000 | |
| Office Equipment .................................... | | 17,500 |

Depreciation for the sixth year would be only $4,750 [10% × ($65,000 − $17,500)] if any replacement calculators are treated as a new group.

Unfortunately, the theoretical justification of the group method decreases as the heterogeneity of the assets in the composite account increases. The concept of an expected mortality dispersion around an average life applies only to groups consisting of large numbers of homogeneous units. The practical advantages of simplified record-keeping, of course, are still present under the composite method.

# QUESTIONS AND PROBLEMS

**9-1.**  Ocean Company bought a machine for $18,000. Its anticipated residual value is $1,500 at the end of an estimated life of five years. The company expects that 66,000 units of output will be produced through use of the machine.

 *scrap value*

*Required:*

a.  Calculate the depreciation cost for each of the first three years of the machine's life, using (1) the straight-line method; (2) the double-declining-balance method; (3) the sum-of-the-years'-digits method; and (4) the activity method (actual units produced in the first, second, and third years were 14,000, 16,000, and 15,000, respectively).

b.  Should depreciation represent the cost of the service potential consumed that period? If so, which of the four depreciation methods considered above should be selected by the firm? Explain your reasoning.

c.  "The activity method is the only way to go. Why get involved with arbitrary cost-expiration assumptions when you have a procedure which, by definition, tells it exactly as it happened?" Indicate whether you agree, and why or why not.

d. Assume that Ocean Company estimates that it will incur no repair costs on the machine until the fourth year and that expenditures for ordinary repairs in each of the last two years will total $2,200. Does this information change any of the amounts you calculated in your answer to part *(a)*? Does it alter your answers to either part *(b)* or part *(c)*? Explain.

e. Which depreciation method would you expect Ocean Company to follow for income tax purposes? Would it be desirable for firms to follow the same methods for both financial reporting and tax purposes? Why or why not?

**9–2.** Westcott Real Estate Corporation acquired a four-year old apartment building on January 1, 1985, for $750,000. On the same day, the firm purchased a maintenance truck for $10,500. Westcott is considering the use of straight-line depreciation for the apartment building and sum-of-the-years' digits for the truck.

*Required:*

a. Assume that Westcott adopts the depreciation methods it was considering. The truck has a six-year life and no residual value. The apartment has a remaining life of 50 years and a $75,000 residual value. Calculate the depreciation for each asset for 1985 and 1986.

b. An alternative set of depreciation methods has been proposed. Under this alternative the apartment building would be depreciated using a declining-balance method, with a rate 150 percent of the straight-line rate, and the maintenance truck would be depreciated on the basis of activity as measured by mileage traveled. Total estimated mileage is 75,000 miles over the six-year life. Travel in 1985 and 1986 was 18,000 miles and 16,300 miles respectively. Calculate the depreciation for each asset for 1985 and 1986 under the alternative methods.

c. "The choice of depreciation methods is influenced by both the quantity and quality of asset services." Explain this quotation. What relation might it have to the choice of which alternative depreciation methods in *(a)* and *(b)* were best?

**9–3.** The Hunt Corporation engaged in the following transactions and events during the year. Indicate how you would reflect each of these events in the accounting records, both initially (capital expenditure or operating expenditure) and in future periods if applicable. What factors did you consider in reaching your decisions?

1. Incurred costs for several projects in the existing factory building, including:
   a. Replacing wood shingles with slate on the roof of one building, $7,600.
   b. Installing heavier grates in the furnace, $2,300.
   c. Waterproofing the walls, $770.
   d. Replacing a window, $230.
   e. Building a new cement foundation to replace an older wooden one that had been eaten by termites, $4,860.
   f. Repainting the entire interior of the factory, $1,800.
   g. Replacing a few shingles that had been blown off in a windstorm, $85.
2. Purchased a used delivery truck from a local dealer for $6,000. Arranged with a garage to have the delivery truck fixed up and to have similar trucks already owned by the company serviced. The following expenditures were made:
   a. License and insurance on the "new" truck, $375.
   b. Replacing spark plugs on the other trucks, $204.

    *c.* Installing a new battery on the "new" truck, $52.

    *d.* Replacing the motor in one of the other trucks, $890.

    *e.* Repainting the "new" truck, $219.

3. Purchased a new machine for $17,000 to replace one that originally cost $19,000. The new machine had a lower-rated capacity than the old one. Removal costs of the old machine were $1,900. The cost incurred to adapt the floor of the factory building for the installation of the new machine was $3,500.

4. Replaced the specially designed lining of a tank used to store acids. The relining cost $14,000, including $1,500 to remove the old lining. The storage tank itself had been built 10 years earlier at a cost of $138,000 and was being depreciated over an estimated life of 50 years. Relining is necessary every 10 years or so.

**9–4.** The president's letter in an annual report to stockholders made the following comments on the company's depreciation policy:

> The depreciation policy of your company has been very sound. The directors realize that it is necessary to charge depreciation in order to value assets correctly. We use straight-line for both tax return and financial statement purposes. Stockholders, therefore, are not deceived by the accounting fraud of having two sets of books—one for the tax authorities and another for the stockholders. In addition, stockholders can be assured that the balance in the accumulated depreciation account assures funds for the replacement of assets when that time arises.

List and describe *all* the misconceptions which are evidenced by the above quotation.

**9–5.** The presidents of the Fast Corporation and the Slow Corporation recently got together for lunch. Both firms had just disposed of identical machines which each had purchased two years ago for $17,000. At the time they were originally acquired, the machines were estimated to have eight-year lives. No residual value was anticipated. Following lunch, a friendly argument broke out concerning which president should pay the check. The president of Fast Corporation told Slow's executive that she should pay because she sold her machine for $12,500—exactly $500 more than he had received for his machine. The president of Slow Corporation disagreed. She felt that Fast's executive was in a better position to pay, as Fast had recorded a gain of $2,083 on the disposal in contrast to a $250 loss on disposal reflected by her firm.

*Required:*

    *a.* Prepare the journal entries made by each firm to reflect the disposal of the machines.

    *b.* Which depreciation method did each firm follow? Show calculations which support your answer.

    *c.* Explain how the firm which received the most money on the machine disposal appears to have made out the worst on that disposal.

    *d.* "Gains and losses on the disposal of plant assets really should not be recorded. They never reflect on the inherent wisdom or lack of wisdom of the disposal decision. As a result, their presentation can greatly mislead the financial statement reader." Do you agree with all or part of this statement? Explain.

**9–6.** The Seth Louis Corporation purchased a new machine on January 1, 1985, and traded in an older machine of a similar type. The old machine was acquired on January 1, 1975, at a cost of $94,000. Both old and new machines had an estimated 15-year life and a $4,000 residual value. The terms of the purchase provided for a trade-in allowance of $48,000 (the fair market value of the used machine was $33,000) and called for either an immediate cash payment of $112,000 or 12 monthly payments of $10,000 each, the first payment due in one month. Seth Louis chose to accept the latter alternative. Other costs incurred in connection with the exchange were:

Wage costs for:
| | | |
|---|---|---|
| Removal of old machine | $1,400 | |
| Repairs to factory floor | 1,000 | |
| Installation of new machine | 1,600 | $4,000 |

Invoices received:
| | | |
|---|---|---|
| Freight-in for new machine | $1,700 | |
| Freight-out for old machine | 1,300 | 3,000 |

*Required:*

a. Why did the firm receive a $48,000 trade-in allowance on a machine whose fair market value was only $33,000?

b. "The list price of the new machine must be $168,000, because Seth Louis will pay $120,000 after receiving a $48,000 trade-in allowance." Is this statement correct? Explain.

c. "Of the five cost items listed above, the repairs to the factory floor pose the greatest problem with respect to proper accounting treatment." Do you agree? Why or why not? How would you account for the floor-repair costs?

d. Prepare journal entries to reflect the exchange of machines on the books of Seth Louis Corporation. The old machine was being depreciated on a straight-line basis.

e. How would your entries in part *(d)* differ if the procedure required for income tax purposes were used? What impact would this difference have in future years? Explain.

f. How would your entries in *(d)* differ if the old machine had been estimated to have a 12-year rather than a 15-year life? Is the change in accounting treatment much greater than the change in facts might seem to warrant? Can the difference in treatment be defended? Explain.

**9–7.** Excerpts from the intangible asset disclosures made by several firms in their 1981 annual reports appear below.

**Buckbee-Mears Company.** "Patents are stated at cost less amortization over 10 years computed on the straight-line method."

**Dresser Industries, Inc.** "Patents are being amortized over an average life of approximately 13 years."

**Philip Morris Incorporated.** "At December 31, 1981, this account (brands, trademarks, patents, and goodwill) included approximately $447 million which is being amortized on a straight-line basis, principally over 40 years. Cost in excess of net assets (goodwill) of companies acquired prior to November 1, 1970, is not being amortized because, in the opinion of management, the related investments have not experienced any diminution in value."

**The Coca-Cola Company.** "Formulae, trademarks, goodwill, and contract rights are stated on the basis of cost and, if purchased subsequent to October 31, 1970, are being amortized, principally on a straight-line basis, over the estimated future periods to be benefited (not exceeding 40 years)."

*Required:*

a. "Dresser Industries's accounting is only slightly better than Buckbee-Mears's reporting. Both firms have violated the matching concept by their failure to amortize all patents over their 17-year legal life." Do you agree? Why or why not? On what basis would one firm conclude that 10 years is an appropriate amortization period while another firm uses a 13-year period?

b. "Because goodwill represents the payment made by the firm for the right to receive excess earnings, goodwill must be amortized in order to properly reflect that those excess earnings were not cost-free." Evaluate this statement and indicate your opinion. Does goodwill amortization facilitate good matching?

c. If Philip Morris believes that it can defend a no-amortization policy for goodwill acquired prior to November 1, 1970, why has the firm decided to amortize all goodwill (and other intangibles) acquired on or after that date? Explain.

d. Philip Morris and Coca-Cola use the straight-line method for amortization over a period not exceeding 40 years. Is this just a coincidence, or were other factors involved in the selection of procedures? How can such requirements be defended?

**9–8.** Two major steel companies, Inland Steel and Wheeling-Pittsburgh Steel, initiated the same type of depreciation accounting change during 1982. The nature of and rationale for the change was addressed in the following excerpts from the firms' 1982 annual reports:

**Inland Steel.** "Commencing on January 1, 1982, the Company revised the estimates of depreciable lives for major production assets, and changed the method of depreciation for certain steelmaking assets from straight-line to a production-variable method. The production-variable modification of depreciation for steelmaking machinery and equipment consists of adjusting straight-line depreciation to reflect production levels at the steel plant. The adjustment is limited to not more than a 25 percent increase or decrease from straight-line depreciation. The new method, which approximates units of production depreciation, recognizes that depreciation of production assets is substantially related to physical wear as well as the passage of time. This method, therefore, more appropriately allocates the cost of these facilities to the time periods in which products are manufactured."

**Wheeling-Pittsburgh Steel.** "In the 1982 second quarter, the Corporation changed its method of depreciation for substantially all machinery and equipment from straight-line to a modified units of production method. The modified units of production method provides for depreciation charges proportionate to the level of production activity thereby recognizing that depreciation of steelmaking machinery is related to the physical wear of the equipment as well as a time factor. The Corporation believes the modified units of production method is preferable in its circumstances to the method previously used and represents a method common to that used by many major steelmakers."

*Required:*

a. Are both firms correct when they assert that depreciation "is substantially related to physical wear as well as the passage of time"? Can steelmakers more plausibly hypothesize such a relation than can other firms? Can use of the straight-line method ever truly reflect the process of depreciation? Explain.

b. Compare and contrast the reasons set forth for the accounting change. Does the change make the firms' financial statements more representationally faithful? Why or why not?

c. 1982 was a year of significant recession in the steel industry. What impact on income would the change in depreciation policy have in such a period?

d. Comment on Inland Steel's 25 percent limit on the magnitude of the adjustment. Would you recommend that Wheeling-Pittsburgh impose such a limit? Explain.

9–9. Wild Cat Oil Corporation specializes in speculative drilling ventures. During 1984 it signed a lease with the owner of a farm, acquiring the rights to drill for oil for the next five years on the land. The terms of the lease called for (1) an immediate payment of $100,000, (2) an additional payment of $10,000 for each year in which the company actually did any drilling or pumping activity, (3) a payment of $1 for each barrel of oil sold during a year, and (4) a provision that Wild Cat would clean up and restore the land to its original condition for farming at the end of the five years (estimated cost to do this is $80,000).

No drilling activity occurred in 1984. Early in 1985 a successful well was drilled at a cost of $400,000. Total oil reserves in the well were estimated to be 1,000,000 barrels. Of these, 250,000 barrels were pumped and sold in 1985, and 280,000 barrels were pumped and sold in 1986. Operating costs were $60,000 in 1985 and $36,000 in 1986. The selling price was $8 per barrel.

*Required:*

a. Calculate the total receipts the lessor (owner of the farm) would receive each year.

b. Prepare an income statement for Wild Cat for 1985 and for 1986. Explain carefully the depletion and other accounting policies you adopt.

c. Indicate what accounts and amounts related to the above items would appear on the position statement as of December 31, 1986. Indicate how they would be classified.

d. At the beginning of 1987, a new geological study indicated that remaining recoverable oil reserves in the well were estimated to be 800,000 barrels. What would the revised depletion rate be?

9–10. Of the 600 large corporations surveyed by the AICPA each year in its publication, *Accounting Trends & Techniques,* 13 made changes in depreciation methods during 1981. Excerpts from the 1981 annual reports of two of those firms appear below.

**Harsco Corporation.** "For domestic plant and equipment acquired subsequent to January 1, 1981, the Company changed its method of depreciation from the declining-balance method to the straight-line method. This change was adopted in order to make its depreciation policies more consistent with other similar industrial companies. Further, the Economic Recovery Tax Act of 1981 introduced a system of depreciation which is not based on the useful life concept; therefore, it is not appropriate to maintain the same system of depreciation for financial reporting and tax purposes."

**Dayton Malleable, Inc.** "The Company changed from accelerated methods to the straight-line method of depreciation for assets placed into service after August 31, 1979. Depreciation on assets placed into service before that date as well as tax depreciation on all assets will continue to be computed on primarily accelerated methods. This change was made to conform to the prevailing depreciation method used by competitors and to provide a more accurate allocation of the cost of fixed assets over their useful lives."

*Required:*

a. Briefly describe the accelerated cost recovery system of depreciation which was incorporated within the Economic Recovery Tax Act of 1981. Why did Harsco choose to mention these *tax* depreciation provisions as part of its explanation of the change in depreciation methods which it instituted for financial reporting purposes?

b. "Harsco is mistaken when it implies that, ideally, firms should use the same depreciation methods for both tax and financial reporting purposes." Has Harsco implied such an ideal? Explain.

c. On what basis might Dayton Malleable have reached the conclusion that the straight-line method provides "a more accurate allocation of the cost of fixed assets over their useful lives"?

d. Which of the two firms did the better job of justifying its change to straight-line depreciation? Explain.

e. How could the firms respond to those critics who might allege that the changes were really made solely to raise net income?

9–11. The 1981 annual reports of two makers of motion pictures contained the following discussions of their accounting treatment of film costs:

**Columbia Pictures Industries, Inc.** "Production, print, pre-release and national advertising costs and related interest are capitalized as incurred. The individual film forecast method is used to amortize these costs based on the revenues recognized in proportion to management's estimate of ultimate revenues to be received. Unamortized film costs are compared with net realizable values on a film-by-film basis, and losses are provided when indicated. The costs of cooperative and local advertising are charged to expense as incurred."

**Warner Communications, Inc.** "Production costs applicable to theatrical and television films are amortized on the basis of management's estimate of the total revenue to be realized. Such estimates are revised periodically, and losses, if any, are provided for in full. Film rights for television exhibition include a portion of the cost of released feature productions which is allocated to television exhibition based generally upon the income expected to be derived therefrom."

*Required:*

a. Explain why Columbia Pictures chose to capitalize pre-release and national advertising costs. Why was a different policy followed for cooperative and local advertising costs?

b. "Warner's policy of allocating a portion of film costs to television exhibition accomplished nothing. Those costs will be amortized whether or not they are allocated to television exhibition." What did Warner gain by making such an allocation? Did the firm increase the accuracy of its financial reporting? Explain.

c. "Motion picture costs should not be capitalized in the first place. Unlike machines or buildings, films can have their revenue-generating potential disappear quickly and suddenly by the receipt of several highly publicized negative reviews." Can motion picture costs be objectively recorded as assets? Should capitalization policies differ for different types of motion pictures?

d. Would you expect to find film costs classified as current or noncurrent assets on the balance sheet? Explain.

**9–12.** Susan Sugarman was not planning to spend her evening deep in thought concerning the accountant's definition of depreciation. Nevertheless, a newspaper ad, a magazine article, and a television commercial all attracted her attention. The references to depreciation were as follows:

1. In the newspaper ad, a major oil company proudly declared its intent to "spend nearly $16 billion over the next four years to help get more energy." The firm went on to explain that the money would come from several sources:

   The largest portion will have to come from corporate earnings. An additional sum will come from capital recovery (depreciation) from our past investments. The balance will come from the world's capital markets.

2. The magazine article reviewed an important accounting change which was instituted in the mid-1970s by the accountants for the Panama Canal. For the first time, they began to depreciate the cost of the canal.

3. The television commercial touted the merits of a particular brand of truck manufactured in Japan. The commercial noted "that a person who had purchased the truck seven years ago would only have experienced $1,400 of depreciation to date."

Susan proceeded to throw the newspaper and magazine in the trash and turn off the television. She then said to herself, "I may not be an accounting genius, but even I know that (1) depreciation does not provide any funds, (2) land is not depreciable, and (3) the $1,400 needs to be adjusted for price-level changes over the seven-year period before it can be said to represent the real depreciation incurred."

*Required:*

a. Is Susan correct in her assertion that "depreciation does not provide any funds"? If so, was the oil company's newspaper ad misleading? Explain.

b. Why is land usually not depreciated? Can the Panama Canal be thought of as land? If so, what factors may have led to the decision to begin depreciation in the mid-1970s? Were the Canal's accountants adhering to generally accepted accounting principles? Explain carefully.

c. "Susan has absolutely no idea what she's talking about. Even if the $1,400 is adjusted for price-level changes, it still would not represent depreciation as that term is defined by the accountant." Do you agree? Why or why not?

**9–13.** During December 1982, a television station paid $300,000 for the local broadcast rights to the Barney Miller sitcom series. Under the terms of the agreement, the station is entitled to 5 runs, or showings, of each of the 200 different programs in the series. All runs must be completed no later than December 31, 1986. Beginning January 1, 1983, the station began showing the episodes in the order in which they originally aired on ABC. The series ran Monday through Friday, so all 200 titles aired at least once during 1983 and 60 of these were shown for a second time.

At the end of 1983, the station's accountants got into a squabble concerning the proper procedure for amortization of the $300,000 contract cost. The chief accountant argued that $75,000 was the proper amortization for 1983, while two other staff members lobbied for $120,000 as the proper amount to charge against that year's operations. Each argued that his method was a generally accepted one.

*Required:*

a. Show how the $75,000 and $120,000 amounts were derived. What arguments might have been set forth by the advocates of each? If you had to choose one of the two amounts suggested, which would you favor? Explain your reasoning.

b. The controller objects to both the $75,000 and the $120,000 because they "failed to incorporate the rate at which the broadcast rights were being used up." He proposed an activity charge of $300 per showing or a total charge of $78,000 for 1983. Is his criticism valid? Evaluate his suggestion.

c. A consultant has suggested that the proper amortization for 1983 is computed in the following manner: $(5/15 \times \$300,000) + (4/15 \times .3 \times \$300,000)$. What do the 5/15 and 4/15 represent? What does the .3 represent? How much would 1983's amortization be? Evaluate the consultant's proposal.

d. Would you expect the viewing audience for each subsequent run of the programs to be smaller? Have you considered this factor in any of your above answers? Should you have?

**9–14.** The OBIPU (Our Business Is Picking Up) Garbage Company purchased an abandoned quarry for $175,000 for use as a dumping ground. Several other garbage-hauling companies bid on it, since the location was favorable and dumping could proceed without exhaustive preliminary preparation of the land. The management of OBIPU anticipated that the value of the quarry land would be considerably less after it was filled, because most people would not want to build on a garbage dump. The quarry land perhaps could only be sold for $15,000 after it was filled. OBIPU's accountant suggested that this quarry land should be depreciated as the hole was filling up with garbage. However, the firm's treasurer objected, citing the "accounting and tax principle that land is not depreciable."

*Required:*

a. Comment on the treasurer's observation that "land is not depreciable." What is the objective of depreciation?

b. Do you believe that the quarry land should be depreciated? Justify your position.

c. If the land is depreciated, how should the accountant determine the rate of depreciation? Explain.

d. "Because accounting reports must be objective, OBIPU really is not in a position to depreciate the land. The firm cannot be reasonably certain that $160,000 is the correct figure for depreciable cost. Future zoning decisions and shifts in public opinion on environmental and health matters could render that amount inaccurate." Do you agree with all or part of this statement? Why or why not?

**9–15.** Owens-Illinois, Inc., included the following among the accounts and amounts which it listed on the Liabilities and Shareholders' Equity side of its balance sheet (amounts in millions):

| | December 31 | | |
|---|---|---|---|
| | *1982* | *1981* | *1980* |
| Reserve for rebuilding furnaces ............... | — | 93.3 | 83.8 |

The reduction in the reserve to zero during 1982 was explained as follows in the firm's 1982 annual report:

> Effective January 1, 1982, the Company's domestic operations adopted the capital method of accounting for the cost of rebuilding glass melting furnaces, where such costs are capitalized and depreciated over the estimated service life of the rebuild. In the past, the Company established a reserve for future rebuilding costs of its glass melting furnaces through a charge against earnings during each period between dates of rebuilds. The Company changed to the capital method for furnace rebuilding costs because that method is used by its major competitors in the glass container industry. The change to the capital method also achieves consistency in accounting for furnace rebuilding costs within the Owens-Illinois consolidated group.

*Required:*

a. Which accounts were debited and credited when Owens-Illinois followed its previous practice of establishing a reserve for future rebuilding costs? How was the reserve account probably classified on the firm's balance sheet? During 1981, was the reserve account credited for either $93.3 million or $9.5 million? Explain.

b. Compare and contrast the old and new approaches with respect to reliability of measurement and the matching of rebuilding costs against revenues?

c. Comment on the rationale given by the company for making the change in accounting method. Has the firm's change served financial statement readers well? Explain.

**9–16.** Barnac and Blake, Inc., has an old milling machine that originally cost $20,000 and has accumulated depreciation of $14,000. Prepare the journal entry to record the exchange of this machine under each of the following six circumstances. Assume each situation is independent of the others and *APB Opinion No. 29* is followed.

1. The machine's fair market value is realistically determined to be $9,000. It is exchanged for a forklift truck with a list price of $15,000. Barnac and Blake pays $4,500 in cash; the truck dealer allows $10,500 for the old machine.

2. The machine's fair market value is realistically determined to be $4,000. It is exchanged for a new milling machine with a list price of $23,000. Barnac and Blake pays $17,300 in cash; the seller allows $5,700 for the old machine.

3. There is no realistic estimate of the fair market value of the old machine. It is exchanged for a forklift truck with a firm cash price of $13,000. Barnac and Blake pays $5,000 in cash.

4. The machine's fair market value is realistically determined to be $4,800. It is exchanged for a forklift truck with a list price of $12,000. Barnac and Blake pays $6,500 in cash; the truck dealer allows $5,500 for the old machine.

5. The machine's fair market value is realistically determined to be $7,500. It is exchanged for a new milling machine with a list price of $16,000. Barnac and Blake pays $8,000 in cash; the seller allows $8,000 for the old machine.

6. There is no realistic estimate of the fair market value of the old machine. It is exchanged for a new milling machine with a price of $25,000. Barnac and Blake pays $20,000 in cash; the seller allows $5,000 for the old machine.

**9–17.** The general ledger of Hoffman Company on December 31, 1985, contains the following accounts under the category Intangible Assets.

| | |
|---|---:|
| Deferred rearrangement costs | $ 24,000 |
| Franchise | 185,000 |
| Trademark | 40,000 |
| Noncompetition agreements | 15,000 |
| Licensing agreement | 216,000 |
| | $480,000 |

The account balances are before year-end entries have been made for 1985. An examination of contracts and records reveals the following information:

1. The balance in the Deferred Rearrangement Costs account consists primarily of payments made to a consulting firm for the design of a more efficient man-machine configuration in one of the firm's branches. Every six years or so, the company undertakes such a study.

2. The firm paid a franchisor $185,000 for the *exclusive* right to use the nationally known name and symbol of the franchisor on a certain line of products distributed in Arkansas, Louisiana, and Mississippi. The agreement calls for Hoffman to pay a fee of 1 percent of its sales of such products. Late in 1985 the district court ruled that such exclusive territories were in restraint of trade. Henceforth, the franchisor must allow its franchisees the right to operate in any of the 50 states.

3. The balance in the Trademark account represents the cost of a trademark purchased early in 1985. Hoffman, Inc., believes that the trademark has an indefinite life and therefore should not be amortized.

4. In 1983 the company acquired all the assets and business activities of a very successful local retailer. As part of the acquisition agreement, $21,000 was paid to the owner in exchange for a promise not to start up any competing retailing business for a period of three years and not to locate a competing retail business within a radius of 20 miles for a period of seven years. The account is being amortized on a straight-line basis over the seven-year period.

5. The Licensing Agreement was purchased on January 8, 1985. It allows Hoffman to use a special manufacturing process patented by another manufacturer. Hoffman needs to use the special process on two of its own contracts. The first contract runs from 1985 to 1988 and is expected to generate $300,000 of revenue. The second contract runs from 1987 to 1990 and is expected to generate $200,000 of revenue. Although the licensing agreement has a perpetual life, Hoffman anticipates no other use for the special manufacturing process except on these two contracts.

*Required:*

Explain how you would report each of these accounts in the financial statements of Hoffman Company for 1985 and in future periods if applicable. Be specific and include dollar amounts whenever possible.

**9–18.** The 1981 annual report of Sundstrand Corporation listed the following balance sheet amounts for net property, plant, and equipment (in thousands):

December 31, 1981 .......................... $284,884
December 31, 1980 ........................ 254,179

Additional detail provided by the firm included the following summary (amounts in thousands):

| | Land and Improvements | Buildings and Improvements | Machinery and Equipment | Equipment Leased to Others | Total Property, Plant, and Equipment |
|---|---|---|---|---|---|
| Cost: | | | | | |
| Balances at December 31, 1978 .... | $12,415 | $ 83,665 | $288,597 | $ 9,341 | $394,018 |
| Additions at cost ................. | 1,239 | 4,549 | 38,674 | 2,556 | 47,018 |
| Retirements ..................... | 644 | 4,198 | 18,211 | 350 | 23,403 |
| Reclassified* .................... | — | — | (19,207) | 19,207 | — |
| Balances at December 31, 1979 .... | 13,010 | 84,016 | 289,853 | 30,754 | 417,633 |
| Additions at cost ................. | 880 | 10,611 | 53,222 | 4,654 | 69,367 |
| Retirements ..................... | 87 | 101 | 10,996 | 641 | 11,825 |
| Balances at December 31, 1980 .... | 13,803 | 94,526 | 332,079 | 34,767 | 475,175 |
| Additions at cost† ................ | 1,488 | 9,456 | 65,947 | 4,337 | 81,228 |
| Retirements ..................... | 4 | 227 | 16,743 | 152 | 17,126 |
| Balances at December 31, 1981 .... | 15,287 | 103,755 | 381,282 | 38,952 | 539,277 |
| Accumulated depreciation: | | | | | |
| Balances at December 31, 1978 .... | 2,272 | 27,585 | 143,189 | 3,767 | 176,813 |
| Additions ....................... | 334 | 2,791 | 26,410 | 3,552 | 33,087 |
| Retirements ..................... | 186 | 1,168 | 14,041 | 284 | 15,679 |
| Reclassified* .................... | — | — | (6,255) | 6,255 | — |
| Balances at December 31, 1979 .... | 2,420 | 29,208 | 149,303 | 13,290 | 194,221 |
| Additions ....................... | 327 | 3,054 | 27,102 | 6,850 | 37,333 |
| Retirements ..................... | 26 | 101 | 10,083 | 348 | 10,558 |
| Balances at December 31, 1980 .... | 2,721 | 32,161 | 166,322 | 19,792 | 220,996 |
| Additions† ...................... | 904 | 3,582 | 38,955 | 5,982 | 49,423 |
| Retirements ..................... | 88 | 21 | 15,816 | 101 | 16,026 |
| Balances at December 31, 1981 .... | 3,537 | 35,722 | 189,461 | 25,673 | 254,393 |

  * During 1979 Sundstrand sold its air conditioning compressor business in a transaction which included the lease of certain assets. The leased assets, originally accounted for as machinery and equipment, were reclassified as equipment leased to others.
  † Includes assets of acquired companies of $13,446,000 and accumulated depreciation on assets acquired of $7,880,000.

*Required:*

a. Why does an amount appear for accumulated depreciation in the column titled "land and improvements"? What types of items might Sundstrand be depreciating? Evaluate the appropriateness of depreciating land items.

b. Comment on the reclassification of $19.2 million during 1979. Is the financial statement reader aided by the firm's distinction between "machinery and equipment" and "equipment leased to others"? Explain.

c. "Sundstrand's 1981 retirements of machinery and equipment were less surprising than its retirements of buildings and improvements during that year, because the former occurred far less prematurely than the latter." Can this statement be explained by reference to the data provided by the firm? Do Sundstrand's retirements of machinery and equipment represent wiser business decisions than its retirements of buildings and improvements? Explain.

d. Can you prepare all or part of the journal entry made by the firm to reflect its 1981 retirements of land and improvements? Does the relationship between certain amounts seem strange? Explain.

**9A-1.** Bumba Corporation owns numerous computer terminals. Every year new machines are added and older ones retired. Although the terminals differ slightly, they all have approximately a four-year service life and are sufficiently similar to be treated together as an open-ended asset group (i.e., new additions are added into the same group). Expected residual value is estimated at 10 percent of original cost. On December 31, 1986, the account balances were:

Computer terminals (at cost) ........................ $ 55,000
Accumulated depreciation .......................... (20,000)

For depreciation purposes, all acquisitions and retirements during a year are treated as if they occurred on January 1. The following schedule sets forth pertinent data concerning subsequent activity in the account:

| | | Retirements | |
| --- | --- | --- | --- |
| | Additions | | |
| Year | at Cost | Cost | Salvage |
| 1987 ................... | $ 8,000 | $ 6,100 | $ 850 |
| 1988 ................... | 16,500 | 15,700 | 1,500 |
| 1989 ................... | 14,700 | 18,500 | 2,000 |
| 1990 ................... | 9,700 | 12,000 | 1,350 |

*Required:*

a. Is the use of a group depreciation method appropriate for the situation faced by Bumba Corporation? Explain.
b. For 1987–1990, prepare journal entries to record the additions and retirements and to reflect the yearly depreciation expense.
c. How would the account balances appear on the December 31, 1990 balance sheet?
d. Would you expect that the depreciation figures from your entries under the group method would be more accurate than those which would have resulted had the unit method been followed? Explain.

**9A-2.** Root Corporation purchases four new machines on January 1, 1984. Although the machines are quite dissimilar, the company decides to depreciate them as a composite group. Relevant information concerning them is given below:

| Machine | Estimated Life | Cost | Residual Value |
| --- | --- | --- | --- |
| 1 ................. | 5 years | $ 32,000 | $ 5,000 |
| 2 ................. | 12 years | 44,000 | 6,000 |
| 3 ................. | 8 years | 30,000 | 2,000 |
| 4 ................. | 10 years | 26,000 | 3,000 |
| | | $132,000 | $16,000 |

*Required:*

a. Compute the composite life and the composite depreciation rate as a percentage of cost for the group of machines.
b. Prepare the journal entry to record depreciation expense in 1984 under the composite straight-line method.
c. If Machine No. 1 were sold at the end of three years for $8,000, what entry would be made?
d. What would the depreciation expense be for the fourth year if Machine No. 1 were sold as in part (c)?

**9A–3.** Presented below are portions of the plant asset disclosures contained in the 1981 annual reports of two well-known corporations.

> **Gulf Oil Corporation.** "Tie cost of properties retired or otherwise disposed of is eliminated from the property accounts and, after adjustment for salvage and dismantling expenses, is charged to accumulated depreciation or depletion. Only gains and losses on extraordinary retirements or retirements involving entire groups of properties are charged or credited to income."

> **Bausch & Lomb Incorporated.** "Upon retirement or disposal of assets, the cost and related accumulated depreciation are removed from the accounts, and gain or loss, if any, is reflected in earnings for the period. Properties are removed from the accounts when they become fully depreciated."

*Required:*

a. Is Bausch & Lomb following a group depreciation procedure? Explain how you arrived at your answer.
b. If the second sentence of the Gulf Oil description had not referred to the group metl.od, how could you still have known that the group method was being used?
c. For what type of firm or assets is the group depreciation method most suited?
d. "Bausch & Lomb should not remove property from the accounts until such plant assets are no longer used. The firm should continue to show on its balance sheet all properties which it is using, even if they are fully depreciated." Evaluate the firm's procedure and comment on this statement. Under the group method, do properties still in use ever become fully depreciated? Explain.

# FURTHER ASPECTS OF FINANCIAL MEASUREMENT— EQUITIES

# CHAPTER 10

# NOTES AND BONDS

This chapter marks the beginning of Section Three, which is devoted to a further development of the concepts and procedures pertaining to the recording of *equities* and their presentation on the financial statements. The treatment accorded monetary claims in the form of notes and bonds constitutes an important part of this area. Normally, notes and bonds are represented by formal documents having definite maturity dates. They bear interest either explicitly, in the form of a specific percentage, or implicitly, through inclusion of the interest in the face amount of the claim (e.g., the U.S. Government Series E bond). Notes commonly involve relatively short-term claims and a single creditor, whereas bonds usually arise out of long-term borrowings, often from a number of individuals.

The procedures associated with bonds are slightly different from those employed with notes, but the general concepts are the same. The major common concepts concern the element of interest and the resultant recording of monetary claims at their *present value*. Indeed, the impact of the present value concept is the connecting thread between the discussions of notes and bonds. Consequently, we begin the chapter with a brief explanation of present value and its relationship to the valuation of liabilities. The next section discusses the use of present value techniques and other procedures in the recording of bond liabilities and investments. The third section extends the analysis to the recording practices for notes payable and receivable. The concluding section discusses the relevant Armco annual report disclosures.

**LIABILITIES AND THE PRESENT VALUE CONCEPT**

In a general sense liabilities represent the debts or amounts that the business entity owes to creditors. They represent both sources of and claims against the assets of the enterprise. Their incurrence brings assets into the firm. At some future time, though, an outlay of assets (usually cash) normally must be made in settlement of each liability. The *timing* of the cash disbursement has an important bearing on the recording of liabilities. In Chapter 2 liabilities are classified as current or long term, according to the date of payment. Even more fundamental, however, is that the date of payment may influence the *valuation* of the liability.

Because liabilities involve future disbursements, the force of interest is often present and should be recognized. Ask yourself the question, "Would I rather have a dollar now or a dollar a year from now?" Obviously, your preference will be for a dollar now. Why? You can earn something with the dollar during the coming year if you have it now. Money is worth more now than at some time in the future because of the interest factor, the earning potential of the money. Put in another way, a promise of money at some future date is not worth that same amount today. Rather, its *present value* is less because the future amount includes the interest element, the charge for delayed payment.

Because money has this time value, the face or contractual amount of most liabilities probably includes some amount of interest. At least theoretically, the liabilities reported should represent the total amount owed at that particular time. If the liability is a promise to pay a future amount, that future amount should be shown currently at its present value, that is, minus the interest element. The real claim against assets is measured by the cash equivalent that would effectively discharge the obligation as of the balance sheet date, even though payment may actually be delayed. We can ascertain this cash equivalent (present value) directly in some cases or measure it by excluding from the face amount of the future payments the amount of interest included therein. The process of reducing future payments to present value is called *discounting*, and the discount rate is the effective rate of interest inherent in the transaction. Discounting is explained more fully in the next section and in the Appendix to this chapter.

Because the waiting period between incurrence of the liability and future payment is very short for many current liabilities, the element of interest is negligible. Usually no explicit recognition is given to it. For these obligations—trade accounts payable, taxes payable, wages payable, and so on—the face values of the liabilities are reasonable approximations of their theoretical present values. However, if the interest factor is specifically recognized in the transaction or if long time spans cause the amount of interest to be significant, liabilities should be recorded at the present value of the future payments necessary for liquidating them.

**Introduction to Present Value**

One of the easiest ways to grasp the concept of present value is to think first about the process of *interest accumulation* or *compounding*. A typical savings account is a good example. Suppose that on January 1, 1985, a person deposits $1,000 in a bank paying 6 percent interest compounded annually. The growth of the bank account is depicted below:

| Year | Amount at Beginning of Year | Interest Earned during Year | Amount at End of Year |
|------|------|------|------|
| 1985 ........... | $1,000.00 | $60.00 ($1,000.00 × 0.06) | $1,060.00 |
| 1986 ........... | 1,060.00 | 63.60 ($1,060.00 × 0.06) | 1,123.60 |
| 1987 ........... | 1,123.60 | 67.42 ($1,123.60 × 0.06) | 1,191.02 |
| 1988 ........... | 1,191.02 | 71.46 ($1,191.02 × 0.06) | 1,262.48 |

During the first year, $60 interest is added on to the principal amount in the account. During the second year, 6 percent is earned not only on the $1,000 but also on the first year's interest. This "interest-on-interest" phenomenon is called compound interest and causes the bank account to grow to $1,262.48 by the end of the fourth year.

Present value is the reverse process. In other words, $1,000 is the present value of $1,262.48 four years from now, discounted at 6 percent. Rather than indicating how much will accumulate in four years if $1,000 is deposited, present value shows how much *has to be deposited now* in order for a specified amount to be reached four years from now. The present value of some future amount is the dollar value you would be willing to accept *now* in lieu of the amount at a later date or the amount you would be willing to pay *now* for a promise of the future amount.

**Present Value of a Future Amount**

There are two present value concepts which relate to interest-bearing liabilities. The first is the one we just discussed—the present value of a promise to pay a single amount at some specific time in the future. For example, how much are you willing to accept now instead of receiving $1,000 in five years? How much would you pay now for a promise of $1,000 in five years?

The answers to these questions depend on what could be earned with the money now. Let us assume an earning rate of 10 percent. If the $1,000 is due in one year, we can determine its present value by dividing $1,000 by 110 percent. Similarly, if we are to receive the $1,000 two years from now, its present value would be $1,000/(1.10)^2$. Thus the present value of $1,000 due in five years at 10 percent annual interest is $1,000/(1.10)^5$. The answer of $621 is the amount which would accumulate to $1,000 in five years if invested now at a 10 percent annual return. Thus, if we could earn 10 percent on our money, we should be indifferent between accepting $621 now or $1,000 five years from now. Similarly, we would be willing to pay $621 now in exchange for a promise of $1,000 in five years.

Fortunately, it is not necessary to compute each figure needed. This type of present value calculation has been worked out in a table, Present Value of $1, which appears for a sampling of interest rates as Table 10A–8 in the Appendix to this chapter. This table gives the present value of $1 due in various periods of time and at various interest rates. To determine the present value of any amount, simply find the present value of $1 for the relevant period and interest rate and then multiply by the specified amount. Notice that the number shown in Table 10A–8 for five periods and 10 percent is 0.6209, signifying that the promise to receive $1 five years from now, discounted at 10 percent, is worth slightly more than 62 cents today. Consequently, a promise of $1,000 would have a present value of approximately $621 ($1,000 × 0.6209).

## Present Value of an Annuity

The second present value concept builds on the first. It deals with the present value of a series of equal amounts due in each of a number of future periods. Such a series is called an *annuity*. The question of the present value of an annuity might be phrased in either of two ways: How much are you willing to accept now in lieu of receiving $1,000 per year for the next five years, or how much are you willing to pay now for a promise of $1,000 per year for five years?

One way of determining the answer is to calculate the present value of each $1,000 payment. The sum of these individual present values would be the present value of the series. For example, at an earning rate of 10 percent, the present value of the first payment, which is one year away, is $1,000/1.10, or $909. The second payment, which is two years away, has a present value of $826 [$1,000/(1.10^2)]. Similar computations for the remaining payments are shown in Table 10–1. Each succeeding payment has a lower present value because it is to be received further in the future.

TABLE 10–1  Present Value at 10 Percent for a Five-Year, $1,000 Annuity

| Present Value (at 10%) | Present Value Factor from Table 10A–8 (10% column) | Amount to be Received at End of Year | | | | |
|---|---|---|---|---|---|---|
| | | 1 | 2 | 3 | 4 | 5 |
| $ 909 ....... | 0.9091 | $1,000 | | | | |
| 826 ....... | 0.8264 | | $1,000 | | | |
| 751 ....... | 0.7513 | | | $1,000 | | |
| 683 ....... | 0.6830 | | | | $1,000 | |
| 621 ....... | 0.6209 | | | | | $1,000 |
| $3,790 ........ | 3.7907 | | | | | |

The total of these present values, $3,790, is the current worth of the series of $1,000 payments. Although the above computations are far simpler to deal with than denominators such as $(1.10)^5$, the calculations can be simplified even further. In Table 10A–9 in the Appendix to this chapter, factors are presented for the Present Value of an Annuity of $1. Table 10A–9 reveals directly that the present value of $1 per period for five periods at 10 percent interest is $3.7908; it is less than the total of $5 to be received by the end of five years because of necessary discounting for the interest factor. The present value of the series of five $1,000 payments is found in Table 10A–9 to be $3,790 ($1,000 × 3.7908); the identical figure is calculated less efficiently in Table 10–1 with the single-period factors from Table 10A–8.

The above present value concepts for a lump sum and an annuity are used in the next section to establish the initial liability for bonds payable. The mathematical formulas for these concepts, as well as a more extensive explanation of their derivations and other applications, are covered in the Appendix to this chapter.

**BONDS PAYABLE**

Bond issues represent the second largest source of corporate capital, being exceeded only by issuance of stock. Investors purchase bonds in much the same manner in which they acquire stock, and ownership of each is evidenced by a certificate. Trading activity is not as extensively publicized in the bond market as in the stock market; this difference probably reflects the fact that fewer individuals can afford to invest regularly in bonds which usually have a $1,000 denomination. Nevertheless, most large firms have issued bonds; in fact, some $488 billion of corporate bonds were estimated to be outstanding on December 31, 1981.[1] Table 10–2 reveals that an important degree of corporate financing has taken place through the issuance of bonds.

It was estimated that the $488.0 billion in Table 10–2 would grow by $24.3 billion during 1982. The $24.3 billion *net* increase in 1982 was estimated to consist of $46.5 billion worth of new bond issues offset by

**TABLE 10–2  Amounts of Various Forms of Corporate Financing Outstanding on December 31, 1981\***

| Forms of Corporate Financing | Amounts Outstanding $ billions—(estimated) | | Percentage |
|---|---|---|---|
| Short-term: | | | |
| Bank loans ..................... | $ 226.7 | | 8.9% |
| Commercial paper .............. | 164.0 | | 6.4 |
| Finance company loans .......... | 89.2 | | 3.5 |
| Total short-term .............. | | $ 479.9 | 18.8% |
| Long-term: | | | |
| Bonds ......................... | 488.0 | | 19.2 |
| Stocks (market value) ........... | 1,300.0 | | 51.0 |
| Commercial mortgages .......... | 280.6 | | 11.0 |
| Total long-term ............... | | 2,068.6 | 81.2 |
| Total .................... | | $2,548.5 | 100.0% |

\* "The Perilous Hunt for Financing," *Business Week,* March 1, 1982, p. 44.

---

[1] "The Perilous Hunt for Financing," *Business Week,* March 1, 1982, p. 44.

some $22.2 billion of bond retirements.[2] If the entire bond issue is taken by a single lender such as a pension fund or an insurance company, the issue is said to be *privately placed*. During the first nine months of 1983, $13.1 billion of the $42.8 billion of new corporate bonds issued were privately placed.[3]

The essence of most bonds is found in a group of legal promises which the issuing company makes in exchange for the receipt of money from the purchasers of the bond issue. The formal bond contract or *indenture* contains provisions, called *convenants*, which the borrower must respect and fulfill. A trustee acts on behalf of the bondholders to assure compliance with these promises. The two most important from an accounting standpoint are the promise to pay a specified sum—the face or maturity amount—sometime in the future and the promise to pay interest periodically on the borrowed money.[4]

The interest rate actually stated in the bond contract is called the *nominal, stated,* or *contractual* rate. In a private placement, the contractual rate is negotiated directly between the individual lender and the borrowing company. When bonds are issued publicly, the firm cannot negotiate with each individual investor. Therefore, it sets the nominal or contractual rate as a percentage of the face amount of the bonds. This rate may or may not equal the *market, effective,* or *yield* rate required by investors in the financial markets.

The market rate is what purchasers of the bond actually earn on their investment. It is set by the interaction of the supply and demand for loanable funds in the investment markets. The market rate of interest varies with general economic conditions and with the riskiness of the investment as perceived by the financial community. Standard & Poor's Corporation and Moody's Investors Service, Inc., are the most visible bond-rating agencies; S&P, for example, utilizes a 12-category scale, ranging from AAA (the highest grade or lowest risk) to D (in default with little salvage value).[5]

Corporations do not deliberately set out to establish a nominal rate which they know in advance will differ from the appropriate market rate at the bond-issuance date.[6] The nominal rate represents the firm's best

---

[2] Ibid., pp. 45 and 47.

[3] *Investment Dealers' Digest,* October 1983.

[4] Most books on business finance contain detailed descriptions of the various types of bonds (e.g., debenture, mortgage, and convertible) and the alternative ways in which they can be issued (e.g., through private placement, through underwriters, and through competitive bidding). Those books also can be consulted for discussions of other convenants, such as restrictions on payment of dividends, provisions for sinking (retirement) funds, restrictions on the issuance of additional bonds, specification of minimum financial ratios, and so on.

[5] For further information on the bond-rating process, see Morton Backer and Martin L. Gosman, *Financial Reporting and Business Liquidity* (New York: National Association of Accountants, 1978), chapter 5.

[6] The deep-discount bond, especially popular during 1981–82, is a specialized exception. For a comprehensive discussion of this debt instrument which had its primary appeal among tax-exempt investors, see *FRBNY Quarterly Review,* Winter 1981–82, pp. 18–28.

estimate of what the market rate will be for investments of similar risk. However, changes in general economic conditions and/or the riskiness of the firm during the three to six months between the date of bond authorization and printing and the date of issuance often create disparities between the two rates.[7] The nominal rate is already printed on the bonds and cannot be changed; at the same time, investors will not purchase bonds that do not offer an appropriate rate of return in light of *current* market conditions. As we shall see shortly, the issue price of a bond in these cases is adjusted so the effective yield for the investor equals the current *market* rate of interest.

In the following sections of this chapter, the accounting for bonds from both the issuer's (seller's) and investor's (purchaser's) perspectives is illustrated. We focus on three accounting and recording areas associated with bonds: (1) the initial issuance/purchase of the bonds, (2) the periodic accrual and payment/receipt of interest, and (3) the possible extinguishment of the bonds prior to maturity. Because of the emphasis on liabilities in this chapter, more attention is given to the bond obligation than to the bond asset. Nevertheless, entries made by the bond purchaser are briefly summarized at an appropriate point in the discussion.

To understand the bond-recording process fully, particularly the issuance/purchase and the accounting for interest, the accountant needs some basic knowledge of the relationship of present value concepts to the valuation of bonds. In the examples which follow, keep in mind that the nominal or stated rate of interest determines only the dollar amount of the interest payment/receipt. It does not enter into the present value calculations. Only the market or effective interest rate measures the time value of money to investors.

## Bonds and Present Value

The connection between bonds and present value is direct and logical. A bond consists of two basic promises—to pay a specified sum (face or maturity amount) at the end of a period of time and to pay a specified sum (interest) in each period for a certain number of periods. If the reasoning in the first section of this chapter is sound, a bond should be worth the total of the present values at the market rate of interest of these two promises.

If the nominal rate of interest is the same as the market interest rate, the bond will initially sell at the face or maturity amount. Take, for example, a $10,000, five-year bond, paying interest annually at a nominal rate of 10 percent. The promises represented by this bond are to repay $10,000 in five years and to pay $1,000 in interest (10% × $10,000) each year for five years. If the *market* rate of interest is also 10 percent, the investor will be willing to pay the present value of these promises at a 10 percent earning rate:

---

[7] For example, the average market rate of interest on new industrial bonds rated AA declined from 15.13 to 12.13 percent during the three-month period from July 16 to October 22, 1982.

Present value of $10,000 due in five years at 10%
($10,000 × 0.6209, Table 10A–8 factor) ................... $ 6,209
Present value of $1,000 per year for five years at 10%
($1,000 × 3.7908, Table 10A–9 factor) ................... 3,791
Total present value ..................................... $10,000

What happens if the rate required by investors in the financial markets differs from that offered in the bond contract? If the market rate is higher than the nominal rate, the investor would insist on a purchase price which is below face amount; the bond sells at a *discount*. This seems only logical; you would be unwilling to pay face value for a bond which gives you a 10 percent return on your investment when you can earn, for example, 12 percent on other investments of equal risk. Rather, you would pay some lesser amount, so that your effective return (yield) would be 12 percent. You can determine this amount by valuing the bond promises above at an interest rate of 12 percent:

Present value of $10,000 due in five years at 12%
($10,000 × 0.5674, Table 10A–8 factor) ................... $5,674
Present value of $1,000 per year for five years at 12%
($1,000 × 3.6048, Table 10A–9 factor) ................... 3,605
Total present value ..................................... $9,279

Having paid $9,279 for this bond, an investor would earn 12 percent each year on the investment. Part of the investor's return would be periodic payments of $1,000 and part would be a payment at maturity date, when the investor receives back $721 more than the amount originally lent ($10,000 − $9,279).

This bond sold at a discount of $721 because of the difference between the market rate of interest and the rate promised in the bond contract. An alternative way of viewing the bond discount is in terms of an interest deficiency. Given the market rate of 12 percent, the issuer would have to offer *$1,200* annual interest in order to sell the bond at its face amount of $10,000. However, the issuer has had a 10 percent nominal rate printed on the bond certificates and, accordingly, *must* pay exactly $1,000 as the annual interest payment. Therefore, the investors attach a discount equal to the present value of the $200 annual interest deficiency. The present value of $200 per year for five years at 12 percent equals the $721 discount ($200 × 3.6048, Table 10A–9 factor).

Conversely, if the market rate of interest is below the nominal rate, the bond will sell for more than face amount, the excess being called a *premium*. An investor who can only earn an 8 percent return on investments of similar risk would be willing to pay more than face value for a bond contract offering a 10 percent rate. The amount paid is calculated as follows:

Present value of $10,000 due in five years at 8%
   ($10,000 × 0.6806, Table 10A–8 factor) ............... $ 6,806
Present value of $1,000 per year for five years at 8%
   ($1,000 × 3.9927, Table 10A–9 factor) .................   3,993
         Total present value ............................ $10,799

     The investor buying this bond will receive an 8 percent return every year on the investment. A portion of the $1,000 received in each period is a return of part of the principal investment the investor has made. The bond sells at a premium of $799 because the nominal rate of interest is higher than the market rate set by competition among borrowers and lenders. With an 8 percent market rate, the issuer would have to offer only *$800* annual interest in order to sell the bond at its $10,000 face amount. Because the 10 percent nominal rate dictates that $1,000 be the annual interest payment, investors will pay a premium equal to the present value of the $200 annual "excess interest." The present value of $200 per year for five years at 8 percent equals the $799 premium ($200 × 3.9927, Table 10A–9 factor).

     Table 10–3 summarizes the three variations in the above bond example. The critical role of the market rate of interest in the determination of the bond's issue price becomes very apparent; the present value factors, used to restate the bond's future promises into present dollars, always come from the table column representing the market rate. An inverse relationship between market rate and issue price is observed, with the bond's selling price decreasing as market interest rates increase. For illustrative purposes only, three different assumptions are made with respect to market interest rate at the date of bond issuance. In an actual situation, there is *one and only one* market rate for a particular bond issue at its date of issuance; as noted earlier, it would reflect both general economic conditions and the risk class of the specific investment.

     In actual investment decisions, bond investors do not use individual present value tables to determine what to pay for a bond. The two present value tables are combined and reflected in *bond tables*. Bond tables indicate the price (expressed as a percentage of face amount) of various bonds,

**TABLE 10–3   Issue Price of Five-Year, 10 Percent Nominal Rate Bond at Various Market Interest Rates**

|  | Market Rate of Interest | | |
| --- | --- | --- | --- |
|  | 8% | 10% | 12% |
| Present value of promise to pay $10,000 at the end of five years ... | $10,000 × 0.6806 = $ 6,806 | 0.6209 = $ 6,209 | 0.5674 = $5,674 |
| Present value of promise to pay $1,000 at the end of each of the next five years ............... | $ 1,000 × 3.9927 = 3,993 | 3.7908 = 3,791 | 3.6048 = 3,605 |
| Issue price ...................... | $10,799 | $10,000 | $9,279 |

depending on their stated interest rate, length of life, and the market rate of interest. For example, a bond table for five-year bonds indicates that a 10 percent, five-year bond would sell for 92.79 percent of face value in a 12 percent market and for 107.99 percent in an 8 percent market.

**Recording the Issuance of Bonds**

Of primary concern to accountants is recording the issuance of bonds after the investor has bought them. The same general principle applies at the time of issuance and throughout the life of the bond. *The liability should be recorded at the present value of the obligations to repay principal and to pay periodic interest.* If the market rate of interest and the nominal rate are the same, present value equals maturity value. The entry to record this case is straightforward:

| | | |
|---|---|---|
| Cash | 10,000 | |
| Bonds Payable | | 10,000 |

**Bonds Issued at a Discount.** A discount indicates that the investor is demanding a higher interest return than the particular bond in question promises to pay. Take, for example, the 10 percent, five-year bond being issued at a time when the investor is demanding a return of 12 percent. The cash received by the company is $9,279, which also represents the present value of its liability. The initial liability is the amount of money committed by investors now, not the $10,000 due in five years. Accountants conventionally record this situation through the use of two accounts—the maturity value is one account and is offset by a *contra liability* called Discount on Bonds Payable:

| | | |
|---|---|---|
| Cash | 9,279 | |
| Discount on Bonds Payable | 721 | |
| Bonds Payable | | 10,000 |

The Discount on Bonds Payable account should be shown on the position statement as a deduction from bonds payable. It is not an asset. Although the liability at maturity will be $10,000, the source of assets at the date the bonds are issued is only $9,279, the amount borrowed. This is the present value of the obligations under the bond contract. The discount represents the portion of the total interest charge that will not be paid or collected until maturity date. Since the discount is a phenomenon of interest, it becomes a liability only gradually, as time passes and interest is earned at the effective rate.

**Bonds Issued at a Premium.** If the 10 percent, five-year bond is sold in a market where the effective return is only 8 percent, the investor would pay more than face value for it, namely, $10,799. Again, the initial liability is the amount borrowed. This liability gradually will be reduced over time, so that at the end of five years it will be only $10,000. Nevertheless, at this moment the equity is the present value of the obligations under the bond contract, $10,799. The face amount is recorded in one liability account and the excess or premium in a *liability adjunct* account, as follows:

| | | |
|---|---|---|
| Cash | 10,799 | |
| Bonds Payable | | 10,000 |
| Premium on Bonds Payable | | 799 |

Premium on Bonds Payable represents the portion of the liability that will be returned to the investor over the life of the bond issue via periodic "interest" payments which are larger than those required by the investor.

**Bond Issue Costs.**   Businesses may incur additional costs in issuing bonds, which in some cases run as high as 5 percent of the principal amount being issued. Examples include fees of auditors, charges for legal services, printing of the bonds, registration and filing fees for the Securities and Exchange Commission and stock exchanges, and commissions and other distribution fees to the underwriters who actually sell the bonds to the investing public. These collectively are called bond issue costs and represent an intangible asset. They are an expenditure of funds for which benefit is received over the life of the bond issue. At the end of each period an adjusting entry is made to amortize a portion of the bond issue costs as an expense of that period.

**Recording Periodic Interest Expense**

Interest is the charge for using money. In the recording of interest the guiding principle is that the *interest cost for each period is the amount of money actually used in that period multiplied by the effective market rate of interest at the time the bond is issued multiplied by length of period*. If the bonds are issued at face value, then the nominal rate of interest equals the actual rate, and face value is the amount actually borrowed. In this case, the total contractual interest payment for the period (Face Value × Nominal Rate × Time) equals the interest charge (Principal × Effective Rate × Time). In each period an entry is made debiting Interest Expense and crediting Interest Payable (or Cash). If the accounting period ends between interest-paying dates, an adjusting entry accrues the interest expense for the elapsed time since the last payment date.

When bonds are issued at a discount or premium, though, the effective interest rate is not the same as the nominal rate being paid in cash each year. Indeed, the existence of a disparity between nominal and market rates of interest is the precise reason why for some bonds the principal does not equal face value. Although this disparity complicates the interest entries, it does not change the basic principle: Interest Expense = Principal × Effective Rate × Time.

**Interest on Bonds Issued at a Discount**

When bonds are issued at a discount, the effective interest rate is greater than the stated rate in the bond contract. As a consequence, the interest expense is more than the contractual interest payment; part of the interest cost in each period is deferred until the maturity date, when the borrowing firm repays more than it originally received. For example, assume that the bond issued at a discount in the previous section is dated January 1, with interest payable once each year thereafter.[8] Although the bond bears a 10 percent coupon rate, the effective interest charge the bondholder makes for lending funds is 12 percent. The total interest for the five years consists of the difference between total payments and the total received, or $5,721:

| | | |
|---|---:|---:|
| Total payments: | | |
| Coupon interest ($1,000 × 5) | $ 5,000 | |
| Repayment at maturity | 10,000 | $15,000 |
| Total received at issuance | | 9,279 |
| Total interest cost for five years | | $ 5,721 |

Knowing the effective rate of interest and the amount borrowed, the accountant can spread the total charge over the five-year period in such a manner that each period's actual interest charges are recorded.

Although the final repayment will be $10,000, during the first year the amount borrowed is only $9,279. Consequently, on December 31, when the company accrues interest for the year, the effective interest charge is $1,113 ($9,279 × 12%). The amount of the lender's money actually invested during the year is multiplied by the market rate of interest inherent in the bond contract. However, the borrower, by contract, is only obligated to pay $1,000 in cash annually. The $113 difference represents interest earned by investors but not paid to them immediately. Because it has been earned and is owed by the borrower, the latter should recognize it as an addition to the long-term liability. The entry to do this is:

| | | | |
|---|---|---:|---:|
| Dec. 31 | Interest Expense | 1,113 | |
| | Interest Payable | | 1,000 |
| | Discount on Bonds Payable | | 113 |

To increase the company's liability, we credit (reduce) the contra liability account, Discount on Bonds Payable. The borrower's liability is always the difference between the main account and the contra liability, so the net liability has increased by $113. It is now $10,000 less $608 (the new balance in Discount on Bonds Payable), or $9,392. The $113 is often called the *amortization of bond discount*.

On January 1 of the second year, the contractual interest would actually be paid in cash:

| | | |
|---|---:|---:|
| Interest Payable | 1,000 | |
| Cash | | 1,000 |

On December 31 of the second year another entry accruing that year's interest would be made. Again, the true interest expense is calculated as

---

[8] Most corporate bonds pay interest semiannually. In that case, we would use half the yearly interest rate and twice the number of yearly periods making up the life of the bond. Interest entries would then be made every six months. To keep our example less complicated, we use yearly periods.

the market rate of interest times the amount of money actually borrowed. However, the amount of the lender's money invested is larger during the second year than during the first because of the addition to the company's liability for the interest earned but not paid to the investor in the first period ($113). The entry would be:

```
Dec. 31   Interest Expense ($9,392 × 12%) ..............   1,127
              Interest Payable .........................              1,000
              Discount on Bonds Payable ..............                 127
```

This same procedure is followed every year for the life of the bond issue.[9] As a result each period is charged for the effective interest cost. Followed consistently, this method will leave Discount on Bonds Payable with no balance at the last interest payment date. At that time the liability will be represented only by the balance of $10,000 in the Bonds Payable account. Table 10-4 shows the effective interest expense for each of the five years, along with the periodic amortization of bond discount and the resulting net liability (amounts have been rounded to the nearest dollar).

**TABLE 10-4   Schedule of Interest Expense and Discount Amortization for $10,000, 10 Percent Bond Sold at an Effective Rate of 12 Percent**

| Year | (a) Interest Expense | (b) Interest Paid | (c) Discount Amortization | (d) Unamortized Discount | (e) Year-End Net Liability |
|------|------|------|------|------|------|
| 0 | — | — | — | $721 | $ 9,279 |
| 1 | $1,113 | $1,000 | $113 | 608 | 9,392 |
| 2 | 1,127 | 1,000 | 127 | 481 | 9,519 |
| 3 | 1,143 | 1,000 | 143 | 338 | 9,662 |
| 4 | 1,159 | 1,000 | 159 | 179 | 9,821 |
| 5 | 1,179 | 1,000 | 179 | — | 10,000 |
|   | $5,721 | $5,000 | $721 | | |

Note: Column (a) is 12 percent of the net liability existing during the year. Column (b) is the face value multiplied by the nominal rate of interest ($10,000 × 10%). Column (c) equals (a) − (b). Column (d) equals the preceding year's unamortized discount less (c). Column (e) is the maturity value of $10,000 less the balance in the Discount on Bonds Payable account (d).

At any time during the five-year period, the difference between Bonds Payable and Discount on Bonds Payable represents the present value of the two promises remaining under the bond contract. For instance, at the end of the third year, according to Table 10-4, the position statement will show:

```
Bonds Payable ......................................   $10,000
    Less: Unamortized discount .........................      338   $9,662
```

---

[9] A slight complication is introduced when the accounting period ends within an interest period. An adjusting entry to accrue interest for the elapsed time is necessary. First, determine what the total entry would be for the *interest* period. Then merely divide this basic entry to conform to the *accounting* period involved.

Inasmuch as the bond has a remaining life of two years, the effective liability should be:

Present value of $10,000 due in two years at 12%
  ($10,000 × 0.7972, Table 10A–8 factor) . . . . . . . . . . . . . . . . . . . . . . . . $7,972
Present value of $1,000 per year for two years at 12%
  ($1,000 × 1.6901, Table 10A–9 factor) . . . . . . . . . . . . . . . . . . . . . . . .   1,690
        Total present value . . . . . . . . . . . . . . . . . . . . . . . . . . . . . . . . . . $9,662

**Interest on Bonds Issued at a Premium**

When bonds are issued at a premium, the nominal interest rate on the bond is greater than the market rate. The interest which the borrower is legally obliged to pay in every period is more than the interest *expense* actually transacted with the investor. The real interest expense can be calculated as the amount of funds used during the particular period in question multiplied by the market rate of interest.

The 10 percent, five-year bond issued in an 8 percent money market serves as a good example. When the bond is issued, cash of $10,799 is received because the investor purchases part of the interest *receipts* in advance. The total interest cost for the five years can be measured by the difference between amounts paid out and amounts received. This difference of $4,201 equals the interest payments less the bond premium:

Total payments:
  Coupon interest ($1,000 × 5) . . . . . . . . . . . . . . . . . . . . . . . . $ 5,000
  Repayment at maturity . . . . . . . . . . . . . . . . . . . . . . . . . . . . .  10,000    $15,000
Total received at issuance . . . . . . . . . . . . . . . . . . . . . . . . . . . .              10,799
Total interest cost for five years . . . . . . . . . . . . . . . . . . . . . .              $ 4,201

On the first interest date the company writes a check for $1,000. However, the true interest expense is only $864 ($10,799 × 8%). From January 1 to December 31 the borrower has used $10,799 of the investor's funds at an effective rate of 8 percent. In this case the borrower is obligated to pay more cash than the actual interest expense. The excess payment represents a return to the lender of a portion of the initial amount borrowed. The liability is gradually reduced in each period by debits to the liability adjunct account, Premium on Bonds Payable:

Interest Expense . . . . . . . . . . . . . . . . . . . . . . . . . . . . . . . . . . . .    864
Premium on Bonds Payable . . . . . . . . . . . . . . . . . . . . . . . . . .    136
    Cash . . . . . . . . . . . . . . . . . . . . . . . . . . . . . . . . . . . . . . . . . . . .              1,000

Table 10–5 summarizes the information which the accountant would use in making entries over the five-year period. Notice that each year the interest expense declines and the bond premium repaid (amortization of bond premium) increases. The interest expense decreases because a portion of the original amount borrowed is returned to the investor with each interest payment, and therefore the amount of money used in each succeeding year decreases. By the end of the fifth year, all of the bond premium will have been returned to the investor. The only liability re-

**TABLE 10-5**   Schedule of Interest Expense and Premium Amortization for $10,000, 10 Percent Bond Sold at an Effective Rate of 8 Percent

| Year | (a) Interest Expense | (b) Interest Paid | (c) Premium Amortization | (d) Unamortized Premium | (e) Year-End Net Liability |
|---|---|---|---|---|---|
| 0 ..... | — | — | — | $799 | $10,799 |
| 1 ..... | $  864 | $1,000 | $136 | 663 | 10,663 |
| 2 ..... | 853 | 1,000 | 147 | 516 | 10,516 |
| 3 ..... | 841 | 1,000 | 159 | 357 | 10,357 |
| 4 ..... | 829 | 1,000 | 171 | 186 | 10,186 |
| 5 ..... | 814 | 1,000 | 186 | — | 10,000 |
|  | $4,201 | $5,000 | $799 |  |  |

Note: Column *(a)* is 8 percent of the net liability existing during the year. Column *(b)* is the face value multiplied by the nominal rate of interest ($10,000 × 10%). Column *(c)* equals *(b)* − *(a)*. Column *(d)* equals the preceding year's unamortized premium less *(c)*. Column *(e)* is the maturity value of $10,000 plus the balance in the Premium on Bonds Payable account *(d)*.

maining at the maturity date is the $10,000 balance in Bonds Payable. At any time until maturity the net liability (the total of the balances in Bonds Payable and Premium on Bonds Payable) is the present value of the remaining obligations under the contract.

## Straight-Line Amortization of Premium and Discount

The above method of recording interest is called the *effective interest, compound interest,* or *scientific* method. It charges each period with an amount of interest directly related to the market rate and the actual amount of money being used.[10] Under this method, the interest expense varies in each period, although the yield rate is constant. Amortization schedules similar to Tables 10-4 and 10-5 can be calculated and printed in a matter of minutes by a computer.

In accounting practice, however, a less accurate procedure is sometimes used. This procedure amortizes the premium or discount over the life of the bond issue on a *straight-line* basis. *Each period receives the same amount of interest expense,* which we determine by taking the nominal interest (cash payment) plus/minus an equal portion of the bond discount/premium. For the five-year, 10 percent bond sold at an effective rate of 8 percent, the annual entries for interest under the two amortization procedures are as follows for Year 1:

|  | *Effective Interest* | | *Straight-Line* | |
|---|---|---|---|---|
| Interest Expense ........... | 864 ($10,799 × 8%) | | 840† | |
| Premium on Bonds |  |  |  |  |
| Payable ................. | 136* | | 160 ($799/5) | |
| Cash ................. |  | 1,000 | | 1,000 |

\* 1,000 − 864.
† 1,000 − 160.

---

[10] The present value calculations throughout the life of the bond continue to use the market rate of interest *at the date the bonds were issued* and are not adjusted for subsequent changes in the market rate yielded by that security.

Although simple to carry out, the straight-line procedure lacks conceptual soundness. Table 10–5 illustrates that the $840 of Interest Expense recorded for each of the five years of the bond's life approximates the true interest charge only in the third year. If the straight-line method is followed, the carrying amount (net liability) shown for the bond in each financial statement will no longer equal the present value of the remaining bond promises; we observed earlier that such equality always results when effective interest amortization is used. Because of these deficiencies in the straight-line approach, the effective interest method is preferred and required in many circumstances. The relevant professional accounting standard states:[11]

> the difference between the present value and the face amount should be treated as discount or premium and amortized as interest expense . . . over the life of the note [or bond] in such a way as to result in a constant rate of interest when applied to the amount outstanding at the beginning of any given period. This is the "interest" method . . . . However, other methods of amortization may be used if the results obtained are not materially different from those which would result from the "interest" method.

**Accounting for Bonds on Purchaser's Books**

Before the procedures for recording the early extinguishment of the bond liability are outlined, it seems appropriate to illustrate how the bond transactions already discussed would be reflected on the purchaser's books. Because the bond purchaser is simply on the other side of the coin from the bond issuer, much symmetry can be expected and, in fact, does exist. The bond represents simultaneously a liability to the issuer and an asset to the purchaser. The issuer incurs interest expense, while the investor earns interest revenue. The cash payments made by the issuer equal the cash received by the investors.

Nevertheless, the symmetry of bond accounting on the issuer's and investor's books is far from complete. In the usual case many different individuals purchase portions of a corporate bond issue; accordingly, the dollar amounts on an investor's books may represent only a small fraction of their counterparts on the issuer's books. Another difference is caused by the investor including in its bond asset cost the amount of the broker's commission incurred upon the purchase. The amortization methods followed by both parties to the bond transaction might be different; perhaps only one of the two could employ the straight-line procedure without materially changing the results obtainable under the effective interest approach. Finally, investors traditionally do not establish a separate account for the bond premium or discount. The amortization takes place through direct adjustment of the bond asset account as opposed to indi-

---

[11] AICPA, *APB Opinion No. 21*, "Interest on Receivables and Payables" (New York: August 1971), par. 15.

**TABLE 10-6  Comparison of Bond Accounting from Perspectives of Issuer and Investor**

*Journal entries:*

| Date | Issuer's Books | | | Investor's Books | | |
|------|----------------|--|--|------------------|--|--|
| Jan. 1 | Cash | 10,799 | | Investment in Bonds | 2,160 | |
| | Bonds Payable | | 10,000 | Cash | | 2,160 |
| | Premium on Bonds Payable | | 799 | ($10,799 × 20% = $2,160) | | |
| | | | | | | |
| Dec. 31 | Interest Expense | 864 | | Cash | 200 | |
| | Premium on Bonds Payable | 136 | | Interest Revenue | | 173 |
| | Cash | | 1,000 | Investment in Bonds | | 27 |
| | $10,799 × 8% = $864; | | | $2,000 × 10% = $200; | | |
| | $10,000 × 10% = $1,000; | | | $2,160 × 8% = $173; | | |
| | $1,000 − 864 = $136. | | | $200 − 173 = $27. | | |

*Dec. 31 Balance sheet amounts for bonds:*

| Issuer's Books—Long-Term Liability | | Investor's Books—Noncurrent Asset | |
|------------------------------------|--|-----------------------------------|--|
| Bonds payable | $10,000 | Investment in bonds | $2,133* |
| Add: Premium on bonds | 663 | $2,160 − $27 = $2,133. | |
| Total | $10,663 | | |
| $799 − $136 = $663. | | | |

\* Notice that $2,133 = 20% of $10,663.

rect adjustment by reduction of a separately established contra or adjunct account.

Table 10–6 compares and contrasts the bond accounting for the issuer's and investor's books. The $10,000, 10 percent bond sold at an effective rate of 8 percent is again used for the issuer's entries. The investor is assumed to have acquired one fifth (or $2,000) of the bonds. To simplify matters, broker's commission and underwriter's fees are assumed away. Both the issuer and the investor use the effective interest method of amortization.

**Extinguishing the Bond Liability Prior to Maturity**

Although bonds are usually issued for relatively long periods of time, the liability can be extinguished prior to maturity. Most bond issues contain a *call provision*, whereby the borrower can redeem the issue at certain set prices during its life. Usually the redemption price includes a *call premium* to compensate the investor for having to give up his or her investment prematurely. In addition to retiring bonds by call, a company also can purchase its own bonds in the securities markets.

Some other bonds, known as *convertible bonds,* contain a provision allowing the bonds to be exchanged for capital stock at the holder's option. The conversion feature offers the investor an opportunity to gain if the market price of the capital stock increases. Until it is converted, though, the bond provides creditor protection and a preferential return.

From the firm's viewpoint, the conversion option may allow the bonds to be issued at a lower market rate of interest or to be used as an indirect way of issuing capital stock. If all or part of a bond issue is converted into capital stock, the liability disappears, and owners' equity replaces it.

Our primary interest lies in analyzing the basic transaction when bonds are extinguished. Regardless of whether this is accomplished by call, by open-market purchase, or through conversion and whether the issue is retired in total or only partially, the analysis remains the same. Therefore, a simple example is used to illustrate redemption or conversion. Assume that the account balances relating to a bond issue are as follows on the date of retirement or conversion:

|  | Debit | Credit |
|---|---|---|
| Bonds payable | | $100,000 |
| Discount on bonds payable | $6,000 | |
| Unamortized bond issue costs | 300 | |

The balances in the contra liability account, Discount on Bonds Payable, and the asset account, Unamortized Bond Issue Costs, are not the original amounts. Each has been partially amortized during the period the bond issue has been outstanding.

**Redemption.**   The redemption price (call price) is usually expressed as a percentage of maturity value. The excess above maturity value is referred to as the *call premium* and is the extra payment required of the business entity for the privilege of retiring the bonds early. If, for example, this bond issue is callable at a price of 104, the company has to pay 104 percent of face value, or $104,000. The entry to record this retirement is:

| | | |
|---|---|---|
| Bonds Payable | 100,000 | |
| Loss on Bond Redemption | 10,300 | |
| Discount on Bonds Payable | | 6,000 |
| Unamortized Bond Issue Costs | | 300 |
| Cash | | 104,000 |

The loss on redemption arises from two factors: (1) we have to pay $10,000 more than the net liability shown on the books [$104,000 − ($100,000 − $6,000)] and (2) an asset of $300 is written off. In many respects the Loss on Bond Redemption account is an adjustment to prior years' earnings. Because the life of the bond issue is shorter than anticipated, the interest charge and amortization of bond issue costs during past years have been too low. The loss is reported as an *extraordinary item* in the period.[12]

**Refunding.**   Issuance of a new bond and use of its proceeds to redeem an old one, often to take advantage of lower interest rates, is called refunding. For instance, an existing 12 percent bond may be called prior

---

[12] FASB, *Statement of Financial Accounting Standards No. 4*, "Reporting Gains and Losses from Extinguishment of Debt" (Stamford, Conn., March 1975), par. 8. See Chapter 16 for a complete discussion of the concept of an extraordinary item.

to its maturity and a new 9 percent bond sold to take its place. In many ways this situation is analogous to an exchange of noncurrent assets. The refunding should be treated similarly—as two separate transactions: (1) retiring the old bond issue as illustrated above and (2) recording the issuance of the new one as illustrated earlier. The old bond issue is being terminated because it has become comparatively uneconomical. The costs, of ending the liability—unamortized discount, unamortized bond issue costs and call premium—are part of the loss recognized upon elimination of the old bond.[13]

**Conversion.**   Two approaches have been suggested to record the retirement of the bond liability and the concomitant increase in contributed capital when bonds are converted into stock. Under one method the current *market value* of the bonds issued is assumed to represent the contributed capital. Under the second method the *book value* of the bond issue is assigned to contributed capital.

Our earlier example can be used to illustrate these two methods. Suppose that the bond issue described above contains a conversion option entitling each $1,000 bond to be converted into stock at a price of $50 per share. The entire bond issue, if converted, could be exchanged for 2,000 shares ($100,000 ÷ $50) of stock. Assume that the bonds are converted at a time when the market value of the stock has risen to $53 per share. At this time the current market value of the bond should reflect its conversion value (equivalent worth in stock), or $106,000.

Some accountants claim that this $106,000 represents what would be necessary to pay off the liability and also the amount that would be received if the stock were issued for cash at the time of conversion. Accordingly, the entry (ignoring bond issue costs) would be:

| | | |
|---|---|---|
| Bonds Payable | 100,000 | |
| Loss on Bond Conversion | 12,000 | |
|     Discount on Bonds Payable | | 6,000 |
|     Capital Stock | | 106,000 |

This method views the conversion as two distinct transactions—the retirement of bonds and the issuance of stock.

The more commonly used procedure increases capital stock by the amount that the bond liability decreases. The entry would be:

| | | |
|---|---|---|
| Bonds Payable | 100,000 | |
|     Discount on Bonds Payable | | 6,000 |
|     Capital Stock | | 94,000 |

Adherents to this position maintain that, unlike a bond refunding, a bond conversion does *not* consist of two independent events. The initial proceeds of the bond issue reflected the fact that the bonds could be converted into stock. Indeed, the convertible bonds may have been designed specifically to serve as an indirect way of issuing capital stock. The actual

---

[13] AICPA, *APB Opinion No. 26,* "Early Extinguishment of Debt" (New York, October 1972), par. 20.

conversion simply completes what was contemplated originally. The bond issue is canceled, and stockholders' equity takes its place. Moreover, to record a "loss" on a transaction with stockholders, as in the first method, appears inconsistent with the nature of capital-raising transactions.

Obviously, total stockholders' equity is the same under either method of recording the conversion. Under the first method, retained earnings is lower and contributed capital is higher. Although individual bondholders may have elected to convert because the market value of the stock has risen, total resources and sources of capital remain constant for the corporate entity.

## NOTES PAYABLE AND RECEIVABLE

Simple, short-term notes payable were discussed in Chapter 5 in connection with the introduction of the Interest Expense account. The liability was recorded at face value, and interest was accrued as time passed. The recording of promissory notes receivable parallels that for notes payable. If the note is explicitly interest-bearing, entries may be made periodically to record the accruing of an asset, interest receivable, and the earning of interest revenue.

This section will discuss notes that bear interest implicitly and some special recording problems associated with measuring interest rates. First, however, we should observe that *notes, like bonds, are recorded at their present value*. The recording procedures may differ somewhat from those employed for bond liabilities. Nevertheless, the amount borrowed on a note is its present value, the amount paid at the due date is its *maturity value,* and the difference is interest, the charge for the use of money. For example, if one were to borrow $6,000 and give a 9 percent, one-year note in exchange, the initial present value of the note is its face value of $6,000. The interest or growth in present value over the year will be $540, and the maturity value is $6,540. That the note is in fact recorded at present value can be demonstrated by discounting the maturity amount (face value plus interest) at 9 percent ($6,540/1.09 = $6,000). There is no premium or discount because the stated rate of interest on the note is assumed to equal the market rate of interest. The transaction is between a single lender and a single borrower. Unless strong evidence exists to the contrary, the rate of interest they agree upon presumably represents a validly transacted effective rate.

### Discount Notes

If a note does not bear interest explicitly, the legal document refers only to the amount due at maturity. Nonetheless, an interest factor is present and included in the maturity value of the note. The amount of money actually borrowed, or the present value, is less than the maturity value. For the implicitly interest-bearing note, the charge for using money is computed by the "bank discount" procedure described below—hence the term *discount note*.

Assume that we sign a promissory note to pay $6,000 one year from now and that the note is valued at a *bank discount rate* of 9 percent. The lender applies the 9 percent bank discount rate to the *maturity* value of the note to get the amount of discount (total charge for using money). In this example the maturity value is $6,000 and the interest charge is $540, but we would receive only $5,460 now. Included in the $6,000 we repay a year from now is the $540 interest charge. We will pay $540 for the use of only $5,460, so we are borrowing at an effective *interest* rate of about 9.9 percent ($540/$5,460).

A 9 percent bank discount rate, then, is not the equivalent of a 9 percent interest rate. We apply the discount rate to the maturity value and subtract the resulting charge to get the present value (the *proceeds*). We apply an interest rate, on the other hand, to the amount actually borrowed. Both interest rates and discount rates, of course, result in the same present value of expected future outlays. The present value of $5,460 derived under the bank discount procedure agrees with the present value calculated with an equivalent interest rate of 9.9 percent ($6,000/1.099 = $5,460).

**Notes Payable.**   A firm borrows money from a finance company on December 1, signing a "noninterest-bearing," 60-day note for $9,000. The finance company discounts the note at 8 percent. The firm employs a calendar-year accounting period. The proceeds are $8,880 ($9,000 maturity value less $120 discount). The entry would be:

```
Dec. 1   Cash ........................................... 8,880
               Notes Payable ..............................        8,880
```

Notice that in this direct approach the liability is recorded at its present value on December 1, not at the ultimate legal liability 60 days in the future. Liabilities represent a source of assets; in this case the source is only $8,880 on December 1.

It is true, however, that the liability will increase as time passes and interest accrues. On December 31 we would make an adjusting entry to record the 30 days' interest applicable to December:

```
Dec. 31   Interest Expense ............................    60
                 Notes Payable ...........................        60
```

Notice that although we are recording interest, we do not use a separate liability account. This procedure is consistent with the legal document, which includes interest in the face amount of the note. The December 31 position statement would show notes payable at $8,940.

On the due date of January 30 the remaining interest is accrued. This brings the note up to its face value of $9,000, which is the amount owed at maturity. The entries would be:

Jan. 30   Interest Expense  ............................  60
             Notes Payable  ...........................          60

           Notes Payable  ..............................  9,000
             Cash  ....................................          9,000

Another common method of recording this type of transaction, found in accounting practice, calls for crediting the note at its face value and making an offsetting debit to a contra liability account:

Dec. 1   Cash  ........................................  8,880
             Notes Payable—Discount  .....................  120
                Notes Payable  ............................          9,000

This approach has the advantage of reflecting the ultimate legal liability in the accounts. It is also easier to use when the general ledger account is a control account for a number of individual notes recorded in a subsidiary ledger. The Notes Payable—Discount account is analogous to the Discount on Bonds Payable account. The market rate of interest, as reflected in the discount rate of 8 percent, is above the stated rate of interest, which in this case is zero. Hence the present value of the note is less than its maturity value. As interest accrues, we debit Interest Expense and credit the contra liability account, thereby increasing the total liability.

**Notes Receivable.**   The holder of a discount note receivable may either record the discounted value directly or use a contra account approach. The finance company in the above example could record the series of entries in either of the ways shown in Table 10-7. The contra account procedure is more common. If this approach is used, Unearned Discount (Notes Receivable—Discount) is a contra asset representing the amount of interest that will be earned if the note is held to maturity. On the position statement it should be subtracted from the face amount of the note.

**TABLE 10-7   Recording of Discount Notes Receivable**

|          |                                   | Direct Approach | | Contra Account Approach | |
|----------|-----------------------------------|--------|--------|--------|--------|
| Dec. 1   | Notes Receivable  .................... | 8,880  |        | 9,000  |        |
|          | Unearned Discount  .............. |        |        |        | 120    |
|          | Cash  ........................... |        | 8,880  |        | 8,880  |
| 31       | Notes Receivable  .................... | 60     |        |        |        |
|          | Unearned Discount  ................. |        |        | 60     |        |
|          | Interest Revenue  ............... |        | 60     |        | 60     |
| Jan. 30  | Notes Receivable  .................... | 60     |        |        |        |
|          | Unearned Discount  ................. |        |        | 60     |        |
|          | Interest Revenue  .............. |        | 60     |        | 60     |
|          | Cash  ........................... | 9,000  |        | 9,000  |        |
|          | Notes Receivable  ............... |        | 9,000  |        | 9,000  |

one year should be reported as a current liability unless there is very convincing evidence that the debt will be refunded or repaid with assets classified as noncurrent (e.g., a bond sinking fund). Also desirable is a schedule summarizing the payments of long-term debt over the next 10 years.

In November 1973, the Securities and Exchange Commission issued *Accounting Series Release No. 148*, requiring disclosure of additional information relating to both short- and long-term debt. Although many of these new disclosures technically are required only in reports like the 10-K filed with the SEC, notes containing them are appearing with increasing frequency in the annual reports to shareholders. The new disclosures include (1) classification of short-term bank borrowings and commercial paper borrowings as separate balance sheet items; (2) the average interest rate and terms for the short-term bank borrowings and commercial paper borrowings at the balance sheet date; (3) the average interest rate, average outstanding borrowings, and maximum month-end outstanding borrowings for short-term debt during the period; and (4) amounts and terms of unused lines of short-term credit and unused commitments for long-term financing arrangements.[15]

*ASR No. 148* also requires disclosure of any compensating balance agreements the firm has. A *compensating balance* is that portion of the asset, Cash in Bank, that a firm agrees to maintain at all times in order to obtain a particular loan or line of credit. Compensating balance arrangements may result from formal agreements or informal understandings. For example, a firm borrows $20,000 from a bank, exchanging a one-year, 9 percent note payable. The agreement calls for a 15 percent compensating balance. Consequently, $3,000 of the amount borrowed cannot be spent by the business entity; it must remain as an idle asset. The impact on the business is twofold: (1) a portion of the cash account is not really a current asset because it cannot be used for normal operating purposes and (2) the effective interest cost on the loan is 10.6 percent, since the firm must pay $1,800 interest for usable funds of only $17,000. Particularly during periods of tight monetary credit, compensating balance arrangements often are significant.

**DISCUSSION OF THE ARMCO ANNUAL REPORT**

Many of Armco's liability disclosures will be surveyed and discussed in this section. Some liability information is more appropriately discussed in later chapters and, accordingly, is minimized or omitted here. Deferred Income Taxes are reserved for Chapter 13, while Long-Term Capitalized Lease Obligations are discussed in greater depth in Chapter 11.

The balance sheet in the Appendix to Chapter 5 shows that total

---

[15] Commercial paper is defined in the money market as all unsecured promissory notes issued by well-established corporations to meet their short-term seasonal borrowing requirements. These notes usually are issued in specific denominations arranged to suit the buyer, with maturities ranging from a few days to nine months.

current liabilities increased during 1981 from $846.7 million to $1,264.3 million. This 49.3 percent rise is not necessarily alarming, especially when note is made of the simultaneous increase in total current assets of 36.8 percent (from $1,685.8 million to $2,306.7 million).

Long-term debt rose during 1981 from $440.4 million to $572.8 million. The increase of $132.4 million far exceeded the relatively minor $8.0 million decline in the balance for long-term capitalized lease obligations. These changes and the $3.9 million growth in the *current portion* of long-term debt and lease obligations can be reconciled with the amounts reported on the statement of changes in consolidated financial position for debt proceeds and debt and lease payments. For 1981, the reconciliation for Armco is presented in Table 10–8 (dollars in millions).

**TABLE 10–8  Reconciliation of Balances of Long-Term Debt and Long-Term Capitalized Lease Obligations**

| | | |
|---|---:|---:|
| Balances, January 1, 1981: | | |
| Current portion of long-term debt and lease obligations | $ 18.7 | |
| Long-term debt | 440.4 | |
| Long-term capitalized lease obligations | 115.4 | |
| Total | | $574.5 |
| Add: Excess of proceeds over payments during 1981: | | |
| Proceeds from issuing long-term debt | 163.0 | |
| Payments on long-term debt | (25.2) | |
| Payments on long-term lease obligations | (9.5) | |
| Total | | 128.3 |
| Equals: Balances, December 31, 1981: | | |
| Current portion of long-term debt and lease obligations | 22.6 | |
| Long-term debt | 572.8 | |
| Long-term capitalized lease obligations | 107.4 | |
| Total | | $702.8 |

Note 3 of Armco's annual report details the composition of the long-term debt. It reveals that the long-term debt issued during 1981 consisted primarily of $100.0 million of five-year notes payable (due in 1986) and over $70.0 million of pollution control and other revenue bonds. These bonds were issued at a significant discount of over $18.0 million, because the nominal interest rates offered undoubtedly were well below the market rate of interest demanded by investors for securities of similar risk.

Despite the large issuance of notes payable during 1981, Armco's long-term debt continued to consist primarily of bonds, especially sinking fund debentures. Historically, a sinking fund provision in the bond covenant meant that the issuer had to make periodic contributions to a bond retirement fund. Notice, however, that the firm's balance sheet lists no bond retirement fund among the assets. Very few actual sinking funds exist today; instead, the required portion of the bonds are retired each period by open market purchase or by call.

Note 3 also serves the very useful purpose of revealing just how long term the long-term debt is. Scheduled maturities for the forthcoming five years (1982–1986) are indicated. On average, relatively small portions of Armco's existing long-term debt mature during 1982–1985. The large amount shown for 1986 is heavily influenced by the $100.0 million of five-year notes issued in 1981. A large proportion of the sinking fund debentures fall due many years from now, between 1995 and 2001.

The discussion of "Financial Condition and Liquidity" on page 167 provides additional insight concerning Armco's existing and planned long-term debt. The company refers to its sound financial condition and notes its ability and intention to issue $100–200 million of intermediate or long-term debt during 1982. Note 3 highlights the existence of some $230 million of unused bank lines of credit. Armco may borrow on these lines at or slightly above the bank prime interest rate. As of December 31, 1981, compensating balances of $5.0 million were on deposit at participating banks. That amount is less than the $11.5 million (5 percent of $230.0 million) required as compensating balances. Accordingly, the firm has opted to pay a fee in lieu of keeping an extra $6.5 million of funds tied up at those banks.

Armco's liability disclosures are fairly extensive; without exception they reveal a corporation which is candidly detailing a debt situation which seems well under control. The reported levels for the debt ratio, interest coverage ratio, and cash flow to long-term debt ratio (see pages 167 and 171) confirm this favorable impression. Those financial ratios are among the measures extensively discussed in Chapter 18.

## SUMMARY

The impact of legal and financial conventions on the recording process is quite evident in the handling of notes and bonds. Examples include the tendency for accountants to record maturity values of discount notes and bonds in the main accounts and to use contra and adjunct accounts to reflect their present value, the recording of interest receivable and payable in separate accounts except in the case of discount notes, and the use of both discount rates and interest rates in calculations of the interest charge. Nevertheless, two basic concepts form the foundation for the accounting for notes and bonds: *interest is the charge for the use of money* and *present value is the valuation basis for monetary liabilities and assets.*

Monetary assets and liabilities initially and at any time until maturity should equal the present value of the payments promised under the contracts. Present value, not the ultimate maturity value, represents the amount of money actually borrowed or lent and the claim as of any specific time. This amount times the *effective* interest rate gives the true periodic interest charge and growth in the liability. As the interest accrues with the

**FIGURE 10-1  Pattern of Changes in Present Value of Various Liabilities**

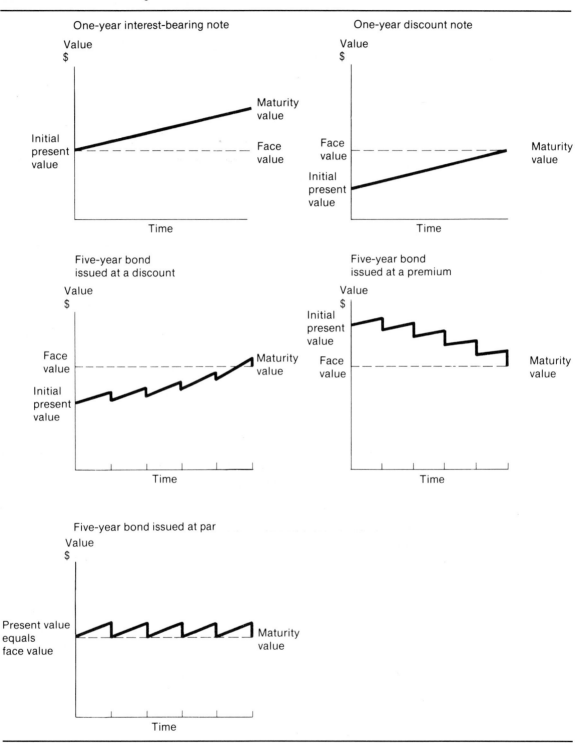

passage of time, the present value of the note or bond moves toward the maturity value. Figure 10-1 shows schematically the change in present value over time for each of the major monetary liabilities we have discussed. The sawtooth patterns on the bonds reflect the yearly accruals of interest and cash payments at year-end. In the case of the discount bond, the payment is less than the yearly interest charge; the residual present value increases to maturity value. With the premium bond, the cash payments exceed the yearly buildup of interest; the residual present value declines to maturity value.

## APPENDIX: Compound Interest and Present Value

This Appendix has two purposes. First, it presents the basic elements of compound interest in a formal manner. Included are discussions of both compound interest and present value formulas, an explanation of the use of present value tables, and some elaboration of the basic concepts. Second, some other uses of present value techniques beyond those described in Chapter 10 are outlined in an attempt to acquaint the reader with this commonly employed analytical aid in decision making.

**Compound Interest**

Interest is the growth of an amount of money during a time period. It is the price that must be paid (received) for the use of money over time. Thus, if $1,000 is deposited at an interest rate of 5 percent, the amount receivable at the end of the year is $1,050. This example illustrates *simple interest*, that is, interest for one time period only. The basic formula is:

$$F = P + iP = P(1 + i)$$

where $F$ equals the future amount of money accumulated, $P$ is the principal or the present amount invested, and $i$ is the rate of interest per time period.

Any growth in amount during the year, if not withdrawn, becomes part of the invested sum. Therefore, in future periods the interest element from past years will also draw interest. This phenomenon is called *compounding*. It lies at the heart of many financial decisions involving sums of money borrowed or invested for more than a single time period.

**Future Amount of $1 Present Value.**   The future amount of $1 at compound interest is the future sum of money that is equivalent to a present sum. To what amount would a sum of money accumulate in $n$ periods if deposited or invested now at $i$ rate of interest? Our knowledge of simple interest would indicate that the amount at the end of a single period would be $1 plus the interest earned on it ($F_1 = 1 + i$). If the amount is left to accumulate, the compound interest phenomenon becomes operative. During the second period, the entire sum at the end of the first period earns interest. Therefore,

$$F_2 = F_1(1 + i) = (1 + i)(1 + i) = (1 + i)^2$$

A continuation of this process would lead to a general formula:

$$F_n = (1 + i)^n = (F/P, n, i)$$

where $(F/P, n, i)$ is the future amount of $1 present sum invested at $i$ rate of interest for $n$ periods, and $(1 + i)^n$ is called the *accumulation factor*.[16]

*Example:* $5,000 is invested for five years at 12 percent compounded annually. The accumulated amount at the end of five years is determined below. A time-line representation of the problem shows the equivalence of the $8,812 future value at the end of five years to the $5,000 present value.

P = $5,000          F = $8,812   $(F/P, 5, 0.12)\$5,000 = \$5,000(1 + 0.12)^5$

$i = 0.12$

0                   5

$$= \$5,000 \times 1.7623,$$
$$\text{Table 10A–6 factor}$$
$$= \$8,812$$

If interest were *compounded semiannually,* we would calculate the amount for 10 six-month periods at 6 percent per period.

P = $5,000          F = $8,954   $(F/P, 10, 0.06)\$5,000 = \$5,000(1 + 0.06)^{10}$

$i = 0.06$

0                   10

$$= \$5,000 \times 1.7908,$$
$$\text{Table 10A–6 factor}$$
$$= \$8,954$$

Notice that the future amount is greater in this case because we have more opportunity to earn "interest on interest" than with annual compounding. A 12 percent interest rate compounded semiannually exceeds an annual 12 percent rate. If interest were only compounded annually, it would take the equivalent of a 12.36 percent annual rate to provide the same future value $(F/P, 5, 0.1236)\$5,000 = \$8,954$.[17]

**Future Amount of an Annuity of $1.** A closely related and natural extension of the concept of the future amount of $1 is the future amount of $1 per period. This concept deals with the growth of a *series* of equal investments made at the end of equal time intervals. The term *annuity* is used to describe a group of periodic deposits, receipts, or payments (generically called *rents*) of this type. The basic question underlying the amount of an annuity might be phrased as follows: to what amount would a periodic deposit of money accumulate in $n$ years if a

---

[16] In deriving and using formulas involving compound interest and present value, users find it easier to work in terms of a single dollar. Expressions and tables for values of $1 provide a generalized form that can be used in problems having different dollar amounts. All that is necessary is to multiply the compound interest or present value factor for $1 by the actual amount in the problem.

[17] The following formula will provide the effective *annually* compounded rate equivalent to a rate compounded more frequently:

$$(1 + i/n)^n - 1$$

where $i$ is the annual interest rate and $n$ is the number of compounding periods within a year.

deposit is made at the end of each of the $n$ years and earns at $i$ rate of interest? We will use the abbreviation $(F/A, n, i)$ for the future amount of an annuity.

The derivation of a generalized formula for the future amount of an annuity is not so straightforward as that for a single investment. However, the general concept is the same. For example, $1 is deposited at the end of each year for four years. The growth of each year's deposit is summarized in Table 10A–1. Being made at the end of the first year, the first year's deposit earns compound interest only for three years—Years 2, 3, and 4.

**TABLE 10A–1  Generalized Formulas for Growth of a Four-Year Annuity**

| End-of-Year Deposit | Accumulated Value at End of Year | | | | For n Years |
|---|---|---|---|---|---|
| | 1 | 2 | 3 | 4 | |
| First | $1 | $(1 + i)$ | $(1 + i)^2$ | $(1 + i)^3$ | $(1 + i)^{n-1}$ |
| Second | | 1 | $(1 + i)$ | $(1 + i)^2$ | $(1 + i)^{n-2}$ |
| Third | | | 1 | $(1 + i)$ | $(1 + i)^{n-3}$ |
| Fourth | | | | 1 | $(1 + i)^{n-4}$ |

The last year's deposit has earned no interest and adds only its original quantity to the total amount.

The amount of this annuity at the end of four years is the total of the accumulated value column for Year 4. The generalized notation at the right indicates that the future amount of any annuity of $1 for $n$ years is:

$$(1 + i)^{n-1} + (1 + i)^{n-2} + (1 + i)^{n-3} + \cdots + (1 + i) + 1$$

This expression is a geometric series, the sum of which is:

$$(F/A, n, i) = \left[ \frac{(1 + i)^n - 1}{i} \right]$$

The formula for the future amount of an annuity of $1 per period can be used in any situation in which there are regular periodic payments or receipts.

*Example:*  A firm has entered into a contract under which it receives $2,000 for its services at the end of every six months for five years. The buyer has asked the firm how much it would be willing to accept in a lump-sum amount at the end of five years in lieu of the periodic fees. Assume that the firm can earn 12 percent compounded semiannually.

$F = \$26,362$

$i = 0.06$

$A = \$2,000$ per period

0                    10

$$(F/A, 10, 0.06)\$2,000 = \$2,000 \left[ \frac{(1.06)^{10} - 1}{0.06} \right]$$
$$= \$2,000 \times 13.1808,$$
Table 10A–7 factor
$$= \$26,362$$

**Future Amount of Annuity Due.**  The preceding discussion assumed that all rents are made at the end of the interest period. Such a series is called more precisely an *ordinary annuity* or *annuity in arrears*. If payments occur at the beginning of the periods, the series is called an *annuity due* or an *annuity in advance*. For the calculations of future amounts, there are five interest periods in a five-year annuity due; this equals the number of interest periods in a *six-year* ordinary annuity, since payments there are not made until the end of the year. Generalizing from this, we can conclude that the amount of an *annuity due* for $n$ years is equal to $(F/A, n + 1, i) - 1$. The last item in the formula reflects the fact that no payment occurs at the end of the $n$th year. The above simple conversion allows us to deal with situations involving receipts or payments either at the beginning or the end of the period through use of the same annuity table. The above formula when applied to Table 10A-7 indicates, for example, that the factor for a five-year annuity due is calculated by subtracting 1.0000 from the factor found on line 6 in the appropriate interest column.

**Compound Interest Tables.** Tables are available for both the future amount of $1 present value and the future amount of an annuity of $1. These tables simplify the calculations by presenting the results for varying interest rates and time periods. Brief extracts from such tables are presented in Tables 10A-6 and 10A-7 at the end of this Appendix. They show the ratio of future values to a present sum or to a series of sums, respectively.

There are essentially four elements—annuity amount, interest rate, number of periods, and future amount—in the above compounding formula. If any three of the four factors are specified, the fourth can be derived from the same basic formula and tables.[18]

## Present Value

The concept of present value is the opposite of compound interest. Instead of showing how much a single payment or series of payments will increase over time, present value indicates how much you have to pay now in order to have a certain amount or series of amounts in future periods. Present value is the current cash equivalent of some designated future amount or amounts.

**Present Value of $1 Future Amount.** The formula for the present value of $1 received $n$ periods in the future at an interest rate of $i$ percent $(P/F, n, i)$ can be derived from the formula for the amount of $1. If we let $x$ equal the present value of $1 $n$ years in the future, we can solve for $x$ as follows:

$$(F/P, n, i)x = x(1 + i)^n = 1$$

$$x = \frac{1}{(1 + i)^n} = (1 + i)^{-n} = (P/F, n, i)$$

In brief, a reciprocal relationship exists between the present value of $1 future amount and the future amount of $1 present value. The *discount factor* is $(1 + i)^{-n}$.

*Example:* A customer owes you $7,500, due in six years, and approaches you about the possibility of paying off the debt early with a single payment now.

---

[18] The explanation and example focused on determination of the future amount of an annuity $(F/A, n, i)$. Another use would be to find the *annuity* that will accumulate to (is equivalent to) a specified future amount $(A/F, n, i)$. This is the reciprocal of the formula derived above.

$$(A/F, n, i) = i/[1 + i)^n - 1] = 1/(F/A, n, i)$$

This reciprocal calculation is sufficiently common to warrant a special name, *sinking-fund factor*, and often the construction of separate tables.

What is the minimum amount you would be willing to accept now if the interest rate is 10 percent?

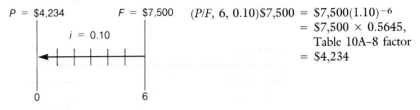

$P = \$4,234$  $\qquad F = \$7,500$  $\qquad (P/F, 6, 0.10)\$7,500 = \$7,500(1.10)^{-6}$
$$= \$7,500 \times 0.5645,$$
Table 10A-8 factor
$$= \$4,234$$

**Present Value of an Annuity of $1.** Commonly, business and financial problems involve a series of equal amounts spaced at approximately equal intervals in the future. What single cash receipt (or payment) now is the equivalent of a series of cash receipts (or payments) to be made at the end of each of $n$ years if the earning value of money is $i$? The abbreviation $(P/A, n, i)$ is used for the present value of an annuity.

The present value of an annuity of $1 is closely related to the present value of $1 and to the future amount of an annuity of $1. It is the sum of a series of individual calculations of the present value of $1. Likewise, the present value of an annuity is the reverse of the future amount of an annuity. Consequently, its formula can be derived from either of these other concepts.

For example, $(F/A, n, i)$, the future amount of an annuity of $1 for $n$ years at $i$ rate of interest, was derived as $([1 + i]^n - 1)/i$. This is the single future amount which is the equivalent of the annuity. If we desire the single present amount which is the equivalent of the annuity, we must take the present value of the future amount. We can determine the present value of any future amount by multiplying it by $(1 + i)^{-n}$. Putting these facts together gives us the following when $A = \$1$:

$$(P/A, n, i) = (P/F, n, i)(F/A, n, i)$$
$$= [(1 + i)^{-n}]\left[\frac{(1 + i)^n - 1}{i}\right]$$
$$= \left[\frac{1 - (1 + i)^{-n}}{i}\right]$$

Using this formula, we can solve for the present value of any annuity or for other variables (interest rate, periodic payment) in which we are interested.[19]

*Example:* A customer owes you $1,250 at the end of each year for the next six years.[20] What is the minimum amount you would be willing to accept now in payment of the debt if the interest rate is 10 percent.

---

[19] The reciprocal of this formula can be used to calculate the *annuity* that is equivalent to a specified present sum $(A/P, n, i)$.

$$(A/P, n, i) = 1/(P/A, n, i) = i/[1 - (1 + i)^{-n}] = \left[\frac{i(1 + i)^n}{(1 + i)^n - 1}\right]$$

$(A/P, n, i)$ is commonly called the *capital recovery factor* and frequently appears in separate tables.

[20] Notice that this example is quite similar to the previous one, except that in this case the $7,500 is payable in six yearly payments rather than in one payment at the end of six years. Because the series of receipts is not as distant as the single receipt, the present value of the annuity is larger than that of the single receipt six years hence ($5,444 versus $4,234), even though the total number of dollars is the same.

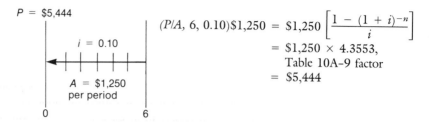

$$P = \$5,444$$

$$i = 0.10$$

$$A = \$1,250 \text{ per period}$$

$$0 \qquad 6$$

$$(P/A, 6, 0.10)\$1,250 = \$1,250 \left[\frac{1 - (1 + i)^{-n}}{i}\right]$$
$$= \$1,250 \times 4.3553,$$
$$\text{Table 10A-9 factor}$$
$$= \$5,444$$

That the present value of an annuity of six payments of $1,250 at 10 percent is $5,444 is shown in Table 10A-2.

TABLE 10A-2  Demonstration of the Present Value of an Annuity

| Period | (a) Amount Invested at Beginning of Period | (b) Interest Earned at 10 percent | (c) Payment | (d) Amount Invested at End of Period |
|---|---|---|---|---|
| 1 ....... | $5,444.00 | $544.40 | $1,250.00 | $4,738.40 |
| 2 ....... | 4,738.40 | 473.84 | 1,250.00 | 3,962.24 |
| 3 ....... | 3,962.24 | 396.22 | 1,250.00 | 3,108.46 |
| 4 ....... | 3,108.46 | 310.85 | 1,250.00 | 2,169.31 |
| 5 ....... | 2,169.31 | 216.93 | 1,250.00 | 1,136.24 |
| 6 ....... | 1,136.24 | 113.76* | 1,250.00 | — |

Note: Column (d) = Column (a) + Column (b) − Column (c).
*Adjusted to compensate for rounding errors.

**Present Value of Annuity Due.**  For the calculation of present value, there are only four interest periods in a five-year annuity due, since payments made at the beginning of Years 2-5 are the equivalent of payments made at the end of Years 1-4. Accordingly, the present value amount of an *annuity due* for n years is equal to $(P/A, n - 1, i) + 1$. The last item in the formula reflects the fact that the initial payment is received immediately (at the beginning of Year 1) and therefore is already stated at its present value. As applied to Table 10A-9, the above formula suggests, for example, that the factor for a five-year annuity due is calculated by adding 1.0000 to the factor found on line 4 in the appropriate interest column.

**Present Value Tables.**  Present value tables for $1 are presented in Tables 10A-8 and 10A-9 and supply us with the factors to use in expressing any dollar figures in terms of their present values. Table 10A-8 gives the amount a person would have to invest now at various interest rates in order to have $1 at the end of various time periods in the future. Table 10A-9 gives the amount a person would have to invest now at various interest rates in order to withdraw $1 at the end of each period for various time periods.

**Infinite Annuity.**  If annuity payments (receipts) continue for a large number of periods, the n in the present value formula below would become very large.

$$(P/A, n, i) = \frac{1 - (1 + i)^{-n}}{i}$$

As a result, the expression $(1 + i)^{-n}$ would become very small. In fact, as n approaches perpetuity, $(1 + i)^{-n}$ would approach zero, and the whole formula would approach the reciprocal of the interest rate $(1/i)$. By dividing the annuity payment (receipt) by the interest rate, we can calculate its present value, assuming an indefinite time period. If *n* exceeds 40–50 periods, the infinite annuity is a very close approximation.

**Continuous Discounting.**    With shorter compounding intervals, the future amount of any given quantity of money becomes greater. The opposite is true with respect to the discounting of amounts to present value: the shorter the interest period, the smaller the present value. With more frequent interest accumulations, more interest is earned on prior interest accumulations. Consequently, it is necessary to invest a smaller sum now if interest is compounded monthly than it if is compounded only annually. In other words, because amounts grow more rapidly with shorter interest periods, the "cost of waiting" for a delayed cash receipt is higher. Consequently, the current cash equivalent or present value is lower.

When the compounding period becomes infinitely short, the entire present value formula becomes $1/e^{in}$. The process giving rise to this formula is called continuous discounting; interest is accumulated and added to principal continuously rather than only intermittently. Some authors rightly contend that continuous discounting is more accurate when future cash receipts or payments consist of continuous flows throughout a time interval rather than of discrete quantities at specified intervals.[21]

Compound interest concepts can be used whenever managerial or investor decisions require a comparison of dollar amounts at two different points in time. In these cases consideration must be given to the time value of money. Conversion of amounts to their equivalents either in future values, or more commonly, present values provides a meaningful base of comparison for decisions involving time as a factor. The examples in the following sections briefly illustrate the application of compound interest techniques in some accounting and financial areas and provide an opportunity for using the interest tables.

## Asset Valuation

Assets are acquired to produce future economic benefits. Presumably, in deciding to acquire an asset, an investor makes a comparison between the present outflow to acquire an asset and the future inflows from the asset. Ideally, the value placed on the asset should be equal to the present value of the expected future net receipts derived from it. Two examples follow.

*Example 1—Bank Loan and Note Receivable:*  A bank is considering lending money through the acquisition of a $50,000 face value, five-year note to be issued by a nearby municipality. The note will be held to maturity as an investment. It bears no interest explicitly, but is being offered to the bank at a price of $30,000. The bank can invest its funds in alternative opportunities yielding 8 percent. Compound interest techniques can be used in a number of ways to help the bank decide whether to lend money on this note. First, if the bank invests its $30,000 in other opportunities, the $30,000 would grow to

---

[21] Continuous discounting (compounding) is more useful in mathematical operations involving calculus. Theoretically it may be more accurate for certain types of investment decisions, but it is not used for most financial transactions—borrowing and lending. Practically, it does not produce results materially different from that of annual or semiannual discounting when interest rates are not unduly high or time periods excessively long. Therefore, tables like those presented in this Appendix are more widely employed and are suitable for most situations.

only $44,079 [(F/P, 5, 0.08) $30,000 = $30,000 × 1.4693 = $44,079], which is significantly less than the $50,000 it would receive from the municipality. Alternatively, the bank could determine the present value of the note to be $34,030 [(P/F, 5, 0.08) $50,000 = $50,000 × 0.6806 = $34,030]. If the bank wishes to earn 8 percent it could lend up to $34,030. Since the bank has to lend only $30,000 to earn the $50,000 dollar return, the value of the asset to management ($34,030) is greater than its cost ($30,000).

*Example 2—Equipment:* Present value techniques play a large role in analyses of capital expenditures on plant assets. Take the following example. By purchasing a new piece of machinery for $70,000, a manufacturing firm could process its product one stage further. The more valuable product would command a higher selling price and cause sales to increase by $22,000 a year. The only other cost would be $12,000 of wages for an operator. The company believes that it can sell the machine for $5,000 at the end of its useful life of 10 years. The company will not undertake this investment unless it can earn a return of 10 percent. The maximum amount that the company should offer for the equipment is the present value of the expected returns from the equipment, discounted at 10 percent. The future values consist of a net return of $10,000 each year for 10 years ($22,000 of additional sales minus $12,000 for wages) and $5,000 at the end of 10 years.

$$\text{Present value of machine} = (P/A, 10, 0.10)\$10,000 + (P/F, 10, 0.10)\$5,000$$
$$= 6.1446(\$10,000) + 0.3855(\$5,000)$$
$$= \$63,374$$

Consequently, the firm would not pay $70,000 for this asset.[22]

**Financing Decisions**

We have already explored the relationship between present value concepts and bonds and notes payable. These same concepts can be extended to the valuation of other types of liabilities, such as leases, pensions, and various alternative forms of financing. Leases and pensions are discussed in Chapters 11 and 12. A few examples of the application of present value to installment contracts and deferred payment plans are given in this section.

*Example 1—Determination of Installment Payments:* A delivery service can acquire a new truck from a dealer by signing an installment note for $7,200. The note is to be liquidated over a 15-month period with interest at a rate of 1 percent per month. For financial planning, management wishes to know what the monthly installment payments will be. The face amount of the note can be viewed as the present value of a series of payments of $x$ amount for 15 periods at 1 percent per period.

$$(A/P, 15, 0.01)\$7,200 = \$7,200/(P/A, 15, 0.01)$$
$$= \$7,200 \div 13.8651$$
$$= \$519.29$$

---

[22] This approach is called the *net present value* method of analysis. For simplicity, we have ignored the many difficulties involved in actually determining future returns in realistic situations, including the impact of income taxes. An alternative approach, called the *discounted or time-adjusted rate of return*, solves for the interest rate that will make the present value of future receipts exactly equal to $70,000. In this case, the rate is approximately 8 percent, substantially below the desired 10 percent rate.

As a separate exercise the reader can verify that 15 payments of $519.29 will, in fact, repay the $7,200 debt plus interest at 1 percent per month.

*Example 2—Calculation of Effective Interest Rates:*   A metal fabricator purchases a stamping press costing $50,000. A deferred payment plan is arranged under which the purchaser will make a $10,000 down payment and a $46,658 payment at the end of the second year. What effective rate of interest is inherent in this arrangement? The general analysis can be set forth in terms of present value formulas as follows:

$$\$50,000 = \$10,000 + (P/F, 2, i)\$46,658$$
$$(P/F, 2, i)\$46,658 = \$40,000$$
$$(P/F, 2, i) = \$40,000/\$46,658 = 0.8573$$
$$i = 8 \text{ percent (on line 2 of Table 10A-8,}$$
$$0.8573 \text{ is found in 8 percent column)}$$

*Example 3—Comparison of Financing Plans:*   A real estate developer owns a piece of land at the edge of the city. Two companies have offered to purchase it under varying financial plans, as described below:

Offer 1:   $10,000 payment at the beginning of each year for five years.
Offer 2:   $15,000 down payment plus a four-year note for $35,000 face amount, bearing interest at the rate of 12 percent payable annually (i.e., $4,200 per year).

Money is worth 18 percent to the company. If the same risk is inherent in each offer, the best one is that which has the greater present value.

Offer 1 = Present value of a five-year *annuity due*
        = $(P/A, 4, 0.18)\$10,000 + \$10,000$(first payment)
        = $(2.6901)(\$10,000) + \$10,000$
        = $36,901
Offer 2 = $15,000 + $(P/A, 4, 0.18)(\$4,200) + (P/F, 4, 0.18)(\$35,000)$
        = $15,000 + $(2.6901)(\$4,200) + (0.5158)(\$35,000)$
        = $44,351

The comparison above involves listing the various cash inflows from each of the financing plans and then determining the present value of each inflow. On this basis, Offer 2 is the more advantageous.

**Depreciation Calculations**

The common accounting procedures for systematically allocating the cost of depreciable assets over their useful lives result in uniform, decreasing, or varying patterns of depreciation over time. One additional possibility is an increasing depreciation charge over time. A procedure called the *capital recovery* or *compound interest method* and based on present value concepts provides such a pattern.[23] This approach employs the assumption that the cost of a depreciable asset represents the present value of a series of future receipts.

For example, if it were known that a piece of equipment would produce net

---

[23] Another approach, called the *annuity method,* also results in the same increasing *net* charge against income. The annuity method includes an imputed interest cost as part of the cost of an asset and records a hypothetical interest revenue based on the interest that could have been earned had the funds not been tied up in the asset. The capital recovery method is more in accordance with conventional GAAP.

cash flows of $9,000 each year for the next four years and that a return of 12 percent should be earned on the investment, management would be willing to pay $27,337 for the asset [(P/A, 4, 0.12)$9,000]. Each periodic cash inflow of $9,000 is then viewed as comprising an income return and a recovery of capital (depreciation expense). For instance, the $9,000 receipt in the first year consists of $3,280 (12 percent × $27,337) income and $5,720 ($9,000 − $3,280) of recovered capital. The latter is the amount debited to Depreciation Expense. Table 10A–3 presents the analysis for the remaining three years as well. The income portion declines over time, since the unrecovered investment is smaller. As a consequence, the capital recovery portion (depreciation expense) increases over time.

TABLE 10A–3 Schedule of Depreciation Expense under the Capital Recovery Method

| Year | (a) Cash Receipt | (b) Portion Assumed To Be Income | (c) Depreciation Expense | (d) Accumulated Depreciation | (e) Year-End Book Value |
|---|---|---|---|---|---|
| 0 ... | | | | | $27,337 |
| 1 ... | $9,000 | $3,280 | $5,720 | $ 5,720 | 21,617 |
| 2 ... | 9,000 | 2,594 | 6,406 | 12,126 | 15,211 |
| 3 ... | 9,000 | 1,825 | 7,175 | 19,301 | 8,036 |
| 4 ... | 9,000 | 964 | 8,036 | 27,337 | — |

Note: Column (b) is 12 percent of the beginning-of-year amount in column (e). Column (c) equals Column (a) − Column (b). Column (e) equals $27,337 − Column (d).

The advantage claimed for the increasing-charge depreciation methods is that they provide a constant return on investment over the life of the asset, as can be seen in the comparison in Table 10A–4 between the capital recovery method and the straight-line expedient.

For external reporting purposes, objections are raised to the automatic *assumption* of a specific, positive earning rate on the asset. Some accountants also feel that the pattern of depreciation increasing over time is contrary to the actual usage of asset services.

Despite its rare use, the present value approach to depreciation does shed additional light on the nature of the investment process and the cost of asset services. Moreover, for the managerial purposes of planning or internal evaluation of divisions, it actually may provide more meaningful information about rate of return on investment. It suggests an alternative view of what matching means—a view stressing the relation of income to investment rather than the relation of expense to revenue.

**Summary**

There is an old adage that time is money. Compound interest and present value concepts simply put this adage into formulas and tables. The fundamental point is that differences in the timing of cash inflows and outflows must be considered when those flows are evaluated and compared. When we are determining the future amount that is equivalent to a given sum now, compound interest is involved. When the focal point is the amount at present (at present, of course, can be any specified point in time) which is equivalent to a given sum in the future, present value is employed. Often a time-line representation similar to those employed in this Appendix helps to organize the cash flows involved and to establish the proper time frame of reference.

Varying symbols and names are used to describe and express compound

**TABLE 10A–4   Comparison of Rates of Return under Alternative Depreciation Methods**

|  | Year 1 | Year 2 | Year 3 | Year 4 |
|---|---|---|---|---|
| Capital recovery method: |  |  |  |  |
| Net revenues ............... | $ 9,000 | $ 9,000 | $ 9,000 | $ 9,000 |
| Depreciation expense |  |  |  |  |
| (see Table 10A–3) .......... | 5,720 | 6,406 | 7,175 | 8,036 |
| Net income *(a)* .............. | $ 3,280 | $ 2,594 | $ 1,825 | $ 964 |
| Asset cost ................... | $27,337 | $27,337 | $27,337 | $27,337 |
| Accumulated depreciation |  |  |  |  |
| as of beginning of year ...... | — | 5,720 | 12,126 | 19,301 |
| Net asset investment |  |  |  |  |
| at beginning of year *(b)* ..... | $27,337 | $21,617 | $15,211 | $ 8,036 |
| Return on investment *(a/b)* ..... | 12% | 12% | 12% | 12% |
| Straight-line method: |  |  |  |  |
| Net revenues ................ | $ 9,000 | $ 9,000 | $ 9,000 | $ 9,000 |
| Depreciation expense |  |  |  |  |
| ($27,337/4 per year) ........ | 6,834 | 6,834 | 6,834 | 6,835 |
| Net income *(a)* .............. | $ 2,166 | $ 2,166 | $ 2,166 | $ 2,165 |
| Asset cost ................... | $27,337 | $27,337 | $27,337 | $27,337 |
| Accumulated depreciation |  |  |  |  |
| as of beginning of year ...... | — | 6,834 | 13,668 | 20,502 |
| Net asset investment |  |  |  |  |
| at beginning of year *(b)* ..... | $27,337 | $20,503 | $13,669 | $ 6,835 |
| Return on investment *(a/b)* ..... | 7.9% | 10.6% | 15.8% | 31.7% |

amounts and present values. Some authors use *s* (sum) or *a* (amount) instead of *F*, *r* (rate) instead of *i*, or *S* (series) instead of *A*. Alternative names include future sum, future value, future worth, compound amount, and present worth. The ones used in this Appendix are either commonly employed and/or recommended by the Standardization Committee of the Engineering Economy Division of the American Society for Engineering Education. The reader should be alert, however, to the use of other symbols. In most instances the context of the problem or the magnitude of the interest factor will reveal whether future amounts or present values are involved.

Table 10A–5 summarizes the four major interest concepts and symbols discussed in this Appendix.

**TABLE 10A–5   Summary of Symbols and Formulas**

| Table | Name | Symbol | Formula | Alternative Symbol |
|---|---|---|---|---|
| 10A–6 | Future Amount of $1 Present Value | *(F/P, n, i)* | $(1 + i)^n$ | a or $a_{\overline{n}i}$ |
| 10A–7 | Future Amount of an Annuity of $1 | *(F/A, n, i)* | $\dfrac{(1 + i)^n - 1}{i}$ | A or $A_{\overline{n}i}$ |
| 10A–8 | Present Value of $1 Future Amount | *(P/F, n, i)* | $\dfrac{1}{(1 + i)^n}$ | p or $p_{\overline{n}i}$ |
| 10A–9 | Present Value of an Annuity of $1 | *(P/A, n, i)* | $\dfrac{1 - (1 + i)^{-n}}{i}$ | P or $P_{\overline{n}i}$ |

**TABLE 10A–6   Future Amount of $1 *(F/P, n, i)***

| Number of Periods | 1% | 6% | 8% | 10% | 12% | 18% | 20% |
|---|---|---|---|---|---|---|---|
| 1 .... | 1.0100 | 1.0600 | 1.0800 | 1.1000 | 1.1200 | 1.1800 | 1.2000 |
| 2 .... | 1.0201 | 1.1236 | 1.1664 | 1.2100 | 1.2544 | 1.3924 | 1.4400 |
| 3 .... | 1.0303 | 1.1910 | 1.2597 | 1.3310 | 1.4049 | 1.6430 | 1.7280 |
| 4 .... | 1.0406 | 1.2625 | 1.3605 | 1.4641 | 1.5735 | 1.9388 | 2.0736 |
| 5 .... | 1.0510 | 1.3382 | 1.4693 | 1.6105 | 1.7623 | 2.2878 | 2.4883 |
| 6 .... | 1.0615 | 1.4185 | 1.5869 | 1.7716 | 1.9738 | 2.6996 | 2.9860 |
| 7 .... | 1.0721 | 1.5036 | 1.7138 | 1.9487 | 2.2107 | 3.1855 | 3.5832 |
| 8 .... | 1.0829 | 1.5938 | 1.8509 | 2.1436 | 2.4760 | 3.7589 | 4.2998 |
| 9 .... | 1.0937 | 1.6895 | 1.9990 | 2.3579 | 2.7731 | 4.4355 | 5.1598 |
| 10 .... | 1.1046 | 1.7908 | 2.1589 | 2.5937 | 3.1059 | 5.2338 | 6.1917 |
| 11 .... | 1.1157 | 1.8983 | 2.3316 | 2.8531 | 3.4786 | 6.1759 | 7.4301 |
| 12 .... | 1.1268 | 2.0122 | 2.5182 | 3.1384 | 3.8960 | 7.2876 | 8.9161 |
| 13 .... | 1.1381 | 2.1329 | 2.7196 | 3.4523 | 4.3635 | 8.5994 | 10.6993 |
| 14 .... | 1.1495 | 2.2609 | 2.9372 | 3.7975 | 4.8871 | 10.1472 | 12.8392 |
| 15 .... | 1.1610 | 2.3966 | 3.1722 | 4.1773 | 5.4736 | 11.9738 | 15.4070 |
| 20 .... | 1.2202 | 3.2071 | 4.6610 | 6.7275 | 9.6463 | 27.3930 | 38.3376 |
| 25 .... | 1.2824 | 4.2919 | 6.8485 | 10.8347 | 17.0001 | 62.6686 | 95.3962 |

**TABLE 10A–7   Future Amount of an Annuity of $1 *(F/A, n, i)***

| Number of Periods | 1% | 6% | 8% | 10% | 12% | 18% | 20% |
|---|---|---|---|---|---|---|---|
| 1 .... | 1.0000 | 1.0000 | 1.0000 | 1.0000 | 1.0000 | 1.0000 | 1.0000 |
| 2 .... | 2.0100 | 2.0600 | 2.0800 | 2.1000 | 2.1200 | 2.1800 | 2.2000 |
| 3 .... | 3.0301 | 3.1836 | 3.2464 | 3.3100 | 3.3744 | 3.5724 | 3.6400 |
| 4 .... | 4.0604 | 4.3746 | 4.5061 | 4.6410 | 4.7793 | 5.2154 | 5.3680 |
| 5 .... | 5.1010 | 5.6371 | 5.8666 | 6.1051 | 6.3529 | 7.1542 | 7.4416 |
| 6 ... | 6.1520 | 6.9753 | 7.3359 | 7.7156 | 8.1152 | 9.4420 | 9.9299 |
| 7 .... | 7.2135 | 8.3938 | 8.9228 | 9.4872 | 10.0890 | 12.1415 | 12.9159 |
| 8 .... | 8.2857 | 9.8975 | 10.6366 | 11.4359 | 12.2997 | 15.3270 | 16.4991 |
| 9 .... | 9.3685 | 11.4913 | 12.4876 | 13.5795 | 14.7757 | 19.0859 | 20.7989 |
| 10 .... | 10.4622 | 13.1808 | 14.4866 | 15.9374 | 17.5487 | 23.5213 | 25.9587 |
| 11 .... | 11.5668 | 14.9716 | 16.6455 | 18.5312 | 20.6546 | 28.7551 | 32.1504 |
| 12 .... | 12.6825 | 16.8699 | 18.9771 | 21.3843 | 24.1331 | 34.9311 | 39.5805 |
| 13 .... | 13.8093 | 18.8821 | 21.4953 | 24.5227 | 28.0291 | 42.2187 | 48.4966 |
| 14 .... | 14.9474 | 21.0151 | 24.2149 | 27.9750 | 32.3926 | 50.8180 | 59.1959 |
| 15 .... | 16.0969 | 23.2760 | 27.1521 | 31.7725 | 37.2797 | 60.9653 | 72.0351 |
| 20 .... | 22.0190 | 36.7856 | 45.7620 | 57.2750 | 72.0524 | 146.6280 | 186.6880 |
| 25 .... | 28.2432 | 54.8645 | 73.1059 | 98.3471 | 133.3339 | 342.6035 | 471.9811 |

Note: For an annuity due, take one more period and subtract 1.0000.

**TABLE 10A-8  Present Value of $1 (P/F, n, i)**

| Number of Periods | | | | Rate of Interest | | | |
| --- | --- | --- | --- | --- | --- | --- | --- |
| | 1% | 6% | 8% | 10% | 12% | 18% | 20% |
| 1 .... | 0.9901 | 0.9434 | 0.9259 | 0.9091 | 0.8929 | 0.8475 | 0.8333 |
| 2 .... | 0.9803 | 0.8900 | 0.8573 | 0.8264 | 0.7972 | 0.7182 | 0.6944 |
| 3 .... | 0.9706 | 0.8396 | 0.7938 | 0.7513 | 0.7118 | 0.6086 | 0.5787 |
| 4 .... | 0.9610 | 0.7921 | 0.7350 | 0.6830 | 0.6355 | 0.5158 | 0.4823 |
| 5 .... | 0.9515 | 0.7473 | 0.6806 | 0.6209 | 0.5674 | 0.4371 | 0.4019 |
| 6 .... | 0.9420 | 0.7050 | 0.6302 | 0.5645 | 0.5066 | 0.3704 | 0.3349 |
| 7 .... | 0.9327 | 0.6651 | 0.5835 | 0.5132 | 0.4524 | 0.3139 | 0.2791 |
| 8 .... | 0.9235 | 0.6274 | 0.5403 | 0.4665 | 0.4039 | 0.2660 | 0.2326 |
| 9 .... | 0.9143 | 0.5919 | 0.5002 | 0.4241 | 0.3606 | 0.2255 | 0.1938 |
| 10 .... | 0.9053 | 0.5584 | 0.4632 | 0.3855 | 0.3220 | 0.1911 | 0.1615 |
| 11 .... | 0.8963 | 0.5268 | 0.4289 | 0.3505 | 0.2875 | 0.1619 | 0.1346 |
| 12 .... | 0.8874 | 0.4970 | 0.3971 | 0.3186 | 0.2567 | 0.1372 | 0.1122 |
| 13 .... | 0.8787 | 0.4688 | 0.3677 | 0.2897 | 0.2292 | 0.1163 | 0.0935 |
| 14 .... | 0.8700 | 0.4423 | 0.3405 | 0.2633 | 0.2046 | 0.0986 | 0.0779 |
| 15 .... | 0.8613 | 0.4173 | 0.3152 | 0.2394 | 0.1827 | 0.0835 | 0.0649 |
| 20 .... | 0.8195 | 0.3118 | 0.2146 | 0.1486 | 0.1037 | 0.0365 | 0.0261 |
| 25 .... | 0.7798 | 0.2330 | 0.1460 | 0.0923 | 0.0588 | 0.0160 | 0.0105 |

**TABLE 10A-9  Present Value of an Annuity of $1 (P/A, n, i)**

| Number of Periods | | | | Rate of Interest | | | |
| --- | --- | --- | --- | --- | --- | --- | --- |
| | 1% | 6% | 8% | 10% | 12% | 18% | 20% |
| 1 .... | 0.9901 | 0.9434 | 0.9259 | 0.9091 | 0.8929 | 0.8475 | 0.8333 |
| 2 .... | 1.9704 | 1.8334 | 1.7833 | 1.7355 | 1.6901 | 1.5656 | 1.5278 |
| 3 .... | 2.9410 | 2.6730 | 2.5771 | 2.4869 | 2.4018 | 2.1743 | 2.1065 |
| 4 .... | 3.9020 | 3.4651 | 3.3121 | 3.1699 | 3.0374 | 2.6901 | 2.5887 |
| 5 .... | 4.8534 | 4.2124 | 3.9927 | 3.7908 | 3.6048 | 3.1272 | 2.9906 |
| 6 .... | 5.7955 | 4.9173 | 4.6229 | 4.3553 | 4.1114 | 3.4976 | 3.3255 |
| 7 .... | 6.7282 | 5.5824 | 5.2064 | 4.8684 | 4.5638 | 3.8115 | 3.6046 |
| 8 .... | 7.6517 | 6.2098 | 5.7466 | 5.3349 | 4.9676 | 4.0776 | 3.8372 |
| 9 .... | 8.5660 | 6.8017 | 6.2469 | 5.7590 | 5.3283 | 4.3030 | 4.0310 |
| 10 .... | 9.4713 | 7.3601 | 6.7101 | 6.1446 | 5.6502 | 4.4941 | 4.1925 |
| 11 .... | 10.3676 | 7.8869 | 7.1390 | 6.4951 | 5.9377 | 4.6560 | 4.3271 |
| 12 .... | 11.2551 | 8.3838 | 7.5361 | 6.8137 | 6.1944 | 4.7932 | 4.4392 |
| 13 .... | 12.1337 | 8.8527 | 7.9038 | 7.1034 | 6.4236 | 4.9095 | 4.5327 |
| 14 .... | 13.0037 | 9.2950 | 8.2442 | 7.3667 | 6.6282 | 5.0081 | 4.6106 |
| 15 .... | 13.8651 | 9.7123 | 8.5595 | 7.6061 | 6.8109 | 5.0916 | 4.6755 |
| 20 .... | 18.0455 | 11.4699 | 9.8182 | 8.5136 | 7.4694 | 5.3528 | 4.8696 |
| 25 .... | 22.0232 | 12.7834 | 10.6748 | 9.0770 | 7.8431 | 5.4669 | 4.9476 |

Note: For an annuity due, take one less period and add 1.0000.

## QUESTIONS AND PROBLEMS

**10–1.** On April 1, 1985, the Lederer Company issued $300,000 face amount of 10 percent, 10-year bonds. The bonds were issued when the market rate of interest was slightly over 12 percent (6 percent each six months). Lederer Company received $265,588 for the bonds. Interest is payable semiannually on October 1 and April 1.

*Required:*

a. Derive the $265,588 issue price by using the present value tables in the Appendix to this chapter.

b. Another person argues that the issue price should have been $266,106, the result of a different calculation in part *(a)*. How was this higher amount calculated? Did the company collect the right amount from the sale of the bonds? Explain carefully.

c. Explain why the company was willing to accept only $265,588 at the date of bond issuance when it will have to pay back the full $300,000?

d. Prepare journal entries for the Lederer Company as follows: (1) April 1, 1985; (2) October 1, 1985; (3) December 31, 1985 (end of accounting period); and (4) April 1, 1986. Use the effective-interest method.

e. If Lederer chose to prepare a balance sheet on April 1, 1990, what accounts and amounts would appear concerning the bonds? Assume the use of straight-line amortization of bond discount.

**10–2.** Refer to your answer to part *(e)* of Problem 10–1. The following alternative presentation has been suggested:

| | |
|---|---:|
| Bonds payable—principal (face amount $300,000 maturing April 1, 1995) | $167,520 |
| Bonds payable—interest ($15,000 per period for 10 periods) | 110,401 |
| Total carrying amount, April 1, 1990 | $277,921 |

*Required:*

a. Derive the above amounts by using the present value tables in the Appendix to this chapter.

b. Ignore the difference in format for the moment and concentrate on the difference in amount. Is the $277,921 carrying amount on April 1, 1990, more or less accurate than the figure you arrived at in *(e)* of Problem 10–1? Explain why.

c. Now ignore the difference in carrying amount and concentrate on the difference in format. Does the alternative format better serve financial statement readers? Explain.

**10–3.** The Hubbard Sales Corporation sold a large piece of machinery to the Elmwood Company. Hubbard received a 120-day, noninterest-bearing $5,000 note from Elmwood. The note was dated July 1 and was discounted by Hubbard at 12 percent. The note was paid at maturity.

*Required:*

a. Make dated journal entries on the books of the Hubbard Sales Corporation relating to the above note. Assume the books are closed on August 31. Record using the direct approach.

b. Make dated journal entries on the books of the Elmwood Company. Record using the contra account approach.

**10–4.** On July 1, 1984, Middleton Construction Company entered into the following two contracts:

1. Purchased land having a $75,000 market value. Middleton pays $15,000 cash now and promises to pay $23,282 on July 1 in each of the next three years.

2. Purchased equipment by issuing a 5 percent, six-year note for $25,000. The interest of $1,250 is paid annually on July 1, and the principal is due on July 1, 1990.

*Required:*

a. Determine the implied interest rate in the first contract and prepare the general journal entry to record the land purchase on July 1, 1984.

b. Prepare the journal entry for the July 1, *1985,* payment on the contract for land.

c. Assume that the best alternative source of funds with which to acquire equipment would entail an interest charge of 10 percent. Record the acquisition of the equipment using a 10 percent imputed interest rate.

d. Prepare the journal entry for the July 1, *1985,* payment on the contract for equipment.

e. How would these liabilities appear on a balance sheet prepared as of *December 31, 1985?* Indicate the accounts with amounts and tell how they would be classified.

**10–5.** The board of directors of South Corporation is trying to decide whether to issue its $5 million of seven-year bonds with a *nominal* rate of 8 percent or 12 percent. The vice president of finance indicates that the current *market* rate of interest for bonds of similar type and risk is 10 percent. Interest would be payable annually.

*Required:*

a. Calculate the proceeds from the bond issue if it is printed with a nominal rate of (1) 8 percent and (2) 12 percent.

b. Should South Corporation select the 12 percent nominal rate, in light of the fact that it produces greater proceeds with no greater face amount of bonds or market rate of interest?

c. What dollar amount of annual interest would have to be paid for the bonds to be issued at their $5 million face amount? Determine the present value for seven years at 10 percent of the difference between this amount and the cash interest paid with an 8 percent nominal rate. What does your answer represent? Why?

d. Calculate the interest expense for the first two years under each of the coupon arrangements. Explain why the interest expense declines in the second year in one case but increases in the second year in the other.

**10–6.** On July 1, 1984, the Scotch Company issued $800,000 face amount of 15-year, 10 percent bonds. The bonds were priced to yield investors an effective, market interest rate of 12 percent. Interest is to be paid *semiannually* on January 1 and July 1. The Scotch Company closes its books annually on December 31.

*Required:*

a. Calculate the price at which the bonds were issued on July 1, 1984.
b. Prepare all journal entries necessary on Scotch Company's books during 1984 in connection with this bond issue. Use effective interest amortization.
c. Repeat *(b)* using straight-line amortization. Which amortization procedure most accurately reflects the facts in this situation? Explain why.
d. If Scotch chooses to prepare a balance sheet on July 1, *1994,* what accounts and amounts would appear there for the bonds? Assume that the effective interest method is used. Calculate the amounts directly; do not prepare a complete amortization schedule year by year.
e. Assume that bonds with similar risk to Scotch's are yielding an effective, market rate of 15 percent on July 1, 1994. Would your answer in *(d)* change?

**10–7.** The following is a partially completed amortization table prepared by Metcalf Corporation to account for its issuance of $100,000 face amount of bonds. Amounts in the table have been rounded to the nearest dollar. These bonds mature in five years and pay interest annually.

| Year | Interest Expense | Interest Paid | Premium Amortization | Unamortized Premium | Year-End Carrying Amount |
|---|---|---|---|---|---|
| 0 | | | | $4,213 | $104,213 |
| 1 | $6,253 | $7,000 | _____ | _____ | _____ |
| 2 | _____ | _____ | _____ | _____ | _____ |

*Required:*

a. Determine the correct amount for each of the eight blank spaces in the table.
b. The vice president of finance has suggested that the issuance of the bonds should be recorded as follows:

```
Cash ........................................... 104,213
    Bonds Payable ............................          100,000
    Gain on Issuance of Bonds .................            4,213
```

Explain why this entry is not appropriate.

c. If *one* investor had purchased all of the Metcalf Corporation bonds at the date of issue, what journal entry would the *investor* have made on that date?

**10–8.** The following is a partially completed amortization table prepared by Murray Company to account for its investment in $100,000 face amount of Sherry Corporation bonds. Amounts in the table have been rounded to the nearest dollar. The bonds mature five years from the date of purchase/issue and pay interest annually.

| Year | Interest Revenue | Interest Received | Discount Amortization | Unamortized Discount | Year-End Carrying Amount |
|---|---|---|---|---|---|
| 0 | | | | $3,991 | $96,009 |
| 1 | $7,681 | $7,000 | $681 | 3,310 | 96,690 |
| 2 | _____ | _____ | _____ | _____ | _____ |
| 5 | _____ | _____ | 926 | _____ | _____ |

*Required:*

a. Determine the correct amount for each of the nine blank spaces in the table.
b. Which amortization method is Murray Company following? How do you know?
c. Why were the Sherry Corporation bonds issued at a discount?
d. Prepare the journal entries necessary at the issue date on the books of Murray and Sherry to record the purchase and sale of the bonds.
e. Prepare all necessary journal entries on both firms' sets of books at the end of Year 1 to reflect interest revenue/expense. Assume that Sherry follows the same amortization procedure as Murray.
f. What would the interest revenue have been for Murray Company for Year 1 if it had chosen to follow the other amortization procedure?

**10–9.** Assume that the following letter from a company president appeared in an annual report to stockholders:

> I am pleased to report that during this year your company sold successfully $1 million of new bonds. The interest rate on the bonds was set at 12 percent, and we sold the bonds at a premium. The premium not only reflects the excellent credit reputation of the company, but it also added significantly to this period's income. Moreover, because market rates of interest declined to only 10 percent, the premium more than offset the entire interest expense this year of $100,000.

Describe *all* the misconceptions which are evidenced by the above quotation.

**10–10.** Included among the listing of bonds trading on the New York Exchange in *The Wall Street Journal* of Thursday, June 16, 1983, were three separate issues of DuPont. A *portion* of the information presented for those bond issues appears below:

| Company | Bond Description | Closing Price—June 15 |
|---------|------------------|----------------------|
| DuPont | 8½%, 2006 | _____ |
| DuPont | 14%, 1991 | 111½ |
| DuPont | — %, 1985 | 103½ |

*Required:*

Comment on each of the following statements. Indicate whether each is true or false and explain the reasoning behind your answer.

a. "The bond issue which has a maturity date in 1985 is selling at 103½ because of the fact that it was originally issued at a small premium."
b. "Apparently persons who trade in DuPont bonds know nothing of present value concepts, because they appear willing to pay almost 8 percent more (111½ versus 103½) for a bond issue they will have to wait an additional six years to collect (1991 versus 1985)."
c. "The DuPont bond issue which matures in 2006 must have been quoted at significantly less than 103½ on June 15."

**10–11.** The Cooper Corporation issued $100,000 of seven-year, 10 percent convertible bonds on January 1, 1985. Interest was payable *semiannually* on July 1 and January 1. The bonds were issued at 90.7 percent of face amount. Each $1,000 bond is convertible into 30 shares of Cooper Corporation common stock. On January 1, 1988, holders of $40,000 face amount of the bonds decide to convert their bonds into common stock. The common stock has a current market value of $40 per share on the conversion date.

*Required:*

a. Assume that the market rate of interest was either 6, 8, or 12 percent on January 1, 1985. Without consulting present value tables, can you reason which of those three percentages was the actual market rate?
b. Use present value tables to derive the bonds' issue price of $90,705.
c. Prepare the journal entries necessary on Cooper's books during 1985 in connection with this bond issue. Cooper's accounting period ends on December 31.
d. Prepare two journal entries to reflect the conversion on January 1, 1988, one under the book value method and the other under the market value method. Which method is generally followed? Which method do you believe is most reflective of the economic substance of the event? Why?

**10–12.** RES Corporation shows the following accounts on its trial balance at the end of 1985:

```
Bonds payable, 10% (due in 1995) .............. $200,000 Cr.
Unamortized bond premium ....................      6,400 Cr.
Unamortized bond issue costs .................      1,800 Dr.
```

The bonds are callable at 104 percent of face value. The company has an opportunity to borrow money from an insurance company. The terms would be a 20-year, 6 percent bond for $220,000 to be purchased by the insurance company for $176,800. Not only does the new bond carry a lower interest rate but it also contains less restrictions on the company's dividend policies.

Accordingly, RES calls in and retires the old bond and issues the new one to the insurance company. The chief accountant makes the following entry:

```
Bonds Payable, 10% .............................. 200,000
Unamortized Bond Premium .........................   6,400
Cost of Successful Refunding .....................  49,600
   Unamortized Bond Issue Costs ..................            1,800
   Bonds Payable, 6% .............................          220,000
   Cash ..........................................           34,200
```

The credit to Cash is the difference between the $208,000 disbursed to call the old bonds and the $176,800 received from the issuance of the new bonds, plus $2,000 costs involved in calling the old bonds and $1,000 fees associated with issuing the new ones.

*Required:*

a. Determine the effective interest rate being charged by the insurance company.
b. Prepare journal entries to record the refunding of the bonds in accordance with generally accepted accounting principles.
c. The chief accountant describes the Cost of Successful Refunding account as an intangible asset to be amortized over the next 10 years, the remaining life of the old bond issue. Based on your entry in (b), determine exactly what elements comprise the $49,600. How should each of these elements be treated and why?

**10A–1.** Compute the future amount for each of the following cases. Use Tables 10A–6 and 10A–7.

a. $700 to be deposited at the end of each of the next four years. Interest is compounded annually at 6 percent. Verify your answer by calculating the size of the fund year by year.

b. $4,000 to be deposited immediately. Interest at 24 percent is compounded quarterly for five years.

c. $100 to be deposited immediately, $200 at the end of the first year, and $300 at the end of the second year. No additional deposits after that. Interest is compounded annually at 8 percent for six years.

d. $2,000 to be deposited immediately. Interest at 12 percent is compounded semiannually for the first four years, and then interest at 10 percent is compounded annually for the next four years.

e. $3,000 to be deposited at the end of each of the next five years. No additional deposits after that. Interest is compounded annually at 8 percent for 10 years.

**10A–2.**   The following exercises concern the understanding and use of present value tables:

a. Determine the present value of $400 under each of the following conditions:

| | Year of Receipt | Interest Rate |
|---|---|---|
| 1 .......... | 3 | 6% |
| 2 .......... | 6 | 10 |
| 3 .......... | 10 | 8 |

Verify your answer to Condition No. 1 by showing that a fund in the amount of your answer will indeed accumulate to $400 at the end of three years if invested at 6 percent.

b. Determine the present value of an annuity of $500 payable *semiannually* under the following conditions (assume *semiannual* discounting):

| | No. of Years | Interest Rate |
|---|---|---|
| 1 .......... | 4 | 12% |
| 2 .......... | 7 | 20 |
| 3 .......... | 10 | 12 |

Verify your answer to Condition No. 1 by preparing a table similar to Table 10A-2.

c. If you invest the sum specified in the first column, you will receive a single or a series of $100 payments in the year or years indicated in the second column. For each case, determine the actual annual rate of interest earned.

| | Invested | Year(s) of Receipt |
|---|---|---|
| 1 ........ | $ 40.39 | 8 |
| 2 ........ | 31.18 | 20 |
| 3 ........ | 624.69 | 1– 9 |
| 4 ........ | 2,202.32 | 1–25 |
| 5 ........ | 91.33 | 21–25 |

d. In Table 10A-8, the present values become smaller as one moves either down or across the table. Explain carefully why.

**10A–3.**   Alan Parmenter faced a dilemma after he found a new car which he wished to purchase for $8,300. The auto dealer offered Alan *either* 9.8 percent financing *or* an instant $300 cash rebate. Alan checked with his local bank and learned that it was charging 11.9 percent on auto loans. At that rate, the bank would require monthly payments of approximately $210 over the next four years in return for lending Alan the $8,000 he desired. The auto dealer informed Alan that the monthly payments with the 9.8 percent rate would be only $203 and urged him to "stay away from the bank and use the $36 savings to take the family out to dinner."

*Required:*

a. What role, if any, should present value concepts play in resolving the dilemma faced by Alan?
b. Should Alan opt for the 9.8 percent financing, or should he take the $300 instant cash rebate? Explain your reasoning.
c. Show how the auto dealer computed the $36 amount. If Alan spent it immediately to celebrate with his family the acquisition of the new car, would he break even?

**10A–4.** One developer of new houses in suburban Chicago knew that the homes, which averaged $250,000 in price, would be very difficult to sell during the 1981–1982 period of particularly high interest rates. Accordingly, prospective homeowners could select *one* of the following three financing incentives with their purchase of one of the new homes:

1. An interest rate of 0 percent, with 50 percent paid down and the balance due in 60 equal monthly payments.
2. A $25,000 cash discount if the customer arranges for his or her own financing.
3. A conventional 25-year mortgage at a 11.9 percent fixed rate.

*Required:*

a. What additional information would be necessary before you could advise an individual as to which financing incentive option he or she should choose?
b. Under what circumstances might the fixed-rate conventional mortgage prove more attractive than the $25,000 cash discount?
c. Under what circumstances might the option of a 0 percent interest rate prove *less* attractive than one or both of the other options?

**10A–5.** Roger Gammon checked his mail recently and found that he had received two interesting offers, one from a national magazine which he currently subscribed to and the other from the bank which held his present home mortgage. The magazine offered Roger special renewal rates of $25 for one year or $46 for two years. The bank wanted Roger to pay off the entire $17,000 remaining balance of his 6 percent home mortgage and was willing to settle for $14,000. The mortgage had 15 years to run. The interest rate on new mortgages was approximately 12 percent.

*Required:*

a. Roger believes that the two-year magazine renewal is the most attractive since he will save $4. If he can earn 12 percent on his investments, are the savings really $4?
b. Calculate the benefit to the bank resulting from an early payoff of the home mortgage. Roger's monthly mortgage payment was $200.
c. Should Roger accept the bank's offer? Explain your reasoning.

**10A–6.** A small, family-held company wishes to build up a fund which can be used, if necessary, to repurchase and retire the stock of a major stockholder upon his demise.

  *a.* How much will accumulate in the fund if deposits of $4,000 at the end of each year for the first five years and $8,000 per year for the next five years are made? Interest is compounded annually at the rate of 6 percent for the first five years and 8 percent for the next five years.

  *b.* If a fund of $90,000 is desired in 10 years, how much should be deposited at the end of each six-month period if interest of 12 percent is compounded semiannually?

**10A–7.**   A warehousing company is negotiating for a building to use for storage. The building can be purchased for $300,000 cash or can be acquired under a 10-year lease at an annual rental of $35,000, payable at the *beginning* of each year. The building's estimated resale value at the end of 10 years is $20,000. Under either arrangement, the warehouse company would pay all operating costs, maintenance, and property taxes.

    Which plan is better if the interest rate is assumed to be 8 percent? (Ignore income taxes.)

**10A–8.**   Assume your firm wishes to earn 12 percent on all investments in new equipment. It has under consideration the following three proposals (ignore income taxes):

| | | Cash Receipts | |
|---|---|---|---|
| Project | Cash Outlay | Amount | Years |
| A ........................ | $ 75,000 | $13,000 | 1–7 |
| B ........................ | 100,000 | { 17,000 | 1–8 |
| | | { 27,000 | 9 |
| C ........................ | 16,500 | { 2,500 | 1–4 |
| | | { 4,000 | 5–9 |

*Required:*

  *a.* Advise the company which of these projects it should accept and which it should reject. Show your calculations.

  *b.* Would your answers in *(a)* change if the desired earning rate was only 8 percent?

  *c.* What rate of return will the company earn on its money if it invests in Project B?

  *d.* What is the maximum amount the company could afford to invest in Project C and still earn 12 percent?

# CHAPTER 11

# LEASES

The discussion of notes and bonds in Chapter 10 explores some of the basic concepts and accounting problems associated with interest-bearing liabilities. Although notes and bonds represent legal claims, we should remember that the concept of a liability extends beyond specifically determinable legal obligations. Liabilities encompass all measurable future outlays of cash or other assets that result from past or current transactions.

When a significant time period exists between incurrence of a liability and its ultimate payment, the total cash payments include an interest charge for the delayed payment. Valuation of a liability at the present (discounted) value of the future payments removes the interest element and records the liability at the current cash equivalent to discharge the debt. This chapter discusses the accounting for leases, another area where present value concepts are extremely useful.

## NATURE OF LEASES

The conventional lease agreement conveys the right to use property from its legal owner (the *lessor*) to a second party (the *lessee*) in exchange for a periodic cash payment (rent). A common example is the typical rental agreement for an apartment between a landlord and tenant. The length of time the property may be used, any restrictions on its use, the amount and timing of lease payments, and other pertinent features normally are specified in the lease contract. In the last decade or so, leasing has become popular as a means for businesses to acquire a variety of asset services. As one might expect, the length of time covered by a lease may vary from a few hours or days (as when one rents an automobile) to the entire life of the asset (as when a store building is leased for 40 years).

The purposes for which items are leased are equally diverse. Some $37 billion worth of equipment was leased in 1980, twice as much as in 1975.[1] For 1982, leasing's share of plant and equipment outlays was $57.6 billion or 16.6% of the $347.6 billion U.S. companies spent that year.[2] Not only are airplanes, computers, and machinery leased, but recently farmers have begun to lease cows, restaurants have leased plants and flowers, and some corporations have even leased clothes for their executives.

Despite the diversity of lease property, terms, and purpose, often the nature of a lease arrangement suggests the economic substance of the transaction. For example, consider the difference between the rental of an apartment by its occupant for one year and the leasing of machinery by a firm for that asset's expected useful life. The former appears to be a straight short-term rental arrangement. The latter, although in form a rental, is in substance a sale by the lessor and an installment purchase by the lessee.

In this chapter we will examine how lease arrangements should be reflected in the financial statements. In particular, in what manner should the accountant recognize the rights to use property and the related obligations to make rental payments that exist under many leases? Certainly the very nature of assets and liabilities needs to be addressed before answers can be formulated. In particular, must a company be the current legal owner of each item which it reports as an asset on its balance sheet? Also, do any differences exist between the obligation to make periodic payments on a note or mortgage payable and the commitment existing under a noncancelable lease?

Because much of the accounting controversy about leases centers on the recording by lessees, slightly more attention is devoted to that side of the arrangement. However, we also look at the counterparts of asset and revenue recognition by the lessor. Specifically, the discussion focuses on five areas:

1. Prior practices in lease recording.
2. Accounting for lessees.
3. Accounting for lessors.
4. Disclosure requirements.
5. Unresolved issues in lease reporting.

The chapter concludes with an analysis of the leasing disclosures contained in Armco's 1981 Annual Report.

---

[1] "Faster Write-Offs May Spur Leasing," *Business Week,* March 23, 1981, p. 96.
[2] "Leasing Means Business," *Fortune,* October 31, 1983, p. 34.

**PRIOR PRACTICES IN LEASE RECORDING**

The reporting requirements and standards for leasing were especially vague and ineffective prior to the November 1976 release of *FASB Statement No. 13,* the current authoritative pronouncement.[3] Although the profession was aware that leases in substance actually fell into several distinct categories and types of transactions, the form of the arrangement was often permitted to govern the accounting recording. Unfortunately, lessees and lessors had a strong incentive to take advantage of the impotent guidelines espoused by the Accounting Principles Board in its four leasing opinions.[4]

As described later in this chapter, given complete freedom, lessors wish to record leases as sales while lessees wish to avoid recording leases as purchases. The prior freedom given to the parties to the leasing transaction resulted, accordingly, in billions of dollars of leased items not being shown or depreciated on *anyone's* books. If the item had been sold, it did not belong on the lessor's books; but it was not shown on the lessee's books either, because it was not viewed as having been purchased. Lessees who could avoid showing leased assets and obligations on their books were said to have engaged in "off-balance-sheet financing."

Faced with this vague and contradictory environment, the FASB issued a relatively comprehensive leasing standard late in 1976. Initially effective for all leases entered into on or after January 1, 1977, and subsequently made retroactive for all prior leases, *Statement No. 13* constituted a significant effort to improve lease reporting for three reasons:

1. It addressed itself to the entire leasing transaction. The previous APB Opinions had been exclusively directed at either lessees or lessors.
2. Perhaps as a result of (1), it established fairly common criteria for use in determining the nature of the lease from the viewpoint of both parties. As a result, far fewer leases now escape everyone's financial statements, for the factors permitting the lessor to view the transaction as a sale generally require the lessee to view it as a purchase.
3. It established additional disclosure requirements to permit the readers of the lessee's and lessor's financial statements to gauge the impact on those statements of the decisions made regarding the classification of leases.

The next two sections describe and illustrate the lease accounting mandated by *FASB Statement No. 13* for lessees and lessors, respectively.

---

[3] FASB, *Statement of Financial Accounting Standards No. 13,* "Accounting for Leases" (Stamford, Conn., November 1976).

[4] AICPA, *APB Opinion No. 5,* "Reporting of Leases in Financial Statements of Lessee" (New York, September 1964); *APB Opinion No. 7,* "Accounting for Leases in Financial Statements of Lessors" (New York, May 1966); *APB Opinion No. 27,* "Accounting for Lease Transactions by Manufacturer or Dealer Lessors" (New York, November 1972); and *APB Opinion No. 31,* "Disclosure of Lease Commitments by Lessees" (New York, June 1973).

**ACCOUNTING FOR LESSEES**

From the lessee's perspective, leases are classified as either *capital leases* or *operating leases*. A capital lease exists when the economic substance of the lease transaction suggests that the lessee is, in effect, acquiring the property being leased under a long-term installment purchase. The operating lease is a residual category; i.e., all leases which do not meet the criteria for being capital leases are considered to be operating leases. The lease-classification decision is important, because it greatly influences several key elements on the financial statements and the resultant financial ratios. The qualitative guideline of representational faithfulness stresses that the economic substance of the lease transaction and not the legal form should govern this classification.

How can capital leases be distinguished from operating leases? The FASB searched for reasonable and practical criteria which could be used in making the classification decision. In *Statement No. 13*, it specified that a lease shall be classified as a capital lease if at its inception it meets *at least one* of the following criteria:

1. The lease transfers ownership of the property to the lessee by the end of the lease term.
2. The lease contains a bargain purchase option.
3. The lease term is equal to 75 percent or more of the estimated economic life of the leased property.
4. The present value at the beginning of the lease term of the minimum lease payments . . . equals or exceeds 90 percent of the . . . fair value of the leased property to the lessor at the inception of the lease.[5]

Although cutoffs such as 75 and 90 percent are inevitably arbitrary, the above four conditions are reasonable and practicable. No lessee is going to receive from an economically rational lessor either a free transfer of ownership or a bargain purchase option unless the lease payments have in essence already paid for most of the asset's services. Similarly, an economically rational lessee who uses property for most of that asset's life or commits itself, in present value terms, to paying close to the outright purchase price of the leased property must, in substance, be acquiring the asset as if by a long-term installment purchase.

The accounting treatment for a capital lease differs greatly from the recording procedures for an operating lease. The economic substance of a capital lease consists of the acquisition of a future economic benefit and the creation of a long-term obligation. Accordingly, an asset and a liability must be reflected in the lessee's accounts. The leased property and lease obligation are placed on the lessee's balance sheet at the lessor of (1) the present value of the minimum lease payments required during the lease term or (2) the fair market value of the leased property at the inception of

---

[5] *FASB Statement No. 13,* par. 7.

the lease. The income statement reflects depreciation of the leased asset and interest on the capital lease obligation.

An operating lease, in contrast, is viewed as a straight rental arrangement. There are no long-term property rights or financing arrangements implicit in the lease agreement. The cash payments for rentals are usually expensed as they become due over the lease term. No balance sheet asset and liability are recognized for operating leases, and no depreciation expense or interest expense is recognized either.

**Illustration**

Suppose that Laural Corporation can acquire some machinery either for an immediate cash payment of $49,173 or for a $10,000 payment each December 31 under a six-year noncancelable lease. The machinery has a useful life of six years and no expected residual value. Calculations reveal that the effective interest rate implicit in the lease is approximately 6 percent [(P/A, 6, .06)$10,000 = $49,173]. If Laural decides to lease the machinery as of January 1, 1984, it would prepare *one* of the sets of journal entries which appear in Table 11–1 for 1984 and 1985, the first two years of the lease.

As you examine Table 11–1, keep in mind that Laural *cannot* choose between those two sets of journal entries. It must follow the left-most set of entries, as this transaction more than qualifies as a capital lease, meeting both Conditions 3 (length of lease at least equal to 75 percent of the life of the leased item) and 4 (present value of minimum lease payments at least 90 percent of the asset's initial fair market value). Prior to the issuance of *FASB Statement No. 13,* Laural probably could have interpreted the then-existing lease pronouncements as permitting recording of the machinery acquisition as a simple rental arrangement. *Statement No. 13* represents a distinct improvement in lease reporting by recognizing here the substance of the transaction rather than its form and, in the process, eliminating a major distortion from Laural's financial statements. For this lease the qualitative guideline of representational faithfulness is adhered to more closely under the treatment as a capital lease.

Table 11–2 reveals why lessees undoubtedly would prefer maximum discretion in their treatment of lease transactions. Note that requiring Laural to recognize the economic event as a capital lease results in its reporting:

1. More expense and, consequently, less income during the early years of the lease.
2. More assets during all six years of the lease.
3. As a result of (1) and (2), a lower return on investment (income/assets) in *all* six years of the lease, with the decline most pronounced in the early years.
4. More liabilities during all six years of the lease.

**TABLE 11-1 Effect of Lease Classification on Lessee's Accounting Entries**

| If Considered a Capital Lease | | If Considered an Operating Lease | |
| --- | --- | --- | --- |
| Jan. 1, 1984—beginning of lease term | | | |
| Leased Property under Capital Leases ................ 49,173 Obligations under Capital Leases ............ | 49,173* | No entry | |
| Dec. 31, 1984—end of first year of lease | | | |
| Interest Expense .................. 2,950 Obligations under Capital Leases ................ 7,050 Cash ...................... 6% × $49,173 = $2,950. | 10,000 | Lease Rental Expense ............ 10,000 Cash ........................ | 10,000 |
| Depreciation Expense ............ 8,196 Accumulated Depreciation .............. straight-line, ⅙ of $49,173. | 8,196 | | |
| Dec. 31, 1985—end of second year of lease | | | |
| Interest Expense .................. 2,527 Obligations under Capital Leases ................ 7,473 Cash ...................... $49,173 − $7,050 = $42,123; 6% × $42,123 = $2,527. | 10,000 | Lease Rental Expense ............ 10,000 Cash ........................ | 10,000 |
| Depreciation Expense ............ 8,196 Accumulated Depreciation .............. | 8,196 | | |

* Per *FASB Statement No. 13,* the liability account is credited for the net (principal) amount owed; $49,173 represents the present value of the lease commitments. Such recording does not reflect the $10,827 of *future* interest expense to be incurred ($60,000 − $49,173). Some accountants would record the initial transaction in a slightly different form:

| | | |
| --- | --- | --- |
| Leased Property under Capital Leases ......................... | 49,173 | |
| Discount on Obligations under Capital Leases ................... | 10,827 | |
| Obligations under Capital Leases ......................... | | 60,000 |

Curiously, as will be seen shortly, this form of recording is specified by the FASB for lessors.

5. As a result of (1) and (4), a higher proportion of total equities consisting of liabilities during *all* six years of the lease.

The figures shown in Table 11–2 for the Lease Obligations account on the balance sheet can be used to illustrate the critical role of present value analysis in the continual valuation of the liability. For example, the $42,123 lease obligation shown at December 31, 1984, can be thought of as more than merely the $49,173 balance at January 1, 1984, less the $7,050 excess of the 1984 cash payment over the 1984 interest expense (Table 11–1). By December 31, 1984, the first lease payment has been

**TABLE 11-2 Effect of Lease Classification on Lessee's Financial Statements**

| Income Statement | Lease-Related Expense | | | |
|---|---|---|---|---|
| | Interest | Depreciation | Rent | Total |
| 1984: | | | | |
| Capital lease ............. | $2,950 | $8,196 | –0– | $11,146 |
| Operating lease ........... | –0– | –0– | $10,000 | 10,000 |
| 1985: | | | | |
| Capital lease ............. | 2,527 | 8,196 | –0– | 10,723 |
| Operating lease ........... | –0– | –0– | 10,000 | 10,000 |

| Balance Sheet | Machinery | Accumulated Depreciation | Machinery (net) | Lease Obligation |
|---|---|---|---|---|
| January 1, 1984: | | | | |
| Capital lease ............. | $49,173 | –0– | $49,173 | $49,173 |
| Operating lease ........... | –0– | –0– | –0– | –0– |
| December 31, 1984: | | | | |
| Capital lease ............. | $49,173 | $8,196 | $40,977 | $42,123 |
| Operating lease ........... | –0– | –0– | –0– | –0– |
| December 31, 1985: | | | | |
| Capital lease ............. | $49,173 | $16,392 | $32,781 | $34,650 |
| Operating lease ........... | –0– | –0– | –0– | –0– |

made, and five remaining payments of $10,000 each are called for. With a 6 percent interest factor, the present value at December 31, 1984, of the remaining lease payments is $42,123 (adjusted for rounding):

Annuity amount .............................................. $10,000
Present-value factor, Line 5, 6% Column, from Table 10A-9 ........ 4.2124
Present value of remaining lease payments ..................... $42,124

**ACCOUNTING FOR LESSORS**

At times, the economic facts surrounding the lease transaction suggest that the lessor is basically a manufacturer or dealer who is using the leasing mechanism as a means of selling a product under a long-term sales contract. On other occasions, the lessor, although not a manufacturer or dealer, is essentially financing the long-term purchase by the lessee of property which that lessor has already acquired from a manufacturer or dealer. At other times, the lessor is merely entering into a short-term rental arrangement. These three different situations involving lessors are referred to, respectively, as sales-type, direct-financing, and operating leases.[6] The operating lease is, once again, a residual category; i.e., all lessor leases which cannot be considered either sales-type or direct-financing leases are considered to be operating leases.

[6] A fourth category of lessor leases, leveraged leases, is too technical for an introductory discussion.

How can sales-type, direct-financing, and operating leases be distinguished from one another for recording purposes? The FASB specifies in *Statement No. 13* that a lease will be *either* a sales-type or a direct-financing lease if:

1. It meets at least one of the four conditions for a capital lease which were previously discussed, and
2. It meets both of the following conditions:
   *a.* Collectibility of the minimum lease payments is reasonably predictable.
   *b.* No important uncertainties surround the amount of unreimbursable costs yet to be incurred by the lessor under the lease.[7]

All leases not meeting the above criteria are operating leases. If the criteria are met, the further classification into sale type or direct financing revolves around whether or not the lease creates for the lessor a manufacturer's or dealer's profit.[8] If it does, the lease is a sales-type. Otherwise, it is a direct-financing one. For example, if a lessor leases a computer under a capital lease, it is likely to be a sales-type lease if the lessor is IBM but a direct-financing lease if the lessor is the leasing department of a bank which bought the computer from IBM.

The conditions specifying the proper classification of lessor leases are, like the lessee criteria, reasonable and practicable. The reference to the capital lease criteria enhances consistency in the recording of the lease by both parties. Assurance of (1) the reasonable predictability of minimum lease payments and (2) the lack of important uncertainties surrounding the amount of unreimbursable costs yet to be incurred by the lessor is important even in nonlease situations for justifying the recording of a receivable and the initiating of revenue recognition.[9]

Great differences are called for in the accounting treatment by lessors of the three types of leases. As its name implies, a sales-type lease is viewed as a sale, so the manufacturer or dealer lessor must record sales revenue and cost of goods sold at the initiation of the lease and then reflect over the lease term the interest revenue (income) earned from the *financing* aspect of the transaction. Because of the treatment as a sale, the lessee, and not the lessor, should depreciate the property.

Under a direct-financing lease a receivable is established, and the property is removed from the lessor's books. The direct-financing lessor is not viewed as having sales revenue and cost of goods sold from the leasing transaction, so the lessor has no gross margin. The lessor's revenue in this case consists only of the interest reflected over the term of the lease.

---

[7] *FASB Statement No. 13,* par. 8.

[8] Ibid., par. 6.

[9] As noted in Chapter 6, it is only the absence of both such conditions that justifies use of the installment method of revenue recognition in lieu of revenue recognition at point of sale.

Under an operating lease, not only is there no sales revenue or cost of goods sold but the leased property is kept on the lessor's books and depreciated there. The only revenue reported is rental revenue, which is generally earned as it becomes receivable over the lease term. Thus treatment of an operating lease by the lessor parallels that by the lessee.

**Illustration**

Refer to the facts previously given concerning the Laural Corporation's six-year lease of some machinery. Assume that the machinery, which had a cash purchase price of $49,173, was manufactured by a lessor, Suma Corporation, at a cost of $40,000. Table 11–3 reveals how Suma would record the lease events under both the sales-type and operating-lease assumptions. Recall that 6 percent was the approximate effective interest rate implicit in the lease. In the far-right column of Table 11–3, the assumption that Suma manufactured the leased machinery is dropped. There it is assumed that Suma is a leasing division of a large bank and has recently made an outright cash purchase of the machinery for $49,173 from the manufacturer.

As noted in the explanation near the bottom of Table 11–1, *FASB Statement No. 13* specifies that lessors should establish any needed receivable account at the total dollar amount of future rentals owed. The $60,000 shown in Table 11–3 as the initial Lease Payments Receivable for the sales-type and direct-financing leases consists of the $49,173 discounted present value of amounts owed and $10,827 of as yet unearned interest revenue. Because the valuation of the receivable is its present value, the Unearned Interest Revenue account must be treated as a contra asset account to the Lease Payments Receivable account on the lessor's balance sheet. Interest revenue becomes earned and recognized over the six-year term of the lease, and it is accompanied by reductions in the Unearned Interest Revenue account. Because the lessor establishes the receivable for the gross payments due (including interest), this account can be reduced each year by $10,000, which is the full amount of the annual lease receipt. The lessee, as noted in Table 11–1, had to divide up each $10,000 payment into its interest and principal components. A comparison of the *net* receivable (Lease Payments Receivable less Unearned Interest Revenue) over the two years reveals that is has declined $7,050 and $7,473 in 1984 and 1985, respectively. These amounts are the same as the decline recorded directly in the liability account in Table 11–1.

As implied by its title, the *sales-type lessor* records sales revenue and cost of goods sold at the lease inception date. Merchandise Inventory is reduced, and $9,173 of gross profit ($49,173 − $40,000) is reflected immediately in income. The *direct-financing lessor* is not considered to have made a sale. Accordingly, no gross profit is recorded, and its revenue from the lease will include only the interest revenue which the sales-type lessor also recognizes. The leased property remains on the books of the *operating lessor,* so it is the only lessor in Table 11–3 which records Depreciation

**TABLE 11-3  Effect of Lease Classification on Lessor's Accounting Entries**

| | If Lease Is Considered | | |
|---|---|---|---|
| | Sales Type | Operating | Direct Financing |
| **Jan. 1, 1984—Beginning of lease term** | Lease Payments Receivable ............ 60,000<br>  Sales ............... 49,173<br>  Unearned Interest Revenue ........... 10,827 | No entry | Lease Payments Receivable ............ 60,000<br>  Machinery ........... 49,173<br>  Unearned Interest Revenue ........... 10,827 |
| | Cost of Goods Sold ......... 40,000<br>  Merchandise Inventory .......... 40,000 | Property Leased to Others ......... 40,000<br>  Merchandise Inventory .......... 40,000 | |
| **Dec. 31, 1984—End of first year of lease** | Cash ............ 10,000<br>  Lease Payments Receivable ...... 10,000 | Cash ............ 10,000<br>  Lease Rental Revenue ...... 10,000 | Cash ............ 10,000<br>  Lease Payments Receivable ...... 10,000 |
| | Unearned Interest Revenue ............ 2,950<br>  Interest Revenue ...... 2,950<br>$60,000 − $10,827 = $49,173<br>net receivable; 6% of<br>$49,173 = $2,950. | Depreciation Expense ............ 6,667<br>  Accumulated Depreciation ...... 6,667<br>straight-line, ⅙ of $40,000. | Unearned Interest Revenue ............ 2,950<br>  Interest Revenue ...... 2,950<br>$60,000 − $10,827 = $49,173<br>net receivable; 6% of<br>$49,173 = $2,950. |
| **Dec. 31, 1985—End of second year of lease** | Cash ............ 10,000<br>  Lease Payments Receivable ...... 10,000 | Cash ............ 10,000<br>  Lease Rental Revenue ...... 10,000 | Cash ............ 10,000<br>  Lease Payments Receivable ...... 10,000 |
| | Unearned Interest Revenue ............ 2,527<br>  Interest Revenue ...... 2,527<br>$50,000 − $7,877 = $42,123<br>net receivable; 6% of<br>$42,123 = $2,527. | Depreciation Expense ............ 6,667<br>  Accumulated Depreciation ...... 6,667 | Unearned Interest Revenue ............ 2,527<br>  Interest Revenue ...... 2,527<br>$50,000 − $7,877 = $42,123<br>net receivable; 6% of<br>$42,123 = $2,527. |

Expense. In the operating lease situation the lessor records Lease Rental Revenue in place of gross profit and interest revenue.

Of course, Suma *cannot* choose among the three sets of journal entries exhibited in Table 11–3. If (1) Suma is the manufacturer of the leased machinery, (2) at least one of the capital-lease conditions are met, (3) collectibility of the minimum lease payments is reasonably predictable, and (4) no important uncertainties concerning future costs remain, then the journal entries in the left-most column of Table 11–3 *must* be followed, because the event qualifies as a sales-type lease. In similar fashion, changed circumstances would dictate treatment as either a direct-financing or an operating lease.

An examination of Table 11–4 illustrates why manufacturers or dealers have a strong desire to treat their lease transactions as sales-types. If Suma had been required to recognize an operating lease rather than a sales-type lease, it would report:

1. No gross profit in the first year of the lease.
2. Depreciation expense in each year of the lease.

**TABLE 11–4   Effect of Lease Classification on Lessor's Financial Statements**

| | Lease-Related Revenues and Expenses | | | | | |
| | Revenues | | | Expenses | | Net |
| Income Statement | Sales | Interest | Rental | Cost of Goods Sold | Depreciation | Income |
|---|---|---|---|---|---|---|
| 1984: | | | | | | |
| Sales type | $49,173 | $2,950 | –0– | $(40,000) | –0– | $12,123 |
| Operating | –0– | –0– | $10,000 | –0– | $(6,667) | 3,333 |
| Direct financing | –0– | 2,950 | –0– | –0– | –0– | 2,950 |
| 1985: | | | | | | |
| Sales type | –0– | 2,527 | –0– | –0– | –0– | 2,527 |
| Operating | –0– | –0– | 10,000 | –0– | (6,667) | 3,333* |
| Direct financing | –0– | 2,527 | –0– | –0– | –0– | 2,527 |

| Balance Sheet | Property Leased to Others (net) | Present Value of Lease Payments Receivable |
|---|---|---|
| January 1, 1984: | | |
| Sales type | –0– | $49,173 |
| Operating | $40,000 | –0– |
| Direct financing | –0– | 49,173 |
| December 31, 1984: | | |
| Sales type | –0– | 42,123 |
| Operating | 33,333 | –0– |
| Direct financing | –0– | 42,123 |
| December 31, 1985: | | |
| Sales type | –0– | 34,650 |
| Operating | 26,666 | –0– |
| Direct financing | –0– | 34,650 |

* Although 1985 income is higher under the operating lease than under the sales-type lease, this would not be true if accelerated depreciation were used. Note also that cumulative 1984–1985 income is $14,650 under the sales-type and $6,666 under the operating lease.

3. Because of (1) and (2), less favorable income performance in the first few years of the lease (the use of an accelerated depreciation method would extend the period of reporting less favorable income performance).

**DISCLOSURE REQUIRE-MENTS**

*FASB Statement No. 13* imposes certain requirements for disclosure of lease information in footnotes to the financial statements. Some of the major disclosures are:

1. A general description of leasing arrangements by both lessees and lessors.
2. Future minimum lease payments to be paid or received in connection with capital leases and operating leases for each of the next five years.
3. Rental expense (lessee) and rental revenue (lessor) under operating leases, with separate amounts for minimum rentals, contingent rentals, and sublease rentals.
4. The gross amount of assets recorded under capital leases by the lessee.

**UNRESOLVED ISSUES IN LEASE REPORTING**

Although many observers regard *FASB Statement No. 13* as improving the quality and quantity of lease disclosures, some believe that the FASB has gone too far, and others feel that not enough progress has been made.

**Objections to Capitalization of Leases**

Numerous objections have been raised to the capitalization of leases on the balance sheet of the lessee. One group of objections centers around potential unfavorable consequences that might result from disclosing leases as assets and liabilities. Fears are voiced that lessees, by reporting more debt and less earnings, would suffer an impairment in their borrowing ability and a decline in their stock prices.

Unfortunately, the above viewpoint ignores the important issue of whether capitalization best reflects the nature of many lease transactions and their impact on financial position and operating performance. Accountants should not be deterred from disclosing economic substance rather than legal form, even if the increased lease capitalizations mandated by *Statement No. 13* have an effect on the lessee's stock and bond prices. Interestingly, a major research study discovered that the capitalization of leases had no such significant effects.[10]

A second objection goes beyond the specific issue of lease reporting and questions whether any accounting pronouncement should be allowed

---

[10] A. Rashad Abdel-khalik, "The Economic Effects on Lessees of *FASB Statement No. 13*, 'Accounting for Leases,'" *Research Report*, (Stamford, Conn.: FASB, 1981).

to cause, rather than merely reflect, economic events.[11] It has been confirmed that *Statement No. 13* did cause changes in management's behavior. These changes included the restructuring of lease transactions (usually to avoid capitalization) and postponement of other debt offerings.[12] Nevertheless, the presence or absence of management responses should not take away from the basic question of whether or not the increased capitalization of leases best reflects economic reality.

A third set of objections to capitalization raises questions about the possibility of measuring the asset and liability amounts accurately. Estimates must be made of the portion of lease rentals which are payments for property rights and the portion representing payments for other services. Similarly, the rate to be used in discounting and the frequency of discounting may not be known with precision. However, the judgments and estimates involved would seem to fall well within the tolerances existing for other areas in accounting. The discount rate, if not explicit in the lease contract, could be determined by a comparison of lease prices and purchase prices, if the latter are available, or through objective determination of the market rate of interest for leases (usually one half to one percentage point higher than what the company is currently paying on other loans). In any case, for most situations the differences in present value caused by different estimates of interest rates or compounding periods are probably acceptable.

The fundamental view that capital leases represent assets and liabilities to the lessee is the point of attack of a fourth set of objections. Some of these objections define assets narrowly, equating them with legal ownership or, at least, eventual ownership. Others claim that lease obligations are not debt because in case of bankruptcy or reorganizations, courts traditionally have treated leases differently from other liabilities. This idea, however, is premised on a liquidation rather than a going concern.

The most perplexing argument in this category states that leases are merely *executory contracts*, both sides of which are equally unperformed. Performance by the lessor is viewed as a continuous concept involving either an implicit approval each period of the use of the asset by the lessee or a replacement of a faulty, destroyed, or obsolete asset. If the lessor does not continuously perform, the lessee has no obligation to pay. Therefore, leases should be recorded as are other executory contracts, for example, long-term employment contracts or purchase commitments. An asset is recorded only if a prepayment is made; a liability is recorded only when services actually are received.

Although some of the above arguments may possess some merit, many observers favor the expansion of existing disclosure requirements, the

---

[11] This argument has also surfaced with regard to accounting rulings on research and development and foreign currency translation and, accordingly, is discussed at several points in this book.

[12] Abdel-khalik, "Economic Effects."

closing of numerous loopholes in *Statement No. 13,* and the capitalization of even more leases than are presently required to be capitalized.

**Support for Increased Capitalization of Leases**

Users of financial statements need adequate information to permit an assessment of the reasonableness of the asset, liability, and net income numbers presented. In addition, knowledge concerning the amount and timing of future cash flows is of great importance. Many users believe that capitalization most often reflects the economic substance of the leasing transaction; they applauded the issuance of *Statement No. 13.*

Some accountants advocate that all long-term leases used as financing devices should be capitalized by lessees. They believe that the noncurrent assets utilized by the lessee should be shown in order for financial statement users to get a correct impression of the scale of the lessee's business and its return on investment (net income/average assets). In similar fashion, the lessee's obligation to make periodic lease payments for the use of leased assets strikes them as no less a liability than the obligation to make periodic payments on a long-term note or mortgage. Certainly knowledge of the commitments made on all long-term noncancelable leases is an essential input to any complete analysis of the magnitude and timing of future cash flows.

The argument of those proposing expanded lease capitalization can be summarized as follows:

> To the extent, then, that the rental payments represent a means of financing the acquisition of property rights which the lessee has in his possession and under his control, the transaction constitutes the acquisition of an asset with a related obligation to pay for it. To the extent, however, that the rental payments are for services such as maintenance, insurance, property taxes, heat, light, and elevator service, no asset has been acquired, and none should be recorded.[13]

This test distinguishes between payments for the *right to use* property and payment for other executory services yet to be performed. Delivery of the leased asset constitutes a service completely performed by the lessor. The lessee has the right to use the leased property for a significant time period. For other services requiring continuous or periodic performance by the lessor in the future, an asset does not exist.

Capital leases provide the lessee with the right to the service potential of the property, conditioned only in that the lessee has no residual rights in the property at the end of the lease period. The lease payments, save for the portion applicable to additional services, constitute a type of installment payment for these user rights. The lessee has an irrevocable obligation to make the lease payments, which include the interest element

---

[13] John H. Myers, *Accounting Research Study No. 4,* "Reporting of Leases in Financial Statements" (New York: AICPA, 1962) p. 5.

inherent in any deferred payment arrangement. Under the above viewpoint, such a lease should be capitalized.

Short of requiring the capitalization of all long-term leases, some steps could be taken to perhaps increase the effectiveness of the existing provisions of *Statement No. 13*. Ambiguities and loopholes in the statement and the ingenuity of lessors eager to please prospective lessees have combined to create a number of lessor sales that have not had to be reflected as lessee purchases.[14] The inherent arbitrariness of such cutoffs as 75 percent of estimated useful life and 90 percent of fair market value has also created situations amenable to noncapitalization by lessees. Efforts to reduce such loopholes are probably worth pursuing.

Another step favored by some would be a requirement that the presently disclosed amounts for future operating lease payments be discounted to their present value, as they would be if those leases had been capitalized. Although not currently disclosed in annual reports, this useful present value information is a required disclosure for statements filed with the SEC.[15] Publication of such data would allow more accurate comparison of the financial statements of two firms, one of which leases extensively while the other leases very little. It would also allow those who favor the capitalization of almost all leases to compute what to them would represent the true present debt obligations of the lessee.

## DISCUSSION OF THE ARMCO ANNUAL REPORT

A description of Armco's leasing activities appears in Note 4 to the financial statements contained in its 1981 annual report. The information presented there for capitalized leases confirms the propriety of accounting for the leased facilities as if they were purchases. Armco has financed the acquisition of those long-term assets through the issuance of Industrial Revenue Bonds. Legally, the bonds were issued by some governmental entity, which built the facilities to Armco's specifications. Armco legally only rents the facilities from the governmental entity. However, the facilities can be purchased at any time during the lease term if Armco is willing to redeem the bonds or can be acquired at the end of the lease for nominal amounts.

In lieu of reporting Leased Property as a depreciable tangible asset, Armco has adopted an acceptable alternative of reporting Lease Rights as an intangible asset. A separate amortization expense is then recorded to reflect use of this asset. Some might take slight exception to the firm's classification, arguing that a lease which in substance represents the pur-

---

[14] For an excellent discussion of such abuses and proposed remedies, see Richard Dieter, "Is Lessee Accounting Working?" *The CPA Journal,* August 1979, pp. 13–19.

[15] SEC, *Accounting Series Release No. 147,* "Notice of Adoption of Amendments to Regulation S-X Requiring Improved Disclosure of Leases" (Washington, D.C., October 5, 1973).

chase of tangible property should be included within the Property, Plant, and Equipment umbrella and depreciated.

Capitalized Lease Rights appear on Armco's balance sheet, net of accumulated amortization, at $59.4 million and $67.2 million at December 31, 1981, and 1980, respectively. The $7.8 million decline in the Lease Rights account during 1981 represents the annual lease rights amortization, as revealed in the operations section of Armco's statement of changes in consolidated financial position. The *original* cost of the lease rights on the balance sheet at the end of both 1980 and 1981 totals $155.8 million. Armco has apparently selected 20 years as the appropriate period for the straight-line amortization ($155.8/20 years = $7.8). Moreover, no new leases were capitalized in 1981.

If $155.8 million represents the cash-equivalent costs of the leased facilities acquired, then the company made the following entry at the initiation of the leases:

```
Capitalized Lease Rights .............................   155.8
       Capitalized Lease Obligations .......................          155.8
```

Although the asset and liability accounts begin with the same balance and someday will both be reduced to zero, they exhibit distinctively different patterns and rates of decline. As noted above, the asset account is reduced in a straight-line pattern over 20 years. At $7.8 million per year amortization, the Lease Rights will be amortized into 1989 ($59.4 million/$7.8 million = 7.6 remaining years). The liability account, on the other hand, has been recorded at the present value of remaining obligations and, due to the interest factor, will decline less in the early years of the lease (when interest is greater) and more later on.

Because Armco's balance sheet reports a decline of $8.0 million in the long-term liability during 1981 and a reduction of $5.6 million in the future interest expense, the firm made the following entry:[16]

```
Interest Expense ........................................    5.6
Capitalized Lease Obligations ..........................    8.0
       Cash ..............................................          13.6
```

Armco will experience the same pattern exhibited by the lessee in the journal entries in Table 11–1. Less of each subsequent lease payment will go for interest, and more will go to reduce the principal owed. As described in Note 4, the Capitalized Lease Obligations account will not be reduced to zero until 1993.

No information is presented concerning the operating leases which Armco has entered into. The disclosure requirements for operating leases, noted earlier in this chapter, are waived when, as is the case here, "amounts applicable to operating leases are not significant." Armco's

---

[16] This journal entry is only an approximation of the recording made by Armco. Changes during 1981 in the current portion of lease obligations would affect the determination of the exact amounts.

capitalized leases do materially affect the amounts shown for long-term debt in the balance sheet. Reported long-term debt of $680.2 million ($572.8 million + $107.4 million) at December 31, 1981, would be understated by 16 percent if the long-term capitalized lease obligations were able to go unreported or to be buried in a footnote.

## SUMMARY

There are normally two parties to a lease transaction. The lessee uses the asset and pays rent for it; the lessor holds legal title to the asset and receives the rental amounts. A critical accounting issue focuses on detecting those leasing transactions that are in substance, if not in form, installment purchases of the leased property from the lessor by the lessee. An asset and a liability must be reflected for such capital leases on the lessee's books. An operating lease, on the other hand, is viewed by the lessee as a straight rental arrangement. The lessee records only rent expense.

From the lessor's perspective, a determination must be made as to whether the leasing transaction constitutes a sale by a manufacturer or dealer, a transfer of property and direct financing arrangement by a lessor who is not a manufacturer or dealer, or a simple operating lease rental situation. In the first two cases the lessor records an interest-bearing receivable. In the first case the manufacturer/dealer records a gross margin on the sale and interest revenue from the financing of the sale through the lease. In the second case only interest revenue is recognized by the lessor. Under an operating lease, the lessor records only rental revenue and depreciation expense on the leased asset.

The FASB, in its *Statement No. 13,* has formulated generally reasonable criteria for use by lessees and lessors in making the lease-classification decision. Those criteria have made it more difficult for a lessee's purchase through the leasing mechanism to escape its balance sheet. The degree of symmetry between lessee and lessor reporting for the same lease has been greatly increased. The arguments put forth for the existing or even expanded capitalization standards seem more persuasive than those calling for capitalization of fewer leases.

The classification decision substantially affects the financial statements of both the lessee and the lessor, particularly of the former. For the lessee, a capital lease in comparison to an operating lease results in greater assets and debt, generally lower net income, and significantly lower return on investment.

Our simplified calculations and examples show the use of present value in the valuation of lease liabilities and, to some extent, of assets and expenses. Dollar amounts to be paid or received over future periods of time can be dealt with effectively only in this manner. Which of these present values are recorded as accounting liabilities (assets) depends on other criteria and definitions, but the valuation methodology is unmistakably clear.

## QUESTIONS AND PROBLEMS

**11-1.** On January 1, 1985, the Pinta Corporation signed an eight-year, noncancelable lease agreement for the use of some equipment. The equipment has a cash cost of $95,000, a useful life of about eight years, and a very nominal residual value. The contract calls for payments of $17,807 to be made at the end of each year. The firm capitalizes the lease rights and related obligations.

*Required:*

a. Under generally accepted accounting principles, is Pinta Corporation required to record this arrangement as a capital lease? Explain.

b. Demonstrate that the effective interest rate implicit in the lease is approximately 10 percent.

c. Prepare all the journal entries necessary on Pinta's books during 1985 and 1986 in connection with the lease. Management selects the sum-of-the-years' digits method for the amortization of the lease rights.

d. Are you troubled by the fact that your entries in *(c)* show the asset account decreasing by less in each successive year while the liability account decreases by larger amounts in each successive year? Explain.

e. What accounts and amounts will appear on the December 31, 1986, balance sheet relative to this lease?

**11-2.** Memorial Corporation manufactures equipment used in demolition work. Fish Company wishes to buy a special type of crane from Memorial but cannot obtain sufficient financing. Memorial offers the crane to Fish on a noncancelable lease for 12 years, which is the crane's useful life.

The lease agreement is signed January 1, 1984, and calls for a $22,000 payment to be made at the end of each year. The crane cost Memorial $120,000 to manufacture and it has a normal sales price of $136,277.

*Required:*

a. Calculate the effective rate of interest implicit in this lease agreement.

b. Prepare all the journal entries needed to properly record the lease on Fish Company's (the lessee's) books during 1984 and 1985. Assume that the firm uses the sum-of-the-years' digits method to amortize the lease rights.

c. Assume that Fish was able to reflect this transaction as an operating lease. Prepare all journal entries necessary during 1984 and 1985.

d. Compare and contrast the expenses reported during 1984 and 1985 as a result of the entries in *(b)* versus the entries in *(c)*. Would Fish Company prefer the *(b)* series of journal entries or the *(c)* series of entries?

e. Which series of entries, *(b)* or *(c)*, best reflects for the lessee the economic reality of the situation? Explain.

**11-3.** Refer to the leasing situation which was introduced in Problem 11-2.

*Required:*

a. Prepare all the journal entries needed to properly record the lease on Memorial Corporation's (the lessor's) books during 1984 and 1985.

b. Assume that Memorial could reflect this transaction as an operating lease. Prepare all journal entries necessary during 1984 and 1985. Memorial uses straight-line depreciation for all of its plant assets.

c. Compare and contrast the revenues and income reported during 1984 and 1985 as a result of the entries in *(a)* vis-à-vis the entries in *(b)*. Would Memorial Corporation prefer the *(a)* series of journal entries or the *(b)* series of entries?

d. Which series of entries, *(a)* or *(b)*, best reflects for the lessor the economic reality of the situation?

**11–4.** The Mineral Point Computer Manufacturing Company makes and sells a computer model, Series 6318. The cost to Mineral Point is $2,000,000. Customers can acquire the computer at a cash sales price of $2,400,000, or they can acquire it under a 15-year lease arrangement. The lease is noncancelable and requires a down payment of $500,000 plus a cash payment of $249,800 at the end of each of the 15 years. On January 1, 1985, the West Company acquired one of the Series 6318 computers under the lease arrangement.

*Required:*

a. "The rate of interest implicit in the lease is slightly more than 6 percent, since $2,400,000/$249,800 equals a present-value factor of 9.608." Is this statement accurate? Explain.

b. Show all the journal entries which would be made on the *lessor's* books during 1985, assuming that the lessor must view the transaction as a sales-type lease.

c. Repeat part *(b)*, but now assume that the recording is for an operating lease.

d. Show all the journal entries which would be made on the *lessee's* books during 1985, assuming that the lessee must view the transaction as a capital lease.

e. Repeat part *(d)*, but now assume that the recording is for an operating lease.

**11–5.** White Corporation reported the following assets and equities on December 31, 1984 (amounts in millions of dollars):

| Assets | | Equities | |
|---|---|---|---|
| Current | $ 20.4 | Current liabilities | $ 11.6 |
| Plant assets (net) | 115.0 | Long-term liabilities | 89.9 |
| | | Common stock | 20.0 |
| | | Retained earnings | 13.9 |
| Total assets | $135.4 | Total equities | $135.4 |

The company recently approached its local bank and requested a loan to finance the purchase of $1.5 million of new equipment having an estimated useful life of 12 years. The bank refused to grant the firm the eight-year loan it had requested, even at the 15 percent interest rate White Corporation was willing to pay. The company had almost given up, when the equipment dealer offered to structure an eight-year lease that "won't mess up your balance sheet and will only carry a 12 percent interest rate."

The firm enters into the lease on January 1, 1985. Payments of $268,741 are due each December 31.

*Required:*

a. Explain why the bank may have been reluctant to approve White Corporation's application for a loan.

b. How could the dealer/lessor afford to offer White a lease interest rate of 12 percent, a full 3 percent below the bank's rate?

c. How could the acquisition of this equipment have "messed up" White's balance sheet? Has the lessor structured the lease agreement so as to avoid such an occurrence? Explain, showing calculations.

d. Prepare all journal entries necessary on White's books for 1985 in connection with the lease.

e. Assume White's 1985 earnings before taxes, interest, and leasing costs were $7.8 million. Calculate the amount of the firm's after-tax earnings (assume a 50 percent tax rate). What would earnings have been if the bank loan had been granted and accepted? (Note: The present value of an eight-year annuity of $1 at 15 percent is 4.4873).

f. Should White be upset that the bank rejected its loan application? Explain. Evaluate the representational faithfulness of its financial statements.

**11–6.** National Trucking Company leased seven trucks to be used in its operations from American Leasing, Inc., on January 1, 1986. The lease is to run for seven years with payments of $15,685 to be made at the *beginning* of each year. National is responsible for all maintenance, insurance, and taxes. However, the trucks revert to the lessor upon termination of the lease. The lessor is to earn a 10 percent return on its investment of $12,000 in each truck.

*Required:*

a. Show how the $15,685 annual lease payment was derived.

b. Assume the lease is treated as a direct-financing lease by American Leasing, Inc. (the lessor), and prepare the journal entries needed during 1986 and 1987.

c. Assume the lease is treated as a capital lease by National (the lessee) and prepare the journal entries needed during 1986 and 1987.

d. Assume the lease is treated as an operating lease by both parties. What entries would be made by *each* company during 1986 and 1987?

e. How should the lease be recorded and why?

**11–7.** A portion of the leasing disclosures contained in Xerox Corporation's 1981 annual report appear below.

The components of the Company's net investment in sales-type leases as of December 31, 1981, and 1980, were (in millions of dollars):

|  | 1981 | 1980 |
|---|---|---|
| Total minimum lease payments receivable | $338.4 | $ 99.8 |
| Less: Amount representing executory costs | (22.8) | (18.3) |
| Net minimum lease payments | 315.6 | 81.5 |
| Less: Unearned income | (91.2) | (19.5) |
| Allowance for doubtful receivables | (7.8) | (2.5) |
| Net investment in sales-type leases | $216.6 | $ 59.5 |

These receivables are collectible as follows (in millions of dollars): 1982—$83.7; 1983—$86.0; 1984—$74.2; 1985—$52.9; 1986—$37.9; thereafter—$3.7.

*Required:*

a. What criteria had to be met before Xerox could consider certain leases to be of a sales-type variety? Are the criteria set forth in *FASB Statement No. 13* reasonable? Explain.

    *b.* What types of executory costs might be involved in these leases? Why did Xerox deduct them?

    *c.* When Xerox entered into sales-type leases, did it debit its Minimum Lease Payments Receivable account for the net (principal) amount due? How do you know? Why did Xerox act in the manner in which it did?

    *d.* What does the Unearned Income account represent, and why is it deducted from the receivable?

    *e.* Assume that Xerox will receive $5.1 million in 1982 as lessee payments for insurance and taxes. If it can also be assumed that $22.9 million of income is earned by Xerox during 1982 on sales-type leases, prepare the journal entry the firm would make to reflect the receipt of the $83.7 million from lessees.

**11–8.** Assume that the following letter from a company's president appeared in an annual report to stockholders:

> I regret to inform you that our earnings per share (EPS) have been greatly reduced as a result of *FASB Statement No. 13.* As you may know, we lease many assets under long-term, noncancelable agreements. Unfortunately, the FASB believes that all noncancelable leases must be reflected as intangible assets and long-term liabilities at an amount equal to the total dollars we will have to pay to the lessors over the lease terms. Although such accounting does increase our return on investment, it artificially lowers our reported EPS and reduces our dividend-paying ability.

List in numerical order and describe all the misconceptions which are evidenced by the above quotation.

**11–9.** Winn-Dixie Stores, Inc., is a major supermarket chain. Excerpts from the leasing disclosures contained in its 1981 annual report appear below.

> **Leasing Arrangements.** "There were 1,230 leases in effect on store locations and other properties at June 24, 1981. Of these 1,230 leases, 114 store leases and 10 warehouse and manufacturing facility leases are classified as capital leases. Substantially all store leases will expire during the next 20 years, and the warehouse and manufacturing facility leases will expire during the next 30 years. However, in the normal course of business, it is expected that these leases will be renewed or replaced by leases on other properties."
>
> **Capital Leases.** "The present value of net minimum lease payments on capital leases totals $77,446,000 (net of $107,016,000 which represents interest)."
>
> **Operating Leases.** "Rental payments under operating leases were $59,588,000 in 1981. The total minimum payments required in future years on operating leases in existence at June 24, 1981, was $813,570,000 ($513,798,000 of which was not due until years after 1986)."

*Required:*

    *a.* Was Winn-Dixie correct in reporting a present value figure for capital lease payments which was net of the interest component? Explain.

    *b.* As a banker or security analyst, would you consider it informative to add $813,570,000 to the total liabilities figure reported by the firm on its balance sheet? Explain.

    *c.* Does the firm's discussion pertaining to the expiration dates of its leases and their probable renewal shed any light on whether or not its treatment of those obligations reflects economic reality? Explain.

**11–10.** The following descriptions of actual lease disclosures illustrate some of the variations which can be observed:

1. Republic Airlines shows its Property and Equipment under Capital Leases as a separate category of assets on its balance sheet, with a deduction then shown for "accumulated amortization."
2. Piedmont Aviation, Inc., lists Leased Property under Capital Leases as a separate item within the Property and Equipment asset category on its balance sheet, with an aggregate deduction shown for "allowances for depreciation."
3. J. C. Penney and Beatrice Foods do not disclose a separate figure for Property under Capital Leases on their balance sheets. Instead, a footnote discloses the portion of plant assets leased under capital leases.
4. Holiday Inns and Federal Express do not disclose a separate figure on their balance sheets for Obligations under Capital Leases. Instead, a footnote discloses the portion of long-term debt that is represented by capital-lease obligations.
5. Mattel and Weyerhaeuser list a separate figure for Capital Lease Obligations in the liabilities section of their balance sheets.

*Required:*

a. Compare and contrast the disclosure approaches of Republic and Piedmont. Should Property under Capital Leases be made a separate asset category on the balance sheet? Is amortization or depreciation a more accurate description for the process of expiration of service benefits from leased assets?
b. Are the leasing disclosures of J. C. Penney and Beatrice Foods inferior to those of Republic and Piedmont? Are the differences in disclosure justified because the former two firms are not in the airlines industry?
c. Compare and contrast the quality of Weyerhaeuser's disclosures vis-à-vis those of Holiday Inns and Federal Express.
d. "There is more need to list the capital-lease obligations as a separate balance sheet item than there is to list the capital-lease assets as a separate balance-sheet item." Do you agree?

**11–11.** Excerpts from the 1981 annual reports of two large airlines appear below:

**Northwest Orient Airlines.** "The Company does not lease any aircraft or related flight equipment. Leased property consists of space in air terminals, land and buildings at airports, and ticket, sales and reservation offices under noncancelable operating leases which expire in various years through 2029. Future minimum rental commitments at December 31, 1981, for noncancelable operating leases were $265.1 million, of which $263.8 million is for air terminal and airport facilities."

**Western Airlines.** "Western leases certain flight equipment and facilities and ground equipment. Equipment under capital leases of $81.8 million (net of depreciation) is included in the balance sheet at December 31, 1981. On that date, the present value of obligations-capital leases was $107.1 million, while the total minimum lease payments for operating leases equaled $199.3 million."

*Required:*

a.  "Without *FASB Statement No. 13,* it would be practically impossible to compare the financial position and results of operation of Northwest and Western." Explain what might be meant by this statement and indicate whether or not you agree with it.

b.  On what basis might both airlines have concluded that noncancelable agreements for air terminal and airport facilities should be considered as operating leases?

c.  Why did Western only calculate a present value for the obligations under capital, as opposed to operating, leases? Would present-value information for *both* types of leases be equally desirable?

d.  Explain how the capital-lease obligations for Western came to exceed its capital-lease assets by $25.3 million?

**11–12.**  The director of accounting policy for a large U.S. firm recently commented as follows:

> We might as well have elected the FASB to our Executive Committee, because the Board often seems to have a greater effect on our business decisions than do our President and Vice President. *FASB Statement No. 2* on "Accounting for Research and Development Costs" has caused a 60 percent decline in the number of research projects which we initiate. We just cannot afford to take all of our research costs to expense immediately. *FASB Statement No. 13* on "Accounting for Leases" has caused a 70 percent decline in the amount of plant assets which we are willing to lease. I ask you: "Is it ever going to end?" When will the FASB realize that accounting should reflect economic activity rather than cause it?

*Required:*

a.  Elaborate on the provisions of the two FASB Statements which may have "caused" the economic activity described by the director.

b.  Did either or both FASB Statements improve the relevance and reliability of published financial statements?

c.  Should accounting only "reflect economic activity rather than cause it?" Does it do both?

# CHAPTER 12

# PENSION COSTS AND OBLIGATIONS

As Chapter 7 points out, the overall cost of acquiring labor services and maintaining a labor force includes the cost of various fringe benefits. Among the most important of these are retirement programs and pension plans. They have grown immensely over the last 25 years and show every sign of continuing.[1]

In its simplest terms a pension plan is an agreement between a business entity and its employees whereby the former agrees to pay benefits to the latter after their retirement. Most pension arrangements also provide for an intermediary, the pension fund, as depicted in Figure 12-1. The employer makes periodic contributions to the pension fund, probably during the working lives of the employees. Those persons in charge of the pension fund have an obligation to invest the contributions and to administer the distribution of benefits to retired employees. In the long run, of course, there should be a correspondence between the cost of the pension program to the employer (the contributions) and the benefits promised to the employees.

**FIGURE 12-1  Typical Relationships between Parties to a Pension Plan**

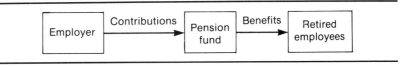

---

[1] The Employee Retirement Income Security Act of 1974 generally requires employers who offer pension programs to make participation available to all employees over 25 who have at least one year of service.

In the short run and in some legal contexts, however, the business is obligated directly to the pension fund and only indirectly to the employees. The pension fund normally is a separate legal and accounting entity.

In economic terms a pension is a type of deferred compensation plan. The employer offers compensation in the future in exchange for employee services rendered in the present. Accordingly, the cost of the pension plan should accrue over the years when employees render service, even though the pension payments are actually made long after. However, the financial accounting procedures and measurements necessary to accomplish this treatment of pension costs involve numerous complexities.

First, there is a great diversity of plans. Some, called *defined-contribution plans,* limit the employer's payments to a fixed sum, for example, so much per ton of coal mined or per hour worked. No specific pension benefits are promised except what the pension fund contributions will provide. The more common form is a *defined-benefit plan,* wherein a specific schedule of pension benefits is established. The employer must contribute amounts sufficient to provide these benefits. Some defined-benefit plans are *contributory plans,* wherein the employer's payments may be augmented by amounts withheld from the employees' earnings. Because our major concern in accounting for pensions is the determination of the cost to the business entity, we shall focus only on noncontributory, defined-benefit plans. Here the measurement problems are the most difficult.

An additional complexity of a financial nature is the *funding* of the pension program. Funding is the actual contributing of cash to some funding agency. Under an *insured* plan the payments go to an insurance company, which invests the funds until they are needed. In *trusteed* plans a bank or trust company receives the payments from the employer. Completely unfunded plans are almost nonexistent, but the pattern of funding varies significantly among plans. Because pension costs, like all business expenses, must be reported on an accrual basis, the amount *funded* in any particular period does not necessarily determine the amount of pension *expense* recognized that period. Nevertheless, we shall see later that the manner in which a firm contributes cash to its pension plan does influence the *total* pension cost and hence influences periodic expense measurement.

Complexities of concept, terminology, and procedure also are introduced into pension calculations by insurance technicalities. Pension calculations necessarily require judgments and estimates about future events. These estimates normally demand the expertise of an actuary—a professional trained in the science of compound interest, probability and mortality distributions, and other aspects of insurance. The assumptions that actuaries tentatively make about future uncertainties affecting the pension cost are called *actuarial assumptions.* Some of the more important have to do with future levels of compensation to the extent that they influence the amount of future benefits; with the proportions of the employee group who will withdraw from the plan, die, become disabled, reach retirement age, and so on; with the rate of interest or earnings to be generated from the pension fund; and with the amount and timing of *vested benefits* (employee benefits the rights to which are no longer contingent on the employee's continuing to work for the employer). The actuary must make assumptions about these and similar subjects in order to estimate the benefits which will be paid under a pension plan. The estimates of benefits, in turn, provide the starting point for calculations of the amount of contribution necessary for funding and the amount of cost necessary for accounting purposes. We will take the actuarial assumptions for granted for the most part, although in practice they represent a whole separate set of potential difficulties and adjustments.

## ACCOUNTING FOR PENSIONS

In spite of these complexities and the profusion of terms and practices, the goals of the accounting procedures are relatively clear and simple. Inasmuch as pensions involve dollar claims payable in the future, the accounting for them should utilize present value concepts. Pension cost each period ideally should be the present value of future benefits earned by employees during the period. The pension liability at the end of any period should be the *unfunded* present value of the benefits that have been earned to date. The practical problem is to accomplish these objectives in a manner that is rational and systematic.

Prior to 1966 the accounting for pension costs and liabilities followed no single pattern. At one extreme, some companies adopted a "pay-as-you-go" approach, charging as expense only the amount actually paid to retired employees. No recognition was given to obligations to workers currently employed. For the majority of companies, the amount paid to a funding agency was considered to be the periodic expense. In some instances the funding pattern also resulted in a reasonable accrual of the pension cost. However, in other cases the amount paid each period was influenced by tax considerations, cash availability, and level of net income. The result was low or no pension expense whenever payments were reduced or stopped in a given accounting period. Similar variations arose if during the year a gain was realized by the trustee on the sale of pension fund assets. Some firms reduced their contributions accordingly, others ignored the gain, and still others recognized the effect of the gain through reduced contributions over a period of years. In short, accounting for pension costs and liabilities was plagued by a diversity of plans, a lack of uniformity of principles among companies having similar pension plans, and an inconsistent application of procedures from one period to the next within a single company.

**Regulatory
Activity**

In November 1966, the Accounting Principles Board issued *Opinion No. 8,* the objective of which was to narrow the range of practices significantly and to prevent distortion in the accounting for pensions.[2] The general approach of the APB is to require that pension costs be systematically accrued by means of rational and consistently applied present value procedures so that pension accounting would be neither discretionary nor governed by cash payments. Even within this general recommendation for accrual accounting, however, definitive guidelines on the amount of pension cost to be accounted for, and specifically how it should be recorded, still require complex answers.

The problems created by the diversity of pension plans and funding arrangements did not go unnoticed by Congress. Employee rights to equitable retirement benefits sometimes were abused. In 1974, therefore, Congress passed the Employee Retirement Income Security Act (ERISA). Technically the law relates to the pension plans themselves and not to the accounting by employers. However, it affects many of the elements that determine the employer's cost of the pension plan, and hence it influences current recording practices. For example, under ERISA, companies must actually fund their pension plans in accordance with sound actuarial methods. In addition to minimum funding requirements, the law establishes minimum vesting provisions, sets requirements for including or excluding employees, and extends an employer's liability in the event a pension plan is terminated.[3] Trustees of pension plans have to make certain financial disclosures and meet other fiduciary responsibilities.

In response to the questions raised and environmental changes made by ERISA, the Financial Accounting Standards Board has done four things. First, it issued *FASB Interpretation No. 3* shortly after the enactment of ERISA.[4] This interpretation affirmed the basic principles of *Opinion No. 8* (which we will discuss in detail later in this chapter). However, in addition, the Board put on its agenda the reconsideration of *Opinion No. 8.* To date, a background paper, a discussion memorandum, a statement of tentative conclusions, and a statement of preliminary views have been issued. Some of these are discussed toward the end of this chapter in the section called Other Problem Areas and Unresolved Issues. It is likely that one of the first changes readers of this book will see in the regulations governing financial accounting will be in the pension area.

---

[2] AICPA, *APB Opinion No.8,* "Accounting for the Cost of Pension Plans" (New York, November 1966).

[3] In addition to a mandatory termination insurance program, up to 30 percent of an employer's net assets could be assigned for the employees' benefit if a terminated pension plan were not fully funded.

[4] FASB, *Interpretation No. 3,* "Accounting for the Cost of Pension Plans Subject to the Employee Retirement Income Security Act of 1974 (an interpretation of *APB Opinion No. 8*)" (Stamford, Conn., December 1974).

In 1980 the FASB issued two statements.[5] *Statement No. 35,* issued in March, contained standards for financial reporting by the pension fund as a separate entity. In May of the same year, the FASB modified the disclosure requirements for employers who have defined-benefit plans. *Opinion No. 8* set forth some requirements for footnote disclosure; *Statement No. 36* expanded them. Employers must include in *their own* financial statements some information prepared under *Statement No. 35* for the pension fund financial statements. The interrelationship between accounting problems and practices of the employer cannot be divorced from those of the pension fund.

The discussion that follows starts from the point that pension costs are a cost of employment associated with the present work force. In accordance with the accrual basis of accounting and the matching concept, pension expense should be recorded in the periods during which the firm benefits from that work force. Through a simplified illustration we examine some of the technical factors and present value concepts which are necessary to an understanding of accounting for pensions. Then we highlight some major aspects. These include (1) the two principal components to a firm's pension cost—*normal cost* and *past service cost,* (2) the effect of different funding patterns, (3) some of the basic entries, and (4) the problem areas and unresolved issues related to the accounting for pension costs and liabilities. Recommendations and reasoning from the aforementioned authoritative guidelines are integrated throughout this discussion so that the reader will have a firm grasp of generally accepted accounting principles in the pension area.

## Basic Data for Illustration

Assume that the employee group of L&B Corporation numbers 100 persons. They all begin work on January 1, 1980, at age 30. The company has established a noncontributory pension plan for its employees. The plan provides that each employee will receive an annual pension check for life beginning one year after mandatory retirement at age 60. Assume that the life expectancy of each employee after retirement is exactly 10 years. The amount of the pension will be 1 percent of the employee's average earnings for each year with the company. If each employee receives average annual compensation of $30,000 over the 30-year period, he or she would receive an annual pension of $9,000 (1% × 30 years × $30,000).

Obviously, the equivalent of some *actuarial assumptions* already has been introduced. Employees do not form a single group. They do not all start to work at the same time and are not all the same age. Neither do they all work the same length of time, earn the same wages, retire at the same

---

5 FASB, *Statement of Financial Accounting Standards No. 35,* "Accounting and Reporting by Defined Benefit Pension Plans" (Stamford, Conn., March 1980); and *Statement of Financial Accounting Standards No. 36,* "Disclosure of Pension Information" (Stamford, Conn., May 1980).

time, and live the same period after retirement. Actuarial or insurance assumptions provide averages for a group. These assumptions cover the factors that determine average working life, average retirement life, and average wage base for pension purposes. Perhaps thinking of our simplified figures as the result of actuarial assumptions may add an element of reality to the illustration.

Pension payments will be $900,000, beginning January 1, 2011. How large a pension fund must be built up over the 30 years of employee working life to permit the withdrawal of $900,000 each year for 10 years? The required size of the fund depends on the interest rate that can be earned on invested assets in the fund. This too is an actuarial assumption; we shall use 6 percent in this example. The desired pension fund equals the present value of an annuity equal to the yearly pensions:

$$\text{Pension Fund on } 1/1/2010 = (P/A, 10, 0.06)\$900,000$$
$$= 7.3601 \times \$900,000$$
$$= \$6,624,090$$

If the firm builds up a fund of $6,624,090 by the end of the 30-year period, it will be able to satisfy its pension obligations.

## PENSION EXPENSE: NORMAL COST

Part of the total fund needs of $6,624,090 will come from interest earned. The rest must come from employer contributions and represents the total pension cost to the employer. The problem of determining periodic pension *expense* involves calculating the portion of this total that is applicable to each of the 30 years.

## Actuarial Cost Methods

Ideally, the recognition of pension expense ought to be related to the amount of pension benefits earned each year. However, one could assume a number of different earnings patterns. These alternative assumptions are called *actuarial cost methods*. Just as actuarial assumptions influence the determination of total pension cost, actuarial cost methods determine how that cost is assigned to the various accounting periods. Specifically, an actuarial cost method is a "particular technique used by actuaries for establishing the amount and incidence of the annual actuarial cost of pension plan benefits . . . and the related actuarial liability."[6] Although developed primarily as funding plans, most of the actuarial cost methods also are appropriate for the determination of accounting cost because they explicitly consider the relevant factors.

A firm must select an actuarial cost method that is reasonable. The Accounting Principles Board specifically endorsed five commonly used methods. Because each makes different assumptions about the circum-

---

[6] *APB Opinion No. 8*, Appendix B.

stances of the pension plan, the different actuarial cost methods can cause the periodic pension cost to vary significantly. One common assumption is that pension benefits are earned equally each year. For convenience, we shall use this assumption, which is called *entry age normal*. Nevertheless, remember that it is only an assumption inherent in a particular actuarial cost method and that, as in the case of depreciation, other rational, systematic assumptions are possible.

**Calculation of Normal Cost**

For our example, then, we want to build an amount of $6,624,090 by the end of 30 years by spreading the cost equally over the 30 years. The $6,624,090 represents *the future amount of an annuity* for 30 years; the annual pension expense is the amount of the annuity.

$$
\begin{aligned}
\text{Normal Cost} &= (A/F, \ 30, \ 0.06)\$6,624,090 \\
&= [1/(F/A, \ 30, \ 0.06)]\$6,624,090 \\
&= \$6,624,090 \div 79.0582 \\
&= \$83,787.51
\end{aligned}
$$

An amount of $83,800 (rounded), set aside each of the 30 years and invested at an earning rate of 6 percent, will permit payments to all retired employees under the plan, provided that the actuarial assumptions are accurate. The $83,800 is called *normal pension cost*. It represents the present value of expected future payments to employees attributable to work performed during each year after the date of the plan (assume that the pension benefits are earned equally each year). The company would accrue $83,800 of pension expense annually.

**PENSION EXPENSE: PAST SERVICE COST**

Now let us make a major change in our example. Assume all conditions as before except that the pension plan is not started until January 1, *1990*. The original employees are still with the company, and no new ones have been added in the 10-year interim. In the determination of the amount of future pension benefits, pension plans commonly recognize years of employee service prior to the adoption of the plan. An employee who has 10 years of service before the pension plan goes into effect and who then works 20 more years before retiring usually would receive retirement benefits based on *30* years of employment. Consequently, in our example the benefits do not change, even though the remaining working life of our employee group is now only 20 years. A fund of $6,624,090 still will be needed by January 1, 2010, to cover the pension obligations.

One way of dealing with this changed circumstance would be to calculate a different normal cost. This would be the annual amount necessary to accrue $6,624,090 over *20* years. The amount obviously would be greater than $83,800. A few actuarial cost methods, in fact, do this. They spread the total pension cost over the time period between the *inception of the plan* and the termination date (actuarially determined) of the employee group.

On the other hand, most actuarial cost methods assign a separate portion of the total cost of pension benefits, called *past service cost,* to the years of service prior to the adoption of the plan. For instance, the entry age normal method assumes a normal cost based on level annual payments from the time employees would have become eligible if the plan had been in existence. However, the plan was not in existence for the first 10 years. Consequently, the accumulated value of what would have been normal cost during the period the company had no plan is the past service cost. In our case, past service cost is $1,104,551, calculated as follows:

$$Past\ Service\ Cost = (F/A,\ 10,\ 0.06)\$83,800$$
$$= 13.1808(\$83,800)$$
$$= \$1,104,551$$

Past service cost is often called the *accrued actuarial liability.* When employers base pension benefits on prior years of service as well as on future years, they assume an obligation to catch up. Past service cost is the present value of the retirement benefits identified with periods prior to adoption of the plan.

If L&B Corporation had started the pension plan at the time the employees first started work, $1,104,551 would have been accrued (and presumably funded) by January 1, 1990. However, although the pension plan formally recognizes service from January 1, 1980, to January 1, 1990, in the granting of the pension benefits, the plan itself does not begin until the latter date. Consequently, the past service cost will have to be accrued separately from normal cost over the remaining employee working life. If normal cost is to be calculated from the time of *initial* service, then normal pension expense in each future year will have to be supplemented by an additional sum in order to provide for the full cost of the pension plan.

A similar problem arises if the pension plan is modified in subsequent years. For example, the company might decide in 1995 to change the pension benefit formula to 1.1 percent of employee average earnings for each year of service. In that case a new actuarial valuation would be made which would recognize the additional 1/10 of one percent for the 15 years of service prior to the date of the modification. The term *prior service cost* applies to the portion of the revised total pension cost that the actuarial cost method identifies with periods prior to the date of plan amendment. It includes any remaining past service cost and any changes in normal cost for years prior to the new actuarial valuation. Prior service cost is determined in basically the same way as past service cost and causes the same accounting problems. Accordingly, the term *past service cost* is used here to encompass amounts arising both upon adoption of the plan and upon amendment of the plan.

The relationship between normal cost, past service cost, and prior service cost can be seen in Figure 12–2.

FIGURE 12-2   Relation of Past Service Cost and Prior Service Cost to Normal Cost

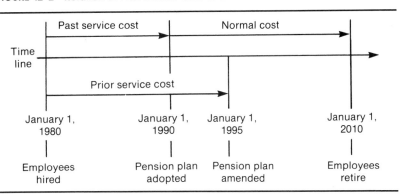

## Alternative Views of Past Service Cost and Expense

To some extent, "past service cost" is a misnomer. The brief illustration above demonstrates that it is, in fact, a future cost. Although the amount of pension cost is measured by past services, pension plans are adopted in contemplation of present and future benefits. The benefits derived from, and therefore the cost of, a pension plan surely cannot precede its adoption. Following this line of reasoning, most accountants conclude that the cost of past service should be spread over future years.

The next obvious question is to what future periods the past service cost should be assigned. Those actuarial cost methods which include past service cost in the calculation of a new normal cost assign it to the remaining years of average employee working life. This procedure seems eminently logical. The cost of pension benefits, whether past costs or normal costs, fundamentally are related to specific individuals. Because they are the ones who will receive the pensions measured by past service, it is reasonable that the period of benefit to the company is related to the time period from the adoption of the plan to retirement of the existing employee group. In our illustration, a strong case can be made for reflecting past service cost in expense over the 20 years of remaining service of the employees covered by the plan.

In contrast, many accountants and business leaders argue that past service cost is a *separate* factor and should be reflected in expense over some reasonable future period not necessarily limited to the service lives of existing employees. For example, one cannot logically argue for the recognition of past service costs applicable to employees already retired over their future period of service. Rather, proponents of this view argue that pension benefits based on past service are granted to older employees for general reasons of improved employee morale, increased productivity, ability to attract and retain better employees, and so on. These benefits extend beyond the remaining service lives of a particular group of employees. Past service costs are related to a *continuing* employee group and pension plan; therefore, the costs should be accrued over a future period somewhat longer than that under the first position discussed.

**Calculations for Recognition of Past Service Cost in Expense**

The process of gradually recognizing the past service cost as an expense is called amortizing the past service cost or accruing the actuarial accrued liability. Let us assume that a decision has been made to spread the past service cost over the next 25 years. At first thought it might appear that $44,182 per year ($1,104,551 ÷ 25) is the appropriate amount. However, we have ignored the interest element. The accrued actuarial liability (past service cost) is $1,104,551 on January 1, 1990, but it will grow unless it is actually set aside in a fund. If we assume that the company funds only those amounts charged to expense, then this $1,104,551 will be funded only over the next 25 years. Consequently, an interest factor must be built into the expense charge to compensate for the lack of an actual fund now. In a sense, the $1,104,551 past service cost can be viewed as the present value of a series of 25 expense charges (and presumably fund deposits). Consequently, the annual expense charge for past service cost for the next 25 years is $86,405.

$$
\begin{aligned}
\text{Annual Accrual (Amortization)} \\
\text{of Past Service Cost} \quad &= (A/P, 25, 0.06) \, \$1,104,551 \\
&= [1/(P/A, 25, 0.06)]\$1,104,551 \\
&= \$1,104,551 \div 12.7834 \\
&= \$86,405
\end{aligned}
$$

The investment of $86,405 per year for 25 years at 6 percent will grow to the same amount that $1,104,551 would achieve if invested today at 6 percent for 25 years.

**EFFECT OF FUNDING**

The entry for periodic pension expense under our example as it now stands will be:

| | | |
|---|---|---|
| Pension Expense | 170,205 | |
| Pension Liability | | 170,205 |

This amount equals normal cost of $83,800 plus accrual (amortization) of past service cost of $86,405. For the calculations giving rise to both parts of the expense figure, funding in the amount of $170,205 each year is assumed. An interest element (present value factor) is implicit in the calculations. Cash payments made to a fund accumulate at compound interest. Therefore, the periodic contributions (accounting cost) need be only the present value of the pension benefits attributable to the period.

However, we must distinguish between the recognition of the proper pension cost for accounting purposes and the actual funding of that cost. The entry above only accrues the period's pension expense. If cash of

$170,205 is transferred from the employer to the pension fund trustee or insurance company, the liability set up each year will be short lived.

However, if for financial or tax reasons a portion of the amount is not funded, the liability becomes a long-term one. More important, the expense in future years is understated. When the periodic expense goes fully or partially unfunded, pension expense in subsequent periods has to be increased by an interest element or *interest equivalent*. An amount of $170,205 each year will not accumulate to the necessary fund unless it is actually invested (funded) each year. An adjustment must be made, increasing future years' expense to compensate for the lack of an actual fund on which interest is earned.

At the extreme, assume that nothing is funded in the first year in our example. Then the entry for the second year would be:

```
Pension Expense ...................................  180,417
     Pension Liability ..............................              180,417
        $170,205 + (0.06 × $170,205).
```

The pension expense accrual in each subsequent year would be increased by an *interest equivalent* equal to the assumed interest that would be earned if the amounts were funded (6 percent of the unfunded balance in the liability account).[7]

In summary, the basic calculation of pension expense assumes funding. Then, whenever the pattern of cash payments differs from that of the expense provision, the effect on pension cost is adjusted for by means of the interest equivalent. Pension expense is increased if funding lags behind cost incurrence and is decreased if funding is faster than cost incurrence.[8]

## AUTHORITA-TIVE STANDARDS

The process of determining pension expense and pension liabilities, although governed by present value concepts, still does not lead to a single precise result. As we have seen in the previous discussion, a number of judgments, any of which can materially influence the amounts shown as pension expense and pension liability, must be made within the overall principles. The following questions indicate some of these judgmental areas:

1. According to what pattern should pension costs be assigned to future periods? The answer to this question involves the choice of an actuarial cost method and affects the calculation of normal cost.

---

[7] Because the interest equivalents arise from a liability not having been paid, some accountants would record them as interest expense rather than pension expense.

[8] Interest equivalents for over- and underfunding are not common. Most firms fund the amounts charged to expense. Under the Employee Retirement Income Security Act of 1974, normal costs must be funded each year. Prior service cost existing on January 1, 1974, must be funded over a period not longer than 40 years. All other prior service cost must be paid into the pension fund over a maximum period of 30 years.

2.  Over what period of benefit should past service cost be charged to expense? What is the fundamental nature of past service cost?
3.  How should the impact of funding decisions be reflected? The amount and timing of funding directly influences the total amount of pension cost. Nevertheless, to conclude that the amount funded each period is the expense of that period is to abandon accrual accounting and to open the door to possible manipulation and erratic swings in income.
4.  What is the appropriate rate of interest in pension calculations? The choice of the interest factor can be significant. For instance, if in our example the assumed earnings rate were 10 percent instead of 6 percent, normal cost would be $33,619 instead of $83,788. More-over, amortization of past service cost would amount to only $59,028 rather than $86,405.
5.  Under what circumstances should a liability associated with pensions appear on the balance sheet? For example, does the existence of unfunded past service costs or vested unfunded past service costs create a recognizable obligation?

**Accounting Principles Board Opinion No. 8**

In 1966 the Accounting Principles Board first attempted to address some of these questions. It did so in a general way instead of formulating detailed rules that would eliminate judgment. The APB said that pension expense must be accrued in a reasonable, rational, systematic manner. Only certain actuarial cost methods are allowable, but the one chosen must be applied consistently. Annual pension expense is not tied directly to funding. Instead, expense determinations are made under the assumption of coincident funding, and then interest equivalents are introduced to adjust for the differences between expense charges and funding.

Having established these broad principles, the APB then defined a procedure for calculating a maximum and a minimum expense charge. If a company's procedure follows the general principles and gives a result that falls within the maximum and minimum, the presumption is that the firm is accruing its pension expense in a rational and systematic manner.

The *maximum* basically includes (1) normal cost, (2) 10 percent of past service cost until fully provided for,[9] and (3) interest equivalents on any difference between amounts charged to expense and amounts funded. The *minimum* basically consists of (1) normal cost, (2) interest on any un-

---

[9] Because of the interest element included in any periodic recognition of past service cost, a period longer than 10 years would actually be necessary to charge all original past service cost to expense. For example, it would take over 15 years to accrue $1,104,551 of past service costs in equal annual amounts, including interest at 6 percent, if the equal amounts were limited to $110,455 ($1,104,551 ÷ $110,455 = 10.0000, which is beyond line 15 in the 6% column of Table 10A–9). See pages 440–441 for a review of the interest factor at work. ERISA changed the maximum past service cost allowable for tax purposes to that which will fully fund these costs over 10 years. This modified maximum has not yet been recognized in GAAP.

funded past service costs, and (3) a provision to accrue the present value of vested benefits within a reasonable period of time. Calculation of the additional charge for vested benefits is complicated and beyond the scope of this introductory discussion. Moreover, because of changes required by ERISA in vesting and funding practices, the minimum practically has become (1) normal cost, (2) accrual of past service costs over 40 years, and (3) interest equivalents.

The maximum and minimum limits differ only as to past service costs. They are not absolute dollar amounts; they depend on the actuarial cost methods and actuarial assumptions applicable to each pension plan. Between them is room for considerable difference in total pension expense.

**Disclosure Requirements**

Because of the complexities and alternatives accompanying pension calculations, *Opinion No. 8* also insisted on full disclosure of some of the significant factors affecting pension costs. *FASB Statement No. 36* modified and expanded the list of items. Currently, the following items must be disclosed in the financial statements or notes to them:[10]

1. A statement that such plans exist, identifying or describing the employee groups covered.
2. A statement of the company's accounting and funding policies.
3. The provision for pension cost for the period.
4. The nature and effect of significant matters affecting comparability for all periods presented, such as changes in accounting methods (actuarial cost method, amortization of past and prior service cost, treatment of actuarial gains and losses, etc.), changes in circumstances (actuarial assumptions, etc.), or adoption or amendment of a plan.
5. For defined benefit pension plans,
   a. The actuarial present value of vested accumulated plan benefits.
   b. The actuarial present value of nonvested accumulated plan benefits.
   c. The fair value of the plans' net assets available for benefits.
   d. The interest rate assumption used in the measurement of accumulated plan benefits.
   e. The date as of which the valuations were determined.

If not intuitively obvious already, the usefulness of these disclosures will become clear as we continue our discussion.

**Financial Accounting Standards Board**

As noted earlier in our discussion, controversy has continued to surround the pension area during the almost two decades since the issuance of *Opinion No. 8*. The passage of the Employee Retirement Income Security Act in 1974 added another element to the controversy.

---

[10] *FASB Statement No. 36*, pars. 7–8.

Nonetheless, except for the increased disclosure mandated under *Statement No. 36* (see above) and for a separate reporting by the pension plan itself mandated under *Statement No. 35,* no major changes have been made in generally accepted principles governing the employer. No definitive answers have been given to the questions raised on pages 441–442. In particular, the fifth question of what liabilities should be required on the employer's balance sheet remains a major conceptual and practical issue.

Many thought that the passage of ERISA would prompt a wholesale revision of *Opinion No. 8* by the FASB. Instead, the FASB's initial response, contained in *Interpretation No. 3,* was that no major changes were necessary in accounting principles. ERISA dealt primarily with funding and vesting requirements. *Opinion No. 8* in principle had already separated the determination of annual pension cost from annual funding. Consequently, changes in funding requirements did not impact directly on accounting principles. To be sure, changes in funding requirements and vesting requirements did change the total pension cost of some companies, but these changes could be accommodated within existing principles.

Two changes affecting liability disclosure were mandated in *Interpretation No. 3.* If the employer does not fund the minimum amount required under ERISA, the unfunded amount must be recorded as a legal liability. If a pension plan is terminated, an estimated legal liability for certain unfunded amounts must also be recorded. However, the FASB concluded that there was no liability associated with unfunded past service costs.

ERISA did trigger the beginning of a closer look at the entire pension area. Numerous suggestions have arisen from this study. Some have been enacted, *Statement Nos. 35 and 36,* for example. Others are still being debated. Some major changes are expected in pension reporting during 1984 and 1985. We shall explore some of these issues in a subsequent section. First, though, let us summarize our discussion so far by looking at the accounting entries.

**SUMMARY OF ENTRIES TO RECORD PENSION COSTS**

Let us return to our example. Past service costs amount to $1,104,551, and normal cost is $83,800 per year. If the firm elects to recognize past service cost (plus interest) in expense over a 25-year period, $86,405 additional expense is required. If the firm also chooses to fund all pension costs accrued, the total expense is $170,205.

Periodic charges to expense would differ if past service costs were recognized over a period other than 25 years or if funding did not coincide with the expense accrual. Recognition of past service cost as expense over a longer or shorter period presents no new problems. If 20 years is chosen, the expense for past service is $96,300 [$1,104,551 ÷ (*P/A*, 20, 0.06)]; if 30 years is chosen, the amount is $80,244 [$1,104,551 ÷ (*P/A*, 30, 0.06)]. Added to the normal cost of $83,800, either of these past service cost figures results in an expense charge between the maximum of $194,255 [$83,800 + ($1,104,551 × 0.10)] and the minimum of $150,073 [$83,800 + ($1,104,551 × 0.06)]. A pattern of funding different from that implicit in the expense accrued gives rise to interest equivalents on amounts over- and underfunded and also to the recognition of prepaid or accrued pension costs.

Table 12–1 summarizes the pertinent information for a continuation of our example. To illustrate the operation of interest equivalents, let us assume that the company elects to *fund* the past service cost over a period of 30 years, even though it is to be recognized in expense over a period of 25 years. We will also modify the illustration to allow for new employees entering the work force as older ones retire, so that normal cost of $83,800 will continue to be expensed (and funded) for the entire 30-year period.

**TABLE 12–1** Financial Statement Information Based on Recognition of Past Service Costs in Expense over 25 Years and Funding of Past Service Costs over 30 Years

| | (a) | (b) | (c) | (d) | (e) | (f) |
|---|---|---|---|---|---|---|
| | | Amount Charged to Expense | | | | Balance Sheet |
| Year | Normal Cost | Past Service Cost | Addition for Interest | Total | Cash Payments | Liability at Year-End |
| 1 ...... | $83,800 | $86,405 | — | $170,205 | $164,044 | $ 6,161 |
| 2 ...... | 83,800 | 86,405 | $ 370 | 170,575 | 164,044 | 12,692 |
| 3 ...... | 83,800 | 86,405 | 762 | 170,967 | 164,044 | 19,615 |
| 9 ...... | 83,800 | 86,405 | 3,659 | 173,864 | 164,044 | 70,800 |
| 10 ...... | 83,800 | 86,405 | 4,248 | 174,453 | 164,044 | 81,209 |
| 19 ...... | 83,800 | 86,405 | 11,425 | 181,630 | 164,044 | 207,999 |
| 20 ...... | 83,800 | 86,405 | 12,480 | 182,685 | 164,044 | 226,640 |
| 24 ...... | 83,800 | 86,405 | 17,373 | 187,578 | 164,044 | 313,080 |
| 25 ...... | 83,800 | 86,405 | 18,785 | 188,990 | 164,044 | 338,026 |
| 26 ...... | 83,800 | — | 20,282 | 104,082 | 164,044 | 278,064 |
| 27 ...... | 83,800 | — | 16,684 | 100,484 | 164,044 | 214,504 |
| 29 ...... | 83,800 | — | 8,828 | 92,628 | 164,044 | 75,714 |
| 30 ...... | 83,800 | — | 4,543 | 88,343 | 164,057 | — |

Note: Column *(b)* is $1,104,551 ÷ (P/A, 25, 0.06). Column *(c)* is 6 percent of *(f)* on the preceding line. Column *(d)* equals *(a)* + *(b)* + *(c)*. Column *(e)* is $83,800 + $80,244 [$1,104,551 ÷ (P/A, 30, 0.06)]. Column *(f)* equals the preceding balance + *(d)* − *(e)*.

The journal entries should be clear from an examination of the table. Any amounts charged to expense but not paid in cash are credited to the Pension Liability account. In later years, when cash payments exceed expense, the liability will be debited. The addition to expense for interest equivalents results from the fact that funding lags behind expense recognition. The $86,405 past service expense assumed funding over a 25-year period. Now, with funding over 30 years, only $80,244 is set aside each year. Therefore, the amount of actual interest accumulation in the fund will be insufficient; hence, the interest element included in the $86,405 is too small. The additional interest element on unfunded accruals included in the expense provision recognizes the increased cost associated with this factor.

**OTHER PROBLEM AREAS AND UNRESOLVED ISSUES**

Undoubtedly, the most troublesome and controversial area in accounting for the cost of pension plans is the treatment of past service cost. However, additional areas also cause problems and disputes. In this section we will discuss four of these in addition to past service costs. For each of the following questions, we will report and analyze current thinking:

1. Under what conditions, if any, should unfunded past service costs be reflected as liabilities?
2. How should pension *fund* assets and liabilities be reported?
3. Should guidelines be issued to limit further the choice of actuarial methods by employers in their measurement of pension amounts?
4. How should actuarial gains and losses be handled in the measurement of pension costs and liabilities?
5. How should unrealized appreciation and depreciation in the value of pension fund investments be treated?

**Past Service Cost as a Liability**

A major question associated with past and prior service costs is whether a liability arises for these costs at the inception of the pension plan or at its subsequent amendment. The Accounting Principles Board took a strict future-accrual approach to both expense and liability recognition. Unfunded past service costs do *not* appear as a liability unless a specific legal obligation exists. The key to nonrecognition of past service costs as an immediate liability lies in the contention that an employee earns pension benefits through future years of work. Employees receive pensions not because they have worked but because they will continue to work until retirement. They cannot earn benefits when there is no pension plan, even though the *amount* of benefits they do earn later may be conditioned by past years of work. For an employee who only has a few years to work before retirement, the future period of earning may be small and the amount of benefits earned each year large. However, fringe benefits like pensions are part of the total cost of labor services. Hence, as with wages, they should be accrued as the employee works. Consequently the only liability normally appearing on the balance sheet would be the difference between the amounts accrued as expense (cost of benefits earned) and the amounts funded.

The foregoing viewpoint reflects a primary emphasis on expense measurement. The only employer liability is to contribute to the pension fund. If more expense is accrued than is funded, then a liability results. However, the accounting by the employer is not concerned with any ultimate obligations to the employees.

An alternative viewpoint stresses liability measurement. This accounting looks through the pension fund to the obligation of providing the defined benefits to employees. An actuarial valuation is made at a point in time. This valuation measures the present value of future pension payments based on years of service already rendered, including past service costs granted when the plan was initiated or amended. To some this represents the employer's gross obligation at that point in time. A fully funded plan is one in which pension *fund assets* equal or exceed this obligation. To the extent that the gross actuarial liability is unfunded, the employer should record a liability.

Recognition of unfunded pension obligations for past and prior service costs as accounting liabilities may result in the recognition of an intangible asset as well. Some accountants contend that an *initial* liability (and simultaneous asset) should be recorded for the *total* past service cost. They argue that the company has acquired an intangible asset (employee goodwill, etc.) upon inception of the plan. The cost of the asset is measured by the present value of the obligation already assumed. The entry might be:

```
Enhanced Future Employee Service  ..................... xxx
      Liability for Unfunded Past Service Costs .............        xxx
```

Expense recognition would be accomplished by amortization of the asset (plus interest) over future periods; liability liquidation would occur when payments actually are made to fund the past service cost.

The above treatment is analogous to that accorded property rights under capitalized long-term leases. However, in our opinion the analogy is weak. Labor agreements are purely executory contracts. If a company were to sign a labor contract under which it agreed to pay hourly wages averaging 10 percent more than the going rate, employee morale, worker efficiency, and the ability to hire and retain employees assuredly would improve. However, few would argue that the present value of the excess wages to be paid under the agreement should be recorded as an offsetting asset and liability. The pension plan is not significantly different.[11]

Some accountants argue that the obligation for unfunded past service costs does not meet the requirements for an accounting liability set forth in Chapter 2. In addition, if a liability is recorded, the resulting debit account does not meet the test of an asset.

There is some evidence that members of the Financial Accounting Standards Board disagree. In its document titled *Preliminary Views on Employers' Accounting for Pensions and Other Postemployment Benefits,* the Board put forth a tentative proposal for discussion.[12] Under this proposal

---

[11] An exception might be *vested benefits,* those pension rights which the employee "earns" without having to continue to work until retirement. It would seem that an immediate pension liability should be recorded equal to the present value of *past service costs that are vested,* and an asset account should present the amount not yet charged to expense.

[12] FASB, *Preliminary Views on Employers' Accounting for Pensions and Other Postemployment Benefits* (Stamford, Conn., November 1982).

employers would have to report on their balance sheets a net pension liability and probably an intangible asset. The net pension liability basically would be the gross actuarial obligation for benefits earned in past periods minus the pension plan assets, valued at fair value. Thus, all unfunded past and prior service cost would be included in the liability.

The intangible asset would be called Deferred Pension Amendment and Initiation Cost. It represents the expected economic benefits to be realized by the employer as a result of the initiation or amendment of the plan. This intangible would be amortized over the average remaining service life of the plan participants.

The FASB proposal has generated considerable opposition. Some opponents believe the type of information discussed by the Board should be disclosed but only in the notes to the financial statements. They feel that the introduction into the formal financial statements of executory obligations offset by fair value pension fund assets is inappropriate. Time will tell which views will ultimately prevail as GAAP.

## Reporting of Pension Fund Assets

The pension fund currently is viewed as a separate legal and accounting entity. Neither its assets nor its liabilities are reported on the balance sheet of the employer. Instead, a separate reporting by the pension plan must be made in accordance with *Statement No. 35,* issued in March 1980.

*Statement No. 35* calls for the annual financial statements of the pension fund to include the following reports:

1.  Statement of net assets available for benefits.
2.  Statement of changes in net assets available for benefits.
3.  Statement of accumulated plan benefits.
4.  Statement of changes in accumulated plan benefits.

The first statement would display the assets of the pension fund—investments in various securities, real estate, receivables for employee contributions, accrued interest, etc. Included among the assets of *insured plans* would be contracts or deposits with insurance companies. The assets would be carried at current market values. The second statement would show the changes in this fund of assets during the year. Investment income, appreciation in the current value of investments, and contributions from employers and employees would augment the stock of assets available for benefits at the end of the year. Payments made to retired employees and operating expenses would reduce the net assets.

The other two statements deal with the "liability" side. The present value of the estimated future benefits are reported in three categories—future benefits for employees already retired, vested benefits of current employees, and nonvested benefits for current employees. These valuations ideally would be made at the beginning and end of the year. Changes in the present value of expected future benefits during the year result from the accrual of interest, the earning of additional benefits by employees, the payment of benefits to retirees, and any modifications of the plan or the actuarial assumptions underlying it.

A few accountants would like to merge the pension fund with the accounts of the employer. The pension fund assets would appear among the assets of the employer. Similarly, the present value of the expected future benefits would show directly as a company liability. They argue that the real economic relationship is between the employer and employee. The pension fund is often only a nonessential intermediary. This might be particularly true with trusteed plans for which the trustees are the officers of the employer corporation. The argument is more difficult to mount when the pension fund is handled by an independent insurance company.

The concept of a complete merging of the pension plan accounts with those of the employer corporation has not gathered general support. However, as we saw in the previous section, the tentative ideas of the Financial Accounting Standards Board lean a little in that direction. For each pension plan there would be a separate accounting and reporting, designed to provide participants with information with which to estimate that plan's ability to pay pension benefits when due. In addition, some of the information reported by the pension plans would also be reflected in the corporate accounts. Specifically, any excess of the present value of expected future benefits over the fair value of pension assets would appear as an employer liability. Currently under *Statement No. 36* it is reported only in the footnotes to the employer's financial statements. It may move to the body of the main statement.

**Choice of Actuarial Cost Methods**

*Opinion No. 8* limited a firm's choice of actuarial cost methods to one of an accepted group. However, much as with varying depreciation methods, different actuarial cost methods can give very different patterns of pension expense recognition.

The discussions of the last decade have raised the question of whether a single actuarial cost method should be prescribed. At issue, in particular, are actuarial cost methods that do not consider future salary changes. Many accountants feel these methods understate current pension expense and, more importantly, current pension liabilities.

The FASB appears to agree. For pension plans that define benefits in terms of future salary levels, salary progression should be considered in measuring pension costs. Projected benefit cost methods explicitly consider future salaries as an actuarial assumption. According to *Statement No. 35,* pension plans must report using projected benefit cost methods if applicable under the plan. Likewise, the supplementary disclosures required under *Statement No. 36* must also be calculated according to one of the projected benefit cost methods.

Consideration is now being given to a requirement that all *employers* use the *same* method (projected unit credit) to measure pension costs and liabilities, regardless of what methods they might use for funding purposes. Ostensibly, this requirement would enhance comparability.

Opponents of the use of a single required actuarial cost method claim that any increase in comparability would be illusory. The actuarial cost method is only one of a number of different actuarial assumptions. Standardization of one assumption does not create comparability. Indeed, different companies have different employee groups and benefit structures. Actuarial assumptions must also be different. Generally accepted accounting principles do not mandate the same depreciation methods for different assets; they should not mandate the same actuarial cost method for different pension plans.

One other advantage to the use of different methods by different employers relates to one of the major objectives of financial reporting—the assessment of future cash flows. Most companies use the same actuarial cost methods to fund their pension costs as to measure pension expense. Requiring a divorce between methods used for funding and those used for expense determination would detract from the achievement of this objective with respect to pension expense. Under current standards, expense measurement follows quite closely the pattern of cash outflows.

## Actuarial Gains and Losses

When the actuarial assumptions underlying the pension calculations are modified to meet changing conditions or when actual experience differs from the original expectations, actuarial gains and losses result. The Pension Reform Act of 1974 (ERISA) called them *experience gains and losses*. They can result from mortality and turnover assumptions as well as substantial gains or losses on the sale of pension investments. Immediate recognition of these actuarial gains and losses could cause significant fluctuations in the year-to-year charge for pension expense. For example, if during the year the funding agency sells securities which have greatly appreciated in value, the gain might more than offset the entire normal pension cost. If the gain is recognized immediately, the result would be no pension expense for the year.

To be sure, actuarial gains and losses do influence the total pension cost; the important question is the *timing* of their impact on expense. The Accounting Principles Board reasoned that such gains and losses should be dealt with in a manner consistent with the long-range nature of pension cost. Actuarial assumptions are only estimates of future events. Actuarial gains and losses may indicate only short-term deviations from the estimates. In fact, they are in the nature of estimates themselves, subject perhaps to further modification. Treating them as adjustments to any particular year's pension expense or even as corrections of prior years' earnings overemphasizes their short-term character. Such changes are an integral part of the framework for estimating pension expense. Accordingly, the APB recommended that actuarial gains and losses should be spread or averaged over the current and future years.[13]

In recent years suggestions have been made to recognize these measurement changes in full immediately. The tentative proposal of the FASB would still recognize them over future periods but in a different manner. A *measurement valuation allowance* would be established as a contra or adjunct account to the net pension liability. As experience gains and losses arise, they would be recognized immediately in the measurement of the gross pension benefit obligation. However, an equal offsetting change would be recorded in the measurement valuation allowance. The balance in the measurement valuation allowance would then be amortized to expense over the remaining service lives of the plan participants. In this manner actuarial gains and losses resulting from changed actuarial assumptions or varying experience would be recognized prospectively. Neither the *net* pension liability nor the current period's expense is affected immediately by experience gains or losses recognized in that period.

**Unrealized Appreciation and Depreciation**

A similar problem is raised by value increases and decreases in pension fund investments which have not been realized by sale. For example, assume that shares of stock are purchased by a pension fund at a price of $5 per share. The stock steadily increases in value each year, much faster than anticipated. The shares are not sold by the pension fund, however, so technically no actuarial gain or loss exists. Should this appreciation be ignored in calculations of pension cost? Should it be offset against the pension expense each year? Should it be recognized as an actuarial gain only when disposed of by the pension fund, perhaps at some later date?

Ignoring unrealized appreciation in a pension fund overlooks the fact that those gains can be realized and thereby be used to reduce the total contribution from, and hence the total cost to, the employer. Changes in the value of these assets do have an ultimate impact on pension cost. Recognition of appreciation and depreciation each year as an adjustment of that year's pension expense is subject to the same criticism as immediate recognition of actuarial gains and losses. It could cause wide fluctuations in annual pension expense by emphasizing short-term fluctuations. Finally, to wait until the gains and losses are realized by sale overemphasizes the turnover of pension fund investment. Moreover, it might result in a material pension-cost reduction (or increase) remaining unrecognized for many years.

The conclusion of the Accounting Principles Board was that unrealized appreciation and depreciation were not significantly different from actuarial gains and losses. Therefore, these value changes "should be recog-

---

[13] The Employee Retirement Income Security Act of 1974 requires that, for legal purposes, actuarial gains and losses be spread over a period of 15 or 20 years.

nized in the determination of the provision for pension cost on a rational and systematic basis that avoids giving undue weight to short-term market fluctuations."[14]

The changes under consideration by the FASB do not disagree with this general principle. Only the method of recognizing the changes differs. If a net pension liability (gross pension benefit obligation minus fair value of pension assets) is set up on the employer's books, any short-term changes in the value of pension fund assets would cause fluctuations in the net pension liability.

Consequently, the Financial Accounting Standards Board is recommending that any net appreciation (above the interest rate assumed in the pension calculations) or depreciation be recognized through a change in the measurement valuation allowance, exactly as actuarial gains and losses are. As the net pension liability goes up or down because of changes in the current value of pension fund assets, a simultaneous change is entered in the measurement valuation allowance. The latter is amortized to expense over the remaining lives of the plan participants. In this way unrealized appreciation and depreciation would be recognized prospectively in a systematic way.

## DISCUSSION OF THE ARMCO ANNUAL REPORT

All of the information that Armco reports about its employee pension plans is contained in a portion of Note 1 to the financial statements (see the Appendix to Chapter 5). Remember that the calculations follow the guidelines set forth in *APB Opinion No. 8*. The disclosures are dictated by that opinion and by *FASB Statement No. 36*.

Pension cost for 1981 was $132.3 million. This cost included current service cost (normal cost) plus amortization of prior service costs over periods of no more than 40 years. Readers of the statement are not told the particular actuarial cost methods used or the precise periods over which prior service cost is expensed. The company has a number of different pension plans. Various actuarial cost methods and periods of amortization are employed. All of the actuarial cost methods must be acceptable ones, however, or a notation would have been made in the auditor's opinion.

Armco states that all pension costs are funded. This means that no pension assets and liabilities, save perhaps for short-term liabilities, appear on the balance sheet. Furthermore, no interest equivalents are involved in the pension cost calculation.

The second paragraph of the pension note contains information about the pension plans themselves. This information is taken from the financial reports of the *pension plan* as governed by *FASB Statement No. 35*. Armco uses an assumed interest rate of 8½ percent in the present value computa-

---

[14] *APB Opinion No. 8*, par. 32.

tions associated with its pensions. An average rate for 100 large companies in 1981 was 7.8 percent; U.S. Steel and Bethlehem Steel both used 10 percent.[15] The higher the assumed rate of return, the less will be the present value of pension benefits and pension cost.

The latest valuation of pension benefits was prepared by Armco's actuaries as of January 1, 1981. The present value of pension benefits promised to all present and former employees, based on all service rendered to date, and including past service costs, was $1,346.6 million on January 1, 1981, and $1,111.6 million on January 1, 1980. These figures reflect not only the 8½ percent assumed rate of return but other actuarial assumptions regarding death, disability, withdrawal, etc., as well. Most of the pension benefits are vested; that is, even if the employee leaves the company before retirement, the vested obligations would still have to be paid. The current values of the assets set aside to pay pension benefits were $1,067.7 million and $832.6 million on January 1, 1981, and 1980, respectively.

As of January 1, 1981, Armco's pension plan contains $278.9 million of unfunded benefits; the vested benefits include only $68.1 million that is unfunded. GAAP do not view these amounts as accounting liabilities primarily because prior service costs are not viewed as an immediate liability upon adoption or amendment of a pension plan. As we pointed out earlier in the chapter, however, some accountants strongly disagree. They would have Armco record an offsetting asset and liability at least equal to the unfunded vested benefits of $68.1 million and probably for the entire $278.9 million.

The $278.9 million figure would constitute the major portion of the net pension liability tentatively being proposed by the Financial Accounting Standards Board. The essence of the FASB proposal would be to move this amount from the financial statement notes directly to the balance sheet itself. The reader is invited to examine the financial statements of Armco for the mid- and late 1980s to see if this suggestion ever reaches fruition.

**SUMMARY**

That the problems of accounting for pensions are complex is apparent from the discussions in this chapter. The area has theoretical controversies, practical compromises, and baffling detail. As in the case of leases in Chapter 11, we illustrate how present value methodology underlies the fundamental nature of pension expense and pension liabilities. Pension expense each period basically is the present value of benefits earned by employees during the period, and the pension liability on the balance sheet is the unfunded present value of benefits earned to date.

Pension expense determinations begin with the concept of a fund of

---

[15] *Business Week,* August 9, 1982, p. 74.

money being accumulated. The amount of benefits granted and the various actuarial assumptions concerning future events determine the ultimate size of the fund. Actuarial cost methods are various methods of funding, systematically setting aside money each period, to accumulate with interest to the desired amount. The actuarial cost methods also serve as reasonable ways of accruing the pension cost. Because the initial calculations assume coincident funding, adjustments to pension expense must be made via interest equivalents whenever the pattern of accrual and funding differ.

The major controversy in pension accounting concerns the treatment of past service cost. Current thinking attributes all pension costs to future periods, even though the size of benefits may be influenced by length of service prior to adoption of the pension plan. Therefore, past service cost is recognized as expense only in future periods, although the determination of the number of future periods involved is still a matter of debate. No pension liability is recognized unless amounts so accrued are not funded.

The accounting for pension expense and liability is an area where only a beginning has been made in the establishment of accounting principles. *APB Opinion No. 8* sets forth some general conceptual guidelines, outlines some broad procedural principles, and establishes a definition of a maximum and minimum expense within which a company's pension expense must fall. There is ample room for a refining of both concept and procedure as the FASB relooks at the pension area. A mastery of the basic principles now will help one to understand future developments.

## QUESTIONS AND PROBLEMS

**12–1.** On January 1, 1984, the Barbarajo Record Company adopted a pension program for employees. Normal pension cost is $150,000 per year; total past service cost is $530,000. The applicable interest rate is 8 percent. The total amount funded at the end of each of the first two years is $170,000.

*Required:*

a. Prepare the journal entry to record pension expense and the payment to the pension trust fund for 1984 and 1985. Assume that past service costs are to be accrued (amortized) over a 20-year period.

b. Calculate the maximum pension expense provision for 1984 and 1985 for this company under *APB Opinion No. 8.*

c. Calculate the minimum pension expense provision under *Opinion No. 8* for both years. Ignore any provision for vested benefits.

**12–2.** You are given below a schedule of financial information for the pension plan of a company which adopted the plan when actuaries estimated its past service costs to be $250,000.

| Year | Normal Cost | Past Service Cost | Adjustment for Interest | Cash Payments | Balance Sheet |
|------|------------|-------------------|-------------------------|---------------|---------------|
| 1 ........ | $20,000 | $25,741 | –0– | $79,349 | $ 33,608 |
| 2 ........ | 20,000 | 25,741 | $ 2,017 | 79,349 | 69,233 |
| 3 ........ | 20,000 | 25,741 | 4,154 | 79,349 | 106,995 |
| 4 ........ | 20,000 | 25,741 | 6,420 | 79,349 | 147,023 |
| 5 ........ | 20,000 | 25,741 | 8,821 | 79,349 | 189,452 |
| 6 ........ | 20,000 | 25,741 | 11,367 | 20,000 | 175,078 |
| 7 ........ | 20,000 | 25,741 | 10,505 | 20,000 | 159,842 |
| 8 ........ | 20,000 | 25,741 | 9,591 | 20,000 | 143,692 |
| 9 ........ | 20,000 | 25,741 | 8,622 | 20,000 | 126,573 |
| 10 ........ | 20,000 | 25,741 | 7,595 | 20,000 | 108,427 |
| 11 ........ | 20,000 | 25,741 | 6,506 | 20,000 | 89,192 |
| 12 ........ | 20,000 | 25,741 | 5,352 | 20,000 | 68,803 |
| 13 ........ | 20,000 | 25,741 | 4,128 | 20,000 | 47,190 |
| 14 ........ | 20,000 | 25,741 | 2,831 | 20,000 | 24,283 |
| 15 ........ | 20,000 | 25,741 | 1,458 | 20,000 | –0– |

*Required:*

a. What interest rate was assumed in pension plan calculations underlying this schedule? How did you arrive at your results?

b. Show how the accrual (amortization) of past service costs was determined.

c. Show how the cash payments were determined.

d. Show how the interest adjustment was determined and explain its relevance.

e. Prepare journal entries to record pension expense and payments in Year 3 and in Year 12.

f. What balance sheet amount would appear at the end of Year 10? What is the nature of the account under which the amount would be reported?

**12–3.** Monpere Corporation established a pension plan for its employees on January 1, 1985. As of that date the company's actuary determined that the past service costs amounted to $1,000,000. Monpere decided to fund normal costs each year and to fund past service costs over a 15-year period. However, it adopted a 10-year amortization period for purposes of determining pension expense. All estimates by the actuary were based on the assumption that the pension fund would earn 10 percent.

The following table contains data based on these estimates for the first three years.

| | 1985 | 1986 | 1987 |
|------|------|------|------|
| Normal cost .................................. | $200,000 | $208,000 | $217,000 |
| Amortization of past service cost ................ | 162,745 | 162,745 | 162,745 |
| Annual payments to trustee for past service costs ............................ | 131,473 | 131,473 | 131,473 |
| Interest equivalents on accrued pension liability ............................ | — | 3,127 | 6,567 |

*Required:*

a. Prepare journal entries to record pension expense for 1985, 1986, and 1987. Ignore any limitations imposed by *Opinion No. 8*.

b. Compute the amount of the accrued pension liability on December 31, 1987. Where would this item appear on the financial statements?

c. Compute the maximum pension expense allowed under generally accepted accounting principles in 1985.

    *d.* Compute the minimum pension expense allowed under GAAP in 1985 assuming that the provision for vested benefits involves the accruing of past service costs over 40 years [$(P/A, 40, .10) = 9.7791$]. Do you see a conflict between your answer to parts *(c)* and *(d)*?

    *e.* Why might normal cost increase each year?

**12–4.** The following disclosures were included in the notes to the financial statements contained in the annual report of Graniteville Company.

> The Company and its subsidiaries have in effect several noncontributory defined benefit and defined contribution employee retirement plans covering substantially all employees. The total expense of these plans for 1981, 1980, and 1979 was approximately $3,727,000, $3,937,000, and $3,600,000, respectively, which includes, as to certain defined benefit plans, amortization of past service costs over 10 years. The Company makes annual contributions to the plans equal to the amounts accrued for pension expense.

| | Information Available as of | | |
|---|---|---|---|
| | January 1, 1981 | January 1, 1980 | January 1, 1979 |
| | (dollars in thousands) | | |
| Total assets available for benefits: | | | |
| At cost ......................... | $39,359 | $36,487 | $32,421 |
| At market ....................... | 48,971 | 40,356 | 34,283 |
| Actuarial present value of accumulated plan benefits: | | | |
| Vested ......................... | 19,680 | 22,084 | 19,212 |
| Nonvested ...................... | 2,938 | 3,350 | 2,898 |
| Total ....................... | 22,618 | 25,434 | 22,110 |
| Gross accrued liability ............... | 48,425 | 45,270 | 39,948 |
| Unfunded accrued liability (assets at cost) ................... | 9,066 | 8,783 | 7,527 |
| Weighted-average, assumed rate of return used in determining the above benefits .................. | 6% | 5% | 5% |
| Actuarial wage rate increase assumption | 6% | 5% | 5% |

> In 1981, the Company changed its investment return assumption from 5 percent to 6 percent and changed its wage rate increase assumption from 5 percent to 6 percent. The net effect of these changes was to reduce pension expense by $666,000 and increase net income by $333,000, or $.08 per share.

*Required:*

    *a.* Explain the difference between defined benefit and defined contribution employee retirement programs.

    *b.* Why might Graniteville Company choose only a 10-year period over which to amortize past service costs?

    *c.* What balance sheet accounts, if any, would you expect Graniteville Company to show? Explain.

    *d.* Do you believe that the Unfunded Accrued Liability should be reflected as a liability on Graniteville Company's balance sheet?

    *e.* Explain how and why each of the changes in actuarial assumptions would be expected to affect pension expense.

**12–5.** The CMA Corporation, which has been in operation for the past 23 years, decided late in 1984 to adopt, beginning on January 1, 1985, a funded pension plan for its employees.[16] The pension plan is to be noncontributory and will provide for vesting after five years of service by each eligible employee. A trust agreement has been entered into whereby a large national insurance company will receive the yearly pension fund contributions and administer the fund.

Management, through extended consultation with the fund trustee, internal accountants, and independent actuaries, arrived at the following conclusions:

1. The normal pension cost will be $30,000.
2. The present value of the past service cost at date of inception of the pension plan (January 1, 1985) is $200,000.
3. Because of the large sum of money involved, the past service costs will be funded over the next 15 years. The first payment will not be due until January 1, 1986.
4. Past service pension costs will be accrued (amortized) over a 20-year period.
5. Where applicable, an 8 percent interest rate was assumed.

*Required:*

a. Give the account titles and amounts which will be reported in the company's (1) income statement for 1985 and (2) balance sheet as of December 31, 1985.
b. Give the account titles and amounts which will be reported in the company's (1) income statement for 1986 and (2) balance sheet as of December 31, 1986.
c. Calculate and label the components which comprise the maximum and minimum 1985 financial statement pension expense limits in accordance with GAAP.

**12–6.** American Telephone & Telegraph incurred over $3 billion in pension costs each year from 1980 to 1982 under its two major pension plans. Contributions under the plans are made to irrevocable trust funds. In its 1982 annual report, AT&T describes its policy as "to make contributions which are equal to the current year cost of the plans determined on a going concern basis by an actuarial method specified by the Employee Retirement Income Security Act of 1974."

AT&T also was required to include the disclosures about the pension plans as mandated by *FASB Statement No. 36*. The following data and company commentary were abstracted from the 1982 annual report (amounts are in millions of dollars).

| | At December 31 | |
| --- | --- | --- |
| | *1981* | *1980* |
| Actuarial present value of accumulated plan benefits: | | |
| Vested | $20,827.4 | $21,455.3 |
| Non-vested | 3,413.4 | 4,050.5 |
| Total | 24,240.8 | 25,505.8 |
| Fair value of net assets available for plan benefits | $35,781.8 | $33,523.7 |

---

[16] Adapted from Examination for the Certificate in Management Accounting, November 1973.

The rates of return used in determining the actuarial present value of accumulated plan benefits are the rates used by the Pension Benefit Guaranty Corporation (PBGC) for determining the value of plan benefits under terminated pension plans and averaged approximately 10.6 percent and 8.9 percent compounded annually at December 31, 1981, and 1980, respectively. If the rates used by PBGC had been 1 percent lower, the actuarial present value of accumulated plan benefits at December 31, 1981, would have been approximately $27,166.9 instead of $24,240.8 as shown above.

The Company believes that misleading inferences concerning the plan's funding status may result from a comparison of the actuarial present value of accumulated plan benefits with the fair value of net assets available for benefits. This is because plan assets have been accumulated by making contributions equal to current year costs determined on a going concern basis as required by ERISA, while the determination of the actuarial present value of accumulated plan benefits required by *Statement No. 36* is essentially a "plan termination" type calculation which uses methods and assumptions which are not the same as those used to determine current year pension costs. The required method for determining the actuarial present value of accumulated plan benefits fails to take into consideration probable future events such as future wage and salary increases and future employee service which have been taken into consideration by the Company and its subsidiaries in determining costs for the plans. Furthermore, the fair value of net assets available for plan benefits will fluctuate which also may create erroneous impressions with respect to long term progress on funding the pension plans.

*Required:*

a. AT&T describes its pension plans as fully funded for actuarial purposes. The data above suggest that the plans are overfunded. Is there a difference in the concept of funding from the perspective of the employer-pension plan relationship and of the pension plan-employee relationship?

b. AT&T's contributions are made to irrevocable trust funds. Is there a difference in the concept of pension liability from the perspective of the employer-pension plan relationship and of the pension plan-employee relationship? Explain.

c. How sensitive are pension "liability" estimates to changes in interest rate assumptions? Does this sensitivity support the argument for or against the use of standardized interest assumptions?

d. Do you agree that "misleading inferences" may result from the comparisons mandated by *Statement No. 36?* What does AT&T mean by a "going concern" basis versus a "plan termination" basis?

e. In light of AT&T's commentary, do you believe that this footnote information should be incorporated into the formal position statements of firms?

12–7. Bubbling Beverage Company first adopted a formal pension plan on January 1, 1983. At that time, the past service cost was actuarially computed to be $900,000, and normal cost was set at $80,000 annually. The company decided to accrue past service costs over a 20-year period. The applicable interest rate is 8 percent. The company funded each year the normal cost plus the amount of past service cost accrued.

Effective January 1, 1988, the pension plan was amended to increase the retirement benefits. As a result, normal cost was increased to $90,000 per year, and $400,000 was added to past service costs. The company decided to accrue all prior service costs over the original 20-year period. This means that the increase in prior service costs will be amortized over 15 years. However, the company decided to continue *funding the same dollar amount* as in the preceding five years.

*Required:*

a. What does the statement that "past service costs were actuarially computed to be $900,000" mean? Explain exactly what the $900,000 represents.
b. What will the total pension expense be each year during the first five years?
c. Prepare the journal entries to record pension expense and the amount funded in 1988 and 1989. Show computations.

**12–8.** P. C. Jason Company, Inc., included the following note to *its* financial statements concerning its pension plan (in millions of dollars).

|  | 1984 | 1983 |
|---|---|---|
| Present value of accumulated benefits: | | |
| Vested | $229 | $184 |
| Nonvested | 29 | 54 |
| | 258 | 238 |
| Net assets available for benefits | $314 | $285 |

In determining the actuarial present value of accumulated benefits, the assumed rate of return used was 8.5 percent. Each 1 percent change in this assumed rate of return would change the present value of accumulated benefits by approximately $26 million. The rate of return used in determining the funding and pension costs of the pension plan was 6 percent.

You also secure a copy of the financial report of the *P. C. Jason Pension Plan* prepared in accordance with *FASB Satement No. 35*. Among the statements in it you find the following two schedules:

P. C. JASON PENSION PLAN
Statement of Changes in Net Assets Available for Benefits
($ millions)

|  | 1984 | 1983 |
|---|---|---|
| Net assets available for benefits, January 1 | $285 | $209 |
| Investment income: | | |
| Interest and dividends | 25 | 22 |
| Net appreciation in fair market value | (35) | 16 |
| Less: Investment expenses | 2 | 2 |
| Contributions from employer | 43 | 41 |
| | 320 | 290 |
| Benefits paid to participants | (5) | (4) |
| Administrative expenses | (1) | (1) |
| Net assets available for benefits, December 31 | $314 | $285 |

P. C. JASON PENSION PLAN
Statement of Changes in Accumulated Plan Benefits

|  | 1984 | 1983 |
|---|---|---|
| Actuarial present value of accumulated plan benefits, January 1 | $303.2 | $300.3 |
| Increase (decrease) during the year attributed to: | | |
| Plan amendment | 19.4 | 4.2 |
| Change in actuarial assumptions | — | (1.1) |
| Benefits accumulated | 6.2 | 3.8 |
| Benefits paid | (5.0) | (4.0) |
| Actuarial present value of accumulated plan benefits, December 31 | $323.8 | $303.2 |

*Required:*

a. Why does the actuarial present value of accumulated plan benefits shown in the financial statements of the pension plan differ from the amount shown in the notes to the financial statements of the employer?

b. In its note, P. C. Jason Company, Inc., states that the present value of accumulated benefits would change by $26 million for every 1 percent change in the assumed rate of return. In what direction would the present value of benefits change if interest rates *declined?* Explain why.

c. Is the P. C. Jason Pension Plan over- or underfunded? Explain. How sensitive is your answer to assumptions about rates of return?

d. What type of actuarial assumptions could have been made in 1983 to have the effect indicated in the schedule on the bottom of page 459?

e. What type of major change in the plan do you think occurred in 1984?

f. Based on this information would you support the recording of information about net plan assets and present value of accumulated benefits as a net asset or net liability in the financial statements of P. C. Jason Company, Inc.? Explain your reasoning.

12–9. Fido Fertilizer Corporation signed a new labor agreement with its union on Janaury 1, 1984. Included in the package of fringe benefits was a newly initiated pension program. Retirement benefits are based on an employee's total length of service, including years prior to adoption of the plan. At the date of an employee's retirement, the pension fund will purchase from a life insurance company an annuity policy which will pay the employee the stipulated monthly benefits.

As of January 1, 1984, the present value at 6 percent of future pension benefits related to years of service prior to January 1, 1984 (past service costs), was $400,000. The increase in present value of the future pension benefits attributable to each subsequent year (normal cost) was $70,000. During 1984 and 1985 retirement annuities were actually purchased for employees retiring in those years in the amounts of $13,000 and $18,000, respectively.

The company is considering a number of funding and expense recognition plans. These include the following:

1. Charge to expense each year only the amount paid for retirement annuities that year.

2. Fund with a trustee the past service cost immediately and each year's normal cost as incurred. Recognize as expense the maximum amount allowed under GAAP.

3. Fund normal cost each year and past service costs over a 40-year period. Recognize as expense normal cost plus past service cost accrued (amortized) over 20 years. $(P/A, 40, .06) = 15.0463$.

4. Fund normal cost each year and past service costs over a 20-year period. Recognize as expense the amount funded each year.

*Required:*

a. Is the first method a suitable way to measure pension expense and liability? Explain your answer.

b. Contrast the second, third, and fourth plans in terms of their impact on the financial statements. For each plan, show the pension expense that would be charged in 1984 and 1985 and any balance sheet accounts related to the pension plan that would appear at the end of each of the two years.

c. After reviewing your figures from part *(b)*, the controller states, "This is a good example of the diversity in generally accepted accounting principles. The financial statements are made to look different depending on which principles we follow, yet the real financial position and performance of the company remain the same." Carefully evaluate this reaction.

**12–10.** The information below has been abstracted from the 1981 reports of Colt Industries, Inc.

> The company and certain of its subsidiaries have in effect, for substantially all employees, pension and retirement plans under which funds are deposited with trustees. As of January 1, 1981, and 1980, the actuarially computed present value of accumulated vested benefits was $337,178,000 and $289,798,000; and of nonvested benefits was $19,974,000 and $13,487,000, respectively, using a 10.4 percent interest factor. The plans' net assets available for benefits, valued at market, were $327,505,000 and $261,868,000, resulting in unfunded vested benefits of $9,673,000 and $27,930,000.
>
> Pension expense of $56,787,000, $52,279,000, and $47,680,000 was charged to earnings in 1981, 1980, and 1979, respectively, and is the maximum annual provision permitted by *Opinion No. 8* of the Accounting Principles Board, including amortization of prior service cost at 10 percent per year or over approximately a 15-year period.
>
> Effective January 1982, in recognition of historically high interest rates, the company changed its portfolio of pension fund assets to match bond maturities with projected benefits for most of its retired employees, principally in its Crucible Inc. specialty steels operations. This dedication of a bond portfolio having an effective yield of approximately 15 percent resulted in a significant reduction in unfunded liabilities related to retired employees. Simultaneously, a review of the company's actuarial policies was made resulting in changes effective January 1982 in the actuarial assumptions used by the company in computing pension liability with respect to active employees. These changes reflect the company's best estimate of future trends and valuation assumptions. The most significant change was an increase in the assumed interest rate of return on investments from 6 percent to 7 percent. Concurrently, the projected wage and salary earnings scales for certain plans were increased 1 percent. . . . The net effect of these changes will be to reduce significantly the 1982 pension expense.

*Required:*

a. Reference is made in the notes to a 10.4 percent interest factor and then later to an interest rate of return of 6 percent and 7 percent. Why are two sets of rates used? What would the impact be on unfunded vested benefits if the 7 percent figure had been used to calculate them?

b. Past service costs are amortized to expense at a rate of 10 percent per year over a 15-year period. Is this contradictory? Would the result not be a charge of 150 percent of past service costs to expense? Explain.

c. Effective January 1982 Colt Industries made two changes in actuarial assumptions and "dedicated a bond portfolio." Explain the nature of each of these changes and why it impacts on pension expense and unfunded vested benefits in the manner described.

d. Do you believe unfunded vested benefits should appear as a liability on the balance sheet of Colt Industries?

**12–11.** The Doleful Company established a pension plan on January 1, 1983. Annual benefits under the plan equal 3 percent of a retiree's average salary times the number of years of employment. Therefore, if an employee had an average salary of $20,000 and had worked for 10 years, the annual pension would be $6,000 ($20,000 × 0.03 × 10).

All costs of the plan are to be born by Doleful. Funding will be accomplished through payments to an independent trust fund. Current plans are to fund normal cost annually and past service cost over a period of 20 years.

The independent actuaries working with Doleful on the plan come up with the following information and actuarial estimates:

1. Number of employees—100.
2. Percentage of employees who will retire under the plan—80 percent.
3. Average age on January 1, 1983—45.
4. Average years of eligible service prior to adoption of the plan—10.
5. Average age at retirement—60.
6. Average life expectancy after retirement—20.
7. Average annual salary anticipated—$12,000.
8. Actuarial cost method—entry age normal.
9. Interest rate to be used in actuarial calculations—8 percent.

In all of your computations, assume that cash payments are made at the end of the year.

*Required:*

a. Calculate the amount that needs to be on deposit at the average date of retirement for the employee group.

b. Without prejudice to your own answer, assume the answer in part *(a)* is $7.4 million. Now calculate normal cost under the entry age normal actuarial cost method. (Note: Entry age normal assumes level annual payments from the time the employees first began eligible service.)

c. Without prejudice to your own answer, assume the answer in part *(b)* is $100,000. Compute the aggregate amount of past service cost as of January 1, 1983.

d. Without prejudice to your own answer, assume the answer to part *(c)* is $1,450,000. For accounting purposes, past service cost is to be recognized as expense over a 15-year period. Prepare entries to reflect the pension plan expense and funding in 1983.

e. Prepare entries to reflect the pension plan expense and funding in 1984.

# CHAPTER 13

# ACCOUNTING
# FOR INCOME TAXES

Corporate income taxes are periodic charges levied by federal and state governments on the taxable income, as defined by law, of incorporated business entities. Such charges are accounted for in Chapter 5 as a reduction in stockholders' equity (a debit to Income Taxes) and an increase in a liability (a credit to Estimated Liability for Income Taxes or Income Taxes Payable). In this accounting the amount of taxes legally owed for the period and the periodic tax expense are assumed to be the same. This assumption, however, may not be valid. Taxable income is a legal concept. The regulations underlying tax accounting do not necessarily coincide with the informational needs of investors and the basic concepts of financial accounting.

This chapter takes a closer look at the problems accountants face when recording the income tax charge for a period. The principal problems fall into five categories.

1. *Permanent differences*—Certain items of revenue and expense enter into either taxable income or accounting income without *ever* affecting the computation of the other. Consequently, they may alter the relationship between income tax expense and net income before tax from what one normally would expect.

2. *Interperiod tax allocation*—Some accounting transactions affect the determination of financial accounting income in one year and the computation of taxable income in another. These *timing differences* cause the income tax charge legally owed for a period to differ from the amount which is related to the events reported on the income statement.

3. *Carry-back and carry-forward of "net operating losses"*—Current tax regulations allow corporations to deduct certain operating losses incurred

in one year from the taxable income of prior and subsequent years. This provision raises the question of when the tax effects of such losses should be recorded—in the period of loss or in the prior and subsequent periods.

4. *Investment tax credit*—Income tax regulations from time to time provide for a credit against income taxes to encourage investment in machinery and equipment. Taxpayers are allowed to reduce their tax payments by an amount equal to a specified percentage of their investment. In what period or periods should this tax reduction appear in the financial accounting records?

5. *Intraperiod or intrastatement tax allocation*—Certain unusual items occurring during a period may be reported in separate sections of the income statement or in a separate statement of retained earnings. These items influence the computation of income taxes as well. How should the tax effects of these unusual items be reported in the financial statements? Because these special items are examined more fully in Chapter 16, the discussion of intraperiod tax allocation is deferred until then.

## DIFFERENCES BETWEEN ACCOUNTING INCOME AND TAXABLE INCOME

On the surface the differences between accounting income and taxable income appear to be minimal. The Internal Revenue Code, in Section 446, requires that taxable income be computed in accordance with the method of accounting regularly employed by the taxpayer, if that method clearly reflects income. However, authorized throughout the Code and in the regulations interpreting the law are many exceptions and special provisions that reflect either policy goals of Congress to be attained through the income tax law or administrative rulings to make implementation of the law convenient. For example, procedures designed to regulate business activity, to encourage or discourage particular industries, to stimulate economic development, to maintain a perceived equity among taxpayers, and to time tax levies to coincide closely with cash receipts have found reflection in the income tax law. The complex income tax rules arise from purposes other than just the measurement of business income. Once these tax options are written into the law, however, companies deliberately take advantage of them to reduce current taxable income. Even if payment is merely postponed, the corporation receives a type of interest-free loan.

Financial accounting, on the other hand, is interested in properly matching costs and revenues to measure business income, not in determining taxable income. Where the two concepts of income are not the same, business firms should, and often do, maintain tax accounting records separate from their financial accounting records. Even if separate records are kept, a financial accounting problem may still arise when the income tax expense and income tax liability are affected by events that are treated in one way on the books and in another on the tax return. Should income tax expense on the income statement be determined necessarily from the legal liability shown on the tax return for the period, or should it be related to the events reported on the income statement? To begin to answer this question, the accountant must separate relatively permanent differences between tax accounting and financial accounting from timing differences.

**Permanent Differences**

Certain items of revenue are excluded by law from the determination of income taxes. Interest revenue from state and municipal bonds, for instance, is not taxed but is properly recognized as accounting revenue. A portion of the dividends received by a corporation from other taxable domestic corporations is treated in a basically similar manner.

Particular deductions also may be treated differently for tax and financial accounting purposes. For example, goodwill is not subject to amortization under current tax regulations but must be written off periodically as an expense on the financial statements. Similarly, life insurance premiums paid on insurance policies of employees are not tax-deductible if the corporation is the beneficiary under the policy. Nevertheless, they are a valid expense on its income statement.

The foregoing examples represent some relatively permanent differences between tax accounting and financial accounting income. Unless and until the statutory provisions of the tax laws are changed, these items will *always* be a cause of difference. There is nothing special to do about them except to reflect them in tax expense and tax liability as they occur. Still, permanent differences may cause difficulties in interpretation because of the lack of reconciliation between the effective tax rate as indicated by the income statement and the statutory federal income tax rate. Consequently, it is important to disclose any material, permanent differences; more is said on disclosure at the end of the chapter.

**Timing Differences**

In contrast, some events are reported for both book and tax purposes but in different accounting periods. These timing differences do raise important financial accounting questions. Over a sufficiently long period, any individual timing difference should disappear and not cause any difference between taxable income and accounting income.[1] Therefore, many accountants argue that periodic income tax *expense* should be based on the amount of income (aside from adjustments for permanent differences) shown on the income statement, regardless of when the tax legally has to be paid to the government.

Let us review some of the major causes of timing differences. The following basic situations can exist:

---

[1] Even though the differences disappear in the long run, the present value of these differences is significant. It is for this reason that companies try to minimize current taxes even though in so doing they may be adding equally to future taxes.

1. Accounting income before tax exceeds taxable income:
   a. *Revenue* is recognized in the accounting records *prior* to its recognition on the tax return.
   b. *Expense* is recognized in the accounting records *after* its deduction on the tax return.
2. Accounting income before tax is less than taxable income:
   a. *Revenue* is recognized in the accounting records *after* its inclusion on the tax return.
   b. *Expense* is recognized in the accounting records *prior* to its deduction on the tax return.

Examples of 1*(a)* include revenue being recognized at the time of sale but being reported for tax purposes in installments, so that the taxation of the revenue is deferred until later periods, when the cash is actually received. A similar situation exists when a company recognizes revenue according to percentage of completion for book purposes but reports revenue for tax purposes only when contracts are completed.

The most prevalent example of 1*(b)*—expenses being deducted earlier on the tax return than in the accounting records—is depreciation. As noted in Chapter 9, firms *must* use the new, super-fast Accelerated Cost Recovery System (ACRS) depreciation for tax purposes for all property placed in service after 1980. For plant assets acquired before 1981, most companies use declining-balance or sum-of-the-years'-digits methods for tax purposes. Because the great majority of firms nevertheless use the straight-line depreciation method for financial reporting purposes (see Table 9–5), the depreciation deductions on the tax return normally exceed those on the income statement in the early years of the asset's life. Taxable income is lower than accounting income in the early years, but there is an offsetting effect in later years. Similar results occur if pension expenditures or other costs are deductible for tax purposes in the year incurred but are spread over some future period for financial accounting purposes.

Timing differences which cause income before tax initially to be less than taxable income do not occur as frequently as the opposite case. However, if a corporation receives prepayments for rent or royalties or advances for goods and services to be rendered over future periods, under certain circumstances such cash receipts are taxable before the services are rendered or the goods delivered—2*(a)*. However, in the accounting statements, some of these receipts are normally treated as liabilities for customer advances and recognized as revenue in future periods as the earning process occurs.

In 2*(b)* the Internal Revenue Service does not allow a *current* tax deduction for certain types of expenses recognized in the current period. Contributions that exceed a certain percentage of income can only be deducted on future years' income tax returns. Similarly, many expenses which create estimated liability accounts or contra asset reserves—for example, *estimated* provisions for product warranties, collection costs, sales returns and discounts, and some deferred compensation amounts—must be reported in the tax return only on a "cash" or "incurred" basis. (Doubtful accounts and depreciation are specific exemptions to this provision.) However, under the matching concept it is proper to reflect these expenses on the books during the period when the related revenue is recognized.

**INTERPERIOD TAX ALLOCATION**

How should a firm account for the income tax charge when, because of timing differences, revenues or expenses are reported on the income statement and on the tax return in different periods? The accounting profession wrestled with this question for more than a decade, finally resolving it in favor of what is called *interperiod tax allocation*. Before investigating the procedures used to implement this concept, let us attempt an intuitive answer consistent with our conceptual framework.

Ignoring permanent differences, we know that in total the same revenues and expenses eventually are reported for both tax and financial accounting purposes. Timing differences merely result in period-to-period variations in reporting these common items. Therefore, we can say that the income taxes paid to the government are caused by the revenues and expenses reported at *some* time for financial accounting purposes. Because of this cause-and-effect relationship, it is a simple extension of our matching and periodicity concepts to say that we ought to record as tax expense this period the tax that sometime has to be paid because of this period's revenues and expenses. Tax expense should be accrued and matched against the income that gives rise to the tax, regardless of when it has to be paid.

It is precisely this logical extension of the matching concept that interperiod tax allocation implements. The tax effects of revenues and expenses are reported in (allocated to) the same periods in which the items are recognized for book purposes. After adjustments have been made for permanent differences, the period's tax expense is recorded in an amount equal to the tax rate applied to the difference between the period's revenues and expenses. To the extent that timing differences cause *taxable* income to be lower in a particular period, this expense exceeds the amount legally owed. The difference represents an increase in a future obligation because eventually the causative timing difference cancels itself through correspondingly increased tax payments. Conversely, timing differences may make this period's legal liability more than the tax expense shown in the statements. In effect, we are paying in this period tax liabilities arising out of prior or future periods' activities. Accordingly, the excess represents a reduction in the deferred taxes established in prior years or a prepayment applicable to operations in future years.

**Accounting for a Timing Difference: A Numerical Example**

Let us take an example in which taxable income initially is lower than accounting income because a firm elects to follow straight-line depreciation for income statement purposes while being required to use ACRS for tax purposes. Assume that a company purchases for $100,000 seven delivery vans with a useful life of five years. If no allowance is made for residual value, depreciation expense will be $20,000 ($100,000/5) each year on the income statement. For tax purposes, the delivery van is considered to be eligible three-year property, so the applicable depreciation recovery percentages are 25, 38, and 37 percent of cost, respectively, for Years 1, 2, and 3, per IRS published schedules.

To focus attention on the relevant tax aspects, we shall assume that the tax return and the income statement are the same in all other respects. The revenues of $200,000 and other expenses of $100,000 remain the same for each year. The delivery vans are the firm's only depreciable assets. Assume that a 50 percent tax rate is applicable.

Table 13–1 shows the company's income statement and tax return for the five years during which the delivery vans are used, in accordance with interperiod income tax allocation. Notice that the amount owed to the government in any particular year is *not* automatically considered to be the income tax expense for that period.

**TABLE 13–1  Income Statement and Tax Return Calculations ($000)**

| | Income Statement | | | | | |
|---|---|---|---|---|---|---|
| | Year 1 | Year 2 | Year 3 | Year 4 | Year 5 | Total |
| Sales ..................... | $200 | $200 | $200 | $200 | $200 | $1,000 |
| Other expenses .............. | 100 | 100 | 100 | 100 | 100 | 500 |
| Earnings before depreciation and taxes ................. | 100 | 100 | 100 | 100 | 100 | 500 |
| Depreciation expense: Books—straight-line, 5 years ................. | 20 | 20 | 20 | 20 | 20 | 100 |
| Net income before taxes ....... | 80 | 80 | 80 | 80 | 80 | 400 |
| Income tax expense (50%) ..... | 40 | 40 | 40 | 40 | 40 | 200 |

| | Tax Return | | | | | |
|---|---|---|---|---|---|---|
| | Year 1 | Year 2 | Year 3 | Year 4 | Year 5 | Total |
| Sales ..................... | $200 | $200 | $200 | $200 | $200 | $1,000 |
| Other expenses .............. | 100 | 100 | 100 | 100 | 100 | 500 |
| Earnings before depreciation and taxes ................. | 100 | 100 | 100 | 100 | 100 | 500 |
| Depreciation expense: Tax—ACRS, 3 years ........ | 25 | 38 | 37 | — | — | 100 |
| Taxable income .............. | 75 | 62 | 63 | 100 | 100 | 400 |
| Taxes currently owed (50%) .... | 37.5 | 31 | 31.5 | 50 | 50 | 200 |

The entries to allocate income taxes would be:

| Year 1 | Income Tax Expense | 40,000 | |
| | Current Income Taxes Payable | | 37,500 |
| | Deferred Income Taxes | | 2,500 |

| Year 2 | Income Tax Expense | 40,000 | |
| | Current Income Taxes Payable | | 31,000 |
| | Deferred Income Taxes | | 9,000 |

| Year 3 | Income Tax Expense | 40,000 | |
| | Current Income Taxes Payable | | 31,500 |
| | Deferred Income Taxes | | 8,500 |

| Year 4 | Income Tax Expense | 40,000 | |
| | Deferred Income Taxes | 10,000 | |
| | Current Income Taxes Payable | | 50,000 |

| Year 5 | Income Tax Expense | 40,000 | |
| | Deferred Income Taxes | 10,000 | |
| | Current Income Taxes Payable | | 50,000 |

The current tax liability is determined from the tax return, but the income tax expense is based on the information shown on the income statement. Each year the income statement shows $40,000 net income after tax. This seems reasonable, because accounting income before tax is a constant $80,000 each year, and the tax rate remains 50 percent. Table 13-2 illustrates how net income after tax would vary each year *if* interperiod tax allocation were not followed. The figures shown there create the false impression that the firm has performed far worse in Years 4–5

**TABLE 13-2   Net Income Amounts ($000) and Effective Tax Rates**

| | With Interperiod Tax Allocation | | | | | |
| | Year 1 | Year 2 | Year 3 | Year 4 | Year 5 | Total |
|---|---|---|---|---|---|---|
| Net income before taxes (Table 13-1) | $80 | $80 | $80 | $80 | $80 | $400 |
| Income tax expense | 40 | 40 | 40 | 40 | 40 | 200 |
| Net income after tax | $40 | $40 | $40 | $40 | $40 | $200 |
| | | | | | | |
| Effective tax rate (Tax expense/Net income before tax) | 50% | 50% | 50% | 50% | 50% | 50% |

| | Without Interperiod Tax Allocation | | | | | |
| | Year 1 | Year 2 | Year 3 | Year 4 | Year 5 | Total |
|---|---|---|---|---|---|---|
| Net income before taxes (Table 13-1) | $80.0 | $80.0 | $80.0 | $80.0 | $80.0 | $400.0 |
| Income tax expense | 37.5 | 31.0 | 31.5 | 50.0 | 50.0 | 200.0 |
| Net income after tax | $42.5 | $49.0 | $48.5 | $30.0 | $30.0 | $200.0 |
| | | | | | | |
| Effective tax rate (Tax expense/Net income before tax) | 46.9% | 38.8% | 39.4% | 62.5% | 62.5% | 50% |

than in Years 1–3 because of an apparent increasing tax burden in those later years.

Interperiod tax allocation views the income tax as a charge caused by the earning of accounting income. Therefore, income taxes should be recognized on the income statement as their causal factor, namely, the earned income, is recorded in the accounting records. Tax regulations determine when the tax liability has to be paid. Because timing differences tend to be temporary and the business entity is assumed to be a going concern, the real question is not *when* the tax is paid but with what items of income it should be reported. A tax reduction in the current period caused by timing differences gives rise to an estimated liability—a future outlay of cash occasioned by events recognized in the current period. In subsequent periods the timing difference reverses (Years 4 and 5 above). Then taxes currently payable exceed the income tax expense accrued and include tax amounts provided for in prior years.

## Classification of Deferred Taxes on Balance Sheet

The preceding example focused exclusively on one specific timing difference which happened to give rise initially to a credit balance in the Deferred Income Taxes account. As noted earlier, other timing differences occur in which the deferred account is established initially with a debit balance. One common example is when a firm accrues an expense on its books for estimated warranty costs even though this item is not deductible for tax purposes until future years.

Of course an individual firm may have several timing differences concurrently. In these cases any deferred tax effects are classified (1) as current or noncurrent and (2) as deferred credits or deferred charges.

The FASB's position on balance sheet classification of deferred tax accounts is as follows:

> A deferred charge or credit is related to an asset or liability if reduction of the asset or liability causes the timing difference to reverse. A deferred charge or credit that is related to an asset or liability shall be classified as current or noncurrent based on the classification of the related asset or liability. A deferred charge or credit that is not related to an asset or liability . . . shall be classified based on the expected reversal date of the specific timing difference.[2]

Within each of these classifications—current and noncurrent—the deferred tax credits and deferred tax debits are combined into single balance sheet accounts having either a *net* debit or credit balance. In the former case, Deferred Income Taxes appears among current and/or noncurrent assets. In the latter and more common situation, it is presented with the current and/or noncurrent liabilities.

---

[2] FASB, *Statement of Financial Accounting Standards No. 37,* "Balance Sheet Classification of Deferred Income Taxes" (Stamford, Conn., July 1980), par. 4.

**Deferred Approach and Liability Approach**

Our initial discussion of interperiod allocation of income taxes treats the problem as an extension of accrual accounting. The resulting debit or credit balances can be analyzed within the conventional asset-liability framework. The Deferred Income Taxes account is classified on the balance sheet as current and/or noncurrent and is often reported among the assets and liabilities.

However, officially the debit and credit balances resulting from tax allocation are treated for position statement purposes as deferred charges and deferred credits rather than as prepaid tax assets and deferred tax liabilities. Such labels reflect the viewpoint of the Accounting Principles Board, which mandated use of the *deferred method* instead of the *liability method*. As noted by the APB:

> Interperiod tax allocation under the *deferred method* is a procedure whereby the tax effects of current timing differences are deferred currently and allocated to income tax expense of future periods when the timing differences reverse. The deferred method emphasizes the tax effects of timing differences on income of the period in which the differences originate . . . The tax effects of transactions which reduce taxes currently payable are treated as deferred credits; the tax effects of transactions which increase taxes currently payable are treated as deferred charges.[3]

This emphasis of APB Opinion No. 11 is almost exclusively on the income statement. Revenues and expenses seem to be viewed in two parts—items themselves and their tax effects. The two parts must be reflected in income during the same accounting period for proper income measurement. Procedures to do this were illustrated in the depreciation timing difference example discussed earlier. If the liability method were used, we would add the word *payable* to the title of the deferred account. Also, if tax rates changed in the future, the "liability" balance would have to be adjusted.

Unfortunately, balance sheet logic is a secondary consideration under the deferred method. The balance sheet should be a statement of assets and equities. Therefore, real accounts having credit balances are classified as either liabilities, part of stockholders' equity, or contra assets. The Accounting Principles Board made it emphatically clear that Deferred Income Taxes (credit balance) is neither part of stockholders' equity nor an offset to some asset. However, it also states, "Deferred charges and deferred credits relating to timing differences represent the cumulative recognition given to their tax effects and as such do not represent receivables or payables in the usual sense."[4] The failure of the APB explicity to come

---

[3] AICPA, *APB Opinion No. 11,* "Accounting for Income Taxes" (New York, December 1967), par. 19.

[4] Ibid., par. 57.

**Evaluation of Interperiod Tax Allocation**

to grips with the nature of this item detracts from the logic of tax allocation.[5]

Accounting for the impact of timing differences has been one of the most controversial issues in accounting since World War II. The *APB Opinion* passed just by the minimum two-thirds vote required.[6] Consequently, it seems appropriate to evaluate the pros and cons of interperiod tax allocation. The case *for* tax allocation has already been made. To summarize, proponents of tax allocation view income tax as an expense that should be allocated to accounting periods in relation to the pretax accounting income included on the income statement for each period. The corporation, by earning income, has occasioned a tax charge that must be paid to the government. This charge should be part of the recording of the period causing it, not of the period in which it is paid.

**Arguments against Tax Allocation.** Opponents of interperiod income tax allocation concentrate on three lines of argument: (1) deferred debit and credit balance are not assets and liabilities, (2) tax allocation may result in a permanent or an ever-increasing deferred tax amount which in the aggregate never has to be paid, and (3) tax charges are unlike other expenses and may be viewed as distributions of income to the government. Let us consider each of these points more fully.

Many accountants have difficulty fitting the deferred tax accounts into the conventional asset-liability framework. Indeed, as seen, *APB Opinion No. 11* had this problem. The government recognizes no legal or contractual claim against the corporation for the deferred liability, and the corporation cannot demand payment from the government for any prepaid asset. Payment of taxes equal to the amount shown on the income tax return effectively discharges all legal claims of the tax authorities. Moreover, even if the lack of legal recognition is ignored, the uncertainties surrounding future tax payments rule out an objective valuation of the "liability." Recognition of the Deferred Income Taxes account as a liability depends, opponents of tax allocation claim, on too tenuous assumptions about future income, stability of tax rates, and the similarity of tax regulations in future periods.

---

[5] A third alternative, called the net-of-tax approach, also achieved considerable attention during this period. However, it has been specifically deemed unacceptable by the Accounting Principles Board. Its name comes from the offsetting of the debit and credit balances resulting from timing differences against the liability or asset accounts involved in the transactions causing the timing differences. The particular asset and liability accounts are reported net of tax on the premise that tax deductibility (or lack of same) influences the valuation of these items.

[6] It appears that the APB's *Opinion No. 11* in favor of the deferred approach was a political compromise. Adherence to either the liability approach or the net-of-tax approach as *the* method could not have captured sufficient support to overcome the votes of those opposing tax allocation. However, some of those supporting the liability and the net-of-tax approaches could unite to accept the middle ground.

This first argument rests on a legalistic concept of liability and measurement. Such a concept is not necessarily employed with other items commonly treated as liabilities. Witness, for example, estimated liabilities for warranties, pensions, and certain leases that are capitalized. These also do not lend themselves to precise measurement, nor are they necessarily legal claims on the firm. However, like deferred taxes, they do fit the broader concept of liability suggested in Chapter 2—a future outlay of cash which can be reasonably estimated, occasioned by some event that has already occurred in a past or present period. The assumptions about the future made for the purpose of measuring the liability do not seem unrealistic in the context of similar assumptions necessary for estimating other liabilities, depreciating plant assets, or adjusting for uncollectibles.

The second objection to tax allocation focuses on whether there will be any future tax payment. Detractors claim that tax deferral very often actually amounts to a permanent tax reduction. For instance, many firms required to use ACRS for tax purposes continually make new investments, replacing old assets or expanding the company. For static or growing firms the higher tax depreciation charges (higher than book depreciation) on new assets will offset or more than offset the lower tax depreciation charges on older assets. Therefore, as long as tax provisions regarding depreciation remain the same and the firm maintains a regular policy of investing in new assets, the deferred tax account *in total* will never be reduced and in fact may grow larger each year. A similar situation arises when the installment method is used for recognizing sales for tax purposes. The current deferred taxes account never declines as long as the *cumulative* timing differences do not decrease, that is, as long as new installment receivables more than replace those collected.

This objection results from the provision of *Opinion No. 11* which dismisses *partial* tax allocation and instead requires *comprehensive* allocation. As implied by its name, tax allocation would occur less frequently under the partial approach. Specifically, tax allocation would apply only to specific nonrecurring timing differences that reasonably can be expected to reverse within a relatively short time. Examples might include a firm which makes only infrequent, isolated installment sales and a smaller company that acquires all of its plant assets in bunches every 10 years. Partial allocation would not reflect as deferred charges or credits those timing differences which are continually perpetuated in the aggregate.

Critics of comprehensive allocation view the deferred tax account as a single amount. In contrast, the account Deferred Income Taxes acts as a control account for the deferral pattern on each *individual* timing difference the firm has. Therefore, although the total balance may remain constant or even grow, tax liabilities caused by specific timing differences are being paid while other tax liabilities caused by new timing differences are being created. This process is somewhat analogous to the continual turnover in other liabilities, such as accounts payable. In a growing firm, total accounts payable may increase, but individual accounts do mature and are replaced by new accounts. The fact that different creditors are involved should not change the principle involved. An expense should not be ignored simply because the related liability may be replaced by another liability in the future, even if this process should go on for an indeterminable time.

The third objection to interperiod tax allocation concerns the fundamental nature of income taxes. The argument states that income tax is *not* an expense similar to other expenses. Income taxes do not make a direct contribution to the generation of revenue. Instead, they are more like a periodic, involuntary distribution of income in recognition of society's contributions to the firm. Furthermore, the continually changing concepts which form the basis of the legal claim are under the control of the government imposing the tax, not the firm itself. These concepts increasingly seem to rest on factors alien to concepts underlying financial accounting income. As a consequence, it is argued, the period tax charge is best measured by the actual levy. If the government levies a reduced amount in a particular year with no explicit future repayment, the accounting statements should reflect a reduced tax charge.

Because factors such as ACRS depreciation have resulted in an increasing divergence between taxable and accounting income, many persons believe that the second and third arguments against interperiod tax allocation have become even more difficult to rebut. For example in 1983, the influential director of the AICPA's accounting standards division urged that "deferred taxes be cast out of the house of GAAP."[7]

Close scrutiny of the tax code reveals that business income and taxable income, except for the permanent differences, basically *are* the same in the *long run*. Nevertheless, a movement by the FASB in the direction of partial allocation certainly might occur in the 1980s because of the renewed interest in and criticism of *Opinion No. 11* and because of the accounting profession's heightened concern for financial statements which are representationally faithful and indicative of future cash flows.

**CARRY-BACK AND CARRY-FORWARD OF OPERATING LOSSES**

Income taxes normally are assessed on an annual basis. A potential inequity can result between a corporation earning taxable income each year and one having a larger taxable income in some years but losses in other years. For the latter firm, taxes could be higher under a strict annual accounting, even if the average yearly earnings of the two firms were the same.

To help alleviate such problems, Congress included in the tax law a deduction for a net operating loss. This loss deduction allows a corpora-

---

[7] Paul Rosenfield and William C. Dent, "No More Deferred Taxes," *Journal of Accountancy,* February 1983, p. 55.

tion to offset the operating loss (unused tax deductions) incurred in one particular year against the taxable income of other years. Specifically, the operating losses can be carried back for three years and offset against the income of those years.[8] If an unused loss still remains, it then can be carried forward for as many as 15 additional years.[9]

This provision creates a slightly different tax allocation problem from that caused by timing differences. The loss deduction creates a claim for a tax refund in the case of the carry-back or a potential tax savings in the future in the case of the carry-forward. The financial accounting question is whether the tax effects of the operating loss should be recognized in the period of loss or in the periods in which income tax is actually reduced. Specifically, with a loss carry-back, should the tax refund be treated as a reduction in the current period's loss (in effect, a negative income tax charge) or as a correction of prior years' taxes? Similarly, should the tax savings associated with a loss carry-forward be recognized immediately as a reduction in the loss or only in future periods when taxes are actually reduced?

**Carry-Back Case**

The guideline developed in the preceding discussion of timing differences is that income tax effects should be reported in the same accounting period as the factors which cause them. Application of this concept to the questions posed above leads to the conclusion that the *tax benefits from carry-forwards and carry-backs should be recognized in the year the causative net loss is incurred.* For operating loss carry-backs, this conclusion has almost universal support. The tax loss causes an allowable, measurable claim for refund. The creation of this asset should be considered in the measurement of the net results of the current period.

For example, assume that a corporation has averaged $40,000 of taxable income in each of the three preceding years. In the current year a net loss of $90,000 is incurred. This loss can be carried back to offset the taxable income of these prior years. If taxes for these years have been paid at a rate of 50 percent, the corporation would enter a claim for a tax refund and make the following entry:

Income Tax Refund Receivable . . . . . . . . . . . . . . . . . . . . . . . . 45,000
    Refund of Income Taxes Due to Loss Carry-Back . . . . .           45,000

The credit account would be closed to Income Summary for the year and appear on an income statement for the current year as follows:

---

[8] A corporation with taxable income during the preceding three years can, if it wishes, elect to carry all of the loss forward and none back. Because such elections are rare, it will be assumed for purposes of this discussion that the carry-back option will be exercised first.

[9] Actually, the accounting loss is subject to various adjustments before it becomes a carry-back or carry-forward operating loss. For most corporations, however, these adjustments are minor and specialized. Consequently, they are ignored in subsequent discussions.

```
Loss before income tax effect ....................... $90,000
    Less: Refund of prior years' income taxes due
        to loss carry-back ............................   45,000
Net loss after income tax effect ..................... $45,000
```

**Carry-Forward Case**

Assume that the loss in the current year is $190,000 instead of $90,000. In this case, $120,000 of the loss can be carried back, completely offsetting the income of the three preceding years and giving rise to a tax refund of $60,000 (50 percent × $120,000). The other $70,000 of the loss can be carried forward as an unused tax deduction to offset taxable income for the next 15 years. Some accountants feel it is proper to recognize this potential tax savings of $35,000 as an asset also and reduce the current year's loss accordingly. The entry they recommend is:

```
Income Tax Refund Receivable ......................... 60,000
Future Tax Benefits—Loss Carry-Forward ............... 35,000
    Reduction in Loss Due to Carry-Overs ..............        95,000
```

The Future Tax Benefits account would then serve to reduce Taxes Payable in future years (but not tax expense). Because the loss in the current year causes the reduction in taxes, the tax savings should be reported now rather than in future years. The net loss in the current year would be $95,000—the $190,000 loss before taxes reduced by the $95,000 positive income tax effect.

This treatment follows the concept illustrated in connection with the carry-back; the tax effect follows the causal items. However, another important factor must be considered—the "realizability" of the carry-forward (the probability that the carry-forward will actually reduce future tax payments). Like any asset, the Future Tax Benefits from Loss Carry-Forward must have future value. Its future value, however, is directly related to the existence of taxable income during the next 15 years sufficient to make use of the carry-forward. The fact that the company has already experienced a loss may cast doubt on its ability to generate income in future years.

The uncertainty concerning the value of a loss carry-forward caused the Accounting Principles Board to prefer a different treatment in most circumstances. The loss in the current year should be reported without consideration of any potential tax savings. If and when taxable income does arise in the future, the tax benefits of the carry-forward should be reported as *extraordinary items*[10] to the extent actually "realized." The tax benefits of loss carry-forwards should be recognized immediately only "in unusual circumstances when realization is *assured beyond any reasonable doubt* at the time the loss carry-forwards arise.[11] Assurance beyond a reasonable doubt exists, in the opinion of the APB, only if:

---

[10] See Chapter 16 for a complete discussion of extraordinary items.

[11] *APB Opinion No. 11*, par. 45.

(a)  the loss results from an identifiable, isolated and nonrecurring cause and the company either has been continuously profitable over a long period or has suffered occasional losses which were more than offset by taxable income in subsequent years, and

(b)  future taxable income is virtually certain to be large enough to offset the loss carryforward and will occur soon enough to provide realization during the carryforward period.[12]

Because firms usually cannot recognize carry-forward tax benefits in the current (loss) year, the journal entry for the above situation would be limited to the following:

```
Income Tax Refund Receivable ........................  60,000
     Refund of Income Taxes Due to
       Loss Carry-Back ...............................          60,000
```

The $70,000 of the $190,000 current year's loss that the firm was unable to carry back will not formally be recognized now but instead will only be reflected if and when the company earns its first $70,000 of net income during the coming 15-year carry-forward period. If $100,000 is earned in the year following the loss and the tax rate remains at 50 percent, the following entry would be made:

```
Income Tax Expense ................................  50,000
     Extraordinary Gain—Tax Loss Carry-Forward .........          35,000
     Current Income Taxes Payable ....................          15,000
```

The soundness of the requirement for "assurance beyond any reasonable doubt" was considered extensively in the financial press during 1982–83 as a result of a controversy which developed between Aetna Life & Casualty Company and the Securities and Exchange Commission. The controversy began after a reporter for *Fortune* discovered, following a careful reading of Aetna's footnotes, that 62 percent of the operating earnings reported by the firm during the first half of 1982 resulted from the inclusion in income of the anticipated benefit of $138 million of tax loss carry-forwards.[13]

Aetna defended its interpretation of *Opinion No. 11,* noting that "the certainty of using the loss carry-forward over a 15-year time span is absolute."[14] The SEC disagreed with Aetna and ordered the firm to stop anticipating tax carry-forward benefits. The Commission felt that Aetna could not be *virtually certain* that future taxable income within the next 15 years would be sufficiently large to absorb the losses.

The SEC's decision may well have been sound. Perhaps Aetna's failure to adequately highlight its accounting practice may have had as great an influence on the Commission's decision as did the issue of whether the insurer's reasoning had merit. Many feel that Aetna's viewpoint rests on

---

[12] Ibid., par, 47.

[13] Carol J. Loomis, "Behind the Profits Glow at Aetna," *Fortune,* November 15, 1982, pp. 54–58.

[14] Ibid., p. 57.

more solid ground with today's 15-year carry-forward period than it might have had in the past when those benefits expired after five or seven years.

It is also true that other assets are often recorded on the books even when their value might not be "assured beyond a reasonable doubt"; these assets are written down only when evidence arises negating their future value. A similar perspective could be taken for loss carry-forwards, with such tax benefits recorded in the loss period *unless* specific doubts exist concerning their future realizability.

## ACCOUNTING FOR THE INVESTMENT CREDIT

Few issues have generated more discussion, argument, and dissension among accountants than the *investment credit*. It represents a direct credit against income taxes and is designed to encourage companies to invest in certain types of assets. Taxpayers are allowed to reduce their tax payments by an amount equal to either 6 or 10 percent of the cost of their "qualified investment."[15] The credit is 6 percent for eligible three-year ACRS property and 10 percent for other eligible property but is limited to $25,000 plus 90 percent of the tax liability over $25,000. However, a carry-back for three years and a carry-forward for 15 years apply to any currently unused investment tax credit. Tax laws also provide for a "recapture" of a portion of the credit if property is disposed of earlier than its estimated ACRS life.

Two major accounting treatments for the investment credit have been argued and practiced. One, called the *flow-through method*, views the investment credit as a selective reduction in taxes of the year in which the credit arises. The alternative view, labeled the *deferral method*, views the credit as a factor which should increase the net income of each year which the asset is used by a pro rata amount. The lines of disagreement are sharply defined and have been acrimoniously defended.

*APB Opinion No. 4* remains the latest expression of GAAP governing the investment credit, and it allows both the flow-through and deferral methods.[16] However, the APB's viewpoint on this issue turned out not to be the controlling factor influencing company accounting practices. In the Revenue Act of 1971, reinstating the investment credit, Congress stipulated that no taxpayer can be required to use any particular method of accounting for the credit in reports subject to the jurisdiction of any

---

[15] "Qualified investment" is specifically defined in the various revenue acts and has been modified slightly over the years as Congress has wished to encourage particular types of investments. Presently, personal and real (other than buildings) property qualifies as long as it is depreciable and has an ACRS recovery period or a useful life of at least three years. A limitation is placed on the amount of used equipment that can be included in qualified investment.

[16] AICPA, *APB Opinion No. 4*, "Accounting for the 'Investment Credit' " (New York, March 1964).

federal agency. This provision effectively bars the Financial Accounting Standards Board from issuing a new standard that would affect very many firms. The inclusion of the provision resulted from intensive lobbying efforts on the part of those who feared that the APB was going to issue a new *Opinion* requiring deferral. Unfortunately, the end result was the setting of an *accounting* principle by political legislation rather than by competent professional judgment.

The treatment of the investment credit for financial accounting purposes depends directly on its fundamental nature. Its intended purpose might have been gleaned from the Revenue Acts or congressional deliberations prior to the enactment or reinstatement of the credit. Unfortunately, the issue there is equally confused. Proponents of both sides have been able to find phrases, statements, or testimony that would imply that Congress intended the credit to be a reduction in income taxes or to be a partial subsidy to reduce the net cost of acquiring the asset. A survey of 600 large corporations revealed that the great majority (531) were following the flow-through method rather than the deferral method in 1981.[17]

**Illustrative Data**

To illustrate the effects of the two treatments of the investment credit on the accounts, the following data are offered:

1. Income before taxes and depreciation ................. $ 86,000
2. Cost of machine acquired which qualifies
   for the investment credit ............................ 180,000
3. Annual straight-line depreciation over
   a 15-year life ...................................... 12,000
4. Amount of investment credit (10% × $180,000) ......... 18,000
5. Normal tax rate ..................................... 50%

Under these circumstances, the firm's normal taxes for the year would be $37,000 (50 percent of $74,000, the net income after depreciation). However, only $19,000 in taxes actually has to be paid this year, since the investment credit of $18,000 reduces the normal income taxes owed. The question is whether income tax *expense* should also be reduced to $19,000 or whether the $18,000 reduction should be spread over the asset's 15-year life.

**Flow-Through Method**

Under this alternative, income tax expense for the current year is reduced to $19,000. Accordingly, net income is higher by $18,000 than it otherwise would have been. The effect of the investment credit has "flowed through" to income via a lower tax expense in the year the asset is acquired. If conditions remain exactly the same in the future and no new assets are acquired, income tax expense will be the normal $37,000 for the

---

[17] AICPA, *Accounting Trends & Techniques,* (New York: 1982), p. 263.

remaining 14 years. Depreciation expense of $12,000 is unaffected throughout the 15-year period.

Accountants and business executives supporting the flow-through treatment base their argument on the theme underlying previous tax-expense discussions. Tax expense should be related to its cause, and this principle is as valid for negative items of tax expense as it is for positive ones. The cause of the *permanent* reduction in tax expense from the investment credit is the acquisition of certain types of depreciable assets. Therefore, the credit should be reflected in income in the same period as its cause. The investment credit is viewed as a periodic reward to the firm for taking a specified action that the government desires.

**Deferral Method**     Under this approach, the $18,000 investment credit is initially deferred and then taken into income over the machine's 15-year life through either a $1,200 annual reduction in depreciation expense or through a $1,200 annual reduction in income tax expense. Depreciation expense is lowered when the investment credit is viewed as a contra asset (reduction in the machine's cost). Income tax expense is lowered when the credit is reported on the balance sheet simply as a deferred credit. The contra asset format is the most logical, because it is more consistent with the underlying rationale for the deferral method. Nevertheless, the deferred credit format is the most common treatment.

Table 13–3 presents a comparison of the journal entries necessary under the flow-through and deferral approaches. The deferral-method journal entries assume the investment credit is viewed as a reduction in asset cost, although the deferred credit approach is discussed near the bottom of the table. Regardless of how the credit is viewed under the deferral method, the total net income reported by the firm over the 15-year period of the machine's life is identical under both the flow-through and the deferral procedures. Table 13–4 reveals that total net income was $573,000 under all approaches. For each of the 15 years, net income before taxes and depreciation was assumed to be $86,000 and the tax rate held constant at 50 percent.

**Evaluation of the Deferral Method.**     Three major points have been cited to support the choice to spread the investment credit over the useful life of the asset:

1.  Earnings arise from the *use* of facilities, not from their acquisition. A firm should not be allowed to increase income simply by purchasing assets, as would be the case under the flow-through method.
2.  The intent behind the credit was to promote increased investment by reducing the cost of the asset. Companies would not purchase the assets unless the credit were available.
3.  If an asset is disposed of before the end of its useful life, part of the

**TABLE 13–3  Comparison of Entries for Flow-Through and Deferral Methods**

| | Flow-Through | | Deferral* | |
|---|---|---|---|---|
| **Year 1:** | | | | |
| Purchase of machinery | Machinery ................... | 180,000 | Machinery ................... | 180,000 |
| | Cash .................. | 180,000 | Cash .................. | 180,000 |
| Income tax expense | Tax Expense ............... | 19,000 | Tax Expense ............... | 37,000 |
| | Taxes Payable ......... | 19,000 | Taxes Payable ......... | 19,000 |
| | | | Accumulated Investment Credit ...... | 18,000 |
| Depreciation expense | Depreciation Expense ......... | 12,000 | Depreciation Expense ......... | 10,800 |
| | | | Accumulated Investment Credit ...... | 1,200 |
| | Accumulated Depreciation ....... | 12,000 | Accumulated Depreciation ....... | 12,000 |
| **Years 2–15:** | | | | |
| Income tax expense ($74,000 of taxable income and 50% tax rate each year) | Tax Expense ............... | 37,000 | Tax Expense ............... | 37,000 |
| | Taxes Payable ......... | 37,000 | Taxes Payable ......... | 37,000 |
| Depreciation expense | Depreciation Expense ......... | 12,000 | Depreciation Expense ......... | 10,800 |
| | | | Accumulated Investment Credit ...... | 1,200 |
| | Accumulated Depreciation ....... | 12,000 | Accumulated Depreciation ....... | 12,000 |

* Entries for deferral method are made consistent with the viewpoint that the investment credit is a contra asset which increases income in all 15 years through an annual reduction of depreciation expense of $1,200. If the $18,000 investment credit had been viewed as a deferred credit under the deferral method, the Tax Expense would have been lowered by $1,200 to $35,800 and the Depreciation Expense would have been the full $12,000.

**TABLE 13-4** Comparison of Total Net Income under Flow-Through and Deferral Methods

| | Flow-Through | Deferral | |
| | | Contra Asset | Deferred Credit |
|---|---|---|---|
| Income before taxes and depreciation ($86,000 × 15) | $1,290,000 | $1,290,000 | $1,290,000 |
| Less: | | | |
| Taxes—Year 1 | $ 19,000 | $ 37,000 | $ 35,800 |
| Taxes—Years 2-15: | | | |
| ($37,000 × 14) | 518,000 | 518,000 | |
| ($35,800 × 14) | | | 501,200 |
| Depreciation—Year 1 | 12,000 | 10,800 | 12,000 |
| Depreciation—Years 2-15: | | | |
| ($12,000 × 14) | 168,000 | | 168,000 |
| ($10,800 × 14) | | 151,200 | |
| Total deductions | 717,000 | 717,000 | 717,000 |
| Total net income for Years 1-15 | $ 573,000 | $ 573,000 | $ 573,000 |

investment credit might be paid back (recaptured).[18] Therefore, its ultimate realization depends on the passage of time.

None of these arguments is overwhelming. The first implies that the investment credit is earned, in the sense of a revenue, by a firm's holding purchased assets a required period of time. Income as conventionally measured in accounting is a residual—the result of matching expenses against revenues for a time period. The real question is the timing of revenue and expense. Clearly, the investment credit is not revenue; it is an expense reduction under either alternative. Therefore, we are back to the original point of the proponents of the flow-through approach: What caused the reduction in expense? The acquisition of "qualified investments," not their use, triggers the granting of the credit.

The second point alludes to an original provision in the Revenue Act of 1962 that required the depreciation base of the asset to be reduced by the amount of the investment credit. Since repeal of that provision, legislative intent behind the credit is not clear-cut. Treatment of the credit as a reduction in the asset's cost implies that the purchaser gets a rebate from the government for a portion of the purchase price. However, it is the *tax liability,* not the liability arising from the purchase transaction, that is reduced. Many argue that Congress granted a *tax reduction as measured by the amount of assets purchased.* Moreover, the established concept of asset cost being a negotiated exchange price would be modified. Asset cost would be dependent on the tax status of the purchaser and not on the agreement bargained at arm's length between the buyer and seller.

---

[18] For example, the credit for five-year ACRS property disposed of after three years would fall from 10 to 6 percent; accordingly, 4 percent would be recaptured.

The third argument is specious. The estimate is certainly no more tentative and may be less so than those normally used in establishing depreciation policy. Few accountants would advocate recording no depreciation until the asset's life is known with certainty and then charging the entire cost as an expense in the year of disposition. In addition, the third argument, even if valid, supports reflection in income not over the life of the asset but only at the end of five years, when recapture provisions specified by law are no longer applicable.

## DISCUSSION OF THE ARMCO ANNUAL REPORT

Information pertaining to Armco's income taxes is found in its three major financial statements and in Notes 1 and 5 of its 1981 annual report. The firm's disclosures concern (1) its accounting treatment for the investment credit, (2) the specific timing differences which contributed to the buildup in the credit balance of its Deferred Income Taxes account, and (3) the factors responsible for producing an effective tax rate which was lower than the statutory rate.

### Investment Credit

Note 1 discloses that Armco accounts for investment and energy tax credits in the manner followed by the overwhelming majority of firms; it uses the flow-through method.[19] Accordingly, Armco's tax expense would normally be lower and its net income would be higher than they would have been if the firm had followed the deferral method. To the extent that Armco is able to purchase significant amounts of "qualified investment" on a regular basis, the flow-through approach could result in a higher net income in practically every year.

### Timing Differences Influencing Deferred Taxes

Armco's income statement reveals a total provision for income taxes (Income Tax Expense) of $188.1 million. The portion deferred and the portion currently payable to various governments are also disclosed. The firm apparently made the following summary journal entry for 1981 income taxes:

| | | |
|---|---|---|
| Income Tax Expense | 188.1 | |
| Federal Income Taxes Payable | | 68.2 |
| Foreign and State Income Taxes Payable | | 55.1 |
| Deferred Income Taxes | | 64.8 |

Deferred Income Taxes appears among the liabilities in Armco's balance sheet. During 1981, the account balance rose from $251.4 million to $322.4 million. The major factor contributing to the $71.0 million in-

---

[19] The business energy investment credit was 10, 11, or 15 percent, depending on the type of energy property. Such property qualified for both the business energy credit and the regular investment credit if it met the qualifications for both. Most energy investment credits were discontinued after 1982.

crease in the account was the $64.8 million credited in the above journal entry; the remaining increase of $6.2 million resulted from the acquisition of other businesses.

As noted earlier in this chapter, capital-intensive firms commonly show increases in the balance for Deferred Income Taxes year after year. This phenomenon occurs when the firm depreciates its plant assets more quickly for tax purposes than for book purposes. Armco reveals in Note 5 that $35.0 million of the $64.8 million increase in Deferred Income Taxes resulted from the excess of tax over book depreciation.

Investment tax credits were an equally significant factor for 1981, but not for 1980 or 1979. The reader may wonder why such credits are even considered to be a timing difference. Because Armco does follow the flow-through method, it would seem that they are reducing their Income Tax Expense in the *same period* that the Income Taxes Payable are lowered (the year of asset acquisition). An analysis of Armco's *1980* annual report reveals that the $35.8 million represents previously unused investment credits which were carried forward to 1981. In previous years, Armco reduced the balance of Deferred Income Taxes to reflect the fact that the unused credits had reduced Income Tax Expense on the books but could not reduce Income Taxes Payable until a later year. When 1981's tax liability was large enough to permit the benefit of the carry-forward, Armco increased Deferred Income Taxes to cancel its previous debit to that account. Therefore, only in this unusual set of circumstances did the investment credit come to appear as a timing difference for a company that employed the flow-through method.

Another timing difference stems from Armco's treatment of the cost of relining blast furnaces. As Note 1 reveals, the firm amortizes such cost over the linings' estimated lives using an activity method. Apparently such costs are written off more quickly for tax purposes, thereby creating an effect on the Deferred Income Taxes account similar to depreciation but of far less magnitude.

Armco's disclosure of the major types of timing differences as well as their individual and total effects on income tax expense represents useful information. Such disclosure is required by the accounting profession and by the SEC. Of course, any reversal of timing differences in the aggregate may exert a significant cash drain in future years. Consequently, the SEC requires that *if cash payments for income taxes* are expected to "substantially exceed" income tax expense because of a *net* reversal of timing differences within any of the next three years, that fact should also be disclosed. Armco apparently had no such net reversals to report for 1981.

## Reconciliation between Effective and Statutory Tax Rate

Another disclosure required by the accounting profession and the SEC is a reconciliation between the effective income tax rate incurred by the company and the statutory income tax rate. As noted earlier, Armco reported $188.1 million of Income Tax Expense for 1981; this amount represents 41.6 percent of the $452.3 million of before-tax income reported on the income statement. Because the corporate statutory income tax rate is 46.0 percent on all amounts over $100,000, the reconciliation presented in Note 5 lists those factors which permitted Armco to incur an effective tax rate that was 41.6 rather than 46.0 percent.[20]

State income taxes were $6.3 million for 1981 and, accordingly, represented 1.4 percent of the $452.3 before-tax income. If the 1.4 percent is added to the 46.0 federal statutory rate, then the difference remaining to be explained is actually 5.8 percent (47.4 − 41.6). We look to the *permanent* differences rather than the timing differences to account for this difference, because interperiod tax allocation was created to prevent timing differences from distorting the real tax rate experienced.

The impact on taxes of investment and energy tax credits becomes readily apparent; such credits had a significant effect on Armco's effective tax rate, lowering it by 4.4 percent. The rate was reduced by an additional 0.5 percent because Armco experienced a tax rate slightly below the U.S. rate on the foreign income included on its income statement. Percentage depletion allowances permit firms to expense more than 100 percent of the cost of certain assets and, accordingly, create an additional favorable permanent difference. In 1980, capital gains income also showed up in the reconciliation. Income tax regulations permit capital gains income to be taxed at lower rates than ordinary income. These capital gains could result from the sale of investments or the disposition of plant assets.

## SUMMARY

An old saying states that nothing in this world is certain except death and taxes. In light of the discussion in this chapter, we might extend the adage to include financial accounting problems caused by taxes. Income tax authorities, admittedly a separate audience for accounting reports, nevertheless provide a source of thorny problems in the preparation of financial statements for other external users.

Three of those problems form the focal points in this chapter. The concept used in approaching all of them is that income taxes are caused by certain transactions and events of the firm. The effect of these transactions and events on the income tax charge should be reported in the same period as the items themselves. Following this concept, we reach these conclusions:

1.  Income tax *expense* should be based on the amount of income subject to eventual taxation that is shown on the current income statement. Any difference between that amount and the amount legally owed should be reflected in the balance sheet as a liability or asset.

---

[20] Corporate statutory tax rates begin at 17 percent for the first $25,000 of taxable income and proceed through several additional brackets before reaching 46 percent.

2. The tax reductions (either refunds or future savings) from net operating loss carry-backs and carry-forwards should be recognized in the year a net loss is incurred. This conclusion does not apply if doubt exists that a carry-forward will actually result in future tax savings because of a lack of future taxable income.

3. The investment tax credit should be recognized as a reduction in income tax expense in the period when the asset is purchased (in line with the flow-through method).

Generally accepted accounting principles presently agree only partially with our conclusions. With respect to timing differences, the deferred approach is required rather than the liability approach. Thus, although the impacts on the income statement basically coincide under the two methods, deferred taxes appear as deferred credits or deferred charges on the balance sheet rather than as liabilities or assets. With tax loss carry-forwards, GAAP probably would apply a stricter realizability test before sanctioning the recording of the tax benefit in the year the loss is incurred. With the investment credit, firms are allowed to use either the flow-through or the deferral method, although the great majority uses flow-through.

The accounting profession can be expected to reconsider its requirement for comprehensive rather than partial tax allocation. Many persons believe that a move toward partial allocation would be consistent with the profession's increased attention to future cash flows and the reporting of liabilities that faithfully represent future cash flows.

## QUESTIONS AND PROBLEMS

**13-1.** In its 1981 annual report, Fairchild Industries includes required disclosures pertaining to the sources of timing differences and the factors causing the firm's effective tax rate to differ from the statutory rate. The following are among the items disclosed (amounts are omitted here):

1. Investment tax credits.
2. Depreciation.
3. Long-term contracts.
4. Capital gains.
5. Amortization expense.

*Required:*

a. Explain the difference between a timing difference and a permanent difference. Indicate whether each of the above five items would normally be a timing difference or a permanent difference.

b. How does a firm's disclosure of the factors causing its effective tax rate to differ from its statutory rate provide useful information to the financial statement reader? Which of the above five items, if any, probably aided in an explanation of such a difference for Fairchild Industries? Explain.

**13–2.** The following figures are taken from the financial accounting records and income tax return of the Gilman Company for the 1985–1987 period:

| Year | Earnings before Taxes on the Income Statement | Taxable Income on the Tax Return |
|------|-----------------------------------------------|----------------------------------|
| 1985 ......... | $360,000 | $300,000 |
| 1986 ......... | 285,000 | 305,000 |
| 1987 ......... | 330,000 | 375,000 |

Revenues and expenses are the same on the tax return as in the financial accounting records in each of the years, with the following exceptions:

1. In 1985 a $60,000 gain was recognized for financial reporting purposes. This gain will be recognized for tax purposes in the amount of $20,000 annually, beginning in *1986*.
2. In 1987 the company accrued a $25,000 expense on its books. For income tax purposes, this expense cannot be deducted until future years when the cash is actually disbursed.

*Required:*

a. Calculate the amount of income tax legally owed for each year, assuming a 40 percent tax rate.
b. Prepare journal entries to record income tax expense in each of the three years under interperiod tax allocation procedures.
c. What account(s) would appear on the balance sheet at the end of 1987? Give amounts and indicate how the item(s) would be classified.

**13–3.** At the beginning of 1984, Prince Corporation acquired for $450,000 some vehicles with an average economic life of five years and no estimated residual value. Income *before* depreciation and taxes was as follows from 1984 to 1988:

| | |
|------|---------|
| 1984 ......... | $300,000 |
| 1985 ......... | 300,000 |
| 1986 ......... | 250,000 |
| 1987 ......... | 250,000 |
| 1988 ......... | 200,000 |

The firm decided to depreciate the $450,000 for financial accounting purposes by the straight-line method. For tax purposes, the vehicles were considered as eligible 3-year property with the resultant depreciation pattern of 25, 38, and 37 percent of cost, respectively, for the assumed life. Assume that the tax rate remained at 40 percent throughout the 1984–1988 period.

*Required:*

a. Compute the annual taxable income and tax liability reported by the firm on its *tax return* for the five years.
b. Compute the book income for each year and make journal entries for tax expense using income tax allocation procedures.
c. Prepare a T-account for Deferred Income Taxes and post the entries in (b) to it for the five years.

    *d.* What would happen to the balance in the Deferred Income Taxes account if Prince Corporation were to spend on vehicles $450,000 per year indefinitely? Assume they begin in 1984 and all vehicles have a five-year life and no residual value.

    *e.* Repeat part *(d)*, only now assume that the company's annual expenditures on vehicles grow by $45,000 each year, after amounting to $450,000 for 1984.

    *f.* What implications, if any, do the results in parts *(d)* and *(e)* have for your interpretation of the nature of the Deferred Income Taxes account? Explain how a security analyst or a banker might be expected to view that account.

**13–4.** Bedford Corporation sells a line of equipment that carries a three-year warranty. The company establishes an Estimated Liability for Warranties (with a corresponding debit to Product Warranty Expense) equal to 12 percent of dollar sales. The percentage is based on past experience and generally has proved quite accurate. The costs of servicing actual warranty claims each year are then charged to this liability account. Sales, expenses, and actual warranty expenditures are given below for the years 1985 to 1987 (in thousands of dollars):

|  | 1985 | 1986 | 1987 |
| --- | --- | --- | --- |
| Sales ...................................... | $350 | $380 | $250 |
| Expenses other than warranty expense and income tax ................................ | 140 | 160 | 110 |
| Actual warranty expenditures ................. | 24 | 29 | 35 |

For tax purposes, warranty expense is not deductible until costs are actually incurred to meet claims. The company's tax rate is 46 percent.

*Required:*

    *a.* Set up a ledger (T-) account for Estimated Liability for Warranty and post entries to it for the three-year period. Determine the balance in the account at the end of each year.

    *b.* Prepare a schedule showing the amount of financial accounting income before taxes and income tax expense and the amount of taxable income and taxes legally owed for each of the three years.

    *c.* Set up a ledger (T-) account for Deferred Income Taxes and post entries to it for the three years. Determine the balance in the account at the end of each year. Where would you show this amount on the balance sheet? Explain.

    *d.* Explain any relationship that exists between the balance in the estimated liability account and the deferred taxes account.

    *e.* "It's a shame to bother with interperiod tax allocation for such an unnecessary timing difference. One can be too concerned with the pursuit of good matching." Explain what might have been meant by this statement and whether or not you agree with it.

**13–5.** Babcock Corporation is engaged in the building of condominiums and apartment houses. Most projects take from two to three years to complete. Consequently, revenue is recognized on a percentage-of-completion basis for external reporting. However, for income tax purposes the firm elects to use the completed-contract method. During its first three years, the company worked on four different contracts. Information related to them is given below:

| | *Contract Number* | | | |
|---|---|---|---|---|
| | *1* | *2* | *3* | *4* |
| Contract price .................... | $300,000 | $900,000 | $600,000 | $700,000 |
| Total cost ........................ | 150,000 | 500,000 | 450,000 | 500,000 |
| Year completed ................... | Year 2 | Year 2 | Year 3 | |
| Percentage of work completed during: | | | | |
| Year 1 ........................ | 80% | 50% | 20% | |
| Year 2 ........................ | 20% | 50% | 60% | 30% |
| Year 3 ........................ | | | 20% | 50% |

General administrative expenses were $35,000, $45,000, and $55,000 in Years 1, 2, and 3, respectively. Assume a tax rate of 40 percent.

*Required:*

a. Determine net income before taxes for each of the three years for financial accounting purposes.
b. Determine taxable income for each of the three years.
c. Prepare journal entries to record income tax expense each year under interperiod tax allocation.
d. What is the balance in the Deferred Income Taxes account at the end of Year 3? Prove directly that this balance is the tax effect of timing differences yet to be reversed.

**13–6.** Allis-Chalmers Corporation in its 1981 annual report showed two accounts related to deferred taxes on the balance sheet.

| | *December 31* | |
|---|---|---|
| | *1981* | *1980* |
| Current assets: | | |
| Prepaid income taxes ................ | $24,666,000 | $13,894,000 |
| Liabilities and shareholders' investment: | | |
| Deferred income taxes ................ | 42,568,000 | 61,875,000 |

Among the timing-difference items which served to increase (decrease) the deferred tax provision were the following:

| | *1981* | *1980* |
|---|---|---|
| Installment sales income .................. | $(1,010,000) | $8,156,000 |
| Long-term contract income .............. | (3,905,000) | 7,472,000 |
| Warranty .............................. | (2,926,000) | 856,000 |

*Required:*

a. "Allis-Chalmers has made its balance sheet unnecessarily complex by showing both prepaid and deferred income taxes. Combining them into a net credit-balance account would hardly prove to be a disservice to financial statement readers." Do you agree with this statement?
b. Which of the above timing-difference items, if any, would you expect to have given rise to the Deferred Income Taxes account? To the Prepaid Income Taxes account? Explain.
c. Which of the timing differences, if any, reversed themselves in 1981? What conditions might have led to such reversals? Explain.

**13–7.** Mineral Corporation began operations in 1983. Earnings for the first four years of operations are shown below:

$$
\begin{array}{ll}
1983 \ldots \ldots \ldots & \$25,000 \\
1984 \ldots \ldots \ldots & 18,000 \\
1985 \ldots \ldots \ldots & 10,000 \\
1986 \ldots \ldots \ldots & 3,000 \\
\end{array}
$$

The income tax rate has been 40 percent for each year, and the firm has no permanent or timing tax differences. The downturn in profits continued during 1987, with Mineral Corporation actually losing $57,000 during that year. At the end of 1987, the chief accountant for the firm made the following income tax journal entry:

| | | |
|---|---|---|
| Tax Refund Receivable ............................ | 22,800 | |
| Reduction in Loss Due to Loss Carry-Overs ....... | | 22,800 |

The accountant's assistant objected, arguing that the correct amount for the above entry was only $12,400.

*Required:*

a. How did the chief accountant come up with the $22,800 amount? What modifications, if any, would you make in the journal entry?
b. Is the assistant correct in stating that the correct amount for the journal entry should be only $12,400? Explain.
c. If the $10,400 in dispute is not reflected in the formal accounts, where, if at all, should the financial statement reader be alerted to it?
d. Assume that Mineral Corporation's fortunes experienced a dramatic turn-around during 1988, with the firm earning a profit of $30,000. Prepare the journal entry necessary to reflect income tax expense for that year under the procedure suggested by the chief accountant.
e. Repeat part (d) under the assistant's procedure.

**13–8.** The business section of a major newspaper included the following item in its issue of July 8, 1983:

> Aetna Life & Casualty Co. ended a dispute with the Securities and Exchange Commission by restating its 1982 earnings to eliminate $203 million in future tax credits. The change lowers the earnings of the largest investor-owned insurance company 38 percent to $319 million, or $3.50 a share.

As noted in the chapter, Aetna agreed reluctantly to discontinue its practice of including expected future tax benefits in current earnings. Nevertheless, Aetna had stated that it would only make the change beginning with the fourth quarter of 1982 and wouldn't restate earlier published 1982 results. As the above news item reveals, the SEC changed Aetna's mind on that matter.

*Required:*

a. What arguments could Aetna advance in support of its practice of including expected future tax benefits in current earnings?
b. What arguments would the SEC advance in support of its decision to prohibit Aetna's accounting procedure?
c. Some failing corporations occasionally are acquired almost solely because of the value of tax loss carry-forward benefits which are useless to the acquired

firm but of great value to the acquiring company. Does this phenomenon lend support to Aetna's position? To the SEC's position? Explain.

d.  Has the SEC's action served to improve the quality of Aetna's financial reporting? Explain.

**13–9.**  The Badger Corporation purchased machinery and equipment which qualify for the 10 percent investment credit on January 1, 1984, at a cost of $200,000. The new assets have an estimated useful life of eight years with no salvage value.

The company's income *before* depreciation and income taxes is $300,000 in 1984 and $325,000 in 1985. The corporate tax rate is assumed to be 46 percent. For financial reporting purposes, the straight-line depreciation method is used.

*Required:*

a.  Prepare the journal entries on December 31, 1984, and December 31, 1985, to record depreciation and income tax expense. Assume the investment credit is accounted for according to the flow-through method.

b.  Repeat part (a) under the assumption that Badger Corporation uses the deferral method and considers the credit to be a contra-asset account.

c.  Should the firm be commended for viewing the investment credit in part (b) as a contra asset rather than as a deferred credit? Explain.

**13–10.**  During 1981, Bell & Howell Co. and Marshall Field & Co. both switched from the deferral method to the flow-through method for accounting for the investment credit. On the other hand, Georgia-Pacific retained the deferral method. Excerpts from relevant portions of the three corporations' 1981 annual reports appear below.

**Bell & Howell Company.**  "In 1981, the Company changed its method of accounting for the investment tax credit. These tax credits are now included in earnings as a reduction of the provision for federal income taxes in the year the related assets are placed in service (flow-through method) rather than amortized over the approximate useful lives of the related assets (deferral method). This change was made to achieve greater comparability with the accounting practices of most other companies. The effect of this change increased earnings from operations by $498,000, or $.08 per share."

**Marshall Field & Company.**  "The Company adopted, as of February 1, 1981, the flow-through method of accounting for investment tax credits. . . . Flow-through is the prevalent method in the retail industry and provides an offset to the start-up expenses of new stores. As a result of this change, income . . . increased by $1,370,000, or 11 cents per share."

**Georgia-Pacific.**  "Investment tax credits realized on the purchase of depreciable assets are recorded on the deferral method as an addition to accumulated depreciation and are amortized to income as a reduction of depreciation expense over approximately seven years. At December 31, 1981, the amount deferred and, to be included in income in future years, was $144,000,000."

*Required:*

a.  Both firms which switched from deferral to flow-through showed an increase in earnings. Was this a coincidence, or would you normally expect this to happen? Explain.

*b.* Bell & Howell and Marshall Field both refer to the popularity of the flow-through method in at least partial defense of their switch in methods. Is that particular reason adequate justification for a switch in accounting methods? Explain.

*c.* Comment on Marshall Field's argument that flow-through "provides an offset to the start-up expenses of new stores."

*d.* *Assume* that groups of stockholders and employees accused Georgia-Pacific of dampening dividend and wage demands by the deliberate understatement of income by $144 million. How could the company respond to those allegations?

**13–11.** Three M.B.A. students recently visited a bar after one of their accounting classes. As you would expect, the discussion quickly centered on interperiod income tax allocation. The students disagreed vehemently concerning the adequacy of present procedures and the direction in which any possible reforms should proceed. If the bartender had not had previous training in sociology, a fullscale barroom brawl might have erupted. The diverse viewpoints of the three students are summarized as follows:

**Student 1.** "The proponents of interperiod income tax allocation have become totally obsessed with the pursuit of good matching. Good matching which must inevitably result in a distorted balance sheet is no bargain."

**Student 2.** "It may have become fashionable to cut down interperiod tax allocation, but the concept and the procedure have really served us well. Show me an opponent of such allocation and I'll show you someone who just might be willing to advocate the violent overthrow of the accrual concept."

**Student 3.** "Give me interperiod tax allocation or give me death. Perhaps we could explore a shift from comprehensive to partial allocation, but our number one priority must remain the inclusion on the income statement of an appropriate amount for income tax expense."

*Required:*

*a.* For each of the above statements, explain what the student probably had in mind when he or she expressed such a viewpoint.

*b.* Which of the three viewpoints seems the *most* justified to you? Explain.

*c.* Which of the three viewpoints seems the *least* justified to you? Explain.

*d.* If you were a member of the FASB when the matter of interperiod tax allocation appeared on the agenda, what advice would you offer to your colleagues on the board?

**13–12.** A number of newspaper articles concerning the deferred taxes of utilities appeared during 1983. Among the facts and opinions contained in the articles were the following:

1. The allegation by the consumer group Fair Share that two major utilities in Massachusetts collected tens of millions of dollars from consumers in 1981 for "phantom" federal taxes that were not paid to the government.

2. The results of a 1981 survey by the Environmental Action Foundation that the nation's 100 largest electric utility companies in that year billed ratepayers for $3.7 billion in income taxes that were not paid to the government.

3. A rebuttal from a utilities spokesperson which noted that "government offers all industries the opportunity to defer, not avoid, taxes in order to encourage

business expansion. The taxes get to be paid eventually . . . on a fixed schedule.

4. A report that the Governor of Wisconsin vetoed a proposal which would have prevented utilities from collecting in their rates state and federal taxes that are accrued but not paid in a given year.

*Required:*

a. Are you surprised that public interest groups and some legislators have begun to question the practice which permits utilities to collect for deferred taxes?

b. Do timing differences for an item such as depreciation ever reverse themselves? Can there be two equally responsible viewpoints concerning this issue? Explain.

c. Are deferred taxes "phantom" taxes, or do they "get to be paid eventually"? Explain.

**13–13.** The following excerpt is taken from the income tax disclosures contained in Deere & Company's 1981 annual report:

> During 1980 the company adopted *FASB Statement No. 37* relating to the balance sheet classification of current and noncurrent deferred income taxes. As a result of adopting this statement, the company reclassified $25.0 million of the beginning fiscal 1980 current deferred income tax balance to noncurrent deferred income taxes.

*Required:*

a. Briefly summarize the text discussion pertaining to the major requirements of *FASB Statement No. 37*.

b. How might Deere & Company have reached the conclusion that a particular $25.0 million portion of its current deferred income tax balance needed to be reclassified as noncurrent?

c. Has *FASB Statement No. 37* served to improve the quality and/or information content of published financial statements? Explain.

**13–14.** The Vermont Apex Corporation reported accounting (book) income before any income taxes of $4,832,000 for 1984.[21] Additional information follows:

1. The corporation's pretax accounting income includes $205,000 of tax-exempt interest from municipal bonds.

2. The corporation's pretax accounting income includes $160,000 of capital gains from ordinary disposals of plant assets. Such gains are subject to a preferential federal income tax rate of 30 percent, instead of 46 percent.

3. During 1984 the corporation purchased $1,800,000 of plant assets eligible for a 10 percent investment credit.

4. Pretax accounting income includes $468,000 earned in Puerto Rico where the corporation is exempt from all federal income taxes until 1990.

5. The corporation's state income tax for 1984 is $230,000. This amount is payable currently but is a deductible expense on the 1984 federal income tax return.

6. The corporation uses straight-line depreciation for accounting (book) pur-

---

[21] Used with permission of Professor Leonard Morrissey of The Amos Tuck School of Business Administration at Dartmouth College.

poses, while it uses ACRS for income tax purposes. In 1984 depreciation was $1,321,000 (accounting) and $1,968,000 (tax return).

7. The corporation guarantees its products for two years following sale to a customer. In 1984 the corporation credited the "Estimated Warranty Liability" account by $623,000, debiting "Warranty Liability Expense." The corporation during 1984 incurred expenditures of $402,000 to meet warranty claims.

8. The corporation's pretax accounting income includes income of $322,000 earned in a foreign country and subject to income tax in that country at 35 percent. (In general, while the regulations are exceedingly complex, a U.S. corporation must pay federal income tax on "overseas" income in the year earned, regardless of the disposition of that income. However, a tax credit against the gross federal income tax liability may be claimed for any foreign income tax payable.)

*Required:*

a. Determine the amount of income tax at the statutory federal income tax rate of 46 percent.

b. Determine the actual federal income tax due for 1984.

c. Determine the provision (expense) for income tax to appear on the income statement for 1984. (This provision should include both federal and nonfederal income taxes.) Given the result, calculate the firm's effective income tax rate for 1984.

d. Prepare a detailed reconciliation of the differences in both dollar and percentage amounts between the results in *(a)* and *(c)*.

e. Prepare a journal entry (or entries) to record *all* income taxes on the books for 1984.

# CHAPTER 14

# STOCKHOLDERS' EQUITY

The accounting emphasis in the recording of equities has been on separating them by source. Hence, liabilities (claims of outside interests) are distinguished from owners' equity (the source of assets from the owners). Because stockholders' equity is a major class of financial interests in a corporation, accountants subdivide it further so that each significant source is identified in a separate account. So far we have made a fundamental distinction between contributed or invested capital (capital stock) and retained earnings. A knowledge of the amount of assets contributed directly by the owners as opposed to the amount arising from the retention of earned assets in the business aids in the interpretation of the historical development and current position of the firm. It also clarifies the status of any asset distributions in the form of dividends, that is, whether they represent earnings or are simply a return of a portion of the originally invested capital.

**THE CORPORATION**

A corporation is a separate *legal* entity. It comes into being when its founders draw up *articles of incorporation* and the corporation receives a state charter. The charter, in conjunction with the applicable state corporation laws, endows the corporation with certain rights, powers, and obligations. One of the most significant of these legal attributes is that of *limited liability* of the stockholders. Creditors' claims are on the assets of the corporation and do not carry over to the assets of the individual stockholders. Unlike partners and single proprietors, the owners of a corporation (stockholders) are not personally liable for the firm's debts.

Stockholders' losses are limited to amounts they have invested in the corporation.

To offer a degree of protection to corporate creditors, most state laws governing corporations require that there be a minimum amount of originally invested capital per share. This *legal* (or *stated*) capital cannot be reduced by voluntary action of the board of directors. Legal capital serves as a buffer to protect the claims of the creditors. Stockholders' equity cannot be reduced below legal capital through the payment of dividends or repurchase of owners' shares by the corporation.[1]

At first glance, one might think that legal capital would automatically correspond to total contributed capital, the relatively permanent investment made by the owners in exchange for shares of stock. This is not the case. The value of a share of stock at date of issue is determined by market forces, not legal considerations, and usually differs from the stated or legal value. Stated capital is a legal concept, specifically and variously defined in each state. This legal concept and the various definitions of stated capital influence the recording procedures for stockholders' equity.

In addition to legal elements in its environment, accounting is also influenced by many financial intricacies, conventions, and policies. Different types of capital stock, varying security provisions and modifications, stock splits, and dividend declarations are more a matter of financial management than of accounting policy. Yet, in the accounting records these matters find their final expression. Consequently, the accounting for stockholders' equity reflects these factors as well.

## ISSUANCE OF STOCK

The legal expression of the owners' investment in a corporation is the share of stock. To the individual stockholders, shares of stock represent personal assets. They give their owners the right to share in earnings through dividends (if and when declared), the right to share in any residual assets in liquidation, the right to share indirectly in management through election of the board of directors, plus other rights specified under corporate law. Usually, these rights have a market value.

To the corporation, on the other hand, shares of stock are merely representations of an ownership interest. The state charter authorizes a corporation to issue a certain number of shares. *Authorized stock,* however, has no accounting significance. Only when assets actually flow into the firm as the result of a stock issue is a record made of the increase in stockholders' equity. In addition, an entry is made in the stockholder ledger, the subsidiary ledger to the capital stock account, for the specified number of shares represented by the stock certificates issued to each

---

[1] Of course, unprofitable operations could deplete the owners' equity in a business. Stated capital is intended to protect the creditor against voluntary withdrawals of capital by the owners, not against dissipation of assets through continued losses.

investor. Therefore, we are interested in *outstanding stock* (or *issued stock*). Of course, the amount of new stock issued can vary greatly from year to year, depending on corporations' needs for capital and investors' desires for such investments. For example, corporations issued $8.7 billion of new stock during the strong bull market which existed during the first quarter of 1983, up 378 percent from the first-quarter 1982 amount.[2]

**Preferred Stock**

Heretofore we have assumed that only one kind of ownership interest is present, that represented by capital stock. Actually, there are two major types of capital stock, *common* and *preferred*. The former corresponds to what we have been calling capital stock. It represents the residual ownership and control of the corporation. Preferred stock represents a special type of ownership interest with certain modifications of the basic rights inherent in common stock.[3]

The term *preferred* originates from two customary provisions of this type of stock. *Preferred stock usually has preference over common stock in the payment of dividends and usually has a prior claim on assets in the event of liquidation*. The latter provision need not concern us here, because we are recording under the going-concern concept. The dividend preference modifies the risk of the preferred stock. *If* dividends are declared, they must first be paid to the preferred stockholders up to the amount stated in the preferred stock contract. Usually the return is fixed, however. Once the preferred dividends are paid, any remaining dividends declared are applicable only to the common stock. Also, in most cases preferred dividends are *cumulative;* that is, before dividends can be paid on common stock, *all* preferred dividends, including any skipped in past years, must be paid.

Preferred stock is a hybrid security. Economically and financially, it is very similar to long-term debt except that dividends are not tax deductible. Preferred stock has less risk than common, as reflected in the prior but limited claim on earnings. It is often callable, like a bond issue. On the other hand, *legally* it resembles common stock. Its claim on earnings is not mandatory; only if dividends are declared does preferred stock have a prior claim. There is neither an accrued liability for the payment of preferred dividends, as is the case with interest, nor a specific maturity date on a preferred stock issue.[4] As a hybrid equity element, it logically could be reported in a separate category between liabilities and common stock equity on the balance sheet. Typically, however, legal convention prevails,

---

[2] "The Rebirth of Equities," *Business Week*, May 9, 1983, p. 121.

[3] The reader is referred to books on business finance for detailed descriptions of various provisions pertaining to preferred stock. Our discussion is limited to some of the basic and more usual differences between preferred and common stock, particularly those which have accounting implications.

[4] An exception exists for those preferred issues that feature a *mandatory* call provision. For all practical purposes, they are debt and should not be included in stockholders' equity.

and preferred is included along with the common in an overall category labeled "stockholders' equity."

## Par Value and No-Par Value Stock

In many cases an arbitrary amount is assigned to each share of stock. This amount, called *par value*, is printed on each stock certificate. Historically, the amount was usually $100. Par value has practically no accounting significance. Obviously, an arbitrary amount printed on a piece of paper does not determine the stock's issue price or its subsequent value. The latter is governed by investors' appraisal of the future earning potential of the business.

The reason for the heavy use of par value stock lies in its legal significance. *Par value defines the amount of stated or legal capital per share.* Creditors can presume that an amount equivalent to the par value of the shares issued is permanently invested by the stockholders. Indeed, in many states anyone buying stock directly from the corporation at less than par value can be held assessable for the difference at some later time if the amount were necessary to pay creditors' claims.[5] Issuing stock initially at a price below par value is illegal in practically all states because of the impairment of legal capital (defined as par value). Many corporations currently use low par value stock ($1, $5, $10), which practically always sells above par.

A share of *no-par* stock simply represents a certain proportionate share of ownership in the business. No-par stock has the advantage of avoiding any implication that par value represents the real worth of the stock. Also, legal capital and invested capital become one and the same. However, many states allowing no-par stock have passed laws permitting or requiring the board of directors to assign a *stated value* to the no-par shares. These laws are designed ostensibly to protect the creditors by insisting that there be some *minimum stated* capital. However, legal capital again becomes something distinct from invested capital. Stated value has the same slight significance as par value.

## Entries to Record Stock Issues

For accounting and financial purposes, the important consideration is the increase in resources arising from the issuance of capital stock. The real increase in stockholders' equity, the amount of contributed capital, is determined by the amount of assets actually invested, not by any par or stated value arbitrarily assigned to the shares. Generally, the issuance of

---

[5] Historically, to avoid issuing stock at less than par value, companies sometimes overvalued noncurrent assets received in exchange for shares of stock by recording the assets at the par value of the stock exchanged for them. Stock issued under these circumstances, when discovered (often with unfortunate consequences for creditors), was called "watered" stock, inasmuch as insufficient real asset value lay behind it. A gradual tightening of generally accepted accounting principles for asset valuation, as well as the introduction of no-par stock, eliminated this practice.

no-par shares involves little difficulty. Cash is debited and Capital Stock is credited for the total amount received, segregated, of course, by common or preferred. When par values or stated values are present, however, they are practically always recognized in the accounts.

The three entries below record the issuance of 2,000 shares of par value common stock, no-par value common stock, and par value preferred stock, respectively. In each instance, investors contribute cash to the corporation according to the value they attach to the ownership interest represented by the 2,000 shares. Assets and owners' equity increase by the amount of assets received. The increase in stockholders' equity is conventionally reflected in two accounts.

Entry 1:  Issuance of 2,000 shares of common stock, each share having a par value of $10, for $30 a share.

```
Cash ................................................. 60,000
      Common Stock—$10 Par  .........................          20,000
      Additional Paid-In Capital—Common  ..............          40,000
```

Entry 2:  Issuance of 2,000 shares of common stock without par value but with a stated value of $15 per share for $20 a share.

```
Cash ................................................. 40,000
      No-Par Common Stock—$15 Stated Value  ..........          30,000
      Additional Paid-In Capital—Common  ..............          10,000
```

Entry 3:  Issuance of 2,000 shares of preferred stock, each having a par value of $50, for $60 a share.

```
Cash ............................................. 120,000
      Preferred Stock—$50 Par  .....................          100,000
      Additional Paid-In Capital—Preferred  ...........           20,000
```

The additional paid-in capital accounts are *equity adjunct* accounts. They represent a part of the total contributed capital of the firm. They are not gains, for a corporation does not generate income by issuing its own shares of stock in a capital-raising transaction. Additional paid-in capital reflects the portion of invested capital over and above the arbitrary amount which has been segregated as legal capital. Other titles are frequently used in accounting practice for this account—Premium (particularly when preferred stock is sold above par) or Excess over Par. At one time Capital Surplus and Paid-In Surplus were also used. However, the connotation of the word *surplus* as indicating something of an unnecessary nature or supplementary funds that can be made available to creditors or stockholders is obviously inappropriate.

## Stock Split

The preceding entries illustrate the issuance of shares in exchange for an inflow of assets. The number of shares outstanding also is increased by a stock split. The corporation distributes additional shares to stockholders for which the latter invest nothing. Contributed capital in total does not change, nor do total assets. The entire stockholders' equity remains constant in dollar amount. However, the equity is now indicated by a larger number of shares, so each share represents a proportionately smaller interest.

The stock split is a financial mechanism used to increase the investor appeal of the stock by reducing its market price and to broaden ownership by having more shares outstanding. If the company has 300,000 shares of stock outstanding, a two-for-one stock split calls for distribution of an additional 300,000 shares. Each shareholder holds two shares for each share previously owned. If the market price of the stock is $70 per share before the split, theoretically it should fall to $35 per share after the split.[6] Because no change in resources or financial interests occurs, no substantive accounting entry is needed. However, if the capital stock has a par value, the stock split suggests a reduction in par value, inasmuch as total legal capital usually is maintained.

```
Common Stock—$20 Par  . . . . . . . . . . . . . . . . . . . . . . .   6,000,000
    Common Stock—$10 Par  . . . . . . . . . . . . . . . . . . . .                6,000,000
    To record issuance of 300,000 additional shares un-
    der a two-for-one stock split and the corresponding
    reduction in par value from $20 to $10 per share.
```

| DETERMINING THE AMOUNT OF CAPITAL RECEIVED | Usually the dollar increase in stockholders' equity is measured by the amount of assets received in exchange for the shares. If the asset received from the issuance of a single security is cash, no problem results. Whether one or more capital accounts are used to record owners' equity, the total net increase is the amount of cash received. In contrast, the measurements sometimes are ambiguous when shares of common stock are issued in exchange for noncash assets, in combination with other securities, or in exchange for other securities. |
|---|---|

**Noncash Assets**

In accordance with the *exchange-price* principle, shares of stock issued when noncash assets are invested should be valued at the fair market value of the asset received. For example, if a stockholder invests land having a fair market value of $50,000 in exchange for 2,000 shares of $20 par value common stock, the entry should be:

```
Land . . . . . . . . . . . . . . . . . . . . . . . . . . . . . . . . . . . . . . . . . . . . . . . .   50,000
    Common Stock—$20 Par  . . . . . . . . . . . . . . . . . . . . . . . .                40,000
    Additional Paid-In Capital—Common  . . . . . . . . . . . . . . .                10,000
```

---

6 Often the market price does not fall exactly this amount. If the dividend amount per share is maintained on the new shares, the stock split is a way of increasing dividend payout. The market price may also rise after the split because the lower price makes the stock attractive to more buyers. Neither of these increases in value is the direct result of the split; they are the result of other factors—increased dividends or greater demand for the stock.

The fair market value of the noncash asset may be determined by reference to quoted market prices, cash transactions for similar assets, or independent appraisals. When accountants encounter difficulty in establishing the fair market value of certain noncash assets, they may look to the market value of the stock issued. Practically speaking, therefore, fair market value may be measured by a valuation of the shares of stock given up in exchange rather than the value of the asset received. The practical measurement problem boils down to a question of relative reliability. Ideally, we should like to determine the value of the asset received and let that govern the amount credited to stockholders' equity. Sometimes, however, we may find more accurate and verifiable measurement in the fair market value of the equity shares and use that in making the debit to the asset.[7]

**Package Issues and Stock Purchase Warrants**

Corporations sometimes issue securities in packages to investors for a single price. Investors buying bonds or preferred stock may also receive some shares of common stock (a package issue) or the right to acquire common stock at a later date (a stock purchase warrant). The same general procedure governs the recording of both types of issues. There are really two separate sources of capital—the senior security (bond or preferred stock) and the common stock or right to acquire common stock (stock purchase warrant). Because these two elements exist independently, they should be accounted for as separate securities. The total proceeds should be allocated between the two elements for accounting purposes, usually in proportion to their market values.

**Package Issuance.** Take, for instance, the following situation. A firm offers a package deal to investors. The package consists of one share of $50 par value preferred stock and two shares of $20 par value common stock. The price of the package is $150, and 1,000 such packages are sold. An attempt should be made to divide the $150,000 between preferred and common stock. This split can be based on relative market values (*proportional method*). For example, if immediately after issue the common stock sells in the stock market at $30 per share and the preferred at $100 per share, 100/160 ($93,750) would be allocated to the preferred and 60/160 ($56,250) to the common. The entry would be:

| | | |
|---|---:|---:|
| Cash ............................................. | 150,000 | |
| Preferred Stock—$50 Par Value .................. | | 50,000 |
| Additional Paid-In Capital—Preferred ............ | | 43,750 |
| Common Stock—$20 Par Value .................. | | 40,000 |
| Additional Paid-In Capital—Common ............ | | 16,250 |

---

[7] Of course, using the market value of outstanding stock is not without its pitfalls. The market price on an organized stock exchange on any particular date may be distorted by temporary influences. Also, one cannot extend a price per share paid for a few shares to determine accurately the fair market value of a large block of stock. Transaction costs need to be considered too. Nevertheless, heavy reliance is frequently placed on the market value of the stock when a firm exchanges stock for the entire net assets of another business. Further discussion of the recording complexities of mergers is contained in Chapter 15.

When a determinable market price exists for only one of the securities, say the common stock, an *incremental method* can be used. An amount equal to the measurable fair market value of the common stock is allocated to it, and the remainder of the issuance price is assigned to the preferred.

**Stock Purchase Warrants.** Assume that a firm wishes to issue 7 percent bonds with a par amount of $100,000. In order to attract investors, the firm offers the purchasers of each $1,000 bond a warrant entitling them to acquire one share of common stock (par value $20) within the next six months at a price of $30. If the current price of the stock is above $30, the stock warrant obviously has a value at least equal to the difference between the market price and the $30 warrant price. Even if the current market price is slightly below $30, the warrant has value because of the possibility that the stock could rise above $30 within the next six months.

In most instances the warrants are detachable. After issuance the warrant can be bought and sold among investors separately from the bond itself. Consequently, an independent market valuation is placed on the worth of the warrant. The price paid for the warrant represents a down payment on the purchase of stock and should be accounted for as contributed or paid-in capital. If after issuance the bonds sell at 99 percent and the warrants at $10 each, the following entry would be appropriate:

| | | |
|---|---|---|
| Cash | 100,000 | |
| Discount on Bonds Payable | 1,000 | |
| Bonds Payable | | 100,000 |
| Common Stock Warrants Outstanding | | 1,000 |

In this case the independent values of the bond and the warrant exactly equal the total amount received by the company. It is quite possible that the total market value could be slightly different, in which case the proportional fair market values would be the basis for the allocation.

Upon exercise of the 100 warrants, the entry would be:

| | | |
|---|---|---|
| Cash | 3,000 | |
| Common Stock Warrants Outstanding | 1,000 | |
| Common Stock—$20 Par | | 2,000 |
| Additional Paid-In Capital—Common | | 2,000 |

Should the warrants lapse without being exercised, a reclassification within stockholders' equity should be made:

| | | |
|---|---|---|
| Common Stock Warrants Outstanding | 1,000 | |
| Additional Paid-In Capital—Common | | 1,000 |

## Stock Option

The measurement of invested capital is also difficult in the case of stock issued in exchange partially or completely for employee services. Assume that the president of a corporation is hired at a salary of $150,000 a year plus the privilege (option) of acquiring 3,000 shares of common stock (par $20) at a price of $30 per share. A year must pass, however, before the option can be *exercised* (the shares actually purchased). The market price of the stock on the date the option is granted is $40 per share.

The stock option agreement clearly is part of the president's compensation. Part of the *total* value of the president's services is paid in cash, and the rest is exchanged for a right to receive stock. The option plan also is an investment arrangement whereby the president invests services during the option period and cash at the end of the period. To obtain a correct picture of both the total compensation and the total investment, we need to place a dollar value on the option and the services represented thereby.

One approach would be to attempt to value the total service of the president directly and assign any difference between the total cash value of the service and the salary paid to the value of the option. Practically, such an approach is extremely difficult. An alternative is to value the option privilege and assign that amount as an addition to the value of services received. For instance, if the president receives the right to buy 3,000 shares at a price $10 below the quoted market value, then $30,000 (3,000 × $10) is deemed to be the best evidence of the amount of services being invested.[8] Accordingly, the following entry would be appropriate:

| | | |
|---|---|---|
| Salary Expense | 150,000 | |
| Compensation Expense—Stock Option* | 30,000 | |
| Cash | | 150,000 |
| Unexercised Options | | 30,000 |

   * If the option plan covers services to be rendered in more than one accounting period, the $30,000 compensation cost would be spread over those periods through appropriate accrual or deferral, depending on when the options are actually exercised.

The credit of $30,000 is made to a special stockholders' equity account. Then, when the option is exercised, the following entry is made:

| | | |
|---|---|---|
| Cash | 90,000 | |
| Unexercised Options | 30,000 | |
| Common Stock—$20 Par | | 60,000 |
| Additional Paid-In Capital—Common | | 60,000 |

The above approach, although required by the FASB, usually causes compensation expense to be significantly understated. Many plans set the option price at or above the existing market price on the grant date in order to provide certain tax benefits for the recipient. Under these circumstances, the required approach would attach *no* value to the option for accounting purposes. Nevertheless, the option offers the recipient an opportunity for great gain by allowing shares to be acquired at a fixed price sometime in the future. This right possesses a value certainly greater than zero.

**Conversion of Preferred Stock**

Often preferred stock, like some bond issues, contains a provision allowing the owners of the stock to convert the preferred stock into common

---

   [8] "Compensation for services that a corporation receives as consideration for stock issued through employee stock option, purchase, and award plans should be measured by the quoted market price of the stock at the measurement date less the amount, if any, that the employee is required to pay." AICPA, *APB Opinion No. 25,* "Accounting for Stock Issued to Employees" (New York, October 1972), par. 10. The measurement date normally is the date of grant. However, if the number of shares or option price is variable, depending on future events, the measurement date is the first date both of these variables become known.

stock. If conversion takes place, the transaction simply involves swapping one kind of equity for another. Common stock equity increases by the amount that preferred stock equity decreases. Total corporate assets remain the same.

On February 11 a corporation issues 2,000 shares of convertible preferred stock at $95 a share. The stock has a par value of $50 and can be converted at any time into five shares of $15 par value common stock. By October 25 the common stock has increased in market value to $20 a share, and holders of 500 shares of preferred elect to convert them to common stock. The entries on February 11 and October 25 are:

```
Feb. 11   Cash .....................................  190,000
              Preferred Stock—$50 Par ..............             100,000
              Additional Paid-in Capital—Preferred  ....          90,000

Oct. 25   Preferred Stock—$50 Par ..................   25,000
          Additional Paid-In Capital—Preferred  ........   22,500
              Common Stock—$15 Par ..............              37,500
              Additional Paid-In Capital—Common .....          10,000
```

Obviously, the preferred stockholders have elected to convert because the market value of the common stock has risen. However, as far as the corporate entity is concerned, no increase in equities or assets is recorded. One fourth of the preferred stock is canceled, and common stock equity takes its place. Total sources of capital remain constant.

**DECREAS-ING STOCK-HOLDERS' EQUITY: DIVIDENDS**

Dividends represent a pro rata distribution of assets to the stockholders. Assets and owners' equity decrease. The declaration and payment of dividends, however, are primarily legal and financial matters. Legal requirements place limitations on which stockholders' equity accounts can be decreased so that dividends will not impair the legal capital of the firm. As a *general* rule, dividends are assumed to arise from earnings. Consequently, a credit balance in Retained Earnings is normally a requisite to dividend declaration.[9] However, the existence of retained earnings does not guarantee that the firm has cash. The *financial* requirement for dividends is that there be some distributable asset, usually cash.

**Dividend Declaration and Payment**

A firm planning to pay dividends would normally follow the procedure outlined below, providing that it has sufficient retained earnings and cash to fulfill the legal and financial requirements. The board of directors makes a formal announcement declaring the dividend; for example, "On July 2, 1985, the Board of Directors of Able Corporation declared a quarterly

---

[9] This is only a very rough guide. Many states allow dividends to be declared out of additional paid-in capital. Because this represents part of the invested capital, sound accounting requires that any decrease in this account caused by dividends be disclosed as a *liquidating dividend,* a return of contributed capital.

cash dividend of $0.50 per share on common stock payable on August 1, 1985, to stockholders of record on July 15, 1985."

Since dividends are discretionary, no liability exists until the *date of declaration*. If 40,000 shares of common are outstanding on July 2, the entry is:

```
Dividends on Common Stock . . . . . . . . . . . . . . . . . . . . . . . . . . 20,000
      Common Dividends Payable . . . . . . . . . . . . . . . . . . . . . .        20,000
```

Dividends on Common Stock is a temporary owners' equity account reflecting the distribution of income; it is closed to Retained Earnings at the end of the year. Sometimes the procedure is streamlined, the initial debit being made to Retained Earnings.

July 15 in this case is called the *date of record*. All stockholders owning stock on that date are entitled to receive the dividend. No additional accounting entries are necessary, however, until the *date of payment*. On August 1 the dividend checks are mailed, and the following entry is made:

```
Common Dividends Payable . . . . . . . . . . . . . . . . . . . . . . . . . . 20,000
      Cash . . . . . . . . . . . . . . . . . . . . . . . . . . . . . . . . . . . . . . . . . . .        20,000
```

Dividends paid in *noncash* assets should be recorded at the fair market value of the assets transferred, and a gain or loss equal to the difference between fair market value and carrying value should be recognized on the disposition.[10]

**Preferred Stock Dividends.** The same general procedure is followed with preferred stock. The dividend rate is stated in the preferred stock contract, usually expressed as a fixed dollar amount per share if the stock is no-par or as a fixed percentage of par for a par value preferred stock. As with common dividends, there is no obligation to pay preferred dividends until they are declared. Therefore, the dividend preference simply states that the preferred dividends have to be paid first.

This fact raises a major question concerning *preferred dividends in arrears*. If the preferred stock is cumulative and dividends in the past have been skipped, these must be paid before common dividends can be declared and paid. However, until they are declared, even preferred dividends in arrears represent only a first claim on any future dividend declaration and not a liability. They therefore are not reflected on the formal financial statements, despite their importance to the common stockholders. Arrearages represent a shadow hanging over any future earnings. A note to the financial statements should disclose this contingency.

**Stock Dividends**

Sometimes corporations declare "dividends" payable in their own shares of stock. Additional shares are issued pro rata to the stockholders without

---

[10] AICPA, *APB Opinion No. 29,* "Accounting for Nonmonetary Transactions" (New York, May 1973), par. 18.

their giving or the business entity receiving anything in return. No distribution of assets is ever involved. The term *dividend* for this situation is a misnomer. Stock dividends really are not dividends at all but a type of small stock split. No change in total assets or total equities results. The dividend shares give nothing to the stockholder that they do not already have. The recipient ends up with more shares, each one representing a proportionately smaller interest. For example, an individual owning 2,000 shares of a corporation with total outstanding stock of 40,000 shares has a 5 percent ownership interest. If the company declares a 10 percent stock dividend, he or she receives an additional 200 shares. However, the total number of shares outstanding is now 44,000; the interest is still 5 percent (2,200/44,000). The investor has received no real income by having the extra shares. Indeed, if the individual sells the dividend shares, he or she is simply liquidating a portion of the investment.[11]

**Capitalization of Retained Earnings.** The factor which differentiates a stock dividend from a stock split in the accounting process is that the former is accompanied by a transfer from retained earnings to the contributed capital accounts. This procedure is called capitalizing retained earnings. The total financial interest of the common stockholder remains the same; all that results is a transfer from one stockholders' equity account to another. The capitalization permanently removes a portion of retained earnings from availability for dividend declaration. The related assets retained in the business probably have been reinvested in the form of buildings, equipment, and other long-term assets. To reflect this relatively permanent commitment, a portion of the retained earnings is reclassified, and the stockholders are given additional shares as separate evidence of their increased investment. However, the stock dividend itself causes a change neither in corporate assets nor in the shareholders' proportionate interests.

How much retained earnings should be capitalized? Possible alternatives include the amounts resulting from a multiplication of the number of shares distributed by the par or stated value, the average contributed capital per share, the average book value (shareholders' equity) per share, or the current market value. State statutes require as a minimum the capitalization of the par or stated value of the additional shares issued to maintain legal capital and may specify more. Beyond that, there is no clear answer in logic; it is a matter of corporate financial policy, not of accounting theory.

The FASB requires the use of *market value* to determine the amount to be capitalized for stock dividends when new shares being issued amount to less than 20 to 25 percent of the outstanding shares. For larger stock dividends, only the legal requirement needs to be capitalized. The reason-

---

[11] As in the case of stock splits, changes in market prices caused by other factors—for example, disguised dividend increases or simply irrational reactions on the part of the investing public—may mask the small decline in market price that logically should accompany a small stock dividend.

ing is that large stock dividends clearly will be interpreted for what they are—stock splits. However, in the case of small stock dividends, stockholders view the dividend shares as income equivalent to their fair market value. Therefore, this should be the amount transferred out of retained earnings.[12] Another argument for the use of market value is that the end result agrees with what the situation would have been had the corporation paid cash dividends and the stockholders turned around and reinvested the cash in the newly issued shares.

If the shares mentioned above have a par value of $5 per share and a market value of $17, GAAP would sanction the following entry when the dividend shares are issued:

```
Retained Earnings (4,000 × $17) .......................  68,000
    Common Stock—$5 Par  ...........................          20,000
    Additional Paid-In Capital—Common ...............          48,000
  To record issuance of 4,000 shares as a 10 percent stock
  dividend to holders of the 40,000 shares outstanding.
```

**DECREAS-ING STOCK-HOLDERS' EQUITY: REACQUI-SITION OF SHARES**

From time to time, a corporation may reacquire shares of its own stock. It may do so because it needs shares for employee stock option and purchase plans, acquisition of new businesses, or conversion of bonds or preferred stock. When a corporation buys back shares of its own stock, essentially the reverse of a stock-issuing transaction occurs.

The reacquired stock is called *treasury stock*. Formally defined, *treasury stock is the company's own stock which has been previously issued and then reacquired but not legally retired.* Economically and financially, it is similar to unissued stock, possessing no basic rights to vote, to receive dividends, or to receive payments upon liquidation. Legally, however, treasury stock is interpreted differently from unissued stock; nevertheless, these slight legal differences should not be allowed to overshadow the fundamental effect on assets and equities. When shares are issued, assets and stockholders' equity increase. Conversely, when shares are reacquired, assets and stockholders' equity decrease. The acquisition of treasury shares represents a contraction of capital—perhaps a partial and temporary one but a disinvestment of capital nevertheless. Similarly, when shares are issued, be

---

[12] It is somewhat ironic that in the AICPA bulletin this particular justification follows a very strong and sound argument that a stock dividend is not income. The result is an inconsistency—an admonition that stock dividends do not constitute income to the recipient, followed by a recommendation that they be treated in the accounting records in a particular way because stockholders may think they are income. See AICPA. *Accounting Research Bulletin No. 43* "Restatement and Revision of Accounting Research Bulletins" (New York, 1953), chap. vii(b), for a complete discussion of the reasoning of the Committee on Accounting Procedure relating to both stock dividends and stock splits. Some authors have suggested that the requirement for capitalization of market value rather than par value was instituted more as a penalty provision than as an accounting principle. It was designed to discourage companies with low earnings from declaring numerous stock dividends, which might mislead investors.

they treasury shares or unissued shares, contributed capital increases. In the following sections, the two acceptable methods of accounting for treasury stock are discussed and illustrated.

**Treasury Stock—Par Value Method**

Assume that on some given date the stockholders' equity appears as follows:

| | |
|---|---|
| Common stock—$2 par, 20,000 shares | $40,000 |
| Additional paid-in capital—common | 15,000 |
| Retained earnings | 25,000 |
| | $80,000 |

A particular stockholder owns 2,000 shares of stock of the corporation. Because all common stock has the same proportionate interest regardless of what the original investment was, the stockholder now has a 10-percent interest in each of the above accounts. The book value of the investment is $8,000 ($80,000 × 10 percent).

If the corporation were to buy back those shares at book value, cash would decrease by $8,000 and total stockholders' equity would drop by a like amount. One way to record this effect is to reduce each account proportionately.

| | | |
|---|---|---|
| Treasury Stock—$2 Par | 4,000 | |
| Additional Paid-In Capital—Common | 1,500 | |
| Retained Earnings | 2,500 | |
| Cash | | 8,000 |

To show that the shares are not permanently retired, the debit of $4,000 is made to a contra account, Treasury Stock—$2 Par, instead of directly to Common Stock. The Treasury Stock account appears as a deduction from Common Stock on the balance sheet. If the stockholder receives more than book value, the adjustment normally takes place in retained earnings.

As treasury stock, the shares can be reissued at some later date. As a potential source of capital, they differ little from unissued stock. If they are reissued later for $9,900, the entry would be the same as with unissued stock. Assets and contributed capital both increase by $9,900:

| | | |
|---|---|---|
| Cash | 9,900 | |
| Treasury Stock—$2 Par | | 4,000 |
| Additional Paid-In Capital—Common | | 5,900 |

This approach to the recording of treasury stock, called the *par value method,* takes the position that treasury stock transactions should be no different in effect from a retirement and later issuance of new shares.

**Treasury Stock—Cost Method**

The foregoing method, although theoretically sound, is not as widely used in current practice as the simpler *cost* method, particularly for shares that remain in the treasury only a short time before they are reissued. Instead of separate debits to each stockholders' equity account, a single debit is made to a *general contra equity account* called Treasury Stock. Under the cost method the entry to reflect reacquisition of the shares of stock at a price of $8,000 would be:

| | | |
|---|---|---|
| Treasury Stock | 8,000 | |
| Cash | | 8,000 |

This method views the acquisition and subsequent reissuance of the treasury shares as a continuous transaction. The corporation serves as an intermediary between the retiring stockholder and the new stockholder. The entry records a temporary contraction in total capital which will shortly be reinstated. Consequently, no need exists to reduce each of the stockholders' equity accounts directly. Treasury Stock is debited in lieu of each account individually as an indirect way of decreasing stockholders' equity through the use of a contra account.

Unfortunately, the Treasury Stock account, on rare occasions, finds its way to the asset side of the position statement, on the ground that the shares can be resold. Such an interpretation is erroneous. Treasury shares are no more an asset than are all the unissued shares. At best, they represent possible sources of additional capital funds. Until they are issued, however, the corporation has received no asset. A firm cannot create an asset by *returning* cash to the stockholders. Treasury stock under the cost method should be shown as a deduction from total common stock equity on the position statement, as an unapportioned contraction of total capital.

**Reissuance of Treasury Stock.** If treasury stock is not an asset, there can be no gain or loss on its reissuance. Income or loss arises from the *utilization* of assets, not the issuance of stock. Issuing shares of stock, whether from unissued or from treasury stock, is a capital-raising transaction. If the treasury shares are reissued for $9,900, the entry is:

| | | |
|---|---|---|
| Cash | 9,900 | |
| Treasury Stock | | 8,000 |
| Additional Paid-In Capital—Common | | 1,900 |

Cash increases by $9,900; contributed capital increases $9,900—part of it recorded as a cancellation of a contra equity and part of it as an increase in the Additional Paid-In Capital account. If the treasury stock is reissued at a price below its acquisition price, the difference can be debited to the Additional Paid-In Capital account, if there is one, or to Retained Earnings. The latter entry is justified on the grounds that the net result of the continuous transaction (reacquisition and reissuance) has been that a part of the entity assets have been distributed as a special kind of dividend.

The acquisition of treasury stock reduces not only contributed capital but also stated or legal capital. Consequently, state laws governing corporations usually place fairly stringent, detailed limitations on when, how, and in what amount a company can repurchase its own shares. Often retained earnings must be restricted (made unavailable for dividends) in an amount equal to the cost of the treasury stock purchased. This requirement is discussed later in the chapter.

### Retirement of Preferred Stock

Normally, when preferred stock shares are acquired by the firm, they are retired rather than held in the treasury for possible reissue. Like bonds, preferred stock issues usually are subject to call, or they can be repurchased on the stock market. Assume that we have $90,000 of par value preferred stock outstanding, which was originally issued at $5,000 over par. By contract, the preferred stock issue can be called in for retirement at a price equal to 108 percent of par value. The following entry would be necessary to record the retirement:

```
Preferred Stock—Par ................................  90,000
Additional Paid-In Capital—Preferred ...................   5,000
Retained Earnings .....................................   2,200
      Cash (108% × $90,000) ..........................          97,200
```

The excess of the $97,200 redemption price over the $95,000 contributed capital is debited to Retained Earnings to reflect the decrease in total common stock equity—a special type of dividend to the preferred stockholders. In practice, the debit to Additional Paid-In Capital would often be made for $7,200, eliminating the need for a debit to Retained Earnings. Likewise, if preferred stock were retired for less than book value, the difference would be credited to Additional Paid-In Capital.

### RESERVES AND RESTRICTIONS OF RETAINED EARNINGS

The equities of a firm consist of its liabilities, invested capital accounts, and retained earnings. Nevertheless, sometimes the balance sheet will include other accounts with credit balances that defy precise classification. We already have seen some of these in Chapter 13—the ambiguous deferred credit accounts. Another is the *reserve* account. This section analyzes some of the accounting problems and complications associated with one particular type of reserve account—*retained earnings reserves.*

### Restrictions (Appropriations) of Retained Earnings

Generally the balance in the Retained Earnings account indicates the maximum amount *legally* available for dividend declaration. Sometimes, however, management may wish to restrict a portion of retained earnings to inform the statement reader that this portion is not available for dividends. Segregation can be accomplished through the establishment of special accounts shown as separate subdivisions of retained earnings. These special accounts sometimes are called Retained Earnings Reserves. Better titles would be Restrictions or Appropriations of Retained Earnings.

Restrictions of retained earnings are sometimes required by contract or law, although they can also be discretionary. Many bond issues, for example, require that dividends in future years be declared only out of future years' earnings. In essence, the retained earnings at the time the bonds are issued become *frozen*. Many states require that retained earnings be restricted for an amount equal to the cost of treasury stock, to prevent the impairment of legal capital. Management sometimes voluntarily uses the restriction procedure to communicate to balance sheet readers about such future events as unspecified contingencies, possible losses on foreign investments, and possible future price declines.

All restrictions of retained earnings can be formally recognized in the accounts through the following journal entry:

```
Retained Earnings  . . . . . . . . . . . . . . . . . . . . . . . . . . . . . . . . . . . . . . . . .   xxx
     Restriction of Retained Earnings for _____  . . . . . . . . . . .          xxx
```

*Notice that no change in assets or in total equities results;* all that occurs is a segregation of retained earnings into a number of different accounts. Ostensibly, the purpose of such appropriations is to alert the financial statement reader that by contract, law, or management discretion, a portion of the retained earnings are not available for dividend declaration.

**Evaluation of Retained Earnings Restrictions**

The entry establishing the retained earnings "reserve" does not make the firm any stronger. No assets are actually set aside. It is possible that dividends *might* be reduced because of this segregation of retained earnings. However, usually this is not the case; the amount restricted is often small in relation to total retained earnings. Moreover, management can cut back on dividends *without making any entry*. The *entry* restricting retained earnings does *not cause* any dividend restriction.

Restrictions of retained earnings are only an attempt to impart information and must be evaluated as a *means of communication*. Unfortunately, their use may tend more often to hinder than to enhance the clear communication of information. The account title Reserve, if used, may mislead some readers into believing that the firm is stronger or that assets have been segregated for the purpose indicated by the reserve.

Any significant information regarding legal restrictions or future contingencies alternatively can be disclosed and described in notes to the financial statements just as easily and perhaps more clearly. Although accounts restricting retained earnings are not theoretically incorrect when they are used properly, a better procedure would be to eliminate them entirely.

**Misuse of Reserves in Accounting for Contingencies**

Doubts concerning the wisdom of using retained earnings restrictions are further heightened when one considers the concealment of information that arises when such accounts are misused. Potential misuses fall into two related categories: (1) charging losses to the restriction account and (2) setting up retained earnings restrictions by means of debits to loss and/or expense accounts. Both of these pitfalls historically have been prevalent in the accounting for future contingencies.

If an account is established by means of a segregation of retained earnings to recognize the possibility of some unfavorable *future* event, the only correct disposition of that account subsequently is to return it to retained earnings. This conclusion follows whether the contingency passes or occurs. In the former case, the amount obviously should be closed back to Retained Earnings from which it came. Even if the future losses do materialize, the restriction account should not be used to absorb them. With the *need for communication* having passed, the restriction should be returned to retained earnings. The losses, themselves, should appear on the income statement of the period in which they become measurable. Unfortunately, sometimes in past business practice the losses were debited directly to those contingency "reserves" and were buried there. Rather than disclose information, this procedure concealed it, screening it from the income statement.

A second abuse occurred when a "reserve" account was established to recognize a specific contingency, such as a possible loss from appropriation of foreign assets or future plant closings, as illustrated below:

```
Provision for Losses on Foreign Investments . . . . . . . . . .  400,000
    Reserve for Appropriation of Foreign Assets . . . . . . .              400,000
```

The debit would appear on the current year's income statement. The credit would appear on future balance sheets outside of the stockholders' equity section and would be charged for any losses that did occur.

A careful look at the nature of the accounts reveals the fallacy of this approach. The Reserve for Appropriation of Foreign Assets is not logically interpretable as either a liability or a contra asset. Appropriation losses do not accrue as a liability, nor is there any measurable impairment of asset values until appropriation actually takes place at some future time (if indeed it ever does). However, if the credit account is interpreted as an owners' equity account, the above entry becomes a debit to owners' equity (provision for loss) and a credit to owners' equity (reserve). In truth, this procedure was nothing more than an indirect way of restricting retained earnings by recording hypothetical losses. The loss was, at best, reported too soon and for an estimated rather than actual amount.

The above points might be summarized as follows: *Credits established by charges to losses or expenses must represent contra assets or liabilities and not segregations of retained earnings; conversely, if the reserves cannot be interpreted as contra assets or liabilities, then the corresponding debit should not be made to an expense or loss account.*

**FASB Standard.** The Financial Accounting Standards Board essentially recognized these points in 1975, setting forth two conditions for the recognition of losses by charges to income. *Both* must be met.

1. Information available *prior to* issuance of the financial statements must indicate that it is probable that an asset *had been impaired* or a liability

*had been incurred* at the date of the financial statements. It is implicit in this condition that it must be probable that one or more future events will occur confirming the fact of the loss.

2.   The amount of loss can be reasonably estimated.[13]

Notice the emphasis in the first condition on the past tense. Events must have occurred already before losses can be recognized, although future events may be necessary to confirm the exact amount of the loss. Also, the future event has to be likely to occur, not just reasonably possible or remote.

*Statement No. 5* does not prohibit restrictions of retained earnings. However, such restrictions must be displayed within the stockholders' equity section of the balance sheet, and no costs or losses should be charged to them.

**DISCUSSION OF THE ARMCO ANNUAL REPORT**

Armco's shareholders' equity data (in the Appendix to Chapter 5) are disclosed in (1) the bottom portion of the statement of consolidated financial position on page 158, (2) the statement of consolidated shareholders' equity following it, and (3) Notes 6 and 7. The statement of consolidated shareholders' equity details the factors causing changes in each of the stockholder accounts during the 1979–1981 period; in effect, it is a glimpse into the various ledger accounts which together constitute Shareholders' Equity. By the bottom of that statement, each ending balance shown in the shareholders' equity portion of the balance sheet has been detailed and explained.

The corporation is authorized to issue two types of preferred stock, denoted as Class A and Class B. When it is eventually issued, the Class B stock will differ from Class A in that it (1) will carry a par value and (2) will not be convertible into common shares. Because the preferred shares issued are of no-par value, the Additional Paid-In Capital relates entirely to the $5 par common stock.

The statement of consolidated shareholders' equity reveals that almost half of the preferred shares have been converted into common during the 1980–1981 period. The par value of the common exceeded the original issue price of the preferred shares being converted. Therefore, a *debit* to Additional Paid-In Capital was necessary; notice that this account was decreased whenever preferred shares were exchanged for common. For example, the 1981 conversions were recorded as follows (in millions of dollars):

| | | |
|---|---|---|
| Preferred Stock | 3.1 | |
| Additional Paid-In Capital | 1.5 | |
| Common Stock | | 4.6 |

---

[13] FASB, *Statement of Financial Accounting Standards No. 5*, "Accounting for Contingencies" (Stamford, Conn., March 1975), par. 8.

Authorized common stock for the company totals 150,000,000 shares, as the balance sheet reveals. The statement of consolidated shareholders' equity shows the reader that only 63,303,247 common shares, or 42 percent of the authorized amount, were outstanding on December 31, 1981. The detail in that statement depicts the factors responsible for the number of outstanding common shares increasing by over 10,000,000 during the 1979–1981 period. In order of importance, these factors were (1) acquisition of businesses, (2) conversion of preferred stock, and (3) exercise of stock options. Although Armco still has an enormous number of authorized but unissued common shares, it reveals in Note 6 that slightly over 5,000,000 shares are reserved for various purposes.

The statement of consolidated shareholders' equity points out wide fluctuations in the number of common shares held in the "treasury" from year to year. The numbers of shares so held was 1,210,524 on December 31, 1979, but only 174, and 171,314 on December 31, 1980, and 1981, respectively. A detailed analysis of the data in that statement reveals that more than half of the shares used during 1980 to acquire businesses, convert preferred stock, and exercise stock options came from the treasury.

Armco is in the minority of firms which account for their treasury stock by utilizing the par value method. Supporting this conclusion is the fact that three different accounts were reduced (debited) whenever common stock was purchased for the treasury. For example, the entry to reflect the purchase of 827,282 shares for the treasury during 1981 was (in millions of dollars):

| | | |
|---|---|---|
| Common Stock | 4.1 | |
| Additional Paid-In Capital | 1.0 | |
| Retained Earnings | 24.1 | |
| Cash | | 29.2 |

You will recall that under the alternative cost method the sole debit would be to a Treasury Stock account, which would then appear as the final deduction within the shareholders' equity section of the balance sheet.

As Note 6 indicates, only $437.0 million of the retained earnings on December 31, 1981, was unrestricted. Inasmuch as the balance sheet amount on that date was $1,862.0 million, a large proportion of Armco's retained earnings were legally unavailable for the declaration of cash dividends and for the purchase or redemption of its capital stock. Armco did not consider it necessary to segregate in a special reserve account the portion of retained earnings which was restricted.

**SUMMARY**

We have discussed a number of problems associated with stockholders' equity. Each has some direct impact on the concepts, accounts, or terminology of the financial statements. Still, only the surface has been scratched. Space does not permit a discussion of all the possible ways certain entries may be recorded in practice. Moreover, variations in terminology are numerous; only a brief sample of commonly used titles has appeared here. The terms *surplus* and *reserve,* in particular, are often used as catchalls for a number of relatively dissimilar items.

Most of the problems in stockholders' equity involve questions of *classification* rather than valuation or measurement. Usually the total change in owners' equity is determined by measurable changes in other assets and liabilities. The primary accounting problem becomes how to divide up this total change among the various accounts comprising stockholders' equity. The fundamental division is between invested capital and retained earnings, even though this distinction becomes blurred in the case of stock dividends. Other desirable objectives in classifying stockholders' equity are to distinguish between the interests of different classes of investor, such as preferred stockholders and common stockholders, and to separate legal capital from any excess amounts. Legal capital consists of the par value amounts, the stated value amounts if shares are no par, or the total contributed capital if the shares are no par with no-stated value.

Usually these classifications can be accomplished without undue complexity. In some special circumstances—conversions, retirements, and treasury stock transactions—the objectives conflict, and the recording problems become more difficult. Perhaps what is needed is a threefold classification of stockholders' equity—contributed capital (by type of stockholder and reflecting legal distinctions), retained earnings, and other sources and adjustments.

Certainly, little doubt exists that major changes in all stockholders' equity accounts should be disclosed and explained. In fact, in *Opinion No.*

**TABLE 14-1   Sample Stockholders' Equity Section of the Balance Sheet December 31, 19—(in $000)**

| | | |
|---|---:|---:|
| Contributed capital: | | |
| Preferred stock: | | |
| 12% cumulative preferred stock (authorized and outstanding, 400,000 shares of $10 par value) . . . . . . . . . . . | $4,000 | |
| Additional paid-in capital—preferred . . . . . . . . . . . . . . . . . . . . . . | 3,322 | |
| Total . . . . . . . . . . . . . . . . . . . . . . . . . . . . . . . . . . . . . . . . | | $ 7,322 |
| Common stock: | | |
| $8 par value (authorized, 1,000,000 shares; issued, 600,000 of which 570,000 are outstanding) . . . . . . . . . . . . . . | 4,800 | |
| Additional paid-in capital—common . . . . . . . . . . . . . . . . . . . | 6,890 | |
| Total . . . . . . . . . . . . . . . . . . . . . . . . . . . . . . . . . . . . . . . . | | 11,690 |
| Total contributed capital . . . . . . . . . . . . . . . . . . . . . . . . . | | 19,012 |
| Retained earnings (Note 1) . . . . . . . . . . . . . . . . . . . . . . . . . . . . . | | 15,780 |
| Total . . . . . . . . . . . . . . . . . . . . . . . . . . . . . . . . . . . . . . . . | | 34,792 |
| Less: Treasury stock at cost (30,000 common shares) . . . . . . . . | | 942 |
| Total stockholders' equity . . . . . . . . . . . . . . . . . . . . . . . . . . . . . . . | | $33,850 |

Note 1: Under the terms of the bond agreements, approximately $8 million of earnings retained on December 31, 19—, is unavailable for dividend declaration, and $.9 million of retained earnings, equal to the cost of the treasury stock, is restricted by state law.

*12* the Accounting Principles Board requires that changes in the individual accounts making up stockholders' equity and in the number of shares of stock be disclosed either in notes to the statements or in separate schedules (as in Armco's 1981 Annual Report). Before changes can be classified, however, the intricacies of some of the common events affecting owners' equity must be understood. From this chapter the reader should acquire a basic ability to analyze stockholders' equity transactions. Such analysis often involves looking behind the facade of legal and financial convention.

The diversity in terminology and procedures that characterizes the area of owners' equity extends to the presentation of stockholders' equity on the position statement. Many formats are employed; some stress legal considerations more than others. Table 14–1 shows one possible arrangement, incorporating most of the preferred views discussed earlier.

## QUESTIONS AND PROBLEMS

**14–1.** The following *selected* transactions affecting stockholders' equity occurred during the first year of the Block Corporation's operations.

1. Issued 3,000 shares of $5 par value common stock for $9 cash per share.
2. On the next day, gave 80 shares of common stock to the corporation's attorneys for legal services rendered in connection with securing the charter and getting the corporation in operation.
3. Issued 400 shares of common stock in exchange for some used equipment. The seller had depreciated the asset down to $3,600 on its books. However, Block's board of directors estimated the equipment's current fair market value to be $4,700. The firm's common stock was currently being traded at $12 per share.
4. Declared a cash dividend of $1 per share.
5. Paid the cash dividend declared in item 4.
6. Declared and issued a 5 percent stock dividend. The current market price of the stock was $14 per share.
7. Purchased 700 shares of Block's stock from one of the original shareholders at a price of $18 per share. The stock was to be held in the treasury.
8. Sold 500 of the shares purchased in item 7 for $19 per share.

*Required:*

a. Prepare journal entries to record the above transactions.
b. Prepare a stockholders' equity section as of the end of the first year. Assume that net income for the year was $17,150.
c. "Both the basic assumption of matching and the constraining criterion of materiality influence the proper recording of transaction 2 listed above." Do you agree?
d. "The gain taken to income as a result of transaction 8 listed above should really be $700 rather than $500." Should a $700 gain be recorded? A $500 gain?

**14–2.** Ownership interests in a corporation are evidenced by shares of stock. Although all corporations must have some common stock, they need not have any preferred stock outstanding. In fact, a survey of 600 large corporations for 1978–1981 revealed that fewer than 230 firms had preferred stock outstanding during any given year.

*Required:*

*a.* What type(s) of preference do holders of preferred stock have over holders of common stock? Is the preference of value to the stockholders? Why do more firms not issue preferred stock?

*b.* In what sense is preferred stock a hybrid security? Should preferred issues with *mandatory* call provisions be considered as stockholders' equity or as debt? Explain.

*c.* What rights, if any, does the cumulative feature convey to a holder of preferred stock? Would the presence or absence of such a feature ever be the determining factor in whether or not you acquire a particular preferred issue? Explain.

*d.* "Cumulative preferred dividends in arrears should be shown as a liability, either current or long-term, depending on how long the arrearage has been." Do you agree or disagree with this statement? Explain carefully.

**14–3.** The president of the Starin Company made the following announcement in a letter to stockholders:

> In years past, the company has paid a cash dividend of 10 percent of par value and purchased new assets with the remaining cash retained out of net income. These reinvestment policies are now beginning to reap additional benefits in the form of increased profits. As a consequence, your board of directors has decided to increase the dividend payout. Beginning this year, a 10 percent stock dividend will be added to the 10 percent cash dividend. In this way, the firm can continue to expand as in the past. Yet, the stockholders will have additional shares that they can convert into cash if necessary. In a sense, by selling dividend shares, an individual stockholder can increase the cash dividend from 10 percent to 20 percent.

*Required:*

*a.* Prepare journal entries to record the declaration and "payment" of the cash dividend and the stock dividend. Assume the firm has 200,000 shares of $20 par value common stock outstanding at the beginning of the year. The market price of the stock is $80.

*b.* Evaluate the president's statement. Comment on *all* the misunderstandings and inaccuracies contained therein.

*c.* One of your close friends has recently purchased 2,000 shares of Starin stock at $75 per share. He said that with the cash dividend of $4,000 (2,000 shares at $2) plus the stock dividend worth $16,000 (200 shares at $80), he will already have earned over 13.3 percent on his investment ($20,000/$150,000). Comment on your friend's reasoning and calculations.

**14–4.** Bird & Son, Inc., included in its 1981 annual report the following description of its dividend activity for the year:

> During 1981, the Board of Directors declared four common stock dividends payable from shares held in the Treasury. A 1 percent stock dividend declared in February, a 2 percent stock dividend declared in May, and a 2 percent stock dividend declared in August have been distributed to share-

holders of record. A 2 percent stock dividend declared on November 24, 1981, was distributed on January 9, 1982, to shareholders of record on December 18, 1981.

The Company has given effect to these distributions by capitalizing $3,701,000 of retained earnings, representing the fair market value of 278,646 shares on the dates of declaration and cash ($54,000) paid or payable in lieu of fractional shares. Additionally, Treasury stock was credited with $1,905,000, representing the cost of these shares, and other capital was credited with $1,742,000, the excess of fair market value over cost.

*Required:*

a. What does it mean to "capitalize" retained earnings? Does capitalization either benefit or harm existing stockholders? Explain.
b. Was Bird & Son following generally accepted accounting principles when it used the fair market value of the dividend shares?
c. Reconstruct the journal entry which the firm made for the stock dividends. Make one aggregate entry for the declaration and distribution of all four dividends.
d. Did Bird & Son voluntarily give out the stock dividends, or are such distributions necessary whenever firms omit cash dividends on their stock?
e. The firm mentions three different dates in connection with the last stock dividend: November 24, 1981; December 18, 1981; and January 9, 1982. On which of these dates, if any, did the stock dividend affect Bird and Son's (1) working capital, (2) paid-in capital, and (3) stockholders' equity? Explain.

**14–5.** Standard Shares, Inc., has adopted a policy of giving to its stockholders, through dividends, stock of *other firms* that has appreciated markedly. In April, 1982, the company distributed one share of Pennzoil Co. for each 100 shares of Standard Shares held by stockholders. Later that year, the firm announced that it would distribute 1.9 shares of MCA Inc. common stock for each 100 shares of Standard Shares held.

*Required:*

a. Does a firm's distribution of a dividend in shares of another company's stock present any special accounting and reporting problems? If so, explain how they should be resolved.
b. Assume that the dividend in MCA stock was declared on August 3 and is "payable" September 3 to stockholders of record on August 13. MCA stock was trading at $65 a share on August 3, although it had been selling as low as $38 in the past year. What accounts, if any, should be debited and credited on each of the three dates? Do you have enough information to come up with all the correct amounts? Explain.
c. "Usually a dividend directly decreases the declaring firm's retained earnings, although this particular dividend will probably indirectly *increase* Standard Shares' retained earnings." Do you agree? Why or why not?

**14–6.** The following were among the common stock disclosures contained in the 1981 annual report of Scope Industries:

On October 28, 1980, the shareowners approved an amendment to the Company's Articles of Incorporation which increased the authorized number of shares of common stock from 1,500,000 to 5,000,000 and eliminated the par value of the stock.

In 1974 the shareowners approved the grant of a nonqualified stock option for 100,000 shares at a price equal to the fair market value ($.8375) at the date of grant. During 1979 the option was exercised, and the proceeds were credited to the common stock account to the extent of par value and the remainder and related tax benefit of $133,904 to additional paid-in capital. No charge was made against income.

*Required:*

a. Why might the firm have decided to increase the authorized number of common shares?
b. Will the elimination of the stock's par value have any positive or negative effect on the firm's stockholders? On its creditors?
c. What accounts were debited and credited as a result of the elimination of the par value?
d. Did Scope Industries violate generally accepted accounting principles when it decided to make no charge against income in connection with the exercise of the stock options? Have those exercising the options really received compensation? Explain.
e. Assume the par value in 1979 was $0.40 per share. Prepare the journal entry which the firm made when the options were exercised (ignore the related tax benefit).
f. Why did Scope include in its 1981 annual report information relating to stock options granted seven years earlier?

**14–7.** The stockholders' equity of Baird Corporation appeared as follows:

BAIRD CORPORATION
Stockholders' Equity
As of December 31, 1984

| | |
|---|---|
| Common stock—$10 par (12,000 shares authorized and outstanding) | $120,000 |
| Additional paid-in capital | 200,000 |
| Retained earnings | 180,000 |
| Total | $500,000 |

On May 1, 1985, the firm purchased 800 of its own shares to hold in the treasury; the cost was $36 per share. On November 1, 1985, it reissued 300 of the shares at a price of $40 per share.

*Required:*

a. Were any shares in the treasury on December 31, 1984?
b. Why might a firm decide to acquire and later reissue treasury shares?
c. Using the cost method of recording treasury shares, (1) make the necessary journal entries on May 1 and November 1 and (2) prepare a schedule of stockholders' equity as of November 2, 1985 (ignore income earned during the year).
d. Repeat part *(c)* using the par value method of recording treasury stock.
e. Which recording method is more commonly used? Is it more representationally faithful than the alternative procedure? Explain.

**14–8.** On January 1, the stockholders' equity of Robinson Corporation consisted of the following items:

| | |
|---|---:|
| 8% cumulative, convertible preferred stock, $100 par value per share | $ 100,000 |
| Premium on preferred stock | 9,000 |
| Common stock—no par ($5 per share stated value) | 1,100,000 |
| Additional paid-in capital—common | 450,000 |
| Retained earnings | 730,000 |
| Total | $2,389,000 |

During the year, the following transactions affecting stockholders' equity took place:

Mar. 20    Declared *quarterly* cash dividends of $2 and $1 per share on preferred and common, respectively.

April. 5    Paid the dividends declared on March 20.

7    Half of the preferred stock was converted into common at the rate of five shares of common for each share of preferred.

May   4    Purchased 3,000 shares of its own common stock for $12 cash per share, to be held as treasury stock.

June 20    Declared *quarterly* dividends identical to those on March 20.

July   5    Paid the dividends declared on June 20.

10    The board of directors authorized an appropriation of retained earnings in the amount of $320,000 for possible future plant expansion.

Aug.   4    Issued the 3,000 shares of treasury stock in exchange for patent rights held by another firm. The market value of the stock was $15 per share.

Nov.   6    In order to raise the stock's market price, the board of directors approved a "reverse" stock split on the common. Each shareholder received one share of new $10 stated value common in place of each two shares of existing common share.

*Required:*

a.    Prepare journal entries to record the above transactions.

b.    Prepare a stockholders' equity section as of December 31. Assume that the net income for the year was $145,000.

c.    What purpose, if any, was served by the July 10 retained earnings appropriation?

d.    Did the fact that the preferred is cumulative influence any of the items or amounts you included in your answer to part (b)? Why or why not? (Recall that quarterly dividends were not declared on September 20 and December 20.)

**14–9.**    The following statement was included in the annual report of Russ Togs, Inc., for the fiscal year ending January 30, 1982:

RUSS TOGS, INC.
Consolidated Statement of Stockholders' Equity
($000)

| | Year Ended | | |
| --- | --- | --- | --- |
| | Jan. 30, 1982 | Jan 31, 1981 | Feb. 2, 1980 |
| Capital stock—$1 par value | | | |
| Preferred: | | | |
| Balance at beginning of year | $ 215 | $ 215 | $ 265 |
| Purchase and retirement of 50,000 shares | | | (50) |
| Balance at end of year | 215 | 215 | 215 |
| Common | 4,114 | 4,114 | 4,114 |
| Additional paid-in capital: | | | |
| Balance at beginning of year | 10,088 | 10,088 | 11,119 |
| Excess of cost over par value of preferred shares acquired and retired | | | (1,031) |
| Balance at end of year | 10,088 | 10,088 | 10,088 |
| Retained earnings: | | | |
| Balance at beginning of year | 54,950 | 49,286 | 44,582 |
| Net earnings (statement attached) | 10,998 | 9,079 | 8,518 |
| Total | 65,948 | 58,365 | 53,100 |
| Less: Cash dividends: | | | |
| Common ($1.00 a share in 1982 and $.88 a share in 1981 and 1980) | 3,416 | 3,007 | 3,311 |
| Preferred ($1.90 a share) | 408 | 408 | 503 |
| Total | 3,824 | 3,415 | 3,814 |
| Balance at end of year | 62,124 | 54,950 | 49,286 |
| Treasury stock: | | | |
| Balance at beginning of year | (7,728) | (4,260) | (3,940) |
| Purchase of common stock for treasury (10 shares in 1982; 331,402 shares in 1981; 31,835 shares in 1980) | | (3,468) | (320) |
| Balance at end of year | (7,728) | (7,728) | (4,260) |
| Total stockholders' equity | $68,813 | $61,639 | $59,443 |

*Required:*

a. Use the information contained in the above schedule to reconstruct the journal entry which Russ Togs made for the purchase and retirement of 50,000 shares of preferred stock.

b. Why is the treasury stock amount deducted in arriving at total stockholders' equity?

c. Did the treasury stock acquired during fiscal 1981 cost more per share than the treasury stock acquired during fiscal 1980? Explain showing calculations.

d. "Russ Togs has paid fewer common dividends than it has declared each year, because the amounts shown for common dividends do not equal the per share dividend multiplied by the number of common shares issued." Do you agree? Why or why not?

e. How many shares were in the treasury on January 30, 1982? Show calculations.

**14–10.** A portion of the stockholders' equity disclosures made by Kerr-McGee Corporation in its 1981 annual report is reproduced on page 522.

**Consolidated Statement of Capital in Excess of Par Value ($000)**

|  | 1981 | 1980 | 1979 |
|---|---|---|---|
| Balance, at beginning of year | $252,579 | $251,023 | $250,276 |
| Par value of common shares issued in two-for-one stock split | (26,028) | — | — |
| Excess of proceeds over par value of common stock issued upon the exercise of stock options | 1,662 | 1,556 | 747 |
| Balance, at end of year | $228,213 | $252,579 | $251,023 |

**Financial Review—Stockholders' Equity (in part)**

At the end of the year, stockholders' equity totaled $1.5 billion, compared with $1.3 billion at the end of 1980. The table below reports the changes in common stock issued and outstanding for the last three years:

|  | 1981 | 1980 | 1979 |
|---|---|---|---|
| Total shares issued, January 1 | 26,009,646 | 25,983,348 | 25,963,723 |
| Exercise of stock options and stock appreciation rights (prior to stock split) | 18,548 | 26,298 | 19,625 |
| Two-for-one stock split | 26,028,194 |  |  |
| Exercise of stock options and stock appreciation rights (subsequent to stock split) | 31,624 | — | — |
| Total shares issued, December 31 | 52,088,012 | 26,009,646 | 25,983,348 |
| Shares held in treasury: |  |  |  |
| January 1 | 106,840 | 106,840 | 106,840 |
| Purchases (prior to stock split) | 546 | — | — |
| Two-for-one stock split | 107,386 | — | — |
| Purchases (subsequent to stock split) | 10,217 | — | — |
| December 31 | 224,989 | 106,840 | 106,840 |
| Shares outstanding, December 31 | 51,863,023 | 25,902,806 | 25,876,508 |

*Required:*

a. Can you use the above information to derive the par value per share of stock?

b. Prepare the journal entry made by the firm to record the two-for-one stock split. Why does it differ from that illustrated in the text?

c. Was it appropriate for the firm to double the number of shares in the treasury at the time of the stock split? Why or why not?

**14–11.** In March 1985, the Murphy Trading Company issued 4,000 shares of preferred stock with a par value of $100 per share. Each share of preferred carried with it one detachable right to acquire one share of the firm's common stock at $27 at any time before July 12, 1985. The average market price of the common stock during March was $34 per share. The preferred stock (with the detachable right) was sold at a price of $106. Both the preferred stock and the rights were traded on the stock market separately. On July 11, 1985, when the firm's common stock was selling for $41 per share, 3,950 rights were exercised. The other 50 rights were never exercised, and they therefore lapsed.

*Required:*

a. "Investors had little enthusiasm for Murphy's preferred stock during March 1985, since they really valued it below par value." Do you agree? Explain.

b. For what price would you expect the rights to be traded at on the stock market immediately following the issuance of the 4,000 preferred shares?

c. Prepare the journal entries to record the issuance of the preferred and the exercise of the rights. Assume that immediately after issue of the preferred stock, it was quoted on the stock market at a price of $99, and the right to purchase one share of common was quoted at $10. Did you make use of the $41 common stock market value in either of your entries? Why or why not?

d. What entry, if any, should Murphy make on July 12, 1985, to reflect the lapsing of 50 of the rights?

**14–12.** Hatfield Corporation was organized on July 1, 1985. In its charter, it was authorized to issue 20,000 shares of 9 percent preferred stock with a par value of $100 per share, and 150,000 shares of common stock with a par value of $15 per share. Each share of preferred was convertible into 10 shares of common stock and was also callable at the firm's discretion at $105 per share. The following are *selected* transactions of the corporation:

1985:
July  2  Issued 7,000 shares of preferred at $102 per share.
       2  Issued 11,000 shares of common; 9,000 were issued for $63,000 in cash, and the remaining 2,000 were issued to lawyers and others who aided in organizing the firm.
Aug. 14  Issued 14,000 shares of common stock to various individuals at a price of $9 per share.
      15  Issued 4,000 shares of common stock in exchange for some used machinery. The seller had depreciated the asset down to $16,400 on its books. The firm has learned that the machinery will be assessed at $17,900 for property tax purposes.
Dec. 31  Declared preferred dividends for six months.

1986:
Jan. 15  Paid the preferred dividends declared on December 31.
Mar.  2  Purchased 2,000 shares of its own common stock to hold in the treasury.
July  1  Announced an imminent call of the preferred stock for retirement at $105 per share plus accumulated dividends. Preferred stockholders owning half of the shares elected to convert their shares into common ahead of the actual call date. The remainder of the preferred was retired by the corporation. The price of the common stock on this date is $12.
Aug. 19  Issued 6,000 shares of common stock at $14 per share. One third of these represented the shares acquired on March 2; the rest were previously unissued shares.
Oct.  4  A two-for-one stock split is declared on the common stock. The par value is formally reduced to $7.50 per share.
Dec. 31  Dividends of $1.20 per share were declared on the common.

*Required:*

a. Journalize the above transactions in 1985 and prepare a stockholders' equity section as of December 31, 1985. (Assume net income from July to December 31, 1985 was $119,000.)
b. Repeat part *(a)* for 1986. (Assume net income in 1986 was $244,000.)
c. Justify your method of valuation in recording the conversion of the preferred

shares on July 1, 1986. What impact would there be on total stockholders' equity if the alternative valuation procedure was used?

d. Redo the October 4 entry assuming it was a 100 percent stock dividend instead of a two-for-one stock split.

**14–13.** You have been called in by the Graves Company to examine its accounts prior to the issuance of financial statements for 1985. In the course of your examination, you learn about the following situations.

1. During 1984 Graves Company was sued by another firm for breach of contract. In 1985 a judgment was rendered against Graves Company. At the end of 1985 the case is still in litigation with respect to the amount of the damages to be awarded. The plaintiff is seeking damages of $1 million, while the lawyers for Graves Company contend that damages should not exceed $400,000.

2. The company owns a manufacturing plant in a foreign country which in 1985 announced its intention to expropriate all property owned by other than its own nationals. The expropriation would affect the Graves Company plant, which has a book value of $1.5 million and a market value of $2 million. The foreign government has announced that it will compensate the owner of expropriated property in an amount equal to 60 percent of fair market value.

3. Because of its large size and diversified operations, the company decided in 1985 to begin "self-insuring" its plant assets. Management felt that in the long run, the losses they would incur by not having insurance would be less than the $450,000 annual insurance premium which they would have to pay for coverage.

4. The company leases over 50 stores which it uses for retail outlets. In 1985 management concluded that 16 of these stores should be discontinued because of their unprofitability. Management estimates that the company will suffer losses of $1.8 million because of this decision. The $1.8 million represents $500,000 write-off of leasehold improvements, $450,000 for liquidation of inventory, $250,000 for penalties associated with lease cancellations, and $600,000 for projected operating losses to dates of closing.

5. A customer filed a claim for $250,000 against Graves Company on October 15, 1985, as payment for injuries sustained in a fall on the company's premises. The customer contends that negligence on the part of the company resulted in the fall. The counsel for Graves Company believes the case is completely without merit and will never be brought to trial. However, if necessary, legal defenses are more than adequate to win the case in the opinion of the lawyers.

*Required:*

Indicate how each of these situations should be reflected on the financial statements for 1985, if at all. If a journal entry is required, indicate the accounts to be debited and credited and where they would appear on the statements. Indicate the nature of any disclosure you would make in notes to the financial statements.

# FINANCIAL STATEMENTS— PROBLEMS OF ANALYSIS, DISCLOSURE, AND INTERPRETATION

# CHAPTER 15

# ACCOUNTING FOR INTERCOMPANY OWNERSHIP AND COMBINATION

Individual investors purchase shares of stock in corporations to hold as investments. Many corporate businesses also acquire substantial holdings of capital stock in other corporations. In some cases corporate investors, like individual investors, acquire shares solely as investments in order to earn a return in the form of dividends and market value appreciation.

In most cases, however, the purpose behind intercorporate stockholdings is for one firm to affect or control the policies and operations of another firm. A corporation, through its substantial ownership of stock of other corporations, may have the ability to *significantly influence* the latter's operating and financial policies. The owner of the shares is called the *investor* corporation; the affected corporations are called *investee* corporations. If the investor corporation owns more than half the voting common stock of the investees, it is called a *parent* company. It has the ability to *determine* the operating and financial policies of the controlled companies, which are called *subsidiary* companies.

A parent company and its subsidiaries (and major investees) often are called *affiliated* companies. Within the affiliate group a subsidiary firm may be a source of supply for raw materials for the parent or an outlet for the parent's finished products. Integration of the operations of the subsidiary with those of the parent may result in production and distribution economies or may allow the parent to penetrate into new markets or enlarge existing ones. In other cases, intercorporate ownership results in a conglomerate of companies in different industries. If the industries have differing risk characteristics, the combination serves as a means for reducing the overall variability and risk of the affiliate group. Still other parent companies invest in subsidiary companies to gain control over new technologies, to acquire management skills, or to obtain legal, political, or tax advantages.

Whatever its reasons for acquiring shares of stock of another company, the parent/investor may exchange for those shares a number of different considerations. The obvious one is cash; the parent/investor simply buys the shares. In addition, however, the parent/investor may distribute its own shares of common stock, issue bonds or preferred stock, or exchange combinations of cash and securities for the voting stock of other companies. Indeed, the acquisition and merger movement of the last three decades has fostered more alternatives than could possibly be described here.

In any event, the initial result of an acquisition is the recording by the parent/investor of an asset, investment in stock of other companies. This chapter explores three aspects of the accounting for the resulting intercorporate relationships and the subsequent handling of the investment account.

1. If Company A owns substantially all of the stock of Company B, it may liquidate Company B and legally transfer all the assets to Company A. Such a combination is called a *merger*. The investment account disappears, and the actual assets and liabilities of the acquired company take its place. The acquired company ceases to exist as a separate *legal* entity, although it often operates intact as a division of the combined company. The first section of this chapter considers the valuation and recording problems encountered when businesses merge or combine through an exchange of shares. Two recording procedures, called *purchase* and *pooling of interests,* constitute the focal point in the section.

2. If Company A owns a controlling interest in the stock of Company B, it may choose to operate B as a separate corporation in harmony with the overall objectives of Company A. There are valid legal, tax, and business reasons to retain separate legal entities for different parts of the business, particularly parts with differing risk characteristics. Still, there may exist a need for financial information for the group of companies operating as a single *economic* entity. The second section of this chapter concerns the preparation of *consolidated financial statements,* which treat the legally separate parent and subsidiary companies as if they were a single company.

3. The third section examines the proper accounting for intercompany investments when the investor and investee companies are treated as separate accounting entities or when the intercompany holding is less than a controlling one. The *equity method* and the *cost method* are contrasted as techniques for recording these relationships.

## RECORDING MERGERS AND ACQUISITIONS

The transaction in which two companies become affiliated is called a merger, acquisition, or combination. When the merger is effected through a parent corporation's acquisition of the outstanding voting stock of a subsidiary for cash, the situation is analogous to a lump-sum purchase of assets (discussed in Chapter 7). The cost assigned to the acquired shares is the amount of cash paid out. This amount in turn is allocated to the individual net assets—tangible and intangible—when the acquired company's shares are retired and its net assets are combined with those of the acquirer. For example, Jeckle, Inc., buys all the outstanding stock of Hyde Company for $960,000 with the intent to merge the two companies. Hyde Company has tangible assets with a book value of $900,000 and a fair market value of $1,020,000; its liabilities are $190,000. The entries are:

| | | |
|---|---:|---:|
| Investment in Hyde Company Stock ................. | 960,000 | |
|    Cash ........................................ | | 960,000 |
|    To record purchase of stock. | | |
| | | |
| Tangible Assets (recorded in detail | | |
|    at their fair market value) ........................ | 1,020,000 | |
| Goodwill ....................................... | 130,000 | |
|    Liabilities ...................................... | | 190,000 |
|    Investment in Hyde Company Stock ............. | | 960,000 |
|    To record the retirement of Hyde Company stock and | | |
|    the merging of its assets and liabilities into Jeckle, Inc. | | |

In brief, the only valuation problem is one of allocating the total cash consideration among the net assets acquired.

In the last two decades, most business combinations have been accomplished through an exchange of shares rather than by an outright purchase for cash. The acquiring company offers to issue a certain number of its shares in exchange for the shares of the acquired company. Under most state laws, if a required percentage of each firm's stockholders agrees to the proposal, the exchange is binding and the firms are legally merged.

The question we are addressing in this section is whether there is a different economic substance to the transaction when the parent corporation exchanges its own shares for those of the subsidiary instead of paying cash. Is a method of accounting different from that illustrated above appropriate?

In some circumstances accountants answer this question in the affirmative. Two methods exist in accounting practice to account for business combinations effected through an exchange of shares. The *pooling of interests approach* is used when the parent company issues its own voting stock in exchange for substantially all the voting stock of the subsidiary. The *purchase approach* is used when any other combination of considerations is exchanged for the subsidiary shares. These two accounting procedures may vary significantly in their impact on the financial statements, because they value the net assets acquired and record the increase in stockholders' equity differently.

**Illustrative Data**    Assume that, instead of making a $960,000 cash payment, Jeckle, Inc., issues 16,000 shares of its common stock to the owners of Hyde Company in exchange for the 10,000 outstanding shares of that company. Jeckle promptly retires the Hyde shares, thereby liquidating and dissolving it as a separate corporation and formally consummating the merger.

Balance sheets for the two corporations immediately prior to the merger are given in Table 15-1. The Hyde Company's inventory of $120,000 is valued on a LIFO basis; its current replacement cost is $170,000. A recent appraisal of its buildings and equipment indicates a current value of about $530,000. The Hyde Company possesses a very fine market reputation. Its brand names are well known, and the company is noted for turning out a quality product. In fact, one of the reasons that Jeckle, Inc., wishes to acquire Hyde Company is to obtain the benefits from this reputation.

**TABLE 15-1   Premerger Balance Sheets ($000)**

|  | Jeckle, Inc. | Hyde Co. |
|---|---|---|
| *Assets* | | |
| Cash | $ 110 | $ 20 |
| Accounts receivable | 770 | 100 |
| Inventory | 1,555 | 120 |
| Land | 305 | 200 |
| Buildings and equipment (net) | 3,360 | 460 |
| Total assets | $6,100 | $900 |
| *Equities* | | |
| Accounts payable | $1,540 | $190 |
| Capital stock—$10 par | 1,000 | 100 |
| Additional paid-in capital | 1,200 | 130 |
| Retained earnings | 2,360 | 480 |
| Total equities | $6,100 | $900 |
| Shares outstanding (thousands) | 100 | 10 |
| Market value per share | $ 60 | Not available |

**Purchase Approach**

The two journal entires below summarize the entries made by Jeckle to effect the merger under the purchase approach.

| | | |
|---|---|---|
| Investment in Hyde Company Stock | 960,000 | |
| Capital Stock—$10 Par | | 160,000 |
| Additional Paid-In Capital | | 800,000 |

| | | |
|---|---|---|
| Cash | 20,000 | |
| Accounts Receivable | 100,000 | |
| Inventory | 170,000 | |
| Land | 200,000 | |
| Buildings and Equipment | 530,000 | |
| Goodwill | 130,000 | |
| Accounts Payable | | 190,000 |
| Investment in Hyde Company Stock | | 960,000 |

Under this approach the assets of Hyde Company, including any intangible assets being acquired, are recorded at their fair market values (their current acquisition costs), and the contributed capital accounts of Jeckle are credited. The net result is the same as if the Jeckle shares had been issued first for cash and then the cash had been used to acquire the Hyde shares. Should the direct exchange of shares without an intermediate inflow and outflow of cash cause the acquisition to be recorded differently?

The purchase approach would say no. The negotiations between the two companies can be reasonably assumed to have been based on an equal exchange of values—the value of the net assets received by Jeckle and the value of the stock issued by it. The fair market value can be measured either by an appraisal of the individual assets or by a valuation of the shares of stock given up in exchange, whichever can be more objectively determined. Because of the likely existence of an intangible asset, goodwill, in the above entry, the market value of the shares being issued is assumed to provide a close approximation of the real substance of the transaction. Jeckle, Inc., has issued shares with a market value of $960,000 (16,000 shares at $60) and therefore values the net assets received at $960,000. Each individual asset is stated at its fair market value, and the excess of $130,000 is assigned to Goodwill. The $960,000 increase in contributed capital is recorded in two accounts—the par value of the shares (16,000 × $10) in the Capital Stock account and the excess over par value in a separate Additional Paid-In Capital account.

**Evaluation of Purchase.** The purchase approach views a business combination, *however consummated*, as primarily an acquisition of one company's assets by another company. The acquisition of assets is the result of a bargained exchange. The basis of accountability relevant to the new ownership is the values implicit in that exchange. The valuation of the assets should not differ from that associated with a cash purchase merely because shares of stock are the consideration exchanged. Similarly, the effect on stockholders' equity should not vary simply because noncash assets are received upon issuance of the stock.

The objections to accounting for business combinations as purchases center on two aspects of the valuation problem. First, some opponents contend that the determination of the values being exchanged is not as clearly evident as the above example might imply. It is difficult to ascertain the fair market value of a group of assets in a going concern, and reliance on the market value of stock places undue emphasis on the vagaries of the stock market. Second, even if values are reasonably determinable, the purchase method merges unlike asset values. The tangible assets of the *acquiring corporation* are *not* revalued to current cost. The goodwill of the acquired company is recognized, but any excess value of the acquiring corporation as a going concern goes unrecorded.

**Pooling of Interests Approach**

This method, as its name implies, calls for a simple combining of assets and equities. In a pooling of interests the Investment account of the parent is valued at the *book value* of the stockholders' equity of the acquired firm. Then, when the investment is liquidated, the assets of the acquired firm are carried over to the acquiring firm at their book values. Likewise, the stockholders' equity amounts of the two firms are combined, including the respective retained earnings.

The entries to record the combination under pooling of interests are:

| | | |
|---|---:|---:|
| Investment in Hyde Company Stock | 710,000 | |
| Capital Stock—$10 Par | | 160,000 |
| Paid-in Capital from Merger | | 550,000 |

| | | |
|---|---:|---:|
| Cash | 20,000 | |
| Accounts Receivable | 100,000 | |
| Inventory | 120,000 | |
| Land | 200,000 | |
| Buildings and Equipment | 460,000 | |
| Paid-in Capital from Merger | 550,000 | |
| Accounts Payable | | 190,000 |
| Additional Paid-In Capital | | 70,000 |
| Retained Earnings | | 480,000 |
| Investment in Hyde Company Stock | | 710,000 |

Pooling of interests assumes a fusion, or marriage, of the two companies instead of an acquisition. The merged company is seen to be little different from the sum of the two companies prior to the merger. Total assets and stockholders' equity after the merger are the sums of the assets and stockholders' equity of each of the companies prior to the merger. The shareholders are also the same, as the Hyde Company shareholders are now shareholders in Jeckle, Inc. Notice that the only adjustment made reflects the par value of the shares issued by the acquiring firm. Because the additional contributed capital is now represented by 16,000 shares of Jeckle, Inc., stock with a total par value of $160,000, instead of 10,000 shares of Hyde Company stock with a total par value of $100,000, $60,000 of the $130,000 in the Additional Paid-In Capital account of Hyde has to be reclassified so that legal capital will conform to the number of shares issued.[1]

**Evaluation of Pooling.** The major justification for the pooling of interests approach is the contention that nothing of substance has occurred in the combination necessitating a new basis of accountability for the Hyde Company assets. The combined entity is nothing more than a combination of the two businesses formerly conducted separately. The assets and stockholders' interests remain the same, but they are now together instead of separate. Useful comparisons with past periods can be made, then, if the accounting for the merged company is only a continuation of the combined accounts of the two companies.[2]

---

[1] If there were insufficient paid-in capital of the acquired company to accommodate the reclassification of stockholders' equity because of the increase in par value, then any excess over par of the acquiring company would be reduced. If all paid-in capital accounts were zero, then retained earnings would be reduced also. Outside of this minor legal adjustment, pooling basically calls for a simple combining of owners' equity accounts.

[2] Pooling also draws practical support from the fact that most exchanges of stock in conjunction with a merger are treated as tax-free exchanges under the income tax law. Consequently, for tax purposes the old asset values must be carried over.

The conceptual arguments against pooling tend to be the same as those in favor of the purchase approach. First, the underlying rationale of pooling—that is, that two groups of stockholders owning businesses are coming together to operate henceforth as partners—just does not fit most business combinations. There is almost always a clearly identifiable acquiring company which is taking over the business of another company. One party to the merger is a continuing entity which exercises dominant control after the merger. Acquisition of another company is simply an alternative means of growth, and the accounting should be consistent with that resulting from internal expansion. Second, something of substance does occur in most combinations. Two independent parties bargain at arm's length to reach agreement on an exchange of values. To record the transfer of assets at book value seems to fly in the face of the real substance of the transaction and agreement between the parties.

**Comparative Impact on the Financial Statements.** The choice between purchase and pooling is an extremely important one because of the impact that each of the two accounting procedures has on the financial statements. The initial effect can be seen in our example. Balance sheets after the merger under the two approaches are presented in Table 15–2. In most instances pooling of interests gives a balance sheet with lower figures than that of the purchase approach.

**TABLE 15–2  Postmerger Balance Sheets under Purchase and Pooling ($000)**

|  | Purchase | Pooling |
|---|---|---|
| *Assets* | | |
| Cash | $ 130 | $ 130 |
| Accounts receivable | 870 | 870 |
| Inventory | 1,725 | 1,675 |
| Land | 505 | 505 |
| Buildings and equipment | 3,890 | 3,820 |
| Goodwill | 130 | — |
| Total assets | $7,250 | $7,000 |
| *Equities* | | |
| Accounts Payable | $1,730 | $1,730 |
| Capital stock—$10 par | 1,160 | 1,160 |
| Additional paid-in capital | 2,000 | 1,270 |
| Retained earnings | 2,360 | 2,840 |
| Total equities | $7,250 | $7,000 |
| Shares outstanding (thousands) | 116 | 116 |

Perhaps even more important is the impact on the measurement of future income. Under the purchase approach, with the newly acquired plant assets recorded at their current market values instead of at book values, subsequent depreciation charges are higher. Straight-line depreciation expense on the *Hyde Company* assets, if we assume that they have a remaining useful life of 10 years, will be $53,000 a year ($530,000/10 years) under the purchase approach but only $46,000 ($460,000/10) when the combination is accounted for as a pooling. Moreover, in accordance with *APB Opinion No. 17*, the acquiring company must also amortize the $130,000 goodwill recognized in the purchase; this step further reduces postmerger earnings. Pooling of interests, in contrast to a purchase, thus gives greater income and lower assets, a double infusion to return on investment.[3] Theoretical reasons aside, one can understand why acquisition-minded companies prefer pooling of interests.

**Purchase-Pooling Issue and the Entity Concept**

Clearly the nature of the accounting entity lies at the heart of this recording problem. Purchase accounting presumes that the relevant entity is the acquiring company and that all recording should be viewed from its perspective. The ownership interests of the stockholders of the acquired company are significantly altered. On the other hand, pooling of interests asserts that a merger effected through an exchange of shares creates no new entity, merely a combination of two old entities. An exchange of shares is solely an arrangement between shareholders; it joins two ownership interests in a combined collection of assets.

Once the entity-identification issue is resolved, many of the other arguments fall into perspective. For instance, *if* the relevant entity is the acquiring company, then the transfer of assets from one corporate entity to another does necessitate a new basis of accountability for the assets. The alleged problems caused by not also revaluing the acquiring company's assets or recording its goodwill are problems of conventional financial accounting in general and not ones unique to business combinations. In *any* acquisition of new assets—cash purchase or otherwise—the new assets are recorded on the entity's books at the current acquisition costs, even though other assets are valued at past purchase prices. Moreover, internally developed goodwill also goes unrecognized in acquisitions for cash. Under the entity concept, transactions between the entity and outside parties give rise to recordable events that appear on the financial statements. Purchased goodwill is real, and its cost is part of the transaction entered into by the entity.

When viewed from the perspective of the acquiring entity, a merger recorded under pooling of interests is unacceptable because of the implication that a firm can generate retained earnings simply by acquiring another firm. Although the acquiring firm can buy another's assets and can assume its liabilities, it cannot generate retained earnings in a capital-raising transaction. Retained earnings bear significance only to the entity which

---

[3] If the merger were a tax-free exchange, neither the amortization of goodwill nor the depreciation on amounts in excess of book values would be deductible for tax purposes. The burden on after-tax earnings would therefore be almost double.

produced the income. Thus, if we accept the *acquiring-entity interpretation of the purchase approach,* the combination of owners' equity accounts under pooling of interests is nonsensical. On the other hand, the combining of all assets and equities at book values is a logical extension of the *shared-entity interpretation of the pooling approach.*

Therefore, the real issue centers on the nature of the entity that ultimately exercises control over the acquired assets and the policies that govern their use. Pooling conceptually would seem to require an entity within which there is a truly mutual exchange of risks and control by more or less equal parties. All previous owners remain with the intention of conducting *together* a combined business.

Except in rare instances, however, most business combinations are characterized by a single identifiable entity acquiring dominant (not shared) control over the assets of another firm. This control is accomplished through an exchange of shares based on an arm's-length bargain. Such an exchange of shares is not solely an arrangement among shareholders. Control over assets passes from one group to another. One of the original entities ceases to exist.

## Authoritative Standards

The accounting profession has long wrestled with the purchase-pooling issue. Authoritative pronouncements, beginning in 1950, attempted to suggest criteria—similarity in size, continuity of former ownership interests, and continuation of existing operations—for distinguishing between purchases and poolings of interest. However, these criteria gradually eroded. The net result was that businesses could account for a merger in whatever manner they found most self-serving, usually as a pooling.

Until the Accounting Principles Board acted in 1970, the pooling of interests approach was widely used and often abused to distort postmerger results. For example, shares of stock were issued for assets of which the market values were significantly higher than the book values. This increased value was suppressed by book-value recording under a pooling. Then, shortly after the merger, some of the acquired assets were sold at their current values. The resultant large gains appeared on the postmerger income statement, even though in an economic sense the increased value was "paid for" through an exchange of equally valued shares.

Presumably, pooling should occur only for combinations consummated by an exchange of common stock and in situations where there is evidence of continuity of ownership interests and operation. Nevertheless, the pooling rationale was sometimes misapplied so that low asset values could be recorded and future earnings boosted as much as possible through pooling. For instance, cash and common stock were issued in the acquisition of another company. The cash portion had to be treated as a purchase, but the stock portion was treated as a pooling. Also, shares of stock were issued in order for the acquisition to qualify as a pooling. However, a separate agreement bound the acquiring corporation to repurchase the newly issued shares for cash later and thus eventually transformed the transaction into a cash acquisition.

Two research studies sponsored by the Accounting Principles Board in the 1960s dealt with business combinations and the related subject of goodwill. Both essentially recommended the abolition of pooling of interests accounting. Instead, in 1970 the APB issued a less extreme opinion, allowing both purchase and pooling but only under differing circumstances. Businesses could no longer choose freely which method to use. In addition, disclosure requirements were expanded for all combinations to include a description of the companies combined, an indication of the method of accounting used, details about the transaction, and comparative earnings information before and after the merger.

**Criteria for Pooling.**[4] Under *Opinion No. 16* business combinations meeting rather specific criteria *must* be accounted for as poolings of interests; all other combinations *must* be handled as purchases. In all, 12 specific conditions are set forth as requisite for the use of pooling of interests accounting. These conditions relate to the nature of the combining companies, the manner in which the companies are combined, and the absence of any plans or contingencies that would negate the concept of two groups of stockholders coming together to significantly share the ownership risks and benefits.

The criteria can be summarized in the following five points: (1) the combination has to result from a single transaction completed within one year between companies that have been autonomous for at least two years and independent of one another, (2) only voting common stock can be issued in exchange for substantially all (at least 90 percent) of the voting common stock of the acquired company, (3) there can be no adjustments or reacquisition of the equity interests of the voting common stock in contemplation of the combination within two years before the merger, (4) there can be no major realignment of voting interests or restrictions on voting rights, and (5) there can be no planned retirement of voting stock or disposition of assets after the combination (except to eliminate duplicate assets). Violation of any of these conditions evidences that one firm is *acquiring* another, in which case the purchase approach is the proper accounting.

Under these criteria our Jeckle-Hyde merger probably would have to be recorded as a pooling of interests. Jeckle is issuing only its voting common stock in exchange for all the voting common stock of Hyde. What if Jeckle issues only 8,000 shares of its stock worth $480,000 for half of the Hyde shares and issues a bond with a present value of $480,000 or pays $480,000 in cash for the rest? In this instance, the merger would have to be recorded as a purchase. In both cases $960,000 of values are exchanged for the Hyde shares. We return to the question posed on page

---

[4] AICPA, *APB Opinion No. 16*, "Business Combinations" (New York, August 1970), par. 45–48.

529: Is there a different economic substance to the transaction? We think not.

## CONSOLIDATED FINANCIAL STATEMENTS

Many times the acquiring firm and the acquired firm do not merge formally. Each retains its legal identity as a separate corporation and continues to maintain its own set of accounting records. Economically, however, the companies may closely coordinate their operations and financial positions as if they were one. Consolidated financial statements provide a comprehensive picture of this economic entity by meshing the accounts of the subsidiary with those of the parent into a single set of statements. Consolidated statements indicate the results that would have transpired if all transactions had been recorded in a single set of accounts.

The purpose of consolidated statements is to provide the management and stockholders of the parent company with an overall view of the activities of their company and its related subsidiaries considered as one unit. This picture typically is more meaningful than separate statements, because the legal entities frequently act in concert to achieve an overall goal for the parent company and its stockholders rather than autonomously to attain individual company objectives. In consolidated statements investors in the parent company can see the results of their investment at work—directly and also indirectly through the parent's investments in other companies. Users of consolidated financial statements can often obtain a better picture of the financial and operating activities of the complex of companies. They get a better idea of the total asset investment subject to common control, the sales volume of the entire group of companies, indirect financial arrangements (e.g., borrowing by subsidiary companies primarily on the credit of the parent company) and so on.

### Consolidation Policy

In consolidated statements the business entity is a group of affiliated companies. Therefore, the consolidated statements are concerned only with the transactions and relationships between the affiliates, viewed as one, and parties outside the family circle. The mere existence of intercompany holdings of securities, however, does not automatically lead to the preparation of consolidated statements. Presentation of the activities and relationships of a number of companies as if they were one can be justified only when there is reason to believe that it would provide more useful information than would separate statements of the parent and the individual subsidiaries. The parent company should therefore adopt a reasonable and consistent consolidation policy governing which subsidiaries are consolidated and which remain as unconsolidated investments. This consolidation policy should be clearly disclosed.

A number of criteria may influence the choice of consolidation policy, but the two most important are *control* and *relatedness of activities*. In order for a group of firms to function as a single company, one of the group must have the ability to determine the operating activities and financial policies of the others. Consolidation of statements is therefore appropriate when there is clearly only one parent company and the parent company owns a majority interest in the subsidiaries.[5] Sometimes foreign subsidiaries are not consolidated because of restrictions on the parent's control over the subsidiary's operations or on the withdrawal of earnings by the parent in the form of dividends.

Even when the criterion of clearly defined control is met, consolidation may offer no advantages if the companies are not operationally related. In fact, it may conceal meaningful differences whenever the types and distribution of assets and liabilities and the sources of revenue are radically dissimilar among the related entities. For instance, consolidated statements for a manufacturing firm and a bank would probably provide less information than would individual reports of each company. On the other hand, the mere fact that the subsidiary is in a different line from the parent is insufficient reason not to consolidate. Careful judgment is required to ascertain whether a particular subsidiary is an organic part of the consolidated entity. Consideration must be given to the objectives of the parent in acquiring the subsidiary, the similarity of their general business activity, the extent of intercorporate transactions, and the degree of uniformity in the structure of their financial statements.

## Consolidated Balance Sheet

When consolidated statements are needed, the accountant works from the individual statements of the companies being consolidated, eliminating items that would not appear if the separate companies had been one company. Let us examine a few typical situations to see what we should eliminate to avoid double-counting or to adjust for the effect of transactions solely within the family.

**Complete Ownership at Book Value.** For the first example, assume that the parent company (P) acquires 100 percent of the common stock of the subsidiary (S) for $10,000 on December 31, 1984; consolidated statements are desired as of that date. Table 15–3 presents the major accounts of each company. Note that the $10,000 amount shown as an asset on the parent company books as Investment in Subsidiary equals the owners' equity (capital stock plus retained earnings) of the subsidiary, because the parent has paid book value for its 100 percent ownership interest in the subsidiary.

The essence of what occurs when P buys the stock of S is that part of the parent's stockholders' equity is now invested in the subsidiary's assets.

---

[5] Both the FASB and the SEC allow and encourage consolidation when one company owns more than 50 percent of the stock in the other companies. For tax purposes, the parent must control at least 80 percent of the voting stock in order to file a consolidated federal income tax return.

**TABLE 15-3  Initial Consolidation Work Sheet**

| Account Titles | Parent | Sub-sidiary | Eliminations Dr. | Eliminations Cr. | Consoli-dation |
|---|---|---|---|---|---|
| Cash | 10,000 | 5,000 | | | 15,000 |
| Accounts receivable | 5,000 | 2,000 | | | 7,000 |
| Land and other assets | 25,000 | 8,000 | | | 33,000 |
| Investment in subsidiary | 10,000 | | | (a) 10,000 | |
| | 50,000 | 15,000 | | | 55,000 |
| Accounts payable | 20,000 | 5,000 | | | 25,000 |
| Capital stock—P | 20,000 | | | | 20,000 |
| Capital stock—S | | 7,000 | (a)  7,000 | | — |
| Retained earnings—P | 10,000 | | | | 10,000 |
| Retained earnings—S | | 3,000 | (a)  3,000 | | — |
| | 50,000 | 15,000 | 10,000 | 10,000 | 55,000 |

P's holding of the subsidiary stock is only a means through which P gains control over S's assets. Viewed from outside the family, the parent's investment account and the book equity attached to P's holdings have no significance. Only P's equity invested in S's assets matter.

In this simple case, then, the Investment in Subsidiary account on the parent's books and the Capital Stock and Retained Earnings accounts on the subsidiary's books need to be eliminated. The investment account as an asset represents an interest in the assets of the subsidiary. However, the subsidiary's assets will be counted as part of the consolidated assets, so it would be double-counting to also consider the investment as a separate asset. Consolidation in essence substitutes the individual net assets of the subsidiary ($5,000 Cash + $2,000 Accounts Receivable + $8,000 Other Assets − $5,000 Accounts Payable) for the single $10,000 balance in the investment account. Similarly, the double counting of assets is accompanied by a double counting of shareholders' equity. Stockholders' equity represents a source of financing. It is clear that both companies are financed only by the stockholders of the parent company. Inasmuch as the capital stock and retained earnings of the subsidiary do not represent relationships with those outside the family, they are eliminated.

**Minority Interest at Book Value.**  Assume now that the parent company purchases only 90 percent of the capital stock of the subsidiary, paying $9,000 for it. The other 10 percent, owned by someone else, is called the *minority interest*. Even though the subsidiary is not wholly owned, the parent company still controls its operation, and consolidation is therefore desirable if the companies are operationally related.

The eliminations are basically the same, except that only 90 percent of the capital stock and retained earnings of the subsidiary is eliminated. This is the only portion represented by intercompany holdings of stock. The remaining 10 percent is not eliminated, because it represents a source of financing from a group outside the family. Because we wish to include all assets under common control in the consolidation, the financial interest of the minority stockholders in these assets rightfully belongs in the consolidated statement.

For analytical purposes, the necessary eliminations can be presented in the form of journal entries. Accountants commonly cast eliminations in a form similar to adjusting entries to take advantage of the self-balancing debit-credit framework. These "elimination entries," however, are not recorded in any company's formal accounting records. Each corporation keeps its own set of books as a separate entity. The eliminations appear only in the accountant's working papers. For this fact situation, the elimination entry is:

```
Capital Stock—S  ...................................  6,300
Retained Earnings—S  ................................  2,700
    Investment in Subsidiary—P  .......................          9,000
    To eliminate the investment account and the internally held
    portion of the subsidiary's owners' equity.
```

The remaining $1,000 of equity interest ($700 capital stock and $300 retained earnings) in the subsidiary is segregated in a single figure called minority interest. For the consolidated entity, it represents a special portion of owners' equity apart from that of the parent stockholders. Often it appears as a separate category between the total liabilities and the consolidated stockholders' equity of the parent company stockholders.

**Investment at More or Less than Book Value.** Acquisition of a subsidiary's stock at book value is likely only when the parent company establishes a new corporation as its subsidiary. When the parent acquires a controlling interest in a going concern, the subsidiary's stock usually does not sell at book value.

How does the consolidated balance sheet appear if the parent company pays $10,800 for 90 percent of the stock in the subsidiary? The parent's investment account has a debit balance of $10,800; however, the subsidiary's books remain unchanged. The subsidiary does not record subsequent resales of its stock between investors. What the parent company has to pay at some later date to purchase shares from the original investors is recorded only in the parent's accounts.

To eliminate the investment account, a credit of $10,800 must be made, but debits of only $6,300 and $2,700 are required to eliminate 90 percent of the subsidiary's owners' equity. The difference of $1,800 represents additional asset value that has no reciprocal element in the subsidiary's underlying equities. If the parent company is willing to pay $10,800 for the stock it acquires, there is reason to believe that it is acquiring an interest in assets worth $10,800. An additional $1,800 of tangible and/or intangible asset value presumably is present in the transaction. When this excess cost of the stock investment to the parent company over its book value is recognized as a *consolidated* asset, the elimination entry shown below does balance.

| | | |
|---|---|---|
| Capital Stock—S | 6,300 | |
| Retained Earnings—S | 2,700 | |
| Excess Cost over Book Value | 1,800 | |
|     Investment in Subsidiary—P | | 10,800 |

This entry is elimination *(a)* on the work sheet in Table 15–4.

The excess may represent undervalued tangible and intangible assets of the subsidiary—for example, LIFO inventory, fully depreciated buildings, appreciated land values recorded at original cost, or the value of unrecorded patents. Alternately, part may represent a general unrecorded intangible asset, "goodwill."[6] Another possibility is that the $1,800 represents payment for benefits expected to arise in the future out of the closer coordination of the two firms—the synergistic advantages springing from the affiliation itself, not ones associated with the subsidiary as a separate entity.

Generally accepted accounting principles require that any portion of the excess attributable to specifically identifiable tangible or intangible assets be allocated to those asset accounts. The rest is treated as a general unidentified intangible asset. If in our example $700 reflects the parent's interest in appreciated land values and the rest represents unidentified intangibles, the reclassification entry *for consolidated statement purposes only* is:

| | | |
|---|---|---|
| Land | 700 | |
| Goodwill | 1,100 | |
|     Excess Cost over Book Value | | 1,800 |

This entry is elimination *(b)* on the work sheet in Table 15–4.

If the parent company pays less than book value, a credit to Excess Book Value over Investment Cost would be required. This item recognizes an overstatement in the subsidiary assets, as measured by what the parent is willing to pay to acquire an interest in them. Unless the specific overvalued assets can be identified, this amount must be treated as a pro rata reduction in the values assigned to the noncurrent assets.

**Consolidation in Subsequent Periods.** Now let us consider preparation of a consolidated position statement after the date of acquisition. The parent and subsidiary may operate as related units, but they maintain separate accounting records as individual entities. For our evolving example let us assume that during 1985 the parent company earns

---

[6] When the excess is attributable to understated subsidiary assets, the possibility exists of also revaluing the minority interest. If 90 percent of the subsidiary is worth $10,800, then 100 percent should be worth $12,000. Logic would suggest adding another $200 to the excess account and a credit of $200 to the minority interest. Although this procedure is sound, it is not done often in practice. The example follows general accounting practice in this matter.

**TABLE 15-4  Consolidation Work Sheet in Subsequent Period**

| Account Titles | Parent | Sub-sidiary | Eliminations Dr. | | Eliminations Cr. | | Consoli-dation |
|---|---|---|---|---|---|---|---|
| Cash | 16,000 | 6,000 | | | | | 22,000 |
| Accounts receivable | 6,000 | 3,000 | | | (e) | 1,500 | 7,500 |
| Land and other assets | 27,000 | 9,000 | (b) | 700 | (f) | 900 | 35,800 |
| Investment in S | 10,800 | — | | | (a) | 10,800 | — |
| Excess cost over book value | — | — | (a) | 1,800 | (b) | 1,800 | — |
| Goodwill | — | — | (b) | 1,100 | (d) | 50 | 1,050 |
| | 59,800 | 18,000 | | | | | 66,350 |
| Accounts payable | 19,800 | 4,000 | (e) | 1,500 | | | 22,300 |
| Capital stock—P | 20,000 | | | | | | 20,000 |
| Capital stock—S | | 7,000 | (a) | 6,300 | | | 700* |
| Retained earnings—P | 20,000 | | (d) | 50 | (c) | 3,600 | 22,650 |
| | | | (f) | 900 | | | |
| Retained earnings—S at acquisition | | 3,000 | (a) | 2,700 | | | 300* |
| Retained earnings—S since acquisition | | 4,000 | (c) | 3,600 | | | 400* |
| | 59,800 | 18,000 | | 18,650 | | 18,650 | 66,350 |

* Would be combined into a single figure for minority interest on the balance sheet.

$10,000 and the subsidiary earns $4,000 and that there are concomitant changes in assets and liabilities in each case. Now, at the end of 1985, another consolidated balance sheet is desired. Table 15-4 illustrates the procedures for this situation as well as for some other intercompany relationships discussed in the next section.

The basic eliminations—entries (a) and (b)—made at the date of acquisition remain the same as in the previous examples. They will be made each year that consolidated statements are prepared. However, the amount added to the subsidiary's retained earnings *since acquisition* must be treated differently in consolidation from the retained earnings on the date of acquisition. The latter is reflected in the investment account on the parent company's books and is eliminated as part of the normal consolidating process in elimination (a). Retained earnings since acquisition are not reflected in the parent's accounts and consequently should appear on the consolidated position statement—divided, of course, between majority (parent company) and minority interests. Ninety percent of the subsidiary's earnings since acquisition inures to the ultimate benefit of the parent company. The remaining 10 percent is the portion of earnings applicable to the minority stockholders. Elimination (c) apportions $3,600 of the increase in subsidiary retained earnings since acquisition to the consolidated retained earnings.

The amount initially recognized as excess cost over book value must be depreciated or amortized to the extent that it is assignable to assets with limited lives. If the excess can be attributed to plant assets, there will be an additional depreciation expense and an increase in accumulated depreciation recorded, although *only* on the *consolidated statements*. In our example, elimination *(b)* ascribes $700 of the extra asset value to land, a non-depreciable asset. On the other hand, the $1,100 allocated to intangibles must be amortized as an expense in the consolidation process according to *APB Opinion No. 17* on intangibles. The amortization entry *(d)* causes a reduction in the goodwill and in consolidated retained earnings. We have chosen an arbitrary amortization period of 22 years.

**Other Intercompany Relationships.** Two other common eliminations are illustrated in Table 15–4. One involves intercompany receivables and payables. The second is for the intercompany sale of assets which have not been resold to outsiders. Let us consider the first type. Whenever one company owes another company, on either a short- or long-term basis, and the two are to be consolidated, the resulting reciprocal asset and liability items should be eliminated. The receivable does not represent an asset to the consolidated entity; it is not an amount owed by an outsider. Neither does the payable represent an amount owed to an outside group. In our example we assume that as a result of intercompany transactions the subsidiary owes the parent company $1,500 on open account. Elimination *(e)* reduces the receivables and payables of the consolidated entity accordingly.

The second situation, that of intercompany sales of assets, is not quite so simple. If the assets are sold at cost, no problem arises. Similarly, if the assets are sold from one company to another and then resold to outsiders, no *balance sheet* problem arises, because the assets no longer appear in the accounts of any member of the consolidation. The problem occurs only when assets are sold by the parent to the subsidiary, or vice versa, at a gain or loss and the assets are not resold to outsiders.

If by consolidating we are to treat the two companies as if they were one, then no gain or loss should be recorded on the intercompany transfer of assets that are not resold to outsiders. For example, assume that the parent sells to the subsidiary for $5,000 land which cost the parent $4,100. From the parent's point of view as a separate entity, a profit of $900 is realized. From the subsidiary company's perspective, an asset which cost $5,000 is purchased. However, from the viewpoint of the consolidated entity the asset has simply gone from one member of the family to another. Consequently, elimination *(f)* is necessary to subtract $900 from other assets. The cost of the land to the consolidated entity is only $4,100 and will be overstated unless the elimination is made. The corresponding elimination is from the parent's retained earnings, where the gain or profit on the sale has been reflected. Consolidated companies can realize gains or losses only on sales to outsiders.

The net result of the consolidation process illustrated above is a balance sheet shown in Table 15–5. It reports the financial position of the

**TABLE 15–5  Consolidated Balance Sheet for Parent Company and Subsidiary as of December 31, 1985**

| Assets | | Equities | |
|---|---|---|---|
| Cash | $22,000 | Accounts Payable | $22,300 |
| Accounts receivable | 7,500 | Minority interest | 1,400 |
| Land and other assets | 35,800 | | |
| Goodwill, net of | | Stockholders' equity: | |
| amortization | 1,050 | Capital stock | 20,000 |
| | | Retained earnings | 22,650 |
| | $66,350 | | $66,350 |

two companies as if they were a single entity. When we think about this balance sheet, we realize that it differs little from that which would result if the companies had formally merged under the purchase approach. The assets of the subsidiary (acquired company) are restated to their fair market values in the consolidation process, and any excess purchase price (excess of the investment account over the value of the identifiable assets) is recorded as an intangible asset. Consolidated retained earnings include the retained earnings of the parent (acquiring company) and the parent's share of the subsidiary's retained earnings since acquisition—just as in the formal merger situation. The only difference is the recognition of minority interest when ownership is less than 100 percent.

**Consolidated Income Statement**

In the same manner that the balance sheet reports only the consolidated assets and equities, eliminating any which represent existing relationships between the individual companies, the consolidated income statement should report only revenues and expenses arising out of transactions with outsiders during the period. If there are no intercompany transactions— sales, dividend payments, interest payments, and so on—the consolidated procedure is a simple combination of the individual income statements.

**Intercompany Revenues and Expenses.**   Normally though, there are intercompany transactions that must be eliminated. The most frequent is the intercompany sale. Take the case of a wholly owned subsidiary which sells 100 percent of its product to the parent company. The parent resells to outsiders all that it buys from the subsidiary (leaving none in ending inventory) and makes no sales other than what it buys from the subsidiary and resells. Assume that the parent also rents a warehouse from the subsidiary for $5,000 a year. The individual income statements, the necessary eliminations, and the resultant consolidated income statement are presented in Table 15–6. Notice that the net income figures have been included along with the expenses so that we can utilize the self-balancing mechanism of the work sheet.

Elimination (*a*) corrects for the overstatement from a consolidated standpoint of revenue and expense related to the warehouse rental. Reve-

**TABLE 15–6  Consolidation Work Sheet for Simple Income Statement**

| Account Titles | Parent | Subsidiary | Eliminations Dr. | Eliminations Cr. | Consolidation |
|---|---|---|---|---|---|
| Sales | 100,000 | 80,000 | (b) 80,000 | | 100,000 |
| Other revenue | — | 5,000 | (a) 5,000 | | — |
| | 100,000 | 85,000 | | | 100,000 |
| Cost of sales | 80,000 | 50,000 | | (b) 80,000 | 50,000 |
| Other expenses | 10,000 | 20,000 | | (a) 5,000 | 25,000 |
| Net income | 10,000 | 15,000 | | | 25,000 |
| | 100,000 | 85,000 | 85,000 | 85,000 | 100,000 |

nues and expenses cannot arise from dealing with oneself. No adjustment is necessary in consolidated net income. The increase in parent income caused by elimination of $5,000 of its rent expense is offset by a decrease in subsidiary net income caused by elimination of its rent revenue of like amount.

The subsidiary sells goods costing $50,000 to the parent for $80,000. The parent, in turn, resells them to outside parties for $100,000. The subsidiary has a gross margin of $30,000 on the goods and the parent a gross margin of $20,000. If the two companies are one, sales to outsiders are only the $100,000 revenue recorded by the parent, cost of sales is only the $50,000 incurred by the subsidiary, and the consolidated gross margin is $50,000. In other words, in this case the income figures are stated correctly; because all goods were currently resold to outsiders, all profits have been realized. Only revenues and expenses are misstated for the consolidated entity. Elimination (b) removes the double-counting effect of the intercompany purchase and sale. From a consolidated viewpoint, these are merely interfirm transfers, not revenue and expense items.

**Incomplete Reselling.**  A more complicated case arises when we assume that the parent company does not resell all it buys from the subsidiary. In addition, let us relax our assumptions that the subsidiary makes no sales directly to outside customers and that the parent has no additional sales of its own. Suppose that a subsidiary, which is only 90 percent owned by a parent, sells only 50 percent of its products to the parent and the other 50 percent directly to outsiders. The parent resells 80 percent of what it purchased from the subsidiary, as well as some merchandise purchased from other sources. The resultant income statements for this example and the consolidation procedures are summarized in Table 15–7.

Before looking at the elimination entries, let us step back and ask intuitively what the consolidated sales and cost of goods sold should be. The total consolidated revenues are only $240,000 ($200,000 sold by

**TABLE 15-7  Consolidation Work Sheet for More Complex Income Statement**

| Account Titles | Parent | Subsidiary | Eliminations Dr. | Eliminations Cr. | Consolidated |
|---|---|---|---|---|---|
| Sales | 200,000 | 80,000 | (b) 40,000 | | 240,000 |
| Other revenue | — | 5,000 | (a) 5,000 | | — |
| | 200,000 | 85,000 | | | 240,000 |
| Cost of sales | 150,000 | 50,000 | (c) 3,000 | (b) 40,000 | 163,000 |
| Other expenses | 30,000 | 20,000 | | (a) 5,000 | 45,000 |
| Net income | 20,000 | 15,000 | | (d) 700 | |
| | | | | (c) 3,000 | 31,300 |
| Minority interest in income | — | — | (d) 700 | | 700 |
| | 200,000 | 85,000 | 48,700 | 48,700 | 240,000 |

the parent and $40,000 sold to outside parties directly by the subsidiary). Similarly, cost of sales for the *consolidated* entity is $163,000, consisting of three elements: (1) $118,000 cost of goods purchased by the parent from outsiders and sold to outsiders (the reported cost of sales of $150,000 on the parent's income statement includes $32,000 for goods bought from the subsidiary and resold); (2) $25,000 cost of goods purchased by the subsidiary and sold directly to outside parties; and (3) $20,000 cost of goods purchased by the subsidiary, transferred to the parent, and sold by it ($20,000 is 80 percent of the other $25,000 cost of sales reported by the subsidiary; the other $5,000 resides in the parent company's ending inventory).

The eliminations in Table 15–7 achieve these desired results. Elimination (a) is the same as in the previous example; it corrects the overlapping revenue and expense associated with rental of the warehouse. Item (b) eliminates 50 percent of the subsidiary's sales ($40,000) because they are not made to outsiders. This same $40,000 was included among the parent company's purchases and thus increased its cost of sales (Beginning Inventory + Purchases − Ending Inventory = Cost of Sales), although the purchases were not made from sources outside the consolidated family.

Item (c) eliminates the impact on income of the ending inventory of the parent which was acquired from the subsidiary. Twenty percent, or $8,000, of the parent's purchases from the subsidiary is on its books in the form of ending inventory. This inventory actually represents a consolidated cost of only $5,000 (the subsidiary's gross margin percentage is 37.5 percent). Likewise, $3,000 ($8,000 × 37.5 percent) of the subsidiary's gross margin is unrealized because the merchandise on which it was earned has not been resold to outsiders. This unrealized subsidiary profit is eliminated by part of (c).[7] The other part reflects the impact of the overstated ending inventory on cost of sales. Because the ending inventory is overstated by the $3,000 profit element, consolidated cost of sales is correspondingly understated.

After eliminations (a), (b), and (c) are allowed for, the consolidated net income is $32,000. However, that is *not* the net income attributable to the parent company shareholders for whom the consolidated income statement is prepared. The minority interest shares in some of that $32,000—specifically, its share of the subsidiary's net income realized from a consolidated view. The income of the subsidiary adjusted for unrealized portions arising from intercompany transactions is $7,000 ($15,000 − $5,000 rent revenue − $3,000 intercompany gain on unsold inventory). Elimination (d) merely segregates 10 percent of that as being applicable to the minority interest. The $700 is the minority's interest in the income of the consolidated entity, not its interest in the income of the legally separate subsidiary.

The figures in the last column of Table 15–7, when rearranged in proper form, constitute the consolidated income statement. Both the net income of the consolidated entity and the net income applicable to the stockholders of the parent company are shown; the minority's interest is treated as a distribution of income. In published financial statements the minority's interest is often buried among the expenses. In theory, though, it is the income of the *consolidated entity*, including the interests of all stockholders, which best measures overall results of operations and which should be related to total assets in the calculation of a return on investment.

The formal income statement appears in Table 15–8. Had the parent company paid more than book value for the subsidiary's stock, an addi-

**TABLE 15-8** Consolidated Income Statement for Parent Company and Subsidiary for the Year 1985

| | | |
|---|---:|---:|
| Sales | | $240,000 |
| Less: Expenses: | | |
| Cost of sales | $163,000 | |
| Other expenses | 45,000 | 208,000 |
| Consolidated income | | 32,000 |
| Less: Minority interest | | 700 |
| Net income | | $ 31,300 |

---

[7] The reader may recall that a corresponding elimination would be called for on the consolidated balance sheet, crediting Inventory for $3,000 for the overstatement of its true cost from the consolidated viewpoint and debiting the subsidiary's Retained Earnings account for the unrealized intercompany profit. Of course, balances in the Retained Earnings account on the position statement come from figures on income statements. Elimination (c) is simply the same one made to retained earnings on the position statement being made to profits on the income statement.

tional *consolidated* expense would be included to reflect amortization of the excess cost. This expense was discussed in connection with the consolidated balance sheet.

## INVESTMENTS IN UNCONSOLIDATED SUBSIDIARIES AND OTHER COMPANIES

Sometimes a parent company owns a substantial stock interest in another company yet does not consolidate that company. First, the investor corporation may lack majority control as in the case of a joint venture, 50 percent owned with another company. Second, the investee corporation's operating activities may have little in common with those of the parent, as in the case of a financial or real estate subsidiary of a parent involved principally in manufacturing or merchandising. The investor company reports these *unconsolidated* affiliates as an investment asset on the balance sheet and income from them as investment income on the income statement. The investor corporation must employ either the equity method or the cost method for recording its investment in the subsidiary and the subsequent earnings of the subsidiary.

Under the *cost method* the parent company's investment is recorded at cost, as is any other asset investment. The investment account remains at cost[8] despite any future increases or decreases in the underlying net assets of the subsidiary resulting from its periodic operations. Likewise, no income is recognized by the parent company unless and until the subsidiary declares and pays a dividend.

## Equity Method

Under the equity method the Investment in Subsidiary account reflects changes in the underlying investment resulting from subsidiary operations, and income or loss also appears on the books of the parent company in the period it is earned by the subsidiary. If the subsidiary operates profitably, the investment account is debited and income credited for the parent company's share of the net income of the subsidiary. The reverse procedure is followed if the subsidiary operates at a loss. A dividend represents a recovery of the investment.

**Entries under the Equity Method.** To illustrate the effect of the equity method on the amount and timing of income and on the valuation of the investment, we offer the following series of events and the journal entries they generate.

1. On January 1, 1985, the parent company acquires 60 percent (30,000 shares) of the 50,000 shares of common stock of a finance company for their book value of $8 per share.

---

[8] If there is a serious, permanent impairment of the investment, the cost basis is often modified to record a decrease in the investment account. If, for example, half of the subsidiary's assets were destroyed, the investment account would be written down. A similar adjustment would be made if the subsidiary were to pay a liquidating dividend.

Investment in Subsidiary ........................... 240,000
  Cash ........................................        240,000

2. During 1985 the subsidiary earns a net income of $50,000 and pays dividends of $20,000. Because the subsidiary is in a completely different line of business, the parent decides not to consolidate the accounts.

Investment in Subsidiary ........................... 30,000
  Equity in Investee Income ........................        30,000

Cash ............................................... 12,000
  Investment in Subsidiary .........................        12,000

3. Assume that the subsidiary operates at a loss of $10,000 in 1986 and pays no dividends, and in 1987 it earns $15,000 and pays $10,000 in dividends.

1986  Equity in Investee Loss ........................... 6,000
        Investment in Subsidiary ......................        6,000

1987  Investment in Subsidiary ........................... 9,000
        Equity in Investee Income ....................        9,000

      Cash ............................................ 6,000
        Investment in Subsidiary ......................        6,000

The Equity in Investee Income appears each year as a separate element of income (or as a deduction in the case of subsidiary losses) on the income statement of the parent company. The account is closed to Income Summary at the end of each year. The equity method recognizes total net earnings of $33,000 ($30,000 − $6,000 + $9,000) over the three-year period. The parent recognizes its share of the income in the period when the income is *earned* by the subsidiary. Dividends received from the subsidiary are credited to the Investment account. For example, inasmuch as $30,000 of subsidiary income in 1985 was recognized by the parent, it would be double-counting to include the $12,000 dividend distribution as additional income. Rather, because the dividends reduce the net assets of the subsidiary, they are shown as a reduction in the parent's investment account.

The Investment in Subsidiary account will appear among the parent's noncurrent assets. Its balance on December 31, 1987, is $255,000. The net increase of $15,000 from January 1, 1985, represents the parent's interest in subsidiary earnings which have *not* been distributed to the parent as dividends. A separate position statement of the subsidiary would show a retained earnings balance $25,000 larger than on January 1, 1985. Because the net assets of the subsidiary have increased $25,000, the investment account properly reflects the parent's 60 percent interest in this increase.

**Analysis of the Equity Method.** Two major arguments are advanced in support of the equity method. First, the results shown by the parent company bear a direct relationship to the periodic operations of the subsidiary. While still treating the investor and investee as separate companies, the equity method recognizes the existence of a significant economic relationship between them. The parent's financial statements, if drawn up according to the equity method, give a more useful picture of this relationship because they reflect the underlying changes in net assets occurring in the subsidiary. The investor's share of investee income is reported on the investor's income statement in the same period as it is reported by the investee.

Second, often the parent company can control or significantly influence the dividend policy of the subsidiary. The cost method, under which income is recorded only when dividends are received, enables the management of the parent company to exercise considerable influence over how much dividend revenue is recognized and when. By taking the subsidiary's earnings onto the parent company's books as earned and treating dividends simply as a reduction in the amount invested, the equity method avoids this possible pitfall. Thus it better satisfies the qualitative guidelines of timeliness and representational faithfulness.

The substance of both these arguments is that dividends poorly measure, in both timing and amount, the periodic benefit from many stock holdings. The equity method acknowledges that subsidiary earnings increase the amount of the parent's investment and that losses and dividends decrease it. The equity method simply extends the concepts of accrual accounting and revenue recognition to substantial intercompany investments. Recognition by the subsidiary of net income measured according to generally accepted accounting principles is deemed to meet satisfactorily the earning criterion for revenue recognition by the parent. Likewise, changes in the underlying net assets of the subsidiary constitute sufficient reliability of measurement. A specific exchange of assets (dividend payment) adds little to the fulfillment of the revenue recognition criteria.

Under the equity method the investor corporation simply recognizes as income its share of the net income of the investee corporation. The share is determined by the percentage of the total common shares held. Part of the total income is reflected as an increase in cash from dividend declaration; the rest is represented by an increase in the investment account. The effect is the carrying of the investment account at cost plus a proportionate share of the subsidiary's *undistributed* retained earnings since acquisition.

When the subsidiary is *wholly owned,* the equity method results in a "one-line consolidation" because it achieves the same consolidated net income and net asset position as if the subsidiary were consolidated. A single item, Equity in Investee Income, reflects the income of the subsidiary instead of a direct combining of its individual revenue and expense accounts with those of the parent company. Similarly, on the balance sheet a single asset, Investment in Subsidiary, appears in lieu of incorporation of the particular asset and liability accounts as with full consolidation.

The similarity between the equity method and full consolidation extends to the treatment of any excess cost over book value and to the elimination of intercompany gains and losses. If the parent company in our example were to pay $280,000 for the 30,000 shares in the financing company, the $40,000 difference between the cost of the investment and the underlying equity of the investee must be written off to expense over future periods. Likewise, the parent company may recognize on its books income from the subsidiary only after any unrealized profits made by the subsidiary from sales to the parent have been eliminated. These steps parallel the procedures used for preparing full consolidated statements.

## Authoritative Standards

The above reasoning caused the Accounting Principles Board to require the equity method for intercompany investments where the investor can significantly influence the operating or financial decisions of the investee. *Opinion No. 10* called for use of the equity method for unconsolidated domestic subsidiaries; *Opinion No. 18* extended the mandate to include *all* subsidiaries and some situations of less than majority ownership.[9]

The ability to exercise considerable influence may of course be evidenced by many factors (e.g., membership on boards of directors, material intercompany transactions) in addition to the amount of voting stock owned by the investor corporation. Nevertheless, the APB concluded that in the absence of compelling factors to the contrary, significant influence is presumed to exist with a 20 percent or more interest in the investee's voting common stock.

Conversely, if the investor corporation owns less than 20 percent of the voting stock, the presumption is that the cost method is the appropriate procedure.[10] The *cost method* assumes that the investor corporation, as only a minor owner of the investee, exercises little or no control over it. Revenue derived from the investment is recognized only in the periods when assets are actually distributed to the investor corporation in the form of dividends and only to the extent of the dividend amount.

Under the cost basis the investment account remains at the amount initially invested. Even though the investee operates profitably over the year, increasing its total net assets, no reflection of this increase is recorded in the investor company's accounts. The reasoning is that only through dividend receipt or sale of the stock can this increased value be realized.[11]

---

[9] AICPA, *APB Opinion No. 10*, "Omnibus Opinion—1966" (New York, December 1966); and AICPA, *APB Opinion No. 18*, "The Equity Method of Accounting for Investments in Common Stock" (New York, March 1971).

[10] See pages 261–264 in Chapter 7 for a discussion of conditions under which marketable equity securities are recorded at market values.

[11] Firms usually use the cost method for tax purposes even when they use the equity method for financial accounting purposes. The difference in the amounts reported for tax and for book purposes may cause tax allocation problems similar to those described in Chapter 13. *APB Opinion No. 23*, "Accounting for Income Taxes—Special Areas," allows this difference to be treated either as a permanent difference or as a timing difference, depending on the probability of the subsidiary earnings being permanently reinvested.

Unfortunately, the existence of relatively arbitrary distinctions between when the equity method must be used and when the cost method must be used has allowed a few companies to manipulate their earnings. For example, intercorporate holdings are kept below 20 percent when the investee is operating at a loss. When the latter begins to show consistent income, the investor increases the ownership to over the magic 20 percent. Examples also exist where investors have used the equity method when the intercompany holdings amounted to less than 10 percent, claiming that effective control exists based on other criteria.[12] Some analysts also object to the large gap that may exist between earnings reported under the equity method and the actual dividends received in cash. They claim that the equity method does not measure actual cash inflow. The prevailing argument, of course, is that, if the investor does control the dividend policy of the investee, then the equity method measures *potential* cash inflows quite accurately.

**Disclosures.** Because common stock investments carried on the equity basis may be significant to an evaluation of the investor corporation, *Opinion No. 18* also imposes some disclosure requirements. In notes or separate schedules, the investor corporation should indicate the percentage ownership of each investee, the accounting policies followed, and the excess, if any, of the Investment account balance over the underlying equity in net assets of the investee. Additionally, in some circumstances the market value of the investment, when available, must be disclosed. In other situations summarized information concerning assets, liabilities, and results of operations of unconsolidated subsidiaries or other investees are included in the notes.

**DISCUSSION OF THE ARMCO ANNUAL REPORT**

Many of the topics discussed in this chapter are relevant to an understanding of Armco, Inc. A careful study of the financial statements and related notes in the Appendix to Chapter 5 reveals a number of events related to intercompany ownership. In 1980 Armco acquired one company which was recorded as a pooling of interests and in 1981 one recorded as a purchase. These and other subsidiaries are combined with the parent company in a set of consolidated financial statements. However, one major subsidiary, the Armco Financial Services Group (AFSG), is not consolidated. It is reported as an unconsolidated investment under the equity method. The equity method is also applied to associated companies, while the cost method is used for other investments.

Each of these major areas is discussed in the following subsections.

---

[12] For a litany of problems and potential abuses of the equity method see Maria Latorraca and Stephen Gilbarg, "Equity Earnings"; and Richard Greene, "Equity Accounting Isn't Equitable," *Forbes*, March 31, 1980, pp. 100–105.

**Pooling and Purchase Acquisitions**

Note 1 provides information about major businesses acquired in 1980 and 1981. NN Corporation was acquired on December 1, 1980, in exchange for 9,424,048 shares of Armco common stock. Because the exchange involved only common stock for common stock, Armco was required by *APB Opinion No. 16* to record the acquisition as a pooling of interests. In accordance with pooling theory, no differentiation is made between operations before and after the merger. Past periods have been restated to reflect the combined activities of the firms. Consequently, the current report offers the financial statement reader no way to measure the impact of this event.

In 1981 Armco acquired Ladish Co. also through an exchange of shares. In this case, however, the exchange was not a single transaction; Armco was obligated to issue additional shares in 1982 under certain conditions. Consequently, the acquisition had to be accounted for as a purchase. We are told in Note 1 that the acquisition was valued at $286.5 million. This is approximately $40 a share in current market value.

The journal entry, in summarized form, to record the acquisition of Ladish was (in millions of dollars):

| | | |
|---|---|---|
| Cash and Marketable Securities | 57.3 | |
| Other Working Capital | 151.5 | |
| Property, Plant, and Equipment | 68.1 | |
| Investments | 10.7 | |
| Common Stock—$5 Par | | 35.8 |
| Additional Paid-In Capital | | 251.8 |

Information about the assets acquired can be found at various locations in the statement of changes in financial position on page 156. These asset amounts have been rounded so the total exceeds the $286.5 million value mentioned in Note 1. Often Goodwill is recognized in purchase situations; however, in this case we are told that the entire value exchanged was attributable to specifically identified assets.

In October 1982 Armco had to issue 1,825,504 additional shares. Additional Paid-In Capital was reduced and par value was increased, as shown in the entry below (per the 1982 Armco Annual Report).

| | | |
|---|---|---|
| Additional Paid-In Capital | 9.1 | |
| Common Stock—$5 par | | 9.1 |

No change occurred in the value of the original acquisition.

If an analyst studies the statement of changes in consolidated shareholders' equity carefully, he or she will notice that shares of common stock were issued in all three years in connection with businesses purchased. These acquisitions are minor ones in relation to the acquisition of NN Corporation and Ladish Co. Accordingly they are not described in detail. However, one result of the other acquisitions in 1981 was the increase in purchased goodwill.

**Consolidation**

The first accounting policy described by Armco in Note 1 is its consolidation policy. Basically, Armco consolidates all subsidiary companies in which it has a majority interest (51 percent or greater). The one exception is the Armco Financial Services Group. Although these subsidiaries are wholly owned, their operations are not similar to those of the consolidated group. Except for AFSG, Armco is a large manufacturing company making carbon steel, heavy industrial equipment for oil fields, and a variety of specialized manufactured products. The accounts of the insurance and finance leasing subsidiaries are very different from those of the manufacturing companies. A quick look at the former's financial statements in Note 2 clearly shows this. Most of the assets, liabilities, revenues, and expenses have no counterpart in typical manufacturing accounts. To combine AFSG through consolidation could significantly distort the components of the income statement and balance sheet.

The total net income would be unaffected, however. The AFSG subsidiaries are accounted for under the equity method. We will discuss this in the next section.

As we noted in this chapter, consolidated statements are prepared by the accountants on worksheets. All we see is the final results of the elimination entries.

Note 1 implies that some subsidiaries with minority interests have been included in the consolidation. However, Armco shows no separate minority interest among the equities on the balance sheet or minority interest deduction on the income statement. The reason is that these items are immaterial. The minority's interest in assets is included in Other Liabilities; the minority's interest in income is included in Sundry Other Expenses. These classifications, although in minor disagreement with the positions advocated in the chapter, are consistent with the viewpoint of Armco stockholders. From their viewpoint total minority equity is a liability and the portion of income applicable to the minority is to be subtracted much as an expense is deducted.

**Equity Method**

Armco uses the equity method for its wholly owned subsidiaries (the Armco Financial Services Group) and for all "associated" companies (those owned between 20 percent and 50 percent). This practice is in accordance with *Opinion No. 18*.

Sufficient detail is available with respect to AFSG to follow the entries made by Armco. First review the separate financial statements of AFSG shown in Note 2. The stockholder's equity of AFSG is equal to the amount Armco shows in its investment asset. Because AFSG is 100 percent owned and was started by Armco, the amount invested by Armco is always equal to the net book value of AFSG.

Because of the pooling of interests with NN Corporation in 1980, certain capital and dividend adjustments were made to the investment account in 1980. These are relatively unusual entries. Let us focus attention on the other events affecting the investment account in 1980 and 1981 (all numbers are in millions of dollars).

1. To record 100 percent of subsidiary earnings under the equity method in 1980.

```
Investment in AFSG ........................................  37.2
    Equity in Net Income of AFSG ...........................        37.2
```

The subsidiaries' retained earnings and net assets have increased this amount as a result of profitable operations. Accordingly, the parent company recognizes a similar increase in its assets and earnings.

2. To record additional investment by Armco in 1980.

```
Investment in AFSG ........................................  20.0
    Cash ...................................................        20.0
```

Armco purchased additional shares of capital stock of the subsidiaries. The subsidiaries would have debited Cash and credited Capital Stock.

3. To record dividends paid by AFSG group in 1980.

```
Cash ......................................................  40.0
    Investment in AFSG .....................................        40.0
```

The dividends received by Armco are not income, only a conversion of part of the investment into cash. The subsidiaries debited Retained Earnings and credited Cash. Their net assets declined; hence, Armco's investment also goes down.

4. To record increases in marketable equity securities for 1980.

```
Investment in AFSG ........................................   1.0
    Net Unrealized Gains on Marketable Equity
        Securities of AFSG .................................         1.0
```

Because the marketable equity securities of AFSG are increased to reflect their rise in market value, the stockholder's equity of AFSG increases. Because the stockholder's equity (net assets) of AFSG has risen, the carrying amount of Armco's investment is also increased. Armco cannot record this increase as income but must show it as a separate adjunct to its stockholders' equity. The net amount is $0.1 million at December 31, 1980, because it had been ($0.9) million at December 31, 1979.

5. To record 100 percent of subsidiary earnings under the equity method in 1981.

```
Investment in AFSG ........................................  30.3
    Equity in Net Income of AFSG ...........................        30.3
```

See the explanation for Entry 1. Notice the direct correspondence between AFSG's net income and Armco's recorded income.

6. To record additional investment by Armco in 1981.

```
Investment in AFSG ........................................   3.4
    Cash ...................................................         3.4
```

7. To record decreases in marketable equity securities for 1981.

Net Unrealized Losses on Marketable Equity
   Securities of AFSG ....................................... 9.7
     Investment in AFSG .................................... 9.7

See the explanation for Entry 4. In this case the marketable equity securities have declined in market value. The $9.7 million loss reduces the net unrealized balance sheet amount from $0.1 million to ($9.6) million. See also pages 268–270 of Chapter 7 for a complete discussion of *FASB Statement No. 12* and its impact on Armco.

8. To record translation adjustments applicable to foreign companies within AFSG.

Net Foreign Currency Translation Adjustments ................ 6.0
   Investment in AFSG .................................... 6.0

The financial services group includes some foreign companies. When the balance sheet accounts of these foreign subsidiaries were translated into dollars at current exchange rates, net assets were reduced. The corresponding reduction in stockholder's equity of AFSG (and hence in the investment asset and stockholders' equity of Armco) was recorded in a special contra equity account. See pages 586–587 in Chapter 16 for a discussion of this entry.

The equity method is also used for investments in associated companies. Here presumably the amounts are sufficiently immaterial that the detail is not reported separately. We are told in Note 1 that the equity in earnings of associated companies is recorded as a reduction in cost of products sold on the income statement. In relation to the over $5 billion of cost of products sold, any income buried there would not distort income statement relationships. On the other hand, the rationale for this treatment is not clear, and whether the amount is significant in relation to other figures reported on the income statement remains unanswered.

**SUMMARY**

We talk about three aspects of intercorporate relationships in this chapter. They all concern the accounting problems encountered when one firm acquires a substantial holding of the voting common stock of another company. If the acquired company is to be dissolved and merged, then is the acquisition a purchase or pooling of interests? If the subsidiary remains a separate legal entity, should a consolidated statement be prepared, or should the acquisition be reported as an investment in unconsolidated subsidiaries? Finally, if the investee remains unconsolidated, how and when can the equity method be employed to account for the intercorporate relationship?

The general conclusions reached are shown below:

| Condition | Accounting Treatment |
|---|---|
| 1. A and B are two independent companies that merge via an exchange of common stock for the purpose of mutually sharing risks and benefits. | 1. Merger recorded as a pooling of interests. |
| 2. A acquires the stock of B through issuance of its own securities, cash payments, or a combination of the two. B is dissolved and becomes an operating division of A. | 2. Merger recorded as a purchase. |
| 3. A acquires between 50 and 100 percent of the stock of B. B is retained as a separate legal entity but as an integral part of A's overall operations. | 3. Subsidiary included as part of a consolidated statement. |
| 4. A acquires between 50 and 100 percent of the stock of B. B is retained as a separate legal entity in a line of business very dissimilar from that of A. | 4. Unconsolidated subsidiary recorded under the equity method. |
| 5. A acquires between 20 and 50 percent of the stock of B. | 5. Investment recorded under the equity method. |
| 6. A acquires less than 20 percent of the stock of B. | 6. Investment recorded under the cost method. |

Procedures for each of these treatments are discussed and illustrated. Under pooling of interests, assets and equities are combined at book values. With a purchase, assets, including any intangible assets implicit in the transaction, are recorded at their fair market values, and only contributed capital accounts are credited. The procedures for consolidation are founded on one underlying objective—to present the situation as if the companies were a single company. They therefore entail the elimination of intercompany relationships and transactions. Finally, the equity method records increases and decreases in the investment account to correspond with changes in the underlying net assets of the investee. Income to the investor is recognized in the periods when it is earned by the investee.

To keep the discussion manageable, we deal with these treatments independently. They may, however, exist together. For example, a company may use the equity method for handling its investment account for a subsidiary and yet still consolidate the subsidiary. Such a practice would require some modification of the eliminations but would not change the underlying concepts or procedures of consolidated statements. Also, on a consolidated statement often other unconsolidated companies recorded under the equity and/or cost methods will appear. Similarly, we imply that purchase versus pooling is an issue concerning only legally merged subsidiaries. This is not always the case. Sometimes a firm will record the acquisition of another company as a pooling of interests but not actually liquidate it. Instead, the statements will show it as a consolidated subsidiary. The valuation of assets and the entries to stockholders' equity are the same, however, as for a merger, and the consolidated effect is the same as under a pooling with a legally merged subsidiary.

These problems and complexities all involve the *entity concept*. The direct consequences of the entity concept are clear—we treat the entity as separate and distinct from groups associated with it. However, the antecedent problems of defining what the accounting entity should be, deciding when it starts and ceases, and identifying the relevant entity in given situations must still be resolved.

## QUESTIONS AND PROBLEMS

**15–1.** Condensed balance sheets of Mammoth Company and Tiny Company as of January 1, 1985, are shown below:

|  | Mammoth | Tiny |
|---|---|---|
| *Assets* | | |
| Cash | $180,000 | $ 36,000 |
| Other assets | 450,000 | 84,000 |
| Total assets | $630,000 | $120,000 |
| *Equities* | | |
| Liabilities | $150,000 | $ 12,000 |
| Capital stock | 300,000 | 80,000 |
| Retained earnings | 180,000 | 28,000 |
| Total equities | $630,000 | $120,000 |

*Required:*

Assume that Mammoth acquires a controlling interest in Tiny under the conditions outlined below. Prepare a consolidated balance sheet for Mammoth and subsidiary as of January 1, 1985, for each alternative situation. Treat each situation independently.

a. Mammoth acquires all the capital stock of Tiny for a cash payment of $114,000 made to Tiny's stockholders.
b. Mammoth acquires 90 percent of the capital stock of Tiny for a cash payment of $90,000.
c. Mammoth acquires 80 percent of the capital stock of Tiny for a cash payment of $96,000.

**15–2.** The North Salem Company has supplied you with information regarding two investments which were made during 1985 as follows:[13]

1. On January 1, 1985, North Salem purchased for cash 40 percent of the 500,000 shares of voting common stock of the Yorktown Company for

---

[13] Material from the Uniform CPA Examinations copyright © (1976) by the American Institute of Certified Public Accountants, Inc., is adapted with permission.

$2,400,000 representing 40 percent of the stockholder's equity of Yorktown. Yorktown's net income for the year ended December 31, 1985, was $750,000. Yorktown paid dividends of $0.50 per share in 1985. North Salem exercised significant influence over the operating and financial policies of Yorktown.

2. On July 1, 1985, North Salem purchased for cash 15,000 shares representing 5 percent of the voting common stock of the Mahopac Company for $450,000. Mahopac's net income for the six months ended December 31, 1985, was $350,000 and for the year ended December 31, 1985, was $600,000. Mahopac paid dividends of $0.30 per share each quarter during 1985 to stockholders of record on the last day of each quarter.

*Required:*

a. As a result of these two investments, what should be the balance in the Investments account for North Salem at December 31, 1985. Show supporting computations in good form.

b. As a result of these two investments, what should be the income reported by North Salem for the year ended December 31, 1985? Show supporting computations in good form.

**15–3.** On September 30, 1984, Mississippi Corporation exchanged 10,000 shares of its $5 par common stock for all of the outstanding stock (50,000 shares, par value $2) of Missouri, Inc. At that time, Mississippi stock was selling at a market price of $40 per share. Missouri Corporation's stock was not widely traded. After the exchange of shares, Missouri was formally merged into Mississippi and became an operating division. Balance sheets drawn up for the two corporations *before* the merger showed the following:

| | Mississippi | Missouri |
|---|---|---|
| *Assets* | | |
| Total assets | $1,300,000 | $290,000 |
| *Equities* | | |
| Liabilities | $ 300,000 | $ 40,000 |
| Common stock—par | 200,000 | 100,000 |
| Common stock—excess over par | 300,000 | 70,000 |
| Retained earnings | 500,000 | 80,000 |
| Total equities | $1,300,000 | $290,000 |

Earnings for the two companies separately for 1984 were:

| | Mississippi | Missouri |
|---|---|---|
| January 1–September 30 | $ 140,000 | $ 30,000 |
| October 1–December 31 | 33,000 | 6,000 |
| | $ 173,000 | $ 36,000 |

The market value of Missouri's noncurrent assets are $60,000 above book value. These noncurrent assets have a remaining life of five years as of the date of the merger. Any goodwill recognized should be amortized over 10 years.

*Required:*

*a.* Fill in the blanks in the following table. Show calculations where necessary.

|  | If Acquisition Were Recorded as— | |
|---|---|---|
|  | *Purchase* | *Pooling of Interests* |
| Total assets, September 30 | | |
| Goodwill, September 30 | | |
| Retained earnings, September 30 | | |
| Common stock—par, September 30 | | |
| Common stock—excess over par, September 30 | | |
| Net income for 1984 | | |
| Goodwill, December 31 | | |
| Retained earnings, December 31 | | |

*b.* Which method do you think would have to be followed in the merger of Missouri, Inc., into Mississippi Corporation? Explain why.

**15–4.** The consolidation policies of five companies are given below. Each statement has been taken from notes to the firm's financial statements for the year indicated.

**Borg-Warner (12/31/81).** "The consolidated financial statements include all subsidiaries except those in Argentina and Brazil, which are carried at cost due to political and economic uncertainty, and the financial and protective services companies. Investments in the financial and protective services companies are carried at equity in underlying net assets. Investment in affiliated companies, at least 20 percent owned by Borg-Warner, and in the Hughes Tool Company, are carried at cost plus equity in undistributed earnings which generally approximates equity in underlying net assets."

**BF Goodrich (12/31/81).** "The financial statements include the accounts of the parent company and all active subsidiaries. BF Goodrich Finance Company (BFGFC) was included on the equity method until July 1981, when it was merged into the parent company. The pretax income of BFGFC is included as a reduction of interest expense and its provision for income taxes is included in the income tax provision. Intercompany accounts, transactions, and profits in inventories of consolidated subsidiaries have been eliminated upon consolidation."

**Marsh Supermarkets (4/2/83).** "The accounts of the Company and all wholly owned subsidiaries are included in the Consolidated Financial Statements. The Company's investment in Convenience Store Distributing Company is accounted for by the equity method for the reasons described in Note C. All significant intercompany accounts and transactions have been eliminated. The Company is principally involved in the retail food business and believes that it has but a single significant business segment."

**Note C.** "Convenience Store Distributing Company, a venture with King Kwik Minit Markets, Inc., operates a distribution facility to service convenience food stores. Marsh contributed 75 percent of the partnership's initial capitalization and is entitled to receive 70 percent of any distribution of accumulated earnings. Marsh shares equally with its partner certain executive powers relative to the management and control of the partnership and, accordingly, Marsh's share of the operating results of the partnership is included in the Consolidated Financial Statements by the equity method of accounting."

RCA (12/31/82). "The consolidated financial statements include the accounts of RCA Corporation and its subsidiaries, except for those engaged in finance-related activities, principally C. I. T. Financial Corporation (C. I. T.) and RCA Credit Corporation (RCA Credit). These subsidiaries, and companies in which RCA has a 20 percent to 50 percent interest, are accounted for on the equity basis."

Sears, Roebuck & Co. (12/31/82). "The consolidated financial statements include the accounts of Sears, Roebuck & Co. and all domestic and significant international companies in which the company has more than a 50 percent equity ownership, except those engaged in manufacturing." (Consolidation includes Sears Roebuck Acceptance Corporation and Sears Overseas Finance N. V.)

*Required:*

a. Evaluate the policy of Borg-Warner to exclude from consolidation subsidiaries in Argentina and Brazil and subsidiaries in the financial and protective services areas. The equity method is used for the latter. Should it also be used for the subsidiaries in Argentina and Brazil?

b. Why might BF Goodrich Company choose to discontinue the use of the equity method for its finance subsidiary? Evaluate the treatment on the consolidated income statement given to income from the finance company.

c. Given that Marsh Supermarkets owns 75 percent of Convenience Store Distributing Company and the two firms operate in similar lines of business, is it appropriate for Marsh to exclude it from consolidation?

d. Contrast the treatment given to the wholly owned finance subsidiaries by RCA and Sears. What impact does the different treatment have on the income statement and balance sheet? Would the total income and total assets of each company be different if the alternative policy were adopted?

e. Borg-Warner states that its investments in affiliated companies "are carried at *cost plus equity in undistributed earnings* which generally approximates *equity in underlying net assets.*" The other companies refer to the use of the *"equity method."* How, if at all, do these three bases of reporting differ? Explain.

15–5. The following represent the ledger account balances of Able Company and its subsidiary, the Baker Company, as of December 31, 1984 (in thousands of dollars):

| | Able | Baker |
|---|---|---|
| Cash | $ 80 | $ 12 |
| Accounts receivable | 116 | 36 |
| Inventories | 140 | 100 |
| Investment in Baker stock | 200 | — |
| Land | 90 | 44 |
| Plant | 300 | 120 |
| Accumulated depreciation | (80) | (26) |
| | $846 | $286 |
| | | |
| Accounts payable | $164 | $ 48 |
| Capital stock | 500 | 160 |
| Retained earnings | 182 | 78 |
| | $846 | $286 |

Able Company acquired 90 percent of the stock of the Baker Company on January 1, 1984, for $200,000 cash. The owners' equity accounts of Baker on that date were: capital stock, $160,000; retained earnings, $40,000.

During the year, the Baker Company sold merchandise costing $12,000 to the Able Company for $18,000. The merchandise was still in the latter's inventory on December 31, 1984. Able Company still owed Baker Company $8,000 in connection with this purchase.

Also, during the year, Able Company sold to Baker Company a piece of land for $10,000 cash which had been carried on the books of Able at $14,000.

*Required:*

a. Prepare a consolidated position statement in good form for the two companies. Assume any excess cost is attributable to intangible assets with a useful life of 10 years.

b. If Able Company had used the equity method of accounting for its investment in Baker, what entries would have been made on Able's books during 1984? How would the consolidation process and the consolidated balance sheet differ?

**15–6.** On January 1, 1984, the Kirkwood Corporation acquired 30 percent of the outstanding stock of Parkway, a newly organized corporation, for a cost of $900,000.

On January 1, 1986, Kirkwood invested another $300,000 for an additional 10 percent of Parkway. The following table gives the results of Parkway's operations in the years 1984–86:

|  | Net Income Reported | Dividends Paid |
|---|---|---|
| 1984 | $180,000 | $150,000 |
| 1985 | 360,000 | 270,000 |
| 1986 | 330,000 | 240,000 |

*Required:*

a. Prepare journal entries to record the original investment and subsequent events, assuming that the equity method of accounting for unconsolidated subsidiaries is used. Assume that any excess cost is to be amortized over 20 years.

b. How much income would Kirkwood have recognized each year if the cost method of recording investments in other companies had been employed?

c. On December 31, 1985, Kirkwood describes its Investment account as being recorded at the underlying book value or equity in the subsidiary's assets. Show that this is true. Is the same description appropriate on December 31, 1986? Explain.

**15–7.** Eastern Inc. owns controlling interest in the common stock of two companies—Albion Company and Murray Inc.[14] Eastern purchased 90 percent of the common

---

[14] Adapted from Examination for the Certificate in Management Accounting, June 1977.

stock of Albion Company for $108 million on January 1, 1982, when Albion's common stock and retained earnings had balances of $100 million and $20 million, respectively. A 60 percent ownership in the common stock of Murray Inc. was acquired on July 1, 1984, for $108 million when Murray's common stock and retained earnings had book balances of $100 million and $80 million, respectively. Both of these investments are recorded at cost in the investment accounts on Eastern's books.

On January 1, 1983, Murray Inc. issued 50,000, $1,000 par value bonds at par (total value, $50 million). The bonds are due January 1, 1993. Interest on the bonds is payable annually on December 31 at the rate of 12 percent. Eastern purchased 10,000 of Murray's bonds on the open market for a total purchase price of $10 million on January 1, 1986.

During 1986 Eastern purchased $20,000 of merchandise from Albion Company. A total of $3,000 of this merchandise still remains in Eastern's inventory on December 31, 1986. Albion has recorded a profit of $1,000 on the merchandise in Eastern's inventory.

All three companies report on a calendar-year basis. Presented below are selected accounts from each of the companies' adjusted trial balances as of December 31, 1986.

Partial Adjusted Trial Balance
December 31, 1986
($000)

|  | Eastern Inc. | Albion Inc. | Murray Inc. |
| --- | --- | --- | --- |
| Inventory (12/31/86) | $ 10,000 | $ 5,000 | $ 15,000 |
| Investment in Albion stock | 108,000 | | |
| Investment in Murray stock | 108,000 | | |
| Investment in Murray bonds | 10,000 | | |
| Bonds payable | | 5,000 | 50,000 |
| Common stock | 200,000 | 100,000 | 100,000 |
| Retained earnings | 120,000 | 50,000 | 150,000 |
| Net operating income | 30,000 | 50,000 | 80,000 |
| Dividend income | 10,500 | | |
| Interest income | 1,200 | | |
| Dividends declared on common stock | | 5,000 | 10,000 |
| Interest expense | | | 6,000 |

*Required:*
a. Calculate the consolidated net income of Eastern Inc. for the year ended December 31, 1986. Show all supporting calculations.
b. Determine the minority interest which would be presented on Eastern Inc.'s consolidated balance sheet as of December 31, 1986. Show all supporting calculations.

**15–8.** The accountant for Rotten Lumber Company has prepared the consolidated work sheet for Rotten Lumber and its subsidiary, Warped Wood, Inc., as of December 31, 1985. It is shown below without any explanations (amounts in thousands of dollars). Rotten Lumber purchased a controlling interest in Warped Wood on January 1, 1985.

| Accounts | Rotten Lumber | Warped Wood | Eliminations Dr. | | Eliminations Cr. | | Consolidated |
|---|---|---|---|---|---|---|---|
| Current assets | 57.0 | 45.0 | | | | | 102.0 |
| Investment in bonds | 8.0 | — | | | (c) | 8.0 | — |
| Investment in subsidiary (cost) | 85.0 | — | | | (a) | 85.0 | — |
| Loans to subsidiary | 10.0 | — | | | (e) | 10.0 | — |
| Land | 23.0 | 13.0 | | | | | 36.0 |
| Plant and equipment | 250.0 | 150.0 | (d) | 16.0 | (d) | 10.0 | 406.0 |
| Accumulated depreciation | (113.0) | (45.0) | | | (d) | 9.0 | (167.0) |
| Excess cost over book value | — | — | (a) | 4.0 | (b) | .4 | 3.6 |
| | 320.0 | 163.0 | | | | | 380.6 |
| | | | | | | | |
| Current liabilities | 47.0 | 36.0 | | | | | 83.0 |
| Bonds payable | — | 12.0 | (c) | 6.0 | | | 6.0 |
| Advances from parent | — | 10.0 | (e) | 10.0 | | | — |
| Capital stock—R | 195.0 | — | | | | | 195.0 |
| Capital stock—W | — | 70.0 | (a) | 63.0 | | | 7.0* |
| Retained earnings—R | 78.0 | — | {(b) | .4 | (f) | 10.8 | 86.4 |
| | | | {(c) | 2.0 | | | |
| Retained earnings—W—at acquisition | — | 20.0 | (a) | 18.0 | | | 2.0* |
| Retained earnings—W—since acquisition | — | 15.0 | {(d) | 3.0 | | | 1.2* |
| | | | {(f) | 10.8 | | | |
| | 320.0 | 163.0 | | 133.2 | | 133.2 | 380.6 |

\* Minority interest.

*Required:*

Answer the following questions related to this consolidation:

a. What percentage of Warped Wood's stock was acquired by Rotten Lumber? How do you know?

b. What period of amortization is being used for any excess cost paid by Rotten Lumber?

c. What is the nature of the intercompany transaction that caused the need for elimination *(c)*? Explain the reason for the debit to retained earnings of $2,000.

d. What is the nature of the intercompany transaction that caused the need for elimination *(d)*? Explain the reason for the debit to retained earnings of $3,000.

e. What is the nature of the intercompany transaction that caused the need for elimination *(e)*?

f. What complications in preparing consolidated balance sheets and income statements will arise in future periods because of the transactions referred to in parts *(c)* and *(d)*? Be explicit in describing the impact of each transaction on future consolidated statements.

**15–9.** At the end of 1984, Alpha Company began negotiations to acquire the net assets and business of Beta Corporation. Condensed balance sheets of the two companies as of December 31, 1984, contain the following accounts:

| Assets | Alpha | Beta |
|---|---|---|
| Cash | $ 180,000 | $ 70,000 |
| Inventory—at FIFO cost | 330,000 | 150,000 |
| Buildings and equipment | 720,000 | 450,000 |
| Total assets | $1,230,000 | $670,000 |

*Equities*

| | | |
|---|---:|---:|
| Current liabilities . . . . . . . . . . . . . . . | $ 200,000 | $145,000 |
| Common stock—$10 par . . . . . . . . | 300,000 | — |
| Common stock—$1 par . . . . . . . . . | — | 100,000 |
| Paid-in capital . . . . . . . . . . . . . . . . . | 500,000 | 200,000 |
| Retained earnings . . . . . . . . . . . . . | 230,000 | 225,000 |
| Total equities . . . . . . . . . . . . . . . . . | $1,230,000 | $670,000 |

Alpha is interested in how the proposed merger would affect its financial statements. Alpha is planning to offer as of January 1, 1985, 12,000 of its previously unissued stock to the stockholders of Beta in exchange for the 100,000 shares of Beta stock outstanding. The market price of Alpha Company shares is $55 per share. Management of Alpha Company attributes any value implicit in the offer in excess of the book values of Beta's net assets to the following assets: (1) inventory understated by $25,000; (2) additional value of equipment, $80,000; and (3) any remainder to goodwill.

Income statement data for the year 1984 for each of the companies appear below:

| | Alpha | Beta |
|---|---:|---:|
| Sales . . . . . . . . . . . . . . . . . . . . . . . . . | $1,350,000 | $720,000 |
| Expenses: | | |
| Cost of goods sold . . . . . . . . . . . . . . | 730,000 | 380,000 |
| Depreciation . . . . . . . . . . . . . . . . . | 72,000 | 35,000 |
| Selling and general . . . . . . . . . . . . . | 420,000 | 250,000 |
| Income taxes . . . . . . . . . . . . . . . . . | 51,000 | 22,000 |
| Total expenses . . . . . . . . . . . . . . | 1,273,000 | 687,000 |
| Net income . . . . . . . . . . . . . . . . . . . | $ 77,000 | $ 33,000 |

Management expects that revenues and expenses for both companies in 1985 will be the same as in 1984 except as affected by the accounting for the merger. If recognized, the additional value of the equipment would be depreciated over a remaining life of 10 years. Goodwill, if recorded, would be amortized over 20 years.

*Required:*

a. Prepare the journal entry Alpha would make to record its investment, on the assumption that the acquisition is to be treated (1) as a purchase and (2) as a pooling of interests.

b. Prepare a balance sheet as of January 1, 1985, on the assumption that the acquisition is treated (1) as a purchase and (2) as a pooling of interests.

c. Prepare a projected income statement for 1985 using the data from 1984 and the assumption that the acquisition is treated (1) as a purchase and (2) as a pooling of interests.

d. Which procedure for recording the merger would have to be followed? How would your answer differ if Alpha were to offer only 8,000 of its shares plus $220,000 for the shares of Beta?

**15–10.** The Big Company owned 80 percent of the stock of the Little Company. During the year Little Company, the subsidiary, sold $120,000 of goods to the parent. These goods had cost Little Company $90,000. The year-end inventories of the Big Company still included 20 percent of the goods it purchased during the year from Little Company.

In addition, Big Company provided managerial services for Little Company, for which it received $3,000. Little Company also paid $1,000 of interest on a note owed to Big Company. On December 31, Big sold some surplus equipment to Little for $20,000. The equipment had a book value of $14,000 to Big.

Income statements, in summary form, for the two companies are given below (in thousands of dollars). Prepare a consolidated income statement in good form.

|  | Big | Little |
|---|---|---|
| Sales | $600 | $200 |
| Interest revenue | 15 | — |
| Gains and other income | 12 | 4 |
|  | 627 | 204 |
| Cost of goods sold | 370 | 140 |
| Other expenses | 183 | 24 |
| Interest charges | 8 | 5 |
|  | 561 | 169 |
| Net income | $ 66 | $ 35 |

**15–11.** Condensed financial information for Parenco and Subsico is given below:

Balance Sheet
As of December 31, 1984

|  | Parenco | Subsico |
|---|---|---|
| *Assets* | | |
| Current assets | $ 70,000 | $ 50,000 |
| Investment in Subsico, at cost | 172,000 | — |
| Other assets | 417,000 | 174,000 |
| Total assets | $659,000 | $224,000 |
| *Equities* | | |
| Liabilities | $130,000 | $ 29,000 |
| Common stock | 350,000 | 150,000 |
| Retained earnings | 179,000 | 45,000 |
| Total equities | $659,000 | $224,000 |

Income Statement
For the Year 1984

|  | Parenco | Subsico |
|---|---|---|
| Sales | $550,000 | $195,000 |
| Dividend revenue from subsidiary | 10,000 | — |
| Total | 560,000 | 195,000 |
| Cost of goods sold | 307,500 | 127,500 |
| Other expenses | 201,500 | 43,500 |
| Total | 509,000 | 171,000 |
| Net income | 51,000 | 24,000 |
| Dividends | (25,000) | (12,500) |
| Increase in retained earnings | $ 26,000 | $ 11,500 |

Parenco had acquired an 80 percent interest in Subsico on January 1, *1983*. At that time, Subsico had common stock of $150,000 and retained earnings of $20,000. The excess of cost over book value is attributable to limited-life intangible assets. Management authorized amortization of these costs over a period of eight years on the consolidated statements.

During 1984, Parenco sold products costing $20,000 to Subsico for $30,000. Half of these were resold during 1984 by Subsico to its customers; the rest is in Subsico's inventory as of December 31, 1984.

*Required:*

a. Prepare a consolidated balance sheet as of December 31, 1984.
b. Prepare a consolidated income statement for the year 1984.
c. The controller of Parenco objects to the consolidation, stating, "Parenco does not own the assets of Subsico nor are we legally responsible for Subsico's liabilities; consolidated statements mask the legal realities." Comment on this objection.

**15–12.** Halen Corporation and Hardy Company have been considering the possibility of a merger of their businesses. As of May 1, 1985, the condensed balance sheets of the two firms were as follows:

| | Halen | Hardy |
|---|---|---|
| *Assets* | | |
| Total assets .................... | $803,700 | $201,200 |
| *Equities* | | |
| Liabilities ....................... | $ 82,900 | $ 56,200 |
| Common stock, $1 par ............ | 100,000 | 50,000 |
| Excess over par ................. | 390,000 | 27,000 |
| Retained earnings ............... | 230,800 | 68,000 |
| Total equities ................... | $803,700 | $201,200 |

The market price of Halen Corporation common stock is very close to $9 a share; Hardy Company common stock is traded at $4.50 per share. An appraisal of the specifically identifiable assets of each company indicates their fair market values to be $875,000 for Halen and $250,000 for Hardy.

Two plans are under consideration. One calls for Halen Corporation to acquire the 50,000 outstanding shares of Hardy Company. Halen would pay $25,000 in cash, issue 200 shares of a new $100 par preferred stock carrying a market dividend rate of 12 percent, and issue 20,000 shares of its own common stock. Hardy Company would be liquidated as a separate legal entity and formally merged into Halen Corporation. The other plan calls for a new company called Halenhardy Corporation to be chartered. Its authorized capital would consist of 50,000 shares of $5 par value common stock. The new corporation would issue its shares to the stockholders of the two existing corporations in exchange for their stock. The exchange ratios would be 1 new share for each 5 shares of Halen and 1 new share for each 10 shares of Hardy. The two existing companies would be dissolved and their assets and liabilities transferred to the new corporation.

*Required:*

a. Under the first plan, which method would have to be used to record the merger? Prepare a combined position statement for Halen Corporation under this plan.
b. Under the second plan, which method would have to be used to record the merger? Prepare a combined position statement for Halenhardy Corporation under this plan.

c. An accounting professor at a nearby university has suggested that if the second plan is followed, the assets of both entities should be revalued and Halenhardy Corporation would start off afresh as a new economic entity. Prepare a position statement under this approach and evaluate the merits of this suggestion.

15–13. The following data relate to Lord Company and its two subsidiaries, Vassel Corporation and Serf, Inc. Lord and Vassel function together as an integral operating unit. Serf, Inc., operates in a completely unrelated line of business.

Balance Sheets
As of December 31, 1985

| | Lord | Vassel | Serf |
|---|---|---|---|
| *Assets* | | | |
| Cash | $ 13,400 | $ 8,400 | $ 2,800 |
| Accounts receivable | 156,500 | 44,200 | 7,000 |
| Notes receivable | 68,000 | — | — |
| Inventory | 102,100 | 86,500 | — |
| Investment in Vassel, at cost | 128,000 | — | — |
| Investment in Serf | 100,000 | — | — |
| Property, plant, and equipment | 127,500 | 64,800 | 100,300 |
| Total assets | $695,500 | $203,900 | $110,100 |
| *Equities* | | | |
| Accounts payable | $ 85,000 | $ 24,200 | $ 3,500 |
| Notes payable | — | 20,000 | 35,000 |
| Capital stock | 380,000 | 100,000 | 40,000 |
| Retained earnings | 230,500 | 59,700 | 31,600 |
| Total equities | $695,500 | $203,900 | $110,100 |

Income Statements
For the Year 1985

| | Lord | Vassel | Serf |
|---|---|---|---|
| Revenues: | | | |
| Sales | $615,000 | $450,000 | — |
| Interest revenue | 5,300 | — | $ 8,000 |
| Other revenue | 14,700 | — | 23,700 |
| Total revenues | 635,000 | 450,000 | 31,700 |
| Expenses: | | | |
| Cost of goods sold | 308,000 | 229,800 | — |
| Operating expenses | 223,400 | 196,900 | 17,200 |
| Interest | 1,500 | 2,000 | 4,900 |
| Total expenses | 532,900 | 428,700 | 22,100 |
| Net income | 102,100 | 21,300 | 9,600 |
| Dividends paid | 45,000 | — | 8,000 |
| Increase in retained earnings | 57,100 | $ 21,300 | $ 1,600 |

*Additional information:*

1. Lord Company owns 70 percent of the outstanding common stock of Vassel Corporation. These shares were acquired on January 1, *1984,* when Vassel's stockholders' equity consisted of $100,000 of capital stock and $20,000 of retained earnings. Of the excess cost, $24,000 is assignable to depreciable plant assets with a useful life of 12 years. The rest is attributable to goodwill and will be amortized over 20 years.

2. Lord Company owns 100 percent of the stock of Serf, Inc. The stock was acquired on January 1, *1985,* at a cost of $100,000. Any excess cost is attributable to unrecognized goodwill of Serf, Inc. The goodwill has a limited life of 30 years. The dividends paid by Serf, Inc., have been included in the other revenue of Lord.

3. During 1985 Vassel Corporation purchased inventory from Lord Company for $85,000. The inventory cost Lord $60,000. The December 31, 1985, inventory of Vassel includes 20 percent of this merchandise.

4. The beginning inventory of Vassel Corporation on January 1, 1985, also included inventory purchased from Lord during 1984 at an intercompany profit of $5,300.

5. The $20,000 note payable of Vassel corporation is owed to Lord Company. During 1985 interest of $2,000 was paid on the note.

Management wishes to issue a set of consolidated statements for Lord Company and Vassel. Serf, Inc., is to be treated as an unconsolidated subsidiary.

*Required:*

*a.* Prepare entries on the books of Lord Company to account for Serf, Inc., on an equity basis rather than on a cost basis.

*b.* Prepare a consolidated income statement and consolidated balance sheet for Lord Company and Vassel Corporation.

*c.* The equity method is sometimes described as a "one-line consolidation." Explain and illustrate with Serf, Inc., the basis for this statement.

15–14. The following descriptions of mergers and acquisitions are taken from five annual reports of actual companies.

**Adams-Russell Company, Inc. (9/30/81).** "On July 9, 1981, the Company acquired all of the outstanding stock of Micro-Tel Corporation in exchange for 442,700 shares of the Company's common stock. On September 29, 1981, the Company also acquired all of the outstanding stock of Microwave Products, Inc., in exchange for 192,100 shares of the Company's common stock and $327,500 in cash paid to shareholders representing less than 10 percent of the outstanding shares of Microwave Products. Both acquisitions were accounted for as poolings of interests and, accordingly, the 1979 and 1980 financial statements have been restated to include the accounts of the acquired companies."

**Bucyrus-Erie Company (12/31/81).** "Effective September 30, 1981, the Company acquired Western Gear Corporation, a manufacturer of aerospace systems and components and industrial machinery and equipment for the power transmission, petroleum, marine, metals, and transportation markets.

The acquisition has been accounted for as a purchase and, accordingly, the purchase price was allocated to assets and liabilities acquired based upon their fair market value at date of acquisition. Allocation of the purchase price is summarized as follows:

| | |
|---|---:|
| Working capital | $ 70,243,000 |
| Property, plant, and equipment | 71,454,000 |
| Intangible assets (including goodwill of $49,814,000) | 77,260,000 |
| Notes payable and other long-term liabilities | (35,786,000) |
| Total purchase price | $183,171,000 |

The Company's consolidated financial statements for the year ended December 31, 1981, include the results of operations of Western Gear Corporation after September 30, 1981. Western Gear Corporation's net shipments and earnings for the three-month period ended December 31, 1981, were $60,969,000 and $1,375,000, respectively.

Pro forma results of operations which follow assume that the purchase had occurred at the beginning of each year presented."

\* \* \* \* \*

"Pro forma financial information presented is not necessarily indicative either of results of operations that would have occurred had the merger been effective on January 1, 1980, or of future results of operations of the combined companies. Pro forma information presented is based on the assumption that the purchase price would have been the same at the beginning of the periods."

**Burroughs Corporation (12/31/81).** "Effective December 3, 1981, Memorex Corporation (Memorex) was merged into a wholly owned subsidiary of the Company pursuant to a Plan and Agreement of Reorganization as of October 30, 1981. The total consideration paid by the Company of $117 million for the outstanding equity of Memorex consisted of $103.1 million in cash and 475,583 shares of Burroughs common stock valued at $13.9 million.

The acquisition is being accounted for as a purchase. The underlying net assets of Memorex as reported in its financial statements exceed the cost of the Company's investment. This excess will be allocated to Memorex assets acquired and liabilities assumed, principally rental equipment and property, plant, and equipment, following completion of an appraisal and an in-depth study. The allocation of the excess will result in lower future costs, principally depreciation and amortization of Memorex assets. The liabilities (including long-term debt at fair value) and current assets of Memorex have been combined with those of Burroughs and included in the 1981 consolidated balance sheet. Pending completion of the aforementioned appraisal and in-depth study, noncurrent assets and the portion of the excess not allocated to debt have been included in Other Assets."

**Freeport-McMoRan Inc. (12/31/81).** "On April 7, 1981, stockholders of Freeport Minerals Company (Freeport) and of McMoRan Oil & Gas Co. (McMoRan) approved a combination of the two companies pursuant to a Plan and Agreement of Reorganization under which Freeport and McMoRan became subsidiaries of Freeport-McMoRan Inc., a new corporation. Each share of Freeport common stock has been converted into 1.795 shares of Freeport-McMoRan common stock, and each share of McMoRan common stock has been converted into one share of Freeport-McMoRan common stock.

The financial statements of Freeport-McMoRan Inc. and Consolidated Subsidiaries (the Company) give effect to the reorganization on a pooling-of-interests basis, the conversion of common stock, and the use of the full cost method of accounting for all oil and gas activities (described in Note 2).

The pooling-of-interests basis essentially adds together the financial information for the combining companies (offsetting any transactions between the two companies) as though they always had been subsidiaries of the Company."

**NCR Corporation (12/31/81).** "On November 7, 1980, NCR completed the acquisition of Applied Digital Data Systems, Inc. This acquisition was accounted for as a purchase, and operations from the date of acquisition have been included in the Consolidated Statement of Income and Retained Earnings. The excess of acquisition cost ($60,964,000) over the net assets acquired, amounting to $20,525,000, is being amortized on a straight-line basis over 20 years.

On June 13, 1979, NCR completed the acquisition of Comten, Inc. This acquisition was accounted for as a purchase, and operations from the date of acquisition have been included in the Consolidated Statement of Income and Retained Earnings. The excess of acquisition cost ($141,486,000) over the net assets acquired, amounting to $118,086,000, is being amortized on a straight-line basis over 40 years."

*Required:*

a. Adams-Russell Company acquired Microwave Products, Inc., through a partial payment of cash and the issuance of common stock. However, the acquisition was treated as a pooling of interests. Is this contrary to GAAP? Explain.

b. Adams-Russell Company and Freeport-McMoRan both used the pooling of interest method. Describe how their implementation of the procedure differed, however. Do you believe that pooling was appropriate in both cases?

c. How does the recording of the acquisition of Western Gear Corporation by Bucyrus-Erie Company differ from recording of the two mergers by Adams-Russell?

d. Why are the operations of Western Gear included for only the last quarter, while those of Adam-Russell's acquisitions are included for 1979, 1980, and 1981? Explain Bucyrus-Erie's comment on the usefulness of the pro forma disclosures. Do you agree?

e. Of the 475,583 shares issued by Burroughs in connection with the acquisition of Memorex, 337,583 were treasury shares that had a cost of $10,736,000. The rest were newly issued shares of common stock with a par value of $5. Reconstruct in summary form the entry made by Burroughs to record the acquisition of Memorex.

f. Why does Burroughs claim that the allocation to be done after a detailed appraisal will result in lower future costs? Would it be appropriate for Burroughs to record a "gain on acquisition" equal to the "excess" being described?

g. Why do NCR and Bucyrus-Erie have substantial increases in intangible assets such as "goodwill" and "excess of acquisition cost" when the other companies do not? Is it appropriate for NCR to use two different periods (20 years and 40 years) to amortize the excess acquisition costs of the two different acquisitions? Explain.

**15–15.** The creation of a meaningful method for recording investments in other companies has not been an easy matter in financial accounting. The following examples taken from actual company situations illustrate some of the problems.

**Amerada Hess Corporation.** The noncurrent section of its balance sheet lists an investment called "Stock of The Louisiana Land and Exploration Company—at cost, $2,262,000." The notes to the financial statements contain the following explanation:

At December 31, 1981, the Corporation owned 2,000,000 shares of the capital stock of The Louisiana Land and Exploration Company. The market value of the 2,000,000 shares aggregated $58,750,000 ($29.375 per share) at December 31, 1981, and $99,250,000 ($49.625 per share) at December 31, 1980.

**Curtiss-Wright Corporation.** Curtiss-Wright owned 14.3 percent of the common stock of Kennecott Copper Corporation, a company which is six times larger than Curtiss-Wright. In 1979 Curtiss-Wright changed from the cost method to the equity method. The company justified the change on the grounds that three Curtiss-Wright directors serve on the board of directors of Kennecott and another four directors serve by the mutual consent of Curtiss-Wright and the majority owners of Kennecott. Having this degree of representation on a board of 18 is enough influence to overcome the usual 20 percent investment necessary for the equity method. The auditors of Curtiss-Wright agreed.

**McLouth Steel Corporation.** McLouth Steel Corporation owned 19.87 percent of Jewell Coal & Coke Co. It included that portion of Jewell's income in its financial statements from 1974 to 1978. The SEC brought suit against McLouth for incorrectly using the equity method, because it did not exercise significant influence over Jewell. The Commission noted that McLouth had tried and failed to get representation on Jewell's Board of Directors and that Jewell had taken numerous actions contrary to McLouth's wishes.

**Jos. Schlitz Brewing Company.** Jos. Schlitz owns 28 percent and 30 percent respectively of two Spanish companies. It received dividend income of $278,000 in 1981 from these companies. The 1981 annual report contained the following note:

> The cost method of accounting is used for the company's Spanish investments because the company does not have the ability to exercise significant influence in matters relating to financial policy and operating control.

> Unaudited information for the year 1981 indicates that La Cruz del Campo and Henninger Espanola were profitable. Accounting practices followed in Spain do not conform to United States principles in some respects.

**Sun Company, Inc.** Among the noncurrent investments in its 1981 annual report Sun Company shows the following (amounts in millions of dollars):

|  | December 31 | |
| --- | --- | --- |
|  | 1981 | 1980 |
| Investments and advances to unconsolidated subsidiaries and affiliated companies | $526 | $458 |
| Investment in Becton, Dickinson, and Company, at cost | 320 | 317 |

Information contained in the notes described these investments in greater detail.

> Sun's net share of the earnings of unconsolidated subsidiaries and affiliated companies included in other income, amounted to $59, $50, and $51 million in the years ended December 31, 1981, 1980, and 1979, respectively. Dividends received from such unconsolidated subsidiaries and affiliated companies amounted to $19, $9, and $18 million in 1981, 1980, and 1979,

respectively. Earnings employed in the business at December 31, 1981, include $163 million of undistributed earnings of unconsolidated subsidiaries and affiliated companies.

Sun's investment in Becton consists of approximately 6,485,000 shares of Becton's common stock at December 31, 1981, representing a 32 percent interest. These shares are held in escrow by a Trustee for exchange under the terms of exchangeable debentures issued by Sun in 1981. Under the terms of the debentures, Sun has relinquished its voting rights with respect to the escrowed shares.

*Required:*

a. Compare the cost per share of stock in Louisiana Land and Exploration Company with its market value. Does this discrepancy suggest a material distortion in the financial statements of Amerada Hess? Are its stockholders being deceived? Would the equity method solve the reporting problem?

b. Evaluate the appropriateness of the equity method for use by Curtiss-Wright. Do you agree with the auditors?

c. Teledyne Corporation owns 32 percent of Curtiss-Wright. If Teledyne uses the equity method, does this mean that 4.58 percent (32% × 14.3%) of Kennecott's income is reflected on Teledyne's books also? Is this appropriate?

d. Evaluate the controversy between the SEC and McLouth Steel. Is the SEC being too picky? If McLouth increased its holding from 19.87 percent to 20 percent, would this make a difference?

e. Evaluate the reasons given by Jos. Schlitz Brewing Company and Sun Company for not using the equity method for subsidiaries in which they clearly own more than 20 percent.

f. Reconstruct the entries made by Sun Company in 1979, 1980, and 1981 related to its investment in unconsolidated subsidiaries and affiliated companies? What other factors could account for the rest of the change in the investment asset account?

# CHAPTER 16

# DISCLOSURE ISSUES IN FINANCIAL REPORTING

As discussed in Chapter 1, completeness in disclosure is a major condition for the qualitative guideline of reliability. According to this concept, accounting reports should disclose fully and fairly the information they purport to represent. Thus, reporting is closely intertwined with accounting theory. As a consequence, most of the authoritative guidelines for financial accounting—APB Opinions, FASB Statements, and SEC Regulations—include disclosure recommendations or requirements. A number of these have been considered at various points throughout the preceding chapters.

In this chapter we examine some important problems of classification and presentation that are not covered elsewhere. The first section discusses the reporting of special changes in retained earnings. Some of these items were mentioned in Chapter 5. However, a discussion of the detailed standards for their presentation on the financial statements was deferred until now. The second section deals with the subject of foreign currency translation. As companies, large and small, become more international in scope, this topic becomes increasingly important. The third section analyzes some extant and proposed recommendations for expanding the usefulness of the data base available to investors. Earnings per share, segment reporting, interim financial statements, and presentation of forecast data are the major topics discussed. The chapter concludes with a discussion of the role of the auditor in the achievement of full and fair disclosure and an examination of Armco's reporting disclosures.

**REPORTING OF SPECIAL ITEMS**

The income statement is the most prominent of the financial statements, and net income probably is the single most important number reported.

Users look to the income statement and the net income figure for a measure of how the firm has performed in the period. A problem arises, however, in that during the period other events happen which cause changes in owners' equity—changes beyond those resulting from revenues, expenses, and dividends. Recurring but nonoperating items, such as interest expense and gains and losses on normal disposals of plant assets, have already been covered in Chapter 5.

In this section we discuss the following additional special items causing increases and decreases in retained earnings:

1. *Extraordinary items*—material events that are characterized by *both* their unusual nature *and* their infrequent occurrence.
2. *Discontinued operations*—the discontinuance and disposal of an entire segment of a business.
3. *Prior period adjustments*—very rare events and corrections of errors that require direct adjustment to retained earnings and retroactive restatement of net income.
4. *Changes in accounting principles*—substitution of one current generally accepted accounting principle (or method of applying it) for another.
5. *Changes in estimates*—modification or adjustment in an accounting estimate as new information becomes available.

Note that the names of these items have rather specific definitions that have evolved over time as authoritative opinions have been issued and revised. Users of accounting data should be careful not to substitute meanings taken from ordinary usage of the terms. Inasmuch as each of these special items may have related tax effects, the proper treatment of the tax impact of these items is presented at the end of this section.

How these changes in retained earnings during a period are presented can have a profound effect on the income statement and net income, so accounting policy makers have spent significant time on these issues. The subsections to follow describe and illustrate the GAAP that have evolved practically to deal with each of these items.

**Extraordinary Items**

Under an all-inclusive approach to income statement reporting, net income basically reflects all items of profit or loss recognized during the period. (The only exception is for prior period adjustments such as corrections of errors, defined and illustrated in a later section.) However, the results of certain transactions called *extraordinary items* are to be shown in a separate section of the income statement as a distinct element of net income for the period. To qualify as an extraordinary item, an event must be *both* unusual in nature and nonrecurring.[1] Consequently, common write-downs of receivables, inventories, or intangibles would not qualify,

---

[1] AICPA, *APB Opinion No. 30,* "Reporting the Results of Operations" (New York, June 1973), par. 20.

nor would such nonoperating events as the disposal of plant assets, the effect of strikes, or the impact of major currency devaluations. The only events that would be classified as extraordinary under these opinions are major casualties, government expropriations, or prohibitions under newly enacted laws.[2] Additionally, under separate standards the realization of a tax loss carry-forward (Chapter 13) and a gain or loss on the retirement of a bond issue (Chapter 10) also are reported as extraordinary items.

If an event qualifies as an extraordinary item, the income statement would highlight it as illustrated below:

| | |
|---|---:|
| Income before extraordinary items | $400,000 |
| Extraordinary item: Earthquake loss of $130,000, | |
| minus applicable income taxes of $50,000 | 80,000 |
| Net income | $320,000 |

Most nonoperating, abnormal, *or* infrequent items will be included in income *before* extraordinary items; only items meeting *all* of these characteristics are now considered extraordinary. Clearly, the APB intended to restrict severely the number of extraordinary items. It succeeded, as a survey of 1981 income statements of 600 large corporations revealed only 53 which listed extraordinary items.[3]

In one sense, the strict criteria for the determination of extraordinary items may have improved the quality of financial reporting by eliminating some past potential for manipulation. When firms were allowed maximum discretion in the classification decision, observers detected a tendency for more losses than gains to be categorized as extraordinary. To many accountants, however, the APB may have overreacted. Items which are unusual but happen to be of a recurring nature can no longer appear as extraordinary. Although *Opinion No. 30* requires that such gains and losses be reported as a separate component of income *before* extraordinary items, they are more likely to be overlooked by analysts when treated this way than when categorized as extraordinary. More than ever, the analyst must closely examine the nature of income before extraordinary items to ferret out unusual but recurring items.

## Discontinued Operations

Although recurring gains and losses on the disposal of individual plant assets are included in income before extraordinary items, the disposal of an entire segment of a business is treated differently. When a significant component of the business—a subsidiary, a division, a separate major line of business—is sold or abandoned, there is likely to be a material impact

---

[2] The environment in which the entity operates must be considered when assessing whether an item is unusual in nature and infrequent in occurrence. For example, a tornado loss is more likely to be viewed as extraordinary in Maine or Oregon than it is in Kansas or Oklahoma.

[3] AICPA, *Accounting Trends & Techniques,* 1982 (New York, 1982) p. 284.

on the financial statements. Consequently, the FASB requires special accounting treatment for discontinued operations, akin to that for extraordinary items. Discontinued operations must be reported in a separate section of the income statement, after income from continuing operations but before extraordinary items.

The income statement disclosure consists of two parts—the periodic income or loss from operating the segment until it was discontinued and the gain or loss on its disposal. For example, the lower portion of the 1981 income statement for Squibb Corporation appeared as shown in Table 16–1. A separate footnote which describes the businesses sold by Squibb is also presented.

**TABLE 16–1   Partial Comparative Income Statement of Squibb Corporation and Related Footnote, Showing Reporting of Discontinued Operations ($000)**

|  | Year Ended December 31 | | |
| --- | --- | --- | --- |
|  | 1981 | 1980 | 1979 |
| Income from continuing businesses ............ | $ 41,098 | $103,373 | $ 89,478 |
| Income from businesses sold (net of tax) ................................. | 12,181 | 24,371 | 34,244 |
| Gain (loss) on sale of businesses (net of tax) ................................. | 58,068 | (318) | — |
| Income before extraordinary charge ............ | $111,347 | $127,426 | $123,722 |

Note: On December 31, 1981, the Company sold the business of Life Savers, Inc., its confectionary products segment, resulting in a gain of $58,068,000 (net of taxes on income of $24,575,000), or $1.16 per share. Pursuant to plans adopted in 1979, the Company sold Dobbs Houses, Inc., Table Talk, Inc., and certain related operations in mid-1980, which resulted in a nominal loss of one cent per share, or $318,000 (net of income tax benefits of $1,712,000).

The first component listed under discontinued operations (businesses sold) represents the functioning of the disposed units up until the date (measurement date) that management committed itself to a formal plan of disposition. The disposed units were profitable for Squibb Corporation for the years of disposal and the earlier years presented for comparative purposes. The next item disclosed pertains to the gain or loss related to the disposal of the businesses. It includes (1) any difference between book value and net realizable value of the assets and liabilities involved, (2) any estimated costs directly associated with the disposal, and (3) any further operating results after the measurement date. The latter could become significant if the plan of disposal were to be carried out over an extended period of time.

As shown in Table 16–1, the gain or loss on the sale of businesses is not considered to be an extraordinary item, although it is listed as a separate component for the interested reader. Squibb Corporation's net income from businesses sold is wisely segregated from the income from continuing operations. The analyst desiring to use the 1981 income figure as a basis for forecasts of future earnings needs the $41,098,000 number, which is not distorted by the $12,181,000 earned from businesses which Squibb no longer owns.

**Prior Period Adjustments and Correction of Errors**

This category of unusual events is rarely encountered. Prior period adjustments are not reported on the income statement. Instead they are added to or subtracted from the opening balance of retained earnings on the separate statement of retained earnings.

*FASB Statement No. 16* specifies that *only* the following events can now appropriately be considered as prior period adjustments:[4]

1. Correction of an error in the financial statements of a prior period.
2. Adjustments that result from realization of income tax benefits of preacquisition operating loss carry-forwards of purchased subsidiaries.

Inasmuch as the second item is too specialized and technical for this book, we now focus exclusively on correction of errors.

*APB Opinion No. 20,* issued in 1971, set forth the initial requirement that corrections of past errors be treated as direct adjustments to retained earnings. The following list illustrates some of the items that fit the classification of correction of errors:[5]

1. *Recognition of oversights*—each year a firm has failed to record depreciation expense on a new machine acquired in 1983.
2. *Correction of mathematical errors*—a company recorded its liability for salaries payable at $120,000 instead of $210,000 in 1984.
3. *Change from the use of an unacceptable accounting principle to one that is acceptable*—a firm has used the cost method for recording its investment in a wholly owned subsidiary and switches to the correct equity method.

Of course, the concept of a subsequent correction of a past error does not apply to adjustments of immaterial or recurring items. Also, the topics discussed in the next two sections, changes from one acceptable accounting principle to another acceptable principle and changes in accounting estimates resulting from new information, are not considered corrections of errors.

The correcting entry for each of the situations qualifying as a correction of errors involves an adjustment to an asset or liability and a corresponding increase or decrease in retained earnings. For example, if the unrecorded depreciation in Item 1 amounted to $250,000 on the new plant since 1983, the correcting entry would be:

```
Correction of Prior Period Unrecorded Depreciation  ....  250,000
     Accumulated Depreciation .......................            250,000
```

---

[4] FASB, *Statement of Financial Accounting Standards No. 16,* "Prior Period Adjustments" (Stamford, Conn., June 1977), par. 11.

[5] AICPA, *APB Opinion No. 20,* "Accounting Changes" (New York, July 1971), par. 13.

The $250,000 debit would be recorded on the statement of retained earnings as a deduction from the balance at the beginning of the year. If comparative statements covering the period of the error are presented, they should be restated in the correct amounts.

## Changes in Accounting Principles

Most financial statements are prepared in accordance with generally accepted accounting principles. However, we have seen numerous examples of alternative procedures that are considered equally acceptable and instances of the failure of GAAP to come to grips with economic realities. Consequently, anyone who analyzes and compares financial statements without comprehending the accounting principles employed runs a risk of error and misinterpretation. Analysts may be unable to change the statements to a comparable set of principles, but at least they should be able to understand the general effects that alternative procedures may have on the statements.

Present-day standards of disclosure require that the policies followed in most of the areas where alternatives exist be indicated to the reader of the statement. *Opinion No. 22* requires that companies identify and describe their significant accounting policies as an integral part of the financial statements, preferably in a separate section preceding the notes or in the first note to the statements.[6] Examples of required disclosures include consolidation policy; depreciation and amortization methods; inventory pricing; revenue recognition practices associated with construction, leasing, or franchising operations; and any other practices that are unusual or peculiar to a particular industry.

The reporting standard of consistency implies that the principles, once selected, will remain the same from period to period. An obvious extension of the disclosure guidelines leads to the requirement that any changes in accounting principle must also be disclosed. *Opinion No. 20* contains that requirement. It goes further, however, and allows changes in accounting principles only if the new principle is preferable to the old. The firm assumes the burden not only of disclosing the change in accounting principle but also of justifying the change. Changes that fall under this requirement include changes in methods of inventory valuation (e.g., from FIFO to LIFO), those in methods of depreciation (e.g., from straight-line to sum-of-the-years' digits), those in methods of revenue recognition (e.g., from percentage of completion to completed contract), and other similar changes. A change in principle refers to principles currently being used and does not include the adoption of a principle for new or substantially different transactions from those previously occurring.

In 1975 the SEC attempted to shift the burden for justifying the accounting change to the firm's auditor. In a very controversial ruling *(ASR No. 177)*, the SEC required that auditors state whether or not in

---

6 AICPA, *APB Opinion No. 22*, "Disclosure of Accounting Policies" (New York, April 1972), par. 15.

their judgment a client's change in accounting principles was *preferable* under the circumstances. Furthermore, the Commission indicated that auditing firms should not accept changes in principles in opposite directions by different clients under similar circumstances. In response to implementation problems and intense opposition from the accounting profession, the SEC revised its preferability rules in *Staff Accounting Bulletin No. 14,* issued in 1977. It restored the fundamental importance of the *client's* judgment and plans in gauging the acceptability of the accounting change.

Disclosure is not the only concern when accounting principles are changed. How should the impact be reported on the financial statements? In general, a change in accounting principle necessitates an adjustment to some asset or liability account and to retained earnings for the effect of the change on prior years' income. Should we record that change as we do a correction of error, that is, as a direct adjustment to the beginning balance of retained earnings with retroactive restatement of all comparative income statements? Alternatively, should we show the effect on retained earnings as a special item on the income statement similar to an extraordinary item?

In *Opinion No. 20* the Accounting Principles Board generally opted for the second alternative. Aware of "the potential dilution of public confidence in financial statements resulting from restating financial statements of prior periods," the APB ruled that *most* changes should be recognized by inclusion of the cumulative effect of the change in the net income of the period of change.[7]

Several specific accounting changes that often are of substantial magnitude (e.g., a change *from* the LIFO method of inventory costing) must, however, be handled retroactively by restatement of the financial statements of prior periods.[8] Apparently the APB's concern was that a substantial cumulative effect, if placed on one income statement, could swamp all other statement items and distort the "bottom line." Also, restatement of past financial statements is sometimes required or permitted for accounting changes mandated by official pronouncements.

For most accounting changes the cumulative effect of the change is reported on the income statement between the captions "extraordinary items" and "net income." Although it is not an extraordinary item, the cumulative effect is reported in a similar manner. A partial income statement of Marshall Field & Company and a related footnote appear in Table 16–2. They illustrate the correct reporting for a cumulative-effect accounting change.

As Table 16–2 shows, Marshall Field speeded up the recognition of

---

[7] *APB Opinion No. 20,* par. 18.

[8] Others include (1) a change in the method of accounting for long-term construction contracts and (2) a change to or from the "full cost" method of accounting for natural resources.

**TABLE 16-2  Partial Comparative Income Statement of Marshall Field & Company and Related Footnote, Showing Reporting of a Change in Accounting Principle**

| | Fiscal Year Ended | | |
| --- | --- | --- | --- |
| | Jan. 30, 1982 | Jan. 31, 1981 | Feb. 2, 1980 |
| Income before cumulative effect of a change in accounting principle ...................................... | $22,602,865 | $20,686,038 | $18,939,967 |
| Cumulative effect on prior years of a change in method of accounting for investment tax credit (note 1e) ......................................... | 6,588,047 | — | — |
| Net income ......................................... | $29,190,912 | $20,686,038 | $18,939,967 |
| Income per common share: | | | |
| Before cumulative effect of a change in accounting principle ................................................ | $1.86 | $1.93 | $1.85 |
| Cumulative effect on prior years of change in method of accounting for investment tax credit (note 1e) ......................................... | .54 | — | — |
| Net income per common share ............................ | $2.40 | $1.93 | $1.85 |
| Pro forma based on revised method of accounting for investment tax credit, applied retroactively | | | |
| Net income ......................................... | $22,602,865 | $21,629,779 | $20,021,881 |
| Net income per common share ........................... | $1.86 | $2.02 | $1.95 |

Note 1e: Investment Tax Credit

The Company adopted, as of February 1, 1981, the flow-through method of accounting for investment tax credits. Prior to this change, the credits were amortized, using the deferred method, over the estimated useful lives of the assets. Credits are now recognized in the year the assets are placed in service. Flow-through is the prevalent method in the retail industry and provides an offset to the start-up expenses of new stores.

As a result of this change, income before the cumulative effect of the change on prior years increased by $1,370,000, or 11 cents per share. If the flow-through method had been used in 1980 and 1979, net income would have been increased by $944,000 (9 cents per share) and $1,082,000 (10 cents per share), respectively.

the investment tax credit by switching from the deferred to the flow-through method, increasing net income and per share earnings. The net income for the fiscal year ended January 30, 1982, was affected in two ways by the accounting change. It increased the income *before* cumulative effect by $1,370,000 and also produced a cumulative effect of $6,588,047. The smaller amount represents the increase in fiscal 1982's income, and the larger number signifies the effect which the accounting change had on the net incomes of years *prior* to fiscal 1982.

Notice that additional disclosures are also shown on the face of the income statement. The net income and earnings per share for all periods are presented on a pro forma basis, that is, as if the newly adopted flow-through method had been applied during the prior periods. Although past financial statements are not completely restated for this type of accounting change, the summary data on net income and earnings per share *are* restated. The pro forma information constitutes more meaningful trend data than do the three-year figures for income before cumulative effect. A comparison of the fiscal 1980 earnings of $18,939,967 and the fiscal 1982 earnings of $22,602,865 is only as accurate as any comparison of apples (deferred method) and oranges (flow-through method). The pro forma net income numbers were derived after accounting methods were held constant and, accordingly, are much superior for trend analysis. For example, the $20,021,881 figure for fiscal 1980 earnings *can* be meaningfully compared with fiscal 1982 income of $22,602,865, because *both* of these numbers assume use of the flow-through method.

## Changes in Accounting Estimates

Financial accounting is rife with estimates. To implement the matching concept, the accountant must estimate the useful lives and residual values of depreciable assets, uncollectible percentages for receivables, recoverable mineral reserves for assets subject to depletion, costs of future services for warranties, various actuarial factors for pensions, and many other figures. In most cases, the need for these judgments stems from the very essence of the accounting process. Therefore, changes in estimates are also a natural consequence of the accounting process. Once adopted, accounting procedures should not be perpetuated if the estimates underlying the procedures are no longer valid. What happens if an accounting estimate is found to be wrong as new information becomes available?

In the preceding sections we have illustrated two major ways of recording and reporting unusual items. One calls for a direct adjustment to retained earnings and a retroactive restatement of the comparative income statements, as in the case of corrections of errors. The second calls for a special charge in the current period's income statement for the cumulative effect of the item, as in the case of changes in accounting principle and extraordinary items. Which of these methods is appropriate for reporting the impact on income (retained earnings) of changes in accounting estimates? In *Opinion No. 20* the Accounting Principles Board ruled that neither approach is acceptable for changes in estimates. Rather, they must be handled *prospectively,* that is, as adjustments to the expenses or revenues of the current and/or future periods. No correction of past periods or cumulative catch-up provision is allowed.

**Illustration of Change in Depreciation Estimate.**   As an example of a change in accounting estimate, let us assume that the original useful life of 10 years for a piece of equipment is being revised to 16 years. The equipment cost $96,000, has an expected residual value of zero, and is being depreciated on a straight-line basis. Near the end of the seventh year, *before* adjusting entries are made, the firm realizes that the equipment will last nine more years. During the first six years annual depreciation of $9,600 has been charged, and the balance in the Allowance for Depreciation account currently stands at $57,600. Based on the revised estimate of useful life, the depreciation expense should have been $6,000 each year ($96,000/16), and the balance, at the end of Year 6 in Allowance for Depreciation should be $36,000 rather than $57,600.

*Opinion No. 20* requires that future depreciation charges be revised to adjust for the overdepreciation in the past. The $38,400 unrecovered depreciable cost (book value) is expensed over the 10 remaining years of useful life (including the current seventh year) at the rate of $3,840 per year. An annual depreciation charge of $3,840 in each of the next 10 years will fully depreciate the asset by the end of the revised useful life.[9]

The conceptual rationale for this requirement rests on the belief that estimation of future events is an inherent part of the process of preparing periodic financial statements. Therefore, the adjustments arising from changes in estimates constitute reactions to new events or experience and not corrections of past mistakes. The practical justifications for the requirement are its simplicity, its required use for tax purposes, and its avoidance of any addition to the number of "unusual" items shown in the income statement. Continuous revision of asset lives would be unnecessarily time-consuming and would undermine the concept of a systematic depreciation policy.

Opponents of this requirement dub it the "compensating-error" approach. They argue that the goal of communicating financial information as accurately as possible is not achieved by a deficient depreciation charge in future years to compensate for an excess charged in the past or vice versa. Opponents would prefer an alternative set of entries at the end of the seventh year:

```
Allowance for Depreciation ...........................  21,600
    Adjustment of Depreciation .......................          21,600
    To correct the accounts for overstatement of deprecia-
    tion charges in prior years due to underestimation of useful
    life ($57,600 − $36,000).

Depreciation Expense ...............................   6,000
    Allowance for Depreciation .......................           6,000
    To record depreciation for the seventh year based
    on revised estimate of useful life.
```

The Adjustment of Depreciation account could appear as a special addition on the current period's income statement. Unfortunately, the APB ruled out this alternative.

As one looks back over the plethora of authoritative standards surrounding the reporting of special items, they seem highly technical and often conflicting. However, some general tendencies are evident. First, an all-inclusive approach to income statement reporting is favored for events occurring in the current period. Second, operations are not to be defined too narrowly or artificially. Third, completed periods generally are to be treated as history.

**Intraperiod Tax Allocation**

In Chapter 13 we discussed tax allocation problems arising from timing differences and from carry-backs and carry-forwards. In both cases the issue is determination of the appropriate tax charge for an accounting period. A separate tax allocation question is the proper *reporting* of the tax

---

[9] The only requirement for disclosure is a note in the year of change indicating the effect on income and earnings per share for a material change in estimate or for one that affects several periods.

charge when special items exist in addition to operating income. As we have seen, according to the guidelines of *APB Opinions No. 20 and No. 30,* the income statement includes all these items except corrections of past errors, which are reported on a separate statement of retained earnings. On the income statement itself, extraordinary items, discontinued operations, and changes in accounting principles are segregated. However, all of these items affect the determination of the taxable income and tax charge for the period. *Intraperiod* tax allocation is the division of the total amount of income taxes for the period among sections of the income statement or between the income statement and the statement of retained earnings.

For instance, it would be quite misleading to report a favorable adjustment of prior years' income in the statement of retained earnings but to include the increased taxes that have to be paid because of the item as part of the tax expense on the income statement. If a special item is shown on a separate statement of retained earnings, then the tax charge or saving related to it should be shown there also. In effect, then, this procedure divides the tax charge for the period between the income statement and the retained earnings statement. The portion shown on the former would be the tax applicable to the income shown there. The additional tax (in the case of a favorable adjustment) or the estimated tax reduction (in the case of an unfavorable adjustment) is reported with the adjustment itself in the statement of retained earnings.

The same idea applies to items reported in separate categories of the income statement. *The tax effect modifies the special item rather than the normal tax provision.* Examples of this type of intrastatement tax allocation can be seen on page 576 for an extraordinary item and in Table 16–1 for discontinued operations. The total tax charge for the period is allocated among different parts of the income statement.

## FOREIGN CURRENCY ACCOUNTING ISSUES

Firms dealing with foreign companies or having subsidiaries or divisions operating in foreign countries frequently enter into transactions expressed in currencies other than the dollar—for example, in francs, marks, or pounds. To be included on the formal financial statements, these transactions must be converted into dollars.

However, the conversion ratios (exchange rates) between francs, marks, pounds, etc., and the dollar are ever-changing. Shifts in the exchange rate lead to problems in the choice of rates to be used for conversion and in some instances to gains and losses. Actually there are two types of foreign currency problems—transaction gains and losses and translation adjustments. The former arise from explicit transactions involving sales or purchases of merchandise and the borrowing or lending of funds during a period when exchange rates change. The latter arise in the process of restatement into dollars of accounts, say of a foreign subsidiary, which are recorded in a foreign currency. Often the two types of problems are discussed together under the general heading of exchange gains and losses, although the treatment of transaction gains and losses has been much less controversial than the treatment of translation adjustments.

**Transaction Gains and Losses**

Let us assume, for example, that a U.S. firm buys equipment from a French seller, promising to pay 6,000 francs at a time when one franc equals $0.167. The equipment account would be debited and accounts payable credited for $1,000, the dollar equivalent. If, however, the exchange value of one franc is $0.184 when payment is due, the U.S. firm will have to spend $1,104 to acquire the 6,000 francs necessary to settle the debt. Its journal entry would be:

```
Accounts Payable .....................................    1,000
Foreign Currency Transaction Loss .....................      104
    Cash ..............................................             1,104
```

These currency adjustments result from explicit transactions denominated in a foreign currency. The domestic firm must settle at a later date a monetary claim expressed in a different unit of measure. In the interim the value of that foreign currency shifts in relation to the dollar.

The FASB's first promulgation on foreign currency accounting issues was *Statement No. 8,* issued in October 1975.[10] Firms were required to report transaction gains and losses in the period in which they occurred. When *Statement No. 8* was replaced by *Statement No. 52* in December 1981, the FASB reaffirmed the need to report such transaction gains or losses in the determination of net income. However, *Statement No. 52* mandates that the gain or loss realized upon the settlement of a foreign currency transaction be apportioned to all of the years which have passed since the transaction was initiated.[11] In the above example, therefore, the $104 foreign currency transaction loss might actually be apportioned to several income statements, if the equipment were paid for in a later accounting period than the period in which it was acquired.

**Translation Adjustments**

These adjustments arise only when a firm has foreign branches or subsidiaries. The accounts on the subsidiaries' books arose at different times when perhaps differing exchange rates prevailed. What rate(s) should be used to restate these accounts to dollars? In the past, the choice of exchange rates has boiled down to either the current exchange rate (the rate in existence at the date of the current statements) or a historic rate (the rate in existence at the time the particular statement item was transacted). Whenever current

---

[10] FASB, *Statement of Financial Accounting Standards No. 8,* "Accounting for the Translation of Foreign Currency Transactions and Foreign Currency Financial Statements" (Stamford, Conn., October 1975).

[11] FASB, *Statement of Financial Accounting Standards No. 52,* "Foreign Currency Translation" (Stamford, Conn., December 1981), par. 15. See par. 20 for two types of transaction gains and losses which need not be included in net income.

rates are used and the rate has changed from a prior period, translation adjustments arise.

Historic exchange rates have the advantage of keeping assets recorded at an amount equivalent to what the *dollar* cost would have been at the date of acquisition. Similarly, contributed capital would be reflected at the equivalent dollar amount originally invested. Current rates, of course, reflect current economic conditions. Translation of foreign accounts into dollars at current rates of exchange would indicate the dollars that would be realized if the foreign *book* values could be liquidated and converted into dollars as of the statement date.

In the United States two common methods of translation have been employed historically:

1. *Current/noncurrent*—current assets and liabilities are restated at current exchange rates; noncurrent assets and equities are converted at historic rates of exchange.
2. *Monetary/nonmonetary*—cash, claims to cash, and monetary payables are restated at current rates; all other items are restated at historic rates.

Prior to the issuance of *Statement No. 8,* translation adjustments were reported in many different ways. Some firms included them in income, others charged or credited them to reserve accounts, and still others followed the conservative practice of recognizing all losses in income but deferring all gains.

*Statement No. 8* required a uniform method of reporting called the "temporal method," which corresponded closely to the monetary/nonmonetary approach described above for translation of balance sheet items. Revenues and expenses were translated at exchange rates prevailing during the year unless they related to assets or liabilities translated at historical rates. Firms were required to report translation adjustments as gains and losses in the income statement for the period in which the exchange rate changed.

Several provisions of *Statement No. 8,* especially the requirement to report translation adjustments as gains and losses directly on the income statement, encountered intense opposition.[12] When firms took steps to limit the resources they invested in foreign countries in order to lower the risk of having to report large translation losses on their income statements, some critics accused *Statement No. 8* of causing economic events rather than merely reflecting them. They often cited the distortion of operating results and the production of misleading information. They did not believe that firms necessarily suffered losses or incurred gains from translation when resources invested abroad were likely to remain there rather than to be transferred home and converted into U.S. dollars.

---

[12] See, for example, "Financial Officers Want *FAS 8* Repealed," *Management Accounting,* August 1978; and FASB, "A Study of the Attitudes toward and an Assessment of the Financial Accounting Standards Board: Executive Summary" (Stamford, Conn., June 11, 1980).

*Statement No. 52* responded to several of the primary concerns voiced by the critics. It required that most firms translate *all* assets and liabilities denominated in non-U.S. currencies by using *year-end* exchange rates.[13] In addition, *translation* gains and losses are no longer to be included in the income statement. Instead, they are "disclosed and accumulated in a separate component of consolidated equity until sale or until complete or substantially complete liquidation of the net investment in the foreign entity takes place."[14] In support of its change, the FASB observed that such translation gains and losses "do not impact cash flows."[15] Recall from Chapter 1 that one major objective of financial reporting was to enable users to assess the cash flows of an enterprise.

**EXPANDING THE DATA AVAILABLE TO INVESTORS**

As a way of responding to audience needs, accountants often take steps to expand the information disclosed in order to make the financial reports more useful for decision making by investors. Some of these presentations are formally incorporated in generally accepted accounting principles as required disclosures; others are under serious consideration by the FASB and/or the SEC as future reporting standards. This section describes four of the most important of these expanded presentations—earnings per share, segment reporting, interim financial reports, and forecasted data.

**Earnings per Share**

In the financial press, the most popular measure of earning power is earnings per share (EPS). Because shares of stock are what investors hold or buy and sell, the earnings per share figure relates the income stream of the corporation directly to the stockholders' investment. Stockholders can see the impact of earnings on their individual interests in the firm. Changes in EPS can be used to evaluate past managerial performance or to project the future growth and potential of the firm. Quite commonly, EPS is compared with the current market price of the stock as an indicator of "inherent" value. If earnings per share are $5.00 and the market price of the stock is $44.25, we say that the *price-earnings ratio* is about 9 times ($44.25/$5.00) or that the stock market values (capitalizes) earnings at over 11 percent ($5.00/$44.25).

**Authoritative Standards.** Because of the importance attached to earnings per share figures, the Accounting Principles Board issued two opinions on the subject, and the FASB issued one statement.[16] As a result, GAAP now explicitly require that earnings per share be reported on

---

[13] *FASB Statement No. 52,* par. 12.

[14] Ibid., pars. 13 and 14.

[15] Ibid., par. 4.

[16] AICPA, *APB Opinion No. 9,* "Reporting the Results of Operations" (New York, December 1966); *APB Opinion No. 15,* "Earnings per Share" (New York, May 1969); and FASB, *Statement of Financial Accounting Standards No. 55,* "Determining When a Convertible Security is a Common Stock Equivalent" (Stamford, Conn., February 1982).

the face of the income statement. For simple capital structures, the calculation of EPS is straightforward. It is computed by division of the net income available to common stock (net income minus preferred dividends) by the average number of shares outstanding during the period. The presentation of EPS figures parallels the general structure of the income statement. Separate EPS figures are calculated for any special subtotals on the statement—cumulative effect of changes in accounting principles, net income before extraordinary items, net income, and so on.

Numerous intricacies are involved when a firm has a *complex financial structure*, one containing convertible securities, stock options, or stock purchase warrants. If these securities would have a *dilutive* effect on earnings per share—that is, if they would *reduce* EPS by 3 percent or more when converted or exercised—the APB requires that two earnings per share figures be disclosed with equal prominence. The summaries below highlight the major ideas underlying *primary earnings per share* and *fully diluted earnings per share*.

**Primary Earnings per Share.** This figure is net income available to common stock (perhaps adjusted) divided by the sum of the average common shares outstanding and the number of *common stock equivalent* shares. Common stock equivalents are securities that have many of the characteristics of common stock but have not yet become common stock. Examples include stock options and warrants and convertible securities which meet certain criteria to be discussed shortly. Very often, the exercise of stock options and warrants or the conversion of bonds or preferred shares will increase the net income available to common by far less, proportionally, than they will increase the average common shares outstanding. Primary earnings per share is a pro forma (hypothetical) calculation intended to provide the financial statement reader with an early warning of the decline in the EPS figure in the future if the complex-structure items do result in the issuance of additional common stock.

**Fully Diluted Earnings per Share.** This per share figure measures the *maximum* dilution in earnings per share that could take place if all contingent issues of common stock that could reduce earnings per share actually do take place. To determine the number of shares used in the denominator, one assumes *full* conversion of bonds and preferred stock, exercise of warrants, and so on, and thus includes all shares that might have a future claim on earnings. It obviously is another prospective calculation showing what would occur under the most conservatively assumed circumstances. Those options, warrants, convertible bonds, and convertible preferred stock which do not meet the criteria for inclusion in the primary EPS number are nevertheless incorporated in the fully diluted number. Accordingly, the latter figure is often significantly lower than the already low primary amount and certainly deserves the title of *fully* diluted.

**Illustration.** Assume the following facts for the Ace Corporation for 1985:

1. 1985 net income after tax is $2,250,000.
2. As of January 1, 1985, 800,000 shares of common stock were issued and outstanding. On July 1, 200,000 additional shares were issued.
3. The market price per share remained at $30 throughout 1985.
4. Options have been granted to executives to purchase 60,000 shares any time prior to January 1, 1988, at $25 each.
5. Eight percent convertible bonds, issued January 1, 1978, at their face amount of $2,400,000, mature in 1989. Each $1,000 bond is convertible into 50 common shares. The average Aa corporate bond yield was 14 percent on January 1, 1978.
6. Seventy-five thousand shares of 11% convertible preferred stock, $50 par, were issued on January 1, 1980. Each share is convertible into four common shares. The average Aa corporate bond yield was 15 percent on January 1, 1980.
7. A 50 percent income tax rate is assumed.

Authoritative pronouncements contain detailed rules for classifying securities as common stock equivalents. Options and warrants are virtually always common stock equivalents, because they derive their value from the common stock. Similarly, convertible bonds that derive their value primarily from the convertibility feature are common stock equivalents. This criterion obviously is quite subjective, and classification might fluctuate from year to year. Consequently, in an attempt to achieve uniformity, the FASB arbitrarily ruled that convertible securities issued at a rate less than two thirds of the average Aa corporate bond yield would be assumed to derive their value primarily from the underlying common stock. The Financial Accounting Standards Board reasoned that investors would accept such a relatively low interest rate on such bonds only if, in fact, they really viewed the security as if it were common stock.

The classification of a common stock equivalent takes place at the date of issuance of the convertible security and is not changed thereafter. For Ace Corporation, the 8% convertible bonds are considered to be a common stock equivalent (8% is less than two thirds of 14%), while the convertible preferred stock is not (11% is *not* less than two thirds of 15%). Accordingly, the convertible bonds enter into the primary earnings per share calculation, whereas the convertible preferred stock is reserved for the fully diluted earnings number.

Of course, the income figure in the numerator of the EPS calculation must be consistent with the number of shares in the denominator. For example, if a convertible bond issue is treated as if it were converted, then the income figure would have to be modified for the interest expense (and related tax effects). Likewise, if stock options are treated as if they were exercised, then some assumption must be made as to the use of the proceeds received upon exercise. To relieve the firm from having to estimate how much extra income would have resulted if the hypothetical option proceeds had been invested, the APB required that the EPS calculation assume that the firm uses those proceeds to reacquire treasury stock.

*If* the capital structure of Ace Corporation had been simple, the computation of earnings per share for 1985 would be relatively easy. The simple EPS would be:

$$\frac{\text{Net Income Available to Common}}{\text{Weighted-Average Number of Common Shares}} =$$

$$\frac{\$2,250,000 \text{ Net Income} - \$412,500 \text{ Preferred Dividends}}{900,000 \text{ Shares } (800,000 + 6/12 \times 200,000)} =$$

$$\frac{\$1,837,500}{900,000} = \underline{\$2.04} \text{ Simple EPS}$$

The capital structure of Ace Corporation is complex, of course. Accordingly, *Opinion No. 15* prohibits Ace from disclosing the $2.04 EPS number, calling instead for the calculation and disclosure of both primary and fully diluted EPS amounts. The simple EPS figure is presented partly to illustrate how a firm with a simple capital structure or with less than 3 percent dilution would calculate EPS. In addition, the above calculation of amounts for net income available to common and weighted-average number of common shares is useful as the starting point for both the primary and fully diluted EPS determinations, as revealed in Tables 16–3 and 16–4.

**Evaluation of Pronouncements.**   Accounting thought is divided concerning the value of the two EPS numbers required by *Opinion No. 15.*

**TABLE 16–3   Calculation of Primary Earnings per Share for Ace Corporation for 1985**

| | | |
|---|---:|---:|
| Net income available to common . . . . . . . . . . . . . . . . . . . . . . . . . . | | $1,837,500 |
| Add: After-tax interest savings from hypothetical conversion of convertible bonds ($2,400,000 × 0.08 × 0.50) . . . . . . . . . . . . . . . . . . . . . . . . . | | 96,000 |
| Earnings applicable to common stock and equivalents . . . . . . . . | | $1,933,500 |
| Weighted-average common shares outstanding . . . . . . . . . . . . . . | | 900,000 |
| Add: Shares issuable upon hypothetical conversion of convertible bonds (2,400 bonds at 50 common shares each) . . . . . . . . . . . . . . . | | 120,000 |
| Add: Incremental shares arising from hypothetical exercise of stock options: | | |
| Shares issuable upon exercise of options . . . . . . . . . . . . . . . . | 60,000 | |
| Less: Assumed buy-back of shares with option proceeds $1,500,000 (60,000 × $25)/$30 . . . . . . . . . . . . . . . . . . . . . | 50,000 | |
| | | 10,000 |
| Total shares for divisor . . . . . . . . . . . . . . . . . . . . . . . . . . . . . . . . . . | | 1,030,000 |

$$\text{Primary EPS} = \frac{\$1,933,500}{1,030,000} = \underline{\$1.88}$$

**TABLE 16-4  Calculation of Fully Diluted Earnings per Share for Ace Corporation for 1985**

| | |
|---|---:|
| Net income available to common .......................... | $1,837,500 |
| Add: After-tax interest savings from hypothetical conversion of convertible bonds ($2,400,000 × 0.08 × 0.50) ................. | 96,000 |
| Add: Dividend savings from hypothetical conversion of convertible preferred shares (75,000 × $50 × 0.11) ...................... | 412,500 |
| Earnings with full dilution ............................... | $2,346,000 |
| Weighted-average common shares outstanding ........... | 900,000 |
| Add: Shares issuable upon hypothetical conversion of convertible bonds (2,400 bonds at 50 common shares each) ............ | 120,000 |
| Add: Incremental shares arising from hypothetical exercise of stock options (see Table 16-3 for calculation) ...................... | 10,000 |
| Add: Shares issuable upon hypothetical conversion of convertible preferred shares (75,000 shares at 4 common shares each) ............ | 300,000 |
| Total shares for divisor ................................ | 1,330,000 |

$$\text{Fully Diluted EPS} = \frac{\$2,346,000}{1,330,000} = \$1.76$$

Some critics object to the hypothetical nature of both the primary and fully diluted EPS numbers. Many believe that Ace Corporation should be permitted to disclose its $2.04 simple EPS for 1985; they feel that it represents the only "true" or "real" EPS amount. Others are willing to accept the primary EPS concept but find the fully diluted EPS number too conservative to be of any significant value.

Perhaps the needs of financial statement readers would be better served by the disclosure of both simple and primary EPS numbers rather than the present combination of primary and fully diluted EPS.

Persons holding Ace Corporation stock options need only pay $25 for common shares, which are currently selling for $30 per share. Those holding Ace's convertible bonds are earning a substandard interest return on those securities. These facts suggest that exercise of the stock options and conversion of the bonds could very well be expected in the near future. Although the "real" EPS may have been $2.04 for 1985, financial statement readers deserve to know that it could decline by 8 percent to $1.88 (Table 16-3) just as soon as the options are exercised and the bonds are converted.

**Segment Reporting**

The last 25 years have witnessed an accelerating trend toward diversification by many companies. Expansion into multiple lines of business has occurred either through internal expansion or through the acquisition of other companies. In some instances, the outcome has been huge conglomerate corporations which operate a number of unrelated businesses. The individual components function, often quite autonomously, in widely diverse industries with separate manufacturing and marketing facilities. They are linked only by top management control and overall stock ownership.

Comparisons of the operating results of diversified companies with industry trends or competing companies are especially perplexing. The reporting of only a single income statement and balance sheet combining all the unrelated businesses causes three potential difficulties for the investor. First, the evaluation of management is made complex, because data for profitable and unprofitable lines may offset each other. One of the risks in management's decision to diversify is the possibility of expanding into unprofitable lines. However, a combined statement allows management to hide its mistakes and avoid external assessment of the costs and benefits from its diversification policy. Second, industry lines are blurred or disappear in conglomerate companies. Industry analysis is an essential element in evaluating past performance and even more crucial in predicting the future. Some industries may be developing at different rates or experiencing different rates of profitability or degrees of risk. The third difficulty concerns the impossibility of making meaningful comparisons among individual companies or competitors. A conglomerate is likely to compete with one or more firms in one line of business but with entirely different groups of firms in its other lines. To what (if anything) does the analyst compare the overall financial statements?

Numerous analysts and accountants have suggested as a solution that diversified companies be required to report separate income statements for each of their major lines of business or segments.

**Difficulties in Segment Reporting.**   Any company attempting to provide financial data by segments encounters numerous difficulties. One obvious problem is identification of the segments on which to report. If each firm were to report according to its peculiar organizational structure (geographic area, customer class, product line), comparability between firms would not necessarily be improved. A second difficulty involves the measurement of income by segment. Some expenses jointly serve a number of segments—advertising, interest costs, home office administrative expenses, research and development, taxes, and so on. Assignment of these common costs to individual lines of business can be accomplished only through the use of allocation procedures, some of which may be highly arbitrary. The assignment of assets and liabilities to segments may be even more difficult. The narrower the segments become, the more arbitrary are the allocated amounts. Accordingly, the results might simply mislead investors and provide them with very unreliable data for predicting the future.

An alternative often suggested is the segmental reporting of some intermediate income subtotal, such as "contribution to earnings before general corporate expenses." Only revenues and expenses directly assignable to segments would be included. This solution might aid in predictability of the future, but resultant figures would, of course, not be comparable to those of other firms operating as separate entities. Additionally, some business executives oppose disclosure of this type of information for fear of aiding competitors or encouraging government regulatory actions.

**Governmental Activity.** In 1974, the Federal Trade Commission ordered most corporations with more than $50 million in assets to start reporting profits, revenue, advertising, and R&D expenses by segments. The segments were specifically defined in terms of the three-digit U.S. Standard Industrial Classification (SIC) code, which consists of over 400 very detailed industry groupings. Partially because firms were not being allowed any latitude in the selection and definition of reportable segments, many firms covered by the FTC order initiated court action, alleging invasion of privacy. Approximately 40 percent of the firms required to file the line-of-business reports during early 1975 refused to do so.[17] Court actions dragged on for many years, and many firms never did submit the required data. The FTC ruling was formally scrapped in the early 1980s.

The Securities and Exchange Commission established less restrictive segment reporting requirements in the early 1970s. Firms were allowed fairly wide discretion in the selection and definition of their segments. Later the SEC made its rules quite similar to the segment ruling enacted by the FASB.

**FASB Statement No. 14.** The need for segment data seems obvious, yet the practical difficulties of drawing up reasonable requirements are large. Since 1967 the Accounting Principles Board and its successor, the Financial Accounting Standards Board, have grappled with the problem. The result is a requirement that companies disclose certain data for all *industry segments* for which the revenue, operating income or loss, *or* identifiable assets are 10 percent or more of the company total.[18] The reportable segments should account for at least 75 percent of the combined sales. Industry segments can be determined by the management of the firm. For guidance in grouping products and services into industry segments, the FASB suggested that companies consider such factors as nature of product, nature of production process, and markets and marketing methods. Most firms have divided their operations into anywhere from three to six reportable segments.

In general, firms must disclose at least the following data for each reportable segment (and in the aggregate for the remainder of the operations):

1. Sales, including sales to unaffiliated customers and intersegment sales and transfers. The latter must be separately disclosed.

---

[17] AICPA, *The CPA Letter,* March 10, 1975, p. 3.

[18] FASB, *Statement of Financial Accounting Standards No. 14,* "Financial Reporting for Segments of a Business Enterprise" (Stamford, Conn., December 1976), par. 15.

2. Operating profit or loss—operating expenses are to include both directly traceable segment expenses and operating expenses reasonably allocated to the segments but not general corporate expenses, interest expense, or income taxes.
3. Identifiable assets.
4. Other related disclosures—depreciation expense, capital expenditures, and so on.

The above information reported by segments must be reconciled with the related amounts shown in the overall financial statements.

In addition, firms deriving 10 percent or more of their sales from a single customer or from a domestic or foreign government must disclose that fact and the revenue amounts. Such information can prove useful in an evaluation of the underlying risk associated with the firm. Consider, for example, the cookie manufacturer which makes 35 percent of its sales to the Girl Scouts or the heavy machinery firm with sizable sales to a foreign government that is undergoing revolution or economic crisis.

**Interim Financial Reports**

The concept of the accounting period establishes the need for the financial accounting process to provide information for time periods shorter than the life of the enterprise. For the last half-century, the most common reporting period has been an annual one, either a calendar year or a fiscal (natural business) year. In the last 15 years, increased attention has been focused on interim reporting, the presentation of accounting information at times other than the end of the year and for periods shorter than a year.

In most instances the concern has centered on *quarterly reports* that many companies issue to external users. In recognition of the fact that a year is too long for investors to wait for information, the New York Stock Exchange requires that companies with stock listed on the exchange supply quarterly reports to stockholders. Additionally, the SEC requires companies under its jurisdiction to file Form 10-Q with the Commission at the end of each quarter.

**Problems in Interim Financial Statements.** As we know by now, the shorter the reporting period, the more the accountant must make estimates to deal with uncertainties. Adjustments for revenue earned under percentage of completion, expense accruals, and sales uncollectibles are more difficult to make for quarterly periods than for annual ones. Similarly, in interim reports the determination of lower of cost or market, the calculation of cost of goods sold under LIFO or in manufacturing firms, and the assignment of period expenses may lead to potentially misleading reports.

This high potential for inaccuracy in interim reports calls into question the more fundamental issue of the purpose of such reports. Is a quarterly statement to present the actual results of that particular three-month period as a separate time span or simply as one part of an annual period?

The answer to this question influences the accounting for income taxes, where the effective rate for the year may differ from the quarterly rate; the accruing of such expenses as bonuses, the existence of which may not be determinable until year-end; the handling of LIFO liquidation (sale of basic inventory layers) during an interim period; and many other accrual and deferral practices.

Closely related is the question of seasonality. Should the interim statements report on each quarter as it occurs or attempt to predict the year's results? Should an investor be able to multiply the quarterly income figures by four to arrive at the best estimate of yearly income figures? The answer to this question influences the amount of smoothing that is done in the recording of sales and particularly in the treatment of period expenses. The more each quarterly period stands alone, the less comparable are the quarters with one another because of seasonal factors and the more unusual they may become because of the irregular occurrences of particular period expenses.

**Authoritative Standards.**   Accounting bodies in both the public and private sectors have addressed themselves to the question of interim reporting. The Accounting Principles Board in *Opinion No. 28* provides guidelines and establishes minimum disclosure requirements.[19] The Securities and Exchange Commission in its *Accounting Series Release No. 177,* issued in September 1975, expands the information that must be contained in the quarterly Form 10-Q and requires that summarized quarterly data must appear in the notes to the annual statement of companies with publicly traded stock and assets exceeding $200 million or income exceeding $250,000.[20]

*Opinion No. 28* begins from the express presumption that each interim period should be viewed primarily as an integral part of the annual period. Revenue is to be recorded in interim reports on the same basis as in the annual report, so seasonal factors do show. Likewise, GAAP are basically the same for expense determination. However, certain modifications are allowed so that the interim results may better articulate with the annual results. The modifications for the measurement of cost of goods sold include use of estimating procedures where physical inventory is taken only once a year, the use of estimated replacement cost when there is a temporary depletion of basic LIFO inventory layers, and the ignoring of write-downs to lower of cost or market when the market decline is thought to be temporary. Similarly, *Opinion No. 28* allows some period costs readily identifiable with more than one interim period to be allocated

---

[19] AICPA, *APB Opinion No. 28,* "Interim Financial Reporting" (New York, May 1973).

[20] The revised instructions for Form 10-Q now require quarterly income statements, balance sheets, and statements of changes in financial position plus a narrative analysis of results of operations. The statements may be presented in summarized form but must otherwise conform to the principles contained in *APB Opinion No. 28.* The quarterly data to be included in the *annual report* notes must include revenue, gross profit, net income, and earnings per share for each quarter of the last two years.

on some reasonable basis such as time expired, benefit received, or activity transpired. Income taxes are to be accrued in accordance with the best estimate of the effective rate for the year.

Although *Opinion No. 28* does not *require* companies to issue quarterly reports, it does set forth the general guidelines that must be followed when they are issued. Similarly, it mandates minimum disclosure requirements for the interim financial reports of *companies whose securities are publicly traded.* Such quarterly reports are to include at least gross revenues, provision for income taxes, net income, and earnings per share. Additionally, any extraordinary, unusual, or infrequently recurring items or any changes in accounting principles, estimates, or provisions for income taxes are to be reported. The foregoing information is to be reported on a comparable basis with the preceding year for the current quarter and year to date. Also, to prevent the possibility that a quarter heavily influenced by seasonal factors will be extrapolated to the whole year, *Opinion No. 28* requires that firms disclose seasonal patterns of revenue or expenses and strongly urges that companies supplement their interim reports with information for the last 12 months to date. The final disclosure requirement specifies that the aggregate effect of year-end adjustments material to the fourth quarter only must be reported in a separate fourth-quarter report or in a footnote to the annual report.

## Financial Forecasts

Chapter 1 sets forth as one major objective of financial accounting the provision of information to enable stockholders and creditors to evaluate the earnings potential and financial strength of the firm. Financial accounting's response to this need traditionally has consisted only of historical information on past performance and existing financial position. Although judgments about earnings potential and future financial strength clearly involve future projections, the provision of any forecast data is deemed to be outside the sphere of financial accounting. The primary responsibility for making projections presumably rests with the investor audience.

During the last 15 years this assumption has come under intense scrutiny. Many analysts and accountants propose that forecasted financial data be included in annual reports to stockholders and in required filings with the SEC. Their arguments are straightforward.

1. Investor decisions are based on the future. Inasmuch as conditions may change in the future, historical information is inadequate for projection of the future. The provision of forecast information would directly facilitate decision making by external users.
2. Most responsible managements do forecast the future for purposes of internal planning. Indeed, these forecasts often are circulated to security analysts. However, the projections are not equally available to all external users and are not subjected to any controls or standards.

**Securities and Exchange Commission Pronouncements.** The SEC issued regulations in 1975 which permitted but did not require certain firms under its jurisdiction to make public projections of future earnings. They also required firms that made public forecasts to file certain information with the Commission. Reaction was so negative the SEC feared that the regulations would discourage companies from making any profit projections—a result directly contrary to the intention of the regulations. Consequently, the proposed *reporting* regulations were withdrawn, although the rules amendment permitting the inclusion of earnings projections in SEC filings stood.

In 1978 the SEC once again urged firms to include management forecasts in company reports and in commission filings. The SEC guidelines for the *voluntary* disclosures suggest that (1) disclosure of the assumptions used in preparation of the forecast would be helpful, (2) projections at a minimum should include revenues, net income, and EPS, and (3) outside reviews of the forecasts may be included.[21] To foster such projections the SEC in 1979 approved a "safe harbor" rule which was designed to limit the liability of firms for their economic projections. A firm is free from liability if the projections are made in good faith and have a reasonable basis.

**Problems with Projected Data**

The controversy over the disclosure of forecast data illustrates the conflict between the qualitative guidelines of relevance and reliability. Earnings projections appear clearly relevant to investors' informational needs. Nevertheless, some doubts exist whether such information can be provided with sufficient reliability that investors will not be misled. The primary concerns center on the behavior of investors and management if forecasts are permitted and on the lack of standards or guidelines for projections.

1. *Investor behavior*—Will investors understand the uncertainties and risks of forecasting, that projections represent only the most probable outcome (within a range) and are often based on tenuous assumptions about future events? Conversely, will they interpret forecasts as precise estimates or even commitments by management and hence suffer disillusionment and lose confidence in management and the financial reporting process if the forecasts turn out to be incorrect? Clearly the answers to these questions beg the more fundamental question of what characteristics are possessed by the investor audience to whom financial reports go. A sophisticated investor presumably already operates in a sphere of uncertainty and fully understands the limitations of forecasting and the crucial role played by assumptions. This type of investor would hardly accept management's projections without qualification. Rather, management's best estimate of the firm's prospects would simply be one of many inputs

---

21 SEC, *Release No. 5992*, "Guides for Disclosure of Projections of Future Economic Performance" (Washington, D.C.: 1979).

to the investor's forecasting model. The naive investor, on the other hand, may well behave as those objecting to the inclusion of forecast data fear.

2. *Management behavior*—Even though management is protected against legal actions or other recriminations when actual results differ from forecasts, might it still be motivated to make conservative forecasts or manipulate operations to create an image of expert forecaster? On the other hand, would a management which cannot be sued by stockholders be inclined to issue overly optimistic or deliberately misleading forecasts?

3. *Standards*—Can standards for the preparation and publication of forecasts be established that will impart a satisfactory degree of reliability to the information? Various organizations, such as the SEC and the AICPA, have proposed guidelines concerning format, time period, adherence to accounting principles, revision, and disclosure of assumptions. The latter area poses the most problems. Forecasts by definition rely extensively on a host of assumptions about external economic events and future management actions. Even if those assumptions most crucial to the forecast were disclosed along with some indication of their rationale, there are no standards by which their reasonableness may be judged. Furthermore, some managements claim that forecasting requirements might force them to disclose confidential information (e.g., anticipated introduction of new products, closing down of a plant, etc.) to competitors.

## THE ROLE OF THE AUDITOR

An auditor's report accompanies the financial statements for most companies. In the report or opinion, the company's independent certified public accountant expresses professional judgment concerning the financial statements. The financial statements are representations by management; therefore, management bears the primary responsibility for the accuracy and fairness of presentation. The auditor, however, provides advice and guidance to management in matters of financial reporting and serves as an independent check on management's presentations.

## Unqualified Opinion

Most financial statements are accompanied by an auditor's report similar to the one presented below. This standard report form or so-called "clean opinion" provides positive assurance that there is a reliable basis for the representations shown on the financial statements.

> We have examined the statement of financial position of X Company as of December 31, 19—, and the related statements of income, retained earnings, and changes in financial position for the year then ended. Our examination was made in accordance with *generally accepted auditing standards* and, accordingly, included such tests of the accounting records and such other auditing procedures *as we considered necessary* in the circumstances.
>
> In our opinion, the financial statements referred to above *present fairly* the financial position of X Company as of December 31, 19—, and the results of its operations and the changes in its financial position for the year then ended,

*in conformity with generally accepted accounting principles* applied on a basis *consistent with that of the preceding year* [italics added].

In the first paragraph, commonly called the *scope paragraph,* the auditor states that the examination of the statements and records was conducted in accordance with professional standards. The auditor reviews the system of internal control operating in the firm and test-checks accounts and reports for the accuracy and legitimacy of the transactions entered in them. Notice that the auditor, not management, has determined the nature and extent of the audit work performed. On the basis of this work, the auditor expresses a professional opinion on the financial statements.

The second, or *opinion paragraph,* attests to two conclusions of considerable importance to the external user. Italics have been supplied to highlight the key words in these conclusions. The first affirms that the statements represent what they purport to represent, undistorted by the value judgments of the persons preparing them. Secondly, the accounting and reporting principles have been applied consistently from one period to the next. Of particular interest are the many affirmations captured in the phrase, "present fairly . . . in conformity with generally accepted accounting principles." To reach this conclusion, auditors must satisfy themselves that:

1. The accounting principles selected and applied have general acceptance.
2. The accounting principles are appropriate in the circumstances.
3. The financial statements, including the related notes, are informative of matters that may affect their use, understanding, and interpretation.
4. The information presented in the financial statements is classified and summarized in a reasonable manner, that is, neither too detailed nor too condensed.
5. The financial statements reflect the underlying events and transactions in a manner that presents the information within a range of acceptable limits.[22]

**Qualified Opinions**

If the CPA cannot attest to all of the above factors or if the scope of the examination has been limited for some reason, the auditor must issue a *qualified opinion.* Such an opinion

> states that, "except for" or "subject to" the effects of the matter to which the qualification relates, the financial statements present fairly financial position, results of operations, and changes in financial position in conformity with generally accepted accounting principles consistently applied.[23]

---

[22] AICPA, *Statement on Auditing Standards No. 5,* "The Meaning of 'Present Fairly in Conformity with Generally Accepted Accounting Principles' in the Independent Auditor's Report" (New York, July 1975), par. 4.

[23] AICPA, *Statement on Auditing Standards No. 2,* "Reports on Audited Financial Statements" (New York, October 1974), par. 29.

Among the circumstances that would cause an auditor to issue a qualified opinion are the following:

1. The scope of the auditor's examination is affected by conditions that preclude the application of one or more auditing procedures considered necessary in the circumstances (e.g., inability to observe physical inventories).
2. The financial statements are affected by a departure from generally accepted accounting principles (e.g., inventories are valued at current cost, which exceeds historical cost).
3. Accounting principles have not been applied consistently (e.g., the firm has switched from FIFO to LIFO).
4. The financial statements are affected by uncertainties concerning future events, the outcome of which is not susceptible of reasonable estimation at the date of the auditor's report (e.g., current litigation may affect the firm adversely and cause a material amount to become payable).[24]

The CPA must make sure that the reason for any qualification is fully disclosed. Normally a middle explanatory paragraph in the report is included for this purpose. For example, if a firm follows an accounting principle at variance with a standard of the Financial Accounting Standards Board, this fact must be indicated. In addition, the explanatory paragraph should disclose the quantitative impacts on financial position, results of operation, and changes in financial position, if these are reasonably determinable.

The AICPA's annual survey of the accounting practices of 600 large corporations offers insight into the frequency of qualified opinions. The findings, summarized in Table 16–5, reveal many more "except for" qualifications for changes in accounting principle than "subject to" qualifications for uncertainties. Most of the former were required responses to newly issued FASB Statements; e.g., almost 100 firms received consist-

**TABLE 16–5** Types and Frequency of Qualified Opinions as Revealed in 1981 Annual Reports of 600 Large Corporations

| Uncertainties | | Accounting Principle Changes | |
|---|---|---|---|
| Litigation | 15 | Foreign currency translation | 98 |
| Going concern | 6 | LIFO adoption | 54 |
| Discontinued operations | 3 | Interest capitalization | 50 |
| Valuation or realization | | Compensated absences | 46 |
| of assets | 2 | Investment credit/depreciation | 25 |
| Other | 5 | Other | 31 |
| Total uncertainties | 31 | Total changes | 304 |
| Companies represented | 28 | Companies represented | 222 |

Source: AICPA, *Accounting Trends & Techniques*, 1982 (New York, 1982), p. 385.

---

[24] Ibid., par. 9.

ency qualifications after changing their accounting for foreign currency translation in line with *Statement No. 52.*

Unqualified and qualified opinions are merely two of four different types of opinions which can be expressed by auditors, although they are the predominant types given. Based on the particular situation and its materiality, the auditor may feel it is more appropriate to issue either a *disclaimer of opinion* or an *adverse opinion.* In a disclaimer situation the auditor declines to express any opinion at all, often because of serious audit scope limitations. An adverse opinion is expressed when the auditor believes that the financial statements are *not* presented fairly in accordance with GAAP.

**Commission on Auditors' Responsibilities**

A significant increase in litigation against auditors in the late 1960s and early 1970s led to increased concern over possible public misconception of the nature of the audit function and the ensuing auditor opinion. In partial response the AICPA established an independent body in 1974; it was referred to as the Commission on Auditors' Responsibilities (CAR). The charge to the Commission was to

> develop conclusions and recommendations regarding the appropriate responsibilities of independent auditors. It should consider whether a gap may exist between what the public expects or needs and what auditors can and should reasonably expect to accomplish. If such a gap does exist, it needs to be explored to determine how the disparity can be resolved.[25]

The CAR issued its 184-page *Report, Conclusions, and Recommendations* in 1978. Evidence of a gap between performance and expectations was discovered by CAR. Its report included a section proposing changes designed to increase the public's understanding of the auditor's task and the respective roles of management and the auditor. Although we cannot do justice to an entire report of such magnitude in the space available here, several proposals that reflect directly on the role of the auditor are now briefly addressed.

The Commission suggested that the public should be informed that the financial statements are and have always been management's and not the auditor's. In 1979 the AICPA issued a report which *recommended* that the annual report include a statement by management in which it affirms its responsibility for the company's financial statements. From 1978 to 1979 the number of firms surveyed in *Accounting Trends & Techniques* which included a Report of Management in their annual report to stockholders increased from 110 to 191; by 1981, 295 of the 600 firms surveyed mentioned their responsibility for the financial information.[26]

---

[25] The Commission on Auditors' Responsibilities, *Report, Conclusions, and Recommendations* (New York: AICPA, 1978), p. xi.

[26] AICPA, *Accounting Trends & Techniques,* 1982, p. 407.

One of the most controversial recommendations called for the elimination of "subject to" qualified auditor opinions. Such qualifications are usually occasioned by the presence of material uncertainties pertaining to pending litigation or serious going-concern problems. The Commission's rationale for proposing the elimination was that the auditor was frequently in no better position than the financial statement user to predict the outcome of many uncertainties. It preferred that financial statement users be provided with enough information to be able to assess the risks faced by the firm and to be able to make their own evaluation of the probable outcome.

Intense opposition from within the accounting profession, the investment community, and the SEC led to the AICPA's decision to reject this proposal. The Canadian Institute of Chartered Accountants, however, accepted the recommendation and implemented it as of November 1980. In March 1982, the AICPA agreed in principle to reverse its earlier position and eliminate the "subject to" qualification. By early 1983 the AICPA again changed somewhat, suggesting that criteria needed to be formulated to aid in the determination of when "subject to" qualifications should be issued.

**DISCUSSION OF THE ARMCO ANNUAL REPORT**

Although Armco made no formal forecast in its 1981 annual report and encountered no extraordinary items, discontinued operations, or prior period adjustments during that year, a significant portion of its annual report is still devoted to the disclosures described in this chapter.

**Changes in Accounting Principles**

Even though the foreign currency translation procedures specified by *FASB Statement No. 52* first became effective for fiscal years beginning on or after December 15, 1982, Armco and most other firms responded enthusiastically to the FASB's encouragement of earlier application of the accounting pronouncement. You will recall that the translation gains and losses which *Statement No. 8* required to be shown immediately as income statement items became translation adjustments as a result of the new standard and are established as a new, separate category of shareholders' equity. Firms experiencing what *Statement No. 8* would have considered translation losses would report improved performance if able to bypass the income statement with such items and take them directly to the balance sheet.

In Note 1 of its annual report, Armco discloses that this accounting change increased its 1981 net income by $10.9 million. Under *FASB Statement No. 52* Armco was permitted but not required to restate its past financial statements; it chose not to, perhaps because of a perceived lack of materiality. As required by *Statement No. 52,* the firm reports its net foreign currency translation adjustments ($40.5 million debit) as a distinct component of shareholders' equity on its balance sheet. This aggregate balance of as-yet-unrealized translation "losses" is dissected in the statement of consolidated shareholders' equity. As noted there, approximately three fourths of the balance on December 31, 1981, arose during 1981.

Also disclosed in Note 1 are amounts for the foreign currency losses recognized in the determination of net income for 1979, 1980, and 1981. The $3.1 million of losses taken to Armco's income statement are of the *transaction,* as opposed to *translation,* variety. Because they represent losses resulting from explicit 1981 events, such as sales, purchases, borrowing, and lending, they cannot bypass the income statement.

Armco made one additional accounting change during 1981. As Note 1 indicates, this one also resulted from the issuance of a new FASB statement. A discussion of compensated absence costs is beyond the scope of this book, so we will not dwell on this second accounting change here.

## Earnings per Share

Because Armco has stock options and convertible preferred shares outstanding, its capital structure is complex. Accordingly, the firm must calculate and disclose amounts for both primary EPS and fully diluted EPS. A simple and understandable explanation of the EPS computation process appears in a separate subsection of Note 1 to the annual report. The primary EPS calculation was affected by the stock options described in Note 7 and the contingent shares discussed in Note 1. Many stock options could be exercised at prices far below the current market price of Armco's shares. Additional common shares were issuable to former shareholders of Ladish Co. under certain conditions. The firm included both complex-structure items in its primary EPS calculation, because the items met criteria suggesting a reasonable likelihood of the issuance of additional common shares which would dilute earnings.

Armco's preferred shares are convertible into common stock and, therefore, also represent a potential source of dilution of earnings per share. The statement of consolidated shareholders' equity reveals that significant conversion took place during both 1980 and 1981. Note 6 discloses that over 2 million common shares were reserved as of December 31, 1981, for conversion by preferred holders. The potential dilution resulting from further conversion was included in the fully diluted EPS calculation only. The convertible preferred apparently did not meet the criterion necessary for classification as a common stock equivalent and, hence, for inclusion in the primary EPS figure.

As it is required to do, Armco discloses its primary and fully diluted EPS numbers on the face of its income statement. Notice that the difference between the two EPS numbers had been narrowing since 1979. By 1981 the fully diluted number was very close to 97 percent of the primary figure. Because significant numbers of convertible preferred shares were being converted each year, fewer of them remained as a factor to distinguish primary from fully diluted. Although the two EPS numbers disclosed were close to each other, Armco did not (and, in fact, could not) disclose what the simple EPS was for 1981. As suggested earlier, many financial statement readers would like to see that factual (rather than hypothetical) earnings number also presented.

**Segment Reporting**

Armco's annual report contains extensive disclosures pertaining to its six distinct segments. As noted earlier, *FASB Statement No. 14* allows firms considerable freedom in establishing and identifying segments for financial reporting purposes. Armco presents financial information at several points for oil field equipment and production, aerospace and strategic materials, specialty steels, fabricated products and services, carbon steel, and financial services. As required by *Statement No. 14,* data by segment are furnished for sales, operating profit or loss, identifiable assets, and depreciation/capital expenditures on pages 171–172.

The segment disclosures provide much insight into just what Armco has been and what it hopes to be. They shed light on the quality of corporate planning and the inherent riskiness of the firm. Profit as a percentage of sales differs markedly for the various segments as does the amount of identifiable assets necessary for generation of a certain level of profit or sales. For example, oil field equipment and production of carbon steel seemed to represent two extremes; the former produced far greater profit per dollar of sales and assets than did the latter. If the drop in world oil prices during 1982 and 1983 had not at least temporarily burst the bubble in oil exploration, Armco's movement into that field and the relative profitability revealed by that segment's data would have augured well for Armco. Certainly its lessening dependence on carbon steel reflects favorably on one aspect of long-range corporate strategy.

**Interim Reporting**

A summary of the data reported quarterly by Armco during 1980 and 1981 appears on page 174. A steady, consistent, upward trend in net sales is apparent during the entire eight-quarter period. Net income, on the other hand, exhibits no steady pattern. For example, the second quarter was the least profitable period during 1980 but the most profitable period during 1981. The footnotes on that page reveal several of the items which contributed to the swings in income from quarter to quarter. The restated EPS amounts represent a disaggregation of the annual amounts reported at the bottom of the firm's income statements. The primary and fully diluted EPS numbers presented there for 1981 can be disaggregated as follows:

|  | Primary EPS | Fully Diluted EPS |
|---|---|---|
| First quarter | $1.21 | $1.17 |
| Second quarter | 1.53 | 1.48 |
| Third quarter | 1.19 | 1.15 |
| Fourth quarter | 1.04 | 1.02 |
| Total for 1981 | $4.97 | $4.82 |

**Reports by Auditor and Management**

The accountants' opinion received by Armco is displayed on page 154 just preceding the presentation of the financial statements. The firm's auditor is Deloitte Haskins & Sells, one of the major independent accounting organizations with offices in most major U.S. and foreign cities. The wording in the scope (first) paragraph is identical to that presented for the "clean opinion" earlier in this chapter.

The opinion (second) paragraph, however, contains a consistency qualification in recognition of Armco's change in the method of accounting for foreign currency translation. Although it is not technically "clean," the auditors' opinion is favorable and carries no stigma, especially since the accounting change was in direct response to a new FASB standard *(Statement No. 52)*. Armco was one of the 98 large corporations shown in Table 16–5 to have received "except for" consistency qualifications during 1981 for such an accounting change.

Armco is included among the half of all large firms responding to an AICPA recommendation to include a statement affirming its responsibility for financial reporting. Such a statement also appears on the same page as the auditor's report. Its positioning there is very desirable, for it allows the annual report reader to ascertain and compare what management is taking responsibility for and what role the auditor has played. Management notes that it has prepared the financial information and selected appropriate acceptable accounting procedures. The auditor notes its use of generally accepted auditing standards, Armco's use of generally accepted accounting principles, and its belief that the firm's financial statements present fairly what they are intended to exhibit.

**SUMMARY**

This chapter considers a potpourri of issues in the disclosure and presentation of financial information. The earlier part of the chapter discusses the accounting for various unusual items and changes that affect retained earnings. Three general approaches have filtered from authoritative bodies.

1.  *Current reporting*—Report the cumulative effect on retained earnings as a separately identified item on the current period's income statement. This approach is used for extraordinary items, discontinued operations, and most changes in accounting principles.
2.  *Retroactive adjustment*—Restate each income statement presented and show the remaining effect as an adjustment of the retained earnings balance at the beginning of the earliest year included in the report. This approach is required for prior period adjustments (e.g., correction of errors) and certain specific changes in accounting principles.
3.  *Prospective correction*—Adjust the operating income of the current and future periods for the effect of the change. This approach applies to changes in accounting estimates.

Whatever approach is used, the principles of intraperiod tax allocation require that the tax effects of these unusual items and changes be reported in the same manner as the causal factors.

Discussion in the latter part of the chapter then turns to issues related to the usefulness of accounting data. Most of these issues have been resolved at least temporarily through authoritative pronouncements. *APB Opinion No. 15* sets forth very complicated and arbitrary procedures for the calculation of earnings per share; *APB Opinion No. 28* lays down only general guidelines for interim financial reporting; *FASB Statement No. 14* establishes rather detailed requirements for segment reporting; and *FASB Statement No. 52* attempts to promulgate a consistent set of concepts and procedures for reporting on the conversion and translation of foreign currencies.

In the discussion of these areas, the reader can sense the dynamic nature of financial accounting. New problems requiring applications of new principles or the development of new concepts continually appear on the horizon. The reader can also see how the qualitative guidelines of completeness, comparability, and consistency and the accounting principles based on our underlying framework of assumptions interact to provide a combined, interrelated approach to the finding of practical solutions to these problems. These problems and others yet to come will provide continual challenges to the auditing profession as it carries out its role of watchdog over the reporting of financial accounting information.

## QUESTIONS AND PROBLEMS

**16–1.** The following items relate to the Winder Corporation for the year 1985:

1. The firm discovered that $9,000 of extra depreciation had to be taken to compensate for the failure to take any depreciation on a machine acquired in 1983.

2. A patent purchased in 1981 for $51,000 was being amortized over its legal life of 17 years. In 1985 this policy was reevaluated, and the decision was made to shorten the life to a total period of 13 years.

3. All of the assets of the firm's foreign subsidiary were expropriated by a foreign government without compensation. The book value of the assets was $219,000.

4. A large portion of the inventory was found to be obsolete and was written down by $80,000 to net realizable value.

5. In 1985, Winder Corporation purchased some new equipment for $70,000. Because of great uncertainty concerning the future benefits to be derived, the firm decided to use sum-of-the-years' digits with a four-year life. Other equipment is depreciated using straight-line.

6. A loss of $82,000 resulted from a very large customer going bankrupt and being unable to pay the account receivable. The bankruptcy was completely unexpected and unpredictable; consequently, the amount was not covered by the normal estimate of doubtful accounts.

7. A cash payment of $70,000 was paid during 1985 to a visitor who was injured in 1982 during a plant tour. Damages of $200,000 were originally assessed by a lower court in 1983. Upon appeal, the state supreme court reduced the amount of damages to only $70,000. A loss and estimated liability for $200,000 had been recognized originally in 1983 when the lower court handed down its ruling.

*Required:*

a. Indicate how each of the above items would be reported on the 1985 income statement or statement of retained earnings. Assume that all amounts are material and ignore tax effects.

b. If the *market value* of the assets at the time of expropriation was $292,000, would your answer for item 3 change? Explain.

c. Is your answer for item 4 a function of how often Winder Corporation discovers that some inventory is obsolete? Explain.

d. "Winder Corporation jumped the gun in 1983. No entry was necessary for item 7 at that point as long as (1) an appeal was initiated and (2) the firm's lawyers were very confident of reversal at the higher-court level." Do you agree? Why or why not?

**16–2.** The following items relate to the Bolton Corporation for the year 1984:

1. Proceeds of $200,000 were received from a life insurance policy on an officer of the firm who died in 1984.

2. Bolton Corporation guarantees its products for a three-year period. It had set up an estimated liability equal to 4 percent of sales. The balance in the account as of January 1, 1984, was $95,000, and applicable sales in 1984 were $450,000. Based on detailed cost studies made in 1984, it was concluded that the estimate should be reduced, starting in 1984, to 2 percent of sales.

3. An analysis of outstanding insurance policies in 1984 reveals that on July 1, 1983, a four-year insurance policy costing $20,000 was debited to Insurance Expense. No adjusting entry was made on December 31 of that year.

4. Early in 1984 the company decided to abandon its sporting goods line which accounted for about 30 percent of the firm's sales volume. The assets directly associated with that phase of activity were sold on August 14, 1984, at a loss of $180,000. Operating losses in 1984 for the sporting goods line were $97,000.

5. The depreciation method on some machinery purchased in 1980 was changed in 1984 from sum-of-the-years' digits to straight-line. The effect of the change was to reduce depreciation by the following amounts: $8,181 for 1980; $6,363 for 1981; $4,545 for 1982; $2,727 for 1983; and $909 for 1984.

6. During November and December, one of Bolton's major suppliers incurred a labor strike. As a result, low-cost LIFO inventory on Bolton's books was liquidated. This liquidation resulted in an $85,000 increase in net income over what would have been recorded if inventory could have been replenished by year-end.

*Required:*

a. Indicate how each of the above items would be reported on the 1984 income statement or statement of retained earnings. Assume that all amounts are material and ignore income tax effects.

b. "Item 2 clearly should be treated as a correction of an error. The warranty cost estimate of 4 percent of sales was simply wrong." Do you agree? Why or why not?

c. "The prescribed treatment for item 4 aids financial statement readers in their prediction of Bolton's future earnings." Indicate what probably is meant by this statement and explain whether or not you agree.

d. Would your answer for item 5 have been less accurate or less precise if the reduction in depreciation had not been broken down by year? Explain.

e. "The prescribed treatment for item 6 constitutes a gross violation of the matching concept." Do you agree?

**16–3.** The Lane Company has the following capital structure on December 31, 1984:

| | |
|---|---|
| Convertible bonds, 7%, issued January 1, 1982, at face amount, convertible into common stock at the rate of 40 shares per $1,000 bond | $150,000 |
| Convertible preferred stock, $10 par value, 9% dividend rate, issued January 1, 1981, convertible into common stock on a one-for-one basis | 300,000 |
| Common stock, $5 par value | 400,000 |
| Common stock, excess over par | 700,000 |

You have obtained the following information:

1. On January 1, 1984, there were only 65,000 shares of common stock outstanding. The other 15,000 shares were issued on September 1, 1984.
2. The average Aa corporate bond yield is assumed to be 11 percent on both January 1, 1981, and January 1, 1982.
3. 1984 net income after interest and taxes is $800,000.
4. The income tax rate is 40 percent.

*Required:*

a. Calculate primary earnings per share for 1984.
b. Calculate fully diluted earnings per share for 1984.
c. Did the information on the average Aa corporate bond yield influence your answers in parts *(a)* and *(b)*? Explain the rationale behind the use of such yield figures.
d. "Accountants are living in a dream world. Lane Company's real earnings per share for 1984 was actually over $11." Explain where the $11 figure came from. Do you agree with the statement?

**16–4.** Crosby Corporation has asked you for guidance in the preparation of its interim report for the first quarter of 1985. *Selected* information concerning the firm follows:

1. An employee strike was forecast for the upcoming second quarter. As a result, Crosby shipped twice as much as normal during the first quarter.
2. Crosby normally incurs approximately 65 percent of its annual heating costs during the first quarter.
3. The annual audit takes place during January.
4. Property taxes are $40,000 for the tax year ending June 30, 1985, and are *reliably* estimated to be $60,000 for the tax year beginning July 1, 1985.

The firm's management proposes to defer half of the sales until the quarter (second) in which they would have occurred had there been no strike. It wishes to assign only one fourth of the audit fee to the first quarter, because it believes that the expenditure benefits the entire year. Similarly, the firm believes that only one fourth of the heating costs belongs on the first-quarter income statement. It reasons that heating the buildings during January to March helps operations throughout the year by "preventing pipes from freezing, machinery from breaking, and employees from quitting." Finally, Crosby proposes to show one fourth of the $50,000 1985 property tax (one half of $40,000 plus one half of $60,000) in each quarter.

*Required:*

a. Which of the four proposals of management do you *most* agree with? Explain why.
b. Which of the four proposals of management do you *least* agree with? Explain why.
c. For the two proposals not discussed in your answers for *(a)* and *(b)*, evaluate management's suggestions.
d. Crosby's management has reviewed your answers to parts *(a)*, *(b)*, and *(c)* and wonders "why we need to report interim data anyway if the reader will be unable to multiply first-quarter earnings by four to get a good estimate of yearly earnings." Respond to management's concern.

**16–5.** A headline in *The Wall Street Journal* on November 1, 1982, proclaimed that "Tymshare's Price Plunged About 23% in Week amid Disappointment and Confusion over Net." The article went on to report the following:

1. About $70 million of Tymshare's market value melted away as a result of "a misunderstanding over 19 cents worth of per share earnings."
2. Analysts had just discovered that the *entire* 19 cents of EPS earned during third-quarter 1982 came from a gain on the sale of a credit-card processing division.
3. Tymshare's earnings announcement did refer to the source of the gain but did not list the gain as a nonrecurring item.
4. The firm's chief executive officer said that "the company wasn't compelled under accounting guidelines to break out the item because the sale was small enough in relation to total revenue to be incorporated in regular earnings."

*Required:*

a. Was Tymshare's gain extraordinary? Was the gain nonrecurring? Explain.
b. Comment on the officer's explanation concerning why the gain was not made a separate line item. Do you believe that Tymshare followed generally accepted accounting principles?
c. "This incident reveals that the accounting profession needs to come up with a multidimensional definition of materiality." Explain what might be meant by this statement and whether you agree with it.

**16–6.** Holiday Inns, Inc., reported the following segment information for 1982 in its annual report of that year (amounts in thousands):

| | Segment | | | |
|---|---|---|---|---|
| | Hotel | Gaming | Restaurant | Other |
| Revenues | $840,698 | $472,792 | $100,584 | $ 11,224 |
| Operating income | 150,205 | 74,595 | 5,029 | 4,999 |
| Identifiable assets | 836,501 | 631,275 | 83,340 | 156,891 |
| Capital expenditures | 173,468 | 85,616 | 695 | 7,634 |
| Depreciation/amortization | 56,003 | 20,663 | 4,410 | 3,957 |

The breakdowns for revenues and operating income appeared directly on the income statement, while the remaining detail appeared toward the end of the Financial Comments section of the annual report.

*Required:*

a.  Are you surprised that the firm focused on those five particular financial statistics for each segment? Explain.

b.  Was the company required to report the breakdowns for revenues and operating income directly on its income statement, or could it have shown them in the Financial Comments section?

c.  Does the division of operations into Hotel, Gaming, Restaurant, and Other segments seem reasonable? How were the segments determined and by whom?

d.  The restaurant figures only reflect the operations of Perkins Restaurants, Holiday Inns's subsidiary. Should the restaurant operations at the hotel and gaming facilities also have been included in those numbers?

e.  "The gaming segment is over three times as profitable as the restaurant segment." Where did "over three times" come from? Do you agree with the statement? Why or why not?

f.  What use might be made of segment information by a financial analyst? By a banker? By a stockholder? Explain.

16-7.  Certain selected items appearing in Pan Am's 1982 Consolidated Statement of Operations are presented below (amounts in thousands of dollars):

| | Year Ended December 31 | | |
| --- | --- | --- | --- |
| | 1982 | 1981 | 1980 |
| Operating revenues | $3,716,025 | $3,797,291 | $3,743,319 |
| Operating income (loss) | (314,465) | (352,643) | (119,198) |
| Gain on sale of subsidiary | | | 294,417 |
| (Losses) on disposal of equipment | (34,305) | (10,569) | (3,636) |
| Income (loss) from continuing operations | (485,331) | (259,620) | 56,664 |
| Income from Intercontinental Hotels | | 18,642 | 23,602 |
| Gain on sale of Intercontinental Hotels | | 222,103 | |
| Net income (loss) | (485,331) | (18,875) | 80,266 |

*Required:*

a.  Distinguish between (1) operating income or loss, (2) income or loss from continuing operations, and (3) net income or loss. What items in addition to those listed in the partial income statement could also account for differences in these three summary amounts?

b.  Which of the items in Pam Am's partial income statement, if any, have been considered extraordinary by the firm? Explain.

c.  Compare and contrast the trends revealed by a focus on the operating income or loss, income or loss from continuing operations, and net income or loss. Which trend is the most accurate and reliable? Which is the least accurate and reliable?

d.  The 1980 gain of $294,417,000 is from the sale of Grand Central Building, Inc., a wholly owned subsidiary whose principal asset was the Pan Am Building in New York City. Would it have been distortive to include that gain in operating income or loss? Why wasn't that gain handled in the same manner as the $222,103,000 gain in 1981 from the sale of a different wholly owned subsidiary? Why wasn't it considered extraordinary?

e. Why does Pan Am separately disclose the *1980* income from the hotel subsidiary it did not sell until *1981*?

f. "There's no need to have so many subtotals on the income statement. Income is income and gains are gains. The important thing is the bottom line." Comment on this statement in the context of this problem.

**16–8.** Allis Chalmers's 1981 annual report contains the following description of its currency translation account:

In the fourth quarter of 1981, the principles of *Statement of Financial Accounting Standards No. 52* were adopted, effective January 1, 1981. Quarterly results for 1981 have been restated; years prior to 1981 have not been restated.

Under the new method, except for financial statements of non-U.S. subsidiaries in highly inflationary economies and in the U.S. dollar economic environment, assets and liabilities denominated in non-U.S. currencies are translated using year-end exchange rates, while revenues and expenses are translated using exchange rates prevailing during the year. In addition, currency translation adjustments are recorded as a component of Shareholders' Investment and are not included in income. Adoption of the new principles resulted in a beginning of year 1981 transitional charge of $35,000 to Currency Translation in Shareholders' Investment. The current year currency translation adjustment was $15,960,000.

This change resulted in increased 1981 income of $8.5 million, or $.68 per share, mainly from remeasuring sales and cost of sales using current exchange rates for contract advances and inventory transactions previously measured at historical exchange rates.

Prior to 1981, assets and liabilities denominated in non-U.S. currencies were translated using year-end exchange rates, except for inventories, property, plant, and equipment and certain other items translated at rates prevailing when these assets were acquired. Revenues and expenses were translated using exchange rates prevailing during the year unless they related to assets or liabilities translated at historical rates. Translation adjustments were included in income.

The statement of income includes currency losses of $10.4 million in 1981, $1.1 million in 1980 and $3.1 million in 1979.

*Required:*

a. *FASB Statement No. 52* first became effective for fiscal years beginning on or after December 15, 1982. Nevertheless, many firms, including Allis-Chalmers, complied with the Statement immediately after its release in late 1981. Can you hypothesize what their motivation may have been for early compliance?

b. Is Allis-Chalmers's statement an accurate comparison and contrast of the major provisions of *FASB Statements No. 8* and *52*?

c. Has the firm excluded all currency losses from income, or just certain types of losses? Explain.

d. "If it were not for *FASB Statement No. 52*, Allis-Chalmers's retained earnings balance on December 31, 1981, would have been $10,400,000 higher and its assets would have been $15,960,000 lower." Do you agree with all or part of this statement? Explain.

**16–9.** As noted in the text, the four types of auditor opinions are: (1) unqualified or clean, (2) qualified, (3) disclaimer of opinion, and (4) adverse. Qualified opinions are of the "except for" and "subject to" variety.

*Required:*

a. Discuss the general circumstances under which it would be appropriate for the auditor to issue each type of opinion. Include in your answer a comparison between "except for" and "subject to" qualified opinions.

b. Distinguish between the scope and opinion paragraphs of an unqualified opinion. Does the auditor, in either paragraph, certify the accuracy of the financial statements and/or the fairness of the generally accepted accounting principles? Explain.

c. For each of the following circumstances, indicate what type of auditor opinion you would expect to be issued and why:

1. A company has been named as a defendant in a price-fixing suit. The firm cannot presently predict the outcome or the range of potential loss, if any, which could result. No provision for any liability has been made in the financial statements.

2. A firm has changed its method of depreciation for existing plant assets from sum-of-the years' digits to straight-line.

3. A firm changed its accounting for foreign currency translation but only after the release of *FASB Statement No. 52.*

4. A firm is in default on its loan agreements with two banks and in arrears on accounts with certain vendor-creditors. These conditions, among other things, cause the balances to become due on demand. The firm is not aware of any alternative sources of capital to meet such demands if they are made.

5. A company reclassifies interest income on its income statement. Previously, interest income was included in sales and other revenue, but now it is being netted against interest expenses. Amounts presented for prior years have been restated.

d. "'Subject to' qualifications are much more serious than 'except for' qualifications." Do you agree? Why or why not?

e. "A disclaimer of opinion is a cop-out. If an auditor has conducted an examination in accordance with generally accepted auditing standards, there is an obligation to issue some opinion." Do you agree?

**16–10.** The financial statement section of Coleco Industries's July 2, 1983, interim report to stockholders appears below.

COLECO INDUSTRIES
Consolidated Statement of Operations
(Unaudited)
($000)

| | Three Months Ended | | Six Months Ended | |
|---|---|---|---|---|
| | July 2 1983 | June 30 1982 | July 2 1983 | June 30 1982 |
| Net sales .......................... | $126,338 | $86,801 | $306,508 | $141,540 |
| Costs and expenses: | | | | |
| Cost of goods sold .............. | 65,933 | 52,419 | 167,529 | 85,614 |
| Selling and administrative expenses ..................... | 39,944 | 18,523 | 85,284 | 30,803 |
| Interest expense ................. | 4,327 | 2,237 | 7,538 | 3,238 |
| | 110,204 | 73,179 | 260,351 | 119,655 |
| Earnings before income taxes ........ | 16,134 | 13,622 | 46,157 | 21,885 |
| Income tax provision .............. | 7,069 | 6,185 | 20,882 | 9,928 |
| Net earnings ..................... | $ 9,065 | $ 7,437 | $ 25,275 | $ 11,957 |
| Net earnings per share* ............ | $ .56 | $ .48 | $ 1.57 | $ .78 |
| Average shares outstanding .......... | 16,317 | 15,400 | 16,150 | 15,374 |

* Earnings per share have been restated to reflect the two-for-one stock split on January 28, 1983.

COLECO INDUSTRIES
Consolidated Balance Sheet Summary
(Unaudited)
($000)

| | July 2 1983 | June 30 1982 |
|---|---|---|
| **Assets** | | |
| Accounts receivable ..................................... | $111,146 | $ 65,185 |
| Inventories ........................................... | 150,704 | 52,023 |
| Other current assets .................................... | 41,870 | 12,234 |
| Total current assets ................................ | 303,720 | 129,442 |
| Property, plant, and equipment (net) ........................ | 40,598 | 24,664 |
| Other assets ......................................... | 2,992 | 3,800 |
| Total assets ......................................... | $347,310 | $157,906 |
| **Liabilities and Stockholders' Equity** | | |
| Notes payable to banks ................................. | $ 86,150 | $ 43,165 |
| Accounts payable ..................................... | 27,018 | 16,329 |
| Other current liabilities ................................. | 40,838 | 19,073 |
| Total current liabilities ............................ | 154,006 | 78,567 |
| Subordinated debentures ................................ | 52,255 | |
| Long-term debt ....................................... | 16,841 | 17,655 |
| Other liabilities ...................................... | 3,081 | 3,475 |
| Stockholders' equity ................................... | 121,127 | 58,209 |
| Total liabilities and equity ............................ | $347,310 | $157,906 |

*Required:*

a. "A useful comparison which is curiously missing from Coleco's report is that of first-quarter results vis-à-vis second-quarter results." Is such a comparison missing, and, if so, is the omission noteworthy? Is such a comparison of great potential use? Does your answer depend on the nature of the company? Explain.

b. Coleco's officers point to record sales and earnings for both the second quarter and the first six months and attribute the success to "the continuing strength of our home video game business." Nevertheless, could the financial statement trends be interpreted in a less favorable light? Explain.

c. Many interim reports to shareholders only provide detailed income statement statistics. Does Coleco's inclusion of equally detailed balance sheet data aid stockholders in their evaluation of the firm?

d. "Stockholders must place less reliance on interim reports vis-à-vis annuals, because the former are clearly labeled as unaudited." Do you agree? Should interim data be audited?

**16–11.** The stockholders' equity section for Piper Corporation was as follows at December 31, 1985:

| | |
|---|---:|
| 9% convertible preferred, $100 par, 100,000 shares authorized; 30,000 issued and outstanding | $ 3,000,000 |
| Additional paid-in capital—preferred | 900,000 |
| Capital from stock purchase warrants | 90,000 |
| Common stock, no par, 500,000 shares authorized; 270,000 shares issued and outstanding | 7,400,000 |
| Retained earnings | 2,300,000 |
| Total stockholders' equity | $13,690,000 |

*Additional information:*

1. Piper issued in 1980 $2,400,000 of 9% convertible bonds at face amount. The bonds are due in 1995 and can be converted until then into 22 common shares per $1,000 bond. The average Aa corporate bond yield was 13 percent when the bonds were issued.

2. The preferred stock was issued in 1981 at $130 per share, when the average Aa corporate bond yield was 14 percent. The preferred is convertible into common at the rate of three to one. No shares have yet been converted.

3. There are 30,000 stock purchase warrants outstanding, which were issued at $3 per warrant in 1980. One warrant plus $15 can be exchanged for a share of common, beginning in 1987. The warrants expire in 1989.

4. Of the 270,000 shares of common, 250,000 were outstanding during all of 1985; the remaining 20,000 shares were not issued until October 1.

5. The market price of the common shares remained constant at $30 throughout 1985.

6. Net income for 1985 was $1,032,000.

7. A 40 percent tax rate is assumed.

*Required:*

a. Are Piper's convertible bonds and convertible preferred considered to be common stock equivalents? Show calculations.

b. Are common stock equivalents ever excluded from the computation of primary earnings per share? How are they treated for purposes of the fully diluted EPS calculation?

c. Calculate primary earnings per share for 1985.

d. Calculate fully diluted earnings per share for 1985.

**16–12.** The student sitting next to you in your accounting class is certain that he has mastered the text's discussion of foreign currency accounting issues. You are not as confident and ask him to summarize all he knows concerning the topic. He claims that *FASB Statement No. 52* is much superior to *Statement No. 8* because it:

1. Delays the recognition of transaction gains and losses.
2. Makes useful changes in the manner in which translation adjustments are handled.
3. Probably will decrease the instability of earnings reported by firms with foreign operations.
4. Unclutters the balance sheet.
5. Makes the financial statements more reflective of the underlying cash consequences.
6. Improves the financial community's opinion of the accounting profession.

*Required:*

a. Is the student correct in observing that *Statement No. 52* in contrast to *Statement No. 8* will have the above six effects? Explain carefully and completely.
b. For those effects which the student *correctly* observed, is it appropriate to view such changes as evidence of *Statement No. 52*'s being "superior"? Why or why not?

**16–13.** Information on major customers is contained in the following excerpts from footnotes contained in the 1981 annual reports of four well-known corporations:

> **Whirlpool Corporation.** "The following percentages of consolidated net sales from continuing operations were to Sears, Roebuck & Co.: 1981— 46%; 1980—46%; 1979—47%; 1978—52%; and 1977—55%."
>
> **The General Tire & Rubber Company.** "Sales to one major customer exceeded 10% of Company sales to unaffiliated customers in 1981 and 1979 and amounted to $251,285,000 and $299,090,000, respectively. Those sales were generated primarily by the automotive business of the 'Tires and related products' segment, the 'Plastics and similar products' segment, and the 'Industrial products' segment."
>
> **Apple Computer, Inc.** "Sales to one retail dealer were 10% and 14% of total sales in 1981 and 1980, respectively."
>
> **Libbey-Owens-Ford Company.** "Sales from all of the company's business segments to domestic and foreign operations of General Motors Corporation and its affiliates were approximately $282.2 million in 1981 and $252.3 million in 1980 and $342 million in 1979."

*Required:*

a. Do generally accepted accounting principles presently require such information concerning major customers? When is a customer considered to be "major"? Should the identity of the customer be a required disclosure? Explain.
b. "The disclosures of Whirlpool and Apple are superior to those of General Tire and Libbey-Owens-Ford." What might the person making this statement have had in mind? Do you agree?
c. "The percentage of income derived from a major customer is at least as

important as the percentage of sales." Do you agree? Should income percentages be required disclosures? What would be the problems associated with making income percentage disclosures?

16–14.  You have been called in to audit the financial records of Penny Company for 1984. You discover that over the past four years certain purchases of new machinery were erroneously charged to repair expense. The machinery so charged should have been depreciated over a useful life of 10 years.

Selected information related to these errors is presented below:

| Year | Net Income Reported | Retained Earnings Balance at Dec. 31 | New Machinery Purchases Debited to Expense |
|------|---------------------|--------------------------------------|--------------------------------------------|
| 1981 | $210,600 | $ 741,100 | $80,000 |
| 1982 | 164,500 | 846,500 | 54,000 |
| 1983 | 161,700 | 963,900 | 60,000 |
| 1984 | 169,500 | 1,078,100 | 38,000 |

*Required:*

a. Prepare a schedule showing the corrected net income for each of the four years. Assume that a full year's depreciation expense is charged on new purchases in the year of acquisition. Ignore income tax considerations.

b. Prepare the adjusting entry necessary to correct the accounts as of December 31, 1984. Assume the accounts have not been closed for 1984.

c. The financial report for 1984 will show comparative income statements and statements of retained earnings for 1984 and 1983. Indicate how this matter should be disclosed in the 1984 report. Be specific as to amounts and manner of presentation.

16–15.  The Rotor Corporation has prepared the following projected income statement for inclusion in its annual report (amounts in thousands of dollars):

| | Low | Likely | High |
|------|------|--------|------|
| Sales | $2,700 | $2,900 | $3,200 |
| Cost of goods sold | (1,350) | (1,450) | (1,600) |
| Operating expenses | (800) | (850) | (900) |
| Income before taxes | 550 | 600 | 700 |
| Income taxes | (275) | (300) | (350) |
| Net income | $ 275 | $ 300 | $ 350 |

*Assumptions supporting the forecast data:*

1. The company's present management and accounting policies will not be changed.
2. Interest rates and income tax rates will not change materially.
3. Sales projections assume that past trends of increase will continue in the future. They also assume that the new West Coast plant will open on schedule on May 1.
4. Current labor contracts expire on July 1. The above projections assume that there will be no strike and that wage increases under the new contract will not exceed 7 percent.
5. Other operating costs are based on a general inflationary increase of 6 percent.

*Required:*

a. Would you advise the company to include the forecast data in its annual report? Explain your reasoning.
b. Do you prefer the three-level forecast or a single-point estimate?
c. What benefit to the investor is gained from the listing of assumptions? Do you see ways in which the statement of assumptions could be improved?
d. Should the company be forced to make a subsequent comparison of the projection with the actual results and to explain material variances?
e. Do you believe that independent auditors could and should attest to forecasts such as this? Explain.

**16–16.** You have been called in to audit the financial records of Nickl Company for 1984. During that year the company decided to change its method of inventory costing from first-in, first-out to average cost. The company was founded in 1981. Inventory computed according to each basis on December 31 for each year is:

| December 31 | Inventory at FIFO Cost | Inventory at Average Cost | Net Income Reported |
|---|---|---|---|
| 1981 ............... | $36,000 | $33,600 | $22,800 |
| 1982 ............... | 52,800 | 49,200 | 30,000 |
| 1983 ............... | 45,600 | 25,200 | 32,400 |
| 1984 ............... | 24,000 | 26,400 | 27,600 |

*Required:*

a. Prepare a schedule showing the adjusted net income for each of the four years. Be sure to include the impact of inventory differences in both beginning and ending inventories. Ignore income tax considerations.
b. Prepare the entry necessary to adjust the accounts as of December 31, 1984. Assume the accounts have not been closed for 1984.
c. The financial report for 1984 will show comparative income statements and statements of retained earnings for 1984 and 1983. Indicate how this matter should be disclosed in the 1984 report. Be specific as to amounts and manner of presentation.

**16–17.** Mason Corporation's capital structure is as follows:[27]

| | December 31 | |
|---|---|---|
| | 1980 | 1979 |
| Outstanding shares of: | | |
| Common stock .................... | 336,000 | 300,000 |
| Nonconvertible preferred stock ..... | 10,000 | 10,000 |
| 8% convertible bonds .............. | $1,000,000 | $1,000,000 |

*Additional information:*

1. On September 1, 1980, Mason sold 36,000 additional shares of common stock.
2. Net income for the year ended December 31, 1980, was $750,000.
3. During 1980 Mason paid dividends of $3.00 per share on its nonconvertible preferred stock.
4. The 8% convertible bonds are convertible into 40 shares of common stock for

---

[27] Material from the Uniform CPA Examinations, copyright © 1981 by the American Institute of Certified Public Accountants, Inc., is adapted with permission.

each $1,000 bond and were not considered common stock equivalents at the date of issuance.

5.  Unexercised stock options to purchase 30,000 shares of common stock at $22.50 per share were outstanding at the beginning and end of 1980. The average market price of Mason's common stock was $36 per share during 1980. The market price was $36 per share at December 31, 1980.

6.  Warrants to purchase 20,000 shares of common stock at $38 per share were attached to the preferred stock at the time of issuance. The warrants, which expire on December 31, 1985, were outstanding at December 31, 1980.

7.  Mason's effective income tax rate was 40 percent for 1979 and 1980.

*Required:*

a.  Compute the number of shares which should be used for the computation of primary earnings per common share for the year ended December 31, 1980.

b.  Compute the primary earnings per common share for the year ended December 31, 1980.

c.  Compute the number of shares which should be used for the computation of fully diluted earnings per common share for the year ended December 31, 1980.

d.  Compute the fully diluted earnings per common share for the year ended December 31, 1980.

16–18.  During the first six months of 1983 John Ross Trading Company engaged in the following transactions with firms in foreign countries.

1.  Purchased goods on open account from a French supplier for 100,000 francs (1 Fr = $0.12).

2.  Sold merchandise to a Portugese customer receiving in exchange a 10 percent, three-month note for 1,200,000 escudos (1 Esc = $0.008).

3.  Sold merchandise to a Spanish customer for 100,000 pesetas on open account (1 Pts = $0.0065).

4.  Received from the Portugese customer 1,230,000 escudos in payment of the note in (2) plus interest. John Ross Trading Company converted the escudos into dollars at the rate 1 Esc = $0.0079.

5.  Purchased 100,000 francs at a bank for delivery to the suppliers in (1) in settlement of the open account. The exchange rate was 1 Fr = $0.122.

6.  Signed an agreement with a Spanish firm. Under the agreement John Ross would use his influence to facilitate shipment of merchandise from the Spanish firm to a Portugese firm. John Ross Trading Company acts only as a facilitator, neither buying nor selling the merchandise. For services rendered, John Ross Trading Company is promised 200,000 pesetas from the Spanish client. No entries are made.

7.  Made payments of 50,000 escudos to appropriate people in Portugal to facilitate the transfer of merchandise referred to in item 6. The payment is debited to Facilitating Expense. Entries to record Service Revenue and Accounts Receivable from the Spanish client are also made at this time. Exchange rates are 1 Pts = $0.007 and 1 Esc = $0.0084.

8.  Received 200,000 pesetas from the Spanish client in items 6 and 7 (1 Pts = $0.0072).

9.  The exchange rate on June 30, 1983, when financial statements are to be prepared is 1 Pts = $0.0073.

*Required:*

a. Prepare journal entries on the books of John Ross Trading Company to record the above transactions and events.

b. If consideration is given to changes in exchange rates, what real rate of interest was earned on the note in item 2?

c. What difference would there be if the purchase agreement in item 1 were denominated as $12,000?

**16–19.** Unusual Enterprises, Inc. is located in the midwestern plains. The following information is taken from its records for the year 1985:

Credits:

| | |
|---|---|
| Sales | $690,000 |
| Rent revenues and other income | 33,000 |
| Gain on sale of building | 24,000 |
| Correction of recording error made in 1982 | 120,000 |
| Income adjustment—change to equity method | 30,000 |

Debits:

| | |
|---|---|
| Cost of goods sold | 350,000 |
| Selling and administrative expense | 150,000 |
| Loss on retirement of bonds | 40,000 |
| Hurricane damages | 280,000 |
| Interest expense | 2,000 |
| Income tax charges | 13,800 |
| Dividends | 25,000 |

Taxable items are subject to a tax rate of 50 percent except (1) the gain on sale of building, which is taxed at a rate of 30 percent; (2) the error correction, which is taxed at 1982's tax rate of 45 percent; and (3) the income adjustment from the change to the equity method, which is taxed at a rate of only 7 percent. The latter item represents the cumulative impact up to January 1, 1985, from a change to the equity method from the cost method for an unconsolidated subsidiary. The equity method was used in 1985. Retained earnings at the beginning of the year were $123,900.

*Required:*

a. Show how the income tax figure of $13,800 was derived.

b. Prepare in good form separate statements of income and retained earnings for 1985. Classify unusual items in their appropriate places and employ proper tax allocation procedures within and between the statements.

# CHAPTER 17

# STATEMENT OF CHANGES IN FINANCIAL POSITION

In Chapter 1 three statements were said to stand at the center of the reporting function in financial accounting. Various aspects of the balance sheet and income statement have been discussed in subsequent chapters. Now we turn our attention to the statement of changes in financial position (SCFP). It summarizes the major *financing and investing* events affecting the entity during the period. The income statement and comparative balance sheet, of course, provide some information about financing and investing activities but only in a limited manner. The income statement deals solely with operations and is affected by asset allocations and net asset changes (gains and losses) that do not necessarily mirror financial flows. Comparative balance sheets show only *net* changes in assets and equities for all activities between balance sheet dates, and these are not classified by cause.

Because an important responsibility of management is adequately to finance the short- and long-run activities of the firm, a special report relating particularly to financing and investing activities seems a desirable addition to the reporting package. Historically, such a statement was commonly referred to as a *funds statement*.

In March 1971, *APB Opinion No. 19* conferred primary status on the funds statement by requiring that it be presented for each period for which income statements are presented.[1] In addition, *Opinion No. 19* changed the title of the statement to statement of changes in financial position, modified its purpose somewhat, and specified guidelines concerning dis-

---

[1] AICPA, *APB Opinion No. 19*, "Reporting Changes in Financial Position" (New York, March 1971).

closure, format, terminology, and treatment of certain kinds of transactions.[2]

**INTERPRETA-TION AND USE OF THE STATEMENT**

In general, the statement of changes in financial position discloses information about how activities are financed, how financial resources are used or accumulated during a period, and how the liquidity position of the firm is affected. An adequate supply of cash or current resources is essential to ensure proper functioning of the business and to maintain its financial soundness. In explaining the basic causes of changes in net current resources, the SCFP reflects the major events and policy decisions made during the period with respect to financing practices and asset expansion. Much of this information about the *causes of changes* in the asset makeup, equity composition, or liquidity structure would not be available or readily apparent from an analysis of other financial statements.

A statement of changes in financial position may be used by external audiences in an evaluation of the firm's past financing policies. It may help answer questions similar to the following: How much reliance has been placed on external versus internal sources of funds? Does the firm have present fund-generating capability for adequate protection against financial risk or embarrassment? How was the firm able to pay large dividends in a period of low earnings or operating losses? How did the firm manage to expand its plant and equipment without borrowing or while at the same time retiring debt? How were additions to plant and equipment financed?

In addition, stockholders and creditors may use a funds statement to see how management has channeled financial resources into alternative uses, particularly expansion. By showing how resources are applied, the statement of changes in financial position sheds some illumination on a number of pertinent questions: What happened to profits? Why did dividends not increase with increased net income? How were the proceeds from a stock or bond issue used? How did the firm use the money it received from selling the plant assets of a particular division? Why did the firm have to borrow money when it had a large income? Is management using its resource inflow for any single purpose, such as plant modernization?

The outside investor also may wish to focus on the *net* result of the inflows and outflows of resources. The maintenance of a satisfactory current financial position is essential to financial health. For example, an adequate amount of working capital provides a financial defense against emerging or seasonal drains on resources, enhances the creditworthiness of the firm, enables management to operate efficiently and flexibly, and

---

[2] For an analysis of this opinion and its impact, see Robert L. Virgil and Earl A. Spiller, "Effectiveness of *APB Opinion No. 19* in Improving Funds Reporting," *Journal of Accounting Research,* Spring 1974, pp. 112–42.

allows the firm to take advantage of special favorable opportunities. Therefore, the investor may be interested in questions such as these: How much did working capital or cash increase, and what factors caused the increase? How does the amount and composition of working capital compare with those of prior years? Is management depleting working capital or cash in order to finance needed expansion or to meet required debt payments? Answers to these questions may provide useful information for measurement of future growth potential. Together with a schedule of changes in individual current resources, a SCFP presents a fairly complete picture of the current area of the business.

A funds statement not only can highlight historical answers to questions like those posed above; it also can be projected into the future. Indeed, the SCFP serves management as a planning tool. Using a forecast (pro forma) funds statement, management can see what financial plans must be made to ensure that the desired future level of operations, dividends, expansion, and so on, is achieved. Some creditors also use forecast funds statements in estimating the firm's ability to pay its debts, and investors project funds flows using prior periods' funds statements in evaluating financial riskiness.

**ALTERNATIVE EXPRESSIONS OF CHANGES IN FINANCIAL POSITION**

The statement of changes in financial position is a statement of flows. It measures and reports those financial events that have caused changes in financial position between two position statement dates. For the accomplishment of this end, a focal point or concept of funds is needed. The object of the statement of changes in financial position then becomes the explanation of changes in the focal point.

Changes in financial position could be expressed in or oriented around any of several different concepts of funds. The term *funds* has never been precisely defined in either accounting theory or practice, partly because different users with varying needs are thought to employ alternative concepts. Two common definitions have gained a large measure of acceptance—cash and working capital (the difference between current assets and current liabilities). *Opinion No. 19* allows either concept but requires that they be interpreted broadly so as not to exclude any significant financing or investing activities of the firm. This broad interpretation is often called the all financial resources concept. We shall discuss and use all these definitions. Also, for the sake of brevity we often will use the term *funds* even though *Opinion No. 19* drops it in favor of the broader term, financial position.

Cash probably comes closest to the everyday interpretation of funds. For short-term financial planning, funds frequently are defined narrowly as cash. With such a definition the funds statement becomes a statement of cash receipts and disbursements. For longer-term planning purposes and for many analyses by external audiences, however, a cash funds statement probably has too much detail. Numerous purchases and sales of marketable securities or borrowings and repayments of short-term bank loans may be important in cash forecasting by management but not in an overall analysis of major sources and uses of resources. Also, cash is subject to short-term fluctuations. A delay in paying an account payable, for example, would decrease the uses of funds (defined as cash) but not really affect the general financial condition of the firm in the eyes of an external analyst. Firms using the cash definition of funds often modify it slightly so that it also encompasses all near-cash items, such as marketable securities. The revised definition is usually referred to as "cash and cash equivalents."

The concept of funds which is most widely accepted for external use by stockholders and creditors is *working capital* (current assets minus current liabilities).[3] During the period a large volume of the following kinds of transactions may occur: payments of current liabilities, purchases of inventory on short-term credit, collections of receivables, and short-term borrowings. These transactions cause changes in individual accounts comprising current assets and current liabilities. However, they do not cause changes in working capital itself. By being based on the working capital concept, a SCFP does not become encumbered with the effects of these detailed fluctuations in the individual current asset and current liability accounts. Inasmuch as these offsetting transactions do not cause working capital to change, their exclusion allows the external analyst to focus on the overall impact of events on the current financial position of the firm.

Changes in working capital reflect normal accrual accounting procedures. Hence, a statement based on this definition of funds articulates well with the other statements. At the same time, working capital also is a measure of the short-term liquidity of a firm (the excess of current assets over current liabilities). An analysis of factors that cause changes in the net amount of current assets and current liabilities during a period of time provides information about the fluidity of current capital, which is relevant for many decisions of stockholders, creditors, and management.

Despite its wide usage, the working capital concept may conceal or exclude too much. Changes in individual current assets and liabilities may be vital to external analysts in their understanding of the firm's financial activities. Examples of potentially significant changes in current accounts include a large buildup of inventory, an increase in accounts receivable caused by a slowdown in collections, and new short-term bank borrowing. A funds statement based on working capital masks these kinds of changes. To overcome this deficiency, the Accounting Principles Board in *Opinion No. 19* set forth the requirement that the net changes in each individual current asset or current liability must be disclosed either on the statement itself or in a supplementary schedule. These disclosures allow the analyst to

---

[3] In a 1981 survey of accounting practices followed by 600 companies, it was discovered that 466 emphasized working capital changes in their funds statement and 134 emphasized cash (or cash and cash equivalents) changes.

detect any significant short-term financing and investing activities and to appraise the impact of the long-term activities on the *composition* of the firm's working capital.

Nevertheless, increasing numbers of individuals and groups have come to question whether the predominance of the working capital funds statement is consistent with the accounting profession's increasing concern for reflecting the *cash* consequences of business events. Recall from Chapter 1 that one of the basic objectives of financial reporting is to provide users with information about cash inflows and outflows to help with assessments of future cash flows. In several places in a November 1981, exposure draft of a *Proposed Statement of Financial Accounting Concepts,* the viewpoint is professed that "reporting meaningful components of cash flow is generally more useful than reporting changes in working capital."[4]

The FASB does admit that "it is conceivable that some benefits might result from the publication of more than one report of funds flows, each using a different definition of funds."[5] However, it then cautions that "additional information about the flows of other types of 'funds' is unlikely to add enough to be cost effective, given that information about changes in other assets and in liabilities can be inferred from information in comparative balance sheets, income statements, and statements of cash receipts and payments."[6]

Is the working capital funds statement, now utilized by the overwhelming majority of firms for their external reporting, likely to become extinct soon? We think not. Certainly the *Proposed Statement of Financial Accounting Concepts,* if enacted in its present form, will encourage firms to *consider* the possibility of preparing a cash funds statement. A firm which chooses to change from working capital to cash or vice versa is not considered to have made an accounting change, which would have required an auditor's qualification. Nevertheless, the working capital funds statement should remain as a popular reporting form in the foreseeable future, for three reasons:

1. The proposal at present is for a Statement of Financial Accounting *Concepts* rather than a Statement of Financial Accounting *Standards.* Although statements of concepts are designed to specify objectives and fundamentals that will lead to the development of appropriate standards, this process is often neither certain nor speedy.
2. As noted earlier, the working capital format retains several significant advantages over the cash approach. Working capital is unquestionably a broader, more comprehensive measure of liquidity than is cash.

---

[4] FASB, *Proposed Statement of Financial Accounting Concepts,* "Reporting Income, Cash Flows, and Financial Position of Business Enterprises" (Stamford, Conn., November 16, 1981), p. xi.

[5] Ibid., par. 138.

[6] Ibid.

Also, it meshes better with the other financial statements prepared by the firm because it reflects accrual accounting.

3. The low incremental costs for the preparation of a second funds statement increases the likelihood that firms inclined or eventually required to issue a cash funds statement will, contrary to the FASB's assertion, find the continued publication of a working capital presentation to be cost effective. As the preparation of both types of funds statements is described later in this chapter, you will note that many items and amounts are completely retained or only slightly modified when we shift from one funds statement format to the other.

Whether the focus of the funds statement is on working capital or on cash, certain items which might seem excludable cannot be ignored, because they are significant to the firm's financing and investing activities during the period. Examples include an increase in land received in exchange for the issuance of shares of stock, the conversion of bonds into stock, and the exchange of noncurrent assets. The APB, in *Opinion No. 19*, required such a broad interpretation in specifying that the *all financial resources approach* be followed, placing emphasis on the substance rather than the form of the transaction. To illustrate, land received in exchange for shares of stock must be viewed as if stock had first been sold for cash and then the cash had been used to acquire the land.

In the next few sections of this chapter we first review the major sources and uses of working capital and cash. Then, we explore the issues and problems involved in the preparation of a statement of changes in financial position, first under the working capital perspective and then from the cash viewpoint. The concluding section examines Armco's funds statement disclosures.

## SOURCES AND USES OF WORKING CAPITAL

With funds defined as working capital, our objective is to determine, classify, and report those transactions that cause the balance of working capital to change between the beginning and the end of the period. Generally, the events in which we are interested must affect both a working capital account (i.e., a current asset or current liability) and another account (noncurrent asset or equity). Only these events can cause working capital to change. Specifically, transactions that cause an increase in working capital are *sources;* those that result in a decrease represent *uses*.

Many transactions during the period will be of no interest to us in this quest, because they do not meet the general rule of affecting both a current and a noncurrent account. One type are the numerous transactions that affect only the current accounts, for example, a cash payment of an outstanding account payable. Although these transactions affect the composition of working capital, they do not change the total amount or balance. Similarly, there are transactions that involve only noncurrent accounts, for example, a stock dividend, depreciation, retained earnings restrictions. These *nonfund* transactions cause no change in any element of working capital.

To our first approximations of sources and uses will be added other events which cause a significant inflow of resources (financing) or outflow of resources (investing). We shall report them on the funds statement as if they simultaneously brought in working capital (source) and used working capital (use). In this way the final statement can both explain the change in working capital *and* show all significant financing and investing activities.

**Sources**

Those events which result in a new increase in funds can be divided into three broad categories—revenues, disposition of noncurrent assets, and financing.

Revenues of a business are the inflow of assets from operations. The asset received is usually cash or a short-term receivable. The corresponding credit is to an owners' equity account (revenue). Because they result in an increase in current assets and, hence, in working capital, revenue transactions are one major source of funds.

On occasion a firm sells one or more of its noncurrent assets. If the sale is made for cash or a receivable, a current asset increases. This transaction is a source of funds. Whether the noncurrent asset is sold at a gain or at a loss does not affect the source of funds (e.g., sale of land) but does affect the amount. For instance, assume that a firm sells for $12,000 in cash some excess land which originally cost $15,000. The journal entry to record this sale would be:

```
Cash .................................................. 12,000
Loss on Sale of Land ...............................  3,000
    Land ..............................................          15,000
```

The loss indicates the decrease in owners' equity because total assets decrease (land decreases more than cash increases). However, the funds viewpoint is concerned with changes in net current assets. This transaction, although reducing total assets, increases *current* assets. Therefore, it should appear on the funds statement as a source of funds of $12,000.

Long-term financing is the third major source. If a company engages in long-term borrowing or issues additional common or preferred stock, cash usually increases. For example, if a company issues for $101,000 bonds with a face value of $100,000, then cash and thus working capital increase $101,000. The offsetting credits are to noncurrent liability accounts, Bonds Payable and Premium on Bonds Payable. This event is a source of funds. The issuance of preferred stock or common stock could be analyzed in a similar manner. The amount of change in the par or face value of all shares outstanding is not governing. The important aspect is the increase in current assets resulting from the transaction.

**Uses**

Four general events affecting a business cause a *decrease* in working capital, either because current assets decrease or because current liabilities increase. Certain expense transactions have this effect. In addition, recurring payments to investors, retirement of noncurrent equities, and the acquisition of noncurrent assets may decrease working capital.

Expenses record decreases in owners' equity as assets are used in the process of generating revenues. However, only those expenses arising from a decrease in current assets (or an increase in current liabilities) are uses of funds. Cost of goods sold (decreases Merchandise), labor expense (decreases Cash or increases Wages Payable), income taxes (decreases Cash or increases Taxes Payable), and rent expense (decreases Cash or Prepaid Rent) are some common examples of fund expenses. Depreciation expense, amortization of patents, and depletion expense represent transactions that decrease owners' equity and decrease a *noncurrent* asset. Although these expenses represent uses of assets, they do not involve a current outlay or decrease in working capital. Therefore, they are called *nonfund expenses,* and care must be taken to see that they are properly interpreted as such.

Similar to the fund expenses are recurring payments to investors—interest expense and dividends. In most cases the transactions giving rise to these items involve a debit to an owners' equity account (Interest Expense, Preferred Dividends, Common Dividends) and a credit to either Cash or a current liability such as Interest Payable or Dividends Payable. Therefore, recurring payments to investors represent another use of funds.[7]

When cash is used to retire bonds or preferred stock or to acquire treasury stock, the opposite situation from financing occurs. In this case funds are being used to reduce long-term equities. Again, the face value or par amount retired is not significant from a funds viewpoint. Only the amount of the decrease in current assets is relevant.

The fourth major type of transaction which should appear as a use of funds is the acquisition of noncurrent assets, such as land, plant assets, or intangibles. These acquisitions frequently cause a concomitant decrease in current assets or increase in current liabilities.

**Statement Form**

Of the three major sources of funds and four major uses of funds named above, the first source (revenues) and the first use (expenses that use funds) both relate to the operations of the business. In preparation of the funds statement, the revenues and fund expenses are offset to yield a net

---

[7] We have considered interest as similar to dividends, because there is conceptual merit in acknowledging both to be recurring payments to investors. This grouping is not made on most published funds statements, however. Rather, interest is usually considered as a fund expense similar to labor, income taxes, and rent.

source, funds from operations. If this is done, the funds statement can be divided into six major sections—three sources of funds and three uses of funds.[8] The form in Table 17–1 is a convenient and useful way to present the major changes in working capital, although this format is only one of many that are used. Appropriate details would, of course, be listed under each of the major subheads. The important objectives of the funds statement are to summarize the major changes that take place during a period of time and to present and classify them in some reasonable manner.

**TABLE 17–1   General Format for Statement of Changes in Financial Position**

SAMPLE COMPANY
Statement of Changes in Financial Position
For the Year 1984

| | | |
|---|---:|---:|
| Sources: | | |
| Funds from operations | $xxx | |
| Sale of noncurrent assets | xxx | |
| Financing | xxx | |
| Total sources | | $xxx |
| Uses: | | |
| Recurring payments to investors | xxx | |
| Return of invested capital | xxx | |
| Acquisition of noncurrent assets | xxx | |
| Total uses | | xxx |
| Increase (decrease) in working capital | | $xxx |

## PREPARATION OF THE STATEMENT—WORKING CAPITAL CONCEPT

Having set forth the general analytical framework for the statement of changes in financial position and discussed the usefulness of the statement, we now illustrate its preparation. Tables 17–2 and 17–3 contain the financial statements of Sentry Corporation. Included are a comparative balance sheet as of the end of 1983 and 1984 and a combined statement of income and retained earnings for 1984.

A thorough knowledge of the material covered in Chapters 1–10 and 13–14 will aid your understanding of this section. Funds statement treatment of more advanced items such as leases (Chapter 11) and parent investments in unconsolidated subsidiaries (Chapter 15), is discussed in the Appendix to this chapter.

### Schedule of Changes in Working Capital

The difference between working capital at the beginning and end of the period is the basic change we are attempting to explain. For Sentry Corporation, the change during 1984 is an increase of $31,000—from

---

[8] *APB Opinion No. 19* requires an additional category whenever extraordinary items which have an impact on funds are present.

**TABLE 17-2**

SENTRY CORPORATION
Comparative Balance Sheet
As of December 31, 1983, and 1984

|  | 1984 | 1983 |
|---|---|---|
| *Assets* | | |
| Current assets: | | |
| Cash .......................................... | $ 80,000 | $ 75,000 |
| Accounts receivable ...................... | 47,000 | 51,000 |
| Inventories ................................. | 110,000 | 100,000 |
| Unexpired insurance ...................... | 2,000 | 3,000 |
| Total current assets ................. | 239,000 | 229,000 |
| Land ......................................... | 120,000 | 100,000 |
| Plant and equipment* ..................... | 360,000 | 355,000 |
| Accumulated depreciation ................ | (75,000) | (68,000) |
| Goodwill (net of amortization) ............... | 24,000 | 25,000 |
| Total assets ........................... | $668,000 | $641,000 |
| *Equities* | | |
| Current liabilities: | | |
| Accounts payable (merchandise) ........... | $112,000 | $140,000 |
| Wages and salaries payable ............... | 3,000 | 2,000 |
| Interest payable .......................... | 4,000 | 2,500 |
| Bank loans payable ....................... | 16,000 | 12,000 |
| Other accrued liabilities .................... | 2,500 | 2,000 |
| Total current liabilities .............. | 137,500 | 158,500 |
| Deferred income taxes ..................... | 7,000 | 5,000 |
| Bonds payable ............................ | 80,000 | 160,000 |
| Preferred stock .......................... | 78,000 | 40,000 |
| Common stock ............................ | 260,000 | 210,000 |
| Retained earnings ........................ | 105,500 | 67,500 |
| Total equities ............................ | $668,000 | $641,000 |

\* Management indicates that the capital expenditures for new plant and equipment during 1984 were $70,000.

working capital of $70,500 on December 31, 1983 ($229,000 current assets less $158,500 current liabilities) to working capital of $101,500 on December 31, 1984 ($239,000 less $137,500).

Additional information is provided in a schedule of changes in working capital, which details the change in each current account during the period. Under *Opinion No. 19*, this type of schedule is a required part of the disclosures associated with the statement; it usually is presented much like a check figure near the bottom of the statement. For the Sentry Corporation, the schedule of changes in working capital appears as Table 17-4.

The schedule reports changes in the balances of the fund accounts (current accounts, since funds are being defined as working capital). Their combined effect is a $31,000 increase in working capital. The SCFP's remaining portions, sometimes referred to as the statement proper, report

**TABLE 17-3**

SENTRY CORPORATION
Combined Statement of Income
and Retained Earnings
For the Year 1984

| | | |
|---|---:|---:|
| Revenues from net sales | | $346,100 |
| Operating expenses: | | |
| Cost of goods sold | $170,000 | |
| Wage and salary expense | 38,000 | |
| Advertising expense | 2,000 | |
| Insurance expense | 2,100 | |
| Depreciation expense | 30,000 | |
| Amortization of goodwill | 1,000 | |
| Other operating expenses | 13,000 | |
| Total operating expenses | | 256,100 |
| Operating income | | 90,000 |
| Nonoperating items: | | |
| Interest expense | 12,000 | |
| Loss on sale of equipment | 9,000 | |
| Total nonoperating items | | 21,000 |
| Income before income taxes | | 69,000 |
| Income taxes | | 24,643 |
| Income before extraordinary item | | 44,357 |
| Extraordinary item: Gain on retirement of bonds of $1,000, minus applicable income taxes of $357 | | 643 |
| Net income | | 45,000 |
| Retained earnings, January 1 | | 67,500 |
| Total | | 112,500 |
| Dividends: | | |
| Preferred | 2,000 | |
| Common | 5,000 | |
| Total dividends | | 7,000 |
| Retained earnings, December 31 | | $105,500 |

any funds impact associated with a change in nonfund accounts (noncurrent accounts in this case). Here, the financing and investment activities which culminated in the $31,000 working capital increase are detailed. The three broad categories of working capital sources (funds from operations, disposition of noncurrent assets, and financing) must sum to exactly $31,000 more than the total of the three categories of working capital uses (recurring payments to investors, return of invested capital, and acquisition of noncurrent assets).

The statement of changes in financial position for Sentry Corporation appears as Table 17–5. Notice that total sources of working capital do indeed exceed total uses by exactly $31,000. The next few pages lead up to Table 17–5 by explaining some of the more complicated items and amounts contained in that table.

**TABLE 17-4**

SENTRY CORPORATION
Schedule of Changes in Working Capital
For the Year 1984

| Account | December 31 Balance | | Increase (Decrease) in Working Capital |
|---|---|---|---|
| | 1984 | 1983 | |
| Current assets: | | | |
| Cash | $ 80,000 | $ 75,000 | $ 5,000 |
| Accounts receivable | 47,000 | 51,000 | (4,000) |
| Inventories | 110,000 | 100,000 | 10,000 |
| Unexpired insurance | 2,000 | 3,000 | (1,000) |
| Total current assets | 239,000 | 229,000 | 10,000 |
| Current liabilities: | | | |
| Accounts payable | 112,000 | 140,000 | 28,000* |
| Wages and salaries payable | 3,000 | 2,000 | (1,000) |
| Interest payable | 4,000 | 2,500 | (1,500) |
| Bank loan payable | 16,000 | 12,000 | (4,000) |
| Other accrued liabilities | 2,500 | 2,000 | (500) |
| Total current liabilities | 137,500 | 158,500 | 21,000 |
| Working capital | $101,500 | $ 70,500 | $31,000 |

* Notice that the Increase (Decrease) column reports the change in *working capital.* Accordingly, the $28,000 decrease in Accounts Payable is not placed in parentheses, because it represents an *increase* in working capital.

**Working Capital from Operations**

A major source of working capital or funds for most companies is operations. Because the income statement summarizes the operations of a firm, we look to it for the information necessary for calculating this first source. Funds from operations itself is a *net* source, consisting of the excess of working capital inflows associated with revenue transactions over those working capital outflows associated with *certain* expense transactions. Extraordinary gains and losses and nonoperating items do not relate to normal operations. Moreover, special analysis is frequently required for determining their full impact on funds. Consequently we focus our attention primarily on the items included in operating income and on income tax expense.

Sentry Corporation's net sales of $346,100 represent the inflow of working capital (cash or accounts receivable) from operations. From this amount should be subtracted the fund expenses, those expenses representing decreases in current assets or increases in current liabilities. Expenses not using funds should be ignored. Depreciation expense and amortization of goodwill are nonfund deductions. They represent decreases in noncurrent assets and do reduce net income, but they do not reduce working capital.

The portion of income taxes which has served to increase the deferred income taxes account also represents a nonfund deduction. As noted in

Chapter 13, a Deferred Taxes account is established at the initiation of a timing difference and is usually credited for the difference between the debit to Income Tax Expense and the credit to Current Income Taxes Payable. If Sentry Corporation recorded a total of $25,000 of income taxes on its 1984 income statement (including the tax resulting from the extraordinary gain) and simultaneously increased its Deferred Income Taxes by $2,000 on its balance sheet, the following entry was made:

| | | |
|---|---|---|
| Income Tax Expense | 25,000 | |
| Current Income Taxes Payable (or Cash) | | 23,000 |
| Deferred Income Taxes | | 2,000 |

Although net income for 1984 is properly reduced by the entire $25,000 of income taxes, the funds effect is only $23,000, because the Deferred Income Taxes is a noncurrent account. Working capital has only been affected by $23,000.

Subtraction of those expenses that use funds ($248,100) from the $346,100 of sales gives $98,000 as working capital from operations:

| | | |
|---|---|---|
| Revenue | | $346,100 |
| Expenses using working capital: | | |
| Cost of goods sold | $170,000 | |
| Wage and salary expense | 38,000 | |
| Advertising expense | 2,000 | |
| Insurance expense | 2,100 | |
| Other operating expenses | 13,000 | |
| Income taxes | 23,000 | |
| Total | | 248,100 |
| Working capital provided by operations | | $ 98,000 |

Interest expense also has been excluded from expenses using funds, because it is to be reported as a separate use under recurring payments to investors.[9] Loss on sale of equipment and gain on retirement of bonds have been excluded here to avoid double-counting. The negative effect of the loss will be reflected elsewhere on the SCFP in the form of a lower reported source of working capital from the equipment sale. The positive effect of the gain will be reflected elsewhere on the SCFP in the form of a lower reported use of working capital in the bond retirement.

An alternative method of computing working capital from operations is usually employed. This method begins with a net income figure and *adds back* those items not related to funds and those to be reported elsewhere in the statement:

---

[9] This classification is a matter of personal preference. As indicated in footnote 7, most statements include interest as an operating expense and hence as a deduction in arriving at working capital from operations. The important point is that, while it does represent a use of funds, it should be deducted only once.

| | | |
|---|---:|---:|
| Net income | | $45,000 |
| Add: Net loss from disposal of noncurrent items: | | |
|     Loss on sale of equipment | $ 9,000 | |
|     Gain on retirement of bonds | 1,000 | 8,000 |
| Net income exclusive of gains and losses | | |
|     on disposal of noncurrent items | | 53,000 |
| Add: Expenses not using working capital: | | |
|     Depreciation expense | 30,000 | |
|     Amortization of goodwill | 1,000 | |
|     Income taxes deferred | 2,000 | 33,000 |
|     Total | | 86,000 |
| Add: Interest expense, reported separately | | 12,000 |
| Working capital provided by operations | | $98,000 |

The advantage of this procedure is that it ties together the income statement and the statement of changes in financial position. The first item appearing on the latter is the bottom line taken from the former. Then the income is converted to working capital from operations by exclusion of (1) income statement items whose funds flow effects are reported in other sections of the SCFP and (2) expenses not using working capital.

The primary disadvantage of this method is the possibility of confusion and misinterpretation. Depreciation, amortization, and taxes deferred are *not sources* of working capital. They are added back because the initial starting figure, net income, is understated from a funds standpoint. Net income arises after all expenses are deducted, including depreciation and amortization, and those income taxes which do not use funds. If the desired goal is working capital from operations, these expenses should not be deducted. If we begin with net income, they have to be added back. Unfortunately, all too frequently these items, particularly depreciation, are looked upon as generating funds simply because they appear to be an addition to net income. The direct method, beginning with sales and deducting only those expenses which use funds, avoids the possibility of this misinterpretation and is more direct in its focus. In 1981 the FASB commented on the direct and indirect options illustrated above. In the *Proposed Statement of Financial Accounting Concepts* referred to earlier in this chapter, the FASB did "not express directly a preference for one of the two methods," because a choice "depends on an assessment of their relative costs and benefits."[10]

**Analysis of Changes in Noncurrent Accounts**

Apart from funds from operations, the statement of changes in financial position primarily conveys information about other investing and financing activities. The very nature of these activities points us to an analysis of the noncurrent accounts. The acquisition or sale of noncurrent assets will

---

[10] "Reporting Income, Cash Flows, and Financial Position of Business Enterprises," par. 167.

affect these accounts, and the noncurrent equity accounts will reflect the issuance or retirement of stocks and bonds. Consequently, a careful analysis of the changes—as revealed by the comparative balance sheet, in noncurrent assets, long-term liabilities, and owners' equity items—is a logical next step in preparing a funds statement.

An examination of Table 17–2 reveals the following changes in noncurrent accounts:

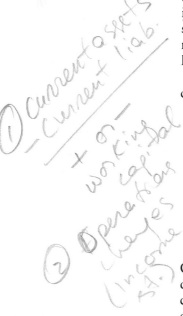

| Account | Increase | Decrease |
|---------|----------|----------|
| Land | $20,000 | |
| Plant and equipment | 5,000 | |
| Accumulated depreciation | 7,000 | |
| Goodwill | | $ 1,000 |
| Deferred income taxes | 2,000 | |
| Bonds payable | | 80,000 |
| Preferred stock | 38,000 | |
| Common stock | 50,000 | |
| Retained earnings | 38,000 | |

Of course, several of these changes result from the netting of increases and decreases. If we can explain each of these changes, we most likely will have considered all the events that have affected Sentry Corporation's working capital.

The earlier discussion of working capital from operations provides explanations for the entire change in Goodwill (amortization of $1,000) and Deferred Income Taxes (expense exceeding current tax payable by $2,000). Also considered there were one component of the change in Accumulated Depreciation (depreciation of $30,000) and one factor influencing the net increase in Retained Earnings (net income of $45,000). Let us take the remaining changes in noncurrent accounts and fit them into our overall framework.

**Sale of Noncurrent Assets.** To determine whether funds have been generated through the sale of noncurrent assets, we have to investigate three areas: (1) noncurrent asset decreases as revealed by the comparative position statement, (2) gains or losses on the income statement indicating that noncurrent assets have been sold, and (3) other information relating to asset acquisitions and retirements that accompanies the financial statements. When we do this for Sentry Corporation, we find only one source, $33,000 from sale of plant and equipment.

The Loss on Sale of Equipment account on the income statement indicates that a sale of equipment has occurred. Furthermore, the net changes in Table 17–2 for the Accumulated Depreciation and Plant and Equipment accounts are less than the Depreciation Expense of $30,000 and the capital expenditures of $70,000 for 1984, respectively. Both of these facts strongly suggest the presence of asset retirements.

However, as we mentioned earlier, it is the net proceeds, not the gain or loss, that is the funds effect. The loss discloses only that total assets decreased as the result of the transaction; funds statement preparation is concerned with the increase in current assets associated with the proceeds from the sale. To find the source of funds we must reconstruct the journal entry that was probably made when the equipment was sold. Combining our information into the normal journal entry made at the time of plant retirements, we can infer that Cash was debited $33,000, the source of working capital from the sale of equipment:

```
Cash . . . . . . . . . . . . . . . . . . . . . . . . . . . . . . . . . . . . . . . . . . . . . . . . . . . . . . . .   33,000
Accumulated Depreciation  . . . . . . . . . . . . . . . . . . . . . . . . . . .   23,000
Loss on Sale of Equipment  . . . . . . . . . . . . . . . . . . . . . . . . . . .    9,000
     Plant and Equipment  . . . . . . . . . . . . . . . . . . . . . . . . . . . . .             65,000
```

The loss on sale is found in the income statement. The rest of the entry, except for cash, is derived from the following reconstruction of ledger accounts:

| Accumulated Depreciation | | | Plant and Equipment | | |
|---|---|---|---|---|---|
| Total depreciation on retirements | $x$ | 68,000 / 30,000 | Beginning balance / Depreciation expense added during 1984 —see income statement | Beginning balance / New equipment purchases— given | 355,000 / 70,000 | $y$ / Original cost of retirements |
| | | 75,000 | Ending balance | Ending balance | 360,000 | |

$$x = \$23,000 \qquad\qquad y = \$65,000$$

In order to account for the net changes of only $7,000 in Accumulated Depreciation and only $5,000 in Plant and Equipment we posit that the former account must have been debited $23,000 and the latter credited for $65,000 when the equipment was sold.

**Acquisition of Noncurrent Assets.**  An analysis of changes in the noncurrent assets during the period as revealed by a comparative balance sheet again is the starting point for this major category of funds application. However, the net change in a noncurrent asset may not reveal the full amount of funds applied. Consideration must be given to the effect of retirements in a computation of the *gross* additions to noncurrent assets.

In the Sentry Corporation example, the gross equipment purchases are given as an additional piece of direct information at the bottom of Table 17–2. Keep in mind, however, that in some cases this figure would become available only through a reconstruction of the entries made in the Plant and Equipment account, similar to that shown above in the determination of the equipment retirements. In addition to the $70,000 purchase of equipment, there was a $20,000 increase in the Land account. We can reasonably assume that working capital was used to purchase land.

**Financing.**  The increase in working capital from financing transactions is usually relatively easy to find. Look at the comparative position statement to see if any long-term liabilities or capital stock accounts have increased. Check to see if the increase is the result of a netting of retirements against new issues or can be explained in another way, such as a reclassification of retained earnings into stock via a stock dividend. Otherwise the net change probably represents a source of working capital.

For Sentry Corporation, long-term debt has actually decreased; only preferred stock and common stock have increased. The two types of stock represent sources of funds, in the amounts of $38,000 and $50,000, respectively. One further caution is in order. You will recall from the discussion in Chapter 14 that the proceeds from stock issuances are usually credited to two balance sheet accounts, the stock account for par or stated value and an additional paid-in capital account for the excess over par or stated value. Under such circumstances, the increase in both of the accounts reflecting portions of the proceeds from the sale of a particular category of stock must be included in the *one* source of funds from the issuance of those shares.

**Return of Invested Capital.** This use of working capital is the counterpart of acquisition of funds through financing transactions. It refers to those events, such as the retirement of bonds or preferred stock or the acquisition of treasury stock, which cause decreases in working capital for the purpose of reducing long-term equities. The procedure to find the information is similar to that described for financing. Look at the comparative position statement to see if long-term liability or capital stock accounts have decreased. If the decrease cannot be explained in another way, then it probably represents a use of funds.

As we noticed earlier, the only long-term equity of the Sentry Corporation to decline is bonds payable. The extraordinary gain on the income statement provides the reason—a retirement of part of the bond issue. A reconstruction of the retirement entry reveals a use of funds for return of invested capital of $79,000.

| | | |
|---|---|---|
| Bonds Payable | 80,000 | |
| Gain on Retirement of Bonds | | 1,000 |
| Cash | | 79,000 |

If the bonds being retired originally had been issued at a premium or discount, any related unamortized valuation account also would have entered the entry above, modifying the amount of cash paid out.

**Recurring Payments to Investors**

Let us now consider the use of funds involved in the periodic distributions to investors. The declaring of cash dividends and the accruing of interest represent decreases in working capital. The amounts of these items can be found on the income statement and statement of retained earnings. For example, Table 17–3 reveals that the Sentry Corporation used $12,000 of funds for interest, $2,000 for preferred stock dividends, and $5,000 for cash dividends to the common stockholders. The $45,000 net income minus the $7,000 of dividends equals the $38,000 net increase in Retained Earnings during 1984.

**Bonds Issued at a Discount or Premium.**  In the case of the Sentry Corporation, the bonds payable were issued at face value. Consequently, the interest expense on the income statement corresponds directly to the use of working capital. However, when bonds are issued at a discount, the current market rate of interest is greater than the nominal rate. In each period, the interest expense exceeds the amount actually credited to Cash or Interest Payable. The remaining credit is made to Discount on Bonds Payable, a contra liability account.

For example, let us analyze the following hypothetical entry made for interest when bonds have been issued at a discount:

```
Interest Expense ....................................    3,300
    Cash (or Interest Payable) ........................          3,000
    Discount on Bonds Payable .......................            300
```

Owners' equity is decreased by $3,300, the amount of the charge for use of the money. The decrease in owners' equity is offset by a $3,000 decrease in working capital and a $300 increase in a long-term liability (actually recorded as a decrease in a contra liability account). From a funds viewpoint the only use is $3,000. Therefore, in reporting as a use of funds "recurring payments to investors," one must take care to adjust the interest charge shown on the income statement for the decrease in Discount on Bonds Payable. Only a portion of the interest charge results in an actual decrease in working capital. If, alternatively, interest is included as part of funds from operations, then adjustment would have to be made for the amortization of the bond discount as a nonfund expense.

When bonds have been issued at a premium, the analysis is the reverse. The effective interest charge for use of the money is less than the actual cash disbursed. Part of the periodic "interest" payment really represents a return of a portion of the bondholders' original investment. Assume the following hypothetical entry for the recording of interest on a bond originally issued at a premium.

```
Interest Expense ....................................    2,800
Premium on Bonds Payable ..........................      200
    Cash (or Interest Payable) ........................          3,000
```

The credit to Cash or Interest Payable represents the use of working capital. Part of it, $2,800, appears under the category of recurring payments to investors. The $200 reduction in Premium on Bonds Payable also reflects a use of working capital, one most appropriately classified under return of invested capital.

**Statement of Changes in Financial Position**

When we put together all the information uncovered in our analysis of the six major areas of sources and uses of funds, the result is the statement in Table 17-5. The decrease in working capital agrees with the change shown on the schedule in Table 17-4. In accordance with *Opinion No. 19*

**TABLE 17-5**

| | | | |
|---|---|---|---|
| SENTRY CORPORATION | | | |
| Statement of Changes in Financial Position (Working Capital) | | | |
| For the Year 1984 | | | |

Sources:
  Funds from operations:
    Sales ................................... $346,100
    Less: Expenses using funds ................ 248,100     $98,000
  Sale of noncurrent assets:
    Equipment .................................              33,000
  Financing:
    Issuance of preferred stock ............... 38,000
    Issuance of common stock .................. 50,000     88,000
        Total sources ........................                          $219,000

Uses:
  Recurring payments to investors:
    Interest .................................. 12,000
    Preferred dividends .......................  2,000
    Common dividends ..........................  5,000     19,000
  Return of invested capital:
    Retirement of bonds .......................              79,000
  Acquisition of noncurrent assets:
    Land ...................................... 20,000
    Equipment ................................. 70,000     90,000
        Total uses ...........................                           188,000
Increase in working capital .....................                      $ 31,000

that schedule would accompany the statement of changes in financial position.

**Other Financing and Investing Activities**

Perhaps not all transactions will fit neatly into one of the three sources or three uses of working capital outlined earlier. Nevertheless, for most situations the direct approach illustrated in this chapter leads to an accurate statement of changes in financial position. Never lose sight of the original transaction; a reconstruction of the journal entry will reveal the effect on funds whenever ambiguity is encountered. Indeed, preparation of the funds statement always entails the reconstruction of some transactions and the analysis of some ledger accounts. However, if we know exactly where to begin looking for each category on the statement and account for all changes in noncurrent assets and equities, the preparation is not difficult. Moreover, the schedule of changes in working capital serves as a check on the result shown by the statement of changes in financial position.

A detailed accounting for the changes in noncurrent assets and equities sometimes reveals the existence of significant financing and investing activities that technically do not affect working capital. When these events provide relevant information about the financing and investing activities of the firm, *APB Opinion No. 19* requires that they appear on the statement of changes in financial position.

Two such events are the acquisition of noncurrent assets through the issuance of securities and the conversion of bonds into stock. For the sake of illustration, let us assume that not all the $38,000 of preferred stock shown in Table 17–5 as a source of working capital was sold for cash. Suppose that $20,000 of it was issued in exchange for land and that $15,000 of preferred stock was issued as part of a conversion or retirement of the bond issue. Only $3,000 was sold for cash. The entries relating to land, preferred stock, and bonds *would have been:*

| | | |
|---|---|---|
| Land ........................................... | 20,000 | |
|    Preferred Stock ................................ | | 20,000 |
| | | |
| Bonds Payable ................................... | 15,000 | |
|    Preferred Stock ................................ | | 15,000 |
| | | |
| Cash .......................................... | 3,000 | |
|    Preferred Stock ................................ | | 3,000 |
| | | |
| Bonds Payable ................................... | 65,000 | |
|    Gain on Retirement of Bonds ..................... | | 1,000 |
|    Cash ......................................... | | 64,000 |

No current assets or current liabilities are involved in the first two entries. Yet, the investment of land in exchange for preferred stock is an important financing step and a major asset expansion. Similarly, the conversion of bonds to preferred stock reflects a change in financial policy and in capital structure. The communication function dictates that these transactions be disclosed on the statement of changes in financial position. *APB Opinion No. 19* requires that the impact of these significant investing and financing activities be included as separate categories on the funds statement. For example, under "sources" we would show:

| | | |
|---|---|---|
| Issuance of preferred stock: | | |
|    Sold for cash ................................... | $ 3,000 | |
|    Issued upon conversion of bonds ................. | 15,000 | |
|    Issued in exchange for land ..................... | 20,000 | $38,000 |

Under "return of invested capital" would appear the following:

| | | |
|---|---|---|
| Retirement of bonds: | | |
|    Redeemed for cash ............................. | $64,000 | |
|    Exchanged for preferred stock ................... | 15,000 | $79,000 |

Under "acquisition of noncurrent assets" would appear:

| | | |
|---|---|---|
| Equipment ...................................... | $70,000 | |
| Land received in exchange for preferred stock ........ | 20,000 | $90,000 |

Presented in this way the extra sources are offset by the extra uses, and the overall change in working capital is not distorted. Still, the detail of two significant financing-investing events—land acquisition and bond conversion—are communicated.

Acquisition of assets in exchange for stock or debt and conversions probably constitute the most common types of significant financing-investing activities not affecting working capital. Other less common ones would include exchanges of long-lived assets (e.g., investments given up in exchange for equipment), dividends paid in kind (e.g., investments distributed to stockholders as a dividend), or capital donations of noncurrent items (e.g., conveyance of title to land from a city to a firm as an inducement to build a plant). In each case the entry can be viewed as a constructive cash transaction.

## PREPARATION OF THE STATEMENT— CASH CONCEPT

A working capital concept of funds disregards offsetting movements among the individual current assets and liabilities. Treating increases in inventories and cash receipts as similar and viewing decreases in prepayments and cash disbursements in the same light may conceal short-term financial movements that have significance to internal and external users. The working capital funds statement may reveal a favorable flow, and yet the firm may be unable to pay its bills. A statement of cash flows provides more detailed information.

This section illustrates how a cash funds statement can be constructed from a basic set of financial statements. Let us take the Sentry Corporation data in Tables 17-2 and 17-3 and try to present in an orderly fashion the major financial events responsible for the increase in cash of $5,000 during 1984. We can again use the framework of three sources and three uses to present the sources and uses of cash.

## Cash from Operations

Many of the transactions reported on the working capital funds statement also may be presumed to have involved cash receipts or disbursements, for example, issuance of preferred stock or sale of equipment. These also appear on a cash funds statement. The major area where the two types of funds statements differ is the flow from operations. Funds from operations under a working capital concept still reflect accrual accounting procedures; for example, sales are a source of working capital, and cost of goods sold is a use of working capital. However, under a cash concept of funds we are concerned with a cash basis of accounting; collections from customers and payments to suppliers for purchased inventory are the source and use of cash corresponding to sales and cost of goods sold, respectively.

To compute cash from operations we must convert working capital from operations from an accrual to a cash basis. This means adjusting each operating item for the effect of changes in the current assets or liabilities operationally related to it. Some common adjustments are outlined in Table 17-6, and other items usually can be handled in a similar manner.

Recall that the determination of the sources and uses of funds requires an analysis of changes in the nonfund accounts. When funds are defined as

**TABLE 17-6  Adjustments to Convert Common Income Statement Items from Accrual to Cash Basis**

| Working Capital Item | ± | Adjustments | = | Cash Item |
|---|---|---|---|---|
| 1. Sales | | − Increase in accounts receivable<br>+ Decrease in accounts receivable | = | Cash collections from customers |
| 2. Cost of goods sold | | + Increase in inventory<br>− Decrease in inventory<br>= Purchases<br>− Increase in accounts payable<br>+ Decrease in accounts payable | = | Cash payments for purchases |
| 3. Insurance expense | | + Increase in unexpired insurance<br>− Decrease in unexpired insurance | = | Cash expenditures on insurance |
| 4. Income tax expense | | − Increase in taxes payable<br>+ Decrease in taxes payable | = | Cash outlays for taxes |

working capital, the fund accounts were, of course, the current assets and current liabilities; the noncurrent accounts were left as the focus of attention for the determination of sources and uses. When funds are defined as cash, the only fund account is Cash; this leaves all noncurrent accounts *plus* all current accounts other than Cash to be considered when we ascertain the sources and uses of cash. The changes in the eight noncash current accounts included in Table 17-4 can no longer be relegated to the schedule at the bottom of the statement of changes in financial position. Instead, they greatly influence the funds from operations as reported in the SCFP proper.

In the Sentry Corporation example, accounts receivable decreased by $4,000 during 1984. Collections from customers (credits to Accounts Receivable) must have exceeded the $346,100 of sales (debits to Accounts Receivable). Consequently, the source of cash from customer collections is actually $350,100 ($346,100 + $4,000). Sales to customers may have produced only $346,100 of *working capital* during 1984, but collections from customers during 1984 for some 1983 credit sales (beginning-1984 balance of accounts receivable) and many 1984 credit sales (all except ending-1984 balance of accounts receivable) produced $350,100 of *cash*.

With merchandise, we note in Table 17-4 that inventories increased $10,000 and accounts payable related to inventory purchases decreased $28,000. These facts indicate that merchandise purchases exceeded goods sold, and cash payments exceeded the amount of purchases. The use of cash can be calculated as follows:

| | |
|---|---:|
| Cost of goods sold | $170,000 |
| Add: Increase in inventory | 10,000 |
| Merchandise purchases | 180,000 |
| Add: Decrease in accounts payable | 28,000 |
| Cash payments for purchases | $208,000 |

Because Wages and Salaries Payable increased $1,000, we can infer that cash payments to employees were only $37,000, $1,000 less than the $38,000 expense. Similarly, the decrease in Unexpired Insurance of $1,000 means that cash disbursements for insurance premiums were only $1,100 ($2,100 − $1,000). Assume that "other accrued liabilities" refers to the various accruals related to advertising, other operating expenses, and current income taxes. Since this liability increased $500 during the period, the total of these expenses must have exceeded the cash expenditures for the items by that amount. Consequently, the use of cash is $37,500 ($2,000 + $13,000 + $23,000 − $500).

The following schedule summarizes the cash flow from operations:

| | | |
|---|---:|---:|
| Cash collections from customers .............. | | $350,100 |
| Cash payments: | | |
|    For merchandise purchases ................. | $208,000 | |
|    For wages and salaries .................... | 37,000 | |
|    For insurance premiums ................... | 1,100 | |
|    For advertising, other operating | | |
|      expenses, and income taxes ............. | 37,500 | 283,600 |
| Cash inflow from operations ................... | | $ 66,500 |

This figure is derived from a restatement of individual revenues and expenses on a cash basis. Notice that it shows only a $66,500 net inflow of cash, even though working capital increased $98,000 as a result of operations.

Practically, it may be difficult to relate specific current assets and current liabilities to particular revenues and expenses on the income statement. The one-to-one correspondence, although helpful in understanding the derivation of the cash funds statement, is not really necessary if we only wish to focus on the single figure of cash from operations. If we can identify those current assets and current liabilities related to operations, an adjustment can be made to the total only, as shown in Table 17–7.

**TABLE 17–7  Derivation of Cash from Operations**

| | | |
|---|---:|---:|
| Working capital from operations* ......................... | | $98,000 |
| Adjustments to convert to cash basis:† | | |
|   Add: Decrease in accounts receivable .................... | $ 4,000 | |
|      Decrease in unexpired insurance .................... | 1,000 | |
|      Increase in wages and salaries payable .............. | 1,000 | |
|      Increase in other accrued liabilities .................. | 500 | 6,500 |
|   Deduct: Increase in inventories .......................... | 10,000 | |
|      Decrease in accounts payable ....................... | 28,000 | (38,000) |
| Cash inflow from operations ................................ | | $66,500 |

* We could start with net income and then adjust for special and nonfund items as well as for changes in noncash current accounts.

† *Opinion No. 19* requires that these adjustments be shown as separate items within the SCFP whenever funds are defined as cash.

**Complete Statement**

The complete cash funds statement is presented in Table 17–8. The analysis of cash events in other major areas is straightforward for the most part. Other new or different items appearing on the cash funds statement in addition to cash from operations are summarized below:

1. During 1984 Sentry Corporation borrowed additional cash from the bank on a *short-term* basis (see increase in Bank Loan Payable account in Table 17–4). Although this $4,000 transaction does not represent a source of working capital (current assets and current liabilities increase by the same amount), it is a source of *cash* from financing.
2. Since interest payable increased $1,500 during 1984, the cash payments for interest are only $10,500 rather than the $12,000 shown for interest expense in Table 17–3.

**TABLE 17–8**

SENTRY CORPORATION
Statement of Changes in Financial Position (Cash)
For the Year 1984

| | | | |
|---|---:|---:|---:|
| Sources: | | | |
| Funds from operations (detail omitted) . . . . . . . . . . . | | $66,500 | |
| Sale of noncash assets: | | | |
| Equipment . . . . . . . . . . . . . . . . . . . . . . . . . . . . . | | 33,000 | |
| Financing: | | | |
| Issuance of preferred stock . . . . . . . . . . . . . . . . . | $38,000 | | |
| Issuance of common stock . . . . . . . . . . . . . . . . . | 50,000 | | |
| Increase in bank loans . . . . . . . . . . . . . . . . . . . . . | 4,000 | 92,000 | |
| Total sources . . . . . . . . . . . . . . . . . . . . . . . . . . | | | $191,500 |
| Uses: | | | |
| Recurring payments to investors: | | | |
| Interest . . . . . . . . . . . . . . . . . . . . . . . . . . . . . . . . . | 10,500 | | |
| Preferred dividends . . . . . . . . . . . . . . . . . . . . . . . . | 2,000 | | |
| Common dividends . . . . . . . . . . . . . . . . . . . . . . . . | 5,000 | 17,500 | |
| Return of invested capital: | | | |
| Retirement of bonds . . . . . . . . . . . . . . . . . . . . . . . | | 79,000 | |
| Acquisition of noncash assets: | | | |
| Land . . . . . . . . . . . . . . . . . . . . . . . . . . . . . . . . . . . | 20,000 | | |
| Equipment . . . . . . . . . . . . . . . . . . . . . . . . . . . . . | 70,000 | 90,000 | |
| Total uses . . . . . . . . . . . . . . . . . . . . . . . . . . . . . | | | 186,500 |
| Increase in Cash . . . . . . . . . . . . . . . . . . . . . . . . . . . | | | $  5,000 |

**The Concept of "Cash Flow"**

One of the currently popular concepts related to funds is that of "cash flow." This term is sometimes used by businesses in reporting on the results of their operations and by security analysts in their evaluations and recommendations concerning the common stock of various companies as investments. As used in these situations, *cash flow* is commonly defined as net income plus depreciation and sometimes amortization and deferred income taxes.

Cash flow is a misnomer for the concept of net income plus depreciation and similar items. As we have just seen, net income computed on an accrual basis does not represent a net cash inflow. Adding back depreciation does not adjust for the other accrual items reflected in net income. Moreover, it carries the false implication that depreciation is a source of cash. All that net income plus depreciation may show is the increase in working capital, *not cash,* arising from the operation of the business.

The cash flow concept may be misleading if not used with care. First, it is incomplete, since it ignores other sources and uses of funds. Operations represent only one source of net current assets and logically should be presented as a part of an overall statement of changes in financial position. The use of funds from operations or "cash flow" by itself may lead to inaccurate judgments concerning dividend, debt reduction, and asset replacement and expansion policies.

Both the APB and the SEC have frowned upon the presentation of isolated statistics of funds from operations outside of the formal statement of changes in financial position. *Opinion No. 19* tried to restrict this practice, without much success. Unfortunately, some users of the cash flow concept suggest it as a substitute for net income, expressing it in per share terms. Cash flow per share falsely implies that depreciation somehow is not a valid expense. When a firm diminishes the service potential of its fixed assets through their use in revenue generation, you have an expense and a determinant of net income. That the resource may have been paid for in a prior period is irrelevant. Only a net income figure that measures the effect of operations on all assets can be meaningfully related to investment in the determination of how well resources have been managed.

Cash flow earnings are a misuse of both the concept of cash and the concept of earnings. To the extent that funds from operations are a meaningful and helpful supplementary measure, cash flow would be also. However, when clothed in a false title, presented in a misleading manner apart from the rest of the funds statement, and used where they do not belong, cash flow figures probably are confusing rather than enlightening.

**DISCUSSION OF THE ARMCO ANNUAL REPORT**

The funds flow disclosures contained in Armco's 1981 annual report consist of (1) the statement of changes in consolidated financial position, (2) an elaboration in the section called "Management's Discussion and Analysis," of many of the major business events reflected in some of the aggregations on the SCFP, and (3) the inclusion of "cash flow from operations" in the Other Financial Data section. Brief mention was made in Chapter 5 of two somewhat unusual aspects of Armco's SCFP; a more lengthy discussion of them is included in the following comments.

**Funds Defined as Cash/Marketable Securities**

The bottom section of the SCFP reveals that Armco defines funds as cash and marketable securities. The 1981 SCFP lists those items and events which explain why the total of Armco's cash and marketable securities increased by $8.2 million during the year. Although the firm is not alone in adopting such a definition of funds, it was certainly in a distinct minority in 1981, given the great predominance of the working capital funds definition (see footnote 3 of this chapter). Armco's selection of a funds definition of cash and near-cash will probably become more common over the next several years as firms feel some motivation to move in the direction of the cash definition recommended in the FASB's *Proposed Statement of Financial Accounting Concepts* issued in 1981.

Although Armco's definition of funds is presently only uncommon, its failure to divide the SCFP into separate sections for sources and uses is almost unique. The interspersing of sources and uses does not affect the accuracy of the statement. Indeed, it may provide potentially useful net source or net use amounts for such broad categories as financing or capital expenditures and investments. Nevertheless, many readers may find such an arrangement more difficult to grasp and interpret. Later, in Table 17–9, Armco's SCFP is recast into the more traditional format; the reader can judge whether it better communicates the major investment and financing activities undertaken by the firm during 1981.

**Alternative Definition of Funds**

An examination of Armco's Statement of Consolidated Financial Position indirectly reveals that the firm's working capital increased during 1981 by $203.3 million; this represents a 24.2 percent increase from the December 31, 1980, total of $839.1 million. In its SCFP Armco reports only an $8.2 million funds increase during 1981. A much different, though not necessarily more accurate, impression of funds flow changes would have been gained by the annual report reader if Armco had defined funds as working capital. The section titled "Change in Working Capital" on page 166 does not adequately substitute for a full-fledged working capital SCFP, especially since that section fails to disclose the $203.3 million increase in working capital.

**"Cash Flow"**

Included in the "Other Data" section on page 171 are amounts of $519.5 million and $460.8 million for "cash flow from operations" for 1981 and 1980, respectively. The relationship between these two numbers is highlighted in "Management's Discussion," where the company states that "cash flow from operations increased 13 percent in 1981."

The top portion of Armco's SCFP shows the items comprising those cash flows from operations. They include net income plus depreciation and other *nonworking* capital items.[11] As we shall see shortly in Table 17–9, the $519.5 million is actually working capital from operations.

---

[11] In a previous section of this chapter, the rationale for the addition of depreciation expense and income taxes deferred in the calculation of funds from operations was discussed. The Appendix to this chapter covers, among other topics, the reasoning behind the addition for lease right amortization and the deduction for equity in net income of AFSG.

**TABLE 17-9  Alternative Format for Armco's Statement of Changes in Financial Position for 1981—Sources and Uses of Working Capital ($ millions)**

Sources:
　Funds from operations:
　　Net income ................................. $294.5
　　Add: Income items not affecting working capital:
　　　Depreciation expense ....................... $166.5
　　　Lease right amortization .................... 7.8
　　　Deferred income taxes ..................... 64.4
　　　Other—net ............................. 16.6
　　　Equity in net income of AFSG .............. (30.3)　225.0

　Working capital from operations ................. $ 519.5
　Sale of noncurrent assets:
　　Book value of property retired ................. 25.5
　　Other items ............................... 38.4　63.9

　Financing:
　　Common stock issued for businesses ............ 297.1
　　Issuance of long-term debt .................... 163.0　460.1
　　　　Total sources ........................... 1,043.5

Uses:
　Recurring payments to investors:
　　Dividends ............................. 103.9
　Acquisition of noncurrent assets:
　　Capital expenditures ........................ 393.6
　　Ladish property acquired ..................... 68.1
　　New investments .......................... 38.4
　　Deferred charges .......................... 11.4
　　Other items ............................. 128.9　640.4

　Return of invested capital:
　　Payments on long-term debt and leases ......... 38.6
　　Purchase of treasury stock .................... 29.2
　　Other items ............................. 28.1　95.9
　　　　Total uses ............................. 840.2
　Increase in working capital ...................... $ 203.3

Every item in the first *two* sections of the report prepared by Armco must be considered before arriving at a number which measures *cash* flow from operations accurately. As we noted in a preceding section of this chapter, net income computed on an accrual basis does not represent a net cash flow. Changes in the balances of all current accounts (other than cash and marketable securities) *which resulted from operations* must be included with Armco's $519.5 "cash flow" number in order to ascertain the real cash flow from operations. As Table 17-10 shows, the real cash flow from operations changes from the reported $519.5 million to only $37.6 million.

**Modifications to Armco's SCFP**

Armco's SCFP has been adjusted and restructured in Tables 17-9 and 17-10 to make it more consistent with the discussion in this chapter. In contrast to the SCFP which Armco presented in its annual report, the

**TABLE 17–10  Alternate Format for Armco's Statement of Changes in Financial Position for 1981—Sources and Uses of Cash and Marketable Securities ($ millions)**

| | | | |
|---|---:|---:|---:|
| Sources: | | | |
| Funds from operations: | | | |
|   Working capital from operations . . . . . . . . . . . . . . . . . | | $519.5 | |
|   Adjustments to convert to a cash basis: | | | |
|     Increase in accounts payable and accruals . . . . . | $ 12.7 | | |
|     Increase in inventories . . . . . . . . . . . . . . . . . . . . . . . | (205.6) | | |
|     Increase in receivables . . . . . . . . . . . . . . . . . . . . . | (137.5) | | |
|     Ladish Co. working capital acquired . . . . . . . . . . . | (151.5) | (481.9) | |
|   Cash from operations . . . . . . . . . . . . . . . . . . . . . . . . . | | | $ 37.6 |
| Sale of noncurrent assets: | | | |
|   Book value of property retired . . . . . . . . . . . . . . . . . | | 25.5 | |
|   Other items . . . . . . . . . . . . . . . . . . . . . . . . . . . . . . . . | | 38.4 | 63.9 |
| Financing: | | | |
|   Common stock issued for businesses . . . . . . . . . . . . . | | 297.1 | |
|   Issuance of long-term debt . . . . . . . . . . . . . . . . . . . . | | 163.0 | |
|   Issuance of short-term notes . . . . . . . . . . . . . . . . . . . | | 282.9 | 743.0 |
|     Total sources . . . . . . . . . . . . . . . . . . . . . . . . . . . . . | | | 844.5 |
| Uses: | | | |
| Recurring payments to investors: | | | |
|   Dividends . . . . . . . . . . . . . . . . . . . . . . . . . . . . . . . . . | | 103.9 | |
| Acquisition of noncurrent assets: | | | |
|   Capital expenditures . . . . . . . . . . . . . . . . . . . . . . . . . | 393.6 | | |
|   Ladish property acquired . . . . . . . . . . . . . . . . . . . . . | 68.1 | | |
|   New investments . . . . . . . . . . . . . . . . . . . . . . . . . . . | 38.4 | | |
|   Deferred charges . . . . . . . . . . . . . . . . . . . . . . . . . . . | 11.4 | | |
|   Other items . . . . . . . . . . . . . . . . . . . . . . . . . . . . . . . | 128.9 | 640.4 | |
| Return of invested capital: | | | |
|   Payments on long-term debt and leases . . . . . . . . . | 34.7 | | |
|   Purchase of treasury stock . . . . . . . . . . . . . . . . . . . | 29.2 | | |
|   Other items . . . . . . . . . . . . . . . . . . . . . . . . . . . . . . . | 28.1 | 92.0 | |
|     Total uses . . . . . . . . . . . . . . . . . . . . . . . . . . . . . . . | | | 836.3 |
| Increase in cash and marketable securities . . . . . . . . . | | | $ 8.2 |

statement formats in these tables clearly distinguish and separate the sources of funds from the uses of funds.

In Table 17–9 the statement of changes in financial position employs a working capital concept of funds. Armco's working capital increased by $203.3 million during 1981. Table 17–10 shows an alternative structure for the explanation of the same $8.2 million increase in cash and marketable securities which Armco depicted in its SCFP. A comparison of the two statements under each of these definitions of funds facilitates an understanding of why cash and marketable securities increased $195.1 million less than the change in working capital. In Table 17–11 the factors that have affected the two funds statements differently are highlighted.

The format presented in Table 17–11 for the conversion of the funds from operations to a cash basis parallels the approach which was illustrated earlier in Table 17–7. Other things being equal, a firm which has built up

**TABLE 17-11  Reconciliation of Armco's Changes in Working Capital and Cash/Marketable Securities for 1981 ($ millions)**

| | | | | |
|---|---|---|---|---|
| Increase in working capital | | | | $203.3 |
| Deduct: Excess of working capital provided by operations over cash provided by operations: | | | | |
| Working capital provided by operations | | | $519.5 | |
| Adjustments to convert to cash basis: | | | | |
| Add: Increase in accounts payable/accruals | | $ 12.7 | | |
| Deduct: Increase in inventories | $205.6 | | | |
| Increase in receivables | 137.5 | | | |
| Ladish Co. working capital acquired | 151.5 | 494.6 | | |
| Net deduction | | | 481.9 | (481.9) |
| Cash provided by operations | | | 37.6 | |
| Add: Issuance of short-term notes payable | | | | 282.9 |
| Add: Excess of working capital used for return of capital over cash used for return of capital—increase in current portion of long-term debt and lease obligations | | | | 3.9 |
| Increase in cash | | | | $ 8.2 |

its inventories and has experienced customers who are incurring new charges at a faster rate than their payment of old charges has less cash than the amount which would have been available had those events not occurred. Similarly, a company which has gone deeper into debt with its suppliers has more cash than the amount which would have been available if this had not occurred.

In Tables 17-10 and 17-11, the amounts used for the changes in accounts payable, inventories, and receivables were taken from Armco's SCFP. Those figures *do not* correspond to the account changes which can be calculated from an analysis of the comparative consolidated balance sheet. In the SCFP, the firm has separately identified the working capital acquired as a result of the purchase of Ladish Co. On the balance sheets, however, that acquired working capital has been disaggregated into the various current items which it represents, namely accounts payable, inventories, and receivables. If the Ladish Co. working capital is dropped as a separate factor, then the current account changes on the consolidated balance sheets can be used to arrive at the same $481.9 reconciliation factor shown in Table 17-11. The calculation is as follows:

| | | |
|---|---|---|
| Increase in accounts payable/accruals | | $ 130.8 |
| Deduct: | | |
| Increase in inventories | $417.7 | |
| Increase in receivables | 195.0 | |
| Total | | (612.7) |
| Net deduction | | ($481.9) |

**Retirement of Property, Plant, and Equipment**

One additional issue emerges when the content of Armco's SCFP is studied carefully. The last item in the section titled "Capital Expenditures and Investments" is a $25.5 million source of funds represented by the

"Book value of property, plant, and equipment retired." In order to achieve more complete disclosure, Armco should have listed the *proceeds* from such retirements as the separate source of funds. All gains and losses from such disposals should have been adjusted out of net income in order to avoid double-counting. Of course, Armco's actual treatment does not destroy the accuracy of the net funds increase of $8.2 million. However, if gains and losses are material, it could distort the dollar amounts attributable to the explanatory events.

Because the discussion of funds statements in this chapter has assumed a thorough knowledge of only the material covered in Chapters 1–10 and 13–14, the nature and placement of several items in Armco's SCFP may be unclear. The Appendix to this chapter discusses some more advanced items in the context of the preparation of a SCFP.

**SUMMARY**

The general purpose of the funds statement is to disclose a firm's major sources of capital during the period and the major areas to which these funds have been committed. In so doing, the statement discloses causes of changes in financial position during the period. In recent years, the statement of changes in financial position has joined the income statement and balance sheet as a primary financial statement in corporate annual reports.

Typical funds statements after *Opinion No. 19* are a curious blend of purposes. On the one hand, the statement usually reports on flows into or out of some corpus of funds, either working capital, cash, or cash and near-cash. Most transactions that affect the firm's long-term assets or capital structure also directly involve cash or other elements of working capital. These investing and financing activities are reported routinely on the statement. On the other hand, the SCFP also serves to classify certain noncurrent and noncash exchanges that occur in designated balance sheet categories or accounts. The FASB requires that those noncurrent and noncash transactions which affect long-term assets or capital structure be viewed constructively, as if offsetting cash or working capital inflows and outflows have occurred. For example, the conversion of debt or preferred stock to common stock should be seen and reported as two separate transactions—the issuance of common stock for cash, then the immediate payment of that cash for retirement of the debt or preferred stock.

In the formats and procedures illustrated in this chapter, we have systematically grouped investing and financing activities according to their causal factors. Intuitively, adoption of this events approach provides to users maximum clarification of the nature of funds activities. It also provides a systematic search procedure in those instances when the analyst must construct or reconstruct the statement.

For sources of funds or financing activities, the user looks at three major areas: (1) operations, as measured by net income adjusted for nonfund expenses; (2) financing transactions, as reflected in increases in long-term equities; and (3) sales of nonfund assets, as revealed by decreases in nonfund assets and/or gains and losses in the income statement. Similarly, there are three broad categories of uses of funds or investing activities: (1) recurring payments to investors, as measured by interest and dividends; (2) return of invested capital, as reflected in decreases in long-term equities; and (3) acquisitions of nonfund assets, as revealed by gross changes in the balance sheet accounts.

A careful analysis of these six areas commonly will reveal the needed information. The analyst has two additional checks. First, a separate schedule of changes in fund accounts should articulate with the differences between sources and uses as well as provide useful information about short-term financing and investing movements within the fund area. Secondly, an investigation to see that all changes in nonfund assets and equities have been explained will preclude the omission of some major event and will identify relevant nonfund exchanges that should be incorporated into the statement of changes in financial position.

The statement of changes in financial position, whether prepared under a working capital or a cash definition of funds, has become an important analytical tool for investors and analysts. Although it also is historical in nature, the SCFP is more forward looking than the balance sheet and income statement. In the process of explaining the causes for the change in the balance of funds, the SCFP provides insight into current investment and financing activities which may very well influence the firm's financial position and net income for many years in the future.

## APPENDIX: Treatment of More Complex Items on the Funds Statement

The purpose of this Appendix is to illustrate how the following four complex and specialized items are handled on the SCFP:

1. Leases.
2. Parent investments in unconsolidated subsidiaries and investees.
3. Amortization of bonds purchased as a long-term investment.
4. Stock dividends.

**Leases**

As noted in Chapter 11, *FASB Statement No. 13* has significantly increased the proportion of leases which must be accounted for as the equivalent of a long-term installment purchase of the leased property. In such circumstances, the lessee makes a journal entry in which Leased Property under Capital Leases is debited and Obligations under Capital Leases is credited.

Table 11-1 summarizes the entire series of journal entries which the lessee makes in such a capital lease situation. The existence of capital leases affects the preparation of the SCFP in several locations. When a capital lease is initially signed, the acquisition of the leased asset and the incurrence of the lease obligation must be shown as a use of funds and source of funds respectively. Although the journal entry technically involves no inflow or outflow of funds, the event is a major financing and investing one that should be disclosed. Accordingly, it is handled on the SCFP as a constructive inflow of funds from financing and use of funds for noncurrent asset expansion.

If the funds from operations section begins with the net income number, depreciation of leased property (amortization of leased rights) must be added. This expense, like amortization of goodwill and depreciation of owned property, is a nonfund item which used neither cash nor working capital. As noted in Table 17-9, Armco added $7.8 million of lease right amortization to its net income number in the operations section of its SCFP.

Because the Lease Obligations account balance constitutes long-term debt, payments which reduce this liability represent a use of funds for the return of invested capital. Many firms, unlike Armco, choose to combine the payments reducing the principal amounts of both lease and nonlease debt and list them as one use of funds. Of course, the interest expense on the financing of capital leases would be treated on the SCFP in the same manner as all other interest expense.

## Parent Company Investments in Unconsolidated Subsidiaries

Included in Chapter 15 was a discussion of the equity method. This method is used by a parent company to record the investment in *unconsolidated* subsidiaries. It is also required whenever a parent/investor exerts significant influence over an investee corporation.

Recall that under the equity method of recording such intercompany investments, the Investment account is debited and Equity in Investee Income is credited each period for the investor's portion of the net income of the investee. The Investment in Subsidiary account is, of course, a nonfund asset. Consequently, only the portion of the investee earnings actually remitted via dividend declaration is a source of working capital. For instance, assume that a 50 percent owned investee earns $90,000 during the year and pays $50,000 in dividends. The following entries would appear on the investor's books:

| | | |
|---|---|---|
| Investment in Subsidiary | 45,000 | |
|     Equity in Investee Income | | 45,000 |
| Cash | 25,000 | |
|     Investment in Subsidiary | | 25,000 |

Only $25,000 of the $45,000 that appears on the income statement should appear as funds from operations. Either only the $25,000 of dividends should be added to sales under the direct approach, or $20,000 should be subtracted from net income as a nonfund adjustment. The funds impact can often be isolated by comparison of the income statement item with the net change in the investment account. If the two are equal, then the entire Equity in Investee Income shown on the income statement is nonfund.

Armco explains in Note 2 of its annual report that it is the sole owner of various insurance and finance/leasing subsidiaries; collectively they are referred to as Armco Financial Services Group or AFSG. The subsidiaries comprising the AFSG are not consolidated, because their operating activities are quite different from those of Armco. Because Armco owns 100 percent of the AFSG firms, the equity method is appropriately used.

In the first section of its SCFP, Armco makes two adjustments to net income to reflect its unconsolidated subsidiaries. Notice that Armco's "Equity in net income of AFSG" is removed from net income and replaced by "Dividends paid to Armco by AFSG." The addition and subtraction accomplish the equivalent of the $20,000 subtraction suggested for the indirect method in the above numerical example.

## Amortization of Bonds Purchased

A previous section of this chapter considered the manner in which discount and premium amortization on bonds *issued* should be reflected on a firm's SCFP. You will recall that the *portion* of interest expense which resulted from discount amortization was treated similarly to other nonfund expenses. It was subtracted from the interest expense in the proper measurement of funds usage. On the other hand, premium amortization was treated as an additional use of funds (return of invested capital), because the total for interest expense understated the use of funds for interest payments. We now will examine the other side of the bond transaction, namely, the *purchase* of bonds at a discount or a premium.

As Table 10–6 illustrated, the investor who purchased bonds at a premium made the following journal entry at the end of the first year:

| | | |
|---|---|---|
| Cash | 200 | |
| Interest Revenue | | 173 |
| Investment in Bonds | | 27 |

Although only $173 was included in the net income of the firm which acquired those bonds, the increase in cash and working capital was $200. Accordingly, the $27 premium amortization on bonds purchased would need to be reported as a source of funds from liquidation of noncurrent assets. Alternatively, it might be *added* to net income in the funds from operations section.

For bonds purchased at a discount, the credit to Interest Revenue will exceed the inflow of cash and working capital. In this instance, the net income figure will overstate the net inflow of funds. Therefore, the discount amortization on bonds purchased would need to be *deducted* from net income in the funds from operations section.

## Stock Dividends

In Chapter 14, the proper accounting treatment for the declaration and issuance of stock dividends was reviewed. Although the amount of the recording could differ depending on the size of the stock dividend, the accounts involved always included Retained Earnings (debit) and Common Stock (credit). When the change in the stock accounts are examined for purposes of preparing the SCFP, the analyst must be careful not to infer too quickly that the entire change in those accounts represents a source of cash and working capital. If evidence of a stock dividend exists, then its amount must be deducted from the changes in the capital stock accounts before the actual source of funds from financing can be ascertained.

The SCFP is intended to reveal the major investment and financing activities entered into by the firm during the year. To aid in the achievement of this objective, an event such as the acquisition of land through the issuance of stock could not be omitted even though it technically did not affect cash or working capital. A stock dividend, on the other hand, involves no new investment or financing; accordingly, once detected it need not be listed on the statement of changes in financial position.

## QUESTIONS AND PROBLEMS

**17-1.** The following list contains some selected accounting events. For each of these items, indicate whether it would result in an increase, a decrease, or no change in *(a)* cash and/or *(b)* working capital. For those items with no effect on either cash or working capital, indicate whether the event would be reported as a constructive source and use under an all financial resources approach.

1. Issuance of a five-year note in connection with the purchase of inventory.
2. Sale of marketable securities for cash at more than their original cost.
3. Issuance of common stock in exchange for shares of preferred stock presented to the company for conversion.
4. Recording of depletion cost.
5. Acquisition of a building through a cash down payment and the assumption of an existing mortgage on the property.
6. Collection of accounts receivable.
7. Reclassification of the currently maturing portion of long-term debt as a current liability.
8. Issuance of shares of stock in exchange for a patent.
9. Write-off of goodwill.
10. Declaration of a cash dividend on common stock on December 15, payable on January 10.
11. Acquisition of new equipment in exchange for some investment securities which had been held for three years.
12. Write-off of a specific uncollectible account.
13. Sales recorded on account.
14. Flood damage to merchandise.
15. Sale of partially depreciated equipment for cash at less than its book value.

**17-2.** The following data relate to the financial information included in the 1985 annual report of UMA Corporation:

UMA CORPORATION
Comparative Balance Sheet
As of December 31

|  | 1985 | 1984 |
|---|---|---|
| *Assets* | | |
| Cash | $ 92,800 | $ 26,900 |
| Accounts receivable (net) | 158,000 | 138,600 |
| Inventories | 113,900 | 88,700 |
| Plant assets | 504,600 | 497,000 |
| Accumulated depreciation | (104,000) | (91,300) |
| Total assets | $765,300 | $659,900 |
| *Equities* | | |
| Accounts payable | $163,400 | $116,500 |
| Mortgage payable | 37,000 | 45,800 |
| Deferred income taxes | 26,600 | 15,900 |
| Preferred stock | 4,000 | — |
| Common stock | 291,100 | 281,700 |
| Retained earnings | 243,200 | 200,000 |
| Total equities | $765,300 | $659,900 |

UMA CORPORATION
Statement of Income and Changes in Retained Earnings
for 1985

| | | |
|---|---|---|
| Sales revenue | | $580,000 |
| Less: | | |
| Cost of goods sold | $397,000 | |
| Selling and general expenses | 30,000 | |
| Depreciation expense | 26,200 | |
| Interest expense | 5,000 | 458,200 |
| Operating income | | 121,800 |
| Less: | | |
| Loss on sale of plant assets | | 8,300 |
| Income before taxes | | 113,500 |
| Income taxes | | 53,500 |
| Net income | | 60,000 |
| Retained earnings, January 1 | | 200,000 |
| Total | | 260,000 |
| Less: | | |
| Preferred dividends | 500 | |
| Common dividends | 16,300 | 16,800 |
| Retained earnings, December 31 | | $243,200 |

*Additional information:*

$65,000 of plant assets were purchased in 1985.

*Required:*

a. Prepare a schedule of changes in working capital for 1985.
b. Prepare the journal entry to reflect the sale of plant assets in 1985.
c. Prepare a statement of changes in financial position for 1985 which will explain the change in working capital.
d. In Chapter 2, the equity side of the balance sheet was described as depicting sources of assets. How does it differ then from the sources of funds shown on the statement of changes in financial position? Do we need both statements?

**17–3.** Elaine Rabin, the distinguished chief executive officer of your firm, calls you on the telephone. Quite irately she says, "The worse we do, the better off we get. We operated at a net loss of over $15,000, but working capital increased by about $1,500 and cash increased by over $12,000. Can anyone around here explain to me what's going on?"

Financial information for the year is summarized below:

Income Statement

| | | |
|---|---|---|
| Sales revenue | | $139,600 |
| Expenses: | | |
| Cost of goods sold | $83,600 | |
| Depreciation expense | 4,100 | |
| Other expenses | 66,200 | |
| Loss on sale of equipment | 900 | 154,800 |
| Net loss | | $ 15,200 |

Statement of Retained Earnings

| | | |
|---|---|---|
| Beginning balance | | $30,000 |
| Net loss | $15,200 | |
| Dividends | 6,000 | 21,200 |
| Ending balance | | $ 8,800 |

Balance Sheet Comparative Data

| | End of Year | Beginning of Year |
|---|---|---|
| *Assets* | | |
| Cash | $30,600 | $18,100 |
| Marketable securities | — | 600 |
| Accounts receivable | 18,400 | 24,300 |
| Inventory | 10,000 | 17,000 |
| Prepayments (current) | 800 | 1,200 |
| Land | 9,500 | 9,500 |
| Plant assets | 40,200 | 45,000 |
| Allowance for depreciation | (24,200) | (22,600) |
| Total assets | $85,300 | $93,100 |
| *Equities* | | |
| Accounts payable | $15,100 | $19,100 |
| Accrued liabilities | 1,400 | 700 |
| Dividends payable | 1,500 | 1,300 |
| Long-term notes payable | 9,900 | 7,000 |
| Common stock | 31,300 | 31,000 |
| Additional paid-in capital | 17,300 | 4,000 |
| Retained earnings | 8,800 | 30,000 |
| Total equities | $85,300 | $93,100 |

*Required:*

a. Prepare a funds statement for the year which will explain the increase in working capital.

b. Prepare a funds statement for the year which will explain the increase in the cash balance.

c. Write a brief memo summarizing your major conclusions and explanations for "what's going on."

**17–4.** The following statement of changes in financial position was prepared by Menon Corporation for 1985:

Sources:
Operations:

| | | | |
|---|---|---|---|
| Net income | $50,000 | | |
| Depreciation expense | 20,000 | | |
| Increase in accounts payable | 10,000 | | |
| Decrease in inventory | 30,000 | | |
| Total | | $110,000 | |
| Issuance of bonds | | 200,000 | |
| Issuance of stock to purchase land | | 40,000 | |
| Total sources | | | $350,000 |
| Uses: | | | |
| Purchase of equipment | | 250,000 | |
| Purchase of land from stock issuance | | 40,000 | |
| Cash dividends declared in 1984 and paid in 1985 | | 5,000 | |
| Total uses | | | 295,000 |
| Net increase in funds | | | $ 55,000 |

*Required:*

a. What concept of funds is being emphasized in this statement? Provide evidence to support your answer. How would the statement differ if the alternative concept had been emphasized?

b. "Depreciation should not be added to the net income number. Menon Corporation is creating the impression that depreciation is not as legitimate an expense as such items as salaries and supplies which it did not add back to income." Do you agree? Is depreciation a source of funds? Explain.

c. "The bottom line of Menon Corporation's statement of changes in financial position is completely unaffected by its inclusion of a $40,000 item in both its sources and uses sections." Does its inclusion make the statement unnecessarily complex? Why is it reported on the statement?

**17–5.** The 1981 annual report of National Service Industries, Inc., contained the following statements of consolidated changes in financial position (amounts in thousands of dollars):

| | For the Years Ended August 31 | | |
| --- | --- | --- | --- |
| | 1981 | 1980 | 1979 |
| Funds were provided by: | | | |
| Operations— | | | |
| Net income ............................... | $50,086 | $45,154 | $39,773 |
| Add: Items not requiring outlay of funds— | | | |
| Depreciation and amortization ............. | 21,809 | 18,567 | 15,362 |
| Provision for deferred income taxes ........ | 380 | 1,841 | 1,739 |
| | 72,275 | 65,562 | 56,874 |
| Increase in accounts payable and accrued liabilities ................................ | 5,436 | — | 17,942 |
| Sales and retirements of property, plant, and equipment .......................... | 2,980 | 1,403 | 1,038 |
| Additional long-term borrowing ................. | 264 | 4,223 | 31 |
| Funds provided ..................... | 80,955 | 71,188 | 75,885 |
| Funds were used for: | | | |
| Additions to property, plant, and equipment (including rental furniture of $6,589 in 1981, $6,495 in 1980, and $9,062 in 1979) ......... | 30,591 | 30,385 | 28,989 |
| Purchase of treasury stock ..................... | 1,678 | — | 1,897 |
| Cash dividends paid on common stock .......... | 16,553 | 15,306 | 13,255 |
| Repayment of long-term debt .................. | 2,042 | 1,581 | 1,667 |
| Increase in— | | | |
| Receivables .............................. | 10,366 | 3,338 | 16,438 |
| Inventories and linens in service, net ........... | 536 | 10,061 | 22,484 |
| Prepayments and other, net ................... | 808 | 372 | 227 |
| Decrease in accounts payable and accrued liabilities ................................ | — | 4,476 | — |
| Funds used ....................... | 62,574 | 65,519 | 84,957 |
| Increase (Decrease) in cash and short-term investments ................................ | $18,381 | $ 5,669 | $(9,072) |

*Required:*

a. Which definition of funds is the firm using? How do you know?

b. Why is $380,000 added in 1981 for "provision for deferred income taxes"? Does that amount represent the August 31, 1981, balance of the Deferred Income Taxes account? Explain.

c. Explain why the increase in receivables is handled differently fom the increase in accounts payable and accrued liabilities.

    *d.* Is the $72,275,000 the actual funds from operations for 1981? Explain what it represents.

    *e.* An alternative calculation of funds from operations is $66,001,000. How was this figure derived and what does it represent?

**17–6.** Presented below are comparative statements of financial position for Kenwood Corporation as of December 31, 1979, and 1978 and Kenwood's income statement for 1979.[12]

KENWOOD CORPORATION
Statement of Financial Position

| | December 31, 1979 | December 31, 1978 | Increase (Decrease) |
|---|---|---|---|
| *Assets* | | | |
| Current assets: | | | |
|   Cash | $ 100,000 | $ 90,000 | $ 10,000 |
|   Accounts receivable (net of allowance for uncollectible accounts of $10,000 and $8,000, respectively) | 210,000 | 140,000 | 70,000 |
|   Inventories | 260,000 | 220,000 | 40,000 |
|     Total current assets | 570,000 | 450,000 | 120,000 |
| Land | 325,000 | 200,000 | 125,000 |
| Plant and equipment | 580,000 | 633,000 | (53,000) |
|   Less: Accumulated depreciation | (90,000) | (100,000) | 10,000 |
| Patents | 30,000 | 33,000 | (3,000) |
| Total assets | $1,415,000 | $1,216,000 | $199,000 |
| | | | |
| *Liabilities and Shareholders' Equity* | | | |
| Liabilities: | | | |
|   Current liabilities: | | | |
|     Accounts payable | $ 260,000 | $ 200,000 | $ 60,000 |
|     Accrued expenses | 200,000 | 210,000 | (10,000) |
|       Total current liabilities | 460,000 | 410,000 | 50,000 |
|   Deferred income taxes | 140,000 | 100,000 | 40,000 |
|   Long-term bonds (due December 15, 1990) | 130,000 | 180,000 | (50,000) |
|     Total liabilities | 730,000 | 690,000 | 40,000 |
| Shareholders' equity: | | | |
|   Common stock, par value $5, authorized 100,000 shares, issued and outstanding 50,000 and 42,000 shares, respectively | 250,000 | 210,000 | 40,000 |
|   Additional paid-in capital | 233,000 | 170,000 | 63,000 |
|   Retained earnings | 202,000 | 146,000 | 56,000 |
|     Total shareholders' equity | 685,000 | 526,000 | 159,000 |
| Total liabilities and shareholders' equity | $1,415,000 | $1,216,000 | $199,000 |

12 Material from the Uniform CPA Examinations, copyright © 1980 by the American Institute of Certified Public Accountants, Inc., is adapted with permission.

KENWOOD CORPORATION
Income Statement
For the Year Ended December 31, 1979

| | |
|---|---:|
| Sales | $1,000,000 |
| Expenses: | |
| Cost of sales | 560,000 |
| Salary and wages | 190,000 |
| Depreciation | 20,000 |
| Amortization | 3,000 |
| Loss on sale of equipment | 4,000 |
| Interest | 16,000 |
| Miscellaneous | 8,000 |
| Total expenses | 801,000 |
| Income before income taxes and extraordinary item | 199,000 |
| Income taxes: | |
| Current | 50,000 |
| Deferred | 40,000 |
| Provision for income taxes | 90,000 |
| Income before extraordinary item | 109,000 |
| Extraordinary item—gain on repurchase of long-term bonds (net of $10,000 income tax) | 12,000 |
| Net income | $ 121,000 |
| Earnings per share: | |
| Income before extraordinary item | $2.21 |
| Extraordinary item | .24 |
| Net income | $2.45 |

*Additional information:*

1.  On February 2, 1979, Kenwood issued a 10% stock dividend to shareholders of record on January 15, 1979. The market price per share of the common stock on February 2, 1979, was $15.
2.  On March 1, 1979, Kenwood issued 3,800 shares of common stock for land. The common stock and land had current market values of approximately $40,000 on March 1, 1979.
3.  On April 15, 1979, Kenwood repurchased long-term bonds with a face value of $50,000. The gain of $22,000 was reported as an extraordinary item on the income statement.
4.  On June 30, 1979, Kenwood sold equipment costing $53,000, with a book value of $23,000 for $19,000 cash.
5.  On September 30, 1979, Kenwood declared and paid a $0.04 per share cash dividend to shareholders of record August 1, 1979.
6.  On October 10, 1979, Kenwood purchased land for $85,000 cash.
7.  Deferred income taxes represent timing differences relating to the use of accelerated depreciation methods for income tax reporting and straight-line depreciation methods for financial statement reporting.

*Required:*

Using the working-capital concept of funds, prepare a statement of changes in financial position of Kenwood Corporation for the year ended December 31, 1979.

**17–7.** Alpha Industries, Inc., included the following consolidated statement of changes in financial position in its 1981 annual report (amounts in thousands of dollars):

| | Years Ended March 31 | | |
| --- | --- | --- | --- |
| | 1981 | 1980 | 1979 |
| Working capital provided from: | | | |
| Net income | $ 2,775 | $1,872 | $1,334 |
| Add (deduct): items not affecting working capital: | | | |
| Contribution of treasury stock to Employee Stock Ownership Trust (ESOT) | 199 | 115 | 65 |
| Depreciation and amortization | 879 | 591 | 488 |
| Deferred income tax | 247 | 58 | 95 |
| Gain on reacquisition of 6% debentures | — | — | (24) |
| Working capital provided from operations | 4,101 | 2,638 | 1,959 |
| Proceeds from sale of common stock | 7,275 | — | — |
| Proceeds from long-term notes payable | 974 | 996 | — |
| Issuance of common stock for 6% debentures | 316 | 252 | — |
| Tax benefit from stock option transactions | 48 | 131 | 74 |
| Provided by ESOT for debt reduction | 43 | 43 | — |
| Guaranteed debt of ESOT | — | — | 218 |
| Total working capital provided | 12,759 | 4,062 | 2,252 |
| Working capital used for: | | | |
| Additions to property, plant, and equipment | 3,804 | 2,538 | 1,218 |
| Purchase of Company's 6% debentures | 43 | — | 31 |
| Decrease in long-term notes payable | 110 | 83 | 83 |
| Cash dividends | 251 | 130 | 123 |
| Conversion of 6% debentures to common stock | 316 | 252 | — |
| Debt guarantee in connection with funds used to acquire Company shares by ESOT | — | — | 218 |
| Other | 20 | 2 | (25) |
| Total working capital used | 4,545 | 3,007 | 1,650 |
| Increase in working capital | $ 8,214 | $1,055 | $ 602 |

*Required:*

a. Prepare the journal entry made by the firm to record the reacquisition of 6% debentures during the year ended March 31, 1979. Explain why the $24,000 gain on reacquisition was deducted in arriving at working capital provided from operations.

b. Added to the net income figure is "contribution of treasury stock to Employee Stock Ownership Trust." What journal entry was probably made to reflect the contribution? Why is the item added to the net income figure?

c. "1981 sources of funds would still exceed the uses of funds by $8,214,000 even if the $316,000 item was totally excluded from the statement." Do you agree? What benefit, if any, results from inclusion of the $316,000?

d. What suggestions would you make to improve the presentation of financing/investing activities by Alpha Industries?

**17–8.** Presented below are the balance sheets of Farrell Corporation as of December 31, 1981, and 1980, and the statement of income and retained earnings for the year ended December 31, 1981.[13]

---

[13] Material from the Uniform CPA Examinations, copyright © 1982 by the American Institute of Certified Public Accountants, Inc., is adapted with permission.

## FARRELL CORPORATION
### Balance Sheets
### December 31, 1981, and 1980

|  | 1981 | 1980 | Increase (Decrease) |
|---|---|---|---|
| *Assets* | | | |
| Cash | $ 275,000 | $ 180,000 | $ 95,000 |
| Accounts receivable, net | 295,000 | 305,000 | (10,000) |
| Inventories | 549,000 | 431,000 | 118,000 |
| Investments | 73,000 | 60,000 | 13,000 |
| Land | 350,000 | 200,000 | 150,000 |
| Plant and equipment | 624,000 | 606,000 | 18,000 |
| Less: Accumulated depreciation | (139,000) | (107,000) | (32,000) |
| Goodwill | 16,000 | 20,000 | (4,000) |
| Total assets | $2,043,000 | $1,695,000 | $348,000 |
| *Liabilities and Stockholders' Equity* | | | |
| Accounts payable and accrued expenses | $ 604,000 | $ 563,000 | $ 41,000 |
| Note payable, long-term | 150,000 | — | 150,000 |
| Bonds payable | 160,000 | 210,000 | (50,000) |
| Deferred income taxes | 41,000 | 30,000 | 11,000 |
| Common stock, par value $10 | 430,000 | 400,000 | 30,000 |
| Additional paid-in capital | 226,000 | 175,000 | 51,000 |
| Retained earnings | 432,000 | 334,000 | 98,000 |
| Treasury stock, at cost | — | (17,000) | 17,000 |
| Total liabilities and stockholders' equity | $2,043,000 | $1,695,000 | $348,000 |

## FARRELL CORPORATION
### Statement of Income and Retained Earnings
### For the Year Ended December 31, 1981

| | |
|---|---|
| Net sales | $1,950,000 |
| Operating expenses: | |
| Cost of sales | 1,150,000 |
| Selling and administrative expenses | 505,000 |
| Depreciation | 53,000 |
| | 1,708,000 |
| Operating income | 242,000 |
| Other (income) expense: | |
| Interest expense | 15,000 |
| Interest income | (13,000) |
| Loss on sale of equipment | 5,000 |
| Amortization of goodwill | 4,000 |
| | 11,000 |
| Income before income taxes | 231,000 |
| Income taxes: | |
| Current | 79,000 |
| Deferred | 11,000 |
| Provision for income taxes | 90,000 |
| Net income | 141,000 |
| Retained earnings, January 1, 1981 | 334,000 |
| | 475,000 |
| Cash dividends, paid August 14, 1981 | 43,000 |
| Retained earnings, December 31, 1981 | $ 432,000 |

*Additional information:*

1. On January 2, 1981, Farrell sold equipment costing $45,000, with a book value of $24,000, for $19,000 cash.

2. On April 1, 1981, Farrell issued 1,000 shares of common stock for $23,000 cash.
3. On May 15, 1981, Farrell sold all of its treasury stock for $25,000 cash.
4. On June 1, 1981, individuals holding $50,000 face value of Farrell's bonds exercised their conversion privilege. Each of the 50 bonds was converted into 40 shares of Farrell's common stock.
5. On July 1, 1981, Farrell purchased equipment for $63,000 cash.
6. On December 31, 1981, land with a fair market value of $150,000 was purchased through the issuance of a long-term note in the amount of $150,000. The note bears interest at the rate of 15% and is due on December 31, 1986.
7. Deferred income taxes represent timing differences relating to the use of accelerated depreciation methods for income tax reporting and the straight-line method for financial statement reporting.

*Required:*

Using the cash basis approach (funds defined as cash), prepare a statement of changes in financial position of Farrell Corporation for the year ended December 31, 1981.

**17–9.** The 1981 annual report of CPC International, Inc., included the following consolidated statement of changes in financial position (amounts in millions of dollars):

|  | 1981 | 1980 | 1979 |
|---|---|---|---|
| Cash provided by operations: | | | |
| Net income | $218.4 | $197.4 | $178.6 |
| Noncash charges (credits) to net income: | | | |
| Depreciation | 87.6 | 74.4 | 67.1 |
| Other noncash items | 22.8 | 8.8 | 8.4 |
| Increase (decrease) in noncurrent items due to changes in exchange rates | (39.1) | (2.9) | 10.5 |
| Changes in working capital: | | | |
| Notes and accounts receivable | 29.1 | (56.5) | (63.0) |
| Inventories | 76.8 | (51.2) | (72.4) |
| Accounts payable and accrued items | (66.0) | 42.3 | 62.3 |
| Cash provided by operations | 329.6 | 212.3 | 191.5 |
| Cash dividends | (91.7) | (81.1) | (71.4) |
| Cash provided by operations and retained in the business | 237.9 | 131.2 | 120.1 |
| Financing activities: | | | |
| Long-term financing | 141.5 | 15.2 | 19.6 |
| Short-term financing—net | (31.0) | 92.9 | 1.0 |
| Payment of long-term debt | (30.6) | (16.8) | (10.0) |
| Net proceeds from financing activities | 79.9 | 91.3 | 10.6 |
| Total cash available from operations and financing activities | 317.8 | 222.5 | 130.7 |
| Investment activities: | | | |
| Capital expenditures | 293.5 | 235.9 | 150.7 |
| Investment in affiliates | 59.9 | 14.5 | 16.5 |
| Sale of plants and properties | (47.6) | (8.7) | (28.9) |
| Net cash used by investment activities | 305.8 | 241.7 | 138.3 |
| Increase (decrease) in cash and temporary investments | 12.0 | (19.2) | (7.6) |
| Cash and temporary investments at beginning of year | 68.7 | 87.9 | 95.5 |
| Cash and temporary investments at end of year | 80.7 | 68.7 | 87.9 |

*Required:*

a. CPC has included the changes in *certain* working capital accounts in its computation of "cash provided by operations." Explain why those accounts were included. Were any working capital accounts not included, and if so, why?

b. Comment on the placement of the amount for cash dividends. Does the location of that item serve to increase the information content of the statement? Explain.

c. Why do most sections of the statement simultaneously have items in parentheses and items not in parentheses? Does this format aid or hinder the reader in his or her attempt to understand the causes of the change in funds?

d. Recast the 1981 statement of changes in financial position so that all sources and uses are each shown in distinct areas.

17–10. Two of your roommates, Melody and Harmony, recently enrolled in an introductory accounting course. They had not ever intended to become business students, but it had just become too expensive to take private music lessons on their first love, the tuba. You recently eavesdropped on the following argument:

**Melody:** Why do they always save the best for last? Here I've struggled through 16 ordinary chapters, and now they've only first begun to excite me with the statement of changes in financial position.

**Harmony:** I simply don't follow your drift, Melody.

**Melody:** It's so simple even you will understand my point, Harmony. The SCFP is the most forward looking of the three major financial statements.

**Harmony:** Hey, Melody! Haven't you heard that we're still operating under the historical cost and realization concepts? The SCFP only records past management actions, so how can you say that it is forward looking?

**Melody:** A careful reading of the SCFP can give me insight into the magnitude of several of the items which will inevitably appear on *future* balance sheets and income statements.

**Harmony:** You sound like you've got your head stuck in a tuba. How is the SCFP prepared? From the other two major financial statements, right? How can something so redundant be of any value?

**Melody:** I am correct, and if you don't agree, that's "tubad."

*Required:*

a. Is the statement of changes in financial position a more exciting financial statement than the balance sheet and income statement?

b. Comment on Melody's observation that the SCFP "is the most forward looking of the three major financial statements." What insight could it provide for *future* balance sheet and income statement amounts?

c. Evaluate Harmony's comment concerning the preparation, redundancy, and value of the SCFP.

d. If the government started rationing financial statements and you could only have access to *one*, which would you choose? Is your choice dependent on whether or not the one statement furnished is comparative or noncomparative?

17–11. Wang Laboratories, Inc., presented the following statements of changes in consolidated financial position in its 1982 annual report (amounts in thousands of dollars):

| | Year Ended June 30 | | |
| --- | --- | --- | --- |
| | *1982* | *1981* | *1980* |
| Provided from operations: | | | |
| Sources: | | | |
| Net earnings | $107,139 | $ 78,073 | $ 52,113 |
| Depreciation | 62,831 | 54,323 | 30,048 |
| Increase (decrease) in deferred | | | |
| income taxes | 20,150 | (650) | 14,500 |
| Other sources—net | (1,108) | 2,402 | 1,478 |
| | 189,012 | 134,148 | 98,139 |
| Less: Net increase in certain working | | | |
| capital items | (59,778) | (160,542) | (131,963) |
| Cash provided from (used in) | | | |
| operations | 129,234 | (26,394) | (33,824) |
| Uses: | | | |
| Investment in property, plant and | | | |
| equipment—net | 146,394 | 124,070 | 74,638 |
| Investment in rental equipment—net | 10,250 | 29,590 | 24,917 |
| Increase in lease installments | | | |
| receivable | 20,281 | 11,813 | 17,276 |
| Cash dividends paid | 6,772 | 5,397 | 3,596 |
| Other—net | 13,891 | 464 | (520) |
| Cash used in operations | 197,588 | 171,334 | 119,907 |
| Net (used in) operations | (68,354) | (197,728) | (153,731) |
| Provided from external financing: | | | |
| Net increase (decrease) in notes payable to | | | |
| banks and portion of long-term debt | | | |
| due within one year | 4,917 | (3,998) | 29,584 |
| Net increase in long-term debt | | | |
| (less $32,000 refinanced in 1980) | 84,279 | 230,123 | 102,939 |
| Retirement of debentures | | (200,000) | |
| Proceeds from sale of Class B Common | | | |
| Stock in public offering | | | 21,928 |
| Issuance of Class B Common Stock on | | | |
| conversion of debentures | 10 | 195,659 | |
| Proceeds from sale of Common Stock to | | | |
| employees | 9,559 | 8,383 | 3,788 |
| Proceeds from sale of warrants | 7,772 | | |
| Purchase of treasury stock | (3,017) | (4,249) | (2,804) |
| Net provided from external financing | 103,520 | 225,918 | 155,435 |
| Increase in cash and short-term | | | |
| investments | $ 35,166 | $ 28,190 | $ 1,704 |
| Analysis of net change in certain working | | | |
| capital items: | | | |
| Increase in current assets: | | | |
| Accounts receivable | $ 23,375 | $ 90,410 | $ 80,837 |
| Inventories | 102,889 | 62,588 | 100,073 |
| Prepaid expenses and other | | | |
| current assets | 5,813 | 23,439 | 4,950 |
| | 132,077 | 176,437 | 185,860 |
| Increase (decrease) in current liabilities: | | | |
| Accounts payable, other payables and | | | |
| accruals | 60,547 | 2,205 | 44,580 |
| Unearned service revenue | 14,382 | 8,418 | 9,442 |
| Income taxes | (2,630) | 5,272 | (125) |
| | 72,299 | 15,895 | 53,897 |
| Net increase in working capital items | $ 59,778 | $ 160,542 | $ 131,963 |

Note B to the firm's financial statements was titled "Change in Presentation" and read as follows:

> The presentation of the Statements of Changes in Consolidated Financial Position has been changed at June 30, 1982, from the previously reported working capital format to a cash format. In the opinion of Management the new format presents a more meaningful analysis of the Company's sources and uses of funds. The Statements of Changes in Consolidated Financial Position for 1981 and 1980 have been reclassified to conform to the new 1982 presentation.

*Required:*

a. Comment on the items that Wang has included under the heading "Provided from operations." Do you agree with the classification of all the items in this section? Where would you classify the various items?

b. Is it appropriate for Wang to devote the bottom one third of its statement to certain working capital items, in light of the shift in format to a cash emphasis? Explain.

c. By how much did working capital increase or decrease in each of the three years covered? Compare and contrast the trends in the change in funds under a working-capital format vis-à-vis a cash format.

d. Do you agree with Wang's management that the cash format "presents a more meaningful analysis of the Company's sources and uses of funds"? Explain.

**17A-1.** The consolidated statements of changes in financial position appearing in the 1981 annual report of Curtiss-Wright Corporation are presented below (amounts in thousands of dollars):

| | For the Years Ended December 31 | | |
|---|---|---|---|
| | 1981 | 1980 | 1979 |
| Sources of working capital: | | | |
| Earnings from continuing operations ......... | $ 51,177 | $ 32,228 | $ 29,646 |
| Items which reduced (increased) earnings but did not affect working capital: | | | |
| Depreciation ........................... | 5,087 | 4,750 | 4,185 |
| Minority interest ........................ | 208 | 162 | 199 |
| Deferred federal and foreign income taxes ............................. | (1,222) | 384 | (710) |
| Equity in net earnings of associated companies, net of dividends: | | | |
| Kennecott Corporation ................. | | (10,227) | (14,970) |
| Other ............................... | (1,732) | (1,859) | (739) |
| Working capital provided from continuing operations: ........................... | 53,518 | 25,438 | 17,611 |
| Gain on disposal of discontinued segment (Dorr-Oliver Incorporated) ............... | 34,131 | | |
| Dividends from discontinued segment ........ | | 1,500 | 12,746 |
| Book value of investment in associated companies sold: | | | |
| Kennecott Corporation ................... | 131,273 | | |
| Dorr-Oliver Incorporated ................. | 77,819 | | |
| Cenco Incorporated ..................... | 11,556 | | |
| Book value of property, plant, and equipment sold or retired ....................... | 284 | 2,156 | 263 |
| Additions to long-term debt ............... | 5,347 | 17,130 | 21,809 |
| Decrease (increase) in long-term receivables ......................... | 3,028 | (3,347) | (404) |
| Other changes, net ....................... | 929 | (594) | 526 |
| Total sources of working capital ..... | 317,885 | 42,283 | 52,551 |
| | | | |
| Uses of working capital: | | | |
| Purchase of minority interest of Dorr-Oliver Incorporated ........................... | | | 22,068 |
| Investment in Kennecott Corporation ......... | | | 27,623 |
| Reduction to long-term debt ................ | 35,120 | 19,284 | 5,461 |
| Acquisition of treasury shares—common ..... | 157,921 | 2 | 218 |
| Redemption of Class A shares .............. | 1,346 | | |
| Increase in restricted cash and investments (included in other assets) ................ | 23,862 | | |
| Dividends ............................... | 4,834 | 8,319 | 7,058 |
| Additions to property, plant, and equipment ... | 11,398 | 11,665 | 13,315 |
| Total uses of working capital ........ | 234,481 | 39,270 | 75,743 |
| Increase (decrease) in working capital ......... | $ 83,404 | $ 3,013 | $(23,192) |

*Required:*

a. What is "minority interest"? Why is it added to earnings in arriving at working capital provided from continuing operations?

b. Why is the equity in net earnings of associated companies reported "net of dividends"? Why is it subtracted in each year? Why does it not appear in 1981 for the investment in Kennecott Corporation?

c. Did deferred federal and foreign income taxes increase or decrease in each of the three years? How do you know? Why is this item reported on the SCFP?

d. What journal entry was made when the investment in Dorr-Oliver Incorporated was sold in 1981? Does the SCFP accurately portray the nature of this event?

e. Why was the change in working capital so different in 1980 from 1979, even though earnings from continuing operations equal in both years? Concentrate on major factors.

**17A–2.** Comparative balance sheet data for the Manual Corporation are:

| | December 31 | |
|---|---|---|
| | 1985 | 1984 |
| Debit-balance accounts: | | |
| Cash | $ 80,000 | $ 50,000 |
| Marketable securities | 14,000 | 18,000 |
| Accounts receivable (net) | 76,850 | 40,000 |
| Inventories | 105,000 | 113,000 |
| Prepaid expenses | 5,000 | 7,000 |
| Investment in Zee Corporation bonds | 48,200 | 48,000 |
| Plant assets | 600,000 | 700,000 |
| Discount on 7% bonds payable | 8,000 | 20,000 |
| Totals | $937,050 | $996,000 |
| | | |
| Credit-balance accounts: | | |
| Allowance for depreciation | $ 81,000 | $118,000 |
| Accounts payable | 55,000 | 115,000 |
| Dividends payable | 7,000 | 5,000 |
| Income taxes payable | 13,000 | 27,000 |
| Deferred income taxes | 4,000 | 12,000 |
| 7% bonds payable | 100,000 | 200,000 |
| Common stock, $5 par | 310,000 | 260,000 |
| Premium on common stock | 230,000 | 140,000 |
| Retained earnings | 137,050 | 119,000 |
| Totals | $937,050 | $996,000 |

*Additional information:*

1. Cash dividends paid during 1985 amounted to $12,000.
2. Manual Corporation purchased 50 Zee Corporation bonds on December 31, 1984, for $48,000. Maturity date for the bonds is December 31, 1994.
3. $20,000 of land was acquired on July 1, 1985, in exchange for 700 shares of Manual Corporation stock.
4. On July 1, 1985, marketable securities costing $4,000 were sold for $2,000.
5. The 7% bonds payable mature on December 31, 1989. However, $100,000 of them were retired early on July 1, 1985, at 110.
6. On September 1, 1985, Manual Corporation received $90,000 in cash when it sold some old equipment at a $30,000 gain.

*Required:*

a. Prepare a schedule of changes in working capital for 1985.
b. Prepare a statement of changes in financial position for 1985. In support of your statement, you should:
   (1) Prepare journal entries for the July 1 bond retirement and the September 1 sale of equipment.
   (2) Set up T-accounts or prepare schedules for:

(i) Cash dividends declared.
(ii) Net income.
(iii) Net loss exclusive of gains and losses on disposal of noncurrent items.
(iv) Depreciation.
(v) Discount amortization on 7% bonds.
(vi) Funds provided by issuance of stock.

**17A–3.** Comparative balance sheet data for the Fortune Corporation follow:

| | December 31 | |
| --- | --- | --- |
| | 1984 | 1983 |
| Debit-balance accounts: | | |
| Cash ................................. | $ 30,000 | $ 50,000 |
| Marketable securities ...................... | 15,000 | 18,000 |
| Accounts receivable ...................... | 77,000 | 40,000 |
| Inventories ............................... | 110,000 | 120,000 |
| Investment in Coe Corporation bonds ......... | 23,500 | 24,000 |
| Plant assets .............................. | 660,000 | 700,000 |
| Totals ............................ | $915,500 | $952,000 |
| | | |
| Credit-balance accounts: | | |
| Allowance for bad debts ................... | $ 9,000 | $ 8,000 |
| Allowance for depreciation ................ | 80,000 | 45,000 |
| Accounts payable ........................ | 55,000 | 115,000 |
| Dividends payable ....................... | 4,000 | 5,000 |
| Income taxes payable ..................... | 13,000 | 27,000 |
| Deferred income taxes .................... | 4,000 | 2,000 |
| 7% bonds payable ....................... | 160,000 | 200,000 |
| Premium on 7% bonds payable ............. | 14,400 | 20,000 |
| Common stock, $5 par .................... | 280,000 | 260,000 |
| Premium on common stock ................ | 170,000 | 130,000 |
| Retained earnings ....................... | 126,100 | 140,000 |
| Totals ............................ | $915,500 | $952,000 |

*Additional information:*

1. Accounts receivable written off as uncollectible were $4,000 in 1984 and $5,000 in 1983.
2. On July 1, 1984, marketable securities costing $3,000 were sold for $4,500.
3. Some equipment was sold during 1984 at its book value of $80,000.
4. Cash dividends paid during 1984 amounted to $9,000.
5. Depreciation expense during 1984 amounted to $70,000.
6. Fortune Corporation purchased 20 Coe Corporation bonds on December 31, 1983, for $24,000. These bonds mature on December 31, 1991.
7. The 7% bonds payable mature on December 31, 1993. However, $40,000 of them were retired early on July 1, 1984, at 110.
8. $10,000 of land was acquired on January 1, 1984, in exchange for 400 shares of Fortune Corporation stock.
9. A $20,000 stock dividend was declared on April 1, 1984, and distributed on May 1, 1984. 500 shares of Fortune stock were involved and the per share market price was $40 on April 1, 1984.

*Required:*

a. Prepare a schedule of changes in working capital for 1984.
b. Prepare a statement of changes in financial position for 1984. In support of your statement, you should:

(1) Set up T-accounts or prepare schedules for:
    (i) Cash dividends declared.
    (ii) Net income.
    (iii) Premium amortization on bonds issued.
    (iv) Funds used to retire bonds.
    (v) Funds provided from sale of stock.
    (vi) Cost of equipment sold.
    (vii) Funds used to purchase fixed assets.
(2) Prepare a journal entry for the July 1 bond retirement.

**17A–4.** The Warren Company's financial statements for fiscal 1985 show the following (all figures are in thousands of dollars):

WARREN COMPANY
Consolidated Position Statement

| | June 30 | |
|---|---|---|
| | 1985 | 1984 |
| *Assets* | | |
| Current assets: | | |
| Cash | $ 936 | $ 604 |
| Accounts receivable, net | 1,502 | 1,221 |
| Inventories | 1,711 | 719 |
| Prepayments | 30 | 50 |
| Total current assets | 4,179 | 2,594 |
| Noncurrent assets: | | |
| Securities held for plant expansion | — | 83 |
| Land | 181 | 122 |
| Buildings and equipment | 2,101 | 2,169 |
| Accumulated depreciation | (640) | (400) |
| Rights to leased property, net | 141 | — |
| Excess cost over book value | 200 | 240 |
| | $6,162 | $4,808 |
| *Equities* | | |
| Current liabilities: | | |
| Accounts payable | $ 180 | $ 178 |
| Wages payable | 100 | 110 |
| Interest payable | 41 | — |
| Income taxes payable | 18 | — |
| Notes payable to banks | 34 | 20 |
| Total current liabilities | 373 | 308 |
| Long-term liabilities: | | |
| Bonds payable | 1,000 | — |
| Discount on bonds payable | (54) | — |
| Lease obligations | 147 | |
| Deferred income taxes | 156 | 210 |
| Deferred contract revenue | 60 | 80 |
| Total liabilities | 1,682 | 598 |
| Minority interest | 304 | 281 |
| Stockholders' equity: | | |
| Common stock | 3,467 | 3,400 |
| Retained earnings | 919 | 913 |
| Cost of treasury shares | (210) | (384) |
| Total equities | $6,162 | $4,808 |

WARREN COMPANY
Consolidated Income Statement
For the Year Ended June 30, 1985

| | | |
|---|---:|---:|
| Sales | | $2,520 |
| Contract revenue | | 129 |
| | | $2,649 |
| Deductions: | | |
| Cost of goods sold | $1,763 | |
| Selling and general expense | 468 | |
| Other expenses, net | 159 | |
| Interest | 76 | |
| Minority interest in earnings | 23 | 2,489 |
| Income before taxes | | 160 |
| Income taxes | | 72 |
| Income before extraordinary items | | 88 |
| Realization of tax loss carry-forward | | 13 |
| Net income | | $ 101 |

WARREN COMPANY
Consolidated Statement of Retained Earnings
For the Year Ended June 30, 1985

| | |
|---|---:|
| Retained earnings, July 1, 1984 | $ 913 |
| Add: Net income | 101 |
| | 1,014 |
| Deduct: | |
| Cash dividends on common stock | (60) |
| Adjustment arising from reissuance of treasury stock below original acquisition cost | (35) |
| Retained earnings, June 30, 1985 | $ 919 |

*Additional information:*
1. Depreciation of $449,000 is included among the various expense accounts.
2. Buildings and equipment acquired during the year cost $458,000.
3. On April 1, 1985, the company entered into a noncancellable capital lease for office equipment. The lease had a present value of $150,000 and was capitalized at that figure. Amortization of lease rights is included in "Other expenses, net."
4. "Other expenses, net" on the income statement include along with other items a loss on sale of securities held for expansion of $15,000 and a gain on sale of equipment of $10,000.
5. Of the treasury stock on hand at the beginning of the year, one half was reissued during the year in exchange for $59,000 worth of land and for cash. The other half is on hand at the end of the year along with additional treasury stock acquired during the year.
6. The bonds were issued on January 1, 1985, at 94 percent of face value.

*Required:*
a. Prepare a statement of changes in financial position for the year. Employ the all financial resources interpretation of working capital.
b. Repeat part *(a)*, employing the all financial resources interpretation of cash.

# CHAPTER 18

# ANALYSIS OF FINANCIAL STATEMENTS

In the preceding chapters we have developed a system for collecting and reporting financial information about the performance and position of the business entity. We have had one major goal in mind—the preparation of reports for external groups interested in the activities of the business. Nearly all decisions made by management ultimately are reflected on the financial statements. Hence, the statements provide major assistance to stockholders or creditors making judgments about the firm.

This chapter studies the financial statements from the viewpoint of an analyst. Our purpose is to develop some analytical procedures to make the statement figures more meaningful. The development of such procedures requires not only a knowledge of particular techniques but also an appreciation of the context in which statement analysis is carried out.

**OBJECTIVES OF STATEMENT ANALYSIS**

The analysis of financial statements serves a number of different objectives—evaluation of past performance, appraisal of present condition, and prediction of future potential. Being basically historical, financial statements are better suited for the first two purposes. However, the majority of statement readers are interested in the future—the capacity of the firm to grow and prosper and the ability of the firm to adapt to varying conditions. Wisely used, financial statement analysis can provide a base for projection of the future and can supply insights as to how the firm may respond to future economic developments.

The Financial Accounting Standards Board reaffirmed these objectives and orientation in 1981:

Users of financial reports are looking primarily at information about the past. They cannot make decisions about the past, though they may change their perceptions of the past. They can only make present decisions that will reflect their assessment of what the future holds. Therefore, a prime characteristic of useful financial information is its value in assisting users' predictions. Financial information, then, should assist the user to evaluate, assess, predict, or confirm the return on an investment and the perceived level of risk involved.[1]

One of the major purposes of this proposal, which was tabled in 1982 but may be considered at a later date, is the addition to the accounting framework of the concepts of *liquidity* and *financial flexibility* in evaluating risk.[2]

Liquidity was used by the FASB to "describe the amount of time that is expected to elapse until an asset is realized or otherwise converted into cash or until a liability has to be paid."[3] Financial flexibility "is the ability of an enterprise to take effective actions to alter the amounts and timing of cash flows so it can respond to unexpected needs and opportunities."[4] Although liquidity is certainly encompassed within financial flexibility, the latter term is broader, for it includes unused borrowing capability and the ability to realize assets other than in the normal course of business.

Regardless of the relative emphasis they place on the past, present, and future, analysts generally desire information about the liquidity, financial strength, efficiency, and profitability of the business under study. Different statement users will employ different analytical procedures and emphasize different information according to their individual purposes. Creditors, for example, may be interested primarily in liquidity and financial strength. However, they cannot entirely ignore profitability, for in the long run a firm that continually operates unprofitably will encounter difficulty in acquiring financial capital to remain solvent. Stockholders, on the other hand, presumably are more concerned with the profitability of the firm. Nonetheless, they are also interested in keeping the business financially sound. Managers are interested in all four areas in making internal operating decisions.

Because of this overlap in interests, it is extremely difficult to talk about statement analysis from the viewpoint of any one user group. This chapter presents statement analysis in a general framework organized around the major areas of liquidity, financial strength, efficiency, and profitability. These areas can be analyzed historically for answers to such questions as: How has the financial condition of the firm changed over time? In what areas has the firm exhibited success or failure? Do the financial statements support management's opinion of the condition of the business? How well

---

[1] FASB, *Proposed Statement of Financial Accounting Concepts,* "Reporting Income, Cash Flows, and Financial Position of Business Enterprises" (Stamford, Conn., November 16, 1981), p. ix.

[2] Ibid., p. xi.

[3] Ibid., p. 12.

[4] Ibid., p. 10.

has management performed as a steward of invested resources? In addition, these same areas can be examined prospectively for answers to questions like: How will management's plans for the future affect the financial statements? Do the statements indicate difficulty in reaching future goals? How will the firm be affected by a contraction or expansion of economic activity? Do any areas show a deteriorating condition that is likely to become critical in the future?

## COMPARISON— THE KEY POINT

Statement analysis entails the analyst's selecting particular items from the financial statements for detailed study. However, statement analysis cannot be done in a vacuum; it requires some basis for comparison. Accounting figures have little meaning by themselves. The way to determine whether an amount is adequate, improving or deteriorating, or in or out of proportion is to relate it to other items. Implicit in much of our earlier discussions on consistency, disclosure, and accounting principles have been the companion ideas of relationships and comparison.

For example, a firm reports operating income of $800,000. Is this satisfactory? If last year the company reported only $700,000 of operating income, then $800,000 looks good, but if industry profits have expanded an estimated 25 percent during the year, 14 percent does not look so good. On the other hand, if the firm generated the $800,000 of income with an asset investment of only $2.4 million, a 33⅓ percent return on investment, even before tax, appears very reasonable. Its reasonableness may diminish, however, if we discover that a major competitor was able to earn $400,000 operating income on an asset investment of $900,000—a before-tax return of almost 45 percent.

The major point is that some comparison is essential to put the analysis into perspective. Different bases of comparison are used in different circumstances, and they do not all necessarily lead to the same judgments. Obviously, the starting point is to relate specific statement items to each other. The study of specific statement relationships is called ratio analysis and constitutes the major part of our subsequent discussion. Nevertheless, this is only the starting point. The ratios themselves must also be evaluated in comparison with similar ratios. Three common bases of comparison are discussed below.

## Comparison with Prior Periods

One customary approach is to compare a firm over time. The company's own past performance serves as the basis for comparison. By looking at changes from year to year, we can spot trends and tendencies as well as appraise current periods in the light of historical relationships. We must make sure, however, that we are dealing with comparable data. Accounting methods may have changed; business entities may have been modified; or the measuring unit, the dollar, may have been drastically altered in size because of changing price levels.

**Comparison with Predetermined Goals**

A second basis of comparison is some type of standard set in advance. Frequently employed by internal management, this type of analysis compares the actual results reflected in the financial statements with what the results should have been or were predicted to be. Actual income is related to budgeted income; actual rate of return on investment is compared to a target percentage. If predetermined goals are carefully formulated, this type of comparison is valuable, particularly when followed up by a detailed study to determine why the actual results differed from expectations.

External analysts sometimes use preestablished "rules of thumb" as guides in their analysis; for example, the ratio of current assets to current liabilities should be at least 2:1. However, in many instances such external guidelines are too general, failing to take into consideration changes in the operating, legal, or economic environment that might invalidate the comparison.

**Comparison with Other Companies**

Another comparison, often made by investors, employs interfirm contrasts. Standards of comparison include ratios calculated from the financial statements of similar companies or average ratios for an industry. A number of organizations publish financial statistics for individual firms and/or industry groups. Robert Morris Associates, a national association of bank loan and credit officers, publishes its *Annual Statement Studies;* for 11 different ratios and approximately 300 lines of business, upper quartile, median, and lower quartile figures are reported. Dun & Bradstreet, Inc., reports similar information on 14 ratios for 125 industry groups. Other sources of such data include investment advisory services, brokerage firms, and trade associations.

Although this type of comparison is valuable, the analyst must be cautious in using the results. The problems of noncomparable data become magnified. Differences in accounting procedures may mask real differences or significant similarities among firms. Mergers and diversification may make tenuous at best the classification of a firm in a particular industry or the identification of the major companies corresponding to it.

**FINANCIAL STATEMENTS— THE RAW MATERIAL**

Before turning their attention to specific methods of statement analysis, analysts first must consider the nature and quality of their "raw material." The depth of analysis possible and the reliability and significance of the results are directly related to the accuracy and soundness of the statements themselves. Any limitations of the financial statements carry over to the analysis.

Some of these limitations are inherent in the basic nature of financial accounting. For instance, most resources on the position statement are listed at amortized cost. Current market values may be more appropriate for the intended purpose, yet they may diverge greatly from the book values shown. Moreover, the position statement represents only one moment in time. Any ratio taken from position statement data represents a relationship that existed on that one date. It may not be a normal relationship if the position statement data were atypical at that one point in time or if they had been influenced by a major recent event. Similarly, the income statement may contain unusual items which could distort the analysis for particular purposes. Inclusion of extraordinary items in net income may be appropriate if the analyst desires to evaluate the overall performance of management in the past, but their inclusion could easily reduce the accuracy of any projection of future operating results.

Still other limitations may be introduced into the analysis through inadequate or misunderstood accounting policies or reporting disclosures. One way to avoid errors and to become cognizant of such limitations is to begin the investigation with an overview consisting of three preliminary steps: (1) read the auditor's report, (2) ascertain the accounting principles employed, and (3) review supplementary disclosures, including notes.

The auditor's report was discussed in Chapter 16. One attestation normally contained in the auditor's report is that the financial statements are prepared in accordance with generally accepted accounting principles. Sound interpretations and meaningful comparisons require, at a minimum, knowledge of the general effects of the accounting principles actually applied in the preparation of the statements. Information concerning accounting policies and principles being followed is often communicated to the analyst in notes to the financial statements.

Additionally, these notes contain other supplementary information. Explanations of extraordinary items and major changes in accounting methods and their financial impact can be found there. Financial commitments, lease agreements, backlogs of sales orders, preferred dividends in arrears, changes in the owners' equity accounts, and descriptions of contingencies are among the examples of footnote disclosure mentioned in previous chapters.

Notes also call attention to material facts occurring after the date of the statements. The statements may be reliable as of the end of the year. However, they are published two or three months later. If major changes in such items as capital stock, indebtedness, dividends, or plant assets have occurred, a note should accompany the statements indicating these. The reader will then be able to interpret the statements in the light of existing conditions which are *materially* different from those reflected in the statements. It behooves the analyst to review these disclosures, to assess their impact on the environment in which the firm operates, and perhaps even to make adjustments to the financial statements to achieve meaningful relationships and comparisons.

Supplementary information of interest to the analyst also includes management explanations. The Securities and Exchange Commission requires that management provide in the annual report a brief description of the general nature and scope of operations, information on lines of business and classes of products and services, and a narrative explanation of period-to-period changes in the major components of operations during the last three years. Such explanations and disclosures provide a meaningful backdrop against which the analyst does his or her investigative work.

## Percentage Comparisons of the Financial Statements

Most analysts begin their quantitative study of the financial statements with an examination of the general percentage relationships and changes shown on the comparative financial statements for a number of years. The two techniques used are called vertical and horizontal analysis, and they direct attention to the entire income statement or position statement. The financial statements of Sebago Company, a hypothetical concern, are presented in Tables 18–1 and 18–2. These tables illustrate the general percentage comparisons. Our subsequent discussion of specific ratios draws upon these statements for illustration also.

**Vertical Analysis.**  Vertical analysis abstracts from the absolute amounts on the statements the relative magnitude of figures expressed as percentages of some base item. On the income statement all the revenue deductions and the net income are usually converted to percentages of net sales. On the balance sheet total assets (total equities) serve as the base, and all individual assets and equities are translated into their relative percentages of the total. The result is a set of financial statements, called *common-size statements,* all expressed in percentages rather than dollar amounts. They provide a means by which the reader can analyze the composition of the statements. Common-size statements tend to highlight relationships that could be masked by changing absolute dollar amounts. For example, for Sebago Company selling expenses absorbed only 15.9 percent of each sales dollar in 1984 but rose to 18.0 percent in 1985. Similarly, long-term debt decreased from 18.2 to 16.1 percent of total equities, even though the proportion of total liabilities in the capital structure remained about the same. The analyst may want to explore why the company appears to be relying more on short-term sources of assets.

The Robert Morris Associates' data mentioned earlier also contain a vertical analysis for each of the 300 industries surveyed. If Sebago Company, our hypothetical firm, is assumed to be a paint manufacturer, then the middle set of columns in Tables 18–1 and 18–2 could be compared with information on 127 similar businesses for a recent year. For example, Sebago would discover that for both 1984 and 1985 it had far fewer funds tied up in receivables than the industry average of 28.6 percent of total assets, and that its cost of goods sold as a percentage of sales was slightly more favorable than the 70.1 percent industry norm.[5]

**Horizontal Analysis.**  Horizontal analysis employs percentages to show how individual items change from *year to year*. A percentage increase or decrease from the prior year is calculated for each component on the

---

[5] Robert Morris Associates, *Annual Statement Studies,* (Philadelphia, 1982), p. 63.

**TABLE 18–1**

### SEBAGO COMPANY
#### Comparative Balance Sheet with Percentage Comparisons
#### As of December 31, 1984, and 1985

| | Amounts | | Percentage of Total | | Increase (Decrease) 1985 over 1984 | |
|---|---|---|---|---|---|---|
| | 1985 | 1984 | 1985 | 1984 | Dollars | Percent |
| **Assets** | | | | | | |
| Current: | | | | | | |
| Cash .............................. | $ 44,600 | $ 42,300 | 10.9% | 10.7% | $ 2,300 | 5.4% |
| Accounts receivable .................. | 57,100 | 49,800 | 13.9 | 12.7 | 7,300 | 14.7 |
| Inventory ........................... | 88,700 | 85,900 | 21.6 | 21.8 | 2,800 | 3.3 |
| Prepaid expenses .................... | 15,700 | 15,300 | 3.8 | 3.9 | 400 | 2.6 |
| Total current assets ............. | 206,100 | 193,300 | 50.2 | 49.1 | 12,800 | 6.6 |
| Land ............................... | 61,000 | 61,000 | 14.9 | 15.5 | –0– | –0– |
| Buildings and equipment .............. | 212,900 | 199,100 | 51.9 | 50.5 | 13,800 | 6.9 |
| Less: Accumulated depreciation ....... | (88,100) | (79,400) | (21.4) | (20.2) | 8,700 | 11.0 |
| Intangibles .......................... | 18,000 | 20,000 | 4.4 | 5.1 | (2,000) | (10.0) |
| Total assets ................... | $409,900 | $394,000 | 100.0% | 100.0% | $15,900 | 4.0 |
| **Equities** | | | | | | |
| Liabilities: | | | | | | |
| Current: | | | | | | |
| Accounts payable.................... | $ 61,600 | $ 54,900 | 15.0% | 13.9% | 6,700 | 12.2 |
| Taxes payable ...................... | 15,400 | 14,000 | 3.8 | 3.6 | 1,400 | 10.0 |
| Other accrued liabilities ............. | 22,000 | 19,600 | 5.4 | 5.0 | 2,400 | 12.2 |
| Total current liabilities ........... | 99,000 | 88,500 | 24.2 | 22.5 | 10,500 | 11.9 |
| Bonds payable—11% ................. | 66,000 | 72,000 | 16.1 | 18.2 | (6,000) | (8.3) |
| Total liabilities .................. | 165,000 | 160,500 | 40.3 | 40.7 | 4,500 | 2.8 |
| Stockholders' equity: | | | | | | |
| 12% preferred stock—$100 par ......... | 30,000 | 30,000 | 7.3 | 7.6 | –0– | –0– |
| Common stock—$10 par .............. | 70,000 | 70,000 | 17.1 | 17.8 | –0– | –0– |
| Additional paid-in capital—common ..... | 90,000 | 90,000 | 21.9 | 22.9 | –0– | –0– |
| Retained earnings .................... | 54,900 | 43,500 | 13.4 | 11.0 | 11,400 | 26.2 |
| Total stockholders' equity ......... | 244,900 | 233,500 | 59.7 | 59.3 | 11,400 | 4.9 |
| Total equities ....................... | $409,900 | $394,000 | 100.0% | 100.0% | $15,900 | 4.0% |

current income and position statements. Such abstraction from the absolute dollar changes may add insights to trends that are developing. As one example, horizontal analysis for Sebago Company reveals that accounts receivable increased 14.7 percent from 1984 to 1985, while net sales increased only 4.7 percent.

A variation of horizontal analysis compares a series of years with a single base year. Each item on the statements in each subsequent year is expressed as a percentage of the same item in the base year. This type of trend analysis of percentages must be used carefully; misinterpretations may result when the choice of base year causes an unusually large or small percentage to appear in a subsequent year.

**TABLE 18–2**

SEBAGO COMPANY
Comparative Statement of Income and Retained Earnings
With Percentage Comparisons
For the Years Ended December 31, 1984, and 1985

|  | Amounts | | Percentage of Sales | | Increase (Decrease) 1985 over 1984 | |
|---|---|---|---|---|---|---|
|  | 1985 | 1984 | 1985 | 1984 | Dollars | Percent |
| Sales .............................. | $502,500 | $480,000 | 100.0% | 100.0% | $22,500 | 4.7% |
| Cost of goods sold ................. | 324,900 | 319,600 | 64.7 | 66.6 | 5,300 | 1.7 |
| Gross margin ...................... | 177,600 | 160,400 | 35.3 | 33.4 | 17,200 | 10.7 |
| Operating expenses: |  |  |  |  |  |  |
| Selling ........................... | 90,700 | 76,300 | 18.0 | 15.9 | 14,400 | 18.9 |
| Administrative .................... | 41,140 | 41,180 | 8.2 | 8.6 | (40) | (0.1) |
| Total operating expenses ........ | 131,840 | 117,480 | 26.2 | 24.5 | 14,360 | 12.2 |
| Operating income .................. | 45,760 | 42,920 | 9.1 | 8.9 | 2,840 | 6.6 |
| Interest expense ................... | 7,260 | 7,920 | 1.4 | 1.6 | (660) | (8.3) |
| Income before taxes ............... | 38,500 | 35,000 | 7.7 | 7.3 | 3,500 | 10.0 |
| Income taxes (40%) ............... | 15,400 | 14,000 | 3.1 | 2.9 | 1,400 | 10.0 |
| Net income ....................... | 23,100 | 21,000 | 4.6 | 4.4 | 2,100 | 10.0 |
| Retained earnings, |  |  |  |  |  |  |
| January 1 ...................... | 43,500 | 32,900 |  |  | 10,600 | 32.2 |
| Total ............................ | 66,600 | 53,900 |  |  | 12,700 | 23.6 |
| Dividends declared: |  |  |  |  |  |  |
| Preferred ........................ | 3,600 | 3,600 |  |  | –0– | –0– |
| Common ........................ | 8,100 | 6,800 |  |  | 1,300 | 19.1 |
| Total dividends ................ | 11,700 | 10,400 |  |  | 1,300 | 12.5 |
| Retained earnings, |  |  |  |  |  |  |
| December 31 .................... | $ 54,900 | $ 43,500 |  |  | $11,400 | 26.2% |

## Ratio Analysis

Ratio analysis is the study of specific relationships and forms the heart of statement analysis. Analysts use ratios to link different parts of the financial statements in an attempt to find clues about the status of particular aspects of the business. Specifically, the four major areas in which ratio analysis is helpful are short-term liquidity, long-term financial strength, efficiency (both investment efficiency and operating efficiency), and profitability. Ratios conveniently capsulize the results of detailed recordings and often complex relationships in these areas.

However, it is easy to get carried away with an oversimplified use of ratios. Wise statement analysis involves knowing the objective of each calculation—the area about which the analysis is attempting to provide information. Each ratio that we discuss has a definite purpose Although our coverage is broad, it is not exhaustive of all the possible ratios that are computed or of the numerous ways the relationships are defined and expressed. Nevertheless, these matters of convention and individual preference are far less important than one's understanding of the purpose of each ratio.

Keep in mind also that ratios merely aid in the evaluation of a business; *they do not substitute for sound judgment.* It is impossible for the financial statements from which ratios are taken to present all the relevant information about the operations, management, and environment of an enterprise. Ratios represent past data and therefore can only hint at the future. Moreover, there are probably no ratios that signify improved performance indefinitely as they move in one direction. When closely analyzed, ratios are "satisfactory" in a middle range and become "unsatisfactory" out of this range in either direction. For example, too few funds tied up in current assets can hinder liquidity, but too many funds tied up in current assets can hinder profitability. Therefore, the best that we can hope for from an analysis of accounting reports is to spot exceptions and variations—relationships which seem out of line or trends which, if continued, might cause trouble. Ratios neither pinpoint precise problems nor indicate causes. They may, however, *aid* in decision making by highlighting areas that may be problems or may require further investigation.

## LIQUIDITY

One group of ratios deals with the business' ability to meet creditors' short-run claims for repayment; we refer to these as liquidity measures.

*Some* indication of liquidity is provided by the working capital number, which equals current assets minus current liabilities. Unfortunately, the absolute nature of this measure precludes meaningful comparison among firms of different size. To obtain a better indication of various companies' relative capacity to meet their short-term obligations as they mature, we calculate two ratios. The *current ratio* divides current assets by current liabilities; the *quick (acid-test) ratio* divides monetary assets by current liabilities. These calculations for both 1985 and 1984 are shown below:

$$
\begin{array}{ccc}
 & \textit{1985} & \textit{1984} \\
\text{Current Ratio} = & \dfrac{\$206,100}{\$99,000} = 2.1 & \dfrac{\$193,300}{\$88,500} = 2.2 \\[2ex]
\text{Quick Ratio} = & \dfrac{\$101,700}{\$99,000} = 1.0 & \dfrac{\$92,100}{\$88,500} = 1.0
\end{array}
$$

Because in the short run a firm must look to its current assets and particularly to its monetary assets—cash, marketable securities, and accounts receivable—for debt-paying ability, these relationships are among the most widely used measures of current financial liquidity. Low or declining current and quick ratios may indicate an insufficient margin of safety between the assets that presumably are or will be available to liquidate claims and the obligations to be paid. On the other hand, an extremely high ratio may indicate the presence of excessive or unproductive inventories and receivables.

The current and quick ratios measure the size of the short-term liquidity buffer. A satisfactory ratio means a low risk that the existing short-term creditors could not be paid even if current assets were to shrink in value. As static measures, both the current ratio and the quick ratio must be interpreted in relation to the character of the business and its industry and to general economic conditions. In industries or firms in which the flow of funds from operations is relatively stable (e.g., utilities), acceptable liquidity ratios are lower than in situations characterized by greater uncertainty. When interest rates reach very high levels, most firms attempt to reduce the levels of cash on hand and funds tied up in receivables and inventories. As a consequence, a current ratio as low as 1.4 or 1.5, while substantially below the 2.0 level normally desired by many, may nevertheless signify good management and compare favorably with industry averages.

**Turnover of Receivables and Inventory**

How well the current and quick ratios indicate short-term debt-paying ability depends on how rapidly inventory and receivables can be converted into cash. Consequently, two supplementary ratios are computed to measure the movement of these current assets.

Inventory turnover is a calculation of how fast inventory on hand normally is sold and converted into accounts receivable. The formula is:

$$\text{Turnover of Inventory} = \frac{\text{Cost of Goods Sold}}{\text{Average Inventory}} = \frac{\$324{,}900}{(\$88{,}700 + \$85{,}900)/2}$$
$$= 3.7 \text{ Times per Year}$$

Many analysts divide the inventory turnover into 365 days to obtain the average length of time units are in inventory—99 days in our example ($365 \div 3.7$) for 1985.

The turnover of receivables provides information on the liquidity of the receivables. How fast are the accounts collected? It is computed as follows:

$$\text{Turnover of Receivables} = \frac{\text{Credit Sales}}{\text{Average Accounts Receivable}} = \frac{\$502{,}500}{(\$57{,}100 + \$49{,}800)/2}$$
$$= 9.4 \text{ Times}$$

The higher the turnover of receivables, the shorter the time between sale and cash collection. Division of the turnover into 365 days yields an estimate of the average collection period. For Sebago Company the estimate for 1985 is 39 days ($365 \div 9.4$). By adding the inventory turnover period and collection period, the analyst gains an idea of the average total elapsed time before an inventory item finally winds up as cash. The longer this time period, the weaker the current ratio becomes as an indicator of debt-paying ability.

**Turnover of Accounts Payable**

Some analysts would argue that the sum of the inventory holding period and the cash collection period overstates the time it takes to go from cash to inventory to cash, because it ignores the financing supplied by current trade creditors. A company can reduce its cash requirements by relying on supplier credit. The extent to which suppliers are willing to wait for cash payment can be approximated by the turnover of accounts payable. If the accounts payable of Sebago Company arise entirely from inventory purchase transactions, the turnover would be:

$$\text{Turnover of Accounts Payable} = \frac{\text{Purchases}}{\text{Average Accounts Payable}} = \frac{\$327,700^*}{(\$61,600 + \$54,900)/2}$$
$$= 5.6 \text{ times}$$

\* Cost of goods sold of $324,900 plus the increase in inventory balance of $2,800.

On average in 1985 the firm took 65 days (365/5.6) to remit cash to its suppliers. This fact is relevant in an appraisal of short-term financial strength and in a projection of cash requirements.

**Coverage of Operations by Quick Assets**

The last measure of short-term liquidity we will discuss concerns the period of time for which operations could be sustained by the monetary assets on hand. For how many days could cash expenditures for operating expenses be paid from the cash on hand, the cash obtained through conversion of marketable securities, and the cash collected from outstanding receivables? A very rough estimate of cash operating expenses can be obtained by subtraction of nonfund expenses like depreciation and amortization from total expenses.

$$\frac{\text{Projected Daily}}{\text{Cash Requirement}} = \frac{\text{Estimated Cash Operating Expenditures}}{365} =$$
$$\frac{\$453,300^*}{365} = \$1,242$$

$$\frac{\text{Number of Days}}{\text{Coverage}} = \frac{\text{Monetary Assets}}{\text{Projected Daily Cash Requirements}} =$$
$$\frac{\$101,700}{\$1,242} = \frac{82 \text{ Days}}{\text{for 1985}}$$

\* Cost of goods sold plus selling and administrative expense plus interest minus depreciation expense of $8,700 ($88,100 − $79,400) and amortization of intangibles of $2,000.

**FINANCIAL STRENGTH**

Another group of ratios focuses on long-term financial solvency. These ratios reflect the business' ability to meet interest payments and to maintain a steady payment of preferred and common dividends.

**Equity Ratios**

The relationship between borrowed capital and owners' equity is one common measure of long-term financial solvency. It can be expressed in a number of ways, including the following:

|  |  |  | *1985* | *1984* |
|---|---|---|---|---|
| Stock-Equity Ratio | $=$ | $\dfrac{\text{Common Stock Equity}}{\text{Total Equities}} =$ | $\dfrac{\$214,900}{\$409,900}$ 52.4% | $\dfrac{\$203,500}{\$394,000}$ 51.6% |
| Debt-Equity Ratio | $=$ | $\dfrac{\text{Long-Term Debt}}{\text{Total Equities}} =$ | $\dfrac{\$66,000}{\$409,900}$ 16.1% | $\dfrac{\$72,000}{\$394,000}$ 18.3% |
| Debt-Stock Ratio | $=$ | $\dfrac{\text{Long-Term Debt}}{\text{Common Stock Equity}} =$ | $\dfrac{\$66,000}{\$214,900}$ 30.7% | $\dfrac{\$72,000}{\$203,500}$ 35.4% |

Sometimes, the total equities denominator is replaced with an amount that represents the *capitalization*. Current liabilities are excluded, and the focus is on the so-called relatively permanent investment in the firm. Because the current liabilities *in the aggregate* can constitute a significant portion of a company's long-term capital that can change from period to period, ratios based on capitalization may be misleading.

The stock-equity ratio tells what portion of the assets has been contributed by common stockholders. A higher ratio generally indicates greater long-term financial strength, because less reliance is placed on debts which have definite maturity dates and mandatory periodic payments and preferred stock. A common stockholder might calculate this ratio to judge the firm's ability to acquire additional funds in the future. A high ratio would indicate room for capital expansion via additional bond borrowing or preferred stock issuance; a low ratio might indicate that the firm is already "borrowed up." A bond holder might use the alternative version, the debt-equity ratio, to obtain an idea of the financial cushion—how much the corporation could lose in assets without the creditors' capital being endangered. The lower the ratio, the more protection the existing bondholders have. As we will see shortly, equity ratios are among the financial measures most stressed by bank lending officers and bond rating agencies. What a proper equity ratio should be, of course, must be judged according to the type and size of the business, the stability of the firm's revenues and earnings, and its susceptibility to general economic fluctuations.

**Ratio of Plant to Long-Term Debt**

One common way to acquire long-term borrowed capital is to issue mortgage bonds, liabilities secured by land or plant assets which have been pledged as collateral for the bonds. The mortgage bondholders would have a prior claim on the proceeds from sale of the property and plant if the firm were forced to liquidate. Consequently, some analysts review the relationship between plant assets (net of depreciation) and long-term debt. If the property and plant are not mortgaged, a high ratio may suggest additional potential borrowing power. If the fixed assets have been pledged, a high ratio may suggest a degree of security for the debt from the bondholders' viewpoint. The ratio for Sebago Company is:

$$\text{Ratio of Plant to Long-Term Debt} = \frac{\$185,800}{\$66,000} = 2.8 \qquad \frac{\$180,700}{\$72,000} = 2.5$$

*1985*                 *1984*

Of course, the reliability of this ratio depends directly on the reliability of book values of plant assets as measures of liquidation values; in many instances, book values prove unreliable.

**Coverage Ratios**

A more direct measure of a firm's capacity to employ large amounts of financial capital from senior securities is its ability to pay the recurring fixed charges imposed. This ability is indicated by coverage ratios which express the relationship between what is normally available from periodic operations and the requirements for interest expense and preferred dividends. The interest coverage is calculated as follows:

$$\text{Interest Coverage} = \frac{\text{Income before Interest and Taxes}}{\text{Interest Expense}}$$

*1985*                 *1984*

$$\frac{\$45,760}{\$7,260} = 6.3 \text{ Times} \qquad \frac{\$42,920}{\$7,920} = 5.4 \text{ Times}$$

The number of times interest is protected (covered) by earnings gives an idea of the firm's ability to handle interest-bearing liabilities in the normal course of events. Because interest is an allowable deduction for income tax purposes, an income figure before income taxes is used in the numerator. Even if Sebago's income before interest and taxes were to shrink to one sixth of its 1985 amount, the firm would still be earning an amount equivalent to the interest expense.

Some bond indentures and loan agreements insist that a specified interest coverage ratio be maintained in future years; otherwise, the amount of the loan or bond becomes due immediately or other default provisions are invoked. To appraise this risk, many analysts calculate times-interest-earned for forecasted income or for the poorest year in the past. The interest coverage ratio is of particular concern to bond raters.

When a firm has both debt and preferred stock outstanding, we can calculate a ratio for the *coverage of total fixed charges*. Failure to pay preferred dividends, while not legally harmful, is viewed as a serious weakness in the financial community. Before-tax earnings of Sebago Company could decline to one third of the 1985 level and still be sufficient to cover its fixed financial charges.[6]

$$\frac{\text{Income before Interest and Taxes}}{\text{Interest Expense} + \text{Pretax Preferred Dividend Requirements}}$$

$$1985: = \frac{\$45,760}{\$7,260 + (\$3,600/0.6)} = \frac{\$45,760}{\$7,260 + \$6,000} = 3.4 \text{ Times}$$

$$1984: = \frac{\$42,920}{\$7,920 + (\$3,600/0.6)} = \frac{\$42,920}{\$7,920 + \$6,000} = 3.1 \text{ Times}$$

**Cash Flow to Long-Term Debt**

Somewhat related to the interest coverage ratio is a financial measure which compares the amount of cash flow with the long-term-debt total. Cash flow generally is defined as simply net income plus depreciation, amortization, and income taxes deferred during the year. Accordingly, it approximates working capital from operations but differs from the real cash flow from operations, the calculation of which was discussed in the previous chapter. Long-term debt includes not only bonds and mortgages payable but also any amounts for long-term capitalized lease obligations. The computation for Sebago Company for 1985 is:

$$\frac{\text{Net Income} + \text{Depreciation/Amortization Expense}}{\text{Long-Term Debt}} =$$

$$\frac{\$23,100 + \$10,700}{\$66,000} = \frac{\$33,800}{\$66,000} = 51.2\%$$

In a later section of this chapter, we see that this ratio is among those financial measures most stressed by both bond raters and bank lending officers. Nevertheless, extreme caution is necessary in the use of this ratio because of possible misinterpretations of the numerator.

**EFFICIENCY**

Two aspects of efficiency may be of interest to an analyst—investment efficiency and operating efficiency. Investment efficiency concerns the degree of asset utilization and relates the size of various asset investments

---

[6] Because preferred dividends, unlike interest charges, are not deductible for tax purposes, the income before tax needed to cover preferred dividends is necessarily higher. Dividing the amount of preferred dividends by (1 − tax rate) gives the before-tax burden of preferred dividends. Note that subtraction of income taxes of 40 percent from the $6,000 of Income before Taxes leaves the $3,600 needed for preferred stock dividends. Many analysts ignore this tax adjustment unless the coverage is low. In fact, for a rough guide, some analysts use aftertax income in calculating all times-charges-earned ratios, although the results are not as logical or interpretable as those presented above.

to volume of activity. Operating efficiency concerns asset consumption in the generation of revenue.

**Investment Efficiency**

The primary mode for expression of investment efficiency is the *turnover*. Various turnovers measure the efficiency with which specific assets or groups of assets are used.

**Turnover of Receivables.**   This turnover is introduced earlier as a supplementary measure of liquidity. It indicates the speed or slowness with which receivables are converted into cash. A firm's average collection period which is significantly longer than that of other firms in its industry may result from a more liberal policy for granting credit and/or a poorer quality of receivables.[7]

The turnover of accounts receivable also serves as a primary indicator of efficiency in this area of investment. For example, comparison of the average collection period with the *selling terms* may reveal poor credit selection or collection efforts. A series of years in which turnover of receivables declines may disclose a situation which is getting out of control. With no change in selling terms, a growing investment in receivables relative to sales volume indicates either a deliberate change in policy, sales to more marginal customers, or insufficient effort being devoted to collection.

**Turnover of Inventory.**   In a manner similar to that employed with receivables, a study of inventory turnovers may reveal an over- or underinvestment in inventory. A steadily decreasing turnover of inventories may denote overstocking, with its unnecessary carrying costs, or obsolescence, with its attendant risks and losses. An unusually high inventory turnover may evidence an inventory investment inadequate to meet the current volume of sales. It may foretell a future loss of sales and customer goodwill because the firm might not be able to deliver promptly or the need for additional funds to rebuild the inventory level.

On page 679 we show the calculation for the turnover of merchandise. Whether this 3.7 times (or 99 days) is satisfactory depends on the type of merchandise. Inventory turnover in a jewelry store is significantly lower than that in a supermarket. The analyst must also be on the lookout for distortions introduced into the turnover calculation by unusually high or low inventories at the beginning and end of the year. If available, average monthly or quarterly inventory figures may serve as a better indicator of overall inventory levels during the year.

Sebago Company appears to be a trading concern (wholesaler or retailer). For a manufacturing concern, an analyst may calculate three separate inventory turnovers—one for raw materials, one for work in

---

[7] The National Association of Credit Management publishes collection periods for many industry groups.

process, and one for finished goods—if the needed data are available. The formulas for the additional two ratios would be:

$$\text{Turnover of Raw Materials} = \frac{\text{Cost of Raw Materials Used}}{\text{Average Raw Material Inventory}}$$

$$\text{Turnover of Work in Process} = \frac{\text{Cost of Goods Completed}}{\text{Average Work in Process Inventory}}$$

As in the case of the turnover of finished goods, the numerator represents the flow variable—the amount of inventory leaving the particular account during the period—and the denominator approximates the average inventory available during the period.

**Turnover of Total Assets.** A measure of overall investment efficiency is the turnover of total assets, computed as follows for 1985:

$$\frac{\text{Sales}}{\text{Average Total Assets}} = \frac{\$502,500}{(\$409,900 + \$394,000)/2} = 1.25 \text{ Times}$$

This relationship shows how many dollars of recurring revenue are generated by each dollar of assets. If a firm's turnover is low compared to that of similar firms or if the trend is downward over a number of years, the analyst may suspect the presence of unnecessary assets (such as idle cash balances) or inefficiently used assets (such as obsolete equipment). On the other hand, a sudden jump in the turnover should not always be interpreted as a favorable sign. It may actually result from a sharp increase in sales volume and a temporary underinvestment in assets. In fact, if the increased volume of sales is to be maintained, additional investment in plant and inventories may be necessary.

**Operating Efficiency**

In this area we are interested in income statement relationships. Most of them are usually expressed as a percentage of sales. A complete set of income statement relationships can be seen in the common-size income statement shown in Table 18–2. We highlight here only a few of the more commonly employed ratios.

**Operating Ratio.** The ratio between *recurring* operating expenses and operating revenues (commonly only sales) measures the proportion of resource inflow from sales that is consumed by normal operating activities—manufacturing, marketing, administration, research, and so on.

Operating Expenses/Operating Revenues

1985 = ($324,900 + $90,700 + $41,140)/$502,500 = 90.9%
1984 = ($319,600 + $76,300 + $41,180)/$480,000 = 91.1%

Definitions of the revenue and expense activities which constitute *normal* operations vary among analysts. For Sebago Company we are excluding interest expense and income taxes from operating expenses;

other analysts, however, might include one or both of them. When defined consistently and applied within industry lines, the operating ratio can provide a rough index of operating efficiency.

**Income or Profit Margins.** Another approach to operating efficiency is to look at what remains after various expenses have been deducted. A number of margin figures can be computed according to the general formula, *income/revenue*. Each attempts to measure what portion of the revenue dollar ends up as income. However, revenue can be defined as sales only or can include all recurring revenues. Even greater diversity exists among possible numerators—gross margin (sales less cost of goods sold), operating income, income before interest and after taxes (the reward to the various suppliers of investor capital), and net earnings to common stockholders. Some of these reflect varying interpretations of operations, some reflect alternative uses or viewpoints, and others simply reflect the personal preferences of individual analysts. The operating income margin is, of course, the complement to the operating ratio—9.1 percent in 1985 and 8.9 percent in 1984 for Sebago Company.

**Gross Margin Analysis.** Another commonly computed margin figure, particularly for retailers and wholesalers, is the difference between sales and cost of goods sold. As shown in Table 18–2, the gross margin percentage (gross margin/sales) increased from 33.4 percent in 1984 to 35.3 percent in 1985. These figures measure the average markup above the cost of the products sold. The level of the gross margin percentage may provide clues to the company's pricing policies and marketing strategies. How satisfactorily this measure performs these functions depends on the inventory method employed. Under LIFO, which matches relatively current costs against current revenues, movements in the ratio primarily reflect how changes in purchase prices are translated into changes in selling prices. Under FIFO, the gross margin reflects both pricing policy and, to a greater extent than under LIFO, the effect on income of holding inventory.

In addition to studying changes in the relationship of gross margin to sales, analysts also like to probe the causes of changes in the dollar amounts. For example, the increase in the gross margin of Sebago Company from 1984 to 1985 was $17,200. This results from an interplay among three major factors—selling prices (price), purchase prices (cost), and number of units sold (volume). Occasionally, an analyst sufficiently familiar with the industry will be able to approximate the separate impact of each factor on gross margin. Alternatively, management may provide information about changes in gross margin in terms of price, cost, and volume in its narrative report on the firm's operations.

**Operating Leverage.** An important aspect of statement analysis is the attempt to shed light on the future, particularly future earnings. The prediction of earnings encompasses more than a simple extension of past trends, important as this may be. Of equal significance is the prediction of environmental changes, particularly industry conditions, and the firm's reaction to these changes. The concept of operating leverage can be helpful in this area as well as in the explanation of historical changes in the operating ratio or in the profit margins. Operating leverage is a measure of the impact on operating profits caused by changes in volume of activity. A change in sales volume may result in a *more than proportional change* in operating income because of the existence of fixed costs among the business' operating expenses.

Broadly speaking, the operating expenses of a business tend to be either fixed or variable in relation to the number of units sold (i.e., volume). Fixed expenses are incurred in approximately the same amount regardless of the level or volume of operations in the period. Salaries, rent, and most depreciation charges are examples of fixed expenses. Variable expenses change in total more or less proportionately with changes in the volume of operations in the period; raw materials, hourly wages, and sales commissions are usually variable expenses.

The rate at which income changes with volume depends on the expense structure. If all expenses are variable and price remains unchanged, income will change at the same rate as volume. There is *no* operating leverage. Because cost of goods sold is a variable expense in a retailing enterprise, one would expect the *gross* margin percentage to remain relatively constant in spite of volume changes. If some expenses are fixed, however, income will change at a rate *greater* than will volume, because not all the expenses rise or fall as volume increases or decreases. The difference in rates of change between income and volume is magnified as fixed expenses become more significant.

Operating leverage, then, deals with the volatility of earnings with changes in volume. External analysts may be unable to measure the precise impact of operating leverage, because under current reporting practices the breakdown of expenses between fixed and variable is not provided in the annual report.[8] Nevertheless, they may make rough guesses based on their knowledge of the firm and perhaps a comparison of expense figures from one year to the next. Even a general understanding of the expense structure and the concept of operating leverage may improve the accuracy of the projections.

**Discretionary Expenses.** A vertical analysis of a comparative income statement reveals changes in the relationships between various expenses and sales. Some of these changes reflect the impact of operating leverage (the expense remains fixed but sales volume changes) or of changing environmental conditions (a new labor contract increases the ratio of labor expense to sales). In other instances, the change may result from deliberate policy decisions by management. *Discretionary expenses are those period costs which management can significantly modify in amount from*

---

[8] In recent years the idea of categorizing expenses as fixed or variable in *external* financial reports has received more serious consideration. See, for example, "Reporting Income, Cash Flows, and Financial Position of Business Enterprises," p. 20.

*period to period.* Research and development, advertising, and repair and maintenance expenses are among the items that fall into this category.

Analysts usually conduct a horizontal analysis of the income statement to keep a close watch on changes in the level of expenditure on the more discretionary expenses. They can be postponed or otherwise manipulated readily in the short run. Thus, an increase in operating income achieved as the result of a substantial curtailment in spending for research and development or repair and maintenance, for example, may be illusory in a longer-run context. For this reason, some analysts calculate the ratio of repair and maintenance expenses to sales or to plant assets each period to evaluate the adequacy or reasonableness of the company's maintenance policy compared to industry averages. The relationship to sales would be more appropriate when the expense is primarily variable, and the comparison to plant assets would be preferred when the expense is not responsive to changes in sales volume.

## PROFITABILITY

Generally the most important overall ratios are those which reflect the earning power of the enterprise. The ultimate test of the economic success of a firm is its ability to earn a return on the resources invested in it. Thus the central measure of profitability is the relationship between income and investment. This relationship is expressed as a percentage rate of return on investment *(income/average investment)*. The precise definitions of income and investment to be used vary with the viewpoint and purpose of the analyst. Some of the more commonly used rates of return are discussed below—along with some other ratios often associated with profitability.

## Rate of Return on Total Capital Investment

In using the concept of return on investment to evaluate overall earnings performance, we usually begin by computing a rate of return on total capital investment. This percentage is useful in the evaluation of operating management, for it measures how productively the total resources of the business have been employed, irrespective of how they are financed. Consequently, it facilitates comparisons between firms with different capital structures and comparisons over time for the same firm when its capital structure has changed.

Two commonly used formulas are illustrated below for Sebago Company for 1985. The first defines investment as average total assets; the second excludes the impact of current liabilities and views average investment as the relatively permanent capital supplied by stockholders and long-term creditors. The reasoning behind the latter approach is that current liabilities usually are a fairly stable, somewhat automatic source of capital arising out of normal accruals and trade credit. Consequently, most managerial decisions concern the employment of assets from long-term sources.

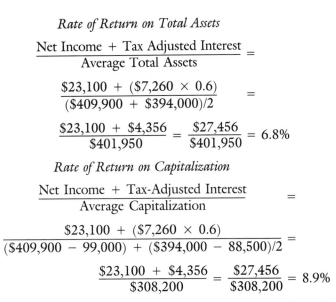

*Rate of Return on Total Assets*

$$\frac{\text{Net Income} + \text{Tax Adjusted Interest}}{\text{Average Total Assets}} =$$

$$\frac{\$23,100 + (\$7,260 \times 0.6)}{(\$409,900 + \$394,000)/2} =$$

$$\frac{\$23,100 + \$4,356}{\$401,950} = \frac{\$27,456}{\$401,950} = 6.8\%$$

*Rate of Return on Capitalization*

$$\frac{\text{Net Income} + \text{Tax-Adjusted Interest}}{\text{Average Capitalization}} =$$

$$\frac{\$23,100 + (\$7,260 \times 0.6)}{(\$409,900 - 99,000) + (\$394,000 - 88,500)/2} =$$

$$\frac{\$23,100 + \$4,356}{\$308,200} = \frac{\$27,456}{\$308,200} = 8.9\%$$

A few words of explanation about the numerator are in order. The income component should be consistent with the investment component. Therefore, if we are concerned with total assets or total long-term investment, the return should eliminate the effect of alternative financing arrangements. That is, the return calculation should be unaffected by how management has chosen to finance the total assets. Seemingly, this figure would simply be net income before the deduction of interest expense. However, if the $7,260 interest expense and related tax deduction were eliminated in 1985, tax expense would increase by $2,904 ($7,260 × 40% tax rate). Therefore, instead of adding back the entire interest charge, we add only $4,356 ($7,260 − $2,904), the after-tax burden of the interest expense, to net income. The resultant figure is the amount of income that would have been generated if all assets (or long-term capital) had been supplied by the common stockholders.[9]

The denominator in this and other ratios consist of a simple average of the beginning and ending balances.[10] This often is the only information available to the external analyst. When there is reason to believe that such a simple average might not indicate the average amount available during the period, the analyst should make appropriate adjustments. For example, new assets invested shortly before year-end obviously were not available for use during the year and should be omitted entirely in the calculation of

---

[9] Many analysts do not worry about tax adjustments or internal consistency. Consequently, the reader will often see the numerator in the rate-of-return calculation defined as net income before interest, net income, or net income before interest and taxes. All of these are theoretically incorrect for measuring a return on total capital; but, employed consistently, they still can provide meaningful information in many instances.

[10] Many analysts ignore the theoretical refinement of averages and simply use investment figures as of the beginning or end of the period.

average total assets. If the objective of the calculation is a rate of return on assets available for *productive* use, then temporarily idle funds and construction in progress might also be excluded from the asset base.

In analyzing differences among firms or changes in the return on investment from one year to the next for the same firm, we may find it helpful to visualize the rate of return as the product of two component parts—a profit margin and the previously discussed turnover of assets. We thus emphasize the fact that overall profitability is dependent upon both *operating efficiency* and *investment efficiency*. The 6.8 percent rate of return on total assets for Sebago Company for 1985 can be broken down as follows:

$$\underset{\text{Average Total Assets}}{\underset{\text{\it Return on Investment}}{\dfrac{\text{Net Income} + \text{Tax-Adjusted Interest}}{\text{Average Total Assets}}}} = \underset{\text{Sales Revenue}}{\underset{\text{\it Margin}}{\dfrac{\text{Net Income} + \text{Tax-Adjusted Interest}}{\text{Sales Revenue}}}} \times \underset{\text{Average Total Assets}}{\underset{\text{\it Turnover}}{\dfrac{\text{Sales Revenue}}{\text{Average Total Assets}}}}$$

$$\dfrac{\$27{,}456}{\$401{,}950} = \dfrac{\$27{,}456}{\$502{,}500} \times \dfrac{\$502{,}500}{\$401{,}950}$$

$$6.8\% = 5.4\% \times 1.25 \text{ Times}$$

Then, by studying the margin and turnover figures separately in the manner discussed earlier, we often can glean additional information about the basic causes of differences or changes in the total return on investment.

## Rate of Return on Common Stock Equity

Another application of the general concept of return on investment takes the viewpoint of the owners of the business. They are interested not only in how well management uses the total assets available but also in the profitability of their particular equity interest in the firm. How well in 1985 has Sebago Co. used the assets *and* modified the capital structure to the benefit of the common stockholders of the business?

$$\dfrac{\text{Net Income to Common Stock Equity}}{\text{Average Common Stock Equity}} =$$

$$\dfrac{\$23{,}100 - \$3{,}600}{(\$214{,}900 + \$203{,}500)/2} = \dfrac{\$19{,}500}{\$209{,}200} = 9.3\%$$

Income in this case is defined as the amount of net income from recurring sources which remains after provision has been made for rewarding sources of capital other than common stockholders. Hence, it consists of net income after taxes, interest, and any *preferred* stock dividends but before common stock dividends. The investment denominator includes all portions of common stock equity—par or stated value of the outstanding common stock, the excess over par or stated value, and retained earnings, less treasury stock.

This rate of return on common stock equity is superior to earnings per share as a measure of the profitability of the owners' investment, for it explicitly considers the increased investment due to retained earnings. It is among the most significant financial measures examined by stockholders and financial analysts.

**Financial Leverage**     Notice in the preceding calculations that the rates of return on investment and on owners' equity differ. Rate of return on total assets is 6.8 percent, while rate of return on common stock equity is 9.3 percent. The difference reflects the impact of *financial leverage*. Financial leverage is the modification of the rate of return on common stockholders' equity from what it otherwise would be through the use of debt or preferred stock capital to finance the acquisition of part of the assets.

Management employs capital supplied by creditors and preferred stockholders in lieu of common stockholders' equity in the expectation that the business will earn more on the noncommon capital than the fixed charges (interest and preferred dividends) associated with this capital. If so, the excess inures to the common stockholders, thereby increasing the rate of return on their investment, and the firm experiences *favorable* financial leverage. On the other hand, the firm may earn at an overall rate that is less than the cost of this capital to the business. Because the return to the bondholders and preferred stockholders is fixed, the deficiency reduces the earnings applicable to the common stockholders' equity. As a result of this negative financial leverage, the rate of return on common is less than the overall earning rate.

The overall effect of favorable financial leverage on the 1985 rate of return on common equity for Sebago Company is illustrated in Table 18–3. Sebago earned an average return of 6.8307 percent on total assets, which were financed in part by current liabilities, bonds, and preferred stock. Because the assets financed from current liabilities (for which no explicit interest charge is made) earned $6,404 during 1985, the common stockholders benefit by that amount. They benefit slightly from bonds-payable financing, since the $4,713 of earnings on the assets provided by bonds exceeds the *after-tax* interest expense ($7,260 × 0.6 = $4,356). The financial leverage from the preferred-stock financing is unfavorable;

**TABLE 18–3  Analysis of Favorable Financial Leverage in Sebago Company**

| Source of Capital | Average Amount Available in 1985 | Overall Earnings Rate of 6.8307% | Payments to Suppliers of Funds | Benefit Remaining for Common |
|---|---|---|---|---|
| Current liabilities ................. | $ 93,750 | $ 6,404 | None | $ 6,404 |
| Bonds payable ................... | 69,000 | 4,713 | $4,356 | 357 |
| Preferred stock ................... | 30,000 | 2,049 | 3,600 | (1,551) |
| Total leverage capital ........ | 192,750 | 13,166 | 7,956 | 5,210 |
| Common stock equity ............ | 209,200 | 14,290 | | 14,290 |
| Total assets ..................... | $401,950 | $27,456 | | $19,500 |

the 12 percent rate paid on such capital far exceeds the 6.8 percent earned on such funds. The $5,210 net amount generated from the current liabilities, bonds, and preferred stock for the benefit of common stockholders adds 2.5 percent ($5,210/$209,200) to the 6.8 percent return on average assets; the result is a 9.3 percent return on common equity ($19,500/$209,200).

The *extent* to which a firm employs financial leverage is a function of the *amount of fixed-charge securities in its capital structure. How advantageous* the financial leverage effect is, though, depends upon the *differential between the earnings rate on total assets and the fixed-charge cost of debt and preferred stock.* Of course, the increased use of debt or preferred stock capital adds to the riskiness of the firm. Therefore, in making capital structure decisions, management must consider the trade-off between potential increases in profitability through financial leverage and potential decreases in long-term financial strength reflected in a higher debt-equity ratio.

## Earnings and Dividend Measures

In Chapter 16 we discussed the most frequently cited measure of earning power—earnings per share. As we noted, quite commonly EPS is related to the current market price of the stock by means of a *price-earnings ratio.* Through a study of movements in the price-earnings ratios of particular stocks or by a comparison of price-earnings ratios among firms in the same risk category, some investors attempt to identify over- and undervalued stock issues. Stock issues are undervalued when the stock market has not fully reflected the value of the firm's earnings in the market price (price-earnings ratios are low).[11] In any case, like many of the widely used measures, extreme price-earnings ratios or sudden changes in relative P/E ratios may signal situations that require further attention by the analyst.

*Dividends per share* supplements the earnings-per-share figure. It measures the *amount* of earnings actually distributed per share in the form of cash dividends to the common stockholders and is reported in most statements as historical fact. Adjustments are necessary only when dividends per share are presented in comparative form over time and the number of shares has been affected by stock dividends or stock splits. Then past years' dividends should be restated in terms of the current equivalent number of shares. As with EPS, analysts commonly divide dividends per share by the current market price to obtain a *dividend yield* rate.

The future dividend stream from an investment in a common stock depends dually on the level of earnings and the *dividend-payout ratio.* The

---

[11] A growing body of research suggests that such searches for undervalued stocks are somewhat futile. In an efficient capital market, the market price of shares fully reflects all publicly available information. Moreover, market prices tend to react rapidly to the availability of new information. What individual investors may perceive as an undervaluation of a stock may only represent a difference in risk evaluation by the market.

payout ratio measures the *proportion* of earnings distributed as cash dividends. It is calculated as follows for Sebago Company for 1985:

$$\frac{\text{Cash Dividends to Common}}{\text{Net Income to Common}} = \frac{\$8,100}{\$19,500} = 41.5\%$$

A company's payout ratio is influenced by its current financial condition (availability of cash), its capital structure (debt-equity ratios), and its need for funds for expansion. To assess the firm's reliance on funds from operations to finance expansion, some analysts calculate an *equity growth ratio* (Earnings retained in business for the period/Average common stock equity) as a measure of internally financed growth.

**PREDICTIVE ABILITY OF FINANCIAL RATIOS**

Since the early 1960s, a large number of studies of financial ratios have been published. Much of this research has focused on the use of ratios in the prediction of business failure or in credit-rating decisions.

Perhaps the best-known studies relating ratio levels to business failure were conducted by Beaver and by Altman.[12] Beaver's definition of failure was very broad, encompassing firms that had either gone bankrupt, omitted preferred dividends, defaulted on bonds, or overdrawn a bank account. The following financial ratios were analyzed for 79 firms which "failed" between 1954 and 1964 and an equal number of firms that had not failed:

1. Cash flow to total debt.
2. Net income to total assets.
3. Total debt to total assets.
4. Working capital to total assets.
5. Current ratio.
6. No-credit interval (quick assets minus current liabilities to fund expenditures for operations).

Beaver looked at each individual ratio's ability to predict financial "failure" for each of the sample firms. The first two ratios had the strongest power; they misclassified only 13 percent of sample firms for the first year before failure. In contrast, the last three misclassified 22–24 percent for the same time period.

Altman gathered information on 22 financial measures for an experimental group of 33 manufacturing companies which filed an involuntary bankruptcy petition between 1946 and 1965 and a control group of 33 nonbankrupt firms, matched by industry and asset size. Unlike Beaver,

---

[12] William H. Beaver, "Financial Ratios as Predictors of Failure," *Empirical Research in Accounting: Selected Studies, 1966,* Supplement to Volume 4, *Journal of Accounting Research,* pp. 71–111; and Edward I. Altman, "Financial Ratios, Discriminant Analysis and the Prediction of Corporate Bankruptcy," *Journal of Finance,* September 1968, pp. 589–609.

Altman examined the ratios simultaneously by using the statistical technique of multiple discriminant analysis to derive the combination of those ratios that allowed the fewest sample firms to be misclassified as bankrupt or nonbankrupt.

The research identified five ratios as having in combination the best predictive ability for the year prior to bankruptcy. Correct classification of 95 percent and 83 percent of the firms for one and two years preceding bankruptcy, respectively, was achieved after analysis of:

1. Working capital to total assets.
2. Retained earnings to total assets.
3. Earnings before interest and taxes to total assets.
4. Market value of equity to book value of total debt.
5. Sales to total assets.

Altman's findings received much attention and generated considerable optimism. It looked as if the cost and complexity of financial analysis would be greatly decreased if bankrupt or nonbankrupt status could be very accurately predicted up to two years in advance on the basis of just five ratios. However, the initial enthusiasm somewhat subsided in later years. Analysts and later researchers discovered that most ratio prediction models, including Altman's, lost significant predictive power when applied years later to a different sample of firms.[13] An additional factor which caused some analysts to view Altman's model cautiously was its inclusion of such ratios as retained earnings to total assets and market value of equity to book value of total debt. Those ratios were not "household words" and could not have been expected intuitively to be among those measures best able to forebode a bankruptcy.

Backer and Gosman focused on the prediction of *financial distress,* as opposed to bankruptcy, in their 1978 research study for the National Association of Accountants.[14] Because changes in the trade credit, bank loan, and bond ratings received by a firm could signal the beginning of financial distress, Backer and Gosman focused on the use of financial measures in the credit-rating decisions of Dun & Bradstreet, federal and state bank examiners, and Standard & Poor's, respectively. Downgradings to a rating of 3 for trade credit, substandard for bank loans, and BB for bonds were considered to be capable of producing varying degrees of financial distress.

Senior executives at Dun & Bradstreet, 24 leading banks, and all 3 bond-rating agencies were asked how important financial ratios are in their credit-rating evaluations. Their unanimous belief was that certain measures were of moderate to strong importance. The ratios stressed by the interviewees are listed in the left column of Table 18–4. They are then

---

[13] For an expanded discussion of this point, see James S. Patel and Kiritkumar A. Ang, "Bond Rating Methods: Comparison and Validation," *Journal of Finance,* May 1975, pp. 631–40.

[14] Morton Backer and Martin L. Gosman, *Financial Reporting and Business Liquidity,* (New York: National Association of Accountants, 1978).

**TABLE 18–4  Financial Ratios Stressed by Credit Raters**

| Ratios Stressed during Interviews | Ratios Exhibiting Significant Deterioration in Actual Credit Downgradings |
|---|---|

*Bonds:*

| Cash flow to long-term debt<br>Long-term debt to capitalization | Cash flow to long-term debt<br>Long-term debt to capitalization |
|---|---|

| Fixed-charge coverage | Net tangible assets to long-term debt<br>Return on tangible net worth<br>Return on sales<br>Return on total assets<br>Cash flow to senior debt<br>Long-term debt to property, plant, and equipment |
|---|---|

*Bank loans:*

| Cash flow to total liabilities<br>Return on sales<br>Total liabilities to tangible net worth | Cash flow to total liabilities<br>Return on sales<br>Financial leverage |
|---|---|

| Working capital to sales | Gross margin<br>Return on equity<br>Fixed-charge coverage<br>Interest coverage<br>Cash flow to senior debt<br>Effective tax rate<br>Percentage sales growth<br>Inventory turnover<br>Current ratio<br>Quick ratio<br>Cash flow growth<br>Percentage profit growth |
|---|---|

*Trade credit:*

| Current liabilities to tangible net worth<br>Total debt to tangible net worth<br>Inventory to working capital<br>Long-term debt to working capital<br>Current ratio<br>Quick ratio | Return on tangible net worth<br>Percentage cash flow change<br>Return on working capital<br>Percentage profit change |
|---|---|

Note: Boxed items signify congruity between interviews and statistical findings.
Source: Morton Backer and Martin L. Gosman, *Financial Reporting and Business Liquidity,* (New York: National Association of Accountants, 1978), p. 19.

compared with the right-column listing of those ratios actually exhibiting significant deterioration prior to the downgrading actions of the credit raters.[15] The findings reported in Table 18–4 reveal that:

1. The levels and trends of certain key financial measures do influence the probability that a firm will experience the downgrading of its bonds, bank loans, and trade credit and consequent financial distress.
2. The ratios stressed in actual credit downgradings were quite con-

---

[15] See Chapters 2 and 5 to 8 of the study for an elaboration of the findings reported in Table 18–4 and a discussion of their implications.

gruous with the bond analysts' and bankers' (but *not* trade credit raters') descriptions of their own decision models.

The above research study is representative of many which strongly suggest that levels of and trends in financial ratios influence organizations and individuals outside the firm who often can significantly affect the company's financial flexibility and future outlook. The accounting profession should continually assess whether the financial statement amounts upon which most ratios are based truly measure what they should be measuring. Individual companies need to closely monitor the trends in their financial ratios and to prominently disclose and candidly discuss in their annual reports the existence and implications of such trends. Armco's efforts in this regard are reviewed in the next section of this chapter.

## DISCUSSION OF THE ARMCO ANNUAL REPORT

Armco's ratio disclosures appear at various points in its 1981 Annual Report. Many financial measures are presented in the "Other Data" section on page 171. For each year from 1977 through 1981, Armco highlights such statistics as:

1. Net income as a percent of sales.
2. Return on average net assets.
3. Return on average shareholders' equity.
4. Dividend payout percentage.
5. Book value per share.
6. Cash flow as a percent of long-term obligations.
7. Long-term debt ratio.
8. Interest coverage ratio.

Several of these ratios are also predominantly featured and discussed in earlier sections of the annual report. Except for certain modifications to be discussed shortly, Armco calculates these ratios in a manner similar to that discussed in this chapter. In the following pages we review these and other financial measures for Armco.

## Liquidity

The financial measures which are indicative of Armco's liquidity are less prominently featured than are the long-term counterparts which gauge financial strength. In the listing of "Other Data," only the statistic on cash flow from operations reflects on short-term liquidity. As we noted in Chapter 17, Armco should not really have labeled the $519.5 million as its 1981 cash flow from operations. That amount represents the total of net income plus noncash expenses, but we must consider changes in various other current accounts in order to arrive at Armco's true cash flow from operations of $37.6 million.

Only in the "Change in Working Capital" section on page 166 does

Armco present information relative to various short-term measures. Since inventory has increased from 15 percent to 19 percent of cost of sales during 1981, we can calculate the inventory turnovers for 1980 and 1981 to be 6.7 times (100/15), or 54 days, and 5.3 times (100/19), or 69 days, respectively. With receivables at 13 percent of sales for both 1980 and 1981, that turnover has remained at 7.7 times (100/13) or 47 days. After calculating the two turnovers for 1981 from the information provided, the analyst can sum them to arrive at 116 days (69 + 47) as the average time for inventory to be turned into cash.

Although Armco's working capital did change during 1981, the amount of the change does not even appear in the "Change in Working Capital" section. The excess of current assets over current liabilities was $203.3 million greater at the end of 1981 than it was at the beginning. Working capital items other than cash, marketable securities, and short-term notes payable increased by much more during 1981 ($482.0 million), but the exclusion of these three significant *current* items leaves one with a concept that is very different from working capital.

**Financial Strength**

**Long-Term Debt Ratio.** The 1981 long-term debt ratio of 21.6 percent is among the most stressed financial measures, being featured on pages 167 and 171. The computation is:

$$\frac{\text{Long-Term Debt and Lease Obligations (LTDLO)}}{\text{LTDLO} + \text{Ending Shareholders' Equity}}$$

$$= \frac{\$572.8 \text{ Million} + \$107.4 \text{ Million}}{(\$572.8 \text{ Million} + \$107.4 \text{ Million}) + \$2,467.2 \text{ Million}}$$

$$= \frac{\$680.2 \text{ Million}}{\$3,147.4 \text{ Million}} = 21.6\%$$

Armco appropriately considers its obligations under capital leases to be exactly what they are—the equivalent in substance of long-term debt. The long-term debt ratio somewhat approximates what we labeled as the debt-equity ratio earlier in this chapter, on page 681. It was noted there that when current liabilities are excluded from the denominator, the result is a capitalization amount rather than a total equities amount. Armco has gone two steps further by also excluding from its denominator the amounts for Deferred Income Taxes ($322.4 million) and Other Liabilities ($83.1 million). Armco's exclusion of the deferred income taxes from its ratio numerator is consistent with the fairly popular viewpoint (noted and explored in Chapter 13) that such taxes *in the aggregate* will never be paid and, hence, are not a real liability.

Armco's reference to its long-term debt ratio at key points throughout its annual report is understandable in light of the very favorable (low) level of that ratio and its implications for the firm's financial flexibility. Many steel companies reported significantly higher (less favorable) long-term debt ratios for 1981; for example, Inland Steel's and U.S. Steel's were 37.3 and 27.2 percent, respectively, while Armco's was 21.6 percent. As noted earlier, a primary source of financial flexibility is provided by the ability to raise new capital quickly through the issuance of debt securities. This flexibility is specifically addressed early in the annual report, where Armco notes, "Our long-term debt ratio at year end was 21.6 percent— well below our acceptable maximum debt level of 30 percent. This leaves us plenty of financing capacity to use when we need to."

**Interest Coverage.**  Closely related to the long-term debt ratio is the interest coverage statistic. It was calculated for 1981 as follows:

$$\frac{\text{Income before Interest and Taxes for Armco and Consolidated Subsidiaries} + \text{Equity in Income of Unconsolidated Subsidiaries}}{\text{Interest Expense}} =$$

$$\frac{(\$452.3 \text{ Million} + \$70.2 \text{ Million}) + \$30.3 \text{ Million}}{\$70.2 \text{ Million}} = \frac{\$552.8 \text{ Million}}{\$70.2 \text{ Million}} = 7.9 \text{ Times}$$

Armco's coverage of 7.9 times for 1981 reflects an interest burden, in relation to net income, that most analysts would consider manageable. The relatively low debt outstanding at Armco directly contributes to the favorable (low) long-term debt ratio and the equally favorable (high) interest coverage ratio.

**Cash Flow as a Percent of Long-Term Obligations.**  Armco's ratio of cash flow to long-term debt was 76.4 percent, as shown on page 171 of its 1981 annual report. The company's relatively low debt level also influences this favorable statistic. The numerator is the $519.5 million working capital from operations, the figure that Armco continually calls cash flow. Presented below is the complete calculation.

$$\frac{\text{Cash Flow}}{\text{LTDLO}} = \frac{\$519.5 \text{ Million}}{\$680.2 \text{ Million}} = 76.4\%$$

The great majority of firms define cash flow for purposes of this ratio in a manner similar to Armco's. Nevertheless, the company's actual 1981 cash flow from operations is only $37.6 million (see Table 17–10 and the earlier discussion in this section on Armco's liquidity). If the $37.6 million figure had been used, the above ratio would have dropped significantly to 5.5 percent ($37.6/$680.2).

**Profitability**

The profitability measures stressed in Armco's disclosures include (1) net income as a percent of sales, (2) return on average net assets, and (3) return on average shareholders' equity. These measures are now considered along with the effect of financial leverage.

**Return on Sales.**  As noted earlier, an income-to-sales ratio (modified to include tax-adjusted interest) is often calculated as the margin component, which is then multiplied by the turnover component to arrive at return on investment. Armco's return-on-sales measure is viewed independently rather than as a component of return on investment and, accordingly, is arrived at (without addition of tax-adjusted interest) as follows for 1981:

$$\frac{\text{Net Income}}{\text{Net Sales}} = \frac{\$294.5 \text{ Million}}{\$6,906.0 \text{ Million}} = 4.3\%$$

**Return on Average Net Assets.** Net assets are usually defined as total assets minus total liabilities and, accordingly, must be equal to total stockholders' equity. Armco, however, shows for 1981 a return on average net assets of 11.1 percent and a return on average shareholders' equity of 13.7 percent. It obviously had deviated from the standard definition of net assets. Although the company indicates very early in its annual report that overall net assets were $3.6 billion on December 31, 1981, the definition used is not revealed in the annual report. The actual calculation of net assets used by Armco is shown below.

|  | December 31 | |
|---|---|---|
|  | 1981<br>($ millions) | 1980<br>($ millions) |
| Total assets .......................................... | $4,817.2 | $3,807.4 |
| Less: Current liabilities ............................ | (1,264.3) | (846.7) |
| Plus: Current portion of long-term debt and<br>    lease obligations ................................ | 22.6 | 18.7 |
| Net assets ........................................... | $3,575.5 | $2,979.4 |

The return on average net assets for 1981 was computed as follows:

$$\frac{\text{Net Income} + \text{Interest Expense} + \begin{array}{c}\text{Minority Inter-}\\\text{est in Income}\end{array}}{\text{Average Net Assets}} =$$

$$\frac{\$294.5 \text{ Million} + \$70.2 \text{ Million} (1 - .5) + \$16.9 \text{ Million}}{\dfrac{1 (\$3,575.5 \text{ Million}) + 3(\$2,979.4 \text{ Million})}{4}} =$$

$$\frac{\$346.5 \text{ Million}}{\$3,128.4 \text{ Million}} = 11.1\%$$

Because almost all current liabilities have been excluded from the denominator, Armco's return on net assets is similar to a return on capitalization. The special treatment afforded the current portion of long-term debt and lease obligations (it is not deducted along with the other current liabilities) seems reasonable, because it is not an automatic source of capital arising out of normal accruals and trade credit. Armco uses a weighted average to arrive at the average net assets, giving the beginning-of-year total three times the weight of the ending amount.[16] It represents an attempt to counter any unrepresentativeness in the end-of-year amount caused by the firm's major acquisition of Ladish Co. on October 16, 1981.

The addition of the minority interest in income to the numerator is one way of ensuring consistency with the denominator. Recall from our discussion in Chapter 15 that Armco has a number of subsidiaries which are less than 100 percent owned. In the consolidated balance sheet, however, the assets of these subsidiaries are included in their entirety. On the consolidated income statement, the minorities' interest in income has been deducted (as an expense) so that the reported net income of $294.5 reflects only Armco's interest. Because assets contributed by both the majority and minority interests are counted in the denominator, *all* the income produced by those assets belongs in the numerator. Accordingly, the $16.9 million of minority interest in income which was previously deducted in the calculation of income must be added back.

Tax-adjusted interest expense is also included in the numerator for the purpose of consistency between numerator and denominator. Many of the assets reflected in the denominator were financed through the use of long-term debt and lease obligations, and, accordingly, the return to those providers of assets (in the form of interest expense) should be considered in the numerator. Although Armco's effective federal tax rate was 41.6 percent for 1981, the company used a 50 percent tax rate to simplify the calculation. The $70.2 million of interest expense is tax deductible and is assumed to have saved Armco $35.1 million in income taxes for 1981. If there had been no interest expense and related tax deduction, after-tax net income would have been $35.1 million greater.

**Return on Average Shareholders' Equity.** In calculating the return on average shareholders' equity, Armco once again gave the beginning-of-year amount three times the weight of the ending amount. The 1981 return of 13.7 percent was calculated as follows:

$$\frac{\text{Net Income}}{\text{Average Shareholders' Equity}} = \frac{\$294.5 \text{ Million}}{\dfrac{1(\$2,467.2 \text{ Million}) + 3(\$2,046.6 \text{ Million})}{4}}$$

$$= \frac{\$294.5 \text{ Million}}{\$2,151.8 \text{ Million}} = 13.7\%$$

Just as the return on investment was dissected into its margin and turnover components on page 690 of this chapter, so can the return on shareholders' equity be disaggregated. The information presented on page 171 in the annual report for the five-year trends in net income as a percent of sales and return on average shareholders' equity offers insight into the relative contribution of margin and turnover. For example, as can be seen

---

[16] The existence of and rationale for such a weighting method and explanations of other specialized adjustments used in this ratio were revealed during a telephone conversation with Armco's accounting department.

below, only an improvement in turnover from 1980 to 1981 prevented the return on average shareholders' equity from deteriorating.

$$
\begin{array}{llll}
\textit{Return on Share-} & & & \\
\textit{holders' Equity} & = & \textit{Margin} & \times & \textit{Turnover}
\end{array}
$$

$$
\begin{array}{lll}
\text{Net Income/Average} & & \text{(Sales/Average} \\
\text{Shareholders'} & = \text{(Net Income/Sales)} \times & \text{Shareholders' Equity)} \\
\text{Equity} & &
\end{array}
$$

| | | | | |
|---|---|---|---|---|
| 1980: 13.6% | = | 4.7% | × | 2.89 Times* |
| 1981: 13.7% | = | 4.3% | × | 3.19 Times* |

\* Equal to Return on Shareholders' Equity/Margin.

**Financial Leverage.**　Up to this point, we have highlighted for 1981 Armco's return on average shareholders' equity of 13.7 percent and its return on average *net* assets of 11.1 percent. In order to make this discussion of financial leverage more comparable to the analysis conducted for Sebago Company on page 691 of this chapter, calculations are necessary for the company's return on average *total* assets and its return on average common stockholders' equity. If Armco's weighting of its beginning-of-year total at three times its end-of-year total is maintained, then the 1981 rates of return are as follows:

*Return on Average Total Assets:*

$$
\frac{\text{Net Income} + \begin{array}{c}\text{Tax-Adjusted} \\ \text{Interest} \\ \text{Expense}\end{array} + \begin{array}{c}\text{Minority} \\ \text{Interest in} \\ \text{Income}\end{array}}{\text{Average Total Assets}} =
$$

$$
\frac{\$346.5 \text{ Million*}}{\dfrac{1(\$4,817.2 \text{ Million} + 3(\$3,807.4 \text{ Million})}{4}} =
$$

$$
\frac{\$346.5 \text{ Million}}{\$4,059.9 \text{ Million}} = 8.5\%
$$

\* See page 699.

*Return on Average Common Equity:*

$$
\frac{\text{Net Income} - \begin{array}{c}\text{Preferred} \\ \text{Dividends}\end{array}}{\text{Average Common Equity}} = \frac{\$294.5 \text{ Million} - \$4.4 \text{ Million}}{\dfrac{1(\$2,459.6 \text{ Million}) + 3(\$2,035.9 \text{ Million})}{4}} =
$$

$$
\frac{\$290.1 \text{ Million}}{\$2,141.8 \text{ Million}} = 13.5\%
$$

A comparison of the 13.5 percent return on average common equity and the much lower 8.5 percent return on average total assets shows that Armco experienced favorable financial leverage for 1981. As was the case for Sebago Company, however, such overall favorable leverage occurred even though preferred stockholders received dividends which exceeded the income earned by the firm from the use of the capital they supplied. Armco's 13.7 percent return on average *shareholders'* equity falls to 13.5 percent after the preferred capital and dividends are removed and the return on average *common* equity is calculated. The overall favorable financial leverage results from the firm carrying a substantial amount of interest-free current liabilities and many long-term liabilities on which it incurred a weighted-average interest charge that was considerably below the 8.5 percent return earned on average total assets.

**Book Value per Share**

Amounts for earnings per share, dividends per share, and book value per share appear at various places in the annual report. Charts (not reproduced in the Appendix of Chapter 5) illustrate that both earnings per share and dividends per share have grown steadily since 1978. Dividends have evidently increased a little more quickly than earnings, for the data on page 171 show a gradual increase in the dividend payout percentage since 1978.

Armco's inclusion of its book value per share on the same page is interesting but not unusual. Many persons would argue that this financial measure (common shareholders' equity/number of common shares) has little relevance, because the shareholders' equity number is, of course, calculated by subtraction of the *book value* of liabilities from the *book value* of assets. In many instances, investors are far more interested in determining what a reasonable *current* valuation of the firm would be, as expressed in market price (rather than historical cost) per share. Nevertheless, if book value *exceeds* market price per share, as in the case of Armco (book value of $38.55 versus market price of $28.00 on December 31) and many other firms during the 1981 recession, some analysts pay attention to the statistic. They feel that the measure could then take on significance as an indicator of probable market undervaluation and a good long-term investment opportunity.

In this chapter, of course, Armco's performance has been expressed in ratios derived from relationships from its historical cost based financial statements. In the next chapter, we will examine whether Armco's results of operations and financial position appear as favorable after adjustments are made to recognize the effect of changing prices.

**A CONCLUDING NOTE**

The analysis of financial statements is truly problematic. On the one hand, it is one major reason for preparing accounting reports and certainly a logical capstone to a study of financial accounting. On the other hand, the area is fraught with difficulties and potential traps. The qualitative considerations pointed out in the first part of this chapter are as important as the quantitative aspects of statement analysis presented in the main portion of the chapter.

As an analyst, you are faced with a variety of ratios and alternative definitions. You must select the relevant information and analytical procedures for your particular purposes. The techniques discussed provide a start in this direction. However, in the computation and use of ratios, keep four points in mind:

1. Ratios are only as valid as the statements themselves. Ratios reflect all the conventions and limitations underlying the basic accounting data. A detailed understanding of the financial statements is essential to an intelligent interpretation of the ratios and a meaningful explanation of changes in ratios.
2. Ratio analysis requires a basis for comparison.
3. Ratios are only a clue to areas needing further investigation. They can serve as screening devices, but they rarely supply answers and can never make decisions.
4. Ratio analysis is meaningful only if there is a clear understanding of the purpose of each relationship—short-term liquidity, long-term financial strength, efficiency, and profitability. The ratios used should make sense; some a priori reason or analytical purpose should exist to support the belief that the financial statement items chosen are related.

# QUESTIONS AND PROBLEMS

**18–1.** The condensed financial data for the Ruggles Company appear below (amounts in thousands of dollars):

RUGGLES COMPANY
Balance Sheet

| Assets | | Equities | |
|---|---|---|---|
| Cash | $ 20 | Accounts payable | $ 56 |
| Marketable securities | 10 | Accrued liabilities | 23 |
| Receivables | 38 | 8% mortgage bonds | 50 |
| Inventories | 90 | 10% preferred stock | 40 |
| Investment securities | 25 | Common stock | 100 |
| Plant assets (net) | 122 | Retained earnings | 36 |
| Total assets | $305 | Total equities | $305 |

RUGGLES COMPANY
Income Statement

| | | |
|---|---|---|
| Net sales | | $475 |
| Cost of goods sold | $372 | |
| Operating expenses | 63 | |
| Depreciation expense | 18 | 453 |
| Operating income | | 22 |
| Other income | 9 | |
| Other expense | (4) | |
| Interest expense | (4) | 1 |
| Income before taxes | | 23 |
| Income taxes (40%) | | 9 |
| Net income | | $ 14 |

Preferred dividends declared and paid during the year were $4,000 and common dividends were $7,000. At the beginning of the year, inventories were $110,000, total common stockholders' equity was $126,000, and the total assets were $275,000. Preferred stock was $40,000 throughout the year.

*Required:*

a. From the above information, calculate the following ratios *and* explain their meanings and uses:
   (1) Current ratio.
   (2) Quick ratio.
   (3) Stock-equity ratio.
   (4) Times-fixed-charges-earned.
   (5) Average number of days' sales uncollected at year-end.
   (6) Turnover of merchandise.
   (7) Rate of return on total assets.
   (8) Rate of return on total stockholders' equity.
   (9) Rate of return on total common stockholders' equity.
b. "Since the current ratio and the quick ratio have identical denominators and similar numerators, it is redundant to calculate both." Evaluate this statement.
c. Why were you provided with beginning-of-year amounts for inventories, total common stockholders' equity, and total assets?
d. Did the firm experience favorable or unfavorable financial leverage from its

use of preferred stock? From its use of bonds? Show calculations to support your answer.

**18–2.** The information presented below is taken from the records of two companies in the same industry:

| | Ken Co. | Caryn Co. |
|---|---|---|
| Cash | $ 23,000 | $ 42,000 |
| Receivables (net) | 43,000 | 53,000 |
| Inventories | 125,000 | 90,000 |
| Plant assets (net) | 199,500 | 260,000 |
| Total assets | $390,500 | $445,000 |
| | | |
| Accounts payable | $ 80,500 | $102,000 |
| Bonds payable | 77,000 | 100,000 |
| Common stock | 120,000 | 160,000 |
| Retained earnings | 113,000 | 83,000 |
| Total equities | $390,500 | $445,000 |
| | | |
| Sales | $590,000 | $910,000 |
| Cost of goods sold | 420,000 | 700,000 |
| Other expenses | 60,000 | 75,000 |
| Interest expense | 8,000 | 9,000 |
| Income taxes | 51,000 | 63,000 |
| Dividends | 11,000 | 17,000 |

*Required:*

a. Answer each of the following questions by making a comparison of one or more relevant ratios:
  (1) Which company is using the stockholders' investment more profitably?
  (2) Which company is better able to meet its current debts?
  (3) If you were going to buy the bonds of one firm, which one would you choose? (Assume you would buy them at the same yield.)
  (4) Which firm collects its receivables faster?
  (5) How long does it take each company to convert an investment in inventory to cash?
  (6) Which company retains the larger proportion of income in the business?
b. Which company is earning the higher rate of return on its total asset investment? Explain the general reasons for the differences in terms of investment efficiency and operating efficiency.
c. Do your answers in parts *(a)* and *(b)* shed any light on which firm represents the better investment opportunity? Explain.

**18–3.** The following ratios have been calculated from the 1981 financial statements of three actual companies. One of the companies is a utility, one is a manufacturer of consumer durables, and the third is a retailer of consumer products.

| | Company | | |
|---|---|---|---|
| | A | B | C |
| Current ratio | 2.86 | 0.85 | 2.01 |
| Stock-equity ratio | 70% | 29% | 47% |
| Turnover of average total assets | 2.21 times | 0.24 times | 1.97 times |
| Margin | 5.3% | 26.9% | 4.2% |
| Return on investment | 11.7% | 6.5% | 8.3% |

*Required:*

a. From the differences in the ratios for the three firms, attempt to identify the utility, manufacturer, and retailer.
b. Explain what industry conditions might account for the differences in the ratios for the three different firms.
c. Could you have calculated one of the ratios on your own if the other four had been given to you? Explain.

**18–4.** The Ali Finance Company is attempting to evaluate an applicant for a *short-term* loan. The following information is furnished by the loan applicant:

| | December 31 | | |
|---|---|---|---|
| | *1986* | *1985* | *1984* |
| Cash ............................ | $ 3,000 | $ 5,000 | |
| Marketable securities ............... | 3,500 | 9,000 | |
| Receivables ..................... | 29,000 | 34,000 | $ 19,000 |
| Inventories .................... | 40,000 | 35,000 | 30,000 |
| Prepayments ................... | 6,500 | 8,000 | |
| Accounts payable ............... | 32,000 | 49,000 | 27,000 |

| | Year Ended December 31 | |
|---|---|---|
| | *1986* | *1985* |
| Sales ......................... | $115,000 | $106,000 |
| Cost of goods sold .............. | 85,000 | 79,000 |

*Required:*

a. Compute for 1985 and 1986 the following ratios: current ratio, quick ratio, inventory turnover, receivables turnover, and accounts payable turnover.
b. Based on your findings in part *(a),* would you recommend that Ali Finance Company grant the loan? Explain.
c. What limitations, if any, do you see in your analysis?
d. Would quarterly data have been helpful in this type of situation?
e. Should Ali Finance Company insist that the financial data presented by loan applicants be audited? Why or why not?
f. If the applicant were requesting a *long-term* loan instead of a short-term loan, is there any additional financial data that the Ali Finance Company should insist on seeing? Explain.

**18–5.** The following statistics for 1981 have been gathered for three well-known brewing companies in the United States (all amounts are in millions of dollars):

| | Anheuser-Busch | Coors | G. Heileman |
|---|---|---|---|
| Sales ......................... | $4,410 | $930 | $807 |
| Interest expense ................. | 90 | 2 | 3 |
| Net income .................... | 217 | 52 | 40 |
| Average total assets ............. | 2,662 | 925 | 306 |
| Average stockholders' equity ....... | 1,119 | 733 | 143 |

*Required:*

a. Compute a rate of return on average total asset investment as a product of margin and turnover for each of the firms. Assume a 46% tax rate.
b. Comment on the differences discovered in part *(a).* Did the firms with lower margins achieve higher turnovers and vice versa?

c. Compute a rate of return on average stockholders' equity for each company.

d. "Each of the three brewers is to be commended, for they all managed to employ favorable financial leverage." Is this true? Should they all be equally commended? Explain.

e. What potential pitfalls do you have to be aware of in making the comparisons asked for in parts *(b)* and *(d)?*

**18–6.** *Selected* financial information from the 1982 annual reports of three airlines is presented below (amounts in thousands of dollars):

|  | Delta | Republic | UAL, Inc. |
|---|---|---|---|
| 1982: |  |  |  |
| Sales revenue | $3,617,523 | $1,530,668 | $5,319,709 |
| Net earnings (loss) from operations | (8,156) | 37,223 | (9,388) |
| Net earnings (loss) | 20,814 | (39,861) | 30,762 |
| Increase (decrease) in working capital | (56,067) | 88,441 | 128,755 |
| December 31, 1982: |  |  |  |
| Receivables | 318,506 | 120,974 | 599,408 |
| Total current assets | 488,198 | 328,640 | 1,074,137 |
| Total assets | 2,657,880 | 1,186,174 | 4,578,894 |
| Air traffic liability | 232,711 | 68,137 | 352,181 |
| Total current liabilities | 743,993 | 306,992 | 1,466,587 |
| Total liabilities | 1,634,229 | 1,130,236 | 3,457,938 |
| Retained earnings (deficit) | 824,280 | (30,286) | 555,954 |

*Required:*

a. Calculate the current ratio and the amount of working capital for each airline at December 31, 1982. Are such levels generally viewed as satisfactory? Are airlines' current ratios really quick ratios in disguise? Explain.

b. The "air traffic liability" is also referred to as "advance ticket sales" and "tickets outstanding." What procedure for revenue recognition is implied by the existence of this current liability?

c. According to Delta, "a negative working capital position is normal for Delta and the airline industry in general and does not indicate a lack of liquidity. The Company maintains adequate current assets to satisfy current liabilities when due, and at year end Delta had unused bank lines of credit totaling $250 million." Is negative working capital normal for the airline industry? If so, what factors contribute to this situation? Is the situation as unimportant and trivial as Delta makes it seem?

d. Compare and contrast the relationship among the airlines' net operating earnings (loss) vis-à-vis their net income (loss) numbers. What factors might have created the observed disparity? Which relationship would you pay more attention to in evaluating the relative profitability of the three firms? Explain.

e. "Republic Airlines is the best managed of the three airlines. The lifeblood of any firm is liquid assets, and Republic's current ratio far exceeds those of Delta and UAL, Inc. Consequently, it has better staying power as the industry attempts to respond to new challenges in the mid-1980s." Do you agree with part or all of this statement? Why or why not?

**18–7.** You are the new small-loan officer at Surety State Bank. Two companies have submitted requests for six-month unsecured loans of $75,000. Because of lending limits imposed by bank policies on this type of loan, only *one* of the loans will probably be granted. Condensed financial information appears below:

|  | Cape Co. | Cod Co. |
|---|---|---|
| Cash | $ 19,500 | $ 5,000 |
| Accounts receivable | 38,400 | 42,800 |
| Inventories | 100,000 | 120,000 |
| Plant assets (net) | 115,000 | 115,800 |
| Total assets | $272,900 | $283,600 |
| | | |
| Accounts payable | $ 41,000 | $120,000 |
| Mortgage payable | 93,000 | 100,000 |
| Stockholders' equity | 138,900 | 63,600 |
| Total equities | $272,900 | $283,600 |
| | | |
| Sales | $320,800 | $250,000 |
| Cost of goods sold | (211,600) | (176,800) |
| Operating expenses | (97,900) | (58,600) |
| Interest expense | (11,300) | (10,000) |
| Net income before tax | –0– | $ 4,600 |
| Income taxes | –0– | (1,840) |
| Net income | –0– | $ 2,760 |

*Required:*

a. As a loan officer considering these requests for six-month loans, are you equally concerned with the four areas of liquidity, financial strength, efficiency, and profitability? Explain.

b. Calculate some ratios that would be helpful to you in assessing the performance of both applicants in the priority areas you cited in your answer to *(a)*. Which *one* of the two companies would you recommend for the loan?

c. One of your assistants suggests that your ratio analysis in part *(b)* should really have been made on a pro forma basis, i.e., assuming that the loan request was granted. Do you agree?

d. Calculate the time it takes each firm to convert an investment in inventory to cash.

e. Another of your assistants says that your calculation in *(d)* is an overstatement of the operating cycle (the time it takes to go from cash to inventory to cash) because it ignores the financing supplied by current trade creditors. Assuming that accounts payable arise entirely from inventory purchase transactions, what is the extent of supplier financing?

f. Which operating cycle calculation (yours or your assistant's) is more realistic and useful? For what purposes?

18–8. *Selected* financial data for Chrysler Corporation appear below. All amounts are in millions and were taken from the annual reports for the respective years.

|  | 1982 | 1981 | 1980 |
|---|---|---|---|
| Year ended December 31: |  |  |  |
| Net sales | $10,045 | $10,822 | $9,225 |
| Income (loss) from continuing operations | (69) | (476) | (1,710) |
| December 31: |  |  |  |
| Cash and marketable securities | 897 | 404 | 297 |
| Accounts receivable | 248 | 430 | 476 |
| Inventories | 1,133 | 1,600 | 1,916 |
| Total current assets | 2,369 | 2,601 | 2,861 |
| Short-term debt | 79 | 164 | 151 |
| Payments due within one year on long-term debt | 16 | 62 | 166 |
| Total current liabilities | 2,113 | 2,419 | 3,029 |
| Total long-term debt | 2,148 | 2,059 | 2,483 |
| Obligations under capital leases | 41 | — | — |
| Paid-in capital | 2,515 | 2,472 | 1,674 |
| Retained earnings (deficit) | (1,524) | (1,692) | (1,215) |

The opinion paragraphs of the auditors' reports received by Chrysler for 1980, 1981, and 1982 read as follows:

> In our opinion, the accompanying financial statements have been prepared in conformity with generally accepted accounting principles applicable to a going concern applied on a consistent basis, except for the capitalization of interest in 1980 with which we concur (see Note 11). The financial statements do not purport to give effect to adjustments, if any, that may be appropriate should the Corporation be unable to operate as a going concern and therefore be required to realize its assets and liquidate its liabilities, contingent obligations and commitments in other than the normal course of business and at amounts different from those in the accompanying financial statements.
>
> In view of the uncertainties and the ongoing restructuring described in the preceding paragraphs, we are unable to express an opinion as to whether or not the accompanying financial statements are presented fairly because we are unable to determine whether or not the use of generally accepted accounting principles applicable to a going concern is appropriate in the circumstances.
>
> TOUCHE ROSS & CO.<br>Certified Public Accountants

February 27, 1981, Detroit, Michigan

---

> In our opinion, subject to the effects of such adjustments, if any, which might have been required had the outcome of the uncertainties regarding the Corporation's going concern status and its investment in Peugeot been known, the accompanying financial statements present fairly the financial position of Chrysler Corporation and consolidated subsidiaries at December 31, 1981, and 1980, and the results of their operations and changes in their financial position for each of the three years in the period ended December

31, 1981, in conformity with generally accepted accounting principles applied on a consistent basis, except for the changes, with which we concur, in the capitalization of interest in 1980 and in depreciation methods in 1981.

TOUCHE ROSS & CO.
Certified Public Accountants

February 24, 1982, Detroit, Michigan

---

In our opinion, the accompanying financial statements present fairly the financial position of Chrysler Corporation and consolidated subsidiaries at December 31, 1982, and 1981, and the results of their operations and changes in their financial position for each of the three years in the period ended December 31, 1982, in conformity with generally accepted accounting principles applied on a consistent basis, except for the change, with which we concur, in depreciation methods in 1981.

TOUCHE ROSS & CO.
Certified Public Accountants

February 24, 1983, Detroit, Michigan

*Required:*

a. Calculate several relevant ratios used to measure liquidity and financial strength. What trends were evident during the 1980–1982 period.

b. Calculate several relevant ratios used to measure profitability. What trends were evident during the 1980–1982 period?

c. Compare your findings for parts *(a)* and *(b)*. Has Chrysler made its greatest improvement in the liquidity and financial strength areas or in the profitability area? Explain.

d. Compare the three auditors' reports. How do they differ? Are the appropriate opinions given in each case? What use does an analyst make of the auditors' opinion?

e. "Adjusted for rounding, the change in Retained Earnings (deficit) during 1981 does equal the $476 million loss shown for 1981. For 1982, however, something must be wrong, because the deficit *decreased* at the same time that a $69 million *loss* was reported." Can you explain this apparent inconsistency?

f. In 1981, Chrysler changed (for financial reporting purposes) from a declining-balance method to the straight-line method of depreciation for new asset acquisitions. This change reduced 1981 depreciation expense by $36.5 million. Is this change worthy of note and consideration in your ratio analysis? Does it invalidate your findings in parts *(a)* and *(b)*? Explain.

18–9. The following descriptive section on working capital appeared in the 1981 annual report of Koppers Company, Inc.:

**Working Capital**
Koppers has maintained its working capital within a narrow range over the past three years. This has resulted from management's efforts to reduce inventories to levels appropriate to weakening business conditions. Further,

management has maintained close attention to accounts receivable so that, in a declining business and financial environment, payments due from customers woud not tie up Company funds excessively. The large increase in 1980 working capital was a temporary condition that resulted when $53 million from the issuance of convertible preference stock in December of 1980 was held in cash at year end. These funds were intended for use in completing the purchase of stock in Richmond Tank Car Company and for the reduction of corporate debt. Excluding these funds temporarily held in cash, working capital at the close of 1980 would have been $272 million.

|  | 1981 | 1980 | 1979 |
|---|---|---|---|
|  | ($ millions) | | |
| Working capital | $270.7 | $325.0 | $265.3 |

Working capital is the surplus of current assets over current liabilities and indicates the amount of financial flexibility a company has to meet day-to-day business obligations, to withstand adversity, to pay dividends, and to build plants.

Shareholders should be cognizant of the way in which the level of working capital has been affected by the Company's use, starting in 1974, of the last-in, first-out (LIFO) method of inventory accounting.

LIFO accounting recognizes the current costs of labor and materials in the cost of sales (on the income statement) and thereby prevents the overstatement of earnings and the overpayment of income taxes that would result from the use of first-in, first-out (FIFO) accounting during inflationary times. The effect of this, however, is an understatement of the Company's current assets, specifically its value of inventories (on the balance sheet). This, therefore, leads to understatement of the level of day-to-day business the Company's working capital can realistically support.

|  | 1981 | 1980 | 1979 |
|---|---|---|---|
|  | ($ millions) | | |
| Inventories: | | | |
| FIFO | $340.6 | $349.6 | $305.0 |
| LIFO | 213.8 | 240.3 | 211.9 |
| Excess of FIFO cost over LIFO | $126.8 | $109.3 | $ 93.1 |

Comparison of the Company's inventories for the past three years, using both the LIFO and FIFO methods of accounting, illustrates the growing disparity between the current value of the Company's inventories (FIFO value) and the value of inventories carried on the Company's balance sheet (LIFO value). This disparity has grown wider every year since the adoption of the LIFO method in 1974.

The fact is that the FIFO value of inventories more closely approximates the purchasing power that the Company actually has to meet short-term business obligations. The following presents what the Company's working capital would be if FIFO inventory values, rather than LIFO, were included in current assets and if the additional tax liability would be reflected in current liabilities. Continued use of FIFO accounting after 1974 would have substantially increased the Company's tax liabilities and would have required greater use of long-term funding to maintain the current level of working capital.

|  | 1981 | 1980 | 1979 |
|---|---|---|---|
|  |  | ($ millions) |  |
| Working capital, including FIFO inventory value | $391.0 | $432.0 | $354.8 |

In the past, a widely accepted rule of thumb within the business and financial community stated that a prudently run corporation should maintain a ratio of current assets to current liabilities of approximately 2-to-1, or better. For the reasons just discussed, this is no longer generally applicable to companies that have been on LIFO accounting for a number of years, and it should be recognized that they can have a strong liquidity position with a current ratio of less than 2-to-1. The following comparison of the Company's current ratio using both types of inventory valuation illustrates this point.

| Current Ratio | 1981 | 1980 | 1979 |
|---|---|---|---|
| Inventory value: |  |  |  |
| FIFO | 2.40-to-1 | 2.34-to-1 | 2.30-to-1 |
| LIFO | 1.99-to-1 | 2.02-to-1 | 1.98-to-1 |

Koppers ability to meet its short-term obligations remains excellent.

*Required:*

a. Calculate the yearly percentage changes in working capital under each of the following:
   1. As actually reported by the firm.
   2. If the $53 million temporarily tied up in cash at December 31, 1980 is ignored.
   3. If FIFO rather than LIFO had been followed.
   4. If FIFO had been followed *and* the $53 million item is ignored.
b. Has Koppers aided your analysis of the firm's liquidity by alerting you to the $53 million item? Explain.
c. How can *FIFO* "more closely approximate the purchasing power that the Company actually has to meet short-term business obligations"?
d. "Koppers has made a mistake. In 1981, for example, $270.7 million + $126.8 million does *not* equal the $391.0 million figure they show." What do each of these numbers represent? Should they add up?
e. "Koppers really cannot say for sure what its working capital would have been if FIFO had been used instead of LIFO, because entirely different business decisions might have been made." What different business decisions might have been made? Could they have significantly affected the level of working capital?
f. Do you agree with Koppers that the 2-to-1 current ratio rule of thumb "is no longer applicable to companies that have been on LIFO accounting for a number of years"? Explain. If a rule of thumb existed for inventory turnover, would it continue to be applicable?

18–10. 1982 was not a good year for the manufacturers of farm equipment and machinery. Massey-Ferguson and International Harvester experienced widely publicized debt-restructuring problems. Deere & Company saw its earnings per share drop from $3.79 to $0.78 and, late in 1982, the firm reduced its cash common stock dividend by 50 percent. Caterpillar recorded its first loss since 1932. *Selected* financial statement data for Deere and Caterpillar are presented below (amounts in millions of dollars):

| | Deere & Company | | Caterpillar | |
|---|---|---|---|---|
| | 1982 | 1981 | 1982 | 1981 |
| Sales | $4,608 | $5,447 | $6,469 | $9,154 |
| Cost of goods sold | 3,822 | 4,274 | 5,334 | 6,933 |
| Interest expense | 267 | 232 | 334 | 225 |
| Income (loss) on consolidated companies | (39) | 160 | (183) | 562 |
| Equity in net income of unconsolidated subsidiaries and affiliates | 92 | 91 | 3 | 17 |
| Net income (loss) | 53 | 251 | (180) | 579 |
| | December 31 | | | |
| Trade receivables | $2,661 | $2,374 | $ 960 | $ 994 |
| Inventories | 761 | 872 | 1,801 | 2,214 |
| Current assets | 3,765 | 3,565 | 3,433 | 3,544 |
| Total assets | 5,936 | 5,684 | 7,201 | 7,285 |
| Current liabilities | 2,396 | 2,305 | 1,197 | 2,369 |
| Long-term debt | 898 | 676 | 2,389 | 961 |
| Total liabilities | 3,547 | 3,234 | 3,705 | 3,428 |
| Retained earnings | 1,905 | 1,971 | 3,231 | 3,622 |

*Required:*

a. Often firms who encounter difficulties in selling their products exhibit reduced gross margin percentages and poorer turnovers of receivables and inventory. Why might this occur? Did it happen for either Deere or Caterpillar? Explain.

b. "Deere's farm equipment business was far more successful than Caterpillar's because Deere generated a $53 million profit while Caterpillar suffered a $180 million loss." Do you agree with this statement? Why or why not?

c. Calculate some ratios which will permit you to assess the relative liquidity of both firms.

d. Calculate some ratios which will permit you to assess the relative financial strength of both firms.

e. The following information applies to two 8% sinking-fund debentures due in either the year 2001 or 2002:

| | Standard & Poor's Bond Rating | |
|---|---|---|
| | January 1983 | January 1982 |
| Bond X | AA − | AA |
| Bond Y | A + | AA − |

One of the bonds was Deere's and the other was Caterpillar's. Was S&P justified in downgrading either or both firms' bonds during 1982? Can you surmise which bond is Deere's? Explain.

**18–11.** Comparative financial statements for Center Awning Company appear below:

CENTER AWNING COMPANY
Income Statements
Year Ended December 31

| | 1985 | 1984 | 1983 |
|---|---|---|---|
| Sales | $60,000 | $49,000 | $45,000 |
| Cost of goods sold | 39,000 | 32,800 | 28,000 |
| Selling expenses | 6,400 | 4,000 | 3,600 |
| Administrative expenses | 9,100 | 5,000 | 7,100 |
| Total expenses | 54,500 | 41,800 | 38,700 |
| Net income before tax | 5,500 | 7,200 | 6,300 |
| Income taxes | 2,200 | 2,880 | 2,520 |
| Net income | $ 3,300 | $ 4,320 | $ 3,780 |

CENTER AWNING COMPANY
Balance Sheets
As of December 31

| | 1985 | 1984 | 1983 |
|---|---|---|---|
| Cash | $ 2,400 | $ 2,800 | $ 1,400 |
| Accounts receivable | 7,000 | 7,200 | 3,100 |
| Inventory | 8,500 | 8,200 | 6,000 |
| Plant and equipment | 9,000 | 11,400 | 12,900 |
| Total assets | $26,900 | $29,600 | $23,400 |
| Current liabilities | $ 6,800 | $ 6,400 | $ 2,900 |
| Bonds payable | 5,000 | 6,000 | 8,000 |
| Common stock | 11,000 | 12,000 | 9,000 |
| Retained earnings | 4,100 | 5,200 | 3,500 |
| Total equities | $26,900 | $29,600 | $23,400 |

*Required:*

a. Express the income statements and balance sheets in common-size percentages. Comment on any significant fluctuations.
b. Prepare a horizontal analysis, 1985 over 1984, for each item. Does this reveal any significant insights?
c. Calculate the following ratios for all three years and comment on your findings: (1) current ratio and (2) quick or acid-test ratio.
d. Calculate the following ratios for 1985 and 1984 only and comment on your findings: (1) rate of return on stockholders' equity, (2) turnover of total assets, (3) turnover of inventories, and (4) turnover of receivables.

**18–12.** Below are the comparative position statements and income statements of United Corporation for the years 1983 to 1985:

UNITED CORPORATION
Comparative Position Statements

|  | 1983 | 1984 | 1985 |
|---|---|---|---|
| *Assets* | | | |
| Current assets: | | | |
| Cash | $ 12,500 | $ 8,800 | $ 12,300 |
| Receivables, net | 30,000 | 30,000 | 36,000 |
| Inventories | 34,500 | 46,200 | 60,800 |
| Total current assets | 77,000 | 85,000 | 109,100 |
| Plant and equipment, net | 52,000 | 95,000 | 151,000 |
| Total assets | $129,000 | $180,000 | $260,100 |
| *Equities* | | | |
| Current liabilities: | | | |
| Accounts payable | $ 17,200 | $ 25,500 | $ 31,500 |
| Accrued liabilities | 800 | 1,000 | 1,200 |
| Other current | 14,200 | 21,500 | 26,000 |
| Total current liabilities | 32,200 | 48,000 | 58,700 |
| Long-term debt | 8,000 | 35,000 | 34,000 |
| Stockholders' equity: | | | |
| Preferred stock | — | — | 40,000 |
| Common stock | 70,000 | 70,000 | 100,000 |
| Retained earnings | 18,800 | 27,000 | 27,400 |
| Total equities | $129,000 | $180,000 | $260,100 |

UNITED CORPORATION
Comparative Income Statements
For the Years Ended December 31

|  | 1983 | 1984 | 1985 |
|---|---|---|---|
| Sales | $150,000 | $175,000 | $225,000 |
| Cost of goods sold | 90,500 | 108,500 | 152,500 |
| Selling expense | 29,000 | 24,900 | 29,500 |
| Administrative expense | 14,900 | 12,000 | 14,800 |
| Research and development | 4,500 | 4,800 | 9,700 |
| Interest expense | 600 | 2,800 | 2,900 |
| Total expenses | 139,500 | 153,000 | 209,400 |
| Income before tax | 10,500 | 22,000 | 15,600 |
| Income taxes | 4,200 | 8,800 | 6,200 |
| Net income | $ 6,300 | $ 13,200 | $ 9,400 |

Preferred dividends were $4,000 in 1985. Common dividends were a constant $5,000 in each of the three years.

The following table shows some statistics representing the average company in the primary industry in which United Corporation operates.

|  | 1983 | 1984 | 1985 |
|---|---|---|---|
| 1. Current ratio | 2.1 to 1 | 2.1 to 1 | 2.2 to 1 |
| 2. Inventory turnover | 2.7 times | 2.6 times | 2.8 times |
| 3. Collection period | 60 days | 59 days | 56 days |
| 4. Total debt/stockholders' equity | 40% | 42% | 45% |
| 5. Fixed-charge coverage before tax | 11.2 times | 10.7 times | 10.0 times |
| 6. Turnover of assets | 1.6 times | 1.4 times | 1.35 times |
| 7. Income before tax/sales | 14.0% | 12.8% | 11.9% |
| 8. R&D/sales | 2.3% | 2.6% | 2.6% |
| 9. Rate of return on stockholders' equity | 10.8% | 11.2% | 10.9% |

*Required:*

a. Calculate yearly ratios for United Corporation that are comparable to the industry statistics. Use year-end balance sheet figures in lieu of averages.

b. What is the purpose (area of interest) of each of these nine ratios? What other ratios would you calculate to aid you in analyzing these areas?

**18–13.** The following *selected* financial information appeared in the 1981 annual report of Rorer Group, Inc. (amounts in thousands of dollars):

|  | 1981 | 1980 | 1979 |
|---|---|---|---|
| Year ended December 31: |  |  |  |
| Net sales | $362,270 | $321,802 | $267,921 |
| Net income | 35,581 | 33,354 | 28,263 |
| December 31: |  |  |  |
| Accounts receivable (net) | 114,136 | 101,999 |  |
| Inventories | 68,495 | 64,707 |  |
| Total current assets | 201,583 | 195,255 |  |
| Total assets | 312,335 | 281,631 |  |
| Short-term debt | 29,723 | 33,789 |  |
| Total current liabilities | 101,462 | 96,872 |  |
| Total liabilities | 134,467 | 120,501 |  |

Rorer's management provided some additional explanation concerning several of the above numbers in the following statement:

> Seasonal factors related to the Company's annual practice of extending longer term payments for the purchase of U.S. pharmaceutical products resulted in a year-end increase in accounts receivable and a corresponding need for short-term borrowings which totalled $28,141,000 in the U.S. at year end. Accounts receivable related to this program become due in the following year in three equal installments during January, February, and March, enabling the company to repay U.S. short-term debt and invest in money market instruments."

*Required:*

a. Did Rorer's liquidity position strengthen or weaken during 1981? Calculate several relevant ratios and explain.

b. How, if at all, did the company's annual practice of extending payment periods affect the following:
   (1) Amount of working capital?
   (2) Trends in working capital?
   (3) Level of accounts receivable turnover?
   (4) Trends in accounts receivable turnover?
   (5) Debt-equity ratio?
   (6) Trends in debt-equity ratio?
   (7) Net income?

c. Two other pharmaceuticals firms, SmithKline and Pfizer, reported accounts receivable turnovers of 6.3 and 4.4, respectively, for 1981. Do Rorer's disclosures aid in intercompany comparisons?

**18–14.** Following a recent accounting class which focused on the analysis of financial statements, a student complained to the professor about the "uselessness of those procedures." The student proceeded to point out the following pitfalls of ratio analysis:

1. It's sometimes impossible to even determine the direction that a ratio would need to take to signify good or bad news. For example, a high inventory turnover ratio is not good news if it resulted from the firm's suppliers refusing to ship any further merchandise on credit.
2. Even when you know the direction which is most favorable for a ratio to take, the existence of both the numerator and the denominator cast a cloud of doubt over the analysis. For example, a higher ratio of inventory to current liabilities is good if it results from the firm being able to pay its debts but is bad if it results from the firm being unable to sell its inventory.
3. Ten different firms can define a ratio in 10 different ways. For example, some firms use average-asset amounts in their denominators while others use ending-asset amounts.
4. Changes in accounting methods can present real difficulties as can differences in accounting methods between firms.
5. It's so easy to come to feel that ratio analysis is an end rather than the means to an end.

*Required:*

*a.* Comment on each of the points raised by the student. Are they illustrative of pitfalls in ratio analysis? Which problem is likely to prove the most difficult to overcome?
*b.* Is it useless to attempt to perform meaningful and accurate financial statement analysis? Explain.

**18–15.** Warford Corporation was formed five years ago through a public subscription of common stock.[17] Lucinda Street, who owns 15 percent of the common stock, was one of the organizers of Warford and is its current president. The company has been successful but currently is experiencing a shortage of funds. On June 10, Street approached the Bell National Bank, asking for a 24-month extension on two $30,000 notes, which are due on June 30, 1980, and September 30, 1980. Another note of $7,000 is due on December 31, 1980, but she expects no difficulty in paying this note on its due date. Street explained that Warford's cash flow problems are due primarily to the company's desire to finance a $300,000 plant expansion over the next two fiscal years through internally generated funds.

The Commercial Loan Officer of Bell National Bank requested financial reports for the last two fiscal years. These reports are reproduced below.

---

[17] Adapted from examination for the Certificate in Management Accounting, June 1980.

WARFORD CORPORATION
Statement of Financial Position

| | March 31, 1979 | March 31, 1980 |
|---|---|---|
| *Assets* | | |
| Cash | $ 12,500 | $ 16,400 |
| Notes receivable | 104,000 | 112,000 |
| Accounts receivable (net) | 68,500 | 81,600 |
| Inventories (at cost) | 50,000 | 80,000 |
| Plant and equipment (net of depreciation) | 646,000 | 680,000 |
| Total assets | $881,000 | $970,000 |
| *Liabilities and Owners' Equity* | | |
| Accounts payable | $ 72,000 | $ 69,000 |
| Notes payable | 54,500 | 67,000 |
| Accrued liabilities | 6,000 | 9,000 |
| Comon stock (60,000 shares, $10 par) | 600,000 | 600,000 |
| Retained earnings* | 148,500 | 225,000 |
| Total liabilities and owners' equity | $881,000 | $970,000 |

\* Cash dividends were paid at the rate of $1.00 per share in fiscal year 1979 and $1.25 per share in fiscal year 1980.

WARFORD CORPORATION
Income Statement
For the Fiscal Years Ended March 31

| | 1979 | 1980 |
|---|---|---|
| Sales | $2,700,000 | $3,000,000 |
| Cost of goods sold* | 1,720,000 | 1,902,500 |
| Gross margin | 980,000 | 1,097,500 |
| Operating expenses | 780,000 | 845,000 |
| Net income before taxes | 200,000 | 252,500 |
| Income taxes (40%) | 80,000 | 101,000 |
| Income after taxes | $ 120,000 | $ 151,500 |

\* Depreciation charges on the plant and equipment of $100,000 and $102,500 for fiscal years ended March 31, 1979, and 1980, respectively, are included in cost of goods sold.

*Required:*

a. Calculate the following items for Warford Corporation:
   (1) Current ratio for fiscal years 1979 and 1980.
   (2) Acid test (quick) ratio for fiscal years 1979 and 1980.
   (3) Inventory turnover for fiscal year 1980.
   (4) Return on assets for fiscal years 1979 and 1980.
   (5) Percentage change in sales, cost of goods sold, gross margin, and net income after taxes from fiscal year 1979 to 1980.

b. Identify and explain what other financial reports and/or financial analyses might be helpful to the commercial loan officer of Bell National Bank in evaluating Street's request for a time extension on Warford's notes.

c. Assume that the percentage changes experienced in fiscal year 1980 as compared with fiscal year 1979 for sales, cost of goods sold, gross margin, and net income after taxes will be repeated in each of the next two years. Is Warford's desire to finance the plant expansion from internally generated funds realistic? Explain your answer.

d.   Should Bell National Bank grant the extension on Warford's notes considering Street's statement about financing the plant expansion through internally generated funds? Explain your answer.

# CHAPTER 19

# INCOME MEASUREMENT AND CHANGING PRICES

Economists have long theorized about the nature of wealth and its relationship to income. Wealth represents the totality of economic values accessible to a person, business, or nation at a point in time. It is a *stock* concept. Income represents the change in wealth between two points of time; it is a *flow* concept, the amount of value coming in (or going out). Income not consumed increases the wealth of the owner. Business income, then, can be viewed as either the increase in business wealth during the period, exclusive of transactions with stockholders, or the amount that the company could distribute to investors during the period and still retain a stock of wealth at the end of the period equivalent to that at the beginning.

In financial accounting, we find the concepts of wealth and income reflected, respectively, in the balance sheet and the income statement. Wealth is commonly measured by the amount of net assets (stockholders' equity), and income is measured by the increase in net assets (stockholders' equity) apart from additional capital investments and dividends. Because the concepts of wealth and income are common to both economics and accounting, one might expect to find accountants using as a guide the measurement ideas suggested by economists. This is not the case.

In this chapter we pursue some of the reasons for this disparity in approach between economics and accounting. The following discussion of alternative valuation (measurement) concepts points up how elusive and tentative any income measurement process is. It also lays the groundwork for a discussion of two useful modifications of the accounting framework—the adjustment of accounts for general price-level changes and the recording of current cost valuations in the accounts.

As we proceed, keep in mind one admonition. Because income and wealth are closely intertwined conceptually, so also are the processes of income measurement and asset-liability valuation. One can look at comparative balance sheets to measure the periodic change and define income to be that change, assuming that accountants can measure all assets. Or one can look to the income statement flows directly and achieve the same results, assuming that accountants can identify all events occurring during the period and measure their effect. We really have but a single concept of income, originating from two different but closely related approaches to measurement. Although users of financial reports may display more interest, at times, in the components of income as reflected on the income statement, that statement's measures have no logical validity apart from the valuations presented on the balance sheet. This fact is forcefully recognized as a basic feature of financial accounting in *Statement No. 4,* issued by the Accounting Principles Board:

> The basic interrelationships between economic resources and economic obligations and changes in them make measurement of periodic net income and of assets and liabilities part of the same process and require that the financial statements be fundamentally related. The measurement bases used to quantify changes in financial position are necessarily related to the measurement bases of the resources and obligations used in representations of financial position.[1]

## ALTERNATIVE VALUATION CONCEPTS

Because of the close association between asset valuation and income measurement, any discussion of one automatically has implications for the other. For convenience in discussing economic wealth and income, we will center our attention in this section on asset valuation. We look at value from a number of perspectives—value in use (the present value of discounted future net cash flows from the use of the resources), exit value (the sale value or net realizable value of resources upon disposition), and various input (entry) values.

## Discounted Cash Flows

In economic theory, the value of assets and liabilities is quantified by the discounting of all expected future cash flows to present value at a rate of interest that reflects risk and the time value of money. This process can be seen in the simple case of a single income-producing asset. Assume that a business owns a $1,000 bond bearing interest at 10 percent and maturing in three years. Also assume that bonds having similar risk characteristics normally carry a 12 percent interest rate. Economic theory (and accounting practice in this case) would establish the worth of the bond at the present value of expected future receipts, that is, the present value of the three interest payments of $100 plus the present value of the $1,000

---

[1] AICPA, *APB Statement No. 4,* "Basic Concepts and Accounting Principles Underlying Financial Statements of Business Enterprises" (New York, October 1970), par. 126.

principal repayment. Using the concepts and notation introduced in the Appendix to Chapter 10, we can calculate the bond's value as follows:

$$(P/A, 3, 0.12)\ 100 = \quad \$100 \times 2.4018 = \$240$$
$$(P/F, 3, 0.12)\ 1{,}000 = \$1{,}000 \times 0.7118 = \underline{\quad 712}$$
$$\$952$$

Initial wealth (asset value) is $952, the amount that the business presumably would pay for the bond. Cash receipts will be $100 at the end of years 1 and 2 and $1,100, at the end of year 3. The bond investment will be revalued at the end of each year to reflect the new present value. Table 19-1 reflects the total wealth position at the end of each year. *Discounted cash flow earnings are the cash received plus the change in present value of future cash receipts.* The income equals the change in wealth.

TABLE 19-1   Present Value of Discounted Cash Flow Associated with Bond Investment

| | | Asset Position—End of Year | | |
|---|---|---|---|---|
| | 0 | 1 | 2 | 3 |
| Cash .................. | — | $  100 | $  200 | $1,300 |
| Bond investment ........ | $952 | 966* | 982† | — |
| Total wealth ........... | $952 | $1,066 | $1,182 | $1,300 |
| Change in wealth (= income) .......... | | $114 (12% × $952) | $116 (12% × $966) | $118 (12% × $982) |

\* (P/A, 2, 0.12)100 + (P/F, 2, 0.12)1,000 = $966.
† (P/A, 1, 0.12)100 + (P/F, 1, 0.12)1,000 = $982.

**Direct Valuation of a Business.**   Theoretically, this same idea could be applied to the entire business. We could calculate this economic value of the entire business (its wealth) by discounting the excess of its expected total cash receipts over total cash disbursements for each future period at the appropriate rate of interest and summing the results. If the excess were expected to be the same each period, wealth or the total value of assets (including going-concern value or goodwill) would be represented by the present value of an annuity.

The usual approach in economics is to value the entire business as if it were a single asset. Alternatively, we could value each individual asset, tangible and intangible, by discounting its *particular* future net cash receipts. The sum of the individual asset values would be, in theory, the value of the business. In practice, cash flows from individual assets are materially interdependent. It would be difficult to value individual assets because of the inseparability of cash flows, except in unique instances such as our bond example. Because all assets contribute jointly to net cash flows, the only value calculable is that of the whole firm.

Under direct valuation, then, income is the change in value; value is the discounted amount of expected future net receipts. Two elements of measurement are inherent in the implementation of a direct valuation theory for a particular business. Future net receipts must be predicted and an appropriate rate of interest chosen to reduce these receipts to their present value. In fact, if these two elements are known with certainty, *income measurement reduces to a simple matter of accruing interest at the discount rate times the balance at the beginning of the period,* as in our bond example. What income will be in future periods is already known now.

**Deficiencies for Use in External Reporting.**   However, the present value approach to income measurement has two defects. First, it may not attribute income to the periods of time when major earning efforts occur. The only economic events given consideration under this method are the amount and timing of cash flows and the interest rate. However, cash flows may not take place in the same time periods as the purchasing, manufacturing, and selling activities traditionally associated with earning efforts. The actual ebb and tide of business activities from one year to the next belie the assumption of a fairly constant earning rate implicit in discounted cash flow. An income figure measured by the amount of change in net present value reveals little information about the temporal occurrence of the basic *causes* of the income.

The second difficulty is that the present value method is almost impossible to apply when uncertainty prevails. Future net receipts have to be estimated by the owners or the managers of the firm. Income and wealth become extremely subjective, being based solely on individual expectations. Moreover, inaccuracies and changes in estimates may cause abrupt fluctuations in present value and, hence, in income that are basically unrelated to actual performance during that period. For example, to the extent that actual net receipts during a period differ from those estimated originally, net income is correspondingly modified. More importantly, actual cash receipts could cause the estimators to revise their predictions of future cash receipts. The *present value of these changes in the amount of estimated receipts* would be part of wealth at the end of the period and, therefore, income for the period. Further, changes in expectations may affect not only predicted cash receipts but also the discount (interest) rate. The interest rate used to derive present value supposedly reflects risk and uncertainty. If risk conditions change from one period to the next, a different discount rate becomes appropriate. A change in rate will change the present value calculation of wealth. The effects of this change, therefore, would also be included in the income measurement for the period of change.

The problems of using direct valuation in financial accounting are apparent from the above discussion. For reporting to external audiences, the degree of possible error and disagreement is too great. However, some alternatives have been suggested that would recognize changes in wealth and still maintain a tolerable standard of reliability.

**Use of Selling Market Prices (Exit Values)**

One suggested alternative relies on the market price at which a firm can sell its assets as the valuation basis. Assets and liabilities would be quantified at "the amounts that would be received or paid currently as a result of non-distress liquidation."[2] The exit-price balance sheet ideally would correspond to the lay interpretation of what the firm is currently worth, "worth" being defined in terms of present realizable selling prices under conditions of an orderly sale. Under this approach income would equal "the change in the exit value of net assets during a stated period, excluding capital contributions and withdrawals."[3]

Two major justifications are advanced for this basis of valuation. The first views exit prices as an objective proxy for discounted cash flow valuation. The price of an asset established in a relatively competitive market presumably reflects the judgments of many individuals concerning the present value of its future cash receipts. Therefore, market values of assets should provide a reliable measure of discounted value. One weakness of this argument is that valuation through the use of market selling prices does not determine the *total* economic value of the firm because it is impossible to measure the value of goodwill (going-concern value); no market exists for this economic quantity. However, output values may come close to the economic model of valuation with respect to many individual assets.

The second conceptual foundation for the use of exit prices focuses directly on the *exchange value* of assets. The value of an asset depends not just on its future service potential but on what others (the market) are willing to exchange for those services. Holding assets in various forms is an alternative to holding cash. The amount of "value" held should be measured by the current cash value (market prices) of the assets. In this way, the financial position of the firm represents the ability of the firm to adapt to or interact with its economic environment. In brief, this concept holds that (1) assets consist only of salable resources in possession of the entity, (2) the amounts of the assets are their present market prices, and (3) financial position is defined as the capacity of an entity at a point in time for engaging in economic exchanges.[4]

**Uses and Advantages.** An exit-price balance sheet has great intuitive appeal as a measure of current financial condition. Exit prices are relevant to an appraisal of financial risk. They measure directly the convertibility of resources into a general medium of exchange. These conversion values represent the potential cash proceeds available to the business

---

[2] AICPA, *Objectives of Financial Statements,* Report of the Study Group on the Objectives of Financial Statements (New York: October 1973), p. 41.

[3] Ibid.

[4] The two major accounting theorists advocating the use of exit prices are Raymond J. Chambers, *Accounting, Evaluation and Economic Behavior* (Englewood Cliffs, N.J.: Prentice-Hall, 1966): and Robert R. Sterling, *Theory of the Measurement of Enterprise Income* (Lawrence: The University Press of Kansas, 1970). The brief discussion above does not do justice to the eloquence of their arguments.

entity in case of financial difficulties. Exit prices provide a value floor to the firm when one appraises financial safety or risk.

Market selling prices also reflect *an* opportunity cost of holding assets in their present form. One alternative open to a business enterprise at any point in time is to dispose of its assets; exit prices measure the value of that option. Exit prices spell out the *current* dollar investment (opportunity cost) necessary for maintaining the existing level of operations. The fact that management elects to hold assets rather than liquidate communicates its judgment that use value as measured by subjectively discounted cash flow exceeds the present exit values.

**Problems and Deficiencies.**   Five deficiencies in using exit prices in financial statements have been advanced. The first three derive from an evaluation of exit-price accounting against some fundamental concepts underlying conventional accounting theory. The last two concern practical problems of implementation and information content.

1.   To the extent that the going-concern concept is a valid assumption about modern business activity, the use of liquidation values seems irrational to many accountants. They argue that companies in fact rarely consider the liquidation of assets on a major scale as a realistic alternative. Some believe that the theory of exit prices presupposes a decision to go out of business periodically rather than one to remain in operation.

2.   Under an exit-price system, assets would be valued at net realizable value (selling price less costs to complete and sell). Income is recorded when net realizable value changes, and this often will be before the efforts necessary to actually generate that income take place. Exit-price income represents a complete departure from income based on a matching of revenue (accomplishment) with services performed (effort). With inventory, for example, income would be recorded when the inventory is produced or acquired as the difference between anticipated selling price and the acquisition cost plus the expected costs to complete and sell the goods. Income would be recorded even though substantial effort still is needed to locate customers and convince them to buy. Net realizable value would anticipate the rewards of accomplishment which many accountants traditionally attribute to the major earning activity—sales.

3.   The net income number derived from a comparison of exit prices of net assets at two different points in time has the advantage of not requiring the arbitrary allocations (e.g., costs of goods sold, depreciation) inherent in the conventional matching concept. However, the approach is basically a balance sheet approach. As with discounted cash flow income statements, useful information about the *causes* of income and their degree of regularity may be lost in an exit-price system.

4.   Another criticism is that there are practical difficulties in applying exit-price valuations. For what resource *groupings* does the firm measure exit values? The liquidation value of all assets may differ significantly from the total of the liquidation values of the individual resources. The exit price of a building plus the exit price of machinery may be more or less

than the exit price of a building-and-machinery package. In accounting theory this problem is called the *aggregation* problem. When the total may not equal the sum of the parts, what level of aggregation (combining) should firms employ in measuring exit values?

5.   Finally, even on an individual asset level, no true selling market may exist for many noncurrent assets. Some exit-market values for plant and equipment probably represent scrap values rather than legitimate attempts by the market to estimate and discount the net future cash receipts resulting from the use of the asset's services. The more unique an asset is, the less likely it is to have an exchange value, although it may have significant use value to the firm owning it for many years to come. The exit-price system would assign little or no value to unique assets; conversely, almost their entire cost would be treated as an income deduction in the year of acquisition. Many accountants object to this result as being distorting and irrational (at least with respect to a going concern). Even for inventory, establishment of net realizable value may require very uncertain estimates of the costs necessary for completion of the product, the costs of selling, the length of time before sale, and the quantity that can be sold at the existing market prices. The further removed the asset is from normal sale, the more numerous and uncertain these estimates become.

**Use of Acquisition Market Prices (Input Values)**

Substantially for the reasons above, accountants for the most part have resisted the use of exit prices. Rather, they have preferred to value assets in terms of acquisition market prices—that is, the amount the assets cost to purchase, not what they can be sold for. *This approach focuses more on a conventional matching or transaction approach to income measurement than on a valuation-of-asset approach.* Under it, the accountant traces inputs through the firm as they are combined into salable products or services. When the product or service is sold, the sacrifice made by the firm for the inputs is compared to the sales price; any excess of output price over input sacrifice is income. Three input values receive prominent attention: (1) historical costs measured in monetary terms, (2) historical costs measured in constant (general purchasing power) dollars, and (3) current (replacement) costs.

**Historic Acquisition Cost.**   The concept of income conventionally used employs historic, dollar acquisition costs as the entry value. It derives from three of the fundamental assumptions studied in Chapter 1—the exchange price, monetary, and revenue recognition assumptions. First, we record assets at their acquisition cost or allocated portions thereof, because this is a monetary expression of the effort the firm has expended in acquiring productive resources via the exchange process. Second, the monetary postulate influences asset valuation and income measurement by specifying the dollar as a stable unit of measurement. Therefore, amounts of and changes in monetary values supposedly reflect real values and changes as well, even over a substantial time horizon. Finally, the revenue postulate sets forth standards for the recognition of new values in the business. Increases in the valuation of total assets are not recorded until they have been earned and can be measured with a reasonable degree of reliability. In most instances, this generally means that no change in asset values is recognized until the point of sale.

As a consequence, conventional financial accounting income is solely a monetary concept. No attention is given to changes in the general price level or to changes in the prices of individual assets. Income under this concept implicitly defines recovery of capital in terms of monetary units only; a firm has maintained its capital if it recovers from revenue the same number of dollars it originally expended on the assets consumed.

**Constant Dollar.** A basic criticism of the use of historical cost as *the* input value is directed against the monetary postulate and arises when the general level of prices changes. When prices on the average have increased, then each dollar can command fewer goods and services than before; that is, the general purchasing power of the dollar has declined. This means that the measuring unit used by the accountant also has changed. Under these circumstances, a sizable number of accountants, including many who accept the matching concept, question whether these changes in the size of the monetary unit can be ignored, as the monetary postulate assumes. They suggest that in the matching of costs against revenues, both must be stated in terms of the same price level. Otherwise, the number of dollars originally expended for an asset is not a realistic representation of cost (effort) in light of the current purchasing power of the revenue stream (accomplishment).

The constant dollar approach would substitute, as input values, original acquisition costs adjusted by means of a general price index to their equivalent in current purchasing power units. Capital is assumed to be recovered only when a firm receives out of current revenues an amount of general purchasing power equivalent to the initial acquisition cost of the asset consumed. When an expenditure is made, part of the firm's pool of general purchasing power has been committed. Alternative purchase opportunities have been foregone. The firm is as well off as it was only if it recovers the same general ability to command goods and services as that represented by the original investment.

*Constant dollar accounting* is the term commonly used for procedures to implement the purchasing power approach. Alternative labels are general price-level accounting and inflation accounting. Such procedures are discussed more thoroughly later in this chapter.

**Current Cost.** A second criticism leveled against the use of historic acquisition cost denies the relevance of such historic costs as a measure of input effort altogether. When changing conditions of supply and demand cause the *current* acquisition cost (replacement cost) of a particular productive resource to increase or decrease, the original cost has lost its economic significance as a measure of the effort involved in the asset's use. A more accurate measure of effort is what it would cost presently to acquire or replace the asset *services* being consumed in the production of revenue. Recovery of capital is viewed in terms of the firm's ability to command goods and services equivalent in service capacity to the particular ones being consumed.

The current cost approach significantly modifies the conventional interpretation of the matching concept. Net operating income is best measured, under this approach, by a matching of the current cost of assets consumed against revenues recognized. The difference between the original acquisition cost and the current acquisition cost represents a revaluation of the assets. The corresponding equity change is a *holding gain or loss,* that is, a change in equity resulting from changes in the acquisition cost of inputs while they are being held for future use in operations. To the extent that holding gains and losses are reflected in income, this approach entails some modifications in the revenue recognition concept as well.

The current cost approach is illustrated at a later point in this chapter.

## THE PROBLEM OF CHANGING PRICES

The preceding discussion of alternative valuation methods highlights two major differences among the methods. One difference is found in the recording of anticipations of future inflows and outflows. Methods like discounted cash flow and exit price changes, which focus on asset valuation, often include a substantial amount of anticipated inflows and outflows in income. Concepts based on input values focus on a matching approach. They generally delay the recognition of operating income until the efforts have been performed and the inflows earned.

The second difference lies in the timing and means of recognizing changing prices. Changes in prices, either of all items in general or of only specific items, have plagued the accountant's measurement process even within a framework that limits the impact of expectations. Consequently, accountants have addressed themselves to this problem more than to the first.

## The Nature of Price Changes

Two types of price changes—general and specific—are of concern to accountants. That they often cannot be separated precisely should not mask the fact that they reflect quite different economic changes and cause quite different theoretical problems.

Prices are quoted in monetary units—the dollar in the case of the United States. The monetary unit in an economic system has three basic functions; it acts as a medium of exchange, a standard of value, and a store of value. To serve effectively as a *medium of exchange,* the monetary unit must be readily acceptable in exchange for goods and services at a particular time. In its capacity as a *standard of value,* the monetary unit must provide a measuring stick for the highly diverse goods and services, the values of which are continually being compared. As a *store of value,* the monetary unit takes on a real value of its own as measured by its purchasing power. In all three functions the dollar serves as a common denominator in which real quantities of goods and services can be expressed. Consequently, it is imperative to distinguish between the number of dollars and the kind and amount of economic quantities these dollars can command.

**Specific Price Changes.** Specific price changes involve the monetary unit in its functions as medium of exchange and standard of value. In economic terms the price of any one item is its exchange value in relation to other goods and services. A specific price, then, becomes the number of dollars of general exchange value required for the acquisition of a particular good or service. The decision to sell a specific item can be viewed as one of electing to exchange the specific item for all other goods and services. The dollar simply serves as a proxy for the exchange values of all other items. A specific dollar price then measures the exchange value of the particular item relative to all other items. Likewise, a specific price change refers to a change in the relative value of an item. Specific price or value changes are caused by changes over time in the interaction of demand and supply for the particular good or service.

**General Price Changes.** The monetary unit serves to measure relative exchange values not only at a point in time but also through time. Moreover, dollars can be accumulated as a store of generalized purchasing power. These functions, of standard of value and store of value over time, are made complicated if the monetary unit itself changes in value. The value of the dollar rests on the real quantities of goods and services that can be exchanged for it. When people exchange less in general each year for a dollar, the purchasing power of the dollar declines. The trends in the consumer price index, shown in Table 19-2, indicate that such purchasing power declines have occurred continually since 1940. A particularly large acceleration began in the early 1970s and did not begin to subside until late in 1982.

**TABLE 19-2  Trends in U.S. Consumer Price Index, 1915–1982**
**(1967 = 100)**

| Year | Average CPI Index | Year | Average CPI Index | Year | Average CPI Index |
|------|-------------------|------|-------------------|------|-------------------|
| 1915 | 30.4 | 1940 | 42.0 | 1965 | 94.5 |
| 1920 | 60.0 | 1945 | 53.9 | 1970 | 116.3 |
| 1925 | 52.5 | 1950 | 72.1 | 1975 | 161.2 |
| 1930 | 50.0 | 1955 | 80.2 | 1980 | 246.9 |
| 1935 | 41.1 | 1960 | 88.7 | 1981 | 272.4 |
|      |      |      |      | 1982 | 289.1 |

Source: U.S. Department of Labor, Bureau of Labor Statistics.

To serve effectively as a stable measuring unit for other economic commodities, the dollar should maintain its own exchange value. If the quantity of things in general which the monetary unit can command varies, the size of the economic yardstick changes. Such shifts in the exchange value of money constitute general price-level changes and reflect a host of factors associated with general inflation and deflation. General price-level changes connote that prices on average throughout the economy are changing. As a result, the exchange value (purchasing power) of the dollar, and, hence, the size of the accountant's measuring unit, shrinks.

It is obvious that both types of price changes probably occur at the same time. The price change for any particular good or service may reflect a change in its real value in relation to all other goods and a general change in the price level. Often, this mixed price change is interpreted to be a specific price change. Such an interpretation is in error, however, because it fails to allow for the effect of a lack of comparability in the size of the measuring unit.

If comparably equipped delivery vans were selling for $7,000 in 1975 and $9,700 in 1980, the $2,700 increase in price must be allocated to both the general and specific price changes before it can be meaningfully understood. The analysis could take the following form:

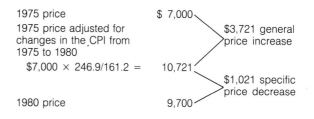

The above analysis reveals that the $2,700 price increase really is a combination of two distinct and somewhat countervailing forces: (1) an *illusory* $3,721 increase, resulting from inflation between 1975 and 1980, which made the 1975 price of $7,000 not comparable in terms of general purchasing power to 1980 dollars, and (2) a *real* $1,021 *decrease* in the value of the delivery van in relation to other goods and services.

## Price Changes and Financial Accounting

Potentially, then, two factors can affect measures of income (changes in wealth)—movements in the prices of particular goods and services and changes in the purchasing power of money. Before World War II, little formal attention was paid to the problems of changing prices. To be sure, upward asset adjustments were not uncommon in the 1920s. These appraisal write-ups supposedly reflected "current values," although, like beauty, the value was sometimes only in the eye of the beholder—management. The write-ups were more than offset by the subsequent write-downs in the early 1930s. The downward adjustments usually were as spotty and subjective as the write-ups had been.

Out of these contortions grew a firm adherence to historic acquisition cost. The American Accounting Association issued the first in its series of periodic statements of accounting principles in 1936. The six-page document strongly urged historical cost for asset valuation and expense determination. More importantly, the Securities and Exchange Commission early in its life took an adamant stand in favor of historical cost and refused to allow filings containing statements in which assets had been revalued.

While the views of the SEC and the American Accounting Association served officially to defuse the price-change controversy at least temporarily, several accounting writers of the 1930s continued to call for the reporting of price-change information. In his 1936 publication, *Stabilized Accounting,* Sweeney illustrated how different the financial statements of three companies would be if adjustments were made for general price-level changes.[5] MacNeal's *Truth in Accounting,* published in 1939, presented the viewpoint that historical cost financial statements "are apt to be worse than no financial statements at all."[6]

The inflation during and after World War II rekindled the accounting profession's interest in the problems caused by the continual shrinking of the dollar's purchasing power and by the disparity in the prices of specific assets before and after the war. Two companion research studies undertaken by Jones were published by the American Accounting Association in 1955 and 1956.[7] He examined in detail the historical cost financial statements of four prominent firms and discovered that the modification for general price-level changes resulted in (1) a much lower return on invested capital and (2) dramatically higher effective tax rates and dividend payout percentages.[8]

During this period both the SEC and the American Institute of CPAs (AICPA) continued officially to oppose the inclusion of price-change information in published financial reports. However, in the early 1960s, the Director of Research of the AICPA did commission two significant research studies. *Accounting Research Study No. 3* recommended the use of net realizable value for inventories and replacement cost for most noncurrent assets.[9] *Accounting Research Study No. 6* recommended supplementary presentation of all financial statement items in units of uniform purchasing power.[10]

Several price-change pronouncements have been issued since 1969. The Accounting Principles Board released its *Statement No. 3* in 1969, and

[5] Henry W. Sweeney, *Stabilized Accounting* (New York: Harper & Row, 1936).

[6] Kenneth MacNeal, *Truth in Accounting* (Philadelphia: University of Pennsylvania Press, 1939), p. 203.

[7] Ralph Coughenour Jones, *Price Level Changes and Financial Statements: Case Studies of Four Companies;* and *Effects of Price Level Changes on Business Income, Capital, and Taxes* (Urbana, Ill.: American Accounting Association, 1955 and 1956).

[8] *Effects of Price Level Changes,* pp. 5–6 and chapter VIII.

[9] Robert T. Sprouse and Maurice Moonitz, *A Tentative Set of Broad Accounting Principles for Business Enterprises* (New York, AICPA, 1962).

[10] Staff of the Accounting Research Division, *Reporting the Financial Effects of Price Level Changes* (New York: AICPA, 1963).

the SEC issued *Accounting Series Release No. 190* in 1976. The Financial Accounting Standards Board issued its *Statement No. 33* in 1979.

**APB Statement No. 3.**[11]  Like all other APB statements, this pronouncement differed from the APB opinions by its recommending rather than requiring certain action. The methodology contained in *ARS No. 6* for presenting supplementary general price-level financial statements was endorsed by the APB, and the resulting information was recommended as useful. However, few firms opted to make such voluntary disclosures.

**SEC Accounting Series Release No. 190.**  After decades of adherence to historic acquisition cost as the *only* allowable basis for valuation of assets and measurement of income, the Commission in 1975 began to rethink its traditional position. Rather than join the movement toward general price-level adjustments, the SEC supported current replacement cost as a supplementary measure. The Commission felt that, when costs change significantly, a matching of historic costs against current selling prices may not be useful to investors in predicting *future* operating results.

Consequently, with annual inflation hovering near 10 percent and no definitive FASB action in sight, the SEC issued *Accounting Series Release No. 190* in March 1976.[12] The ruling required either footnote or special section disclosure of replacement cost numbers for inventories and productive plant on the balance sheet and cost of goods sold and depreciation expense on the income statement. The positive benefits from such disclosures have been discussed to some extent in Chapters 8 and 9.

*ASR No. 190* applied to the approximately 1,000 firms whose total of inventories and gross plant exceeded $100 million *and* 10 percent of total assets. Disclosures were only required in the annual Form 10-K reports filed with the SEC, as long as the report to stockholders at least contained a general description of inflation's impact and a reference to the Form 10-K data. One study revealed that nearly 80 percent of the firms elected to follow such a differentiated disclosure approach.[13]

After *FASB Statement No. 33,* to be discussed next, became effective, the Commission repealed its separate disclosure requirement.[14] Not only were its disclosures included among the data mandated by *Statement No. 33,* but they also had to be presented in the annual reports to stockholders.

**FASB Statement No. 33.**  The SEC's issuance of its *ASR No. 190* in 1976 did not silence those within the accounting profession who believed that the Financial Accounting Standards Board needed to take action on the price-change issue. Some felt that the profession had been

---

[11] AICPA, *APB Statement No. 3,* "Financial Statements Restated for General Price-Level Changes" (New York, June 1969).

[12] SEC, *Accounting Series Release No. 190,* "Disclosure of Certain Replacement Cost Data" (Washington, D.C.: March 23, 1976).

[13] Arthur Young & Company, *Disclosing Replacement-Cost Data* (New York, 1977), p. 21.

[14] SEC, *Accounting Series Release No. 271,* "Deletion of Requirement to Disclose Replacement Cost Information" (Washington, D.C.: October 23, 1979).

harmfully upstaged by the SEC and needed to act forcefully to reassert its traditional role as the originator of accounting principles and policies. Others were primarily concerned about the content, rather than the source, of *ASR No. 190*. They felt that the SEC was remiss in only requiring specific price-level change disclosures and then only in reports filed with the Commission.

*Statement No. 33*, issued by the FASB in September 1979, represented the profession's first set of price-change disclosure requirements.[15] Qualifying firms have to disclose the following:[16]

1. Income from continuing operations adjusted for the effects of general inflation.
2. The purchasing power gain or loss on net monetary items (to be explained later).
3. Income from continuing operations on a current cost basis.
4. The current cost of inventory and property, plant, and equipment at the end of the fiscal year.
5. Increases or decreases in current cost amounts of inventory and property, plant, and equipment, net of inflation.

Companies are also required to include a five-year summary of such financial data as net income, sales, and dividends and market price per share, all adjusted to reflect changing prices. In the computation of net assets, only inventory and property, plant, and equipment need to be adjusted. Similarly, only cost of goods sold and depreciation expense on the income statement must be changed.

In contrast to *ASR No. 190, Statement No. 33* covers approximately 200 more firms, a total of 1,200. It applies to companies with *either* assets in excess of $1 billion or inventories and gross plant totaling more than $125 million. The specific formats used by most companies to disclose the information required by *Statement No. 33* are highlighted later, when Armco's inflation disclosures are examined in detail.

Nobody should expect *Statement No. 33* to be the final official word on accounting for changing prices. Advocates of complete restatement of all financial statement items find that the FASB ruling falls far short. Persons who erroneously believe that constant dollar and current cost accounting are competing alternatives were only frustrated by the FASB's inclusion of *aspects* of both systems among the required disclosures. One member of the FASB who dissented to *Statement No. 33* described the ruling as "having something for everybody" and "offering a smorgasbord of data."[17] The following passage from the pronouncement may have been intended to address the dissenter's views:

---

[15] FASB, *Statement of Financial Accounting Standards No. 33*, "Financial Reporting and Changing Prices" (Stamford, Conn., September 1979).

[16] *FASB Statement No. 33*, par. 29–30.

[17] *FASB Statement No. 33*, p. 28.

The requirement to present information on both a constant dollar basis and a current cost basis provides a basis for studying the usefulness of the two types of information. The Board intends to study the extent to which the information is used, the types of people to whom it is useful, and the purpose for which it is used. The requirements of this Statement will be reviewed on an ongoing basis and the Board will amend or withdraw requirements whenever that course is justified by the evidence. This Statement will be reviewed comprehensively after a period of not more than five years.[18]

The two major systems for recognizing price changes on a continuing basis, constant dollar accounting and current (replacement) cost reporting, remain under serious consideration. Neither complete system is presently mandated by the FASB; instead, only a small portion of each is required by *Statement No. 33*.

The next two sections discuss the two models and their quite different objectives and procedures in a comprehensive manner. Hopefully this analysis will allow you to reflect upon whether the FASB chose the most important and useful aspects of each model for its required public disclosures. The discussion is also pertinent because the accounting profession, following the five-year period of experimentation, might decide to require complete adoption of either or both of the price-change reporting models.

## CONSTANT DOLLAR ACCOUNTING

Constant dollar accounting deals with general purchasing-power changes only. It adjusts solely for changes in the size of the measuring units used in accounting. In conventional financial statements asset and equity items and changes are measured in terms of dollars of the period in which the transactions arise. These dollars represent varying amounts of purchasing power when general inflation or deflation occurs. In contrast, financial statements restated for general price-level changes reflect these same items and changes in terms of dollars with a uniform purchasing power. The dollar at a specified date, often at the end of the current period, is selected as the measuring unit.[19]

Therefore, constant dollar accounting differs from conventional financial accounting only with respect to the unit of measure employed. It modifies the monetary postulate from units of money to units of purchasing power. All other assumptions, conventions, principles, and procedures remain the same. In this sense, it is not a departure from traditional accounting but rather a *restatement* of original transactions in terms of constant dollars.

---

[18] Ibid., par. 15.

[19] The FASB, in *Statement No. 33* (par. 43), specified use of the average price index for the current year for the limited price-change disclosures required. However, the end-of-year index is allowed for any *comprehensive* restatement of financial statements a firm might voluntarily choose to make.

Changes in the price level typically are measured by some index of general prices. As the prices of items in general increase, the purchasing power of the dollar decreases. Because it is impractical to measure the price increases of all items, a price index of a general sample of items is used.[20] The index expresses the relationship between an average of all prices at a point in time and those same prices in some base year. The changes in a general price index—or more precisely, the reciprocal of the index—over time provide a reasonably accurate indication of movements in the value of the dollar in relation to that set of goods and services.

**Restatement of Nonmonetary Accounts**

By means of general price indices, dollar amounts recorded at any particular point in time can be restated in dollars as of any other point in time. We normally wish to express the financial statements in terms of the measuring unit existing during the current accounting period. We can do so by means of the following general conversion formula:

$$\frac{\text{Cost of Item}}{\text{Recorded in}} \times \frac{\text{Index of Current Period}}{\text{Index at Date Item Originated}} = \frac{\text{Cost Restated in}}{\text{Dollars of Current}}$$
$$\text{Accounts} \qquad \text{or Was Acquired} \qquad \text{Purchasing Power}$$

For example, land was purchased for $8,000 in 1960, when the general price-level index (as shown in Table 19-2) was 88.7. The equivalent amount of purchasing power invested expressed in 1982 dollars, when the index was 289.1, is $26,072, calculated as follows:

$$\$_{(60)}8,000 \times \frac{289.1}{88.7} = \$_{(60)}8,000 \times 3.259 = \$_{(82)}26,072$$

Because prices have increased over three times, $26,072 is needed in 1982 to provide the same general purchasing power which $8,000 provided in 1960.

The restatement procedure used above for land and earlier in the delivery van example can be used for all *nonmonetary* assets and equities. Nonmonetary items are those which can retain their initial purchasing power even after the general level of prices has changed.

Other examples of nonmonetary items include inventory, buildings, liability for warranties, and capital stock. Inasmuch as nothing specifies that the ultimate resolution of such items must involve the transfer of a fixed number of dollars, they may be adjusted to retain the initial purchasing power.

To recognize the effect of general price-level changes we merely restate their acquisition costs (or financial interests therein, in the case of equities) in terms of the purchasing power of the current-year dollar. The restate-

---

[20] The FASB, in *Statement No. 33* (par. 39), required use of the Consumer Price Index for All Urban Consumers. Nevertheless, the Gross National Product Implicit Price Deflator has its share of proponents, because it is inherently more comprehensive.

ment for machinery and equipment involves aging the book costs by year of acquisition. Then the balance of each year's costs remaining on the books is expressed in constant dollars by means of the index appropriate for each year. In a similar manner, the capital stock account is subdivided according to the year of origin of the various stock issuances. Each subdivision is then converted to current-year dollars, and all are added together. Other examples of the restatement process can be found in the comprehensive illustration presented later.

It is important to realize that conversion of nonmonetary items involves merely a change to a different-size measuring unit. No change in *value* (gain or loss) results from the adjustment. In this sense, the restatement procedure is directly analogous to the translation of foreign currencies. Accountants would *not* add land costing $8,000 in Canadian dollars to $8,000 of land measured in U.S. dollars and arrive at a total asset of $16,000. First, the $8,000 Canadian dollars would have to be restated in terms of their U.S. equivalent. The attribute being measured (cost of land) does not change, only the unit of measure in which it is expressed. It is argued that when general price levels change, the size of the accountant's yardstick changes also. Land costing $8,000 expressed in *1960 U.S. dollars* cannot be added to assets measured in *1982 U.S. dollars* without undergoing a similar process of restatement.

**Monetary Assets and Liabilities**

The situation is different for *monetary* assets and liabilities. These items represent cash or claims to cash. Their amount is established contractually at a specified number of dollars; the number cannot change with changes in economic conditions. Take, for instance, an account receivable. This is a contractual right to receive a fixed number of dollar units. It does not require the customer to remit a certain amount of general purchasing power. Thus, the realistic figure at which to record the current balance of receivables is the number of dollar units originally transacted. Current payables, being merely the opposite side of the coin, can be analyzed similarly. Monetary claims, in essence, require no restatement. By their very nature they always show the number of units of *current* purchasing power to be received or paid.

On the other hand, the *value* of the stock of dollars on hand, receivable, or payable depends on what the number of monetary units will purchase. Because the *number of dollars is fixed,* the value of the dollars changes as general price levels change. Therefore, a business in fact can gain or lose purchasing power as a result of inflation or deflation. Assume that a firm has $2,000 in cash in the bank at the beginning of the year and holds it until the end of the year. In the interim, a general price index moves from 100 to 108. It takes $2,160 year-end dollars ($2,000 × 108/100) to equal the purchasing power originally represented by $2,000 one year before. However, at the end of the year the firm has only 2,000 dollar units. As a result of having held cash (or claims to cash) during inflation, the business has suffered a loss of $160 in purchasing power.

Conversely, assume that the same business is liable throughout the year for an account payable of $700. In terms of the year-end dollar, the initial $700 liability is actually equivalent to $756 of purchasing power ($700 × 108/100). However, at year-end the business contractually owes only 700 dollar units and therefore has gained $56 of general purchasing power at the expense of the creditor.

Financial statements prepared under the conventional monetary postulate fail to measure and report such gains and losses in purchasing power. A comprehensive application of the constant dollar accounting system will include the highlighting of the net gain or loss resulting from the firm's holding of monetary items. Most larger firms with a significant liability for bonds payable achieve a net purchasing power *gain* on holding monetary items. During these inflationary times, the holding of more monetary liabilities than monetary assets creates such a net gain.

**Comprehensive Illustration**

The Huron Corporation presents the financial information shown in Tables 19–3 and 19–4, unadjusted for general price-level changes. In addition, you have become aware of the following information (hypothetical rather than real price indices were used for the various years to simplify the calculations):

1. The general price index to be used in the restatement process stood at 100 and 108 at the end of 1984 and 1985, respectively. Inflation

**TABLE 19–3**

HURON CORPORATION
Comparative Balance Sheet
As of December 31

| | 1984 | 1985 |
|---|---|---|
| *Assets* | | |
| Cash | $ 50,000 | $ 40,000 |
| Receivables | 65,000 | 85,000 |
| Inventory | 45,000 | 80,000 |
| Land | 30,000 | 30,000 |
| Plant and equipment | 200,000 | 200,000 |
| Accumulated depreciation | (48,000) | (68,000) |
| Total assets | $342,000 | $367,000 |
| *Equities* | | |
| Current payables | $ 75,000 | $ 40,000 |
| Bonds payable | 50,000 | 50,000 |
| Capital stock | 175,000 | 175,000 |
| Retained earnings | 42,000 | 102,000 |
| Total equities | $342,000 | $367,000 |

**TABLE 19-4**

HURON CORPORATION
Statement of Income and Changes
in Retailed Earnings
For the Year Ended
December 31, 1985

| | | |
|---|---:|---:|
| Sales revenue | | $850,000 |
| Expenses: | | |
| Cost of goods sold | $600,000 | |
| Selling and administrative | 99,000 | |
| Depreciation | 20,000 | |
| Interest | 9,000 | |
| Taxes | 48,800 | |
| Total expenses | | 776,800 |
| Net income | | 73,200 |
| Add: Retained earnings, January 1, 1985 | | 42,000 |
| Total | | 115,200 |
| Less: Dividends | | 13,200 |
| Retained earnings, December 31, 1985 | | $102,000 |

occurred at a steady pace during 1985, and, accordingly, the average index for 1985 was 104.

2. The business was started four years ago, when the general price index was 85. All of the capital stock was issued then. The land and $140,000 of the plant and equipment also were acquired at that time. The rest of the plant and equipment was acquired two years ago, when the general price index was 95. All plant and equipment has a 10-year useful life and is depreciated on a straight-line basis.

3. The bonds were issued at the end of 1984.

4. Sales, purchases, selling and administrative expenses, interest, and taxes occur evenly throughout the year. Dividends are declared and paid each December 31.

5. The firm uses the FIFO inventory flow. The inventory on hand at December 31, 1984, and 1985, was acquired when the general price index was 99 and 106, respectively.

The procedures for restating the balance sheet amounts at December 31, 1985, and 1984, for changes in the general level of prices are illustrated in Tables 19-5 and 19-6, respectively. The restatements for the December 31, 1985, balance sheet items are presented first, for they are somewhat less complicated than the year-earlier restatements.

In Table 19-5, no conversion factor is used for the two monetary assets (cash and receivables) and the two monetary liabilities (current payables and bonds payable). As noted earlier, these four items represent either cash or contractual claims to a fixed number of dollars, without regard to the current purchasing power of those dollars. Because the commitments represented by monetary items are not automatically ad-

**TABLE 19-5**

HURON CORPORATION
Balance Sheet
As of December 31, 1985
(restated to dollars of ending-1985 purchasing power)

| | Transaction Amount | Conversion Factor | Restated to 12/31/85 Dollars |
|---|---|---|---|
| *Assets* | | | |
| Cash | $ 40,000 | — | $ 40,000 |
| Receivables | 85,000 | — | 85,000 |
| Inventory | 80,000 | 108/106 | 81,509 |
| Land | 30,000 | 108/85 | 38,118 |
| Plant and equipment | { 140,000 / 60,000 | 108/85 } / 108/95 } | 246,093 |
| Accumulated depreciation | { (56,000) / (12,000) | 108/85 } / 108/95 } | (84,795) |
| Total assets | $367,000 | | $405,925 |
| | | | |
| *Equities* | | | |
| Current payables | $ 40,000 | — | $ 40,000 |
| Bonds payable | 50,000 | — | 50,000 |
| Capital stock | 175,000 | 108/85 | 222,353 |
| Retained earnings | 102,000 | Table 19-7 | 93,572 |
| Total equities | $367,000 | | $405,925 |

justed for changes in the general level of prices, no conversion is appropriate. The inability of those monetary items to respond to inflation creates a net purchasing power loss for Huron Corporation for 1985, given that monetary assets held exceeded monetary liabilities held. The calculation of such net purchasing power loss will be illustrated shortly in Table 19–8.

Each nonmonetary item in Table 19–5 is converted into its equivalent expressed in the purchasing power of December 31, 1985, dollars. The numerator of each factor is 108, the general price index existing on December 31, 1985. The denominator ranges from 85 to 106, depending on how long before December 31, 1985, the transaction amount originated. The $93,572 restated amount for retained earnings is calculated in the manner shown in Table 19–7.

The restatements for the December 31, 1984, balance sheet amounts are shown next in Table 19–6. Here the adjustments were done in two stages. First, the balance sheet was recast into the purchasing power of December 31, 1984, dollars, by the same general procedure already illustrated in Table 19–5 for the year-later balance sheet. Retained earnings was entered as a *balancing* figure rather than as a separate restatement, which would have required the restating of all prior years' income statements. Second, the balance sheet which had been recast into the purchasing power of December 31, 1984, dollars was *rolled forward* to the purchasing power one year later by means of an 8 percent (108/100) increase

**TABLE 19–6**

HURON CORPORATION
Balance Sheet
As of December 31, 1984
(restated to dollars of ending-1985 purchasing power)

| | Transaction Amount | Conversion Factor | Restated to 12/31/84 Dollars | Conversion Factor | Restated to 12/31/85 Dollars |
|---|---|---|---|---|---|
| **Assets** | | | | | |
| Cash | $ 50,000 | — | $ 50,000 | 108/100 | $ 54,000 |
| Receivables | 65,000 | — | 65,000 | 108/100 | 70,200 |
| Inventory | 45,000 | 100/99 | 45,455 | 108/100 | 49,091 |
| Land | 30,000 | 100/85 | 35,294 | 108/100 | 38,118 |
| Plant and equipment | { 140,000 / 60,000 | 100/85 / 100/95 | 164,706 } / 63,158 } | 108/100 | 246,093 |
| Accumulated depreciation | { (42,000) / (6,000) | 100/85 / 100/95 | (49,412) } / (6,316) } | 108/100 | (60,186) |
| Total assets | $342,000 | | $367,885 | | $397,316 |
| **Equities** | | | | | |
| Current payables | $ 75,000 | — | $ 75,000 | 108/100 | $ 81,000 |
| Bonds payable | 50,000 | — | 50,000 | 108/100 | 54,000 |
| Capital stock | 175,000 | 100/85 | 205,882 | 108/100 | 222,353 |
| Retained earnings | 42,000 | To balance | 37,003 | 108/100 | 39,963 |
| Total equities | $342,000 | | $367,885 | | $397,316 |

in every item to reflect the increase in prices and decrease in purchasing power which occurred during 1985. The land, for example, was increased from $35,294 to $38,118 in recognition of the fact that one would need $38,118 on December 31, 1985, to have the same general purchasing power that only $35,294 would have provided one year earlier. The roll-forward procedure makes possible the preparation of a comparative balance sheet adjusted for general price-level changes; the figures in the final column of *both* Tables 19–5 and 19–6 are now restated to dollars of ending-1985 purchasing power.

Table 19–7 presents the adjustments for the 1985 statement of income and changes in retained earnings. The conventional net income calculation of $73,200 reported in Table 19–4 does not represent the net gain from operations in purchasing power adjusted dollars. The dollars in the individual revenue and expense accounts are not all comparable and, as a result, cannot meaningfully be added to or subtracted from each other. Because sales, selling and administrative expenses, interest, and taxes were assumed to occur evenly throughout the year, they were on balance transacted at the 1985 average general price index of 104. Depreciation represents the allocation of the cost of plant and equipment. Accordingly, it has traditionally been expressed in dollars entered on the books when the index was 85 and 95. Given the FIFO inventory flow, the cost of goods sold figure includes dollars at the 99 index for late 1984 purchases and the 104 index for 1985 purchases.

**TABLE 19-7**

HURON CORPORATION
Statement of Income and Changes in Retained Earnings
For the Year Ended December 31, 1985
(restated to dollars of ending-1985 purchasing power)

| | Transaction Amount | Conversion Factor | Restated to 12/31/85 Dollars |
|---|---|---|---|
| Sales revenue | $850,000 | 108/104 | $882,692 |
| **Expenses:** | | | |
| Cost of goods sold: | | | |
| Beginning inventory | 45,000 | 108/99 | 49,091 |
| 1985 purchases | 635,000* | 108/104 | 659,423 |
| Goods available | 680,000 | | 708,514 |
| Ending inventory | 80,000 | 108/106 | 81,509 |
| Cost of goods sold | 600,000 | | 627,005 |
| Selling and administrative | 99,000 | 108/104 | 102,808 |
| Depreciation | { 14,000 / 6,000 | 108/85 } / 108/95 } | 24,609 |
| Interest | 9,000 | 108/104 | 9,346 |
| Taxes | 48,800 | 108/104 | 50,677 |
| Total expenses | 776,800 | | 814,445 |
| Net operating income | 73,200 | | 68,247 |
| Net purchasing power loss | — | Table 19-8 | 1,438 |
| Net income | 73,200 | | 66,809 |
| Add: Retained earnings January 1 | 42,000 | Table 19-6 | 39,963 |
| Total | 115,200 | | 106,772 |
| Less: Dividends | 13,200 | 108/108 | 13,200 |
| Retained earnings, December 31 | $102,000 | | $ 93,572 |

\* $80,000 Ending Inventory + $600,000 Cost of Goods Sold − $45,000 Beginning Inventory = $635,000.

The proper relating of revenues and expenses requires a restatement to a uniform unit of measure. In Table 19-7, all components of net income are converted to dollars of ending-1985 purchasing power (general price index of 108). Sales revenue for 1985 really was $850,000 (measured in average 1985 dollars), and depreciation expense really was $20,000 (measured in 1981 and 1983 dollars). The adjustments are not intended to dispute these facts. Sales are changed to $882,692 and depreciation to $24,609 so that they both are in dollars of common purchasing power and can be meaningfully combined. The restatement changes the relationship between those two income statement items; depreciation increases from 2.3 to 2.8 percent of sales. Such relative changes among the income statement components are inevitable, since many conversion factors have dissimilar denominators.

The restated 1985 net income of $66,809 reconciles with the restated retained earnings of $39,963 on January 1 (Table 19-6) and $93,572 on December 31 (Table 19-5). The adjusted *net operating income* was actually

$68,247, but a $1,438 net purchasing power loss from the holding of monetary items was then deducted for the final determination of *net income*. Table 19–8 presents the detailed calculation of this loss.

**TABLE 19–8**

HURON CORPORATION
Schedule of Net Purchasing Power Loss
from the Holding of Monetary Items in 1985

| | Trans-action Amount | Conver-sion Factor | Restated to 12/31/85 Dollars | Trans-action Amount | Gain (G) or Loss (L) |
|---|---|---|---|---|---|
| Net monetary liabilities, 1/1/85 | $(10,000) | 108/100 | $10,800 | $10,000 | $ 800G |
| Excess of 1985 sales over the total of 1985 purchases, S&A expenses, interest, and taxes | 58,200* | 108/104 | 60,438 | 58,200 | 2,238L |
| 1985 dividends | (13,200) | 108/108 | 13,200 | 13,200 | –0– |
| Net monetary assets 12/31/85 | $ 35,000 | | | | |
| Net purchasing power loss for 1985 | | | | | $1,438L |

* $850,000 Sales less ($635,000 Purchases + $99,000 Selling and Administrative Expenses + $9,000 Interest + $48,800 Taxes) = $850,000 – $791,800 = $58,200.

The Huron Corporation began 1985 with $10,000 of net monetary liabilities. Current payables and bonds payable totaled $125,000, while cash and receivables amounted to $115,000. We begin Table 19–8 by asking how the firm would have fared *if* that net monetary position had been maintained throughout 1985. The $10,000 of net monetary liabilities would have had to increase by 8 percent to provide Huron's creditors with as much purchasing power as they had lent earlier to the firm. Since Huron can repay the net $10,000 borrowed with that same quantity of dollars, without regard to their purchasing power, the company would have realized a $800 gain.

Matters become complicated when it is realized that the net monetary position *did not remain* at $10,000 of liabilities throughout 1985. Table 19–3 shows that Huron Corporation ended the year with $35,000 of net monetary assets. Dividends were declared and paid each December 31; they help explain the change in the net monetary position by year-end but do *not* affect the total of monetary items held *during* the year. Accordingly, the December 31 dividends do not change the net amount of Huron's purchasing power gain or loss.

The total of monetary items held during 1985 was affected by the firm's sales, purchases, selling and administrative (S&A) expenses, interest, and taxes. Because sales brought in $850,000 of monetary assets (cash or receivables), Huron Corporation did not maintain the January 1 net monetary-liabilities position throughout 1985.

On the other hand, expenditures totaling $791,800 for purchases, S&A expenses, interest, and taxes either used monetary assets (cash) or created monetary liabilities (various payables). The $58,200 excess of sales over the combined cost of the four items signified the extent to which the $800 "gain" does not really reflect the firm's gain or loss from the holding of monetary items. All five items were assumed to be spread evenly throughout 1985. Therefore, Huron lost approximately 4 percent of its purchasing power (4/104 = 3.8 percent) on the $58,200 excess, or $2,238. As Table 19-8 reveals, the company's net monetary position shifted from $10,000 of *liabilities* on January 1 to $35,000 of *assets* on December 31. As a result, the $2,238 loss more than offset the $800 "gain," producing a $1,438 net loss in purchasing power.

In this section, the traditional financial statements of a hypothetical firm were presented in Tables 19-3 and 19-4 and restated in accordance with the constant dollar accounting model in Tables 19-5 through 19-8. The pros and cons of such restatements will now be discussed.

**Advantages and Uses of Constant Dollar Accounting**

The user of accounting statements adjusted for general price changes must be careful not to interpret them as reflecting current values or costs. Constant dollar accounting makes no attempt to measure what it would cost currently to replace the assets or what the business is worth. It seeks only to restore comparability in terms of general purchasing power among the dollars originally recorded in the accounts. It converts original transaction prices to equivalent numbers of dollars of purchasing power as of a particular date. The assets on the balance sheet show the amount of current purchasing power committed to them. The equities show the amounts of current purchasing power owed to creditors and the amount of general purchasing power represented by the stockholders' investment, which presumably is to be preserved and enhanced. Finally, the income statement represents a measurement in current dollars of the company's gain or loss in general purchasing power during the year.

Perhaps the greatest contribution of procedures that adjust for general price-level changes is the introduction of *comparability of measurement*. It is inherently logical that any measurement system should have a unit that does not change between measurements. By standardizing the accountant's measuring unit, constant dollar accounting should provide more meaningful summations of data within the generally accepted framework.

Constant dollar adjustments often have a significant effect on financial statement amounts. Even in years when inflation is relatively modest in the United States, the cumulative effect on such items as depreciation and asset restatements over a period of years can cause major changes in many financial accounting variables. Moreover, the investor cannot, in the absence of restatements, apply any general formula to approximate the adjustments which would have taken place if constant dollar accounting had been followed. Different firms and industries are affected unevenly because of variations in capital intensity, financing policies, and inventory turnover.

Table 19-9 reports the results of *Business Week's* annual "Inflation Scoreboard" for both 1981 and 1982; both unadjusted and constant dollar earnings were tracked for 400–500 of the largest industrial firms in over 30 key industries. The data were taken from corporate annual reports and, accordingly, reflects the less comprehensive *Statement No. 33* disclosures. As we noted earlier, the FASB requires firms to show the changes in *net operating income* caused by adjustments only to cost of goods sold and depreciation expense; the net purchasing power gain or loss is excluded and shown as a separate item.

**TABLE 19-9  Magnitude of Constant Dollar Adjustments Reported by Large Corporations for 1981 and 1982 (constant dollar net operating income as a percent of unadjusted net operating income)**

| | The Best Off | | The Worst Off | |
|---|---|---|---|---|
| | *Industry* | *Percent* | *Industry* | *Percent* |
| 1981: | Publishing, TV | 82 | Trucking | 27 |
| | Oil service and supply | 80 | Containers | 21 |
| | Aerospace | 76 | Building materials | 14 |
| | Leisure time | 75 | Paper | 10 |
| | Beverages | 71 | Retailing (food) | 8 |
| | Drugs | 71 | Airlines | Loss |
| | Instruments | 70 | Automotive | Loss |
| | Food and lodging | 69 | Real estate | Loss |
| | Special machinery | 65 | Steel | Loss |
| | General machinery | 64 | Tire and rubber | Loss |
| | Tobacco | 64 | | |
| | All-Industry Average = 46% | | | |
| 1982: | Drugs | 82 | Airlines | Loss |
| | Publishing, TV | 81 | Appliances | Loss |
| | Leisure time | 76 | Automotive | Loss |
| | Aerospace | 75 | Building materials | Loss |
| | Instruments | 73 | Containers | Loss |
| | Oil services | 70 | Metals and mining | Loss |
| | Personal care products | 70 | Paper | Loss |
| | Food and lodging | 68 | Real estate | Loss |
| | Beverages | 62 | Special machinery | Loss |
| | Office equipment | 60 | Steel | Loss |
| | Services | 60 | Tire and rubber | Loss |
| | All-Industry Average = 22% | | | |

Sources: "How 400 Companies Really Performed in 1981," *Business Week,* May 3, 1982, p. 84; and "A Real Look at Earnings: 1982 Was a Dismal Year," *Business Week,* May 2, 1983, p. 76.

Certainly the *Business Week* findings demonstrate the often-significant, differential magnitude of constant dollar adjustments. On average, constant dollar net operating income was only 46 and 22 percent of unadjusted net operating income for 1981 and 1982, respectively. The magazine reported that, even if the net purchasing power gain or loss (most often a gain) was added back, adjusted profits on average would still not exceed 66 and 50 percent of unadjusted earnings for 1980 and 1981, respectively. Because 1982's inflation rate of 6.1 percent was far below 1981's rate of 10.3 percent, initially it might seem strange that a greater portion of 1982's earnings (vis-à-vis those of 1981) disappeared after adjustment for constant dollar accounting. This apparent irony resulted because unadjusted earnings for 1982 were considerably less than for 1981. As a consequence, the similar *absolute* downward adjustment for both years to reflect inflation constituted a greater relative portion of the year whose unadjusted earnings were lower.

Many advocates of constant dollar accounting claim that the use of financial statements restated for general price changes is a necessity for *sound investor evaluation of managerial efforts* in an inflationary economy. Financial policies with respect to a firm's use of borrowed capital and the relationship between its monetary assets and liabilities can be appraised better if data are available which reveal the losses or gains from the holding or owing of monetary items. Current dividend policy could be evaluated in relation to the increases in purchasing power represented by net income and retained earnings.

*Interpretations of trends* in financial accounting information over time also are facilitated and clarified when that information is in dollars of uniform general purchasing power. For example, trends depicting growth in sales, net income, plant, retained earnings, net working capital, and the like will already be adjusted for their inevitable upward biases during inflationary periods if they are developed from price-level accounting information. Certainly, *comparative statements or statistics* encompassing periods of substantial general price changes (e.g., 5- or 10-year summaries included in annual reports) should be restated so as to reveal the real economic changes that have occurred. An increase in dollar sales of 50 percent is misleading as an indicator of sales growth if the general price level has increased 40 percent.

Ratios calculated from historic accounting data likewise can be distorted by changes in general price levels. *Rate of return on investment* is one example. Conventional net operating income (the numerator) is usually overstated in terms of general purchasing power, and the average investment (the denominator) is understated when expressed in historic dollars. Working together, they commonly result in an overstated rate of return. The use of restated data to calculate rates of return and other ratios ensures against distortions of this kind, because the dollars contained in the numerators and denominators are comparable. This issue will be illustrated in some detail in the last section of this chapter, on Armco's price-change disclosures.

**Objections to Constant Dollar Accounting**

Over the many years that the need for constant dollar adjustments has been debated, primary opposition has appeared to center on five points:

1. No legal or tax recognition is accorded to general price-level adjustments.
2. It is not the purpose of financial accounting to deal with other than money values and cash movements.
3. Constant dollar accounting reports would be misunderstood by users.
4. Introduction of constant dollar procedures may inhibit efforts to implement a true current cost system.
5. The cost of constant dollar adjustments may exceed the benefits.

Our contractual and tax system is based on dollar units and not purchasing power units. Neither the Internal Revenue Service nor most other legal agencies use accounting data restated for general price-level changes. Although this fact may be regrettable, financial accounting's main job is to report economic data to stockholders and creditors. Uniform dollar accounting, particularly if done through supplementary statements, is not hampered by legal or tax considerations. Besides, recognition of these restatements may reveal information useful on a macro level in the legal, regulatory, or tax systems.

The second objection assumes that the goal of financial accounting is to provide a net income figure that relates very closely to cash flows—past, present, or future. Reporting in terms of units of general purchasing power introduces items and adjustments that have no ultimate correspondence to actual cash movements. General price-level accounting is premised on the idea that *real* values rather than money values should be reported to investors. However, real values have significance only to the ultimate users of money for *consumption* purposes. Since the investors in a firm are a heterogeneous group, each might have a different measure of real value (purchasing power). Therefore, opponents of restatement argue that financial accounting should report money values and then let each individual stockholder make purchasing power adjustments consistent with their particular situation. Accounting only for *dollars* of cost and *dollars* of revenue presumably provides enough information for evaluating and predicting cash flows associated with stockholder *investments*.

Many have claimed that restated accounting data would serve only to confuse and possibly mislead statement readers. The conventional reports embodying historic acquisition costs are well understood. People are used to thinking in terms of dollars, not in terms of units of purchasing power. Reports adjusted for general price-level changes, on the other hand, are complicated and require expert interpretation. Although it is true that the *method* of adjusting statements for general price-level changes is complex, the extension of these arguments to the resultant statements posits the existence of a rather unsophisticated user of financial information. With full disclosure and explanation, stockholders familiar with the fluctuating value of the dollar should be able to understand changes in the "corporate cost of living" as well as they comprehend changes in the consumers' cost of living.

The fourth objection stems from critics' fears that the introduction of constant dollar adjustments will lull the profession into falsely believing that the entire problem of price-change reporting has been resolved. As we mentioned earlier in this chapter and will illustrate shortly when Tables 19–9 and 19–12 are compared, individual firms and industries are not affected equally by each type of price-change procedure. Most of us are aware of the price trends in calculators and many electrical component parts during the 1970s; the cost of such items actually dropped at the same time that the general price-level index was rising consistently. The action of the FASB in experimenting with *both* types of price-change adjustments in *Statement No. 33* has, for now, lessened the critics' fears that one procedure will rule out the other.

Finally, some allege that the cost of either or both types of price-change adjustments exceeds any benefits claimed by proponents. Winn-Dixie Stores grudgingly made the *Statement No. 33* disclosures in its 1982 annual report, noting that "the cost incurred to develop this information far exceeds any benefit derived." Certainly the costs incurred will be greatest in the first few years in which the procedures are implemented. The fact that the benefits provided usually accrue to persons other than those who are incurring the costs considerably clouds the issue. Then too, the degree of benefit will depend on the ultimate validity of several of the objections previously listed; e.g., does the average annual-report reader have the capacity to fully understand the constant dollar adjustments? Further research and experimentation should aid in resolving this cost-versus-benefits issue.

Now that the procedures for implementing constant dollar accounting and the pros and cons attributed to that model have been explored, our attention turns to the other major price-change system.

## CURRENT COST (REPLACE-MENT COST) ACCOUNTING

The incorporation of changes in *specific* prices of assets and liabilities into the measurement of income and financial position divides period income into two categories—current operating income and holding gains (losses). The basis for the representation of assets on the position statement becomes their current acquisition (replacement) cost.

Traditionally, the entire difference between revenue and the historic acquisition cost of expired assets is recognized as income in the period of sale. The impression is given that the entire difference, with the exception of specifically designated extraordinary gains and losses, reflects operations. In fact, a significant portion of this value increase may be attributable to the holding of asset inputs during a time of specific price change. Moreover, some of these holding or price gains may have occurred before the period in which the asset is consumed.

To correct these perceived defects in conventional accounting, many theorists have argued for a procedure which would separate holding activities from operating activities.[21] Operating activities comprise the production activities in a broad sense, the conversion of asset inputs to outputs. Income from operating activities is measured by the difference between revenue and the *replacement cost* of asset services at the time they are consumed in operations. It represents the difference between the value of goods and services provided by the firm, as reflected in the marketplace, and the value of goods and services used by the firm, as determined by the current marketplace. Operating income is recognized as it occurs.

The procedure also recognizes that income can arise from the firm's buying resources when they are low priced and holding them while they increase in value. These holding gains may result from shrewd buying or conscious speculation on the part of the firm or simply from fortuitous circumstances. Moreover, the holding gains may be tied up in higher levels of inventory and plant and thus not be available for dividends. In any case, the gain or loss results from decisions concerning the timing of acquisition rather than from decisions concerning effective use in operations.

**Illustration**

To illustrate how an accounting system can measure management's success in both holding and operating activities, the following simplified but fairly complete model of current cost reporting is depicted. Liner Company is assumed to have experienced the transactions listed below during its first year of operations:

1. January 1:
   a. The company issues common stock in exchange for $90,000 cash.
   b. A delivery van costing $9,000 is purchased for cash. It has an estimated useful life of three years.
   c. Six units of merchandise, each costing $12,000, are purchased for cash.
2. June 30:
   a. Two units are sold for cash at a price of $18,000 each.
   b. The company pays sales commissions of $3,600 on these sales.
   c. Three more units of merchandise, each costing $11,000, are purchased on credit.
3. December 31:
   a. Five units, the four remaining from the January 1 purchase and one acquired on June 30, are each sold for $19,000 cash.
   b. Sales commissions amounting to $9,500 on these sales are paid in cash.

---

[21] The two foremost works that deal comprehensively with both the theoretical and practical aspects of current cost accounting are Edgar O. Edwards and Philip W. Bell. *The Theory and Measurement of Business Income* (Berkeley: University of California Press, 1961); and Lawrence Revsine, *Replacement Cost Accounting* (Englewood Cliffs, N.J.: Prentice-Hall, 1973).

Assume that the trends in the current (replacement) cost of the delivery van and a unit of merchandise were as follows:

|  | Merchandise (per unit) | Delivery Van |
| --- | --- | --- |
| January 1 | $12,000 | $ 9,000 |
| June 30 | 11,000 | |
| Average for year | | 9,900 |
| December 31 | 14,000 | 10,800 |

**Entries.**  Each of the above transactions will now be recorded in accordance with a current cost system. Only two modifications to the historical cost model are necessary. Asset expirations must now be measured in terms of current costs, and differences between acquisition and current cost at the time of use or at the end of the period must be isolated as holding gains or losses.

| | | | | |
| --- | --- | --- | --- | --- |
| Jan. 1 | Cash | | 90,000 | |
| | Common Stock | | | 90,000 |
| | | | | |
| | Delivery Van | | 9,000 | |
| | Merchandise Inventory | | 72,000 | |
| | Cash | | | 81,000 |
| | | | | |
| June 30 | Cash | | 36,000 | |
| | Sales Revenue | | | 36,000 |
| | | | | |
| | Sales Commissions Expense | | 3,600 | |
| | Cash | | | 3,600 |
| | | | | |
| | Holding Loss—Merchandise | | 2,000 | |
| | Merchandise Inventory | | | 2,000 |

For each of two units sold on June 30, a $1,000 holding loss is represented by the excess of the $12,000 January 1 purchase price over the $11,000 current cost at June 30.

| | | | | |
| --- | --- | --- | --- | --- |
| | Cost of Goods Sold | | 22,000 | |
| | Merchandise Inventory | | | 22,000 |

For each of two units sold, expense is equal to the $11,000 *current* cost of the asset consumed.

| | | | | |
| --- | --- | --- | --- | --- |
| | Merchandise Inventory | | 33,000 | |
| | Accounts Payable | | | 33,000 |
| | | | | |
| Dec. 31 | Cash | | 95,000 | |
| | Sales Revenue | | | 95,000 |
| | | | | |
| | Sales Commissions Expense | | 9,500 | |
| | Cash | | | 9,500 |
| | | | | |
| | Merchandise Inventory | | 17,000 | |
| | Holding Gain—Merchandise | | | 17,000 |

For four of the units sold on December 31, a $2,000 holding gain is measured by the excess of the $14,000 current cost as of December 31 over the $12,000 January 1 purchase price; for all three units purchased on June 30 (one of which had been sold by December 31), a $3,000 holding gain is measured by the excess of $14,000 over the $11,000 June 30 purchase price.

| Cost of Goods Sold | 70,000 | |
| Merchandise Inventory | | 70,000 |

For each of five units sold, expense is equal to the $14,000 current cost of the asset consumed.

| Depreciation Expense | 3,300 | |
| Accumulated Depreciation | | 3,300 |

Average current cost of delivery van for the year is $9,900; $9,900 divided by three years gives the current cost depreciation.

| Delivery Van | 1,800 | |
| Accumulated Depreciation | | 300 |
| Holding Gain—Delivery Van | | 1,500 |

To raise balance in Delivery Van account to the $10,800 current cost as of December 31 from the $9,000 purchase price, to raise Accumulated Depreciation by $300 to total one third of the $10,800 current cost or $3,600, and to show balancing element which is the holding gain.*

\* Gain could be directly calculated as follows: ($9,900 − $9,000) × 1/3 + ($10,800 − $9,000) × 2/3 = $300 + $1,200 = $1,500.

**Financial Statements.** Table 19–10 and Table 19–11 present the income statement and balance sheet for our simplified example. Notice that in measuring current operating performance on the former, asset expirations are quantified at their replacement cost at the time of use. Additionally, operating and holding activities are segregated, although the impact of all cost changes during the period is included in the determination of net income. The balance sheet reports assets at their current input values as of the end of the year.[22]

**TABLE 19–10**

LINER COMPANY
Statement of Income
Using Replacement Costs

| | | | |
|---|---|---|---|
| Current operating income: | | | |
| Sales revenue | | $131,000 | |
| Expenses: | | | |
| Cost of goods sold | $92,000 | | |
| Sales commissions expense | 13,100 | | |
| Depreciation expense | 3,300 | 108,400 | $22,600 |
| Holding gains: | | | |
| Merchandise | | $ 15,000 | |
| Delivery van | | 1,500 | 16,500 |
| Net income | | | $39,100 |

[22] In this example, the entire amount of holding gain has been included as part of retained earnings. One logically could argue that since these are *real* value changes, this income will eventually be subject to taxation. If the holding gains are to be recognized on the books before they are recognized for tax purposes, a provision for deferred income taxes should be established (see Chapter 13).

**TABLE 19-11**

---

LINER COMPANY
Balance Sheet
Using Replacement Costs

*Assets*

| | | |
|---|---:|---:|
| Current assets: | | |
| Cash | $126,900 | |
| Merchandise | 28,000 | $154,900 |
| Noncurrent assets: | | |
| Delivery truck | 10,800 | |
| Less: Accumulated depreciation | 3,600 | 7,200 |
| Total assets | | $162,100 |

*Equities*

| | | |
|---|---:|---:|
| Current liabilities: | | |
| Accounts payable | | $ 33,000 |
| Stockholders' equity: | | |
| Common stock | 90,000 | |
| Retained earnings | 39,100 | 129,100 |
| Total equities | | $162,100 |

---

**Measurement of Current Costs**

In the foregoing example, replacement cost is determined for each specific asset at the time it is used. It would probably be more practical to determine the current cost as of the end of the period and use it for all transactions during the period. This shortcut would be appropriate for plant assets in particular. For instance, in our example the holding gain on the delivery truck would be $1,800 (replacement cost at year-end of $10,800 less cost at beginning of the year of $9,000), and the depreciation expense would be $3,600 ($\frac{1}{3}$ of $10,800). Use of year-end replacement costs tends to overstate holding gains and understate operating income in a period of increasing prices but does not change the "bottom line" net income number. Accordingly, the shortcut approach is acceptable unless dramatic price changes have occurred.

A more difficult measurement problem than *when* to measure replacement cost is *how* to measure it. Current input costs should be the cost of the same or equivalent asset services. These specific prices can be noted from three sources: (1) an established market price for the particular good or service, (2) purchase price of an asset providing equivalent service potential, and (3) an adjustment of acquisition cost by means of a price index restricted to assets of like kind. Each of these has its shortcomings.

Most discussions, including our simple example, focus solely on changes in asset values. However, if replacement costs are to be used in the preparation of financial statements and changes in these values are to be recognized as holding items in income, should not the same concepts be applied to interest-bearing liabilities? Assume that a firm issues a long-term debt obligation at an effective interest of 8 percent and that subsequently the market rate of interest rises to 9 percent. The value of the bond declines because of the increase in the market rate of interest. The present value of the future payments under the bond at the *replacement cost rate of 9 percent* are less than the present value at the transacted rate of 8 percent. The firm has gained from holding a long-term debt at 8 percent when the market rate is 9 percent. If the bonds are traded in the open market, the firm could realize this gain by repurchasing the bond issue. Logically, the gain should be included as a holding gain for the period and used in the evaluation of management's timing of its borrowing decisions. Similarly, the liability on the balance sheet should be shown at the lower figure, and interest expense should be based on the current rate of 9 percent. Much of the literature on replacement cost accounting ignores its applications to liabilities.

## Advantages and Uses of Current Cost Recording

The total dollar income over the life of a business is not modified under replacement cost recording. Its difference from income under historical-dollar cost accounting lies in its *timing* and *sources*. Through the valuation of assets at current input cost, significant changes in asset values are not deferred until sale or consumption takes place. These value increases and decreases are reported in the period in which they occur. As a result the balance sheet reports costs at current input values, the income statement reports expenses at the current values of the resources consumed, and holding gains/losses are reported separately from operating income.

This separation of operating income from holding income constitutes one of the major advantages claimed for current cost accounting. It is argued that because different kinds of decisions give rise to these two types of income, the decision-making framework can be improved if we distinguish between success or failure in operations on the one hand and gains or losses from speculation or holding of resources on the other.

Recall that Liner Company on June 30 sold two units for $18,000 each. Each unit had been acquired on January 1 at a cost of $12,000, although Liner Company only paid a unit price of $11,000 to acquire identical merchandise on June 30. Under the system of unadjusted historical cost, the firm would report on June 30 $36,000 of Sales Revenue reduced by $24,000 of Cost of Goods Sold for a $12,000 gross margin. The current cost journal entries for Liner Company *also* produced a $12,000 net advantage, but it consisted of a $14,000 gross margin ($36,000 sales revenue minus *$22,000* current cost of goods sold) and a $2,000 holding loss for merchandise ($24,000 historical cost less $22,000 current replacement cost).

**Current Operating Income.** Ostensibly, one of the purposes of financial information is to predict future earnings. Operating income based on current costs provides a better measure of future earning power for two reasons: (1) It excludes gains and losses that might not occur again and (2) the profit margin between revenues and current costs probably constitutes the best estimate of future operating conditions.

As we have previously mentioned, advocates of replacement costing maintain that operating income should measure the amount that can be distributed without contraction of the level of capacity. If a business entity is to operate as a *going concern* at the same level of capacity, it must recover from revenues the cost of restoring the resources consumed. Expenses should therefore be measured at replacement cost. Then investors will have a better basis for assessing dividend policy. When income is measured by conventional accounting methods, management may have to retain some of these earnings in the business just to *maintain existing capacity*. Ideally, when replacement cost methods are used, a dividend payout significantly more or less than current operating income would indicate an intention on the part of management to contract or expand the level of operations.

**Holding Gains and Losses.**   However, current operating income, by itself, is not satisfactory for another use of accounting information, the complete evaluation of managerial performance. Here the holding income becomes important, because it gives credit for the favorable acquisition of resources when prices are low. Of course, management may or may not be directly responsible for all gains and losses from holding activities. Even so, separately disclosed information about holding activities can reveal the costs or benefits arising from policy decisions. For example, holding gains or losses on inventory indicate the impact from a firm's carrying inventory in a period of price change rather than being able to buy and sell instantaneously.

**Ratio Analysis.**   The procedures outlined above provide income statement information useful for the evaluation of both operating and holding aspects of management's activity. On the replacement cost balance sheet, assets are valued at the amount the firm would need currently to replace the asset services. Together, the financial statements provide a more meaningful and more comparable basis for ratio analysis. Safety margins for liquidity and financial strength, as revealed in current ratios or debt-equity ratios, would be measured in a more realistic manner. Inter-firm comparability would be improved, because assets for all companies would be stated at current costs. Investment bases would not be distorted by differences in the timing of plant acquisitions or by the choice of arbitrary inventory flow assumptions (e.g., FIFO, LIFO, etc.). Similarly, net income would reflect value changes occurring *during* the period and would not differ artificially from one firm to another simply because of the timing of sale or realization.

Table 19–9, presented earlier during our discussion of constant dollar accounting, depicted the magnitude of the general price-level adjustments reported by large corporations for 1981 and 1982. In Table 19–12, the magnitude of the *current cost* adjustments are highlighted; once again, the *Business Week* annual "Inflation Scoreboard" is the source. It is clear that the current cost adjustments required by *Statement No. 33* have had widely differing effects on the net operating income reported by firms in various

**TABLE 19-12  Magnitude of Current Cost Adjustments Reported by Large Corporations for 1981 and 1982 (current cost net operating income as a percent of unadjusted net operating income)**

| | *The Best Off* | | *The Worst Off* | |
|---|---|---|---|---|
| | *Industry* | *Percent* | *Industry* | *Percent* |
| 1981: | Office equipment | 93 | Metals and mining | 25 |
| | Publishing, TV | 83 | Retailing (food) | 21 |
| | Drugs | 81 | Paper | 16 |
| | Leisure time | 80 | Building materials | 14 |
| | Instruments | 79 | Railroads | 5 |
| | Aerospace | 77 | Airlines | Loss |
| | Oil service and supply | 73 | Automotive | Loss |
| | Food and lodging | 72 | Real estate | Loss |
| | Electrical | 71 | Steel | Loss |
| | Beverages | 69 | Tire and rubber | Loss |
| | Tobacco | 69 | | |
| | All-Industry Average = 44% | | | |
| 1982: | Office equipment | 89 | Airlines | Loss |
| | Drugs | 85 | Automotive | Loss |
| | Publishing, TV | 84 | Building Materials | Loss |
| | Leisure time | 78 | Containers | Loss |
| | Aerospace | 77 | General machinery | Loss |
| | Instruments | 74 | Metals and mining | Loss |
| | Tobacco | 73 | Paper | Loss |
| | Food and lodging | 71 | Railroads and trucking | Loss |
| | Beverages | 69 | Real estate | Loss |
| | Electrical | 69 | Special machinery | Loss |
| | Oil services | 69 | Steel | Loss |
| | Personal care products | 68 | Tire and rubber | Loss |
| | All-Industry Average = 27% | | | |

Sources: "How 400 Companies Really Performed in 1981," *Business Week,* May 3, 1982, p. 84; and "A Real Look at Earnings: 1982 Was a Dismal Year," *Business Week,* May 2, 1983, p. 76.

key industries. Current cost adjustments for both 1981 and 1982 have lowered the operating net income of *all* industries surveyed, however.

**Objections to and Limitations of Current Costing**

The arguments opposing the recognition of current costs appear to fall into three groups. One group asserts that replacement cost recording violates the fundamentals of the exchange-price concept, the realization principle, and the stewardship of financial resources. This class of objection states the obvious. It is clear that replacement cost recording *is* premised on different concepts of cost, value recognition, and stewardship. The major issue is to determine which theoretical structure provides more useful information to the external audience of financial accounting.

The second type of objection addresses this issue and concludes that replacement cost is deficient. A replacement cost system, while avoiding the problems of selection of inventory methods, still relies on arbitrary allocation schemes for depreciable assets. A replacement cost balance sheet does not show present financial position in terms of exit or liquidation values. Replacement cost is not an accurate measure of the opportunity cost of using an asset when future use value is *less* than replacement cost. In this instance, the valuation method implies replacement when replacement is not, in fact, contemplated. Furthermore, the distinction between holding activities and operating activities, many critics argue, is artificial. They contend that the buying and holding of assets are absolutely essential to a continuance of operations. A business cannot operate from hand to mouth as the separation of operating from holding activities might imply.

The last set of objections concerns measurability. Some accountants feel that there is insufficient reliable information concerning replacement costs of assets. Wholesale markets are imperfect; appraisal values display wide variance, as shown by experiences in the 1920s and 1930s. Revaluations according to specific index numbers measure only reproduction cost of a physical asset, not replacement cost of the asset's services, because they fail to consider technological improvements. These problems of measurability are particularly evident for special-purpose assets, such as technical machinery; complex assets, such as buildings and manufactured inventory; and unreproducible assets, such as land. In the minds of some, these measurement problems are too staggering to overcome, and piecemeal application—that is, revaluation of some assets but not others—could be considered both inconsistent and confusing by some. The FASB's *Statement No. 33* supplementary disclosure requirements for only key items on the financial statements might, accordingly, be labeled a piecemeal approach. Nevertheless, such required experimentation by the FASB should produce more evidence concerning the reliability of current cost estimates and the difficulties of making them.

**CURRENT COST/ CONSTANT DOLLAR ACCOUNTING**

In our Huron Corporation example, we concentrated solely on general price-level changes. The Liner Company illustration looked solely at specific price-level changes; changes in the general price index were assumed to be either nonexistent or not relevant. It is hoped that the examination of each price adjustment model in a separate and distinct manner aided the reader to comprehend each. Actually, the current cost and constant dollar reporting models can be combined. The reporting system incorporating both procedures is referred to as current cost/constant dollar accounting. Our forthcoming discussion of Armco's price-change disclosures will reveal that certain data mandated by *Statement No. 33* are of such a combined nature.

A comparison of the *Business Week* findings in Table 19–9 for constant dollar and Table 19–12 for current cost shows that the use of either price-change model caused approximately the same adjustments to the net operating income for such industries as publishing/TV and aerospace. On the other hand, the results for such industries as office equipment and railroads varied greatly, according to which price-change procedure was utilized. Railroads did much worse when evaluated on the basis of current cost rather than constant dollar, while office equipment performed much better. Obviously both models capture their own unique trends; they may therefore need to be combined before a completely meaningful assessment can be made.

The integration of current cost with constant dollar is not as complicated as one might expect. The major differences are in the stockholders' equity section of the balance sheet and in the income statement. Assets stated at replacement cost at the end of the year are already stated in dollars of year-end purchasing power. Items of current revenue and *current* expense would be restated in year-end dollars from, say, year-average dollars, if the annual general price-level change were material.

Holding gains and losses would have to be recalculated in terms of year-end dollars. The amount of *real* holding gain or loss generally would be reduced to reflect general price-level increases. The rest is simply part of the *restatement* of stockholders' equity and not a change in value. A firm can experience *real* holding gains by holding only those assets with price increases greater than that of the general price level. Finally, a gain or loss in purchasing power from the holding of monetary items would appear along with the other elements of holding income.

The reader may wish to experiment with the example of the Liner Company by assuming a general price-level change during the period and preparing financial statements encompassing both general and specific price changes.

| **DISCUSSION OF THE ARMCO ANNUAL REPORT** | Armco is one of the approximately 1,200 firms which are required to comply with the disclosure requirements of *FASB Statement No. 33*. The mandated information on price changes is presented on pages 168–170 in the Appendix to Chapter 5. The two schedules presented at the bottom of the first two of those pages have become fairly standardized in format among firms; the FASB illustrated such formats as an appendix to *Statement No. 33* as examples of ways to disclose the required information. |
|---|---|
| **Restatement of 1981 Amounts** | The first schedule compares and contrasts three distinct income statements for the firm for 1981. Column 1 features the major categories reported in the unadjusted historical cost income statement presented earlier in the annual report. It, of course, is the only reporting model which can be utilized in the primary income statement. Columns 2 and 3 recast the cost of products sold and depreciation/amortization amounts in order to approximate net income under the constant dollar and current cost reporting systems, respectively. Because the FASB did not require restatement of more than those two items from the income statement, far fewer of the |

amounts in Column 2 are adjusted than of the Huron Corporation's figures in our comprehensive example shown in Table 19–7.

Armco's net operating income of $294.5 million plummets to $137.9 million after the constant dollar adjustments and to $134.5 million as a result of the current cost restatements. The entire $3.4 million difference between the two adjustment procedures comes with respect to depreciation; apparently the specific prices of the depreciable property held by Armco increased slightly more than the general rise in prices during 1981. As noted previously in Chapter 8, the cost of products sold amount for Column 3 was actually within 1 percent of the Column 2 adjusted figure, so Armco felt justified in reporting the same $5,769.0 million for both columns.

Although the firm's net operating income as restated has dropped to 47 percent (constant dollar) and 46 percent (current cost) of the unadjusted figure, it should be realized that the decline would have been even greater if Armco had not been using LIFO. As Tables 19–9 and 19–12 reveal, most steel companies reported a net operating *loss* in Columns 2 and 3 for 1981.

Certainly the figures on page 168 dampen enthusiasm concerning Armco's performance. Even if the FASB were to allow the addition of the purchasing power gain from the holding of net monetary liabilities to the net income number, a practice which makes theoretical and practical sense, Armco still would have had a drop in income of approximately $100 million. The actual effective tax rate experienced by the firm approached 65 percent when expressed in relation to the much lower restated income. The firm uses this fact to argue for "a more enlightened tax policy."

The effects of price-change adjustments on the current cost of inventory and net property, plant, and equipment (PPE) are revealed near the bottom of the schedule. The $756.2 million increase in the current cost of such assets held during at least some portion of 1981 (even if not held on December 31) is disclosed and then divided into the portions attributable to general price changes and to specific price changes. The analysis is similar to our dissection of the delivery van's price change earlier in this chapter. It is *only a coincidence* that exactly half of the price increase, or $378.1 million, is a result of each type of price change.

Restated balance sheet amounts for inventory and net property on December 31, 1981, are also presented. For inventories, the $1,143.1 million unadjusted figure reported on the regular balance sheet needed to be raised by 70 percent to the $1,942.4 million amount before it approximated current cost. Armco's use of LIFO made the price-change adjustment particularly large. For net property, the current cost of $3,046.1 million was 68 percent higher than the reported balance sheet amount of $1,812.7 million. The significance of such adjustments for financial ratio analysis becomes apparent from a study of the summary trend data in the schedule on page 169.

**Five-Year Comparative Data**

Valuable information for gauging the effects of changing prices on financial trends reported by Armco is presented in the second price-change schedule. The unadjusted historical cost data show a trend of steady increases in net sales and cash dividends per common share since 1977 and equally promising trends in net income, net income per common share, and shareholders' equity over the 1979–1981 period examined. A significantly different picture emerges when the trends are recast in accordance with the constant dollar (general inflation) and current cost models. The unadjusted historical cost record of continual and steady improvement is shown to be a facade which hides a large downturn experienced by Armco in 1980.

The financial ratios reported by Armco and analyzed by us in the concluding section of Chapter 18 undergo a major transformation when adjusted for changing prices. For example, the 1981 return on average shareholders' equity of 13.7 percent that Armco reports becomes 3.4 percent and 3.2 percent after constant dollar and current cost adjustments, respectively. The calculation expressed in constant dollar terms is as follows:

$$\frac{\text{Net Income}}{\text{Average Shareholders' Equity}} =$$

$$\frac{\$137.9 \text{ Million}}{\dfrac{1(\$4,272.6 \text{ Million}) + 3(\$4,020.7 \text{ Million})}{4}} =$$

$$\frac{\$137.9 \text{ Million}}{\$4,083.7 \text{ Million}} = 3.4\%$$

When the above computation is compared to its unadjusted historical cost equivalent (see page 700 in Chapter 18), we can see that the huge drop in the return on shareholders' equity from 13.7 to 3.4 percent had two causes. First, the net income used as the numerator was more than halved when adjusted to a constant dollar basis. Second, the average shareholders' equity used as the denominator simultaneously almost doubled. The lower numerator in combination with the higher denominator created double downward pressure on this financial measure.

Armco notes on page 169 that "comparing dividends per share and earnings per share when both are adjusted for general inflation shows we have paid out substantial percentages of our income in dividends." When the constant dollar cash dividends per common share is divided by the constant dollar net income per common share, the trend in and absolute level of the dividend payout percentage changes dramatically:

|  | Dividend Payout Percent | | |
|---|---|---|---|
|  | 1981 | 1980 | 1979 |
| Unadjusted historical cost* ............... | 34.6% | 33.2% | 31.7% |
| Constant dollar reporting ................. | 75.1 | 99.4 | 55.6 |

* See page 171.

For all three years, the constant dollar adjustments are large, with Armco in 1980 actually distributing cash dividends equal to its net operating income adjusted for general price changes.

Our brief examination of Armco's price-change disclosures reveals the large potential value of such information. New insights into the absolute levels and trends in a firm's performance and financial position can result from such constant dollar and current cost adjustments. The disclosures required by *Statement No. 33* appear to possess significant information content. The tone of Armco's price-change discussion is most salutary. The company seems to have approached the issue of adjustments positively and has candidly acknowledged the illusory profits and distorted financial ratios and trends which often result from the unadjusted historical cost reporting model.

## SUMMARY

The discussion in this chapter ranges over a number of topics. The economic model of direct valuation through the discounting of expected future net receipts is explored. It is rejected as a general framework because of a lack of reliable measurements and because of the incorporation of expectations and changes in expectations into the income calculation. Quantification based on current exit values is a viable alternative, although it is criticized for some of the same reasons. A concept of income measurement stressing individual flow elements is assumed to be more valuable than the comparative balance sheet approach underlying exit value accounting.

From the study of theoretical models and the nature of price changes come two ideas that can be incorporated into the theories and procedures of financial accounting as they currently exist: (1) the measurement of dollar values in *real* terms, in terms of the general command over goods and services, and (2) the recognition of changes in the current input values of the firm's resources. Attempts to deal with these ideas are discussed under the headings of constant dollar and current cost accounting, respectively. The first reexamines the validity of the monetary postulate; the second modifies the exchange-price, matching, and recognition (realization) concepts. Stated in another way, constant dollar accounting modifies the dollar amounts of income reported but not their timing. Current cost reporting, on the other hand, changes the timing of recognition but not the total amounts.

Information about why prices and values change would seem intuitively to be important both for evaluations of the earnings potential and financial strength of a firm and for judgments about the effectiveness of management. Still, the accounting profession took until 1979 to require price-change disclosures and then specified only limited data in supplemental form. When Louis Harris and Associates polled 415 persons interested in financial reporting during March 1980, *Statement No. 33* was felt to be "sound and wise" by only a relatively narrow 48–37 percent plurality.[23] The less than overwhelming mandate can perhaps be explained in terms of more fundamental considerations.

Financial accounting lacks any clear-cut objectives or criteria for a theory of income. For example, how much do we really know about the informational needs of the audiences of financial accounting reports? Have we adequately identified the primary audience and its purposes, analytical abilities, preferences, level of sophistication, and so on? The fundamental judgment that must be made concerns which theory provides the most meaningful information to users. How do they define wealth? What criteria should we use in evaluating measurements? If the measurements are to be "reliable," precisely what does this concept imply? Because it is a relative concept, what minimum standards must be met? To what extent are accountants, or more accurately the ultimate users of financial statements, willing to sacrifice reliability to achieve greater relevance?

Until questions like these can be answered, the controversies probably will continue. There are, however, some hopeful signs. The accounting profession's progress in developing and issuing statements of financial accounting concepts, such as those noted in earlier chapters, is evidence of a real concern for addressing such large, conceptual issues. In addition, the FASB's commitment to review *Statement No. 33* comprehensively no later than 1985 raises the possibility that the relative costs and benefits of each major price-change model will be carefully evaluated.

## QUESTIONS AND PROBLEMS

**19–1.** The John Lewis Company reports a net income of $280,500 in 1982. Dividends declared and paid amounted to $214,000. Depreciation expense of $208,000 is included among the deductions from revenue. Straight-line depreciation was calculated from the following schedule:

| Year of Acquisition | Asset Cost | Years of Useful Life | Depreciation Expense |
|---|---|---|---|
| 1975 | $940,000 | 8 | $117,500 |
| 1980 | 220,000 | 11 | 20,000 |
| 1981 | 282,000 | 4 | 70,500 |
| | | | $208,000 |

The CPI index applicable to each year was as follows (1967 = 100):

| | |
|---|---|
| 1975 | 161.2 |
| 1980 | 246.9 |
| 1981 | 272.4 |
| 1982 | 289.1 |

---

[23] FASB, "A Study of the Attitudes toward and an Assessment of the Financial Accounting Standards Board: Executive Summary" (Stamford, Conn., June 11, 1980), p. 6.

*Required:*

a. Restate the depreciation expense in uniform dollars of 1982 purchasing power. Determine the related net income figure.

b. Comment on the company's dividend policy in light of your answers in part *(a)*.

c. Assume that in addition to the book value of the plant assets, there are $186,000 of current assets. Calculate and compare net income as a percent of total assets in (1) unadjusted dollars and (2) restated dollars of 1982 purchasing power. Which statistic is more realistic? More accurate?

**19–2.** In September 1979 *Statement of Financial Accounting Standards No. 33,* "Financial Reporting and Changing Prices," *(FAS No. 33)* was released.[24] This statement applies to public enterprises that have either (1) inventories and property, plant, and equipment (before deducting accumulated depreciation) of more than $125 million or (2) total assets amounting to more than $1 billion (after deducting accumulated depreciation). No changes are required in the basic financial statements, but information required by *FAS No. 33* is to be presented in supplementary statements, schedules, or notes in the financial reports.

*Required:*

a. A number of terms are defined and used in *FAS No. 33.*
   (1) Differentiate between the terms *constant dollar* and *current cost.*
   (2) Explain what is meant by *current cost/constant dollar accounting* and how it differs from *historical cost/nominal dollar accounting.*

b. Identify the accounts for which an enterprise must measure the effects of changing prices in order to present the supplementary information required by *FAS No. 33.*

c. *FAS No. 33* is based upon *FASB Concepts Statement No. 1,* "Objectives of Financial Reporting by Business Enterprises," which concludes that financial reporting should provide information to help investors, creditors, and other financial statement users assess the amounts, timing, and uncertainty of prospective net cash inflows to the enterprise. Explain how *FAS No. 33* may help in attaining this objective.

**19–3.** Bebe Jay is a confused person. He had always thought that it was better to lend money than to borrow money. "Interest income" always had a much nicer ring to it than "interest expense." This philosophy had been reflected in the operation of his business; in particular, he always sold on very liberal credit terms. Recently, however, Bebe heard a friend remark that "the only way to beat inflation is to borrow heavily and pay back your loans in cheaper dollars." A schedule of *selected* balance sheet accounts for Bebe's CB Store appears below (amounts in thousands of dollars):

|  | Jan. 1, 19x1 | Dec. 31, 19x1 | Dec. 31, 19x2 |
|---|---|---|---|
| Cash | $160 | $175 | $190 |
| Receivables | 280 | 425 | 600 |
| Inventories | 450 | 500 | 625 |
| Accounts payable | 130 | 140 | 155 |
| Wages payable | 80 | 90 | 100 |
| Mortgage payable | 100 | 95 | 90 |

[24] Adapted from Examination for the Certificate in Management Accounting, June 1981.

Assume that a standard index of the general level of prices was as follows:

|  | 19x1 | 19x2 |
|---|---|---|
| January 1 | 100 | 116 |
| Average for year | 108 | 120 |
| December 31 | 116 | 124 |

*Required:*

a. Explain to Bebe how creditors lose and debtors gain during inflation. What did his friend mean by paying "back your loans in cheaper dollars"?

b. Calculate the net purchasing power gain or loss experienced by Bebe's CB Store over the two years. Express the gain or loss in dollars of uniform purchasing power as of December 31, 19x2. Assume that any changes in account balances occurred evenly throughout the year.

c. Bebe examines your findings in part *(b)* but remains unconvinced. "How can one improve their own position by borrowing money they don't even need and alienating good customers with very restrictive credit terms?" Is Bebe correct? Explain.

**19–4.** The following information is available for the Berry Corporation:

|  | December 31 | |
|---|---|---|
|  | 1985 | 1984 |
| Monetary assets | $130,000 | $70,000 |
| Monetary liabilities | 60,000 | 40,000 |
| Merchandise inventory | 90,000 | 75,000 |

|  | 1985 |
|---|---|
| Sales revenue | $800,000 |
| Purchases | 500,000 |
| Depreciation expense | 200,000 |
| Operating expenses | 250,000 |

*Additional information:*

1. Sales, purchases, and operating expenses were incurred evenly during 1985.
2. Depreciation expense is 10 percent of the cost of the fixed assets, all of which were acquired on January 1, 1978.
3. Goods remaining on hand each December 31 were acquired during the previous three months.
4. A $10,000 dividend was declared and paid on November 15, 1985.
5. The consumer price index was assumed to be as follows:

| | |
|---|---|
| January 1, 1978 | 100 |
| Fourth quarter 1984 | 150 |
| December 31, 1984 | 160 |
| Average for 1985 | 175 |
| Fourth quarter 1985 | 190 |
| December 31, 1985 | 200 |

*Required:*

a. Calculate the net purchasing power gain or loss experienced by the Berry Corporation during 1985.

*b.* Prepare a 1985 income statement for the Berry Corporation on a constant dollar basis, expressed in terms of December 31, 1985, dollars.

*c.* Is the income statement you prepared in part *(b)* less objective than the traditional income statement prepared by firms? Is it less consistent with generally accepted accounting principles? Explain carefully.

**19–5.** R. Company acquires a warehouse and plans to rent space in it to various customers. Annual gross rentals of $35,000 are expected over the building's 15-year life. Cash operating expenses will be $11,000 each year. Assume that 12 percent is the proper discount factor and that all cash flows occur at the end of the year.

*Required:*

*a.* Determine the value of the warehouse now and a year from now, using direct valuation. How much income was attributable to the first year?

*b.* At the end of the second year, you anticipate that cash operating expenses will be $12,300 for each year in the future. What is the value of the warehouse at the end of the second year and the income attributable to that year? What factors influenced the income for the second year?

*c.* The warehouse originally cost $105,000. Its resale value at the end of the second year is $140,000, and its replacement cost new is $150,000 at that time. What asset amount would appear on a balance sheet at the end of the second year under (1) historical cost, (2) exit-price accounting, and (3) replacement cost accounting?

*d.* Which of the balance sheet amounts you arrived at in part *(c)* would be most useful to an investor in the firm? To a banker considering lending money to the firm? Explain.

**19–6.** A sampling of firms' editorial comments pertaining to the required price-change disclosures contained in their 1981 or 1982 annual reports appears below:

> **International Harvester Company.** "Net loss as computed under the current cost method is not necessarily an indication of what the results would be if the existing assets were replaced, because the new assets would be expected to generate operating efficiencies which would partially offset the increased depreciation expense."
>
> **Federal Express Corporation.** "Although the Company recognizes the importance for readers of financial statements to understand the impact of inflation, management believes that the user should continue to focus on the historical financial statements in assessing the Company's results of operations and financial condition. The supplemental data contained in this section may not be a fair presentation of the effects of inflation, and the Company cautions the reader against accepting it as such."
>
> **Weyerhaeuser Company.** "The information provides useful insights into the erosive effects of inflation on the Company's earnings and return on invested capital. However, because the information deals with only certain aspects of inflation and because the compilation of the data by its nature is imprecise, an analysis of the Company's performance and an assessment of its

future prospects based solely on the information given is incomplete and likely misleading."

**Koppers Company, Inc.** "Koppers does not believe, however, that the impact of inflation on the Company's 1981 performance and financial condition was as severe as the inflation-adjusted income data, taken alone, would indicate. Koppers bases its operating and investment decisions on cash flow considerations."

**Pennsylvania Power & Light Company.** "The FASB recognizes, and the Company cautions users of this information, that there is no consensus on the general practical usefulness of this supplementary information."

**Corning Glass Works.** "Corning does not totally agree with the methods required to explain the impact of inflation. Like any other analytical tool, current cost adjusted data present a partial picture, which should be used in conjunction with other financial and economic indicators."

*Required:*

a. Has International Harvester discovered a flaw in the price-change reporting requirements? Explain.

b. Is Weyerhaeuser correct when it asserts that "the information deals with only certain aspects of inflation"? If so, which aspects are not dealt with? Does their omission justify the pessimism contained in the firm's statement? Explain.

c. Discuss how, if at all, inflation-adjusted income data might overstate the effect of inflation on a firm (such as Koppers) which "bases its operating and investment decisions on cash flow considerations."

d. Do you agree with Pennsylvania Power & Light that "there is no consensus on the general practical usefulness of this supplementary data"? If not, why not? If so, does this represent a critical deficiency of *Statement No. 33?*

e. What other financial and economic indicators might Corning Glass have had in mind when it made its statement? Explain.

f. Evaluate the comments of Federal Express. Are you in agreement with all or part of them? Be specific.

g. "The FASB should immediately ban all such editorial comments. What good are tough disclosure requirements if the firms are permitted to take the wind out of their sails." Do you agree? If you were a stockholder in all of the above firms, would your reading of their price-change comments cause you to place less reliance on the dollar adjustments? If so, with which firms would this be most likely to happen? Does this bode ill for the potential effectiveness of future accounting pronouncements?

19–7. Apple and Wang Laboratories are two well-known manufacturers of computers and related equipment. Both firms revealed in their 1982 annual reports that they compute depreciation for financial reporting purposes principally by use of the declining-balance method. A portion of the *Statement No. 33* disclosures included in their reports appear below (amounts in thousands of dollars):

|  | Reported in Primary Statements | Adjusted for General Inflation | Adjusted for Changes in Specific Prices |
|---|---|---|---|
| Apple: | | | |
| Depreciation ........... | $ 14,400 | $ 15,200 | $ 14,800 |
| Net income ............ | 61,300 | 54,700 | 60,900 |
| Wang: | | | |
| Depreciation ........... | 62,831 | 45,761 | 43,665 |
| Net income ............ | 107,139 | 101,271 | 113,472 |

*Required:*

a.  "The depreciation adjustments shown by Apple are somewhat surprising, but those shown by Wang are mind-boggling." Do you find the depreciation numbers resulting from the adjustments to be "somewhat surprising" or "mind-boggling"? Explain.

b.  Why did Wang's adjusted net income numbers change by an amount which is significantly smaller than the decline in its adjusted depreciation expense?

c.  Wang included the following statement in its annual report:

Depreciation expense computed under the constant dollar and current cost methods is substantially lower than that computed under historical cost accounting. This is attributable to the use of the straight line method for constant dollar and current cost accounting instead of the declining balance method generally used for historical cost purposes. Had the same depreciation methods been used, depreciation expense under both the constant dollar and current cost methods would have been greater than under the historical cost method. Accelerated depreciation methods were chosen in the primary financial statements partly to compensate for changing prices. Accordingly, the application of such methods under constant dollar and current cost accounting would have overstated the effect of changing prices.

Is Wang's rationale valid, or does it represent a poor attempt to justify a departure from the true intent of the FASB's disclosure requirements?

**19–8.**  A comparative balance sheet as of December 31, 1984, and 1983, and an income statement for 1984 for Madeline, Inc., are presented on page 766:

Balance Sheet

|  | As of December 31 | |
|---|---|---|
|  | 1984 | 1983 |
| **Assets** | | |
| Cash | $ 108,000 | $ 94,000 |
| Accounts receivable | 292,000 | 195,500 |
| Inventory, at LIFO cost | 222,000 | 200,000 |
| Land | 95,000 | 95,000 |
| Building | 320,000 | 320,000 |
| Less: Allowance for depreciation | (80,000) | (70,000) |
| Equipment | 600,000 | 600,000 |
| Less: Allowance for depreciation | (250,000) | (200,000) |
| Total assets | $1,307,000 | $1,234,500 |
| **Equities** | | |
| Current liabilities | $ 189,000 | $ 151,100 |
| Common stock | 700,000 | 700,000 |
| Retained earnings | 418,000 | 383,400 |
| Total equities | $1,307,000 | $1,234,500 |

1984 Income Statement

| | | |
|---|---|---|
| Sales (80,000 at $7.50) | | $600,000 |
| Cost of goods sold: | | |
| Beginning inventory (40,000 at $5) | $200,000 | |
| Purchases (84,000 at $5.50) | 462,000 | |
| Goods available | 662,000 | |
| Ending inventory (40,000 at $5; | | |
| 4,000 at $5.50) | 222,000 | 440,000 |
| Gross margin | | 160,000 |
| Operating expenses: | | |
| Depreciation on building | $ 10,000 | |
| Depreciation on equipment | 50,000 | |
| Other | 65,400 | 125,400 |
| Net income | | $ 34,600 |

*Additional information:*

1.  The replacement cost of the inventory was $5.20 on December 31, 1983, and $5.80 on December 31, 1984. Of the units sold, 70,000 occurred when the replacement cost was $5.50 and the rest when it was $5.80.
2.  The land had an appraised value of $105,000 and $112,000 on December 31, 1983, and December 31, 1984, respectively.
3.  An index of nonresidential construction costs was 120 when the building was acquired. It stood at 150 on December 31 of both 1983 and 1984.
4.  The replacement cost of similar new equipment on December 31, 1983, was $640,000, and it was $675,000 on December 31, 1984.

*Required:*

a.  Prepare a comparative balance sheet and an income statement for Madeline, Inc., using a replacement cost system of reporting. On the income statement, separate operating activities from holding activities.
b.  Prepare a schedule showing the calculation of holding gains and losses. What has happened with respect to holding gains on the building?

c. How much holding gain was "realized" in 1984 when the inputs to which the gains attach were used in operations?

d. How, if at all, would your above answers probably have differed if Madeline, Inc., had been under FIFO rather than LIFO? Explain.

e. "Management is responsible for doing a good job with respect to both operating activities and holding activities. Therefore, there's no need to distinguish the two activities in an accounting reporting system." Do you agree? Why or why not?

**19–9.** Retail Showcase Mart was organized on December 15, 1980. The company's initial statement of financial position is presented below.[25]

RETAIL SHOWCASE MART
Statement of Financial Position
December 31, 1980

*Assets*

| | |
|---|---|
| Cash | $200,000 |
| Inventory (at historical cost which equals market value; FIFO; periodic) | 400,000 |
| Furniture and fixtures | 200,000 |
| Land (held for future store site) | 100,000 |
| Total assets | $900,000 |

*Liabilities and Stockholders' Equity*

| | |
|---|---|
| Accounts payable | $300,000 |
| Capital stock ($5 par, 200,000 shares authorized; 120,000 issued and outstanding) | 600,000 |
| Total liabilities and stockholders' equity | $900,000 |

The statement of income and the statement of financial position prepared at the close of business on December 31, 1981 are presented below.

RETAIL SHOWCASE MART
Statement of Income
For the Year Ended December 31, 1981

| | | |
|---|---|---|
| Sales | | $1,100,000 |
| Cost of goods sold: | | |
| Inventory 1/1/81 | $ 400,000 | |
| Purchases | 1,000,000 | |
| Goods available | 1,400,000 | |
| Inventory, 12/31/81 | 600,000 | 800,000 |
| Gross profit | | 300,000 |
| Operating expenses: | | |
| Rent | 36,000 | |
| Depreciation | 20,000 | |
| Other (all required cash expenditures) | 44,000 | 100,000 |
| Income before taxes | | 200,000 |
| Income tax expense | | 80,000 |
| Net income | | $ 120,000 |
| Earnings per share | | $1.00 |

---

[25] Adapted from Examination for the Certificate in Management Accounting, December 1981.

RETAIL SHOWCASE MART
Statement of Financial Position
December 31, 1981

*Assets*

| | |
|---|---:|
| Cash ......................................... | $ 240,000 |
| Accounts receivable ........................... | 400,000 |
| Inventory (at historical cost; FIFO; periodic) ........ | 600,000 |
| Furniture and fixtures (net) ...................... | 180,000 |
| Land (held for future store site) ................... | 100,000 |
| Total assets ................................ | $1,520,000 |

*Liabilities and Stockholders' Equity*

| | |
|---|---:|
| Accounts payable ............................. | $ 800,000 |
| Capital stock ($5 par, 200,000 shares authorized; 120,000 issued and outstanding) ............... | 600,000 |
| Retained earnings ............................ | 120,000 |
| Total liabilities and stockholders' equity ............ | $1,520,000 |

Retail Showcase Mart rents its showroom facilities on an operating lease basis at a cost of $3,000 per month. The rent would be $5,000 per month if it were based on the current cost of the facility. All sales and cash outlays for costs and expenses occur uniformly throughout the year.

The following information is indicative of the changing prices since Retail Showcase Mart began its operations.

1. The Consumer Price Index for All Urban Consumers for the following times is:

| | |
|---|---|
| December 31, 1980 | 200 |
| October 1, 1981 | 216 |
| December 31, 1981 | 220 |
| Average for 1981 | 212 |

2. The ending inventory was acquired on October 1, 1981.
3. Inventory at current cost on December 31, 1981, is $700,000.
4. Cost of goods sold at current cost as of date of sale is $875,000.
5. Current cost of the land on December 31, 1981, is $150,000.
6. There has been no change in the current cost of furniture and fixtures in 1981.
7. The sales and purchases occurred uniformly throughout 1981.
8. The "net recoverable amounts" for inventories and fixed assets have been determined by management to be in excess of the net current costs.

The accounting manager of Retail Showcase Mart has decided to comply voluntarily with the reporting requirements presented in the *Statement of Financial Accounting Standards No. 33*, "Financial Reporting and Changing Prices."

*Required:*

a. Calculate Retail Showcase Mart's purchasing power gain or loss for 1981 in terms of December 31, 1981, dollars. Round all computations to the nearest $100.
b. Prepare a constant dollar income statement for 1981 for Retail Showcase Mart in terms of December 31, 1981, dollars. Round all computations to the nearest $100.

   *c.* Prepare a current cost income statement for 1981 for Retail Showcase Mart.

   *d.* Prepare a schedule showing the historical cost, the constant dollar cost, and the current cost of inventory on December 31, 1981.

   *e.* Calculate the unrealized holding gain on inventory in 1981. How much of this is attributable to general price inflation?

**19–10.** Assume that the following president's letter appeared in an annual report to stockholders:

> I am pleased to report to you about the ways your company has voluntarily modified its accounting reports to reflect the environment of escalating prices. We have decided to show the impact of general price-level changes on our accounts. We made this change reluctantly, because it constitutes such a radical departure from all the principles that underlie the conventional financial statements. However, such disclosures clearly show the extent to which the company loses by holding current assets during inflation. Currently, regulatory authorities in accounting permit a company to disclose either general price changes or specific price changes. We have chosen the former because the prices of almost all of the goods and services we purchase have increased dramatically during the last few years. As soon as we are allowed, we intend to expand our disclosures to include current cost information.

List and describe all the misconceptions which are evidenced by the above quotation.

**19–11.** Presented below is a portion of the *Statement No. 33* disclosures which appeared in the 1981 annual reports of two airlines (amounts in thousands of dollars):

|  | *Delta* | *Piedmont* |
|---|---|---|
| Net income (loss): |  |  |
|  As reported in the primary statements | $146,474 | $32,585 |
|  Adjusted for general inflation | 44,147 | 22,277 |
|  Adjusted for change in specific prices | (15,462) | 16,919 |
| Net purchasing power gain (loss) | $ 46,910 | $17,652 |

*Required:*

   *a.* Are you surprised that both firms reported significantly worse performance when the net income figures were adjusted for general inflation and the change in specific prices? Can you hypothesize why Piedmont's earnings erosion was less severe than Delta's?

   *b.* What factors probably contributed to the net purchasing power gains reported by both companies? Are those gains real gains or merely paper gains? Were they included in the adjusted net income results? Why or why not?

   *c.* One friend of yours remarks that "both firms did equally well in 1981, since Delta had profits of $31,448,000 and Piedmont had profits of $34,571,000." A second friend rejects that comparison, claiming that "it's only the two firms' success at operating an airline that should be compared." How were the two above-profit numbers arrived at? Explain the comment of your second friend and indicate whether or not you agree with it. Did both firms do equally well in 1981?

*d.* Are the required *Statement No. 33* disclosures likely to change the viewpoint of a prospective stockholder concerning the relative attractiveness of each airline as a potential investment? If so, is the statement inconsistent with the desirable goals of unbiased and neutral accounting and reporting pronouncements? Explain.

**19–12.** The following are among the comments made by firms in their 1981 annual reports in conjunction with their reporting of a net purchasing power gain or loss:

> **Allegheny International, Inc.** "For purposes of this calculation, net monetary liabilities include the carrying values of Allegheny's redeemable preferred stocks which have mandatory redemption provisions. The purchasing power gain should not be viewed as providing funds for reinvestment or distribution to shareholders."

> **International Minerals & Chemical Corporation.** "Although that gain has not been included in the determination of either current cost or constant dollar net earnings, it should be considered in the evaluation of the effect of inflation on IMC."

> **Ogden Corporation.** "By holding a monetary asset, a theoretical holding loss results; conversely, by holding a monetary liability, a theoretical holding gain results in a period of inflation."

> **Engelhard Corporation.** "By requiring that these gains be shown separately, the FASB ignores the connection between the rise in normal interest rates during periods of inflation and the gains associated with the decline in purchasing power of amounts owed. The increase in nominal interest rates compensates creditors for the decline in purchasing power for amounts owed them, and, accordingly, that portion of the interest expense recorded on historical cost financial statements could be "matched" against the purchasing power gain from net amounts owed."

*Required:*

*a.* Comment on Allegheny's treatment of its redeemable preferred. Did such treatment increase or decrease its purchasing power gain?

*b.* Is Allegheny correct in asserting that a purchasing power gain "should not be viewed as providing funds for reinvestment or distribution to stockholders"? If not, why not? If so, is Ogden Corporation correct in labeling the purchasing power gains and losses as "theoretical"? Explain.

*c.* Should the purchasing power gain be included in the determination of adjusted net income as IMC seems to suggest? What does it tell the reader about the impact of inflation?

*d.* Briefly describe in your own words the "connection" and need for "matching" referred to by Engelhard Corporation. Does the firm have a point? Are the adjusted income numbers mandated by *Statement No. 33* inaccurate due to mismatching? Explain.

**19–13.** While waiting in line to tour the U.S. Mint, you decided to ask those around you to comment on the subject of accounting for changing prices. Among the comments you received were the following:

1. "The constant dollar approach is far superior to the current cost approach. After all, why go out of your way to violate the historical cost and realization concepts when you don't have to?"

2. "The current cost approach is far superior to the constant dollar approach. At least with the current cost approach, you don't run the risk of using grossly inappropriate indices and having continual, confusing changes in the reported figures for such items as sales revenue."

3. "I'm on vacation. Would love to comment, except that I left my mind at home."

4. "If given a choice between current cost and current cost/constant dollar, I'd take current cost/constant dollar. It gives you everything current cost does and then some. It furnishes the most possible insight into the way in which changing prices have affected the firm."

5. "There's really no need to discuss the subject anymore. *FASB Statement No. 33* has attacked the reporting problem head-on and has solved it."

*Required:*

*a.* Explain what the author of each statement probably had in mind when he or she made the statement.

*b.* Restricting your response to the first, second, and fourth comments received, indicate which viewpoint you most agree with and which viewpoint you least agree with.

*c.* Has *Statement No. 33* "attacked the reporting problem head-on and solved it"? Explain.

**19–14.** The Cwagmire Realty Company speculates on land prices. It buys parcels of undeveloped land and holds them for a number of years. It subsequently either sells the undeveloped land or develops it by putting in streets and clearing trees and sells individual lots to subdivision builders.

In 19x1 the company bought a piece of land for $100,000 when the general price index was 150. In 19x9 the value of the undeveloped land was $150,000, and the general price index stood at 180.

*Required:*

*a.* If the company pays taxes at a rate of 30 percent of conventional accounting income, how much would it have to sell the undeveloped land for in order to recover the original purchasing power invested?

*b.* In 19x9, Cwagmire spends $50,000 on developing the land and sells the lots for $217,000. How much of the $67,000 profit ($217,000 − $100,000 − $50,000) is an illusory gain from general price changes? How much is attributable to the actual development work (operating activity), and how much is the result of speculation (holding activity)?

**19–15.** Holiday Inns, Inc., included the following comparison in its 1982 annual report:

**Five-Year Comparison of Selected Supplementary Financial Data Adjusted for Effects of Changing Prices**

|  | 1982 | 1981 | 1980 | 1979 | 1978 Restated |
|---|---|---|---|---|---|
| Revenues ($000): |  |  |  |  |  |
| As reported | $1,425,298 | $1,351,775 | $1,156,615 | $ 834,576 | $ 780,819 |
| In 1982 dollars | 1,425,298 | 1,434,648 | 1,354,852 | 1,109,825 | 1,155,244 |
| Income from continuing operations ($000): |  |  |  |  |  |
| As reported | $97,219 | $98,706 | $69,892 | $61,687 | $50,676 |
| In 1982 dollars | 64,779 | 71,392 | 50,713 | 55,839 | 49,850 |
| At current cost in 1982 dollars | 51,082 | 60,133 | 37,991 | 42,935 | — |
| Income per common and common equivalent share-continuing: |  |  |  |  |  |
| As reported | $2.50 | $2.68 | $1.94 | $1.94 | $1.64 |
| In 1982 dollars | 1.65 | 2.00 | 1.48 | 1.76 | 1.62 |
| At current cost in 1982 dollars | 1.29 | 1.72 | 1.16 | 1.35 | — |
| In 1982 dollars, including gain from decline in purchasing power of net amounts owed | 2.18 | 2.93 | 2.81 | 2.54 | 2.41 |
| At current cost in 1982 dollars including gain from decline in purchasing power of net amounts owed | 1.82 | 2.64 | 2.48 | 2.13 | — |
| Net assets at year-end ($000): |  |  |  |  |  |
| As reported | $ 942,962 | $ 772,377 | $ 707,961 | $ 624,491 | $ 550,080 |
| In 1982 dollars | 1,392,029 | 1,265,658 | 1,232,576 | 1,160,806 | 1,118,347 |
| At current cost in 1982 dollars | 1,591,606 | 1,489,362 | 1,473,057 | 1,354,973 | — |
| Gain from decline in purchasing power of net amounts owed in 1982 dollars ($000) | $20,363 | $36,550 | $52,038 | $24,581 | $24,652 |
| Cash dividends declared per common share: |  |  |  |  |  |
| As reported | $.80 | $.74 | $.70 | $.66 | $.56 |
| In 1982 dollars | .80 | .79 | .82 | .88 | .83 |
| Market price per common share at year-end: |  |  |  |  |  |
| As reported | $36.63 | $28.00 | $26.75 | $18.25 | $16.38 |
| In 1982 dollars | 36.21 | 28.76 | 29.93 | 23.00 | 23.33 |
| Debt-to-invested-capital ratio (percent): |  |  |  |  |  |
| As reported | 29.6% | 40.3% | 39.4% | 26.8% | 27.9% |
| In 1982 dollars | 22.5 | 30.6 | 30.1 | 20.2 | 21.7 |
| At current cost in 1982 dollars | 20.4 | 27.4 | 26.7 | 17.9 | — |
| Average consumer price index | 289.1 | 272.4 | 246.8 | 217.4 | 195.4 |

*Required:*

a. Explain why the two amounts for revenues are identical for 1982 and not identical for all other years.

b. Most items in the chart have three amounts shown for each year. Explain why revenues, cash dividends, and share market price have only two amounts provided.

c. What effect do the price-change adjustments have on the five-year trend in revenues? Is that effect smaller or larger than the effect which the price-change adjustments have on the five-year trend in income from continuing operations? Are you surprised by this result? Explain.

*d.*  Compare and contrast the trend in the dividend payout ratio as reported and the trend(s) when price-change adjustments are made. Which trend best represents what has really occurred between 1978 and 1982?

*e.*  Compare and contrast the trend in the return on average stockholders' equity as reported and the trend(s) when price-change adjustments are made. Which trend best represents what has actually happened?

*f.*  Assume the president of the firm just called you and wants your help in deciding what the "true EPS" was for 1982? Would your answer be $2.50, $1.65, $1.29, $2.18, $1.82, or some other number. Explain, defending your answer.

*g.*  The debt-to-invested-capital ratio is significantly lower when price-change adjustments are made. Explain why that particular measure showed improvement when price changes were taken into consideration.

**19–16.**  Lisi Golden is the major stockholder of Commack Company. The business was founded on January 1, 1984, with a cash investment of $30,000. Comparative balance sheets prepared according to generally accepted accounting principles are shown below:

|  | December 31 | |
| --- | ---: | ---: |
|  | *1985* | *1984* |
| **Assets** | | |
| Cash | $14,500 | $12,000 |
| Accounts receivable | 22,000 | 11,000 |
| Inventory | 12,000 | 9,000 |
| Prepaid insurance | 1,000 | 2,000 |
| Prepaid rent | 2,000 | 4,000 |
| Equipment | 25,000 | 25,000 |
| Allowance for depreciation | (5,000) | (2,500) |
| Total assets | $71,500 | $60,500 |
| **Equities** | | |
| Accounts payable | $17,000 | $14,000 |
| Bonds payable | 10,000 | 10,000 |
| Common stock | 30,000 | 30,000 |
| Retained earnings | 14,500 | 6,500 |
| Total equities | $71,500 | $60,500 |

Ms. Golden would like the balance sheets recast in terms of exit values. You are provided with the following information:

1.  The historical cost valuations for cash and accounts payable are exactly equal to the exit-price valuations of those items.

2.  Accounts receivable can be sold to a finance company at 97 percent of face amount.

3.  Inventory quantities are 800 units and 600 units, respectively, on December 31, 1985, and 1984. The firm's selling price per unit was $23 during 1985 and $21 during 1984. Additional selling costs average 15 percent of selling price.

4.  Prepaid insurance represents a three-year policy purchased for $3,000 on January 1, 1984. If Commack Company cancels the policy, it would receive $1,400 at the end of the first year and zero at the end of the second year.

5.  Prepaid rent represents the unamortized cost of a $6,000 prepayment on a

three-year lease. The lease can be canceled upon 30 days' notice; however, Commack Company would receive only one half of the unamortized cost as a refund.

6. Equipment is being depreciated on a straight-line basis over a useful life of 10 years. One quarter of this equipment is so specialized that it is of little use to anyone else. Its resale value is only its $300 scrap value. The firm has calculated that the remainder of the equipment could be sold for $13,000 on December 31, 1984, and $10,700 on December 31, 1985.

7. The bonds can be retired by call at 104 percent of face amount. However, because of an increase in the general level of interest rates during 1985, the company estimates that it could repurchase the bonds on the open market for $9,400 on December 31, 1985.

*Required:*

a. Prepare comparative balance sheets as of December 31, 1985, and 1984, using exit-price valuation for both assets and liabilities.

b. Calculate the net income for 1984 and 1985 under the exit-price system. No dividends were paid in either year. How do these figures compare with the historical-cost net income numbers? Which set of numbers is more accurate? Which is of greater use to financial statement readers? Explain.

c. One of the criticisms of the exit-price system is that it anticipates the rewards of productive activity. Illustrate this criticism using data from Commack Company.

d. Ms. Golden is delighted with the recast balance sheets, because "we finally have some balance sheet numbers that will provide us with an accurate return on investment ratio. After all, isn't our investment at any point in time what we are forgoing by not selling the business"? Evaluate Ms. Golden's statement.

19–17. Lee V. Plant purchased a tract of land with standing timber on it at a cost of $800,000. The residual value of the land is negligible. The timber was estimated to contain one million board feet. The following statistics relate to operations during the first three years:

Board Feet

| Year | Beginning of Year | Yearly Growth | Amount Cut |
|------|-------------------|---------------|------------|
| 1 ......... | 1,000,000 | 40,000 | 100,000 |
| 2 ......... | 940,000 | 30,000 | 120,000 |
| 3 ......... | 850,000 | 25,000 | 150,000 |

Financial Data

| Sales of Cut Timber | Cash Operating Expenses | Value per Board Foot of Standing Timber |
|---------------------|-------------------------|------------------------------------------|
| $150,000 ....... | $40,000 | $0.80 |
| 192,000 ....... | 50,000 | 0.90 |
| 255,000 ....... | 60,000 | 1.00 |

Lee has suggested measuring income in two segments: (1) income from cutting—sales of cut timber minus (Cash operating expenses plus Current value of the standing timber cut), and (2) income from growth and appreciation (Current value of standing timber at end of year plus Current value of standing timber cut minus Current value of standing timber at the beginning of the year).

*Required:*

a. Prepare an income statement for each of the three years under Lee's proposed system.

b. Comment on the usefulness of this system of income measurement. What are its strengths and weaknesses?

c. Does this system employ input or output values? Explain.

# GLOSSARY

*Note:* The number in parentheses after each definition refers to the chapter in which the term is prominently discussed.

**Accelerated cost recovery system (ACRS):** Extremely accelerated method of depreciation which must be used for tax purposes for all tangible assets purchased after December 31, 1980. It normally would not be acceptable for financial reporting purposes. (9)

**Accelerated depreciation:** Depreciation methods which take proportionately more of the asset's cost to depreciation expense in the earlier years of the asset's life. (9)

**Account:** Summarizing device prepared for each asset, liability, owners' equity, revenue, and expense item. Collectively they constitute the firm's ledger and are used to accumulate and maintain current balances for all items. (3)

**Accounting:** The concepts and processes by which financial and economic data, primarily quantitative in nature, are gathered and summarized in reports that are useful in decision making. (1)

**Accounting cycle:** The established order in which the procedures in an accounting system are performed. (4)

**Accounting equation:** Refers to the equality of assets and equities, or the equality of assets and the sum of liabilities and owners' equity. (2)

**Accounting period concept:** Assumption that economic activity can be meaningfully divided into time periods which will facilitate the communication of relatively timely information. Also referred to as periodicity concept. (1)

**Accounting Principles Board (APB):** Organization created by the AICPA in 1960 to issue authoritative opinions and to publish research studies. Dissolved in 1973 upon the establishment of the FASB. (1)

**Accounting Series Releases (ASRs):** Policy statements issued by the SEC in which the Commission articulates standards for the reporting of financial information in SEC reports and firms' annual reports to stockholders. (1)

**Accrual accounting:** Basis of accounting which recognizes revenues when they are earned and recognizes expenses when they are incurred in earning revenue. The timing of the cash receipts and cash payments does not control the recording of revenues and expenses. (4)

**Accrued actuarial liability:** Another term used to refer to pension past service costs. (12)

**Accrued liability:** Liability which grows progressively in amount until a payment date is reached, at which time the debt is liquidated. Wages Payable is an example. (2)

**Accumulated depreciation:** Contra asset account which reflects the total depreciation expense which has been taken on a plant asset since its date of acquisition. Also referred to as allowance for depreciation. (4)

**Acquisition cost:** All reasonable and necessary costs of acquiring an asset, getting it to the place of business, and rendering it available and ready for the intended use. (7)

**Activity method:** Depreciation method whereby the cost of the plant asset is first related directly to some unit of asset service and then to periods of time. Depreciation expense will only be constant from period to period if the asset's use is constant from period to period. Also referred to as units of production method. (9)

**Actuarial assumptions:** The assumptions that actuaries tentatively make about future uncertainties affecting the pension cost. Examples include estimates of employee turnover and the interest rate earned on pension fund assets. (12)

**Actuarial cost methods:** Alternative techniques used by actuaries for establishing the amount and incidence of the annual actuarial cost of pension plan benefits and the related actuarial liability. (12)

**Actuarial gains and losses:** Gains and losses which occur when the actuarial assumptions underlying the pension calculations are modified to meet changing conditions or when actual experience differs from the original expectations. (12)

**Adjunct account:** An account whose balance is on the same side (debit or credit) as that of another related account to which it is added. Premium on Bonds Payable is an example. (10)

**Adjusting entries:** Those entries made at the end of the accounting period to record internal events that have taken place but have not yet been recorded and to revise entries that were made incorrectly. (4)

**Aging the receivables:** The process of classifying accounts receivable balances according to the length of time they have been outstanding. Then, a different estimated uncollectible percentage is applied to each age group. (6)

**All financial resources concept:** Broad interpretation required for the preparation of the statement of changes in financial position whereby all significant financing and investment activities are included even if they did not affect the balance of cash or working capital. The issuance of stock for the acquisition of land is one such event which this concept would require to be reflected. (17)

**All-inclusive income statement:** Income statement which reflects all transactions and events, normal or unusual, affecting stockholders' equity during the period—except, of course, transactions in capital stock and dividends. (5)

**Allowance for doubtful accounts:** A contra to the Accounts Receivable account. Credited in adjusting entry for bad debts and measures firm's estimate of amount of receivables which will probably prove to be uncollectible. (6)

**Amortization:** The process of rationally and systematically allocating the cost of intangible assets over their useful service lives. (9)

**Annuity:** A series of equal amounts due in each of a number of future periods. If the amounts are exchanged at the end of each period, it is referred to as an ordinary annuity. Examples include payments for lease obligations and the interest on bonds. (10)

**Annuity due:** A series of equal payments/receipts occurring at the beginning of each period. (10)

**Appropriations of retained earnings:** Establishment of separate accounts as a segregation of retained earnings in order to inform the reader that a portion of retained earnings is not available for dividends. (14)

**Assets:** Probable future economic benefits obtained or controlled by a particular entity as a result of past transactions or events. Assets consist of economic resources which arise in a transaction, can be measurable in monetary terms, and hold future economic benefit. (2)

**Auditing:** The function of verifying and appraising the accuracy, integrity, and authenticity of the financial statements. (1)

**Auditors' report (opinion):** Report in which the company's independent certified public accountant expresses professional judgment concerning the financial statements. It accompanies the financial statements in a firm's annual report. (16)

**Balance sheet:** Financial statement which presents the financial condition of the entity (assets, liabilities, and owners' equity) as of a moment in time. Also referred to as statement of financial position. (1)

**Book value:** The excess of the original cost of the asset over the balance in the Accumulated Depreciation account. (9)

**Book value per share:** Total stockholders' equity (or net assets) divided by number of shares of common stock outstanding. (18)

**Bookkeeping:** The system for recording and classifying accounting data. (1)

**Call provision:** Provision in bond agreement which specifies that bonds can be redeemed by the issuer at certain set prices during their life. Many call provisions do not become operative until the bonds have been outstanding for a period such as five years. (10)

**Capital expenditures:** Expenditures which increase the quantity or quality of service provided by an asset. They are treated as assets since they benefit future periods. Examples include a major engine overhaul and an addition to an asset. (9)

**Capital lease:** Leasing transaction whose economic substance suggests that the lessee is, in effect, acquiring the property being leased under a long-term installment contract. Leases meeting at least one of four specified criteria are considered to be capital leases from the lessee's perspective and are reflected on its books as an asset and a related obligation. (11)

**Capitalization of interest:** Practice of charging some of the period's interest cost to an asset account. The interest cost will be taken to expense over future periods as the completed, financed asset is used in the business. (7)

**Cash flow:** Normally calculated as the sum of net income, depreciation, amortization, and income taxes deferred during the year. Excludes the effects of many nonoperational uses and sources of cash and does not even represent total cash provided by operations. (17)

**Cash flow to long-term debt:** A widely used measure of financial strength. Calculated by dividing cash flow by the long-term debt. (18)

**Change in accounting estimates:** Changes which are implemented to adjust the accounting records in light of new information concerning the adequacy of previous estimates. They are not considered changes in accounting principles or corrections of errors. Examples include a change in either the estimated useful life of a machine or the anticipated bad debt losses from credit sales. (16)

**Change in accounting principles:** Changes initiated by firms such as switches from FIFO to LIFO and from straight-line to sum-of-the-years' digits depreciation. Firms must disclose the changes and justify the switch. (16)

**Chart of accounts:** A list which identifies the accounts required by a particular company as the components of its ledger. (4)

**Closing entries:** Necessary entries prepared at the end of the accounting period to clear the revenue and expense accounts to zero and to transfer the net income or net loss for the period to the Retained Earnings account. (4)

**Commercial paper:** All unsecured promissory notes issued by well-established corporations to meet their short-term seasonal borrowing requirements. These notes usually are issued in specific denominations arranged to suit the buyer with maturities ranging from a few days to nine months. (10)

**Common-size statements:** Financial statements resulting from vertical analysis, where all items are expressed in percentages rather than dollar amounts. (18)

**Common stock:** All capital stock which is not preferred stock. (14)

**Common stock equivalent:** Securities which have many of the characteristics of common stock but have not yet become common stock; important in EPS calculations. (16)

**Comparability:** Qualitative guideline which calls for like events to be reported in the same manner and unlike events to be reported differently; facilitates analysis among firms and between accounting periods. (1)

**Completed production method:** Revenue recognition procedure (point) permitted when a ready market exists to absorb all completed production at a quoted price. Examples include the extraction of precious metals or the harvesting of grains. (6)

**Completeness:** Quality which suggests that financial accounting information should be fully disclosed; one of the three conditions which contribute to the existence of reliability. (1)

**Complex financial structure:** A financial structure which contains convertible securities, stock options, or stock purchase warrants. Its existence requires the calculation of primary and fully diluted earnings per share. (16)

**Compound interest:** Phenomenon whereby interest earned on an investment is not withdrawn but rather remains invested and earns interest itself. (10)

**Comprehensive income:** The change in equity (net assets) of an entity during a period from transactions and other events and circumstances except those resulting from investments by owners and distributions to owners. (5)

**Comprehensive tax allocation:** Procedure for interperiod income tax allocation whereby all timing differences must be accounted for, even if they will be continually perpetuated in the aggregate. It can result in a balance for Deferred Income Taxes which will either never decrease or never stop increasing. (13)

**Conservatism:** When a decision requires judgment, accountants tend to select those procedures which result in smaller measures of assets or income. The consequences of overstating these items are more risky than those associated with an understatement. (1)

**Consistency:** Qualitative guideline which calls for accounting practices not to be changed unless a change would facilitate more accurate or correct reporting; an essential ingredient of comparability over time within a single firm. (1)

**Consolidated financial statements:** Financial statements which treat a legally separate parent company and its subsidiary companies as if they were a single company. (15)

**Constant dollar accounting:** Asset valuation and income determination procedure which recognizes changes in the general level of prices and the net purchasing power gain or loss incurred from the holding of monetary items. Many large firms are required to present limited constant dollar data in a supplementary format. (19)

**Contingent liabilities:** Potential liabilities whose existence is solely dependent upon future events. They do not presently appear on the balance sheet but are referred to in the footnotes to the financial statements. An example would be the guarantee of another's debts. (2)

**Contra account:** An account whose balance is on the opposite side of another related account from which it is subtracted. Examples include Accumulated Depreciation and Discount on Bonds Payable. (4)

**Contributed capital:** The portion of stockholders' equity which arises from the contribution of capital by stockholders. (14)

**Control account:** A general ledger account for which detailed information is maintained in a subsidiary ledger. Examples are accounts receivable and accounts payable. (4)

**Convertible bonds:** Bonds which contain a provision allowing them to be exchanged for capital stock at the holder's option. (10)

**Cost method of accounting for investment in stock:** Procedure used to account for an investment of less than 20 percent of the stock of another corporation. The acquiring firm maintains the Investment account on its books at acquisition cost and only reports income from its investment when dividends are received. (15)

**Coverage of total fixed charges:** A measure of the firm's ability to meet its interest obligations and the normally declared preferred dividends. Calculated by dividing income before interest and taxes by the sum of interest expense and normally declared preferred dividends. (18)

**Credit:** Right side of ledger account and right-hand amount column in a journal. Credits occur (amounts are entered on the right side) whenever assets decrease and liabilities and owners' equity increase. (3)

**Current assets:** Cash and other resources which will be converted into cash or used in the normal operations of the business within a relatively short period of time (usually one year). Examples include accounts receivable and merchandise inventory. (2)

**Current cost accounting:** Asset valuation and income determination procedure which recognizes changes in the specific level of prices and the gains and losses incurred from the holding of certain assets. Many large firms are required to present limited current cost data in a supplementary format. (19)

**Current liabilities:** Obligations that will be paid within one year (or within the operating cycle when that is longer). Examples include accounts payable and taxes payable. (2)

**Current operating performance income statement:** Income statement which reflects only those changes in retained earnings (other than dividends) which have arisen from normal, recurring operating activities. (5)

**Current ratio:** A widely used measure of liquidity; equal to current assets divided by current liabilities. (18)

**Debit:** Left side of ledger account and left-hand amount column in journal. Debits occur (amounts are entered on the left side) whenever assets increase and liabilities and owners' equity decrease. (3)

**Debt-equity ratio:** A widely used measure of financial strength. Calculated by dividing long-term debt by total equities. (18)

**Declining-balance depreciation:** An accelerated depreciation procedure whereby a constant percentage (150 percent or 200 percent) of the straight-line depreciation rate is applied to the decreasing book value of the asset in order to calculate depreciation expense in successive years. (9)

**Deferral method for investment tax credit:** Procedure for accounting for the investment credit that views the credit as a factor which should increase the net income of each year that the asset qualifying for the credit is used by a pro rata amount. Income is increased by reducing either depreciation expense or income tax expense. (13)

**Deferred income taxes:** An account which arises and is adjusted whenever the income tax expense reported on the income statement differs from the income tax payable in the current period because of timing differences. (13)

**Deferred method of tax allocation:** Method of interperiod tax allocation whereby the tax effects of current timing differences are deferred currently and allocated to income tax expense of future periods when the timing differences reverse. It emphasizes the tax effects of timing differences on income of the period in which the differences originate. (13)

**Deficit:** Term used to describe a debit balance in the Retained Earnings account. (3)

**Defined-benefit plans:** Pension plans which establish a specific schedule of pension benefits. The employer must contribute amounts sufficient to provide these benefits. (12)

**Defined-contribution plans:** Pension plans which limit the employer's payments to a fixed sum. No specific pension benefits are promised except what the pension fund contributions will provide. (12)

**Depletion:** The process of rationally and systematically allocating the cost of natural resources (wasting assets) over their useful service lives. (9)

**Depreciation:** The process of rationally and systematically allocating the cost of plant assets over their useful service lives. (9)

**Depreciation base:** The asset cost to be allocated to the various periods in which the asset provides service. In most cases, it is equal to the acquisition cost minus the net residual value. (9)

**Direct-financing lease:** Leases meeting certain criteria from the lessor's perspective without creating a manufacturer's or a dealer's profit. Lessor removes leased item from its books and reports interest revenue over the term of the lease purchase which it is financing. (11)

**Direct write-off method:** Procedure whereby an expense for bad debts is recorded only when specific uncollectible accounts are identified. No Allowance for Doubtful Accounts is established. Results in less accurate and perhaps less objective financial statements. (6)

**Disbursement:** The payment of money. (3)

**Discontinued operations:** The sale or abandonment of a significant component of the business. A separate income statement section is created to report (*a*) the periodic income or loss from operating the component until it was discontinued and (*b*) the gain or loss on its disposal. (16)

**Discount notes:** Notes which do not bear interest explicitly. Nonetheless, the interest factor does exist and must be calculated. (10)

**Discount on bonds:** Excess of face or maturity amount of a bond over its issue price. Occurs when the market rate of interest demanded by investors exceeds the nominal rate of interest offered by the corporation. Accounted for as an addition to the interest expense over the life of the bond. (10)

**Discounted cash flows:** The present value of the net future cash inflows. (19)

**Discretionary expenses:** Those period costs which management can significantly modify in amount from period to period. Examples include research and development and advertising. (18)

**Dividend payout ratio:** Measures the proportion of earnings distributed as cash dividends; calculated by dividing cash dividends to common stockholders by the net income available to common stockholders (after preferred dividends). (18)

**Dividends:** A pro rata distribution of assets by a corporation to its stockholders. Usually they are in the form of cash and represent a distribution of a portion of the firm's earnings. (5)

**Double-entry bookkeeping:** Method of recording in which every transaction has at least two aspects—a debit and a credit. (3)

**Earning criterion:** Criterion which asserts that revenue should not be recognized until it has been earned. In conjunction with measurability criterion, influences the recognition of revenue. (6)

**Earnings per share (EPS):** The earnings available for common stockholders divided by the number of shares outstanding. In more complex situations, very complicated calculations are made for primary and fully diluted earnings per share. (16)

**Effective interest bond amortization:** Interest-recording procedure which charges each period with an amount of interest directly related to the market rate and the actual amount of money being used. The interest expense varies in each period of the bond's life, but the yield rate is constant. Also referred to as compound-interest or scientific amortization. (10)

**Entity concept:** Assumption which states that accounting reports and records pertain to a specifically defined business entity, separate and distinct from the people or groups concerned with it. (1)

**Equities:** Representing the source of assets, they measure the financial investment in or claim on the business by creditors (liabilities) and owners (owners' equity). (2)

**Equity method of accounting for investment in stock:** Procedure used to account for an investment of between 20 to 50 percent of the stock of another corporation. The acquiring firm increases the Investment account for its share of the other firm's income and reduces it for its share of any dividends from that company. It reports income in relation to earnings reported, regardless of the extent to which earnings were distributed as dividends. (15)

**ERISA (Employee Retirement Income Security Act):** Act passed by Congress in 1974. Affects funding, vesting procedures, and various other aspects of an employer's pension plan. (12)

**Exchange price (cost) concept:** Establishes the valuation measures to be applied as data enters the accounting process. The assets held by a firm and its liabilities are recorded at the prices (values) agreed upon or inherent in the exchanges in which they originated. Results in most assets being reported on the financial statement items at their historical cost. (1)

**Executory contracts:** Contracts which are traditionally not reflected in the formal accounting records as they depend on equal future performance from both parties to the contract. Examples are long-term employment contracts and purchase commitments. (11)

**Exit values:** The market prices at which a firm can sell its assets in an orderly liquidation. (19)

**Expenditure:** A monetary sacrifice to acquire a productive resource. Does not become an expense until the productive resource is consumed in the generation of revenues. (3)

**Expenses:** The consumption of assets or creation of liabilities in the generation of revenues. (3)

**Extraordinary items:** Material events which are characterized by both their unusual nature and their infrequent occurrence. Such items are shown in a separate section of the income statement as a distinct element of net income for the period. Examples include major casualties and government expropriations. (16)

**FIFO (first-in, first-out):** Inventory costing procedure which assumes that the ending inventory consists of those goods which were most recently purchased. During a period of rising prices, it produces higher income than LIFO and a relatively current balance-sheet amount for ending inventory. (8)

**Financial accounting:** Accounting activity whose primary concern is the provision of information to investors and other groups not directly involved in operating the business or empowered to dictate the presentation and content of the reports prepared for them. (1)

**Financial Accounting Standards Board (FASB):** The authoritative force, since 1973, in the private sector for the setting of standards for financial accounting reports. (1)

**Financial flexibility:** The ability of an enterprise to take effective actions to alter the amounts and timing of cash flows so that it can respond to unexpected needs and opportunities. (18)

**Financial leverage:** The modification of the rate of return on common stockholders' equity from what it otherwise would be through the use of debt and/or preferred stock to finance the acquisition of part of the assets. (18)

**Financial strength (solvency):** Measure of firm's ability to meet its long-term obligations. (18)

**Finished goods:** Inventory of merchandise for which the manufacturing process is completed. Merchandise is awaiting sale to customers. (7)

**Fiscal year:** Another term for natural business year. (2)

**Fixed expenses:** Expenses which are incurred in approximately the same total amount regardless of the level or volume of operations in the period (as long as it remains within the relevant range). Examples include depreciation charges and many salaries. (18)

**Flow-through method:** Procedure for accounting for the investment credit which views the credit as a selective reduction in taxes of the year in which the credit arises. This is the procedure followed by most firms. (13)

**Foreign currency transaction gains and losses:** Gains and losses which result from explicit transactions denominated in a foreign currency. The value of the foreign currency, vis-à-vis the dollar, has changed between the initial recording and the eventual settlement of a business event. Such gains and losses appear on the income statement in the year in which they occurred. (16)

**Foreign currency translation adjustments:** Adjustments arising when the accounts on the books of a foreign branch or subsidiary are translated at current year-end exchange rates, which differ from the exchange rates in effect when the items arose. Such gains and losses no longer appear on the income statement. Instead, they appear as a contra or adjunct stockholders' equity item. (16)

**Form 10-K:** Annual report which firms under SEC jurisdiction must file with the Commission; includes a complete set of financial statements audited and prepared in accordance with guidelines set forth by the SEC in its Regulation S-X. (1)

**Full costing:** Procedure whereby all expenditures for exploration and drilling, whether associated with productive or unproductive ventures, are treated as necessary asset costs. (7)

**Fully diluted earnings per share:** A measurement of the maximum dilution in earnings per share that could take place if all contingent issues of common stock that could reduce earnings per share actually do take place; a more conservative and hypothetical number than primary earnings per share. Examples of such contingencies include the conversion of bonds and the exercise of stock options. (16)

**Funds statement:** Former name of financial statement now known as statement of changes in financial position. (17)

**Future value:** The future sum of money which is the equivalent of a smaller present amount. (10)

**Gains:** Events favorable from the stockholders' perspective and not connected with the main earning activities of the firm. Examples include the excess of selling price over acquisition cost of noncurrent assets or the advantageous settlement of liabilities. (5)

**General price changes:** Changes in the overall level of prices for goods and services in the economy; caused by general inflation rather than shifts in the supply/demand relationship for particular goods or services. Such price changes are the focus of the constant dollar supplementary disclosures. (19)

**Generally accepted accounting principles (GAAP):** Elements in the framework on which financial accounting rests. GAAP consist of concepts and conventions that act as general guides in the identifying, measuring, classifying, and reporting processes. (1)

**Going-concern concept:** In the absence of evidence to the contrary, the entity is assumed to remain in operation sufficiently long to carry out its objectives and plans. Also referred to as continuity concept. (1)

**Goodwill:** Excess of the total purchase price over the sum of the separate market values of the tangible assets and the specifically identified intangible assets acquired in a business transaction; a general intangible which represents the cost of the unidentified intangible assets. (9)

**Gross margin (profit):** The excess of sales revenue over the cost of goods sold. (5)

**Group depreciation:** Depreciation procedure whereby the individual costs of all units in a group are combined and treated as a single asset. There is only one Accumulated Depreciation account and one depreciation rate based on the average expected life. No loss is recognized on the retirement of individual units. (9)

**Holding gains and losses:** The value increase or decrease attributable to the holding of asset inputs during a time of specific price change. Such holding activities are separated from operating activities under a full-fledged, current cost (replacement cost) reporting system. (19)

**Horizontal analysis:** Analysis which employs percentages to show how individual financial statement items have changed from year to year. A percentage increase or decrease from the prior year is calculated for each component on the current income and position statements. (18)

**Imputed interest:** Interest rate inferred when the evidence suggests that the stated interest rate on a note does not represent the effective rate. (10)

**Income statement:** Financial statement which summarizes the major changes in the resources of the business as a result of the operating or earning activities (revenues, expenses, gains, and losses). (1)

**Installment method:** Revenue recognition procedure (point) whereby revenue is recognized later than the sale and then only in proportion to the cash received each period. It is widely used for tax purposes but cannot be used for financial reporting except where enormous uncertainty exists concerning amount and probability of payment. (6)

**Intangible assets:** Nonphysical rights and privileges. Examples include patents and copyrights. (9)

**Interest coverage:** A measure of the firm's ability to meet its interest obligations; calculated by dividing income before interest and taxes by interest expense. (18)

**Interest equivalent:** Element which will increase or decrease pension expense whenever the amount funded differs from the originally computed expense amount. Necessary to compensate for the pension fund earning less or more than was originally contemplated due to under- or over-funding. (12)

**Interim financial reports:** Accounting reports prepared for periods shorter than a year, usually every three months. They contain some meaningful income statement data, but very little balance sheet and funds statement information. Even the income statement disclosures are nowhere near as complete as those contained in the annual financial statements. (16)

**Internal control:** The procedures and techniques used to safeguard assets, to promote operational efficiency and compliance with prescribed policy, and to achieve accurate reporting of information. (4)

**Interperiod tax allocation:** Procedure to relate the income tax expense reported on the income statement to the income reported there, even if a different amount of taxes is currently payable. The taxes not currently payable are assumed to be only temporarily deferred and payable in another accounting period. (13)

**Intraperiod tax allocation:** The allocation of the total tax expense of a given period among the various sections of the income statement, with a portion perhaps going directly to the retained earnings statement. (13)

**Inventoriable cost:** All costs necessary for acquiring inventory and placing it for sale. Examples include net invoice price, freight charges into the firm, and handling costs incurred in unloading and storage. (7)

**Inventory formula:** Beginning inventory plus net purchases equals cost of goods available for sale. Cost of goods available for sale less ending inventory equals cost of goods sold. (8)

**Inventory profits:** The realized inventory holding gains; calculated by subtracting cost of goods sold at historical cost (using FIFO, LIFO, or weighted average) from cost of goods sold at replacement cost. (8)

**Inventory turnover:** A measure of how fast inventory on hand normally is sold and converted into accounts receivable; calculated by dividing cost of goods sold by the average inventory balance. (18)

**Investee corporation:** The corporation whose shares are owned by another corporation (the investor). (15)

**Investment efficiency:** Concerns the degree of asset utilization and relates the size of various asset investments to the volume of activity. Inventory and receivables turnovers are examples of such investment efficiency measures. (18)

**Investment tax credit:** A credit allowed against income taxes to encourage investment in machinery and equipment. (13)

**Investor corporation:** The owner of the shares of stock of another corporation (the investee). (15)

**Journal:** Recording medium which facilitates a separate record of each event so that a chronological history of the transactions that affected the business is preserved. (3)

**Lease:** An agreement conveying the right to use property from its legal owner (the lessor) to a second party (the lessee) in exchange for a periodic cash payment (rent). (11)

**Ledger:** Recording medium which facilitates the accumulation of the effects of various transactions on individual asset, liability, owners' equity, revenue, and expense items. (3)

**Legal (stated) capital:** The minimum amount of originally invested capital which state laws specify may not be reduced by voluntary action of the board of directors. Because it is not available for dividends, it serves as a buffer to better protect the claims of creditors. (14)

**Lessee:** Party which receives the right to use the leased property from the lessor in the lease transaction. (11)

**Lessor:** Party which grants the right to use the leased property to the lessee in the lease transaction. (11)

**Liabilities:** The debts and other amounts owed by the business to its creditors; one of the two major sources of assets and, accordingly, categories of equities. (2)

**Liability method of tax allocation:** Method of interperiod tax allocation whereby the deferred taxes are considered to be a liability or asset rather than a deferred credit or charge. The account balance would be adjusted in the future if tax rates changed prior to the reversal of timing differences. It is not presently permitted under GAAP. (13)

**LIFO (last-in, first-out):** Inventory costing procedure which assumes that the ending inventory consists of those goods which were purchased first. During a period of rising prices, LIFO produces the lowest income and income taxes and an unrealistically low balance-sheet amount for ending inventory. It may be used even if actual physical flow is not last-in, first-out, and it must be used for financial reporting if it is used for tax purposes. (8)

**LIFO reserve:** A contra asset account which measures the excess amount of a firm's inventory valued at either FIFO or some approximation of replacement cost over its LIFO cost. (8)

**Liquidating dividend:** Dividends which are not paid out of retained earnings and, accordingly, represent a return of contributed capital. (14)

**Liquidity:** Measure of firm's ability to meet its short-term financial obligations. (18)

**Losses:** Events unfavorable from the stockholders' perspective and not connected with the main earning activities of the firm. Examples include the excess of acquisition cost over selling price of noncurrent assets or cost of inventory destroyed in a fire. (5)

**Lower of cost or market:** Procedure whereby inventories or marketable equity securities are assigned either a historical cost amount or a current market valuation, whichever is lower. (8)

**Managerial accounting:** Accounting activity whose primary concern is the provision of information to management; consists of the additional procedures and techniques for supplying detailed operating data and projections. (1)

**Manufacturing overhead:** All manufacturing costs except raw materials and direct labor. (7)

**Market bond interest rate:** The interest rate actually incurred by the corporation issuing the bonds. A function of the supply and demand for loanable funds of a given risk. It will differ from the nominal rate of interest in many cases, giving rise to bond discounts or premiums. Also referred to as the effective or yield interest rate. (10)

**Marketable equity securities:** Marketable securities which are to be reported in the balance sheet at the lower of acquisition cost or current-market value. (7)

**Matching concept:** The central operational assumption of financial accounting—net income is best measured by a matching (deduction) of costs against (from) the revenues to which the costs have given rise. (1)

**Materiality:** Refers to the relative importance or magnitude of a piece of accounting information; any amount or transaction that has a significant (material) effect on the financial statements should be recorded correctly and reported. (1)

**Maturity value:** The specified sum which the corporation must pay to the bondholder or noteholder at the maturity date. (10)

**Maximum pension provision:** The maximum amount of pension expense which a firm can report. It is calculated as the sum of (*a*) normal cost, (*b*) 10 percent of past service cost until fully

provided for, and (*c*) interest equivalents on any difference between amounts charged to expense and amounts funded. (12)

**Measurability criterion:** Criterion which asserts that revenue should not be recognized until it can be measured with a reasonable degree of reliability. In conjunction with earnings criterion, it influences the recognition of revenue. (6)

**Minimum pension provision:** The minimum amount of pension expense which a firm can report. It is calculated as the sum of (*a*) normal cost, (*b*) interest on any unfunded past service cost, and (*c*) a provision to accrue the present value of vested benefits. (12)

**Minority interest:** The portion of the subsidiary company which is not owned by the parent company. It often appears on the consolidated balance sheet as a separate category between liabilities and stockholders' equity. (15)

**Monetary concept:** Assumption containing two basic ideas about the unit of measurement used in accounting. First, because money is the common denominator for the expression of economic activity, it should be used to measure and analyze accounting events and transactions. Second, fluctuations in the value of the dollar can be ignored without significant impairment of the usefulness or validity of the financial statements. (1)

**Monetary items:** Assets and liabilities which are presently cash or represent future sources or uses of a fixed number of dollars, without regard to their purchasing power. Examples include accounts receivable and accounts payable. (19)

**Natural business year:** Accounting period which ends during some month other than December. (2)

**Net assets:** Excess of assets over liabilities; equal to owners' equity. (2)

**Net price:** The price calculated by deducting the discount offered for prompt payment from the invoice price. (7)

**Net purchasing power gain or loss:** Gain or loss resulting from the holding of monetary assets and monetary liabilities during a period of general price-level changes. A net gain results if more monetary liabilities were held than monetary assets during a period of rising prices. (19)

**Net realizable value:** Selling price reduced by the anticipated costs of completing and selling the item. (8)

**Nominal bond interest rate:** The interest rate actually stated in the bond contract; multiplied by the bond's maturity amount to determine the cash interest paid each year. Also referred to as the stated or contractual interest rate. (10)

**Nonfund expenses:** Expenses which do not involve a current outlay or a decrease in funds. An example would be depreciation expense, which has no effect on funds defined as either cash or working capital. (17)

**Nonfund transactions:** Transactions which do not affect the balance of funds and, therefore, are appropriately excluded from the statement of changes in financial position. Examples include a stock dividend and an appropriation of retained earnings. (17)

**Normal cost:** The present value of expected future payments to employees attributable to work performed during each year after the date of adoption of the pension plan. (12)

**Operating cycle:** The time needed by the business to acquire the product or service, sell it, and collect the receivables. (2)

**Operating efficiency:** Concerns asset consumption in the generation of revenue. The operating ratio and profit margins are among the factors calculated and examined. (18)

**Operating expenditures:** Expenditures which simply keep the asset in good working condition but in no better condition than when it was purchased; are expensed immediately as they are deemed to benefit only the current accounting period. Examples include lubrication and other routine maintenance procedures. (9)

**Operating lease:** A residual category. It covers all leases from lessee's perspective that are not capital leases and all leases from lessor's perspective that are not sales-type or direct-financing leases. The depreciable leased item remains on the lessor's books, and only the periodic rental payments are reflected by the lessee. (11)

**Operating leverage:** A measure of the impact on operating profits caused by changes in volume of activity. It is greatly influenced by the proportion of fixed vis-à-vis variable expenses present in the firm. (18)

**Operating ratio:** The ratio between recurring operating expenses and operating revenues (commonly only sales). It measures the proportion of resources inflows from sales that is consumed by normal operating activities. (18)

**Owners' equity:** The residual interest in the assets of an entity that remains after deducting its liabilities. It is one of the two major sources of assets and, accordingly, categories of equities. Referred to as stockholders' equity in a corporation. (2)

**Par value:** An arbitrary amount printed on each stock certificate and assigned to each share. In many states, it represents the legal or stated capital per share. The par value of shares issued is credited to the stock account directly. (14)

**Parent company:** A company which owns more than half of the voting stock in another corporation referred to as a subsidiary. (15)

**Partial tax allocation:** Procedure for interperiod income tax allocation whereby only those timing differences which will not be continually perpetuated in the aggregate are recognized on the books. (13)

**Past service costs:** The present value of expected future payments to employees attributable to the credit they have received for work performed prior to the adoption of the pension plan. (12)

**Percentage of completion method:** Revenue recognition procedure (point) used for individual projects involving substantial amounts of revenue and considerable periods of time from inception of the project to its completion. Revenue is recorded as work progresses in proportion to the percentage of estimated total costs incurred. The method is useful for such businesses as airplane manufacture and highway construction. (6)

**Period costs:** Expenses that cannot be traced directly to units of product and, accordingly, are expensed in the period in which they are incurred. Examples include rent expense and the president's salary. (5)

**Periodic inventory system:** Cost of goods sold is recorded only at the end of the accounting period in the form of an adjusting entry removing the cost of goods sold from the inventory account. (8)

**Permanent differences:** Differences between taxable income and accounting income created by certain items of revenue and expense, which enter into either taxable or accounting income without ever affecting the computation of the other. (13)

**Perpetual inventory system:** Cost of goods sold is recorded each time the inventory is decreased through sale or use. (8)

**Pooling of interests approach:** Procedures used to account for business combinations where the parent company issues its own voting stock in exchange for substantially all the voting stock of the subsidiary. All the subsidiary's asset accounts are carried over at book value, and no goodwill is recognized. The retained earnings of both firms are combined. (15)

**Posting:** Transcribing the component parts of the journal entries to the individual ledger accounts. (3)

**Preferred dividends in arrears:** Dividends which have been skipped in past periods on cumulative preferred stock. They do not represent a liability of the corporation but must be paid along with current preferred dividends before any common dividends can be declared. They are usually disclosed in a footnote. (14)

**Preferred stock:** A special type of ownership interest with certain modifications of the basic rights inherent in common stock. It usually has a preference over common stock in the payment of dividends and usually has a prior claim on assets in the event of liquidation. (14)

**Premium on bonds:** Excess of issue price of a bond over its face or maturity amount; occurs when the nominal rate of interest offered by the corporation exceeds the market rate of interest demanded by investors. It is accounted for as a reduction in interest expense over the life of the bond. (10)

**Present value concept:** The current cash equivalent of some designated future amount or amounts. It is based on the observation that a smaller amount today is the equivalent of a larger amount in the future, because today's amount can be invested and earn compounded interest. (10)

**Price-earnings ratio:** A measure relating earnings per share to the current market price of the stock. (18)

**Primary earnings per share:** The net income available to common stock (perhaps adjusted) divided by the sum of the average common shares outstanding and the number of common stock equivalent shares. (16)

**Prior period adjustments:** Very rare events and corrections of errors that require direct adjustment to retained earnings and retroactive restatement of net income. (16)

**Prior service costs:** The portion of the revised total pension cost that the actuarial cost method identifies with periods prior to the date of amendment of the pension plan; very similar to past service costs except that prior service costs arise upon the amendment, rather than the adoption, of the plan. (12)

**Product costs:** Costs which can be traced directly to units of product. Examples include the direct purchase price of merchandise and such indirect items as freight charges. (5)

**Profit margin:** One component of return on assets (investment). Calculated by dividing net income plus tax-adjusted interest by sales revenue. (18)

**Proportional performance method:** The service counterpart to percentage of completion for revenue recognition. Total revenue is apportioned and recognized in relation to some measure of performance (e.g., magazines provided under the terms of a subscription). (6)

**Purchase approach:** Procedure used to account for all business combinations where it is not possible to use the pooling of interests approach. Usually at least some cash is exchanged for the subsidiary's shares. The balance sheet items of the subsidiary are revalued, and goodwill is usually recognized. (15)

**Qualified opinions:** Issued by the auditor whenever the scope of the examination has been limited or some other factor has prevented the issuance of an unqualified opinion (e.g., a switch in accounting methods). (16)

**Quick (acid-test) ratio:** A widely used measure of liquidity. It has the same denominator as the current ratio, current liabilities, but uses only monetary assets rather than all current assets in the numerator. The major current assets excluded from the numerator are inventory and prepaid expenses. (18)

**Rate of return on common stock equity:** A widely used measure of profitability that reveals how well the firm has used the assets and modified the capital structure to the benefit of the common stockholders. It is calculated by dividing net income available to common stockholders (after deduction of any preferred dividends) by the average common stockholders' equity balance. (18)

**Rate of return on total assets:** A widely used measure of profitability. Calculated by dividing net income plus tax-adjusted interest by the balance of average total assets. It can be broken down into its profit-margin and turnover-of-assets components. Also referred to as return on investment. (18)

**Raw materials:** Inventory of materials which has not yet entered the manufacturing process. (7)

**Receivables turnover:** A measure of how fast accounts receivable are turned into cash. Calculated by dividing net (credit) sales by the average accounts receivable balance. (18)

**Refunding:** Issuance of a new bond and use of its proceeds to redeem an old bond. (10)

**Relevance:** Qualitative guideline which states that accounting information should be responsive to the audience's information needs and be capable of affecting its decisions. To be relevant, information must have either predictive or feedback value to the user and be timely. (1)

**Reliability:** Qualitative guideline which states that financial accounting information should be reasonably free from error and bias and should faithfully represent what it purports to represent. Three conditions which contribute to the existence of reliability are (*a*) representational faithfulness, (*b*) completeness, and (*c*) verifiability. (1)

**Replacement cost:** The current acquisition cost of a previously purchased and currently held asset. (19)

**Representational faithfulness:** One of several qualitative guidelines which contributes to the existence of reliability. It implies a correspondence between accounting measures and the underlying economic events they are representing. (1)

**Residual value:** Portion of the asset's cost which is expected to be recovered at the end of its useful life to the firm. (9)

**Retained earnings:** The additional owners' equity arising from the retention of earnings in the corporation. It is increased by net income and decreased by net losses and dividends. (2)

**Revenue recognition concept:** Revenue should be recognized only when it has been earned and can be measured with a reasonable degree of reliability. (1)

**Revenues:** Inflows of assets from the sale of goods and services. (3)

**Sales-type lease:** Leases meeting certain criteria which also create for the lessor a manufacturer's or dealer's profit. Lessor removes property from its books, reflects gross margin on sale immediately, and reports interest revenue over the term of the lease purchase which it is financing. (11)

**Securities and Exchange Commission (SEC):** Federal agency established in the 1930s to regulate the nation's securities markets and to ensure that investors receive adequate information on which to base their investment decisions. (1)

**Segment reporting:** Disclosure requirements that result in firms reporting certain data for all industry segments for which the revenue, operating income or loss, or identifiable assets are 10 percent or more of the company total. Firms have considerable discretion in their definition of segments. (16)

**Special journals:** Separate books of original entry which are introduced to facilitate the recording of major, recurrent types of transactions.

Examples include special journals for sales and cash disbursements. (4)

**Specific identification:** Inventory costing method under which the various purchases made are segregated so that the goods remaining on hand at the end of the period can be specifically identified as having come from certain lots purchased. (8)

**Specific price changes:** Changes in the number of dollars of general exchange value required for the acquisition of a particular good or service; caused by changes over time in the interaction of supply and demand for the particular good or service. Such price changes are the focus of attention in the current cost supplementary disclosures. (19)

**Statement of changes in financial position (SCFP):** Financial statement designed to disclose the major financing and investing transactions undertaken by the firm and their effect on the balance of funds, usually defined as cash or working capital. (17)

**Statement of retained earnings:** A statement which reconciles the period's change in retained earnings with the balances on the comparative balance sheets. It begins with the beginning-of-period balance, adds income and deducts dividends, and ends up with the end-of-period balance. (5)

**Statements of Financial Accounting Concepts (SFAC):** Publications issued by the FASB which attempt to lay the groundwork for a conceptual framework for financial accounting and reporting. (1)

**Statements of Financial Accounting Standards (SFAS):** Authoritative statements issued by the FASB which spell out the current generally accepted accounting principles. (1)

**Stewardship:** The responsibility of management for protecting funds and other properties committed to the firm, for using the resources for the purposes intended, and for periodic reporting. (1)

**Stock dividends:** Dividends declared by corporations where the "payment" is made in additional shares of the firm's stock. They usually involve far fewer shares than do stock splits. (14)

**Stock-equity ratio:** A widely used measure of financial strength; calculated by dividing the common stock equity by total equities. (18)

**Stock option:** An agreement whereby recipients, usually the firm's chief executives, can acquire shares of stock after some date in the future at the specified price per share. (14)

**Stock split:** The corporation distributes additional shares of stock to stockholders for which the latter invest nothing. It represents a financial mechanism to reduce market price per share and increase the stock's appeal to investors. A stock split usually involves far more shares than a stock dividend. (14)

**Stock warrants:** Rights given outright to stockholders or included with the sale of other securities such as bonds. Holders of the warrants are permitted to acquire new shares of common stock at a specified price, even if the market price per share is in excess of that amount. (14)

**Straight-line bond amortization:** Interest-recording procedure which charges each period for the cash interest adjusted for a pro rata share of any bond premium or discount. The interest expense will be constant for each period of the bond's life. (10)

**Straight-line depreciation:** Depreciation procedure whereby a uniform charge for depreciation expense is taken during each year of the asset's life. (9)

**Subsidiary company:** A company which has more than half of its voting stock owned by another corporation, referred to as the parent. (15)

**Subsidiary ledger:** A group of accounts in which detailed information about a particular general ledger account (a control account) is kept. (4)

**Successful efforts:** Procedure whereby only those exploration and drilling costs traceable to successful wells or fields are set up as assets. The cost of dry holes or unproductive fields is immediately charged to expense. (7)

**Sum-of-the-years' digits (SYD) depreciation:** An accelerated depreciation procedure whereby a smaller fraction of the asset's depreciation base is taken to depreciation expense in each successive year. (9)

**Tax loss carry-backs and carry-forwards:** Provisions in the tax code which permit firms to offset a current tax loss against taxable income of the prior 3 years and the following 15 years. (13)

**Timing differences:** Differences between taxable income and accounting income which are created by certain items of revenue and expense which affect the computation of taxable income in one year and the computation of accounting income during another period. (13)

**Transactions:** Those financial activities and events involving the business entity which cause a measurable change in asset or equity accounts. (3)

**Treasury stock:** A corporation's own stock which has been previously issued and then reacquired but not legally retired. (14)

**Trial balance:** A listing of ledger accounts and their balances, classified as debit or credit; a procedure to ascertain whether the equality of debits and credits has been maintained in the accounting records. Making a trial balance is the first step of the accounting cycle to be undertaken at the end of the accounting period. (4)

**Turnover of assets:** One component of return on assets (investment); calculated by dividing sales revenue by average total assets. (18)

**Uncollectible accounts (bad debts):** Accounts receivable which will never be collected because the customer is unable or unwilling to pay. (6)

**Unit depreciation:** Depreciation procedure whereby the cost of each asset is assigned individually to the accounting periods in which it is used. (9)

**Unqualified ("clean") opinion:** An auditors' report which provides positive assurance that there is a reliable basis for the representations shown by management on its financial statements. (16)

**Variable expenses:** Expenses which change in total amount more or less proportionally with changes in the volume of operations in the period. Examples include raw materials and sales commissions. (18)

**Verifiability:** Quality which suggests that accounting information and measurement models can be independently confirmed by other competent measurers. It is one of three conditions which contribute to the existence of reliability. (1)

**Vertical analysis:** Analysis which abstracts from the absolute amounts on the financial statements the relative magnitude of figures expressed as percentages of some base item. Total assets and net sales are usually the bases used for the balance sheet and income statement, respectively. (18)

**Vested benefits:** Employee benefits the right to which are no longer contingent on the employee's continuing to work for the employer. (12)

**Weighted-average cost:** Inventory costing method which assumes that the ending inventory is representative of all units available for sale during the period. It produces ending inventory and cost of goods sold figures which are between those resulting from FIFO and LIFO. (8)

**Work in process:** Inventory of products for which the manufacturing process has been begun but has not yet been completed. (7)

**Work sheet:** A columnar device employed as a convenient and orderly way of organizing information to be used in the preparation of adjustments and financial statements. (4)

**Working capital:** Excess of current assets over current liabilities. (17)

# INDEX

*This book has been set Linotron 202, in 10 and 9 point Galliard, leaded 2 points. Section numbers are 20 point and section titles are 30 point Avant Garde Book. Chapter numbers are 20 point and chapter titles are 24 point Avant Garde Book. The size of the type page is 34½ by 48 picas.*